sociology
a canadian perspective

edited by

Lorne Tepperman

and

James Curtis

OXFORD
UNIVERSITY PRESS

1904 ❖ 2004

100 YEARS OF
CANADIAN PUBLISHING

OXFORD
UNIVERSITY PRESS

70 Wynford Drive, Don Mills, Ontario M3C 1J9
www.oup.com/ca

Oxford University Press is a department of the University of Oxford.
It furthers the University's objective of excellence in research, scholarship,
and education by publishing worldwide in

Oxford New York
Auckland Bangkok Buenos Aires Cape Town Chennai
Dar es Salaam Delhi Hong Kong Istanbul Karachi Kolkata
Kuala Lumpur Madrid Melbourne Mexico City Mumbai Nairobi
São Paulo Shanghai Taipei Tokyo Toronto

Oxford is a trade mark of Oxford University Press
in the UK and in certain other countries

Published in Canada
by Oxford University Press

National Library of Canada Cataloguing in Publication Data

Sociology: a Canadian perspective/edited by Lorne Tepperman and
James Curtis.

Includes bibliographical references and index.

1. Sociology. 2. Canada—Social conditions. I. Curtis, James E., 1943–
II. Tepperman, Lorne, 1943–

HM586.S62 2004   301   C2003-907338-6

Cover and text design: Brett Miller

2 3 4 - 07 06 05
This book is printed on permanent (acid-free) paper ∞.
Printed in Canada

Contents

Detailed Contents

Preface

From the Editors

The two of us have been writing and publishing textbooks intended for first-year sociology students since the early 1980s, often together.

In all this work, we have aimed to provide up-to-date pictures of Canadian society and Canadian sociology, written by Canadian experts in the important subfields of sociology for students at Canadian colleges and universities. In short, our goal has been to teach Canadians about Canada and about sociology, and, in that way, make a modest contribution to both Canadian society and Canadian sociology.

A lot has happened since 1980, in every area of life. Just think about a few of those changes. For example, many readers of *Sociology: A Canadian Perspective* had not yet been born, and of those alive in, say, 1985, almost none would have known how to read yet. At that time, televisions were in every home, but VCRs, CD players, DVD players, and computers were not. Try to imagine a world without e-mail, the Internet, or Game Boy!

Health problems and health possibilities were different then. AIDS barely registered on people's consciousness. There was no SARS, no Ebola virus, and little or no concern about antibiotic-resistant "super bugs." Genetic engineering was still a dream (or a nightmare); no one had yet mapped the human genome. What we call the "new reproductive technology" was in its infancy.

Twenty years ago, the Soviet Union—billed in a *Time* magazine cover story of the era as "Earth's last empire"—still existed. So did Yugoslavia and the Berlin Wall and communism as a functioning political system in many societies. The Cold War continued, as did a balance of power between the United States and the USSR. Novels and movies about communist espionage were still popular. Aside from the hostage-taking at the American embassy in Teheran, Islam scarcely registered on Westerners' attention span. Fears of Japan as an economic superpower were growing, but awareness of the rest of East Asia was just starting to infiltrate our consciousness.

We feared different things then. For example, overpopulation was a greater world concern; fertility rates were high and still rising in many "developing" countries of the world. Ecology and pollution were new and growing concerns, but there was little concern with homelessness. People knew the Canadian population was aging, but few expressed much concern about mandatory retirement or how Canada could support the retired elderly population.

Back in the early 1980s, when we first began writing first-year sociology textbooks, tattooing and body piercing were rare and still considered bizarre. Homosexuality was still hidden. Marriage was common, as was divorce. Cohabitation was relatively rare and not socially acceptable among middle-aged middle-class people. Clearly, most people shunned childbirth and parenting outside of marriage. Women were slowly gaining equality with men, as they still are, but many more men than now expressed ridicule at the idea of gender equality, which they characterized as mere bra burning or bitchiness.

Quebec separatism was a much bigger cultural concern in the mid-1980s than it is today. Now, globalization is a bigger worry. Canada was multicultural in those days, but less multicultural than it is now. The large-scale immigrations from Asia, Africa, South America, and the West Indies had yet to reach a peak. Since then, international trade has also grown dramatically, and globalization has assimilated Canada into a worldwide trading network dominated, more completely than in the past, by the United States. Contending for influence in this new global economy are a growing European Economic Community and various aggressive new economies, many of them in Asia—Japan, China, Taiwan, and Singapore, among others.

So, as you can see, a lot has changed in the last 20 years both in terms of people's behaviours and in terms of their shared understandings of things. No wonder our sociology textbooks have changed too. Some of the contributors to our first textbooks also contributed chapters to this new book, but at least half of the contributors to this volume are new. Likewise, various topics—globalization, for example—are new here.

We think you will find that *Sociology: A Canadian Perspective* provides an up-to-date picture of Canadian society and Canadian sociology at the beginning of the twenty-first century. As always, we remain committed to providing the best, most reader-friendly presentation of social facts and theories. Our publisher, Oxford University Press of Canada, has helped us do so, and we are grateful for this help. *Sociology: A Canadian Perspective* has received strong support from the topmost levels of Oxford University Press Canada, including Joanna Gertler, President of the Canadian branch, and David Stover, head of the Higher Education Division. Thank you, Joanna and David.

Oxford knows that it wants a Canadian sociology list and knows how to produce it.

One person very central to this enterprise, and to the production of this book in particular, was Megan Mueller. In every practical and creative sense, Megan guided, prodded, jollied, coerced, and encouraged us. Megan knows what she is doing and does it with great humour and energy. She has a keen eye for quality in books for the undergraduate audience. It was a great pleasure working with Megan on this project, as on our *Social Problems* textbook.

Also working with us on *Sociology: A Canadian Perspective* was copy editor Stephanie Fysh, another veteran of the *Social Problems* textbook. Like Megan, Stephanie is a true professional, incredibly thorough, and one of the best Jim and I have met in decades of writing books. Stephanie had as many great ideas as Megan; her assistance has been supportive, enlightening, and provocative. We also thank Stephanie for her endless patience. Finally, we want to thank managing editor Phyllis Wilson for taking care of the backstage practical matters at Oxford—making sure that all the pieces come together when and where they are supposed to—and those talented people who took the photos and painted the pictures that appear in this great-looking book. Most particularly, we want to thank Brett Miller, who designed the incredible cover.

We are also grateful for help received from Lorne's University of Toronto work-study undergraduates, who this year comprised Maja Jovanovich, Maria Karasyova, Evan Kazolis, Iris Lazaro, Ha Luu, and Nicola Torma. Victrine Tseung and Michelle Wong, heading up this group, oversaw many aspects of the manuscript production. In particular, Victrine and Michelle made sure our authors produced what they were supposed to produce, on time. Additionally, prize-winning undergraduate Amy Withers rooted out materials for boxed inserts and helped create learning aids for chapters 1 and 5. It's been a pleasure to work with these talented young people. Julie Dembski also provided very valuable assistance to Jim at the University of Waterloo.

Our main thanks go to the contributing authors, without whom this book simply would not exist. They put up with our (seemingly endless) demands and cavils, and somehow we all got from A to B without any homicides or other untoward emotional displays. It has been a great privilege working with this distinguished group of top Canadian scholars from all over the country. Thank you, authors.

Finally, in closing, we dedicate this book to our friend and colleague, Jack Richardson, who passed away a year ago, when our work on this book was just beginning. Over the years, we were fortunate enough to work with Jack on numerous editions of texts intended to introduce the fundamentals of sociology to undergraduates. Jack, we miss you. However, the ideas that you espoused in the various books we wrote with you—that they might contribute to Canadian sociology and the education of young Canadian scholars—remain alive and in good hands. We think the readers of this book will agree.

Lorne Tepperman, University of Toronto
James Curtis, University of Waterloo

From the Publisher

In preparing *Sociology: A Canadian Perspective*, the general editors, chapter authors, and publisher have from the start kept in mind one paramount goal: to produce the most authoritative, comprehensive, yet accessible and interesting introduction to sociology available for Canadian students.

Among the features of the text designed to enhance usefulness and interest for students and instructors alike:

Top Canadian contributors. Sociology is a global discipline, but one to which sociologists working in and studying Canada have made unique contributions. Not merely an adaptation of a book originally written for American undergraduates, this text was conceived and written from the ground up as a Canadian perspective on this fascinating field. Experts in their particular sub-disciplines examine not only the key concepts and terminology of sociology as an academic subject, but also use those concepts to shed light on the nature of Canadian society and Canada's place in the world.

Global perspective. Although this is a book written by and for Canadians, the editors and authors never forget that Canada is but one small part of a vast, diverse, and endlessly fascinating social world. Along with Canadian data, examples, and illustrations, a wealth of information about how humans live and interact the world around is presented in every chapter. To cite just one example, Chapter 7, "Families," presents not only a cutting-edge picture of the state of Canadian families today, and the sociological theories that help us understand them, but also fascinating snapshots of family life in other countries, including chapter author Maureen Baker's poignant vignette about the life of a New Zealand Maori single mother and her family (page 165).

Theoretical balance. The very mention of the term "theory" seems calculated to make first-year undergraduates uneasy, but the overriding goal in *Sociology: A Canadian Perspective* has been not only to make the theories that underpin the discipline comprehensible, but to show how they inform one's understanding of the data that sociologists gather— and how the choice of which theoretical perspective to employ can yield new and surprising insights. The field's major paradigms (including the increasingly important feminist perspective) are introduced in Chapter 1, "What is Sociology?" Chapter 22, "Sociological Theory," provides a more detailed discussion of the different schools of sociological thought and how they relate to theoretical constructions in the other social and natural sciences. Throughout the text, emerging paradigms are also discussed where they shed new light on long-standing questions.

Aids to student learning. A textbook must fulfill a double duty: while meeting instructors' expectations for accuracy, currency, and comprehensiveness, it must also speak to the needs and interests of today's students, providing them with an accessible introduction to a body of knowledge. To that end, numerous features to promote student learning are incorporated throughout the book. These include:

- *Learning Objectives* at the start of each chapter, which provide a concise overview of the key concepts that will be covered.
- *Theme Boxes* illustrating important points and providing examples of how sociological research sheds light on the "real world." These are discussed in greater detail below.
- *Graphs and Tables.* Though qualitative research methods have grown in importance in recent years, one of the characteristics that still distinguishes sociology from some of the other liberal arts and social sciences is its emphasis on using quantitative data and analysis as a crucial tool for understanding society. Colourful graphs and charts make such data clear in a way that sometimes text cannot. See, for instance, the chart illustrating various ways young people use the Internet (page 72).
- *Annotated Recommended Readings* lists at the end of each chapter point students toward useful sources for further research and place those sources in the broader context of the field.

- *Annotated Recommended Web Sites* direct readers to additional resources available on the Web, with useful commentary that helps students learn how to sort the wheat from the chaff as they sift through the overwhelming volume of information available through the Internet.
- *Questions for Critical Thought* at the end of each chapter draw out key issues and encourage readers to think deeply about them and draw their own conclusions.
- A *Glossary* located at the end of the book defines important terms, which are highlighted in **boldface** in the text, and provides a concise, convenient dictionary of sociological terms for future reference.

Contemporary design. The advent of new media technologies has meant that today's students live in a world that is much more visually cluttered and complex than did their predecessors of a generation or two ago. As a result, textbooks have had to change with the times in order to remain appealing and useful to the readers of today. To borrow and modify a tag line from a General Motors advertising campaign for its ailing Oldsmobile division, "This is not your father's first-year sociology text." Or, we hasten to add, your mother's, either; nor your older brother's or sister's. We have striven for a look that is contemporary yet clear and clean, a design that reflects the vibrancy and excitement of sociology today without sacrificing content or authoritativeness. The use of colour and novel design elements is a necessary acknowledgement of the changes wrought by new media in how readers expect information to be packaged and presented. At the same time we remain well aware that this is indeed a printed book, with both the limitations and the very real and enduring strengths that are a product of print's long history as the preeminent method of codifying and transmitting knowledge.

Theme boxes. "Why study sociology?" is a question frequently asked by students enrolled in their first sociology course. There are all kinds of reasons, of course, many of which are touched on in Chapter 1, but among them are the undeniable fact that sociology provides a unique insight into the nature of the human world; that it shows us things about society and ourselves that we might not otherwise know; and that the lessons of sociology can be intriguing, touching, tragic, even fun. The dozens of theme boxes scattered throughout the text illustrate all these dimensions of the discipline. Four series of boxes run throughout the book:

- *Sociology in Action* shows how sociological research can help us better understand the everyday world, from the ways in which Halloween has been revolutionized by high-tech (page 4) to the outcome of the unionization movement at that most ubiquitous symbol of today's consumer society, the local McDonald's (page 243).
- *Open for Discussion* boxes use contemporary social issues and debates to focus understanding of core sociological concepts. For instance, can racism be promoted through inaction as well as action (page 15)?
- *Global Issues* draws upon examples from around the world to illustrate the effects of globalization and show what sociologists have to say about it, as, for instance, in the contentious matter of the health consequences of global climate change (page 28).
- *Human Diversity* boxes recognize the overwhelming and unavoidable fact of human diversity, and seek to introduce students to the ways of life and world views of different cultures and social groups, whether it be the question of whether Canadian society is bilingual or "centilingual" (page 55) or the profound questions raised by new standards of "environmental justice" and the disproportionate price paid by the poor for environmental pollution (page 563).

Sociology as a human pursuit. Finally, *Sociology: A Canadian Perspective* celebrates the fact that while sociology is an academic discipline with a distinguished pedigree, it is also a very human pursuit—a fact that becomes clear in the brief *In the First Person* narratives included in many chapters, in which the authors discuss why they chose careers in sociology. The text's contributors first encountered the discipline while the same age as many of you now using this text in "intro soc." What was it about the study of sociology that, for example, led general editor Lorne Tepperman to abandon both his father's desire that he become a doctor and his own decision that (in his words) "I'll get a BA in sociology, like my friend Jerry, and then become a lawyer"? How did "growing up in the border city of Niagara Falls, [where] I became aware early of some of the more peculiar eccentricities and excesses of human behaviour," lead contributor Vince Sacco to a lifelong study of how society defines deviance? Sociology is, above all, the study of human beings interacting within society in all their wonderful complexity, and the *In the First Person* boxes provide an intriguing glimpse of why this particular group of humans chose to make that study their lifework.

Supplements

Today's texts no longer are volumes that stand on their own but, rather, the central element of a complete learning and teaching package. *Sociology: A Canadian Perspective* is no exception. The book is supported by an outstanding array of ancillary materials for both students and instructors.

For The Instructor

Instructor's manual. The instructor's manual includes comprehensive outlines of the text's various parts and chapters, additional questions for encouraging class discussion, suggestions on how to use videos to enhance your classes, and extra material for use in lectures.

Test item file. A comprehensive test item file, available both in printed and computerized form—the latter employing cutting-edge test generator technology which allows instructors a wide array of options for sorting, editing, importing, and distributing questions—provides more than 2400 questions (more than 100 per chapter), including multiple choice, short answer, true/false, and essay formats.

PowerPoint ® slides. Hundreds of slides for classroom presentation are available to adopters of the text. The slides incorporate graphics and tables from the text, summarize key points from each chapter, and can be edited to suit individual instructors' needs.

Colour transparencies. The PowerPoint® slides can also be made available as colour acetates to qualified adopters.

Instructors should contact their Oxford University Press representative for details on these supplements as well as additional ancillaries which may be made available.

Student Supplements

Companion Web Site. Visit www.oup.com/ca/he for details about the innovative Companion Web Site that accompanies *Sociology: A Canadian Perspective*. Resources available include automatically graded study questions, annotated links to other useful Web resources, and much else.

Study Guide. A comprehensive printed *Study Guide* to accompany the text is also available. The *Study Guide* includes review questions, applied exercises, and other material designed to enhance student learning.

part **one**

> > >

Introduction:
The Sociological Approach

1

James Curtis and
Lorne Tepperman

> > >

What Is Sociology?

© PhotoDisc, Inc.

☐ Learning Objectives

In this chapter, you will:

- learn about the purposes of sociology and the types of questions sociologists attempt to understand and answer

- examine the difference in perspective between macrosociology and microsociology

- clarify the difference between sociology and other academic fields that also study human behaviour

- explore the meanings of the two basic phenomena studied by sociology—social structure and culture—and how the two relate to each other

- study the development of sociology, its major founders (Karl Marx, Émile Durkheim, and Max Weber), and their main ideas and contributions

- learn the basic elements of four major approaches in sociology: functionalist, conflict, symbolic interactionist, and feminist

- consider the role of sociology in social and cultural change

Introduction

Why does someone become a sociologist? There are many answers to this question, but some of them can be summarized with the expression, "It is a wonder that everyone doesn't want to become a sociologist." We say this because all people experience peculiar facts of social life that affect their opportunities, and they try to understand them. This is where **sociology** begins for most people. When people proceed from here, there is even more motivation to do sociology. What can be more fascinating, more empowering, and more personal than to begin to understand the society that shapes our lives? For these reasons, sociology is an inherently attractive area of study, and many people do study it.

Maybe as a child you noticed that

- parents sometimes treat their sons differently from their daughters
- teachers often treat pretty little girls better than plain-looking ones
- adults treat well-dressed children better than poorly dressed children
- movies typically portray people with "accents" as strange or ridiculous

If you noticed these things, you may have wondered why they happen. They may even have affected you, as a daughter or son, a plain-looking or attractive person, a poorly dressed or well-dressed person, or a person with or without an "accent." You may have felt ashamed, angry, or pleased, depending on whether you identified with the favourably treated or the unfavourably treated category of people.

Perhaps as a child you grew up in a neighbourhood that was dangerous, where

- people were often nervous about walking down the street
- someone had killed people you knew, for no good reason
- men had attacked or humiliated women who lived nearby
- children were afraid to go to school for fear of bullying

If you noticed these things, you may have wanted to understand them better. These are the kinds of circumstances in which sociological curiosity begins. All sociologists somehow, sometime or another, got hooked on trying to better understand their own lives and the lives of people around them. They came to understand that common sense gave them only incomplete explanations about what happened to people, about people's behaviour and the society in which they live. They were not satisfied with the incomplete explanation and wanted to know more.

For many people, and for much of what we do, common-sense understanding is just fine. Still, for anyone who *really* wants to understand how society works, it is not good enough. You may already realize that there are many questions common sense cannot answer adequately. For example,

- Why are some people so different from you, and why are some so similar?
- Why do apparently similar people lead such different lives?
- How is it possible for different people to get along?
- Why do we treat some people as if they are more "different" than others?
- Why do we often treat "different" people much worse than others?
- What do people do to escape from being treated badly?
- Why do some aspects of society change very quickly and others hardly at all?
- What can citizens do to make Canadian society a more democratic place?
- What can young people do to make their elders think differently?
- Can we bring about social change by changing the laws of the country?

Sociologists try to answer these questions by studying societies methodically. In fact, they study people's lives—their own and others'—more carefully than anyone else. Sociologists want to understand how societies change and how people's lives change with them. Social changes, inequalities, and conflicts captivate sociologists because such issues—war and peace, wealth and poverty, environmental destruction and technological innovation, for example—are very important for people's lives. However, sociologists always see two sides to these issues: a macro side and a micro side. They know that "personal problems" are very similar across many individuals. They know that many of our personal problems are the private side of public issues. As such, we need to deal with them collectively and, often, politically—with full awareness that we share these problems and their solution with others.

However, solving problems entails clear thinking and careful research. Consequently, they have developed

Sociology in Action
The Technology of Night Fun

Many of the wee goblins and ghouls roaming the streets last night in search of sweets used the latest in communications technology to maximize their candy-earning potential.

Cellphones helped children turn trick-or-treating into a fine art as they traded information on which houses had the best loot so they could fill their pillowcases in record time.

"I'm using my phone to tell my friends what houses have the best candy and what houses are handing out apples, and which ones give the most candy," said Katrina Proulx. The 13-year-old devil and her costumed friends turned up on select doorsteps in Langley, BC, last night courtesy of her Fido cellphone. "A lot of my friends have them."

Some groups of children worked the streets in tandem, taking opposite sides of a roadway and calling each other to let them know which houses to hit when it was time to swap sides. Those equipped with free text-messaging, like Katrina, were able to fire messages to each other, giving specific addresses of houses too good to miss.

Rogers AT&T Wireless even got into the act by circulating a Top 10 list of Halloween-related text messages before the night began. Their suggestions included cryptic communiqués such as GR8 CNDY @ SUZ'S (great candy at Susan's) and XLNT TRTS @ No. 67 (excellent treats at house number 67).

"I think it's great," said Paula Proulx, Katrina's mother. "Who wants to get toothbrushes and apples when they can get a big bucket of candy? It's smart trick-or-treating. It's all about the smart strategy to get to the houses in the least amount of time."

The Halloween trend has more significance than merely boosting candy counts, said Rebecca Grinter, a research scientist at Xerox's Palo Alto Research Center who studied teenage use of text messaging.

"It's part of forming closer friendships and trying to make connections with people," said Ms Grinter, who co-authored a study titled "y do tngrs luv 2 txt msg?" (Why do teenagers love to text message?).

Other trick-or-treaters, however, scoffed at the idea, saying the only reason to carry a cellphone last night was to keep in touch with parents and stay safe.

Halloween is not about the candy, said David Goroztieta, a Grade 9 student at Kitsilano Secondary School in Vancouver. "It's just about going out, having fun and just being with your friends."

SOURCE: Mary Vallis, "Trick-or-Treaters Go High-Tech for 'gr8 cndy' Using Cellphones, Text Messaging," *National Post*, 1 Nov. 2002. Reprinted by permission of National Post.

concepts, theories, and research methods that help them investigate the social world more effectively. Our goal as sociologists is to be able to explain social life, critique social inequities, and work toward effecting social change. In this book, you will learn how sociologists go about these tasks, and some of what sociologists have found out about the social world.

Our starting point in this chapter is a formal definition of *sociology*, comparisons of sociology with other related fields of study, and a discussion of sociology's most basic subject matter.

A Definition of Sociology

Scholars have defined **sociology** in many ways, but most practising sociologists think of their discipline as the systematic study of social behaviour in human societies. Humans are intensely social beings and spend most of their time interacting with other humans. That is why sociologists study the social units people create when they join with others. As we will see in the following chapters, these units range from

IN THE FIRST PERSON

I got into sociology in a roundabout way. My father wanted me to become a doctor, so I went into general science at the University of Toronto, but I didn't really care about the natural sciences. I thought, I'll get a BA in sociology, like my friend Jerry, and then become a lawyer. So I went into sociology, which was interesting but not very challenging—until third year, when I had a theory class with a young professor, Jan Loubser, just down from Harvard. Jan was passionate and smart and funny. The material he taught, Parsonian general theory, was hard to understand, but I found it fascinating. In fourth year, though I still planned to go to law school, I applied to graduate school in sociology. I figured that if someone gave me a scholarship to study somewhere interesting, I'd go (I really wanted to get away from home). I applied to nine schools, Harvard among them. What I didn't know was that Jan had written my idol, Talcott Parsons, about me. How surprised I was to receive a handwritten letter from Parsons, urging me to come to Harvard. I couldn't refuse. – LORNE TEPPERMAN

For as long as I can remember I was always puzzled, and annoyed, about why many people were poor and had few opportunities for a good life. Upon reaching university in Montreal my work-study scholarship required that I register in courses in the social sciences, and one of these turned out to be a large introductory sociology course taught by Hubert Guindon. He proved to be an exceptionally insightful and inspirational teacher and I became "hooked on" sociology for a lifetime. I began to understand what I was annoyed about and what I could do about this as a researcher and citizen. I continue to find these yields of sociological research as important today as I did in those early university years. I wonder what life would have been like if I had not been placed in that course? How would those puzzles and annoyances have played out for me? – JIM CURTIS

small groups—comprising as few as two people—to large corporations and even whole societies (see, for example, chapter 5, on groups, cliques, and bureaucracies). Sociologists are interested in learning about the ways in which group membership affects individual behaviour and, reciprocally, the ways in which individuals change the groups of which they are members. In most social life, at least in Canadian society, there is a visible tug-of-war between these two forces: the group and the individual.

However, it is impossible for any sociologist to study all social issues or to become an expert in all the subareas of sociology. As a result, most sociologists specialize in either macrosociology or microsociology—two related but distinct approaches to studying the social world—and choose problems for study from within these realms.

Macrosociology is the study of large social **organizations** (for example, the Roman Catholic Church, universities, corporations, or government bureaucracies) and large social categories (for example, ethnic minorities, the elderly, or college students). Sociologists who specialize in the macrosociological approach to the social world focus on the complex social patterns that people form over long periods (see many examples in parts III and V of this volume, on social institutions and global society, respectively).

On the other hand, *microsociology* focuses on the typical processes and patterns of face-to-face interaction in small groups. A microsociologist might study a marriage, a clique, a business meeting, an argument between friends, or a first date. In short, he or she would study the common, everyday interactions and negotiations that together produce lasting, secure patterns (see many examples in chapters 3 and 4, on socialization and on roles and identities, respectively).

The difference in names—*macro* versus *micro*—refers to the difference in size in the social units of interest. Macrosociologists study large social units—organizations, societies, or even empires—over long periods of time: years, centuries, or millennia. Microsociologists study small social units over short periods of time—for example, what happens during a conversation, a party, a classroom lecture, or a love affair. As in nature, large things tend to move (and change) slowly and small things move more quickly. As a result, macrosociologists are likely to stress how slowly things change and how amazingly persistent a social pattern is as it plays itself out in one generation after another. An example is the way society tends to be controlled by its elite groups, decade after decade. The connection between business elites and political elites is amazingly persistent. By contrast, microsociologists, are likely to stress how quickly things change and how very elusive is that thing we call "social life." In their eyes, any social unit is constantly being created and reconceived by the members of society. An example is the way one's friendship group changes pretty much yearly, if not more rapidly, as one moves through the school system or the world of work. Some people remain our close friends over years, but many are close friends for only a short while.

Combining macro and micro approaches improves our understanding of the social world. Consider a common social phenomenon: the domestic division of labour—who does what chores around the home. From the micro perspective, who does what is constantly open to negotiation, a result of personal characteristics, the history of the couple, and other unique factors. From a macro perspective, different households tend to have pretty similar divisions of labour, despite differences in personal history. This suggests that the answer lies in a society's history, culture, and economy. It is far from accidental that, across millions of households, men enjoy the advantage of a better salary and more social power both in a great many workplaces and at home.

While these approaches are different, they are also connected. They have to be: after all, both macro- and microsociologists are studying the same people in the same society. All of us are leading somewhat unique lives within a common social context, faced by common problems. The question is, how can sociologists bring these elements together? The great American sociologist C. Wright Mills (1959) gave the answer when he introduced the notion of the **sociological imagination** as something that enables us to relate personal biographies—the lives of millions of ordinary people like ourselves—to the broad sweep of human history. The sociological imagination is what we need to use in order to understand how societies control and change their members and, at the same time, are constantly changed by the actions of their members.

All of this is the subject matter of sociology. We may chose to focus on problems of microsociology or macrosociology because of our preference to understand one or the other, but a proper or full understanding of most problems will require that we consider elements of both, because the two types of processes are closely connected.

Sociology Goes Beyond and Corrects Common Sense

Accomplishing the tasks of sociology requires systematic research, not merely **common-sense knowledge.** Some students studying the subject for the first time think that sociology is nothing more than common sense. After all, so many of the principles sociologists discover about everyday life seem familiar; we know these principles already because we live with them all the time. Yet, for all that familiarity, few people are able to guess correctly how a marriage, a friendship, a business partnership, or a political campaign will turn out. True, our experience gives us "rules of thumb"—guidelines for accomplishing everyday life. They often even become folk wisdom, for example, "If you lead a good life you will be rewarded in the next life" or "Anyone can get whatever success they try hard for." However, sociologists would not consider these to be scientific statements, even if they make sense to us and seem true. Most of the time, scientific research finds they are not true; in fact, they're usually false. They're false because they are rooted not in careful research but in wishful thinking.

One of the problems with common-sense explanations of social life is that they are often based on a *voluntaristic* view of life. This point of view suggests that people live as they want to, get the lives they *want*. Supposedly, people with good ideas, attitudes, and values get good lives, while people with bad ideas, attitudes, and values get bad lives. This view implies that what you make of your life is up to you and that people who lead bad lives probably deserve to.

Yet most sociologists would deny that. Consider the following facts; they all pose a problem for the so-called voluntaristic approach:

- Certain kinds of people (such as people who are poor) get sick more often and die at younger ages than other kinds of people.
- Certain kinds of people (such as job applicants who are black) are less likely to get hired for jobs than other kinds of people.
- Certain kinds of people (such as young women) are more likely than other kinds of people to be presented semi-nude in the **mass media**, or in sexually provocative poses.

Is it really true that poor people *want* to die younger? Or that black job seekers *want* to be unemployed? Or that young women are mainly worth knowing as sex objects? Would their lives improve overnight if only they adopted the right attitudes and values, as the common-sense argument seems to suggest? Or are there social forces that push these people into certain kinds of lives, putting harm in their way and limiting their choices, despite their deepest wishes to the contrary?

This last question of choice—of free will—is at the heart of sociology. It raises additional questions—for example, why do some people get more choices and better chances than others? Why do some people keep getting a bad deal? And, given these unpleasant facts of life, and despite plenty of personal experiences to the contrary, why do so many people believe in the "common-sense" ideas of free will and happy endings?

By the time you finish reading this book, you will have the beginnings of an answer to all these questions. For now, take it as given that because of their voluntaristic bias and untested character, common-sense explanations are more likely to be wrong than right. Sociology—both macro and micro—is about seeing beyond such popular beliefs. That is why sociologists take a systematic and studied approach to understanding everyday life. When we do, we often find the unexpected.

Sociologist C. Wright Mills said that the sociological imagination is the ability to see connections between large and small, fast-changing and slow-changing, portions of our social world. The sociological imagination is what enables us to relate personal biography to the broad sweep of human history. (Photo © Megan Mueller)

The Example of Job Searches

To get a better idea of sociology's approach, consider a debate about how people find jobs. Common sense might tell you to talk to close friends and relatives to get a job. They have the greatest motivation to help you find a job. However, sociological research shows that this common-sense approach can be misleading.

Imagine you are searching for a full-time job, a good one if possible—something related to what you studied at college, with good pay, good working conditions, and prospects for advancement. Now, imagine too that you can search in any of three ways:

- *Strategy 1.* You can ask your best friend for information, help, or advice.
- *Strategy 2.* You can randomly pick a name out of the telephone book, phone that person, and ask him or her for information, help, or advice.
- *Strategy 3.* You can work your request for information, help, or advice into a conversation with an acquaintance at school or work; you are on a first-

name basis with this acquaintance, but you don't consider him or her a close friend.

Common sense would tell you to avoid Strategy 2, the random phone call. That strategy is unlikely to land you a job, though it has one thing in its favour: you are likely to reach someone you have never talked to before. In 10 random telephone calls, you are likely to reach very different kinds of people. Random calling maximizes the variety and range of information you might possibly receive. However, the people you reach in this way are not likely to be useful. They have no motive for helping you find a good job. After all, they don't even know you.

Common sense says Strategy 1 is more promising. Your best friend, like your mother, father, brother, and sister (and perhaps a few other relatives), is motivated to help you: he or she likes you. However, if you think about it, you will realize we tend to choose friends who are like us. Because of this similarity, our close friends, though motivated, are not very helpful. They tend to form *cliques*. In cliques, our best friends—and their best friends— know the same things, which are often things that we already know. The information reaching our best friends, whether about jobs or about drugs, is not very different from the information already reaching us. So while close friends are motivated to help us, they can't help us much if we need varied or obscure information.

That leaves Strategy 3, the use of acquaintances. We all have dozens, if not hundreds, of people we know on a first-name basis. They are people with whom we have casual conversations from time to time. Some of them know each other; they may even be kin, friends, neighbours, or acquaintances of each other. A great many of our acquaintances, however, do *not* know each other. Thus, the information reaching a dozen of our acquaintances is quite varied—not as varied as the information reaching a dozen randomly selected people, but much more varied than the information reaching our dozen closest friends and relatives.

At the same time, because we know our acquaintances and they know us, we are willing to ask them for information or advice and they are likely to be willing to provide it. What's more, our experience with these acquaintances gives us some basis on which to evaluate the quality of the information they are providing. So we might very well tell an acquaintance we are looking for a job, and listen for suggestions about where to look.

In our society, we like to believe that people who are talented and work hard will—somehow—get the best jobs, and that the best jobs will—somehow— find the best employees. There is supposedly a job market with an "invisible hand" operating. People who get bad jobs, by this reasoning, probably deserve bad jobs. They lack the qualifications, or even the skills of self-presentation that are important when interviewing for a job. Likewise, jobs that fail to find good candidates probably also deserve to fail. They haven't advertised effectively or presented candidates with a positive corporate image or an attractive employee package.

Yet research finds that there is little merit in this commonsensical analysis. In a systematic study of managers in Boston, sociologist Mark Granovetter (1974, 1982) found that a significant number of the managers he studied had found their job through an acquaintance—what Granovetter called a *weak tie* (to distinguish it from a close friend or relative, which would be a *strong tie*). In fact, managers found the *best* jobs in that way.

Why do weak ties pay off in this way? Granovetter argues that acquaintances provide the best combination of awareness, or information quantity, and evaluation, or information quality. Networks of acquaintances are large, and the information that flows through them is much more varied than that through networks of friends or relatives. Yet networks of acquaintances provide more reliable information than you can obtain from a random selection of names, or even (which is similar) from the job applications and résumés of hundreds of strangers.

How does the average Canadian search for her or his job? While we know of no data source with complete information on how the overall job search process takes place for the average worker, we can report data on how Canadians found their current job. The data come from those with full-time jobs who answered a national survey in 2000. We have data for all types of jobs and for males and females (recall that Granovetter's US community study was for males with management-level jobs only). As Table 1.1 shows, the largest proportion of workers, whether male or female, found out about their jobs from a family member or friend, suggesting that the "common-sense" approach was very popular, if it is not the most efficient. This approach was followed, in order of frequency, by answering an advertisement, sending or dropping off an application, asking an acquaintance, and following up with an agency of some sort. Only

Table 1.1   **How Canadians Find Out About Their Jobs, by Gender and Level of Job[a]**

Source of Job Information[b]	Professional/Managerial		Other White-Collar		Blue-Collar	
	Male %	Female %	Male %	Female %	Male %	Female %
Family member or friend	24.1	14.1	26.6	25.0	33.0	31.5
Acquaintance	12.4	9.9	12.1	10.8	10.5	10.8
Agency	11.7	11.3	6.4	10.0	8.6	12.3
Advertisement	23.7	27.7	24.3	20.0	24.6	16.7
Prior employment	4.9	6.2	6.4	7.5	3.2	4.0
Résumé sent in or dropped off	10.2	15.3	9.8	20.0	8.4	14.4
Other	13.2	15.3	14.5	6.7	11.8	10.4
(N)	(266)	(354)	(173)	(120)	(570)	(480)

[a] Columns may not add up to 100 because of rounding.
[b] "How did you learn about the job opening for your main job?"

SOURCE: Based on unpublished data from a survey conducted in 2000 for the Economy, Security and Community Project, University of British Columbia, Jon Kesselman, Project Director, 2002.

a small minority, about 11 per cent, used the help of an acquaintance. As the table shows, job seekers were more likely to have used family members and friends for lower-level blue-collar jobs than for professional and managerial or other white-collar jobs. They used acquaintances slightly more often to get the better jobs (for males) than for other jobs.

Males were generally more likely than females to have acquired their professional and managerial jobs through contacts with family and acquaintances. Females were more likely to have followed up on ads, used an agency, or dropped off applications.

Thus, these Canadian data suggest that there are some important **gender** differences in the job-search process. For better jobs, apparently both strong ties (family and friends) and weak ties (acquaintances) seem to pay off better for males than for females. These data do not appear to completely support Granovetter's findings. However, Granovetter was looking at how people find the best jobs—not merely their current jobs.

How Sociology Differs from Other Academic Fields

Sociology is just one of several fields of study designed to help describe and explain human behaviour; others include journalism, history, philosophy,

and psychology. How does sociology differ from these other endeavours? Canadian sociologist Kenneth Westhues (1982) has compared sociology's approach with those of the other fields. He emphasizes that journalism and history describe real events, as does sociology. However, journalism and history only sometimes base their descriptions on a **theory** or interpretation, and then it is often an implicit theory. Sociology is different. It strives to make its theories explicit in order to test them. Telling a story is important for sociologists, but less so than the explanation on which the story is based. Sociology may be good preparation for doing history or journalism, but it differs from these disciplines.

Sociology also differs from philosophy. Both are *analytical*—that is, concerned with testing and refining theory. However, sociology is resolutely *empirical*, or concerned with gathering evidence and doing studies, while philosophy is not. Philosophy has greater concern with the internal logic of its arguments. Sociological theories must stand up logically, but they must also stand up to evidence in a way philosophical theories need not. Sociologists, no matter how logical the theory may be will not accept a sociological theory whose predictions are not supported by evidence gathered in a sound way.

Finally, sociology differs from psychology, which is also analytical, empirical, and interpretive. The difference here lies in the subject matter. Psychologists

day in and day out. Imagine travelling in an automobile across one of our cities if we did not share such understandings!

We can take this conception of culture as shared too far, though. Some parts of a culture are exclusive to some members of the society: some aspects of culture are learned and known by most of us, but other cultural items are shared by only a choice few. In addition to the rules of traffic, most of us know the meanings of such concepts as "money" (such as what a dollar will buy today), "work," "family," and "education." Very few of us, however, are privy to the information shared in the federal cabinet or in the boardrooms of major corporations. Only some of us know much about classical music, jazz, or bluegrass; and very few know how to fly a jet plane, perform a heart transplant, or build a house. In other words, much of the culture that has been accumulated within a society resides within **subcultures**.

These subcultures share some of the common culture with others, but not all of it. Without some shared culture, though, there can be no society because we would no longer have the social relationships that are requisite for society. And without social relationships and society, there can be no culture.

Social Structure and Culture Influence People Together

Social structure and culture both limit and change people's behaviours. First, they both cause different kinds of people to act in similar ways in the same social situation. They shape people's actions in a way that the situation dictates and, in that sense, limit their actions. Given the same situation—for example, a church, a classroom, a theatre, or a bus queue—people with very different histories, attitudes, and lifestyles will all behave similarly.

Second, social structure and culture both cause the same people to act differently in different social situations. In that way, they are change-producing. So, for example, people in authority—police officers, bank presidents, judges, and schoolteachers—who may behave carefully and even stiffly while on duty, cut loose when they are among friends or at a party. Then they are likely to make as much noise and tell as many dumb jokes as your friends do in the same situation. Social situations change us—even the stiffest of us—in similar ways.

The social forces that limit and change us are both outside and inside us. During childhood, we learn the norms, values, and beliefs that are part of our culture, and we internalize them—take them inside ourselves. We will consider in chapter 3 how this occurs through the process of **socialization**. In chapter 6, on deviance, we will see how external social sanctions are also brought to bear to limit and change people's behaviour.

Note that our description of the consequences of social structure and culture is precisely opposite to the assumptions that underlie genetics, biology, and personality psychology. According to sociology, people's behaviours vary according to the social structural context and subculture in which they find themselves. According to genetics, biology, and personality psychology, people do not vary much from one situation to another—a view that is hard to defend in the light of observable reality.

Consider the sociological approach to problem gambling—a topic that is gaining ever more public attention and concern. Problem gambling is kind of addiction—like an addiction to drugs or alcohol—and as such it is intensely personal. Yet sociological research shows that the risk of problem gambling varies from one social group to another. Young men run the highest risk. Certain ethnic groups run a higher than average risk, for reasons that are not yet fully understood. People who live near to casinos run a higher than average risk, for reasons that are not as hard to understand. What this tells us is that personal behaviour is subject to social and cultural influences. We learn how to behave—even how to misbehave—in social situations, and practise our knowledge in other social situations. As a result, to a large degree our behaviour can be predicted by looking at situational characteristics.

The reason we behave predictably in social situations is because otherwise, social interaction becomes impossible. No one knows what to say or do. Social life rests on situational predictability, especially when strangers are interacting with other strangers. This is obvious in many settings. Consider the university or college classroom. There, surrounded by 50, 100, or even 500 students, the professor cannot deal with students in a personalized, intimate manner. He or she must act according to the students' (and institution's) expectations—specifically, to act "professionally," in a serious, concerned, and knowledgeable manner. The students, in return, must also act "professionally," or else the classroom interaction breaks down. Both teacher and student start wondering what to say and do next.

We learn to value stable relationships. Often, we don't know how to change them. Sometimes, the people who hold power in our society are strongly invested in maintaining these relationships and oppose changing them. People with the most to gain urge us to meet other people's expectations. We will discuss all the reasons for this throughout the course of this book.

Researchers have found that what we learn about one social relationship—for example, the teacher–student relationship—can help us understand other, quite different social relationships. The similarities and differences between relationships fascinate sociology. The structures they form when fitted together also fascinate sociology. Sociologists love to study the relationship between small structures and large structures—their similarities, differences, and interconnections. And they love to apply insights and concepts developed in studying one social situation to understanding a different situation. For an example of this, see chapter 5 on small groups and large organizations.

This willingness to generalize is one of sociology's most distinctive features. In the end, sociology is the study of all social structures and cultures—from two-position (or dyadic) relationships, such as doctors and patients or marriages, to business enterprises or political campaigns, all the way up to total societies and global empires.

The Reason for Society and Culture

Our society and culture are undergoing major changes, as we shall see, but they are also persistent. Why do society and culture exist, and why do they persist over time? Perhaps it is foolish to ask this question. After all, nobody has suggested they are about to disappear, except in observations that the Canadian and American societies and cultures are becoming more similar, moving toward one culture and one society. Most of us take the survival of Canadian society and culture for granted. Yet it will be useful to pursue the matter briefly, because understanding why society and culture exist helps us to understand what they are.

There are two basic arguments for the necessity of society and culture, one based on a conception of human nature, the other on the problem of human survival. First, the individual organism is helpless to meet its own needs at birth and for quite a while afterward. People must protect and sustain it; otherwise it will quickly perish. What is required of the human organism is a complex learning process: to acquire the culture, to learn the things necessary to

live. This must come from prolonged association with others, which means at least an elementary form of society.

From this, in turn, we can derive another point: through prolonged association with others (and especially after interaction is facilitated by the acquisition of language), the person begins to become attached to interaction itself. The individual is bound more firmly than ever to relations with others. The person comes to need to be loved and to love, to need to give and receive respect and consideration. We all come to feel that it is painful not to be respected and not to have people close to us. Thus, becoming human means sharing in a social and cultural existence that is always more than physical survival.

The second reason for the persistence of society and culture is survival. Human survival in a sometimes capricious, often hostile, environment can only be accomplished if human beings act collectively. Co-operation can accomplish things no one could manage alone. From this perspective, society is a collective adaptation to a natural environment, a process of finding how to live co-operatively to make the natural order yield enough to sustain life. Through co-operative activity among an aggregate of people, skills are acquired, knowledge is accumulated, techniques and tools are developed, and all are transmitted to the next generation through the culture.

From this argument come two other observations: for any society to exist it must organize people, and sustaining organization makes additional demands on people to accept the requirements of a collective existence. Social organization requires co-ordination and control processes, procedures for assigning individuals to roles and tasks, and means to teach the culture in order to produce people who can fill the roles well. A society is carried on by the actions of its members; each new member must learn what the necessary actions are.

Human beings, then, cannot even survive physically except through co-operation to produce food, protection, and care. This means that work is a central human activity. Many sociologists believe this is sufficient reason for concluding that the economy is the basic form of organization of any society, from which all else is derived—the activity necessary to provide the material basis for life that is required before anything else can occur in the society.

French sociologist Pierre Bourdieu has done the most important work in the sociology of culture. Bourdieu (1930–2002) was one of the best-known

French sociologists. His work was grounded in everyday life. Bourdieu extended Karl Marx's term *capital* into categories of economic capital, **social capital**, symbolic capital, and **cultural capital**. He was also known as a politically engaged, socially progressive intellectual. He will be best remembered, however, for his research into subcultures of taste and distinction, examining the relationship between social status, cultural consumption, and social connectedness (Bourdieu, 1984).

The Development of Sociology

Sociology developed during the nineteenth and twentieth centuries as people attempted to grapple with new changes and challenges. Two revolutions were critical to the growth of sociology. The Industrial Revolution, starting around 1776, changed people's lives by drawing them into harsh urban conditions and new kinds of exploitive, impersonal work relationships. The French Revolution, starting in 1789, convinced people throughout the West that new kinds of social and political arrangement were possible and should be pursued. Both revolutions provided a fertile ground for the study of social change and social problems. We typically credit three individuals with founding sociology as a scientific discipline: Karl Marx, Émile Durkheim, and Max Weber.

Karl Marx

Karl Marx (1818–83) was not, strictly speaking, a sociologist. Nevertheless, sociology derived many of its key concepts—such as the term **class**—from his work. Marx explains most social phenomena in terms of class struggles and economic processes ([1867] 1967; Marx and Engels, [1848] 1948).

According to Marxist theory, in a capitalist society like Canada the **bourgeoisie**—the social class comprising the owners of the **means of production**—is in control. As the controllers of factories and business establishments, the bourgeoisie can decide the nature of the work for the second, lower class of society, the **proletariat**. This latter group, lacking the means to produce merchandise on their own, must resort to selling the only remaining commodity they have: their labour power. The bourgeoisie, recognizing the proletariat's dependence on the wages earned from work, are free to exploit the labour of the working class and to amass more wealth for themselves. They keep wages low to ensure that their workers remain dependent on them for economic survival. By manipulating the schools and mass media, they ensure that popular thinking continues to support the unequal distribution of wealth and power in society.

This practice, which began with the rise of industrial capitalism, continues in the present era, Marxist theory argues. Those who control the means of production continue to control the market system, although in a post-industrial economy the controllers are no longer just local factory owners. Today, multinational corporations—or, more precisely, the powerful executives who run them—continue to amass huge annual profits that are grossly inconsistent with the payment offered to their employees.

Marx and Friedrich Engels ([1848] 1955) contended that a revolution that would eliminate ruling and subordinate classes forever by eliminating private property—by placing the means of production in the hands of **the state**—would bring better conditions for all. With the eventual "withering away" of the state, communism would end history as we have known it, for it would end social classes and class conflict.

A twentieth-century sociologist working in the neo-Marxist tradition, Gerhard Lenski, deserves special mention. It was Lenski who pointed out that social inequalities have big consequences for societies only when there is a large surplus to divide. In early pre-industrial (and even pre-agricultural) societies, there was little surplus, so there was little inequality. Factors that led to a growth in food surplus (such as new hunting and farming technologies) indirectly led to more social distinctions (such as the growth of aristocracy, warrior classes, priestly classes, and the like) and more inequality (Lenski, 1966; Lenski, Nolan, and Lenski, 1995).

Lenski does not view ownership of the means of production as the only factor that influences inequality and social change. Inequality and social change are also influenced by technological development and the resulting development of new social classes and social forms that produce even more growth in surplus. Changes in population and the environment, which also affect the amount of food surplus, also affect inequality and change. Finally, the cultural factors that promote and legitimate all these changes also stimulate the growth of surplus, the translation of surplus into social difference, and the translation of social difference into inequality. The overall result is a continuing evolution of

1.2

Open for Discussion
Racism Through Inaction

Cutting Toronto's school community advisers is tantamount to racism, a former trustee charged last night.

"How else can we describe it? The direct impact of losing these people is going to fall on the ethno-racial community," Tam Goossen told a committee room packed with concerned parents gathered to discuss the effects of Paul Christie's recently-announced cuts to the Toronto District School Board.

"This is the only group of people here that bring the school system and diverse community groups together," said Goossen, a former chair of the board's race relations committee.

More than 40 people jammed the Toronto District School Board committee room last night, representing groups such as the Iranian Parents Organization, the Vietnamese Parents Organization and Parents of Black Children. They were united by a fear that the loss of the board's 24 full-time community advisers would hamper access to the education system for immigrant and low-income families.

As recently as last year, there were 40 school community advisers, working in high-needs neighbourhoods to help parents navigate the school system and communicate their concerns to the school board.

They do everything from translating meetings for parents who don't speak English, to helping them understand how the Toronto school system works, and even helping create separate parent groups.

That's what they did for the Toronto Federation of Chinese Parents, said co-chair Philip Wong.

"If you want your kid to have better academic behaviour, you've got to get involved as a parent in the school system—by going to forums, meeting with counsellors, learning what the school does and how the school system operates," said Wong, who arrived in Canada 25 years ago from Hong Kong.

Christie was appointed by Education Minister Elizabeth Witmer in August after the board failed to pass a balanced budget. Elimination of the community advisers' jobs will save $700,000. It was just one of the $90 million in cuts Christie proposed last month.

SOURCE: Catherine Porter, "Parents Lobby for Advisers," *The Toronto Star*, 18 Dec. 2002. Reprinted with permission Torstar Syndication Services.

---

human societies in relationship to technology and the natural environment.

Marx, for his part, viewed all social differences and social inequalities in terms of relations to the means of production. The master difference in every society is whether a person owns the means of production or has to sell his or her labour to its owner. All other differences pale in importance beside this difference, and all the important social inequalities flow from this difference. For Marx, the only way to eliminate harmful differences and inequalities is to eliminate private ownership of the means of production.

Marx's work was noteworthy for many reasons. He tried to uncover **objective**, scientific laws with which to understand society. He also tried to use his-tory to predict the future course of economic and social change. Marx's questions about how society works remain relevant today, even for scholars who reject his answers.

Émile Durkheim

One of those who rejected some of Marx's answers and modified others was the French scholar Émile Durkheim (1858–1917). Durkheim was one of the first European academics to describe himself as a sociologist, and he devoted much of his career to establishing sociology as a distinct and respected form of social research.

Durkheim was remarkable in a great many ways, not least for the breadth of his interests and scholarship. To win his professorial position—as the first Jew to hold a professorship in the French university system—Durkheim had to write not one but two doctoral theses. One thesis, written in Latin on the French seventeenth-century thinker Charles-Louis de Secondat, baron de Montesquieu, showed the line of intellectual development from political philosophy to what we today think of as sociology. It asked about the social conditions that give rise to different kinds of laws. A second thesis, written in French on the topic of industrialization, was the classic work still read today, *The Division of Labor in Society* ([1893] 1964). It discussed the problems associated with an increased social differentiation that results from industrialization. Durkheim asks, how is social order possible in a highly differentiated secular society?

Other classic works mapped out the direction the sociological discipline would go in the next century. *Suicide* ([1897] 1951) showed how intensely personal troubles—and solutions such as suicide—are socially structured. For example, Durkheim showed that single people and Protestants are much more likely to commit suicide than married people and Catholics, and he provided a theory to explain why. *Rules of the Sociological Method* ([1895] 1964), as the name suggests, set out a strategy for sociological (as distinct from psychological or philosophical) research, and includes a remarkable speculation on the "normality of crime." In *The Elementary Forms of Religious Life* ([1912] 1965), Durkheim addresses the social nature of religion, arguing that religion—including the use of gods and other ritual objects—is a celebration of society itself, with the effect of producing social cohesion.

Durkheim is remembered for his attempts to develop rigorous and consistent sociological research methods, such as his use of suicide rates to uncover the link between suicide and social factors. Though some of Durkheim's assumptions and findings are rejected today, his image of sociology continues to inspire sociologists.

In relation to the central sociological questions we mentioned earlier, Durkheim believed that social differentiation was a natural—and acceptable—result of the complex division of labour that accompanies industrialization. For Durkheim, the central sociological questions of interest are, how can we prevent extreme differentiation from isolating everyone and causing anomie (normlessness)? How can we prevent it from creating extreme, exploitive inequality? How can we build cohesive communities that take advan-

tage of the wide differences between people? In connection with this last question, Durkheim spent a great deal of time looking for the basis of "organic solidarity" in complex societies ([1893] 1964).

A twentieth-century sociologist who follows, loosely, in the tradition of Durkheim is Daniel Bell, who studied the rise of what he called *post-industrial society* (1979). What is different about post-industrial society is that wealth is produced by the combination of capital, knowledge, and information. Service industries and professions are the dominant forms of occupation. Compare this with an *industrial society*, in which wealth is produced by the combination of capital, labour, and raw materials. There, manual workers and managers (or supervisors) are the dominant forms of occupation.

What is unchanged since Durkheim's time is the need to pull culture into conformity with the new social, political, and economic forms that result from this new, complicated mode of production. Cultural "contradictions" can result. For example, Bell writes of modern Western societies that

> the social structure today is ruled by an economic principle of rationality, defined in terms of efficiency in the allocation of resources; the culture, in contrast, is prodigal, promiscuous, dominated by an antirational, anti-intellectual temper. The character structure inherited from the nineteenth century—with its emphasis on self-discipline, delayed gratification, restraint—is still relevant to the demands of the social structure; but it clashes sharply with the culture, where such bourgeois value have been completely rejected—in part, as we shall see, and paradoxically, because of the workings of the capitalist system itself. (1979: 432–3)

For Bell, as for Durkheim, there is a question about how to bring together the forces of social, economic, political, and cultural change.

Max Weber

Like Durkheim, Max Weber (1864–1920) modified or rejected much of Marx's approach, but he did so for different reasons. In particular, Weber rejected the idea that any single factor or set of factors determines either society or the individual. Weber saw society as an extraordinarily complex set of social relationships. In his view, we can never completely explain society and predict its course. All we can do is try to understand the more important factors and identify the impact these factors have had on history (Weber, [1923] 1961).

Like Durkheim, Weber had a remarkable breadth of knowledge and interests. Trained in the law, Weber naturally had a far greater interest in structures of authority than either Marx or Durkheim. Accordingly, he wrote seminal works on the sociological bases of law, business, bureaucracy, and political organization. He studied structures of domination and power in a variety of historical settings. Weber was particularly interested in social change and social innovations. He saw the development of cities, of bureaucracy, and of institutional science as key elements in the transformation of Western civilization; they had all made a significant contribution to social and economic change. Not everything was due to the rise of capitalism, as Marx had argued.

In fact, the rise of capitalism was itself dependent on other social factors, Weber argued. These factors included the development of supportive religions such as Protestantism. Thus, Weber turned Marx on his head: religion was not a mere handmaiden of economics, an opiate to dull the senses of oppressed workers—it was a key motivation for capital accumulation. Like Durkheim, Weber viewed religion as a central expression of people's social structure and culture—their deepest beliefs and aspirations. Accordingly, he wrote books comparing humanity's key religions—Hinduism, Confucianism, Judaism, and Christianity, among others—to explain why capitalism arose when and where it did.

Weber addressed the questions of difference and inequality in yet another way. He was particularly interested in how ruling parties and classes used beliefs—including ideologies, religions, and **rational-legal** strategies—to support and legitimate advantageous differences. Inequalities do not make and maintain themselves. People need to be persuaded that they are natural, inevitable, or even desirable before they will co-operate in their own subordination. Neither Marx nor Durkheim was sufficiently systematic in recognizing and studying the "idea content" of social inequality.

Unlike Marx, who saw scholarship as an instrument for revolution as well as understanding, and Durkheim, who saw scholarship as a means of addressing current social problems, Weber did not view scholarship in a practical, instrumental light. He felt that human societies were too complex and subject to continuous change to permit successful prediction, much less social engineering.

Sociology is just one of the fields of study designed to help describe and explain human behaviour. Others include history, journalism, philosophy, and psychology. Sociology differs from psychology in that it studies social relationships or groups observed in society. (© Bill Wittman)

Weber's impact on modern sociology is immense. He opened up new areas of research, on organization, urbanization, and politics. He refined the sociological approach to understanding religion, stratification, and economic life. Most important, Weber argued for a careful historical scholarship that avoided easy answers and simple, universal explanations.

Four Sociological Paradigms

Today there are four major theoretical approaches to the study of society and social behaviour, and two of them were developed from the works of Durkheim, Marx, and Weber. The **structural functionalist** approach and the **conflict approach** emphasize research at the macrosociological level of the whole society or its major institutions, although these perspectives are sometimes applied to social behaviour in small groups too. The **symbolic interactionist** perspective features microanalysis of small groups and interpersonal interaction. The **feminist** perspective is rooted in macrosociological analysis, but it also has been effectively applied to research on small groups and interpersonal interaction.

These four approaches have also been called *sociological perspectives* or **paradigms**. A *perspective* or *paradigm* is a general way of seeing the world. It embodies broad assumptions about the nature of society and social behaviour. It suggests which questions to ask in research and how to interpret the answers obtained from research. We will briefly describe each of the four approaches here, and then you will see them applied repeatedly to different subjects in the various chapters of this textbook. In chapter 22, which focuses on sociological theory, you will find a more detailed summary of the elements of these theories.

Structural Functionalism

The structural functionalist perspective is based on Émile Durkheim's work. It views society as a set of interconnected elements that operate together in equilibrium to maintain the overall stability and efficiency of the society as a whole. For example, the individual social institutions—families, the economy, government, education, and others—are each said to make a vital contribution to the functioning of the larger society. Families operate to reproduce and nurture members of society; the economy regulates the production, distribution, and consumption of goods and services; government controls conflict between groups and contributes to the sharing of values and norms; and education socializes young people, teaching them things they will need to know for adult life.

Robert Merton (1957), a key figure in the development of this perspective, argued that social institutions perform both manifest and latent functions. *Manifest functions* are outcomes that are intended and easily recognized; *latent functions* are unintended and hidden from participants. Education, for example, is manifestly responsible for providing students with the knowledge, skills, and cultural values that will help them to operate effectively in society. Both the school system and its participants formally recognize these functions. At a latent level, however, education also functions as an institutional "babysitter" for young children and teenagers not yet ready to work full-time or to roam the streets independently while their parents are at work, and as a "matchmaker" where older high school and university students socialize with potential future lovers or marriage partners. These functions, though important to society and

accomplished with equal success, are considered latent because they are not the intended consequences envisioned by designers of the educational system, nor are they acknowledged in any official way by school administrators, students, or parents.

Structural functionalists argue that because society is a system of interrelated parts, changes in one part of society always produce changes—unintended—in another part. Society is always reacting and readjusting to new inputs, even when people do not intend the changes that occur. This fact is important for both sociology and social planning. Unless we are aware of the likely consequences of a planned change—the latent and the manifest functions—we are likely to end up with changes we did not want. One sociologist (Sieber, 1981) has coined the term *fatal remedies* to describe attempts at social planning that fail to think through the consequences. In the end, they may do more (unintended) harm than they do (intended) good. At the least, they produce new, unforeseen problems. This is because any society is an extremely complex, unpredictable social system.

Functionalists argue that sometimes there is a failure of institutions to fulfill their functions, particularly during times of rapid change. They believe that sudden and major social change sometimes disrupts traditional values and common ways of doing things. For example, during the phases of industrialization and urbanization in Western Europe and North America in the late nineteenth and early twentieth centuries, crime, poverty, unsanitary living conditions, environmental pollution, and other forms of social disorganization increased sharply. Durkheim ([1893] 1964a, [1897] 1964b, [1912] 1965) introduced the term *anomie*, or normlessness, as a name for this condition in which social norms are weak and different values are in conflict with one another. As traditional forms of guidance break down, social control declines, and people bond less with one another; they become more likely to commit non-conforming, deviant acts (crime, drug use, and so on). The general solution to this situation, according to the functionalist perspective, is to strengthen social norms and slow the pace of social change.

The functionalists' emphasis on the interconnectedness of society has been useful in highlighting the ways in which one part of the society influences other parts. For example, recent changes to the family, such as the rise in divorces and in single parenting, have important consequences for work and education, particularly with respect to time constraints among those juggling the dual—and conflicting—roles of employee and parent.

Functionalists would emphasize the unexpected consequences of easier divorce laws and more births to unwed mothers. Ever more Canadian children are experiencing parental separation by ever younger ages (see Figure 1.1); this experience is particularly common among children whose parents were cohabiting, not legally married. The resulting lone parenthood, in turn, increases the likelihood of financial hardship, emotional stress, and worse parenting. These in turn can hinder the children's mental and physical health and can result in worse school outcomes.

Functionalists also assume that there is considerable agreement among people in the society on *values*—the valued goals that individuals believe they should pursue—and on the way the society and its institutions operate. Thus, functionalists would expect there to be considerable consensus on family values, the best type of political system to live under, the best form of economy, and so on, and within Canadian society the dominant value preferences would reflect the types of institutions that do exist.

In summary, the basic principles of the structural functionalist perspective are these:

1. Society is a system of interrelated parts, a social system, with each part contributing to the whole.
2. A social system tends to be stable, in equilibrium; when it changes, it changes gradually, especially if the change is for the better.
3. A society cannot remain stable unless there is considerable sharing of values and norms among people.
4. Societies persist through time because their parts, such as institutions, serve the survival needs of the whole.

Conflict Theory

Conflict theory has its roots in the basic division between the "haves" and the "have-nots" of society. Conflict theorists take exception to the structural functionalists' assumption of consensus in values among members of society and to the limited attention given to power struggles and competing interests within the population. The conflict perspective instead views society as largely a collection of disparate groups struggling over a limited supply of resources and power. Some have more resources and power than others, and this helps the haves to dominate and coerce the have-nots.

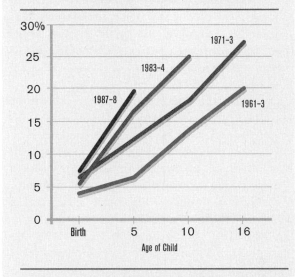

Figure 1.1 **Children Born to a Lone Parent or Who Have Experienced Parental Separation by Age and Year of Birth, Canada**

SOURCE: Adapted from Statistics Canada, *Social Trends in Canada* Seminar, Catalogue 10H0052, April 2002.

Conflict theory has its origins particularly in the works of Karl Marx (see, for example, [1844] 1970, [1867] 1965). As we have suggested, Marx believed that as societies make the transition from an agricultural to an industrial economy, the predominant social concerns of the people shift from survival to earning a living wage. In an industrialized, capitalist system, two broad classes emerge: the bourgeoisie and the proletariat. The Marxist conflict perspective argues that many of the social ills of society stem from the economic inequalities that exist between these two classes. Obviously, to hold wealth and power is to be in an enviable position, since one reaps the financial, political, and social benefits of a system that works in favour of one's own group over others. However, for the capitalist class to maintain its wealthy, privileged status, it must also ensure that those below it in power do not have an opportunity—and if possible, even the desire—to encroach upon the power of the bourgeoisie. Because the bourgeoisie reap so much economic gain from the system without giving much back in the form of social welfare support, there are sizeable minorities who live in poverty. This poverty of the less fortunate working and lower classes is a problem since it is unjust and conflict-producing. Economic inequality also underlies many other social problems, including crime, unemployment, homelessness, racism, and physical and mental health problems.

Marxists also contend that labourers in a capitalist system experience a feeling of **alienation** from the processes and products of their labour since these processes and products are highly fragmented and specialized. They have narrow job functions and are therefore powerless to control or change the conditions of their work.

Besides exploiting their workers, boardroom executives—the post-industrial successors to the factory owners of the industrial era—sometimes maximize profits through the perpetration of *corporate violence*: actual and potential harm caused to workers, consumers, and the public for the sake of the company's efficiency or success. Examples of this include failing to remedy unsafe working conditions, exposing employees to hazardous materials, knowingly marketing dangerous or inferior products, and releasing industrial pollution into the environment.

Two main criticisms of the Marxian conflict theory approach are that, historically, communist societies founded on Marxism have failed either to prosper or to eliminate inequality and that the approach overemphasizes the importance of one type of inequality—class inequality—at the expense of other types of inequality and social injustice. Non-Marxist conflict theories argue that there are several forms of inequality. While they recognize the value people place on differences in income and class, proponents of this perspective believe that other divergent interests and characteristics can also lead to conflict and oppression. Thus, conflict theorists have noted that women and men have competing interests and that this is a cause of social conflict and social problems too. Others cite the conflicting interests of various ethnic groups, for example, Aboriginal and non-Aboriginal groups in Canada or blacks and whites in North America. Still other dimensions of social conflict involve, for example, heterosexuals and homosexuals, the young and the old, liberals and conservatives, urbanites and rural-dwellers, and enviro-nmentalists and industrialists.

Conflict theorists do not consider conflict a destructive force. Instead, they believe it focuses attention on social problems and brings people together to solve these problems. Sociologists working within this perspective would emphasize that conflict has been central to the women's movement, the civil rights movements, and trade unionism, among other beneficial social movements. Conflict is more common than consensus, and conflict can serve as the vehicle of positive social change, conflict theorists say.

This outlook on social life also focuses attention away from shared values and toward ideologies. An *ideology* is a coherent set of interrelated beliefs about the nature of the world and of people. It guides a person's interpretation of and reaction to external events. *Dominant ideology* is the ideology of the dominant group, justifying its power and wealth. The rest of us do not rebel because we have come to believe in the dominant ideology. We teach young people this ideology in the schools, churches, and media; we hear it repeated throughout life. Ideas included in the dominant ideology of this society are "people are poor because they are lazy; they could get ahead more if they were not so lazy" and "women who get less pay than men for the same job don't want to be paid at a similar rate to men." Sociological research has shown that these forms of "common sense" are patently false.

The work of Max Weber also inspired sociologists who follow the conflict approach. Weber argued that conflict arises as much over values, status, and a sense of personal honour as economic status. From Weber's point of view, even modern corporations with no identifiable owner experience conflict. The bureaucratic managers of the corporation come to think of themselves as a **status group** and act to further their own group interests. That is why, Weberian theorists argue, conflict can be found in *any* large society, not only in capitalist societies.

A key modern proponent of conflict theory today is Jürgen Habermas. In his critical analysis of Western institutions and rationality, Habermas stresses the humanist side of Marx's work as a critic and examines tensions between theory and practice in philosophy. Bridging the connections between sociology and philosophy, Habermas's major work, *The Theory of Communicative Action* (1984), addresses not only philosophies of agency and rationality, but also the theories of sociologists such as Max Weber, George Herbert Mead, Émile Durkheim, and Talcott Parsons.

We can summarize the basic assumptions of the conflict perspective as follows:

1. Societies are always changing.
2. Conflict and power differentials are always present in society as groups pursue their interests.
3. Conflict is a major contributor to social change.

Symbolic Interactionism

Whereas the structural functionalist and conflict perspectives focus on large elements of society such as social institutions and major demographic groups, symbolic interactionists focus on the opposite end of the sociological spectrum: on small groups and interpersonal interactions.

Symbolic interactionism sees society as a product of face-to-face interaction between people using symbols. In simple terms, a *symbol* is something that meaningfully represents something else. It can be a written or spoken word, a gesture, or a sign (such as a raised fist). Thus, the language that humans share and use in their interaction is a system of symbols and their understood meanings. *Interaction* refers to the ways in which two or more people respond to one another. Most interaction between human beings is symbolic, in the sense that it depends on words and actions that have meanings beyond themselves. A frown, a kiss, and a smile all have meanings that we learn, share, and change through interaction. Some acts even have hidden meanings and double meanings.

One of the outstanding works in this tradition is *The Social Construction of Reality*, by Peter Berger and Thomas Luckmann (1966). These authors claim that the job of sociology is to understand "the reality of everyday life"—how it is experienced, co-ordinated, and organized. They point out that the everyday world is an *intersubjective* world, meaning that we must all work to find communicative meeting places for common or shared understanding. They also emphasize that the everyday world is "taken for granted," and it is the job of the sociologist to make us aware of the socially constructed nature of the world.

Symbolic interactionism focuses on the processes by which people interpret and respond to the actions of others. It studies the way social structures, as patterns of behaviour, arise out of these processes. When naming the approach "symbolic interactionism" in 1937, Herbert Blumer described the basic elements of the paradigm in terms of three propositions: (1) "human beings act toward things on the basis of the meanings that things have for them"; (2) these meanings "arise out of social interaction"; and (3) social action results from a "fitting together of individual lines of action" (1937: 172). This perspective was strongly promoted by Blumer, but it also has roots in the work of a group of scholars centred at the University of Chicago in the early twentieth century,

among them George Herbert Mead, W.I. Thomas, and Robert Park.

One forerunner of the interactionist approach was German sociologist Georg Simmel ([1943] 1997), who investigated the effects of urbanization on group relations at the community level. He found the urban lifestyle to be relentless and ultimately alienating, with inhabitants numbing their emotional contacts with others in order to cope with the excessive stimulation that city life offered. The fragmentation of urban life leads to a reduction in shared experience, Simmel argued. It is within such a framework of distinctive, isolated, and isolating experiences that urban people must work out their social lives.

The symbolic interactionist sees society as the product of interaction between people in their everyday social relationships. In these relationships, the culture of the larger society is adapted to daily life, and sometimes new ways of doing things are developed. Culture is fluid rather than static; it is always open to revision. It is especially situated in specific relationships and occasions for interpersonal interaction. Thus, society and its social relationships are always changing, always being reconstructed by people (Blumer, 1937).

One of the types of shared meanings emphasized in the symbolic interactionist approach is "the definition of the situation." It is this that guides the course of interaction in social relationships. A *definition of the situation* is a person's understanding of the package of norms governing and regulating a social situation, such as a classroom, a hockey game, or an office. It includes norms defining the appropriate reasons for people's participation in the situation and the goals one may properly pursue within it. It also spells out how these goals may be achieved, as well as regulating the relationships among the various participants. Because definitions are also shared, they permit people to co-ordinate their actions in pursuing their goals. Seen this way, a definition of a situation is a source of meaning for participants because it permits them to make sense of the situation (Thomas and Thomas, 1926).

Definitions of the situation emerge out of interpersonal negotiations. Negotiations may be formal and explicit (for example, when a contract is drafted between a union and an employer). However, most agreements are less dramatic and tangible, as people informally and tacitly communicate with each other about the situations in which they find themselves. Communication is verbal, but it may also consist of gestures, body language, and people's attire.

One way people communicate involves the impressions they create, sometimes intentionally and other times unintentionally, when they first encounter each other. Wearing a clerical collar, highly polished shoes, or jeans, having one's hair in a bun, or introducing oneself as "doctor"—all have consequences for how people regard one another. **Impression management** and first impressions foster understandings about the meaning people attach to their relationships, their goals, and what actions are acceptable and unacceptable to them. People have many motives governing how they present themselves and the kinds of interpretations they invite. They may or may not be conscious of these motives, and they may or may not be sensitive to the cues they convey to others. Symbolic interactionists also study these social processes.

Society is fluid and dynamic, according to interactionists, but this does not mean that it is unlicensed except for the whims of the people involved. Situations physically and socially constrain what can reasonably be done in them and therefore limit the kinds of definitions that are effectively available. It is difficult to play ice hockey, for example, where there is no ice. Likewise, what we do in the classroom is surely constrained by the facts of organizational life outside the classroom. **Sexual harassment** policies, for instance, remind those who are forgetful that the larger community has a continuing interest in what transpires within the classroom as well as the workplace.

A definition of the situation constrains interaction, but it is not rigid. Relationships between fellow workers or between customers and clerks sometimes turn into romantic relationships, which is to say that the relationships have been redefined. Symbolic interactionists are therefore interested in the tactics used to redefine and reconstruct relationships. *Seduction*, for example, refers to a class of interpersonal manoeuvres that bring about a redefinition of the relationship between a man and a woman. The possibility of such redefinitions underscores the fact that people are actively involved in exploiting and modifying the social situation and are not merely its puppets. The interactionist studies such redefinitions of the situation and how they came about.

The structural functionalist and conflict perspectives do not necessarily contradict the symbolic interactionist approach, or vice versa. For one thing, the meanings studied by symbolic interactionists are not at all unique or original to a particular relationship.

Much of it has its origins in the larger society and is reworked for the immediate requirements of a particular relationship. We can also easily imagine interpersonal negotiations begin studied by sociologists working within the structural functionalist and conflict perspectives, even though this would not be a priority for them. Structural functionalists might analyze what is functional in such negotiations, while conflict theorists might consider the different forms of conflict in such negotiations. The structural functionalist and conflict viewpoints emphasize, though, that there are important shared meanings beyond those found in small groups. In addition, these meanings are seen as less transitory and localized than the symbolic interactionist view might lead us to expect.

In relation to the central sociological questions we raised earlier, symbolic interactionists are enormously interested in the **social construction** of differences and inequalities. They would hold that understanding perceptions of difference and similarity, inferiority and superiority, is central to the sociological enterprise. Likewise, they would say that similar people lead different lives because they have been socially construed as different, thus deserving different opportunities. Why we treat some people as if they are more "different" than others and why we treat "different" people much worse than others are most important questions in the symbolic interactionist's library, starting with the classic statement of this problem by Erving Goffman, in *Stigma* (1964).

Summarizing, basic principles of the symbolic interaction perspective include these:

1. People are, above all else, symbol users; they acquire these symbols and their shared meaning through social interaction with others.
2. People respond to others and others' actions based on their understandings of meaning in the particular situation—their definition of the situation.
3. Society and the social groups within it are processes whereby people have constructed meanings and have negotiated social interaction.

The Feminist Perspective

A fourth paradigm that is ever more influential in sociology is the feminist perspective. It can be traced back two centuries, to work in philosophy by Mary Wollstonecraft, in *A Vindication of the Rights of Woman* ([1792] 1986).

Since the nineteenth century, there have been at least three waves of feminist activity and research.

The first wave of feminism occurred from the middle of the nineteenth century through the early twentieth century. It culminated in women's gaining the right to vote in many Western countries. Then two strands of feminism emerged: one concerned with the objective of gaining equal rights with men in the public sphere, the other with gaining recognition of women's difference from men and improving their position in the private sphere of the family. This second wave, or re-emergence, of feminism crystallized in the 1960s. It saw the development of the modern women's movement, which has greatly influenced sociology. Modern feminism has focused research on the oppression that women commonly experience. In addition, recent feminist scholarship has emphasized the diversity of women's experience as members of different countries, classes, and racial and ethnic groups.

One widely accepted distinction is that between *radical feminism* and *materialist (socialist or Marxist) feminism*. Radical feminism—perhaps the dominant form of feminism in the United States—is characterized by a belief that **patriarchy** is the main and universal cause of women's oppression, owing to the superior power of men over women. This view has promoted the notion that women must organize separately from men to protect their own interests and foster a distinct women's culture. Materialist feminism—which is equally important in Canada and dominant outside North America—traces its roots to **Marxism** and, like Marxism, views gender relations in a historical, economic context. It sees social class relations as determining the conditions women experience within capitalism. This approach calls for women to organize alongside men of the same social class to solve the problems women are suffering.

The two main types of feminism have in common a belief that the domination of women is a result not of **biological determinism**, but of socio-economic and ideological factors. Though they differ in thinking about the ways we might achieve this, both types are committed to eliminating the continued social inequality of women. Feminists view most, if not all, gender differences as socially constructed, and all gender inequalities as socially constructed. For feminists, patriarchy is the cultural mechanism that translates differences of biology into differences of social condition and opportunity.

Feminism emphasizes that women and men have different experiences in the same social interaction. For example, men and women typically have differ-

Canadian society is made up of all the families, clubs, groups, corporations, and so on in which its members participate. Seeing the boundaries between the Canadian and American societies is sometimes difficult. But Canadians have different national symbols; we have a different culture. (© Bill Wittman)

ent views about divorce because the experience of divorce is different for men and women. For men, it means a brief reduction in the standard of living, if any reduction at all, and a huge reduction in parenting responsibilities. For women, it means a dramatic, long-term loss in income and standard of living. Poverty is common among single mothers and their children. Divorce also means an increase in parental responsibilities for women, since mothers retain custody of the children. For all these reasons, divorce has a different meaning for women than it does for men. Similarly, sex, love, marriage, housework, child care, and leisure time all have different meanings for men and women, as we will see in later chapters.

To be a woman in our society is to act out a role that others have defined, feminists emphasize. The "feminine" role tends to be a subservient one, in which women are sometimes degraded or victimized. Along with children, women are comparatively powerless and in danger of their lives (men far more kill women and children than women and children kill men, for example). Thus, women's acceptance of the female role is far more costly, even more dangerous, than men's acceptance of the male role.

Feminism is also a form of political activism, with an emancipatory goal. If gender relations always reflect the larger pattern of male-dominated social relations in a society, then changing gender relations requires changing those social relations as well. In this respect, feminism is one of the *new social movements*, which include the anti-war, youth, civil rights, and anti-racism movements that have in the last three decades reshaped modern politics. Like these other movements, feminism has appealed to the social identity—the personal life experience—of its supporters. More than that, by arguing that "the personal is political," feminism opened up new domains of social life—sexuality, housework, child rearing, and so on—to political debate and legislation. It also forces us all to examine the roots of our being as gendered subjects—that is, how we get to be, and to think of ourselves as, men or women, mothers or fathers. Thus, in a century, feminism has moved dramatically from demanding an equal access to social positions defined and dominated by men to demanding that we re-examine the organization of roles, identities, even knowledge about reality in a gendered society.

We can summarize essential characteristics of the feminist approach as follows (see Sydie, 1987):

1. All personal life has a political dimension.
2. The public and private spheres of life are both gendered (that is, unequal for men and women).
3. Patriarchy, or male control, is present in society.
4. Because of routinely different experiences and differences in power, women's and men's perceptions of reality differ.

Using the Four Sociological Perspectives

As we have seen, there are many differences between the four major approaches to research in sociology. Moreover, there is no simple relationship between the four main perspectives and the two broad levels of analysis—macrosociology and microsociology. True, symbolic interactionism specializes in microsociological analysis, functionalism and conflict theory in macrosociological analysis. The feminist approach calls for work at both levels of analyses, although it is especially rooted in understandings about macro-level processes that are underpinnings for the greater power of males. All four perspectives have something to contribute at both levels of analysis.

These four perspectives will keep reappearing in the chapters that follow, applied to the subject matter of the chapters wherever this helps the authors with explanations and descriptions of their topics. Sometimes the authors are explicit about their use of one or more of the theoretical perspectives; other times the matter is more implicit as the authors draw from studies conducted within each research tradition. Throughout this book, we will see that each of the four perspectives provides explanations for many of the same aspects of the social world. However, they lead us to look at different dimensions of the problem under study. Their answers concerning the topic are complementary.

There is no conclusive evidence that one paradigm is always or never appropriate, or that combining paradigms is misleading and fruitless. The clear implication of your further reading of this book will be that we gain nothing by ignoring one or more of the perspectives. Therefore, the best course one can follow in one's own research is to keep an open mind and consider the insights and evidence provided by any of the theoretical approaches applied to one's particular problem for study. A more holistic understanding of a topic is always to be preferred over a narrow consideration of the problem, because we learn more. Each of the perspectives is just that—a "perspective"; it directs our attention to particular issues, to the relative neglect of other issues. Therefore, giving some attention to the contributions of more than one perspective on the same research topic should add new data and new insights to our work. There are no better illustrations of this principle than the discussions chapter after chapter in this textbook.

We can illustrate the point with a brief example from microsociology where each approach might be used fruitfully. Consider how the four perspectives might be applied to studying university or college classes. The conflict theorist might look at the effects of authority and power differences between the teacher and students. The structural functionalist might study the functions of lectures, examinations, or term papers. The symbolic interactionist might study students' changing perceptions of their classes over the term and how these changes came about, or patterns of interaction during class and possibly before and after class. The feminist researcher might compare classes and look at the effects of having a female versus a male instructor upon class interaction by female and male students, and whether the content of the course materials was affected by the gender of the instructor. Obviously, the more of these perspectives we draw upon, the more we learn about the classes. The same is true of virtually any sociological topic we might want to study, micro or macro.

Sociologists will not always use different perspectives in their research because they are interested in analyzing a specific topic or because they want to execute the work quickly. A multi-perspective approach requires more research time. A sociologist will use his or her best estimate of the most useful approach, at least to begin with, always mindful that there is more research that can be done on the topic. In addition, it is common for sociologists to choose research problems suggested by their preferred theoretical perspective or the perspective that they is most familiar with. This being the case, it is all the more important that when we review others' published studies, we look at research done from different perspectives.

Sociology and Social Change

Social Change Is Constant

All sociologists, regardless of the theoretical perspective they work with or the research problems they study, will agree that societies and social institutions are changing all the time. First, routine change occurs because people flow through roles. People are born, grow up, and die. As individuals, generations, and members of different subcultures, these people play their roles differently. In addition, norms and roles change. They change because different kinds of people play the same roles and, as the symbolic interactionists emphasize, "negotiations" are constantly taking place.

Think of this more concretely, in terms of doctors and patients. Today, doctors are more specialized than in the past: this represents a change in the doctor role. However, the people playing doctor roles are changing too. Compared with 30 years ago, more doctors are women. More are immigrants. More are racial minorities. More have research experience as well as clinical experience. These facts all affect the ways they play the role and how they interact with patients.

Roles and institutions also change because people flow through them more quickly or in larger numbers and because institutions grow and shrink more rapidly. Think of this in terms of families. In the last 30 years, families have become smaller, have taken on

a wider variety of forms, and have been subject to much more rapid changes through higher rates of separation, divorce, cohabitation, and remarriage. These facts all affect the ways children experience childhood and family life compared with 30 years ago.

The Key Role of Social Innovations

Additionally, societies change because of changes in the ways that roles process flows of people, which happens because of material innovations, social and cultural innovations, and knowledge use and planning. A medical check-up today means interacting with many machines, few of which existed in anything like their present form 50 years ago. Likewise, family life has been changed by technology. Much of our family time is spent interacting with, or around, machines and substances that did not exist 50 years ago (computers, VCRs, microwave ovens) or that existed in drastically different forms (televisions, frozen foods). (See also Table 1.2.)

If we take a longer period, we can see that social innovations have been just as important as technological innovations in changing social life over the ages. Just think of the enormous importance of the following inventions, all of which involve numeracy— that is, numbers, numbering, or counting (Duncan, 1985):

- Voting
- Censuses
- Money and banking
- Competitions and examinations to measure competence
- Graduated rewards (for example, grades) and punishments (for example, prison sentences)
- Modern ideas of probability
- Random sampling to assure fairness in selection
- Public opinion polling
- Aptitude testing
- Measures of public well-being (for example, GNP per capita)

Not only were these innovations important in their own right, they also had important secondary effects, for example, increases in efficiency, productivity, and social engineering.

Consider also social inventions of a larger kind, such as representative government, the modern corporation, the bureaucracy, and the modern city. Max

Table 1.2   **Percentage of Internet Users Who Say Their Time Use for Various Activities Has Changed or Stayed the Same Since They Started Using the Internet, Canada, 2000**

Activity	Increased	Decreased	Stayed the Same
Watching TV	1	27	72
Reading books, magazines, newspapers	4	15	81
Sleeping	1	11	88
Doing leisure activities at home	2	11	87
Doing household chores	1	10	89
Shopping	2	8	90
Doing leisure activities outside the home	2	7	91
Visiting with and talking to family	3	7	90
Visiting with and talking to friends	5	6	89
Spending time with children	3	4	93

SOURCE: Adapted from Heather Dryburgh, *Changing Our Ways: Why and How Canadians Use the Internet* (Ottawa: Statistics Canada, 2001); Catalogue 56F0006, March 2001, and from the Staticstics Canada web site <www.statcan.ca/english/IPS/Data/71-542-XIE.htm>, accessed 15 May 2003.

Weber has a lot to say about the importance of each of these for the transformation of human social life. Weber also addressed himself to a variety of what we might call "moral inventions," such as new religions (for example, Protestantism), which were important in their own right and for their effects on capitalism and science, and political ideologies, such as liberal democracy, fascism, and communism, for their effects on industrialization. (See, for example, Weber, [1904], 1958; [1923] 1961).

A key sociologist in the tradition of Weber is Norbert Elias, who has studied the processes of state formation and nation-building, relating these to cultural and legal shifts in history. Elias (1994) has argued, for example, that the development of etiquette and good manners—which we associate with civility and civilization—was closely associated with the development of state-imposed order. That the proper use of knives and forks should be associated with the growth of central government is indeed a novel idea.

Sociologists Value Particular Forms of Change

Not all sociologists attempt to achieve social change through their research, but most sociologists place a high value on improving the lives of human beings. Whatever theoretical perspective a sociologist uses in his or her research, improvements in peoples' lives and in society as a whole are what he or she hopes will result from the research, even if the application of the research is left for others to do. And most research that leads to better understanding of how society

operates can be useful for improving social life in some way. Research on some topics, such as social problems, is, of course, more directly useful for the betterment of peoples' lives than other research.

Sociology is, for the most part, an engaged, progressive, and optimistic discipline founded on the notion that people can improve society through research and the application of research-based knowledge. Consistent with this, we find that much of the research that sociologists do is guided by one or more of these seven value preferences (Alvarez, 2000):

- Life over death
- Health over sickness
- Knowing over not knowing
- Co-operation over conflict
- Freedom of movement over physical restraint
- Self-determination over direction by others
- Freedom of expression over restraint of communication

In this sense, sociology may be said to be a "moral enterprise," and a humanistic one. Sociologists value the outcomes listed above and pursue these outcomes. As a result, much research in sociology criticizes the existing social order. Much of the sociological literature shows a desire to change society, protect the vulnerable, and redress injustices.

Researchers are concerned with combating myths, ideologies, and stereotypes—for example, about women, visible minorities, poor people, the elderly, or youth—that perpetuate harmful conditions for vulnerable peoples. A related concern is the frequently observed tendency for "public issues" to be turned into "private troubles." The public and public officials wrongly see a social problem as the personal responsibility of the sufferers, who are blamed for having these problems.

Consider as an example research on depressive disorders, which are a major public health problem today. The general public and health practitioners see depressive disorders as personal problems of individuals. However, depression occurs frequently and produces severe suffering for the people affected and their families, leading to higher risks of death, disability, and secondary illness. For various reasons, including the aging of the population and the extended life expectancy of people suffering from chronic physical disorders, the frequency of depressive disorders has been increasing and will increase in years to come. Sociologists have been emphasizing how ideological thinking about these disorders, which blames the victims, should be questioned, and they have been making clear the social nature of these disorders to policy makers and the public (Sartorius, 2001).

Like many other sociologists today, and just like two centuries ago when sociology began, we assume that the purpose of sociology is to use knowledge to improve social life. Thus, one of the goals of a book like this is to aid our understanding of how people's lives may be improved by better understanding how society and culture operate.

The Individual, Organizations, and Social Change

We need good, sound knowledge of society to be well equipped to change things. Then we as individuals can pursue changes to better the life circumstances in which we find ourselves, or we can work to improve the lives of others. There are important individual actions and actions of groups and organizations to be considered for these tasks. For social change affecting large numbers of people, we must mobilize actions of groups or organizations. For some changes in our own daily lives, certain individual actions will be sufficient.

C. Wright Mills's (1959) point in describing the sociological imagination in the way he did was that knowledge can be power—if individuals or groups choose to act upon it. That is to say, when we know what is going on in society and then act accordingly and in our best interests, we stand some chance of maximizing our opportunities. Under individual-level solutions, we can act to "work the system" to our specific benefit.

A good example of this is our earlier discussion of how people find jobs. Armed with the results of sociological analysis of what types of job searches turn out to be most successful, you can better maximize your chances of finding a good job, being careful to draw on both strong and weak ties as sources of information, not de-emphasizing the latter. As a second example, if you learn that some sections of the workforce are shrinking while others are expanding, you can consider preparing yourself for a job you would like in one of the expanding sectors. We all have choices of this type to make. Your power to choose means that while society and culture may constrain your options, they do not entirely determine your life. What you choose to do at certain points in life can make a difference. Opportunities can be exploited or squandered, difficulties overcome or compounded. The trick is to know what is occurring and how to help your chances. Information and understanding can lead us to individual solutions for personal problems, as we will see repeatedly in the remaining chapters.

You can also consider getting involved in groups or organizations—there are political parties and interest groups of all sorts. Some of them will have goals for social changes that you would like to see realized. Here, too, knowledge of your society and culture is a prerequisite for making good decisions about which groups and organizations are most appropriate to your interests. Your values and ideologies (which are socially derived, remember) will also determine your choices of goals and organizations.

People acting in groups and organizations make history. The chapters that follow will demonstrate this many times through different examples. Consider, for example, the changes in health care legislation, family law, and unemployment insurance and minimum-wage legislation that have been forced by reform groups over the past several decades. Be warned, though, that this strategy of political action through groups and organizations can be a slow road. Moreover, many of your journeys may be unsuccessful. The analyses to come in other chapters will indicate, too, that dominant groups oppose certain solutions to improve peoples' lives because they are not particularly in their own interests. As Marx and Weber, along with other scholars, have emphasized, such dominant groups will have considerable organizational and ideological power.

However, political struggles can be won. There are many examples in Canada and the United States

1.3

Global Issues

The Health Challenges of Climate Change

Pollution Probe released a report in October 2001, with Health Canada looking into the impact of climate change on the health of people in the Toronto and Niagara regions. Here is an edited excerpt.

The impact of the health effects of climate change will be determined, in large part, by how well the health infrastructure is able to cope.

Until recently, the prevailing view of many experts was that both Canada and the United States are well protected against adverse health outcomes due to a strong public health-care system (especially in Canada), a high standard of living, and high levels of public awareness.

Evidence emerging from climate change and human health research suggests that this may be an optimistic view for a number of reasons.

First, changes in the frequency, intensity and severity of extreme weather events may pose a greater challenge than small changes in mean temperatures. This may be especially true for vulnerable groups, whose health is already being affected by current climate conditions.

Extreme weather events—such as the Saguenay-Chicoutimi flood in 1996 and the 1998 ice storm in Ontario and Quebec—clearly demonstrated the vulnerability of municipal infrastructures in Canada to climate stresses, with harmful consequences for human health. Similarly, the illnesses and deaths due to a highly virulent strain of E. coli in Walkerton in spring, 2000, were triggered by weather conditions (drought followed by intense rainfall).

The Walkerton disaster has heightened public concern over the quality of our water and the ability of municipal infrastructure to deliver clean water. Ongoing health concerns over periodic heat waves, severe cold spells

and, especially, intense smog episodes continue to attract the attention of politicians from all levels of government, as well as members of the health-care community.

Second, the health-care system has been able to cope relatively well with most climate stresses in the past. However, this is not a guarantee that the health of Canadians will be well protected in the future. In many regions of Canada, the health-care system is already becoming overburdened.

In Ontario, for example, there is growing concern that emergency hospital departments and home care services are in a state of crisis. Further, the vulnerability of Canadians may also be increasing. The population is getting older, and in some urban centres, such as the Greater Toronto Area and the city of Hamilton, the disparities between rich and poor are on the rise, with areas of poverty becoming increasingly marginalized from the more affluent suburban communities.

Consequently, the ability of the health infrastructure to respond effectively to climate change impacts, such as new and emerging diseases, and ensure the health of Canadians is by no means certain and, at the very least, demands closer attention.

In order to reduce the vulnerability of Canadians to the health effects resulting from climate change, it is necessary that decision-makers have a strategy for developing an effective adaptation action plan.

Such a plan requires a clear understanding of the health risks associated with current climate and climate change, the options that are available and the capacity of health infrastructure to adapt to future climate change impacts.

SOURCE: Excerpts from Part 1 – Introduction, *Towards an Adaptation Action Plan: Climate Change and Health in the Toronto-Niagara Region, Summary for Policy Makers,* Pollution Probe, 2002. Reprinted by permission of Pollution Probe.

alone of successful protest movements by subordinate groups: the civil rights movement in the United States, the Quiet Revolution in Quebec, the women's movement in both countries, to name only three. Another important example is the success of the labour movement in Canada and the United States, fighting over many decades to secure better wages and job conditions for the working class. This textbook will refer to many instances of social change initiated by social organizations, including many examples initiated by government agencies. Such developments should give us heart concerning the possibilities of joint action to resolve societal problems. Many problems will be shown to be formidable in their social causes and social consequences, but there is room to effect social change if we work at it.

Conclusion

Sociology is a good idea. It pays off in enlightening us, and it has worthy goals. It is the systematic study of how society and patterns of social behaviour within society are structured and change.

It is a broad field of study. This is evident in the four broad theoretical perspectives used to guide much sociological research. The breadth of the field of study is further evident in the idea that sociology emphasizes both micro- and macro-level analyses and the complex relationships between the two as emphasized in Mills's discussion of the sociological imagination. Sociology also covers a broad subject matter—consider the subject matter of the following chapters, ranging across deviance, family, education, religion, politics, the economy, health, and beyond.

Sociology allows people to move beyond a purely common-sense approach to better understanding social life. It allows them to use more powerful methods of investigation that reveal the multi-faceted and elaborate ways that aspects of social life are interconnected. In the process, much common-sense knowledge is shown to be faulty. Sociology will help you see that things are not always what they seem.

Sociology emphasizes the relationships among individuals, social structure, and culture. Social structure and culture are shown to constrain greatly the behaviour of individuals, yet they are essential for the persistence of human life and society. In addition, social structure and culture are shown to be creations of humans through social interaction, which are, therefore, subject to future change by individuals acting in group settings. Strong constraints are placed upon certain forms of social and cultural change, however, by virtue of the actions of powerful interest groups.

Sociology has obvious personal relevance, since it addresses everyday life issues. And, finally, sociology has an important goal overall: to contribute positively to the future of humanity.

Appendix	The Top Ten Sociology Books of the Twentieth Century, as Voted by the Members of the International Sociological Association	
		Votes Received (%)
1	Max Weber, *Economy and Society*	20.9
2	Charles Wright Mills, *The Sociological Imagination*	13.0
3	Robert K. Merton, *Social Theory and Social Structure*	11.4
4	Max Weber, *The Protestant Ethic and the Spirit of Capitalism*	10.3
5	P.L. Berger and T. Luckmann, *The Social Construction of Reality*	9.9
6	Pierre Bourdieu, *Distinction: A Social Critique of the Judgment of Taste*	9.5
7	Norbert Elias, *The Civilizing Process*	6.6
8	Jürgen Habermas, *The Theory of Communicative Action*	6.4
9	Talcott Parsons, *The Structure of Social Action*	6.2
10	Erving Goffman, *The Presentation of Self in Everyday Life*	5.5

Source: International Sociological Association, "Books of the Century" (1998); available at <www.ucm.es/info/isa/books/>, accessed 15 May 2003.

□ Questions for Critical Thought

1. Thinking about the roles that you have in your life (student, worker, mother, father, daughter, son, and so on), choose one role and examine your patterns of interaction from a macro and a micro perspective. How does this role influence your current behaviours? From what sources in society did you learn this role?

2. How can we build cohesive communities that take advantage of the wide differences between people? This is one of Émile Durkheim's central sociological questions. Come up with some ideas of how we could best answer this question for our society today, using concepts discussed in the chapter.

3. Which of the four sociological paradigms do you think best fits your own ideas about how society is arranged? Explain why this particular paradigm is most applicable and how you might use it in some of your own research.

4. Consider the issue of discrimination (racial, gender, age, and so on). Using one of the four theory paradigms, brainstorm about the sources and consequences of this type of behaviour.

5. Standardized testing for children in elementary and high school is becoming more common in Canada. Consider the manifest and latent functions of this type of testing. In addition, using a conflict perspective, consider who has the most to gain in the implementation of this testing.

6. Think about dominant ideologies that exist in our society today. Examine two ideologies that you accept and one that you reject in your own personal value system. Consider how you may have come to hold these ideologies.

7. Sociological research can provide important information about how people could have effectively deal with many situations in their daily life. Consider how we could make sociological research and information more accessible to the common person than is currently the case. In addition, could we increase the use of sociological knowledge by members of the general public?

□ Recommended Readings

Randall Collins and Michael Mayakowsky, *The Discovery of Society* (New York: Random House, 1989).
   A brilliant short history of the development of sociology, set against the backdrop of nineteenth- and twentieth-century social and political change.

Anthony Giddens, *Sociology: A Brief but Critical Introduction* (San Diego, TX: Harcourt Brace Jovanovich, 1987).
   A short, interesting book on one central debate in sociology: whether contemporary social problems are due to capitalism (as Marx would say), industrialism (as Durkheim would say), or bureaucracy (as Weber would say).

Charles C. Lemert, *Social Things: An Introduction to the Sociological Life*, 2nd edn (Lanham, MD: Rowman & Littlefield, 2002).
   An easy-to-read book for introductory sociology students, this text examines how local and global forces influence individuals' lives, with particular attention paid to political and economic events and trends.

C. Wright Mills, *The Sociological Imagination* (New York: Oxford University Press, 1967).
   This classic work in sociology is written from the conflict perspective. It emphasizes the close connection between personal troubles (private experience) and public issues (the wider social context). This is perhaps the best-known, most often quoted sociological work in the world.

Robert A. Nisbet, *The Sociological Tradition* (New York: Basic Books, 1966).

Wonderfully written, this long book organizes much of the history of sociology around the "unit-ideas of sociology," or its founders' key concerns: community, authority, status, the sacred, and alienation.

R.J. Rummel, *The Conflict Helix: Principles and Practices of Interpersonal, Social, and International Conflict and Cooperation* (New Brunswick, NJ: Transaction, 1997).

This book is written for the general public and introductory students, organized in terms of the fundamental principles necessary to understand conflict and co-operation between people, in society, and in international relations. It is a non-technical presentation of a unified theory of co-operation, conflict, and its resolution based on three decades of accumulated research.

□ Recommended Web Sites

The Émile Durkheim Archive

www.durkheim.itgo.com

This site presents information related to Durkheim's life, his work, and the concepts he used in his research. It provides a sound understanding of his perspective and main concepts.

Marxism Page

www.anu.edu.au/polsci/marx/marx.html

An introduction to Karl Marx's ideas and original works, as well as to basic concepts of Marxism politics.

Metafuture.org

www.metafuture.org

Metafuture.org provides information and articles about issues related to our future, such as globalization, multiculturalism, and corporatization. The section called "Articles by colleagues" provides articles on many sociological problems and questions.

A Sociological Tour Through Cyberspace

www.trinity.edu/~mkearl/

An excellent set of links to sociology resources on the Internet.

Sociorealm

www.digeratiweb.com/sociorealm

This excellent site provides students with links to the work and history of many sociologists, to sociological terms, and to books.

SocioSite

www.pscv.uva.nl/sociosite

Sociologists, dead and very much alive, with links to biographies, works, and research in sociology.

Verstehen: Max Weber's HomePage

www.faculty.rsu.edu/~felwell/Theorists/Weber/Whome.htm

This site explores Weber's sociological insights in a clear and concise manner, providing students with an excellent overview of his life and work.

Voice of the Shuttle

http://vos.ucsb.edu

Voice of the Shuttle offers links to sites about women's studies, feminist theory, queer studies, the men's movement, cybergender, and techgender, as well as minority and cultural studies.

part **two** > > >
Major Social Processes

We emphasized in chapter 1 that people's behaviours, and even their personal identities, are greatly influenced by two types of processes—culture and social structure—in which they find themselves embedded. Both culture and social structure are always all around us, and they continually shape our behaviours and views. At the same time, culture and social structure are produced and maintained by individuals. In short, the sociological perspective points out that there are very close and dynamic relationships among individuals, culture, and social structure. Part II focuses on the ways in which individuals, culture, and social structure mutually affect each other.

2

Shyon Baumann

> > >

Culture and Culture Change

☐ Learning Objectives

In this chapter, you will:

- see that *culture* has many meanings, and that we need to specify a particular cultural dimension when raising questions about culture

- observe that culture is ubiquitous: it is thoroughly a part of our lives, and we would not have societies without it

- learn that culture is powerful: it integrates members of society but can also cause great conflict

- learn that one of the quintessential elements of culture is its ability to carry meaning and facilitate communication

- see that change in culture is inevitable: it is within the nature of culture to evolve and to build on its own previous configurations

- find that the reasons and mechanisms behind culture change are various—some are social-structural, while sometimes cultural changes spur on other cultural changes

Why Study Culture?

What do we mean by the word **culture**? And why do we want to know? To answer the second question briefly, we want to know because culture is an amazingly powerful social force that influences events as diverse as whom we marry and whether we go to war. Marriage and war are interesting examples—while they seem unrelated, they are similar insofar as they both involve the bonds between people, in one case bringing people closer together and in the other pushing them further apart.

Let us consider for a moment how culture is implicated in each of these events. How we choose whom to marry is incredibly complicated, but what is clear is that in general people like to marry other people with whom they share interests and experiences. Such shared ideas and preferences create a feeling of comfort and familiarity, which are things we enjoy about being with other people. If we like the same music and the same kind of movies, if we share a belief in the importance of family and the role of religion in our lives, if we share a notion of the different roles and responsibilities of men and women, if we support the same political ideals, then we feel more connected to each other. In all these ways, culture is influencing how we relate to others. Culture includes all these preferences and ideas and notions, and these are the things that allow us in our daily lives to feel connections to other people. Cultural similarities influence our decisions not only about getting married, but about all kinds of connections—with whom we become and stay friends, even with whom we work.

Just as we are often brought closer to other people, so too we often experience social divisions, some relatively minor and others quite significant. Like marriage, war is an enormously complicated phenomenon; it can result from a wide array of social, economic, and geopolitical factors. But it is also clear that culture can play a role in creating or worsening the divisions between groups or societies that can lead to war. While a conflict of material interests is usually the basis of war, culture can play a large role in determining whether war is the ultimate outcome. If we differ in fundamental **beliefs** about such things as democracy and human rights, if we speak different languages and cannot easily communicate, if we cannot understand others' religious concepts and practices, if we do not share preferences for what we consider to be the normal and good ways to live our lives,

then we feel less connected to each other. In all these ways, culture plays a role in dividing us from others, and it is only in the presence of such divisions, when we feel essentially different and disconnected from others, that we are able to pursue as drastic a course of action as war. In addition, culture plays a role in many more minor social divisions that are not as significant as war, the various social cleavages between many **social groups** within the same society.

Culture, then, is important because it is the key to understanding how we relate to each other; specifically, it is behind both what unites us and what divides us. Our cultural differences and similarities are continually coming into play, in our daily face-to-face interactions and on a global scale. To truly understand the dynamics of war and peace, love and hate, and more, we need to look at the way that culture facilitates or inhibits the bonds and the rifts between us.

The goals of this chapter are to review the many nuances to the meaning of *culture* and to explain how culture is implicated in many important social processes. To achieve this goal this chapter will first further specify what culture is through a clear conceptualization of culture's many dimensions. With the many connotations of *culture*, we need to pay heed to various aspects of it. In addition, this chapter will summarize how culture is used in sociological theorizing about society. It examines how culture fits into causal explanations about the way society works. In this chapter, we are also interested in a description of those realms of social life that are primarily cultural—the loci of culture. The nature of culture change is another focus of this chapter, and we will examine the reciprocal relationship between culture change and social change. Finally, we will discuss the insights of this chapter as they pertain to Canadian culture.

What Is Culture?

Think of the many ways that you might use the word *culture* in casual conversation. You might use it to refer to the way that an entire society lives, visible most clearly when it is foreign to you, as in "Thai culture." You might use *culture* to refer to the refined aesthetic productions that "highbrow" people enjoy. *Culture* takes on a still different meaning in a phrase such as "consumer culture," which focuses on a major pattern of people's behaviour and a set of economic institutions in contemporary society. Or you might use *culture* to refer to the practices and preferences of a subgroup of people (for example, "jock culture," "geek culture," or "skater culture") who are nonetheless part of the larger society, in whose culture they also participate.

Perhaps no term in the sociological vocabulary has as many meanings as *culture*. Although some of these meanings are closely related to each other, others are remarkably divergent. For a concept that has traditionally been viewed as central to much sociological analysis, this is a strange state of affairs and one that complicates any attempt to provide a succinct and definitive summary of the sociology of culture.

To begin defining *culture*, we can recognize that at its most expansive, culture can be conceived of as the sum total of human creation: everything that is a product of a human mind, no matter how small or large, how concrete or abstract, how individual or widely shared, constitutes an element of culture. Of course, for a concept to be useful, it must allow us to distinguish what it is referring to from what it is not referring to. The first clear distinction, then, is that between culture and the natural world as it exists apart from human interaction. For the purposes of sociological analysis, when we speak of *culture* we do not refer to the physical reality of our natural environment, the complex ecological system billions of years in the making. This first distinction, however, still leaves quite a lot under the rubric of culture, namely all of social reality, and this begs for further clarification.

Distinctive Elements of Culture

Defining *culture* as the sum total of the human-influenced and human-created environment, anything and everything that is the product of a human mind, leaves us with a rather bloated notion of the term's meaning. This expansive definition rests on the notion that all of our thought processes are conditioned and shaped by the **social environment** into which we are socialized. Without this social environment, without this culture, we would have nothing to form our thoughts except for our natural instincts and desires. All human societies, however, develop a cultural way of life that can significantly shape the minds of individuals and allow them to develop into socialized members of that society. Insofar as this **socialization** process influences all that we do—if not directly then at least indirectly—we can plausibly call all of social life *cultural*.

Although *culture* can mean all of this, the concept is really only useful for helping us to make sociolog-

ical arguments and draw sociological insights if we can limit it. In practice, we are usually interested in determining the relative influence or functioning of cultural factors in society compared to other, non-cultural factors. We therefore often employ various, more restricted senses of the term and strive to set apart certain elements of social life as "cultural" from those elements that are not. To add to the complicated nature of defining *culture*, it so happens that there is a certain amount of disagreement over which elements of social life are properly "cultural."

For the sake of giving initial form to the idea of culture as it is discussed here, we can create a list of specific things that are always or usually classified as "culture" in sociology. Languages, symbols, discourses, texts, knowledge, values, attitudes, beliefs, norms, world views, folkways, art, music, ideas, and ideologies are all "culture." In sociological analysis, these social phenomena are differentiated on the basis of inherent cultural qualities. To better understand why these things are "culture," we need to think about their characteristics.

We can do that by first examining how culture is dependent on specific locations and times. That is to say, culture is different between places and at different times. Examining the nature of those changes is a first step in providing a full description of culture. Second, to better understand what makes the above list of the elements of culture conceptually coherent, we need to examine the ways that sociologists distinguish between the cultural and the non-cultural. We will review two major distinctions employed in the sociological literature to specify the elements of culture: the difference between culture and structure, and the difference between the symbolic and the non-symbolic.

Culture in Place and Time

Culture is quite often used to refer to the entire social reality of particular social groups in comparison to other social groups. Perhaps the largest cultural groupings frequently in use differentiate between large regions of the globe—Western culture, for example, while encompassing tremendous variation, is a notion that coheres in contradistinction to the history and present reality of, for example, Eastern and Near Eastern cultures. Such a distinction obscures the many similarities and historical continuities between these cultures and instead emphasizes how they differ. Nonetheless, it is a first step in limiting the concept of "culture" to a more helpful definition, namely the social environment, in its entirety, of people from within a circumscribed physical space.

It should be immediately clear that we often think of culture in more specific geographic terms than just Western or Eastern. We frequently think in national terms, with fairly strong ideas of what we mean by, for example, Japanese culture, Italian culture, or Mexican culture. These ideas exist in our minds as stereotypes or generalizations about the kind of lives inhabitants of these countries choose to lead. We might think of, among many other things, Japanese rituals of politeness and a preference for sushi, the sights and sounds of Italian opera and the speed of Vespa scooters, and small Mexican towns where elaborate, solemn Catholic ceremonies can give way to lively and colourful festivals. Likewise, you might have noticed when talking to people from other countries that they sometimes impose expectations on you based on stereotypes of Canada and Canadians: "Do you play hockey?" "Do you drive a snowmobile?"

Whatever the accuracy or generalizability (frequently low) of such stereotypes as images of the typical culture of these countries, their pervasiveness points to the reality that culture can vary systematically between nations, even if it is often in ways of which we are commonly unaware. There is good reason for this: nation-states have often coalesced around a common cultural foundation, or if one was not clearly defined from early on, they have tended to promote such a cultural foundation for the sake of national unity and cohesion.

Despite the definitional clarity that a notion of national culture offers, upon closer inspection we can see that, like the larger generalizations of "Western culture" or "Eastern culture," national cultures also entail a great deal of regional and local variation. For example, in a large country such as the United States, the culture of the politically liberal, highly urbanized, and economically successful northeastern region can be contrasted with the culture of certain of the politically conservative and less affluent states in the South. Such a contrast points to the differences between the whole way of life of Northeasterners and Southerners; however, we need to be mindful that both share a culture that is more generally "American" and that they therefore share countless cultural features.

We can continue to spatially limit our concept of culture by pointing to the general social differences between various cities and even between parts of cities. The culture of downtown Toronto, for example, brings up notions of a lifestyle and a built environment that are business-oriented, cosmopolitan, and culturally rich. Toronto's **urbanism** is often cited for its impersonality and inward-lookingness, and contrasts with the particular habits, manners, and interaction styles of, for example, St John's, Newfoundland, among other places. Remember, though, that just as with the differences in regions, such local cultural variations belie more similarities than differences.

Just as with the differences between regions, however, we must be careful not to overstate the precision with which we can delineate a concept of culture based on physical space. Cultural similarities are bound to exist between various physical spaces—no matter how narrowly we draw our boundaries—on account of shared *social* spaces. Just as we can identify culture as the human environment of specific geographic locations, so we can also identify culture as the human environment of groups who are similar socially despite being geographically disparate. Therefore, we can think of the culture of, for example, adolescent males as distinct from adolescent females or from adult males, no matter whether their geographic location is Vancouver or Halifax. (See also Table 2.1 on the cultural activities of adult Canadian males.) Acknowledging culture's social, not just physical, boundedness provides us with a second dimension for understanding and limiting the meaning of culture.

Age and **gender**, the social groupings in the above example, are just two of many social boundaries that can differentiate between cultures. Other social lines along which cultural features may fall include **race** and **ethnicity**, sexual orientation, religion, and many other ways that people see fit to distinguish themselves. Another social space with important cultural implications is that of social **class**. Stereotypes of distinct working- and upper-class cultures are at least as pervasive as national stereotypes. We have firm ideas about the typical speech, mannerisms, dress, culinary preferences, occupations, and leisure activities of the working class and the upper class.

At this point it is necessary to point out again that, just as the cultures of urban Ontario and rural Alberta share more similarities than differences, the culture of different social groups within a society likewise share more similarities than differences. By enumerating the ways in which, for example, social classes in

Table 2.1   **Participation in Cultural Activities, Canadians and Male Canadians, 1998**

	Both Sexes		Male	
	Thousands	**%**	**Thousands**	**%**
Read a newspaper	19,851	81.8	9,915	83.1
Read a magazine	17,264	71.2	8,166	68.4
Read a book	14,881	61.3	6,478	54.3
Use library services	6,688	27.6	2,845	23.8
Borrow materials	6,036	24.9	2,432	20.4
Use Internet	583	2.4	296	2.5
Do research	1,898	7.8	964	8.1
Attend a program	277	1.1	81	0.7
Other	107	0.4	49	0.4
Go to a movie	14,340	59.1	7,216	60.5
Watch a video on VCR	17,690	72.9	8,921	74.7
Listen to cassettes, records, CDs	18,625	76.8	9,166	76.8
Use Internet	7,171	29.6	4,117	34.5
Research	5,412	22.3	3,248	27.2
Communicate	5,478	22.6	3,081	25.8
Read a newspaper, magazine, book	2,322	9.6	1,432	12.0
View video, film, TV, listen to music	1,204	5.0	799	6.7
View art or museum collections	1,011	4.2	611	5.1
Create artistic compositions, designs	983	4.1	601	5.0
Electronic banking	1,437	5.9	942	7.9
Download software, other	2,714	11.2	1,864	15.6
Total population (15 and over)	**24,260**		**11,937**	

SOURCE: Statistics Canada, "Participation in Cultural Activities by Sex, Canada," General Social Survey, 1998; available at <www.statcan.ca/english/Pgdb/arts36a.htm>, accessed 15 May 2003.

Canada differ, we neglect myriad ways in which they are similar: difference in accent is trivial to the overall nature of a language; a similar reliance on automobiles overshadows any consideration of whether those automobiles are foreign or domestic; and a propensity to vote for different political parties cannot diminish the tremendous importance of a shared faith in parliamentary democracy.

In addition, it is necessary to point out that the dimensions of physical and social space are relatively but not entirely independent. In some instances there is considerable overlap, when a social grouping exclusively or almost exclusively inhabits a physical space. For example, if we were to study the culture of retirement communities, we would see that these are physical spaces populated mostly by a specific social group defined by age. The social boundedness of culture by age (the culture of an older generation) maps onto a physical boundedness of culture by residential location (the culture of a retirement community). Likewise, there is a great deal of overlap between the physical space of Anglican churches and the social space of Anglicans.

Notice that cases in which the physical and social spatial dimensions of culture intersect to the exclusion of other social groups are fairly narrowly circumscribed. For the most part, our social lives are messier, and different **subcultures** interact with each other all the time. Sometimes the young visit their grandparents in their retirement homes; quite frequently individuals of various social classes occupy the same classrooms, malls, arenas, and workspaces (although with different functions within those workspaces); segregation on the basis of race sometimes occurs residentially, though for the most part the common venues in which daily life is played out are racially integrated.

Finally, we can recognize that culture varies over time. The temporal dimension is an important qualifier because of the magnitude of differences that accumulate to produce cultures that are vastly different from what came before. In other words, culture evolves.

Leaving aside the precise mechanisms of cultural evolution for now, we can recognize that for the most part culture is never static. It is always developing new features and characteristics. Therefore, Western culture of today is remarkably different from 500 years ago and is in many ways quite different from even 10 years ago. The temporal dimension of culture is independent of its physical and social locations—culture changes over time in all countries and regions and for all social groupings. Norwegian culture today is different from what it was in 1900; French Canadian culture, irrespective of actual geographic roots, has evolved over the century as well; and the culture of Canadians in their sixties has changed dramatically over time—the leisure and work options and the values and ideals of elderly Canadians bear little resemblance to what they were in earlier time periods. It is worth noting that many observers of culture argue that cultural changes are occurring more frequently in recent time periods: the rate of cultural change is increasing. When we turn to the specifics of cultural dynamics, we will learn more about the reasons behind this increase in the rate of change.

Culture and Structure

While a description of culture's dependence on time and location shows us the changing nature of culture, we also need a clear idea of what "counts" as culture and what does not. To help us to draw this boundary,

we can consider the distinction between *culture* and **structure**, two terms that have specific meanings within formal sociology. This distinction, as described by Philip Smith, sees culture primarily as the realm of the "ideal, the spiritual, and the non-material" and opposed to the "material, technological, and the social-structural" (2001: 3–4).

The meanings of these terms merit further elucidation. One might characterize the *ideal*, the *spiritual*, and the *non-material* as things that exist primarily in people's heads, limited to an essentially mental existence. That is to say, this version of culture privileges the distinction between thoughts, emotions, beliefs, and the more abstract elements of organized social life on the one hand and the "concrete" elements of society that are literally embodied and enacted by actual things and people on the other hand. Drawing the boundaries of culture in this fashion allows us to classify, for example, attitudes about gender roles and about the kinds of work that are appropriate for men and for women as "cultural." Such attitudes are shared modes of thinking, and to the extent that they are only mental constructs, they are properly cultural.

At the same time, the fact that there exists a high degree of occupational segregation by gender, with some jobs (for example, elementary school teachers)

 2.1

Open for Discussion
Animal Liberation

The first time I opened Peter Singer's "Animal Liberation," I was dining alone at the Palm, trying to enjoy a rib-eye steak cooked medium-rare. If this sounds like a good recipe for cognitive dissonance (if not indigestion), that was sort of the idea. Preposterous as it might seem, to supporters of animal rights, what I was doing was tantamount to reading "Uncle Tom's Cabin" on a plantation in the Deep South in 1852.

Singer and the swelling ranks of his followers ask us to imagine a future in which people will look back on my meal, and this steakhouse, as relics of an equally backward age. Eating animals, wearing animals, experimenting on animals, killing animals for sport: all these practices, so resolutely normal to us, will be seen as the barbarities they are, and we will come to view "speciesism"—a neologism I had encountered

before only in jokes—as a form of discrimination as indefensible as racism or anti-Semitism.

Even in 1975, when "Animal Liberation" was first published, Singer, an Australian philosopher now teaching at Princeton, was confident that he had the wind of history at his back. The recent civil rights past was prologue, as one liberation movement followed on the heels of another. Slowly but surely, the white man's circle of moral consideration was expanded to admit first blacks, then women, then homosexuals. In each case, a group once thought to be so different from the prevailing "we" as to be undeserving of civil rights was, after a struggle, admitted to the club. Now it was animals' turn.

————

SOURCE: Michael Pollan, "An Animal's Place," *New York Times Magazine* (10 Nov. 2002), 58, 60. Copyright © 2002, Michael Pollan.

primarily done by women and others (for example, elementary school principals) primarily done by men, is not cultural. Rather, this segregation is "structural." It is an enduring pattern of social behaviour, existing primarily not at a mental level but at a level of lived experience. The idea that it is normal or proper for men to be principals and women to be elementary school teachers is a cultural value. The fact that this pattern exists in our society (however changing) is a structural property of our society.

We can find another example in the realm of **politics**. The widely held preference for representative democracy and a belief that it is a legitimate and necessary form of self-government in Canada represents a deep-rooted aspect of Canadian culture. This political orientation is related in a significant way to many other beliefs about authority, individual rationality, and justice, and so it is an element of culture that is clearly enmeshed in a web of other important cultural elements. In contrast, representative democracy is not merely an idea, it is a practice that involves a tremendous amount of material resources and engenders long-standing patterns of social behaviour. Known in the sociological literature as **the State**, our

The Centre Block of the Parliament buildings is immediately evocative of Canada. It is an effective symbol of the nation, and its image is both a part of and representative of Canadian national culture. Library of Parliament/Mone's Photography.

democratic government is a structural dimension of social life. It is related in significant ways to many aspects of citizens' daily existence; it influences, among other things, our work lives, our consumption patterns, our health outcomes, and our educational outcomes, and so it is a material element of social life that is clearly enmeshed in a web of other important structural elements.

Culture as Symbolic

A second way in which *culture* is frequently defined in sociology is according to the role that it plays in creating meaning. In this view, culture is those elements of social life that act as symbols and are subject to interpretation. These elements are produced in order to be received and understood by individuals who derive meaning—a personal understanding—through the reception process. Any element of society that has meaning for both its creator and its audience, even if there is a discrepancy between the intended and the perceived meanings, is part of the symbolic order. Culture, then, is both a product of **social interaction** and the social force that enables social interaction because it allows people to communicate meanings to each other.

In contrast, culture is *not* those things that serve *no* communicative or expressive role. This is a fine distinction because meaning can often be found wherever we look hard enough, especially by those with a postmodern sensibility. However, it is important to limit culture to those things that are intended to be interpreted and to have meaning, even if the nature of those eventual interpretations might vary.

Going back to the political example demonstrating the difference between culture and structure, we can see the State as an instrumental **social institution** designed to achieve governance. It does not qualify as "culture" because it is not in itself a symbol: it does not exist to be received and understood as having a meaning. However, there is no shortage of politically oriented culture or of political symbols, existing in a wide array of forms. Political ideologies of the left, centre, and right, expressed in political discourses, in conversations, newspaper articles, and books, both fiction and non-fiction, are squarely in the realm of culture. The national anthem and the Canadian flag are both explicit political symbols. The neo-Gothic Parliament buildings in Ottawa, while serving as the venue for federal politics, also serve as a political symbol, not only through the "messages" associated with their stately, traditional, European appearance (they are not pagodas or pyramids), but also because they are widely known to conjure up an association with the federal government and so can represent the wider country. Their very image has gained interpretive currency and so can be effectively used as a tool for communication.

The symbolic view of culture bears much similarity to the view that opposes culture to structure. In both views, the roles of ideas and mental states are important elements of culture. The two views do differ, however. Where the opposition between culture and structure emphasizes the distinction between the material and the non-material, the symbolic view of culture, with its focus on the expressive function of culture, recognizes that meaning is often conveyed through symbols that take material form. By combining the insights of each perspective, we can recognize that culture is ideas, beliefs, emotions, and thoughts *and* their direct physical embodiments.

A few interesting features of this combination of insights are worth noting. First, the two views together provide a more comprehensive description of what constitutes culture than either does individually, but without being unduly or impracticably broad. Second, those topics that are clearly "culture" from both perspectives are generally closer to the core of the concerns of the sociology of culture. For example, language—non-material words spoken to convey meaning—is a phenomenon that is a cultural subject *par excellence*. Third, the two perspectives show us that there are multiple ways of viewing social phenomena. It is possible that certain things can be analyzed as culture while they are simultaneously understood as being outside the realm of culture.

To take a technological example, the automobile can be analyzed on different levels. On the one hand, automobiles are material objects that are instrumental in facilitating social needs. They are part of the structural side of social life, namely, our transportation system. On the other hand, automobiles are designed with an aesthetic dimension to them, and as such they are the embodiment of ideas about taste and style, which are cultural elements. They play a role in self-expression for many people. On a deeper level, attitudes toward automobile use and the kind of lifestyle that their use engenders are known as "car culture," and in this sense automobiles are implicated in the realm of culture in a second way.

A Detailed Picture

Following the above descriptions and distinctions, our view of culture is one in which, on the one hand, we can separate the cultural from the non-cultural and, on the other hand, we can recognize the contingency of the cultural on physical and social location and on time. We can be very specific now about what we mean by *culture* and how it is represented in sociological work.

The sociology of culture has tackled topics such as the reading experiences of middle-class women in the American Midwest in the 1980s (Radway, 1984); the influence of religion on civic engagement and individualism in the United States (Bellah, 1996); the attitudes, values, and morality of French and American upper-middle-class males (Lamont, 1992); the tension between morality and economic imperatives in the late-twentieth-century West (Bell, 1979); and the organizational and economic foundations for the ideology that developed after 1800 in Vienna to distinguish the "serious" music of genius from ordinary classical music (DeNora, 1991).

As in any subfield of sociology, studies within the sociology of culture often gain analytical leverage through comparisons. We can increase our understanding of current values, for instance, by comparing them to values of a different time, to values of a different social group, or to values of a different place. Comparative work exists in many forms and covers many topics within the sociology of culture. Cross-national comparisons, which sample across physical space, help to outline the contours of national cultural features, such as political values. Sociologist Seymour Martin Lipset (1990) has helped us to understand Canadian values through work that contrasts Canada with the United States. Comparisons of men and women, across social space, can highlight the gendered nature of language use (Weatherall, 2002). Historical studies, by comparing present-day and historical elements of culture, can provide tremendous insight into the time-contingent nature of such things as our ideas about human rights or appropriate and inappropriate public behaviour (Elias, 1994).

The Role of Culture in Social Theory

Now that we have a clear idea of what culture is, we can gain an understanding of how it has figured in the works of some of the major sociological theorists. In this section, we will outline how these thinkers have employed culture in their writings about the fundamental driving forces of society.

Above all else, theories explain things. That is to say, the defining feature of a **theory** is that it tells why or how something is the way it is. *Social theory*, then, is explanations of social things—it tells us why certain aspects of society are the way they are. A great deal of social theory, it turns out, is strongly concerned with culture. This concern, however, appears in different forms: social theories are concerned with culture for a variety of reasons. Below we will review the place of culture in five major social theoretical perspectives.

Orthodox Marxist and Neo-Marxist Theories

One of the most influential theoretical perspectives in sociology is **Marxism**. In developing his theory of society, Karl Marx was responding directly to previous philosophical arguments about the central role of ideas (squarely cultural) in determining the path of history and the nature of social reality. In such arguments, the general cultural environment worked at the level of ideas to shape people's thoughts and actions, and so was in principle the root cause behind events and social change. This "spontaneous unfolding" of the spirit or culture of a given time could explain the course of history (Smith, 2001: 13).

By contrast, in Marxism, social reality is seen as determined primarily by the prevailing **mode of production**, evolving through history from agrarian societies to slave ownership to feudalism and then to industrial **capitalism**. This perspective posits that the best way to explain social facts—and all of history—is by recognizing that they are outcomes, direct or indirect, of the economic organization of society.

Societies shift from one mode of production to the next in a historical progression, with the current state being industrial capitalism. The economic organization of society forms the *base* upon which the rest of society, the *superstructure*, is founded. In a strict reading of Marxism, the superstructure responds to but does not cause changes in the base. Culture, in all its forms—ideas, beliefs, values, art, religion, and so on—is part of the superstructure and must be understood as essentially a product of the base.

In today's society, then, all aspects of our culture are shaped by the needs and dictates of industrial capitalism. One of the most important cultural productions of capitalism is the **dominant ideology**. This ideology is a system of thoughts, knowledge, and beliefs that serves to legitimate and to perpetuate capitalism. Our mental lives and our entire thought modes are shaped to minimize criticism of capitalism and to maximize participation in and support of capitalism.

Neo-Marxist perspectives do not adhere so strictly to the view that culture is entirely dependent on society's mode of production. While they borrow extensively from Marx's insights, they also modify these insights, and in so doing they provide a significantly different view of culture. These perspectives share with Marxism a focus on the role of culture in maintaining and supporting capitalism, but they differ from Marxism insofar as they seek to explain culture as more than simply the reflection of the underlying economic base.

Neo-Marxists recognize that culture can be shaped by specific groups and individuals who seek to achieve certain social outcomes. For example, Antonio Gramsci (1992) argued in the 1920s and 1930s that intellectuals within spheres such as politics, religion, the mass media, and education provide knowledge, values, advice, and direction to the general population that serve to perpetuate the status quo and to suppress revolutionary tendencies. To take another example, members of the Frankfurt School, who began writing in the 1920s, identified pro-capitalist functions in much of popular culture, which promotes capitalist ideals and stifles critical, independent thinking. The groups responsible for the creation and promotion of popular culture within the entertainment industry are themselves significant members of the **bourgeoisie**. In the view of the Frankfurt School, the entertainment industry is of great use to the capitalist order through the cultural products it creates.

It is important to note that neo-Marxists make a fundamental advance in their view of culture insofar as they see it as more than simply an artifact of the economic base. Culture, they argue, can also help to determine other facets of social reality—not merely reflective of other things in society, it also helps to shape society. A significant continuity between Marxist and neo-Marxist views of culture is that culture is implicated in the essentially conflictual nature of society. Culture, in a sense, supports dominant groups in their efforts to maintain their dominance.

Cultural Functionalism

A contrasting approach to understanding culture can be found in work that is based on the theoretical insights of Émile Durkheim. In contrast to the conflictual emphasis of the Marxists and neo-Marxists, the views on culture that are based on Durkheimian sociological insights focus on the integrative ability of culture. Rather than pointing to the ways in which culture can create social fissures, Durkheim ([1912] 1995) identified the ways in which culture can create social stability and solidarity, focusing on how culture unites us rather than on how culture divides us.

Culture, in terms of norms, values, attitudes, and beliefs, is not reflective of the economic mode of production. Instead, these cultural elements are generated according to the needs of society by its form as a more or less complex system. Culture rises up out of a particular society's **social structure** to produce a general consensus about the goals and nature of society. As such, our values about, for example, the importance of education evolve in response to the changing needs of a modernizing society in which higher general levels of education allow for a more smoothly functioning society. In this sense, culture serves a necessary function: through common values and beliefs, society is able to remain coherent and all the different parts of society can effectively carry out their specific purpose.

Durkheim paid special attention to the role of religion as a motivating force in society, one that made possible the affirmation of collective sentiments and ideas, and one that therefore could play an important role in strengthening social bonds that then strengthened and reinforced the fabric of society.

Symbolic Interactionist and Dramaturgical Perspectives

A third important perspective treats culture as a product of individuals' interactions. In **symbolic interactionist** thought, culture plays the role of a vehicle for meaning (hence "symbolic") and is generated by individuals in face-to-face encounters (hence "interactionist"). Culture is the enacted signals and attitudes that people use to communicate effectively in order to go about their daily lives. Body language and the signals we send through it, however subconsciously, are a clear element of culture in this perspective. The decisions we make and carry out to reveal or to suppress certain pieces of information about ourselves are also culture.

Social interaction can be analyzed to reveal layers of meaning behind routine actions. It becomes evident that there is a communicative element in a great deal of our interactions although we are not always conscious of its presence or of the nature of the messages we send. The result of our interactions is (usually) the successful management of our relationships with others.

In terms of its view on culture, the symbolic interactionist approach contrasts with Marxist and functionalist approaches insofar as it attributes more responsibility to individuals as the active creators and implementers of culture. Rather than originating from an economic order or indirectly from the general social structure, culture is a product of creative individual agents who use it to manage their everyday tasks and routines.

One of the most influential theorists to write about the interactions of individuals was Erving Goffman. Goffman developed an analytical framework that analogizes social interaction to what goes on in a theatre. For that reason, it is known as a *dramaturgical* perspective. In a theatre, there are actors with roles to play for an audience. Likewise, when we interact with people, we assume a role for the situation we find ourselves in and perform that role according to a well-known script that defines the boundaries of what is expected and acceptable for the role. We learn these rules of social behaviour through the ordinary process of socialization. We use these rules to create meaningful and effective interaction with others. When we are interacting with others and are in our roles, we are managing impressions and performing in a *frontstage* area. When we let down our guard and behave informally and in ways that would embarrass us in front of others, we are in the *backstage* area.

Culture plays a part in the dramaturgical perspective that is in one sense quite central: social order is constituted by the creation and use of meanings embodied in interaction. The sending and receiving of signals and messages is the key to understanding why society functions at all when there is so much potential for chaos. When you think about it, we are remarkably efficient at maintaining social order most of the time, and this achievement is made possible through the shared meanings in face-to-face interactions.

This view of culture, however, is one that is perhaps less rich than that offered by the cultural functionalist perspective. Rather than playing a fundamental role in shaping individuals' very consciousness, as the functionalist perspective would argue, the dramaturgical perspective sees culture as just a tool for creative individuals to manipulate strategically. Rather than being fully subject to the influence of culture, culture is subject more to the influence of individuals.

The Cultural Studies Tradition

Cultural studies is a field with roots in British literary scholarship and in sociology. Much of the work accomplished in this tradition builds on the work of Marxism and neo-Marxists. The specific insight that cultural studies borrows from neo-Marxists is that culture can be shaped and manipulated by dominant groups and employed to maintain hegemony. Cultural studies practitioners agree that culture can function to maintain social divisions, keeping some groups dominant over others. Where they break from Marxists and early neo-Marxists is in the recognition that class conflict is only one of many sites of ideological dominance. As Smith writes of cultural studies, "a move has gradually taken place away from Marxism toward an understanding of society as textured with multiple sources of inequality and fragmented local struggles" (2001: 152). Dominant groups can be defined not only by class position, but also by race, gender, geography, and sexual orientation.

In addition to a focus on the multiple forms of domination, cultural studies has provided a more sophisticated understanding of the ways in which meaning functions in society. One of the main figures in this tradition is Stuart Hall, who has produced some of the seminal concepts of cultural studies. As Hall (1980) explains, communication of meaning requires both **encoding** and **decoding**. By this he means that such things as an advertisement or a television show are created in such a way as to convey a particular perspective. The predominant beliefs of the creators are encoded into these cultural productions (or *texts*) in subtle and sometimes subconscious ways. A fresh, critically informed reading of such texts is required to see how they encode assumptions and messages about such things as gender and social class relations. Another significant insight of Hall's is that meaning does not simply exist as part of cultural creations, but instead is constructed by individuals through the process of receiving and interpreting culture. Meaning is created by people while they make sense of the culture they consume or take in.

As evidence, note how the very same cultural products may carry very different meanings for different individuals or for different groups. For example, a study of the meaning of Hollywood Westerns showed that the movies were interpreted quite differently by "Anglos" and by Native Americans: the films' messages about the frontier, Native–European relations, and the value of authority and independence were construed quite differently by the Anglo and the Native viewers (Shively, 1992). While those who create cultural products may intend them to convey a certain meaning, there is, nonetheless, opportunity for individuals to read or understand messages, texts, and symbols in oppositional or idiosyncratic ways, deriving meanings through a process that is influenced by the individuals' backgrounds and interpretive abilities.

The "Production of Culture" Perspective

The "production of culture" perspective takes as an object of study those aspects of culture that are created through explicit, intentional, and co-ordinated processes. There is, therefore, a focus on material culture, and studies taking this perspective focus on mass media, technology, art, and other material symbol-producing realms such as science and law. The guiding insight of this perspective is that culture is a product of social action in much the same way as non-cultural products are. The implication of this view is that culture is best studied according to the same methods and analysis that are standard in other fields of sociology.

A key figure in the development of the production of culture perspective, Richard A. Peterson (1994), notes that the perspective developed to account for perceived shortcomings in the prevailing "mirror" or "reflection" view that posited that culture was somehow a manifestation of underlying social-structural needs or realities. This view, held by orthodox Marxists and by functionalists, is quite vague about the specific mechanisms through which culture is created. The metaphor of a mirror is descriptive of the content of culture—it represents the true nature or character of society—but is mute about culture's production.

Such a view would find that, for instance, the contours of Canadian national identity are visible through studying the literary output of Canadian authors. As a body of work, Canadian literature takes on the characteristics of and "reflects" the essence of Canadian society. Likewise, Baroque art forms are seen as expressions of society in the Baroque period, and modernist art is explained as an expression of societal sentiments and values in the early decades of the twentieth century.

By contrast, the production of culture perspective is insistent on specifying all the factors involved not only in cultural production per se, but also in how culture is "distributed, evaluated, taught, and preserved" (Peterson, 1994: 165). Through a thorough analysis of all these processes, we can better account for the specific content of culture. We need to examine the resources and constraints that specific actors were working with and that influenced the kind of art or other symbols that they created. In this way, the production of culture perspective provides us with the means of explaining the shape of culture.

Conflict, Integration, Origin, and Autonomy

It is useful to compare these various perspectives according to their views on several key features of culture. Marxists and neo-Marxists are clear in their argument that culture is a tool of conflict in society, a view that contrasts with functionalists, who emphasize the integrative function of culture. Functionalists are interested in explaining social order, and they see culture as a key factor in creating social stability.

For symbolic interactionists, culture is primarily the means by which individuals create order out of potentially chaotic and unpredictable social situations, and so they support an integrative view of culture. The cultural studies tradition, building on the work of neo-Marxists, has an explicit focus on the many ways in which culture is implicated in various forms of domination and conflict in society.

The production of culture perspective has little to say about characterizing culture as integrative or as implicated in conflict. But while it has the least to say about that dimension of culture, it says the most about another dimension, the origin of culture, because it developed out of dissatisfaction with the views of Marxism and functionalism on the origin of culture. While these older perspectives relied on a "reflection" metaphor to explain where culture comes from, the production perspective locates cultural origin in "purposive productive activity" (Peterson, 1994: 164). Cultural studies does not provide quite so articulate an account of cultural origin, but neither does it merely rely on vague notions of reflection. Instead, it sees culture as originating in the work of hegemonic leaders who create the texts,

symbols, and discourses that embody particular ideologies. Symbolic interactionists also provide an explanation for the origin of culture: it is produced in the meanings that people create through social interaction at the micro level.

Finally, the various perspectives place different emphases on what we can call the "autonomy of culture." *Autonomy of culture* refers to the place for culture within causal explanations. Is culture primarily a dependent **variable**, something that deserves to be explained but does not warrant recognition as a fundamental cause of social outcomes? Or is culture autonomous—does culture merit a place at the core of sociological explanation, wherein it is the key to understanding the contours of social reality?

Marxism clearly denies the autonomy of culture by making it a reflection of the economic base of society. Functionalism views culture as far more autonomous: culture is, in and of itself, the predominant stabilizing force in society and can account for social order. Symbolic interactionists are less sympathetic to the autonomy of culture, preferring instead to privilege the role of spontaneous human creativity in understanding how social order is maintained; culture is more appropriately viewed as the product of action than as the motivator of action. The cultural studies tradition gives us a view of culture as enjoying a significant degree of autonomy; the crucial role of ideology in various forms of dominance portrays culture as primarily shaping the conflictual nature of social life. The production of culture perspective, to conclude this summary, is largely concerned with the ways in which myriad social processes create cultural products, and so finds little room for the autonomy of culture.

Cultural Realms

The stage is now set to discuss some of the attributes of those realms of social life most commonly located at the core of the sociology of culture. Although we could discuss the cultural dimension of almost any area of society, we will limit our discussion to the realms of language and discourse, the mass media, religion, and art. Within each realm, we will highlight the insights that the sociology of culture can bring to bear.

Language and Discourse

As mentioned above, language is a cultural subject par excellence. But before describing the interest of sociology in language more fully, it will be useful to distinguish it from the related concept of communication. *Language*, a system of words both written and spoken, is but one means of communication. **Communication** is the sharing of meaning, by which the thoughts of one person are made understandable to another. Communication can occur through a variety of signs and symbols, but we reserve a special place for the study of language because it is the primary means by which our communication takes place.

Languages are complicated systems of many symbols deployed according to a set of rules, and their use gives rise to a number of interesting social phenomena. It is argued, for instance, that the presence of language structures our very thoughts and consciousness, that without a vocabulary with which to label events (as is the case for infants) we cannot remember them. The character of social reality is tied to language insofar as we make sense of all our experiences in terms of the linguistic devices of and the logic made available through the language we speak.

As evidence of the consciousness-determining nature of language, we can point to examples of concepts and thoughts that exist in one language and are not entirely translatable to other languages, such as the German concepts of *Kultur* and *Geist*, or the French concepts of *ennui* and *savoir faire*. Speakers of a language are said to share a certain *mentalité* that differentiates their mindset and world view. Likewise, it has been argued that the advancement of science in the West was in part related to the structure of European languages that encourages linear, causal thought patterns.

Discourse is a linguistic phenomenon that refers to a set of ideas, concepts, and vocabulary that recur in texts. A *text* can be broadly defined as any material or non-material communication act. Discourse is a habitual way of speaking about and understanding a topic or issue. Discourses abound in society. We encounter them constantly, but rarely do we explicitly recognize their features even when we are ourselves employing them. That is because it is natural for us to adopt a singular way of understanding an issue, and so a singular way of discussing or talking about an issue.

Take, for example, the issue of crime. In talking about crime, we might employ an *individualist discourse* that understands crime as the actions of a self-interested individual who is presented with options and makes certain choices. Crime in this discourse is conceived as something that one person does to one or more others, and it occurs in discrete instances.

This discourse of crime encourages an understanding of the psychological factors involved in criminal behaviour and leads to solutions that work at the level of the individual. An individualist solution might suggest that if we alter the attractiveness of the option of committing crime by making penalties harsher for those who are caught, the individual will, we hope, no longer choose to commit crime.

In contrast, a *collectivist discourse* of crime also exists. This discourse views crime as a social problem. Crime is conceived as a feature of society that can be more or less prevalent. The focus is on crime rates and on the social conditions that influence the likelihood that crime will be committed in society. This discourse encourages a view more sociological than psychological of the factors contributing to crime, focusing on the social level rather than the individual level. Just as the problem is conceived at the group level, so the ideas and terminology of a collectivist discourse promote a conception of solutions at the group level. For example, an effort to reduce crime might be based on information gained from a comparison of low- and high-crime societies to determine how certain social differences influence crime rates.

As the example of discourses about crime shows, discourses have the potential for great influence. The promotion of certain discourses throughout society, by those with the power to do so, can have the effect of setting the public agenda for certain issues. A discourse of abortion as an issue of privacy, for example, portrays the central concern as autonomy. It privileges the discussion of government impingement on the right of women to control their own bodies. But an opposing discourse surrounding abortion privileges a discussion of the need to uphold the value of all human life, no matter how inchoate that life appears to be. In this discourse, the primary concern is the religiously based idea that human life is sacred and cannot be compromised.

Such discourses play a role in the **social construction** of the categories and definitions we use to understand and to analyze social life. In our daily lives, we constantly refer to these categories and definitions in order to make judgments about good and bad, right and wrong, desirable and undesirable, how to distinguish between "us" and the "other," as well as to understand the very nature of things—Is abortion murder? Are movies an art form or entertainment? Is eating animals a question of morality? Is race about biological differences? Is crime an individual failing? For all these questions, our answers will be influenced

2.2

Sociology in Action
Patients with AIDS

AIDS presented a serious challenge to established identities—and patterns of trust and control—in the treatment domain. A knowledge and treatment vacuum emerged as a result of a very public display of scientific uncertainty and institutional impotence in the face of this new crisis. Suddenly, old understanding about who was knowledgeable, who could and could not be trusted, and who should and should not be granted control, were open to contestation. For example, early on in the epidemic, the expertise of the "doctor" was in doubt. Not only did physicians *not* have the expertise to deal with this new challenge, some were patently unwilling to acquire it or even to act in the interests of their patients. Many early AIDS patients were abandoned, as discrimination, bigotry and fear led to some doctors "dumping" their patients.

PWAS ["persons with AIDS"] began to reject the identity of "patient" and the victimhood it implied. "Patients" (from the French "patienter," which means to wait, as in a physicians' wait-ing room, and originally from the Latin, where it means "to suffer") would be "patient" and suffer in silence no longer. "*Silence = Death*," an expression made popular by the activist group ACT-UP, became the call to action for HIV/AIDS patients seeking to re-define themselves and their role within the domain. Community members stressed that they were neither "patients" nor "victims," but "people living with AIDS." . . .

The identity of PWAS, collectively, is thus very different from that of traditional patient groups. The notion of patients as passive, ignorant, requiring the medical expertise of an elite was successfully deconstructed and replaced with a notion of a patient group as empowered, informed and organized decision makers.

SOURCE: Steve Maguire, Nelson Phillips, and Cynthia Hardy, "When "Silence = Death", Keep Talking: Trust, Control and the Discursive Construction of Identity in the Canadian HIV/AIDS Treatment Domain," *Organization Studies*, 22, 2 (2001): 296. Reprinted by permission of Sage Publications Ltd.

by the way that predominant discourses shape and frame our notions of the core issues at play.

Mass Media

The mass media are a powerful social force. They constitute a key realm of cultural production and distribution and can be seen to play a variety of social roles. The **mass media** are those technologically based methods and institutions that allow a single source to transmit a message to a mass audience. The mass media in Canada include print (newspapers, magazines, books, and journals), film, radio, television (broadcast, cable, and satellite), and the Internet. The Internet is a special case because although it can function as a mass medium, it is also much more: it is a *network* medium by virtue of its ability to allow multiple message sources. Every person on the Internet can potentially be a source of mass media content.

The mass media are a core cultural concern because of the nature of the content that they bring to the vast majority of people. That content can be categorized as *information* and *entertainment*.

Let us first consider the mass media as the primary source of news information in society. They are the means by which we find out about important political, economic, and social happenings. We rely on them for the information we need to understand our local, regional, national, and global contexts. In addition to information that is delivered as news per se on news programs and in newspapers, the mass media provide us with a wealth of other information about the world that we might never have access to through first-hand experience. Through the mass media, we can read about the modernization of industries in China, we can see what the skyline of Buenos Aires looks like, and we can hear about the best way to invest money in a sluggish economy. In short, the mass media bring a world of information to us, and their capacity to do so has greatly increased with the advent of the Internet, which allows us to access only the information we desire, when we desire it.

As the providers of so much information, the mass media have an enormous amount of influence on people's attitudes and behaviours, which are dependent on the state of our knowledge. For example, some people will alter their eating habits based on information they learn from magazine articles about the dangers and benefits of certain foods. And some people will form an opinion about strengthening environmental protection regulations based on stories they watch on television news programs. Because the mass media select a limited amount of information to present to audiences from a virtually infinite supply, they serve as informational gatekeepers (White, 1950). This gatekeeping function can account for much of their influence. However, just as important as what they present is the question of how they present media content. There is a connection here to the preceding discussion of discourses, because it is through the mass media that most discourses are disseminated to the general public.

The mass media are also the primary source for popular culture. While high culture is only rarely made available through the mass media, popular culture is everywhere. We will discuss the aesthetic dimension of culture in a later section, on art and aesthetics. Here we can outline how the popular culture productions brought to us by the mass media are argued to be linked to deep-seated social problems. This link is specified as the ability of the mass media to warp or corrupt our culture: television shows, movies, music, and so on are argued to have a profoundly negative impact on our entire way of life.

An important criticism of mass media content finds fault with the materialistic values the mass media explicitly and implicitly advocate. By constantly connecting depictions of happiness and success to material wealth, the mass media have been a key cause of the development of a consumer culture that focuses our attention and energies on gaining and spending money and away from spiritual, moral, ethical, and social issues. The mass media are also often blamed for a culture of violence: it is argued that they contribute to high levels of violence in society insofar as portrayals of violence incite violent acts and desensitize people to the presence of violence. At the same time, it is argued that the mass media contribute to an unhelpful, unrealistic, and shallow understanding of and response to this violence. The list of social problems linked to the ways in which the mass media may distort and negatively influence our culture is long, including such serious issues as body consciousness and eating disorders, racism, and sexism, exacerbated through stereotypical and misleading depictions.

Religion

Religion is a sociological subfield of its own, but it merits inclusion in a discussion of culture because it has had such a large impact on the development of values and social traditions in most countries, Canada included. The case for the importance of religion as a cultural force was strongly made by Durkheim ([1912] 1995), who saw religion as providing the basis for social solidarity, as noted earlier in this chapter. More generally, we often characterize Western countries as belonging to a Judeo-Christian tradition, a tradition that denotes a specific history and related social institutions and dominant values. It is important to realize that it does not require a specifically religious mindset to be influenced by general Judeo-Christian values. Rather, these values permeate our culture and are seen in such things as predominant views of the role of authority, beliefs in the value of punishment and of rehabilitation, and attitudes toward work and leisure.

Perhaps the best-known thesis regarding the influence of religion on culture is Max Weber's argument in *The Protestant Ethic and the Spirit of Capitalism* ([1904] 1958). Weber argues that several specific aspects of Protestant (specifically Calvinist) doctrine encouraged the values and behaviour of economic rationalism, thereby promoting the rapid advancement of capitalism in Protestant societies. The accuracy of this argument has been questioned, but its importance for an understanding of the cultural role of religion remains.

Art and Aesthetics

In common usage, *culture* is often synonymous with *art*, though for the reasons described in this chapter so far, there is good reason for distinguishing between the two. Art is best seen as one element, albeit a unique element, of our larger culture. The realm of art is, above all, an expressive area of social life. Whereas much of our behaviour is oriented toward the practical achievement of a useful goal, art stands out as an activity that is done for its own sake.

The essence of art is communication through **aesthetic** means. *The New Shorter Oxford English Dictionary* (1993) defines *aesthetics* as "a system of principles for the appreciation of the beautiful." Art, then, employs a set of rules or principles pertaining to our notions of what is beautiful. This makes art a special form of communication: it is those thoughts and emotions that we find difficult to communicate through ordinary language. Instead, it relies on the much more implicit and intuitive rules that people in general use to assess beauty.

Art is an inherently imprecise form of communication, in which particular works carry implicit messages that require a sense of appreciation for the aesthetic principles at play in order to be received. That is why we can read a novel and generate many different ideas about what the novel "is really about" or what the author "is really saying," just as we can for paintings, sculpture, plays, and so on. Moreover, we like to think of truly good art as the expression of artistic genius. Masterpieces, we believe, are the works of geniuses, special people whose ideas and forms of self-expression represent models for human creativity and thought. The very best of art, we believe, represents the very best of humanity, and so art occupies an honoured place in society.

As discussed above, we often distinguish between "popular culture" and "high culture." This distinction points to the existence of a *cultural hierarchy*, in which certain forms of culture are granted greater legitimacy and prestige. Oil painting is higher on the hierarchy than filmmaking, which in turn is higher than television. It is important to recognize that such status distinctions are themselves cultural productions. That is to say, our categories of "high" and "low" are socially constructed. These categorizations represent more than just real differences in the characteristics of cultural productions. They also reflect differences in the social contexts in which high and popular culture are produced, distributed, and received.

Take, for example, Italian opera. We have a clear notion of opera as a high art. The dominant discourse of art portrays art as the product of artistic minds and as inherently special—there is something about art that allows us to recognize it when we see it. So long as we are informed about the value of art, we will never confuse Italian opera with popular culture. This discourse neglects the reality that our definitions of "high" and "popular" reflect an entire social process involved in bringing art to audiences. Our ideas about Italian opera as high art are based partially on an array of cues, such as its high cost, the status of its audiences, the physically distinct and opulent venues in which it is performed, its non-profit status (we like

to oppose art to commerce), and intellectual analyses of Italian opera to explain why it is great art.

This approach to art highlights several of art's sociologically significant features. First, as explained by the production of culture perspective, art does not just spring out of a **collective consciousness**, or even out of an individual's consciousness. Instead, art is a collective activity that requires collaboration between many actors in an art world (Becker, 1982). It is this collective activity that helps to determine how legitimate or prestigious artistic genres are.

Second, the socially constructed nature of distinctions between high and low in art also points to the significance of art in helping to determine the contours of social stratification. This link is rooted in the notion of **cultural capital**: the knowledge, preferences, and tastes that people have concerning art and aesthetics. Having high cultural capital means sharing the knowledge, preferences, and tastes that are common among those of high status in society (see Figure 2.1 on the size of this group). The link between cultural capital and stratification is based on the power of high cultural capital to provide access to informal interpersonal connections that can influence our occupational and economic prospects. Sharing similar artistic tastes and consumption patterns with those in economically privileged positions provides us with access to networks and opportunities not open to those who do not have the necessary aesthetic preferences and expertise. In sociological terms, our cultural capital can increase our economic capital. (This is an interesting inversion of the Marxist logic whereby the cultural realm is determining, or influencing, the economic realm.)

Third, and perhaps even more significant, is the role that artistic consumption plays in creating social groupings in society. The enjoyment of aesthetic products is deeply related to our conceptions of our own identities, of who we really are, and of the kind of people with whom we wish to be associated. In this way, our tastes are profoundly implicated in how our lives are structured. We've already seen how artistic tastes can interact with our class position, but just as important, tastes can also be a way of expressing racial, gender, regional, and age-based identities.

Take the example of youth culture. Although this term refers to many aspects of how young people live their lives, one important way in which adolescents and young adults set themselves apart is through the music they listen to, the publications they read, the television shows and channels they

Figure 2.1 **Attendance Rates of Canadians over 15 for Cultural Activities, 1998**

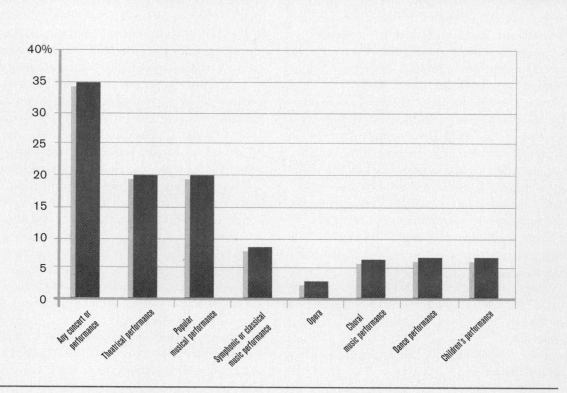

SOURCE: Data derived from Statistics Canada, "Performing Arts Attendance," based on General Social Survey, 1998; available at <www.statcan.ca/english/Pgdb/arts08a.htm>, accessed 16 May 2003.

watch, the films they see, and, increasingly, the Web sites they visit and create. Knowledge of and participation in this particular set of aesthetic preferences allows young people to experience group belonging. Through aesthetics, they can distinguish themselves from prior generations.

Cultural Dynamics

We have already seen that culture changes over time, but we have yet to fully consider any specific mechanisms of cultural change. There are various perspectives we can take to understand why and how culture changes over time. First, we can view changes in culture as responses to particular social-structural changes; we will focus on the cultural ramifications of economic changes and of technological changes. Second, we can also view changes in culture as responses to other cultural developments, a view that emphasizes the weblike, interconnected nature of culture.

Economic, Technological, and Cultural Change

At the most basic level, all of culture can be seen as human adaptation and ingenuity to better control and survive in the physical environment. Beyond that most basic level, but in keeping with the premise that culture allows us to deal with our surroundings, it also gives us the means to function effectively in our social environment, in our dealings with other people. Changes in that social environment, then, encourage and enable corresponding cultural changes.

The discussion of Marxism earlier in this chapter reviewed the case for the economic foundation of culture. In Marxism, culture is a reflection of the underlying economic basis of society. But it is not necessary to adopt Marxists' assumptions of culture as merely a reflection of economics to see that important economic changes are capable of provoking specific changes in culture. An example of such a change is the liberalization of attitudes toward women and

Sometimes art is employed to achieve ideological ends. This painting by Franklin Carmichael, a member of the Group of Seven, depicts the landscape of the Canadian north. The Group sought to express their nationalistic sentiments through paintings of scenes that were uniquely Canadian. (Franklin Carmichael [1890–1945] *Northern Tundra* 1931. Oil on canvas. 77.4 x 92.5 cm. Gift of Col. R.S. McLaughlin. McMichael Canadian Collection. 1968.7.14)

work. In the mid- to late nineteenth century and in the first half of the twentieth century, there was a strong belief in Western societies that it was most appropriate for women, especially married women, not to work outside the home but rather to fulfill their roles as mothers and housewives. While the reasons for the change that has occurred in this attitude are many, it can be argued that an important cause of the change was economic. Maintenance of a middle-class standard of living increasingly required a second income. Changing attitudes about women and work, in this view, were an adaptive response to a changing economic reality.

Over the same period of time, rising levels of affluence made it possible for teenagers to possess a certain amount of disposable income. The development of youth culture, while deriving from various causes, was facilitated by the economic changes that created consumers out of young people and thereby encouraged cultural producers to target and cater to youth. The continued growth in spending power of teenagers has also allowed them to become the primary demographic target of Hollywood film studios. Because young people see films in theatres more often than do older groups, a great deal of film production is tailored to their tastes and expectations. This dynamic is representative of the more general dependence of the content of cultural industries on economic conditions.

Technological change can also be viewed as the source of a great deal of the change in our culture. Perhaps the clearest and most significant technological influence on culture has been the development of the mass media. The printing press, invented by

Johannes Gutenberg in 1452, has been credited with transforming European culture in diverse ways. For example, the press allowed many people to personally own bibles, a precondition for the Protestant Revolution. The invention of the telegraph, which vastly hastened the speed with which information could travel over great distances, has been cited as changing our attitudes concerning the pace of life and punctuality, and even our very definitions of the proportions of space and time.

Television is arguably one of the most powerful technologies ever invented. It has wrought profound cultural changes. First, a specific form of cultural content has developed for the purposes of the medium, shaping our tastes for and expectations of dramatic entertainment, but also, and more fundamentally, influencing our perceptions of social reality and of the nature of the world outside our daily lives. Second, this technology has brought a major leisure activity into our homes, promoting the growth of television culture, in which we spend our free time in a one-way relationship with a screen rather than interacting with others or engaging in community-based activities.

It would be impossible to enumerate all the ways in which technology has created cultural change. To take an example of a broad cultural pattern, the very idea of "nightlife" and all its attendant activities is predicated on the existence of electric light. Much more narrowly, the technological innovation of the electrification of musical instruments has influenced tastes in musical styles. Suffice it to say that technological change frequently has the potential to create cultural reverberations, sometimes of limited significance and other times life-transforming.

Before moving on, it is important to note that recognition of the influence of technological, economic, and other (for example, demographic) changes on the shape of culture is in no way a denial of the transformative power of culture. The relationship, to be sure, is reciprocal. Cultural changes can at times influence these very same structural features of society.

Change for the Sake of Change

Despite the strength of the relationship between culture and social structure, culture also has internal dynamics that can account for cultural change. In this view, cultural change is inevitable because culture, as representative of individual and collective self-expres-

sion, is inherently progressive, evolutionary, volatile, and unstable: it is the nature of culture to evolve.

The validity of this view is perhaps best exemplified by the phenomenon of fashion. *Fashion* is change for the sake of change in the realm of aesthetics. Ongoing change is built into the very idea of fashion. Moreover, fashion is not just the styles of clothes that are popular, although that is one of its most visible manifestations. Rather, elements of fashion can be found in a many areas of social life.

Consider, for instance, how vocabulary choices acknowledge that some words are "in" while others are "out." To express approval, one might have heard adjectives in the past such as *swell*, *groovy*, or *mod*, words that sound dated now despite the fact that the need to express approval has not gone away. New, more fashionable words do the job today. Consider also how changes in furniture and interior design occur gradually but consistently enough to evoke associations with particular decades. Few of these changes are linked to changes in function or technological innovations. Finally, consider how fashion operates to change the popularity of first names (Lieberson, 2000). The Ethels, Mildreds, and Eunices of today are the Emilys, Hannahs, and Madisons of tomorrow (see Table 2.2). The function of naming remains constant, while the aesthetic element of naming reveals continuous modification. The kinds of aesthetic modifications that are made today are dependent on the nature of the aesthetic modifications of the past.

Although aesthetic changes do not serve any practical or functional purposes, they may still be related to a social purpose: they satisfy needs for self-expression. In this sense, the aesthetic dimension of life is symbolic—we communicate to others and articulate (however obliquely) for ourselves certain thoughts, values, identities, and senses of group affiliation. Change in aesthetics results from shifts in the meanings or understandings commonly attributed to certain aesthetic elements, such that they no longer connote what they used to.

To see how this is so, consider Georg Simmel's theory of fashion (1957). This argument has become known as the *trickle-down model*. In this model, fashion is triggered by the status concerns of high-status groups who seek to distinguish themselves by adopting a new fashion. Those elements of fashion that they adopt then come to connote high status on account of their association with a high-status group—that is the symbolism of the fashion. Lower-

Table 2.2   **Top 20 Names for Baby Girls Born in Illinois by Race, 1989, 1940, and 1920**

1989		1940		1920	
Shared by Blacks and Whites		**Shared by Blacks and Whites**		**Shared by Blacks and Whites**	
Ashley	Jessica	Barbara	Joyce	Alice	Helen
Brittany	Michelle	Beverly	Margaret	Anna	Margaret
Christina	Nicole	Carol	Mary	Catherine	Marie
		Dorothy	Patricia	Dorothy	Mary
		Joan	Sandra	Elizabeth	Mildred
			Shirley	Evelyn	Ruth
				Frances	Virginia
White Only	**Black Only**	**White Only**	**Black Only**	**White Only**	**Black Only**
Amanda	Alicia	Carolyn	Betty	Betty	Ethel
Caitlin	Amber	Donna	Brenda	Eleanor	Gladys
Catherine	Ariel	Janet	Dolores	Florence	Lillian
Elizabeth	Bianca	Judith	Gloria	Lorraine	Louise
Emily	Candace	Karen	Gwendolyn	Marion	Lucille
Jennifer	Crystal	Linda	Helen	Marjorie	Thelma
Kelly	Danielle	Marilyn	Jacqueline		
Lauren	Dominique	Nancy	Loretta		
Megan	Ebony	Sharon	Yvonne		
Rachel	Erica				
Rebecca	Jasmine				
Samantha	Kiara				
Sarah	Latoya				
Stephanie	Tiffany				

SOURCE: Stanley Lieberson, *A Matter of Taste: How Names, Fashions, and Culture Change* (New Haven, CT: Yale University Press, 2000), 204. Reprinted by permission of Yale University Press.

status groups then adopt this fashion for themselves to share in the high status, but in doing so they change the meaning of the fashion: it no longer expresses what it used to. High-status groups thus no longer find the fashion appealing or useful, and so they adopt a new fashion. Although this model cannot in fact explain much of the fashion world, which often appropriates the symbols of lower-status groups, it is nonetheless a clear illustration of how culture can evolve according to an internal set of principles that do not reflect social-structural change.

Canadian Culture

The concepts and arguments reviewed in this chapter can help us to understand the current state of Canadian culture, along with some of the more contentious issues facing Canadian society. Because of its unique history, Canadian culture is unlike any other national culture, with a unique set of challenges and a unique set of opportunities.

Distinct Societies

One of the defining features of Canadian culture is its basis in "two founding peoples," French and English. The term *peoples* refers, of course, not only to the actual members of the French and English colonies, but also to their respective ways of life—their cultures. How different or similar are the cultures of French and English Canada? On a global scale, they are quite similar to one another in comparison with, for example, Pakistani or Indonesian culture. However, there are still important ways in which they differ. Most obvious is the linguistic basis for the distinction (see Table 2.3). As discussed earlier, language is a core component of culture, with significant implications for social life. The ability to communicate with verbal and written language is a key element to social bonding—without this form of communication, opportunities for social interaction are limited. Differences in other cultural traditions exist as well, ranging from cuisine and leisure activities to political values and views on marriage and family.

Table 2.3 **Population by Language Spoken Most Often at Home, Canada, 1991, 1996, and 2001**

	1991	1996	2001
English	18,440,535 (68.3%)	19,294,835 (67.6%)	20,011,535 (67.5%)
French	6,288,425 (23.3%)	6,448,615 (22.6%)	6,531,375 (22.0%)
Non-official language	2,265,075 (8.4%)	2,784,645 (9.8%)	3,096,110 (10.5%)

SOURCE: Adapted from Statistics Canada, *Profile of Languages in Canada: English, French and Many Others* (Ottawa: Statistics Canada, 2002); available at <www12.statcan.ca/english/census01/products/analytic/companion/lang/contents.cfm#nine>, accessed 17 May 2003.

The challenge for Canada has been and continues to be the need to forge a unified Canadian culture that respects the unique characteristics of both traditions. To this end, we employ a policy of **official bilingualism** and we foster cultural events and new traditions that embrace both French and English cultural elements. The great concern over the success of this endeavour has been with us for decades and remains. The movement for sovereignty within Quebec is to a large extent based on the belief that the health of French Canadian culture, and especially the vigour of the French language in Quebec, can only be adequately maintained and nurtured separate from a wider Canadian culture. The challenge for our country is to capitalize on the potential for Canadian culture to unite us rather than to divide us.

Multiculturalism

The conception of two founding peoples can be seen as primarily a legal construct rather than an accurate historical depiction. In reality, there have always been more than two cultural traditions in Canada. The Aboriginal cultures of **First Nations** and Inuit peoples were, of course, present before the idea of a Canadian society or culture was ever proposed.

More recently, increased immigration from a large number of countries and the formation of an equally large number of ethnic communities in Canada have added to the number of cultural traditions we have to work with (see Figure 2.2 on Canada's increasing linguistic diversity). As a society, we have adopted a stance of official **multiculturalism**, although the merits of this position engender a good deal of debate. We should distinguish between multiculturalism as a fact of contemporary Canadian society—there are ethnic subcultures that are thriving—and multiculturalism as a policy—the tolerance and

encouragement of the maintenance of the national cultures that immigrants bring with them from their countries of origin.

Proponents of multiculturalism point to its helpfulness in easing the transition of new immigrants into Canadian society. This happens through the fostering of ethnic communities that can provide social support. In addition, proponents argue that multiculturalism is a policy that is properly respectful to all Canadians and that enriches the wider Canadian culture. Detractors, on the other hand, argue that multiculturalism only makes it more difficult to create a unifying Canadian culture. Moreover, they question the wisdom of a policy that encourages, to however small a degree, self-segregation rather than facilitating the full cultural integration of immigrants into Canadian life. Again, just as with the question of two founding peoples, the challenge here is to balance culture's potential for unifying us with our desire to maintain certain cultural partitions.

Globalization and American Cultural Imperialism

Globalization typically refers to the fact that goods, services, information, and labour, now more than ever, can easily flow between distant countries. Of particular concern for us is the cultural influence that globalization brings. There are various implications of globalization for Canadian culture. Technological advancements in mass media have made possible easy and abundant access to the sights and sounds of geographically distant locales. Through media representations we can be made aware of cultural elements from across the globe, and the potential exists to incorporate these elements into Canadian culture. In a sense, one effect of globalization is the internationalization of national cultures as they are increasingly exposed to one another. The mass media, then, are the key channels of the cultural diffusion occurring through the mutual influence of many national cultures.

Globalization, however, can bring with it many difficult cultural challenges. Chief among these challenges is the need to manage the global export of American popular culture. Popular culture, in the form of films, television shows, music, and Web sites, is one of the largest American exports, reaching every corner of the globe. The sheer volume of American cultural export has led to the term *cultural imperialism*, describing the scope of the global dominance of American culture.

The reaction to this state of affairs in Canada has been one of alarm and a concerted effort has been mounted to maintain the integrity of Canadian culture. The importation of American cultural products is seen as dangerous to Canadian culture because the many pre-existing similarities with American culture threaten to overwhelm the differences by which we recognize our culture as distinct and, for us, preferable. In order to promote Canadian cultural production, the federal government has for several decades enacted policies that require Canadian broadcasters to make a sizeable proportion of their content of Canadian origin. In addition, a variety of programs exist to subsidize Canadian film, television, music, and book production (see Figure 2.3 on the relative costs of production).

This policy of Canadian cultural protectionism has clearly achieved some measured successes. Scores

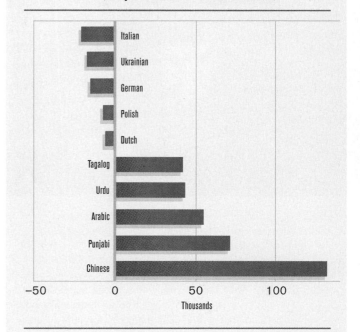

Figure 2.2 Allophone Groups[a] That Increased or Decreased the Most from 1996 to 2001, Canada (Population in Thousands)

[a] Groups of people who possess the same non-official language as their mother tongue.
SOURCE: Adapted from Statistics Canada, *Profile of Languages in Canada: English, French and Many Others* (Ottawa: Statistics Canada, 2002); available at <www12.statcan.ca/english/census01/products/analytic/companion/lang/contents.cfm#nine>, accessed 17 May 2003.

2.3

Human Diversity
Canadians Bilingual? How About Centilingual?

The image of a bilingual Canada is becoming less accurate because Canadians speak more than 100 languages, a report from Statistics Canada says.

The report, released on Tuesday, is based on data from the 2001 national census. It says Canadians reported 100 different mother tongues—the first language they learned and still understood at the time of the census.

Most Canadians, nine out of 10, said they speak either English or French at home, but more than five million people, a sixth of the population, said they learned another language first.

The number of those people grew by 12.5 per cent since 1996, far eclipsing the general population growth rate of four per cent.

After French and English, Chinese was the third most common mother tongue.

SOURCE: "Canadians Bilingual? How About Centilingual?" CBC News Online, 10 Dec. 2002; available at <www.cbc.ca/stories/2002/12/10/statscan_021210>, accessed 17 May 2003.

The smaller Canadian market makes it difficult for Canadian cultural industries to compete with their US counterparts, who can generate vast profits from the American market. Nonetheless, there are occasional inversions of the usual patterns, whereby Canadian artists find success in the United States, such as the rock band Sum 41. While certainly welcome, these successes tend to draw attention away from the fact that Canadians consume vastly more American culture than Americans do Canadian culture.
© Tim Mosenfelder/Corbis/Magmaphoto.com

Figure 2.3   Relative Costs and Revenues of Canadian Content and US Simulcasts in Television

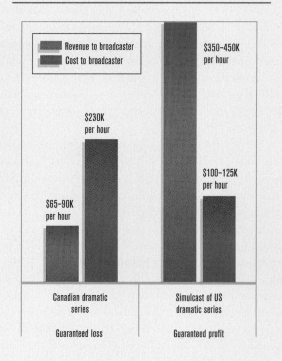

SOURCE: CBC, *The Economics of Canadian Television* (CBC Fact Sheet) (2002); available at <http://cbc. radio-canada.ca/htmen/pdf_rtf/CBCfacts-economics-finale.pdf>, accessed 17 May 2003.

of Canadian artists have achieved a level of success that would have been unlikely if left to compete on the unequal playing field with American artists who are promoted by vast media conglomerates. Yet despite these successes, and despite the strict requirements of Canadian content regulations, Canadians consume tremendous amounts of American popular culture. There is no question that the continuing distinctiveness of Canadian culture and identity is threatened by the extensive consumption of American cultural products. There is an unfortunate contradiction between Canadians' preference for their own national norms, values, attitudes, and beliefs on the one hand and their preference for American popular culture on the other.

Conclusion

Culture is undoubtedly one of the most difficult sociological terms to pin down—it has many meanings—but through careful analysis sociology can bring those

multiple meanings into focus and can explain why we have them. Many different social phenomena can be called "cultural." We need to understand what those various phenomena have in common to cause them all to be considered "culture." Culture is always evolving and is intimately tied to other social changes and to other cultural changes. Finally, we need to be aware of the role of culture in social life because it is the key to understanding some of the most important events in our society and in the world today. Culture is implicated in the social dynamics both of conflict and of people coming together, and for that reason as well as others it is an essential subject for sociological analysis.

☐ Questions for Critical Thought

1. What is Canadian culture, and what are its most important or distinctive facets?
2. What subcultures are you a member of? What are the characteristics of those subcultures, and how did you enter them?
3. How much do you know about other cultures and how did you learn about them? How do you know if your impressions are accurate?
4. Where does culture come from? How could you begin to research such a question? What dimensions of culture are particularly amenable to such a research question?
5. What role do art and music play in your life? Do your friends like the same art and music that you like? Do these art forms bring you together?
6. Who gets to decide what is good literature, painting, films, television, or music, and on what bases? Should you listen to experts on these matters, or can you decide for yourself?
7. How would you go about measuring cultural change? Moreover, how would you try to explain such change?
8. Is cultural change beneficial to society? Is it conceivable to have no changes in our culture?

☐ Recommended Readings

Jeffrey Alexander and Steven Seidman, eds, *Culture and Society: Contemporary Debates* **(New York: Cambridge University Press, 1990).**
This book touches on many of the central issues in the sociology of culture and deals with fundamental issues concerning culture in social theory.

Peter Berger and Thomas Luckmann, *The Social Construction of Reality: A Treatise in the Sociology of Knowledge* **(Garden City, NY: Doubleday–Anchor, 1966).**
This is a seminal work in the sociology of culture, laying the groundwork for social constructionist thought.

Laura Desfor Edles, *Cultural Sociology in Practice* **(Malden, MA: Blackwell, 2002).**
Edles's book is a good survey of many issues and studies, both old and new, in cultural sociology.

Gary Alan Fine, *Gifted Tongues: High School Debate and Adolescent Culture* **(Princeton, NJ: Princeton University Press, 2001).**
Fine employs an analysis of many key cultural sociological concepts to illuminate in a fascinating way a particular subculture.

Wendy Griswold, *Bearing Witness: Readers, Writers, and the Novel in Nigeria* **(Princeton, NJ: Princeton University Press, 2000).**
This is an excellent demonstration of the complexity of cultural analysis, examining cultural production, subculture, and the influence of national values and beliefs.

Michele Lamont, *The Dignity of Working Men: Morality and the Boundaries of Race, Class, and Immigration* **(Cambridge, MA: Harvard University Press; New York: Russell Sage Foundation, 2000).**
This is a thoughtful analysis of the complex ways in which the many dimensions of culture act to shape the lives of working-class men.

Nelson Phillips and Cynthia Hardy, *Discourse Analysis: Investigating Processes of Social Construction* **(Thousand Oaks, CA: Sage, 2002).**
This short book provides a concise and insightful review of the theory and research in sociology and related fields on the role of discourse in social life.

Lyn Spillman, ed., *Cultural Sociology* **(Malden, MA: Blackwell, 2002).**
Spillman provides an entertaining overview of many excellent empirical studies in the sociology of culture as well as many intriguing theoretical works.

☐ Recommended Web Sites

Canadian Broadcasting Corporation (CBC)

www.cbc.ca

In addition to finding the news, you will also find links to the corporate history of the CBC, the broadcasting entity charged with strengthening Canadian culture and identity.

Canadian Heritage

www.canadianheritage.gc.ca

There are many agencies within this federal government department actively involved in promoting the health of Canadian culture.

Canadian Radio-television and Telecommunications Commission (CRTC)

www.crtc.gc.ca

Here you'll find the public policy behind our broadcasting regimes. The CRTC is the quasi-independent agency responsible for regulating the entire broadcast industry.

Culture & Tradition

www.ucs.mun.ca/~culture/

The bilingual journal Culture and Tradition focuses on Canadian folklore and folk culture, both French and English.

Culture/Online

www.ncf.edu/culture/

This is the site of the American Sociological Association's Section on the Sociology of Culture. Here you can find links and news about new work done in the field.

National Film Board of Canada (NFB)

www.nfb.ca

There are countless interesting links at the Web site of the NFB, which is especially renowned for its documentary and animated productions.

Poetics

www.elsevier.nl/inca/publications/store/5/0/5/5/9/2/

The electronic version of the journal Poetics: Journal of Empirical Research on Culture, Media and the Arts is here.

UNESCO

www.unesco.org

The United Nations Educational, Scientific and Cultural Organization deals with, among others, issues of cultural diversity and preservation.

3

Sue Wilson

> > >

Socialization

© Bill Whittman

☐ Learning Objectives

In this chapter, you will:

• gain an understanding of the process of socialization

• understand and develop the capacity to apply basic concepts in the study of socialization

• reflect on personal experiences growing up in terms of socialization

• think about ways the hidden curriculum in educational institutions reproduces inequalities of gender, class, and race

• think critically about the ways in which the mass media both shape and reinforce social values

• learn about the National Longitudinal Survey of Children and Youth as a resource for studying Canadian children

Introduction

Peter Berger (Berger and Berger, 1975) defined **socialization** as the process by which people learn to become members of society. For every individual, this process starts at birth and continues throughout life.

The most intense period of socialization is infancy and early childhood. Almost from the moment of birth, children begin to learn the basics of **social interaction**; they learn to recognize and respond socially to parents and other important people in their lives. In the process of interacting with parents, siblings, and other caregivers, children typically acquire the necessary cognitive and emotional skills to get along in their society. Moreover, as they adjust to daily routines, they learn to conform to adult expectations about a wide range of behaviour: where and when to sleep and eat, what to wear and play with, what is funny and what is serious, and so on. At the same time, children develop an individual **identity**, a self-concept.

Language is an important aspect of socialization. As children learn to understand words and later to use them, they simultaneously learn to categorize their experience. Children also begin at an early age to evaluate their own behaviour and that of others. Indeed, one of the first words many children say is NO!

In time, children learn to identify social **roles**—first the roles of family members, and later, as their experience broadens, those of others with whom they interact. They begin to identify consistent patterns in how they should act around relatives, teachers, doctors, religious leaders. They also develop an understanding of status differences, and the ways in which roles interact with **race**, **class**, and **gender** to create a complex social structure. When children respond appropriately, conforming to social expectations, they are said to have internalized behavioural **norms**.

Socialization patterns vary with class, ethnicity, family structure, gender, and birth order. The way people are socialized is therefore affected by whether they grow up in Vancouver or Moncton; whether they speak English or Cantonese at home; whether they worship at a church, a synagogue, or a mosque; whether they grow up in a single-parent or a two-parent household; and whether their parents are strict or lenient in their discipline, among many other factors. Despite such differences, the research cited throughout this chapter shows that there are certain interesting patterns in socialization practices and outcomes. According to Eleanor Maccoby, for example, as a result of socialization, most people acquire a package of attitudes, skills, and behaviours that enable them to "(a) avoid deviant behaviour; (b) contribute, through work, to the economic support of self and family; (c) form and sustain close relationships with others; and (d) be able to rear children in turn" (1992: 1006).

Parents (or parent substitutes) control much of the early learning environment of their children. But children are not simply passive receptors in the processes of socialization. Because of individual differences, some children thrive on routine; others resent it. Some grow up wanting to be like their parents; others react against parental models. Even within the same family, children will experience socialization differently.

Socialization, then, occurs in the process of social interaction. The two major accomplishments of

Socialization is a life-long process. Almost from birth, children begin to learn the basics of social interaction. They adjust to daily routines and they learn to conform to adult expectations about a wide range of behaviour. (Photo © Megan Mueller)

Family is the most important agent of primary socialization. Parents socialize their children in a wide variety of ways. They teach them how and what to eat, what to play with, what is funny. (Andrew Stawicki/Photosensitive)

children intentionally in countless ways as they teach them how and what to eat, what to wear, what to play with, what is funny, what is sad, how to address and treat others, which behaviours are rewarded and which punished, and so on. At the same time, unintentional socialization takes place as children learn about power and authority; gender, age, class, and ethnic differences; love, affection, and intimacy. Furthermore, the family's status in the community will affect the responses of others to the child, as well as where and with whom the child will play or go to school.

Although it is not entirely a "top-down" process, primary socialization *is* largely imposed, because children have less power and are less competent than adults. Yet, although the relationship is far from equal, there will be some elements of reciprocity in parent–child interactions. On the other hand, the relative power of parents will not guarantee socialization outcomes: children do not simply absorb life lessons from their parents.

Secondary Socialization

Secondary socialization is an ongoing process of "recalibrating" throughout the life cycle as people anticipate and adjust to new experiences and new situations. In changing jobs, marrying, having children, coping with life crises, and so on, people are continually being socialized.

In many ways, socialization is a reciprocal process: children learn from their parents, but parents also learn from their children. Thus, as children learn social interaction from their parents, parents learn how to parent. Reciprocal socialization is not confined to parents and children. Students learn from teachers, teachers from students. Family members, friends, and co-workers also socialize one another. In learning related to digital media, children are typically far more sophisticated than their parents and teachers. Much of this high-tech learning will involve children teaching adults.

Adult socialization differs from childhood socialization because it is based on accumulated learning and previous experience. Frances Waksler likens the difference between primary and secondary socialization to the difference between being born into a religion and converting from one religion to another: "In the latter process, one has both more choice (e.g., the very choice of converting or abandoning the endeavour) and more limits (e.g., the difficulty or

socialization are the development of a self-concept and the internalization of social expectations. This chapter will examine some of the processes by which the complex learning that is socialization occurs and will discuss a number of theories of socialization. As you will see, families, schools, peer groups, and the media all play a part in socializing children. Moreover, adolescent socialization is a process that prepares young people for adult family and employment responsibilities. The chapter closes with a brief look at future directions in socialization.

Forms of Socialization

Socialization is complex and multidimensional. In many ways, socialization is an umbrella concept: it takes in all social contacts and continues from birth to death. This section will consider the various forms of socialization experienced throughout life.

Primary Socialization

The most intense learning, **primary socialization**, occurs from birth through adolescence. The family is the most important agent of primary socialization. This socialization is both intentional and unintentional, imposed and reciprocal. Parents socialize their even impossibility of coming to believe something that one had previously thought unbelievable)" (1991: 14).

Anticipatory Socialization

In most situations, previous experience provides the capacity to imagine new experiences, so people become adept at **anticipatory socialization**. People mentally prepare themselves for future roles and responsibilities by means of anticipatory socialization, which Robert K. Merton defined as "the acquisition of values and orientations found in statuses and groups in which one is not yet engaged but which one is likely to enter" (1968: 438–9). Many college and university students, for instance, are engaged in anticipatory socialization as they acquire necessary academic skills and credentials for their future occupations.

The effectiveness of anticipatory socialization will depend on the degree of ambiguity of a new situation, as well as on its similarity to previous experience. According to Diane Bush and Roberta Simmons, "if the individual is prepared ahead of time for a new role, in the sense of understanding the norms associated with the role, having the necessary skills to carry it out, and becoming aware of expectations and rewards attached to the role . . . he or she will move into the new role easily and effectively" (1981: 147). This sums up very well the assumption underlying the concept of anticipatory socialization.

Many vehicles exist to ease the process of anticipatory socialization. Familiar examples include high school and university initiation, new employee orientation programs, parenting courses, and pre-retirement courses.

Resocialization

Most people would not be able to anticipate successfully what it would be like to join the Armed Forces or a religious cult, to experience the sudden death of a loved one, or to be fired. When people encounter such situations, they must learn new rules. When new situations are so unique that people cannot rely on their previous experience to anticipate how to act, they may encounter a period of **resocialization**.

Some institutions, such as prisons and psychiatric hospitals, are specifically designed to resocialize "deviants." Timothy Seiber and Andrew Gordon (1981) introduced the idea of *socializing organizations*

as a way of understanding socialization. Socializing organizations include total institutions such as prisons, as well as schools, job-training programs, counselling centres, and voluntary associations. These organizations are formally mandated to bring about some change in their members, but often the explicitly stated aims are less important than the latent messages they impart. In the words of Seiber and Gordon, "as recruits participate in the organization they learn its social and speech etiquettes, modes of self-presentation, rituals, routines, symbolic codes of deference, and other patterns of social relations" (1981: 7).

Theories of Socialization

The questions sociologists ask, and often the methods they use, depend on which theoretical perspective they adopt. Some sociologists take **social structure** as their point of departure; others begin with individual interaction. Alan Dawe calls these two approaches, respectively, the *sociology of social system* and the *sociology of social action*: "One views action as the derivative of system whilst the other views system as the derivative of action" (1970: 214).

These two contrasting views of socialization are the focus of this section. The sociology of social system—"action as the derivative of system"—is best represented by the functionalism of Talcott Parsons (1955), who was interested in the ways in which individuals internalize social norms and become conforming members of society. **Symbolic interactionism**, by contrast with functionalism, explains how individual self-concepts develop in the process of social interaction.

The Functionalist Perspective

Sociologists who take the functionalist perspective, such as Talcott Parsons, describe socialization as a process of internalizing socially approved norms and behavioural expectations. People who grow up in a particular culture internalize a similar set of norms and values. The more widespread their acceptance, the more smoothly the group will function. Sociologists refer to a smooth outcome as *social integration*.

According to functionalist thinking, conformity is the consequence of internalizing behavioural expectations. This sounds very deterministic—as if norms necessarily make individuals conform. Indeed, the functionalist emphasis on individual conformity to group norms amounts, as Dennis Wrong (1961) put it, to "an oversocialized view" of humankind. To say that people are socialized does not imply that they have been completely moulded by the norms and values of their culture.

3.1

Global Issues
In China, Conformity Begins Early in Childhood

It's playtime at the Tongren Kindergarten. As three-year-olds run relay races in the schoolyard, the teacher suddenly calls out to one girl.

"You didn't run on the dotted line," the teacher says disapprovingly. The girl, pigtails bobbing, immediately retraces her steps on faded red spots painted on the concrete. The teacher smiles and nods. No one else makes the same mistake.

Children in China learn early the importance of conformity and obedience. Here in the world's most populous country, the highest praise for a child is to be called *guai*—well-behaved and obedient.

To be sure, Chinese kids are loved and pampered by their parents. Indeed, because of a family planning policy begun in late 1979 that limits each couple to one child, spoiled only-children have become so common that Chinese have dubbed them "the little emperors."

But practically from the moment they are born, Chinese babies are conditioned to conform. They are swaddled in blankets and tied up with string to prevent their arms and legs from moving. They sleep only on their backs, never on their stomachs.

Thumbsucking, pacifiers, security blankets and cuddly stuffed animals are not allowed. Toilet training starts within months of birth. Crawling, the main way infants learn new skills, is discouraged. Left-handedness is a no-no.

"Parents like best for their children to be obedient," says Wu Feng-gang of the Child Development Research Centre of China.

Western child-development experts say such practices may teach children to rely not on themselves, but on an outside power, whether their parents or society.

"I think it would make them learn very early that they didn't have any control over their environment," says T. Berry Brazelton, a pediatrics professor at Harvard Medical School who has also studied child development here.

"I think a child who was feisty or individualistic would have a very hard time in China."

After a Chinese baby is born, nurses and doctors swaddle it so tightly in layers of cloth that its arms and legs cannot move. Only the head is exposed. Chinese say the purpose is to re-create the security and warmth of the womb.

Swaddling has been linked to increased incidence of respiratory disease and hypothermia and hinders breastfeeding.

Although some hospitals in Beijing have stopped the practice, swaddling is still widespread in much of China, and in some poor rural regions it is taken to an extreme. In parts of Shandong province and Hobei province—areas plagued by water shortages—an estimated 700,000 to 800,000 peasants are wrapping their babies in sandbags for as long as five years after birth, UNICEF says.

Babies are packed into bags with about 4 kilograms of sand—covered to the waist so that they cannot bend, sit up, roll or move about. Parents then leave their children at home in these bags while they work in the fields.

But it is in day care and preschool that the most rigorous socialization takes place. Working parents often have no choice but to board their children—sometimes just a few months old—in day care for several days at a time.

———

SOURCE: Lena Sun, "For Chinese, Conformity Begins Early in Childhood," *Toronto Star* (20 Aug. 1993), C1, C20. © 1993 *The Washington Post*. Reprinted with permission.

The Feminist Critique

Sexist socialization practices were one of the first targets of **feminist** critiques of sociology, in the 1970s. Feminists were very critical of Parsonian analysis because of the implication that differences between men and women could be understood as differences in socialization. In the first place, to describe inequities as the result of socialization avoided the issue of the structural barriers faced by women. Secondly, the socialization approach begged the question of change: how could parents socialized in traditional ways adopt non-sexist child-rearing practices? Therefore, feminists typically do not use socialization to explain gender differences, viewing them instead as consequences of systemic inequalities.

Gender socialization will be discussed in more detail later in the chapter. There is an extensive literature documenting differential socialization practices, both implicit and explicit, and the ways these contribute to establishing gender differences in adolescents and adults.

The Symbolic Interactionist Perspective

The symbolic interactionist approach, in contrast to the functionalist perspective, assumes that individuals actively participate in their own socialization. George H. Mead and Charles H. Cooley, two American sociologists who were active around the beginning of the twentieth century, were key influences in developing the symbolic interactionist perspective. Perhaps more than any other theorists, these two men influenced the way in which most sociologists understand socialization.

Both Cooley and Mead were interested in the way individuals develop a sense of **self**, and in the importance of family interaction in this process. Cooley believed that children were born with an instinctive capacity for self-development, which matured through interactions in *primary groups*, which he defined as "characterized by intimate face-to-face association and cooperation" ([1909] 1962: 23).

Adults communicate their attitudes and values to their children primarily through language, and children develop a self-concept on this basis. In other words, people begin to see themselves as they imagine others see them. This feeling, "I feel about me the way I think you think of me," Cooley called the **looking-glass self**. The looking-glass self has three elements, according to Cooley: "the imagination of our appearance to the other person; the imagination of his judgment of that appearance; and some sort of self-feeling, such as pride or mortification" (1902: 184). The reaction of others, then, is important in determining how people feel about themselves.

Mead (1934) was also interested in the development of self-concept, which he considered to have two components: the Me, the socially defined self that has internalized society's norms and values, and the I, the spontaneous, creative self. The I is what makes every person different from others. The Me induces people to conform to behavioural expectations.

Mead emphasized the importance of children's imaginative play in early socialization, believing that it is through play that children become sensitive to the responses of others. He believed that people learn symbolically, by taking roles, to present themselves in different social situations. This process consists of four stages. At first, children's behaviour is a combination of instinctive behaviour and imitation. This Mead called the *pre-play stage*. Later, when children pretend to be a parent, teacher, doctor, and the like, they are in effect role-playing. Mead called this the *play stage*, in which children learn to assume the roles of others and to objectify that experience by seeing themselves from the point of view of others. In the next stage, the *game stage*, children learn to handle several roles at once, to anticipate the behaviour of others and the expectations others have of them. Finally, children learn to internalize general social expectations by imagining how any number of others will act and react. At this **generalized other** stage, a child has a sense of self and can react in a socially approved way.

Marlene Mackie (1987) regards the pre-play stage as lasting until the age of about two, the play stage as extending from two until the entry to school, and the game stage as continuing until puberty. Judy Dunn (1986), however, argues that children have an early and sophisticated sense of the emotional states of family members, and respond appropriately. On the basis of her study of British families, Dunn asserts that by two years of age, children have developed "powers to anticipate the feelings and intentions of other family members" and "powers to recognize and transgress social rules and to understand that jokes about such transgressions can be shared with other people" (1986: 112). Nonetheless, because social meanings are based on assumptions concerning the understanding and intentions of others, they are always more or less ambiguous and subject to ongoing interpretation and reinterpretation.

Psychological Theories of Socialization

Sociologists owe a considerable debt to psychological theories of development, including the psychoanalytic theories of Sigmund Freud (1856–1939). According to Freud ([1938] 1973), the emotional development of children can be measured as a progression through five stages: oral, anal, phallic, latent, and genital.

The *oral stage* occurs in the first year when children are satiated, and experience positive sensations through suckling. At this stage too, children begin to explore the world by putting objects in their mouths. The *anal stage* focuses on toilet training and is the child's first experience with self-control (Collier, Minton, and Reynolds, 1991). Gender differences in development begin at the phallic stage, when children become aware of sex differences. This is followed by a latent period during which a child's sex drive is dormant before being awakened in adolescence.

Phase theories of development that focus on particular life tasks accomplished at specific stages in the life cycle inevitably build on Freud's work. Erik Erikson (1982), for instance, identified eight stages, or "turning points," from infancy to old age. Each stage involves a conflict whose resolution creates a specific human capacity. For example, in the first phase, infants resolve the conflict between trust and mistrust, developing hope in the process. In the final stage, old age, the conflict is between integrity and despair, and people develop wisdom from the resolution of this conflict.

Another way Freud influenced the thinking of social psychologists was through his theory of personality development (Freud, [1923] 1974). Indeed, awareness of the three components of personality (the id, the ego, and the superego) has seeped into popular culture and become part of everyday parlance. For Freud, the ego mediates between the id—our basic instincts—and the superego—internalized values. The insight for sociologists is that both the ego and the superego develop socially—in other words, in the process of socialization: "One of Freud's central theses is that society forces people to suppress basic human impulses such as sex and aggression, so that they must find expression in indirect and often distorted ways" (Collier, Minton, and Reynolds, 1991: 105).

Behavioural theories, by contrast, describe socialization as a process of learning through identification or reinforcement. Reinforcement, typically by parents, encourages some behaviours and discourages others. Albert Bandura (1973) whose work on children's imitation of violence has been very influential, developed his social learning theory based on observations of children imitating parents and other models. While we have all seen children imitating parents, and may have family stories that centre on such imitative behaviour, it is hard to explain all learning in terms of this model.

There are, then, two views of socialization: action as derivative of system, and system as derivative of action. Those who focus on ways individuals *internalize* social norms and values fall into the first group. This perspective was the focus of early feminist critique of socialization theories. Mead and Cooley, in contrast, focus on ways individuals are active participants in socialization—that infants are born with the capacity for self-development. Students interested in understanding more about this topic are encouraged to read original versions of the work of Freud, Mead, Cooley, and Erikson.

Agents of Socialization

Agents of socialization are those social institutions in children's environments that have the greatest effect on their socialization. The principal agents of socialization are the family, friendship or peer groups, the education system, the media, religious institutions, and the neighbourhood or community. The socializing effect of these agents varies over time, and are different for different children.

For most children, the family is the most important agent of socialization. Although it is reasonable to assume that children today spend fewer of their preschool years in the exclusive care of a family member, it is still the case that children learn basic life skills and develop their values and beliefs in the course of family interaction. The other important agents of socialization to be discussed here are schools (including daycare centres and preschool), friendship or peer groups, and the media. Parents and schools have legally defined responsibility for socializing children; peer groups do not.

The Family

Most children today have early and extensive experience of the world around them. Nevertheless, the family is still the most impressive agent of socialization. In families, children learn how to relate to other people, express intimacy, and resolve conflict. Parents play a major part in the lifelong social adjustment of their children. To cite Maccoby, "successful socialization of children involves not only bringing about their outward conformity to parental directives, but also enabling them to become self-regulating, and motivating them so that they become willing to cooperate with parental socialization efforts" (1992: 171).

How do parents encourage their children to internalize social norms and values and to behave in socially appropriate ways? On the surface, it might seem that parental control of scarce resources would be sufficient inducement. However, asserting parental power is only effective in the short term. Longer-term effects are achieved when children have a say in setting the standards with which they are expected to comply (Maccoby, 1992). The parenting style which seems to be most effective in developing high self-esteem and encouraging self-regulating skills is a combination of warmth and discipline. Diana Baumrind (1971) called this style *authoritative parenting*. Authoritative parents are affectionate, but clear in their expectations for prosocial, responsible behaviour. An authoritative parenting style is balanced between the two extremes of authoritarian and permissive parenting.

The family is the child's window to the world. A child's experience of the world will be framed by his or her family's social class, religion, ethnicity, and so on.

Families today are also far more varied structurally than families in the past. More children are born to single women, live in single-parent households, or enter reconstituted families. What effect do these outcomes have on socialization? Do socialization practices differ by type of family? Many researchers have considered these questions. Sociologists Elizabeth Thomson, Sara McLanahan, and Roberta Curtin, for instance, argue that "the most consistent findings from studies of family structure and socialization are that single parents exert weaker controls and make fewer demands on children than married parents" (1992: 368). The researchers wondered why this was so. Was it because one parent can exert only half as much control as two, or because single mothers have not been socialized to display traditional paternal control behaviours? They concluded that socialization differences are determined primarily by the structural conditions of being a single parent, not by gender. In other words, the primary reason for the greater leniency of single parents is their lack of time.

Does parenting style matter? According to the National Longitudinal Survey of Children and Youth, it does indeed. Sarah Landy and Kwok Kwan Tam

3.2 Sociology in Action
The National Longitudinal Survey of Children and Youth

The National Longitudinal Survey of Children and Youth (NLSCY) was initiated in 1994. Its purpose is to follow Canadian children by interviewing them every other year until 2018. The initial national sample comprised 22,500 individuals aged newborn to adult.

Information is gathered about the children and their families from the "person most knowledgeable"—usually the child's mother. Teachers and school principals also contribute information about school performance. Children aged 10 and 11 are asked about their experiences with friends, family, and school.

The study was designed to support the analysis of child and youth characteristics over time and to allow for the investigation of the

impact of social and physical environments on outcome measures such as sociability and success in school.

Longitudinal studies such as this one allow researchers to identify factors in a child's environment that affect later life abilities, capacities, health, and well-being. The NLSCY includes key development indicators such as family composition, employment, economic well-being, parenting styles, and community resources. Some of the research cited in this chapter is taken from this survey. To find out more about the survey, go to the study Web site: <www.hrdc-drhc.gc.ca/sp-ps/arb-dgra/nlscy-elnej/home.shtml>.

(1996) looked at the effect of parenting style on children who were also at risk because of family characteristics. Four styles were identified: ineffective, aversive, consistent, and positive. *Ineffective parents* are often annoyed with their children and prone to telling the child he or she is bad, or not as good as others. *Aversive parents* raise their voices when children misbehave and use physical punishment. *Consistent parents* discipline the same way for the same behaviour. *Positive parents* praise their children and play and laugh together. Risk factors that might negatively affect physical or mental development include family dysfunction, low social support, and low income. Fewer than 4 per cent of the children in the survey were significantly at risk, and these children had four or more risk factors. The authors found that parenting practices had a greater impact on outcomes than risk factors. Indeed, positive parenting practices significantly contribute to child outcomes and protect children who are at risk: "Children in at-risk situations who enjoyed positive parenting practices achieved [outcome] scores within the average range for children in Canada" (Landy and Tam, 1996: 109). The parenting style that most strongly predicts delinquent behaviour in children aged 8 to 11 is the ineffective style, followed by the aversive and inconsistent styles (Stevenson, 1999). (See also Table 3.1.)

Children gradually move beyond their experience of the family. As they become involved in groups in the neighbourhood—other families, play groups, school classes, church groups, and the like—they gain social experience, deal with conflicting demands, and become increasingly sophisticated social actors.

Nevertheless, at the base of this experience of the world is their initial experience of family, which acts as a benchmark throughout life.

Mass Media

The **mass media**, including newspapers, magazines, television, radio, films, and the Internet, are more than sources of entertainment or information. They are influential agents of socialization. The mass media are instrumental in transmitting and reinforcing certain values, social behaviours, and definitions of social reality. By focusing on some groups and not others or by stereotyping social characteristics, the media provide important lessons about power and influence. In this way, the media contribute to racial and sexual stereotypes. Stereotyped portrayals of men and women, racial or ethnic minorities, homosexual men or women, older people, or those with varying abilities both reflect and socialize. The impact is circular. Media representations are indicative of "who counts" in our society, and in turn provide lessons in who counts.

One of the first targets of feminist critique was the mass media, for contributing to the stereotyping of men and women. One would expect that there would be less stereotyping now than in the past because of this criticism and because women have made economic and political gains in the last four decades. It is therefore surprising to find that television commercials continue to reflect a gender imbalance. Robert Bartsch and colleagues (2000) replicated two earlier studies of stereotyping in television

Table 3.1 **Poor Parenting Practices**

Parenting Style Used	Children with Conduct Disorder	
	Frequency	%
Ineffective	Rarely	4
	Sometimes	24
	Very often	63
Aversive	Rarely	7
	Sometimes	22
	Very often	40
Consistent	Rarely	38
	Sometimes	24
	very often	16
Positive	Rarely	27
	Sometimes	19
	Very Often	14

SOURCE: Adapted from Kathryn Stevenson, "Family Characteristics of Problem Kids," *Canadian Social Trends* (Winter 1999), Catalogue 11-008, 4.

3.3

Human Diversity
More Immigrant Children Enjoy Good Mental Health Than Canadian Children

Children in recent immigrant families have better mental health than Canadian children according to a study conducted by Beiser, Hou, Hyman, and Tousignant (1999) using the National Longitudinal Survey of Children and Youth. Canadian children are more likely to have severe symptoms of hyperactivity, emotional, or conduct disorders when compared to the children of new immigrants.

This is an interesting finding in that a higher proportion of immigrant families are poor, and poverty is an important risk factor for children. In addition, both children and parents in immigrant families suffer from the stress of relocation. The authors of the study suggest the following explanation:

> Unemployment and poverty are initial conditions of adversity in a new land—the promise of a better life sustains immigrant families. For poor Canadian families, poverty tends to be part of a negative spiral of family dysfunction, single-parent family structure, alcohol abuse and parental mental illness—all of which affect parenting practices as well as the mental health of children. The context of poverty modifies the effect that it has on the mental health of immigrant and Canadian children, resulting in different rates of well-being.

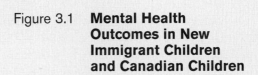

Figure 3.1 **Mental Health Outcomes in New Immigrant Children and Canadian Children**

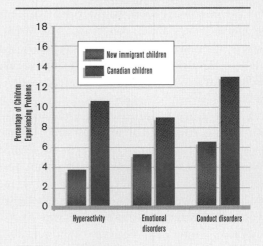

SOURCE: Morton Beiser, Feng Hou, Ilian Hyman, and Michel Tousignant, "Immigrant Mental Health," Human Resources Development Canada, *Applied Research Bulletin* (Fall 1999), 21.

SOURCE: Exerpts from 'Immigrant Mental Health' by M. Beiser et al, *Applied Research Bulletin*, Human Resources Development Canada, Fall 1999. Reproduced with the permission of the Minister of Public Works and Government Services Canada, 2003.

commercials and found that most voice-overs continue to be male, and men are still more likely to appear in all commercials except those advertising domestic products. The authors did find some movement, however. The proportion of male voice-overs dropped from approximately 90 per cent to approximately 70 per cent, and the proportion of women advertising non-domestic products increased (2000: 739–40).

What about advertisements in non-Western media? In India, magazines, not electronic media, are the primary vehicle for advertising. Mallika Das (2000) studied changes in portrayals of men and women in Indian magazine advertisements in 1987,

1990, and 1994. Interestingly, the results showed that the 1990 ads portrayed women in less traditional situations than the earlier or later ads. At the same time, men were portrayed in more traditional ways in 1990 than before or after. In North American media, men and women are most typically shown in athletic roles in advertisements. This is far less evident in India. On the other hand, Indian women are less likely to be portrayed as sex objects than women in British media. Das writes, "In India the trend seems to be to portray women less often as housewives or concerned with looks, but not more often in non-traditional, career-oriented, or authority figure roles" (2000:

713). Das suggests that this may reflect the patriarchal values of Indian society.

Concern about media violence has been long-standing. Today, concern focuses on violence and pornography in digital media; 20 years ago it was television, particularly music videos; but movies, comics, and magazines have all been considered potentially dangerous sources of influence, especially for young people. In the 1950s, Frederic Wertham published his book *Seduction of the Innocent* (1954) to protest violence in comic books, as there was a concern regarding the rise of comic books and the rise of violence in the United States. Those concerned about media violence feel that the negative effects of the media are self-evident, that the sheer amount of violence speaks for itself. They are concerned that children will imitate what they see on television or on the Internet. A second, more subtle, more pervasive problem is the media's role in creating definitions of social reality. For example, we may tolerate high levels of violence because we have come to think that "that's the way life is."

Media effects have been studied by psychologists in laboratory experiments. Under laboratory conditions, subjects display more aggressive behaviour than control groups when exposed to television portrayals of violence (see Bandura, 1973). It is not clear, however, whether the kinds of imitative behaviour that occur in the laboratory also occur in normal social interaction. Experiments may confidently conclude that the response (aggressive behaviour) was triggered by the stimulus (violent media portrayals) but not that it will also occur outside the lab (Singer and Singer, 2000). In natural settings, the difficulty lies in controlling extraneous variables. In other words, how can we be sure that the behaviour we observed was, in fact, triggered by the media and not by something else?

Television is the third largest time allocation in our lives, after work or school and sleep. It is interesting that the number of hours Canadians spend watching conventional television has decreased over the past two decades. Canadians watched television for an average of 21.5 hours a week in the fall of 2000. The average ranged between 23 and 24 hours a week during the 1980s. Young men (aged 18–24) spent the least amount of time watching television—only 13.2 hours a week. Women watched an average of 5 more hours of television than men, although for both sexes, viewing time increased with age (Statistics Canada, 2001d).

Television is the primary medium accessible to children and is a potent agent of socialization. While we might worry about the amount of television children watch and about the way television contributes to a sedentary lifestyle, the amount of time children spend watching television has, like adult viewing, decreased. According to Statistics Canada figures, adolescents watch an average of 14.1 hours a week and children watch 15.5 hours. Part of the decline is due to the increased use of VCRs. However, the main reason for the change in television behaviour has been pay-TV and specialty service. Almost 84 per cent of Canadians had access to cable or satellite services in 2000 (Statistics Canada, 2001d; see also Figure 3.2).

In 1997, Statistics Canada began to collect data about Internet use. The 2000 General Social Survey, with over 25,000 respondents, provides an interesting picture of Internet use in Canada. In this survey, use was defined as at least once in the past year. As we might predict, Internet use is related to age, income, and education. Only 30 per cent of low-income Canadians (with a household income of below $20,000) said that they used the Internet in the previous year, compared to 81 per cent of those with household income over $80,000. The education gap is even more dramatic. Only 13 per cent of adults over 20 with low education (less than a high school diploma) used the Internet, compared to 79 per cent of those with university degrees (Statistics Canada, 2001c: 3).

In his book *Growing Up Digital*, Don Tapscott (1998) refers to what demographers have called the *baby-boom echo generation* (born between 1977 and 1997) as the *Net generation*. The media sometimes call this group *screenagers*. While their parents, the baby-boom generation, were shaped by television, which influenced their values, their political beliefs, and how they spent their leisure time, the Net generation are immersed in digital media, with perhaps more far-reaching effects, for digital media is an educational tool in a way that television was never able to be. The Net generation also use the Internet to communicate with friends and to establish and maintain community. Young people have, according to Tapscott, become bored with the unidirectional medium of television, preferring the engagement required by digital technology. Indeed, they watch far less television than their parents did when they were young. The Net generation are also sophisticated users of the new technology, far surpassing their parents or their teachers.

Two aspects of shifting media use are worth noting. The first is that media use is increasingly a solitary activity. Today there are more televisions and

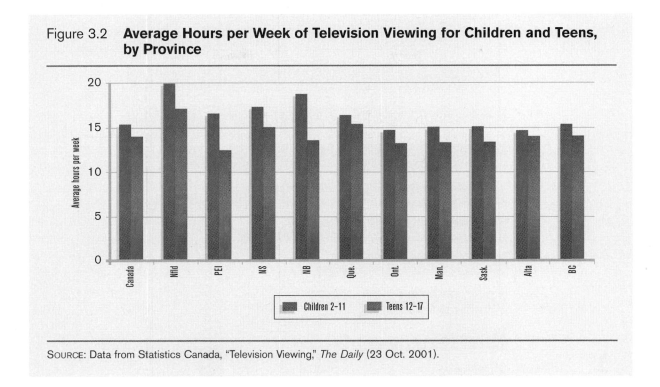

Figure 3.2 **Average Hours per Week of Television Viewing for Children and Teens, by Province**

SOURCE: Data from Statistics Canada, "Television Viewing," *The Daily* (23 Oct. 2001).

fewer people per household. In other words, more people are watching television alone. We also watch more videos and go to fewer movies. Again, going to the movies is usually a social activity; video viewing may not be. Typically, entertainment and communication on the Internet are solitary. The second point concerns what Tapscott (1998) calls the *digital divide*: the class and educational difference in digital media use. This has created a system of information haves and have-nots. The digital divide occurs within societies like Canada and the United States, and it occurs between societies where dramatic differences in access distinguish the developing and the developed world.

The Statistics Canada General Social Survey of 2000 asked Canadians about their Internet use. There were 3,300 young people (aged 15–24) among the respondents, 56 per cent of whom were connected to the Internet at home. Almost half of these young people used the Internet every day. Frequent users also access the Internet at school and at work. Nevertheless, those with home access indicated far more hours of use than those without home access. Men use the Internet for more hours per week than women. E-mail is the most popular Internet activity for young Canadians (Rotermann, 1999: 5–6; see also Figure 3.3). Internet use for 15- to 24-year-olds is lower in Quebec than in the rest of Canada. This is

presumably because much of the content of the Internet is in English only, a factor that affects usage worldwide.

The Peer Group

Patricia Ramsey writes, "For both children and adults, friends enhance our pleasure, mitigate our anxieties and broaden our realm of experience" (1991: 3). As you have seen, the family is the first reference group for most people, that is, the group with which children compare their behaviour, ideas, and values. But starting at an early age, the peer group also becomes very important. Because so many parents are now in the labour force, more children are spending more time with children of the same age, and at a younger age. Peer groups have therefore gained increasing recognition as important socializing agents for even very young children. The success of children's peer relationships is linked to their later psychological development and to school success. It has also been suggested that children with poor peer relationships may experience job-related and marital problems in later life (Ramsey, 1991).

Play groups provide important opportunities for children to learn to relate to others and increase their social skills. By interacting with their peers in play groups, children develop a frame of reference not

Figure 3.3 **Young People's Use of the Internet (Ages 15–24)**

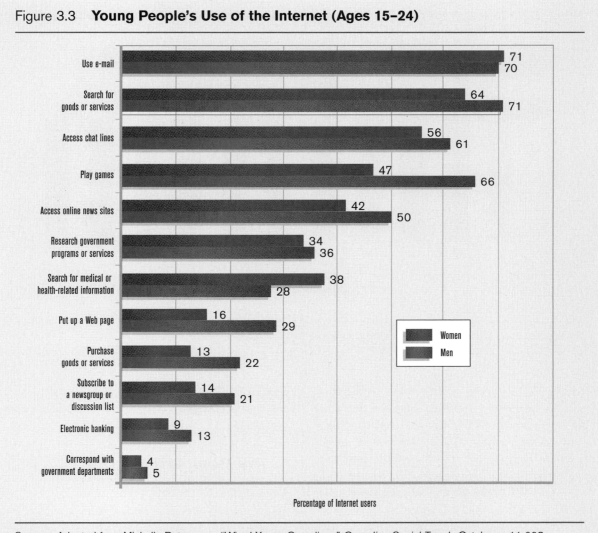

	Women	Men
Use e-mail	71	70
Search for goods or services	64	71
Access chat lines	56	61
Play games	47	66
Access online news sites	42	50
Research government programs or services	34	36
Search for medical or health-related information	38	28
Put up a Web page	16	29
Purchase goods or services	13	22
Subscribe to a newsgroup or discussion list	14	21
Electronic banking	9	13
Correspond with government departments	4	5

Percentage of Internet users

SOURCE: Adapted from Michelle Rotermann, "Wired Young Canadians," *Canadian Social Trends* Catalogue 11-008 (Winter 2001), 6.

based on adult authority. Gerald Handel asserts that "it is in these peer groups that a child learns to function more independently, to acquire and test skills and beliefs that earn him a place among people of the same generation, to develop new outlooks that reflect youthful interests rather than adult ones" (1988: 17).

The peer group assumes great influence in adolescence. In developmental terms, the task of adolescents is to begin to establish emotional, social, and economic independence. By the age of 13 or 14, adolescents typically spend most of their leisure time with peers. In an international survey, Klaus Hurrelmann found, for example, that Western adolescents report spending more time talking to peers than on any other single activity—and are happiest doing just this (1989: 16).

Adolescence is commonly depicted as period of testing limits. It is not a surprise that more adolescents

are killed in accidents than die from health-related problems. If we were to rely on the mass media, we might be persuaded that youth violence is increasing in this "age of Columbine." Certainly there have been a few spectacular incidents of adolescent violence in Canada and in the United States. On the other hand, official statistics suggest that the incidence of violent crime is declining and that only a small proportion of young people are involved in physical violence. When Canadian sociologist Reginald Bibby surveyed Canadian young people, he found that many were fearful of encountering violence: 22 per cent of young people did not feel safe in school—a smaller proportion than found in comparable US studies (2001: 84, 88). (See also Table 3.2.)

Why is it that some adolescents resort to physical violence and others do not? The National Longitudinal Survey of Children and Youth (NLSCY) provides some interesting information about aggressive behaviour among Canadian pre-adolescents. Indeed, children become less, not more, violent as they become older. The age at which children are most likely to hit, bite, or kick was 27 to 29 months (Tremblay et al., 1996: 129), suggesting that most Canadian children "benefit from the socializing impact of their families and other socialization agencies" (Tremblay et al., 1996: 130). Children who are physically aggressive are also often hyperactive and suffer inattention problems. They also have lower self-esteem, tend to exhibit high levels of indirect aggression and high emotional disorder, and tend not to help other children (Tremblay et al., 1996: 132).

Families have an important impact on the aggressive behaviour of pre-adolescents. Boys and girls who have siblings with behavioural problems are more likely to be aggressive themselves. They are also more likely to live in families with high levels of parent–child conflict and sibling conflict. Aggressive children have poor peer relationships and are more likely to be victimized by other aggressors (see Table 3.3). Will these young people outgrow their adolescent behaviour? Richard Tremblay and colleagues (1996) suggest that because the aggression stems from

Peer play groups provide important opportunities for children to learn and relate to others and increase their social skills. Peer groups have gained increasing recognition as important socializing agents even for very young children. (Photo © Megan Mueller)

family interaction problems, this appears unlikely. Without support, these children are more likely to continue aggressive behaviour into adulthood. It is, however, important to keep in mind that these children represent a small proportion of all Canadian

Table 3.2 **Teens' Concern About Violence by Region, Community Size, and Birthplace (Percentages)**

	School Violence a Very Serious Problem	Close Friend Attacked at School	Not Safe at School	Not Safe at Home	Close Friend Physically Abused at Home
Nationally	50	32	22	7	31
British Columbia	51	30	19	7	30
Prairies	49	32	17	5	30
Ontario	53	32	22	7	32
Quebec	43	33	27	7	33
Atlantic	54	30	21	8	27
North	53	34	19	2	31
Cities, towns					
<30,000	53	29	21	8	33
30,000–99,999	56	36	28	7	31
100,000–399,999	51	32	21	7	34
>400,000	44	35	21	5	32
Rural					
Non-farm	52	32	18	7	27
Farm	50	24	19	6	25
Born in Canada	50	31	21	7	32
Born outside Canada	47	35	26	6	28

SOURCE: Reginald W. Bibby, *Canada's Teens* (Toronto: Stoddart, 2001), 84.

Table 3.3   **Prevalence of Bullying and Victimization in Canada (Percentages)**

	Parent's Report		Children's Self-Report[a]	
	Boys	Girls	Boys	Girls
Ages 4–6				
Bullying	14.4	9.4	–	–
Victimization	4.9	4.4	–	–
Ages 7–9				
Bullying	14.8	7.9	–	–
Victimization	4.0	7.4	–	–
Ages 10–11				
Bullying	13.0	9.2	17.2	8.7
Victimization	8.6	9.1	13.6	8.1

[a] Self-report data were not collected in the 4–6 and 7–9 age groups.
SOURCE: Wendy Craig, Ray Peters, and Roman Konarski, "Bully and Victim: Child's Play or Unhealthy Schoolyard Behaviour?" *Applied Research Bulletin* (Fall 1999), 17. Reproduced with the permission of the Minister of Public Works and Government Services Canada, 2003.

children. Most children are not inappropriately aggressive. In addition, they are, as Bibby (2001) points out, highly resilient. In the face of family problems and economic and educational disadvantage, Canadian adolescents are optimistic about the future.

Although much is made of the idea of adolescent rebellion, there will generally be considerable correspondence between parental and adolescent values. Because parents want their children to be well liked and want good relationships with them, they are generally supportive of their children's activities. Peer-group influence is tempered by parental influence because parents control scarce and valued resources, including their approval. Certainly some adolescents rebel, but for most young people learning to be independent adults, adolescence is not a particularly turbulent time. In fact, research suggests that the majority of teenagers experience adolescence positively. Daniel Offer's 1988 study of 6,000 adolescents in 10 countries (Australia, Bangladesh, Hungary, Israel, Italy, Japan, Taiwan, Turkey, the United States, and West Germany) revealed surprising similarities in the experience of growing up. Most adolescents (about 80 per cent in each country) were well adjusted and confident, enjoyed life, had a positive self-image, and liked their parents (Offer et al., 1988). They had positive expectations about the future and felt emotionally able to cope with it.

School

Schools do more than instruct students in the three R's; they also provide an important environment for the transmission of social values. Next to the family, the school is probably the most important locus of childhood and adolescent socialization, because it is central to a young person's social life and acts as a filter for future occupational choice. A key component here seems to be the effect of positive reactions by parents and teachers on a child's self-concept. Doris Entwisle and Leslie Hayduck (1988) report that parental and teacher reactions measured in Grade 3 had a significant effect on achievement almost a decade later. As they explain, children in the early grades are building their "academic self-images." During transitions, children depend on significant others for support: "getting off to a good start gives them a competitive advantage from then on" (Entwisle and Hayduck, 1988: 158).

Self-concepts are particularly fragile when adolescents are in middle school (senior public or junior high). David Kinney (1993) reports that older adolescents remember this as a difficult time. Students universally recall a rigid social structure dominated by a popular (and powerful) group. Unpopular adolescents remember being ridiculed, shunned, and ignored by their popular classmates. Fortunately, the impact of popularity is short lived. In high school, student culture is more open and more diverse. There are far more reference groups with which to identify, and the social structure is less hierarchical (Kinney, 1993).

As children mature, they increase their experiences and contacts. However, these events and associations will be not random, but rather largely compatible with earlier experience. It is therefore unlikely that the school environment will promote values that are different from those already learned by a child. For example, middle-class children will attend school with other middle-class children, who for the most part will value school achievement.

Yet much of what is learned in school is implicit, sometimes referred to as the **hidden curriculum**. The hidden curriculum comprises unspoken rules and practices such as the acclaim given by students and teachers alike to academic versus athletic endeavours and the behaviours that are punished versus those that are excused; the age, sex, race, and ethnic structure of the administration, the teaching staff, and the student body; and the similarity or difference between a student's friends' and his or her family's expectations for the student's success. The greater the disjunction between the behaviours reinforced at school and those reinforced by the family or the peer group, the smaller the likelihood that the student will see success in school as relevant.

Parental involvement, including helping children with homework, encouraging them to study, having contact with the school and teachers, and attending events at the school, has a positive effect on children's academic performance. This relationship holds for younger as well as older students.

Many immigrant parents in particular have high expectations for their children regarding education. As shown in Table 3.4, the majority are actively involved in their children's education and want their children to go to university. Canadian-born children of Canadian-born parents are much less likely to want to choose their children's career or to expect their children to go to university. They are, however, among the most likely parents to help their children with school. L.P. Salazar and colleagues (2001) studied the family socialization processes used by Filipino Canadian parents living in Winnipeg to motivate their children in school. The children who were in Grades 7 through 12 completed a self-report questionnaire about parenting styles, parent involvement, the importance of family reputation, attribution of success, and student involvement. The results suggest that student involvement in school was promoted by parental involvement (as perceived by their adolescents) and authoritative (not authoritarian) parenting. Authoritative parents encourage psychological autonomy and exert firm behavioural guidelines. Authoritarian parents, in contrast, are strict, demand obedience, and are emotionally distant. Adolescents indicated that they felt obliged to do well in school in order to maintain their family reputation. Those

Next to the family, school is probably the most important locus of childhood and adolescent socialization because it is central to a young person's social life and acts as a filter for future occupational choice. (Andrew Stawicki/Photosensitive)

students who were concerned about family reputation were inclined to believe that effort and interest, not academic ability, were the basis of student success. That these findings corresponded very closely to findings of a study done of Filipino immigrants in San Francisco suggests that, indeed, the emphasis on family reputation as a mediating factor in school success may be characteristic of Filipino adolescent immigrants.

In schools throughout the world, adolescents are "sorted" during secondary schooling. High school grades and course selection will determine whether a student attends a postsecondary institution or enters the labour force upon graduation. One of the most important variables influencing which of these paths is taken is gender.

Socialization Outcomes

This section will look at the effects of gender, race, and class on socialization practices. It will also examine how children learn to make gender, race, and class distinctions and how to understand their implications. For children, adolescents, and adults alike, gender identity and perceptions of socio-economic status are fundamental aspects of the development of self-concept. Gender and class infuse social interaction as children develop physically, cognitively, and

Table 3.4 **Parental Expectations About Education and Career (% of Teens Agreeing)**

	Caribbean[a]	Chinese[a]	East European[a]	Latin American[a]	South Asian[a]	Canadian[b]	All
My parent(s) want to choose a career for me	15	26	17	19	26	8	19
My parent(s) expect me to go to university	69	89	70	68	77	45	70
My parent(s) think high marks in school are important	92	87	91	81	90	75	84
I feel a lot of pressure from my parent(s) to do well in school	50	55	49	52	60	45	52
If I have problems at school, my parent(s) are ready to help me	76	64	71	81	78	80	73

[a] Children not born in Canada or whose parents were not born in Canada.
[b] Children born in Canada to Canadian-born parents.
SOURCE: Barbara Helm and Wendy Warren, "Cultural Heritage and Family Life," *Transition Magazine* (Ottawa: The Vanier Institute of the Family, Sept. 1998), 7.

emotionally and as they anticipate adult family and economic roles.

The Social Reproduction of Gender

Individuals develop an understanding of gender through a complex interweaving of individual and environmental factors, predispositions, and expectations. In the course of gender socialization, children are exposed to many models of behaviour and gain a sense of masculinity or femininity from a variety of sources. Furthermore, individuals receive inconsistent messages even from the same sources.

How much of what we are is determined by socialization, and how much is inborn? This question is often referred to as the *"nature versus nurture" debate*. The assumption that nature dominates is called **biological determinism**. The opposite of *biological determinism* is what is described as "an oversocialized view" of human nature (Wrong, 1961) that implies that people are largely moulded by their socialization experiences.

In the past, people believed that behavioural differences were largely genetically determined, that people were born with certain aptitudes and dispositions—including a predisposition to good or evil. This assumption of inherent characteristics was taken to apply to differences between races as well as between men and women. This line of reasoning is now regarded as fallacious. It is one thing to suppose that nature helps explain individual differences, quite another to say the same thing about group differences. Nevertheless, the question of nature versus nurture remains a focus of continuing research, with much attention given to differences between females and males. Are sex distinctions in adults better explained in terms of biological differences or in terms of differential socialization?

Gender differences have been the subject of thousands of studies. Much of the research has focused on the behaviour of infants and young children. Reviews of this body of work, including an early review by Eleanor Maccoby and Carole Jacklin (1974) of 1,400 studies, find few behaviours that consistently differentiate males and females. In many cases, studies investigating similar behaviours have had contradictory results. For instance, consistent gender differences have been reported in aggression and in a preference for certain toys. In fact, most studies have found that the actual distinctions between boys and girls are minor. Most children are not aggressive, and they spend most of their time playing with toys that are not gender related. Furthermore, since boys are handled more roughly from birth onward, it is predictable that there will be some sex-related differences in behaviours such as level of activity or aggressiveness; however, these differences may have more to do with socialization practices than with biology. Most adult behaviours do not have clear antecedents in early childhood. The important differences between adults—**status** distinctions, for example—are unrelated to the differences typically found in children.

Some researchers argue that gender differences develop because of parental reaction to innate differences (see Ruble and Martin, 1998). That is, girls become more verbally skilled because they are more receptive to verbal interactions, while boys become more physically aggressive because they respond more positively to aggressive play. Others argue that parents reinforce behaviour in a way that is consistent with their own expectations and stereotypes. Parents have different expectations of their infant boys and girls in language, cognitive, and social development (see Ruble and Martin, 1998). This may or may not also extend to motor development. E.R. Mondschein, K.E. Adolph, and C.S. Tamis-LeMonda (2000) measured mothers' expectations regarding crawling and compared this to crawling ability. Mothers of boys had higher expectations of their sons than did mothers of daughters regarding the crawling tasks. Although the infant boys and girls in the study did not differ in motor abilities, mothers expected them to differ. This difference in expectation has significant implications for later motor development and risk-taking.

Very young children show sex-stereotyped toy preferences and sex-stereotyped activities. Research evidence seems to favour a socialization explanation. Television ads, catalogue layouts, toy packaging, and the organization of toy departments all seem to collude to steer the toy purchaser in the direction of stereotyped choices. It is no surprise that toys and other aspects of the physical environment of very young children are differentiated according to gender. Andrée Pomerleau and colleagues (1990) found that boys under the age of two tended to be given sports equipment, tools, and large and small vehicles, while girls were presented with dolls, fictional characters, child's furniture, and other toys for manipulation. They also observed the traditional pink–blue differences in the room decoration of the children in their sample.

Socialization is, to a large extent, based on nuance and subtlety. By the age of two, children are perceptive readers of their **social environment**. They observe patterns of interaction in the home, including the gender-relatedness of household tasks. Even in homes where both parents are gainfully employed, women take greater responsibility for housework and child care than men. Socialization to such divisions of labour presumably affects the family and occupational choices of young people. Children grow up with gendered names, toys, clothes, games, and room decorations. By the time they get to school, then, **gender stereotypes** are well established. The structure and practices of education, then, reinforce rather than challenge these earlier perceptions.

As argued earlier in the chapter, the media are a significant source of gender stereotyping. Studies of media content continue to find that women are underrepresented, stereotyped, and trivialized. Susan Losh-Hesselbart (1987) made the interesting discovery that heavy television viewers show more rigidity in gender stereotyping than occasional viewers. It is hardly surprising, then, that one of the women's movement's first targets among traditional socialization practices was the gender stereotyping in children's books and television programming. These criticisms have met with some success. A study of children's picture books by Carole Kortenhaus and Jack Demarest found that newer books show a greater representation of female characters: "Prior to 1970, children's literature contained almost four times as many boys as girls in titles, more than twice as many boys in central roles, almost twice as many boys in pictures, and nearly four times as many male animals as female animals" (1993: 225). After 1970, there were more female characters in all categories—but still not an equal number. Kortenhaus and Demarest also noted that activities depicted in books were strongly stereotyped by sex, with males dominating in instrumental behaviours and females in passive, dependent roles. Again, however, they found some improvement over time.

Childhood experiences have lifelong implications. Patricia Coats and Steven Overman (1992) compared childhood play and other early socialization experiences of women in traditional and non-traditional professions. They found that women in non-traditional fields had received different forms of parental encouragement than women in traditional professions. Women in non-traditional (business) professions participated in more competitive activities as

3.4

Open for Discussion
Do the Media Contribute to Disordered Eating Among Young Adolescent and Pre-adolescent Girls?

Most women in fashion magazines, movies, and television are pencil-thin. Indeed, the media create an impression that thinness is highly valued in Western society. Viewers of all ages use these images as points of comparison when evaluating their own body image. No wonder body dissatisfaction is universal. Kevin Thompson and Leslie Heinberg (1999) connect exposure to unrealistically thin images in magazines and television with body dissatisfaction and disordered eating among girls and women. Their solution is to counter these extreme images: "The media itself is one potential vehicle for communicating pro-ductive, accurate, and deglamorized messages about eating and shape-related disorders" (339).

What do you think about this issue? Are girls susceptible to images of ultra-thin models? Are girls more susceptible than young boys? In what other ways besides the mass media is thinness reinforced? How do we reconcile media images with reports of increased numbers of obese children and youth? Does the solution lie, as these authors suggest, in changing the images in the media, or is it a larger and more complex problem?

children and continued to seek competitive recreational activities as adults. The members of this group also had more male companions when they were children. Interestingly, the fathers of all the professional women encouraged their daughters' competitiveness. Mothers of women who entered non-traditional professions echoed that encouragement, whereas mothers of women who entered traditional professions encouraged more traditional values.

Data from a US intergenerational panel study of parents and children provide an opportunity to see the effect of childhood socialization practices regarding household division of labour on the next generation (Cunningham, 2001). Women in this sample were interviewed first in 1962 and again in 1977, and their 18-year-old daughters were interviewed in 1980. Indeed, the mothers' attitudes during their children's early years had a strong influence on the children's ideal division of household labour at 18. The family division of labour also had an important impact: adolescent women whose fathers had shared housework were more apt to support men's participation in stereotypically female household tasks.

Gender stereotypes continue to frame our understanding of the social behaviour of males and females from infancy to old age. Minor behavioural and attitudinal differences in childhood are reinforced through adolescence and become pronounced in adults. However subtly, people react to boys and girls, men and women, differently, and in the process encourage different behavioural responses. The differential reactions may be quite unintentional. Parents tend to say they have similar expectations for their children with regard to dependency, aggression, school achievement, and so forth, although fathers are typically more concerned than mothers about gender-typed behaviour in their children.

The gender stereotyping of occupational choices has important implications for a young person's future. Occupational stereotypes frame educational, occupational, and interpersonal choices, especially for women, and are the basis of discriminatory practices in education and the workplace. Nonetheless, it is clear that significant changes have occurred in the family and occupational responsibilities of both women and men during the past three decades. These changes indicate that behaviour can be modified, even for those whose primary socialization was highly traditional.

The Social Reproduction of Race and Class

Racial socialization refers to all of the ways parents shape children's learning about race and race relations (Hughes and Johnson, 2001). Racial socialization is an important component of child rearing among ethnic and racial-minority families. It appears that efforts to instill racial pride are successful. Generally, children whose parents have emphasized racial pride have higher self-esteem and greater knowledge of their ethnic or racial group (see Marshall, 1995).

Racial socialization, like gender and class socialization, is an iterative process. Children are not simply sponges. Their reactions and needs interact with their parents' own experiences of being socialized and with their parents' experiences in the world to determine parental racial socialization strategies.

D. Hughes and D. Johnson (2001) used reports of 94 dyads of African American parents and Grade 3, 4, and 5 children to see whether socialization practices were influenced by whether or not children had experienced racial **discrimination**. Most parents reported that they talked to their children about their own and other ethnic groups, and most talked to their children about the possibility that the child might experience discrimination. Only about one-fifth of parents reported that they had cautioned or warned their children about other racial or ethnic groups. Hughes and Johnson refer to this strategy as "promotion of mistrust." Not surprisingly, promotion of mistrust was related to parents' reports that their children had received unfair treatment from adults as well as to children's reports of unfair treatment from peers. Interestingly, parental promotion of mistrust was not related to their own experiences of discrimination.

How does racial socialization work when parents and children are of different races? Tracy Robinson (2001) studied this issue by analyzing interviews of white mothers of mixed race (white–Maori) children in New Zealand. These mothers described the importance of exposing their children to both white (*Pakeha*) and Maori culture and their frustration in the face of the discrimination their children experienced. One woman discussed tearfully the difficulty her child encountered in finding an apartment. Her daughter had phenotypical characteristics (brown skin, dark hair, and brown eyes). One day the daughter said, "Mum, you come along with me so that I can get the apartment" (Robinson, 2001: 180).

Another important context of socialization is socio-economic class. The kinds of work adults perform and the coping strategies they employ to make sense of their work have fundamental implications for the socialization of their children. As in gender socialization, children begin at a very young age to absorb the implications of class in society. They learn early "who counts" and where they fit into the social hierarchy.

Child-rearing practices and socialization contexts change over time and reflect cultural, ethnic, and class differences. Melvin Kohn was a pioneer in researching the relationship between social class and socialization values and practices. His research has important implications for understanding cross-cultural variations as well. Kohn argues that attitudes to child rearing vary by social class because of important class differences in occupational experiences. According to Kohn (1977), the key variables are closeness of supervision, routinization, and the substantive complexity of work. Blue-collar workers are more closely supervised, perform more routine tasks, and work primarily with physical objects rather than with people or ideas. Parents who hold these kinds of jobs emphasize conformity, neatness, and orderliness. Typically, middle-class parents are more permissive and place greater emphasis on self-reliance. White-collar parents focus on behavioural intentions, blue-collar parents on consequences. Attitude studies done in the United States support these findings. Duane Alwin (1990) observes that, typically, the middle and upper classes emphasize self-direction, while working-class families emphasize obedience and conformity to tradition or authority.

Alwin (1990) argues that there was a general shift in North American parental values over the five decades leading up to his study. Whereas parents used to want their children to be obedient and conforming, they were now more inclined to want to instill a sense of independence or autonomy. He looked at five studies measuring parental socialization values from the 1920s through the 1980s. Public opinion surveys done in Detroit in 1958, 1971, and 1983 revealed some interesting differences (Alwin, 1984). Parents were asked the following question:

> If you had to choose, which thing would you pick as the most important for a child to learn to prepare him for life?
> (a) to obey
> (b) to be well-liked or popular
> (c) to think for himself
> (d) to work hard
> (e) to help others when they need help (Alwin, 1984: 365)

Respondents were asked to rank their top four choices. Alwin found that "to think for himself" was the most preferred quality and that the number of parents citing it as most important increased over time. "To be well-liked or popular" was the least preferred and became even less important over time. Obedience also decreased in importance, while hard work increased. The number of parents who valued the quality of helpfulness remained stable. In other Western countries, too, there seems to be a similar parental concern for developing independence in children (Alwin, 1990).

What accounts for this shift in focus? Alwin feels it results partly from increased education, partly from increased secularization. Predictably, increased education is associated with the valuation of autonomy and with a decrease in the value of conformity. Parental preference for obedience is linked to levels of church attendance, which have declined over recent decades. Finally, it is interesting that some evidence exists that the youngest cohorts are slightly more inclined toward conformity and obedience than older cohorts. Nevertheless, parental values are only one part of the equation. Myriad factors combine to influence children's behaviour. The fact that parents claim to value self-reliant behaviour does not necessarily imply that children will respond accordingly.

The Social Reproduction of Adult Family and Work Roles

Childhood, adolescence, and adulthood are social constructs that broadly define periods of social, psychological, and biological development. They are generally, but not absolutely, determined by age. Because life-cycle stages do not follow a predictable or orderly track, there is no specific point at which an adolescent is declared to be an adult, for example. Some young people will have assumed adult roles of marriage, parenthood, or economic independence before their 18th birthday. Others remain in school and financially dependent on parents well into their twenties. Still others return to the parental home after divorce or job loss. Some of these adult children will have children themselves, thus creating a temporary three-generation household. During the past quarter-century, the transition from adolescence to adulthood has been altered by such trends as increased schooling and a rise in the age at first marriage. Now, young adults enjoy a period of independent living before marriage. Two or three decades ago, this period of independence was shorter, as both men and women typically married in their early twenties. Ceremonies such as graduation or marriage may therefore be more appropriate than age as signals of the transition to adulthood.

José Machado Pais (2000) has argued that the transition to adulthood takes longer now than in the past. One of the reasons for this is uncertainty about future education, work, and family roles. The transitional process from youth to adulthood is affected by past socialization experiences and by expectations about the future. To the extent that the future appears uncertain, the transition to adulthood is stalled. Leaving school, starting a job, or making a commitment to a relationship does not necessarily signal permanent departure or the assumption of adult responsibilities.

A second characteristic of the transition to adulthood today is that it is reversible. Education, employment, relationships, and living arrangements all are more transitory than they were in the past; young people may return to school, or again live with parents at the end of a romantic or employment relationship. Pais (2000) calls this reversibility the "yo-yo-ization" of the transition to adulthood. Parents of youth in transition are also affected by this pattern because of the societal dominance of youth culture. Parents adopt aspects of youth culture in an effort to forestall aging.

One of the greatest challenges of adolescence is preparation for adult family and work responsibilities. Dating is one of the vehicles for this learning. Even though dating is much less formal than it was in the past, it still helps develop social and communication skills and contributes to the development of self-esteem. In our culture, dating provides opportunities for anticipatory socialization for future cohabitation or marriage.

Adolescents are also required to make decisions about educational options that will affect their future opportunities in the labour force. While not irreversible, decisions such as quitting school or selecting math and science rather than languages and history will open some doors and close others.

Not all of the socialization children receive for adult roles is positive. For instance, violent or abusive adults have internalized this inappropriate response to stress or frustration through socialization. In the area of family violence, researchers have just begun to clarify the links between experiences in childhood and adult behaviour. Judith Seltzer and Debra Kalmuss predicted that people who have experienced violence in their homes as children "may incorporate abuse into the behavioural repertoires they bring to intimate relationships that they establish in adulthood" (1988: 475). Their findings support this prediction: "Early childhood exposure to family violence has a substantially greater effect on spouse abuse than does . . . exposure to recent stressful experiences or chronic economic strain" (1988: 487). Furthermore, observing parents' marital aggression has more of an effect on children than being hit by a parent.

However, the relationship is not absolute. Some adults have violent marriages even though they did not grow up in violent homes. Moreover, not all children growing up in such homes become abusive adults. Extra-familial socialization agents, including peer groups, dating partners, and the media, explain the discrepancies (Seltzer and Kalmuss, 1988).

Socialization for Parenthood

Do adolescent boys and girls anticipate parenthood differently? A New Zealand study by Barbara Calvert and Warren Stanton (1992) found considerable evidence to support the conclusion that adolescent males and females were equally committed to becoming parents. Among the respondents, 89 per cent answered "Yes" to the question, "Would you like to have children of your own?" When asked whether they would want to adopt if they were unable to have children, 83 per cent of the girls and 72 per cent of the boys answered in the affirmative (Calvert and Stanton, 1992: 317). Both boys and girls wanted to have their first child when they were in their mid-twenties, and both genders listed "fond of children" as an important quality in a spouse. All the young people in the study expected to combine family and employment responsibilities, although the majority thought that, ideally, one parent should stay home with young children. Interestingly, 82 per cent of the boys and 85 per cent of the girls said it did not matter whether the mother or the father was the care-giving parent (Calvert and Stanton, 1992: 319). Other responses indicated that both girls and boys expected both parents to nurture and perform child care tasks.

The major gender difference between these teenagers was not in attitudes, but in experience; the boys had considerably less exposure to young children and less experience in caregiving. As Calvert and Stanton suggest, this difference could result in a definition of the women as more expert and promote a gendered division of labour when the adolescents form families of their own. The study also found strong evidence to suggest that children will be strongly influenced by the child-rearing practices to which they were exposed when growing up: "Most

respondents expected to do pretty much as their parents had done" (Calvert and Stanton, 1992: 325).

Studies of new parents find that many are ill prepared for the time and energy demands of caring for a newborn. Not surprisingly, Renee Steffensmeier (1982) found that anticipatory socialization had a significant effect on the transition to parenthood. The more previous experience new parents had, or the better they were prepared by training for the experience of parenting, the more satisfying they found it. Jay Belsky (1985) found that women were more likely than men to experience a disjunction between their expectations and their experiences regarding childbirth and, consequently, to report less satisfaction. Since women hold the greatest responsibility for infant care, this is hardly surprising. While the household division of labour tends to become more traditional following birth, the mothers in Belsky's sample were more involved in infant care relative to the fathers than either the mothers or the fathers had anticipated, and this was a major source of dissatisfaction.

While most men marry, and while attitude surveys indicate that men give high priority to family life, early socialization does little to prepare them to be fathers. To some extent, low involvement by fathers is a self-fulfilling prophecy. Men have very little preparation for the care of infants or young children, and they are likely to feel awkward; they therefore experience failure in their attempts to help. Alice Rossi's investigations of interactions between fathers and infants suggest that men "tend to avoid high involvement in infant care because infants do not respond to their repertoire of skills and men have difficulty acquiring the skills needed to comfort the infant" (1984: 8). She sees a solution in teaching fathers about parenting and so encouraging their participation. Rossi assumes that men are not more active parents because they have not been socialized to anticipate this role.

In recent years, it has become more the rule than the exception for fathers to attend pre-natal classes, to assist during labour, and to be present during the birth of their child. Other trends, such as high divorce rates, have brought about an increase in the number of "weekend fathers"—divorced men who have periodic responsibility for their children. Such parenting experiences seem to pave the way for increased male involvement in child care.

However, no amount of compensatory socialization will alter the structural barriers to equal involvement in child care and other domestic tasks. Primary caregiving fathers in a study in Australia had made a decision to be involved in child rearing and house-hold tasks, although only half the sample defined housework and child care as their primary tasks (Grbich, 1992). In Australia, the role of caregiver is not considered appropriate for men. The fathers all recognized that parenting and housework have low status, and one-third of them were uncomfortable with their role for this reason. Some of the fathers mentioned that they received verbal put-downs from neighbours, shopkeepers, and others. They reported a number of subtle tactics used to marginalize them, including sexual labelling, avoidance, ostracism, active confrontation, lowered expectations of their perform-ance or capabilities, and non-payment of child allowances (Grbich, 1992). Clearly, it will take much more than changes in individual behaviour to change the structures of sexual inequality.

Socialization for Employment

Professional schools are important socializing agents for adults. Medical schools in particular have been studied in this regard. What students learn during their years in medical school goes well beyond the acquisition of technical skills: they are learning to behave like doctors. Some researchers, however, feel that the similarities in attitudes and values among medical school graduates have more to do with selec-tive recruitment of middle- and upper-class students than with any training they receive. In their panel study of Canadian medical students, Neena Chappell and Nina Colwill (1981) found that students recruit-ed to medical schools shared certain attitudes at the outset. Interestingly, these viewpoints seemed unrelat-ed to either social class or gender. Although the researchers do not discuss their findings in terms of anticipatory socialization, it seems that a medical stu-dent's orientation to the profession begins long before he or she enters medical school.

Frederic Jablin (1984) describes three stages of socialization to employment. The first is the period of *anticipatory socialization*. Prospective employees form expectations about the job on the basis of their edu-cation, training, and previous employment. The sec-ond stage is the *encounter phase*, during which the employees "learn the ropes"—what the organization and its members consider to be normal patterns of behaviour. If anticipatory socialization experiences have created an accurate sense of the work environ-ment, the encounter phase will be a relatively smooth

transition. From the organization's point of view, effective socialization of new employees is a key to organizational stability. Most organizations therefore formalize the encounter phase in a new employee orientation. The final *metamorphosis stage* continues throughout each employee's career in the particular organization.

Much adult socialization is self-initiated. Some is formal, such as the training provided in professional schools or work-related courses; some is informal. Increasingly, formal training is available in areas pre-viously left to the family, the schools, or other agents of socialization, or in areas for which socialization was once taken for granted. Thus, prospective parents can take pre-natal and, later, parenting courses, while people anticipating retirement can sign up for cours-es in retirement planning. When adults join such organizations as Weight Watchers or Parents Without Partners, they do so because they seek the social sup-port these groups provide. It is during transition peri-ods that this support is most needed.

Future Directions

It is not new to suggest that family life has undergone major changes over the past few decades. Marriage rates have declined, while divorce rates have increased. More couples live together instead of mar-rying, and more children are born to single mothers. When social policy catches up to social attitudes, we will presumably give legal recognition to same-sex marriages. More children live independently, too, many of them on the street. At the same time, work demands and economic insecurities create stressful situations for many families. In the past decade, increased concern has been expressed for the plight of children worldwide, much of it arising from a con-cern about family instability and change. Thus, in the future, we might expect more research to focus on understanding the dynamics of early childhood development and socialization in order to provide the kind of support to families that will optimize their positive development.

Sociology has been criticized for not paying suffi-cient heed to children, but this inattention is likely to change in the future. In an aging society such as that of Canada (and Western nations generally), with well below replacement birth rates, children will become an increasingly valued resource. An important goal for the future, then, is to create a central place in the dis-cipline of sociology for children. This place should be based on a deeper understanding of the role of children, not just as recipients of adult socialization practices, but as active agents in the lifelong socialization of the people with whom they interact.

Conclusion

Sociologists view socialization as a lifelong process, one that is influenced by all of an individual's social interactions. The two main accomplishments of socialization are the development of a self-concept and the internalization of social expectations.

Sociologists who take the functionalist perspective have tended to describe socialization as being imposed on individuals. By contrast, symbolic interactionists such as Cooley and Mead have helped to shed light on the active engagement of individuals in their own socialization.

All socialization takes place in a social context. For most people, the enduring and intimate nature of family relations makes socialization in the family the most pervasive and consequential experience of childhood. Parent–child interactions are differentiated by class, race, and ethnicity and are framed by the relationships between the family and the community. They are further affected by family size, birth order, family structure, and household composition. Patterns of influence are extremely complex, and become more so as children increase their contacts to include friends, neighbours, and schoolmates. The messages people receive from others are inconsistent and sometimes contradictory, and all draw their own conclusions from these competing influences.

Individual life chances are also strongly influenced by structural variables, the most important of which are gender and social class. Gender and social class have considerable influence on socialization and on the development of self-concept throughout life. The socialization of children and adolescents anticipates their adult work and family responsibilities. The competencies people develop in the course of primary socialization enable them to anticipate, prepare for, and deal with the ups and downs of adulthood.

☐ Questions for Critical Thought

1. Far too many children grow up in the face of societal conflict. When so many children are socialized in this way, is there a realistic hope for peace?
2. What are the implications of the research finding that there are few characteristics that consistently differentiate very young females and males?
3. Why do gender stereotypes persist in the media despite the women's movement, the rise in female labour force participation, and other signs of structural change?
4. Talk to your parents and other family members about what they considered to be important values in your early development. What differences do you anticipate in raising your own children?
5. Ask students who have come to your university or college from another country to describe the resocialization they experienced in making the transition.
6. Can you link early socialization experiences to your decision to attend a postsecondary institution? to the courses you have chosen to focus on? to your anticipated career?
7. Are children's cartoons too violent? Watch a variety of cartoons, and document the type and frequency of violent action. What about video games? Are these more or less violent than cartoons?
8. What, if anything, can be done to protect children from exposure to inappropriate content on the Internet?

☐ Recommended Readings

Reginald Bibby, *Canada's Teens: Today, Yesterday and Tomorrow* (Toronto: Stoddart, 2001).

Canadian sociologist Reginald Bibby has written a number of books based on his analysis of national surveys. This book documents attitudes and experiences of Canadian teenagers regarding violence, sex, and drugs and compares current patterns to past trends.

Kathleen Guy, *Our Promise to Children* (Ottawa: Health Canada, 1997).

This book, sponsored by Health Canada and the Canadian Institute of Child Health, takes seriously the notion that raising healthy children is a community responsibility and requires a national commitment.

Margaret Norrie McCain and J. Fraser Mustard, *Reversing the Real Brain Drain: Early Years Study: Final Report* (Toronto: Canadian Institute for Advanced Research, 1999).

This report, commissioned by the Government of Ontario, argues that without positive nurturing and stimulation before the age of six, children suffer emotionally, socially, and economically in later life. This is not simply a class problem. The authors argue that many of the approximately 15 per cent of Ontario children who are at risk are middle-class children. The study is available on the Canadian Institute for Advanced Research Web site or from the Children's Secretariat of the Ontario Government.

Mary Pipher, *Reviving Ophelia: Saving the Selves of Adolescent Girls* (New York: Ballantine, 1994).

This book, written by a clinical psychologist, examines the roots of young adolescent women's angst. Pipher addresses the question of young girls' feelings of low self-esteem and the high incidence of depression, suicide, and eating disorders among adolescent girls.

William Pollack, *Real Boys: Rescuing Our Sons from the Myths of Boyhood* (New York: Henry Holt, 1998).

This book is in many ways a companion to *Reviving Ophelia*; it too is written by a clinical psychologist. Pollack documents the "silent crisis" affecting young boys in the United States. Stereotypical expectation of manliness are as damaging to young boys as are stereotypically feminine expectations to young girls.

Statistics Canada, *Growing Up in Canada* (Ottawa: Human Resources Development Canada and Statistics Canada, 1996).

This first volume of research from the National Longitudinal Survey of Children and Youth (NLSCY) includes an overview of the first published findings, as well as chapters on parenting, school performance, and aggression in children.

Marvin B. Sussman, Suzanne K. Steinmetz, and Gary W. Peterson, eds, *Handbook of Marriage and the Family*, 2nd edn (New York: Plenum Press, 1999).

An excellent and comprehensive resource for students of marriage and the family, this book looks at parent and child socialization, adolescent socialization, and the development of gender roles, among other topics.

Don Tapscott, *Growing Up Digital: The Rise of the Net Generation* (New York: McGraw-Hill, 1998).

This book is an examination of the 88 million children of the baby boomers in the United States and Canada to have grown up with the Internet. This generation, Tapscott argues, is destined to be a force for social transformation.

☐ Recommended Web Sites

Canadian Research Policy Networks
www.cprn.org/cprn.html

The family network at this site is dedicated to advancing public debate on policy issues that have an impact on Canadian families and on the circumstances in which they live. Its research ranges from public values about children and families to broader concerns of social cohesion within communities and society as a whole.

Childcare Resource and Research Unit (CRRU), University of Toronto
www.childcarecanada.org

> Here you will find links to information about published and ongoing research, policy developments, and print materials related to child care policy. The Resources section contains print and Web resources, including bibliographies, complete texts of CRRU publications, and links to useful child care, social policy, and research Web sites.

Growing Up Digital
www.growingupdigital.com

> This Web site is a companion to Don Tapsott's book *The Net Generation*, about those children and youth who have grown up surrounded by digital media. This, according to Tapscott, makes them a force for change. The Web site includes summaries of the main themes of the book and links to discussion groups related to this topic.

Health Canada
www.healthcanada.ca

> Health Canada's Web site provides links to a wide range of information, including research reports about the health and well-being of Canadians of all ages, including children and youth.

Human Resources Development Canada (HRDC), Applied Research Branch
www.hrdc-drhc.gc.ca/sp-ps/arb-dgra/nlscy-elnej/child_youth.shtml

> One of HRDC's mandates is to supply information to governments to inform policy relating to children and youth; this is done in part by supporting research about children and youth. HRDC is one of the sponsors of the National Longitudinal Survey of Children and Youth (NLSCY), a comprehensive longitudinal survey designed to measure and track the development and well-being of Canada's children and youth over time. The second longitudinal survey in this area is the Youth in Transition Survey (YITS), with a special focus on the school-to-work transition of young adults.

Statistics Canada
www.statcan.ca

> The Statistics Canada Web site is a fundamental tool for all students of sociology. It provides links to volumes of current information about all aspects of Canadian economic and cultural life. Here is where you will find current data on demographic trends, labour force patterns, consumption, media use, and more.

Today's Parent
www.todaysparent.com

> This is the Web site for the Canadian magazine *Today's Parent*. Despite the advertising, the site contains practical and useful information for parents presented in an accessible way.

Vanier Institute of the Family
www.vifamily.ca

> The vision of the Vanier Institute of the Family is to make families as important to the life of Canadian society as they are to the lives of individual Canadians. The Institute advocates on behalf of Canada's 8.4 million families because it believes that families are the key building block of society. This Web site is designed to help build public understanding of important issues and trends critical to the well-being and healthy functioning of Canadian families.

4

Cheryl Albas and
Dan Albas

> > >

Roles and Identities

☐ Learning Objectives

In this chapter, you will:

- learn what *roles* and *identities* are and how they relate to each other

- understand how it is possible to interpret roles and identities from different theoretical perspectives

- see how theoretical perspectives concerning role and identity can be used to understand face-to-face interaction in everyday life

- see how roles and identities constrain us and shape us

Introduction

The subject matter of sociology is **social structure**, that invisible thing with the power to constrain us and change us. This chapter is about some of the ways that social structure exerts its influence.

This chapter argues that sociologists view **roles** and **identities** as the main ways in which social structure constrains and changes us. Roles and identities are the parts of social structure that we enact and internalize. Just as they form the basic elements of social structure, they are also the basic elements of who we are and how we lead our lives. Roles and identities are, therefore, the meeting point of social structure, culture, and personality. You cannot understand social life unless you understand roles and identities, the building blocks of social structure.

One central question in sociology, then, is where roles and identities come from. Sociologists who espouse the different schools of theory or **paradigms** disagree about this, as we shall see. Specifically, they disagree about whether roles are imposed on people from "above" or are invented and negotiated from below. Additionally, they disagree about the answers to other difficult questions. Do we more or less automatically adopt the identities attached to roles we play? Or do our identities combine a variety of influences from past and present roles, plus a good deal more? These are some of the questions this chapter will address.

The Social Nature of Identity and Role

Prior to birth, humans may have life, but it is not social: before birth, humans have neither status nor identity. The subjects of this chapter—identities and roles—are things we acquire over the course of our lives as we interact with others. **Identities** are the names we give ourselves (female, male; child, adolescent, adult; friend; athlete; "nice person") or who we announce ourselves to be in word, manner, and appearance that enables others to respond to or place us (Stone, 1981).

Our first placement by others is at the moment of birth, when we are introduced to the expectant audience with the words "It's a girl" or "It's a boy." As children learn the meaning of this placement, they usually identify with it and begin to present (or "announce") themselves accordingly. Throughout a lifetime of establishing identities, we act parts in the

Does this person announce her identity via apperance, manner, and setting adequately to place her? (© Bob Adelman/Magnum Photos)

game of life by playing out organized scripts in the form of normative expectations, called **roles**, that are attached to social positions, or **statuses**. These roles include gender roles, age roles, occupational roles, and a multiplicity of others.

On the one hand, roles are scripts that permit and oblige us to behave in certain ways. For example, at a party everyone can say, "It's getting late, I've got to go to sleep"—except the host. On the other hand, roles can be thought of in a more dynamic fashion, as expectations that emerge in the give and take of **social interaction**. For example, a student reports that during an exam, he was passed a note by his friend sitting in the next seat requesting "help" for a particular question. Terrified that the invigilator might notice the interaction, the student attempted to resolve the dilemma by eating the note, mercifully "very short and written on a small piece of paper" (Albas and Albas, 1995: 219).

Thus, *role enactment*, or *role-playing*, can be viewed either structurally (that is, as fixed expectations) or interactionally (that is, as changing and dynamic). We can, accordingly, view social behaviour as the learned performance of scripts that follow agreed-on rules or as negotiated arrangements that people work out with one another to solve unique problems of spontaneous interactions.

What is the use of studying the concepts of role and identity? The answer is that, as agreed-to expectations for behaviour, roles help to smooth interaction

"Let's play you're a guest, and I'll think of ways of trying to get rid of you."

in society. We don't realize just how dependent we are on **role expectations** to co-ordinate our acts with others until those expectations are violated. Similarly, in order to play roles, we need to know the identities of others as well as our own.

As we will see, roles and identities are complementary and intertwined. The roles we play give us a sense of what and where we are relative to others with whom we interact. This sense of identity allows us to act in ways that are both coherent and purposeful. Every role we play has an identity awaiting us, and taking on that identity makes the role come to life. When role expectations are breached, it is as if trust is betrayed, and we feel bewildered and insecure. It leads us to question who we—and others in the situation—really are.

Consider an example of how roles and identities work. The American sociologist Harold Garfinkel (1997) believed that we could best understand the constraints of social structure by breaking the hidden rules. To do this, he instructed his university students to return to their homes and behave in ways that breached the normal expectations of their family lives, by acting as if they were boarders and their parents were the landlords. Students were to be extreme-

ly polite, addressing their parents formally as "Mr" and "Mrs" and speaking only when spoken to.

The result: approximately 80 per cent of students who actually went through the experiment reported that their parents were stupefied, shocked, and embarrassed. Many worried that their children had "lost their minds"—that the pressures of school, work, and everyday life had "gotten to them." Others thought their children were being mean, inconsiderate, and impolite. In short, they couldn't make sense of this deviant, rule-breaking behaviour.

In one instance, a father even followed his son to the bedroom and said in a very concerned tone of voice, "Your mother is right. You don't look well and you're not making sense. You had better get another job that doesn't require such late hours." The son replied that he appreciated their [parental] concern but that he felt fine and only wanted a little privacy. The father went into a rage: "I don't want any more of that out of you," he shouted. "And if you can't treat your mother decently, you'd better move out" (Garfinkel, 1997: 401–2).

How can we understand these strange, disturbed reactions to **deviance**? As was noted in chapter 1, sociology is a discipline with a variety of perspectives. Also called *theoretical frames of reference* or *paradigms*, these perspectives vary from theorist to theorist and from time to time. A number of different problems can be analyzed within the same paradigm, and any one problem can be analyzed from the standpoint of more than one paradigm. All discussion of problems involves concepts—their definitions, the ways they relate to each other, and the logical sense these relationships make for solving problems or answering questions that arise—in effect constructing theory.

In this chapter, the focal issues to be theorized about are role and identity, and the major paradigms to be used to address them are **structural functionalism**, **symbolic interactionism**, and **conflict theory**.

Role

The Structural-Functional Approach to Role

The structural-functional approach generally stresses the part played by factors that exist independent of individuals and that constrain individuals to act, think, or feel in particular ways. In this perspective, the roles of actors in "real life" are described as expected behaviour corresponding to their positions in the "real world," positions that, in turn, are termed *statuses*.

In this view, individuals are evaluated in terms of how successfully they enact roles and are then accorded varying levels of esteem. Thus, "actors" earn high esteem if their performances are praiseworthy and low esteem if they are not. For example, one of the Manitoban authors of this chapter consumed several cups of wonderful coffee at breakfast one morning in Regina and then headed north for the several-hour-long drive to Saskatoon. Unfortunately, there were few stops along the way that offered relief in the form of washroom facilities, and by the time Saskatoon appeared on the horizon, the situation had become quite desperate. He pulled up to the first available public facility, which happened to be in a shopping mall. In great haste he parked the car—not within the bounds of the marked parking stalls, but more diagonally, so that the car crowded the then-empty stall next to it—and rushed off to find the closest public washroom. When he returned, he found a note was tucked under the windshield wiper on the driver's side: "In Saskatchewan we park properly. In Manitoba you can't f— any better than you park" (but more explicit). The note clearly implied low esteem.

The term *status* is also used to describe society's ranking of tasks relative to each other, which, in turn, determines a corresponding amount of prestige for the individual involved. For example, in Canada, high-status occupations such as law or medicine bestow high levels of prestige on doctors and lawyers.

Émile Durkheim's initial orientation to the concepts of role and status was considerably elaborated, systematized, and reinforced by the anthropologist Ralph Linton (1936) as follows: Status is a position to which are attached specific rights and duties, which, in turn, confer reciprocal rights and duties on actors who occupy other, interacting statuses. For example, in the case of students and teachers, teachers have the right to expect that students come to classes, are attentive during class, join class discussions, and study conscientiously: these are student duties.

An example of this mutual interplay of status and roles between teacher and students was observed in a large introductory-level university class. Two students started conversing with each other in tones loud enough to interrupt the order of the classroom and to distract the professor; that is, their behaviour constituted a breach of courtesy to the professor, a lack of consideration for other students, and a violation of

their duty as students to be attentive. The professor's response to the miscreants was a polite inquiry as to whether they had a question—that is, a reminder that they were not living up to their duties. When the professor returned to lecturing, the students returned to their chatter. After class, the professor stopped them and reminded them of the requirement of considerate behaviour in class and of their duties to the other students in the class, to themselves as students, and to himself (the professor). The professor's suggestion that they no longer sit together in the class was met with the aggressive complaint that "we weren't doing anything"—a clear breach of the students' duties of basic courtesy to the status of professor and a clear indication that they were failing in their own responsibilities to themselves as university students by engaging in immature behaviour typically associated with high school. Their disruptive behaviour was indeed role enactment, but certainly not "ideal" role enactment, and as such, it was dysfunctional.

Students have reciprocal rights and expectations regarding their teachers. They can, for example, expect teachers to demonstrate expertise, mastery, and patience, to show up for class well prepared, and to treat them with respect and civility. These rights and obligations are well known and accepted by everyone. Problems arise when people do not fully know or embrace these agreed-on rights and duties. Then the interaction breaks down, and the situation becomes chaotic and confusing.

However, such breakdowns are remarkably rare. Sociologist Talcott Parsons (1949), perhaps the best-known structural-functionalist theorist, explains this by emphasizing that society is filled with common values that are the source of stability and social order; this is Durkheim's concept of *exteriority* ([1893] 1964). It is only when **socialization** is imperfect or inadequate that people break the rules. Then others reinforce conformity by public sanctions, such as shame—Durkheim's ([1893] 1964) concept of *constraint*—as in the faulty parking example.

One of Parsons's students, sociologist Robert K. Merton (1957), makes more explicit this structural aspect of society in general, and of roles in particular. In fact, the problem facing us is that we all play so many different roles and, therefore, take on many different rights and responsibilities. Merton terms the specific collections of statuses we occupy *status sets*, and the collections of roles in a specific single status (which Linton did not identify), a *role set*: "By role-set I mean that complement of role-relationships in which persons are involved by virtue of occupying a particular social status" (Merton, 1957: 110). The multiplicity of statuses and, consequently, of roles individuals occupy and play, respectively, in their lifetimes follow recognizable patterns that Merton terms *status sequences*.

These concepts of role-sets, status sets, and status sequences underlie the recognition of order and structure in society as structural functionalists view it. More specifically, for example, a physician's status set may include the collection of statuses of a spouse, a parent, an administrator, and a soccer coach as well as a medical specialist. For each status in this status set, the physician has a number of roles to play, every one of which requires considerable expertise, tact, and discretion for its performance. This collection of roles is termed a *role set*.

For example, a physician's role in a hospital or medical office involves interaction with a variety of other roles—nurses, paramedics, janitorial staff, clerks, medical colleagues, and patients—each interaction demanding different role behaviour. Consequently, physicians interact differently with each other than they do with other members of the medical team or with patients. Whereas physicians must routinely request that patients remove clothes so that their bodies can be examined, the same request to a ward clerk or nurse would be completely out of role.

The norms governing the role of physician also demand professional decorum, no matter how dramatic the circumstances. For example, years ago a plane carrying a soccer team crashed high in the Andes mountains of South America. The flight was intended to be a short one, so the chartered plane carried no supply of food. The passengers not killed in the crash survived only because they ate the flesh of the others who died during and subsequent to the crash. When rescued and asked by the attending physician what he had been eating during the ordeal, one survivor responded "human flesh." The physician indicated that his "stomach turned" and he felt extreme "revulsion"—a completely normal reaction to the situation. However, the physician also noted that professional protocol required that he not allow the "normal" reaction of revulsion to show, so he simply continued with the examination as if it were a routine event.

A good synonym for Merton's concept of status sequence is *career*. An individual progresses from high school student to university student to medical intern to medical resident to qualified physician. Each phase

of the sequence carries with it specific rights, duties, and associated prestige—generally, medical students do not have the right to carve up patients' bodies without supervision until they become fully fledged surgeons, at which time the carving process will be termed "surgery" and the knife will be designated a "scalpel."

When individuals occupy a number of different statuses and accordingly play a number of different roles, they consequently acquire varying amounts of prestige and esteem attached to each. Nonetheless, there is normally a single status and accompanying prestige that most distinctly characterizes each one. Everett C. Hughes (1945) terms the overarching, distinguishing status a **master status** and the other statuses in the status set *auxiliary statuses*. This distinction was originally used to distinguish occupational statuses from other ones. As Hughes indicates, if we know nothing about people, the status that tells most about them as a whole is their occupation, which, in turn, probably provides a very good idea of their level of education, their income, and their lifestyle. The term *master status* is now used not only to cover occupational "achieved" statuses, which are arrived at by our own efforts, but also "ascribed" statuses, over which we have no control and which are attributed to us on the basis of characteristics such as race, sex, and age.

Role Strain

Despite the tendency toward order just described, there is also a tendency toward disorder in every society, and in every life. When roles compete and even conflict with each other, they produce *role strain* for actors. Strain above a critical level results in distress that we may describe simply as "stress." William Goode, Merton's student and a structuralist in the Mertonian tradition, states, "Role strain—difficulty in meeting given role demands . . . is normal. In general, the individual's total role obligations are overdemanding" (1960: 485). Role strain may undermine the tendency to order and interfere with people's ability to play their roles as expected.

The major sources of strain that constantly challenge the established order include *inadequate socialization*, when people simply do not know the appropriate rules of behaviour. Consider this example: Almost three decades ago, a northern trapper came to the "big city," and his son took him to a relatively posh restaurant for dinner. On the way home, the father admonished his son, saying, "You're pretty careless with your money. You left some on the table but I took care of it." His isolated northern way of life at that time and his socialization had taught him nothing about the convention of tipping. As a result, he violated the posh city restaurant rules. Both parties in this interaction then experienced a degree of strain—the father because of his unfamiliarity with the restaurant setting, the son because he is now responsible for **resocializing** his father, who was originally his mentor.

Another illustration of role strain comes from first-year university students who are inadequately socialized to the "looseness" of their new role. High schools have fairly tight institutional structures, in that the rules students must follow are laid out explicitly, specifically, and clearly. Students are constantly observed and supervised by teachers who keep them "in line" with a variety of sanctions, ranging from mild to severe reprimands and to the ultimate threats of reporting them to their parents or expelling them. This tight role is reinforced by daily attendance taking, specific directions as to pages and paragraphs to be read, and frequent testing.

By contrast, universities are loose institutions. Students frequently find themselves unrecognized by instructors who rely heavily on course outlines that specify broad topics to be covered and due dates for exams and assignments. Given the impersonality of it all, many students feel as if their instructors don't care how they are doing until the time comes to assign a final grade based on highly weighted, infrequent exams and a major term paper. In the context of this loose structure, many students fail to keep up and fall by the wayside.

Sometimes, role strain is due to a bad fit between personality and the requirements of a role. In this instance, people's natures and personalities clash with the duties they are called upon to perform. For example, tender-hearted employees may experience personality–role conflict when ordered by their bosses to call customers with outstanding debts and put "the squeeze" on them even though both are aware that the customer is in dire economic straits. Likewise, highly extroverted students may experience more personality–role conflict than introverted students when it comes to studying because serious study is usually a solitary activity. W. Furneaux notes in a 1957 report that university students who score high on extroversion on personality inventories do not perform as well on examinations as do those who score high on introversion. These differences in perform-

ance are not evident in high school. He suggests that stricter supervision (that is, "tight" role) in high school checks the socializing tendencies of extroverts. (See Entwhistle and Entwhistle, 1970.)

Role conflict occurs when individuals are called upon to play two or more roles that make incompatible demands such that conformity to one role necessarily means violation of the other. For example, an athlete who becomes the coach of the team and is required to select members for the next year will experience role conflict when choices must be made whether to select outstanding new players or buddies and friends from the previous year. A former student working for her father during the summer formed friendships with other employees. When those new friends disparaged her father, she found it particularly difficult to cope with both roles.

Role competition, which can also cause strain, exists for almost everyone on a regular basis because our many and varied roles compete continually for our energy and our time. For example, students might plan to spend a night in with their books when friends call and ask them to go out. As long as there is enough time before the exam to study and catch up with work, they think they can do both. However, the night before the exam, they face role overload and must prioritize their roles as student and as friend and decide which role to honour.

The same principle applies to workers—especially, in our society, women, who are trying to balance multiple tasks, such as paid work, parenting, elder care, and household work. They too are faced with choices between competing tasks and competing loyalties. They experience role overload when they run out of time or energy and must choose to honour the demands of one role at the expense of others. Some women in a study by Hochschild spoke longingly of sleep "the way a hungry person talks about food" (Hochschild and Machung, 1989: 9).

Merton (1957) identifies some social mechanisms that help to articulate role sets and status sets more clearly, thus reducing strain. For example, people can appeal to hierarchies already established in society that distinguish between roles and order them in terms of institutional priority. In our society, the student role is valued and given high priority, so families and workplaces often give special concessions to students that allow them more study time.

Another way to reduce role strain is to abide by recognized **power** differences between roles. In schools, for example, principals, who must mediate altercations between teachers and students, are almost always expected to support and defend teachers unless teachers' behaviour breaches the legal code for that role (for example, through sexual misconduct). Few principals who fail to publicly support their teachers survive in their role for very long. At the same time, the underlying authority structure of society is publicly confirmed and reinforced.

Role strain is reduced when roles can be compartmentalized. Thus, families may separate and isolate the affectionate parent role from the affectionate spouse role and compartmentalize them into separate spaces in the home by installing locks on "master," parental bedrooms.

Finally, role strain can be reduced by providing opportunities for relinquishing a role. When parental roles become overwhelming, some workplaces allow employees to take time off. Likewise, it is increasingly the case that when life circumstances become generally overwhelming, employees may be granted some form of stress leave or offered compensation if they completely relinquish the role.

In performing their multiple roles, actors must learn what the roles really are about, what they involve for themselves and others, the strains inherent in the roles, and, finally, the societal mechanisms that can lessen some of those strains. Few of us in modern life have learned to play all our roles as smoothly and effortlessly as we should.

The Interactional Approach to Role

The concept of *role* in sociology was first borrowed from the world of the theatre to describe the behaviour of actors playing parts in the drama of life. As Shakespeare wrote in *As You Like It*,

All the world's a stage,
And all the men and women merely players.
They have their exits and their entrances;
And one man in his time plays many parts.

This analogy suggests two possible avenues of interpretation for the concept of role. In the theatre, an actor speaks or behaves in a particular way that produces a response from other actors on the stage. These responses were "set pieces"—scripts, originally written on rolls (which later came to be called "roles"), the contents of which are spoken and acted out in such a way as to appear dynamic, changing, and spontaneous.

However, the emphasis is upon the word "appear." There is a difference between roles in the theatre and the roles actors play in everyday life. From the interactional perspective, in everyday life, actors' roles are not completely set pieces: there is opportunity for mutual and reciprocal action and reaction to what other actors say and do. Thus the "script," or role, is really a dynamic, constantly changing drama. George Herbert Mead (1934), the first social scientist explicitly to use the concept of role, refers to this ongoing drama as **role-taking**.

Mead and Turner

George Herbert Mead's outstanding contributions to role theory (1934) incorporate the concepts of significant **symbols** (language), role-taking, mind, self, and society. The concepts are linked together theoretically as follows: First, intelligent human interaction rests upon mutual understanding of the current symbols of meaning in society. Second, during interaction our (that is, our ego's) response to others' (called by Mead *alters*) behaviour toward us is based on our interpretation of their behaviour (that is, the process of role-taking). Third, a further aspect of role-taking is the impression of self provided by the other's reaction to us (to our self). Fourth, when we have a distinct sense of **self**, we can name and recognize objects in the environment and make decisions about the appropriate reaction to them. We make these decisions in the process of an internal conversation with self—what Mead terms a **mind**.

Mead postulates that, as humans, we are universally vulnerable and our only hope for survival rests upon our co-operation with others. In new situations, we use ingenuity to develop new ways of co-operating. During a major mine disaster a few years ago in Pennsylvania, nine miners were trapped together underground in one part of the mine. Soon they became hungry, started to suffer from hypothermia, and were in real danger of being swept away by a strong current in the underground river that had broken through the mine wall.

The miners' story of survival made headlines all over the world. We can translate their story into Mead's concepts to understand how their co-operation made survival possible. For example, when, after 18 hours, their hopes for rescue seemed bleak, one miner took out a pen, wrote a letter to his wife on the side of a cardboard box he found, and passed the pen around to the other eight miners in turn so they could do likewise, the process of role-taking enabled him to know that they needed and wanted to do the same thing. As experienced underground workers, they were able to relate meaningfully and successfully to all the objects surrounding them in the mine shaft (that is, symbols). The man's generous gesture, in turn, generated a strong feeling of camaraderie in the group and created an image of himself as a significant contributor to the enterprise of survival—something that might not have happened without that contribution.

As the hypothermia became more pronounced, it was obvious that the men had to find a way to warm themselves or they would perish. Among the multiplicity of tools, gadgets, and work paraphernalia in the mine shaft was a long piece of rope. Despite the fact that in our society males are frequently uncomfortable being in too close bodily contact with each other, the exigencies of survival in this instance overcame any reluctance the miners might have felt and they tied themselves closely together to generate as much body heat as possible to lessen the hypothermia. Thus, according to Mead's terminology, "mind" was brought to bear on the problem and the most rational alternative employed to solve it. The miners overcame traditional expectations and created new ones through meaningful interaction. They all survived.

Meadian theory as we have discussed it has been considerably refined and extended by Ralph Turner (1962), who regards the more structuralist approach put forth by Linton and Merton as being far too rigid and static. According to Turner, "The actor is not the occupant of a status for which there is a neat set of rules—a culture or set of norms—but a person who must act in the perspective supplied in part by his relationship to others whose reactions reflect roles that he must identify" (1962: 23). In effect, Turner shifts the focus from role-playing to the reciprocal joint processes of role-taking and **role-making**.

In role-making, we "devise" performances on the basis of an imputed other role. In turn, role-taking is the gestalt (the organized whole that is more than the sum of its parts) that we impute to be the role the other appears to be devising. As we might expect, in this process of self-presentation (role-making) and the imputation of the projected role (role-taking), there is the possibility of considerable inaccuracy and attempts to reinterpret the imputations involved. Turner (1962) refers to this process as "shifting axes," which, in turn, involves us continually in testing the validity of our presumptions. Actors involved in role-making attempt to create a gestalt for each other so

that they can more effectively role-take. To this end, they use the symbolism involved in things such as clothing, gestures, eye contact, and tone of voice to communicate clearly with each other.

A former student illustrated the role-making/role-taking process involving a relationship between herself and a male friend, a relationship that, to this point (as she inferred from role-taking) had been on a casual level. They frequently attended movies together, visited in each other's homes, and engaged in games like pool. She assumed it was a non-romantic relationship and that he was a friend (this is the gestalt implied by his actions toward her to that point). Then one evening, as they walked toward a movie theatre, the axis shifted and the friend appeared to transform his role of friend into a role of lover. Instead of just walking side by side, he suddenly placed his hand on her upper hip. This unaccustomed and unexpected action on his part shocked her and presented her with a problem of how to validly interpret his role: he was clearly role-making, and she was attempting to role-take accurately but was uncertain.

Was it an accidental slip of the hand, or was he attempting to demonstrate to approaching friends that they had become an "item" (that is, a couple)? Had the relationship changed from mere friendship to romance? She looked for cues to help her define an accurate, valid interpretation of the situation: she glanced at him, he looked embarrassed and glanced away quickly, and when he finally did speak it was in a hoarse croak; she then noted with surprise that he was better dressed than usual; and, contrary to their custom of "going dutch," he paid for her ticket to the movie. Confirmation of the transformation of the relationship into a romantic one occurred when the movie began and he reached for her hand to hold.

Thus, Turner's approach to the concept of role is interactive and symbolic; it involves mutual testing of the images projected by symbols. Because of the tentativeness of meanings, interaction is always highly fluid. Although Turner's role theory deals mainly with interpersonal interaction at the individual level, it can also have a macro aspect in that the "other" (alter) may be the "**generalized other**" constituted by society at large. Even "ego" can be thought of as a group (for example, industrial workers) carrying on role-taking. Relationships between groups, like relationships between individuals, shift constantly and effect changes in the social order (shifting axes).

For example, there is a strong debate in Canada about the amount of painkillers physicians should be allowed to administer to dying patients and whether large doses constitute merciful relief as implied by some physicians and members of the public (role-making) or murderous euthanasia (role-taking) as implied by some other physicians and other members of the public. In at least one instance a physician was prosecuted in the courts for this difference in perception of the therapy. However, a more recent shift in the axes of perception has resulted in a decrease in the distance between the two points of view. This concordance has been partly achieved by the creation of slightly more clear-cut regulations drawn up by the medical profession for medical personnel to follow—a process that represents a definite change in the public order.

Both theoretical approaches to role—structural and interactional—have weaknesses. The **structural approach** faces difficulties explaining change, and the interactional has difficulty explaining stability. As a result, it is useful to employ them both when analyzing sociological problems.

The Conflict Approach to Role

The *conflict paradigm* emanates from the theoretical thinking of Karl Marx ([1867] 1967). Marx believed that the control of the distribution of material goods and the ownership and control of the instruments of production, along with family heritage, produced divisions between the two major classes that, under **capitalism**, came to be termed the **bourgeoisie** and the **proletariat**. The bourgeoisie owned and controlled the **means of production** and employed the proletariat, who were sometimes compelled by force to contribute to the maintenance and enhancement of the capital accumulations of their employers. This situation of forceful exploitation of one class by the other maintained by power and exemplified by contrasting lifestyles (aristocracy versus peasantry) led to hostility on both sides. The aristocracy feared the loss or reduction of their profits because of the resentment, lack of co-operation, and even rebellion by the workers who contributed to their profits.

W. Peter Archibald (1976, 1978) deals with the micro aspects of role from a conflict perspective and focuses on Marx's concept of **alienation** from others (Marx, 1964). According to Archibald, alienation from others is characterized by four features: (1) we feel indifference or separation; (2) when we approach others, it is for narrow egoistic purposes; (3) when we interact with others, we are more controlled than in control; and (4) when we relate to others, it is with

feelings of dissatisfaction and even hostility. Archibald develops these four features in generalizations that can also be considered aspects of the symbolic interactionist paradigm as it is elaborated by Erving Goffman in his chapter "Nature of Deference and Demeanor" in *Interaction Ritual* (1967).

In the case of indifference or separation—really a detachment generalization—Archibald (1976) notes that people of different classes, statuses, and power groups tend to avoid each other. In factory settings, for example, management tends to have separate maintenance facilities, such as entrances, elevators, washrooms, and cafeterias. Similar principles apply in a **macrosociology** realm. For example, in her historical study of urban transformation, Lyn Lofland indicates that zoning ordinances emerged in the nineteenth century as a "result of a desire on the part of the upper and middle classes to separate themselves from the 'dangerous classes'" (1973: 74). Developers took these sentiments to heart and did their best, creating district after district of similarly valued homes and "protecting" those values through covenants and "gentlemen's agreements."

Archibald (1976) argues that the two classes avoid each other because each feels threatened by the other. The position of the privileged depends on continued deference from the underprivileged. But such compliance is not always assured, and when it is not forthcoming it signals a loss of **face** and questions one's superiority. In addition, revealing slips in the presence of subordinates give evidence that one is not a superior person. People in lower positions feel even more threatened by those in higher positions. Studies (see, for example, Cohen and Davis, 1973) demonstrate that performing in front of high-status audiences is more anxiety-producing (as measured by the Palmar Sweat Index) than performing before an audience of peers. Interacting with, or at least within hearing distance of, bosses may result in giving out information that can be used against one. Consequently, avoidance is a useful strategy in dealing with enemies and rivals. As Goffman states, "The surest way for a person to prevent threats to his face is to avoid contacts in which these threats are likely to occur" (1967: 15). Archibald concludes that "avoidance as a self-protective strategy is . . . a very plausible explanation for the 'detachment generalization'" (1976: 822).

Archibald's second principle is the *means–ends generalization*. That is, when the two classes do interact there is a tendency (especially on the part of subordinates) for it to be on a role-specific basis rather than

Open for Discussion
Philip Zimbardo's Stanford Prison Experiment

Commonly held stereotypes portray prisons as pathological places because of the personalities of the prisoners (low impulse control, problematic character structure, sociopathologies) and guards (surly, sadistic, megalomaniac). However, psychologist Philip Zimbardo and colleagues (1972) thought otherwise and suspected that social roles were the major factors in determining prisoner–guard interactions.

To test their hypothesis, they set up a mock prison and advertised in a local newspaper for subjects to participate in a two-week experiment on prison life in return for modest remuneration. All of the more than 75 male applications were subjected to a rigorous screening process to ensure that they were mature, emotionally stable, and "normal." From this original group, 21 college students from middle-class homes were selected to participate in the experiment. Approximately half of the subjects (11) were randomly assigned to the status of prison guard, the remainder (10) to the status of prisoner. Guards were issued khaki uniforms, billy clubs, whistles, and handcuffs. Prisoners were dressed in smocks resembling hospital gowns and in nylon stocking caps.

Initially, subjects approached their role-playing in a light-hearted fashion, but it did not take long before they began to fall into stereotypical behaviour characteristic of their roles. The guards became increasingly callous and began to demonstrate inventiveness in the application of arbitrary power (Zimbardo, 1972). They refused prisoners permission to go to the toilet and forced them to do tedious and useless work (such as moving cartons back and forth, and picking thorns out of blankets that had been dragged through thorn bushes). Guards issued commands to prisoners to do push-ups and occasionally stepped on their backs in the process. They also forced prisoners to do humiliating tasks such as scrubbing toilets with bare hands.

As early as the second day, the prisoners began to rebel, and the guards responded with increased force and threats of violence. In turn (given the reciprocal nature of roles), prisoners became increasingly passive and began to "adopt and accept the guards' negative attitude towards them. . . . The typical prisoner syndrome was one of passivity, dependence, depression, helplessness, and self-depreciation" (Haney, Banks, and Zimbardo, 1973: 79).

The result was that prisoners began to develop serious pathologies. One prisoner developed a psychosomatic skin rash over his whole body, and others developed symptoms of severe depression and acute anxiety. The experiment had to be aborted after six days. As Zimbardo states,

> At the end of only six days we had to close down our mock prison because what we saw was frightening. It was no longer apparent to most of the subjects (or to us) where reality ended and their roles began. The majority had indeed become prisoners or guards. . . . There were dramatic changes in virtually every aspect of their behavior, thinking, and feeling. . . . We saw some (guards) treat others as if they were despicable animals, taking pleasure in cruelty. While other boys (prisoners) became servile, dehumanized robots who thought only of escape, of their own individual survival, and of their mounting hatred for guards. (Zimbardo, 1972: 5)

on a personal basis. As one former student said of his summer job, "I am a very conscientious worker. When my boss asks me questions pertaining to work I'm happy to answer them . . . they make me look responsible . . . but I don't like him asking questions about my life outside of work. It's none of his business . . . it makes me look less responsible and reliable because I'm a teenager who loves to party and drink on weekends."

This emphasis on role specificity is hypothesized to be the result of a desire, especially on the part of workers, for predictability. When subjects in J.L.

Cohen and J.H. Davis's study (1973) described earlier were told what high-status audiences were looking for (that is, when they experienced role specificity), their anxiety levels were lower than when they were told nothing (that is, when they experienced role diffuseness). Archibald states, "restricting the number of roles and the scope of activities associated with each role permits one to get some of what one wants from the person in a different class or power position while at the same time minimizing threat" (1976: 820–1).

Once again drawing on Goffman, Archibald (1976) explains that high-status individuals' reliance on the formalities of role relationships helps maintain the status quo. As for the low-status role point of view, Goffman states that "adherence to the formalities one owes others can be a relatively protective matter, guaranteeing that one's conduct will be accepted by others" (1961b: 128). For example, one former student reported that her boss at her summer job always asked her how her weekend was, and she always said something general like "fine" or "too short." This way she was sociable enough to show respect and guarded enough to maintain her privacy. Thus, she not only protected her privacy and smoothed her relationship with her boss (the micro aspect of the interaction) but also maintained the macro system by demonstrating her acceptance and approval of the expected convention. This seemingly insignificant personal interaction can and does have an impact on the wider social system.

Archibald's third principle is the *control–purposiveness generalization*. Archibald maintains that higher-class, higher-status, and higher-power individuals are more likely than lower-class, lower-status, and lower-power ones to initiate activity and influence others. Goffman notes that "in American business organizations, the boss may thoughtfully ask the elevator man how his children are, but this entrance into another's life may be blocked to the elevator man, who can appreciate the concern but not return it" (1967: 64). This point about the control–purposiveness generalization is further illustrated by experiments showing that drivers of expensive, high-status cars are more likely to honk at low-status cars in front of them (Diekman et al., 1996). Anthony Doob and Alan Gross (1968) report that when low-status cars stall and block traffic behind them, they are more likely to be honked at than are high-status cars and, in a couple of cases in their study, stalled low-status cars were actually bumped by obviously impatient drivers behind them. The fact that drivers of low-status cars

are less likely to initiate such action illustrates conformity with the principle of the control–purposiveness generalization.

On the other hand, William Whyte's study of the social structure of the restaurant (1949) presents an apparent contradiction of Archibald's generalization. In one busy restaurant, the workforce consisted of cooks, other kitchen workers, service pantry workers, bartenders, supervisors, and waitresses. The waitress group was submitted to the greatest level of stress because they came in contact with anywhere from 50 to 100 customers a day, who were frequently in a hurry, impatient, and sometimes abusive; the waitresses also had to deal with the other categories of workers, who were predominantly male. In order to satisfy the urgent customer demands, waitresses (females, assumed to be subordinates, and not expected to be aggressive) were often forced to shout orders urgently—something the predominantly male cooks (assumed to be superordinate in the institutional hierarchy of the restaurant) and other workers took as an affront from the subordinate females. In response, cooks often turned a deaf ear to the orders, frustrating the waitresses even more and causing angry customers to exert even greater pressure when food orders were not forthcoming.

At this point it might be noted that whereas in the study by Diekmann and colleagues (1996), the generalization of the initiation of activity (that is, honking) by drivers of high-status cars is taken for granted, in Whyte's restaurant study the converse appears to be true: when lower-status waitresses shouted orders to cooks, they were objected to and ignored. This anomaly illustrates what happens when interaction is organized in a manner contrary to the generally accepted principles of everyday life.

Whyte relates that one restaurant solved the problem by installing a spindle wheel on which orders were placed, thus eliminating the necessity for personal contact and potential animosity between waitresses and cooks. One cook stated that never in all his life had he worked in such a "wonderful place." He described earlier experiences in other restaurants where there was no such insulating mechanism: "The girls could call their orders in—an ordeal to which no man should be subjected" (Whyte, 1949: 308).

Archibald's fourth principle is the *feelings generalization*: an element of hostility underlies much and perhaps most interaction between non-equals; occasionally there is outright rebellion. An example would be low-power workers who rejoice at a manager's misfortune. In one instance told to the authors, a lawyer had his parking privileges at work revoked because he used his wife's parking pass and attempted to gain the use of two spaces for the price of one. His misfortune gave so much satisfaction to his clerk in the law firm that she said she felt like a cat who just caught a mouse. Expressions of these feelings of hostility become particularly virulent during strikes.

The conflict paradigm provides a light by which to view role in its perhaps less acceptable, institutional aspects and to examine its underside of dissatisfaction, turbulence, and coercion—even its tendency to violence and revolution. So, while the structural-functional paradigm asserts that order in society is achieved by wide cultural consensus and achieves considerable stability and longevity, the conflict paradigm suggests that stability and any degree of permanence is achieved by the dominance of one group over the other and by the force used to maintain this dominance.

Identity

The Symbolic-Interactionist Approach to Identity

We turn now to the second element of interest in our discussion of social structure and the way it constrains us. *Identity* is the way in which people define themselves and, in turn, are defined by others. It is a result of the things people do (their roles) and the ways in which their acts are evaluated (accorded prestige) and reacted to. As John Hewitt says, "A role in itself is lifeless—an unplayed part that has no substance until the individual claims it for his or her own and breathes life into it through identification with it" (2000: 97).

Hewitt (2000) classifies several aspects of identity. **Situated identity** focuses on identity as it emerges through and affects face-to-face interaction with others. *Social identity* is based on identification with groups (for example, family, ethnic, and occupational

4.2

Sociology in Action
Seymour Lieberman's Workplace Study

Seymour Lieberman (1956) studied the attitudes (that is, orientations toward a person, group, or social process) of 2,354 rank-and-file workers in an appliance factory toward unions and management. He demonstrated, as did Peter Archibald (1976) later, the Marxian hypothesis concerning the effect of status on attitudes and the resulting attitude of mutual hostility between upper and lower classes in society.

After the initial survey was completed, the usual workplace processes continued; 23 men were promoted to the rank of foreman and 35 people were elected by their work groups as shop stewards. After 15 months, promoted foremen and shop stewards whose attitudes had originally been recorded in the first survey were retested and the results compared with their answers on the first survey. The results of the second test showed an increase in pro-management attitudes on the part of the promoted foremen and an increase in the pro-union attitudes on the part of the shop stew-

ards. However, the increase in the pro-management attitudes of foremen was greater than the increase in pro-union attitudes of the shop stewards. Lieberman says that these differences should have been predicted because the move from rank-and-file labourer to foreman is greater than that of worker to shop steward.

After two more years, business conditions for the company changed and fewer foremen were needed in the plant, so eight of them were demoted to their former positions. Lieberman then conducted a third survey to compare the attitudes of foremen who were demoted with those who retained their positions. The results indicated that individuals who were demoted now had much stronger pro-union than pro-management attitudes—a clear reversal compared to the situation when they were at the level of foreman. In effect, all of the test results in Lieberman's study support Archibald's (Marxian) theories of inter-class, particularly Industrial World, attitudes.

groups) and significant social categories (for example, age and gender), which, in turn, define us in terms of our similarities with some groups and our differences from other groups. *Personal identity* consists of factors that make us unique from others (including physical characteristics such as height, weight, and looks) as well as aspects of our past based on the manner in which other people have reacted to us and typed us. Personal identity and social identity are parts of our *biographical identity* and, as such, provide continuity as we step into and out of various situated identities. Identities are established by the processes of our announcement of ourselves and by others' placement of us. If one or both are compromised or less than complete, the result is identity trouble.

Classical Theorists on Identity: Cooley and Mead

Charles Horton Cooley (1902) is best known for formulating the concept of the **looking-glass self** to describe how identity is formed. Cooley states, "Each to each a looking glass / Reflects the other that doth pass" (1902: 52). In effect, then, our identity is what we think others think of us. This reflected (hence "looking-glass") self emerges as we imagine how we appear to others, then imagine how others judge that appearance, and finally come to some self-feeling such as pride or mortification.

In one incident told to the authors, a male student once sat at the back of a crowded classroom. There were three vacant seats between him and the next person. Three female students came to class late and entered through the back door, then struggled over the knees of the students already seated. The first one in stopped at the empty seat farthest from him; the next passed her to the seat beside her, and the third latecomer passed those two to sit beside the male student. On the surface it seemed far more logical to him had they reversed their seating order and saved themselves from having to crawl over each other's knees, so he began to reflect on their perception of him. He felt embarrassed and mortified, and he hoped that other students would not notice this "real putdown."

Of course, the female students may have had no particular reason for their seating procedure and may have been completely unaware of its "reflective" effect upon him. Similarly, professors experience much the same effect when their students walk out of the room while they are still lecturing. Not surpris-

ingly, according to Cooley ([1909] 1962), this self-image is reflected most strongly in primary, intimate face-to-face groups such as play groups, family, or even work groups.

Cooley anticipates later work by Goffman on the dramaturgical model of identity not only by asserting that "the imaginations people have of each other are the solid facts of society" (1902: 107), but also by noting that children quickly learn how to control their appearance so as to be seen and treated as they wish: "The young performer soon learns to be different things to different people. . . . If the mother or nurse is more tender than just, she will almost certainly be 'worked' by systematic weeping" (197).

Mead extended Cooley's ideas by emphasizing the cognitive skills acquired through role play and through learning the rules of games. Mead's best-known distinctions in the area of self-development are the definitions of the *play stage* and the *game stage* (1934). In the play stage, children "play at" being, for example, a mother or father and speak to themselves as the mother or father might. Consequently, they assume for themselves the identity of the label applied by parents. For example, a little girl fiddling with the television dial—an explicitly forbidden act—might tap her own extended hand with the other and say "bad girl"—an assumed identity, at least temporarily.

In the game stage, according to Mead (1934), there is a clear-cut, and in some circumstances intricate, organization of roles to be played. This complexity involves reciprocity on the part of the players. Overall, there is a set of rules that structure the game, but players must nevertheless respond appropriately to the specific acts of other members of their own team as well as to members of the opposing team. As the game progresses, these conditions, acts, and reciprocal acts change constantly and must be adjusted to and coped with by effective role-taking.

For example, in the game of baseball, when the pitcher throws the ball to the batter, the first reaction is by the batter. The batter's reaction determines the reaction of the fielders, depending on whether it is a hit or not. After a hit, the batter runs to first base, and the first fielder, to gain control of the ball, throws it to the first base player (or second or third—whichever would be most strategically effective) according to the rules of the game.

Games involve a number of players having to enact expected roles quickly and efficiently, anticipating others' actions and reacting to their own acts and to the anticipated outcomes of those acts. This com-

4.3

Human Diversity
Karen March: "Who Do I Look Like?"

Karen March's study "Who Do I Look Like? Gaining a Sense of Self-Authenticity Through Physical Reflections of Others" (2003) focuses on the components of identity and identity trouble that emerge when there is a disjunction between announcement and placement. She describes the situation of adoptees who lived during the period when it was illegal to reveal who their biological parents were. The adoptees describe feelings of a "deep gap" in their personality and an "incompleteness" of self-image (that is, personal and social identities).

To understand the phenomena, March contrasts the table-talk experiences of individuals from biologically intact families with those of adoptees. In biologically intact families, it is not unusual for people to hear casual comments about how so-and-so has the nose, eyes, ears, body, or build of their parent, aunt, uncle, or grandparent. This seemingly trivial talk builds family bonds and constructs identity in family terms. In the case of adoptees, however, there is rarely such talk, and if it does occur, it is often problematic. A 35-year-old female adoptee put it very well: "You come into a room, or you're sitting there, and they talk about how so and so looks like Uncle Jim. They ignore you. Or they notice you and stop talking. Or they change the subject. It makes you [feel that] a piece is missing. . . . You feel a bit on the outside. I feel phoney" (March, 2003: 319). These experiences of incomplete placement

marginalize adoptees and contribute to their feelings of inauthenticity. As the adoptee notes, "It makes you want something that is biologically yours."

When secrecy laws were eventually relaxed and face-to-face contacts achieved, adoptees reported feelings of completeness, authenticity, and relief, especially if there was biological matching. They said things such as "I immediately knew I belonged there," "I felt real for the first time," and "It made me feel connected." In essence, contact provided adoptees with a more complete framework for further development of their social and personal identities. As March states, "It validates the source of self as a physical being. Furthermore, biological matching substantiates one's unrivaled position within an intergenerational group of physical beings possessing unique characteristics" (2003: 321).

March's article on the identity troubles of adopted children is echoed by a 40-year-old test-tube baby, who bemoans the fact that not only does she not know her father as a person, but she knows only that he "is a glass jar [with] a blob of sperm in it": "If my mum had had an affair at least there would have been sex and lust, something human rather than something so cold, scientific and clinical. My parents never even met." The effects on her identity are dramatic: "I feel like a freak, a fake, I don't feel I know who I am any more" (Woodward, 2003: 24).

---

plexity of organization, interreaction, and outcome within us develops a concept of society at large that Mead refers to as the *generalized other* (1934).

The development of identity, particularly biographical identity, is the result of a series of impulses to act and the resultant actual responses to those impulses. For the most part, the impulses are spontaneous and even unconscious, whereas reactions are more deliberate. Mead terms the spontaneous motivations of the individual the "I" aspect of the self and the deliberate chosen behaviour the "Me" aspect of self. Over time, the chosen behaviour characteristic of an individual comes to characterize that individual's self. Thus, identity corresponds to the Me—to that part of

self most sensitive to the expectations of others; the I is based more on impulse and provides energy and propulsion to the act. There is a continuing dialogue (and frequently an outright struggle) between the I and the Me and, as such, **social control** is usually a matter of self-control. Think of the Motown song "Will You Love Me Tomorrow" by Gerry Goffin and Carole King, in which the singer says, "Tonight the light of love is in your eyes"; this is the I—in this case the internal "urge to merge." The song then asks, "But will you love me tomorrow?"—the Me agonizing over whether yielding to the impulse of the I will result in a loss of self-esteem and to lack of respect from the other person.

Contemporary Theorists on Identity: Blumer, Stone, Goffman

The structural view of interaction, as we have seen, emphasizes the relative stability and permanence of the social world. Symbolic interactionism, on the other hand, views social life as *processual*, involving continual interaction out of which emerge new situations and new interaction within them, producing, in turn, different identities and coping strategies. Herbert Blumer (1969) named this mode of thinking (that is, interaction as an exchange of meanings through symbols), which had been initiated by Cooley and Mead, *symbolic interactionism*, and is considered its predominant exponent. These situated coping strategies and identities rest upon and are recognized by symbols, for example, the uniform identifying a police officer or the vestments identifying a priest.

In this ongoing process, Gregory Stone (1981) recognizes two kinds of identity: *identification of*, when placement coincides with announcement, and *identification with*, when there is a comfortable compatibility between the person who does the announcing and the one who does the placement; an identification of the other is necessary before role-taking can occur, which, in turn, makes possible an identification with the other.

One example of identification of and identification with is the process sometimes called "gaydar," by which some lesbians, in public places, signal their identities to each other (for example, short cropped hair, no make-up, masculine appearance). When lesbians recognize each other (identification of), it leads to the expression of feelings of **solidarity** (identification with). As one of Tracy Nielsen's respondents stated, "I find most lesbians seem to be pleased seeing other lesbians in public (you don't feel freaky and alone)—and so you treat each other accordingly" (2002: 32).

A novel twist that has developed out of technology and that relates to the process of identification of and identification with is the text-based chat site. Here couples or groups use computers to chat with each other about a variety of matters, particularly the social and personal aspects of their lives. During these conversations, they identify themselves—sometimes truthfully, but often, also, fictitiously (Wolejszo, 2002). Identity announcement in this context is completely textual and the participants never see each other, so identification with, if it ever happens, is entirely in the mind. Almost invariably, participants develop a strong urge for more material (that is, face-to-face) contact in the form of photographs, which may be embarrassing and not willingly agreed to by the original identity announcer. When exchanges occur, they are frequently followed by feelings of disenchantment: "It's almost invariably disappointing. I like knowing what people look like, but . . . well, I'd rather they were more attractive, and less stereotypically computer-useresque" (Wolejszo, 2002: 53). One recent remedy for this disappointment is the compulsory exchange of photos prior to online identity announcement, something that emphasizes the importance Stone (1981) places on the universe of appearance and not merely that of **discourse**.

Erving Goffman's is perhaps the most lucid and imaginative exponent of identity analysis (though he does not label it as such); significantly for this discussion, it also involves the concept of role. Goffman places the concept of role squarely back on the stage, thus suggesting its structural aspect while, on the other hand, also explicitly indicating an interactionist orientation. In the case of the structuralist aspect of self-presentation, Goffman (1959) uses the theatrical analogies of "front stage" and "back stage" to distinguish the two zones of open and explicit role-making in the front stage from the hidden role-making in the back stage. Between the front stage and the back stage are "barriers to perception" that buffer one arena from the other.

Presentation of self in the front stage is analyzed in terms of three factors: (1) setting—the spatial aspects of things, such as sets and props; (2) appearance—the actor's age, sex, race, clothing, appearance; and (3) manner—behaviour indicating how one intends to perform the role, for example, haughtily or friendlily, formally or informally. These three factors combine to create *front*—a set of abstract, stereotyped expectations that prepare audiences for the ensuing performance and help them come to an appropriate definition of the situation (Goffman, 1959). Front adds "dramatic realization" to performances because it helps performers convey everything they wish to convey on any given occasion.

Goffman also indicates that whether performances are honest or dishonest, they still have the same general characteristics: "Whether an honest performer wishes to convey the truth or whether a dishonest performer wishes to convey a falsehood, both must take care to enliven their performance with appropriate expressions, exclude from their performances expressions that might discredit the impression fostered and take care lest the audience impute unintended meanings" (1959: 66). In addition, "impressions given" are intended and designed to convey a desired identity, whereas "impressions given off" are accidentally conveyed (for example, by a slip of the tongue or an uncontrolled gesture) and represent actors in an undesirable light from their own point of view (Goffman, 1959: 7). These aspects of front must be consistent to produce a convincing identification of the actor.

One example of interaction gone awry because of such inconsistencies involves the case of Ahmed Ressam, the so-called Millennium Bomber, who, in 1999, was stopped at the Canada–US border by a US customs officer. The culprit attempted to identify himself to the officer as a routine commuter. The first inconsistency that emerged was that the car carried British Columbia licence plates but the driver was from Montreal. Furthermore, it could be logically presumed that, as a "regular commuter," he would be fully familiar with British Columbia and matters pertaining to that province. When questioned, though, he seemed completely ignorant of both. In addition to these inconsistencies, his manner was diffident and faltering. He soon began to sweat, a strong cue that something was untoward. The setting was an international border crossing where the drug trade was a serious problem. The customs officer became very suspicious and, in Turner's terms (1962), "imputed the role" of drug dealer to him. She asked him to open the trunk of the car, where, instead of the drugs she had suspected, she discovered a stock of explosives. In effect, then, the three aspects of front (setting, manner, and appearance) were present, leading to impressions "given off" that contradicted an identity Ressam tried to project and with which the customs officer did not identify.

The back stage is a region characterized by privacy that hides accidents, disagreements, and conflicts between actors on the team (that is, those who cooperate to present a performance). In one instance told to the authors, for example, a waiter in a restaurant accidentally dropped a plate of food, destined for a customer, on the kitchen floor. Disgusted and frustrated with himself, he uttered a stream of profanities, then scooped up the food, neatly rearranged it on a clean plate, and presented it with a big smile to the customer. Another waiter reported the incident to the owner, who told her to mind her own business. The customer, left unaware by these "barriers to perception," expressed verbal satisfaction with the service and left a generous tip. In this example, the interaction in the respective areas of kitchen and dining room dramatize the distinctions between backstage and frontstage behaviour.

Goffman's treatment of presentation of self and the establishment of identity involves the concepts of role, status, and prestige presented by actors and recognized by an audience. Goffman states emphatically that the recognition and granting of high status and the accompanying prestige it deserves are an actor's "moral right": "Society is organized on the principle that any individual who possesses certain characteristics has a moral right to expect that others will value and treat him in an appropriate way" (Goffman, 1959: 13). In the process of self-presentation to others, Goffman says that we overplay the two basic strategies of self-revelation and concealment. Self-revelation allows us to project ourselves in the best possible light when our worthy qualities might not be fully apparent to others, while concealment allows us to hide aspects of ourselves that could be discreditable.

Another aspect of identity projection is **altercasting** (Weinberg and Deutschberger, 1963). Altercasting is the strategy of projecting a characteristic of some kind—favourable or unfavourable, obligatory or privileged—onto another person with the object of achieving some advantage for oneself. It is the counterpart of Goffman's concept of **impression management**, whereby, in effect, actors engage in self-casting.

In altercasting, this process of fixing an identity upon another in order to elicit a specific role could be considered role-making in reverse. In essence, the other person is put on the spot, forced to interact in a way he or she may not wish to but that forces the drama into the pattern intended. For example, Premier W.A.C. Bennett, who had dominated British Columbia's legislative assembly for years, attempted to put down Dave Barrett, the new, admittedly upstart, leader of the opposition, by responding to the young member's first attempt at government criticism with the accusation, "You are a Marxist." The response, which came with great alacrity, was "Which one, Harpo, Groucho, or Chico?" Members roared with laughter and the premier was cast, perhaps deservedly, into the role of a fool. The premier—not yet aware that he had met his match—then went doggedly on and accused the opposition leader of being a "Waffle" (a member of the well-known radical wing of the New Democratic Party in the early 1970s), to which came the quick response, "That makes you, Mr Premier, a pancake." The identity negotiation continued over time with the premier almost always on the losing end, which probably ultimately contributed to his political downfall in the next election.

Another illustration of the concept of altercasting concerns the case discussed earlier in this chapter of a young couple, initially only friends, whose relationship was transformed into that of lovers. In that instance, Turner's concept of "shifting axis" was discussed, and we noted how the male "friend" moved the axis from one of friend to one explicitly of lover. The first phase of the altercasting act was putting his hand on her upper hip, the second was paying for the movie, and the final phase was taking her hand. One other, common, well-known example of altercasting is when some acquaintance becomes uncommonly friendly. Experience shows that such occasions often presage the request for a special favour.

Identity Troubles: Embarrassment

Embarrassment occurs when an announced identity is not supported or is even distorted, resulting in unsatisfactory placement (Gross and Stone, 1981). Typical instances of embarrassment resulting from dissonance between announcement and placement are a result of bodily accidents, which cause embarrassment because they project a less than fully mature persona, or possibly a careless one.

A dramatic illustration occurred when a female university student went to Banff with her church youth group. She was particularly attracted to one of the young men in the group and was delighted when he invited her to climb partway up one of the mountains. They reached their destination and were sitting close together enjoying the splendour and romance of the setting sun, when he leaned over to kiss her. As their lips met, the strong emotional arousal combined with the excitement and tension were just too much for her to cope with, and she lost control of her sphincter. Mortified and humiliated, she raced down the mountain with her friend in hot pursuit. When he finally caught up to her, he assured her that it really didn't matter and leaned over to give her another kiss; once more she lost control. This was clearly a case of distorted announcement and unsatisfactory placement.

A second cause of embarrassment is insufficient support for identity announcement. Consider a self-confident "ace" student who consistently receives A's emerging from the exam room proclaiming "I aced

it" only to find out when grades are posted that the performance was worthy of merely a B. Or consider what happens when you go to a cashier's counter and announce yourself as a paying customer only to discover that you've left your wallet at home. (Incidentally, the frequency of this event was one of the reasons leading to the invention of credit cards.) Yet another example occurred to a university student who relates that when she was about 10 years old, she got her hair cut very short and was pleased with the result, but when she boarded a bus for the trip home she struck up a conversation with some peers, one of whom mistakenly took her for a boy. She was so ashamed and embarrassed that she became a virtual recluse for the time it took her hair to grow back.

A third source of embarrassment is *mistaken identity placement*, in which a person may adequately document an identity but fail to have others place it because of distraction or inadequate attention. For example, a former student, a young woman who worked as a waiter, once went to serve two customers seated at a table. She placed napkins on the table and, without observing the customers very closely, greeted them with "Hi there, ladies." Only then did she glance up and realize to her horror that one of them was clearly a man, who pointedly said, "Excuse me!" Both she and the customers were deeply embarrassed. She apologized quickly and tried to smooth things over with humour, but neither technique seemed to work. The customers did not leave a tip. Mistaken identity placement also occurs when we forget a person's name when introducing her or him to someone else, or when we say something disparaging about someone to a third party only to discover later that the two of them have a close relationship.

Mismanagement of superfluous identities is a fourth cause of embarrassment. In most encounters, there are more activities (roles) and identities than are necessary for ensuing transactions. For example, at parties people eat and drink (subordinate role) while they converse (dominant role). The subordinate roles and identities must be managed so that they remain in the background and don't interfere with what people have come together to do—their dominant roles. A misalignment of these subordinate and dominant roles and identities can result in embarrassment. This occurs when subordinate roles and identities impose themselves on dominant ones. A subordinate activity that properly belongs to a situation may suddenly become the dominant focus of the occasion. For example, at one dinner party the guests were engaged in serious discussion. As they munched on their salads, which contained small cherry tomatoes, one guest, who related this story to the authors, bit into an especially ripe specimen and accidentally squirted the host, who was sitting across the table. The shocked guests and host all noted the misdeed, which superseded the main objective of the occasion and caused great embarrassment for all.

Embarrassment also occurs when reserve identities inappropriately surface on the dominant identity (Gross and Stone, 1981). For example, one of Gross and Stone's respondents, a judge, said that he stumbled on the way up to the platform, exposing his golfing clothes (reserve identity) beneath his robes. Similarly, if a student's cell phone rings during a lecture, a reserve identity (friend) imposes itself on the dominant identity (student).

We also experience embarrassment when a *relict identity*—an element of our biographical identity we no longer wish to announce—resurfaces (Gross and Stone, 1981). For example, a former student whose new girlfriend admired his sweater and asked where he got it blurted out spontaneously that his ex-girlfriend had knitted it for him. The new relationship was short lived. A more extreme case was that of a student who took his new girlfriend home to meet his parents for the first time. His mother was obviously attempting to dazzle the girlfriend, and at one point she produced a small formaldehyde-filled vial and proudly announced that it contained the remains of her son's foreskin from when he was circumcised as an infant.

Identity Management: Defensive Practices

Goffman (1971) says that embarrassment causes us to "lose **face**," and that when we do, we attempt to compensate for the loss by engaging in *remedial work* (that is, *face-work*, or face-saving). Remedial work manifests itself in a variety of forms, including avoidance, accounts (justifications or excuses), and disclaimers, all of which are designed to prevent or remedy damage to our identity (Goffman, 1971; Scott and Lyman, 1968; Stokes and Hewitt, 1976).

Avoidance

Goffman's term for face-saving work to prevent identity damage in the first place is *avoidance*. For example, university students who know for certain they have failed an exam frequently do not attend classes on the day the tests are to be returned, and students who do attend class and find that they have received very low or failing grades generally attempt to avoid students who received high grades. In other words, we attempt to avoid situations wherein we are likely to be embarrassed. Test bombers not infrequently make remarks like "You want to avoid them [Aces] because you emerge looking like the 'dumb one,'" or "It makes you feel like you're lazy or unreliable." Understandably, bombers become particularly sensitive to the signs of success aces display—things like "sitting tall" at their desks, "broad grins," "sparkling eyes," and "jaunty walks." Bombers often use these signs as cues to identify whom to avoid (Albas and Albas, 2003).

Disclaimers and Accounts

Two related defence strategies to save face are disclaimers and accounts. *Disclaimers* are excuses that come before the act for which face-saving is expected to become necessary. *Accounts* are excuses and justifications that follow embarrassing acts. According to Stone (1981), both disclaimers and accounts can be verbal, in what he terms the *universe of discourse*, or they can be non-verbal mannerisms, in the *universe of appearance*. In the past, almost all research in this area of identity has focused on verbal disclaimers and accounts in the universe of discourse. More recently, however, there has been increased interest in the non-verbal mannerisms we employ in public places where talk is difficult or out of the question.

Verbal disclaimers—excuses that come before a potentially problematic act that may damage our identity—come in a multitude of forms. For example, when a professor asks a university class an "open question," students who do take the risk and respond when they are not entirely certain they have the "right" answer may attempt to set up the situation to defend their identity beforehand, using verbal disclaimers such as hedging: "I may be wrong on this, but. . . ."

Another verbal disclaimer comes in the form of *sin licence*, when, if we know we are going to break a rule, we argue that we have good reason to do so. Thus, students state that they do not study for tests in advance because "if I study early I'll only forget it" or "I study best under pressure." Verbal disclaimers, especially hedging, are rampant just before exams, when students offer many excuses why others should not expect too much from them. In fact, it's not unusual for a sort of contest to emerge as to why each will do worse than the other—"I'm going to outfail you!"

Verbal accounts are offered following a faux pas, and are "statements made to explain unanticipated or untoward behavior" (Scott and Lyman, 1968: 46). Accounts, in turn, can be subdivided into excuses and justifications.

Excuses are "accounts in which one admits that the act in question is bad, wrong, or inappropriate but denies full responsibility" (Scott and Lyman, 1968: 47)—for example, "I did not know," "I was coerced," or, in the case of one of the authors of this chapter, who committed a parking violation and appealed to a biological drive, "I had to 'go' so badly."

Justifications are statements wherein we accept responsibility for an act but deny the negative implications associated with it. For example, students who cheat on an exam may admit that they did so but argue that it "was okay because no one was hurt." People may mistreat others but argue that "it's okay because they're not important enough to worry about anyway," or that they "deserve" what they get. In all cases, accounts serve to "repair the broken and restore the estranged" (Scott and Lyman, 1968: 46).

Actors can also use accounts to negotiate a more positive identity for themselves after a disruptive interaction. Two students persisted in talking to each other during lectures. After the first request by the professor (not one of the authors), the talking ceased, and there was compliance for the next couple of classes. In subsequent classes, though, the talking resurfaced, and when confronted once again by the professor, the students offered the account that they were only doing what "everyone else" was. One of the students accused the professor of "picking on him." In this case, the students attempted to switch their identity from that of troublemaker to that of innocent victim by condemning the condemner.

Non-verbal forms of disclaimers and accounts are termed *motive mannerisms*; these occur within a universe of appearance when talk is difficult or out of the question (Stone, 1981). As noted earlier, this is an area of identity management that is increasingly being recognised.

An illustration of an account "face-saving" mannerism occurred to a former student who, at a high school social, emerged from the bathroom unaware that she had caught the end of the toilet paper in her skirt and that she was trailing it behind her. The startled looks of others soon alerted her that something was amiss. When she realized what was happening, she had the presence of mind to gather up the toilet paper behind her and wrap it around herself

while dancing in perfect step with the music. She received a loud round of applause and managed to salvage heroism from embarrassment.

Disclaimer mannerisms (that is, excuses) prior to the problematic act can be seen regularly in traffic when a driver cuts in front of another vehicle and the offender then waves to the other driver, implying that the latter has generously allowed the privilege. It is possible that in this process ruffled feathers are smoothed and chances of road rage are decreased.

Other sites rich in the display of motive mannerisms are the labelling-liable locales of university examination rooms, where students go to elaborate lengths to demonstrate that they are not cheaters. In the study "Avoiding the Label of Cheater During Exams" (Albas and Albas, 1995), some of the strategies classified included "actions to be avoided." Placement of books and notes is important, for example: not infrequently, students report that any such items are placed under a pile of books from other courses, usually on the floor and under the desk. It is also important to observe the *morality of place*. Knowing that locations are invested with varying degrees of trustworthiness, students avoid areas of the room they believe to be occupied by troublemakers and known cheaters.

On the other hand, some "actions to be taken" include demonstrations that students are beyond reproach by "hunching" and "draping" themselves over their exam papers to offset potential cheaters. If they must reach for or retrieve something, they use exaggerated movements purposefully designed to attract attention, thus demonstrating there is nothing to hide (Albas and Albas, 1995).

Exaggerated shows of innocence are also important. Some students always wear clothing without pockets to exams so it is obvious there is no place to conceal cheat notes. Others become friendlier than usual, suggesting to the invigilator that they are on the "same side" and therefore are not to be regarded as objects of suspicion (Albas and Albas, 1995). Similarly, shoppers often take self-conscious precautions to avoid looking suspicious by making exaggerated shows of innocence, for example, by tying a knot at the top of every bag they are carrying to give a clear message that nothing else is being added.

Identity Management: Protective Practices

Protective practices are to some extent altruistic and show consideration of the other. They also function

Sociology in Action
Jack Haas and William Shaffir's Medical Students

Jack Haas and William Shaffir's study of medical students (1978) graphically illustrates the principles of identity announcement, placement, and management. Identity announcement occurs in a "universe of appearance"—students, from the first few weeks of medical school, are issued white lab jackets, name tags, and stethoscopes—and in a "universe of discourse"—they are trained and required to "talk the talk." These universes of appearance and discourse constitute the media providing "identification of" the neophyte medical students.

This is followed by a phase of "identification with," which for the medical students is somewhat paradoxical. Because of role overload and other forms of role strain, the personal humanitarian ideals that brought them into the profession in the first place tend to become diluted; consequently, "identification with" becomes more with colleagues and the profession than with patients. At times, patients are referred to solely by their maladies: "the gall bladder in room 317." The more idealist orientation to patients eventually returns in professional practice.

Another way of coping with role strain is to establish a hierarchy of priorities in the concentration upon particular subjects. This is an example of a defensive practice because it reduces the likelihood of students' being publicly embarrassed before an audience of significant others. Thus, students almost inevitably focus more on subjects such as anatomy and pathophysiology, in which they are more likely to be called upon to answer questions and so be able to impress professors and other significant audiences with their professional competence. They spend less time on psychosocial areas, in which they are not so likely to be questioned.

An additional coping strategy for role strain is to put forth a "front" or mask that exudes enthusiasm and keenness. This disclaimer mannerism implies that even though students may not be all-knowing, they are at least doing everything in their power to achieve their potential.

Some students employ avoidance as a defensive mechanism to deal with their role strain. When the possibility arises of being submitted to a session of uncomfortable questioning, they strive to steer the situation into some more pleasant and comfortable area in which they feel more expert. Conversely, where they feel expert and comfortable, they seize opportunities to dramatize and show off their competence.

Finally, to demonstrate competence, students employ altercasting as a strategy by raising with a professor a question for which they already know the answer. In the repartee that follows, they can impress others: "The best way to impress others with your competence is asking questions you know the answer to. Because if they were ever to put it back on you: 'Well what do you think?' then you tell them what you think and you'd give a very intelligent answer" (Haas and Shaffir, 1978: 219).

Clearly, this account of the medical-training program involves, as do all such training programs, (1) clear-cut physical identification (for example, white lab jackets and name tags) as announcements; (2) placement (for example, by other students, colleagues, and patients); (3) the inevitability of embarrassment at times and the necessity to employ defensive strategies as part of identity management; and (4) the learning of not only biology, chemistry, and medical ethics, but also how to project a reassuring image of competence that is just as important when interacting with patients.

to protect the user as well as the communal assembly in which these practices are used because gaffes by a single person disrupt the interactional tone and thereby embarrass the entire group. Protective practices provide the user with some degree of self-protection because everyone is always vulnerable and considerate people are more likely to have consideration directed to them than are people who are thoughtless and unsympathetic. As Goffman (1959) notes, actors form a moral pact to support each other's fostered impressions of themselves.

Protective practices include studious inattention to small lapses in appropriate behaviour of others. For example, we might pretend not to notice a quiet burp emitted by the person next to us. Goffman (1959) refers to this face-saving device as *studied non-observance*. Studied non-observance can also be active; imagine a professor entering a large lecture theatre with his zipper down; a considerate student might prevent his embarrassment by rushing around the professor, back to the blackboard so that the professor's back is to the class, to let the professor know.

The previous illustrations are of small lapses in appropriate behaviour. However, the process applies just as well when the lapses are much more significant. A dramatic illustration of pretended non-observance to a large lapse in appropriate behaviour comes from the fable of the emperor's new clothes, in which of all the crowds who surround the emperor, it is only an unsophisticated child who blurts out that he is wearing no clothes. In some versions of the story, the child is scolded for being so observant. As Goffman states emphatically in regard to nakedness, "When bodies are naked, glances are clothed" (1971: 46). It is also taboo in nudist colonies to stare at the intimate parts of other people's nude bodies (Weinberg, 1997). Similarly, there are general rules of civil inattention expected in bars and restaurants where waitresses are topless (Goffman, 1971).

Protective practices also come in the form of being considerate and refraining from possibly embarrassing the other. A student once approached one of the authors of this chapter after a lecture and asked how to spell a word (*Kamikaze*) she had used. When asked why the request had not been made at the time the word was used, the student, a former teacher, said, "I didn't want to embarrass you in case you didn't know." It is also common for students to inform professors before class that they have to leave early; in so doing, the students remove the implication that they are leaving because the lecture is boring.

Refraining from gloating over our own successes and providing feasible excuses to the unsuccessful for their failure to do as well is also a protective practice. It happens when, after an exam is returned in class, high-scoring "aces" merely gloss over their grade ("I did okay") when talking to low-scoring "bombers." Aces also often offer bombers face-saving excuses such as the difficulty or unfairness of the test, or remind them of disclaimers: "As you said, you hardly had any time at all before the test to study."

Self-mockery (Ungar, [1986] 1992) is yet another frequent protective practice we use to save our own image, but it is also a protective practice to save the image of the other. For example, on a visit to Canada, US president Ronald Reagan was heckled by a particularly vocal crowd. To prevent then prime minister Pierre Elliott Trudeau from being embarrassed by the rude treatment his guest was receiving, the president quipped, "They must have been imported to make me feel at home" (*U.S. News and World Report*, 1981, cited in Ungar, 1992: 50).

Where Role and Identity Come Together

Three concepts that demonstrate strikingly how role and identity overlap are role distance, role embracement, and role exit. *Role distance* (Goffman, 1961b) designates the behaviour of actors who play roles in such a way as to announce identities that will have others place them at a distance from the identities they are seemingly announcing. *Role embracement* occurs when actors attempt to convey by their role-making actions the specific and correct self-images by which they wish others to identity them.

Goffman's examples of these concepts are based on his observations of boys on a merry-go-round. First, role embracement begins at about age 4 or 5, when they have to expend every effort just to hang on to the reins, and often also to the horse's neck or ears, and so, literally as well as metaphorically, embrace the role of rider. As Goffman states, "to embrace a role is to disappear completely into the virtual self available in the situation, to be seen fully in terms of the image, and to confirm expressively one's acceptance of it" (1961b: 106).

Role embracement represents the polar opposite of role distance; it can be observed when boys reach the age of 11 or 12 years. By this point, maleness "has become a real responsibility. . . . It is necessary to stay away or exert creative acts of distance" from childhood (Goffman, 1961b: 108). Boys accomplish role distance by treating the wooden horse as if it were a race horse, or by pretending that they are stunt riders or comedians, jumping from horse to horse, all the while making faces at friends and passersby. The purpose of these acts, of course, is to display distance from the role of a merry-go-ground rider.

A contemporary example of role distance is practised by teenagers who no longer wish to be viewed as children and instead want to establish an identity of independence and maturity, and do so in part by insisting that parents drop them off around the corner from their destination. Imagine also a computer science student who says she enjoys the challenge that comes with mastering the subject area of her role but does not like the nerdish identity that comes with it. To demonstrate that she is not a nerd, she sits in the very back of the classroom and fools around with similarly motivated others. David Snow and Leon Anderson also found that role-distancing is common among the homeless, especially the recently homeless; they quote one man as saying, "I'm not like other guys who hang down at the Sally [Salvation Army]. If you want to know about the street people, I can tell you about them; but you can't really learn about studying street people from studying me, because I'm different" (1993: 349).

Role exit, as distinct from role embracement, is the disengagement from a role that is central to one's self-identity (Ebaugh, 1988). This relinquishment usually brings with it a continuing identity "hangover" from the past, which influences the playing of a new role. Helen Ebaugh, a former nun, used her own case as an example in her study and also interviewed 69 other former nuns as well as another 116 "exe's," including transsexuals, police officers, convicts, doctors, divorced people, and air traffic controllers. Drawing on Robert Prus (1987), she formulates a generic social process involved in becoming an "ex."

First, there are feelings of frustration, unhappiness, uncertainty, and burnout, which Ebaugh (1988) terms *first doubts*. This uncertainty on the part of people about to exit a role leads to what she terms *unconscious cueing*, whereby they begin to change the image they project to others. For example, nuns in this early phase of becoming an "ex" begin to let their hair grow. Consequently, their announcement leads to a tacit placement, which accordingly encourages or discourages the contemplated move.

Second, dependent upon whether there has been encouragement or discouragement in the first phase,

role alternatives are considered and weighed, and a new role identity is tentatively decided upon. In this process, the person inevitably chooses and begins to identify with a new reference group, which will help to consolidate and confirm the new identity. For example, transsexuals, who identify with the opposite sex, cross-dress and take on new mannerisms before (often) undergoing sex-change surgery (Ebaugh, 1988). Role exit occurs after this anticipatory socialization in and by the contemplated new reference group, and finally the new reference group and the new membership group become one.

A fourth and final stage involves accommodating the new identity to the old one. This process is always problematic because the old identity constantly intrudes itself upon the new one. Ebaugh (1988) cites examples of former police officers who find it difficult to interact affably with people they knew in their previous lives to be involved in shady activities.

Role exit is a predominant characteristic of modern society. In the past, people generally lived their entire lives in one community, gender, occupation, marriage, and religion. In today's society, these statuses and their accompanying roles are taken on and shed with increasing frequency.

Conclusion

The concepts of role and identity can be viewed and analyzed from a variety of theoretical perspectives: structural functionalism, interactionist theory, and conflict theory. Role and identity are complex, far-reaching, and yet related entities.

Role is related to identity in that role involves a script of action, and that identity is a result of actions and how they are categorized, judged, and evaluated by others. Every role has an accompanying identity, and playing the role shapes both action and actor. We usually become that which we play at. Identity troubles, as manifested in episodes of embarrassment, make continued role performance difficult, if not impossible, raising the question of embarrassment management, which in turn involves strategies such as avoidance.

The study of roles and identities stands at the intersection of society, culture, and personality. As such, it is inevitably connected with socialization—the process by which infants become socially competent—and with the formation and maintenance of communities. The process is social because it is through interaction with others and in response to social pressures that people acquire the culture—the language, perspective, and skills, the likes and dislikes, the cluster of **norms**, **values**, and **beliefs**—that characterizes the group to which they belong.

Society determines many of the ways we think and act, much of what we say, and the values and norms we live by. At the same time, we—all of us together—constitute society. We are both the actors and the acted upon. Freedom and determinism, transformation and constraint, are all central features of social life. *Socialization*, accordingly, is often defined as the social learning process a person goes through to become a capable member of society. As people go through the socialization process, they actively participate in learning. They generalize, apply rules, and use language in a creative way. They continue to invent roles and invent identities, and they struggle with the conflict between their various roles and identities.

Having a concept of the generalized other is possible because there is a rough consensus among members of the **society** or **subculture** to which we belong. The I is spontaneous, impulsive, and self-interested. All of us also have a Me, a part of the self

that is the result of socialization and is therefore conscious of social norms, values, and expectations. The most difficult stage of a child's development is the stage at which the child begins to develop a sense of self and to differentiate itself from others.

In the first few years of life, we also learn such basic facts about ourselves as whether we are male or female and what that means about who or what we are or should be. In this sense, gender socialization stands as an example of all **primary socialization**. Gender roles and gender identities are among our most complicated and most central defining roles and identities. Throughout this book, in chapters on socialization and gender, work and family, we will return again and again to the themes of role and identity discussed in this chapter.

As we have also seen, the creation and transmission of roles and identities is shaped by technology—currently, by new information technology. The result is a new set of problems and opportunities, and the need for a continual improvement in our theories about how social structure works and about the place of roles and identities in this.

□ Questions for Critical Thought

1. What do you think are proper professor–student expectations and obligations?
2. How is it possible to interact smoothly with a complete stranger?
3. In the work world, what are the differences between workers and management? How are these differences expressed in roles?
4. What is the difference between the interactionist view of role and the structuralist view of role?
5. Where does one's sense of identity come from?
6. How is identity related to role?
7. What is the difference between "identification of" and "identification with"? Can you illustrate this from your own life?
8. How does embarrassment relate to role and identity?

□ Recommended Readings

Kathleen Charmez, "The Body, Identity, and Self: Adapting to Impairment," in *Health, Illness and Healing: Society, Social Context and Self*, **edited by Kathleen Charmez and Debora Paterniti (Los Angeles: Roxbury, 1999), 95–112.**

> This study reveals that the stable nature of self-concepts makes them resistant to change. Experience (in this case, illness) changes more rapidly than self-concept, and so self-concept frequently lags, especially when the experience is overwhelming.

Helen Ebaugh, *Becoming an Ex: The Process of Role Exit* **(Chicago: University of Chicago Press, 1988).**

Ebaugh details how people disengage from social roles that previously were central to their self-identity.

Victor Gegas and Peter Burke, "Self and Identity," in *Sociological Perspectives on Social Psychology,* **edited by Karen S. Cook, Gary Alan Fine, and James S. House (Boston: Allyn and Bacon, 1995).**

This article is a review of the literature concerning self and identity.

Erving Goffman, "Role Distance," in *Encounters: Two Studies in the Sociology of Interaction* **(Indianapolis, IN: Bobbs-Merrill, 1961), 85–152.**

Goffman describes how people use distancing techniques (here, role distance) when they do not wish others to identify them with a "self" implied in a particular role, especially if the role in question is considered beneath them.

David A. Snow and Leon Anderson, *Down on Their Luck: A Study of Homeless Street People* **(Berkeley: University of California Press, 1993).**

The authors describe how people with low self-concept cope with themselves and with everyday life.

Vered Vinitzky-Seroussi, *After Pomp and Circumstance: High School Reunion as an Autobiographical Occasion* **(Chicago: University of Chicago Press, 1998).**

The author provides a touching account of how people's experience of high school reunions leads them to reflect on themselves.

Kath Woodward, *Understanding Identity* **(London: Arnold, 2003).**

This work explores personal and collective identities by drawing upon experiences that highlight the importance of ethnicity and race, gender, and place in the production of meanings about who we are.

☐ Recommended Web Sites

ALS Survival Guide

www.lougehrigsdisease.net/index.html

This Web site discusses how disability is a master status that supersedes gender, race, and religion. It details the social, medical, emotional, and psychological aspects of Lou Gehrig's disease (amyotrophic lateral sclerosis).

Erving Goffman: The Presentation of Self in Everyday Life

www.cfmc.com/adamb/writings/goffman.htm

Adam Barnhart's article here elaborates upon Goffman's influential book.

ETHNO/CA NEWS

www.pscw.uva.nl/emca/index.html

This site has a great deal of very basic information about all aspects of contemporary work in the field in ethno-methodology and conversation analysis.

The Presentation of Self in Electronic Life: Goffman on the Internet

http://ess.ntu.ac.uk/miller/cyberpsych/goffman.htm

Hugh Miller's article relates Goffman's description of face-to-face interaction to interpersonal communication in cyberspace.

5

R. Jack Richardson and
Lorne Tepperman

> > >

Groups and Organizations

© Bill Whitman

☐ Learning Objectives

In this chapter, you will:

- distinguish between spontaneous and formal organizations
- learn the history of the bureaucratic form of organization
- see outlined the characteristics of a bureaucracy
- identify the discrepancies between the model or ideal bureaucracy and the real-world bureaucracy
- read about the significance of the Hawthorne studies
- distinguish between the main points of organizational theories
- identify recent changes in the structure of organizations

Introduction

This chapter is about some basic elements of **social structure**—namely, groups and organizations. In fact, you could say that, along with the previous chapter on roles and identities, this chapter maps the most fundamental elements of social structure, the subject matter of sociology itself. Wherever you turn these days, you come face-to-face with **organizations**. People work, study, and teach in organizations, and often play and pray in them, too. We spend more and more of our lives dealing with large organizations—with colleges, governments, hospitals, department stores, and so on. Yet few of our experiences with these organizations, whether as workers or as "customers," are particularly pleasant. In fact, often they make us feel fake and inhuman. This is because large organizations have their own impersonal **cultures**, which will be discussed in this chapter. And because they bring together large numbers of strangers, large organizations devise special ways of maintaining social control. To do this, they invent large bodies of rules and regulations. Often, large organizations are so complex that no one knows all the rules. The result—a huge, powerful collection of strangers following rules that almost nobody knows—can be frightening. It was this image of the "organization" that terrified novelist Franz Kafka; he captured it in his surrealist novel *The Trial*, first published in 1925.

We begin the chapter by discussing different *sets* or ways of organizing people; they include networks, groups, and cliques. We start small and build up to bureaucracies, because the two sizes of organization—large and small—are more similar than you might think.

First, as we shall see, all bureaucracies contain networks, groups, and cliques. These small, informal organizations actually accomplish much of the work of large, formal bureaucracies. Under some circumstances, they also subvert the plans and efforts of these bureaucracies. Second, many of the same organizational principles that shape small groups, cliques, and communities also shape large, formal organizations. As we shall see, processes of leadership, commitment, control, and exchange, among others, shape all organizations, whatever their size. That means that what you already know about families, classrooms, and clubs can be applied—with some ingenuity—to things you know less about, like bureaucracies, societies, and empires (for example).

Large organizations of the kind we see today (and discuss in this chapter) are still relatively new to human history, and in some ways they are a major human accomplishment. Yet somehow this great ambition has gone wrong. This chapter discusses the paradox of large organizations: namely, that they are so effective and yet so dangerous. Large organizations are as likely to frustrate and disappoint as they are to satisfy our wishes. Moreover, they sometimes control us, not us them. Next we trace the development of organizational theory from its crude beginnings at the turn of the twentieth century. In general, this development reflects the growth of sociological knowledge about human groups. The chapter ends with an examination of the ways that large organizations actually work, compared with the ways they are supposed to work.

Sets of People

Imagine 5 sets of 20 people each. Call them *categories, networks, communities, groups,* and *organizations*. Sociologists will study these five sets differently, because they are organized differently and have different effects on their members. This section will briefly discuss these sets and explain briefly why they would interest sociologists in different ways.

Categories

Imagine, first, that these 20 people are a mere aggregate or collection of people who are unconnected with one another—say, a random sample of Canadian 19-year-olds—but fall into the same category: they are the same age. These teenagers do not know one another and are not in contact with one another, but they have their age in common.

This *aggregate*, or sample, of teenagers is of interest to sociologists if they represent the attitudes and behaviours of 19-year-olds across the country. Knowing these attitudes and behaviours may help us predict the future behaviour or explain the current behaviour of 19-year-olds. It will be of particular interest to market researchers who want to sell products to 19-year-olds and to political pollsters who want to shape their voting preferences. However, for the most part, sociologists will not be interested in such an aggregate of people. Since they are unconnected, people in categories possess no social structure of interest, and it is **social structure**—the invisible feature of social life that controls and transforms our behaviour—that is mainly of interest to sociologists.

There is no social structure to study in an aggregate or set of 20 unconnected teenagers. The same will be true of any category of people—people who live in Toronto, drive snowmobiles, eat yogurt, read *Sports Illustrated* magazine, go to church every week, or whatever. Categories, though interesting to market researchers, are relatively uninteresting to sociologists.

There is one major exception to this rule: categories become sociologically interesting when societies dramatize (or socially construct) meanings for the boundaries between one category and another. No such meaningful boundaries exist for 19-year-olds, compared with 18- and 20-year-olds. However, important cultural boundaries exist between the categories named "male" and "female," "young" and "old," and, in some societies, "white" and "black." As a result, *these* categories assume social importance. However, they assume importance only when the categorical differences are dramatized, the boundaries are enforced, and categorical differences give rise to social and cultural differentiation—for example, in the form of communities or **social movements**.

Networks

Sets of people who are more interesting are organized in what sociologists call *networks*, or **social networks**. Imagine the same 20 people all connected to one another, whether directly or indirectly. By *direct connections*, we mean links of kinship, friendship, and acquaintanceship or otherwise among all 20, each connected to the other. In a set of 20 people, there can be [20(19)]/2 = 190 such pairwise connections—obviously, a lot of interesting relationships and combinations of relationships to study.

Indirect connections are also of interest to sociologists. In fact, some sociologists—such as Mark Granovetter (1974), whose work on job seeking was discussed in chapter 1—believe that *weakly tied* networks, based largely on indirect links, may be even more useful than *strongly tied* or completely connected networks. Information, social support, and other valuable resources all flow through incompletely connected, or weakly tied, networks. Likewise, rumours, diseases, innovations, and job information all spread geographically through (indirectly linked) networks of weak ties. This is because weakly tied networks have a huge outreach. They connect very large numbers of weakly tied people (for example,

acquaintances) at a few removes, unlike tightly connected networks, which tend to circulate the same information or resources repeatedly through the same set of people (for example, close friends).

The pairwise connections (which sociologists call *dyadic relationships*) that make up social networks are based on regular patterns of social exchange. In stable dyadic relationships, people give each other things they want and need. So long as these relationships satisfy their needs, people stay in these relationships. People usually act in their own best interests—when they are aware of these interests. They are rational and sensible, and they maintain **social relationships** that are useful to them. Accordingly, people enter, leave, and stay in the social networks in which their valued dyadic relations are embedded. Over time, as people enter and leave relationships, networks change in their size and composition. This, in turn, affects the resources flowing to other members of the network.

As you can see from this glimpse, social networks are important and interesting. There is a huge and growing sociological literature on social networks. However, much of social life is not well understood in terms of networks. That is because networks lack several key characteristics. First, people in networks lack a sense of collective identity, such as a community would possess. Second, people in networks lack a complete awareness of their membership and its characteristics, such as a group would possess. Third, people in networks lack a collective goal, such as an organization would possess.

Communities

Sets of people with a common sense of identity are typically called **communities**, and there is a long history of community studies in sociology. Imagine for the sake of consistency that we are thinking of a community of only 20 people—say, a commune of like-minded people living together on the land (perhaps a hippie commune in 1960s British Columbia or a utopian farming community in nineteenth-century upstate New York) or in the city (perhaps a community of anarchist or bohemian youth living in a dilapidated squat in twenty-first-century Amsterdam).

These are likely to be people drawn together by common sentiments; or they may be people who have grown up together and share strong, unusual values. The nineteenth-century German sociologist Ferdinand Tönnies ([1887] 1957) took great pains to

5.1

Open for Discussion
Essentializing in Communities

The concept of community is central to recent discussions of multiculturalism. Among the ties that bind a community together is a sense of identity. One important question that has raised concerns whether positive essentializing is possible. *Essentializing* means taking a characteristic of a person, applying it broadly to a group, and claiming that it is intrinsic to that group of people. Essentializing serves to create strong bonds between people and distinguishes one community from another. In a multicultural society, is the use of differences to define identity useful or harmful?

Pnina Werbner and Stuart Hall take different stances on this question. Agreeing that, in fact, people—the components of communities—are fluid and change their own identities, Hall and Werbner differ as to the extent to which a community can be objectified in a positive way. Werbner (Werbner and Modood, 1997)

claims that there are two forms of essentializing: negative and positive. Negative essentialism typically shows itself as racism and stereotyping. Positive essentialism is strategically created by the groups themselves for a particular cause.

Hall (2000) does not buy Werbner's distinction between negative and positive essentializing. He argues that demarcating *any* difference between groups of people in a multicultural society risks leading to stereotyping and racism. Werbner's model creates boundaries between groups, making it more difficult for a universal identity—one that crosses boundaries—to exist in a multicultural society. Accordingly, for Hall, when equality is missing and sought in a multicultural society, instead of advocating a competition between fixed community identities, communities should avoid essentializing altogether and turn outward, open to differences both within and among communities.

---

distinguish the foundations of community life, or what he called *Gemeinschaft*, from the foundations of non-community life, which he called *Gesellschaft*. Tönnies also associated community life with rural areas and non-community life with urban areas. At least since medieval times, the city has represented in the popular mind a place distinct from both rural communities and from the natural environment.

Gemeinschaft refers to the typical characteristics of rural and small-town life. These characteristics include a stable, homogenous group of residents with a strong attachment to one particular place. Residents of the community interact around similar qualities and lead similar lives. Not only are their lives similar, they are also linked by intimate, enduring relationships of kinship, friendship, neighbouring, and (often) working together. Because rural people share so much, it is not surprising they also share similar moral values, and moral custodians such as the Church, school, and local upper classes protect these values. In terms of social structure, the *Gemeinschaft* is marked by dense or highly connected networks, centralized and controlling elites, and multiple social ties.

By contrast, the ties among people in a city take the form of a *Gesellschaft*. This includes a fluid, heterogeneous group of residents with a weak sense of place. According to Tönnies ([1887] 1957), the residents have different personal histories and impersonal, brief relationships. They interact around similar interests, not similar characteristics or histories. There are few shared moral values and few moral custodians to enforce a common moral code. In terms of social structure, city networks are less connected, less centralized, less cliquish, and less redundant. In short, there is less cohesion and less control in the *Gesellschaft*.

The question that several generations of sociologists have debated since Tönnies is whether *Gesellschaft*—or city life—represents a loss of community or a new kind of community. Most sociologists in the first half of the twentieth century believed the former: they saw city life as disorganized and lacking in the cultural and social benefits of community. However, in the second half of that century, sociologists came around to another view. They demonstrated that people are not isolated and atomized in large cities. Rather, the majority form small communities based on residential proximity and social similarity, or on friendship and support networks among geographically dispersed people.

Communities, whether urban or rural, real or virtual, are important because people are conscious of their membership in them. They want the community to survive and may make large personal sacrifices to see that it does.

Groups

In some cases, groups can be like small communities: highly engrossing and very demanding of loyalty. In other cases, groups are much less so. What all groups have in common is an awareness of membership. Additionally, members are all connected with one another (directly or indirectly), and they communicate, interact, and conduct exchanges with one another, to varying degrees. To continue our example, a 20-student classroom would be one kind of group. It is more highly connected than a 20-person category, more self-aware than a 20-person network, but less solidary (or based on common values) than a 20-person community.

Since Charles Horton Cooley ([1909] 1962) in the early twentieth century, sociologists have distinguished between primary groups and secondary groups. *Primary groups* are small and marked by regular face-to-face interaction; an example is a family household. Cliques, which we will discuss shortly, and work groups also fall into this category of primary group. *Secondary groups* are larger, and many members may not interact with one another on a regular basis. However, even in secondary groups there is a clear membership, at least some members interact, and there is an identifiable normative system and some shared sense of collective existence (as in a community).

Typically, groups are less engrossing than communities. However, they have organizational structures and do what social structures are expected to do: namely, control and transform their members. All groups, even small groups, have clearly defined familiar **roles**: for example, husband–wife, parent–child, or brother–sister in families, leader–follower in cliques, or teacher–student–teacher's pet in classrooms. These roles, as was seen in the chapter on roles and identities, carry interactional expectations, and people are identified (and identify themselves) with the roles they play. Even in small groups, behaviours become scripted. Robert Bales, in the 1950s, found that in the

discussion groups he studied, three roles—task leader, emotional leader, and joker—regularly emerged. Bales (1950) concluded that groups seem to "need" these roles, in order to survive.

As will be discussed later in this chapter, informal work groups emerge within large formal organizations. Within these work groups, informal leadership roles and group norms emerge. These control and transform the behaviour of group members, sometimes to the consternation of the people who manage the formal organization. This discovery is one of sociology's most important contributions to the study of organizations.

Secondary groups, though less strongly integrated than primary groups, are no less important. We spend most of our waking hours as members of secondary groups, interacting, communicating, and exchanging resources with other people. Secondary groups are also the staging area for much social learning. They bind people together in relatively stable patterns of **social interaction**. Formal organizations, which will be discussed at length later, are subtypes of secondary group, and bureaucracies are subtypes of formal organization. So, in the end, almost everything in this chapter—except the discussion of cliques—is about secondary groups.

Organizations

As just noted, **organizations** are secondary groups that have a collective goal or purpose. An organization can be a giant **multinational corporation**, such as General Motors, or a small corner variety store; a political party or a government; a church, a school, a sports club, or a search party. Given the endless variety of organizational forms (see Figure 5.1 on social network analysis to understand why this is so), and the millions of specific examples, what do all organizations have in common?

Every organization is a group of people working together and co-ordinated by communication and leadership to achieve a common goal or goals. Within this general definition, however, organizations vary considerably. The group of people in question—that is, the **social group**—may come together spontaneously or deliberately. The division of labour within that organization may be crude or complex. The communication and leadership may be *informal* or *formal* (these terms will be defined these terms shortly). The organization may have one specific goal or a range of loosely related goals.

Figure 5.1 **Social Network Analysis**

The study of networks, whether cliques or the weak ties people have with each other, is a powerful explanatory tool for sociologists. *Social network analysis* has been used to discuss topics as wide ranging as adolescent behaviours and the pro-democracy protests in 1989 in Beijing. At the same time, social network analysis is something that many people do without thinking of it as social science. For example, when planning a party you may try to ensure either a homogenous or a heterogeneous group—perhaps only people from work, or at least two people from each activity and stage of your life. In a way, you are gathering the initial data for a social network analysis.

Hypothesis: When two people establish themselves in a long-term relationship, their social networks change by becoming smaller and cliquier. True or false?

Try it out: Do a "before" and "after" analysis of one of your parents or a friend.

Whatever question you ask will likely give you different results, so consider your choice of question carefully. Instead of asking, "Who are you close to?" ask, "Who would you talk to about something very important?" or "Who do you call at least once a week?"

Then draw the networks: Each person is a node, or dot, and each connection is a line between nodes. If the hypothesis above is correct, the pictures should look like this:

Before:

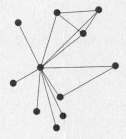

After:

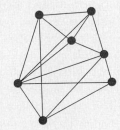

One important distinction to make concerning organizations is between **spontaneous** and **formal organizations**. Both types fit the general definition of an organization, yet the two are different in important ways. A *spontaneous organization* is one that arises quickly to meet a single goal and then disbands when the goal is achieved or thought to be beyond reach or when the organization is absorbed by a formal organization. A clique, though informal, is not a spontaneous organization. Perhaps the most commonly cited examples of spontaneous organizations are bucket brigades and search parties. Each has a single goal—keeping a barn from burning down or finding a lost child. Each arises spontaneously, and its leaders emerge informally, without planning. Each has a crude division of labour—for example, filling buckets, passing them along, emptying them on the fire. Nevertheless, each is much more likely than an unco-ordinated mob to achieve its goals. Compare the chance that a mob, running off in one direction, has of finding a lost child with that of a group conduct-ing a co-ordinated search pattern. Spontaneous organizations disband as quickly as they form. The bucket brigade will scatter when it achieves its goal of putting out the fire or the barn has burned down or the fire department arrives on the scene.

Organizations that have loosely related goals and are relatively unstructured, with little differentiation between their members, are considered **informal organizations**. One familiar example of informal organization is the clique. Cliques seem very different from the formal organizations to be discussed in most of this chapter, yet, paradoxically, they share some common features. Moreover, as we will discover later, cliques and other informal organizations can usually be found nested within formal organizations, doing much of the work.

Cliques

Sometimes it helps to view the familiar through unfamiliar lenses. The first thing we learn when we study cliques in this way is that they satisfy human needs for interaction and support. Lloyd Siegel and Arthur Zitrin (1978), for example, in a classic study of New York male-to-female transsexuals on public welfare, found that all the people they were studying lived with one or more transsexual friends. Moreover, a transsexual community had apparently come into existence, creating its own **subculture**. A citywide informal network provided transsexuals with information concerning particular needs, and reportedly worked to create a feminine environment and appearance for clique members. The community, made up of multiple cliques, was stable, cohesive, and supportive. Transsexual friends often accompanied clients to welfare centre interviews and provided other practical assistance. The authors conclude that this subcultural community helped transsexual men to foster their illusion of being female, often without their having to undergo surgery.

The second thing we learn when we study cliques and communities is that they tend to produce new roles, rules, and cultural values. An example is the supposedly anarchic world of "bohemians." *Bohemians* are people who, for artistic or other reasons, have rejected the middle-class lifestyle. Paradoxically, once freed from middle-class conventions, they create their own conventions. In a classic study of bohemians, Patricia Nathe (1978) writes that although "Bohemia" is a classless society, there are distinct circles of membership: at the core are the true career artists and intellectuals; then their disciples, known as *pseudo-* or *professional bohemians*; then the weekend or part-time bohemians; then the entrepreneurs who profit from the bohemian scene; and in the "outer circle," the voyeurs, relatives, reporters, detectives, and groupies. These various "types" interact in cliques regularly, filling recognizable roles and playing out scripts based on the romance of art, poverty, self-expression, and identification with other socially vulnerable groups.

These two aspects of clique and community formation—the provision of social support and the production of new rules and roles—are familiar to us from our own experience of cliques at school. Everyone reading this book has, by now, suffered the savagery of school life—especially the cruelty of cliques. William Golding's classic novel *Lord of the Flies*, first published in 1954, has schoolboys tormenting, killing, and then eating the weakest on a desert island. This is a mere exaggeration of children's behaviour in schoolyards. Some might imagine that the cruelty the boys display in Golding's novel is a result of unvarnished human nature—Hobbes's state of nature ([1651] 1968), perhaps. In fact, their cruelty grows out of the operation of a hierarchical society controlled by a ruthless leader. Children's social structures can be just as cruel as nature, Golding tells us.

Cliques, though often supportive, offer an excellent example of structured cruelty, and they can be found everywhere. No one escapes childhood without becoming a member of a clique or feeling isolated because of exclusion from one. Though seemingly without goals, cliques have an unstated "mission" or purpose: to raise the status of clique members at the expense of non-members. Though lacking an organizational chart or stated division of labour, school cliques have a clear hierarchy of influence and popularity, with the leader on top surrounded by his or her favourites. In this sense, then, a clique is a group of people working together and co-ordinated by communication and leadership to achieve a common goal or goals.

Defining the Term Clique

Dictionaries variously define *clique* as "a small exclusive set," a "faction," a "gang," a "noisy set." This meaning comes from the French *cliquer*, meaning "to click," or "to make a noise." People in cliques—especially the most popular ones—make a lot of noise, pumping themselves up and ridiculing others.

To come closer to our current sociological meaning, we would define *clique* as a group of tightly interconnected people—a friendship circle whose members are all connected to one another, and to the outside world, in similar ways. Usually, clique members feel strong positive sentiments or liking for one another and contempt for outsiders. They spend more time with one another than with non-clique members, share their knowledge with one another, and think and behave similarly. They tend to ignore or exclude outsiders—people not like themselves, and not friends of their friends.

In short, *cliques* are groups that are characterized by friendship, similarity, interaction, exclusion, and the flow of valuable resources: information, support, and opinions, among others. In these respects, cliques are mini-communities, like mini-states. Like states, they accumulate **power** and resources. They receive, censor, and direct information flow. Like states, cliques remain distinct; resources (such as information) flow readily within the clique and less readily outside its borders. Cliques accumulate and redirect information. They also distort information, generate it, and send it out as gossip and rumour. Cliques, like other organizations, create and concentrate information flow. Because they generate and control the flow of information effectively, cliques are stable structures (on this, see Carley, 1989, 1991). They survive largely through what psychologist Irving Janis (1982) called *groupthink*.

Cliques in School Settings

Cliques form in every area of life, even within bureaucracies and other formal organizations. However, cliques are most familiar to us from our childhood school experience. In school settings, cliques typically have a well-defined membership. Clique members are typically similar to one another in background and behaviour (Ennett and Bauman, 1996). Cliques typically have rituals that exclude outsiders and integrate insiders. Cliques also have a leader, who is the most popular member of the clique and who dominates the other members. Usually, the leader defines the group boundaries, invents group rituals, and chooses the membership.

Cliques are not only organizations: they are communities and miniature societies, just as Golding suggested. In cliques, children first learn the rules and expectations of society outside their family home. Through games and play with clique members, children internalize the beliefs, values, and attitudes of their group. By these means, children also come to form judgments of themselves. For example, they learn what it means to be "good-looking," "sexy," and "popular," to be chosen or passed over. Children's activities, their friendships, and their feelings about themselves are tied up with their involvement in the cliques that organize their social landscape (Crockett, Losoff, and Peterson, 1984).

How Cliques Form

Cliques form when people meet others like themselves. The social structuring of activity itself—for example, the age grading of activities such as education, entertainment, or work—increases the likelihood that people will meet others like themselves (Feld, 1982). Additionally, since class or ethnicity often segregates neighbourhoods, and since children usually attend neighbourhood schools, they are likely to meet other children of the same class and ethnic background. The more homogeneous the people they meet, the more children will form relationships with others who are similar. It is, first of all, this structuring of acquaintanceships that leads to the creation of cliques.

Cliques teach young people the dynamic of power, manipulation, and conformity. They create a hierarchical social organization of students, with top-ranking, middle-ranking, and bottom-ranking groups. Ranking the clique strongly affects children's social experiences at school. Membership in a low-ranking clique can be humiliating or painfully isolating. (www.harrycutting.com)

However, an element of choice is also involved. Cliques carefully screen people for membership. Once formed, cliques maintain themselves by continuing to ensure that members remain similar. Cliques evolve as individuals enter and leave the group. Those at the clique's centre—the leaders—are most influential in the recruitment process. They use their power, based on their popularity, to decide which potential members are acceptable and which are not.

Cliques control their members by defining the behaviours that are appropriate and acceptable. Leaders are particularly skilled in exercising control. They often do so by building up the clique members and then cutting them down (Adler and Adler, 1995). One technique is to draw new members into an elite inner circle, allowing them to enjoy brief popularity, then humbling them by turning the group against them. Leaders also take advantage of quarrels to divide and conquer the membership. They degrade and make fun of those who are lower in the hierarchy or outside the group. All of these tactics allow leaders to build up their own power and authority. Such rites of degradation also foster clique solidarity by clarifying the norms for acceptance and rejection.

The cohesion of a clique is based mainly on loyalty to the leader and loyalty to the group. This loyalty, in turn, is based as much on exclusion as it is on inclusion. First, group members hive themselves off from non-members. Lack of contact with outsiders permits members to believe that outsiders are different and less socially desirable than themselves. Additionally, clique members use gossip to reinforce their ignorance of outsiders and maintain social distance from them. They also use gossip to ridicule and spread nasty rumours about outsiders. Finally, they may pick on or harass outsiders. Doing so instills fear, forcing outsiders to accept their inferior status and discouraging them from rallying together to challenge the power hierarchy.

Cliques and the rituals of inclusion and exclusion on which they rely are more than mere children's games. They are small-scale models of how organizations state, teach, and enforce rules; as such, they provide a lesson in social control. Cliques remind us that every inclusive action is, at the same time, an exclusive action. Organizations like cliques can have shared goals that are unstated but real, norms that are unwritten but compelling, hierarchies that are undocumented but powerful, divisions of labour that are effective but unplanned.

Bureaucracies

Formal Organizations

Organizations are *formal* if they are deliberately planned and organized. This planning may occur at the outset, when people found a new university, for instance. Or it may occur gradually, as happens when the people who form a bucket brigade find that enough fires are starting that they would do better to organize themselves into a volunteer fire department.

Within formal organizations, communication and leadership are provided through consciously developed and formalized statuses and roles. Often formal organizations have multiple goals, and they usually have a long lifespan. The Roman Catholic Church is a formal organization that has lasted nearly 2,000 years. Besides this, formal organizations normally have access to far greater resources and more complex technologies than spontaneous organizations.

As a result, we can define a *formal organization* as a deliberately planned social group in which people, resources, and technologies are consciously coordinated through formalized roles, statuses, and relationships to achieve a division of labour intended to attain a specific set of objectives. This is very similar to the general definition of organizations. A formal organization will have an overarching set of goals formulated by its leaders and more or less accepted by its members. But we cannot assume that these are the only goals of the membership. Workers, professionals, and managers will all have their own occupational goals as well.

There is a huge literature, containing many lively debates, that addresses the question of why some organizations are more successful and powerful than others. The most common explanations cite the degree to which an organization fills a social need (either real or successfully promoted by the organization itself), controls or has access to needed resources and technologies, tailors its goals to match the goals of its members, and adapts to or causes changes in its environment. The main form of the large, powerful, and long-lived formal organization of the twentieth century is the **bureaucracy**.

"Bureaucracy" is a negative word for most people. It calls to mind images of red tape, an overemphasis on rules and regulations, inefficiency, and unwieldy government organizations moving at a tortoise-like pace. To sociologists, however, a bureaucracy is merely a particular type of formal organization that thrives in both the public and the private sector, in capitalist and socialist societies alike. The very fact that bureaucracy is the main organizational form taken by competitive corporations shows that it can be very efficient.

The Emergence of the Bureaucratic Form of Organization

In a bureaucracy, the *superordinate*, or boss, personally owns none of the resources. All resources belong to the organization. Further, all resources are meant to flow from superior to inferior on the basis of authority or office holding alone—not on the basis of personal attachment. In turn, office holding is (ideally) based on expertise and effectiveness alone.

In bureaucracies, people move through positions, or *offices*, in the organization, based on their merit. The resources remain attached to offices; they do not follow the individual movers. Moreover, there are elaborate written rules to govern many (if not all) of the relationships in the organization. *Organization charts* are constructed to show the (ideal) chains of responsibility, authority, and communication between superiors, subordinates, and equals.

It was obvious to Max Weber ([1908] 1978)—the first sociologist to study bureaucracies—that this form of organization held enormous advantages over earlier organizational forms, such as *clientelism*, in which clients are tied to their boss or patron by personal loyalty. First, bureaucratic organization holds the potential for rational planning. In bureaucracies, goals are stated explicitly, strategies are planned and communicated, the most capable people are hired and trained, resources are mobilized, effectiveness is evaluated, and organizational improvements are implemented. How very different this makes IBM or the University of Toronto—both bureaucracies—from the Italian Mafia or the court of Louis XIV—both patron–client organizations.

A highly developed, though imperfect, form of bureaucracy apparently existed in medieval China. There, highly trained mandarins carried out the wishes of the emperor in a relatively systematic fashion. However, in the end this was a patrimonial system in which the emperor's wishes—however irrational—interfered with the rationality of the mandarins. It was not what we today would consider a bureaucracy.

Bureaucracy in its modern form arose under three important historical conditions: European nation-building, capitalism, and industrialization. The modern state is a bureaucratic apparatus of rule that rests on a particular structure of legitimation, leadership, and policy, complete with symbolic instruments—signatures, offices, seals, and registers—to establish impersonal, interchangeable power (Bourdieu, 1997b). Nation-building—and by extension imperial conquest and colonization—created the need for effective tax collection and military capability. Kings cannot run countries, or wars, without taxes. They cannot raise taxes without the help of honest and hard-working tax collectors who are loyal to the king. An honest and effective military is needed to beat down the local aristocrats, and also to fight the armies of other countries.

With nation-building and international warfare—especially in the eighteenth and nineteenth centuries—rulers quickly discovered that their armies were not properly organized, provisioned, and led. The weakness of command, in most instances, was due to the filling of officer positions through patronage or the purchase of commissions. There was no assurance that military officers were competent to lead, or that authority was linked in any way to competence. The results were ineffective, often disastrous, as witnessed by Britain's lengthy failure to control Napoleon's armies. Eventually one nation after another—Prussia, Great Britain, France, and others—realized there was a need to reorganize the military and the civil service along bureaucratic lines, else the nation could never achieve its ruler's goals. (See Bensman, 1987; Gorski, 1995; Kiser and Schneider, 1995; Spittler, 1980; Tyrell, 1981.)

Capitalism imposed similar demands. Under capitalism—a system devoted to the pursuit of maximum profits—people quickly discover that some forms of social and economic organization yield higher rates of profit on investment than others. The rationality of bureaucratic organization is well suited to the rationality associated with a pursuit of profits. The bureaucratic structure is capable of growing as large as necessary, through a proliferation of roles, yet remain highly controlled from the top. This is less possible, if possible at all, in clientelist systems based on personal loyalty. The legal concept of "limited liability" allows a bureaucracy to manage investment and profits impersonally, in a way that protects both the owners and the workers. This impersonality also makes bureaucracy quite different from clientelist systems.

Finally, industrialization also favoured the rise of bureaucracies. Bureaucracies are good at controlling large workforces—even highly educated and differentiated workforces. As the size of an organization grows, its degree of differentiation typically increases. Related problems of co-ordination and control—formalization, decentralization, and supervision—must be solved (Marsden, Cook, and Kalleberg, 1996). Often reorganization is called for, especially if the number of personnel is growing rapidly (Raadschelders, 1997).

As industrial enterprises grew larger with the mechanization of work, control structures (that is, for management and administration) had to grow correspondingly larger. This has been equally true in post-industrial enterprises that process information and turn out services (or other information) rather than manufactured goods. The twentieth-century development of professional management and administration activities reflects the enormous importance of bureaucratic organization in modern work life. Modern organizations—embedded in diverse networks of ties to external sources, growing rapidly, and responding to continuous changes in the environment—became continuous adopters of new technology and administrative technique (Kelley and Helper, 1997).

On a broader scale, Weber ([1908] 1978) traced the rise of bureaucracy, capitalism, and the modern state to the **rationalization** of human activity. Indeed, rationalization is central to Weber's general conception of history. For Weber, *rationalization* refers to the movement away from mystical and religious interpretations of the world to the development of human thought and belief based on a methodical accumulation of evidence. Also associated with rationalization is the rise of impersonal authority based on the universal application of a codified set of rules and laws.

The value system associated with rationalization prizes efficient, effective administration in government and in the production of goods and services. In Weber's view, these values spurred the growth of bureaucracy, because bureaucracies organize human activity in a logical, impersonal, and efficient manner. Or so he thought.

The Characteristics of Bureaucracy

Weber first analyzed the particular features of the bureaucratic form of organization. In his study of the major organizations of his day, Weber ([1922] 1958) identified six essential characteristics of bureaucracy:

- a division of labour,
- a hierarchy of positions,
- a formal system of rules,
- a separation of the person from the office,
- hiring and promotion based on technical merit, and
- the protection of careers.

Division of Labour

In earlier eras, workers generally handcrafted specific articles from start to finish to produce society's goods. Gradually, this type of production process gave way to specialization and the division of labour. Adam Smith noted the overwhelming productive superiority of specialization as long ago as 1776 (Smith, [1776] 1976). A specialized division of labour became the foundation of modern industry and bureaucratization. An automotive assembly line is perhaps the typical modern example of such a division of labour. An assembly-line worker may perform one highly specialized operation every 36 seconds of the working day (Garson, 1972).

As on an assembly line, every member of a bureaucracy performs specified and differentiated duties. The bureaucracy itself provides the facilities and resources for carrying out these duties. Workers work with equipment they do not own; in other words, they are separated from the **means of production**. Moreover, administrators administer what they do not own. The goals of this combination—task specialization based on technical competence plus the centralized provision of resources—are increased efficiency and productivity.

Hierarchy of Positions

We can visualize the structure of an organization as a pyramid, with authority centralized at the top (see, for example, the organizational chart in Figure 5.2). Authority filters down toward the base through a well-defined hierarchy of command. Thus, the structure explicitly identifies both the range and the limits of authority for people in each position. Within this hierarchy, each person is responsible *to* a specific person one level up the pyramid and *for* a specific group of people one level down.

The organizational chart of any large corporation is shaped roughly like a Christmas tree, in that the number of workers increases (and the division of labour specializes) as you move down toward the base

Figure 5.2 **City of Kingston Organizational Chart, 2002**

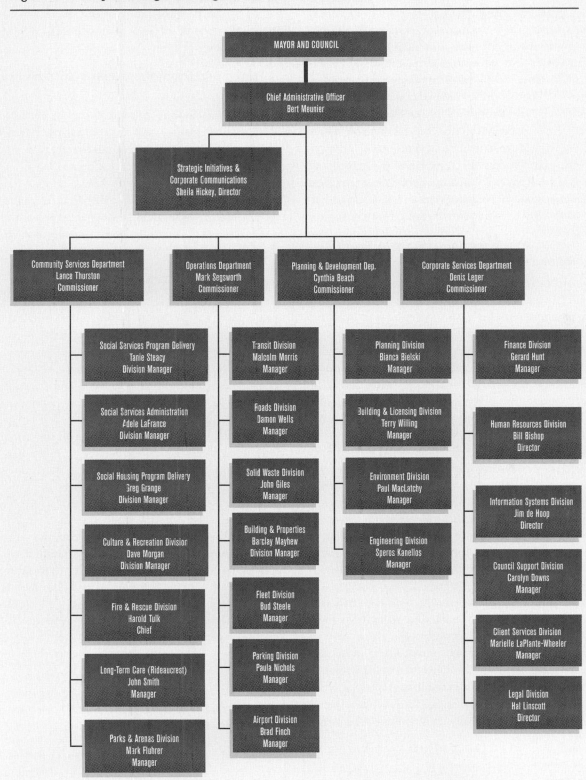

SOURCE: City of Kingston, "City of Kingston Organizational Chart" (2002); available at <www.city.kingston.on.ca/pdf/CityOrgChart2002.pdf>, accessed 21 May 2003.

of the hierarchy. Together with the other characteristics of bureaucracy, this feature serves to increase efficiency: all communications flow upward to control central from large numbers of workers "at ground level." However, formal communication within a bureaucracy can be extremely awkward. What if a Halifax, Nova Scotia, sales representative wishes to discuss a special order with a craft worker in the Moncton, New Brunswick, plant? Does the sales rep really have to communicate through intermediaries, all the way up and down the structure, until he reaches the craft worker in Moncton? No. In real life, people work to avoid such unwieldy communication channels, often forming informal communication networks, which will be examined later in the chapter.

Rules

Bureaucracies operate according to written rules. The rules permit a bureaucracy to formalize and classify the countless circumstances it routinely confronts. For each situation, decision makers can find or develop a rule that provides for an objective and impersonal response. The rules therefore guarantee impersonal, predictable responses to specific situations. This impersonality and objectivity in turn helps the organization to achieve its objectives.

Separation of the Person from the Office

In a bureaucracy, each person is an office holder in a hierarchy. The duties, functions, and authority of this office are all explicitly defined. That is, the rights and responsibilities of a Level 3 supervisor are all spelled out, in relation to a Level 4 supervisor (her superior) or Level 2 supervisor (her subordinate). The relationships between positions in a bureaucracy are, therefore, impersonal relationships between roles, not personal relationships between people. This separation of person and office means that people are replaceable functionaries in the organization: people come and go, but the organization remains intact. It also means that personal feelings toward other office holders must be subordinated to the impersonal demands of the office. Equally, relationships are confined to the official duties of office holders and ideally do not invade their private lives.

To illustrate: Charlie Brown, as sales manager, has the right to issue specific orders to his sales force. The sales representatives follow these orders because they come from the sales manager, not because they come from Charlie per se. And they follow the orders only

to the extent that these relate to each salesperson's official duties. Next week, if Charlie is transferred to a different job, he can no longer issue the same orders to the same people, because he now holds a different office.

Hiring and Promotion Based on Technical Merit

A properly functioning bureaucracy hires on the basis of impersonal criteria such as technical competence, not on the basis of ascribed, inborn characteristics such as gender, race, or ethnicity. Promotion is likewise based on technical competence, or sometimes on seniority. People are neither discriminated against nor favoured because of such personal criteria as their personalities or their kinship with someone at the top of the hierarchy.

Protection of Careers

The final characteristic of bureaucracies is that people's careers are protected within them. People can look forward to long careers in a bureaucracy because they are not subject to arbitrary dismissal for personal reasons. So long as they follow the rules attached to their office or position, they are secure in their jobs. Generally speaking, their income will continue to arrive at the end of each month.

Compare these characteristics with the cliques considered earlier. In a bureaucracy, we find a much more detailed division of labour and a much longer hierarchy of positions than one finds in the typical clique. The system of rules in a bureaucracy is formal, or written, unlike the informal rules in a clique. A bureaucracy separates the person from the office, whereas there are no offices in a clique, only distinct individuals. Hiring and promotion in a bureaucracy are based on technical merit; in a clique, they are based on popularity, friendship with the leader, toughness, or attractiveness. Finally, a bureaucracy provides people with secure, often lifelong careers; as we have seen, clique memberships may be brief and insecure.

Merton's Bureaucratic Personality

Robert Merton's analysis of bureaucracy (1957) focused on the pressure placed on bureaucrats to act in ways that serve to weaken the organization. Merton compared bureaucrats to overtrained athletes. Bureaucracies place immense pressure on their members to conform. This pressure, combined with intensive training, overemphasizes members' knowledge of the bureaucracy's rules. This, in turn, makes it easy for bureaucrats to act habitually in routine ways. In Merton's words, they follow rules in a methodical, prudent, and disciplined way. Inevitably, the routines become similar to blinkers on a horse, keeping bureaucrats from recognizing new situations in which the old rules are inappropriate. Thus, Merton argued, bureaucrats develop a "trained incapacity" for dealing with new situations.

Additionally, the routine application of rules requires that all situations must somehow be classifiable by objective criteria so that they may be made to fit the appropriate pigeonhole. The result is that bureaucrats cannot see their clients as people with unique wants and needs, only as impersonal categories. This viewpoint is harmful to the organization since it causes bureaucrats to fail to meet the unique needs of individual clients. The result may be efficient but not effective, seemingly productive but unsatisfying and inhumane.

Informal Organizations in Bureaucracies: The Hawthorne Studies

Although bureaucracy is intended to be an impersonal form of organization, actual people fill the bureaucratic roles. As human beings, workers resist becoming faceless cogs in the bureaucratic machine (replaceable cogs, at that). Consequently, they develop complex personal and informal networks that function within the formal organization. Collectively, these networks constitute the informal organization—bureaucracy's human face. Within formal organizations, we find informal organizations, even cliques of the kind discussed earlier in this chapter.

Informal networks among people who interact on the job serve many purposes. First and foremost, they humanize the organization. They also provide support and protection to workers at the lower levels of the hierarchy, serve as active channels of information (the grapevine), and become mechanisms for exchanging favours and exerting influence. They provide people with a sense of community, a sense of inclusion. They also direct the flow of information, enforce moral standards, and exclude people whom they consider inferior. All of these informal processes affect the operation of formal organizations. Paradoxically, informal networks within formal

organizations—though similar to cliques in many ways—can serve to liberate people from the limitations of formal organization and, occasionally, allow them to protest and subvert their working conditions. They also confer human meaning on otherwise impersonal settings, as we see from the classic Hawthorne studies.

The Hawthorne studies were conducted between 1927 and 1932 at the Western Electric plant at Hawthorne, Illinois, under the direction of Elton Mayo. Mayo held the view that workers were non-rational, emotional beings. His studies provided a massive database that social scientists are still using to test a wide variety of hypotheses. They also spawned a huge literature, of which the account by George Homans (1951) is probably the most readable. The Hawthorne studies first revealed the importance of the informal organization in formal organizations.

Early conclusions drawn from the Hawthorne studies provided the foundation of the human relations school. One of the first conclusions became known as the **Hawthorne effect**. This proposition holds that when people know they are subjects of an important experiment and receive a large amount of special attention, they tend to behave the way they think the researchers expect them to. The Hawthorne effect has influenced the design of social-psychological experiments ever since, as researchers try to control for this distortion.

Other conclusions drawn from the studies dealt with the social aspects of work: the relationships among the members of the informal group, the norms developed by the informal group, and types of supervision. The relationships among the women in Phase II of the research were happy and supportive—and associated with higher productivity—while those among the men in Phase IV were not. This finding led human relations theorists to conclude that happy group relationships may even increase productivity. The Hawthorne studies also found that group relationships can limit productivity, particularly in the absence of rigid, formal supervision.

Decades later, further analyses of the Hawthorne studies by Perrow (1972) and others modified the original conclusions. In fact, they produced a very different idea of informal groups. Starting from the premise that people will respond rationally to the constraints placed on them by organizations, Perrow and other researchers investigated the objective conditions surrounding the original Hawthorne studies. They

Sociology in Action
"Emotional Labour": Is Marx's Concept of Alienation Relevant Today?

Arlie Hochschild has appropriated Marx's concept of alienation, making it more relevant today by applying it to service employees. Hochschild re-examines alienation by comparing Marx's vignette of a factory worker's arm pressing a lever all day and thereby becoming a machine with a flight attendant's alienation from her tools of production, her smiles.

In her analysis of flight attendants, Hochschild refers to "emotional labor," meaning "the management of feeling to create a publicly observable facial and bodily display" (1983: 7). One of the pillars of Hochschild's argument is that a flight attendant's smile is appropriated or alienated from the individual flight attendant, through airline advertising that stresses smiling flight attendants. Hochschild describes the smile as the emotional tool used by flight attendants to complete their jobs. Not smiling is not "okay." In Hochschild's words, "emotional labor

is sold for a wage and therefore has *exchange value*" (1983: 7). Flight attendants, like Marx's factory workers, do not own the means of production and so the seller/labourer does not reap the profits.

Hochschild's concept of emotional labour is a mutation and extension of the concept of alienation. Hochschild is concerned with the psychological consequences of emotional labour and the alienation of emotions. She argues that the alienated labour cannot be utterly faked, which leaves flight attendants not as actresses, but as the "givers" in a non-reciprocal relationship with customers. In short, they feel emotionally drained. Hochschild's work may be of particular concern in future because evidence suggests that the service industry will continue to be a key industry while manufacturing will continue to decrease in wealthier nations.

---

found that the Hawthorne plant, like most others, had a long history of raising the productivity standard once workers had consistently attained a certain level. As a result, workers had achieved an increasingly fast pace to maintain their incomes. It is entirely logical, then, that workers would try to keep a balance between productivity and earnings, protecting their jobs by not producing too much. This analysis forces organizational theorists to reject the early human relations idea of non-rational workers and group norms.

This later research has led to the conclusion that informal organization can either help the formal organization to attain its goals or hinder it. Which it does will depend largely on the quality of the relationship between the workers and their managers. Frequently cited examples of hindrance are the British coal industry and Canada Post, both of which have a long history of bitter labour–management conflict.

The Evolution of Organizational Theory and Research

Scientific Management

Why was the assumption that workers might rationally seek to improve their well-being so very radical? Perhaps the answer lies with the primitive state of organizational thinking in the early twentieth century. Shortly after the turn of the century, Frederick W. Taylor's view of workers as mere machine cogs became enormously influential.

One of the earliest approaches to organizational theory was Taylor's 1911 publication *Principles of Scientific Management*. It attracted great attention in North America and Western Europe during a period of industrial strife. Taylor's intention was to end labour–management conflict over "shares of the pie" by providing a bigger pie. Taylor saw the worker as *homo economicus*: an economically rational being who works solely for economic rewards, that is, for money. Therefore, reasoned Taylor, if the worker is shown how to produce more and is paid more as profits increase, everyone will be happy—workers, managers, and corporate shareholders alike.

To accomplish this end, Taylor and his followers rigorously trained time and motion study experts to break down every task into its essential motions. In the process, they hoped to strip away all non-essential motions. The experts then trained each worker to perform specific tasks in the precise way their studies showed was the most efficient. Then they timed them with a stopwatch to develop a "standard time," which became the basis of their piecework rates. The result was often a spectacular, but short-lived, increase in productivity.

Taylor's **scientific management** approach developed the specialized division of labour to the fullest extent. It produced an extreme vertical division of labour within which workers repeated their narrowly defined tasks over and over again. It also introduced a new horizontal division of labour. No longer could workers use their experience to improve the efficiency of their task performance. Instead, the workplace was now divided into thinkers (managers and experts) and doers (workers).

The mindless, repetitive work advocated by Taylorism and the alienation it produced is one reason scientific management gradually faded from prominence. The underlying reason is that human beings are too complex and too resilient to be treated simply as *homo economicus*. When the last trace of their autonomy is removed, they will act together to preserve their humanity. Equally important is the fact that, in the words of Reinhard Bendix, "many employers regarded [Taylor's] methods as an unwarranted interference with managerial prerogatives" (1956: 280).

The Human Relations and Behavioural Schools: The Happiness Era

In the early 1930s, organizational theory shifted away from seeing organization in terms of structure (in the tradition of Taylor) to viewing it in terms of people. This new focus dominated the field through the 1960s.

Growing out of the famous Hawthorne studies, the early human relations school focused on relationships within informal groups. It assumed that happy group relationships produced job satisfaction, which, in turn, produced high productivity. The school

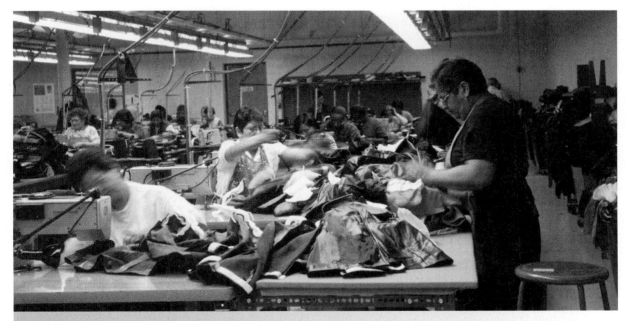

Taylor's scientific management divided the workplace into thinkers and doers. The doers repeated their narrowly defined tasks over and over again. The mindless, repetitive work advocated by Taylorism and the alienation it produced is one more reason scientific management gradually faded from prominence. (© Dick Hemingway)

studied the effects of supervision on this equation. Since workers were seen as emotional and non-rational, management's task was to instill both happiness and rationality in work groups. The fundamental objective, though, was productivity. Happiness and rationality were viewed as means to this end.

The **behavioural school** developed out of a fusion of human relations theory and a psychological conception of human needs. In 1940s and 1950s, the psychologist Abraham Maslow (1954) developed his idea of the hierarchy of needs, which changed the view of workers forever. No longer were organizations seen as being composed of just two groups, workers and managers. They were now viewed as associations of complex human beings, who responded to inner drives that Maslow ranked in the following hierarchy, from lowest to highest: physiological needs, security, social needs, esteem, and self-fulfillment.

Douglas McGregor developed and popularized Maslow's path-breaking work. His 1960 publication *The Human Side of Enterprise* is probably the most influential book ever written for managers. McGregor and other members of the behavioural school concluded that the predominant leadership style of their era was autocratic and task centred. They proposed that managers should adopt a participative employee-centred leadership style instead.

The cumulative result of the ideas of these two schools was the rapid increase of management-training programs aimed at improving the relationship between superior and subordinate and increasing the happiness of workers.

Systems Theory: The Organization as Organism

Sociological influence on organizational theory re-emerged with **systems theory**, an approach in which organizations are viewed as open systems. An organization receives inputs from its environment, processes them, and produces outputs for consumption. These outputs must be acceptable to the environment if the organization is to survive. Survival is a basic theme of systems theory, which sees organizations and their goals as shaped by the interests of their participants and their environments.

Philip Selznick's justly famous 1949 study of the Tennessee Valley Authority (TVA) showed how this particular organization co-opted important elements of its environment to gain support for its operations. However, support came at a price, as these elements became participants in the TVA's decision-making processes.

Systems theory stresses the effects of the environment on organizations. However, as critic Charles Perrow (1972) has correctly charged, it tends to ignore the effects of large and powerful organizations on their environments.

Systems theory also regards organizations as similar to organisms—that is, as intricately interdependent systems of functional parts. Consider this analogy: just as blood poisoning from an infected cut on the hand affects the whole body, so an ineffective sales department or a hostile workforce can endanger the success of an entire organization. This approach produces an almost inevitable emphasis on the uniqueness of organizations. It also often focuses on the *ripple effect*, that is, how changes in one part produce (often unforeseen) changes in other parts of an organization.

Labour Process Theory: Worker Exploitation

Arising in the 1970s, **labour process theory** is a neo-Marxist approach to organizations and the conduct of work. It focuses on the alienation of the worker and on power relationships between capitalists and workers.

Alienation is an important concept in Marx's analysis of capitalism. It comprises four elements, which have been summarized by James Rinehart (2001) as follows:

- *Alienation of workers from the products of their labour.* As soon as workers sell their capacity to work to their employers, they receive wages in return rather than any interest in the products they produce. The products belong solely to the employer.
- *Alienation of workers from the labour process.* Wage workers must surrender to their employer the control of how and when a product will be produced.
- *Alienation of workers from themselves.* Because of the first two elements of alienation, work is no longer a central life activity or a means of self-expression. It becomes, instead, merely a means to the end of obtaining income for life satisfaction off the job.
- *Alienation of workers from others.* Under capitalism, workers are separated from their employers because the two sides hold opposing interests in the control of and benefits from the labour process. Workers are also alienated from each other as they compete for jobs.

From these premises, it logically follows that rational workers will resist efforts by capitalists and management to convert the labour time they purchase into increased effort. This perspective sees the "human engineering" of the behavioural school as a misguided and superficial effort that does nothing to change the power relations of the wider society or those at the point of production (Braverman, 1974). Indeed, Rinehart suggests, the ultimate solution would be worker control within a socialist economy.

An important strand in the labour process perspective is the intensification of management control over the workplace that has occurred since the turn of the century. Taylor's scientific management, the introduction of assembly lines, and the use of technology to convert workers into tenders of machines all exemplify this trend. Labour process theorists regard all these as elements of a strategy to replace the skilled craftsperson of a bygone era with a modern unskilled, easily replaceable counterpart (Braverman, 1974). Many historical studies have generally supported the idea of the decline of the craftsman. However, as Wallace Clement (1988) points out, the deskilling process is very complex, with new skills replacing old ones in many instances.

Another central element of labour process theory has been an analysis of the evolution of different forms of control exercised by capitalists over the workplace. Richard Edwards's influential study (1979) concluded that the first of these was the simple person-to-person domination of the owner or supervisor over the worker. As firms grew, this type of control became impractical. Edwards suggests that capitalists then consciously developed technology that enhanced their ability to govern the pace and execution of work. Thus, technological control replaced face-to-face domination. The automotive assembly line, first implemented by Henry Ford in 1913, would be a clear example of this form of control. Technological control made power relations more impersonal but did nothing to motivate the workers.

The increasing worker resistance that resulted led to the advent of today's bureaucratic control, which represents the institutionalization of control. Rules and procedures now govern the conduct of each specific task, the penalties for poor performance, and the rewards for good performance. In this form of control, power relations became impersonalized and embedded in the structure of the organization. Still, to quote Edwards, "top-echelon managers retain their control over the enterprise through their ability to determine the rules, set the criteria, establish the structure, and enforce compliance" (1979: 173).

Edwards proposes that this transformation of forms of workplace control has been driven by capitalists' imperative to extract the maximum possible effort from the wage worker. Critics of labour process theory argue, in contrast, that alienation, deskilling, and the advent of bureaucratic control occur in socialist and capitalist societies alike. While deplorable

Some believe that people have blindly let technology shape the whole concept of work. Engineers develop the most efficient technology, completely ignoring this dehumanizing effect. (Photodisc/Getty Images)

and even demeaning, they are really specific aspects of Weber's more general concept of bureaucracy. This criticism may have validity. Nevertheless, we can learn much from labour process theory about the reality of work and the problems faced by workers in repetitive, mind-numbing jobs.

The Structural Approach: The Organization Makes the Person

Another prominent perspective that seems to offer great promise is the **structural approach**. In the Weberian tradition, it focuses on the structural characteristics of organizations and their effect on the people within them. One objective of contemporary **structural analysis** is to devise changes in organizational structures that will make bureaucracies more effective by making them more humane. Perrow (1972), for example, concludes that structural analyses of the famous Hawthorne studies show that bureaucratic effectiveness depends on the degree to which a bureaucracy can implement structural changes that will increase the congruence between the goals of the formal and the informal organizations.

Nobel laureate Herbert Simon (1986, 1997) was an important pioneer of the structural approach. Noted primarily for his work on decision theory, Simon also pointed out the importance of structural constraints on organizational decision making. In doing so, he provided "the muscle and flesh for the Weberian skeleton" (Perrow, 1972: 146). Simon's studies led him to conclude that Weber's six elements of bureaucracy define the situation for decision makers and shape the premises upon which they make organizational decisions. Thus, bureaucratic structures impel their members to make decisions that are consistent with those made at the top of the hierarchy.

An influential structural analysis of modern bureaucracy is Rosabeth Moss Kanter's *Men and Women of the Corporation* (1977). Kanter explains the behaviour of people in organizations in light of three key variables: the structures of power, of opportunities for advancement, and of proportional representation. Her evidence suggests that those who have power make good leaders—not because of the nature of their relationship with subordinates, but because they can obtain for their whole group a favourable share of the organization's resources. On the other hand, "accountable but powerless" people react rationally to their unfortunate situation in ways detri-

mental to both the organization and their leadership. Those who are upwardly mobile support the organization and its goals. Those whose mobility is blocked salvage their dignity by withdrawing their support from the organization and attempting to gain recognition elsewhere (for example, from subordinates or from sources outside the organization).

Finally, Kanter suggests that those who make up a small proportion of a group—for instance, women and ethnic minorities among managers—are treated as tokens. The results, which include stereotyping, exclusion from leaders' networks, and intense scrutiny, produce a self-fulfilling prophecy. Tokens perform moderately well at best because of structural constraints, not individual deficiencies. Thus, their numbers fail to become large enough to break the bonds of tokenism. Needless to say, Kanter advocates modifying the structures of power, mobility, and proportions.

Feminist Perspectives: Gender Matters

Until two decades ago, most organizational theorists seem to have ignored the fact that organizations comprise women as well as men. A notable exception is Rosabeth Moss Kanter (1977). However, Kanter takes a structural approach in accounting for the disadvantaged positions of women. Women are, indeed, disadvantaged because they are heavily overrepresented in lower-level clerical and service occupations and underrepresented in management (Armstrong and Armstrong, 1984).

A new wave of feminist theories has developed to address this organizational issue, using gender as a crucial explanatory concept. Earlier theorists either ignored gender or assumed that organizations were gender-neutral. However, feminist theorists, including Joan Acker (1991), have pointed out that historically, men have dominated organizations, with the result that the organizational image of the manager and the worker is a male image. This bias has several important consequences.

First, the hierarchical structure of bureaucratic organizations and the accompanying sets of rigid rules and procedures are incompatible with female gender characteristics. Kathy Ferguson (1984) has suggested that women press for more open and democratic organizational systems not only for their own sakes, but also because they believe such changes would make their organizations more effective.

However, women are rarely in positions of sufficient power and authority to change the organization. Thus, organizations remain bastions of oppressive male power.

Second, as Acker (1991) asserts, the dominant male image excludes and marginalizes women. Almost by definition, women cannot achieve the qualities of a "real" worker because to do so is to become like a man. Moreover, women's bodies and sexuality are often stigmatized in organizations and used as grounds for control and exclusion.

Third, the male image of the organizational worker causes women's gender roles to be regarded as deviant. Women are seen as being incompatible with organizational life because of their (assumed) ties to marriage and responsibility for children (Cuneo, 1990). As Cynthia Cockburn charges, even attempts to make organizational adjustments to ease women's role conflicts are unproductive: "The more women are permitted various kinds of flexibility in relation to work to enable them to cope with motherhood and other domestic responsibilities the more they can be dismissed as 'different,' less serious than male employees" (1990: 92). Cockburn goes on to point out that all women become dismissed as deviant because of the potential role conflicts of some.

How Bureaucracies Actually Work

Weber's concept of bureaucracy, as we have seen, is a very useful model for the study of this complex form of organization. It calls our attention to central features of bureaucracy. But it is a simplification, an idealization. It is like the notion of a perfect vacuum in physics, or of a feather falling through space without meeting any wind resistance. Such images are good for starting to think theoretically, but they are not the real world. In the real world, bureaucracies have flaws, and sociologists since Weber have spent a great deal of time discussing these flaws. This section presents some of the more obvious and troubling discrepancies between ideal bureaucracies and actual bureaucracies.

Ideally, every member of a bureaucratic organization is knowingly enmeshed in a network of reporting relationships. In graphic form, a bureaucracy is a Christmas-tree-shaped structure that repeatedly branches out as you go down the hierarchy. Thus, at the bottom of the hierarchy there are a great many people whose job it is to (1) carry out orders from above and (2) report work-related information up the

tree to their superiors. At the top of the hierarchy, there are a few people whose job it is to (1) issue orders to their subordinates, (2) process information received from below, and (3) maintain linkages between the organization and its (political, economic, and social) environment. Also at the top, information is shared between the heads of planning, manufacturing, shipping, public relations, and other sectors of the organization.

In practice, organizations do not work this way, as sociologists since Weber have pointed out. They could not afford to work this way, and human beings aren't constructed to work this way. Thus, alongside the ideal or formal structure—which prescribes how a bureaucracy *ought* to work—there is an actual or informal structure, which is how it *really* works.

Actual Flows of Information

In theory, a failure to report information up the hierarchy would never occur. In practice, it occurs all the time. That is because workplaces are politically "contested terrains" (Edwards, 1979), and controlling the flow of information from below is a means of changing the balance of power between superiors and subordinates. And, as the French sociologist Michel Crozier (1959) showed, bureaucracies work differently in different societies. This is because people raised in different cultures have different ideas about inequality, deference, openness, and secrecy. For example, people raised in France or Russia will be much more alert to the inequality of bureaucratic relations and the power of information control to equalize relations than workers raised in the United States will be. They will therefore behave differently, and as a result bureaucracies will work differently in these countries.

Bureaucracies also appear to work differently for men and women, as has already been noted. When playing a managerial role, women adopt a collaborative, relational approach derived from qualities used in familial relations, whereas men emphasize purely economic considerations. Women's managerial styles emphasize the establishment of good employer–employee relations and the sharing of information and power (Occhionero, 1996).

In practice, workers everywhere form friendships and acquaintanceships. As a result, they casually share work information. Much of the information that flows within an organization is shared orally, not in writing, to introduce civility and negotiation between work teams (Grosjean and Lacoste, 1998). In many cases, workers use information purposefully to help one another. In a few cases, they may even leak information for personal gain or to subvert their boss or the organization as a whole.

Thus, within organizations based ideally on strangers relating to other strangers on the basis of written rules, we find workers forming what amount to secret organizations or subcommunities that obey their own rules. Political actors below the top level cannot employ routine channels or resources to negotiate in the idealized manner. There is a "politics from below" that includes all the actions that defy, oppose, or sidestep the rules or roles of the organization (Brower and Abolafia, 1997).

The basis of this informal organization is trust, which relies on friendship, acquaintanceship, and gossip about third parties that strengthens existing ties (Burt and Knez, 1996). In the end, the same materials that build cliques build the informal, often hidden infrastructure of bureaucracies.

As in cliques, trust in bureaucracies is built gradually, maintained continuously, and easily destroyed (Lewicki and Bunker, 1996). When trust is violated, the result is often revenge or another disruptive response—confrontation, withdrawal, or feuding, for example (Bies and Tripp, 1996). Trust is easier to generate *within* organizations than across organizations, since it is within organizations that managers, serving as third parties, can monitor and enforce reciprocity. The result is that organizational boundaries work effectively to restrict intellectual diffusion (Zucker et al., 1996). Within organizations, the flow of information is harder to contain.

Often team structures are purposely created to cut across the bureaucratic hierarchy, enabling workers to co-operate in the solution of a cross-branch problem. This is done with the recognition that requiring all information to flow to the top and then across is a slow and ponderous way of solving problems. Thus, increasingly, organizations have adopted horizontal, as well as vertical, reporting relationships. In many instances, this has improved organizational learning and given the organization a competitive advantage (West and Meyer, 1997).

Such temporary, cross-cutting groups rely on what is called *swift trust*. In these temporary systems, a premium is placed on making do with whatever information is available and in which swift judgments of trust are mandatory. Generally, trust develops most rapidly when (1) there is a smaller labour pool and

more vulnerability among workers; (2) interaction is based on roles, not personalities; (3) behaviour is consistent and **role expectations** are clear; (4) available information allows a faster reduction in uncertainty; and (5) the level of interdependence is moderate, not high or low (Meyerson, Weick, and Kramer, 1996).

New information technology also makes it easier for horizontal groupings to form, since distant employees can easily exchange information through a large organizational computer network (Constant, Sproull, and Kiesler, 1996). New cultures emerge when computers, linked together to form intra-organizational networks, create a virtual organization parallel to but independent of the traditional bureaucratic hierarchical organization (Allcorn, 1997). As well, telecommuting, or teleworking, now occupies an important place in the world of information work, posing new problems (Di Martino, 1996). It may reduce costs by externalizing or delocalizing work, but we are far from knowing how it will affect work organization and productivity (Carre and Craipeau, 1996). For example, the increased use of computer-mediated communication appears to increase user satisfaction in task-oriented organizational cultures and to decrease user satisfaction in person-oriented organizational cultures (Kanungo, 1998).

Organizational Cultures and Flexibility

In temporary or other horizontal groupings, a worker reports to more than one superior, which may create conflicts or inconsistent demands. In some cases, it becomes unclear where a worker's main duties lie and, therefore, how that person's work should be evaluated and rewarded. This means that greater flexibility and co-operation must be sought from the workers as well as built into the organizational structure itself.

Organizations require increasingly more flexibility from workers, which is possible only if those workers receive continuing education and training and participate in planning (de la Torre, 1997). Yet worker motivation, recruitment, and training all pose problems for bureaucracies. The motivational problem is greatest in organizations where professional expertise and judgment are most required, as in universities, law firms, and technology-development firms. There we find the greatest attention given to matters of organizational culture and career development. It is only by giving these workers considerable autonomy and rewards for strong identification with the firm that the most able workers can be induced to join, stay, and carry out their duties in conformity with organizational goals. Along with this comes a need for thorough organizational **socialization**, which begins at the stage of recruitment and interviewing and is never completed (Edwards, 1979).

Some organizational cultures are more effective than others in creating a high level of worker commitment and high rates of employee retention, and societies vary in their use of one or another kind of organizational culture. For example, in Japan, Korea, and China, there is more receptivity to a collective (or group) culture than we find in North America. (See also Table 5.1.)

Some organizations manipulate organizational culture to apparently tackle the perceived shortcomings of bureaucracy and empower the workers. They espouse open management, teamwork, continuous improvement, and partnership between customers and suppliers without replacing bureaucratic principles of standardization, differentiation, and control through a single chain of command. In the end, senior management has merely used these techniques to restructure management roles, justifying increased corporate control and intensifying work.

However, people usually form stronger attachments to other people than they do to "the organization" as an abstract entity. Thus, patterns of clientelism develop even within bureaucracies. In the end, bureaucracies are organizations in which two principles—rule-based rationality and person-based clientelism—contend for dominance, with neither being able to win decisively at the expense of the other.

The Problem of Rationality

Bureaucracies are thought to be rational in the ways they make and execute plans. They are indeed more rational—in a limited sense—than patron–client relations. This is because, over the long term, by making impersonal decisions and rewarding excellence, they are more able to pursue long-term organizational goals with huge amounts of wealth and power.

However, the sheer size of large bureaucracies and their long-term outlook introduces certain types of

---

Table 5.1   A Diversity of Organization Styles: Aboriginal and Mainstream

In the article that this chart originally accompanies, Ian Newhouse, Don McCaskill, and Ian Chapman argue that the differences in organization outlined here are important for Aboriginal people to maintain their cultural identities as distinct from mainstream North American culture.

Aboriginal	North American Mainstream
Group orientation. The interests and functioning of the group are more important than those of the individual.	*Individual.* The interests and functioning of the individual are paramount over the group.
Consensual. The organization respects employees and expects them to contribute to decisions in an equitable process.	*Majority rules.* Decisions are generally made by voting in which the majority wins the right to choose the course of action.
Group duties. Roles are not specialized, and the organization relies on peer support, team work, task delegation.	*Specialized duties.* Each person is expected to have a well defined job with a set of well defined duties.
Holistic employee development. The organization is concerned with all aspects of the employee's life, both inside and outside the organization.	*Organization employee development.* The organization is concerned only with those aspects of the employee which directly have a bearing upon the ability to do the assigned task.
Elder involvement. Elders are included formally and informally in the organization as advisers and teachers.	*No elder involvement.* Employees retire at the age of 65 and expertise and knowledge is lost to the organization.

SOURCE: Ian Newhouse, Don McCaskill, and Ian Chapman, "Management in Contemporary Aboriginal Organizations," *Canadian Journal of Native Studies*, 11 (1991): 341; available at <www.brandonu.ca/library/cjns/11.2/McCaskill.pdf>, accessed 22 May 2003.

irrationality that, in the end, may undermine the organization. A concern with the mere survival of the organization may undermine shorter-term concerns with the quality of decisions, products, and services the organization is providing to its customers. The much-hated "red tape"—or administrative delay—by bureaucracies persists not because of inadequate technology or personnel, but because it serves positive (as well as negative) functions for the organization (Pandey and Bretschneider, 1997). The bureaucratic demand to eliminate subjectivity and individuality actually undermines the productivity of institutions. By creating boundaries between the institution and outside influences, the institution loses touch with the individuals who are both the subjects and the objects of their efforts (Imershein and Estes, 1996).

Managerial tools such as corporate statements, corporate culture, performance appraisal, and reward systems are means for the **social construction** of homogeneity. Obedience is valued because it is interpreted as the willingness to adopt and internalize dominant ideas, values, rationality, and, more generally, normative systems (Filion, 1998).

In bureaucratic organizations, the presumption of knowledge, heavy reliance on official records and procedures, and the predominance of routine all cushion "papereality"—a world of **symbols**—from other forms of representation. This inhibits both forgetting and learning (Dery, 1998). Another result is the creation of a *bureaucratic personality*, which substitutes proceduralism at the expense of any moral impulse or ethical concern with outcomes (Ten Bos, 1997). Anonymity and distance from decision making make moral indifference likely, if not inevitable. Rule making and record keeping proliferate, particularly in private organizations. There is some evidence that managers who are more alienated and more pessimistic make more rules (Bozeman and Rainey, 1998).

Rule by offices undermines personal responsibility for decisions the organization may take. No member of the bureaucracy is asked, or obliged, to take responsibility for collective decisions. As a result, so-called collective decisions—typically taken by the top executives—are liable to be foolish, harmful, or even criminal. Corporate and government entities are unique in that their deviant behaviour may be caused by systemic patterns in their organizations rather than only by individual malfeasance. However, once deviant behaviour has occurred, they are well positioned to evade responsibility. Managers may often

refuse responsibility, by hiding behind organizational structures, or by adopting the view that they were merely following orders. The deviant behaviour of big business and big government occurs because of limited information, the establishment of norms and rewards that encourage deviant outcomes, or the implementation of actions by organizational elites.

Such deviance is usually initiated by managerial elites and subsequently institutionalized into organizational culture. It will normally continue unchecked until it is challenged from inside or outside the organizations. Organizations themselves are rarely penalized for deviant behaviour (Ermann and Lundman, 1996).

As a legal person, the corporation is able to employ many more resources than individuals who are seeking redress for their injuries by the corporation. The result may be fraudulent practices, dangerous commercial products, or even, as in Nazi Germany, death camps.

The administrative bureaucracies that carried out the extermination of the Jews progressed through several steps ending in incarceration in concentration camps, starvation, and eventual annihilation. Once the machinery had been put into place, it was not confined to Jews but spread to treatment of other groups, including Gypsies, asocial individuals, and Polish prisoners of war. It is true that the managers responsible for this program experienced psychological repulsion. However, most managers rationalized their behaviour in terms of their duty in the bureaucratic system and the supposedly evil nature of the Jewish race (Hilberg, 1996).

Relations with the Outside World

Ideally, the bureaucratic organization relates to the outside world as though it is looking through one-way glass. The outside world, composed of competitors, customers, and other bystanders, cannot see into the organization. However, the organization can see out as well as it needs to. In principle, the main contact between the organization and the outside world is by means of its top executive. It is the top executive, in full possession of organizational intelligence, who can act publicly in the organization's interests.

The separation of decision-making authority from front-line experience is also likely to create an "us versus them" point of view within the organization. As customers criticize the organization for

5.3

Global Issues
Rational Means Can Lead to Irrational Ends

At the turn of the century, German sociologist Max Weber called attention to the dominant process underlying Western culture—rationalization. In Weber's view, the economic revolution and the Industrial Revolution combined to produce the Protestant Ethic and the Spirit of Capitalism. The driving force underlying both was rationalism—a quest for and the implementation of the most rational means for goal achievement. In order for capitalism and industrialization to reach their goals, a system of production and organization would emerge based on the principles of efficiency, predictability, calculability and control. The emergent result of this driving force is the bureaucracy.

While Weber certainly recognized the importance and the positive potentialities of rationalization, he also recognized its dangerous potential to erode individual liberties and to dehumanize. Weber feared the long-range consequences of a process which focused exclusively on means–end rationality to the exclusion of any concern with the human element of social organization. He expressed these fears in his concept of the "Iron Cage of Rationality," i.e., a process so rational that (a) it is irrational and (b) [it] creates an inevitable cage from which there is no escape.

Contemporary sociologist George Ritzer (The McDonaldization of Society, 1996) has extended Weber's analysis to virtually every segment of modern society (the fast food industry, education, health care, child care, recreation and the work place). In a particularly penetrating analysis, Ritzer applies this analysis to the Holocaust. Drawing upon Weber and Holocaust scholar Zigmunt Bauman (Modernity and the Holocaust, 1989) Ritzer argues that the Holocaust displays all the characteristics of rationality: efficiency, predictability, calculability, control and the ultimate dehumanization of its victims by treating death as a unit of production.

The experiences of the Einsatzgruppen and the mobile gas vans served as the impetus for the Nazis to seek a more rational and efficient killing process.

SOURCE: Ben S. Austin, "The Camps," *The Holocaust/Shoah Page* (n.d.); available at <www.mtsu.edu/~baustin/holocamp.html>, accessed 22 May 2003.

unresponsiveness to their concerns, the organization takes a stance of embattled resistance to change. Union-based protest and organized citizen or customer protest movements put pressure on the bureaucracy. The result may be *groupthink*, a resistance within the organization to taking criticism seriously, considering a wide variety of options, or conceding the need for change. Nowhere is this organizational strategy more starkly depicted than in what Erving Goffman (1961a) has called *total institutions*.

Total Institutions

As Goffman (1961a) pointed out, mental hospitals, convents, prisons, and military installations have a lot in common as organizations. True, they have different institutional goals and provide different services to society; they also employ different kinds of experts and oversee different kinds of "customers." However, what they have in common organizationally far outweighs these differences.

First, they are all organizations that have total control over their "customers"—whether mental patients, nuns, convicts, or soldiers-in-training. Twenty-four hours a day, seven days a week, they are able to watch and, if desired, control behaviour within the institution. Though they can see their customer pool perfectly, none of them—whether as psychiatrists or nurses, priests or mothers superior, guards or officers—can be watched unknowingly or unwillingly. Thus, their relationships in the flow of information are highly unequal.

Total institutions offer an extreme example of the bureaucratic organization and the bureaucratized society. They are founded on principles of efficiency and procedural rigidity that are potentially in conflict with the values to which public organizations are expected to assign priority: particularly, democratic participation by employees and by those affected by organization practice (Davis, 1996).

What Goffman (1961a) tells us about mental institutions and prisons reminds us of what we have heard about life in **totalitarian** societies like Nazi Germany and Soviet Russia. Under both Nazism and communism, governance is further complicated by the competition between two bureaucratic hierarchies: the government (based on expertise) and the party (based on loyalty). (For details on East Germany, see Bafoil, 1996, 1998; on China, see Zang, 1998.) Moreover, in practice, both are dominated by a patrimonial ruler, making neither a true bureaucracy (Maslovski, 1996).

In fact, totalitarian societies are not only like total institutions, they also make liberal use of total institutions to punish, brainwash, and **resocialize** uncooperative citizens. Thus, as Weber warned, modern bureaucratic society is an "iron cage" in which we are all trapped by aspirations to career, efficiency, and progress ([1904] 1958: 181). Bureaucracy has an enormous potential for enslavement, exploitation, and cruelty. It also has an enormous potential for promoting human progress through economic development and scientific discovery, high-quality mass education, and the delivery of humane social services to the needy. It is to gain the second that we have risked the first. The jury remains out as to whether, in the twentieth century, the gain justified the cost.

Indeed, Blau (1963), drawing on the work of Michels (1962), points out a paradox in the relationship between two essentially different forms of social organization: bureaucracy and democracy. *Bureaucracy* is an organization formed to achieve set objectives. Its organizing principle is efficiency, and its organizing structure is the hierarchical relationship of dominance and subordination. *Democracy*, on the other hand, is an organization established to find out the objectives of a human group. Its organizing principle is the freedom of dissent necessary to permit majority opinions to form, and its organizing structure is essentially egalitarian.

Democratic forms of social organization are well suited to making choices between alternative policies, but they are not well suited to implementing them. This is the role bureaucracy fills so efficiently. Hence, the two forms of organization complement each other: democracy depends on bureaucracy to implement its policies. But paradoxically, as Blau recog-

nized, by concentrating power in the hands of a very few, bureaucracy is a constant threat to the very survival of democratic institutions.

In the end, Weber was ambivalent about bureaucracy. Its superiority over other organizational forms—for example, organizations based on friendship or kinship, charismatic leadership or tradition—greatly impressed him. He concluded that a bureaucracy is an extremely powerful tool for whoever controls it. For that very reason, Weber ([1908] 1978) expressed disquiet over the immense power a bureaucracy can wield in society, citing the domination by Otto von Bismarck's bureaucracy of the weak German parliament of the day. The fate of "grey-faced bureaucrats" was also of concern to Weber in his writings about bureaucracy ([1908] 1978, [1922] 1958). Bureaucracies posed problems because they shared many of the shortcoming of cliques, yet they were infinitely more dangerous since more likely to achieve their goals.

Conclusion

As we have noted, wherever you turn these days, you see organizations. Large organizations are daunting: they have their own impersonal cultures, they bring together large numbers of strangers, and they devise special ways of maintaining social control. However, it is unclear whether small tightly connected organizations, such as cliques, are any better than large tightly connected organizations, such as bureaucracies.

This chapter has reviewed a variety of different "sets" of people. These included categories, networks, communities, groups, cliques, and organizations. Sets of people with a common sense of identity are typically called *communities*, and there is a long history of community studies in sociology. Communities, whether urban or rural, real or virtual, are important because people are conscious of their membership and make personal investments in remaining members. Formal organizations combine many of the features of networks, groups, cliques, and communities.

The main form of the large, powerful, and long-lived formal organization of the twentieth century is the *bureaucracy*. The goals of bureaucracy—task specialization based on technical competence plus the centralized provision of resources—are increased efficiency and productivity. Owing to its social importance, the chapter has discussed bureaucratic organization at some length.

Theories about formal organization, in turn, mirror changes in society and changes in organizations over the twentieth century. This chapter has reviewed a variety of theories about organization, starting with Taylorism. Taylor's intention was to end labour–management conflict over "shares of the pie." However, the mindless, repetitive work advocated by Taylorism and the alienation it produced is one reason scientific management gradually faded from prominence. The human relations approach was more humane. Since workers were seen as emotional and non-rational, management's task was to instill both happiness and rationality in work groups. This approach, however, ignored real inequalities of power in the workplace. Labour process theory paid attention to problems of exploitation in the conduct of work. Under capitalism, workers are separated from their employers, because the two sides hold opposing interests in the control of and benefits from the labour process. More recent feminist theories pay attention to the importance of gender differences and inequality in formal organizations.

Finally, this chapter considered total institutions. As Goffman pointed out, mental hospitals, convents, prisons, and military installations have a lot in common as organizations. These are all organizations that have total control over their "customers"—whether mental patients, nuns, convicts, or soldiers-in-training. Myths and **ideologies** are propagated to justify the differences between rulers and ruled. Total institutions offer an extreme example of the bureaucratic organization and the bureaucratized society.

□ Questions for Critical Thought

1. Given the goal of fair treatment for all, argue that bureaucracy in the real world is better or worse than a spontaneous organization at achieving this goal.

2. This chapter has touched on our most frequent response to an encounter with a bureaucracy: total frustration. We are frustrated because getting something done through a bureaucracy is slow. Respond to the following assertion: bureaucracies' slowness is a benefit in government and corporations where the party in power or the top-level management changes frequently, altering the goals of the organization.

3. Blau is cited in this chapter as having found that people feel less demeaned by following impersonal rules. Argue whether or not this is true, using a case example from your own or someone else's experience.

4. We have talked about groups as communities with identities. Is it useful for a group to essentialize its identity? Where do you stand on the debate between Werbner and Hall? The broadest question raised in their debate is whether a multicultural society ought to help groups keep their culture or to help individuals to make connections above and beyond their cultural group(s). Where do you stand? Does essentializing always lead to stereotyping and discrimination?

5. Referring to Hochschild's work on "emotional labour" and to Marx's concept of alienation, apply these concepts to your own job, detailing, as Marx and Hochschild do, the precise actions, like smiling, that you sell. More broadly, can you or can anyone perform emotional labour without, for example, smiling without meaning it? Try it.

6. Total institutions have a utterly different environment from the norm in which to socialize inmates. Do some research: do prisons teach inmates how to live "inside," or resocialize them to obey the rules of the outside world? Identify a few key procedures or values and argue your perspective.

7. Consider your own interactions with organizations, either at work or at school or in a community group. How does the goal of the organization—whether it be profit or helping the homeless—effect the organizational style employed?

8. Are some styles of decision making more legitimate than others within a democracy? Rank different types of decision making, such as consensus, majority rule, and incremental decision making by bureaucrats, and explain your ranking of them.

□ Recommended Readings

Holly Arrow, Joseph E. McGrath, and Jennifer L. Berdahl, *Small Groups as Complex Systems: Formation, Coordination, Development and Adaptation* **(Thousand Oaks, CA: Sage, 2000).**
This text takes a micro approach. It adheres to the interactionist view while covering the impact of cliques and teams within workplace environments.

David Beetham, *Bureaucracy* **(Minneapolis: University of Minnesota Press, 1996).**
This theoretically informed volume pays particular attention to the bureaucracies in democratic states. Beetham asks if public-sector bureaucracies can be controlled by politicians and if bureaucracies are more or less responsive to citizens.

Linda Davies and Eric Shragge, eds, *Bureaucracy and Community: Essays on the Politics of Social Work Practice* **(Montreal: Black Rose, 1990).**
This collection focuses on the Canadian case. The articles look at bureaucracy within democratic states in terms of community concerns, and cover welfare and the administration of welfare in Canada as well as social workers.

Paul du Gay, *In Praise of Bureaucracy: Weber, Organizations, Ethics* **(Thousand Oaks, CA: Sage, 2000).**
Weber is a starting point for many sociologists' studies of organizations. This text focuses on the moral and ethical aspects of bureaucracy and examines Weber's contributions to these concerns.

Neil Garston, ed., *Bureaucracy: Three Paradigms* **(Boston: Kluwer Academic Publishers, 1993).**
This collection looks at bureaucracies, how they work, and their effects on society. Readers of this text may find part 2, which examines a range of organization styles in bureaucracies, of particular interest.

Aida Y. Hasaballa, *The Social Organization of the Modern Prison* **(Lewiston, NY: Edwin Mellen, 2001).**
This text examines a prison in Washington, DC. Hasaballa looks at the social behaviour in prisons, the patterns of everyday life, and the social problems that exist in prisons, such as drugs and gang-organized violence. Although the author focuses on the Lorton Central Prison, she provides a thorough overview of prisons through the ages.

Andrew Ross, *No Collar: The Humane Workplace and Its Hidden Costs* **(New York: Basic Books, 2003).**
This text focuses on the changes in the American workplace over recent years. The changing structure of workplace organizations is one product of downsizing and workers' increased mobility. Ross examines the implications of these changes by looking at employees' quality of life and satisfaction with their work environment. He used the participant observation technique to carry out first-hand research that takes two organizations through the technology boom and 9/11.

Daniel A. Silverman, *Queen Victoria's Baggage: The Legacy of Building Dysfunctional Organizations* **(Lanham, MD: University Press of America, 1999).**
This book offers a cross-cultural analysis of what the author calls "dysfunctional" organizations. Silverman focuses on the classroom and community as a site in which he examines different cultural concepts of discipline.

Guy van Gyes, Hans de Witte, and Patrick Pasture, eds, *Can Class Still Unite? The Differentiated Work Force, Class Solidarity and Trade Unions* **(Burlington, VT: Ashgate, 2001).**
This recent collection focuses on the interactions between labour unions and social classes. The text is drawn from a 1998 conference in Belgium where academics and trade unionists discussed what relevance the concept of class still held. Although academics have long held that as class is too static a concept to be useful today, trade unionists have a long history of using the term. The broad questions of the political uses of solidarity within and between classes are addressed.

Robert Westwood and Stephen Linstead, eds, *The Language of Organization* **(London: Sage, 2001).**
Taking a more micro approach, the articles in this collection focus on language as a form of social control. The volume looks specifically at the kinds of words we use to describe organizations generally, the day-to-day interactions within organizations, and the components of organizations. This book will interest those curious about language-based research.

□ Recommended Web Sites

Chinese Immigration Research Network

www.chass.utoronto.ca/~salaff/chineseimmigration.html

University of Toronto professor Janet Salaff has a long history of research on the instrumental uses of social networks within the Toronto Chinese community and the Chinese community in Hong Kong. Papers and abstracts are available to read. Her recent research focuses on immigrant's social networks and on finding jobs.

Correctional Service Canada

www.csc-scc.gc.ca

The Web site of Correctional Service Canada, like all Canadian government Web sites, offers a wealth of literature on a variety of topics, including prisons as total institutions.

Ellen Balka

www.sfu.ca/~ebalka/index.html

Professor Balka's research includes cross-cultural examinations of organizations that assume a more collectivist model. Check out her publications on participatory design, including "Political Frameworks for System Design: Participatory Design in Non-profit Women's Organizations in Canada and the United States" (1995).

Inside Canada's Prisons

www.cbc.ca/prison/index.html

The CBC offers an interactive tour of a Canadian prison, giving clues to how it would feel to be a prisoner. As well, this link offers articles and analysis concerning prisons and further links for those interested.

Managementlearning.com

http://managementlearning.com/index.html

This commercial site aims to educate users about behaviour within an organization. The main goal of the literature the site supplies is efficiency. Try following any of these sublinks: Research, Library, Articles, or Topics.

PROFITguide.com

www.profitguide.com

This Web site has a clear objective: profits. Focusing on this goal, the site has articles and step-by-step guides to help managers increase their profits by organizing their workplace according to certain principles. Try the "How To" link.

Social Networks and Social Capital

www.soc.duke.edu/~xioye/abstract.html

This is a link to a conference, primarily of sociologists, concerning social networks and social capital. In some cases, both the abstracts and the full text of presented papers are available to read. Many of the papers are concerned with the uses to which groups put their social networks and social capital.

Statistics Canada

www.statcan.ca

Statistics Canada is likely the most useful Web site for students. Try clicking on "Our Products and Services," and, at the bottom of the page, click on "In Depth." Click on the journal called *Perspectives on Labour and Income*, and under the Subject index click "Unemployment" and see the article "Obtaining a Job." This is one of many useful and accessible articles available on the Statistics Canada Web site. Statistics Canada also has data in chart form at the local, provincial/territorial, and federal levels concerning many interesting aspects of Canadians' lives.

Treasury Board of Canada

www.tbs-sct.gc.ca

The Treasury Board of Canada is the secretariat of the Government of Canada that helps the federal government manage itself. If you are curious about general government hiring policies, procedures, and preferences, this site will interest you. Try the Public Service Modernization Act, and search using the keyword "students" for recent changes to student hiring policies within the federal government.

6

Vincent F. Sacco

> > >

Deviance

© Digital Vision

☐ Learning Objectives

In this chapter, you will:

- learn to define deviance and social control as sociological concepts
- think critically about the images of deviance that we regularly encounter in the popular media
- learn to describe the major problems confronting researchers who study deviance
- identify the major questions that sociological theories of deviance and control are intended to answer
- compare and contrast various sociological explanations of deviant behaviour
- examine some of the social and demographic factors that are related to particular forms of deviant conduct
- learn how behaviours and people come to be categorized as deviant
- study the ways in which people who are labelled "deviant" cope with stigma

Introduction

On a quiet, tree-lined street, two suburban teenagers sit in a kitchen and discuss how they will spend Friday night. They decide that one of them will try to get a fake ID in order to buy some beer for a party they are planning to attend. An older brother of one of the teenagers approaches the house. He picks the daily newspaper off the front step and glances at the front page, where there is a very prominent story about the mayor's resignation—it was discovered that the mayor had been giving untendered contracts to a construction firm owned by someone who made large and regular contributions to her recent political campaign. The teenagers stop discussing their plans when the older brother, a student at the local university, enters. He instructs them to stay off the computer because he is waiting for a "very important" e-mail. What he doesn't tell them is that the e-mail is from a friend at another university who has promised to send a copy of an A+ essay, which the recipient plans to submit as his own work in a course he is failing.

Across town, in a gleaming corporate office, several key members of a clothing company meet to consider the bad press they have been getting since it was revealed that their clothing lines are made by children in sweatshops in Third World countries. Rather than considering how they might improve employees' working conditions, they decide to launch a publicity blitz that denies the charges and calls into question the honesty and motivations of their accusers. One of the executives finds it difficult to concentrate on business because she is distracted by the situation at home. Her husband's occasional violent outbursts have become more frequent, and she worries that she and her children may be in some real danger.

What do all of these situations have in common? On the surface, it might seem that the answer is very little. However, some important common themes run through these examples. These common themes relate to the central concerns of this chapter: the sociological nature of deviance and control. All of these situations raise questions for us about the nature of disvalued social action, why some people engage it, and why others might react to it in particular ways.

This chapter will attempt to accomplish several specific objectives. First, it will talk about what the terms **deviance** and **social control** mean when they are used in sociological discourse. Next, it will consider some of the major problems faced by researchers who are interested in the empirical investigation of

deviance and social control. Finally, it will focus on the three major theoretical questions that occupy the time and attention of sociologists who are interested in the study of deviance.

What Is Deviance?

Any discussion of the sociology of deviance and social control must begin with some consideration of precisely what these terms mean. This is not a straightforward task. These terms can be, and have been, defined in many different ways, both within and beyond the discipline of sociology.

Formal sociological conceptualizations of deviance can be contrasted with more popular views of what this concept means. These more popular views define *deviance* by illustration, statistically, and in terms of a notion of harm.

By Illustration

When students are asked in a classroom to define *deviance*, a first response is typically to list types of people or types of behaviours that they think deserve the label. Most of us would have no trouble coming up with a long list of deviants, which could include (but would not be restricted to) criminals, child molesters, drug addicts, alcoholics, the mentally ill, members of religious cults, liars, and more. Of course, who makes the list and who does not is very much a function of who is doing the listing and when and where the listing is being done.

The major problem with these stand-alone lists is that they are incomplete. On their own, they tell us nothing about why some types of people and behaviour are (and why other types are not) included. In short, we are left in the dark regarding the nature of the definitional criteria being employed.

In Statistical Terms

Statistical rarity suggests a more explicit way of thinking about the meaning of *deviance*. In this sense, deviant behaviour and deviant people are identifiable on the basis of their rarity. On the face of it, this makes a certain amount of sense. Many of the kinds of people we are think of deviant are, in a relative sense, statistically unusual.

A major problem with statistical definitions of deviance is illustrated by Figure 6.1. The areas between points X_1 and X_2 represent typical performance

6.1

Human Diversity
Who Are the Deviants?

In 1969, the sociologist J.L. Simmons (1969) reported the results of a small study in which he asked 180 respondents to list people and things they regarded as "deviant." His respondents varied by gender, age, and other socio-demographic characteristics.

The list of people and behaviours nominated was extensive, with more than 250 items. Many of the categories suggested by respondents were expected, including (in the language of the day) homosexuals, prostitutes, drug addicts, radicals, and criminals.

However, the list also included liars, career women, reckless drivers, atheists, Christians, the retired, card players, bearded men, artists, pacifists, priests, girls who wear makeup, divorcées, perverts, smart-aleck students, know-it-all professors, modern people, and Americans.

It might be interesting to conduct a small follow-up survey to see what sort of list that question might generate (among your classmates, for example). As well, it worth speculating what such a list teaches us about everyday understandings of deviance and what the list generated by Simmons might reveal about the historical period during which it was made.

---

levels across some task. The shaded area on the far left represents that minority of cases that are statistically rare and that fall well below the average. On an examination, for instance, the people who fail very badly would be represented there. We might tend to think of such people as "deviants" in a conventional sense.

However, the shaded portion on the far right-hand side also suggest a statistically rare performance—but in the positive direction. On an examination, these people would be receiving very high A's. Statistical definitions thus obscure distinctions between people who exceed and people who fall short of expectations.

As Harmful

Another popular way of defining *deviance* is in terms of harm. In this sense, we equate deviant action with action that produces destructive outcomes. Once again, many of those who would make most shortlists of deviants would also seem to be scoped in by this definitional criterion. Murders, thieves, liars, sexual abusers, and wife assaulters can all be said to be authors of real and tangible harm.

But any attempt to equate deviance with harm is also fraught with difficulties. First, while many of the people we treat as deviant in this society are the authors of harm, it is also true that many are not. The developmentally delayed, the mentally ill, gays and lesbians, and many others are often treated as deviant although it is difficult to document the harm that they cause. In contrast, greedy corporate executives and unethical politicians are often able to quite effectively manage how others see them even though their actions may result in considerable damage to life and property. We tend to reserve the label of "deviant" in our society for other categories of people (Pearce and Snider, 1995; Simon and Hagan, 1999).

In many ways, harm is as much a matter of judgment and opinion as is deviance. There is considerable

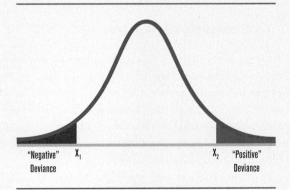

Figure 6.1   The Normal Curve

"Negative" Deviance X_1 X_2 "Positive" Deviance

Statistical definitions of deviance make it difficult to distinguish "negative" deviance from "positive" deviance.

IN THE FIRST PERSON

I have been interested in sociology—especially the sociology of crime and deviance—my entire life. Growing up in the border city and tourist destination of Niagara Falls, I became aware early of some of the more peculiar eccentricities and excesses of human behaviour. Like many students, I majored in sociology because I thought the subject matter was, as we used to say, "pretty cool" and because I did reasonably well in my first-year course. My fascination with the discipline was nurtured by many dedicated and patient teachers and mentors who showed me the real value of careful sociological analysis. However, it was not until I read C. Wright Mills's *The Sociological Imagination* that I began to think seriously about the links between the lives we live and the social structures within which we live them.—VINCE SACCO

disagreement in our society about what is and what is not harmful and whom we do and do not need to fear (Glassner, 1999). Indeed, historical and anthropological evidence shows that judgments about harm change over time and from one culture to another.

Deviance as a Sociological Concept

As sociologists, we are interested in trying to understand deviance as a product of **social interaction** and group structure. Simply put, we understand the study of deviance to be the study of people, behaviours, and conditions that are subject to social control. Conversely, we can define social control as the various and myriad ways in which members of **social groups** express their disapproval of people and behaviour. These include name calling, ridicule, ostracism, incarceration, and even killing. The study of deviance is about ways of acting and ways of being that, within particular social contexts and in particular historical periods, elicit moral condemnation.

When sociologists talk about deviance in this way, it sometimes creates confusion for those who are used to thinking about the subject in a more conventional manner. When the sociologist says, for instance, that homosexuality is an appropriate subject matter for the scholar interested in the study of deviance, the implication is not that the sociologist thinks of homosexuality as deviant. Rather, the point is that homosexuality is subject to various forms of social control in our society. As sociologists, we are interested in why those with the power to exert social control regard gays and lesbians in this way and what the consequences of such actions are (Herek, 2002).

In the study of deviance, it is important to distinguish between the *objective* and the *subjective* character of deviance (Loseke, 1999). The former refers to particular ways of thinking, acting, and being, the latter to the moral status accorded such thoughts, actions, and characteristics. It is important to keep this distinction in mind at all times. The "deviant" character of certain behaviours or world views or physical features is not implicit in those behaviours, world views, or physical features but is conferred upon them. Deviance thus requires both aspects of the phenomenon: there must be things (actions and so on) that can potentially be labelled as "deviant," and there must exist deviant labels and powerful others who are willing to use them.

Of course, as sociologists, we recognise the need to focus our attention on both sides of the deviance coin. We need to be alert to the fact that not everything that could be labelled "deviant" *is* labelled "deviant." The ability of some in society to use available resources in order to resist the efforts of others to consider them deviant is also of sociological interest.

Researching Deviance

Sociologists who undertake empirical studies of deviance attempt to make use of all of the same methodological tools that are employed in other areas of the discipline. These include, for instance, experiments, surveys, content analyses, and field research. However, attempting to study the degree to which people might be engaging in behaviours that excite widespread disapproval can create some rather formidable problems. While the problems discussed in this section represent challenges to all forms of social research, they suggest special difficulties when the subject matter of the research is deviance.

Secrecy

By its nature, deviant behaviour is often behaviour that people wish to keep secret. How then do sociologists undertake valid research in a way that does not intrude into the lives of those under study? Of course, there is no simple answer to this question.

Sometimes the researcher attempts to gain the confidence of the subjects by posing as one who shares their deviant status (Whyte, 1943). This involves some extremely hazardous ethical dilemmas. One much discussed case in this respect is an early study by sociologist Laud Humphreys. His book *Tearoom Trade* (1970) is a study of impersonal sexual encounters between homosexual men in public washrooms ("tearooms"). In order to familiarize himself with the social character of these sexual encounters, Humphreys presented himself to "tearoom" participants as someone who was willing to play the role of voyeur/lookout. This deception allowed him to observe the interaction between sexual partners in a way that did not arouse their suspicion. To compound the ethical problem, Humphreys recorded the licence plate numbers of the men who frequented the "tearoom" and was able to determine their addresses. After disguising his appearance, he went to their homes, under the guise of conducting a public health survey, in order to learn more about them. Needless to say, this provoked a firestorm of controversy. Generally, sociologists do not believe that such deception is ever excusable.

Discovery of Reportable Behaviour

If research subjects confide in the researcher and reveal information about troublesome circumstances, does the researcher have an obligation to report that wrongdoing to authorities? The problem is brought about by the cross-pressures that the researcher experiences. On the one hand, the researcher has a professional obligation to respect the confidentiality of information that research subjects divulge. On the other hand, there is a social and moral obligation to protect the safety of the public or, even more, of the research subject.

Some of the complexities relating to reportability are illustrated by the case of Russel Ogden, who in 1994 was an MA student in the School of Criminology at Simon Fraser University in British Columbia. Ogden's study involved an investigation of the process of assisted suicide among terminally ill HIV/AIDS patients. Shortly after he defended his thesis, he was summoned by a coroner's inquest, which asked to him to reveal the sources of his information. Ogden refused, citing the pledge of confidentiality he had provided to his research subjects. He was subsequently charged with contempt of court, but, in spite of having little formal support from his university, he was able to win the case. The court later ruled that social science researchers have a qualified privilege to maintain confidentiality because such research contributes substantially to Canadian society (Palys, n.d.).

Safety

Closely related to the problems of reportable behaviour are those related to the safety of respondents. In short, researchers should take no action that results in harm to those who participate in the research. While we tend to think only of physical harm in this respect, the injunction is much broader and includes emotional, mental, and economic harm.

There are many ways in which research could produce harmful outcomes. In the case of one major survey of female victims of male violence, for instance, there was a real concern on the part of researchers that calling women out of the blue and asking questions about violence in their lives could put them in danger if, for instance, a woman's abuser might be sitting next to her when she received the phone call (Johnson, 1996). As a result, it was necessary to take several special precautions, for instance, training interviewers to be sensitive to cues that the respondent might be under some immediate stress.

There is, as well, a more general sense in which research can put study subjects at risk. It is important to remember that, by definition, research into the disvalued nature of people and behaviour often involves research into the lives of the most vulnerable members of society. These could include the poor, the homeless, and others with whom society associates designations of deviance. The sociologist needs to remain aware that research findings can often be used against these vulnerable groups, especially when due care is not taken to qualify conclusions or to suggest appropriate interpretations of research evidence.

The Sociology of Deviant Behaviour

We have defined *deviance* as ways of thinking, acting, and being that are subject to social control—in other words, as kinds of conditions and kinds of people that are viewed by the members of a society as wrong, immoral, or disreputable. In so doing, we recognize that deviance has two distinct yet related dimensions: objective and subjective. *Objective* refers to the behaviour or condition itself, *subjective* to the placement of that condition in the system of moral stratification.

To choose a simple example, it is important that we not confuse the physical act of smoking marijuana with the designation of marijuana smoking as a deviant act. While each suggests a distinct realm of experience, each is an appropriate object of sociological attention. It is one thing to ask why people smoke marijuana, and it is quite another to ask why this is considered deviant conduct (in the law, for example). However, both types of questions are important and interesting.

We can identify several key problem areas that have been the focus of theoretical attention in the sociology of deviance. These include questions about (1) the causes and forms of deviant behaviour, (2) the content and character of moral definitions, and (3) the struggle over labels of deviance.

While sociologists are interested in a broad array of questions, questions about why deviants do what they do have always attracted the lion's share of attention. However, the "Why do they do it?" question contains a number of important (if unstated) assumptions. By implication, it assumes that most of us share

6.2

Open for Discussion
What's Deviant and What Isn't?

- We tend to distinguish in our language between "drugs" and "alcohol" as though they are two different kinds of substances, but the nature of this difference isn't clear. The major distinction is really only a legal one—alcohol is not a prohibited substance, but marijuana and cocaine are. This invites a question: why is it legal to drink alcohol but illegal to smoke marijuana? Or, even more pointedly, why is it legal to smoke cigarettes but illegal to smoke marijuana? These distinctions do not derive from any logical assessment of the harm to self or others associated with consumption. Far more people die as a result of tobacco and alcohol use than as a result of the use of prohibited substances.
- We make distinctions between "religions" and "cults" as though these differences exist in nature. Some writers argue, however, that the world *cult* is typically used to describe a religion we do not approve of (Bromley and Shupe, 1981). Many of the contemporary mainstream religions (such as Roman Catholicism or Mormonism) have been accused in the past of doing what contemporary cults are accused of doing (for example, brainwashing new members, exploiting believers, or covertly encouraging violence). Some critical writers maintain that our contemporary dislike of cults merely reflects the latest manifestation of long-standing religious intolerance.
- Women who are engaged in sex work (for example, prostitutes) have traditionally been the object of derision and ostracism (Brock, 1998; Larsen, 2000). The police, the courts, and the prisons have been directed toward the suppression of the prostitute. Interestingly, though, the societal attitude toward the seller of sexual services has always been much harsher than the attitude toward the buyer. This, too, defies logic.
- Especially after the events of 9/11, we have tended to use the words *terrorist* and *terrorism* as though their meanings were not problematic. Of course, terrorism, like any other deviant category, is socially constructed. Whom we see as a terrorist depends largely upon our political positions and national loyalties. One person's terrorist is another person's soldier of liberation.

a conformist view of the world and that the important thing to understand is why some deviant minority refuses to act the way that *we* act. The moral status of deviant behaviour is never called into question. In a sense, the "Why do they do it?" question proceeds from the assumption that—by and large—society is a pretty stable and orderly place, that there is generally widespread agreement about what is right and what is wrong, and that we therefore need to understand what pushes or pulls some off the path the rest of us travel.

Quite obviously, most (but not all) of the theoretical thought in this respect reflects the influence of functionalist perspectives. Three major strands of thought can be identified—strain theory, cultural support theory, and control theory.

Strain Theory

Strain theory derives from the writings of the famous American sociologist Robert Merton, who in 1938 published a very influential paper entitled "Social Structure and Anomie." Merton sought to understand why, according to official statistics, so many types of non-conformity are much more pervasive among members of the lower social classes. Crime, delinquency, drug addiction, alcoholism, and other forms of deviance, Merton recognized, seem to emerge as more significant problems the further one moves down the socio-economic structure. As a sociologist, Merton was interested in trying to understand this issue in a way that made the structure of society—rather than the personalities of individuals—the central explanatory mechanism.

Merton argued that the answer could be found in the malintegration of the cultural and social structures of societies. In other words, it is the lack of fit between the cultural goals people are encouraged to seek and the means available to pursue these goals that creates a kind of social strain to which deviant behaviour is an adjustment. Merton's logic is elegant and compelling. In a society like the United States, there is little recognition of the role that **class** barriers play in social life. As a result, everyone is encouraged to pursue the goal of material success—and everyone is judged a success or a failure in life based on his or her ability to become successful.

Merton knew though that there are many people near bottom of the class hierarchy who because of their ethnic or regional or class origins may not be able to achieve that overpowering goal of success.

This, Merton said, is a type of socially induced strain to which people must adjust their behaviour, and often these adjustments take deviant forms. When people steal money or material goods, for instance, it can be said that they are attempting to use "illegitimate means" to achieve the trappings of success. When they take drugs (or become "societal dropouts"), they can be seen to have pulled out of the race for stratification outcomes. For Merton, these problems are most acute in the lower social classes because it is there that people are most likely to experience the disjuncture between the things they aspire to and things that are actually available to them (see Table 6.1).

Later critics have pointed out several problems with Merton's arguments (Kornhauser, 1978; Vold, Bernard, and Snipes, 2002). For instance, Merton proceeds from the assumption that the distribution of crime and deviance that we find in official statistics is accurate, which it may not be. In a related way, the argument is not very successful in explaining acts of crime and deviance within middle- and upper-class populations.

Despite these limitations, this argument has had a great deal of influence on the way in which sociologists think about the causes of deviant behaviour (Laufer and Adler, 1994). For example, sociologists Richard Cloward and Lloyd Ohlin (1960) expanded upon Merton's ideas in an effort to explain lower-class gang delinquency. They agree with Merton that juvenile crime was prompted by the inability of lower-class youth to achieve the things that their culture encouraged them to seek. However, they suggest that there is a need to explain why different kinds of delinquent behaviour patterns emerge in different types of neighbourhoods.

For these researchers, delinquency patterns are like rare plants that require specialized conditions to flourish. Cloward and Ohlin identify three specific kinds of delinquent adaptations. The first, which they refer to as the *criminal pattern*, is characterized by instrumental delinquency activities, particularly delinquency for gain, in which those involved seek to generate illegal profits. We might think of drug selling or the stealing and fencing of stolen goods as examples of this kind of crime. The second, the *conflict pattern*, is characterized by the presence of "fighting gangs" who battle over turf and neighbourhood boundaries. The third, the *retreatist pattern*, is organized around the acquisition and use of hard drugs.

A more recent version of strain theory has been proposed by Robert Agnew (1985; Agnew and

Table 6.1   Robert Merton's Paradigm of Deviant Behaviour

Robert Merton argued that there are essentially five ways of adjusting to a social structure that encourages large numbers of people to seek objectives that are not actually available to them. Four of these adaptations represent types of deviance. Each type can be understood in reference to the goals and means of the culture.

	Attitude to Goals	Attitude to Means	Explanation/Example
Conformity	accept	accept	Most people accept as legitimate the culturally approved ways of achieving those goals. In Merton's example, most strive for material success by working hard, trying to get a good education, etc.
Innovation	accept	reject	The bank robber, drug dealer, or white-collar thief seeks success, too, but rejects the conventional means for achieving that success.
Ritualism	reject	accept	Some people seem to simply be going through the motions of achieving desired social goals. In large organizations, we use the term *bureaucrat* to describe people who are fixated on procedures at the expense outcomes.
Retreatism	reject	reject	Some people adjust to strain by "dropping out" of the system. Such dropping out could include losing oneself in a world of alcohol or illegal drugs or adopting some unconventional lifestyle.
Rebellion	reject/accept	reject/accept	Rebellion includes acts intended to replace the current cultural goals (and means) with new ones. In this category we might include the radical political activist or even the domestic terrorist.

Broidy, 1997). Agnew theorizes that the inability to achieve the things we want in life is only one type of socially induced strain and that there are at least two others. A second source of strain involves an inability to avoid or escape some negative condition. For example, the youth who cannot avoid an abusive parent or a bully at school might turn to drugs, run away, or become aggressive with others as ways of coping with the strain that the situation creates. A third kind of strain results from conditions in which individuals lose something that they value. Strain in this sense can result, for example, when a child is forced to move and thus to leave behind old friends, when a parent dies, or when a breakup with a boyfriend or girlfriend occurs.

Despite their differences, these arguments share certain features in common. First, they all take as their point of reference the need to explain why some individuals rather than others behave in ways that invite social sanction. Second, they share in common an explanatory logic that focuses on the ways in which the organization of our social relations creates problems that require solutions. In this sense, the causes of deviant behaviour are located in patterns of social life that are external to but impact upon individuals.

Cultural Support Theory

A second explanation of deviant behaviour, **cultural support theory**, focuses on the way in which patterns of cultural beliefs create and sustain such conduct (Cohen, 1966). According to arguments of this sort, people behave in ways that reflect the cultural values to which they have been exposed and that they have internalized. In this way, it can be said that you are attending university or college because you value education and learning. If conventional values support conventional behaviour, it should also follow that deviant values support deviant behaviour. The important task of such theories is to understand how the cultural meanings people associate with deviant conduct make that conduct more likely.

One of the earliest explicit statements of this position was provided by a sociologist associated with the University of Chicago, Edwin Sutherland (see Sutherland, 1947). Writing in the 1930s, Sutherland proposed that people become deviant because they have been exposed to learning experiences that make deviance more likely. In short, people end up deviant in the same way that they end up as Catholics, as stamp collectors, as saxophone players, or as French film fans—that is, as a result of exposure to influential learning experiences. People become deviant because they have learned in the context of interpersonal relationships how to become deviant.

But what does learning to be deviant actually involve? Most important, according to Sutherland, is the learning of what he called the "specific direction of drives, motives, attitudes and rationalizations" (1947: 7). In other words, we must learn to think about deviant conduct as acceptable to ourselves. Why do we not kill people who make us angry? It can't be because we don't know how (most of us do) or even, in many cases, because we fear getting caught. Most commonly, we refrain from murderous violence because we have come to define such action as morally repugnant, that is, as unacceptable to ourselves. For Sutherland, it was this learning to accept or to value criminal or deviant action that in a very real sense made such action possible.

Sutherland's cultural insights help us to understand how people come to value actions the rest of the society might despise. But other writers in this tradition have shown that the culture of deviant action is even more complicated. The complication concerns the fact that we live in a society that seems simultaneously to condemn and to support deviant behaviour. Is it possible to simultaneously believe in and break important social rules? Most of us think, for example, that stealing is wrong, and we have learned to be wary of thieves. However, most of us have also stolen something of value (perhaps at work, perhaps from a corner store or a family member). This is possible because we have learned to define these deviant situations as ones to which the rules really do not apply. When we steal at work, for instance, we might not really see this as theft. We tell ourselves (and others) that we are underpaid and deserve whatever fringe benefits we can get or that our employers actually expect people to steal and build it into their budgets. The broader culture, from this perspective, both condemns deviance and makes available for learning the techniques to neutralize the laws that prohibit deviant action (Coleman, 1987; Matza and Sykes, 1957).

Like strain arguments, cultural arguments have been very influential in the sociological study of deviant behaviour. Some critics have charged, however, that arguments that use culture to explain deviance are ultimately tautological (Maxim and Whitehead, 1998). This means that these arguments are accused of employing a kind of circular reasoning. Cultural theories tell us that deviant beliefs and values are the source of deviant conduct. Yet how do we ever really know what people's beliefs and values are? Usually, we observe how people behave and then, on the basis of their behaviour, infer that they hold certain values. Is it appropriate, then, to use the value we have inferred from observations of behaviour to explain that behaviour? If we observe people stealing and then infer that they have come to acquire values that are supportive of stealing and that these values explain the stealing, we have gone in a very large circle and have really explained nothing at all.

Control Theory

The logic of the strain and cultural support theories contrasts quite sharply with the logic of a third type of view known as **control theory**. Advocates of control theory argue that most types of deviant behaviour do not really require a particularly sophisticated form of explanation. People lie, cheat, steal, take drugs, or engage in sexual excess when and if they are free to do so. Lying and cheating can be the most expeditious and efficient ways of getting what we want in life. Experimenting with drugs and sexual promiscuity can be more fun than working or studying. The important question we need to ask, according to control theorists, isn't "Why do some people break rules the rest of abide by?" Instead we need to ask, "Why don't more us engage in forbidden behaviour?" For control theorists, deviant behaviour occurs when it is allowed to occur. Thus, we expect to find deviance when the social controls that are supposed to prevent or check it are weak or broken. Seen in this way, deviance is not a special kind of behaviour that requires a special kind of motivation. Rather, it is behaviour that results from the absence of pressures that would normally check or contain it.

This idea is a very venerable one in sociology—it can be traced back to the writing of Émile Durkheim ([1897] 1966). In his classic study of suicide, Durkheim sought to explain why some groups in society experience higher suicide rates than others and why suicide rates very over time. Catholics, he found, have lower suicide rates than Protestants, and married people have lower rates than single people. As well, suicide rates increase in times both of economic boom and of economic depression. What is it that is varying in all of these cases? Durkheim suggested that the crucial variable might be social regulation (or what we might call *social control*). Social regulation forces people to take others into account and discourages behaviours that are excessively individualistic. So Catholicism—with its mandatory church attendance and practices such as confession—might suggest more social regulation than various strands of Protestantism. Married life implies more external regulation (in terms of obligations, duties, and so on) than single life. Periods of both boom and depression throw large numbers of people out of the customary social grooves in which they have been living their lives and disconnect them from social regulations. In short, suicide is more likely when people are left to their own resources.

In more recent times, sociologist Travis Hirschi (1969) has been the most influential social control theorist. Like many other sociologists interested in the study of deviant behaviour, Hirschi focused on the study of juvenile crime. In a very influential book published in 1969, Hirschi attempted to use social control logic to explain the conduct of youthful offenders. For Hirschi, the problem of juvenile crime could be understood in reference to the concept of the bond to conventional society. Each of us, to a greater or lesser degree, has a bond or connection to the world of conventional others. In the case of youth, the world of conventional others is the world represented by their parents, teachers, and members of the legitimate adult community. Hirschi reasoned that if youthful bonds to conventional others are strong, youths need to take these others into account when they act; if the bonds are weak, however, they are free to act in ways that reflect much more narrow self-interest. Much of what we call crime and deviance, Hirschi reasoned, is evidence of this self-interested behaviour.

More recently, in collaboration with Michael Gottfredson (Gottfredson and Hirschi, 1990), Hirschi has proposed a general theory of crime and deviance that has been the object of a great deal of attention. Gottfredson and Hirschi argue that crimes of all types tend to be committed by people who are impulsive, short-sighted, non-verbal risk takers. The underlying social-psychological characteristic of such people, they maintain, is low self-control. Further, individuals who have low self-control not only are more likely to commit crime, they are also more likely to engage in a wide range of deviant practices, including drinking, smoking, and activities that result in getting into accidents (Junger, van der Heijden, and Keane, 2001; Nakhaie, Silverman, and LaGrange, 2000). For Gottfredson and Hirschi, the problem of low self-control originates in inadequate child rearing that fails to discourage delinquent outcomes.

Social control theories remain very influential, but they have been criticized for their assumption that motivation is essentially irrelevant to the study of crime and deviance (Bohm, 1997). As well, some writers argue that while these ideas make a certain amount of sense when we are talking about crime and deviance among the more marginalized segments of society, they do not do a very good job of explaining why those members of society whose bonds to the conventional world seem strongest also engage in prohibited acts (Deutschmann, 1998).

The Transactional Character of Deviance

Despite their sociological character, strain, cultural support, and social control arguments tend to focus our attention on the individual: people, according to these theories, commit deviant acts because they respond to strain, because they are exposed to learning environments that support deviance, or because they are free from social constraints. Other writers, however, encourage us to understand deviant behaviour as an interactional product. From this perspective, we understand deviant behaviour as a joint or collective, rather than individual, outcome.

Murder provides an interesting case in point (see Figure 6.2 for homicide rates in Canada). When most of us seek to explain murder, we tend to focus on the murderous acts of the individual. As sociologists, for instance, we might try to understand how people who commit acts of lethal violence do so in response to social strain (Messner and Rosenfeld, 1997) or as a result of an affiliation with a culture of violence (Wolfgang and Ferracuti, 1967). Alternatively, though, we might try to understand how murder results from particular kinds of interactions.

David Luckenbill (1977), for example, has attempted to show how murder can in many cases be understood as a **situated transaction**. This means that murder is seen not as an individual act, but rather as a interaction sequence in which the participants (the eventual murderer, the eventual victim, and, perhaps, an audience) interact in a common physical territory. Based on a study of 70 homicides in the state

Figure 6.2 **Provincial Variations in Rates of Homicide (Number of Homicides per 100,000 Population), 2001**

For reasons that are not entirely clear, the rate at which the situated transaction we refer to as *homicide* varies from province to province.

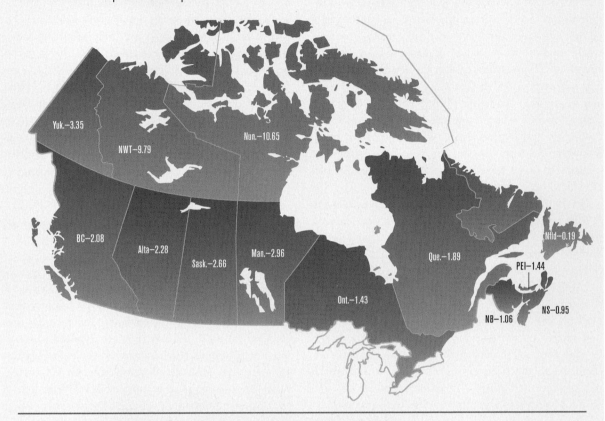

SOURCE: Mia Dauvergne, "Homicide in Canada: 2001," *Juristat*, 22, no. 7 (2001): 3.

of California, Luckenbill concludes that many murders move through six common stages:

- *Stage 1*. The transaction starts when the person who will end up the victim does something that the person who ends up the offender could define as an insult or as an offence to "face." This could be quite trivial. The victim might call the offender a liar, refuse to share a cigarette, or make a sexually suggestive comment about the partner of the eventual offender.
- *Stage 2*. The offender defines what the victim has said or done as threatening or offensive.
- *Stage 3*. The offender makes an countermove intended to respond and save face. This could involve a verbal response or a physical gesture.
- *Stage 4*. The victim responds in an aggressive manner. At this point, a working definition of the situation as one that will require a violent resolution seems to be emerging. The problems may be aggravated by the presence of onlookers who jeer the participants, offer to hold their jackets, or block a convenient exit.
- *Stage 5*. At this stage, a brief violent exchange occurs. It may involve a fatal blow, a thrust with a knife, or the pulling of a trigger. Typically it is over quickly.
- *Stage 6*. The battle, such as it was, is over and the offender either flees or remains at the scene.

Luckenbill's work show us how murder can be understood as a social product. This does not imply an absence of guilt on the part of people who murder, and it is not offered as an excuse for killing. It does show that acts of deviance can be quite complex and can involve significant interactional dimensions.

Making Sense of the "Facts" of Deviant Behaviour

Sociologists interested in the study of deviant behaviour have repeatedly demonstrated that deviant acts—especially the kinds of acts that seem to concern the average member of the society most—are not randomly distributed in the population. Instead, people with some kinds of social and demographic characteristics seem much more likely to be involved in such behaviour than others. The task for sociological explanations that focus on the deviant act is to explain these levels of differential involvement.

Gender

It is well known that **gender** tends to correlate closely with a wide range of behaviours. This is no less true in the study of deviance than in the study of other areas in sociology. Males and females differ in terms of the amounts and the kinds of disapproved behaviours in which they engage.

Males, for instance, are more likely to be involved in a wide range of behaviours of which most members of Canadian society would say they disapprove. As illustrated by Table 6.2, males are much more likely to be involved in most types of criminal activity (crimes related to prostitution are one notable exception in this regard). The differential is most sizeable in the case of violence but is also very large in the case of other kinds of crime. While there has been some narrowing of the gender gap in recent years, crime remains very much a male-dominated activity (Hartnagel, 2000).

Table 6.2	**Adults Charged in Criminal Incidents, by Gender, 2001 (Percentages)**	
	Males	**Females**
Violence	85	15
Property	78	22
Other	85	15
Total	**83**	**17**

SOURCE: Statistics Canada, *Canadian Crime Statistics 2001* (Ottawa: Canadian Centre for Justice Statistics, 2002), 16–17.

Males are also more likely to consume both legal and illegal drugs, including tobacco, alcohol, marijuana, and cocaine (Miethe and McCorkle, 1998). In addition, males are more likely to commit suicide, and when they do so, they are more likely to use guns or explosives (Thio, 1998). Overall rates of mental illness do not differ markedly between men and women, although there are significant variations by type. Women are more likely to be diagnosed as suffering from depression and anxiety, while men are more likely to experience problems relating to various forms of addiction and psychosis (Blackwell, 1992).

Several feminist writers have argued that there has been a marked tendency in the sociological literature to systematically ignore the deviant behaviour of women (Belknap, 1996; Boritch, 1997; Chesney-Lind, 1997). To be sure, most of what is written about crime and deviance concerns the behaviour of men, both as the deviants and as the police and other agents of social control. Moreover, many sociologists have assumed that female deviant behaviour could be explained using the same theoretical ideas and models that have been used to make sense of male behaviour—a position with which many feminists do not agree (van Wormer and Bartollas, 2000).

The failure to be sufficiently attentive to the gendered nature of criminal and deviant behaviour has also been an empirical problem. Most research has dealt with the actions of men, either explicitly or implicitly. In the former case, sociologists tended, historically, not to be terribly interested in acts of crime or deviance that did not have a significant male dimension (Boritch, 1997). It was only through the work of feminist social critics that researchers came to focus on problems that affect women more directly. These include, for instance, various forms of deviance that tend to uniquely victimize women, such as intimate violence and sexual harassment (Chasteen, 2001; Loseke, 1992; Rose, 1974).

Age

Age, liked gender, tends to be strongly associated with many kinds of deviant behaviour (Tanner, 2001). Crime rates, for instance, tend to be greatest during the late teens and early adulthood and to decline very sharply after that (Hirschi and Gottfredson, 1985). This pattern characterizes even violence in the home: young husbands (those under 30) are much more likely than older husbands to treat their wives violently (Johnson, 1996). Of course, this pattern does not hold for all kinds of crime. White-collar crimes (professional fraud, cheating on taxes, and so on) tend to occur somewhat later in the life cycle (Gottfredson and Hirschi, 1990).

Alcohol use and illicit drug use are also more heavily concentrated among young people (Tremblay, 1999). But while suicide rates among young people are a cause of considerable concern, such rates actually tend to be lower among younger Canadians (see Figure 6.3). And though it has traditionally been argued that older people in society are most likely to experience a variety of forms of mental illness (Gomme, 2002), recent research casts doubt on that generalization and suggests in some cases that the elderly may be the least likely members of society to suffer from various types of mental disorder. These more recent studies indicate that rates of some forms of mental illness (especially depression) have increased substantially among teenagers and young adults in the last few decades (Thio, 1998).

Class and Ethnicity

As with gender and age, relationships between indicators of socio-economic disadvantage and various garden-variety forms of deviant behaviour are of considerable interest to sociologists. Many of the

studies on this subject say that poorer people and people from minority groups are more likely to be involved in many forms of crime and delinquency, to use drugs and alcohol, and to develop various kinds of mental illness. Indeed, a great deal of sociological theorizing about the "causes" of deviant behaviour has taken as its central issue the need to explain why social and economic precariousness is related to deviant outcomes. This is very clear, for instance, in most versions of strain theory.

However, there does not really exist a consensus in the research literature regarding how concepts such as poverty, economic inequality, ethnicity, or minority-group status should be measured for research purposes (Braithewaite, 1979; Hagan and Peterson, 1995; Wortley, 1999), and there is less consistency in research findings. While some studies seem to say that working-class youth are more likely to be delinquent, other studies tell us the opposite. As well, while minority-group status seems to be related to higher rates of crime in some cases, as with **First Nations** people, it seems to be related to lower rates of crime in others, as with Asian immigrants in British Columbia (Gordon and Nelson, 2000; LaPrairie, 2002).

Other interpretations of the significance of the relationship between social disadvantage and deviant behaviour point in the direction of a more general fault line that runs through the sociology of deviance. These other interpretations encourage us to ask different types of questions. Are poorer or minority people more likely to be deviant, or are they just more likely to get caught and labelled as "deviant"? Even more profoundly, do our definitions of what constitute crime and deviance themselves reflect class biases? Poor people, for instance, are less likely to commit many kinds of crimes, such as fraud and embezzlement. They are even less likely to manufacture faulty products, to engage in false advertising, to profit from political corruption, or to engage in various kinds of stock market swindles.

These observations suggest that while questions about who commits deviant acts and who does not are interesting and important, there is a need to move beyond them and to ask questions about the subjective character of deviance. Why are some ways of thinking, acting, and being more likely than others to excite indignation and disapproval, and why are some people more likely than others to become the objects of social control attention? It is to these questions that we now turn our attention.

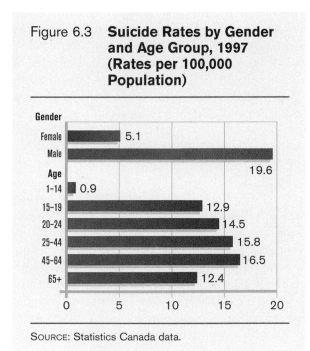

Figure 6.3 **Suicide Rates by Gender and Age Group, 1997 (Rates per 100,000 Population)**

Gender
- Female: 5.1
- Male: 19.6

Age
- 1-14: 0.9
- 15-19: 12.9
- 20-24: 14.5
- 25-44: 15.8
- 45-64: 16.5
- 65+: 12.4

SOURCE: Statistics Canada data.

The Sociology of Deviant Categories

As stated at the beginning of the chapter, the sociology of deviance is also the study of moral stratification. To call something or someone "deviant" is to articulate a judgment that that thing or person is disreputable. An important set of issues in the sociology of deviance relates to the creation of categories—some deviant and some not—in which people and actions are sorted (Loseke, 1999).

In the course of living our lives day to day, we tend to treat these distinctions as common sense. The deviant qualities of people and acts, we tend to convince ourselves, reside within the people and acts themselves. However, judged from another standpoint, known as **social constructionism** (Miller and Holstein, 1993; Spector and Kitsuse, 1977), this logic is flawed. Acts and people are not inherently deviant but are defined as such by those in society with the power to do so.

Proceeding from this assumption, we are led to another set of questions. For example, how do we make the moral distinctions that we make? This perspective maintains that there is nothing self-evident or commonsensical about the deviant quality of people and their behaviour. Instead, the deviant quality assigned to people and behaviour is itself problematic and requires investigation.

Further, we need to recognize that the character of social condemnation is fluid and dynamic over time (Curra, 2000). It is easy to think of behaviours that were once widely viewed as deviant but that have come to be seen as much less deviant in recent years. "Living together," having a child outside of marriage, or being gay might only a few years ago have been widely seen as grounds for social exclusion. While there is some resistance to these behaviours in the society at large (and a great of deal of resistance in some particular sectors of society), societal attitudes have moderated considerably.

At the same time, it is equally easy to think of many of example of ways of acting or ways of being that were once widely tolerated but that now seem to draw considerable disapproval. One clear example is cigarette smoking (Troyer and Markle, 1983; Tuggle and Holmes, 1999). Only a few decades ago, cigarette smoking was widely approved of, even seen as glamorous. People smoked on elevators, in restaurants, and around children—even while attending sociology classes. That view of smoking contrasts sharply with the present-day view. Today, smokers are pariahs in many circles, and their habit is the object of scorn. Increasingly, they are the objects of a variety of forms of legal and extra-legal control (Wagner, 1997). Other examples include drinking and driving (Gusfield, 1981), wife assault (Johnson, 1996), and sexual harassment (Rice, 1996).

The moral status of tobacco use has changed markedly over the years. Once considered largely harmless, even romantic, cigarette smoking is now viewed by many as highly deviant. (© Dick Hemingway)

Deviance as a Claims-Making Process

What are the sources of the distinctions that the members of a society make between what is and what is not deviant? Social constructionist writers understand this to be a **claims-making** process (Best, 2001; Spector and Kitsuse, 1977). This refers to the process by which groups assert grievances about the troublesome character of people or their behaviour. Claims-making thus involves the promotion of a particular moral vision of social life. In a practical sense, we recognize claims-making in many different sorts of activities. It includes voting for "reform" candidates in a local election, a debate about some exotic sexual practice on a daytime talk show, a protest march to call for the police to do something about local crime, and the testimony provided by experts before a parliamentary committee. In short, claims-making is anything anybody does to propagate a view of who or what is deviant and what needs to be done about it (Loseke, 1999).

As a social process, claims-making is directed toward the achievement of three broad types of objectives:

1. *Publicizing the problematic character of the people with the behaviour in question.* Before they come to see people as troublesome, the members of a society generally need to be convinced that there is some tangible reason to regard those in question as troublesome. Claims-makers may endeavour to convince us that deviants are dangerous or irresponsible or that their behaviour is contagious (Best, 1999). In many cases, there is no objective basis to the claim, but this does not mean that it is not understood by many as a valid statement about the world.

2. *Shaping a particular view of the problem.* Deviants can be defined in many different ways, and it matters greatly whether we see people as troubled or as troublesome (Gusfield, 1989). Generally, claims-makers not only want to convince us that certain people are a problem, they also want to convince us that they are problems of a particular type. "Problem drinking" for instance, can be constructed in many different ways (Holmes and Antell, 2001). We might see it as a sin, which implies that it is a religious problem. We might see it as a crime, which implies that it is a legal problem. Or we might see it as a sickness, which implies that it is a medical problem. In all cases the behaviour in question remains the same, and in all cases it is seen as deviant. What changes is the kind of deviant the problem drinker is understood to be. These differing constructions have very different implications for what it is we think we need to do about the deviant person.

3. *Building consensus around the new moral category.* Claims-makers endeavour to build widespread agreement about the correctness of a particular moral vision (Heimer, 2002). This is accomplished by winning the support of the media, officialdom, and the general public (Hilgartner and Bosk, 1988). As consensus is built, dissenting views become relegated to the margins of legitimate discourse. It is precisely the establishment of consensus and the marginalization of dissenting views that give the deviant categories in our society their common-sense character.

Who Are Claims-Makers?

The movement to "deviantize" (Schur, 1979) people and behaviour originates in the perceptions (however narrowly shared at the outset) that something is troubling and needs correction. Howard Becker (1963) coined the term *moral entrepreneur* to describe those who "discover" and attempt to publicize deviant conditions. Becker says that moral entrepreneurs are crusading reformers who are disturbed by some evil that they see in the world and who will not rest until something is done to correct it.

In the early stages, definitions of deviance are often promoted by those who have some direct connection to the problem. In the case of drinking and driving, for instance, claims-making to heavily criminalize this conduct originated with victim groups such as MADD (Mothers Against Drunk Driving), whose members had a powerful emotional stake in the issue (Reinarman, 1996). In contrast, many of those involved in the construction of deviance have no vested interest in or emotional connection to the problem or the outcome. Lawmakers, journalists, daytime talk show hosts, and the producers of television drama often play a very significant role in the promotion of particular designations of deviance (Altheide, 1997; Hilgartner and Bosk, 1988). However, their social distance from the issue is often greater that that of victims' groups, and for many of them, the construction of deviance is just another day at the office.

What Are *Claims*?

When social constructionists speak of *claims*, they are talking about the actual message content that conveys a moral vision of deviance and non-deviance. What do claims-makers say, for example, in interviews on television talk shows, in pamphlets, in newspaper editorials, and on picket signs to convey the message that something or someone deserves the appellation of "deviant"? The study of claims is the study of rhetorical communication, since such communications—by design or in effect—persuade audiences.

Successful claims-making rhetoric can demonstrate the gravity of a problem in several ways, including these:

- *Using compelling statistics.* Statistics are often used to impress upon consumers of the media the size of a problem and that the problem is getting worse over time (Best, 2001; Gilbert, 1997). Statistical estimates of a problem's dimensions that suggest that a large problem is getting worse legitimate concern and provide compelling evidence of the urgency of a problem.
- *Linking an emergent concern to problems already on the public agenda.* In this way, familiar moral language can be used to provide ready reference points for the emergent problem. For instance, because addiction is well recognized as a problem in North America, new problems are often described as "addictions." We use the term *addiction* in a very liberal way and speak of, for instance, "pornography addicts," "gambling addicts," and "Internet addiction" (Butters and Erickson, 2000).
- *Using emotionally compelling examples to typify the seriousness and character of the threat posed by the behaviour.* (See Bromley and Shupe, 1981.) For example, the killings at Columbine High School in Colorado are often used in a rhetorical way to exemplify the problem of school violence even though such incidents are extremely rare and most school crime in no way resembles this incident (Fox and Levin, 2001).

Deviance Ownership

Claims-making is not just about seeing particular types of people or behaviour as problems, it is also about seeing them as particular *kinds* of problems (Gusfield, 1989). What is at stake is the "ownership" of the problem: how a problem is framed determines who will be responsible for responding to or dealing with the problem (Sasson, 1995). If problem drinking is understood as a legal problem, we might expect the courts and police to do something about it. If it is understood as a religious problem, then we look to the clergy for solutions. If it understood as a medical problem, we turn to doctors and psychiatrists.

One dominant trend in the way we think about deviance solutions concerns *medicalization* (Conrad and Schneider, 1980; Green, 2000). Increasingly, we have come to think about a very wide range of behaviours as forms of medical disorder that require treatment rather than punishment (Dworkin, 2001). More and more, it seems we have come to use the language of sickness, health, and disease when talking about conditions as diverse as violence, gambling, obesity, drug use, underachievement, and rampant consumerism. It can be argued that this shift suggests a more benign approach to deviants, since it implies that individuals are not to blame for their behaviour; the stigma associated with deviant conduct is therefore reduced (Appleton, 1995). At the same time, it can be argued that medicalization encourages us to ignore structural contexts when we think about various kinds of deviance. In other words, medical models imply that these problems occur because individuals get "sick" and not because social structural conditions make some kinds of behaviour more likely.

Deviance and Social Conflict

Moral differentiation suggests processes of social conflict. Disagreement exists in society regarding who or what should be seen as disreputable (Hier, 2002). These conflicts are evident in the battle over abortion, the movement to legalize marijuana, and efforts to control cigarette smoking. In other cases, the conflict is less evident only because effective claims-making has resulted in consensus.

While sociology makes available to us a large number of versions of **conflict theory**, two broad types can be distinguished: conservative and radical (Williams and McShane, 1994). These theories suggest different ways of understanding the wider social dynamic of the claims-making process.

From the perspective of conservative conflict theory, social conflicts regarding the moral meaning of conduct emerge from diverse sources (Turk, 1976; Vold, 1958). As members of various ethnic, religious, professional, lifestyle, or cultural groups seek to pursue their social interests, they may come into conflict with other groups over scarce resources. In the context of such models, **power** is seen as relatively diffuse and thus not concentrated in any one sector of the

Deviance has both objective and subjective dimensions. It is one thing to ask why people smoke marijuana, another to ask why doing so is considered deviant. CP/Maclean's (Phil Snell)

society (Gusfield, 1963). Instead, various **status groups** come into conflict, often over specific issues. From this perspective, the study of moral differentiation is the study of how some groups in society are able to influence systems of social control so as to allow them to compete more effectively in their struggle to achieve their goals.

There may be many ways in which the creation of new categories of deviance may facilitate the pursuit of social goals. Social control bureaucracies may find that the resources made available to them become more plentiful when they can identify new forms of danger that require control (Becker, 1963; Jenkins, 1994). Alternatively, new or struggling medical specialities can find their social status enhanced if the members of a society become convinced that they are indispensable to the solution of some pressing social problem (Pfohl, 1977).

Often the struggle to define deviance reflects a much more evident cultural difference regarding what is or what is not moral. Contemporary debates over abortion, for instance, can be seen as debates about who will, in the end, get to call whom a "deviant." In a similar way, those whose cultural or religious beliefs lead them to oppose a movement for gay rights may think of gay people as deviants. At the same time, gays and lesbians (and others in society) may think of those who actively (or even violently) oppose the movement for gay rights as suffering from a psychological malady known as *homophobia*. Both examples suggest status struggles over whose moral vision shall prevail

and, conversely, over who shall be thought of as deviant.

In contrast, radical conflict theory draws on the Marxian understanding of society (Spitzer, 1975). Thus, it views the economic organization of society as the key to understanding moral stratification. From this point of view, the **social construction** of deviance must be understood as reflecting the economic realities of capitalism and the class exploitation capitalism engenders.

It is important to note that, from a Marxian position, it is the internal logic of capitalism that gives deviance both its objective and its subjective character. For example, capitalism requires a large pool of labour that can be exploited by keeping wages low. But this means that there will always be more workers than jobs and that some people will of necessity be marginalized. These marginalized populations will have little stake in the system and will be at greater risk of criminal involvement and of being labelled as criminal.

The Sociology of Deviant Stigma

A third key area of study in the sociology of deviance concerns the ways in which deviant stigmas are applied to people and how stigma is managed (see, for example, Table 6.3). This body of research and theory focuses our attention on the social interaction between those who exercise social control and those who are thought of in society as disreputable. In this respect, questions about the application and consequences of deviant stigma tend to be more microthan macrosociological.

The Process of Labelling

People come to be seen as deviant because of what others believe they have done or what others believe them to be. The labels of "deviant" that are assigned to people are not benign. Rather, they are charged with a great deal of emotion. Such labels sort through the thousands of acts in which a person has engaged and indicate that the person's identity is best understood in terms of the act according to which the label is affixed (Erikson, 1966).

The assignment of stigma suggests what sociologists refer to as a **master status**. This means that the label of deviant overrides all other status considerations (Becker, 1963). To be known as a murderer, for example, is to possess a status characteristic that

Table 6.3 **Types of Deviant Behaviour**

Howard Becker (1963) suggested that once we recognize that deviant stigma is separable from the deviant act, it is possible to recognize at least four types of deviants. These types are created by the contrast between what people actually do (breaking rules or keeping them) and what they are perceived as (deviant or not deviant).

| | | Behaviour | |
		Obedient	Rule-Breaking
Perception	Perceived as deviant	Falsely accused	Pure deviant
	Not perceived as deviant	Conforming	Secret deviant

trumps any other status characteristics the person might have. Whatever else one might be (bright, interesting, poor, blond, left-handed), one is a murderer first.

Sociologists use the term **status degradation ceremony** to refer to the rituals during which the status of "deviant" is conferred (Garfinkel, 1956). These ceremonies, like other public ceremonies such as marriage or graduation, publicly and officially acknowledge a shift in social **roles** and the emergence of a new identity. Status degradation ceremonies, including incompetency hearings, psychiatric examinations, and courtroom trials, mark the movement from one social position to another as the individual at the centre of the ritual is officially declared deviant. While we have designed ceremonies to move people into the status of "deviant," we don't have comparable ceremonies to move them out of these statuses and back to "normality."

Resistance to Labelling

Of course, many people do not submit willingly to the imposition of labels of deviance. The ability of some in society to confer the status of "deviant" on others reflects differentials in social power. When people have access to power resources, they are able to more effectively negotiate the status of "deviant" (Pfuhl and Henry, 1993). A high-priced legal team (like the O.J. Simpson "dream team") can effectively counter-challenge efforts by the state to impose the status of "deviant." Plea-bargain negotiations, as the name implies, suggest straightforward attempts to negotiate moral status.

People might use a range of other strategies to avoid or negotiate a label of deviance. One obvious method involves efforts to undermine social control efforts through evasion. Such statuses are negotiated most effectively, perhaps, by avoiding their assignment in the first place. "Successful" deviants learn to engage in prohibited conduct in ways that decrease the likelihood of getting caught (Becker, 1963).

Individuals also try to avoid or negotiate stigma through what Goffman calls *performance* (Goffman, 1959). Many of us are quite explicitly aware of the dramatic roles we might perform if we are stopped by the police officer who suspects we have been speeding; the performance is intended to neutralize the efforts of the police to impose a deviant designation (Piliavin and Briar, 1964). Under some conditions, people use what are called *disclaimer mannerisms*. These are actions intended to signal to agents of social control that they are not the appropriate targets of deviant attribution.

Deviant Careers and Deviant Identities

One important potential consequence of the labelling process is what is known as *deviancy amplification*: the ironic situation in which the very attempt to control deviance makes deviance more likely (Lemert, 1951; Tannenbaum, 1938).

Efforts to describe how labelling processes result in more rather than less deviance usually distinguish between primary and secondary deviance (Lemert 1951; McLorg and Taub, 1987). *Primary deviance* is the deviance in which we all engage from time to time and that has no real consequence for the ways in which we see ourselves or for the ways in which other people see us. For instance, all of us from time to time might lie, might cheat, might drink too much, or might engage in some other prohibited behaviour. *Secondary deviance*, in contrast, is marked by a life organized around the facts of deviance. Secondary deviance suggests emergence in a deviant role rather than ephemeral acts of deviance. It is one thing to steal on

6.3

Sociology in Action
Disclaimer Mannerisms in University Examinations

Sociologists Daniel Albas and Cheryl Albas (1993) undertook a study of how students attempt to distance themselves from charges of academic dishonesty while writing examinations. Data of several sorts were collected, including interviews with students and observations of students writing exams. The authors note that people writing examinations are at high risk of stigmatization. Invigilators patrol the rooms on the lookout for suspicious behaviour. Too often, neither the professor (who may or may not be at the exam) nor graduate assistants have any direct knowledge of the individuals writing the exam. For these reasons, students take many steps to ensure that they will not be falsely accused of cheating.

The authors were able to define two major types of strategies: actions that students take and actions that they attempt to avoid taking.

Actions taken include the following:

- *Picayune overconformity with regulations.* This involves the demonstration of conformity with even the most minor examination rules. Students are careful, for instance, to hand in their papers before gathering up their possessions to leave. In this way, there can be no suspicion that anything untoward is occurring. A student who needs to blow his or her nose will be sure to wave the tissue around first so it is clear that it is nothing other than a tissue.

- *The expression of repression of creature releases.* Creature releases are those aspects of the self that steal through the facade of social control, including sneezes and yawns. A student who needs to use the bathroom during the exam might make very exaggerated gestures to impress upon invigilators the urgency of the situation.

- *Shows of innocence.* Students know, for instance, that a lack of activity might be read as indicative of a lack of preparation. So when they are not writing, they might be underlining or circling words or phrases on the exam sheet.

Actions avoided include these:

- *Control of eyes.* Students know that they are not supposed to have roving eyes, so they are careful where they look. One preferred strategy is to stare at the ceiling or the head of the person behind whom the student is sitting.

- *Control of notes.* Students might frisk themselves before they enter the exam room to ensure that they are not carrying anything with them that could get them into trouble.

- *Morality of place.* Students worry that where they sit can send a message about their trustworthiness. A student might be careful, therefore, not to sit next to a very good student or someone whom they believe is perceived as a potential cheater.

occasion; it is quite another to be a thief. While all of us might tell an occasional lie, most of us do not think of ourselves or are thought of by others as liars.

Some researchers have asked what is it that sometimes turns primary deviance into secondary deviance. The answer is societal reaction. It is argued that the ways in which agents of social control respond to initial acts of deviance—through stereotypes, rejection, the degradation of status—can actually make future deviance more rather than less likely (Tannenbaum, 1938).

One of the key intervening mechanisms in this process, it is argued, is the transformation of the **self**. Consistent with social psychological theories (such as the one advanced by Charles Horton Cooley, 1902) of how the self emerges and is maintained, labelling theorists have argued that individuals who are consistently stigmatized may come to accept others' definition of their deviant identity. To the extent that individuals increasingly come to see themselves as others see them, they may become much more likely to behave in ways that are consistent with the label of "deviant."

In a sense, individuals become committed to a life of deviance largely because others have expected them to. Deviance becomes a self-fulfilling prophecy (Tannenbaum, 1938).

Managing Stigma

How do those who have been labelled "deviant" manage these labels? People may employ a wide variety of strategies that allow them to control information about their deviant identity or to alter the meaning of their stigma so as to reduce the significance of the deviance in their lives (Miller and Kaiser, 2001; Park, 2002).

In any discussion of stigma management, it is important to distinguish between the *discreditable* and the *discredited* (Mankoff, 1971). In the former case, we are talking about people who might become discredited if knowledge about their stigma were to become public. In the latter case, the stigma is either evident or it can be assumed to be known.

Because the discreditable and the discredited face different sorts of problems, they have differing options available to them for the management of stigma (James and Craft, 2002). For the discreditable, the pressing need is to control information others have about them. If people have a kind of stigma others may not know about, they face the constant worry that others they care about may reject them if information about this stigma becomes public (James and Craft, 2002). Victims of a sexual crime, those suffering from certain stigmatized diseases, and those who hold unpopular religious beliefs need, in many cases, to keep aspects of their lives secret because they fear the rejection of others.

In other cases, the discreditable may attempt to "pass"—to fraudulently assume an identity other than the one for which they might be stigmatized. A gay man, for instance, might "stay in the closet" and so hope to convince others that he is "straight." An individual whose unpopular political opinions are kept secret may laugh publicly at the jokes directed at people who think the same way that she does.

The discredited face a different problem. Their stigma tends to be apparent, so there is no need to keep it secret. Rather, they need to restrict its relevance to the ways in which others treat them. One obvious way in which this might be accomplished is through some form of purification, in which the stigmatized individual attempts to convince others that he or she has left a deviant identity behind (Pfuhl and Henry, 1993). Some sort of redefinition of the self is intended to restrict the interactional rele-

vance of the stigma by locating it in the past. This occurs when stigmatized individuals tell others that they "got religion" or that they have "finally grown up." One of our contemporary definitions of a hero is someone who has left a deviant stigma behind. Helen Keller and Christopher Reeves, for instance, are thought of as heroes largely because they rose above the stigmatizing character of particular physical conditions.

The discredited may also invoke some collective form of stigma management. This means that individuals who are the bearers of stigma may join together to form some sort of association intent on changing public perceptions of their disvalued character. Organizations intended to "undeviantize" behaviour have been formed in recent years, including the National Organization for the Reform of Marijuana Laws (NORML) and COYOTE (Call Off Your Old Tired Ethics), which promotes the rights of sex workers. Collective stigma management may involve attempts to influence media coverage of the group in question or the use of terms used to describe members of the group (Bullock and Cubert, 2002). For instance, groups organized around collective stigma management have advocated that the terms "disabled," "retarded," and "AIDS victim" be replaced in popular and official discourse with "differently abled," "developmentally delayed," and "AIDS survivor," respectively (Titchkosky, 2001).

Conclusion

Our experience with deviance reflects the influence of the cultural context and the historical period in which we live. As times change, so do the categories of people and behaviour society finds troublesome. While gay and lesbian lifestyles were once viewed as highly deviant, today they are seen as less so. While drunk driving, wife assault, and cigarette smoking were once regarded as normal, they are now viewed as highly deviant. Deviance is thus a dynamic process, and the future will present further permutations and innovations. By way of example, we need only think about the large number of newly constructed forms of deviance that we already associate with computer usage, such as cyberporn, cyberstalking, and Internet addiction.

In the most general terms, the sociology of deviance is concerned with the study of the relationships between people who think, act, or appear in disvalued ways and those who seek to control them

(Sacco, 1992). It seeks to understand the origins, the character, the consequences, and the broader social contexts of these relationships.

Deviance can be thought of as having two dimensions: the objective and the subjective. The objective aspect is the behaviour, condition, or cognitive style itself. The subjective aspect is the collective understanding of the behaviour, condition, or cognitive style as disreputable. A comprehensive sociology of deviance needs to consider both dimensions. Thus, we want to know why some people rather than others act in ways the society forbids, but we also want to know why some ways of acting rather than others are forbidden.

Correspondingly, it is possible to identify three major types of questions around which theory and research in the sociology of deviance are organized. First, how do we understand the social and cultural factors that make prohibited behaviour possible? Strain theory argues that people engage in deviant behaviour because it is often a form of problem solving, cultural support theories focus on the ways in which people acquire definitions of deviant conduct that are supportive of such behaviour, and control theories maintain that deviance results when the factors that would check or contain it are absent.

Second, what is and what is not viewed as disreputable is not obvious and there is a need to explain the prevailing system of moral stratification. Definitions of deviance emerge from a process of claims-making. It is the establishment of consensus around such definitions that gives categories of deviance such a taken-for-granted quality.

Finally, we need to ask questions about the application and management of deviant stigma. Being labelled "deviant" is a complex process that creates a large number of problems for the person who is the object of social control attention. It is important, therefore, to understand who gets labelled and how people cope with social control. In particular, we need to be alert to the manner in which the imposition of labels can worsen the very problems that the application of social control is meant to correct.

☐ Questions for Critical Thought

1. What images of crime and deviance dominate coverage in the local media of the community in which you live? What sorts of images do they create of troubled and troublesome people?

2. Why do people cheat on university examinations? How might this question be answered by proponents of strain, cultural support, and control theories?

3. In your view, why are young males so much more likely than other groups in society to engage in a wide range of behaviours that many in society find troublesome?

4. What evidence do you see in your own social environment of the disvalued character of cigarette smoking and smokers?

5. Aside from the examples given in the text, can you suggest behaviours or conditions that have undergone a shift in moral status in the last few years? How would you account for these changes?

6. How might Marxian and Weberian conflict theorists differ in their interpretations of the legal and moral battle in our society regarding the use of "soft" illegal drugs, such as marijuana?

7. How might you explain to an interested layperson the difference between the ways in which sociologists think about deviance and the ways in which journalists do?

8. In your opinion, does it make sense to speak of something called "positive deviance"? Why or why not?

□ Recommended Readings

Joel Best and David Luckenbill, *Organizing Deviance* **(Englewood Cliffs, NJ: Prentice-Hall, 1982).**

This book offers a systematic treatment of how deviance is organized. The authors discuss both the organization of deviants and the organization of deviant transactions.

Deborah Brock, *Making Work, Making Trouble: Prostitution as a Social Problem* **(Toronto: University of Toronto Press, 1998).**

This study provides a very comprehensive treatment of the social problem of prostitution in Canada. The author's analysis illustrates the value of a constructionist approach to the study of specific forms of social deviance.

John Curra, *The Relativity of Deviance* **(Thousand Oaks, CA: Sage, 2000).**

The aim of this book is to show that deviance cannot be considered an absolute and that what is subject to social control varies by time and place. The analysis of necessity calls into question many common assumptions about the nature of problematic people.

Barry Glassner, *The Culture of Fear: Why Americans Are Afraid of the Wrong Things* **(New York: Basic Books, 1999).**

An informed and highly readable discussion of why people fear what they fear. The author attempts to demonstrate that there is a disjunction between the harms we perceive and the harms our social environments actually present to us.

Erving Goffman, *Stigma: Notes on the Management of Spoiled Identity* **(Englewood Cliffs, NJ: Prentice-Hall, 1963).**

This is the classic discussion of how people who are defined as "deviants" by the society in which they live manage stigma. The book was formative in the development of the sociology of labels of deviance.

John Hagan and Bill McCarthy, *Mean Streets: Youth Crime and Homelessness* **(Cambridge: Cambridge University Press, 1998).**

Hagan and McCarthy present an empirical study of the problem of crime and violence among homeless youth in Toronto and Vancouver. The study draws insights from the major theories of deviant behaviour discussed in this chapter.

Kevin D. Haggerty, *Making Crime Count* **(Toronto: University of Toronto Press, 2001).**

This is a field study of the agency within Statistics Canada that produces crime statistics. The study nicely illustrates that the counting of deviants, like the making of deviants, is a social process.

Holly Johnson, *Dangerous Domains: Violence Against Women in Canada* **(Scarborough, ON: Nelson Canada, 1996).**

Johnson pays considerable attention in this detailed treatment to the Statistics Canada Violence Against Women Survey.

□ Recommended Web Sites

Access to Justice Network
www.acjnet.org

The Access to Justice Network provides comprehensive discussions of a wide range of issues relating to social control and social justice in Canada.

Canadian Criminal Justice Association
http://home.istar.ca/~ccja/angl/index.shtml

This site contains a great deal of useful information relating to the operation of the Canadian criminal justice system.

Canadian Sociology and Anthropology Association
http://alcor.concordia.ca/~csaa1/

This Web site contains the rules, regulations, and principles relating to the ethics of professional sociological research.

Crimetheory.com

http://crimetheory.com

> This site provides a very comprehensive discussion of deviance and crime theory for educational and research purposes.

Florida State University School of Criminology and Criminal Justice

www.criminology.fsu.edu/cjlinks/default.htm

> This collection of links relating to the sociologies of crime, deviance, and social control is extremely comprehensive.

Prostitution Issues

www.bayswan.org/student.html

> This "student-friendly" page offers educational materials regarding prostitution. Of particular interest are the documents that offer a redefinition of the moral character of such behaviour.

Society for the Study of Social Problems

http://itc.utk.edu/sssp/

> This is the main page for the Society for the Study of Social Problems (SSSP). The journal of this society, *Social Problems*, has been very influential in the development of the sociology of deviance.

Statistics Canada

www.statcan.ca

> This is the main page for Canada's national statistical agency, Statistics Canada. Many different sorts of reports, tables, and graphs relating to a variety of forms of deviance can be located at this site.

part three

> > >

Social Institutions

In this section we will see that society's major social institutions—families, the educational system, the economy and workplaces, health issues, politics, and religion—persist, change, and interconnect with one another in complicated patterns. As always, the sociological imagination helps us see these linkages and the ways that large changes often result from millions of much smaller changes.

7

Maureen Baker

> > >

Families

© Bill Whittman

☐ Learning Objectives

In this chapter, you will:

- learn to differentiate popular myths about family life from actual research results

- gain a clearer understanding of variations in family life

- understand how sociologists have conceptualized and explained family patterns

- gain some insight into several contentious issues in Canadian families

- identify current demographic trends in Canadian families

- understand how predictions are made about family life in the future

Introduction

The media often dwell on the negative side of family life by highlighting child abuse, custody disputes, adolescent behavioural problems, and overstressed parents. Yet both public polls and sociological research indicate that most Canadians value their families and that young people expect to develop a meaningful relationship with an intimate partner, raise children, and live within a stable family for most of their lives (McDaniel and Tepperman, 2000). Ideally, family life can contribute to personal development and can provide companionship, love, sexual expression, children, care, a sense of belonging, and shared resources. Yet some people spend years of their lives with people they resent and seem to fight more with family members than with friends or acquaintances.

Governments typically encourage heterosexual marriage and childbearing because they need future citizens, taxpayers, voters, consumers, and labour-force members to continue the nation. Both governments and employers rely on parents to produce children, to socialize and discipline them to become future citizens and employees, to encourage both young people and adults to live law-abiding lives, and to provide the necessary recuperation that enables people to return each day to school or work.

Intimate relationships remain important both to individuals and to the larger society, but family life for most Canadians has changed considerably during the past 30 years (Baker, 2001a). Demographic research indicates that since the 1970s, young people have been delaying marriages while they gain an education and prepare for paid employment. More couples now live together without legal marriage. Couples are producing fewer children, who spend more daytime hours with non-family care providers while their parents work for pay. Remarriages form a larger percentage of all marriages as relationships now have a higher probability of ending in separation or divorce, and an increasing proportion of children are raised in stepfamilies. People tend to live longer, but more people are living alone, especially before marriage, after separation and divorce, and after widowhood.

This chapter defines *families* and outlines some of the variation in family structure and practices. The different ways that sociologists have discussed and explained family patterns are introduced before we turn our attention to five issues in family life: sharing domestic work, low fertility and assisted conception, child care concerns, the impact of divorce and repartnering on children, and wife abuse. Some general comments are made about family policies before turning to a prediction of what families will be like in the future.

Family Variations

What Are Families?

Many different definitions of *family* have been used in academic and government research, as well in as the delivery of government programs. Most definitions focus on legal obligations and family structure rather than on how people feel about each other or on what services programs provide. These definitions always include heterosexual couples and single parents sharing a home with their children, but not all definitions encompass same-sex couples. Most definitions include dependent children, while some also take into account childless couples or those whose children have left home. Still others extend the definition of family to grandparents, aunts, uncles, and cousins who are sharing a dwelling.

Sociologists and anthropologists used to talk about "the family" as a monolithic **social institution** with one acceptable structure and common behavioural patterns (Eichler, 1997). Academic researchers used to assume that family members were related by blood, marriage, or adoption and that they shared a dwelling, earnings, and other resources; that couples maintained sexually exclusive relationships, reproduced, and raised children together; and that family members cherished and protected each other. Nevertheless, academics have always differentiated between **nuclear families**, which consist of parents and their children sharing a dwelling, and **extended families**, which consist of several generations or adult siblings with their spouses and children who share a dwelling and resources. Both kinds of families continue to be a part of Canadian life.

The most prevalent definition used in policy research is Statistics Canada's **census family**, which includes married couples and cohabiting couples who have lived together for longer than one year, with or without never-married children, as well as single parents living with never-married children. This definition says nothing about the larger kin group of aunts, uncles, and grandparents, or about love, emotion, caring, or providing household services. Yet a common definition must be agreed upon when taking a **census** or initiating policy research.

IN THE FIRST PERSON

I first became interested in sociology after I worked for a sociologist as a research assistant at the University of Toronto in 1968. I was just completing my second year of university. That work experience and more undergraduate sociology courses led to several similar jobs working for sociology professors, who encouraged me to continue with graduate studies. Since completing my doctorate in sociology at the University of Alberta in 1974, I have worked in three different countries (Australia, Canada, and New Zealand) as a university teacher, freelance consultant, parliamentary researcher, and social policy advisor. – MAUREEN BAKER

The Canadian government also uses the concept of **household** in gathering statistics relating to family and personal life. *Household* refers to people sharing a dwelling, whether or not they are related by blood, adoption, or marriage. For example, a boarder might be part of the household but not necessarily part of the family. A gay or lesbian couple might also be considered by the government to be a household, even though they might be living as a married couple. Table 7.1 shows how the Canadian government categorizes families.

In a culturally diverse society such as Canada, it is inaccurate to talk about "the family" as though a single type of family exists or ever did exist. In fact, different cultural groups tend to organize their families differently, depending on cultural traditions, religious beliefs, socio-economic situation, immigrant or indigenous status, and historical experiences, though most Canadians live in nuclear families comprising parents and their children (Vanier Institute of the Family, 2000).

Nevertheless, the extended family, in which several generations (or siblings and their spouses and children) share a residence and co-operate economically, remains important as a living arrangement as well as as a support group, especially among recent immigrants from the Middle East or South Asia. Even when family members do not share a residence, relatives may live next door or in the same neighbourhood, visit regularly, telephone daily, assist with child care, provide economic and emotional support, and help find employment and accommodation for one another (Paletta, 1992). When relatives do not share a household but live close by and rely heavily on one another, they are said to be a **modified extended family**.

In the 1950s, American sociologists lamented the isolation of the modern nuclear family, suggesting that extended families used to be more prevalent prior to industrialization (Parsons and Bales, 1955). Since then, historians have found that nuclear families were always the most prevalent living arrangement in Europe and North America (Goldthorpe, 1987; Nett, 1981), but extended families were and still are quite prevalent among certain cultural groups, such as some **First Nations** peoples, Southern Europeans, and some Asians. They are also more prevalent among those with lower incomes and at certain stages of the family life cycle, for example, in order to provide low-cost accommodation and practical support for young cash-strapped couples, lone mothers after separation, or frail elderly parents after widowhood.

Table 7.1	**Percentages of Families in Canada by Type, 1996ª**
Married couples with children	45.1
Married couples without children	28.5
Common-law couples with children	5.5
Common-law couples without children	6.2
Lone parents with children (total)	14.5
Male lone parents	2.5
Female lone parents	12.0

ª Percentages do not add up to 100 because of rounding.
SOURCE: Vanier Institute for the Family, *Profiling Canada's Families II* (Ottawa: Vanier Institute of the Family, 2000), 31.

Many immigrants come to Canada from countries where people live in extended families, yet the percentage of "multi-family households" (a term used by Statistics Canada that approximates an extended family) declined from 6.7 per cent in 1951 to 1.1 per cent in 1986, when immigration rates were high (Ram, 1990: 44). The explanation for this decline is that most Canadians considered living alone more acceptable and feasible and that immigrants tend to change their family practices to fit in with the host country. In a recent study of immigrants who came to Canada in 1985, 43 per cent lived with established relatives in 1986, but this declined to 26 per cent by 1996 (Thomas, 2001: 18). In contrast, only 11 per cent of Canadian-born people lived with relatives in 1986 compared to 13 per cent in 1996. Living with relatives was more prevalent among female immigrants and among those with lower educational qualifications and lower incomes (Thomas, 2001: 21).

In this chapter, the term *families* will be continually used in the plural to indicate the existence of different family structures and many acceptable sociological definitions. Qualified phrases, such as "male-breadwinner families," "lesbian families," and "stepfamilies," will be used for clarification. Although sociological definitions formerly focused on *who* constitutes a family, more researchers and theorists now emphasise *what* makes a family. This approach downplays the sexual preference of the couple and the legality of the relationship, focusing instead on patterns of caring and intimacy (Eichler, 1997).

Monogamy Versus Polygamy

When George Murdock completed his *World Ethnographic Sample* back in 1949, he noted that only about 20 per cent of the 554 societies he studied could be designated as strictly monogamous. In Canada and most industrialized countries, monogamy—being legally married to one spouse at a time—is both social custom and law. Yet many Canadians marry more than once over their lifespan, which is called **serial monogamy**. In Murdock's study, most societies permitted **polygyny**—being legally married to more than one wife at a time—and were characterized by a mixture of polygyny and monogamy.

In some African and Islamic nations, polygyny continues to be practised by wealthier men who can afford to support more than one wife. Wives in polygynous marriages may welcome a new wife to help with household duties and child care, to share work in the fields, or to provide companionship (Leslie and Korman, 1989).

Polygyny is much more prevalent than **polyandry**, the practice of being legally married to more than one husband at a time. The underlying reasons are probably that only one male is needed to impregnate several wives, that questions of paternity and inheritance would arise with more than one husband, and that men have the power to ensure that family practices suit their interests (Baker, 2001a). In recent years, **polygamy**—marriage to more than one spouse at a time—has been prohibited by law in all

7.1

Global Issues
A Maori Lone-Mother Family on Social Assistance, New Zealand

"From Friday to Sunday it's pretty much mayhem here. I can have anything up to thirteen kids. Nieces, nephews, the *mokos* [grandchildren], the neighbours. Last weekend I had their baby, a 15-month-old baby from next door. Because they were having a big party and they were out of babysitters and I said, well, just chuck him over the fence and we'll be right and she can sleep here the night so you can . . . pick her up in the morning. So they did that. My niece had to go to a funeral and she's got a 3-week-old baby and she popped her over to me with a little bottle of breast milk as well. So I had those two babies and . . . my son had his friend over for the night because his mother was next door partying and so while everybody does their thing, I have the kids and I had another little girl 'cause her mother was there too and I don't really know them."

———

SOURCE: Maureen Baker, personal interview, 2002.

Western nations because of the assumed difficulties of providing adequate financial and emotional support for more than one partner and because of Christian ideas of sexual exclusivity.

Arranged Versus Free-Choice Marriage

Marriages continue to be arranged in many parts of the world in order to enhance family resources, reputation, and alliances and because parents feel more qualified to choose their children's partners. The family of either bride or groom may make initial arrangements, but marriage brokers or intermediaries with extensive contacts are occasionally used to help families find suitable mates for their offspring.

Marriages are sometimes arranged for Middle Eastern and East Asian immigrants living in Canada. These arrangements may involve returning to the home country to marry a partner selected by family members still living there, or a man and a woman from the same cultural group, living in Canada, may be introduced to each other by family members and may be encouraged to marry. Young people expect to have veto power if they strongly object to their family's choice, but in the home country considerable pressure exists to abide by the judgment of elders (Nanda, 1991).

Family solidarity, financial security, and potential heirs are more important in arranged marriages than

sexual attraction or love between the young people (Baker, 2001a). New marital partners are urged to respect each other, and it is hoped that love will develop after marriage. Often, arranged marriages are more stable than free-choice unions because both families have a stake in marriage stability. Furthermore, divorce may be legally restricted, especially for women, and may involve mothers relinquishing custody of their children. In addition, women cannot always support themselves outside marriage in some of these societies.

A **dowry** is sometimes used to attract a higher-status husband, to clinch a marriage agreement between the two families, to contribute to the establishment of the new household, and to furnish a married woman with "insurance" money in case of divorce or premature widowhood. Under this system, families with marriageable daughters must show families with eligible sons that they can provide money or property upon their daughter's marriage. If a woman has a large dowry, she can find a "better" husband, which usually means one who is relatively wealthy, healthy, well educated, and from a respected family. However, the dowry system has been a financial burden for poorer families with several daughters and tends to encourage a preference for sons. For these reasons, the dowry system has been outlawed in some countries, such as India, though it continues to operate clandestinely in rural areas (Baker, 2001a; Nanda, 1991).

Marriages continue to be arranged in many parts of the world in order to enhance family resources, reputation, and alliances. Family solidarity, financial security, and potential heirs are important in arranged marriages.
(© Dick Hemingway)

In other societies that practised arranged marriage (such as eastern Indonesia), the groom's family was expected to pay the bride's parents a **bride price** for permission to marry their daughter. If the bride was beautiful or came from a wealthy or well-respected family, the price would rise. If the groom and his family were short of cash or property, the bride price could sometimes be paid through the groom's labour.

Although dowries and bride prices are associated with arranged marriages, free-choice marriages have retained symbolic remnants of these practices. For example, trousseaus, honeymoons, and the wedding itself are remnants of dowries. The engagement ring and wedding band given to the bride by the groom are remnants of a bride price.

Patterns of Authority and Descent

Most family systems designate a "head," who makes major decisions and represents the group to the outside world. In both Western and Eastern societies, the oldest male is typically the family head, in a system referred to as **patriarchy**. An authority system in which women are granted more power than men is a *matriarchy*, but matriarchal systems are rare. Some black families in the Caribbean and the United States have been referred to as matriarchal, or at least **matrifocal** (Smith, 1996), as has been the Tchambuli people of New Guinea (Mead, 1935). In both examples, wives and mothers make a considerable contribution to family income and resources as well as to decision making. Although Canadian families used to be patriarchal, men and women now have equal legal rights and men are no longer automatically viewed as family heads. However, in some cultural communities, men are still regarded as family heads.

When young people marry, they usually consider their primary relationship to be with each other rather than with either set of parents or siblings. In most cases, however, the newly married pair is expected to maintain contact with both sides of the family and to participate in family gatherings, and could inherit from either side of the family. This situation is termed a **bilateral descent pattern**. In other cases, the bride and groom are considered to be members of only one kin group, in a system called **patrilineal descent** if they belong to the groom's family, **matrilineal descent** if they belong to the bride's. Patterns of descent may determine where the couple live, how they address members of each other's family, what surname their children will receive, and from whom they inherit.

In Canadian families, bilateral descent is common for kinship and inheritance, but patrilineal descent has been retained for surnames in some provinces. The surname taken by a wife and by the couple's children has traditionally been the husband's name—a symbol of his former status as head of the new household. This tradition has been changed in Quebec, where brides are required to retain their family name. In Ontario, brides have a choice between keeping their family name and taking their husband's name. Where there is some legal choice, couples may also abide by their cultural traditions.

Explaining Family Patterns and Practices

All social studies are based on underlying philosophical assumptions about what motivates human society and what is important to emphasize in research. These assumptions, often called *theoretical frameworks*, cannot be proven or disproven but guide our research and help to explain our observations (Klein and White, 1996). In this section, several theoretical frameworks used to study families will be examined, including their basic premises, strengths, and weaknesses.

The Political Economy Approach

The basic thesis of the political economy approach is that people's relation to wealth, production, and power influences the way they view the world and live their lives. Family formation, interpersonal relations, lifestyle, and well-being are all affected by events in the broader society, such as economic cycles, working conditions, laws, and government programs. This perspective originates in the nineteenth-century work of German political philosophers Karl Marx (1818–83) and Friedrich Engels (1820–95). In *The Origin of the Family, Private Property and the State* ([1882] 1942), Engels discussed how family life in Europe was transformed as economies changed from hunting-and-gathering societies, to horticultural, to pre-industrial, and finally to industrial societies.

The political economy approach has been debated and modified over the years. Political economists argue that social life always involves conflict, especially between the people who have wealth and power and make social policies and people who do not.

Conflicting interests remain the major force behind societal change. In the nineteenth century, men's workplaces were removed from the home, which gradually eroded patriarchal authority and encouraged families to adapt to the employer's needs. Furthermore, many of the goods and services that people formerly had produced at home for their own consumption were eventually manufactured more cheaply in factories. This meant that families eventually became units of shared income and consumption rather than units of production. Once the production of most goods and services took place outside the home, people began to see the family as private and separate from the public world of business and politics. Nevertheless, unpaid domestic labour helps keep wages low and profits high (Bradbury, 2001; Fox, 1980; Luxton, 1980).

The impact of industrialization and workplace activities on family life become the focal point of the political economy approach, as well as the belief that economic changes transform ways of viewing the world. Political economists would argue, for example, that the surge of married women into the labour force after the 1960s occurred mainly for economic rather than ideological or feminist reasons. The service sector of the economy expanded with changes in domestic and foreign markets, requiring new workers. While married women had always worked as a reserve labour force, the creation of new job opportunities, as well as inflation and the rising cost of living, encouraged more wives and mothers to accept paid work. These labour market changes led to new **ideologies** about family and parenting. Political economists focus on the impact of the economy on family life, on relations between **the state** and the family, and on the social conflict arising from these political and economic changes. In doing so, they downplay voluntary behaviour and interpersonal relations.

Structural Functionalism

The basic assumption of **structural functionalism** is that behaviour is governed more by social expectations and unspoken rules than by personal choice. Individuals cannot behave any way they want but must abide by societal or cultural guidelines learned early in life. Deviant behaviour that violates rules is always carefully controlled.

Within this approach, "the family" is viewed as a major social institution that provides individuals with emotional support, love and companionship, sexual expression, and children. Parents help to maintain social order through socializing and disciplining their children. Families co-operate economically and help each other through hard times by sharing resources. They often protect their members from outsiders. Finally, people acquire money and property through inheritance from family members, which suggests that social **status** is largely established and perpetuated through families.

Talcott Parsons and Robert F. Bales (1955) theorized that with the development of industrialization and the shift to production outside the home, the small and relatively isolated nuclear family began to specialize in the **socialization** of children and in meeting the personal needs of family members (Thorne, 1982). These authors assumed that the family has two basic structures: a hierarchy of generations, and a differentiation of adults into instrumental and expressive **roles**. Parsons and Bales argued that the wife necessarily takes the expressive role, maintaining social relations and caring for others. The husband, on the other hand, assumes the instrumental role, earning the money for the family and dealing with the outside world (Thorne, 1982).

Structural functionalists have been criticized for their conservative position, as they often write about "the family" as though there is one acceptable family form rather than many variations. They believe that behaviour is largely determined by social expectations and family upbringing, and therefore difficult to alter. Structural functionalists have also implied that a gendered division of labour was maintained throughout history because it was "functional for society," when it may have been functional mainly for heterosexual men (Thorne, 1982). In addition, change is seen as disruptive rather than as normal or progressive, and individual opposition to social pressure has been viewed as "deviance." Consequently, the structural functionalists have not dealt with conflict and change as well as have those taking a political economy approach. Nor have they focused on the dynamic nature of interpersonal relations. For these reasons, many researchers who want to examine inequality, conflict, and change find this theoretical perspective less useful than others to explain the social world.

Systems theory accepts many of the basic assumptions of structural functionalism but focuses on the interdependence of family behaviour and the way that families often close ranks against outsiders, even when they are in trouble. This approach has been particularly useful in family therapy.

Social Constructionist Approach

The **social constructionist** approach refutes the idea that people behave according to unwritten rules or social expectations. Instead, it assumes that we construct our own social reality (Berger and Luckmann, 1966). Life does not just happen to us—we make things happen by exerting our will. This approach, also called **symbolic interactionism**, originated with the work of Americans Charles H. Cooley (1864–1929) and George Herbert Mead (1863–1931), who studied how families assist children to develop a sense of **self**. Within this perspective, the way people define and interpret reality shapes behaviour, and this process of interpretation is aided by non-verbal as well as verbal cues. Social constructionists also theorized that part of socialization is developing the ability to look at the world through the eyes of others and anticipating a particular role before taking it (called **anticipatory socialization**).

Studies using this approach often occur in a small-groups laboratory, using simulations of family interaction and decision making. Researchers observe the interaction in this kind of setting between parents and children, among children in a playgroup, and between husbands and wives. Sometimes behaviour will be videotaped and the subjects will be asked to comment on their own behaviour, which is then compared to the researchers' observations. Research is often centred on communication processes during everyday experiences, but it is not enough to observe what people *do*. In addition, it is essential to understand how they *feel* and why they feel this way. People's perceptions and their definitions of the situation influence their actions or behaviour. This perspective could be seen as the precursor of postmodernist theory, to be discussed later in this chapter.

Feminist Theories

Feminist theorists have focused on women's experiences, on written and visual representations of women, and on socio-economic differences between men and women. These perspectives developed and proliferated as more researchers concluded that women's experiences and contributions to society have been overlooked, downplayed, or misrepresented in previous social research.

Some feminist researchers have used a **structural approach** to analyze the ways in which inequality is perpetuated through social policies, laws, and labour market practices (Baker, 1995; O'Connor, Orloff, and Shaver, 1999). Others have concentrated on interpersonal relations between men and women, examining non-verbal communication, heterosexual practices, and public discourse (Baines, Evans, and Neysmith, 1998). Still other feminist theorists are attempting to create a more interpretive feminist analysis that takes women's experiences and ways of thinking and knowing into consideration (Butler, 1992; D. Smith, 1999).

Feminists typically argue that **gender** differences are social and cultural, are developed through socialization, and are maintained through institutional structures and practices. Most argue that differences in interests, priorities, and achievements between girls and boys grow out of their unique psychological and sexual experiences, which are shaped by different treatment by community leaders, relatives, parents, teachers, and employers (Brook, 1999). Nancy Chodorow (1989) combines psychoanalysis and feminist theory, showing how unconscious awareness of self and gender, established in earliest infancy, shapes the experiences of males and females as well as the patterns of inequality that permeate our culture. Carol Gilligan argues in *In a Different Voice* (1982) that women's moral development is quite different from men's: while men tend to focus on human rights, justice, and freedom, women's sense of morality is typically based on the principles of human responsibility, caring, and commitment. Feminist scholars have also argued that whatever is considered "feminine" in our culture is granted lower status than "masculine" achievements or characteristics.

Feminists note that housework and child care are unpaid when performed by a wife or mother but paid when done by a non-family member but that, in both cases, the work retains low occupational status and prestige. Although most adult women now work for pay, they continue to accept responsibility for domestic work in their own homes (Bittman and Pixley, 1997; Fox, 2001a; Hochschild, 2001). The unequal division of labour within families, as well as women's "double day" of paid and unpaid work, is considered to interfere with women's attempts to gain employment equity.

Post-feminists question the very nature of feminist analysis by arguing that vast differences remain between individual women depending on their unique experiences, social position, and cultural background (Fraser and Nicholson, 1990). Others criticize the feminist perspective because it glosses over men's experiences or fails to compare men with women, but feminists argue that men's experiences and views are already well represented by traditional social science. Much of social science is now permeated by feminist ideas, especially the work of female scholars. The incorporation of this perspective into mainstream academic theory has been promoted by greater acceptance of the idea that there is no absolute truth and that perception and knowledge depend on one's social position (Seidman, 1994).

Postmodernist Approaches

The postmodernist analysis of families argues that "truth" is relative and depends on one's social position, gender, race, and culture. Furthermore, vast differences exist in family life, and "the traditional nuclear family" is more a myth than a historical reality. In contemporary OECD (Organisation for Economic Co-operation and Development) countries, sexuality is increasingly separated from marriage, and marriage is being reconstructed as a contract that can be ended. Childbearing and child rearing are no longer necessarily linked with legal marriage, and the division of labour based on gender is continually renegotiated (Elliot, 1996). These demographic and social trends have led to a theoretical reworking of what defines *family* in the twenty-first century.

Another focus is on how families are constructed in everyday language and policy discourse (Muncie and Wetherell, 1995). By deconstructing—or analyzing the origins and intended meanings of **beliefs** about—"the family," researchers are able to see how images of this institution have been socially constructed and are historically situated. Nancy Fraser (1997) argues that historical conceptions of the nuclear family, upon which many Western countries built their welfare systems, were premised on the ideal of the male-breadwinner/female-caregiver family. Labour market changes (including the casualization and feminization of the workforce) and changing expectations for both men and women have questioned this gender order. Fraser suggests that we need major changes to conceptions both of gender and of the organization of work in order to facilitate a new order based on equity and on recognition of the interdependence of work and family.

The legal assumption of the heterosexuality of couples has also been criticized, and Martha Fineman (1995) proposes a reconceptualization of family away from the current focus on sexual or horizontal intimacy (between spouses or partners). She argues for abolishing marriage as a legal category and placing greater emphasis on a vertical or intergenerational organization of intimacy (between parents and children). This would redirect attention away from sexual affiliation and encourage policy discussions about support for caring. Elizabeth Silva and Carol Smart (1999) suggest that "normative heterosexuality" is being challenged by lesbians and gays who dispute the old saying, "You can choose your friends, but you can't choose your relatives." These families embrace friends, lovers, co-parents, adopted children, children from previous heterosexual relationships, and offspring conceived through alternative insemination (Weeks, Donovan, and Heaphy, 1998). Critics of the postmodernist approach often argue that too much emphasis is placed on communicating messages and meanings and on minority family situations, rather than on discussing the ways that most people actually live or the influence of socio-economic forces on families (Nicholson and Seidman, 1995).

Recent Issues in Canadian Families

In the past few decades, many aspects of family life have come to be seen as conflictual or even as social problems. In this section, we consider a number of these, with specific reference to Canadian families. First, we examine issues relating to the gendered division of labour.

Sharing Domestic Work

Over the past 20 years, patterns of paid work between husbands and wives have changed dramatically. While 50 per cent of families depended only on the husband's income in 1975, by 1996 only 20 per cent had a single male earner because so many wives have entered the job market (Statistics Canada, 1998a: 22). Families relying on a single wage earner experienced a $4,200 decline in real average income between 1989 and 1996, but the combined income in dual-earner families increased slightly (Statistics Canada, 1998a: 10). Table 7.2 shows that fathers are still more likely than mothers to be working for pay, regardless of the age of their children.

Canadian adolescent women expect to have paid jobs in the future. They tend to perceive household

What defines a family? "Normative heterosexuality" is being questioned by lesbians and gays who seek to legally marry and whose families embrace friends, lovers, co-parents, adopted children, and offspring conceived by alternative insemination. (Donald Weber/*Globe and Mail*)

tasks as "women's work," but not as a viable option for themselves, except among working-class girls (Looker and Thiessen, 1999). Furthermore, both adolescent males and adolescent females see jobs normally done by women as less desirable than those typically performed by men.

Research typically concludes that most heterosexual couples divide their household labour in such a way that husbands work full-time and perform occasional unpaid chores around the house, usually in the yard or related to the family car. Most wives are employed for fewer hours per week than their husbands, but they usually take responsibility for routine indoor chores and child care, even when employed full-time. Wives are also expected to be "kin keepers"

(Rosenthal, 1985), which includes maintaining contact with relatives, organizing family gatherings, and buying gifts. In addition, wives and mothers usually retain responsibility for "emotional work," such as soothing frayed nerves, assisting children to build their confidence, and listening to family members' troubles (Baker, 2001a).

Despite this prevalent division of labour, wives who are employed full-time tend to perform less housework than those who work part-time or who are not in the labour force (Marshall, 1993). Wives employed full-time may lower their housework standards, encourage other family members to share the work, or hire someone to clean their houses or care for their children. Yet women continue to retain all or most of responsibility for indoor housework and child-rearing tasks, including the hiring and supervision of cleaners and care providers (Bittman and Pixley, 1997; Luxton, 2001). Many employed mothers report feeling exhausted and drained by their attempts to earn money and take most of the responsibility for child care and homemaking (Beck-Gernsheim, 2002; Fox, 1980; Hochschild and Machung, 1989).

Younger, well-educated couples with few or no children are more likely to share domestic work more equitably. Some wives in dual-earner families are employed full-time but still retain sole responsibility for housework, especially older women and those who did not complete high school (Marshall, 1994). Wives' bargaining power may increase slightly when they earn an income comparable to their husbands', as these wives are better able to persuade their husbands to do more housework and they tend to be less willing to relocate with their husbands' jobs (Marshall, 1993).

According to the 1998 Canadian Time Use Survey, married men aged 25 to 44 with children and employed full-time spent 23.1 hours a week on unpaid work (including volunteer work), compared to

Table 7.2	Labour-Force Participation Rates of Mothers and Fathers with Children Under 15 Years of Age, 1996 (Percentages)		
Family Type		**Mother**	**Father**
Lone parent with youngest child under 6		55	83
Married parent with child under 6		69	94
Lone parent with youngest child 6–14		75	86
Married parent with youngest child 6–14		79	94

SOURCE: Vanier Institute for the Family, *Profiling Canada's Families II* (Ottawa: Vanier Institute of the Family, 2000), 87

34.3 hours for the same category of women; at the same time, women spent about 10 hours less per week than men on paid work (Vanier Institute of the Family, 2000:79). An unsatisfactory division of housework with their partner was given as a valid reason for divorce by 17 per cent of respondents in a 1995 Canadian study, but men were more likely to hold this attitude than women (Frederick and Hamel, 1998).

Why do wives accept the responsibility for housework even when they work for pay and prefer more sharing? Lorraine Davies and Patricia Jane Carrier (1999) examined the division of labour in dual-earner Canadian and US households using 1982 data, which allows them to say little about the current division of labour. Nevertheless, they concluded that the hours of work and the income earned by marital partners are less important than marital power relations in determining the allocation of household tasks. These power relations are influenced by gender expectations, opportunities, and experiences in the larger society, and gender intersects with race, ethnicity, and social class to influence these relations.

Based on 66 interviews with Australian women in and around Melbourne, Ken Dempsey (1999) concluded that few wives want to retain control over the domestic realm but that most are unable to persuade their husbands to take more responsibility for indoor household tasks. Husbands use a variety of tactics to avoid doing housework, such as waiting to be asked each time by their wives, saying they do not know how to do the task, arguing that it does not really need doing yet, and delaying completion of the task.

Only 1 per cent of Canadian families have adopted a role reversal, with the husband performing domestic work and child care at home while the wife works full-time (Marshall, 1998). In these families, most of the men are unemployed and have not necessarily chosen this lifestyle. Other North American research suggests that unemployed husbands feel that they would lose power in their marriages if their wife earned most of the household income, and that this view is shared by the wider community (Potuchek, 1997). Considerable research suggests that even when men have time available, they do not choose to spend it on domestic work (Shelton and John, 1996). Husbands will lend a hand if their wives are pressed for time, but housework and child care remain the responsibility of wives (and female relatives) throughout much of the world. Furthermore, women who have attempted to resist the gendered consequences of marriage by living in common-law arrangements find that they often slip back into conventional arrangements (Elizabeth, 2000). Cohabiting couples seem to have a less gendered division of labour than legally married couples (Wu, 2000), but relative power differences in heterosexual relationships continue to influence patterns of housework.

An uneven division of labour has many implications. More mothers than fathers develop close ties with their children, through years of physical and emotional caring work. In addition, some wives supported by their husbands are able to pursue hobbies and friendships during the day. At the same time, accepting most of the responsibility for housework and child care reduces the likelihood of obtaining employment qualifications, of working full-time or overtime, or of being promoted to higher-paying or more responsible positions. Furthermore, the consequent lack of income may reduce women's confidence in their ability to earn a living outside marriage. This may translate into reduced decision-making power in marriage and less income in the event of widowhood or divorce (Baines, Evans, and Neysmith, 1998). And when women accept responsibility for domestic work, they also reinforce traditional role models for their children (Duffy and Pupo, 1992). Many women feel they have little control over the household division of labour but would like their husbands to accept a larger share of household and caring work (Dempsey, 2002).

Low Fertility and Assisted Conception

The emergence of common-law marriage, same-sex partnerships, divorce, and remarriage has complicated marriage and family relationships in the twenty-first century, but reproductive and genetic technologies may be in the process of fundamentally reshaping families (Eichler, 1997). This reshaping includes separating biological and social parenthood, changing generational lines, and creating the possibility of sex selection. A wide range of procedures have now become routine, such as egg retrieval, in-vitro fertilization, and reimplantation into a woman's womb. Frozen sperm and embryos make conception possible after their donors' death, postmenopausal women can bear children, and potential parents can contract surrogates to bear children for them (Baker, 2001a).

Eichler (1996) argues that reproductive technologies tend to commercialize human reproduction: we can now buy eggs, sperm, embryos, and reproductive services—all of which are produced and sold for profit. These technologies tend to raise the potential for eugenic thinking and enable us to evaluate embryos on their genetic makeup. Prenatal diagnoses allow us to determine whether or not a fetus is worthy of being born (Eichler, 1996). However, we have very little research on the impact of these technologies on family life, such as how parents involved in artificial insemination reveal their children's background to them and how children deal with this knowledge.

Most men and women intend to reproduce, as Figure 7.1 indicates. Fertility is important for social acceptance and gender identity, and conception problems contribute to feelings of guilt, anger, frustration, and depression and to marital disputes (Doyal, 1995). Low fertility may be caused by many factors, including exposure to sexually transmitted diseases, long-term use of certain contraceptives, workplace hazards, environmental pollutants, hormonal imbalances, and lifestyle factors such as tobacco smoking, excessive exercise, a large consumption of caffeine or other drugs, and prolonged stress (Bryant, 1990). The probability of conception also declines with women's age. Some couples spend years trying to become pregnant, while others place their names on adoption waiting lists. The number of infants available for adoption, however, has dramatically decreased in the past two decades with more effective birth control and with social benefits that enable single mothers to raise their own children. Consequently, more couples with fertility problems are turning to medically assisted conception.

Infertility is usually defined as the inability to conceive a viable pregnancy after one year of unprotected sexual intercourse, although many fertile people take longer than that to conceive. This short-term definition encourages some fertile couples to seek medical attention prematurely. Access to reproductive technologies is often limited to those considered most acceptable as parents: young heterosexual couples in a

Figure 7.1 **Number of Children that Women and Men Intend to Have, by Age Group, 1995[a]**

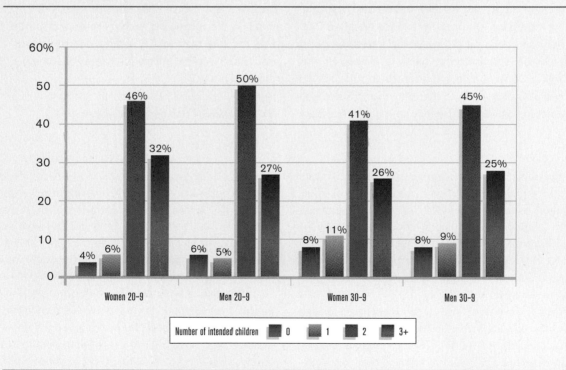

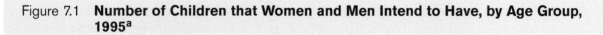

[a] As measured by the question, "What is the total number of children you intend to have, including those you have now and are currently expecting?" The proportion responding "don't know" ranged from 12 per cent among women aged 20–9 and men aged 30–9 to 14 per cent among women aged 30–9.
SOURCE: Adapted from Dave Dupuis, "What Influences People's Plans to Have Children?" *Canadian Social Trends,* Catalogue 11-008 (Spring 1998).

Open for Discussion
Medically Assisted Conception

"We tried IVF [in-vitro fertilization] and we got pregnant the first time. So it was very successful and obviously we are very pleased. I would say the IVF process was very cruel, even though we succeeded. I take my hat off to people who have it two or three times because it was extremely tough. It is very impersonal. You can't fault the treatment or the staff, but all the injections, different phases—it's like a roller coaster. You think you're ahead. Then you have a setback, bad news.

"One of the most stressful times for me was when I was in the room and they were harvesting the eggs from [my wife's] ovaries the first time—one egg. It felt terrible because we were hoping to get twelve. We got five off the second, so that was great but you still feel pretty disappointed. Then they fertilize and you only get two embryos and we were pretty depressed. Then a day later, we were up to four, so we were elated. Their goal was to try for five or six to choose. We had four, but one was a bit dodgy so we had three good embryos—you get that news a day later and you're down a little bit. Then during the IVF we had always envisaged that they would insert two embryos, which is extremely common—most peo-

ple have two put in. We only had one because [my wife's] uterus is a bit dodgy and they didn't want twins with a uterus shaped like that. They didn't want a prem [premature] baby, so all of a sudden you think that your chances are halved, which wasn't quite true. Then we had three great embryos and they chose the best one and it took, which is very pleasing. The other two are cryogenically frozen just like Austin Powers, waiting for their day in the sun."

(Interviewer: "Amazing isn't it, when you think of the technology?")

"Yes it is, and we wouldn't have got pregnant otherwise. . . . One of the senior doctors said that this was just the start and there were plenty more ups and downs. We are in the process now where there is lots of worry. [My wife] is worried about what she should and shouldn't eat. She worries that the baby will be born with some fault because she didn't take enough care. I'm very much in the reassuring mode—I'm sure it will be fine. I'm sure that once it is born then more worries start. It is an intriguing game, becoming a parent, I'd say."

SOURCE: Maureen Baker, personal interview, 2002.

stable relationship with no previous children. Private clinics charging fees, however, may be less selective, and many women around 40 years of age approach fertility clinics for assistance. Most treatments last for several months and involve the use of drugs that can produce side effects such as depression, mood swings, weight gain, and multiple births. Some treatments continue for years.

Fertility treatments are also expensive, although those who end up with a healthy baby may find these costs acceptable. And although many individuals pay privately for medically assisted conception, any complications will probably be treated within the public health system. The chances of complications following IVF are higher than with natural conception; about 25 per cent of IVF pregnancies end in miscarriage (Baird, 1997). Furthermore, the success rate is

not always as high as couples anticipate. British research indicates that in vitro fertilization ends in success for fewer than one-third of those who embark on it (Doyal, 1995: 149) and for only about 15 per cent per treatment cycle. The probability of producing a live birth from IVF declines substantially with age, and among women aged 40 to 44 the chance is only 5.5 per cent. With donor eggs, however, the probability of having a live birth increases to 17.7 per cent per IVF cycle for women aged 40 to 44 (HFEA, 1997). A higher number of multiple births also results from medically assisted conception. Medical births and their complications tend to use greater public health resources and also place financial and time constraints on new parents.

Those unable to reproduce even with the assistance of medical technology have sometimes turned to surrogacy arrangements. Surrogate mothers are usually low-income women who view pregnancy and childbirth as a relatively easy way to earn money, while the childless couple is often financially well off (McDaniel, 1988). P. Baird (1997) suggests that commercial surrogacy arrangements are unethical because they are premised on the idea that a child is a product that can be bought on the market and because they allow women to be exploited. In the United States, the substantial cost of surrogacy arrangements means that the commissioning couple is likely to be of a much higher economic and educational status then the woman gestating, and the brokers work on behalf of the paying couple (Baker, 2001a).

Eichler (1997) argues that reproductive and genetic technologies represent a quantum leap in complexity by blurring the role designations of mother, father, and child. For the child in a surrogacy relationship, who is the mother—the woman who gave birth or the woman who was part of the commissioning couple? What does it now mean to be a father? Does a man become a father if he impregnates a woman but has no social contact with the child? Does he become a father when he contracts another woman to use his sperm to make a baby, which he then adopts with his legal wife? Although sociologists have always been interested in the impact of absent fathers on family life, they are now talking about the "new absent fathers": sperm donors (Jamieson, 1998: 50). Social researchers are also interested in the increasing number of lesbian couples who are using self-insemination to create families without men (Albury, 1999; Nelson, 1999).

Sociologists and feminists have been ambivalent about medically assisted conception. On the one hand, it offers hope and opportunities for parenthood for those who might otherwise be excluded. However, some of the technologies are experimental and intrusive. These technologies also medicalize the natural act of childbearing, reinforce the pressure for all women to reproduce, and provide costly services unavailable to the poor. Feminist scholars have also been concerned that patriarchal societies will use sex selection to reinforce the cultural preference for sons rather than daughters and that working-class women will be exploited, both financially and emotionally, through surrogacy arrangements. These scholars seem to be most supportive of new reproductive technologies when they discuss self-insemination within lesbian relationships (Nelson, 1999), perhaps because of

the assumption that unequal power relationships and coercion are minimized (Baker, 2001a).

Sociologists are also concerned that the widespread availability of medically assisted fertility treatments could place additional pressure on childless women, who are already perceived to be either unfortunate or "morally flawed" (Morell, 1994). Research suggests that adoptive mothers are not always seen as "real" mothers, even by other women. These persistent attitudes help explain why some women and couples go to extreme lengths to reproduce or acquire a baby.

The Cost and Regulation of Child Care

The dramatic increase in the proportion of employed mothers within the past 40 years has led to a higher demand for non-family child care and to public concerns about the need to regulate the quality of care. Yet the demand still outstrips the supply, the assurance of quality continues to be a problem, and child care costs are unaffordable for many parents.

Since the 1960s, Canadian governments have provided subsidized spaces for low-income and one-parent families, generally in not-for-profit centres or licensed homes. However, there are insufficient spaces for eligible families. Two-parent families with higher incomes must pay the full cost, but the Canadian government provides income-tax deductions for employed parents requiring child care to maintain their employment. These tax deductions, however, cannot be used by a substantial minority of parents because they are unable to obtain receipts from caregivers working informally within the underground economy (Clevedon and Krashinsky, 2001).

Many not-for-profit child care centres have long waiting lists. Furthermore, they do not usually accept children under the age of two unless they are toilet-trained. Even if space is available, parents want to ensure that the centre employs an adequate number of staff to keep the infants clean, fed, and stimulated. In addition, some parents are concerned about the spread of infectious diseases in centre care. Finding a qualified babysitter to come to the child's home or who will welcome an extra child in her home is also difficult. Although licensed family homes are available in most jurisdictions, sitters usually operate outside these regulations (Doherty, Friendly, and Oloman, 1998).

In two-parent families, employed parents may be able to share child rearing if they work on different shifts. In the past, the majority of physical care and emotional support was given to the child from the mother, but today's fathers are taking a more active role in child care and nurturing. (www.harrycutting.com)

Sitter care is unregulated by any level of government, yet it remains the most prevalent type of child care for employed parents. Grandparents (usually grandmothers) are sometimes able and willing to provide child care while the parents are at work, and care by grandmothers can save money, provide culturally sensitive care, and create a more solid bond between generations. Yet it could also lead to disagreements about child-rearing techniques between the parents and the grandparent, who is likely to have retained more traditional cultural values. Child care concerns have encouraged some mothers to remain at home to care for their own children, although most can no longer afford this option.

Most centre-based care operates during regular office hours, but some parents need child care in the evening and weekends. In two-parent families, employed parents may be able to share child rearing if they work on different shifts, but it is difficult to maintain their own relationship or to engage in family activities. Parents whose children have special needs also experience problems. Before institutions and hospitals were built in the 1960s, mothers were

the main caregivers of these children. This source of unpaid labour is once again being examined as a way to reduce health and chronic care costs with policies of deinstitutionalization since the 1980s. Yet many mothers are now in the labour force, and without some remuneration and community assistance, they will be unable to supervise their disabled children (or frail relatives) because of their own work responsibilities.

Many parents and activists are concerned about the quality of care both in licensed centres and by babysitters in private homes. In some jurisdictions (such as Alberta), neither the employees of child care centres nor babysitters are required to have special training. These jobs pay the minimum wage or less and have difficulty attracting and retaining trained workers. A number of advocacy groups have formed around child care concerns. These groups have asked governments to tighten regulations; to improve training, fringe benefits, and pay for child care workers; and to allocate more public money to child care for employed parents. However, the extent of government involvement in the funding and regulation of child care remains contentious in many jurisdictions.

Some conservative politicians assert that child care is a family matter that should be of no concern to governments or employers. Yet conservative women's lobby groups, such as REAL Women of Canada, have argued for more income-tax relief for single-earner families and for higher social benefits to allow women to make a choice about working for pay or caring for their children at home (Baker and Tippin, 1999). For governments to provide mothers with a real choice, however, the social benefits would need to approximate women's potential earnings. This suggests that taxes would have to rise considerably.

Divorce and Repartnering: The Impact on Children

When divorce rates increased in the 1970s and 1980s, researchers began to devote their attention to the social consequences, especially for children. Many studies concluded that children from one-parent families experience more negative outcomes than do children from two-parent families, including lower educational attainment, behavioural problems, delinquency, leaving home earlier, premarital pregnancy for girls, and higher divorce rates when they marry among many others. The main research question typically focused on whether negative outcomes result from the parental conflict during marriage, the trauma of separation, the absence of a father, or some other factor. As Figure 7.2 shows, mothers typically retain custody of the children.

Despite negative media attention given to single-parent families, most children from these families do not experience problems, although they have a higher risk of problems than do children from two-parent families. Furthermore, when studies control for changes in family income after marital separation, the incidence of problems declines, although it does not disappear (Elliott and Richards, 1991; Kiernan, 1997). The Canadian National Longitudinal Survey on Children and Youth (NLSCY) found that about 19 per cent of children from low-income families headed by a lone mother experience a conduct disorder, compared to 9 per cent of children from two-parent families. For those from higher-income families, this percentage drops to 13 per cent for lone-mother families and 8 per cent for two-parent families (Lipman, Offord, and Dooley, 1996: 8). Socio-economic conditions, however, are not always held constant.

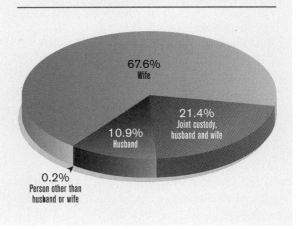

Figure 7.2 **Dependent Children by Party to Whom Custody Was Granted, 1995**

Many lone-parent families experience economic disadvantage *before* divorce as well as after, as people from lower socio-economic groups tend to have higher rates of bereavement, separation, and divorce (Rodgers and Pryor, 1998). When children are raised in low-income families, they are likely to suffer disadvantages that continue into adulthood. Furthermore, more children live in poverty in English-speaking countries than in Nordic nations, as Table 7.3 indicates. Using British National Child Development Study data, Kathleen Kiernan (1997) found that children from separated families were more likely than those from intact families to experience low earnings, low family income, unemployment, and social housing as adults.

Distinguishing between the impact on children of low socio-economic status and of parental separation is difficult for researchers. Lower status after separation seems to be a mediating factor for some outcomes but not for others. It accounts for a decline in educational attainment but not for rates of delinquency, psychosomatic illnesses, cigarette smoking, or heavy drinking in adulthood (Hope, Power, and Rodgers, 1998). Even in intact families, being raised in lower socio-economic households is associated with negative behavioural outcomes. These include delayed school readiness, lower educational attainment, a greater number of serious childhood illnesses, childhood accident rates, premature death, high rates of depression, high rates of smoking and alcohol abuse as young adults, and more trouble with school authorities and the law, to name only a few (NLSCY, 1996). For this reason, social researchers and theorists

Table 7.3   **Percentage of Children Living in Poverty in Various Countries, 2000**

	Lone-Parent Families	Other Families
United States	55.4	15.8
Canada	51.6	10.4
United Kingdom	45.6	13.3
Australia	35.6	8.8
Netherlands	23.6	6.5
Finland	7.1	3.9
Sweden	6.7	1.5

SOURCE: United Nations Children's Fund (UNICEF), *Innocenti Report Card*, no. 1 (June 2000), 10.

must consider socio-economic status as an important variable in all discussions of the outcomes of children after divorce.

Many studies indicate that children who live with their mothers after divorce are likely to experience diminished contact with their fathers and to suffer distress from this loss (Cockett and Tripp, 1994; Funder, 1996; Furstenberg, Morgan, and Allison, 1987). As children grow older, the time they spend with the non-resident parent decreases, and some lose contact completely. The amount of access that non-resident fathers have to their children is not the deciding factor in children's adjustment after their parents separate, however, as access is mediated by inter-parental conflict. Frequent contact with their father may negatively impact on children's well-being if there is a high amount of conflict between father and child or between parents over the children (Amato and Rezac, 1994). If conflict is absent or contained, children both want and benefit from frequent contact with both parents (Mitchell, 1985). In general, a close relationship with both parents is associated with a positive adjustment in children after divorce (Rodgers and Pryor, 1998). Furthermore, whether or not the father continues to pay child support may influence both the children's adjustment and the socio-economic status of the lone-parent family.

Adult children of divorced parents are more likely than those from intact marriages to end their own marriages with divorce (Beaujot, 2000). This may result from poor role models in childhood, from the simple observation that there is "life after marriage," or from the fact that divorce becomes more personally acceptable as a solution to an unhappy marriage if it has already happened in one's own family.

There is no simple or direct relationship between parental separation and children's adjustment, although many studies do find differences between children from intact and separated families. Parental separation clearly adds stress to children's lives through changes in relationships, living situations, and parental resources. Although most studies find that psychological and behavioural stress are prevalent for children from separated parents, few studies conclude that psychological disturbance is severe or prolonged (Emery, 1994). Instead, most research finds that the first two years after separation require adjustments by both parents and children.

Never-married mothers who become pregnant before their education is completed are particularly vulnerable to low income as well as to disciplinary problems with their children (Dooley, 1995). These mothers often repartner within a few years of the child's birth, but the socio-economic disadvantages of bearing a child at a young age may linger. Their children are most likely to spend their childhood in one or more stepfamilies, which are often conflictual (Marcil-Gratton, 1998). These factors may partially account for higher rates of behavioural problems in the children of never-married mothers.

Research suggests that stepfamilies are difficult to establish and that considerable negotiation is required to maintain them. Children living in stepfamilies are at the same risk of behavioural problems and distress as children growing up in lone-parent families. Neither increased household income nor having two adults in the home ensures good outcomes for these children (Pryor and Rodgers, 2001). One explanation is that parental conflict and separation have a lasting effect on children. Another is that stepparents do not relate to their stepchildren with the same warmth and concern as they do with their biological children because they do not share their genes and have not spent their formative years together.

Although researchers usually study separation and divorce as negative life events, parents often experience relief and contentment after the initial adjustment of leaving an unhappy marriage. This is reflected in their general outlook and in their interactions with their children. Consequently, most researchers agree that children living in stable lone-parent families are better off than children living in conflict-ridden two-parent families (Booth and Edwards, 1990). Furthermore, children of employed lone mothers tend to accept more egalitarian gender roles, as they see their mothers supporting the family and managing tasks that were previously defined as "men's jobs" (Baker, 2001a). This suggests that separation and divorce could have positive as well as negative outcomes for both parents and children.

Wife Abuse

Beginning in the 1980s, when domestic violence appeared to be on the increase, sociologists became more interested in studying this phenomenon. Feminist sociologists argue that the very term *family violence* implies that this behaviour is randomly distributed within families, when men actually are the perpetrators in the vast majority of cases that come to the attention of police and social workers (Dobash et al., 1992).

The Canadian Urban Victimization Study found that in cases of "spousal violence," physical abuse is not an isolated event. Some abused women are assaulted on numerous occasions by their male partners and have sought help many times from friends, neighbours, social workers, and the police. Furthermore, separated women are more likely to be assaulted than divorced or married women (Johnson, 1990). Women are more vulnerable if they see their partner as the head of the household and if they are financially dependent on him. The larger society also condones such behaviour: violence is used as a form of entertainment in films and sports events. This tends to normalize violence as a means of resolving conflict.

Longitudinal US survey research by Murray Strauss and Richard Gelles (1990) concluded that marital violence actually decreased in the United States throughout the 1980s even though the reporting of this behaviour increased. They argue that reporting was influenced by the women's movement, by police campaigns to prosecute perpetrators, and by the availability of more options for women wishing to leave violent marriages. Yet they also make the controversial claim that women are as likely as men to abuse their partners, although they acknowledge that this behaviour is less likely to be reported to the authorities, is less consequential in terms of physical harm, and is often is a form of self-defence. Walter DeKeseredy (2001) criticizes the conflict tactics scale used by Strauss and Gelles, which counts incidences of violence but fails to examine their social context. He agreed that women's "violence" against men is often in self-defence.

Wife abuse may represent men's rising concern that they are losing authority in their families, especially those men who are experiencing unemployment or other personal problems. This kind of violence is also aggravated by alcohol and substance abuse but represents much more than an interpersonal problem. The fact that most victims of reported violence are women and that separated women are often the targets indicates important social patterns in this behaviour relating to gender and power.

In the past, the police failed to respond in a serious way to calls about violent wife abuse because they thought women did not want charges laid or would later withdraw them (Johnson, 1990). Policies have now been implemented in most jurisdictions for police to charge men who batter. Yet many wives remain with abusive partners because of shortages of low-income and temporary housing, an inability to support themselves and their children, and a lack of knowledge about where to turn for assistance. Abuse is also permitted to continue because some women feel that they deserve it, especially those abused as children and those who suffer from low self-esteem. In addition, many women fear reprisal from spouses or former spouses who have threatened to kill them if they go to the police or tell anyone about an incident. The enormous publicity recently given to women killed by their partners indicates that, in many cases, fear of reprisal is entirely justified.

Women's groups, social service agencies, police, and researchers have developed new ways of dealing with violence against women in intimate relationships. Many of the programs are crisis oriented and focused on women, helping them develop a protection plan that could involve laying charges against a spouse or ex-spouse, finding transitional housing, engaging a lawyer, and, if necessary, acquiring social assistance to cover living costs. Through either individual counselling or group therapy, battered wives are also helped to restructure their thinking about

7.3

Sociology in Action
The Emotional Scars of Family Violence

"I was raped by my uncle when I was 12 and my husband has beat me for years. For my whole life, when I have gone to the doctor, to my priest, or to a friend to have my wounds patched up, or for a shoulder to cry one, they dwell on my bruises . . . that's for sure. . . . I don't look like anything like I did 15 years ago, but it's not my body that I really wish could get fixed. The abuse in my life has taken away my trust in people and in life. It's taken away the laughter in my life. I still laugh, but not without bitterness behind my laughter. It's taken away my faith in God, my faith in goodness winning out in the end, and maybe worse of all, it's taken away my trust in myself. I don't trust myself to be able to take care of the kids, to take care of myself, to do anything to make a difference in my own life or anyone else's. That's the hurt I would like to fix. I can live with my physical scars. It's these emotional scars that drive me near suicide sometimes."

SOURCE: Walter S. DeKeseredy and Linda MacLeod, *Woman Abuse: A Sociological Study* © 1997. Reprinted with permission of Nelson, a division of Thomson Learning: www.thomsonrights.com. Fax 800-730-2215.

violence and to view it as unacceptable regardless of their own behaviour.

The male abuser is now more often charged with an offence. He is also given opportunities for counselling, including accepting responsibility for his acts of violence rather than blaming his partner, learning to control his emotions, developing better communication skills, and learning non-violent behaviour from male role models. Action against family violence has also included sensitization workshops for professionals, such as teachers and judges, to increase their knowledge of program options and of the implication of this form of violence for women, their families, men who batter, and the wider society (DeKeseredy, 2001). In addition, support services have been provided for families in high-risk circumstances.

Money is a major impediment to establishing new programs and transitional housing, even though governments at all levels have voiced their concern about violence against women and children. Transition houses are usually funded by private donations, staffed by volunteers, and operated with uncertain resources. Follow-up therapy and counselling may also be necessary for the entire family, but these services also cost money to establish and maintain. Despite the serious nature of marital violence, new program funding for the rising number of reported victims and their abusers is difficult to find.

A correlation has been noted between "courtship" violence and marital violence. K. O'Leary and colleagues (1989) found that the probability of spouse abuse in the United States was over three times greater if violence had also occurred during courtship. They also found that adults who abuse their spouses or children have often come from families where their parents engaged in similar behaviour.

Three broad explanations of marital violence arise from these studies. The intergenerational theory suggests that solving conflicts through physical or verbal violence is learned from early family experiences. The solution within this perspective focuses on improving conflict resolution and parenting skills in order to reduce marital violence. A second theory sees marital violence as a misguided way of resolving conflicts that is used by husbands who feel that their authority within the family is being threatened. The solution to the problem within this systems framework is to offer therapy sessions to men or couples to improve their communication skills, learn to control emotions, and become more assertive about their feelings and needs without resorting to violence.

In contrast, feminist theories argue that "marital violence" is actually violence by men against their female partners. This behaviour is symptomatic of women's lack of interpersonal power in families, the way in which the patriarchal state has permitted husbands to control their wives, and the social acceptability of violence toward those considered most vulnerable (Baker, 2001a). Changing public attitudes toward physical and sexual abuse means that more people now report such activity and that social services are needed to assist them. Consequently, this kind of behaviour, which always existed, now appears more prevalent.

These theories are not entirely incompatible: not everyone becomes abusive who has witnessed abuse or who feels threatened by lack of power in their workplace or at home. Furthermore, everyone lives in a society that condones certain kinds of violence and a lower status for women. None of the theories can explain by itself the perpetuation of violence in intimate relationships. Yet it is clear that violence against women and children cuts across national, cultural, and class boundaries and that it is not confined to marriage or cohabitation. In fact, women who are separated appear to be more vulnerable than married women (Johnson, 1990).

Overview of Canadian Family Policies

Late in the nineteenth century and early in the twentieth century, Canadian governments (both federal and provincial) developed ways to count their citizens and to register marriages, births, adoptions, divorces, and deaths. They also established child welfare legislation, offered married women more political rights and control over their property, equalized the guardianship rights of mothers and fathers over their children, and established basic social services. As Table 7.4 indicates, income security programs for families were developed mainly from the 1940s to the 1970s, and governments tightened abuse and neglect laws as well as the enforcement of child support during the 1980s and 1990s (Baker, 2001a; Ursel, 1992).

There will always be a need for governments to regulate certain aspects of family life, especially to protect vulnerable family members and to assist those in serious financial difficulty. Families also require health and social services to ensure healthy and safe pregnancy, childbirth, and childhood, and these services need government regulation and financial support. Regulation of life events by the state is designed to prevent incestuous and bigamous marriages, adoptions by "inappropriate" parents, and hasty divorces

Table 7.4 The Establishment of Social Benefits in Canada

Family Allowance	• A universal allowance created in 1945 and paid to mothers for each child • Replaced by the targeted Child Tax Benefit in 1993
Old Age Pension	• Established in 1926 as a pension for those with low incomes • Converted to a universal pension in 1951
Mothers/Widows Pensions	• Developed around 1920, but date varies by province
Unemployment Insurance	• Established as a federal social insurance program in 1941 • Maternity benefits added in 1971 • Now called Employment Insurance
Hospital/Medical Insurance	• Hospital insurance established nationally in 1958 • Medical insurance established in 1966 (commonly called "medicare")
Canada Pension Plan	• Established in 1966, and financed by contributions from employees, employers, and government • Also pays survivors benefits and disability benefits to contributors
Spouses Allowance	• Established in 1975 as an income-tested pension for spouses aged 60–4 of old age pensioners, mainly women
Child Tax Benefit	• The former Family Allowance and tax deductions and credits for children were rolled into this targeted tax benefit for lower- and middle-income families in 1993 • Replaced by the Canada Child Tax Benefit in 1998
Parliamentary resolution to end "child poverty"	• All-party agreement in 1989
Canada Child Tax Benefit	• The Child Tax Benefit and the Working Income Supplement were rolled together to form this benefit in 1998

and to ensure that spouses and parents understand and fulfill their basic support obligations. Governments also gather basic statistics about populations in order to plan future social services and facilities. They need to be able to predict the size and structure of the future labour force and the numbers of future voters, taxpayers, and consumers. Some of these statistics also prove useful for the business sector in their marketing and growth plans.

Since the mid-1970s, unemployment rates have increased and have resisted attempts at reduction. At the same time, marriage has become less stable and more lone mothers now need assistance to support themselves and their children without a male breadwinner. Throughout the 1980s and 1990s, more people experienced unemployment, underemployment, and marriage dissolution. This raised the cost of social programs for governments (Baker and Tippin, 1999). Consequently, more taxpayers and politicians expressed concerns about the high levels of taxes needed to maintain the welfare state at existing levels and questioned the effectiveness of anti-poverty strategies. In addition, many politicians and researchers are concerned about the state's ability to sustain social programs with an aging population, growing structural unemployment, and high rates of marriage dissolution.

Throughout Canadian history, the extent of government involvement in the "private" realm of the family has been debated, although these debates have usually focused on the provision of income support. Recently, federal and provincial governments have trimmed the costs of social services and focused more on "personal and family responsibility" rather than on social support or the payment of social benefits. At the same time, they have tightened laws on spousal and child abuse, but these laws have been difficult to enforce because this behaviour often occurs within the privacy of people's homes and without witnesses. The careful monitoring of at-risk families suggests that the state regulates family life as a form of **social control** as well as merely for information gathering or future planning.

Future Families

Sociologists often look at current family trends and make assumptions about family life in the near future. Predicting the future, however, is always risky. Nonetheless, from what we know about patterns in family formation, we might assume that cohabitation will become more prevalent in the future (Wu, 2000). As a result, and as the distinction between common-law and legal marriage becomes socially and legally blurred, the average age of legal marriage will increase slightly and legal marriage rates will continue to fall. Living together will become more socially acceptable as a preliminary step to the commitment of legal marriage. In particular, young people from divorced families and older divorced adults will be reluctant to enter legal marriage without some previous experience of living with their partner. Furthermore, those who are ideologically opposed to traditional gender roles will continue to see cohabitation as a preferable alternative to legal marriage, even though research suggests that the differences in gender roles between cohabiting and married couples become minimal over time (Baxter, 2000).

As more families rely on two incomes, men's opportunities to move to jobs in new locations may be limited by their wives' employment. These husbands could find it harder to encourage their wives to give up their jobs because their families could not survive on one income. More couples may be forced to live apart for short periods in order to further their education or obtain work. Commuter marriages could become more prevalent as professional and managerial positions become harder to find, as the labour market becomes more globalized, and as women become more career oriented.

Delayed marriage and delayed childbearing are definitely on the increase in Canada. This suggests that more couples will live for longer periods in non-family households, in a lifestyle that focuses on work, career development, leisure pursuits, and travel. Some will become accustomed to this lifestyle and will choose a marriage without children. If substantial numbers of Canadians make this choice, however, policy makers will become concerned about the future of the nation's population. An increase in child-free marriages could also lead to higher divorce rates, as it is easier to divorce without children. Higher rates of cohabitation also suggest greater marriage instability in the future because couples who lived together before legal marriage have a higher probability of divorce than those who have not lived together. In addition, children from divorced parents have a higher probability of divorce, suggesting the greater impermanence in marriage in the future.

Most demographers suggest that declining birth rates will continue because children are increasingly costly in modern urban environments and because combining work and family life is difficult when both parents are employed. Many working parents experience problems finding affordable and high-quality child care services. Although government reports have said that children are our "greatest future resource," little has been done in North America to help parents combine paid work and child rearing.

Young people tend to remain at home with their parents for longer periods now than in the 1970s. The greater need for higher education, the longer time required to find a secure job, and the higher cost of housing prolong the period of active parenting. At the same time, more women are in the full-time labour force in mid-life, which means that they have neither the time nor the energy to supervise their young adults adequately.

As **life expectancy** increases and fertility declines, more people will live long past the age of 65 and more frail elderly people will continue to require care. Middle-aged people, especially women, could be caught in the middle, trying to provide attention, emotional care, and domestic services for both children and aging parents. Furthermore, middle-aged people will have fewer siblings to help them care for frail parents. In the future, they will also need to remain in the labour force longer to counteract job insecurity throughout their lives and lower employment pensions. To deal with rising public pension costs as well as employees' need for more income in later life, an increasing number of governments are proposing to end or change mandatory retirement regulations.

As more people remarry in later life, attitudes toward aging, marriage, and leisure may gradually change. Family relationships will become more complicated, with stepchildren and ex-partners and with older men repartnering and reproducing with younger women. A global economy and high rates of migration could also mean that more elders remain in their home communities while their children migrate to find work, taking the grandchildren far away. This may lower the frequency of family activities, but it could also strengthen friendship ties for both generations. Yet keeping in touch will become even easier with e-mail, long-distance telephone, and text messaging, as well as new, as-yet-unforeseen communications technologies.

Conclusion

Family life has changed substantially over the past few decades, but intimate relationships remain central to most people's lives. At the same time, cultural variations are becoming more prevalent with new immigration sources. More people are creating their own intimate arrangements, but governments continue to clarify the rights and responsibilities of family members in these new arrangements. Cohabitation and divorce are now more prevalent that a generation ago, while legal marriage and fertility are declining. Nevertheless, popular support for intimate relationships remains strong.

Social scientists have used different theoretical frameworks to study the similarities and variations in family life, each emphasizing different aspects and issues. The five theoretical frameworks presented in this chapter suggest that theorists differ in their focus within family studies. This chapter also discussed five of the many conflictual issues in family life. The first is the sharing of domestic work; despite dramatic increases in women's paid work, wives still do the lion's share of housework and child care. The second issue relates to the apparent rise in infertility and to feminist and sociological concerns about medically assisted conception. The third issue relates to the high cost and quality of care of the children of employed parents, making it difficult, especially for mothers, to combine paid work and child rearing. The fourth discusses the contradictory evidence of the impact of separation, divorce, and repartnering on children, suggesting that remarriage is not always the best solution for children. And the fifth issue relates to wife abuse and why it continues.

☐ Questions for Critical Thought

1. In your opinion, does the way in which *family* is defined make a difference? Why or why not?
2. Would you expect societies that practise arranged marriages to have more stable and happier marriages than societies that allow free-choice marriage? Why or why not?
3. How would you explain the perpetuation of family violence, with reference to (a) feminist perspectives, (b) structural functionalism, and (c) political economy theory?
4. Why are more young people living together without legal marriage? Does this behaviour indicate a rejection of family?
5. Is parental divorce detrimental to children?
6. Should the services of fertility clinics be covered by government health care systems? Give reasons for your viewpoint.
7. Should governments contribute more or less than now to child care services for employed parents?
8. Is there any reason to believe that Canadian birth rates will rise again in the near future?

☐ Recommended Readings

Maureen Baker, *Families, Labour and Love* (Vancouver: University of British Columbia Press, 2001).
This comparative book examines the similarities and differences between Canadian families and those in Australia and New Zealand. It focuses on the impact of immigration, culture, labour market trends, and changing laws on and practices of family life.

Bettina Bradbury, "Social, Economic, and Cultural Origins of Family Life," in *Families: Changing Trends in Canada*, 4th edn, edited by Maureen Baker (Toronto: McGraw-Hill Ryerson, 2001), 69–95.
This chapter discusses the competing visions of family among indigenous peoples and early French and English settlers from Canada's earliest history to post-war society.

Walter DeKeseredy, "Patterns of Family Violence," in *Families: Changing Trends in Canada*, 4th edn, edited by Maureen Baker (Toronto: McGraw-Hill Ryerson, 2001), 238–66.
This chapter discusses recent research and theorizing about various forms of family violence, including wife abuse, child abuse, sibling violence, and elder abuse.

Margrit Eichler, *Family Shifts: Families, Policies, and Gender Equality* (Toronto: Oxford University Press, 1997).
Eichler examines major new shifts affecting families today, including gender equality as a legal and moral principle and the potential impact of biotechnology.

Lynn Jamieson, *Intimacy: Personal Relationships in Modern Societies* (Cambridge, MA: Polity, 1998).
The author discusses whether a new type of intimacy is being sought in Western societies or if relationships are still fundamentally shaped by power and economic considerations.

Susan A. McDaniel and Lorne Tepperman, *Close Relations: An Introduction to the Sociology of Families* (Scarborough, ON: Prentice-Hall Allyn and Bacon, 2000).
This Canadian text provides an overview of research on and theories of family life.

Jan Pryor and Bryan Rodgers, *Children in Changing Families: Life After Parental Separation* (Oxford: Blackwell, 2001).
This book, which covers international research on the impact of parental separation and stepfamily formation on children, offers insights into why some survive family change better than others.

Vanier Institute of the Family, *Profiling Canada's Families II* (Ottawa: Vanier Institute of the Family, 2000).
This book contains numerous tables and charts about family trends and patterns, accompanied by a discussion of their relevance.

☐ Recommended Web Sites

Campaign 2000

www.campaign2000.ca

Campaign 2000, created in 1989 to monitor "child poverty" in Canada, publishes an annual report card.

Centre for Families, Work and Well-Being

www.worklifecanada.ca

The Web site of the Centre for Families, Work and Well-Being at the University of Guelph contains information about research projects.

Child & Family Canada

www.cfc-efc.ca

This Web site offers public education from numerous non-profit organizations.

Childcare Resource and Research Unit

www.childcarecanada.org

The Web site of the Childcare Resource and Research Unit at the University of Toronto includes Canadian and cross-national research and other material on child care issues.

Early Canadiana Online

Nineteenth-century documents pertaining to marriage and families can be found on this site.

National Association for the Education of Young Children (NAEYC)

www.naeyc.org

This US-based association publishes the journal *Young Children*, which includes reviews of research and practical information.

Statistics Canada

www.statcan.ca

Statistics Canada provides a wide range of census documents and statistics relating to families and households.

Vanier Institute of the Family

www.vifamily.ca

The Vanier Institute of the Family in Ottawa provides educational material, news items, and research on Canadian families.

8

Terry Wotherspoon

> > >

Education

© Bill Whittman

☐ Learning Objectives

In this chapter, you will:

- understand how and why formal education has become a central social institution in Canada and other nations

- identify the main dimensions associated with the growth of formal education systems

- gain a critical understanding of various forms of lifelong learning beyond formal education

- understand the major theoretical perspectives and theories that sociologists employ to explain educational institutions, practices, and outcomes

- understand the relationships between education and social inequality

- explore how education and educational outcomes are shaped by relationships between educational institutions and participants and the social contexts within which those institutions operate

- critically understand contemporary debates and controversies over major educational issues

Introduction

The chief economist for the World Bank recently highlighted the importance of education as "critical to participation and productivity in economic life." "A healthy, literate labor force," he said, "will both increase the amount of growth realized from establishing a sound investment climate and strongly reinforce the poverty reduction benefit from that growth" (Stern, 2002: 21). Probably few people would take issue with these comments. What do they mean, though, to people in different situations? Consider the following cases of students in a Canadian high school:

- a recent immigrant who speaks little English or French
- a teen who has difficulties with reading comprehension but has stayed in school until now because of friends or opportunities to play on sports teams
- new arrivals who find the school much larger and more regimented than elementary schools in nearby **First Nations** and rural communities
- a student pressured by parents who feel the school's poor academic and disciplinary standards are impeding the student's ability to gain entry into a prestigious university
- a youth whose repeated conflicts with students and teachers in a previous school, combined with substance abuse and domestic problems, have made regular school attendance difficult

These situations reveal much about education's significance in the context of what is often called the *knowledge* or *learning society*. Education has been thrust into a central role as individuals, organizations, and nations struggle to keep pace with demands for new knowledge and credentials regarded as essential for jobs, career advancement, and economic and social development. We expect educational institutions to educate and prepare learners with a wide range of technical, social, and personal competencies for changing, often uncertain futures. We also look to schools to respond to the needs of diverse students and communities.

Sociologists are interested in several issues associated with educational processes and outcomes and in the environments within which education operates. This chapter examines several key questions that sociology addresses in its concern to understand education:

- Why is formal education so important in contemporary societies, and how did it get to be that way?
- What are the main dimensions of education and education systems in Canada and other nations?
- How do sociologists explain the growth of education systems and the outcomes associated with education for different groups?
- What are the main educational experiences and outcomes for different social groups?
- What are the main challenges facing education systems in Canada and other nations?

The Changing Face of Education

Education is generally understood as the formal learning that takes place in institutions such as schools, colleges, universities, and other sites that provide specific courses, learning activities, or credentials in an organized way. *Informal learning* also occurs as people undertake specific activities to learn about distinct phenomena or processes. Both formal and informal education are part of the broader process that sociologists typically call **socialization**, which refers to all direct and indirect learning related to humans' ability to understand and negotiate the rules and expectations of the social world.

Nearly all Canadians engage in formal education for extended periods of time, a situation that was not always the case. In the late nineteenth century, educational participation tended to be secondary to other pressing concerns. Ian Davey observes that factors such as "cyclical depressions and crop failures affected school attendance because in good times more parents sent more of their children to school and sent them more regularly. Yet, lower attendance during bad times resulted largely from a magnification of those factors which caused irregular attendance throughout the nineteenth century—transience and poverty" (1978: 230). At the beginning of the twentieth century, only three out of five pupils enrolled in public school attended on a regular basis, and many of those were not in school for extended periods during the school year. Many communities lacked schools or qualified teachers. Children often did not begin their **schooling** until they were seven or eight years old, and typically left school by their early teen years (Guppy and Davies, 1998).

Many aspects of schooling have changed dramatically over time, although the core structure of classroom life has also retained some constant elements. In the early twentieth century, only three out of five children attended school, often for limited periods of time. Both teachers and students, like those depicted here in a Model School in Vancouver in about 1907, were supervised closely to emphasize routine habits, discipline, conformity, and common values. Most people today have more educational options that are considered essential parts of lifelong learning. (City of Vancouver Archives, SGN 1586, Photographer C. Bradbury)

A comparison of today's educational settings and classrooms with those of a century ago yields both striking similarities and profound differences. Massive, architecturally designed complexes have replaced self-contained one- or two-room wooden buildings; sophisticated equipment often takes the place of chalk and slate boards; and most students are exposed to a diverse range of teachers, subject choices, and work projects unthinkable in 1900. Today's students and teachers are likely to exhibit a far greater array of personal, stylistic, and cultural variation than was apparent a century ago and have access to many more learning and community resources.

Despite these changes, the casual visitor to classrooms in either time period is not likely to mistake schools for other settings. Groupings of children and youth, under the instruction and regular scrutiny of adult teachers, are guided through both regimented activities—at least for part of the time in rows or other arrangements of desks—and periods allocated for recreation or personal expression. Education is a unique **social institution** at the same time as it reveals characteristics that are integral to the society in which it operates.

Dimensions of Educational Growth

Educational expansion accelerated rapidly after World War II. In 1951, over half (51.9 per cent) of all Canadians aged 15 and over had less than a Grade 9 education, while just under 2 per cent had a university degree and only about 1 in 20 aged 18 to 24 was enrolled in university (Clark, 2000: 4–6; Guppy and Davies, 1998: 19). At the beginning of the twenty-first century, by contrast, Canadians have unprecedented levels of education, distinguishing Canada with one of the most highly educated populations in the world.

Table 8.1 provides an overview of the increasing educational attainment of Canadians in the last half of the twentieth century. The proportion of the population who had less than a Grade 9 education diminished rapidly, especially in the 1960s and 1970s. And while very few had taken or completed postsecondary studies at the start of the period, over half of the population had at least some postsecondary education by 2001. The average number of years of formal education held by Canadians rose from just under 12.5 at the beginning of the 1990s to nearly 13 by 1998, ranking Canada second only to Germany, where the average was just over 13.5 (Organisation for Economic Co-operation and Development [OECD], 2001: 19). Growing emphasis on the importance of formal education and credentials has been matched by three interrelated factors: the overall expansion of educational opportunities and requirements, increasing levels of educational attainment among people born in Canada, and recent emphasis on the selection of highly educated immigrants.

The fact that many people did not have substantial amounts of formal education in the late nineteenth and early twentieth centuries was not as significant as it may seem in retrospect because only a few occupations required educational credentials. Most people relied on schools to provide some basic skills and knowledge, discipline, and social training, and as a service to provide something for children to do when their parents were too busy to attend to them. Formal learning was often subordinate to other concerns. School superintendents and other educational authorities devoted their efforts to enforcing school attendance and improving the quality of instruction in schools. Annual reports and other documents maintained by provincial education departments are filled with references to concerns such as the need to maintain proper order and discipline in the classroom; attention to habits and duties; routine procedures and daily records of pupil attendance, school visitors, and recitations drawn from various subjects; and the desire for teachers who were not so much good instructors as proper role models with good manners and high moral standing. (See Lawr and Gidney, 1973, for examples.)

Early advocates of public schooling undertook a mission to convince the public, and especially members of influential groups, of the merits of the educational system. They promoted schooling as an efficient enterprise that would serve the public or general interest. Other institutions or sites, such as families, churches, and businesses, were by contrast more narrow and selective in scope.

The education system adopted a degree of flexibility that made it possible to integrate new tasks and curricula. School authorities had to make concessions when funds to build and run schools or hire the preferred quality of teachers were scarce. Some people resented having to pay or be taxed for schooling. Schools could also be victims of their own success, as demands for education or population growth in communities outpaced the ability to provide school facilities, textbooks, teaching materials, and qualified teachers. In many parts of Canada, especially in smaller communities and rural areas, school operations remained highly uncertain or irregular until well into the twentieth century because of sporadic pupil attendance, resignation of or inability to attract teachers, lack of funds, or disputes between school board and community members. A single teacher provided the schooling for all grades that were offered in rural one-room schools, whereas cities and larger districts tended to have better equipped schools with a full range of programs and a complement of trained, more specialized teachers.

Gradually, centralized schools and districts replaced smaller units across Canada. School district consolidation began in 1900, though amalgamation into larger schools and school districts did not fully take hold until the period between the mid-1940s

Table 8.1 **Educational Attainment in Canada, by Percentage of Population Aged 15 and over, Selected Years, 1951–2001[a]**

	Less than Grade 9	Grades 9 to 13	Some Postsecondary	University Degree	Median Years of Schooling
1951	51.9	46.1	–	1.9	–
1961	44.1	53.0	–	2.9	–
1971	32.3	45.9	17.1	4.8	10.6
1981	20.1	44.3	27.6	8.0	11.8
1986	17.3	43.0	30.2	9.6	12.2
1991	13.9	43.0	31.7	11.4	12.5
1996	12.1	40.7	34.0	13.3	12.7
2001	9.8	39.0	35.7	15.4	–

[a] Figures may not add up to 100 because of rounding.
SOURCE: Compiled from Statistics Canada, census data and *Education in Canada*, annual series.

and the late 1960s. Amalgamation has continued since then, accelerating in the 1990s when the number of school boards in some provinces, including Alberta and Quebec, was cut by over half. In New Brunswick, all school boards were abolished between 1996 and 2001. Consolidation was hastened by financial and administrative difficulties in many districts and by the development of transportation networks and support linkages that made it easier to concentrate schools in selected centres. By 1970/1, there were just over 16,000 public schools in Canada (a figure that has declined moderately into the early twenty-first century), nearly 10,000 below the number that had operated a decade earlier (Statistics Canada, 1973: 104).

Pressure to build and maintain larger schools intensified as more people began to stay in school longer, extending into and beyond the high school years. The **baby boom** that occurred after World War II resulted in unprecedented cohorts of children who were entering and moving through the school system. The figures in Table 8.2 demonstrate that, while total enrolment in Canadian public elementary and secondary schools in 1950 was just over double what it had been in 1900,

enrolment doubled again over the next decade and a half. The average number of pupils per school increased in Canada from 66 in 1925/6 to 156 in 1960/1 and nearly doubled over the next decade to reach 350 in 1970/1, a level that has remained relatively stable since then (Manzer, 1994: 131).

The data in Table 8.2 demonstrate how formal education has expanded throughout the life course. Children have begun their schooling at progressively younger ages over the past five decades. Kindergarten is now compulsory in most Canadian jurisdictions, and many children also attend various preschool and early childhood education programs.

Meanwhile, people have been extending their formal education well past high school into postsecondary studies. The larger cohorts of students moving through schools and completing high school, combined with increasing emphasis on higher education in particular fields and more general reliance on educational credentials as a means for firms to select employees, contributed to massive growth in postsecondary studies. The data in Table 8.2 demonstrate that, in 1950/1, only about 69,000 people were enrolled in full-time university studies, but university

Table 8.2 **Full-Time Enrolment in Canada, by Level of Study, Selected Years, 1870–2000 (in Thousands)**

	Pre-elementary	Elementary and Secondary	Non-university Postsecondary	University Undergraduate	University Graduate
1870	–	768	–	2	–
1880	–	852	–	3	–
1890	–	943	–	5	<1
1900	–	1,055	–	7	<1
1910	–	1,318	–	13	<1
1920	–	1,834	–	23	<1
1930	–	2,099	–	32	1
1940	–	2,075	–	35	2
1950	–	2,391	–	64	5
1955	103	3,118	33	69	3
1960	146	3,997	49	107	7
1965	268	4,918	69	187	17
1970	402	5,661	166	276	33
1975	399	5,376	221	331	40
1980	398	4,709	261	338	45
1985	422	4,506	322	412	55
1990	473	4,669	325	468	64
1995	536	4,895	391	498	75
2000	522	4,867	407[a]	591[a]	–

[a] 1999.

SOURCE: Compiled from various editions of Dominion Bureau of Statistics/Statistics Canada, census data and "Education at a Glance," *Education Quarterly Review*.

enrolment exploded to over 200,000 by the mid-1960s and approached 600,000 by 2000.

A similar pattern followed in other postsecondary institutions, which until the 1960s had encompassed mostly specific occupational and vocational certification programs in areas such as nursing and teacher education as well as pre-university studies in Quebec and other provinces. However, the introduction and expansion of the community college system in the 1960s and 1970s provided numerous options for postsecondary study both for students seeking certification in specialized trades or vocations and for students taking courses that could be employed for university credit. Sociologists have been concerned with issues related to the bureaucratic organization of education and educational inequality as school size and complexity increased.

Education in the Learning Society

The organization and nature of schooling across Canada remain varied. Initiatives to implement greater conformity and consistency across jurisdictions run parallel with increased numbers of alternative schools and educational services. Educational diversity is a product, in part, of the fact that elementary and secondary education is a formal jurisdiction of the provinces under constitutional legislation, while other forms of education, including adult and postsecondary education and vocational training, are controlled, operated, or funded by a variety of governments (federal, provincial, and First Nations) and by private sources. Increased emphasis on education and training has been accompanied by considerable expansion of educational opportunities and programs offered at all levels. Many people are turning to additional sources, such as distance education and Web-based course offerings that originate both within and outside Canada.

Formally, schooling is compulsory for Canadians aged 5 to 16 in most provinces. However, most people engage in education well beyond these limits. The widespread use of terms such as *information society*, *learning society*, and **lifelong learning** signifies the central place that education holds within the context of what is commonly designated as the **new economy** or *knowledge-based economy*. The new economy has gained prominence through increasing reliance on rapidly changing information technologies and scientific advancements that have affected not only business and the workplace, but virtually every major sphere of social life. Learning is central to all dimensions of the new economy, including the need to train qualified personnel; to conduct research for continuing innovation; to develop, test, and market new products and services within firms; to process the vast amounts of new information being created; and to ensure that people have the capacities to employ new technologies at work and at home (Wolfe and Gertler, 2001). In this climate, what counts is not so much the knowledge that we acquire as the capacity to learn and apply that knowledge to emergent situations. People are expected not simply to learn more, but to develop different ways of learning.

These expectations have contributed to extensive levels of and variations in educational qualifications and experiences. With respect to formal learning, nearly 6.4 million Canadians (about one-fifth of the entire population) identified in Table 8.2 are engaged in full-time schooling, and well over 300,000 more are involved in part-time studies. Between one-quarter and one-third of the population that has completed initial education indicate, as well, that they are involved in some adult education, whether in the form of in-person, correspondence, or private courses, workshops, apprenticeships, or arts, crafts, or recreation programs (Statistics Canada and HRDC, 2001: 13).

The phenomenon of informal learning has also attracted growing attention. *Informal learning* involves distinct efforts arranged and undertaken by individuals or groups to acquire new knowledge that can be applied to work, personal, or community circumstances. Such activities include initiatives to learn a new language on one's own or with other people, to learn computer skills or software programs, or to gain competencies that can be used for volunteer work or family situations. Surveys in Canada and the United States estimate that over three-quarters of the adult population undertake well over 300 hours of informal learning projects per person every year. Even among adults with a university degree, nearly half (48 per cent) report that they are engaged in adult education, and nearly all people, regardless of education, are heavily involved in informal learning activities (Livingstone, 1999: 36–7; Statistics Canada and HRDC, 2001: 18).

Canada ranks high on international comparisons of education, although Canadians are not unique in their growing pursuit of education and training. Among the nine Organisation of Economic Co-operation and Development (OECD) nations represented in Figure 8.1, Canada has the highest proportion of the population with formal educational credentials beyond high school and ranks second, behind the United States, with respect to the percentage of the population with a university degree.

Emphasis on formal training and lifelong learning is a phenomenon associated with **globalization** and competitiveness across national settings. Throughout the twentieth century, the degree to which a population was educated came to be recognized as a significant indicator of modernization and development status. The more education one has, the higher the chances are to have a good job, better income, good health status, and many other factors positively associated with a high standard of living. Conversely, rates of poverty, unemployment, crime, serious illness and injury, and other less desirable indicators rise when formal education is limited.

Many nations are accelerating the pace of educational advancement as they undertake economic and human resource development strategies aimed at the production of new knowledge and a more highly trained workforce. The importance of education for the new economy is highlighted in the titles of numerous recent research reports and discussion papers produced by governments; Canadian examples include *High School May Not Be Enough* (Human Resources Development Canada and Statistics Canada, 1998), *Learning a Living in Canada* (Skill Development Leave Task Force, 1983), and *Knowledge Matters: Skills and Learning for Canadians* (Human Resources Development Canada, 2002). Consequently, governments, businesses, and agencies concerned with economic development stress the need to expand education well beyond compulsory levels in order to foster both economic growth and non-economic benefits such as improved health, the ability to use skills for non-monetary purposes, and the intrinsic desire to learn (OECD, 2001). The prevailing sentiment is that, with a few variations, "overall, individuals will need more and more knowledge and skills, and our society will need a class of highly educated and trained people to prosper" (LeBlanc, 1994: 15).

Regardless of the widespread acceptance of and participation in education as an essential feature of contemporary life, not everyone encounters and benefits from education in the same way. Educational experiences, outcomes, and achievements differ considerably among individuals and groups and are interpreted in different ways.

Figure 8.1 **Level of Education and Functional Literacy in Selected OECD Countries, 1996[a]**

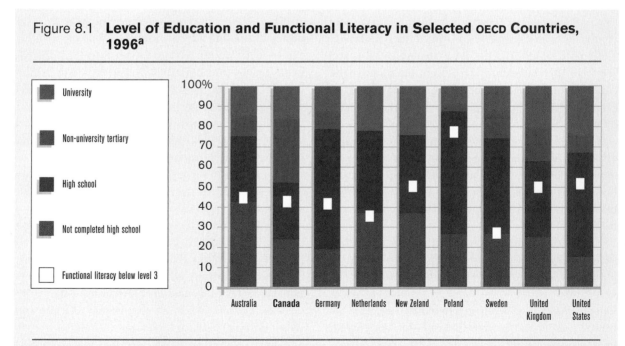

[a] Percentage distribution of the population 25 to 64 years of age, by the highest completed level of education (1996) and level of functional literacy proficiency (1994–5).
SOURCE: Adapted from Statistics Canada, *Learning a Living: A Report on Adult Education and Training in Canada*, Catalogue 81-856, May 2001.

Alternative Accounts of Educational Growth and Development

There are various ways of understanding education, just as there are diverse orientations to what education should be like. These orientations are concerned with the politics of education or represent different ideological positions that outline specific visions related to issues such as what kinds of education a society should have, who should control and pay for education, and what should be taught in schools. Sociological theories of education, by contrast, are more concerned with describing and explaining education systems, educational processes, and educational change, although they sometimes draw from or influence educational **ideologies**.

Several major theoretical perspectives that have been applied to an understanding of the education system are outlined here: the structural-functionalist approach, symbolic interactionist and interpretive theories, conflict theory, feminist theories, and more recent integrative orientations to the analysis of education.

Structural Functionalism

Structural functionalism is concerned primarily with understanding how different parts of the entire social system are interconnected in order to keep the system going. It addresses questions of how societies perpetuate themselves, how individuals come to be integrated within social frameworks, and how social change can occur without upsetting the social order. Structural functionalism examines education, like any other aspect of society, in terms of its contributions to social order and stability. Education gains importance in modern societies as an institution that provides participants with the core understandings, capabilities, and selection criteria necessary to enable them to fit into prescribed social and economic roles. As society becomes more complex and specialized, schools and other educational institutions take on many of the functions previously managed by families, communities, and religious organizations to ensure that children and youth—and eventually adult learners, also—are equipped for work and adult life.

The structural-functionalist perspective presents an image of the properly functioning society as one in which the **transition** from early childhood and family life into schooling and eventually the labour force is relatively seamless, relying upon the co-ordination and integration of all key components. Disruptions and changes are posed as problems of adjustment, either within the social system or by individuals who do not "fit." Social pathologies, like the need for periodic automobile maintenance or health check-ups, must be repaired through proper diagnosis and treatment in order to maintain the system in a state of healthy balance.

Émile Durkheim, who wrote extensively about education in his efforts to establish sociology as a distinct scientific discipline in the early twentieth century, described education as "the means by which society perpetually re-creates the conditions of its very existence" ([1922] 1956: 123). Education cultivates within each person knowledge as well as moral obligation and commitment to other members within a social framework governed by definite rules, regulations, and expectations.

Talcott Parsons (1959) later extending this analysis to a North American context, highlighting the two central functions that schooling fulfills within contemporary societies. First, schooling allocates individuals into selected occupational pathways and social positions in order to match social requirements with the available pool of skill, talents, and interests. Second, it socializes people by providing them with the general aptitudes and knowledge that they need to operate successfully in their society and preparing them more specifically for the adult roles that they will occupy. Schooling is organized in such a way that people move in the primary grades from home environments where highly personal, emotional ties prevail, through the senior grades, which are marked by progressively greater degrees of competition, merit, and instrumentality intended to prepare the individual for integration into work and other institutional settings crucial to adult life.

Robert Dreeben (1968) shows further the importance of school practices, in and out of the classroom, in cultivating characteristics essential for contemporary work and public life. Four essential **norms** are independence (acting by oneself), achievement (actions to meet accepted standards of excellence), universalism (treatment of others in an impartial way based on general categories), and specificity (emphasizing selected important individual characteristics as opposed to the person as a whole).

Structural functionalism offers a possible explanation of educational expansion both by connecting schooling with the growth of complexity in the occupational structure and by highlighting its increasing importance to citizenship in industrialized societies. A related form of analysis, sometimes referred to as *technical functionalism*, links educational growth with the increasing technical sophistication of jobs and knowledge production (Bell, 1973). Functionalist analysis typically assumes a broad social consensus about what should be taught in schools and how educational institutions should be organized. Moreover, it tends not to question either the legitimacy of educational credentials to determine entry into specified labour market positions or the fairness of the way the education system operates.

Functionalist analysis also tends to portray deviation from these ideals as abnormalities or temporary problems that warrant minor reforms rather than challenges to the education system as a whole. It offers more of a description of what schools should be like, within liberal democratic ideologies, than an explanation of how schooling came about. Functionalism presents education as a meritocratic ideal, a means to enable people to gain opportunities for social or economic success regardless of their social backgrounds. Societies require a careful fit among capability, talent, effort, training, and jobs as social tasks become more complex and specialized. These claims have led to subsequent research into the definition and measurement of educational inequality, calling into question the degree to which educational realities match the needs of industrial democratic societies.

Human capital theory, an approach with some affinity to structural functionalism, emphasizes education's role as a critical tool for developing human capacities to create and apply new knowledge. The human being is regarded as an input, along with material and economic resources, that contributes to economic productivity and development. **Human capital** can be enhanced when adequate investment is made in the form of proper training, education, and social support; this approach has been used to justify massive investment by governments that contributed to the significant enrolment growth in postsecondary education observed in Table 8.2 (p. 190). More recently, human capital theory has been revisited as attention turns to the importance of advanced training and educational credentials in the "knowledge" society.

Despite evidence that levels of employment, income, and other benefits improve with educational attainment, structural functionalism and related theories, such as human capital theory, are unable to account for the presence of persistent inequalities in educational opportunities, outcomes, and benefits. The theoretical emphasis on consensus limits consideration of differences in educational values, content, and practices; of how some things get incorporated into schooling while others do not; and of how these differences affect people from different social backgrounds. Alternative theoretical approaches to education attempt to address some of these issues.

Symbolic Interactionism and Microsociology

In contrast to structural functionalism's focus on education systems and institutional arrangements, *microsociology* or *interpretive theories* are concerned more with interpersonal dynamics and how people make sense of their **social interactions**. The term **symbolic interactionism**, applied to one of the most influential branches of microsociology, reveals its focus on the ways in which meanings and **symbols** are integral to social activity. Symbolic interactionism moves the analysis directly into the lives and understandings of social participants.

Interpretive analysis examines diverse questions central to the sociological study of education, such as how schooling contributes to the development of personality and **identity**, how some forms of knowledge and not others enter into the curriculum, and how students and teachers shape the learning process in and out of the classroom. This work stresses the importance of examining the meanings and possibilities that social actors bring to social settings. Willard Waller depicts schools as "the meeting-point of a large number of intertangled social relationships. These social relationships are the paths pursued by social interaction, the channels in which social influences run. The crisscrossing and interactions of these groups make the school what it is" ([1932] 1965: 12). Peter Woods (1979) explores schooling as a series of **negotiations** among teachers, students, and parents, expressed in phenomena such as how pupils select the subjects they take, the role of humour and laughter in the classroom and staff room, and teacher reports on student progress. Howard Becker (1952) shows how teachers' backgrounds influence their construction of images of the ideal pupil, which in turn affect how they treat and assess students.

These examples illustrate symbolic interactionists' depictions of societies and institutions as fluid rather than fixed entities. Institutional patterns are the result of recurrent daily activity and of people's capacities to shape, interpret, reproduce, and modify social arrangements through their social relations. *Ethnomethodology*, a variant of interpretive sociology, examines in detail the methods or approaches that people draw upon to construct a sense of reality and continuity in everyday life. Understood this way, the likelihood that classrooms in one place resemble those in another is less a product of a given model of schooling than an outcome of actions based on images about what is expected of us and how we are supposed to act.

Symbolic interactionism and ethnomethodology offer interesting insights, but they tend to fail to account for broader concerns and limiting factors by focusing too much on the details of ongoing social activity. Classroom dynamics or how one interprets the curriculum cannot be understood fully without reference to educational policy, power structures, social change, and persistent social inequalities that strongly influence educational processes and outcomes.

Some researchers have combined interpretive sociology, with its insights into practical social activity, with other approaches that pay greater attention to the social contexts within which social action takes place. Several British sociologists, under the banner of the "new sociology of education," extended this analysis by attempting to break down barriers between **micro-** and **macrosociology**, and by shifting attention away from educational problems defined by educational administrators and policy makers. Their concern is with how educational knowledge and practices are socially constructed and become part of the "taken for granted" assumptions that guide the actions and understandings of teachers and other educational participants. This work has focused "on the curriculum, on the 'educational knowledge' imparted by the school, and on the school's conception of 'what it is to be educated'" (Blackledge and Hunt, 1985: 290). Furthering this analysis, Basil Bernstein (1977) highlights the various ways that **power** and control enter into the authority structure of schools and classrooms as well as through the expectations and assumptions around which the curriculum and educational policies are framed. Bernstein's contributions to a systematic understanding of micro and macro levels of analysis have influenced writers working within diverse theoretical traditions (Sadovnik, 1995).

Conflict Theory

Conflict theory encompasses approaches to social analysis that emphasize competition between and power relations among social actors, groups, or forces. There is much greater concern than in other approaches with how institutional structures and social inequalities are maintained or changed through conflict and struggle.

Samuel Bowles and Herbert Gintis (1976), like structural functionalists, emphasize schools' role as mechanisms to select and prepare people for different positions in labour markets and institutional life. Their Marxist orientation, however, reveals schools' inability to fulfill the democratic ideology that all people have fair chances to succeed. The labour market is conditioned more by capitalist interests than by general consensus about social values and needs. Bowles and Gintis posit education, historically, as "a device for allocating individuals to economic positions, where inequality among the positions themselves is inherent in the hierarchical division of labor, differences in the degree of monopoly power of various sectors of the economy, and the power of different occupational groups to limit the supply or increase the monetary returns to their services" (1976: 49).

Conflict theorists emphasize that education-related inequalities are not simple imbalances that can be eradicated with minor modifications or reforms. Deeply rooted relations of domination and subordination create persistent barriers to opportunity and advancement. This critical sociological orientation denies the functionalist and human capital theory accounts of educational expansion as being a result of rising technical requirements of jobs. Different **social groups** are understood to employ education and educational ideologies as tools to pursue their own interests. Employers rely on formal educational credentials, regardless of the skills demanded by the job, to screen applicants and assess a person's general attributes. Professions control access to education and certification as a way to preserve the status and benefits attached to their occupations. New knowledge and technological advancements in areas such as medicine, nursing, teaching, engineering, and information processing may appear to produce a demand for increasingly more advanced, specialized training. But more often, credential inflation occurs as occupations preserve special privileges by simultaneously claiming the need for superior qualifications and restricting entry into these kinds of jobs (Collins, 1979).

Technological developments are not necessarily accompanied by increasing skill requirements for many jobs. Machines and information technology often substitute routine technical operations for human input or lead to new jobs in which people are required to do little but read gauges, respond to signals, or input information. Under these conditions, schools can function more as warehouses to delay people's entrance into the labour force and dissipate dissatisfaction with the economy's failure to provide sufficient numbers of satisfying jobs than as places where effective learning and occupational training take place. Harry Braverman suggests that "there is no longer any place for the young in this society other than school. Serving to fill a vacuum, schools have themselves become that vacuum, increasingly emptied of content and reduced to little more than their own form" (1974: 440). **Capitalism**, in this view, has contributed less to skills upgrading through technological advancement than to an ongoing process that erodes working skills, degrades workers, and marginalizes youth.

Other conflict theorists highlight the biases and inequalities that are produced directly or indirectly through the curriculum and classroom practices. Students and parents have different understandings, resources, and time that affect the extent to which they can participate in and benefit from educational opportunities. Government cutbacks and changes to school funding formulas exacerbate many of these inequalities. In Ontario, for instance, many schools report difficulty raising funds even for basic school materials and supplies: "funding levels are so low, parents are having to make up for programs that aren't paid for—so then it depends on where you live and who you are. . . . There is a growing concern about equity. There is a growing gap between the 'have' and 'have-not' schools" (L. Brown, 2002: A1, A26).

In postsecondary education, decreased government funding has led to rising tuition fees, which, accompanied by higher costs for textbooks and technology support, living expenses, and other factors, make it increasingly difficult for students without sufficient resources or unable or unwilling to take on mounting student loans to attend colleges and universities. Conflict analysis also points to concern about the growing reliance by educational institutions on corporate donations and sponsorships to make up for shortfalls in government funding.

Conflict theories of education, in short, stress that expectations for schooling to fulfill its promise to offer equal opportunity and social benefits to all are unrealistic or unattainable within current forms of social organization. Barriers that exist at several levels—access to schooling, what is taught and how it is taught, ability to influence educational policy and decision making, and differential capacity to convert education into labour market and social advantage—deny many individuals or groups the chances to benefit from meaningful forms and levels of education. Conflict theories offer varying assessments of what must be done to ensure that education can be more democratic and equitable. Some analysts stress that educational institutions and organizations themselves must be transformed, while others suggest that any kinds of school reform will be limited without more fundamental social and economic changes to ensure that people will be able to use, and be recognized for using, their education and training more effectively.

Feminist Theories

Feminist analyses of schooling share similar observations with other conflict theories, though with an explicit emphasis on the existence of and strategies to address social inequalities based on **gender**. Feminist theory stresses that social equity and justice are not possible as long as males and females have unequal power and status though **patriarchy** or gendered systems of domination. In the eighteenth century, Mary Wollstonecraft ([1792] 1986) saw access to education as a fundamental right for women; by being denied such a right historically, women were degraded as "frivolous," or a "backward sex." Later waves of feminism have continued to look to education as a central institution through which to promote women's rights, opportunities, and interests.

There are multiple "feminisms" in the analysis of education, rather than a single feminist orientation; each poses different questions for educational research and proposes different explanations and strategies for change (Gaskell, 1993; Weiner, 1994). In general, though, feminist analysis shows that influential mainstream studies of schooling have often concentrated on the lives of boys and men, with little recognition that girls and women have different experiences and little chance to voice their concerns. Much research in the 1970s and 1980s focused on how such things as classroom activities, language use, images and examples in textbooks and curriculum

Sociology in Action
Dimensions of Educational Participation

In Canada and most other nations, educational participation rates and attainment levels are increasing, regardless of social background. Sociologists have debated the extent to which these trends do or do not reflect education's ability to fulfill its promise to provide social and economic opportunity, especially in relation to demands associated with labour markets that require more skilled and highly qualified workers.

Exploration of these issues offers a useful opportunity to apply a *sociological imagination*, described by C. Wright Mills (1959) as the ability to link one's personal biography or background and circumstances with historical sensitivity to wider social structures and processes.

Begin by examining your own educational and career pathways. What level of formal education have you attained so far? What level would you like to attain? What other kinds of education (such as informal learning through self-directed or group study, special interest courses, adult education, or on-the-job training) have you engaged in? Have there been any gaps or interruptions in your studies? What experiences (positive or negative) have affected your interest and ability to gain the level of education you desire or have completed? What jobs (if any) have you been engaged in? What is the relationship between your educational background, including any specific skills, knowledge, or credentials you have, and the job itself? (Examine both the starting

qualifications for the job and the actual tasks involved in the job.) What future employment do you desire, and how is this related to your educational plans and qualifications?

Second, consider your own educational experiences in relation to your social background and context. How typical or different are your own educational and work experiences in comparison with your family and members of other social groups you have associated with (such as your grandparents, parents, childhood peers, and community members) or those you consider yourself part of now? Relate your educational experiences and aspirations to other important characteristics or aspects of your social background (including your gender, race, ethnicity, family income, regional and national origin, place of residence such as urban or rural, age, and other factors your consider important).

Third, engage in broader comparisons between your own education and working experiences and those of others. Examine data from various studies cited in this chapter, and from extensive records maintained on the Statistics Canada Web site. What is the relationship between your experiences, those of other persons from your family and home community, and wider trends evident from these data?

Finally, explain the major patterns and conclusions derived through your inquiries. What do these findings reveal about the nature of education and its social and economic importance?

material (including the absence of women and girls in many instances), treatment of students by teachers, and patterns of subject choice reflected gender-based stereotypes and perpetuated traditional divisions among males and females (Kenway and Modra, 1992).

Feminist analysis seeks to do more than simply demonstrate how these social processes contribute to inequalities, in order to change the conditions that bring these practices about. This focus has shifted as some aspects of the agenda on women's rights a nd issues have advanced successfully while specific barriers continue to restrict progress on other fronts. For instance, school boards have policies, enforced through human rights legislation, to restrict sexist curricula and to prohibit gender-based **discrimination** in educational programs and institutions. Educational participation rates of and attainment by females have come to exceed those for males. Yet there remains a need for greater progress in getting girls to take courses or programs in areas such as computer programming, engineering, and some natural sciences and to remove gender-based barriers in other areas of schooling.

Feminist analysis of education also explores the gender structure of the teaching force. The feminization of teaching, as female teachers came to outnumber male teachers by the end of the nineteenth century, carried significant implications for the occupation and its members. Teachers often lack the professional recognition that might otherwise accompany the demands and training their work involves. Teachers—and women teachers in particular—have been heavily regulated by governments and by school boards. During the early part of the twentieth century, guidelines often specified such things as what teachers could wear, with whom they could associate, and how they should act in public (Wotherspoon, 1995). Until the 1950s, legislation in many provinces required women to resign their teaching positions upon marriage. Although today's teachers have much greater personal and professional autonomy than those of the past, teachers' lives and work remain subject to various forms of scrutiny, guidelines, and informal practices that carry gender-based assumptions or significance. Female teachers predominate in the primary grades, while men tend to be overrepresented in the upper grades and in postsecondary teaching positions, especially in the most senior teaching and educational administrative positions.

Feminist analysis also addresses interrelationships among gender and other social factors and personal characteristics. Gender-based identities, experiences, and opportunities are affected by race, region, social class, and competing expectations and demands that people face at home, in the workplace, and in other social spheres (Acker, 1999). Students and teachers from different backgrounds encounter diverse experiences, concerns, and options, even within similar educational settings, which in turn affect subsequent educational and personal options.

Emerging Analysis and Research in the Sociology of Education

Educational researchers make distinct choices about which theoretical positions are most useful or relevant to their analysis. Since theory is also a tool to help understand and explain phenomena and guide social action, sociologists commonly employ insights from a variety of models or orientations.

Critical pedagogy is an approach that draws from different theoretical positions, including conflict theory and feminist theory, both to explore how domination and power enter into schooling and personal life and to seek to change those aspects that undermine our freedom and humanity (Giroux, 1997; McLaren, 1998). Anti-racism education shares similar orientations, stressing further the ways in which domination builds upon notions of racial difference to create fundamental inequalities among groups that are defined on the basis of biological differences or cultural variations (Dei, 1996).

Pierre Bourdieu (1997a; Bourdieu and Passeron, 1979) has explored how **social structures** (the primary focus of both structural functionalism and conflict theory) become interrelated with the meanings and actions relevant to social actors (the main concern of symbolic interactionism or interpretative sociology). Bourdieu, as a critical theorist, emphasizes that education contributes to the transmission of power and privilege from one generation to another as it employs assumptions and procedures that advantage some groups and disadvantage others. Educational access, processes, and outcomes are shaped through struggles by different groups to retain or gain advantages relative to one another. However, the mere fact that people hold varying degrees of economic, social, and cultural resources does not guarantee that these will be automatically converted into educational advantage. Competition for educational access and credentials increases as different groups look to education to provide a gateway into important occupational and decision-making positions.

Canadian research, influenced by Bourdieu's analysis and other integrative approaches such as life course theory, demonstrates the complex interactions among personal and social structural characteristics that affect the pathways that children and youth take through education and from schooling into work and other life transitions (Andres Bellamy, 1993; Anisef et al., 2000). In order to understand schooling fully, it is necessary to take into account several interrelated dimensions, including

- how educational systems are organized and what happens inside schools
- how school experiences are made sense of and acted upon by various educational participants
- the relationships between internal educational processes and external factors, including governments and agencies that set and administer educational policy, employers that demand particular kinds of education and training and that recognize particular types of credentials, political frameworks composed of competing values and ideologies about what education should be all about and how resources should be allocated for education in relation to other priorities, and broader structures of social and economic opportunity and inequality
- the relations among transformations that are occurring on a global scale with more specific economic, political, and cultural structures that alternatively provide opportunities for, and systematically exclude, democratic participation by specific social groups (Apple, 1997; Torres, 1998)

Educational Participants

Educational institutions reveal considerable complexity in their organization and composition. Comprehensive schools may have 2,000 to 3,000 students and dozens of teachers and support staff, while colleges and universities can exceed the size of small cities. Consequently, sociologists are interested in questions related to the changing nature of who attends and works in these institutions (with respect to gender, racial, ethnic, religious, socio-economic, and other factors), what positions they occupy, and what barriers and opportunities they encounter.

Increasing diversity in education is a consequence of several factors. The educational participation of girls and women has increased significantly since World War II, especially at the postsecondary level. Immigration has also contributed to changing educational profiles, particularly in the largest cities. The immigrant population, in turn, contains increasing numbers and proportions of students classified as visible minorities and of those who speak languages other than English or French upon their arrival to Canada. Combined processes of rural-to-urban migration, policy changes, and population growth have increased the concentrations of Aboriginal students in elementary and secondary schools, especially in western and northern Canada. Economic changes have exacerbated many inequalities, including the perpetuation or magnification of gaps between high- and low-income families. Poverty and economic marginalization affect up to one-quarter of Canada's children. Classrooms also integrate students who historically have been excluded, such as those with physical or learning disabilities and teen parents. Numerous additional factors such as religious orientations, the health of regional economies, and distance to essential educational and support services affect educational participation and outcomes.

Significant questions arise concerning how educational institutions attend to the diverse circumstances and needs of their student bodies. Sociologists are interested in much more than simply how the curriculum and formally structured activities affect students' learning and chances for success. Educational organization, rules, expectations, and practices also contain a **hidden curriculum**, the unwritten purposes or goals of school life. School life has a daily rhythm, through repeated variations between structured learning situations and informal interactions, channelling students into selected directions and contributing to taken-for-granted understandings about order, discipline, power relations, and other aspects of social life (Lynch, 1989). These educational processes are likely to reflect selected interests or issues while they ignore others. Benjamin Levin and J. Anthony Riffel observe that "low socio-economic status is more strongly associated with poor educational outcomes than any other variable. Yet educators are quite ambivalent about the meaning of poverty for their work and the conduct of schooling" (1997: 117). Schooling often has limited connection with—and produces negative consequences for—the students and communities it is intended to serve (Dei et al., 2000; Royal Commission on Aboriginal Peoples, 1996).

Two mechanisms—referred to as *silencing* and the *banking model*—illustrate how common educational practices can have indirect and unequal consequences for students, their identities, and their educational experiences and outcomes. *Silencing* refers to practices that prevent educational participants from raising concerns that are important to them (such as when teachers do not give students the opportunity to talk about current events or matters of student interest), as well as to indirect processes that make students question their own cultural background or that discourage parents from talking to teachers because of their discomfort with the authority represented by the school. The *banking model* of **pedagogy** (Freire, 1970) refers to educational practice in which material is pre-packaged and transmitted in a one-way direction, from the educator to the student. This practice limits the forms of knowledge that are presented as valid, leaving students from alternative backgrounds with a sense that their experiences, questions, and capacities are invalid or irrelevant.

Many educators have modified their approaches as they have gained sensitivity to the impact of their actions on students and have responded to new skill priorities in areas such as critical thinking. However, educators are under considerable pressure to balance public demands for improvement in the quality of education with attention to the multi-faceted problems and interests they must deal with in their work. As resources and energies are directed to special needs students or to programs to accommodate students from diverse cultural backgrounds, there tends to be less time and funding for core areas that must also be covered.

The high profile given to concerns such as bullying and violence in the classroom and schoolyard is in part symptomatic of tensions encountered by both staff and students. Teachers are becoming increasingly frustrated with many aspects of their jobs as they find they are given little time and recognition for all that they are called upon to do (Council of Ministers of Education Canada, 1996). While teachers are considered to be professionals, with the expectation that they are responsible for planning and carrying out educational functions, their professional status is constrained by extensive regulations and scrutiny.

Educational Policy, Politics, and Ideologies

Educational policy is established and administered in a variety of ways across jurisdictional settings. Many nations, such as Sweden and Japan, have highly centralized systems of education. Canada and the United States, by contrast, do not have uniform or centralized education systems because education is constitutionally defined as an area of provincial and state authority. Canada exhibits what Paul Axelrod describes as an

"educational patchwork, particularly in comparison with the more uniform approaches of other countries" (1997: 126). In nearly all nations, however, competing demands for more co-ordinated educational planning, national standards, and consistency across jurisdictions coexist with competing reforms seeking greater responsiveness and **accountability** to local concerns (Manzer, 1994).

Provincial and territorial governments in Canada have the authority to create legislation and guidelines that outline virtually all aspects of the education system, including how it is organized, the school-year length, curriculum and graduation requirements, teacher qualifications and certification, and educational funding. The specific details related to setting and carrying out educational policies and operating schools are normally delegated to elected local school boards or similar regional bodies.

Almost all provinces and territories have begun in recent years to propose and initiate significant changes in the ways in which education is organized and administered, particularly at the school board or district level. Since the early 1990s, for instance, many provinces (Newfoundland and Labrador, Quebec, Alberta, and, for a five-year period, New Brunswick) have cut the number of school boards by more than half, while new bodies, including parents' advisory councils, have been established to replace or supplement school boards' roles in these and other jurisdictions (Council of Ministers of Education Canada, 2001).

Public education at elementary, secondary, and postsecondary levels have experienced significant financial changes since the early 1990s. Total educational expenditures in Canada dropped by more than $760 million between 1995 and 1996, with an overall decrease from 8 to 7 per cent of the nation's gross domestic product (GDP, or total expenditures) between 1992 and 1996 (Statistics Canada, 2002a: 49). Since the mid-1990s, renewed levels of educational spending have become more selective or targeted in nature. Selected educational priority areas, such as materials, innovation, and training related to new technologies, have expanded, whereas other areas have languished. Figure 8.2 shows that provincial and territorial governments are the predominant source of education funding in Canada but that there is growing reliance on private and individual sources.

These fiscal trends have also placed higher burdens on students and others who have come to be defined

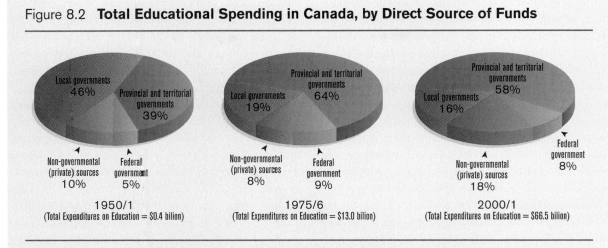

Figure 8.2 **Total Educational Spending in Canada, by Direct Source of Funds**

SOURCES: Based on data from Statistics Canada, *Historical Compendium of Education Statistics: From Confederation to 1975* (Ottawa: Statistics Canada, 1978); Statistics Canada, *Advance Statistics of Education* (Ottawa: Statistics Canada, annual); and Statistics Canada, *Education Quarterly Review* (2002), 8: 3.

as "educational consumers." Educational inequalities increase when students from less privileged backgrounds cannot afford to enrol and remain in advanced educational programs. Postsecondary tuition fees doubled during the 1990s and have continued to grow dramatically. Increases in the numbers of students incurring student debt and in the extent of student debt loads have accompanied rising costs of education and living expenses (Bouchard and Zhao, 2000).

Similarly, elementary and secondary schools are often forced to choose between having to pay higher costs, fundraising to cover educational expenses, and cutting school programs and services. An advocacy group in Ontario has expressed concern about what it views as the "growing gap between the 'have' and 'have-not' schools" following changes to the school funding formula in that province; among their findings from responses from 841 schools,

- Fifty-two per cent of schools said that they fundraise for classroom supplies, up from 31 per cent in 1997.
- Twenty-four per cent of schools fundraise for textbooks, up from 21 per cent in 1997.
- Sixty-two per cent of schools say they fundraise for library books, compared to 56 per cent in 1997 (L. Brown, 2002: A26).

Educational funding decisions are accompanied by growing concern over the extent to which education systems are able to prepare learners for contemporary economic and social conditions. There are competing viewpoints (often expressed through concerns about educational quality and excellence) about what role governments should play within this changing environment.

Neo-conservative critics have advocated for governments and the services they deliver, including education, to operate more like businesses guided by market principles. High-quality education is defined in terms of the excellence of educational "products," measured by such things as standardized test scores, parental choice, and public accountability. Parents and learners are commonly viewed, in this way, as "consumers" who should have the opportunity to approach education (like decision making about other purchases, with the added importance that it is their children and not some material object that is of concern) with the tools to make personal choices about the kinds of schooling they desire.

These criticisms have had some impact on education systems, particularly as governments look for ways to restrict expenditures and reorganize public services. Some observers view the recent directions in educational reform as a dangerous shift in public priorities to serve the needs of vocal interest groups who are more concerned with preserving the narrow interests of their own families or groups rather than a commitment to community participation and high-quality education (Osborne, 1999). Matters of educational quality, accountability, and choice are often framed by a focus on a limited number of factors that can be measured in quantifiable terms, such as standardized test results. These kinds of indicators, and the manner in which they are interpreted, can be misleading when they do not account for the full range of activities and competencies encompassed by schooling. Ironically, many reforms that claim to increase educational "choice," public accountability, and decentralization of educational decision making in fact concentrate control over such matters as finance, curriculum, and provincial testing at the provincial or territorial level or in central bodies outside of formal education systems (Gidney, 1999; Kachur and Harrison, 1999).

Education is the focus of intense debate in part because of its social and economic importance. It is both a central institution in the lives of children and youth and a strategic focus for policy related to emerging economic realities. Given these concerns, it is important not to forget that there has been fairly consistent consensus over time about the general nature and purposes of education: schooling is to be responsive, as much as possible, to the needs and interests of the communities it serves while it must also prepare people for effective participation in broader social, cultural, and economic contexts.

Education, Work, and Family

Changes in the nature and composition of learners' families and the varied demands from workplaces for particular kinds of qualified labour-force participants have made it even more crucial to understand how education systems interact with other institutions.

The nature of childhood and adolescence is changing profoundly as students and their families experience various life challenges. Few people experience traditional linear pathways from home to school to work. Periods of work and study often overlap. Children and their parents undergo substantial stress as they experience family breakdown, economic crises induced by job layoffs or persistent poverty, or difficulties in securing adequate child care arrangements. Family, work, and community responsibilities create multiple demands on both children's and parents' time, often making it difficult to provide strong support for learning and extracurricular activities that rely on extensive student–parent interaction. Tensions often spill over from one site of social life to another, expressed in public concern over phenomena such as bullying, violence, gang warfare, and "risk" among

children and youth. Unfortunately, these issues are often regarded in a highly sensationalist way that distorts the true nature of childhood and youth activity and that ignores the strong motivations and positive contributions to leadership and mutual support prevalent among much of the student population.

Students, teachers, and educational environments face additional stresses through the growing general emphasis on education as an entry point to subsequent occupational and economic success. Taking their cue from the market model of education, many parents view their children's education as an investment, making significant demands on both their children (in order to guarantee high performance) and on teachers and educational administrators (in order to deliver a high-quality product that will yield the best results in the marketplace). Parents and community members from diverse backgrounds often have divergent expectations about the way education should be organized and delivered. Some immigrants, for instance, may feel the Canadian education system is too unstructured and undemanding in comparison with the systems they were familiar with prior to arriving in Canada, while others take the opposite view (Campey, 2002). Aboriginal people look to schools to reconcile the need to prepare youth for a meaningful place in global society with the need to make strong connections with indigenous people, their cultural heritage, and their contemporary circumstances (Royal Commission on Aboriginal People, 1996).

Education and New Technologies

Education, like other institutions, has been significantly affected by the introduction of computers and other new technologies. Information technology, in a few cases, has indeed revolutionized education. Some institutions have replaced traditional instructional settings with fully wired teaching/learning centres in which participants can not only communicate with each other, but also draw upon material and interact with individuals on a global basis (Gergen, 2001). Schools in remote regions have gained access to varied learning resources and connections through the Internet and through initiatives such as SchoolNet, which aims to provide Web-based learning resources to all Canadian schools. Adults can subscribe to an unprecedented range of continuing and post-secondary study options. Schools and universities are just beginning to explore fully the opportunities that new technologies are making available to them (even though the origins of the World Wide Web lie, in part, in the development of a tool that could be used to produce and share new knowledge among university-based researchers).

New technologies and their use in and impact on education give rise to several important questions. Levin and Riffel, reviewing different perspectives on the role that new technologies play in school settings, conclude that "it may be that technology is not living up to its promise because it has been seen as an answer to rather than a reason to ask questions about the purposes of schools and the nature of teaching and learning" (1997: 114). Two issues are especially critical in this respect.

First, a significant "digital divide" separates those who have access to computers and electronic connections—and the skills and know-how to use and take advantage of new technologies—and those who

do not. This divide is most commonly posed in global terms, distinguishing richer, more technologically developed nations, such as those in North America, Europe, parts of Southeast Asia, and Australia and New Zealand, from developing nations in Asia, Africa, and Latin and South America. Canada, in this regard, is in a highly favourable situation in comparison to all or nearly all other nations, with one of the highest proportions of its population who use and own computers and employ Internet connections at home and at work. However, even within regions and nations, regular access to computers and the ability to employ them regularly at higher levels depend on such factors as a steady job, income and education levels, gender, social class, and racial characteristics (see Figure 8.3).

A second issue related to the impact of new technologies on education arises from an examination of how and why new technologies are being adopted as tools and expectations in education. Clearly, informa-

Figure 8.3 Internet Home Access Among Households by Income Level

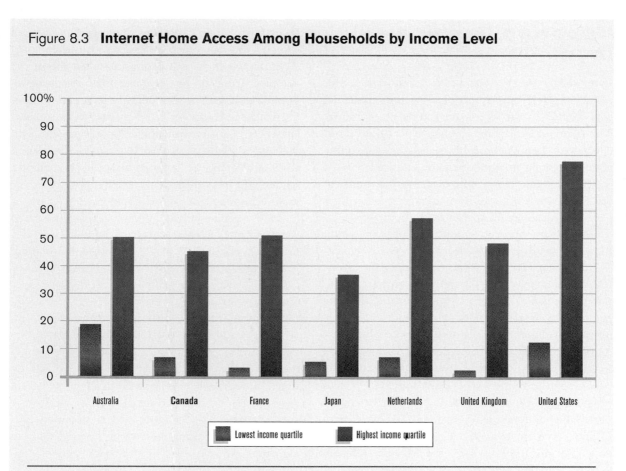

Lowest income quartile   Highest income quartile

SOURCE: Organisation for Economic Co-operation and Development, *The New Economy: Beyond the Hype. The OECD Growth Project* (Paris: OECD, 2001), 68. Reprinted by permission.

tion technology offers many advantages to users, contributes to important educational innovation, and may provide greater employment and economic opportunities outside of school. However, students and teachers are not always equipped and supported to use such technologies to their advantage or in ways that may benefit their education and training.

Issues related to the adoption of computer technologies in education reflect more enduring concerns about the relationship of what happens in the classroom with structures and processes outside of schooling. Educational practices are strongly influenced by social, technological, and economic developments and innovations, though they also reveal their own peculiarities and rhythms. Demands for education to prepare people for the changing workplace sit side by side with parallel demands for producing better citizens and persons with multiple competencies to function in a global society.

Educational Opportunities and Inequalities

Questions about the relationship of education with social inequality and opportunity structures have long been central to the sociological study of education. This is due, in large part, to public expectations about education's contributions to social and economic advancement in post-industrial or knowledge-based societies. Despite compelling evidence that much of this promise has been fulfilled, significant inequalities persist in educational experiences and outcomes.

Differences between groups are apparent within the significant increases in levels and rates of educational participation and attainment across the population as a whole. One of the most striking trends within the general pattern of educational growth has been the strong advancement of educational opportunities for women, particularly in postsecondary education. With respect to the increase in overall education levels during the period between 1951 and 1991, Neil Guppy and Scott Davies point to two key trends related to gender: "First, at the low end of the educational distribution, men remained less likely than women to complete at least Grade 9 and this difference did not narrow over the 40-year interval. Second, at higher education levels, women have surpassed the lead that men clearly held in 1951" (1998: 87). Among persons most likely to have completed

their education recently, the proportion of the population in the 20- to 29-year-old age cohort with a postsecondary degree or diploma increased from 37 per cent for both men and women in 1981 to 51 per cent for women and only 42 per cent for men in 1996 (Statistics Canada, 1998b: 1). By 1999, nearly three out of five (57.6 per cent) of all persons who received university degrees were women, although the reverse was true at the highest end, where 61 per cent of PhDs were awarded to men (based on Statistics Canada, 2002a: 43; see also Table 8.3).

The shift in the gender balance of educational attainment has drawn attention to other aspects of education. Findings from numerous surveys that girls have begun to outperform boys on a number of indicators have generated controversy over suggestions that gender inequality has reversed to the point that the education system is now "failing" boys. For example, the comprehensive Programme for International Student Assessment (PISA), conducted in 2000 to compare student performance in core areas, posed a concern for policy makers that girls in Canada and the 31 other participating nations consistently demonstrated stronger test outcomes in reading (Bussière et al., 2001). However, the PISA findings also demonstrate the complex nature of gender inequalities in education. Few pronounced gender differences appear in performance in areas of mathematics and science. Moreover, the survey highlights how similarities and differences based on gender cannot be understood without reference to a broad array of other family, school, and individual characteristics, notably family socio-economic background (Bussière et al., 2001).

Many gender-related differences are obscured through simple comparisons between boys' and girls' test results (Epstein et al., 1997). Women outnumber men in postsecondary enrolment and graduation, but there are strong gender differences in fields of study and types of training programs (see Table 8.3). Programs in areas such as business, management, and commerce, some arts and social sciences, protection and correction services, and languages are relatively popular among both men and women. Women are much more heavily concentrated in a few fields such as education, nursing, and social work or social services. Men tend to be more widely dispersed over more fields but outnumber women considerably in areas such as engineering and electrical technologies, computer science, and primary industries.

Differences in fields of study reflect a combination of personal choices and circumstances, institutional characteristics (such as cues or levels of comfort and discomfort that direct students into some areas and away from others or the compatibility between particular programs and responsibilities to care for dependent children), and broader socio-economic factors (Statistics Canada, 1998b; Wotherspoon, 2000). Employment options and life pathways are generally associated with the kinds of education and credentials that people attain. Nonetheless, rising levels of education do not always translate fully into gains in labour market positions, incomes, and other equitable outcomes for women (Kenway et al., 1998).

As the case with gender comparisons, educational differences between racial and ethnic groups appear to have disappeared or diminished significantly in recent decades (Guppy and Davies, 1998). Immigration policies have simultaneously emphasized the recruitment of immigrants with high educational credentials and made Canada less dependent on immigrants from Western Europe and the United States. These policies have contributed to a growing proportion of highly educated or professionally qualified visible-minority immigrants who place a high value on their children's educational advancement.

Table 8.3 **Top Fields of Study by Gender, Postsecondary Graduates, Canada**

Community College Diplomas Granted in Career Programs, 1997–8[a]

Women

Rank	Field of Study	Number of Graduates	Women Graduates in Field as % of All Women Graduates	Women as % of All Graduates in Field
1	Management and administration	9,198	17.4	62.3
2	Social services	5,271	10.0	86.7
3	Nursing	4,952	9.4	88.0
4	Secretarial science	4,471	8.5	93.0
5	Arts	4,365	8.3	58.4
6	Health-related technologies	4,156	7.9	77.5
7	Educational and counselling services	3,665	6.9	93.3
8	Protection and correction services	2,233	4.2	48.8
9	Arts and sciences	1,966	3.7	58.7
10	Computer science and mathematics	1,748	3.3	32.0
Total Women Graduates		**52,909**	**79.4**	**57.9**

Men

Rank	Field of Study	Number of Graduates	Men Graduates in Field as % of All Men Graduates	Men as % of All Graduates in Field
1	Management and administration	5,566	14.5	37.7
2	Computer science and mathematics	3,718	9.7	68.0
3	Electrical/electronic technologies	3,542	9.2	92.8
4	Arts	3,109	8.1	41.6
5	Protection and correction services	2,341	6.1	51.2
6	Arts and sciences	1,384	3.6	41.3
7	Merchandising and sales	1,364	3.5	47.3
8	Health-related technologies	1,210	3.1	22.5
9	Environmental and conservation technologies	1,079	2.9	61.0
10	Primary industries	894	2.3	81.1
Total Men Graduates		**38,450**	**63.0**	**42.1**

(continued)

Table 8.3 **(cont.)**

University Bachelor's and First Professional Degrees, 1998

Women

Rank	Field of Study	Number of Graduates	Women Graduates in Field as % of All Women Graduates	Women as % of All Graduates in Field
1	Education	11,435	15.5	74.2
2	Business, management, and commerce	7,045	9.6	48.5
3	Psychology	6,756	9.2	78.0
4	Languages	5,595	7.6	75.5
5	Sociology	4,290	5.8	76.0
6	Biology	3,834	5.2	60.4
7	Nursing	3,084	4.2	93.0
8	Physical education	2,244	3.0	56.7
9	Social work	2,096	2.8	84.9
10	Law	1,830	2.5	52.4
Total Women Graduates		**73,593**	**65.5**	**58.9**

Men

Rank	Field of Study	Number of Graduates	Men Graduates in Field as % of All Men Graduates	Men as % of All Graduates in Field
1	Business, management, and commerce	7,466	14.6	51.5
2	Engineering	6,598	12.9	80.1
3	Education	3,983	7.8	25.8
4	Computer science	2,530	4.9	79.4
5	Biology	2,515	4.9	39.6
6	Economics	1,930	3.8	60.2
7	Psychology	1,900	3.7	22.0
8	Languages	1,818	3.5	24.5
9	Physical education	1,712	3.3	43.3
10	History	1,686	3.3	51.2
Total Men Graduates		**51,268**	**62.7**	**41.1**

[a] Figures have been rounded.
SOURCE: Data derived from Statistics Canada, *Education in Canada, 2000* (Ottawa: Statistics Canada, 2001), 126–46.

Racial diversity has been accompanied by increasing sensitivity to the impact of racial discrimination and other mechanisms that historically have excluded or discouraged racial minority students from advancing through the Canadian education system.

Nonetheless, as in the case of gender inequalities, much of the analysis of racial and ethnic inequality in education points to a complex series of factors and interactions that do not lead to any straightforward conclusions. The short answer to the question of whether some groups are advantaged or disadvantaged in relation to racial and ethnic criteria is, "It depends." Guppy and Davies (1998), in common with many other commentators who have reviewed census data and education indicators over time, observe that Canadians in most categories (based on gender, race, region, age, class, and other factors) have benefited from the expansion of education systems. However, specific groups, including Aboriginal people, those from working-class backgrounds, francophones within Quebec, Portuguese Canadians, and the disabled, continue to face strong disadvantages relative to most other groups. Social class has a strong impact on postsecondary attendance and educational attainment. These general trends are compounded by considerable variation in educational success and attainment within groups.

Research on education for Aboriginal people is instructive in this regard. Many significant initiatives have been undertaken as researchers, policy makers, and educators have come to acknowledge the combined impact of significant barriers to educational advancement faced by Aboriginal people. Education has long been regarded by Aboriginal people, as for any other group, as an important vehicle for gaining meaningful employment and social participation. Many First Nations, for instance, expressed their desire in the treaty-making process in the nineteenth century to have access to formal education in order to keep pace with contemporary social and economic demands.

However, subsequent developments, including the often damaging legacy of residential schooling, lack of acceptance or discriminatory treatment in provincial schools, and other social, cultural, and economic factors, have left Aboriginal people's overall education levels (especially for Registered Indians who live on reserve) well below national levels (Schissel and Wotherspoon, 2003). Data from the 1996 census reveal that "despite general improvements in educational attainment, Aboriginal people in [the 20- to 29-year-old] age group remained only one-half as likely to have a postsecondary degree or diploma, one-fifth as likely to have graduated from university and over twice as likely not to have completed high school" (Statistics Canada, 1998b: 7).

Sociologists and other researchers have identified numerous factors, such as cultural differences, lack of individual motivation and family or community support, and social and educational discrimination, to explain these educational inequalities. In fact, a complex chain of interrelated cause-and-effect mechanisms is usually involved. Increasing attention has been paid to the importance of early childhood development and to the family and social environments in which children are raised for the development of literacy and language skills, thinking processes, and other capacities that are central to educational success. These conditions, in turn, depend on the socio-economic circumstances of parents, the availability of support networks in the home and community,

labour market opportunities for parents and students coming out of the education system, the extent to which people in particular communities or regions have access to high-quality educational programs and services, and numerous other factors. There are strong associations between social class or socio-economic background and educational attainment. Parents' education levels and household income are strong predictors, both independently and in combination with one another, of the likelihood that a person will continue into postsecondary education (Knighton and Mirza, 2002).

Educational institutions are implicated in these broader processes in several ways. Schooling makes a difference in many ways, such as how well institutions are equipped to deal with students from diverse cultural and social backgrounds; the kinds of relationships that prevail between and among teachers, parents, and students; curricular objectives and materials; standards for assessing and evaluating students; and the general social climate within educational institutions. Social class and cultural differences are evident, for instance, in the grouping and **streaming** of students into specific educational programs that contribute, in turn, to diverse educational pathways.

There is general agreement, in the context of global economic developments that place a premium on knowledge and learning, that education is important for all people. The same consensus does not exist, however, with regard to how education should be arranged to fulfill its promise on an equitable basis.

Conclusion

This chapter has examined several dimensions of education and its relevance for sociological inquiry. It has highlighted the phenomenal growth of formal systems of education since the nineteenth century and the accompanying increases in general levels of education throughout the population. It has linked that growth to a strong degree of public faith in the ability of education to contribute simultaneously to individual development and to address social needs for knowledge, innovation, and credentials. Educational growth, processes, and outcomes have been understood from four major theoretical perspectives: structural functionalism, which analyzes education in terms of its contributions to dominant social and economic requirements; symbolic interactionism and microsociology, which highlight the roles and interactions of various participants within

8.2

Human Diversity
Education for Canada's Aboriginal People

The educational experiences of Aboriginal people in Canada are instructive for an understanding of how education can both advance and restrict social and economic opportunities. Historical practices and inequities have contributed to a legacy of widespread failure, marginalization, and mistrust, but considerable optimism also accompanies many new initiatives.

Many Aboriginal people in the late nineteenth century looked to schooling as a way to ensure integration into contemporary societies. Tragically, while some education-related treaty promises were fulfilled, the residential school system and continuing problems with other forms of educational delivery had devastating consequences that many Aboriginal communities and their members are still struggling to cope with. The report of the Royal Commission on Aboriginal Peoples (1996) endorsed the long-standing principle of First Nations control over education along with other measures to ensure that all educational institutions would provide more receptive schooling for Aboriginal people.

Mixed results have been accomplished so far, as one of the co-chairs of the Royal Commission has observed:

> Considering the primary importance of children in aboriginal cultures, it is not surprising that education was one of the first sectors where aboriginal nations and communities are now administered locally, and where possible they incorporate aboriginal languages and cultural content in the curriculum. . . .

More young people are staying in school to complete a high-school diploma, though a gap still exists between graduation rates of aboriginal and non-aboriginal people. . . . Aboriginal youth are especially vulnerable. They are less likely than mature adults to have attained academic and vocational credentials and they are hardest hit by unemployment. (Erasmus, 2002: F6–7)

The accomplishment of educational improvement is a difficult one in the context of considerable diversity among Aboriginal populations and their educational options, aspirations, and circumstances. Some successful schools or programs, for instance, have developed strong foundations in Aboriginal cultures and indigenous knowledge systems, while others have been more concerned to provide services oriented to students' immediate needs and future plans. Marlene Brant Castellano, Lynne Davis, and Louise Lahache, reviewing recent trends, conclude that

> the promise of education is that it will enable Aboriginal people to sustain well-being while meeting their responsibilities in the circle of life. Those responsibilities are seen to reach further today than in any previous generation. Fulfilling the promise will require preparing successive generations to participate fully in their own communities and to assume their place as Aboriginal citizens and peoples in global society. (2000: 255)

Historical developments, including the often damaging legacy of residential schooling, lack of acceptance or discriminatory treatment in provincial schools, and other social, cultural, and economic factors, have left Aboriginal people's overall education levels well below national levels. In February 2003, the *Globe and Mail* reported that Ottawa would make $35 million available over the next two years for issues such as stopping the high turnover among teachers in some First Nations schools. (Patti Gower/*Globe and Mail*)

educational processes; conflict theories, which emphasize education's contributions to social inequality and power relations; and feminist theories, which stress gender-based educational differences. The chapter has also addressed the changing significance of formal schooling to the experiences and social and economic opportunities of different social groups, particularly with respect to gender, race and ethnicity, and social class. All groups have benefited from educational expansion, though in varying degrees. Adequate sociological analysis of education requires an ability to integrate an understanding of what happens in and as a result of formal education with the social context in which education is situated.

☐ Questions for Critical Thought

1. Why is education in most nations organized formally through schools and related institutional structures rather than through some other arrangement, such as families or community-based agencies? To what extent should education be a private as opposed to a public responsibility?
2. Explain how and why employers and other agencies have come to rely on formal educational credentials or qualifications as legitimate mechanisms to determine applicants' eligibility for positions in their organizations.
3. Compare and contrast schooling (formal education) with other major social institutions, including businesses, families, prisons, and religious organizations. Describe and explain the major similarities and differences.

4. What is the impact of emerging emphases on lifelong learning and the new economy on education systems? Explain and critically discuss the changes (or lack of change) you have identified.

5. What factors account for the rising levels of education in Canada and other, similar nations? Discuss and explain the extent to which increasing levels of education are required to perform essential tasks associated with new technologies and information systems in a global economic framework.

6. Discuss the extent to which education is, and should be, organized in the interests of the communities in which educational institutions are located as opposed to interests shaped by national and global concerns. Illustrate this with reference to your own educational experiences.

7. To what extent has education in Canada fulfilled its promise to provide greater opportunities for social and economic advancement to all social groups? Explain your response with reference to at least three different theoretical frameworks.

8. Discuss the relative impact that particular social groups or forces (including students, teachers, administrators, parents, policy makers, and selected interest groups) have had upon educational decision making and processes. To what extent are the arrangements you describe satisfactory, and to what extent should they be changed? Justify and explain your answer.

☐ Recommended Readings

Paul Anisef, Paul Axelrod, Etta Baichman-Anisef, Carl James, and Anton Turrittin, *Opportunity and Uncertainty: Life Course Experiences of the Class of '73* (Toronto: University of Toronto Press, 2000).

A comprehensive account of the life transitions that people undergo after high school, this book traces for a period of over two decades the educational, work, and family dynamics experienced by Ontario students who were in Grade 12 in 1973. General findings from the data are interwoven with selected case studies and discussions of broader social, economic, and educational transformations in order to highlight the shifting implications that educational choices and outcomes have for life prospects.

Madeleine Arnot, Miriam David, and Gaby Weiner, *Closing the Gender Gap: Postwar Education and Social Change* (Cambridge, UK: Polity, 1999).

This book highlights the closing and apparent reversal of the gender gap in education, detailing the processes by which girls' and boys' educational experiences and outcomes have changed in recent decades. The authors detail (primarily from a British perspective) the interconnections both in and out of school among personal choices and circumstances, gender identities, and life prospects.

Sandro Contenta, *Rituals of Failure: What Schools Really Teach* (Toronto: Between the Lines, 1993).

Contenta discusses how schools' hidden curricula both restrict future prospects for many students and limit the extent to which true education is accomplished through schooling. Tracing the damage that schools can inflict on students and their communities, the author concludes with a proposal to reorient schools to foster critical thinking and social change.

George J. Sefa Dei, Irma Marcia James, Leeno Luke Karumanchery, Sonia James-Wilson, and Jasmin Zine, *Removing the Margins: The Challenges and Possibilities of Inclusive Schooling* (Toronto: Canadian Scholars' Press, 2000).

Diverse research and experiential backgrounds highlight the authors' call for a more inclusive form of education. The work moves beyond simple critique of the ways that schools can marginalize and undermine students from particular social or cultural environments, outlining a series of strategies that can enable schools to benefit all students by drawing from the varied resources and capacities available in diverse community settings.

Neil Guppy and Scott Davies, *Education in Canada: Recent Trends and Future Challenges* (Ottawa: Statistics Canada, 1998).

> This book analyzes census data for a comprehensive overview of major trends and indicators in education and related areas, and presents a concise discussion of the relevant literature employed to interpret and explain the findings. The authors cover a wide range of important educational issues, including demographic and enrolment patterns, regional and social inequalities, student outcomes and returns to schooling, and the changing profile of the teaching profession, highlighting where possible historical trends as well as contemporary developments.

A.H. Halsey, Hugh Lauder, Phillip Brown, and Amy Stuart Wells, eds, *Education: Culture, Economy, and Society* (New York: Oxford University Press, 1997).

> This is one of the most comprehensive collections of analyses of education from various perspectives in sociology and other disciplines, containing influential chapters from different national settings. The book examines educational transformations in detail, including the impact of political and economic changes on education, cultural diversity, new conceptions of knowledge and curricula, the reshaping of teaching, and the dynamics of inequality and exclusion in relation to formal education.

D.W. Livingstone, *The Education–Jobs Gap: Underemployment or Economic Democracy* (Toronto: Garamond, 1999).

> Livingstone systematically analyzes the relationships between education and work in the current economic context. Both education and the extent to which it is related to actual employment situations are explored through several dimensions, integrating statistical data with people's accounts of their own education and work experiences. The book contrasts common rhetoric about the mismatch between education and jobs with the reality that many people do not have sufficient opportunities to apply the capacities they have gained through a combination of formal education and informal learning.

Terry Wotherspoon, *The Sociology of Education in Canada: Critical Perspectives* (Toronto: Oxford University Press, 1998).

> Various dimensions of Canadian education are explored from a critical orientation that emphasizes inequalities based on class, race, gender, region, and other factors. The book addresses contemporary aspects

☐ Recommended Web Sites

> of Canadian education in the context of an overview of varying theoretical perspectives and historical factors. Core issues include the nature of educational processes and teaching; relations between schooling, work, and economic change; educational opportunity and inequality; and emerging educational debates and reforms.

Council of Ministers of Education, Canada
www.cmec.ca

> The Web site of the Council of Ministers of Education, Canada provides access to major reports and studies conducted through that organization, as well as links to each of the provincial and territorial ministries of education and other important Canadian and international education bodies.

Educational Resources Information Center (ERIC)
www.eric.ed.gov/searchdb/searchdb.html

> The ERIC database is a comprehensive collection of information (mostly abstracts of journal articles and reports) on various aspects of and fields related to education, including sociology of education. It is a valuable reference tool and starting point for research into both contemporary and historical educational issues.

Indigenous Education Network (IEN)
www.oise.utoronto.ca/other/ien/ienpage.html

> The Indigenous Education Network, started in 1989 by Aboriginal students at the Ontario Institute for Studies in Education (OISE), University of Toronto, includes both Aboriginal and non-Aboriginal students, faculty, alumni, community members, and others to organize events, foster collaborative work, and provide

support for and public information related to Aboriginal education. Its Web site is oriented primarily to postsecondary education, but it also contains links to numerous sites for those interested in historical and contemporary dimensions of Aboriginal people and their education.

Organisation for Economic Co-operation and Development (OECD)

www.oecd.org

The OECD Web site provides useful and up-to-date information for major international comparisons and developments. It includes report summaries, statistics, and links to major documents on education and related thematic areas that highlight significant trends and issues for 30 member countries and several dozen other nations.

SchoolNet

www.schoolnet.ca

SchoolNet was established by the Government of Canada in the late 1990s. In 1999, Canada became the first nation in the world to link all public schools and libraries to the Internet in order to provide ready access for educators, students, and numerous educational partners to common sites and to an extensive resource base to support teaching/learning and educational activities.

Section on Sociology of Education, American Sociology Association

www.asanet.org/soe

This site is directed primarily to professionals and researchers engaged in the field. However, it contains a summary description of the sociology of education and emerging issues and many useful links to other databases and relevant sites.

Social Science Information Gateway

www.sosig.ac.uk/roads/subject-listing/World-cat/soceduc.html

The Social Science Information Gateway, based in the United Kingdom, offers a substantial and useful set of links to significant reports, databases, journals, publishers, government bodies, and other organizations pertinent to the sociology of education in numerous national settings.

Statistics Canada

www.statcan.ca

Statistics Canada provides a comprehensive body of data and information on education and numerous relevant areas on its Web site and through its links with other sites. The site includes census data, diverse databases and reports on both current and historical dimensions of Canadian social and economic life, and learning resources for students and educators.

9

Pamela Sugiman

> > >

Work and the Economy

© PhotoDisc, Inc.

☐ Learning Objectives

In this chapter, you will:

- come to understand the different types of paid and unpaid work that people carry out in this society

- examine the different ways in which work has been socially organized by employers

- be introduced to some of the main concepts that are used in the sociological analysis of work

- learn some of the recent trends in employment

- highlight the ways in which workers experience work and sometimes resist

- recognize the impact of the new flexibility strategies on workers who are located differently in a society stratified by race, gender, and class

Introduction

In the last decade, we have witnessed a waning interest, if not a discernible disinterest, in the study of work in Canada. Many students have abandoned courses on work, labour, and occupations in favour of the seemingly sexier topics of deviance, popular culture, sport, and sexuality. The first step in confronting this challenge has been to pose the question, Why does the sociology of work no longer seem inspiring? Perhaps the answer is that we have moved too far away from the original sources of inspiration: the workers and workplaces. Perhaps scholars have placed too much emphasis on impersonal forces, numbers, and aggregate trends. In doing so, they have taken people and agency out of the picture. How then to bring people back into the analysis and thereby re-engage students in a discussion of work?

Let us begin by making three straightforward assertions. These assertions are the premises on which this chapter is based. First, most of us will spend the better part of our lives working, because work is central to our economic well-being. Second, work is a social product and, as such, it is subject to **negotiation** and change by human actors. And third, people seek meaning in the work that they perform: there is a close relationship between work, life, and **identity**. Let us look more closely at each of these points.

1. *Work remains central to our existence.* In recent years, some social commentators have predicted the demise of work. In this view, people will invest more time in leisure activities and will be shaped primarily by their relationship to the consumer economy. But try to imagine a life without work. What would it be like if you never held a job? Unless you were incredibly wealthy, unable to work as a result of disability or poor health, or willing (or forced) to live on social assistance or handouts on the street, it is unlikely that you could live without work. If you are like most people, you have no choice but to work in order to secure for yourself the basic necessities (food, clothing, a hospitable living environment). Most of us will spend the bulk of our days working; the majority will work for someone else, on another's terms. This holds true whether you bus tables, drive a truck, trade on Bay Street, or teach in a school. The very wealthy rely heavily on investment income for their economic well-being, and the extremely poor depend on social welfare (transfer payments). But the majority of people in the middle- and highest-income groups in Canada (from $50,000 to over $100,000 household income per year) count on wages and salaries (Jackson and Robinson, 2000: 11). A recognition of the strong link between work and life calls for a critical examination of the world of work. It is imperative that students today confront the topic for it has strong implications for how you will live your lives.

2. *Work is a social product.* The second point emerges from the observation that most Canadians view the work they do as a given. Work is something that we either have or do not have (Gorz, 1999), that we must prepare ourselves for, that we must escape at the end of a day or the end of a career. Discussions of work therefore tend to revolve around a specific, narrowly circumscribed set of concerns, namely, job growth, unemployment, and job-related training (Lowe, 2000). But just as we need to face up to the fact that work is what we will do for the good part of our lives, it is also important to understand that there is nothing inevitable about the way in which work is presently organized. Work is a social product. The way work is structured, the nature of jobs, the rewards of work—these are all the products of **social relationships** between different groups of people. As such, over time and across cultures, work has taken varied forms. Students need to critically examine its current form and organization with the knowledge that it can be questioned and perhaps even transformed.

3. *People seek meaning in their work.* Although most of us work in order to survive, to live comfortably, we also work for more than mere economic survival or comfort of living. Sociologist Graham Lowe (2000) highlights the importance, therefore, of moving discussions of the quantity of work (unemployment statistics, job counts, and work hours) to its quality. After all, the quality of work matters to workers, young and old. According to *Workplace 2000*, this country's first national work-ethic study, when Canadian workers were asked what they would do if they won a million dollars, only 17 per cent said that they would quit their jobs and never work again; 41 per cent of respondents claimed that they would remain in their current job, 17 per cent would embark on a different career, and 24 per cent would start their own business (Lowe, 2000: 52). Canadians still have a strong attachment to work.

In order to fully understand work, it is necessary to think about the wider economy in which it is situated. We may define the *economy* as a social institution in which people carry out the production, distribution, and consumption of goods and services. Discussions of the economy are sometimes presented in an inaccessible language that easily mystifies those untrained in the discipline. Talk of gross domestic product, gross national product, inflation, and recession can be confusing. Yet it is critical that we understand how economic systems function, for they have a direct bearing on how we live. The economy and our location in it shapes, for instance, the quality of health care, housing, diet and nutrition, consumer spending, and lifestyle. The economic system is, furthermore, linked to a nation's political system, to people's conceptions of democracy and citizenship, and to general measures of success and failure.

World Economic Systems

Economic systems are not abstract entities. They are structured and contested, shaped and reshaped, by the people who inhabit them. They further reflect relations of **power** and inequality. In Canada, we presently live in a society that is based on a system of **capitalism**. As such, it is one in which there are blatant as well as subtle manifestations of inequality. We observe extremes of wealth and poverty every day. On the highway, a shiny new Porsche whirs by a 1989 Chevy Impala. A businessman rushing to pick up a $1,500 suit from Holt Renfrew walks quickly past a homeless person squatting on the corner. A Filipino nanny on a temporary work permit spends her days taking someone's children to Montessori school, piano lessons, and dance class. On her way home, she buys their groceries. At night, she returns, tired, to her small room beside the furnace in the basement of the family's well-appointed home. We live in a society in which economic inequalities are complexly wound up with inequalities based on **gender**, **race**, and **ethnicity**.

The power of capitalism is so pervasive that we tend to take for granted many of its central premises. Few of us notice, much less question, the kinds of inequalities that characterize a capitalist society. Concerned about how we, as individuals, can make our way upward through the capitalist hierarchy, we seldom stop to question the system itself. But by looking more closely, with a sociological lens, we can see how our present society is historically specific and is very much a product of conflicting interests and struggles. We may recognize that there are different ways of organizing the economy and society.

Pre-industrial, Pre-capitalist Societies: Hunting and Gathering

Early human societies rested on a system of production and exchange called *hunting and gathering*. Hunting-and-gathering (also called *foraging*) societies were characterized by a simple *subsistence economy*—relatively small groups of people lived off the land (gathering nuts, berries, and other forms of wild vegetation), hunting game, and, in some cases, fishing. Such societies were characterized by considerable physical mobility as groups would move from one geographic location to another in accordance with the food and water supply. Production among hunter-gatherers was largely for *consumption*, or immediate use. In other words, food gathered would be divided among people and eaten with little excess, or *surplus*. Without the accumulation of surplus, a system of exchange was minimal, and there was no private accumulation of wealth. Hunting and gathering societies are thus considered to be among the most egalitarian in human history.

Furthermore, the division of labour among hunter-gatherers was simple, based on sex and age. Women tended to perform gathering activities, often with children in tow, while men hunted. Some anthropologists have argued that this sex-based division of labour did not translate, however, into inequalities between the sexes. While men and women performed different functions, the divisions were not as rigid as they are currently. As well, the work that women performed was not devalued. Indeed, insofar as hunting-and-gathering societies looked largely to vegetation (and not scarce meat) for their dietary needs, women made a greater productive contribution to the maintenance of the group than did men.

Agricultural Societies

The development of *agriculture* (the breeding of animals, the cultivation of plants, and human settlement) brought about many changes in the social and economic organization of societies. These changes were connected to an increase in productive power, a more dependable and stable food supply, and the accumulation of surplus and establishment of market exchange.

Prior to the nineteenth century, Canada was largely an agricultural society based on a *family econ-omy*: most economic activities were located in or nearby family households. The **household** thus served as both a place of work and residence. This type of economy, furthermore, featured a more elaborate division of labour (than in the past) based on age and sex (Nelson and Robinson, 2002). Family survival during this period, though, depended on the interdependent and collective labours of household members. Work was organized according to the market, but also according to nature, seasonal cycles, and personal need.

Capitalism

Unlike earlier economic systems, capitalism is based on private ownership of the **means of production**, an exchange relationship between owners and workers, an economy driven by the pursuit of profit, and competitive market relations.

In order to understand capitalism, let us turn to the ideas of the social theorist Karl Marx. Marx ([1867] 1967) wrote about the profound changes that he observed in nineteenth-century England. He witnessed in England a gradual but dramatic transition from a feudal agricultural society to an industrialized, capitalist economy. Under capitalism, the capitalist class (or **bourgeoisie**) owns the means of production, while the majority of people, the working class (or **proletariat**), does not. *Means of production* is a concept that refers to wealth-generating property, such as land, factories, machines, and the capital needed to produce and distribute goods and services for exchange in a market. While many of us own a car, a computer, or perhaps a house, these items do not constitute the means of production insofar as they are for our personal use only (a place to live, a tool for writing your research papers) and not for the production of wealth.

In a capitalist society, furthermore, capitalists and workers are engaged in a relationship of unequal exchange. As workers do not own the means of production, they have no choice but to sell their labour to a capitalist employer in exchange for a wage. Working people are forced into this relationship because in this type of economy, it is almost impossible to survive without money. One can try to feed a family with the produce of a home vegetable garden, wear home-made clothes, and live without electricity, but at some point it is necessary to purchase market goods and services. For example, you will need to buy fabric, sewing needles, seeds, and a plot of land.

The capitalist class organizes production (work) with the specific goal of maximizing profits for personal wealth. For this reason, it structures work in the most efficient way imaginable, pays workers the lowest possible wages, and extracts the greatest amount of labour from the worker within a working day. And, lastly, capitalism is based on a freely competitive market system and therefore a *laissez-faire* ("hands-off") government. Under capitalism, the market forces of supply and demand are supposed to determine the production and distribution of goods and services, with no government interference.

Capitalism and Industrialization

People sometimes use the terms *capitalism* and *industrial society* interchangeably. However, conceptually, they are distinct. While *capitalism* is a broad economic system, *industrialization* refers to a more specific process that has consequences for the nature and organization of work as well as for the division of labour.

In Canada, as in England, industrialization resulted in a transformation of capitalist production. The rise of industrial capitalism in the late nineteenth and

Industrialization refers to a specific process that has consequences for the nature and organization of work, as well as for the division of labour. This process contributed to the rise of the factory system of production and the manufacture and mass production of goods, and led to the introduction of time discipline ("by the clock") and a more specialized division of labour. (© Vincenzo Pietropaolo/CAW)

early twentieth centuries constituted one of the most fundamental changes in our society. Industrialization involved the introduction of new forms of energy (steam, electricity) and of transportation (railroads), **urbanization**, and the implementation of new machine technology, all of which contributed to the rise of the factory system of production and the manufacture and mass production of goods. These changes greatly facilitated and heightened capitalist production. As well, and in profound ways, they have shaped the ways in which people worked and organized their lives.

The proliferation of factories led to the movement of work from homes and small artisanal workshops to larger, more impersonal sites, to the concentration of larger groups of workers under one roof, and to the introduction of *time discipline* (by the clock), in addition to a more specialized division of labour.

This movement of work, furthermore, resulted in the departure of men from the home and family. While single women were employed in some textile factories, married women were prohibited from most factory jobs. Many women thus continued to work in the home or were employed as domestics in private households, took in boarders, or did other people's laundry in exchange for a small cash sum (Bradbury, 1993). These changes in the economy had far-reaching consequences for the construction of femininity and masculinity, marriage, and family life.

As well, it was during the period of industrial capitalism that economic inequalities became increasingly visible and conflict between classes grew. While successful capitalists made huge amounts of money, working-class men toiled in factories or mines for a pittance, women combined long hours of domestic drudgery with sporadic income-generating activities, and children were sent off to factories or domestic work. Many people lived in poverty and misery.

Family Capitalism

In the mid- to late nineteenth centuries, industrial capitalism was in its early stages. Throughout this period, a small number of individuals and families owned and controlled most of the country's wealth—major companies and financial institutions. Because wealth accrued from business enterprises was passed on within families, from generation to generation (for example, the Fords and Rockefellers in the United States and the Eatons and Seagrams in Canada), this era is aptly termed that of *family capitalism*.

Corporate Capitalism

The subsequent phase of economic development, occurring in the late nineteenth to mid-twentieth centuries, is called *corporate* (or *monopoly*) *capitalism*. This phase witnessed the movement of ownership from individuals and families to modern corporations (and their shareholders). A *corporation* is defined as a legal entity distinct from the people who own and control it. As an entity, the corporation itself may enter into contracts and own property. This separation of enterprise from individuals has served to protect owners and chief executives from personal liability and from any debts incurred by the corporation.

Insofar as the Canadian economy has traditionally been resource intensive, many of the corporations that have dominated our industrial development have been American owned. Consequently, Canadians have witnessed the establishment of numerous branch plants of companies whose head offices are located in the United States (for example, IBM Canada and GM Canada). This fact has raised important concerns about our political sovereignty, our culture, and our distinctiveness as a people and a nation.

Under corporate capitalism, furthermore, there has been a growing concentration of economic power (that is, power in the hands of a few large corporations). One way in which capitalists have increased their economic power is through mergers. By merging, large corporations have been able to create situations of monopoly and oligopoly. We have a *monopoly* when one corporation has exclusive control over the market. Obviously, this situation is undesirable for consumers, as it restricts their market "choices." The Canadian government has, as a result, implemented various controls to curb the monopolization of an industry.

An *oligopoly* exists when several companies control an industry. The insurance, newspaper, and entertainment industries are all characterized by oligopolistic control. Increased revenues by way of mergers and acquisitions is obviously desirable to corporate owners but may occur at the expense of industrial development and employment. In 1996, profits of the top 500 firms internationally increased by 25.1 per cent, while assets grew by 3.5 per cent and the number of employees grew by a mere 1.1 per cent (International Labour Organization, n.d.). (See also Table 9.1.)

Welfare Capitalism

In the real world, of course, examples of pure capitalism and pure socialism cannot be found. In Canada, as well as in parts of Western Europe, the economy is market based while, at the same time, there is government intervention in the form of regulations and controls. Economists call this type of system *welfare capitalism*. Under this system, state-sponsored programs such as universal health care and public education address the needs of different groups of people within the country. Many government controls, such as tax credits for corporations, act in the interest of business.

As well, in our society, the means of production are owned by both private citizens and governments. In spite of moves toward their **privatization**, we still have a number of *Crown corporations* (businesses owned by the federal or provincial governments) such as Canada Post, the Canadian Broadcasting Corporation (CBC), and the Canada Mortgage and Housing Corporation (CMHC).

Socialism

Marx (Marx and Engels, [1848] 1986) believed that in a capitalist society, workers would eventually revolt against their **exploitation**, develop a consciousness of themselves as a class, and overthrow the system of capitalist production, replacing it with a socialist economy. It was not clear how this revolution was to proceed (except that it would be led by a communist party). In the first stages after victory, workers would establish a "dictatorship of the proletariat" and the economy would be socialized. This would involve the elimination of private property and public ownership of the means of production (in other words, workers' control). Once this had been accomplished, the state would gradually wither away and socialism would give way to *communism*. Under communism, work would be organized on the basis of a radically different division of labour. In particular, the production and distribution of goods and services would be in accordance with ability and need within the population, rather than shaped by market forces and the pursuit of profit for individual gain.

Like capitalism, socialism and communism have never existed in a pure form. Many revolutions, successful and not, have been attempted in its name (for example, the Bolshevik revolution in Russia in 1917,

Table 9.1   **The 25 Largest Employers in Canada, 2001**

Rank	Company (Year End)	Location of Head Office	Number of Employees	Revenue per Employee ($)	Profit per Employee ($)
1	Loblaw Companies (De01)	Toronto	114,000	118,912	4,939
2	Onex Corp. (De01)	Toronto	87,300	275,968	9,141
3	Bombardier Inc. (Ja02)	Montreal	80,000	272,555	4,886
4	BCE Inc. (De01)	Montreal	75,000	343,947	6,973
5	Hudson's Bay Co. (Ja02)	Toronto	71,000	105,037	1,025
6	Magna International (De01)[a]	Aurora, Ont.	67,000	165,985	8,657
7	Royal Bank of Canada (Oc01)	Toronto	57,568	443,337	41,881
8	Sears Canada (De01)	Toronto	56,000	120,114	1,680
9	Quebecor Inc. (De01)	Montreal	54,000	216,254	−4,476
10	Nortel Networks Corp. (De01)[b]	Brampton, Ont.	52,600	324,030	−521,787
11	Brascan Corp. (De01)	Toronto	52,100	26,046	5,969
12	Alcan Inc. (De01)[b]	Montreal	51,800	243,996	97
13	Bank of Nova Scotia (Oc01)	Toronto	46,804	449,833	46,342
14	Toronto-Dominion Bank (Oc01)	Toronto	45,565	459,080	30,352
15	Thomson Corp. (De01)[b]	Toronto	44,500	169,865	17,438
16	Bell Canada (De01)	Montreal	43,724	336,177	37,051
17	Canadian Imperial Bank of Commerce (Oc01)	Toronto	42,315	505,424	39,844
18	Canadian Tire Corp. (De01)	Toronto	41,000	131,092	4,309
19	Celestica Inc. (De01)[b]	Toronto	40,000	250,803	−995
20	Air Canada (De01)	Dorval, Que.	38,440	251,015	−32,622
21	Extendicare Inc. (De01)	Markham	37,000	46,068	−984
22	Bank of Montreal (Oc01)	Toronto	33,842	508,894	43,467
23	Cara Operations (Ap01)	Mississauga, Ont.	32,100	35,188	3,199
24	Sobeys Inc. (My01)	Stellarton, NS	32,000	355,328	1,313
25	Fairmont Hotels & Resorts (De01)[b]	Toronto	30,000	19,947	2,320

[a] Figures reported in $US and annualized in previous 3 through 5 years.
[b] Figures reported in $US.
SOURCE: Excerpted and adapted from "50 Largest Employers," *Globe and Mail Report on Business Magazine* (2002); available at <http://top1000.robmagazine.com/2002/employers/employers.htm>, accessed 29 May 2003. Reprinted with

China's in 1949, and Cuba's in 1959), but these societies have never reached the vision laid out by Marx. During the 1980s, the Soviet Union experienced a series of economic and political crises that ultimately led to the disintegration of its economic base and political structures. This economic crisis was based on the inability of this form of "command economy" to adapt rapidly to the changing global economy. The last two decades have witnessed the breakup of the Soviet empire and attempts by Russia and the various "new" countries, such as Hungary, Czechoslovakia, Poland, Ukraine, Latvia, Estonia, and Lithuania, to make the transition from command economies to capitalist one, or some variation in-between the two (Storey, 2002).

According to Robert Storey, "for the present, capitalism seems triumphant. If so, however, given the historical and contemporary inequalities, not to mention capitalism's intimate association with war and environmental degradation, it is a triumph that has many human and natural costs" (2002).

The Global Economy

Today, economic activity knows no national borders. Most large companies operate in a global context, setting up businesses in Canada, the United States, and various parts of Asia, Africa, and India. These companies may be called *transnational* (or *multinational*). The head offices of transnational corporations are located in one country (often the United States), while production facilities are based in others. We see the products of the global economy everywhere we turn. Look at the clothes you wear, the car you drive, the food you eat. Where are they from? Products of the new global economy typically move through many nations.

Clearly, the goal of transnational corporations is profit. Capitalists are rapidly moving beyond national boundaries in an effort to secure the cheapest available labour, low-cost infrastructure (power, water supply, roads, telephone lines), and production unencumbered by health and safety regulations, minimum-wage and hours-of-work laws, maternity provisions, and the like. Unprotected by legislation and typically without union representation, labour in **developing countries** is both cheaper and easier to control than workforces in Canada.

Critics have pointed to the negative cultural, social, and economic consequences of **globalization**. Some argue, for example, that globalization has resulted in a homogenization of **culture**. Media giants AOL Time Warner and Disney, for instance, distribute many of the same cultural products (television shows, films, videos, books) to audiences across the globe. Among many other holdings, AOL Time Warner owns more than 1,000 movie screens outside of the United States and the second largest book publishing business in the world. Admittedly, corporate capitalists of the early twentieth century wielded great power, but the power of transnational firms in the current era is immense. According to Anthony Giddens, "half of the hundred largest economic units in the world today are nations; the other half are transnational corporations" (2000: 315).

Furthermore, global capitalism has had an uneven impact on different groups of people both within Canada and around the world. Media exposés of children sewing Nike soccer balls in Pakistani sweatshops for the equivalent of six cents an hour have brought worldwide attention to sweatshop abuses in the garment and sportswear industries. More hidden, says the Maquiladora Solidarity Network, are the teenage girls, often single mothers, who sew clothes in the maquiladora factories of Central America and Mexico for major North American retailers such as Wal-Mart, The Gap, and Northern Reflections (Maquiladora Solidarity Network, 2000). Some of these are 12- and 13-year-olds working illegally, while others, 15- and 16-year-olds, are legal employees. Both groups of young people, however, work 12- to 18-hour days, often without overtime, under unsafe conditions and in the face of physical, verbal, and sometimes sexual abuse.

It is no coincidence that many sweatshop employees are women, and of colour—people who have no choice but to endure these conditions in order to survive. Garment manufacturers in Central America's free trade zones, Mexico's maquiladora factories, and Asia's export processing zones say that they prefer to hire young girls and women because "they have nimble fingers. Workers suspect that children and young people are hired because they are less likely to complain about illegal and unjust conditions. And more importantly, they are less likely to organize unions" (Maquiladora Solidarity Network, 2000). We are seeing the intensification of divisions of labour, globally, along the lines of class, sex, and race.

These developments, furthermore, have direct consequences for the organization of work, and for the collective power of working people in Canada. Many Canadians now work under the constant threat of company relocation to lower-cost areas. And this has resulted in a weakening of the political power of workers and their unions. In light of this threat, many people in Canada have agreed to concessions (that is, giving up past gains) such as pay cuts, loss of vacation pay, and unpaid overtime. In a study of clerical workers employed at a major telecommunications firm, Bonnie Fox and Pamela Sugiman (1999) found that top management relied on television monitors in the employee cafeteria to broadcast warnings that jobs would be lost if the workers did not make special efforts (including concessions) in the interest of the firm's survival. One employee explained, "the axe is falling. People are afraid. . . . They'll do what they need to do to keep their jobs" (Fox and Sugiman, 1999: 79). In the long term, the lingering threat of job loss affects the standard of living in the country as a whole.

The Capitalist Economy: Where People Work

Most of us contribute to the economy in one way or another. And just as the economy undergoes change throughout history, so too does our relationship to work. With the expansion of some economic sectors and the contraction of others, our opportunities for certain kinds of jobs also change. Social scientists identify four major economic sectors in which people in this country find employment: primary and resource industries, manufacturing, the service sector, and social reproduction (see Figure 9.1).

9.1

Global Issues
Global Sweatshops: Nike in China

Nike's presence in China is estimated at 50 contracted factories, manufacturing sneakers and clothing and employing approximately 110,000 workers. Forty percent of Nike's footwear is produced in China. The Sewon factory is a South Korean investment that has produced exclusively for Nike since 1989. Average wages for a worker in a shoe factory in South Korea are US $2.49/hour, or more than twelve times the cost at Sewon. Is it any wonder that Nike produces such a considerable amount of shoes and garments in China?

The New York–based National Labour Committee (NLC) researchers uncovered that working time is excessively long and three factories show evidence of gender and age discrimination. These factories prefer to hire young, single women, specifically stating in job recruitment advertisement that proof of marital status is necessary for the application. One company fires employees at the age of 25 when they become "used up" (exhausted).

Nike's Code of Conduct guarantees that ". . . partners share the best practices and continuous improvement in . . . management practices that recognize the dignity of the individual" and that "there shall be no discrimination based on race, creed, gender, marital or maternity status, religious or political beliefs, age, or sexual orientation." Obviously, on these points, Nike has failed in China.

———

SOURCE: Canadian Labour Congress, "Nike in China," *Sweatshop Alert* (November 2000), 9; available at <www.clc-ctc.ca>, accessed 16 July 2003.

Nike in China: Five Factories

Factory	Location	No. of Workers	Wages ($US)	Working Hours	Time Off	Remarks
Sewon	Jiaozhou City, Shandong Prov., Liuhizai Ind. Area	1,500, mostly women aged 18–25	Base wage: 20¢/hr	11- to 12-hr shifts, 6 days/wk	1 day/wk	Sewon would not hire 27 yrs of age
Hung Wah & Hung Yip Keng Tau	Huijou City, Guangdong Prov.	2,000–2,500, mostly women aged 16–32	Average: 22¢/hr	Peak season: 15-hr shifts, 7 days/wk	1 day/mo.	Workers never heard of Nike's Code of Conduct; 12/room
Keng Tau	Keng Tau Industrial Zone	1,000–1,200	11–36¢/hr	Peak season: 14 hrs/day, 7 days/wk	1 day/mo.	No overtime premium; 16/room
Tong Ji	Chongzhan Prov.	500 migrant workers	Average: 27¢/hr	57.5 hrs/wk	1 day/wk	Nov. 1999: 72.5 hrs/wk
Wei Li	Guangdong Prov.	6,100, mostly women aged 16–25	Average: 56¢/hr	Normal: 8 hrs/day, 5 days/wk; Peak: 12-hr shift	Normal: 2 days/wk; Peak: 1 day/ 2 wks	Employs only single women; require certificate of marital status

Figure 9.1 **Employment by Industry and Sex**

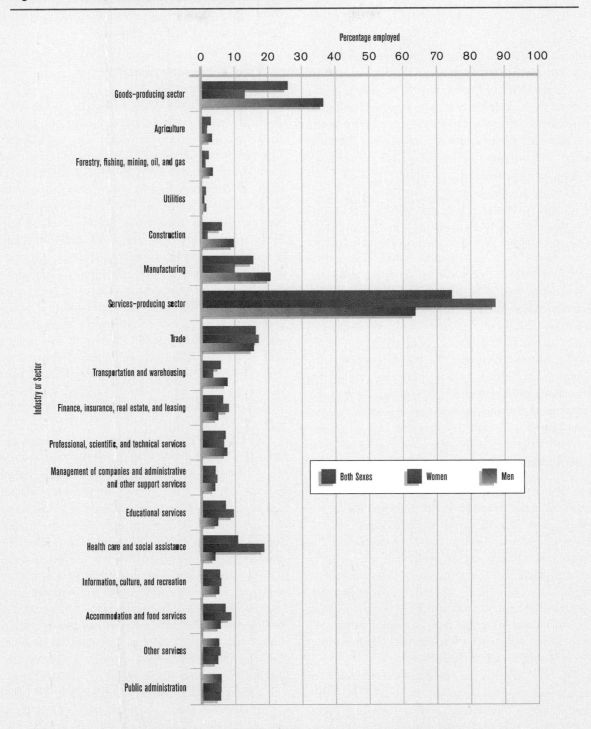

SOURCE: Adapted from the Statistics Canada CANISM database <http://cansim2.statcan.ca>, Table 282-008.

Primary Resource Industry

Years ago, most Canadians worked in *primary* (or *resource*) *industry*. It is likely that your grandparents or great-grandparents performed primary-sector work. Though not always for pay, **First Nations** people have had an important history in the resource industry (Knight, 1996). Work in the primary sector involves the extraction of natural resources from our environment. Primary-industry jobs may be found for instance, in agricultural production (farming, skilled and unskilled agricultural labour), ranching, mining, forestry, hunting, and fishing.

Throughout the eighteenth and nineteenth centuries, the primary sector represented the largest growth area in Canada. However, in the twentieth century, it began to experience a dramatic decline. Many forces have contributed to its contraction, notably the demise of small family farms and small independent fishing businesses, along with a corresponding rise in corporate farming (or "agribusiness") and large fishing enterprises. These developments have resulted in dwindling opportunities for many people. Moreover, because of the geographic concentration of primary-sector jobs, this decline has devastated some towns (for example, Elliot Lake, Ontario) and entire regions (for example, Atlantic Canada).

Manufacturing

Into the twentieth century, growing numbers of Canadians began to work in the *manufacturing* (or *secondary*) *sector*. Manufacturing work involves the processing of raw materials into usable goods and services. If you make your living by assembling vans, knitting socks, packing tuna, or piecing together the parts of Barbie dolls, you are employed in manufacturing. Though the popular image of a manufacturing employee is a blue-collar male, the industry's workforce now reveals much more diversity along the lines of sex, as well as race and ethnicity.

On the whole, the manufacturing sector in Canada has experienced a slower decline than primary industry. The decline in manufacturing began in the early 1950s. In 1951, manufacturing represented 26.5 per cent of employment in Canada, but by 1995, the employment share of manufacturing had been cut nearly in half, to 15.2 per cent (Jackson and Robinson, 2000: 11). The industry nonetheless continues to be an important employer of Canadians. Job losses in manufacturing are largely attributable to technological change and the relocation of work to various low-wage sectors in Mexico, parts of Asia, and the southern United States.

The Service Sector

In *The End of Work* (1995), Jeremy Rifkin wrote about the relationship between job loss and technological change. Rifkin predicted that technological innovation would result in the loss of a great many jobs (except for an elite group of knowledge workers such as computer technicians and scientists) and would thus constitute an end to work. For various reasons, Rifkin's predictions have not come true. First, many employers prefer to hire dirt-cheap human labour rather than purchase expensive machines. Second, unions have exerted some power in resisting the wholesale implementation of technological change. And third, a massive number of new jobs have been created in the rapidly expanding *service* (or *tertiary*) *sector*. Study after study demonstrates that employees who lost jobs in manufacturing have been absorbed by the service industry. Indeed, many of you are no doubt currently employed in part-time or temporary service jobs. If so, you are not unlike many Canadians.

In recent years, the service sector has expanded dramatically. From 1951 to 1995, the employment share of this sector more than doubled, from 18 per cent to 37.1 per cent. The rise of the service industry has been linked to the development of a post-industrial, information-based economy and to the rise of a strong consumer culture. All of this has resulted in a growing need for people to work in information processing and management, marketing, advertising, and servicing. In the course of a day, you will encounter dozens of service-sector employees. Airline reservation agents, taxi drivers, teachers and professors, daycare staff, bank employees, computer technicians, crossing guards, librarians, garbage collectors, and Starbucks barristas—these are all service workers.

As you can see from these examples, the service sector embraces a wide range of jobs. So dissimilar are these jobs that some people speak of a *polarization of work*. In other words, there are some "good," highly skilled, well-paid jobs at one end of the spectrum and many "bad," poorly paid, dead-end jobs at the other. Jobs in retail trade and food services are at the low end of the hierarchy, while those in finance and business, health, education, and public administration tend to be at the high end.

The experience of service work is also qualitatively different than that of manufacturing. Much service employment involves not only the physical performance of a job, but also an emotional component. In the face of an intensely competitive market, how does a company vie for customers? Service. And service rests on a big smile and (artificially) personalized interactions. In *The Managed Heart* (1983), Arlie Hochschild explored the emotional work of flight attendants. According to Hochschild, emotional labour, typically performed by women, is potentially damaging to workers because it involves regulating one's emotional state, sometimes suppressing feelings and often inventing them.

Also problematic is the frequently tense relationship between workers and their bosses. Low-end service work is characterized by low-trust relationships. With the expectation that their workforces will have only weak loyalties to the company and its goals, managers attempt to control employees largely through close direction and surveillance (Tannock, 2001). It is now common practice for employers to use electronic equipment to monitor telephone conversations between employees and clients and to install video security cameras to keep an eye on retail clerks. Another form of surveillance, more common in the United States than Canada, is drug testing (through urinalysis) of prospective employees. Such testing is standard, for example, at Wal-Mart stores (Ehrenreich, 2001). But at the same time that such work is subject to routinization and close surveillance, it necessitates high levels of self-motivation and investment on the part of the workers. In consequence, the most common complaint among workers in low-end service jobs is a high level of stress (Tannock, 2001).

Social Reproduction

All of the work we have discussed so far is conducted in what social scientists call the *sphere of production*. Production typically occurs in the public world of factory, office, school, and store. Moreover, it involves monetary exchange. The study of work in this country has largely been biased toward production. When we think of work and workers, who comes to mind? Steelworkers, garment workers, plumbers, secretaries, farmers, and lawyers. What is common to all of these

occupations? They are all done in exchange for money—a wage, salary, or income.

However, in Canada as well as in other parts of the world, many people spend hours and hours each day doing work that is not officially recorded as part of the economy. This type of labour may be called **social reproduction**. Social reproduction involves a range of activities for which there is no direct economic exchange. Often, though not always, this work is performed within family households. Typically, it is done by women. We do not view as economic activity the hours women (and less often men) spend buying groceries, planning and cooking meals, washing dishes, folding laundry, chauffeuring children, buying clothes, vacuuming, managing the household budget, caring for aging relatives, supervising homework, and cleaning the toilet bowl. The instrumental value of such activities has long been hidden. Rather than viewed as work, they are deemed a labour of love (Luxton, 1980).

But what would happen if women and other family members no longer performed this labour? How would it get done? Equally important, who would pay for it? If capitalist employers or the state had to ensure that workforces got fed, clothed, nurtured, and counselled, what would be the cost? These kinds of questions perplex economists and social statisticians. Says economist Marilyn Waring, breastfeeding, for example, is "a major reproductive activity carried out only by women, and this thoroughly confuses statisticians' and economists' production models. The reproduction of human life also seems conceptually beyond their rules of imputation. But bodies most certainly have market prices" (1996: 86). In the United States, the cost of reproducing another life ranged from $1,800 for artificial insemination to $36,000 for a surrogate mother to carry the child. This, notes Waring, is the equivalent of $5.35 (US) per hour over a 280-day pregnancy (1996: 86). According to a Canadian estimate, if unpaid work were replaced for pay, it would be worth $275 billion to the Canadian economy (GPI Atlantic, n.d.).

The system of capitalism benefits tremendously from the performance of unpaid labour. Yet the unpaid services of housewives and other family members are not only excluded from traditional economic measures, for many years sociologists did not even consider them to be "work." This is perplexing insofar as such work is essential to basic human survival and to the quality of our lives.

The Informal Economy

Also hidden from official growth figures—as well as from public conscience—is a wide range of economic activities that are not officially reported to the government. These activities make up the **informal** (or *underground*) **economy**. Some are legal; others are not. They include, for example, babysitting, cleaning homes, editing a book manuscript, sewing clothes, peddling watches, playing music on the streets, gambling, and dealing drugs. As you make your way through the downtown areas of most major cities in Canada and the United States and almost anywhere in the developing world, you will see people of all ages trying to eke out a living in the informal sector. The so-called squeegee kids who can be found at congested intersections of Canadian cities are also part of this world of work.

Of course, we do not know the precise size of the underground economy. We have only estimates of its share of officially recognized economies. Here, we see much variation across the globe. In Africa, the informal economy has been estimated to involve 60 to 70 per cent of the labour force and to produce close to one-quarter of the continent's output. According to the International Labour Organization (ILO), the informal sector absorbs three-quarters of new entrants into the African labour force. In Mexico, beginning in the 1990s, the informal economy was estimated to contribute between 25 and 40 per cent of the country's gross domestic product (GDP), providing work for roughly one-quarter of the economically active population (Kilgour, 1998: 2–3).

There have long been informal economies in most nations. However, this sector has been growing in importance, largely because of economic hardship related to restructuring, globalization, and their effects of dislocation and forced migration. Increasingly, people are turning to "hidden work" in order to survive in the midst of contracting opportunities in the formal economy. It has become a safety net of sorts for the poorest groups in society. Without doubt, workers in this sector have had to be enterprising. Some are highly motivated and possess valuable skills; others lack formally recognized credentials. Unfortunately, most people who rely on the informal economy for a living face precarious, unstable "careers" in unregulated environments.

Managerial Strategies of Control

Scientific Management

In order to assess the new world of work, it is important to first understand the old one. So let us briefly go back in time. Since the days when Marx observed the rise of the factory system, capitalist goals of efficiency and profit making have shaped the organization of work. Writing in the nineteenth century, Marx declared that work should be a central source of meaning and satisfaction in a person's life. In his words, "the exercise of **labour power**, labour, is the worker's own life-activity, the manifestation of his own life" (cited in Rinehart, 2001: 13). But he noted that for most labouring people, work had lost meaning and creativity. Under capitalism, the worker "works in order live. . . . Life begins for him where this activity ceases" (cited in Rinehart, 201: 3).

By the early twentieth century, with the spread of mass production, much work (most notably in manufacturing) was being further divided into ever more unconnected and meaningless parts. The twentieth century witnessed the large-scale implementation of **scientific management**, one of the most influential and long-lasting managerial strategies. Scientific management was a method of organizing work and controlling workers that was introduced by American engineer Frederick Winslow Taylor. After its founder, scientific management is also referred to as *Taylorism*.

Taylor applied the principles of "science" to the performance of human labour. On the basis of his close observations of workers performing their jobs, he broke work processes down into simple tasks, each of which could be timed and organized into formal rules and standardized procedures. Taylor believed that once the work was subdivided, workers did not need to understand the entire process of production. Scientific management, in this sense, resulted in the separation of mental and manual labour, the conception of work from its execution. In short, it contributed to the deskilling of the worker.

Also in the twentieth century, Henry Ford, founder of the Ford Motor Car Company, applied the principles of scientific management (in tandem with the bureaucratic organization of work) to mass production of the automobile. Even if you have never stepped foot in an auto manufacturing plant or other mass production facility, you are probably familiar

The assembly line has been called an example of technical control. This refers to the control of the workforce not directly by supervision (for example, a foreperson), but rather indirectly by a machine. This photograph depicts an autoworker in Windsor, Ontario. (© Vincenzo Pietropaolo/CAW)

with the assembly line. Richard Edwards (1979) called the moving assembly line an example of "technical control." *Technical control* refers to the control of a workforce not directly by supervision (for example, by a foreperson), but rather indirectly by a machine.

While early researchers highlighted the application of Taylorism to manufacturing, this principle is now applied to many different types of work. In one form or other, scientific management has been implemented in offices (Lowe, 1987), schools, hospitals, and restaurants. Esther Reiter (1991) describes how the fast food industry has carefully broken the process of serving a burger down from laying down the buns to evenly spreading the ketchup to distributing precisely half an ounce of onions. The total preparation time for a Burger King Whopper is 23 seconds—no more, no less.

Though efficient and rational, critics have argued that work that is broken down into simple parts results in degradation and dehumanization (Braverman, 1974). Marx introduced the concept of alienation to describe the consequences for working people. **Alienation** is a structural condition of powerlessness that is rooted in a worker's relationship to the

means of production. Insofar as workers have little or no control over their labour, work is no longer a source of fulfilment. According to Marx, under these conditions, workers become estranged from the products of their labour, from the work process itself, from each other, and from themselves (Rinehart, 1996).

Faced with the problem of alienated workforces, some employers have attempted to motivate workers with financial incentives. In the 1930s, Henry Ford introduced the "Five Dollar Day." In that era, five dollars constituted a relatively high rate of pay that would supposedly cover the living costs of not only the male autoworker but also his (dependent) wife and children. Decades later, J.H. Goldthorpe and colleagues' study of workers' orientations to work (1969) further supported the view that some people have an instrumental relationship to work. In this view, people can be compensated for meaningless work. Work can be a means to an end rather than an end in itself.

But there are two central problems with the assumption that money makes up for the meaninglessness of work. First, only a minority of employers do in fact compensate their employees for performing degraded and dehumanized work. In the popular media, we hear stories about $30 hourly wage rates for auto and steelworkers. But we must keep in mind that Ford, GM, and Stelco workers represent the privileged of the working class. The fact is that most employers are not willing to pay high wages—though they can be forced to do so, under the pressure of strong unions such as the Canadian Auto Workers and the United Steelworkers of America. Consequently, the majority of people do not receive high monetary compensation. Most Canadians perform boring jobs and are not paid handsomely for doing so.

Second, this view overlooks the importance of workers' needs for *intrinsic satisfaction*—the need of human beings to find meaning in the work that they perform. As stated, whether they be Supreme Court judges, car assemblers, letter carriers, caretakers, or retail clerks, people need to find meaning in the work that they perform day in and day out. We have a basic human need for respect and dignity at work (Hodson, 2001). This holds whether you are a man or woman, Canadian-born or a recent immigrant or a migrant labourer, in middle age or youth, in a part-time job or a career.

The Early Human Relations School

In the 1930s, social psychologists and managerial consultants began to recognize this basic human need. In a series of experiments at the Western Electric Company's Hawthorne plant in Chicago, an industrial psychologist named Elton Mayo discovered that attention to workers resulted in a significant improvement in their productivity. The Hawthorne studies played an important role in spawning a new school of management thought known as the **human relations** approach. The basic idea on which the human relations approach rests is that if managers want productive, motivated workers, they should recognize workers' social needs.

In contemporary workplaces, many early human relations principles are embedded in an array of organizational initiatives such as "human resource management," "total quality management," and "quality of work life" programs. Employee-of-the-week schemes, employee suggestion boxes, quality circles, and job enrichment all reflect such managerial methods. All of these schemes highlight employee motivation by promoting a discourse of co-operation (rather than conflict) between managers and workers, with the belief that happy workers are better workers.

A fundamental problem with the human relations approach to managing, however, is that such programs do not constitute real workplace democracy. Under such schemes, employers often create the illusion that workers are important and respected, their ideas valued and rewarded, but there is no real redistribution of power and control. Over time, employees begin to recognize the limits of their involvement. Moreover, some research has demonstrated that workers' suggestions for organizing work may backfire against them, resulting in layoffs for some and in the further rationalization of the work process for those who remain (Robertson et al., 1993).

The Social Organization of Work Today

Revolutionary New Technology

Today, popular writers and scholars alike are talking about the emergence of a new world of work, one that is rooted in a "knowledge society"—a world that offers opportunity, an increase in leisure time, an experience of work that is far more positive than in the past. Are these assertions founded? Do people now have better jobs than their parents and grandparents? Have we rid the economy of many of the low-paying, dead-end, and routine jobs that characterized the past? In short, has work been transformed?

According to Daniel Bell (1973), the answer to these questions is "Yes." In *Post-industrial Society*, Bell argues that we are now living in a post-industrial era, a new information economy, one based on the use of sophisticated microelectronic technology. With the decline of Taylorized manufacturing jobs and the rise of knowledge work, argues Bell, people are becoming highly skilled and jobs are becoming intrinsically rewarding.

Admittedly, most people agree that the new technology may eliminate routine, repetitive tasks, thereby freeing people to perform more challenging work. Think, for example, about preparing a research paper without a computer, printer, and access to the Internet. Moreover, the technology has had a positive impact on job creation. In fact, in Canada, information technology has created more jobs than it has eliminated. In a comparison of firms that relied extensively on sophisticated information technology with other, low-tech firms, the Conference Board of Canada found that the former produced more jobs than the latter (Lowe, 2000).

Notwithstanding these findings, some sociologists argue that, at the same time, the technology has created new forms of inequality and exacerbated old ones. While it has resulted in new, more challenging jobs for some people, many others have lost their jobs (or skills) as a result of technological change in the workplace. In the **service economy**, for instance, employers have relied extensively on computers and the new microelectronics to streamline work processes. In banking, many of the decisions (such as approving a bank loan) that used to be made at the discretion of people are now computer governed. And the introduction of automated bank machines has made redundant the work of thousands of tellers. As well, in various industries, computers have taken over the supervisory function of employee surveillance. With state-of-the-art computer equipment, and without the direct intervention of a supervisor, firms can now effectively enforce productivity quotas and monitor workers, especially those who perform highly routine tasks (Fox and Sugiman, 1999).

Another problem is that the technology is rapidly changing. Competence with the technology thus necessitates continually learning new skills and making ongoing investments in training. Often workers themselves assume the costs of such training. In the past, says Graham Lowe, employment was based on an implicit understanding of loyalty in exchange for job security; today, this idea has been replaced with a system based on "individual initiative and merit." Workers who go above and beyond, who contribute what managers sometimes call "value added," who hone their skills—these are the workers who will be recognized and rewarded (2000: 61).

Moreover, opportunities for extra job-related training are unequal. Not surprisingly, they are closely linked to an employee's income and level of education. Lowe notes that only 3 in 10 Canadian workers annually receive training related to their present or future employment (2000: 65). University graduates are twice as likely as high school graduates to be involved in such training. One in 5 workers who earns less than $15,000 participates in training, compared to half of those earning in excess of $75,000.

Flexible Work

Alongside information technology, some writers are extolling the benefits of related innovations in management methods. In business circles today, one hears buzzwords such as "workplace restructuring," "down-sizing," and "lean production." All of these concepts are part of a new managerial approach called *flexibility*. Flexibility (most often in tandem with technological innovation) has, as they say, "held out the hand of promise." It has been promoted as an improvement over the old human relations approach and an alternative to the Taylorist and Fordist methods that have long stripped workers of control and dignity (Sennett, 1998). Critics, on the other hand, say differently. Smart, young managers trained in the postmodern language of flexibility may introduce seemingly new forms of managing and organizing work and adapt them to an increasingly competitive and precarious global context, but on close inspection, they claim, such strategies are firmly grounded in earlier approaches.

Most contemporary flexibility strategies are based on one or a combination of two approaches: *numerical flexibility* and *flexible specialization* (also called *functional flexibility*).

Numerical Flexibility

Numerical flexibility involves shrinking or eliminating the core workforce (in continuous jobs, and full-time positions) and replacing them with workers in *non-standard* (or *contingent*) *employment*. **Non-standard work** is a term used to describe various employment arrangements such as part-time work, temporary (seasonal and other part-year) work, contracting out or outsourcing (work that was previously done in-house), and self-employment. Non-standard work is, in short, based on an employment relationship that is far more tenuous than those of the past (Jackson and Robinson, 2000).

When you hear about non-standard work, what comes to mind? If you are like most Canadians, you think of jobs in the fast food or retail industries—"McJobs." But in the current economy, non-standard work arrangements now characterize most spheres of employment. We need look no further than the university or college, for example, to see the employment of people in non-standard jobs. In these institutions of higher learning, you may discover that many of your courses are taught by part-time or sessional instructors, some of whom hold PhDs, others of whom are graduate students. These are individuals who are paid by the university to teach on a course-by-course or session-by-session basis. Sessional or part-time instructors typically do not work on a full-time basis, and they seldom receive assurances of stable employment.

According to the Economic Council of Canada, non-standard labour represents the fastest growing type of employment in this country (Duffy, Glenday, and Pupo, 1997: 53). While 6 per cent of all employed persons worked part-time (fewer than 30 hours per week) in 1975, that proportion had risen to over 18 per cent by 1997 (Nelson and Robinson, 2002: 239). Today, non-standard work represents about one-third of all jobs. Though this form of employment may be found in all industries, it is most typical of sales and service.

Many writers have cogently argued that the growth of non-standard work is closely linked to the corporate goals of flexibility and global restructuring (Harvey, 1989). Not unlike the "reserve army of labour" described by Karl Marx, non-standard employees provide owners and managers with a ready supply of labour to "hire and fire" as the market demands. Employers invest minimally in these workers and offer them only a limited commitment. In order to remain competitive in the global market, it is argued, corporations must reduce labour costs through downsizing (that is, laying off permanent, full-time workers and replacing them with part-time, temporary, and contract labour; Duffy, Glenday, and Pupo, 1997).

Yet, unyielding market forces notwithstanding, there is also evidence that "precarious jobs have become the norm much faster in some countries than in others" (Jackson and Robinson, 2000: 50). For example, in the United States, non-standard work grew quickly in the 1980s, but in comparison to Canada, in the 1990s, its growth has been limited by low unemployment. Moreover, in much of Europe, unions and employment laws have (until recently) limited the growth of contract work and substandard part-time work. In the Netherlands, a country known for having one of the most flexible labour markets in continental Europe, part-timers receive equal wages and benefits with full-time employees, and contract workers must be given a permanent job within a specified time period (Jackson and Robinson, 2000).

Another offshoot of the increasingly precarious relationship between employers and workers is the growth in self-employment. In the 1990s, one driving force behind self-employment was the move of large firms and governments to contract out work that had formerly been performed in-house by a core workforce (Jackson and Robinson, 2000). In fact, throughout the 1990s, growth in self-employment was a leading labour market trend. In 1998, self-employed individuals accounted for 18 per cent of all employment in Canada, and between 1989 and 1997, self-employment constituted about 80 per cent of all job growth (Lowe, 2000).

Contrary to romantic images of the self-employed as benefiting from flexible work schedules, autonomy, and economic success, research indicates that they are not always better off than their waged or salaried counterparts. Most self-employed people work alone, often in small enterprises. Only a minority run companies that employ others (Lowe, 2000). Furthermore, they tend to work excessively long hours and, on average, accrue about the same earnings as regular employees. In addition, gender-based pay differentials are more pronounced among the self-employed, and work is highly polarized. In other words, recent growth in self-employment has been especially strong at the top of the job hierarchy (for example, among engineers and accountants) and at the bottom (for instance, among domestic cleaners and salespeople).

Part-time and temporary workers tend to be women and young people, though not exclusively (see Table 9.2). Because of these demographics, people assume that the casual employment relationship is not problematic; indeed, some believe it to be desirable. Admittedly, there are individuals who choose non-standard work in the hope that it will offer heightened flexibility to facilitate the competing demands of job and family or job and school. Yet many other people accept these employment terms on an involuntary basis, largely because they have no alternatives. Moreover, studies suggest that many non-standard work arrangements do not in fact provide employees with greater flexibility (Vosko, 2000) or that they offer flexibility to favoured employees only (Sennett, 1998).

Furthermore, non-standard workers as a whole receive relatively low wages and few benefits. Consequently, many people who rely on this type of work must resort to holding multiple jobs in an effort to make ends meet. People carve out a living by stringing together a host of low-paying, part-time, and temporary jobs. Often this involves moonlighting or doing shift work, situations that no doubt put added strain on families.

Interestingly, along with the expansion of the non-standard workforce, there has been an increase in overtime work for full-time employees. And while there has been a significant rise in overtime hours for both sexes, men are especially likely to work beyond

Table 9.2 **Full- and Part-Time Employment by Gender and Age, 1997–2002 (Thousands)[a]**

	1997	1998	1999	2000	2001	2002
Both sexes						
Total	13,774	14,140	14,531	14,910	15,077	15,411
15–24 years	2,043	2,102	2,206	2,289	2,313	2,367
25–44 years	7,468	7,577	7,635	7,704	7,681	7,679
45 years and over	4,263	4,462	4,690	4,917	5,082	5,366
Full-time	11,140	11,467	11,849	12,208	12,345	12,528
15–24 years	1,110	1,143	1,223	1,281	1,296	1,292
25–44 years	6,452	6,577	6,660	6,760	6,732	6,718
45 years and over	3,578	3,747	3,967	4,167	4,317	4,518
Part-time	2,635	2,674	2,682	2,702	2,732	2,884
15–24 years	933	959	983	1,008	1,017	1,075
25–44 years	1,016	999	975	943	949	961
45 years and over	685	715	723	750	765	848
Men						
Full-time	6,717	6,851	7,052	7,220	7,266	7,362
15–24 years	663	669	713	741	742	747
25–44 years	3,806	3,873	3,908	3,946	3,911	3,888
45 years and over	2238	2,310	2,432	2,532	2,612	2,727
Part-time	792	810	814	830	844	900
15–24 years	404	413	429	437	441	462
25–44 years	200	200	184	181	193	200
45 years and over	188	197	201	212	211	239
Women						
Full-time	4,432	4,615	4,797	4,989	5,080	5,166
15–24 years	447	474	511	540	554	545
25–44 years	2,636	2,705	2,752	2,814	2,820	2,830
45 years and over	1,340	1,437	1,535	1,635	1,705	1,791
Part-time	1,843	1,864	1,868	1,872	1,888	1,984
15–24 years	530	547	555	572	576	613
25–44 years	817	799	791	762	757	762
45 years and over	497	518	523	538	555	610

[a] Figures may not appear to add up to totals because of rounding.
Source: Adapted from Statistics Canada, "Full-Time and Part-Time Employment" (2003); available at

the standard 40-hour week. As well, the lengthening of the work day has been more pronounced among managers than among employees. And on the whole, more of this overtime is unpaid. Paid overtime tends to be concentrated in unionized workplaces and in blue-collar manufacturing and construction jobs (Jackson and Robinson, 2000). Unpaid overtime, in comparison, is more marked in the female-dominated public sector such as in teaching and social work (suggesting that women are more likely to put in overtime without pay), as well as among managers and professionals.

There are many reasons for the recent increase in overtime work. First, as a result of downsizing and restructuring, people simply must put in longer hours to get the job done. Say Andrew Jackson and David Robinson, "the survivors have to pick up the work of those who have left as a result of layoffs or early retirement" (2000: 86). Fear of future job loss is also a potent factor behind putting in extra hours. In a "survival-of-the-fittest" corporate culture, long hours are viewed as evidence of effort and commitment. Undoubtedly, many workers also internalize the ethic of doing more with less, particularly those who are serving the public and helping to make up for cuts through unpaid work. In short, in the face of general labour market uncertainty, many core employees feel pressured to work overtime, whether or not they so desire. As a result, we now have, "side by side, under-employment and overemployment, with high levels of insecurity and stress on all sides" (Duffy, Glenday, and Pupo, 1997: 57).

In light of these trends, for most Canadians, the concept of a career is a remnant of the past. The gold watch for 50 years of continuous service to the same company is not attainable in the new workplace scenario. Says Richard Sennett, "flexibility today brings back this arcane sense of the job, as people do lumps of labor, pieces of work, over the course of a lifetime" (1998: 9). Living in this era of economic uncertainty, with the attendant worry about layoffs and job loss, is, not surprisingly, a major source of stress for people in Canada (Jackson and Robinson, 2000).

Flexible Specialization

Another component of the new flexibility is **flexible specialization** (or *functional flexibility*, often called *flex spec*). Flexible specialization involves multi-skilling, job rotation, the organization of workers into teams, and the concentration of power—without the centralization of power. Flexible specialization has been called the antithesis of the system of production embodied in Fordism (Sennett, 1998). Under the new system, the old auto assembly line has been replaced by "islands of specialized production." These new work units, or *islands*, allow businesses to respond quickly to fluctuations in market demand, especially in industries such as fashion and textiles where there is a short product life.

Typically, flex spec is also accompanied by a goal of co-operation and flexible arrangements between labour and management rather than adversarial relations based on strict contractual agreements. Where Taylorist management strategies have rationalized production by eliminating the need for workers to make decisions, a flex-spec organization attempts to eliminate "waste" by employing workers' knowledge of their jobs in the rationalization process. Working in teams, employees are given responsibility for scheduling, planning the work, rotating workers among jobs, and meeting quotas (Fox and Sugiman, 1999). By increasing workers' responsibility, team organization diminishes the need for supervision—although it provides employees with no added authority.

Finally, information technology has been an integral component of flexibility strategies. Flexible specialization is suited to high technology: "Thanks to the computer, industrial machines are easy to reprogram and configure. The speed of modern communications has also favoured flexible specialization, by making global market data instantly available to a company" (Sennett, 1998: 52). Unlike the earlier mechanization, the new telecommunications technology enables employers to easily relocate work from one site to another, thereby scattering workforces to various parts of the country, continent, or world. As a result of teleworking, you can make a hotel reservation or check your credit level from Hamilton, Ontario, and be speaking to a reservation agent or debt collector in Tennessee. Likewise, with the availability of portable computers, fax machines, cell phones, and e-mail connections, some people may simply do their work from home rather than in an office or factory. Work can now follow people home.

Flexibility for Whom?

We may now point to a polarization of jobs. At one end of the spectrum are the good jobs, at the other the bad. There is no bulging middle. There has, in other words, been a widening of inequalities. Good jobs offer decent pay and intrinsic rewards (fulfilment, autonomy, the opportunity to exercise knowledge and acquire skill). But while the new information society has created some good jobs, these are not held by all, or even most, people in this country.

And whether they work in the primary, manufacturing, or service economy, as manual labourers or as professionals, people are facing increasing uncertainty in the labour market.

Downsizing, the resulting increase in non-standard employment, and the **globalization of work** have all contributed to this uncertainty. Says Sennett, "What's peculiar about uncertainty today is that it exists without any looming historical disaster; instead it is woven into the everyday practices of a vigorous capitalism. Instability is meant to be normal" (1998: 31).

The Changing Face of Labour: Diversity Among Workers

Just as places of work have changed dramatically over time, so too has the workforce itself. Workplaces

9.2

Sociology in Action
Don't Work Too Hard

Hard work never killed anyone! This is an old and familiar phrase. Teenagers are likely to hear it from their parents when they are asked to shovel the snow. Steelworkers, miners, and loggers hear it bellowed at them by their supervisors when they do not want to clean out the steel-making furnace, work overtime to dig out extra coal, or climb a steep hill to get to the next stand of trees.

But hard work does injure and kill. In 1998, just over 3 Canadian workers died every working day from an occupational injury, and 1 in 18 workers was injured at work. This represented one occupational injury every 9 seconds. In 2002, the Ontario Workplace Safety and Insurance Board registered over 350,000 claims for workplace-based injuries.

Canadian workers are injured and killed on the job in at least three ways. First, some jobs, such as mining, logging, and fishing, are very dangerous, and accident and fatality rates are unacceptably high. Second, accident rates are related to how fast and how long a person works at a job. The more hours a person works in a day, the greater the likelihood of an accident. Why? Fatigue. If you get tired shovelling snow, you can stop. If you are paid according to the number of widgets you produce, you are likely to push yourself beyond safe limits. And if you are manipulating a fast-paced machine with sharp cutting tools, even a brief lapse in attention can result in serious injury. Third, years of working hard can lead to various work-related diseases that are both debilitating and fatal.

The change from an industrial to a "post-industrial" or "information" society has altered the patterns of accidents somewhat. Over 30 years ago, the dominant form of injury compensated by provincial compensation boards involved crushed or severed limbs. Now it is various forms of strains and sprains, especially of the lower back and upper limbs. These injuries now represent approximately half of all workplace injuries, and their severity is increasing.

But this is just the tip of the iceberg. These numbers apply overwhelmingly to injuries caused by workplace accidents. But what about occupational disease? Numerous studies link long-term exposure to toxic substances and chemicals such as asbestos, lead, benzene, and arsenic to cancer and other deadly or debilitating diseases.

The problems associated with compensating occupational diseases are many and complex. How does a worker prove that exposure to a toxic chemical caused their cancer—especially if they changed jobs over the years and they smoked cigarettes? While some researchers believe that upward of 25 per cent of all cancers can be linked to the workplace, only about 2 per cent of all compensation claims are for occupational diseases. Every year, thousands of Canadians get ill and die from a work-related illness. The problem is that they don't know it.

Workers and unions in Canada have protested this alarming health and safety situation. In the late 1970s, these protests resulted in the passage of occupational health and safety laws that gave workers the right to know about the substances they were working with, the right to participate with management in identifying unsafe and unhealthy working conditions, and the right to refuse to do work they believed to be unsafe. While these rights apply to the majority of workers, unionized workers are most knowledgeable about their health and safety rights and are most likely to exercise them on a regular basis.

In 1994, Sean Kells, a 19-year-old from Mississauga, Ontario, was killed when flammable liquid he was pouring into a vat was ignited by electricity. It was his third day on the

continued

job. The plant in which he was working was not unionized. He had received no safety training or safety information from his employer. He was not aware of his health and safety rights, including his right to refuse unsafe work. He might still be alive if his employer had obeyed the law.

Know your rights. And don't work too hard.

———

SOURCE: Robert Storey, Labour Studies Program and Department of Sociology, McMaster University (2003). Printed with permission of the author.

today, whether they be offices, factories, hospitals, or classrooms, are becoming increasingly diverse. Only a minority of families relies on a single paycheque. First Nations people make up a growing proportion of the paid labour force in certain geographic areas. People of colour, some of whom are immigrants to this country, many Canadian-born, currently have a stronger-than-ever presence, particularly in big cities such as Vancouver, Toronto, and Montreal. As well, the workforce has become more highly educated and younger. As a result of these changes, students of work must turn their attention to some pressing new problems.

Gendered Work

The participation of women in the paid labour force has increased steadily over the past four decades. In Canada today, women constitute approximately 45 per cent of the labour force (Statistics Canada, 2001b: 8). Most striking has been a rise in the employment rates of married women and mothers of children under the age of six. Recent census data indicate that the two-breadwinner (also called *dual-earner*) family is now the norm. Gone are the days of *Ozzie and Harriet*.

Decades—indeed, over a century—of struggle and activism by feminists have resulted in important gains. Paid work is one arena in which these gains have been most prominent. In Canada, we now have employment equity legislation (albeit limited) in the federal government and laws enforcing equal pay for work of equal value. It is important to remember, though, that many of these breakthroughs are relatively recent. Into the 1950s, companies and governments still restricted the employment of married women, overtly defined work as "female" and "male," and upheld gender-based seniority systems (Sugiman, 1994).

Today, many young women and men entering the labour force are unaware of the blatant sexual inequalities of the past. Whether or not they self-identify as feminists, women today are building their careers on a feminist foundation. If not for the challenges posed by women's rights activists, university lecture halls would be filled exclusively by men, women would not be permitted entry into the professions or management, and paid employment would simply not be an option after marriage.

But just as women's historical breakthroughs are instructive, so too are the persisting inequalities. In spite of a dramatic increase in female labour-force participation, women and men are by no means equal in the labour market. The **social institution** of work is still very much a gendered one. It is important that women have made inroads in non-traditional fields of manual labour, the professions, and management and administration, but the majority of women remain concentrated in female-dominated occupations such as retail salesperson, secretary, cashier, registered nurse, elementary school teacher, babysitter, and receptionist, while men are more commonly truck drivers, janitors, farmers, motor vehicle mechanics, and construction trade helpers, for example. Particularly troubling is the finding that Canadian women who have completed university or community college are three times more likely than their male counterparts (24 per cent and 8 per cent, respectively) to move into a clerical or service job (Nelson and Robinson, 2002: 226). To the extent that occupational segregation by sex has lessened somewhat over time, it is more because of the entry of men into female-dominated occupations than the reverse.

As well, women (as well as youth of both sexes) are more likely than men to be employed on a part-time and temporary basis. For years now, women have made up approximately 70 per cent of the part-time workforce in Canada. And while the majority of the self-employed are men, the 1990s witnessed a rapid growth in women's self-employment. In comparing the sexes, we also see that self-employed men are more likely than self-employed women to hire others—male employers outnumbered females three to one—and that businesses operated by men are more likely to be in the goods sector whereas female-run businesses are likely to be in the less lucrative service sector (Nelson and Robinson, 2002: 242).

These trends—labour market segregation by sex and the overrepresentation of women in precarious employment—have contributed to gender-based differences in earnings. From 1967 to 1997, the pay gap between women and men employed full-time and full-year narrowed from 58 per cent to 72 per cent (Jackson and Robinson, 1997: 19), yet the narrowing of this wage gap was largely the result of an increase in time worked for women and of falling or stagnant wages for men, with only a modest increase in women's earnings. In addition to this, gender-based earnings differentials may, to a large degree, be attributed to women's concentration in part-time and temporary work. When we compare women employed on a full-time basis with their male counterparts, the gap narrows—though, as noted above, it does not disappear.

All women are not, of course, in the same position. Immigrant women, women of colour, and First Nations women bear the brunt of income and occupational polarization by sex. In consequence, their average annual earnings are disproportionately low. In her research on various categories of women, Monica Boyd (1999) concludes that earnings differentials increase between Canadian-born women and foreign-born women, especially when the latter group are of colour and when they are not fluent in English or French. In addition, foreign-born women who are currently residents of Canada are more likely than Canadian-born women to be employed in particular segments of the service sector—namely, those that are typically labour-intensive, poorly paid, and dominated by small firms (Vosko, 2000). While men of colour are concentrated in either professional occupations or service jobs, women of colour are more likely than Canadian women as a whole to perform manual labour. First Nations women likewise are concentrated in service or clerical work (First Nations men are more likely to perform manual labour than other kinds of work).

Faced with multiple forms of **discrimination**, working-class women of colour and some female immigrants have come to occupy job ghettos. Indeed, many of the jobs that are typically performed by working-class people of colour have a "hidden" quality: the work they do is not noticed; the workers are

Many of the jobs in job ghettos are performed by working-class people of colour. This work has a hidden quality: the work is not noticed. All too often, we regard these workers—nannies, maids, taxi drivers, dishwashers—simply as part of the backdrop. (© Vincenzo Pietropaolo/CAW)

rendered invisible. All too often, we regard private domestic workers and nannies, hotel and office cleaners, taxi drivers, health care aides, and dishwashers—all of whom perform indispensable labour—as simply part of the backdrop (Arat-Koc, 1990; Das Gupta, 1996). Not only are they physically out of sight (in basements, in kitchens, working at night when everyone else has gone), they are out of mind.

In documenting sex-based inequalities in employment, social scientists have produced reams of statistics. But there are many other ways in which we may speak of the gendering of work, some not easily quantifiable. Joan Acker (1990) writes about the process by which jobs and organizations come to be gendered, regardless of the sex of job holders. The bureaucratic rules and procedures, hierarchies, and informal organizational culture may rest on a set of gender-biased assumptions, for example. In her book *Secretaries Talk* (1988), Rosemary Pringle highlights the ways in which gendered family relationships are reproduced in workplace relations between bosses (fathers) and secretaries (wives, mistresses, daughters). Pringle describes how male bosses determine the boundaries between home and work, public and private, whereas "secretaries do not have this luxury. Male bosses go into their secretaries' offices unannounced, assume the right to pronounce on their clothes and appearance, have them doing housework and personal chores, expect overtime at short notice and assume the right to ring them at home" (1988: 51).

There are many formal and informal mechanisms that prevent women from entering male-dominated occupations. Cynthia Cockburn (1983) explores the ways in which a culture of manhood became very much a part of the printing trade. For years, the link between masculine identities, masculine culture, and the printing trade was so strong that it made the occupation completely impenetrable to women. Sugiman (1994) describes how women attempted to carve out for themselves "pockets of femininity" in the male-dominated auto plants of Southern Ontario during World War II. By the war's end, however, women's presence was no longer welcome. Most were hastily dismissed from the industry.

Today, many young women plan to both have a professional career and raise a family, but they are not quite sure how they will combine the two. Feminist researchers have demonstrated how the very concept of "career" is gendered. It is one that has been built on a masculine model. Career success depends on the assumption of a wife at home—a helper who will pick up the children from school, arrange dinner parties, and generally free the "breadwinner" to work late

at nights or on weekends and for out-of-town business travel.

Feminist analysis has, furthermore, called attention to the complex link between paid and unpaid labour, employment and family. With two breadwinners, both of whom are spending increasing hours in their paid jobs, families are under enormous pressure (see Figure 9.2). While the demands of paid work have risen over time, so too have pressures on family life. Government restructuring and cutbacks in resources have affected public daycare, after-school programs, special needs programs, and care of the elderly and the disabled. Who picks up the slack? The family. One consequence has been an intensification of (unpaid) family work and growing tensions within families as people try to cope.

In a study of working-class families in Flin Flon, Manitoba, Meg Luxton (1980) introduced the concept of a *double day* of labour—the combination of paid and unpaid labour that must be performed in the course of a day. Usually, notes Luxton, this double burden is carried by women. Every day, millions of people put in a "second shift" of unpaid labour after they get home from their paying jobs. According to Hochschild (Hochschild and Machung, 1989), this second shift amounts to one extra month of 24-hour

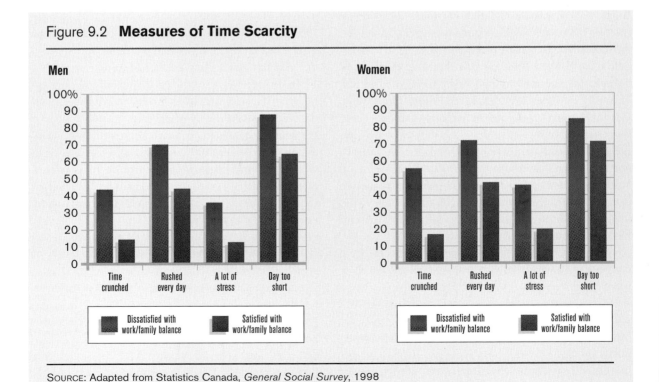

Figure 9.2 **Measures of Time Scarcity**

SOURCE: Adapted from Statistics Canada, *General Social Survey*, 1998

days of work per year. Hochschild (1997) also speaks to the experiences of millions of North American families in her study of the "time bind." The time bind has resulted in overworked, stressed people and in the downsizing and outsourcing of family responsibilities. Children are cranky, parents are rushed, and the concept of "leisure" is laughable. Hochschild suggests that rather than leave families with the "leftovers" of paid work, people should start challenging employers to more seriously consider the conflicting needs of family and employment.

Race and Racialized Work

The trends we have so far discussed (precarious work, heightened job insecurities, and underemployment) have clearly had a disproportionate impact on groups who have long faced discrimination in the labour market and in society as a whole: women, people of colour, and Native people. But though we now have an abundance of research on the gendering of work, sociologists in Canada have paid far less attention to the relationship between race, citizenship, and employment.

Barriers faced by people of colour, by Native people, and by immigrants are most often demonstrated in unemployment and earnings disparities. Native people comprise only a tiny percentage of the working-age population (2.3 per cent), yet this group is growing rapidly and already constitutes a sizable share of the labour force in some cities (Jackson and Robinson, 2000: 70). **Unemployment rates** for Native people are disturbingly high, more than double that for the Canadian population as a whole (24 per cent for Native men and 22 per cent for Native women; Nelson and Robinson, 2002: 228). In addition, only one in three Native people was employed in a full-time, continuous job in 1996, and this proportion was even lower for those who live on reserves (Jackson and Robinson, 2000: 71). Close to half of the off-reserve Native population lives in poverty.

The category "people of colour" is quite diverse, containing significant differences according to class, education, and citizenship status. In Canada, about 1 in 10 workers is defined as being of colour (the official census term is *visible minority*), and over 80 per cent of this group are relatively recent immigrants (Jackson and Robinson, 2000: 69). Today, immigrants of colour (compared to earlier generations of immigrants) are finding it extremely difficult

to close the employment gap with native-born Canadians (see Figure 9.3). In 1996, the average employment income for immigrants who arrived between 1986 and 1990 was 18 per cent lower than the earnings of non-immigrants. For those who immigrated after 1990, earnings were 36 per cent lower. And these gaps persist even when we control for age and education. On average, recent immigrants are younger than the labour force as a whole, but they also have more schooling. One problem is that foreign credentials are not always respected in Canada, thus contributing to a high concentration of immigrants of colour in low-wage jobs (Jackson and Robinson, 2000: 69–70).

Likewise, in 1995, the unemployment rate for workers of colour was 14.2 per cent compared to 10.1 per cent for all workers. Black Canadians in particular experienced a relatively high unemployment rate of 19.3 per cent, almost double the Canadian average (Jackson and Robinson, 2000: 70). It is not surprising then that roughly 45 per cent of black households in Canada live in poverty. Furthermore, there is evidence of race-based inequities in earnings. On the whole, people of colour earn about 15 per cent less than the total Canadian workforce (Jackson and Robinson, 2000: 70). And among this group, the pay gap is much

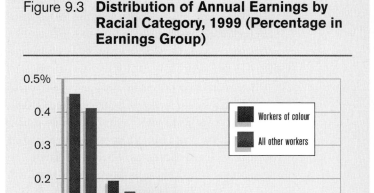

Figure 9.3 **Distribution of Annual Earnings by Racial Category, 1999 (Percentage in Earnings Group)**

SOURCE: From 'Workers of Colour' by Andrew Jackson, in *Falling Behind: The State of Working Canada, 2000*, Andrew Jackson, David Robinson, Bob Baldwin, and Cindy Wiggins (Ottawa: Canadian Centre for Policy Alternatives/Canadian Labour Congress, 2000). Reprinted by permission.

Human Diversity
Migrant Farm Workers in Canada

Summer brings the promise of warm, sunny days and the prospect of fresh Ontario-grown produce. Tempting supermarket produce displays belie the fact that thousands of invisible hands, more than 100,000 workers in Ontario's agricultural sector, including many migrant workers, have been hard at work planting and harvesting these crops. . . .

Agriculture is a staple in Ontario's economy, but its mainstay is no longer the family farm. Farming is big business. Leading Canada, Ontario shipped more than seven billion dollars of agrifood to the world in the first 11 months of 2001, a 13 per cent increase over the same period in 2000. In the last decade, Ontario's agrifood exports have tripled. . . .

While the structure of the agricultural industry may have changed, the nature of the work has not. Planting and harvesting is labour intensive, some would say back-breaking. Exposure to toxic substances, like pesticides, and the potential to contract disease from biological hazards are daily health threats. For some the work can be deadly. . . .

Last May, 20 migrant agricultural workers from Leamington spoke out about their working and living conditions. They didn't call the Ministry of Labour office but instead contacted the nearest Mexican consulate. Within days they were sent back to Mexico. . . .

For more than 30 years, migrant workers like these have been regularly employed on Ontario farms to meet short-term labour demands during peak seasons. Farm owners have traditionally failed to find sufficient Canadian labour to perform the work many characterize as poorly paid, unskilled, but most likely rejected for its gruelling nature.

The Seasonal Agricultural Workers Program (SAWP), created in 1996, was a response to farm owners' appeal for government assistance to address these ongoing labour shortages. The program, administered by Human Resources Develop-

ment Canada (HRDC), provides migrant workers for a period of six weeks to eight months from Mexico and Commonwealth Caribbean countries. An agreement between the participating countries also includes guidelines and an employment contract entered into by the worker, employer, the Canadian government and the worker's home country.

The program currently operates in Alberta, Manitoba, Ontario, Quebec and Nova Scotia. Of the 16,705 migrant workers employed in Canada under the program in 2000, 90 per cent worked on Ontario farms, 60 per cent are from Mexico.

Farm work in Ontario pays little more than minimum wage at $7.25/hour. Other legal rights, however, are less than minimum. While some may be entitled to health benefits, Ontario agricultural workers are not entitled to overtime pay and are exempt from hours of work legislation. Like other workers they pay Employment Insurance premiums. In 2000, $11 million was deducted from migrant farm workers and their employers yet they do not qualify to collect the benefit.

Toiling almost invisibly on farms, migrant workers are part of the community but have few social, economic or legal support systems. . . . Last December [2001] the Supreme Court of Canada in Dunmore v. Ontario (Attorney General) ruled agricultural workers' exclusion form the *Labour Relations and Employment Statute Law Amendment Act* violates workers' right to freedom of association guaranteed by the *Charter of Rights and Freedoms*.

———

SOURCE: Workers Health and Safety Centre, Ontario, Canada. Excerpts from 'Cultivating Health and Safety: Labour and community partners extend a hand to agricultural workers' from <www.whsc.on.ca/Publications/atthesource/summer2002/cultivatinghs.pdf>, accessed 28 May 2003. Reprinted by permission.

greater for men than women (though we must consider that women generally have much lower earnings than men). These lower earnings are in part a result of

this group's concentration in low-paying, relatively low-skilled jobs, their underrepresentation in skilled jobs, and their higher rates of unemployment.

Though telling, these statistics reveal only one dimension of the research on disadvantaged groups. It is equally important to recognize that because of racial and cultural differences, people experience the work world in distinct ways. In their study *Who Gets the Work*, Frances Henry and Effie Ginzberg (1985) found striking incidences of discrimination directed at job seekers. For example, when whites and blacks with similar qualifications applied for entry-level positions than had been advertised in a newspaper, whites received job offers three times more often than did black applicants. Similarly, of the job seekers who made inquiries by telephone, those who had accents (especially South Asian and Caribbean) were often quickly screened out by employers.

There is, furthermore, much historical documentation of the role played by the Canadian state in promoting or facilitating racialized work (Schecter, 1998). Agnes Calliste (1993) notes that between 1950 and 1962, Canadian immigration authorities admitted limited numbers of Caribbean nurses, but under different rules than white immigrant nurses. Black nurses were expected to have nursing qualifications superior to those demanded of whites. Several scholars (Arat-Koc, 1990; Bakan and Stasiulis, 1994) have also discussed the role of the Canadian state in addressing the need for cheap child care workers by importing women from the developing world (the Caribbean and the Philippines, in particular) to perform domestic labour without granting them full citizenship rights.

Often, jobs and occupations come to be racialized (that is, to adopt a racial label) as a result of formal and informal barriers that prevent their holders from exiting (Calliste, 1993; Das Gupta, 1996). In a study of black workers in automotive foundries, Sugiman (2001) found that after years of intense discrimination, workers themselves may come to circumscribe their "choices." Over the course of many decades, most black men remained where they had started—in the foundry. In the words of one foundry worker, "Their idea was, 'well, the white man don't want you up there no how, so why . . . put yourself in a position where you know you're not wanted'" (Sugiman, 2001: 102).

Youth

In Canada today, youth (persons between the ages of 15 and 24) constitute a much smaller share of the population than in past years (Lowe, 2000: 110). Yet the youth labour market is expanding at a significant rate. Curiously, young people still receive relatively little attention in studies of work. But young people today are facing harsh economic conditions, with the youth unemployment rate roughly 50 per cent higher than that of the population as a whole. Throughout the 1990s, in Canada, the overall high unemployment rate, government deficit-cutting, public- and private-sector downsizing, and various other wage-reduction strategies resulted in a contracting job market. In consequence, large numbers of youth withdrew from the labour market, returning to school or staying in school for longer periods (Lowe, 2000: 109).

The research presents us with a woeful picture. Study after study suggests that young people are in important ways no different from the majority of Canadian workers. They want high-quality work—work that is interesting and challenging and that provides a sense of accomplishment (Lowe, 2000). And youth have been increasing their human capital to acquire such jobs. Notably, young people are acquiring more education. (While a university degree does not guarantee a job, young people are still better off if they have the formal credentials.) But while Canadian youth are better schooled on the whole, they are also working less, and in jobs for which they feel that they are overqualified. Young people are most likely to be employed in low-paying service-sector jobs such as fast food restaurants, clothing stores, and grocery stores. For most students, contingent work is all that is available.

Some writers argue that the youth labour market makes a perfect accompaniment to the new goals of managerial flexibility. Employers invest in the belief that young people will have a limited commitment to the goals of the firm and that they expect to stay in jobs temporarily, as a stop-gap measure discontinuous with their adult careers and identities (Tannock, 2001). Stuart Tannock explains that youth themselves partially accept the popular **ideology** that positions them "as a separate class of workers who deserve less than adult workers do. Good jobs are predominantly the privilege of adulthood. Young workers must be content at first to spend their time in a tier of lower-quality service and retail employment. Dreams of meaningful work must be deferred" (2001: 109). Many young people compare themselves not to other workers across the spectrum, but exclusively to other youth workers (Sennett, 1998). Consequently, youth are more pliable and passive. Also, because their jobs

9.4

Open for Discussion
"We Don't Need No Education"

At an individual level, the command to "get educated" is like a mantra, repeated ad nauseam to hapless teenagers, the unemployed, displaced workers and any other unfortunates who appear to need free advice from their more comfortable acquaintances. At a policy level, meanwhile, the clarion call to educate, educate, educate provides a handy catchall solution for just about any economic or social problem imaginable: poverty, low productivity, globalization, inequality.

[But] the claim that Canada is being held back by a shortage of skills and knowledge is absurd. On the contrary, there is a vast and wasteful underutilization of the abundant skills and knowledge that our citizens already possess. . . . Close to two-thirds of young adults in Canada now complete a college or university degree program by the time they turn 30. According to the World Bank, our post secondary enrollment rates are the highest in the world.

Yet millions of Canadians are employed in positions that do not come close to fully utilizing their existing skills and knowledge. One-quarter of the 8 million Canadian workers with post secondary education report that they are over qualified for their jobs; one-quarter of all university and college graduates in Canada are employed in clerical, sales and menial service positions; and close to 30 per cent of all Canadians living in poverty have at least some post secondary education. So much for education being a one-way ticket to prosperity.

. . . Self-righteous hectoring about education and the knowledge economy is especially disingenuous when we remember that the well-educated, comfortable classes actually require vast output of unskilled, low-paid labour in order to continue living in the style to which they have become accustomed. Imagine, for example, what would happen if the entire low skill workforce suddenly went back to school and then burst back into the economy with Internet startups and consulting practices. Who would then do the dishes, clean the professional offices and mind the children? The age-old lament of the wealthy, "it's hard to find good help these days," would resonate with a dramatic urgency. Ultimately, both the employers of unskilled workers and the consumers of their services benefit from their lousy salaries, and their lack of formal education is simply a convenient excuse for their poverty.

If the great unskilled proletariat actually followed the nominal advice of those above them and bettered themselves through further education, then the system would need to quickly recreate another unskilled proletariat—through immigration and/or through the recruitment of new internal pools of "disempowered" labour. If we are genuinely concerned about ditch diggers, we'll save the lecture about how they should invest in their human capital. Our economy needs more ditch diggers—and dishwashers and janitors and labourers and secretaries and cashiers and manufacturers and waiters and drivers.

Further education may be extremely valuable for these Canadians, but they don't need it to do their jobs well and it won't guarantee them a better standard of living. Higher minimum wages, more effective unions, and other efforts to directly regulate and improve the wages and conditions of their work will do a lot more for them than investing in human capital.

We need the labour of these workers. And there's no inherent economic reason (other than the greed of their employers and their customers) that they shouldn't receive a decent income.

———

SOURCE: From Jim Stanford, "We Don't Need No Education," *This Magazine* (July/August 2001), 15–16.

are viewed as transient, youth are not as likely to become unionized. All of these features render them an extremely exploitable source of labour.

But as Tannock (2001) points out, youth are not stop-gap workers simply because they are young: they are also stop-gap workers because of the poor conditions under which they have to labour—conditions that have been created by employers in the service sector. But despite the popular view that young people are not especially concerned about their conditions of work, there is now much evidence that points to the contrary: "Teenagers and young adults working in these industries, who expect to have long lives ahead of them, worry that their jobs, which are supposed to be meaningless, stop-gap places of employment, will have lasting and detrimental effects on their bodies and future life activities" (Tannock, 2001: 54).

Workers' Coping and Resistance: The Struggle for Dignity and Rights

Finding Meaning in Work

Regardless of the many differences among Canadian workers today, one point remains clear: most Canadians want work that is personally fulfilling (Lowe, 2000). People have a powerful desire to maintain dignity at work (Hodson, 2001). Some of us are fortunate to hold jobs that offer challenge, jobs in which we can exercise autonomy and from which we can reap fruitful economic rewards. But even the "good jobs" are not always meaningful. And there are many jobs that are rarely rewarding. How do people cope with their work?

Sociologists have found that no matter how meaningless the job, people seek meaning in their work. Sometimes this is done through the culture of the workplace. People who have boring, routine jobs, for example, may make a game out of their work, varying repetitions, altering pace and intensity, imagining the lives of customers. As well, the social component of work (peer relations) is frequently a source of pleasure. In some workplaces, employees regularly exchange gossip, flirt, engage in sexualized play, share personal problems, debate politics, ridicule management. Relationships with co-workers often make the job itself more bearable, if not meaningful. In cases where the organization of work permits such exchanges, the lines between employment and leisure can become blurred.

Job satisfaction studies suggest that work is not all that bad. Most people report that they are generally satisfied with their jobs (Lowe, 2000). On close exam-

ination, though, discontent broods near the surface. At the same time that they report satisfaction, a majority of workers say that their jobs are somewhat or highly stressful, that they are not sufficiently involved, recognized, and rewarded, and that their talents are underutilized (Lowe, 2000). In addition, there are high rates of absenteeism, oppositional attitudes, slacking off, pilfering, and even destruction of company property. Some workers simply quit their jobs. But in the face of a competitive job market, family responsibilities, consumer debt, and, for some, few marketable skills, this is not a viable option. Furthermore, it is telling that even though they themselves claim to like their jobs, many people add that they do not want their own children to end up doing the same kind of work (Sennett, 1988).

Faced with unfair, unsafe, and sometimes unchallenging work, there will be discontent. Workers will find ways to make changes, to resist. The question is how. Individual acts of coping and resistance may give workers the feeling of agency and control, but insofar as they are individual acts, they rarely result in a fundamental or widespread change in conditions of work. In order to effect large-scale change, people must resort to collective measures.

Professions and Negotiating Professional Control

Securing professional control is an option for middle-class people who possess formally recognized credentials and can claim expertise in an area. When we think of a *professional*, who comes to mind? Physicians, psychiatrists, dentists, lawyers, engineers, accountants. Some sociologists (proponents of trait theory) have attempted to define *professionals* with reference to a checklist of characteristics (Freidson, 1970). This checklist includes, for example, possession of a body of esoteric or abstract knowledge, reliance on a specialized technical language or vocabulary, and membership in associations that control entry and membership in the occupation through licensing, accreditation, and regulation.

Critics, however, argue that trait theory does not fully explain how and why some occupations come to be defined as professional while others do not. Rather than list a series of traits that define a profession, Terence Johnson (1972) highlights the resources available to different occupational groups. It is these resources that have enabled physicians, psychologists, and lawyers to define themselves as distinct from other groups such as managers, clerical workers, and massage therapists. In focusing on the process of professionalization, critical theorists have noted that at the heart of the struggle to professionalize are relations of power and control. Feminist scholars have recently offered a more nuanced analysis of the ways in which **patriarchy** (a system of male dominance), too, structures the process of securing professional authority and control (Witz, 1991).

Labour Unions and Labour's Agenda

But the struggle to professionalize is not one in which many Canadians will be engaged—it is largely an exclusive one. Greater numbers of people in Canada, and globally, turn to another form of collective action to secure their rights and dignity in the workplace: they look to unionization. Just as campaigns to secure professional control have had a middle-class base, the struggle to unionize in this country has traditionally been one of white men in blue-collar jobs. In the latter part of the twentieth century and into the present time, however, increasing numbers of women, people of colour, white-collar workers, and middle-class employees have joined the ranks of the labour movement.

When most of us think of unions, strikes come to mind. Some of us may view trade unionists as just a bunch of greedy, overpaid workers demanding higher wages and, in the process, disrupting our lives, transportation, communication—even our garbage collection. We may owe this perception to dominant media representation of unions, their members, and their leaders.

But the labour movement in this country goes far beyond this narrow and unfair characterization. The basic premise of the organized labour movement is to take collective action through the process of bargaining a contract. This *collective agreement* is the outcome of days, weeks, or even months of negotiations between two parties: worker representatives and company representatives. The contract is a legally binding document, an agreement that has been signed by both the employer and the union. Only if the two parties cannot reach an agreement is there potential for strike action. The actual incidence of strikes in Canada is, in fact, low. In 2001, the estimated work time lost through strikes and lockouts was 0.07 per cent, one-sixth the level of 20 years earlier (Statistics Canada, 2002f: 3). The strike is usually a measure of

last resort. The vast majority of contracts that come up for renewal are settled without resorting to strike action. Indeed, some would argue that the leadership of unions acts to contain militancy on the part of its rank-and-file membership.

Workers in the nineteenth century first struggled to secure union representation in an effort to protect themselves against excessively long work days, extremely hazardous work environments, low pay, and blatant favouritism on the job. Critical to the survival of the labour movement in Canada was the passage of the Rand formula at the end of World War II. The Rand formula, named after Supreme Court Justice Ivor Rand, ensured the automatic deduction of union dues by the employer in a unionized workplace.

Today, labour–management conflict arises over a host of issues. Not only are wages an item of dispute, but companies and union representatives also negotiate benefits packages, job security, the implementation of technological change, outsourcing, concessions, and anti-harassment policies. It is because of the struggles of union members that Canadian workers in offices, stores, and factories now have the right to refuse unsafe work, the right to participate in company-sponsored pension plans, and, in some cases, access to on-site daycare centres.

The gains of unionized workers, moreover, spill over into the wider society. Both unionized and non-unionized workers now have employment standards, (un)employment insurance, a standard work day of eight hours, a five-day work week, overtime premiums, vacation pay, health benefits, and sick-leave provisions. Unions have been pivotal in lobbying governments to introduce worker-friendly provincial and federal legislation.

Union Membership

In the first half of 2002, union membership in Canada was 3.9 million (of 12.8 million paid employees). This represented a slight increase from 3.8 million in 2001. Women accounted for nearly all of this increase. In 2002, the rate of union membership among women was 30.2 per cent, for the first time matching that of men (at 30.3 per cent; Statistics Canada, 2002f: 1). In part, growth in female membership reflects the high rate of unionization in the (female-dominated) public service (for example, in Crown corporations, public schools, and hospitals). It is also, in part, a result of recent union organizing in private services (Jackson and Robinson, 2000). In comparison, the unionization rate for men has

9.5

Sociology in Action
McDonald's and Unions

A Quebec trade union has signed a labour contract with a McDonald's fast-food franchisee, the first in North America and only the second in the world.

"We had so many problems, so much repression," said Jean Lortie, a division president with the Quebec Confederation of National Trade Unions in Montreal. "But we didn't give up."

It took more than a year of often bitter negotiations to get a contract with the fast-food outlet in the tiny resort town of Rawdon, in the Laurentians north of Montreal. The process, Mr Lortie said, was so unpleasant and lengthy that by the time the union won only two of the 25 original signatories were still on staff.

The CNTU nearly became the first union in the world to get a labour contract with McDonald's, but a French union signed up a McDonald's restaurant only six weeks ago, said Len Ruel, area director of the Canadian Auto Workers in British Columbia.

The French union had to strike for six months to get a contract. By contrast, the Quebec contract was negotiated through the normal arbitration channels without a work stoppage. "All parties negotiated in good faith," said Maureen Kitts, a spokeswoman for McDonald's Restaurants of Canada Ltd in Toronto. She said McDonald's pays fair and equitable wages. Employees often start at the minimum legal wage with merit increases that are based on performance.

Rawdon is the first Canadian McDonald's outlet to sign a labour contract. Several other Canadian outlets have been certified by provincial labour authorities, but were unable to reach a first contract.

Ms Kitts said an outlet in Squamish, BC, was the first to be certified in North America. But Mr Ruel said the company decertified that union before he was able to negotiate a first contract.

Unions have organized other outlets in recent years, notably in Orangeville, Ont., in Montreal and in St-Hubert, Que.

But Mr Lortie said those outlets were closed or decertified shortly after. Another outlet, in the United States, was bulldozed by the franchisee shortly after it was certified, Mr Ruel said. "The company does everything it can to stop the union," he said.

With the first contract, the McDonald's workers in Rawdon will get a base pay of $7 an hour and a raise of 10 cents every six months on the job. "It's not a very good deal, but it's a start," Mr Lortie said. "This is the first time that everybody will get the same wage. There will be no favouritism."

More important, he said the workers will get seniority rights and layoff protection, a key factor in a resort town where the work is highly seasonal. The company has also agreed to stiffer safety regulations, a contentious issue in a restaurant that fries potatoes in boiling oil.

The labour contract in Rawdon will not apply to other McDonald's outlets because it is owned by an independent franchisee.

The two union leaders said McDonald's fought hard to stop the union coming in. They say the company and the franchisee harassed the union leaders by moving them to midnight shifts, giving them dirty jobs or by neglecting to call them into work.

"They had so many problems, they quit," Mr Lortie said. "They were only getting $7 a hour, so it wasn't worth it for them.

"We had to rebuild the union from scratch after they pushed out the union officers," he added. "It was a tough job to implement the new agreement."

SOURCE: Oliver Bertin, "Quebec Union's Labour Contract with McDonald's Is Landmark," *The Globe and Mail*, 18 Apr. 2002. Reprinted with permission from The Globe and Mail.

dropped since the 1960s. This is largely attributable to a shrinking proportion of jobs in traditionally male-dominated and heavily unionized sectors such as primary/resource, manufacturing, and construction (Jackson and Robinson, 2000).

Union membership also varies with terms of employment. Almost one in three full-time employees belongs to a union, compared to one in four part-time workers. Similarly, close to one in three permanent employees is a union member compared to about one in four non-permanent employees (Statistics Canada, 2002f: 2). We can, furthermore, see variations by age. Employees aged 45 to 54 (41.6 per cent) are more likely to be unionized than those aged 15 to 24 (13.3 per cent). Education is also a factor. A higher-than-average unionization rate can be found among men with postsecondary credentials (34.7 per cent) and those with less than a Grade 9 education (34 per cent). For women, the highest rate is for those with a university degree (40 per cent), reflecting unionization in health care and teaching (Statistics Canada, 2002f: 3).

Global comparisons reveal that the rate of union membership in Canada is higher than those in the United States and Japan and lower than those in most Western European nations. The dramatic decline in union membership in the United States has been a particular source of concern. The US unionization rate fell from 30 per cent at the end of the 1960s to less than 15 per cent in the current period (Jackson and Robinson, 2000: 25). This drop can be explained by a variety of forces, not the least of which are the electoral success of anti-union governments and the growth of anti-union employers such as Wal-Mart and Radio Shack. The assault on trade unions has been blatant in the United States.

The Union Advantage

There is absolutely no doubt that unionization benefits workers (see Table 9.3). Collective bargaining has secured for employees advantages in wages, benefits, job security, and extended health plans. This has been called the *union advantage*. The union wage premium in particular is greatest for (traditionally disadvantaged) workers who would otherwise be low paid. Unionization tends to compress wage and benefit differentials and thereby promote an equalization of wages and working conditions among unionized workforces (Jackson and Robinson, 2000). In 2001, for example, average hourly earnings of unionized workers in Canada were $20.29, while for non-unionized workers, they were $17.22. For part-time unionized

and non-unionized workers, the figures were $17.31 and $10.60, respectively. Unionized part-time workers also tended to work more hours per week than their non-unionized counterparts. Consequently, their average weekly earnings were nearly double ($343.94 compared to $181.65; Statistics Canada, 2002f: 3).

The advantages of unionization to women are perhaps the most obvious. In 2001, unionized women working full-time received on average 90 per cent of the hourly earnings of their male counterparts, and female part-time workers earned 9 per cent *more* than men who were in part-time work (Statistics Canada, 2002f: 3). It is also notable that women in unionized jobs are more than twice as likely to be included in pension plans than are women in non-unionized jobs (Jackson and Robinson, 2000).

According to the 1995 *World Employment Report* of the International Labour Organization (ILO), it is erroneous to believe that unions or good labour standards are the "fundamental cause of unemployment, and it is important to recognize the positive impacts for society in terms of greater equality and less poverty"; collective bargaining efforts should be regarded as an "important source of social well-being" (Jackson and Robinson, 2000: 96).

Conclusion: Work in the Future, Our Future as Workers

Workers and unions, of course, have limited powers. While newspaper headlines promote the "big" collective bargaining gains of the most strongly organized unions, most unionized workers across the country are still struggling to attain basic rights that others managed to secure years, if not decades, ago. Every day, in small workplaces, employees (unionized and non-unionized) negotiate their rights. More often now than in the past, these are women, people of colour, the disabled—not members of the dominant groups in this country.

These struggles have been difficult, and continue to be so, particularly in the context of the current assault on unions. In Ontario, the Harris-led Conservative government, for example, curbed the power of the Ontario Labour Relations Board by introducing legislation that removes the board's right to give union certification to workers who have faced (illegal) intimidation by anti-union employers. The power of workers and their movements is being even

Table 9.3   **The Union Advantage: Average Earnings and Usual Hours by Union and Job Status, Canada, 2001**

	All Employees	Union Members	Union Coverage[a]	Non-union Members[b]
Both Sexes				
Average hourly earnings	$17.18	$19.88	$19.84	$15.92
Full-time employees	$18.25	$20.29	$20.27	$17.22
Part-time employees	$12.23	$17.31	$17.16	$10.60
Average weekly earnings	$634.30	$724.94	$724.89	$591.31
Full-time employees	$723.85	$786.51	$786.58	$691.89
Part-time employees	$221.07	$343.94	$339.69	$181.65
Average usual weekly hours, main job	35.70	36.10	36.20	35.50
Full-time employees	39.70	38.80	38.90	40.10
Part-time employees	17.40	19.40	19.30	16.80
Men				
Average hourly earnings	$18.95	$20.91	$20.90	$18.00
Full-time employees	$19.31	$21.23	$21.23	$19.07
Part-time employees	$11.39	$16.19	$16.02	$10.18
Average weekly earnings	$744.19	$809.26	$809.92	$711.93
Full-time employees	$806.60	$842.93	$844.28	$786.92
Part-time employees	$193.13	$310.76	$305.94	$163.76
Average usual weekly hours, main job	38.40	38.50	38.50	38.40
Full-time employees	40.90	39.80	39.90	41.50
Part-time employees	16.40	18.40	18.30	15.90
Women				
Average hourly earnings	$15.29	$18.74	$18.65	$13.75
Full-time employees	$16.24	$19.04	$18.97	$14.89
Part-time employees	$12.59	$17.66	$17.53	$10.78
Average weekly earnings	$517.31	$631.45	$629.96	$465.74
Full-time employees	$616.99	$711.06	$709.19	$571.52
Part-time employees	$232.74	$354.37	$350.57	$189.74
Average usual weekly hours, main job	32.80	33.50	33.50	32.50
Full-time employees	38.10	37.40	37.50	38.30
Part-time employees	17.90	19.70	19.70	17.20

[a] Union members and persons who are not union members but who are covered by collective agreements (for example, some religious group members).

[b] Workers who are neither union members nor covered by collective agreements.

SOURCE: Adapted from the Statistics Canada web site <http://www.statcan.ca:8083/english/indepth/75-001/online/00802/fsfi_200208_02_a.pdf>.

more severely circumscribed by the aggressiveness of global capitalists, many of whom are openly supported by networks of governments in both developing and developed nations. Whether you work part-time at The Gap, labour a 60-hour week in a steel factory, freelance as a consultant, or find sporadic office employment through a temporary help agency, you are faced with a challenge.

Regardless of theoretical perspective or political agenda, scholars today are debating the nature of the challenge of the transformation of work. Young people entering the labour market for the first time and middle-aged people confronting reconfigured jobs and refashioned workplaces are both part of this transformation. Workers, young and old, must work in order to survive, to nurture families, to participate in life. Given this reality, it is crucial to know the debate, engage in it, and perhaps transform the world of work according to your own vision.

☐ Questions for Critical Thought

1. Think about where you are located in the economy. If you are not currently employed, where do you plan to find work? How does this depart from your parents' and grandparents' work histories? What factors have shaped (or constrained) your work-related aspirations?
2. Some employers believe that if you pay a worker more money (and offer better benefits), then you can compensate her or him for the boredom of work, loss of control, and lack of autonomy on the job. What do you think about this belief?
3. Think about the work that you perform in the course of an average day. What proportion of this is paid and what unpaid? Do you believe that we should define unpaid domestic activities as "work" that is of economic worth? If you were asked to calculate the economic worth of unpaid domestic labour, how would you begin? What factors would you take into account?
4. Most people in Canada today take the new computer technology for granted. But as a sociologist, you must take a closer, critical look. Consider some of the ways in which computer technology has reshaped employment opportunities and the nature of work.
5. A prevailing view is that the youth today are merely "stop-gap" workers. They are young and resilient. As they mature, they will move on to better, more secure and fulfilling employment. Thus, their conditions of work are not problematic. Young people themselves are not concerned about the nature of the jobs that they perform. Why should sociologists bother writing about youth at work?
6. Do you believe that who you are (that is, female or male, Aboriginal, of Asian or European or African descent, young or middle-aged, working-class, educated) is an important indicator of the type of work that you will perform? If so, in what ways? If not, explain.
7. Even though women's labour-force participation rate is now almost the same as men's, there are many persisting gender-based inequalities in employment. Identify some of these inequities. What are some of the formal and informal barriers to equality between women and men in the labour market today? How would you confront them?
8. Labour unions have long faced challenges in capitalist societies. Some people would argue that today union leaders and members face *new* challenges, perhaps more formidable than those of the past. Identify and discuss some of the new challenges that confront the labour movement in this country.

☐ Recommended Readings

Gillian Creese, *Contracting Masculinity: Gender, Class, and Race in a White-Collar Union, 1944–1994* (Toronto: Oxford University Press, 1999).

A carefully researched case study of the white-collar office workers' union at BC Hydro. Creese uncovers the negotiation of gender, class, and race in collective bargaining.

Barbara Ehrenreich, *Nickel and Dimed: On (Not) Getting By in America* (New York: Henry Holt, 2001).

An extremely readable sociological (and personal) comment on "getting by" as a low-wage worker in the **new economy**. Ehrenreich, a sociologist, travelled throughout the United States, working as a hotel maid, a waitress, a cleaner, and a Wal-Mart clerk. She describes the hardship and indignity of it all.

Ann Eyerman, *Women in the Office: Transitions in a Global Economy* (Toronto: Sumach, 2000).

In presenting the stories of 12 women office workers in Canada, the author makes a highly accessible critique of new managerial approaches in the context of global competition, corporate restructuring, computer technology, and the rise of contingent work arrangements.

Randy Hodson, *Dignity at Work* (Cambridge: Cambridge University Press, 2001).

Based on an examination of 109 organizational ethnographies, Hodson sensitively highlights the ways in which workers search for dignity and self-worth on the job.

Graham S. Lowe, *The Quality of Work: A People-Centred Agenda* (Toronto: Oxford University Press, 2000).

A refreshing and informative empirical analysis, by one of Canada's experts on the sociology of work, of the quality of work that is performed by Canadians today.

Meg Luxton and June Corman, *Getting By in Hard Times: Gendered Labour at Home and on the Job* (Toronto: University of Toronto Press, 2001).

Based on a series of interviews with women and men in families having one member employed at Stelco's manufacturing plant in Hamilton, Ontario, the authors demonstrate how working families are coping in the face of the economic restructuring that began in the 1980s.

Richard Sennett, *The Corrosion of Character: The Personal Consequences of Work in the New Capitalism* (New York: Norton, 1998).

A meaningful, eloquent critique, by one of America's finest sociologists, of the consequences of the new flexible workplace on individual lives and moral identity.

Stuart Tannock, *Youth at Work: The Unionized Fast-Food and Grocery Workplace* (Philadelphia: Temple University Press, 2001).

An excellent, engaging study of youth at work. Tannock gives voice to young people themselves, their experiences and concerns, while at the same time offering a rigorous critique of the low-end service economy today.

☐ Recommended Web Sites

Canadian Auto Workers (CAW)

www.caw.ca

The CAW is the largest private-sector union in Canada. For most of its history, the union represented only auto workers. Since the 1980s, though, the CAW has broadened its membership to include fishers, fast food workers, Starbucks employees, health care workers, and thousands of other workers in many different sectors.

Canadian Centre for Occupational Health and Safety (CCOHS)

www.ccohs.ca

The CCOHS, based in Hamilton, Ontario, promotes a safe and healthy working environment by providing information and advice about occupational health and safety issues.

Canadian Centre for Policy Alternatives (CCPA)

www.policyalternatives.ca

The CCPA offers an alternative to the message that we have no choice about the policies that affect our lives, by undertaking and promoting research on issues of social and economic justice.

CorpWatch

www.corpwatch.org

CorpWatch is a San Francisco–based organization that monitors and critiques corporate-led globalization through education and activism. It seeks to foster democratic control over corporations by building grassroots globalization—a diverse movement for human rights, labour rights, and environmental justice.

European Foundation for the Improvement of Living and Working Conditions

www.eurofound.ie

The foundation is a tripartite European Union body set up in 1975 to contribute to the planning and establishment of better living and working conditions.

International Labour Organization (ILO)

www.ilo.org

The ILO was founded in 1919 and is now an agency of the United Nations. Its mandate is to promote and realize standards, fundamental principles, and rights at work.

Labour/Le Travail
www.mun.ca/cclh/llt/

Labour/Le Travail is the leading academic journal for labour studies in Canada. In operation since 1976, the journal publishes historical and contemporary articles on all aspects of work in Canada.

LabourStart
www.labourstart.org

LabourStart is a Web-based news organization that provides up-to-the-moment information on a wide variety of labour-related issues and developments around the globe. Visitors to this site can find anything from job advertisements in Australia to the latest strikes in the United Kingdom to recently published books.

No Sweat
www.nosweat.org.uk

No Sweat is a UK-based activist campaigning organization that fights sweatshops around the world. It stands for a living wage, safe working conditions, and independent trade unions. No Sweat is an open, broad-based campaign that aligns with anti-capitalist protest movements and the international workers' movement.

2

10

Juanne Clarke

> > >

Health Issues

© Digital Vision

☐ Learning Objectives

In this chapter, you will:

- see how health, illness, and disease are distinct in the sociology of health, illness, and medicine

- learn that health, illness, disease, and death are integrally related to the social world through a number of intermeshing levels

- examine medicare as a system that embodies five principles: portability, universality, comprehensive coverage, public administration, and accessibility

- see how privatization is increasing in the Canadian medical system

- learn that medicalization is a powerful cultural force

- discover that there are significant problems in the medical profession

Introduction

This chapter is an investigation of health and medical issues from the perspective of sociology. What do you think are some significant health issues facing you today as a student, as a young man or woman, as a Canadian? Do you think immediately of HIV/AIDS, cancer, or heart disease? Do you think of eating disorders, depression, unwanted pregnancies, or sexually transmitted diseases (STDs)? Or do you jump to thinking of the medical care system and topics in the news such as long waiting lists for emergency service, the lack of available physicians, or home care services? This chapter will introduce you to a sociological perspective on topics such as these that are related to the sociology of health, illness, and medicine.

Health is inextricably linked to the social order. Its very definition, its multitudinous causes, and its consequences are all social. What is considered healthy in one culture may not necessarily be considered to be healthy in another. What was thought of as good health at one time is not the same as what is considered to be good health at another. Rates of sickness and death vary across time and place. Social classes differ in their definitions of good health. What a woman considers health may be different from a man's definition of health. Moreover, **class** and **gender** seem to operate in ways that lead to different levels of health and sickness and different rates of death.

One example of cultural differences in the experience of health and illness comes from a tale told by the early Canadian writer Catherine Parr Traill in *The Backwoods of Canada* ([1836] 1966). This account is based on Traill's letters home from 1832 to 1835, while she and her husband were homesteading near what is now Peterborough, Ontario. She wrote,

> My dear husband, my servant, the poor babe, and myself, were all at one time confined to our beds with ague. You know how severe my sufferings always were at home with intermittents, and need not marvel if they were no less great in a country where lake-fevers and all kinds of intermittent fevers abound. Few persons escape the second year without being afflicted with this weakening complaint; the mode of treatment is repeated doses of calomel, with castor-oil salts, and is followed up by quinine. Those persons who do not choose to employ medical advice on the subject dose themselves with ginger-tea, strong infusion of hyson, or any other powerful green tea; pepper, and whiskey;

with many other remedies that have the sanction of custom or quackery. (Traill, [1836] 1966: 107)

I doubt that you have heard of or suffered from lake-fever or intermittents. I also doubt that you have used quinine, pepper, or whiskey as a treatment when you were ill, although many of you may have your own family healing traditions, such as chicken soup, mustard plaster, or brandy for a cold. Yet the diseases and the treatments described by Traill were believed in as fervently as we believe in treating cancer with chemotherapy, radiation, and surgery today.

Similar stories of the experiences of new immigrants from various parts of the world to all of the provinces in Canada would provide interesting insights into some of the culturally distinct threads of the Canadian "mosaic" of health's meanings. The interpretation of health varies not only historically and culturally, but also between men and women, people of different educational and social class backgrounds and religious traditions, and so on. Think a little about how your male and female friends, your brothers and sisters, and your parents differ with respect to how they think about and act with regard to what they consider sickness. Think too about how illness and medicine are portrayed on television programs such as *ER*. The first part of the chapter will examine several health issues: the changing health of Canadians over the nineteenth and twentieth centuries, HIV/AIDS, the Walkerton water crisis, social inequality, **social capital** and health, the sense of coherence, obesity and eating disorders, and health among Aboriginal Canadians.

However, the sociology of health issues is not only about health, **illness**, and **disease**, but also about medical or health systems of diagnosis, prognostication, and treatment. Conventional medicine—sometimes called **allopathic medicine** because it treats by means of opposites, such as cutting out or killing germs, bacteria, or other disease processes through chemotherapy, surgery, or radiation—is taken for granted in much of the Western world. In fact, much of the history of the sociology of health and medicine is based on assuming the primacy of the work of the allopathic system and its practitioners. However, naturopathic (treatment through "natural" remedies and procedures, such as herbs or massage), chiropractic (treatment through spinal adjustment), and homeopathic medicine (treatment with similars), all examples of *CAM*, or *complementary and alternative medicines*, are of increasing importance in the Western world.

The second part of this chapter will investigate some of the most important trends and social policy issues in the area of medical sociology, including **medicalization**, the future of the health care system, and **privatization**.

Theoretical Perspectives

Four theoretical **paradigms** are conventionally considered to be the most significant ways of approaching and understanding health and medicine sociologically: structural functionalism, conflict theory, symbolic interactionism, and feminism.

Structural Functionalism

From the **structural functionalist** perspective, health is the normal and normative position or behaviour in the social system. In a stable society, all institutional forces work together to create and maintain good health for the population. Your university or college assumes your good health as it organizes its courses and exams—you probably have to get a letter from a doctor for exemption from writing a test or an exam. The smooth functioning of societies depends on the good health of its members. Societies are organized to support a population up to an average **life expectancy** and at a given level of health and ability. This normative standard of health and normative age at death are reinforced by political, economic, cultural, and educational policy.

It has been suggested, for example, that the reason that governments continue to allow cigarette smoking is because to do so reaps economic benefits, through the high levels of taxation, for **the state**. Not only does the availability of cigarettes with their high taxation rate contribute to the income of the state, but the relatively fast death from lung cancer as compared to other cancers, for instance, saves the government in health care costs. Although this may be too cynical an analysis, it does make clear that there are interesting and thought-provoking social structural ways of thinking about the potential relationships between the health and life expectancy of a population and the institutional and political forces of the population.

Assertions about the interrelationships among institutions all fit within the structural functionalist theoretical perspective. A classic statement of this perspective is found in the work of Talcott Parsons

(1951), in particular in his concept of the *sick role*. The sick role is to be thought of as a special position in society. It exists to prevent **sickness** from disrupting the "ongoingness" of social life. The sick role also provides a way of institutionalizing what might otherwise become a form of deviant behaviour. It does this by articulating certain rights for those who claim sickness in a society so long as they fulfill certain duties.

Specifically, in Parsons's thinking, there are two rights and two duties for those who wanted to claim sickness and engage in the sick role. The rights include the right to be exempted from normal social **roles** and the right to be free of blame or responsibility for the sickness. The duties are to want to get well and to seek and co-operate with technically competent help. However, that these theoretically derived ideas do not always have empirical support is evident in a number of ways. For example, it is well known that the right to be exempt from the performance of social roles depends in part on the nature of the sickness. A hangover, for instance, may not be considered a good enough reason to claim the sick role as an excuse for an exam exemption. There is also a great deal of evidence that people with AIDS were seen as culpable, especially in the early days of the disease in North America—in fact, it was called the "gay plague" by some (Altman, 1986). And not everyone is expected to want to get well. Indeed, those with a chronic disease such as multiple sclerosis are expected to accept their condition and to learn to live with it. Parsons assumed the dominance of allopathic medicine in his statement that a sick person was to get technically competent help. Today, however, many people believe that the best help may not always come from allopathic medicine even though it is the state-supported type of medical care. Indeed, a substantial minority—approximately 40 per cent—of North Americans now rely on complementary and alternative medicines, or CAMS (Statistics Canada, 2001a: 17; Eisenberg et al., 1998).

Conflict Theory

From the perspective of **conflict theory**, health and ill health result from inequitable and oppressive economic conditions. The primary focus of analysis is the distribution of health and illness across the **social structure**. Questions driving this perspective include, Are the poor more likely to get sick? Is the **mortality rate** (the frequency of death per a specified number of people over a specified period of time) among the poor higher than among the rich? Are women more likely than men to get sick? Do men die at younger ages? Does racism affect the **morbidity** (sickness) **rate** (the frequency of sickness per a specified number of people over a specified period of time)? Health is seen as a good that is inequitably located in society.

A classic statement of this position is found in the work of Friedrich Engels, who often wrote with Karl Marx. In his book *The Condition of the Working Class in England* ([1845] 1994), Engels demonstrates the negative health consequences of early **capitalism**. He describes how the development of capitalism advanced mechanism in agriculture and forced farm workers off the land and into the cities to survive. Capitalists in the cities sought profit regardless of the costs to the well-being of the workers. Owners maintained low costs for labour through poor wages and long hours of back-breaking work in filthy and noisy working conditions. Even children worked in these unhealthy circumstances.

As a consequence, poor labourers and their families lived exceedingly rough lives in shelters that offered little or no privacy, cleanliness, or quiet. They had very little money for food, and the quality of the

foodstuffs available in the cities was poor. The slum-like living conditions were perfect breeding grounds for all sorts of diseases, and because of the high density of living quarters, the lack of facilities for toileting and washing, and the frequent lack of clean drinking water, the morbidity and mortality rates in the slums were very high. Infectious diseases such as tuberculosis (TB), typhoid, scrofula, and influenza spread quickly and with dire results through these close quarters and malnourished populations.

Epidemics were almost common in nineteenth-century industrial cities, where overcrowding, overflowing cesspits, garbage piled all around, and unsafe water were the norm. It was only when there were new discoveries in bacteriology and it became clear that many of the worst diseases were spread by bacteria and viruses in the water, air, and food that governments enacted public health measures. These new prevention policies included sewage disposal, garbage removal, clean filtered drinking water, and hygienic handling of food. The death rates began to abate (Crompton, 2000). Table 10.1 shows how, even in the 1920s in Canada, infectious diseases such as influenza, bronchitis, and pneumonia, TB, various stomach and digestive ailments such as gastritis, and communicable diseases were important causes of death.

Table 10.1 **Leading Causes of Death, Canada, Twentieth Century**

	Cause of Death[a]	Rate per 100,000
1921–5	All causes	1,030.0
	Cardiovascular and renal disease	221.9
	Influenza, bronchitis, and pneumonia	141.1
	Diseases of early infancy	111.0
	Tuberculosis	85.1
	Cancer	75.9
	Gastritis, duodenitis, enteritis, and colitis	72.2
	Accidents	51.5
	Communicable diseases	47.1
1996–7[b]	All causes	654.4
	Cardiovascular diseases (heart disease and stroke)	240.2
	Cancer	184.8
	Chronic obstructive pulmonary diseases	28.4
	Unintentional injuries	27.7
	Pneumonia and influenza	22.1
	Diabetes mellitus	16.7
	Hereditary and degenerative diseases of the central nervous system	14.7
	Diseases of the arteries, arterioles, and capillaries	14.3

[a] Disease categories are not identical over time.
[b] Rates are age-standardized.
SOURCE: Adapted from the Statistics Canada publication, *Canadian Social Trends*, Catalogue 11-008, Winter 2000, p.13.

Conflict theory has also been given a feminist emphasis, as in the work of Hilary Graham. In *Women, Health and the Family* (1984), Graham documents how inequality affects the various types of home health care work done by women in order to protect the good health of their families. In particular, she articulates four different components of women's home health care work: (1) maintaining a clean, comfortable home with an adequate, safe, and balanced diet as well as supportive social and emotional intra-familial relations; (2) nursing family members when they feel ill or are debilitated; (3) teaching family members about health and hygiene, including such things as sleeping, bathing, cleaning, and toileting; and (4) liaising with outsiders regarding the health care needs of family members, such as taking children or a partner to the doctor, clinic, hospital, or dentist.

As Graham notes, the ability of women to fulfill these four roles varies significantly depending on the educational, socio-economic, health, spiritual, emotional, and financial resources that women have or to which they are able to gain access. Moreover these resources are inequitably distributed over the socio-economic hierarchy.

Symbolic Interactionism

Interpretation and meaning are the hallmarks of sociology within the **symbolic interactionist** perspective. What is the meaning, for example, of anorexia and bulimia? Are they medical conditions? Are they the result of a moral choice? Or could they be thought to be "socio-somatic" conditions, that is, caused by society (Currie, 1988)? Various authors have attributed them to women's "hunger strike" against their contradictory positions, against culturally prescribed images, and against lack of opportunities in contemporary society. They have been conceptualized as a means "through which women, both unconsciously and consciously, protest the social conditions of womanhood" (Currie, 1988: 208). There is often a stigma attached to the person with HIV/AIDS, cancer, depression, inflammatory bowel disease, diabetes, or asthma. By some, they are thought to have connotations of morality or immorality. Good health is even associated with being a good person.

One contemporary study that uses the symbolic interaction perspective is Michael Hardey's discussion of illness stories on the Internet (2002). In this investigation, Hardey argues that the illness home page accounts demonstrate the processes whereby, in a

global economy, ill people have transformed themselves from mere passive recipients of diagnosis and medical treatments at the behest of the powerful doctors into consumers and producers of health information and care. Home pages offer explanations for illness, advice, solutions, and products and services to those who read them. They provide space for people to portray themselves as experts with regard to particular diseases. These pages can be read for the meanings that people associate with illness and other topics related to a symbolic interactionist perspective.

Feminism

Feminist health sociology recognizes the centrality of gender to social life as well as to inequity in the worlds of and in relations between men and women. Feminist health sociology investigates whether, how, and why men and women have different health and illness profiles, as well as different causes and average ages of death. Feminist health sociology also includes consideration of such things as **ethnicity**, sexual preference, and ability/disability as fundamental characteristics of social actors and social life. These axes of inequality are therefore central issues to be included in designing research, uncovering social injustice, and planning and making social change.

Women's health has been a central issue and in many ways a major impetus for the recent women's movement. The health-related book *Our Bodies, Our Selves* became, when first published in 1971, a major rallying document for women. Translated into many languages, and more recently revised and updated, the book offers a radical critique of medical practice and medicalization as well as women's views of their own health, sickness, and bodies.

Another example of work within the feminist paradigm is Anne Kasper and Susan Ferguson's *Breast Cancer: Society Shapes an Epidemic* (2000), which suggests that among the reasons for the growing incidence (number of new cases in a year) and prevalence (number of cases within a given population) of the disease is that it is primarily a women's disease and is therefore not given the serious and systematic research attention that it would have received had it been primarily a male disease. Contributions to this book by scholars and practitioners from a wide variety of fields, including sociology, zoology, social and health policy, anthropology, law, and biology, examine the social and political contexts of breast cancer as a social problem, arguing that gender, politics, social class, race, and ethnicity have affected the type of research that is done, the types of treatments that have become dominant, the rates of growth in the morbidity and mortality of breast cancer, and even the ways in which the disease is experienced by women. Indeed, they suggest that one of the reasons for the continuance of the epidemic is that it is not only primarily a women's disease but it is located in their breasts.

Kasper and Ferguson's collection provides a thought-provoking look at one of the major causes of worry, sickness, and death among women in Canada and the United States. Despite the fact that both heart disease and lung cancer are more frequent causes of death for Canadian women, women in Canada fear breast cancer more and even think of their breasts as essentially flawed and vulnerable to disease (Robertson, 2001). This is undoubtedly related to the enormous mass media attention the disease has received in the last 15 years or so. During this time, first in the United States and then in Canada, powerful lobby groups of women activists founded highly successful breast cancer advocacy coalitions, lobbied governments and corporations, and received substantial increases in the funding levels for research into the disease and its treatment. There is, of course, a painful irony in the fact that the increased attention and financial investment have been coupled with a proliferation of stories in the mass media that have served to increase anxiety and fear of risk of disease among Canadian women.

The Sociology of Health, Illness, Disease, and Sickness

At the broadest level, sociologists compare within and between societies around the world and over time with respect to the rates of, causes of, and treatments for health and sickness and to rates and causes of death. Here, factors such as wars, famine, drought, epidemics, natural disasters, air and water quality, quantity and quality of foodstuffs, transportation safety, level and type of economic development, technology, available birth control, immunization, antibiotics, medicalization, culture, and political economy all are all considered relevant.

At the next level, sociologists examine morbidity and mortality within societies and cultures and compare people of different social class backgrounds, educational levels, genders, religiosity, rural/urban

locations, occupations, ethnicities, family statuses, and so on. Another level of investigation down concerns the way socio-psychological factors such as level of stress and sense of coherence are implicated in illness, disease, and sickness.

The next level is an examination of the relationships between various "lifestyle" behaviours, such as smoking, seat-belt use, alcohol consumption, diet, risk-taking behaviours, sexual activity and protection, and drug use. Finally, the existential considerations, including the meaning and the experience of morbidity and mortality to individuals, are studied. Figure 10.1 shows these links, beginning from the person.

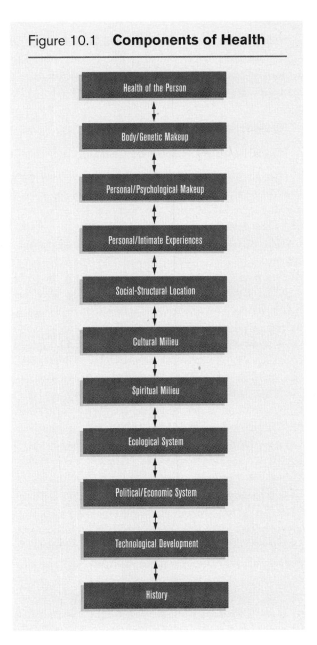

Figure 10.1 **Components of Health**

Health of the Person

Body/Genetic Makeup

Personal/Psychological Makeup

Personal/Intimate Experiences

Social-Structural Location

Cultural Milieu

Spiritual Milieu

Ecological System

Political/Economic System

Technological Development

History

In this chapter, we will look at specific and limited topics within each of these levels of analysis, beginning with the changing health of Canadians over the nineteenth and twentieth centuries, HIV/AIDS in Canada and around the world, and the water crisis in Walkerton, Ontario, as examples of the first level. At the second level, we will look at social inequity and social capital, along with Aboriginal health issues. At the third level, the focus will be on sense of coherence. Fourth, we will investigate eating-disordered behaviour and attitudes, including obesity. The fifth and final level will be illustrated by a discussion of popular conceptions of illness as well as an illustration of the experiences of one mother when her child had cancer.

I doubt that you will be surprised to learn that this separation into levels is artificial and done only for reasons of analytical clarity. In fact, each of the levels influences all the other levels.

Comparative Analyses

The Changing Health of Canadians

People are generally living longer and healthier lives today than they did in the past. The increase in health and the decrease in mortality rates over the past 150 years has been substantial. In the nineteenth century, infectious and communicable diseases such as cholera, typhoid, diphtheria, and scarlet fever were responsible for enormous levels of suffering and death for early Canadians. Wound infections and septicemia were frequent results of dangerous and unhygienic working, living, and medical conditions. Puerperal fever killed many women during and after childbirth. The health experiences of early Canadians have been well described in some general non-fiction (see, for example, Bliss, 1991, 1992) and in personal memoirs, such as Susannah Moodie's *Roughing It in the Bush* ([1852] 1995), on settler life in the 1800s. Even fiction can help us understand how people have experienced health. Margaret Atwood's *The Edible Woman* ([1968] 1994), for example, foreshadows the contemporary issue of eating-disordered attitudes and behaviours.

In 1831, the average life expectancy for Canadian men and women was 39.0 years—38.3 for women, and 39.8 for men (Clarke, 2000: 50). Today, life expectancies are about double this for Canadian men and women. Today's women can expect to live to 81, men to 75 (Crompton, 2000: 12). What has happened to cause this dramatic shift? You might think first of medical interventions and vaccinations. However, the most important causes of the increase in life expectancy are related to public health measures that were able to forestall the spread of disease. These included improved nutrition, better hygiene through sanitation and water purification practices, and advances in birth control. Interventions such as these brought the average life expectancy to 59 in the 1920s and, largely because of dramatic declines in infant mortality, to 78 in 1990–2 (Crompton, 2000: 12).

In the 1920s, the most common causes of death became heart and kidney disease, followed by influenza, bronchitis, and pneumonia, and the diseases of early infancy. Widespread use of newly discovered vaccines and antibiotics (vaccines against diphtheria, tetanus, typhoid, and cholera were developed in the late nineteenth and early twentieth centuries, and antibiotics were introduced in the 1940s) made a significant difference in the twentieth century (Crompton, 2000). While heart disease remains the most common cause of death, it has declined dramatically over time, probably as a result of lifestyle changes such as declines in smoking and dietary fat, improvements in exercise, and better medical treatments. Lower infant death rates today have resulted primarily from better nutrition and improved hygiene in pregnancy, secondarily from medical and technological advances. For example, prematurity, a frequent cause of infant death in the past, is now both more often prevented through educational programs and prenatal care and well managed in hospital.

The incidence of diseases such as measles, scarlet fever, and whooping cough was all but cut to zero until some people abandoned the vaccines in the 1990s. For a short time, the incidence of these diseases increased, but by the late 1990s they had declined again when public health authorities became alerted to the issue and became more diligent about universal vaccinations in Canada.

One other important feature of the declines in mortality or gains in life expectancy is the gap between men and women and how this gap has changed over time (see Table 10.2). From 1920 to 1922, women lived an average of two years longer than men; from 1990 to 1992, they lived an average of six years longer than men. Part of the explanation for women's greater benefit from the changes of the twentieth century relates to the decline in maternal mortality over this period. Another part of the explanation is the greater tendency for men to engage in risk-taking behaviours such as cigarette smoking and drunk driving.

Table 10.2 **Life Expectancy at Birth (Years), over Time, by Province, and by Gender**

	Both Sexes	Males	Females	Difference
Canada				
1920–2	59	59	61	2
1930–2	61	60	62	2
1940–2	65	63	66	3
1950–2	69	66	71	5
1960–2	71	68	74	6
1970–2	73	69	76	7
1980–2	75	72	79	7
1990–2	78	75	81	6
1990–2				
Newfoundland and Labrador	77	74	80	6
Prince Edward Island	77	73	81	8
Nova Scotia	77	74	80	6
New Brunswick	78	74	81	7
Quebec	77	74	81	7
Ontario	78	75	81	6
Manitoba	78	75	81	6
Saskatchewan	78	75	82	7
Alberta	78	75	81	6
British Columbia	78	75	81	6

SOURCE: Adapted from Statistics Canada web site <www.statcan.ca/english/Pgdb/health26.htm>, accessed 17 July 2003.

Today, among the most important causes of death are, for men, cardiovascular disease, followed by diseases of the heart and then cancer, and for women, cardiovascular disease, followed by cancer and then diseases of the heart. The rates per 100,000 for men are 316.9, 238.7, and 234.7, and for women, 193.8, 150.3, and 134.8, respectively (Statistics Canada, 2001a).

But these rates do not take age into account. Potential years of life lost, or **PYLL**, is a statistical representation of death that does take age into account: the younger the average age of death for a given disease, the greater the number of years of life lost. PYLL allows us to see the years of life lost by disease type, taking 70 years as the cut-off age point. Here the rank order of the top four causes of death changes: all cancers were responsible for 302,585 deaths, accidents for 228,106, diseases of the heart for 145,394, and suicide for 108,488 (Statistics Canada, 1996a: 116).

These two sorts of information have different implications for such things as government health promotion planning. For example, the PYLL figures tell us that younger people are more likely to die of accidents and suicide and that the numbers of deaths in these categories are large. One can then consider what sorts of things might be done to prevent different sorts of accidents and suicides as compared to the chief causes of death—those sometimes called "diseases of civilization"—cancer and cardiovascular and heart diseases?

HIV/AIDS

We have all heard of HIV/AIDS. It is a disease of pandemic proportions around the world today (see Figure 10.2). Many people in North America have come to associate the disease with certain categories of other people. In particular, North Americans tend to think of HIV/AIDS as the "gay disease" (Crossley, 2002). In an international context, however, HIV/AIDS is almost as common among women as among men: in 1997, 59 per cent of those diagnosed internationally were male and 41 per cent were female; by 2000, 53 per cent were male and 47 per cent female (UNAIDS, 2001b: 1). In sub-Saharan Africa, however, more women than men are HIV-positive (this means that they carry the precursor virus but have not yet developed AIDS). In some of the sub-Saharan African countries where the disease has taken its highest toll, teenage girls are five to six times as likely to be infected as boys. Whether because they themselves are diagnosed with the disease or because they are much more likely to act as caregivers to others when they are sick, women are substantially more affected by the AIDS epidemic than men in Africa. Already, too, in Africa, more than 1 million children are living with HIV and 12.1 million children have been orphaned by the disease. The number of orphans is expected to double by 2010. Children who are orphaned because of AIDS bear additional burdens of stigma and decreased access to health and education. In turn, they are more susceptible to becoming infected by HIV/AIDS (UNAIDS, 2001a: 2).

What is this disease that has caused so much havoc in the last 20 years? AIDS (acquired immune deficiency syndrome) is a disease of the immune system that most scientists believe comes from HIV (human immunodeficiency virus). It is spread from person to person through bodily fluids such as semen, blood, vaginal fluid, and breast milk. Sexual intercourse, needle sharing, and mother-to-fetus transmission are currently the most common means of transmission. In the end, though, it is not HIV/AIDS that causes death, but rather such diseases as cancer, pneumonia,

and tuberculosis that the vulnerable immune system is too weak to resist.

Even though the incidence and prevalence of HIV/AIDS are much lower here, Canada is not exempt from this epidemic. By 2002, there had been a cumulative total of 18,124 AIDS cases in this country. Of these, 7.9 per cent were among women. However, the rate among women is growing, from 5.6 per cent prior to 1992 to 8.3 per cent in 1995 and 16.4 per cent in 1999 (Health Canada, 2003: 1).

The most common means of transmission in Canada has been among men who have sex with men (MSM)—75.6 per cent of cases have been attributed to MSM, an additional 9.9 per cent to men who inject drugs (this category also includes other high risk behaviour i.e., MSM). Among women, 59.6 per cent of cases are attributed to heterosexual contact, 21.9 per cent to injection drug use, and 9.6 per cent to receipt of blood and blood products (UNAIDS, 2002: 6).

HIV/AIDS is especially prevalent among Aboriginal people. Between 1996 and 1999, the number of Aboriginal people infected with HIV grew from 1,430 to 2,740—almost doubling. In 2000, a study

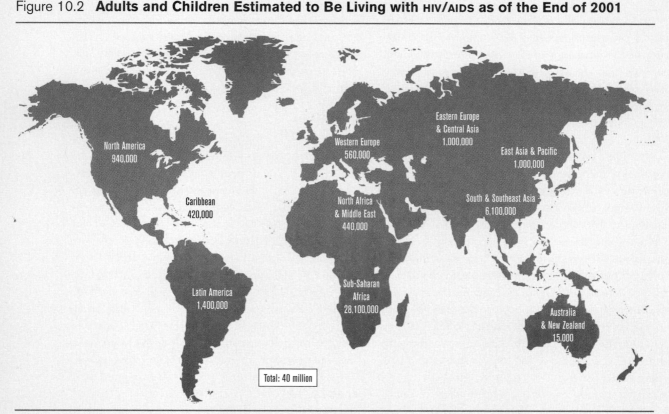

Figure 10.2 **Adults and Children Estimated to Be Living with HIV/AIDS as of the End of 2001**

Source: From <http://www.unaids.org/worldaidsday/2001/EPIgraphics2001/EPIcore_en.ppt>. Reprinted with permission from UNAIDS.

by the Canadian Aboriginal AIDS Network concluded that Native people were five times more likely than non-Native people to become HIV-positive (Ottawa Citizen, 2000: A7).

The Walkerton Water Crisis

At the broadest level, our health is dependent on the natural environment and the ways in which we as societies maintain the health of the natural environment. Water, air, and soil are among the basic and determinate issues. How safe is your drinking water? How is it purified? How much is available? Is there enough for your generation, for your children and their children, and so on? Water is fundamental to our good health. Walkerton, Ontario, has been mentioned in this chapter in passing already. Where is Walkerton, and why does it deserve to be the topic of discussion in a chapter on health found in an introductory sociology textbook?

Walkerton is a small, pretty town, nestled among rolling hills beside the Saugeen River in southwestern Ontario. It was, at least from the outside, a picture-perfect postcard town—until May 2000. That was when the drinking water became polluted with a virulent strain of *E. coli* bacteria that came to be ingested repeatedly by the townspeople, leading to the death of 7 of those people and to illness in 2,300 others. The report of the Walkerton Inquiry, written by Justice Dennis R. O'Connor (2002), details the causes of these tragic deaths and sicknesses and suggests that individual behaviours, cultural values, and social structural arrangements were all causes of the suffering of the people of Walkerton.

Let us examine these causes. First, what were the causes at the level of individuals? Two brothers, Stan and Frank Koebel, were particularly implicated in the tragedy. According to the O'Connor report, Stan Koebel neglected several essential aspects of his job as the general manager responsible for water chlorination and safety with the Public Utilities Commission (PUC). In addition, he repeatedly lied to officers in the health unit and, even after many people had taken sick, reported that the water was "okay." Some of his actions were the result of his lack of understanding of the health consequences of his work. Some were due to the fact that the norms in the PUC culture had been lax for at least 20 years, before Koebel was hired. As the report states, "It had been the practice of PUC employees not to measure the chlorine residuals on most days and to make fictitious entries for residuals in the daily operating sheets" (O'Connor, 2002: 7).

Additionally, there were structural causes for this tragedy. These included the fact that Stan and Frank Koebel were certified on the basis of their experience ("grandfathered") and were not required to take any courses or pass any examinations for continued certification. Another structural deficiency related to the fact that the Ministry of the Environment failed in its responsibility to regulate and enforce regulations pertaining to the construction and operation of municipal water systems. Budget reductions at the provincial level were also implicated because they led to the privatization of lab testing and to failure to regulate the reporting responsibilities (to the Ministry of the Environment and the local medical officer of health) of private labs whenever unsafe water was detected, and to ensure that proactive water treatment interventions were made.

Intra-societal Analyses

Social Inequality and Health

The degree of inequality has been increasing in Canada, especially recently, in the last decade of the twentieth century and into the twenty-first century. As an illustration, consider the following statistics. In 1996, the top 20 per cent of the Canadian population earned 43.2 per cent of the total income, while the bottom 20 per cent earned 2.3 per cent (Ross and Roberts, 1999: 26). Over the decade of the 1990s this disparity grew substantially (Yalnizyan, 1998).

What you might be less familiar with is that there is a direct link between income inequality and ill health. A classic illustration of this relationship can be found in the Whitehall studies, which followed the health of more than 10,000 British civil servants for nearly 20 years and found that both the experience of well-being and a decline in mortality rates were associated with increases in the ranks in the occupational hierarchy of the British civil service (Marmot et al., 1978, 1991). Positive health benefits were found in each increase in rank. Remember, too, that this is a study of the civil service. Thus, all jobs were white-collar, office jobs with "adequate" incomes. It is interesting to highlight that this finding held true even among people who engaged in health-threatening behaviours such as smoking. Thus, for instance, "researchers found that top people who smoked were much less likely to die of smoking-related causes" than those nearer the bottom who did not smoke (National Council of Welfare, 2001–2: 5).

Poverty exacerbates health problems from birth onward. In 1996, the poverty rate in Canada was

One of the most troubling health issues faced by Canadians today is the relatively poor health and shorter lives of Aboriginal Canadians. For example, in the Northwest Territories, where more than half of the population is Aboriginal, the life expectancy is five years less for women (at 75) and four years less for men (at 70) than that of other Canadians (Helwig, 2000: 681). This is largely due to the higher mortality rates among Aboriginal people.

Among the factors that have been used to understand this difference are the higher rates of alcohol use and cigarette smoking, and higher rates of certain infectious diseases, including tuberculosis and some sexually transmitted diseases. While the higher level of physical activity among the Inuit confers some cardiovascular benefits, it also contributes to their accident rate, which is twice the national average.

Following are some highlights of the *NWT*

Health Status Report (1999), covering territory that is now the Northwest Territories and Nunavut:

- More NWT residents reported (self-perceived) very good or better health status (91 per cent) than other Canadians (85 per cent).
- The incidence of binge drinking in the Northwest Territories is three times the frequency in the rest of the population, and 26 per cent of NWT residents are heavy drinkers, compared with 9 per cent in the rest of Canada.
- Forty-five per cent of the population smoke tobacco, compared to 30 per cent in the rest of Canada.
- The tuberculosis rate is nine times, the chlamydia rate seven times, that of the rest of Canada.
- The chief cause of injury-related deaths in the Northwest Territories are, in order, vehicular accidents, suicide, and drowning.

18 per cent, the child poverty rate 21 per cent (Raphael, 2001: 226). Poor women are more likely to bear low-birth-weight babies. Low birth weight is associated with myriad negative health, disability, learning, and behavioural effects. Children born in the poorest neighbourhoods in Canada (the lowest 20 per cent) live shorter lives, by 2 to 5.5 years. They also tend to spend more of these shorter lives with some degree of disability. Individuals living within the poorest neighbourhoods are also more likely than the well-off to die of almost every disease (Wilkins, Adams, and Brancker, 1989). *The Health of Canada's Children* (Canadian Institute of Child Health, 1994) noted that children at the lower end of the social hierarchy have a greater variety of both health and development deficits than those higher up on the socio-economic status ladder. It is also important to note that these results, like the Whitehall study results, are situated in the context of a nationally funded medical care system.

Even though there are substantial links between income inequality and both ill health and death, Canadian health policy continues to involve substantial investments in the health care system rather than

community-level interventions such as a guaranteed annual wage, job creation, a national daycare program, or proactive prenatal care for low-income mothers. This is despite the fact that repeated studies have documented that interventions at these levels would have more widespread effects on the health of the population than do medical initiatives directed toward individuals.

The ways in which economic inequality affects health outcomes are complex and contested. Certainly, material needs are part of the explanation. For example, differential ability to pay for ample healthy foodstuffs and for clean, quiet, and temperature-appropriate living quarters are a part of the explanation. What the Whitehall studies suggest, however, is that there is likely something beyond material differences contributing to the explanation. One finding of the Whitehall studies was that while all levels of the civil service had elevated stress levels while at work, blood pressure levels of the senior administrators dropped when they went home; in contrast, the stress levels remained high for those lower in the hierarchy (National Council of Welfare, 2001–2). Socio-psychological issues related to perceptions of well-being and of relative advantage and disadvantage also appear to be implicated in inequities in health outcomes. In other words, people also feel stress and appear to have consequent health difficulties as a result of comparing their socio-economic positions (negatively) to those of others (Marmot et al., 1978, 1991).

Social Capital

It is clear from all types of research done both today and in the past, and in this and in other societies, that social **status** and health are related. Much of this analysis compares individuals who differ in health and social status. However, when the level of analysis moves from the individual to the society as a whole, the link between status and health remains. Societies with greater degrees of inequality have poorer overall health outcomes regardless of their overall wealth. Thus, for rates of health and illness, the overall wealth of a society appears to be less important than the degree of inequity among societal members with respect to rates of health and illness.

This interesting paradox needs explanation. Explanations for the individual-level correlation have suggested that people with higher incomes, higher occupational prestige scores, and higher educational levels are more able to prevent ill health through eating and drinking wisely, avoiding serious threats to health such as cigarette smoking and excessive alcohol consumption, and engaging in prescribed early detection such as mammograms and PSA (a test for prostate cancer). When those in these higher levels are

sick, they are able to get immediately to the doctor and take advantage of the most sophisticated and effective new treatments. They are also, as the Whitehall studies intimated, able to maintain a sense of well-being through various socio-psychological processes.

But why would the degree of inequality in a society be more important than the average living standard and income of persons in a society in predicting health and illness outcomes? A recently developed theoretical explanation is that it is the degree of social cohesion, social capital, or trust that is the link between inequity and health (Mustard, 1999). A society characterized by inequity is one in which "there is a pronounced status order" (Veenstra, 2001: 74). As people compare themselves to one another, it is possible—indeed, likely—that those lower in the status hierarchy "will feel this shortcoming quite strongly, given the width of the gap, and consequently will suffer poorer health" (Veenstra, 2001: 75). This may result from "damaging emotions such as anxiety and arousal, feelings of inferiority and low self-esteem, shame and embarrassment, and recognition of the need to compete to acquire resources that cannot be gained by any other means" (Veenstra, 2001: 75).

A number of researchers have suggested that societies with high degrees of inequality are also low in *social cohesion* (or *social capital*), and it is social cohesion that mediates between social status and illness. Social cohesion is thought to be evident in societies to the extent that people are involved in public life and volunteer to work together for the good of the whole.

 10.2

Sociology in Action
Canada's Guide to Health?

Canada's Guide to Health?
1. Don't smoke.
2. Exercise regularly.
3. Drink alcohol only in moderation.
4. Minimize the amount of fat in your diet.
5. Reduce stress.
6. Don't use marijuana or other street drugs.
7. Get eight hours of sleep a night.
8. Follow Canada's Food Guide.
9. Have a yearly check-up.
10. Reduce the amount of sugar in your diet.

A Sociologist's Version
1. Don't be poor.
2. Don't be born to a teenage mother.
3. Don't be born into a poor family.
4. Don't be a member of a racialized group.
5. Don't live on the streets or in temporary or poor housing.
6. Don't drop out of school.
7. Don't live in a polluted environment.
8. Don't lose your job.
9. Don't work at manual labour.
10. Don't be a woman.

A society with little social cohesion might, for instance, be dominated by market values and characterized by transactions in the interest of profit. Current social policies in Canada that favour market dominance over state intervention exacerbate the degree of inequity in society.

Many researchers are now looking at the processes whereby societies in which there is a high degree of citizen involvement, communication, and community feeling (social cohesion or social capital) maintain relatively high levels of good health.

Socio-psychological Factors: The Sense of Coherence

The *sense of coherence* is a socio-psychological concept articulated first by Aaron Antonovsky (1979). Rather than asking what makes people sick, Antonovsky wondered about what kept people healthy. Having thought about this and reviewed available research, he defined *sense of coherence* as an orientation to the world and to one's place in it that leads a person to a long-lasting and dynamic feeling of confidence that "things will work out" because (1) life is basically comprehensible, understandable, and predictable; (2) there are sufficient resources for the individual to be able to cope with whatever circumstances arise; and (3) life makes sense or has meaning. These three components of the sense of coherence enable individuals to manage life experience in a positive manner and to establish a basis for resisting disease and handling suffering.

Lifestyle Behaviours: Obesity and Eating Disorders

A number of recent articles in the *Canadian Medical Association Journal*, and indeed in the mass media, have reported on seemingly opposite health concerns: obesity, on the one hand, and eating disorders such as anorexia and bulimia, on the other. It seems that both are increasing among children and adults and that both herald other serious medical problems. Why are so many young people facing such problematic and contradictory issues related to food, body image, and control of eating?

Obesity is now pandemic (Katzmarzyk, 2002), affecting millions of people around the world, especially in rich countries, where between 10 and 20 per cent of the population is obese. In poor countries there are few obese people. *Obesity* is defined as an

excess of fatty or adipose tissue; it "results from unbalanced energy budgets. An overweight person consumes food energy in excess of expenditure and stores the surplus in body fat" (Obesity Canada, 2001). Excess body fat is associated with higher rates of premature morbidity and death from diseases such as coronary heart disease, stroke, type 2 diabetes mellitus, gallbladder disease, and some cancers. Adult obesity is associated with 2.4 per cent of total direct medical costs (Katzmarzyk, 2002). Children are vulnerable too, and obesity's incidence among children is growing because of both an increase in calories and a decrease in exercise (Tremblay and Willms, 2000). The rate of growth from 1981 to 1996 is estimated at 92 per cent in boys and 57 per cent in girls (Tremblay and Willms, 2000). Our sedentary lifestyle, typified by television viewing and computer games, has a role to play in this growing health concern. Children who watch four or more hours of television a day have higher body mass indices and thicker skin folds than those who watch fewer than two hours per day (Tremblay and Willms, 2000). In addition, caloric intake is positively associated with television viewing (Tremblay and Willms, 2000).

While some children are gaining too much weight, others are losing or trying to lose too much. For example, in a survey of 1,739 adolescent females, 23 per cent were dieting to lose weight (Jones et al., 2001: 549). Binge eating was reported by 15 per cent, self-induced vomiting by 8.2 per cent, and the use of diet pills by 2.4 per cent. Disordered attitudes toward eating were found in over 27 per cent of the young women surveyed. Consistent with other studies, disordered eating behaviours and attitudes seemed to increase gradually during adolescence and were more common among girls with higher body mass indices (BMI), an international standard for measuring being overweight and obese (Jones et al., 2001: 549–50). This link between obesity and disordered eating attitudes and behaviours is confirmed by studies showing that dieting on and off ("yo-yo" dieting) frequently leads not to weight loss but to obesity, partly because people use diet pills and laxatives to achieve weight loss.

The Existential Level

How do you experience illness? What sorts of illnesses have you had? Have you always gone to the doctor when you have felt ill? Have you gone to a naturopath, chiropractor, or acupuncturist? Have you always been able to get a diagnosis when you have sought to find out what is wrong with you? People around the globe and even within the variety of cultures and classes within Canada experience illness in different ways. There are competing and overlapping popular conceptions of illness, too. One compilation of popular notions of illness includes illness as choice, illness as despair, illness as secondary gain, illness as a message of the body, illness as communication, illness as metaphor, illness as statistical infrequency, and illness as sexual politics (Clarke, 2000).

Illness as choice refers to the notion that we choose when to become sick, what type of illness we will have, and so on. In other words, illness episodes are a reflection of the deep tie between the mind and the body. That illness is a sort of despair is a related notion. Here, however, the idea is that illness results from emotional misery. It reflects unresolved grief and unhappiness.

The notion of secondary gain emphasizes the idea that people sometimes benefit from illness—for instance, an ill student might not be able to write an exam for which he or she also happens to be unprepared. Closely related to this notion is the philosophy of illness that suggests that physical symptoms are a means through which the body is trying to communicate a message to the world. And related to this, in turn, is the idea that the symptoms are meant to reflect a particular message, a particular set of unmet needs. For example, a cold, with its running nose and eyes, may be said to represent a frustrated desire to cry.

Susan Sontag (1978) has described some of the metaphors attached to diseases such as tuberculosis, AIDS, and cancer. One illustration of disease metaphor is the idea of a disease as an enemy and the subsequent necessity for a war against the disease. Illness as statistical infrequency, in contrast, is simply a numerical definition that names as "illness" a bodily functioning or symptom that is infrequent in the population.

Finally, the idea that illness reflects gender politics is related to the **patriarchy** of the medical profession and its consequent tendency to see women's bodies as basically flawed and women's behaviours as more likely to be pathological (for example, meriting psychiatric diagnosis) than those of men. These medical views reflect gender and gender roles in society (see Clarke, 2000). All of these different popular conceptions of illness have been taken up at one time or another by Canadians.

The existential level of analysis also now includes a new way of sharing research findings through art

Many women with eating disorders see themselves as much bigger than they are. What social forces do you think contribute to this? (GettyImages/ Tony Latham)

and poetry. The following prose poem was written to express the feelings of a mother whose child had cancer and whose symptoms (which immediately after this excerpt almost killed him) from the side effects of treatment were not taken seriously. The prose poem is in the words of the mother and taken from a transcript of an interview in a recent study on the home health care work of mothers whose children have cancer (Clarke and Fletcher, 2001). The poem, in this context, is a means of expressing a key theme in a qualitatively based sociological study (the significance of chicken pox is that it is the one disease that parents are told that they must avoid or get immediate treatment for during the time that their child is sick with cancer and undergoing chemotherapy).

A Mother's Lament

When we were sent home on a weekend
Benjamin was having abdominal pains
Severely

We called and it was the other oncologist
And it wasn't ours.
She said,
He is just constipated
And
to keep him at home
I ended up with a counter full of medications
   and . . .
      Finally
Rich rushed him into emergency in the
   middle of the night.
The child
was
like a woman
in labour
Without an epidural.
His eyes were dilated and you could see the
   contractions coming on . . .

We brought him in
And we found chicken pox on his abdomen
Rich brought him in
At 4 o'clock
in the morning . . . and
Emergency sent him home with a
   prescription . . .

We were sent home.

The experience of illness has been portrayed in theatre, movies, poetry, and other art forms. Perhaps
these may also be effective means for the transmission
of social science findings.

Sociology of Medicine

The sociology of medicine examines the location,
definition, diagnosis, and treatments of disease. It
includes an examination of the various health care
institutions such as hospitals, clinics, co-operatives,
and home care, along with medically related industries and the training, work, and statuses of medical
and nursing professions and other health care
providers today and in historical context.

Because the history of the twentieth century has
been characterized by the increasing dominance of
allopathic medicine and its spreading relevance to
more and more of life (Zola, 1972), the term *medicalization* (the tendency for more and more of life to be
defined as relevant to medicine) has provided an
important conceptual framework for critical analysis.

In this part of the chapter we will discuss the medical
care system in Canada today.

The Canadian Medical Care System

Our present medical care system was first implemented in 1972 after a Royal Commission on
Health Care (Hall, 1964–5), under Justice Emmett
Hall, recommended that the federal government
work with the provincial governments to establish a
program of universal health care. While hospitaliza-
tion and some medical testing had been covered
before that, the new program was designed to cover
physicians' fees and other services not already covered under the Hospital Insurance and Diagnostic
Services Act (1958).

Four basic principles guided the program. The
first was universality. This meant that the plan was to
be available to all residents of Canada on equal
terms, regardless of prior health record, age, income,
non-membership in a group (such as a union or
workplace), or other considerations. The second was
portability. This meant that individual benefits would
travel with the individual across the country, from
province to province. The third was comprehensive
coverage: the plan was to cover all necessary medical
services, including dentistry, that required hospitaliza-
tion. The fourth was administration. This referred to
the fact that the plan was to run on a non-profit basis.

The Canada Health Act of 1984 added a fifth
principle, accessibility. The costs of the plan were to
be shared by the federal and provincial governments
in such a way that the richer provinces paid relatively more than the poorer provinces; thus, the plan
would also serve to redistribute wealth across
Canada. Doctors, with few exceptions (found
mostly in community health clinics), were not
salaried by the government. Instead, they were and
continue to be private practitioners paid by the government on a fee-for-service basis.

Privatization

Despite the presence of the universally available and
federally supported national medical care system,
there is considerable evidence of privatization within
the system. Moreover, the degree of privatization
varies across the provinces. Approximately 75 per
cent of the Canadian system is presently public, 25
per cent private (Fuller, 1998). These figures, however,

These older women seem to be energetic and engaged in life. They are providing one another with social support. (Photo, Health Canada © Minister of PWGSC, 2001)

exclude physicians, who are in a somewhat anomalous position because though most receive money from the state, they do so as private entrepreneurs compensated on the basis of the number of patients they see and the type of diagnosis and treatment they offer.

The private aspects of the Canadian system are dominated by multinational corporations involved in providing a variety of health-related goods and services, including additional medical insurance, information technology services, food and laundry for hospitals, long-term and other institutional care, drugs, medical devices, and home care (Fuller, 1998). The most important impetus for growth in the medical system is in the private sector, particularly in drugs and new (and very expensive) technologies such as MRI, CAT scan, and mammography machines and other increasingly popular diagnostic technologies, such as the PSA test for prostate cancer (Fuller, 1998).

Table 10.3 portrays the increase in personal expenditures on medical care from 1989 to 1999. Notice especially the dramatic increases in private expenditures for other health care professionals (for example, providers of complementary and alternative health care) and for drugs.

There is considerable debate today about whether or not Canada can continue to afford a publicly funded and universally available medical care system. The mass media are full of stories of overcrowded emergency rooms and impossibly long waiting lists (Canadian Health Services Research Foundation, 2002). These sorts of concerns often seem to lead to the argument that the problem is the publicly funded

system. Consistent with the move to the political right both in Canada and throughout the Western world is an emphasis on the value of the free market, arguing that a private health care system would be both more efficient and more cost-effective. However, evidence from a wide variety of sources does not support this point of view (Canadian Health Services Research Foundation, 2002). For example, Calgary, Alberta, recently moved to some degree of privatization: cataract surgery services are now bought from private companies. This has resulted not only in more costly cataract surgery but also in longer waiting times than in the nearby cities of Lethbridge and Edmonton.

US studies on the effect of governments' buying of medical services from private companies also demonstrate problems with privatization. For instance, dialysis and kidney transplants are funded through the federally run Medicare program, which buys services from both for-profit and not-for-profit dialysis centres. Johns Hopkins University researchers compared over 3,000 patient records and found that the for-profit centres had higher death rates, were less likely to refer patients for transplants, and were less likely to treat children with the dialysis method most likely to be of benefit to them (Canadian Health Services Research Foundation, 2002).

Most US-based research suggests that for-profit (private) care costs more, pays lower salaries to staff, and incurs higher administrative costs but does not provide higher-quality care or greater access. Between 1990 and 1994, for-profit hospitals billed approximately $8,115 (US) for every discharged

Table 10.3 **Total Health Care Expenditures by Category, 1989 and 1999**

	Percentage of Total Expenditures		Percentage Privately Funded	
	1989	1999[a]	1989	1999[a]
Hospitals	39.9	31.6	8.9	8.1
Other institutions	9.1	9.7	25.5	30.6
Physicians	15.1	13.9	1.0	1.2
Other professionals	10.6	12.8	85.0	89.6
Drugs	11.0	15.2	69.0	68.1
Capital	3.7	2.6	18.7	12.0
Other health care spending[b]	10.6	14.1	17.8	18.5
Total	100.0	99.9[c]	25.2[d]	30.4[d]

[a] Forecast.

[b] Includes prepayment administration, public health, health research, and other.

[c] Column does not add up to 100 because of rounding.

[d] Represents percentage of total spending.

SOURCE: *In Search of Sustainability: Prospects for Canada's Health Care System* (Ottawa: Canadian Medical Association, 2001), 7; available at <www.cma.ca>, accessed 10 July 2003.

patient, whereas not-for-profit hospitals charged $7,490 per person even though quality of care, according to some indices, was better in not-for-profit institutions. For instance, not-for-profits tend to provide higher rates of immunization, mammography, and other preventive services (Canadian Health Services Research Foundation, 2002). People lose, on average, two years of life when they are treated in for-profit hospitals (Devereaux et al., 2002: 1402).

It has also been claimed that private systems offer more choice. The inference is that public systems are restrictive because of bureaucratic government interference. In fact, however, the interference by insurance companies in medical decision making in private, for-profit systems appears to be more problematic than state interference. The other aspect of the argument for choice is that a combined system would allow individuals the possibility of choosing between private and public services for different services. This argument flies, by and large, in the face of the repeatedly confirmed value orientations of Canadians, who continue to identify medicare as one of Canada's most important social programs.

Medicalization

Medicalization is the tendency of more and more of life to be defined as relevant to medicine. Irving Zola (1972) is one of the social theorists who has been critical of this process. He defined *medicalization* as including the following four components:

1. an expansion of what in life and in a person is relevant to medicine
2. the maintenance of absolute control over certain technical procedures by the allopathic medical profession
3. the maintenance of almost absolute access to certain areas by the medical profession
4. the spread of medicine's relevance to an increasingly large portion of living

The first area of medicalization is the expansion of medicine from a narrow focus on the biomechanics of the human body to a broader concern by medicine with the "whole" person. The second area refers to the fact that there are things that only doctors are allowed to do to the human body, such as surgery. The third refers to the fact that doctors, through medicine, have been able to transform into medical problems areas of life such as pregnancy and aging that were formerly viewed as normal, neither as pathological nor as medically relevant processes. The fourth pertains to the way in which medicine increasingly has jurisdiction in areas formerly considered to be of relevance to the criminal justice or religious systems, such as criminality and alcohol addiction.

Medicalization has been shown to be evident in the tendency for more and more of life to be defined by the medical profession. Ivan Illich (1976) attributes the growth of medicalization to bureaucratization. Véase Navarro (1975) claims that medicalization, or medical dominance, is more related to class and class conflict, in particular the upper-class background and

10.3

Sociology in Action
Population Aging

You have probably heard the concern voiced that as the population ages in the next several decades in Canada as a result of the aging of the baby-boom generation, the strain will be felt in our health care system. In fact, people over 65 are more likely to be ill than adults at other ages. Moreover, they are also more likely to use the health care system when they are ill.

Recent research from the Canadian Health Services Research Foundation demonstrates that the increasing use of the health care system by seniors is not the result of their increasing numbers in the population, but rather of their relatively higher utilization rates. There is evidence that it is not the sick seniors who are responsible for the increase in costs, but rather *healthy* seniors. For example, the rate of doctor visits by the well in Manitoba increased by 57.5 per cent for visits to specialists and by

32.0 per cent for visits to general practitioners between the 1970s and 1983. Rates for unhealthy seniors increased by only 10 per cent or less (Canadian Health Services Research Foundation, 2001: 1–2). It appears, then, that the elderly routinely receive more care than they formerly did. The cost of health care increases because of the simple aging of the population is estimated to be only 1 per cent of total health care costs. The significant impact of population aging, then, appears to be the result of overtreatment of the elderly, including such interventions as flu shots, hip replacement, and cataract surgery (Canadian Health Services Research Foundation, 2001).

Examine the accompanying figure. What is the obvious explanation for what is portrayed? What do you think are the more complex and interesting explanations?

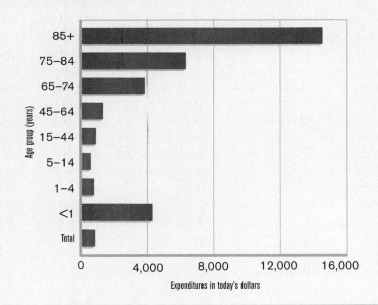

Estimate of Total Provincial Government Per Capita Health Care Expenditures by Age Group, Canada, 1998–9

SOURCE: *In Search of Sustainability: Prospects for Canada's Health Care System* (Ottawa: Canadian Medical Association, 2001), p. 26.

position of physicians. He also relates medicalization to the work of physicians who operate as entrepreneurs in the definition of health and illness categories and their relevant treatments.

Disease Mongering

Furthering this argument about the role of capitalism in the growth of medical dominance is the instrumental role that the pharmaceutical corporations play in "disease mongering." Through a series of suggestive anecdotes, Ray Moynihan, Iona Heath, and David Henry (2002) argue for critically examining the ways in which the pharmaceutical industry plays a significant role in defining as diseases conditions for which they have developed an effective drug. The researchers illustrate this practice through descriptive case histories of a process whereby a drug is manufactured and then a disease is newly highlighted as problematic. Three cases are highlighted: a baldness tonic for men, a drug for "social phobia," and osteoporosis in aging women.

Ostensibly involved in public education about new diseases and treatments, and often working alongside doctors and consumer groups, the pharmaceutical industry has promoted as problematic conditions that may well be better seen as part of life. For example, the medicalization of baldness by Merck occurred after the development of their anti-baldness drug, Propecia, in Australia. Around the time of the patenting of the drug, a major Australian newspaper reported on a new study that indicated that about one-third of men experienced hair loss (Hickman, 1998). Further, the article emphasized, hair loss sometimes led to panic and other emotional difficulties and had a negative impact on job prospects and well-being. At the same time, the paper featured news of the establishment of an International Hair Study Institute. What the newspaper failed to report was that both the study and the institute were funded by Merck and that the "expert" quotations were from the public relations firm hired by Merck.

GlaxoSmithKline, another pharmaceutical company, along with the medical communications firm In Vivo, developed a three-year "medical education program" to create a new belief about irritable bowel syndrome (IBS) as a specific and treatable disease. According to documents from In Vivo, one of several companies specializing in corporate-backed medical "education," the key aim of the education program was to ensure the following: "IBS (irritable bowel

syndrome) must be established in the minds of doctors as a significant and discrete disease state" (Moynihan et al., 2002: 886). The steps for this education program were all laid out, beginning with the establishment of an advisory board comprising key opinion leaders from each state in Australia, who would provide information about what was currently believed about IBS and how this could be changed. Another strategy was to produce and distribute a newsletter that would reinforce the seriousness of the syndrome.

These two steps are just illustrations of some strategies used by pharmaceutical industries who have been advised in Britain's *Pharmaceutical Marketing* magazine to "establish a need and create a desire" (Cook, 2001, cited in Moynihan et al., 2002). The report cited is based on several anecdotes. More and systematic research on the extent of these practices is needed, but even these few examples raise questions about what may be invisible and unregulated attempts to "change public perceptions about health and illness to widen markets for new drugs" (Moynihan et al., 2002: 891).

Morale and Bullying Among Doctors

Recent research in the United Kingdom has identified workplace bullying as a major source of stress at work for health care professionals (Quine, 2002). One study among doctors who worked for the National Health Service found that one in three reported that they had been bullied in the year previous to the study (Quine, 1999). Another study found that bullying, racial harassment, and discrimination were everyday occurrences in the work lives of Asian and black doctors in the United Kingdom (Coker, 2002). In the United States, too, a few studies have identified mistreatment and bullying experienced by medical students, interns, and residents (Kassebaum and Cutler, 1998).

Lyn Quine (2002) developed a "bullying" scale that includes 21 bullying behaviours, then sent a questionnaire containing this scale, a definition of bullying, and socio-economic information questions to 1,000 doctors randomly selected from the British Medical Society list of doctors and representing various levels of responsibility and status. Thirty-seven per cent of the doctors surveyed reported that they had been bullied in the previous year, and 84 per cent had experienced at least one of the behaviours included on the "bullying scale"; 69 per cent reported that they had observed others being bullied (Quine, 2002: 878–9). Asian, black, and female doctors were significantly more likely to report having been bullied than white male doctors. The experiences of being bullied occurred all of the way up and down the job hierarchy.

Thus, even though doctors tend to be recruited from higher social class and educational backgrounds, they are not immune to discrimination on the job. While these studies of bullying have not been done in Canada, there is reason to think that the patterns might be generalizable to this country. However, the research needs to be done. It is particularly important as increasing numbers of Canadian-educated doctors are both female and from visible-minority backgrounds.

Bullying is not the only cause of increasingly poor morale among doctors around the world (Edwards, Kornacki, and Silversen, 2002). Poor morale is partly the result of doctors' increasing workload accompanied by a relative decrease in remuneration. However, according to extensive research, the declining morale of doctors is also, and perhaps more importantly, related to the changing social compact between doctors and the societies in which they practise. Doctors who were previously sole practitioners and operated as independent entrepreneurs within a private—even, many suggest, "sacred"—doctor–patient relationship are now under intense surveillance by governments and corporations (such as insurance companies). They are presently faced with strict and pervasive accountability to organizations that not only monitor their work, but may even decide whether or not certain prescribed treatments are justified.

Evidence-based medicine may also contribute to decreasing morale. This new approach to medical practice removes the clinical judgment from the doctor and puts it into the hands of epidemiologists and other scientists who determine best-practice principles that doctors are expected to follow. In these conditions, medical decisions are not the sole purview of individual doctors working their craft and exercising their clinical experience in the midst of a "sacred" professional relationship, but rather the result of research findings. Moreover, best-practice findings are not published only in arcane medical journals, but are often easily accessible to insurance company personnel and to individual patients through numerous, often disease-specific Internet sites.

The Socio-economic Background of Medical Students in Canada

There are substantial differences between the backgrounds of medical students and those of the rest of the Canadian population. Doctors are not drawn, in a representative way, from all across the socio-economic and socio-demographic variation of the whole population of citizens.

Specifically, medical students have been more likely to have had fathers who were doctors. This continues to be true today. In 1965, 11.8 per cent of medical students had fathers who were doctors. Today, 15.6 per cent do (Dhalla et al., 2002: 1032). Rural students, in contrast, were underrepresented in the mid-1960s and continue to be underrepresented today. Whereas 30.4 per cent of Canadian high school students lived in rural areas in 1965/6, only 8.4 per cent of the medical students did. Rural students are slightly better represented today (Dhalla et al., 2002: 1032). In 1965/6, the fathers of 7.5 per cent of the population had attended university, while 38.0 per cent of the fathers of medical students did so. Today, 39.0 per cent of the fathers of medical students had graduate or doctoral degrees, compared with only 6.6 per cent of the whole population of the same age (Dhalla et al., 2002: 1032). With respect to gender, however, significant changes have occurred. In 1965/6, 11.4 per cent of the medical students were female. Now about half are (Dhalla et al., 2002: 1032). Medical students continue, however, to be less likely than the general population to be Aboriginal or black (Dhalla et al., 2002).

These findings are important in practical terms as well. For example, medical students who are from rural areas are more likely to practise in (underserviced) rural areas. And poorer people have poorer health outcomes, yet students from the poorest neighbourhoods are seven times less likely to attend medical school than those from the richest neighbourhoods (Dhalla et al., 2002).

The trend toward privatization in Canadian universities can only exacerbate these discrepancies in adequate representation of medical students. Rising tuition fees in Ontario since 1997 have already affected the equitable representation of doctors such that there has been an increase in the self-reported family incomes of students in medical schools while they are graduating with more debt, are more likely to consider finances when choosing a place to practise, and are more likely to report financial stress while in school (Kwong et al., 2002).

Conclusion

In many ways, health issues are fundamentally social issues. The rates, definitions, and meanings of illness, sickness, disease, and death have varied and continue to vary around the world and over time. Within Canadian society, these differences, particularly in rates, reflect culture and social structure and mirror inequality and marginalization. They are affected by large external physical forces such as characteristics of the physical environment and by smaller lifestyle, existential, and psycho-social factors.

Medical care is dominated by allopathic medicine today. However, a sizeable minority of Canadians are now choosing complementary and alternative care. Still, there is continuing evidence of the dominance of medical definitions of reality (*medicalization*) in many parts of life. There is as well increasing evidence of the manipulation of medicalization by the pharmaceutical industry and its entrepreneurial disease-defining work. While there is substantially more privatization in the Canadian medical care system today, it has tended not to reduce costs or to provide better medical service but the reverse. Finally, it appears that doctors in the system are experiencing low levels of job satisfaction and morale today.

□ Questions for Critical Thought

1. What are the implications of developing health policy on the basis of the mortality rate from the chief causes of death in Canada as compared to PYLL?
2. Discuss the evidence for an increasingly medicalized society.
3. What are the costs and benefits of medicalization?
4. Assess the opportunities for social cohesion in your college or university. Are there things available to you to do in class or extracurricularly that give you chances to get to know and trust people from different programs and years at your university?
5. What challenges to your health are evident in your school? Include challenges related to the physical plant, the organization of learning and testing, and the social life available to students in your answer.
6. Discuss the water or air quality of the town where you are going to school. Discuss the strategies that you have used to get information about the air or water quality. Assess the quality of the information to which you have gained access.
7. Examine three magazines that you commonly read for their health-related messages. Include both articles and advertisements in your analysis. Consider the portrayal of issues such as gender, ethnicity, and social class in your discussion.
8. Compare the sense of coherence and social cohesion. To what extent are these concepts related to one another?

□ Recommended Readings

Pat Armstrong and Hugh Armstrong, *Wasting Away: The Undermining of Canadian Health Care* **(Toronto: Oxford University Press, 1996).**
This book is based on interviews, observation, and documentary evidence regarding the effects of the "cuts" to and privatization of health care in Canada. The focus here is especially on the effects of the changes on workers and patients.

Pat Armstrong, Hugh Armstrong, and David Coburn, eds, *Unhealthy Times: Political Economy Perspectives on Health and Care in Canada* **(Toronto: Oxford University Press, 2001).**

This is a fascinating book on the ways that economics and politics influence health in Canada and globally. Topics covered include globalization and its impact on health and the health care system, the pharmaceutical industry, health-related ideologies such as neo-liberalism, the impact of capitalism on the curriculum of pharmaceutical sciences, women's health issues related to health care reform, the relationship between work and health globally, environmental contamination and political ecology, and poverty, social disintegration, and health among Canadians.

Sharon Batt, *Patient No More: The Politics of Breast Cancer* **(Charlottetown, PEI: Gynergy, 1994).**

This is an award-winning story of the politics of breast cancer in Canada and the Western world. Batt begins with the experience of her own diagnosis and moves from this through the larger world of breast cancer science, medicine, and charities. She critically discusses what is known and debated about prevention, radiation, surgery, chemotherapy, hormones, and alternative medicine.

David Coburn, Carl D'Arcy, and George Torrance, eds, *Health and Canadian Society: Sociological Perspectives*, **3rd edn (Toronto: University of Toronto Press, 1998).**

This excellent reader on the topic of medical or health sociology in Canada provides an overview of the socio-historical development of the medical system, health care costs, and the health status of Canadians. It also provides a number of empirically based commentaries on various social factors that are known to be related to health and illness, including income, gender, Aboriginal status, ethnic differences, and tranquillizer and sedative-hypnotic drug use. It includes a number of articles on contemporary issues in the provision of medical care.

Daniel Drache and Terry Sullivan, eds, *Market Limits in Health Reform: Public Success, Private Failure* **(London: Routledge, 1999).**

The essays in this collection are written largely from the perspectives of political economics. The book focuses on the tensions between a nationally funded medical care system and a growing move toward a market-driven economy. It compares the United Kingdom, the United States, and Canada with respect to the effects of privatization and rationalization on health and on health costs.

Nicholas J. Fox, *Postmodernism, Sociology and Health* **(Toronto: University of Toronto Press, 1994).**

This book takes up poststructuralism and modernism in social theory and examines how they might change our conventional understandings of health, illness, the human subject, the body, and so on.

Colleen Fuller, *Caring for Profit: How Corporations Are Taking Over Canada's Health Care System* **(Vancouver: New Star, 1998).**

Fuller is a health care activist and researcher who wrote this book while she was a research associate at the Canadian Centre for Policy Alternatives. After discussing the beginnings of the medicare system in Canada, Fuller charts medicare's history up to the current period of privatization. She documents examples of privatization across the country to demonstrate that medicare is no longer a universal system.

Anne Kasper and Susan J. Ferguson, eds, *Breast Cancer: Society Shapes an Epidemic* **(New York: St Martin's Press, 2000).**

This reader is written with a multi-disciplinary perspective, including sociology, women's health activism, environmentalism, medicine, health policy, and health management. It makes the case that the breast cancer epidemic is socially constructed from the very diagnosis to ideas about treatment and early detection. It points out that prevention has not received the attention or the scientific investment that it should have, and suggests that this is because of the economic and professional interests of pharmaceutical companies and medical oncologists in maintaining current chemotherapeutic treatments as normative.

Michael Rachlis and Carol Kushner, *Strong Medicine: How to Save Canada's Health Care System* **(Toronto: HarperCollins, 1994).**

This is a critique of the current medical care system written by a physician and a journalist. The book is a very accessible account of various problems in the Canadian system. The authors advocate fundamental structural reform in the interests of quality and efficiency while maintaining universal medical care.

☐ Recommended Web Sites

The Cancerweb Project
http://cancerweb.ncl.ac.uk/

This is a cancer resource site with information on many different aspects of cancer, with sections devoted to the needs of patients and families, health care professionals, and scientific researchers.

Gilford Health Online
www.gilfordlibrary.org

This Web site provides links to a number of other sites under the topic headings of Alternative Medicine, Mental Health, Nutrition, Diseases, Fraud and Quackery, National Organizations, Pharmaceuticals, References, Family Health, Government, News, and Prevention. This is not a sociology Web site, but one that can be used to consider what topics and sites are thought today to be relevant to the category of health. This is a place to go to get health-related information.

Health Canada
www.hc-sc.gc.ca

Health Canada, a government department, provides health-related information on topics such as healthy living, health care, diseases and conditions, health protection, and media stories. You can also find here the latest statistics regarding health, illness, death, PYLL, medical care system characteristics, and current issues.

The Hunger Site
www.thehungersite.com

This is a site for those who are concerned about world hunger, who want to keep up on the situation and to take action.

My Morning Journal
www.mymorningjournal.com

This site provides links to numerous medical, science, and news journals and to magazines and radio and television program contents that are available online, including *Canadian Family Physician*, the *Canadian Medical Journal*, *Nature*, *Family Practice*, the BBC, the CBC, *Newsweek*, *Time*, and *Science*.

National Network on Environments and Women's Health
www.yorku.ca/nnewh/english/nnewhind.html

This is one of the five federally funded Centres of Excellence for Women's Health. It focuses on the impact of three key environments on women's health workplaces, including paid and unpaid work, unemployment and labour force restructuring and adjustments, health systems (both conventional and unconventional forms of health care), formal and informal practices, women's understandings of health and health risks, and policy.

The National Women's Health Information Center
www.4woman.gov

This is the Web site of the Office on Women's Health and the Department of Health and Human Services of the US federal government—an excellent site for the latest findings regarding health research, particularly as it pertains to women (there is also an internal link to men's health issues included on the home page). It includes topics such as screening and immunization information, advice on how to quit smoking, action strategies regarding breastfeeding, information about violence against women, body image, women with disabilities, and health information for "minorities." This site would also be of use as a document for content analysis regarding current definitions of significant health issues and their treatments.

Statistics Canada
www.statcan.ca

Statistics Canada publishes myriad studies on Canadian society, including statistics relevant to morbidity, mortality, disease incidence, birth rates, and so on. The journal *Canadian Social Trends*, census data, and *The Daily* can all be accessed here.

United Nations Statistics Division
http://unstats.un.org/unsd/

This site provides global statistics on the populations, families, health, education, communication, work, human rights, and political decision making of people in nations around the world.

11

Religion

Lorne L. Dawson

> > >

© Bill Whittman

☐ Learning Objectives

In this chapter, you will:

- learn how the great sociological theorists thought religion played a crucial role in the operation of all societies

- see why it is particularly difficult to study religion sociologically

- discover that the apparent demise of religion in modern societies may be misleading

- learn that the forms in which religion is expressed in modern Western societies may be changing but that the basic demand for religious answers persists

- study how the religious life of Canadians has changed since the middle of the twentieth century

- find out how the Internet and non-European immigration are changing the face of contemporary religious life in North America

Introduction: Why Study Religion?

The sociology of religion requires students to exercise their **sociological imagination**. To borrow the evocative phrase of the philosopher Thomas Nagel (1986), Canadians are prone to mistake their experience of religion in the late twentieth century for "the view from nowhere." We tend to see our situation as universal and to overlook how it actually is a very specific view from somewhere. We are inclined to think that what has happened here will soon happen everywhere, and hence that we need not pause to consider the singularity of our experience and how it might bias our understanding.

But contrary to initial expectations, the experience of Canadians is not very typical of most of the rest of the world. In fact, it is atypical in some important regards, and quite culturally specific. We are inclined to overlook this fact because the changes in the practice of religion in Canada over the last 50 years seem to be in line with the expectations of the great modern commentators on religion, from Karl Marx (Marx and Engels, 1957) and Sigmund Freud ([1927] 1961) through to Peter Berger (1967).

The role of religion in our social life seems to be in sharp decline, a process that sociologists call **secularization**. Where once much of community life was centred on the church and its activities, today people dedicate most of their time, money, and energy to other pursuits and institutions. The religious symbols and leaders that once shaped the conscience and habits of most Canadians have been displaced by other leaders and influences of a decidedly more secular nature, whether political, economic, or social. As Canada has developed into a modern nation, the public presence of religion has dissipated. With the spread of modernization, secularization theory assumes, the same fate awaits religion in the rest of the world. For many Canadians then, especially among the young and the cultural elites in education and the media, religion may not seem that important anymore.

But this immediate view is easily called into question when the Canadian experience is analyzed in greater detail and placed in comparative perspective with what is happening elsewhere. The reality is much more complex and interesting than secularization theorists envisioned, and most sociologists of religion speak now of the changing face of religion in societies living with the conditions of late modernity, not of its simple demise. In fact, there is evidence of considerable religious resurgence around the world, and perhaps in Canada as well.

To the best of our knowledge, humankind has always been religious. Until very recently, every aspect of human social life was regulated and imbued with meaning by religious systems of beliefs and practices. Time and space were organized by religious principles and marked by ritual activities. The cycle of the year followed the calendar of holy days and festivities, while the temple or cathedral lay at the physical heart of every town or city. The time and space dedicated to establishing contact with and preserving the integrity of the sacred served to give structure to the profane time and space around them. Birth, death, and every major life transition in between were understood in terms of religious **rites of passage** (for example, baptisms, marriages, and funerals) that made these events meaningful and legitimate. The great events of the world, from wars to the coronation of kings and the launching of ships, were marked by ceremonies designed to curry the favour of supernatural powers, while the events of daily living, from planting crops to cursing an uncooperative neighbour, were suffused with words and gestures that acknowledged and invoked a spiritual presence.

With the rise of science and the material comforts and security that came with industrialization, much of this has changed for the prosperous nations of Europe, North America, parts of Asia (such as Japan), and elsewhere. We live in much less manifestly religious societies. Yet as the great sociologist Max Weber reasoned, the root causes of religious belief have not been significantly displaced by our recent progress in achieving either prosperity or knowledge.

Weber ([1920–] 1963) suggested there is an inner compulsion on the part of humanity to understand the world as a meaningful cosmos, and a consequent desire to take a consistent and unified stance toward this cosmos. This compulsion, which has taken on a life of its own in human history, is fundamentally driven by the need of humans, as a species and as individuals, to cope with the graphic realities of suffering in their lives.

In this sense, Weber finds at the heart of all religious systems what Christian theology calls **theodices**. A *theodicy* is an attempt to explain and justify why God or other supernatural forces would allow the suffering we all experience, from both natural and human causes. In particular, many people need some way to account for the suffering of the

IN THE FIRST PERSON

I was on my way to becoming a lawyer when I took some courses in religious studies, especially a fourth-year seminar in the sociology of religion. Within a year I was doing graduate work in the latter. Perhaps my interest stems from the fact that religion is one of the most difficult subjects to study sociologically; yet almost all societies are shaped profoundly by their religious heritage. What does it mean to be human? What is the ultimate purpose of the societies we build? The answers to these basic questions are codified in our diverse religious visions. I wanted to understand the nature, wisdom, or folly of these visions, and their consequences for everyday life. I was intrigued by the sheer intellectual challenge of determining how such a subjective phenomenon could be studied scientifically. The mysteries of religious life continue to make its study a stimulating challenge. The things people do in the name of religion—good and bad—leave us no end of important issues to investigate. –LORNE DAWSON

innocent and of the righteous. The object is not so much to explain this suffering away as to place it in a framework of meaning that renders it bearable and that strengthens our resolve to face even more suffering in the future.

Over the course of human history, religious beliefs have changed, prompting sweeping changes in the social conditions of life. The changes are instigated, Weber argues, when our desire for greater meaning, order, and justice is frustrated. This frustration is the result of the discrepancies between the expectations and explanations we learn from our societies and our actual experiences. In the face of the seeming irrationality of so much that happens to us, the suffering experienced at the hands of nature and our fellow human beings, a plethora of religious views have arisen, gained acceptance, spread, or disappeared forever.

The collapse of certain forms of religious expression in some societies of the advanced industrial West is indicative of a growing discontent with the existing religious institutions. The church-centred Christianity that satisfied the needs of so many Canadians from the founding of our nation through to about the 1960s appears to be losing its relevance. But the data collected by sociologists continue to reveal a strong and ongoing need for some meaningful response to the ultimate issues of life. We undoubtedly live healthier and more materially happy lives than our predecessors, so our religious orientations have changed accordingly. But the kinds of

suffering that Weber saw as fundamental to the religious impulse remain an all too regrettable presence in our lives. Illness, accidents, heartbreak, loneliness, and death still punctuate and disrupt, and sometimes even define, our lives, and with the advent of the **mass media**, every Canadian is now embroiled, if only emotionally, in the catastrophic or senseless suffering of thousands of others around the world.

The force of this state of affairs was driven home recently by the public response to the tragic events of 11 September 2001. A hundred thousand Canadians gathered spontaneously on Parliament Hill in Ottawa three days after members of the terrorist group al-Qaeda crashed the planes they hijacked into the twin towers of the World Trade Center and into the Pentagon. Canadians gathered to share their grief and show their solidarity with their American friends and allies. Similar memorial services, redolent with religious symbols, prayers, and other invocations of God, happened across Canada.

In the United States, a much more religious society to begin with, the shocking attack upon innocent Americans spurred public officials from the president to the mayor of New York City to set aside the constitutional separation of church and state and call upon their citizens to pray as a nation for the salvation of the thousands who had lost their lives and for the future safety of their country. Levels of church attendance rose markedly for weeks after, and throughout Manhattan shrines of candles, flowers, and pictures honouring the dead were created spontaneously in

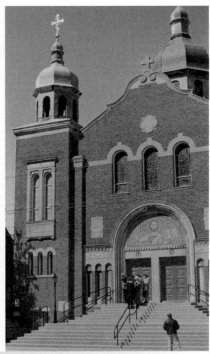

Canada's Christian heritage is reflected in the thousands of prominent churches built in every community. (Photos © Megan Mueller)

parks, on church steps, and around the lampposts where pictures of missing loved ones had been posted.

It would be difficult to imagine how either Canadians or Americans could have responded to this disaster without religion, and a year later people turned to their faith in a higher order, no matter how implicit or vague, to seek the appropriate words of solace and significance to commemorate this tragedy. The anniversary began with a moment of silence in the United States and ended with a plea from President George W. Bush to pray that God "will see us through and keep us worthy." The citizens of the most powerful and modern nation in human history struggled to cope with what had happened while listening to the stirring sentiments of traditional hymns such as "Amazing Grace" and "The Battle Hymn of the Republic." These songs, known by almost everyone, related those who grieved to one another, to the struggles of their nation's past, and to the promise of a better future—in line with God's providence.

In making these introductory comments, it is not my intention to suggest that religion is simply about coping with pain, fear, and the unknown. Most of what passes for religious activity in this world happens at a more mundane and daily level, and religions serve many other important functions in society, in intended and unintended ways. But in the contem-porary Canadian context, in a society in which secularization has made deep inroads and much of the conventional church-oriented religion that people experience seems increasingly tangential to their daily lives, it is important to stress the ways in which a primal need for religion persists. Moreover, there is reason to believe that even in Canada we may be on the cusp of a great shift in the form and functioning of religion as an integral part of social life. Most sociologists of religion are now convinced that the outward appearance of secularization in many modern Western nations belies a deeper truth of continuity in the ways people will be religious, one that assures a significant, though somewhat different, role for religion in humanity's future. To paraphrase Mark Twain, the rumours of religion's demise have been much exaggerated. But, then, there also are some sociologists who disagree, and, as we will see, much depends on how the data are interpreted.

To understand the parameters of the debate over the fate of religion in modernity, we must discuss some of the basic methodological dilemmas that mark the social scientific study of religion; discuss the influential insights into the nature and functioning of religion found in the work of the great classical figures of sociology, Karl Marx, Émile Durkheim, and Max Weber; discuss some important recent changes

11.1

Sociology in Action
"The Battle Hymn of the Republic"

The stirring words of this classic American hymn were sung by the soldiers of the Union Army as they marched into battle in the US Civil War. It was set to the tune of the anthem of the American anti-slavery movement, "John Brown's Body." The verses refer to the second coming of Christ to defeat evil and judge humanity, as foretold in the last book of the Bible, the Book of Revelation. It is easy to see why contemporary Americans could still find comfort in these words in the face of threats to their nation.

Mine eyes have seen the glory of the
coming of the Lord;
He is trampling out the vintage where the
grapes of wrath are stored;
He hath loosed the fateful lightning of his
terrible swift sword;
His truth is marching on.
Glory, glory, hallelujah! His truth is marching on! [repeat after each verse]

He hath sounded forth the trumpet that
shall never call retreat;

He is sifting out the hearts of men before
his judgment seat.
O be swift, my soul, to answer him; be
jubilant, my feet!
Our God is marching on!

In the beauty of the lilies Christ was born
across the sea,
With a glory in his bosom that transfig-
ures you and me;
As he died to make men holy, let us live
to make men free,
While God is marching on!

He is coming like the glory of the morning
on the wave;
He is wisdom to the mighty, he is succour
to the brave;
So the world shall be his footstool, and
the soul of time his slave:
Our God is marching on!

–Julia Ward Howe (1819–1910)

in the way sociologists are conceptualizing religion and the process of secularization; and discuss how the face of religion seems to be changing in Canada, the United States, and elsewhere around the world. Religion is likely to continue to be a significant force for both good and evil in human affairs in the twenty-first century, compelling us to learn more about its nature and functioning.

Three Methodological Dilemmas of the Sociology of Religion

Sociologists of religion confront three interrelated methodological dilemmas that most of their colleagues in other subfields are spared: (1) the people they study often claim that their actions are motivated by super-natural forces that science cannot explain; (2) it is

extremely difficult to define the term *religion*; and (3) it is equally difficult to measure people's religiosity.

The Experiential Dilemma

Sociologists have long recognized the importance of religion as a **social institution**. The great founding figures of the discipline argued that an understanding of the social functions of religion was instrumental to the study both of the processes by which social order is created and maintained and of the processes of social change. The study of religion poses problems, however, not encountered in the analysis of other basic social concerns. People's religious faith is often associated with their most intimate and hard-to-articulate thoughts and experiences. As such, it is difficult to access, conceptualize, measure, categorize, and compare people's religious sensibilities.

Many of the greatest scholars of religion (Eliade, 1969; Otto, 1923; Smith, 1959) insist that the experiential core of religious faith is unique. It cannot be grasped by comparison with other kinds of social and psychological phenomena. The sacred is "wholly other" and non-empirical, and attempts to grasp the nature of encounters with it in the light of other known social processes are destined to be incomplete and misleading. Such explanations, it is argued, are excessively reductive. In obedience to the strictly empirical dictates of science, these reductionist explanations sacrifice any explanatory consideration of what is most true and historically significant about the presence of the divine or transcendent in people's lives. The proper study of religion requires, some scholars insist, that the researcher have some prior personal experience of the unique and mysterious wellsprings of religious faith. But how, others ask, are we to test the credibility of the claims made by those who would appeal to such privileged and idiosyncratic sources of knowledge (see, for example, Flood, 1999; Idinopulos and Yonan, 1994; McCutcheon, 1999)?

Most sociologists are content to admit that their claims about religion are strictly limited to those aspects of people's religious life that can be observed or perhaps even measured in some way. They acknowledge that they are not qualified to comment on the truth or falsity—or the reality—of assertions about the supernatural made by the people they study. In most instances, it is sufficient to maintain a position of what we might call methodological agnosticism, tempered by a healthy suspicion that the religious themselves can benefit from the application of a measure of detached reason to their emotional commitments. An element of mystery remains, however, as the possible causal role of uniquely religious forces in the affairs of humanity cannot be logically discounted by the use of logic or empirical analyses alone.

The Definitional Dilemma

When we refer to something as a "religion," what precisely to we mean? Regrettably, there is no easy answer to this question because there is no definitional consensus in sociology. The diversity of things that people have held sacred through the centuries and the practices they have adopted relative to these sacred things are so vast as to defy easy inclusion under any one definition. When pressed, most sociol-ogists revert to a pragmatic definition suited to their immediate empirical task or theoretical interest. These definitions tend to reflect a range of possibilities configured along a continuum anchored by substantive definitions at one end and functional definitions at the other.

Substantive definitions try to delineate some presumably crucial feature of all religious activity. They focus on what religion "is." A classic and simple example is provided by the eminent British anthropologist Edward Tylor (1903), who defined religion as "belief in Spiritual Beings." Functional definitions focus, alternatively, on what religion "does," and a simple and classic example is provided by the American sociologist of religion Milton Yinger: "Religion [is] a system of beliefs and practices by means of which a group struggles with [the] ultimate problems of human life" (1970: 7). Each approach has its well-known limitations, and many sociologists have devised definitions that attempt to blend the two perspectives while minimizing their liabilities.

Substantive definitions tend to be too exclusive. Tylor's definition, for example, has been criticized on two counts. First, the definition suggests that religions are primarily sets of **beliefs**. Yet this is often not the case in any strict sense for the religious practices of most preliterate peoples and even followers of some more contemporary forms of religious expression, such as neo-pagans and Wiccans (adherents of various forms of witchcraft). Their beliefs are quite fluid and not encoded in any definitive set of texts accepted by all as authoritative. Moreover, holding certain beliefs is often secondary in some traditions to participating in specific rituals and other shared activities (for example, Hinduism and Daoism). Orthopraxis (right practice) may take precedence over orthodoxy (right belief). The stress on belief may manifest an **ethnocentric bias** since it is so characteristic of the great religions of the West: Judaism, Christianity, and Islam—the so-called religions of the book (that is, the Bible and the Qur'an)—most particularly the Protestantism dominant in Britain at the time Tylor framed his definition.

Second, the specification of "Spiritual Beings" would also work to questionably exclude some forms of religion. Contemporary neo-pagans and some Buddhists, for example, either see such a belief as optional or formally deny it. There is no absolute God, or strictly any gods at all, for the Theravada Buddhists living throughout southeast Asia. In all other regards, however, most observers would wish to identify these groups as religious, and little is gained empirically by excluding them from the category.

Finally, Tylor's substantive definition of religion raises a third problem very common to almost all definitions of religion: it relies on terms that are themselves in need of definition. In this case, we might ask just what constitutes a "spiritual" being.

Functional definitions suffer from the opposite tendency: they are often too inclusive. Their terms of reference tend to be so broad that it is difficult to distinguish true religions from what sociologists call *functional equivalents*. Plus they too frequently invite an infinite regress of definitional questions. Yinger's definition focuses on struggles with the ultimate problems of human life, but what constitutes an "ultimate" problem? Further specification is needed, and disagreements are likely with any list of problems or criteria of "ultimacy." Is it appropriate to suggest that the world view of radical environmentalists is their religion? What if they display an abiding concern with being a good environmentalist, perhaps even at the cost of laying down their lives to protect some endangered species or ecological niche? Does the inclusion of such activities within the bounds of religion help, or does such talk simply blur the boundaries between phenomena in a way that is analytically unhelpful? Too many things become religious, critics charge, when the functionalist perspective is adopted.

In framing their definitions of religion, sociologists must seek to balance the relative strengths and limitations of these options in the service of their immediate research objectives. Some of the most famous definitions of religion have incorporated elements of both the substantive and the functional approaches. Émile Durkheim, for instance, defined religion as "a unified system of beliefs and practices relative to sacred things . . . which unite into one single moral community . . . all those who adhere to them" ([1912] 1965: 62). The substantive element is concern with the sacred, which is used to differentiate religion from other activities. The functional element is reflected in the identification of religion with the creation of normative societies. Does this approach dissolve the definitional dilemma or merely compound it? It is difficult to say.

The Measurement Dilemma

Clearly, if it is so difficult to define *religion*, and many argue that a strictly empirical grasp of the phenomenon is inevitably deficient, then measuring the degree to which people are religious—what sociologists call *religiosity*—is going to be problematic. Being religious is a multi-dimensional process, and as such it is not measured readily by means of a few questions on a survey. As most of us know from personal experience, being affiliated with a church or attending services regularly may not be very sound indicators of an individual's piety or spirituality. There are many ways to be religious, and the most religious among us may actually be motivated by their convictions to avoid or reject such conventional expressions of religiosity.

Consequently, sociologists have sought to devise composite measures of religiosity that address many different aspects of religious beliefs, attitudes, and behaviour. Charles Glock and Rodney Stark (1965), for example, favour gathering data on at least eight different dimensions of religious life:

1. *The experiential*—whether people think they have had contact with the supernatural
2. *The ritualistic*—whether people participate in public rites
3. *The devotional*—whether they participate in more private rites, such as praying or saying grace before eating
4. *Belief*—whether they agree with the doctrines of their stated faith
5. *Knowledge*—whether they recognize and understand the beliefs of their religion
6. *The consequential*—whether their religion effects their daily life
7. *The communal*—whether they socialize with other members of their faith community
8. *The particularistic*—whether they believe that their religion is the one true path to salvation

Ideally, the higher a person scores on each of these dimensions, the greater that person's religiosity.

This multi-dimensional approach has been widely emulated in the research literature. But the research shows that it is rare for anyone to score high on all counts. Most often, individuals score high on some measures while scoring low on others. For example, high levels of church attendance among Canadians and Americans are not matched by a sound grasp of the basic tenets and texts of Christianity: there is a very weak correlation between the ritualistic and the knowledge dimensions of religiosity. Application of the measures can tell us something important, then, about the nature and the degree of religiosity of individuals, groups, or whole societies. But there is no way to truly measure the relative religiosity of different groups of people, since the differences detected may often be more reflective of different ways of being religious (that is, different styles of religiosity; see Davidson and Knudsen, 1977). Moreover, it has proven notoriously difficult to devise criteria for making the measurements characteristic of each dimension without introducing some implicit religious bias. Glock and Stark's original efforts appear to display an unintended bias in favour of more conservative styles of Christianity, resulting in devote Quakers scoring lower than indifferent Baptists (1965).

In every case, moreover, research into the religiosity of groups is hampered by the problems of self-reporting. In most societies it is still considered preferable to display a degree of religiosity. Thus, people are inclined to exaggerate their religiosity when approached by social scientists. In the United States, for example, C. Kirk Hadaway, Penny Long Marler, and Mark Chaves (1993, 1998) found serious discrepancies between the head counts they did on Sunday mornings in a sample of Protestant and Catholic churches and the levels of church attendance commonly reported by Americans.

The Importance of Religion in Classical Sociological Theory

The great founding figures of sociology, Karl Marx (1818–83), Émile Durkheim (1858–1917), and Max Weber (1864–1920), were not personally very religious. In fact, Weber declared himself to be "religiously unmusical," while Marx was a scornful critic of the Christian heritage of Europe. Yet each saw the analysis of religious life as being essential to his work. Durkheim and Weber, indeed, dedicated much of their lives to its study. The great common concern of these theorists was the investigation of the sweeping changes in social conditions gripping their societies as they were transformed into modern industrial states.

The traditional social order of every society prior to the modern era had been suffused with religious institutions, symbols, and sentiments. Religions legitimated the dominant institutions of the day and provided a cosmic sanction for the **norms** that guided almost every aspect of daily life. One of the seeming marks of modernity, as first experienced in Europe, was the declining presence and influence of religious

symbols and institutions. Nationalism and a pragmatic stake in economic interests seemed to be displacing religion as the unifying forces of society. Religion became an increasingly private matter, a personal concern, of diminishing significance in the lives of an ever-growing number of people. Secularization appeared to be a hallmark of modernization.

Comprehending the social functions of religion, Marx, Durkheim, and Weber realized, might improve their grasp of the causes of the social discord and **alienation** so characteristic of modern life. To know the contours of the emerging new social order and to ease the sufferings it imposed, they sought to understand the foundations of order on which societies had always relied—which most certainly included religion. Could societies be strong without the presence of a common religion? To answer this question, one must first understand the operation of religion.

In simple terms, it can be said that the studies of Marx, Durkheim, and Weber enhanced our appreciation of religion's intended and unintended contributions to three fundamental aspects of social life: Marx examined the ways in which religion can act as an agent of **social control**, Durkheim examined the role of religion in promoting social solidarity, and Weber showed how religious beliefs and practices may prompt sweeping social changes.

Marx and Social Control

Contrary to the Biblical view of the world, Marx ([1844] 1957) insisted, God did not make humanity, humanity made God. This atheistic proposition was nothing new when Marx penned it. But few others had expressed it more forcefully or stipulated so well the social sources of the human need for an illusion like God. Religions exist, Marx argued, to legitimate the right to rule of wealthy and powerful elites and to make that rule possible by distracting the poor and oppressed masses from grasping the real causes of their suffering. The **ideology** and rites of religion provide people with a harmless way of venting the fears, hopes, and grief they feel in the face of the hardships imposed on them. In the pithy and famous phrase of Marx, religion is "the opium of the people" (Marx, [1844] 1957: 38). The promises of rewards for good behaviour in the next life and the admonitions to cultivate humility and forgiveness in the face of hardship act like a powerful sedative, subduing and diverting the people's attention from the social and economic sources of their lowly lot in life. Religion gives voice to the distress of the oppressed, and its communal bonds provide some much-needed comfort. But the struggles with temptation and sin, and the worship of God or gods, do little to end the political and economic **exploitation** that is the true reason for their suffering.

Yet, Marx argues, those who rule, the classes that "owned the **means of production**," are equally deluded. They tend to fervently support the religious institutions of their day, believing in a cosmology that conveniently justifies their authority and comfort as either their God-given right or just part of the natural order of things. Church and state (the instruments of the ruling class of any society) collude to the mutual benefit of the ruling classes.

The first step, Marx asserts, to the communist revolution that will usher in the classless society that will finally liberate humanity is the critique of religion. Enough people must realize that their religious beliefs and practices are fantasies in the first place, and that they constitute a harmful system of social control, for the revolution to even begin. But only with the overthrow of the political tyranny founded on the wage slavery of the modern capitalist state will the suffering of humanity be relieved sufficiently to end the condition of need that fosters the illusory compensations of religion. When equality is achieved, the church will wither away.

Durkheim and Social Solidarity

Durkheim, like Marx, was essentially an atheist. But he was more keenly aware of the role played by religion in holding societies together in the face of adversity and, even more, of the destructive antisocial impulses of their own members. Religious beliefs and practices, he argued (Durkheim, 1965), have been instrumental in protecting the moral integrity of social relations and hence assuring the very survival of societies. Divine sanctions serve to suppress the natural selfishness of individuals and to encourage the unselfish behaviour that all groups need to prosper. The members of any society must be willing to make personal sacrifices, perhaps even lay down their lives, for the benefit of others or of future generations if that society is to survive in the struggle for resources with others. Religion provides the ultimate reasons and justifications for such sacrifices.

These reasons, with their supernatural cast, may well be illusory. But Durkheim thought he had discovered why people continue to believe in the special powers of the sacred to protect humanity. At the heart of religion lies a real experience of power, he argues, that people find exhilarating and comforting. They may attribute this feeling incorrectly to the various sacred objects they worship. But the experience is real, as are its benefits. In fact, Durkheim proposes, it is the experience of society itself, in its most fundamental form, that inspires the religious convictions that serve society's needs so well.

Durkheim's theory of religion rests on a set of interrelated observations and assumptions. He begins by stipulating that the unique mark of the religious world view is the division of reality into two kinds of phenomena, the sacred and the profane. *The sacred* is that which is thought to possess tremendous power, and it is set apart and treated with special awe and respect. Throughout the course of human history, a great many things have been deemed sacred, from natural phenomena like trees, rocks, streams, and stars to objects crafted by human hands. The sacred is not marked by any intrinsic features. What marks the sacred is our attitude toward it, and its consequences. It acts as the fixed and eternal, yet volatile, focal point of reality, around which the chaos of the profane world happens. Religious rites and the institutions that provide them offer people a stable and safe way to contact this power and to harness it to stave off the threatening uncertainties of profane existence. But how, Durkheim asks, could this extraordinary division of reality into the sacred and the profane have arisen "though nothing in sensible experience seems able to suggest the idea of so radical a duality?" (1965: 57). The answer lies, he proposes, with two other observations derived from his study of (what he took to be) the most primitive religion in the world: that of the Australian aborigines. In studying these seemingly simple beliefs and practices, he thought he had gained an insight into the core nature of all religious experience.

When the aborigines perform their sacred rites, Durkheim notes, they are moved by feelings of heightened strength. In his words, "The believer who has communicated with his gods is not merely a man who sees new truths. . . . He is a man who is stronger. He feels within him more force, either to endure the trials of existence, or to conquer them" (1965: 464). This feeling of empowerment, Durkheim argues, is marked by three features: the strength is felt to come from a source greater than themselves, from outside of themselves, and independent of their will. It has a kind of sovereignty over them. These features provide a crucial clue, Durkheim reasons, to the true source of their experience. If as scientists we discard the possibility of a supernatural source, then we must find the cause in the religious activity itself. By participating collectively in the performance of religious rites of worship and sacrifice, people are brought into dramatic contact with two powerful aspects of social life: **collective conscience** and **collective effervescence**.

Religion, unlike magic or mere superstition, Durkheim insists, is always a social undertaking. It is a shared activity. In fact, for most of human history, the enactment of religious rituals marked one of the few regular occasions when relatively large numbers of people would purposefully gather together. In the performance of solemn and elaborate rituals, often entailing specific attempts to induce ecstatic states through rhythmic drumming, chanting, and the use of incense and colourful imagery, people would be lifted out of their ordinary existence and worries. Through symbols and myths they would be exposed to a larger horizon of understanding and the cumulative wisdom of their society—to the collective conscience. They would be imbued with a profound sense of their participation in a cultural whole that transcends them and that seeks to instruct and protect them. The reassurance this provides is reinforced by a contagious emotional enthusiasm set in motion by the sheer presence of so many people united in an activity of celebration. They are gripped by a collective effervescence that inspires a sense of power and possibility far outstripping their solitary experience. Like soldiers marching to battle or participants in political rallies or large sporting events, they feel transported for a time to a place where their personal woes are of little consequence and their collective strength is unimpeachable.

People mistakenly believe that the mythic entities they are worshipping are the source of these feelings, of their strength. So at the heart of religion, for Durkheim, lies a great error. But the illusion serves a worthy and most important social function: it boosts and maintains the social solidarity of a people. It is the unifying result that counts. In circular manner, the practice of religion bonds people together; these bonds fortify the strength of every individual, and this feeling of empowerment helps to perpetuate the belief in the sacred that in turn bonds people together. By Durkheim's reasoning, society is the "soul of religion," but then religion is the soul of society. This makes it difficult to imagine a stable society in the absence of religion.

Weber and Social Change

Weber devised a comprehensive sociological theory of religion encompassing an encyclopedic range of historical information. He wrote books and essays on the religious history of the Western, Chinese, and Indian civilizations, as well as on ancient Judaism and Islam. In the introduction to this chapter, the basic principles of his understanding of religion were discussed, but in its scope and critical insight, Weber's analysis of religion defies easy summary. At the core of his thought, however, is a famous and reasonably simple argument that has become part of the canon of sociological knowledge, what is known as the **Protestant ethic thesis**. We will confine our attention to this important argument.

Weber's chief concern was the origin and nature of modernity. Like Marx before him, he identified modernity with the emergence of **capitalism**. He recognized that many factors contributed to the creation of the capitalist economic, social, and political order of Western Europe—the driving force of modernity around the world. The capitalist system was dependent on the discovery of everything from double-entry bookkeeping to the steam engine. There could have been no capitalism without the growth of a large pool of labourers free to leave the land and take jobs in the new factories of the eighteenth and nineteenth centuries, or without the new resources and markets opened up by colonialism. But capitalism, and modernity in its diverse forms (such as bureaucratic administration and autonomous legal systems), was also marked by an attitude, a motivational pattern, that was equally unique and essential. Weber identified this "spirit of capi-talism" as the "ascetic ethic of vocation" (Weber, [1904] 1958).

In his famous book *The Protestant Ethic and the Spirit of Capitalism* ([1904] 1958), Weber argues that the early capitalists were distinguished from their more traditional predecessors by a proclivity to resist spending the profits of their labour on the luxuries of life. They favoured instead reinvesting their profits in their businesses. In other words, they peculiarly chose to deprive themselves in the present—to be ascetic—in order to establish ever-growing businesses, and hence more profits to invest as capital. With constant reinvestment, their enterprises prospered, and the substantial capital required to lay the foundation for the modern industrial economy accumulated.

But what could have led people to adopt this new approach to their work, to turn to an ascetic ethic of vocation? Prompted by studies indicating that Protestants, when compared with Catholics, were disproportionately employed in business and other related professions, Weber turned to the legacy of the Protestant Reformation for an answer (Weber, [1904] 1958). He traced the spirit of capitalism to the unique influence of two religious doctrines advanced by the Protestant reformers in their rebellion against the Catholic Church. The first was Martin Luther's concept of the calling. The second was John Calvin's doctrine of predestination.

Seeking to return people to the purity of the primitive Christian church, free of what he saw as the institutional corruption of Catholicism, Luther proposed that all people are called, in their ordinary walks of life, to the service of God. He announced "the priesthood of all believers," whereby each person, in completing their calling to the best of his or her ability, as farmer, lawyer, carpenter, or whatever, was doing the bidding of God. The religious virtuosi—the monks praying in their cells or the bishops ruling the church—no longer had a special status in the eyes of God. Everyone was elevated in importance, in principle, while the church's role in intervening with God was demoted.

But this change had two unforeseen and related consequences. First, it made Protestants more acutely aware of the significance of all their daily deeds, most particularly their work. They became more methodical in their labours and more careful and honest in all their dealings. If one should fall into sin, there was no escape from the consequences, because the Reformation had cast off the rites of confession and priestly absolution in rejecting the Catholic Church. Second, this inducement to dedication to one's calling understandably helped businesses to thrive. But other factors limited the impact of these developments until later in the Reformation, when the social consequences of Luther's innovations were reinforced by Calvin's doctrine of predestination.

If God is all-knowing, present everywhere, and all-powerful, Calvin reasoned, then all things must have been determined by him from the beginning of time. God knows who is saved or damned, and all efforts to influence our fate are not only futile, they are an affront to God, calling into question his majesty. Our fate lies in his hands alone; it is predestined. Our duty, as prescribed by his teachings, is to have faith in God and to believe in our salvation. Doubt of our salvation reveals that we are susceptible to temptation and may be evidence that we are not

saved. Faced with this spiritual conundrum, Weber surmises (Weber, [1904] 1958), the very devout and sincere Protestants of the early modern era were driven to find some psychological relief in the discovery of covert signs of salvation. Agonizing over their fate, Protestants were advised by their pastors to allay all doubts by redoubling their labours at their callings. Idle hands, as the saying goes, are the devil's helpmates. With time, success in one's calling became an unofficial sign of salvation, while the humility required of true believers helped to further assure that the wealth accrued from this success was ascetically reinvested and not squandered on ostentatious displays of self-importance or the corrupting pleasures of the flesh.

Thus, the conditions required for the accumulation of capital sufficient to lay the foundations of the modern industrial order grew out of the religiously motivated desire to secure peace of mind and social prestige in the community of believers. By this means, Weber concludes, religion unintentionally played an instrumental role in the birth of capitalism, and thus in the eventual spread of modernity around the world. It had become a world-transforming agent of social change, but in ways quite contrary to the original intentions of any of the leaders of Christianity. In this instance, religion was the agent of a series of unintended and sweeping changes that would ironically push religion itself to the periphery of social life. Or so most sociologists have believed until recently.

Religion vs Modernity: The Ambiguous Legacy of Secularization Theory

Over the course of the twentieth century, a vast research literature has accumulated exploring aspects of religion's role as an agent of social control in society, a force for social solidarity and order, and a source of social change. In these studies, religion has been both the independent variable—the cause of other social events and developments—and the dependent variable—a phenomenon significantly affected by other events and developments in society. In characteristic manner, religion has been shown to be both a force for the maintenance of systems of social stratification and inequality, or racial **prejudice** and sexism, and, simultaneously, a key influence in efforts to reform society and correct its ills (see, for example,

Christiano, Swatos, and Kivisto, 2002; Roberts, 1995). Everything depends on the style of religion being examined, the social and historical circumstance of its practice, and numerous other factors, such as the leadership exercised by individuals in the groups studied.

In the southern United States, for example, the same evangelical Christianity that fostered the civil rights movement in the 1960s also served to undergird the white segregationists fervently opposed to the extension of civil rights to blacks. Extremist groups such as the Ku Klux Klan operate as quasi-religious organizations, invoking a Christian heritage to legitimate their discriminatory beliefs. But the great leaders of the civil rights movement, such as Reverend Martin Luther King, Jr, and Reverend Jesse Jackson, employed a Christian rhetoric to rally opposition to the Klan and all that it stands for. Both sides claim the sanction of God for their cause and revert to the Bible to support their views.

In Canada, the Christian churches played a leading role in helping the government to suppress and assimilate the Native population, running the residential schools that ultimately did so much physical and mental harm to generations of young Native people. Yet many of the same churches were in the forefront of efforts to raise the consciousness of Canadians about the rights of Aboriginal peoples, the value of their culture, and the need for the government to redress their grievances (Lewis, 1993; Miller, 1996). Religions interact in diverse and complex ways with their surrounding societies. There is no set agenda or predictable pattern.

Beneath all the research, however, the assumption of the classical theorists that the significance of religion would diminish in the modern world persisted. By the 1970s, although there were significant variances in the patterns emerging in Western Europe, Canada, and the United States, it seemed clear that the citizens of the most advanced nations on earth were turning their backs on organized religion in ever-increasing numbers. In Europe, the numbers of churchgoers had been declining for decades, and though various official state churches continue to be supported with tax dollars (for example, the Lutheran Church in Germany and Sweden), these societies have become more or less completely secular. In Canada and the United States, there was a great surge of religious activity following World War II, as the soldiers returned home, got married, had children, and moved to the suburbs. Thousands of new churches were built throughout the land, and people flocked to Sunday services as never before. But by the time their children, the baby-boom generation, began to come of age, many denominations had begun to experience serious declines. In Canada, the slide has been constant, with levels of church attendance dropping from 50 per cent in the 1950s to about 20 per cent in 2000 (see Table 11.1).

In the United States, the so-called mainstream and liberal denominations (for example, Congregationalists, Episcopalians, and Methodists) took the hit, with overall levels of membership and attendance declining quickly for a time. During the 1960s, things were beginning to look bleak, and the United States, a very religious nation by most standards, seemed destined to replicate the secular trajectory set by Europe. By the late 1970s and the early 1980s, however, the US numbers began to reverse themselves. Taken as a whole, over the last 50 years, the United States has maintained a remarkably constant level of reported church involvement of about 40 per cent (Greeley, 1989).

Table 11.1 **Weekly Service Attendance in Canada, 1957–2000 (as Percentage of Whole Population)**

	1957	1975	1990	2000
Total	53	31	24	21
Protestant	38	27	22	25
Conservative	51	41	49	58
Mainline	35	23	14	15
Roman Catholic	83	45	33	26
Outside Quebec	75	48	37	32
Quebec	88	42	28	20

SOURCES: Reginald Bibby, *Restless Gods: The Renaissance of Religion in Canada* (Toronto: Stoddart, 2002), 73; Gallup poll, March 1957; for 1975, 1990, and 2000: Bibby, Project Canada surveys.

Berger's Theory of Religion and Secularization

In 1967, the American sociologist Peter L. Berger published a highly influential book called *The Sacred Canopy*. In this work, he laid out a theory of religion and a theory of secularization. By examining each argument briefly, we can get a sense of why a consensus formed on the inextricable links between the processes of modernization and of secularization. By the 1990s, however, Berger had reversed himself, declaring his earlier pessimism about the future of religion to have been a mistake (Berger, 1999). This change of heart is characteristic of a broader shift in sensibilities among sociologists of religion. Looking briefly at the debate set off by Berger's ideas, we can come to understand how many sociologists now think that religions can coexist with modernity, perhaps even thrive in some instances.

Religion finds its roots, Berger (1967) proposes, in a simple yet fundamental human predicament. Humans, unlike most other animals, are born unfinished. We lack the biological programming, the instincts, to survive. Each of us requires a long period of instruction and protection to learn how to cope with our environment. Our species created **culture** to provide for this possibility. It is the humanly fashioned realm of culture that stands protectively between us and the cruel realities of nature. It is culture that constitutes the true ecological context of most of our behaviour, and the quality of our lives depends on the stability of our cultural creations. Social order is a necessity.

But human cultures are a product of a dialectical process of world construction that is inherently unstable. People's thoughts are externalized: they are embodied in the things that we make and do in the world. Once in the world, these products of our thoughts—these physical, social, and cultural objects—take on an independent existence. They are, to use Berger's word, "objectivated" and can exert a coercive influence on our lives. Machines, ideas, and institutions guide and structure what we do. We internalize them and the norms associated with them in the process of being socialized. Thus, while we are ultimately the creators of our world, we are also just another of its creations, objects in the world that humanity has collectively fashioned. But because the world we live in is the ongoing product of human externalizations, it is subject to constant flux and change. This is our predicament. We are biologically driven to create culture in order to secure a stable and hence safe environment, yet our cultures are at heart only fragile **social constructions**.

Religions, Berger suggests, are cultural constructs designed to curiously hide the constructed and hence unstable nature of our social worlds. The human drive to create a meaningful world order—what Berger calls a *nomos*—is totalizing; that is, it wishes to encompass all things to assure its stability. But it cannot. On the margins of life there are always experiences that resist being incorporated, that threaten some primal chaos. Death, nightmares, and unanticipated twists of fate plague us. They threaten us with *anomie*, an anxiety-inducing sense of normlessness. Religions assert that the *nomos* is in fact one with the cosmos. They assert that the social order is in fact the natural order, the way things are meant to be. And they seek to provide an account for those extreme and chilling aspects of life that otherwise defy comprehension. Religions are the "ultimate shield against the terror of anomie" (Berger, 1967: 25). They place the creation of the world in the hands of others (that is, the gods) and socialize us to a "forgetfulness" of our ongoing creative role. In this sense, Berger says, religions are the consummate agents of alienation. They estrange us from an important aspect of our own nature in order to harbour us from the effects of another, the experience of anomie. In traditional societies, religions functioned as sacred canopies sheltering and unifying groups.

The plight of religion in the modern world is a plausibility crisis brought on by social and cultural pluralism and the privatization of religion. Following Weber, Berger thinks that the roots of these two closely related yet analytically distinct processes can be traced to historical features of the Biblical religions of the West that reached their natural culmination in the Protestant Reformation. In casting off the religious monopoly of the Catholic Church, the Protestant reformers placed a premium on the faith and practice of the individual believer. With time, this emphasis transmuted religion into a private matter.

In principle, at least, religious beliefs have become a matter of individual choice. Such beliefs cannot be legitimately imposed on populations from above, and people should not take the beliefs to which they have been socialized for granted. Religious beliefs can and probably should be subject to critical scrutiny. These new norms, in combination with the exposure to other cultures that accompanied the universal spread of Western capitalism, made it possible for a plurality of religious systems to either develop in or be imported into the cultures of North America and Europe. So we live in societies where there are a large number of quite different and seemingly equally valid religions. But the relative plausibility of all religious systems today impairs the ability of any one religion to offer the kind of absolute protections against anomie that Berger thinks brought religion into being in the first place. And privatized conceptions of religion will not support a common universe of meaning for the members of a society, a lack of support that severely ruptures the traditional function of religion. The sacred canopy of the past has been dissolved, Berger laments, by the acidic rain of new and voluntary religions.

In the face of these corrosive effects, Berger stipulates that religions in the modern world are compelled to choose between two options: (1) they can accommodate themselves to the dominant social order and seek to find their place in the growing leisure and service economy, serving the needs of spiritual consumers in piecemeal fashion, or (2) they can "entrench themselves and continue to profess the old objectivities as much as possible as if nothing had happened" (1967: 153). In other words, they can adapt to modernity or reject it. Neither option sounds promising for the future of religion as a significant feature of social life. Many mainstream Christian denominations appear to have pursued the first course of action and watched their memberships shrink because these institutions have lost their distinctiveness and cannot compete with other sources of knowledge, fellowship, entertainment, and comfort in the modern world. The latter option appears to be characteristic of various separatist and fundamentalist religious groups that have risen in stark opposition to the dominant **values** and behaviour of modern societies (for example, Hasidic Jews, Jehovah's Witnesses, forms of Pentecostalism). These groups have grown in numbers and strength, surprising the proponents of secularization. Yet, in the last analysis, some sociologists argue, they will be more or less permanently confined to the margins of society (Bruce, 1996; Wilson, 1982).

Many were convinced by Berger's arguments, but by the 1990s Berger himself was expressing strong doubts. He continued to state that modernization had some very real secularizing effects. But the effects varied greatly from place to place, and he stressed that modernization "has also provoked powerful movements of counter-secularization" (Berger, 1999: 3).

Three developments led him to suspect that his reading of the options available to modern forms of religion had been too limited and pessimistic: (1) the revival of religion in the United States, particularly what is called the "New Christian Right," (2) the resurgence of conservative forms of religion around the world, and (3) the apparent survival of religion, even in secularized societies, at the level of individual consciousness.

In the 1980s, evangelical forms of Protestantism began to systematically assert themselves on the US scene, setting off what came to be know as the "cultural wars" (Hunter, 1991). Aligning themselves with conservative elements in US politics, a rising tide of born-again Christians reasserted the role of Christian values in American public life. They sought to reverse court decisions and laws such as those banning prayers in the schools or banning the posting of the Ten Commandments in courts and other public buildings. They sought to end the support for such things as more liberal abortion laws and gay rights. In the end, the relevant laws did not change, but a broadly Christian and conservative social agenda has achieved prominence in much of American political life. For decades now, every president has sought to curry the favour of the religious right as conservative denominations continue to grab an ever-greater share of the US religious market.

Elsewhere in the world, much the same has happened, with the sharp rise in fundamentalist movements in Islam and the creation of Islamic states following the successful Iranian revolution of 1978, the revival of the Orthodox Church in Russia following the collapse of the Soviet Union, the spread of conservative forms of Catholicism in Africa and elsewhere in the developing world, the insurgence of evangelical Protestantism in Latin America, and the rise of Hindu nationalism in India. Throughout the world, the role of religion as a focal point for group and national identity is increasing rather than diminishing. Likewise religion has re-emerged as a significant factor in many social conflicts around the world, from the violent clashes between Muslims and Hindus in India and between Christians and Muslims in Bosnia-Herzegovina, Nigeria, and the Philippines to the persecution of thousands of members of the Falun Gong spiritual movement in communist China.

Most important, though, it also appears that the public decline in the membership and influence of the traditional Christian institutions of the modern

West has not been matched by a decline in the religious concerns, inclinations, and even practices of the majority of people in modern secular societies (see, for example, Bibby, 1993, 2002; Davie, 1994, 2000; Roof, 1999). People continue to believe in God, to worry about life after death, and to pray with regularity, even if they have stopped going to church. We must distinguish, it seems, between secularization at the institutional and individual levels.

Stark's Theory of Religion and Secularization

Before exploring this matter further, in the context of contemporary Canadian society, we must pause to consider another theory of religion and secularization that has exerted a powerful influence on the sociology of religion since the late 1980s. The American sociologist Rodney Stark, in conjunction with several colleagues (Finke and Stark, 1992; Stark and Bainbridge, 1985, 1996; Stark and Finke, 2000) has proposed a theory of religion that accounts for—that even anticipated—these exceptions to the conventional consensus on secularization.

Like Weber, Stark based his theory of religion on the assumption that the need for religion is probably a constant of the human condition, and that consequently the current secularization of parts of the world is more of a historical aberration than a permanent feature of all future societies. The theory is based on four simple assumptions, borrowed in part from exchange theory and rational choice theory in sociology.

The first premise is that religions are about the operation of the supernatural in people's lives. Many social involvements may become quite all-consuming for individuals and hence play a religious-like role in their lives. But it is the reference to the supernatural that truly distinguishes a religious phenomenon. The second premise is the simple utilitarian principle that most of human behaviour, including religious behaviour, is governed by the pursuit of what we perceive to be rewards and by the avoidance of what we perceive to be costs. The third premise is that the rewards most highly prized by people are usually scarce and that the rewards at the heart of the religious quest seem to be the things least readily available, like true peace of mind or life after death.

The fourth premise is that in the absence of these most valued real rewards, people are inclined to create, exchange, and accept what Stark and William

An 18-metre granite figure of the Jain saint Bahubali is anointed with scented waters, milk, rice flour, and flowers during a *mahapuja* performed in the year of its thousandth anniversary. Jainism is one of the world's oldest religions. This figure is located at Shravanabelagola in Karnataka, southern India. (Courtesy of Darrol Bryant)

Bainbridge (1985, 1996) call **compensators**. In daily life, we often appease people for incurring some sacrifice today by promising some appropriate reward in the future—every household and work environment in the world operates on this basis. In many cases these promised rewards are quite specific—in the case of children, an ice cream cone for good behaviour at the mall; in the workplace, a good pension for loyal employees. But religions deal in the most general of compensators: ultimate relief from suffering, immortality for the virtuous, and knowledge of the meaning of life. These compensations require belief in the operation of a supernatural agency or force in this world.

Religions, then, are organizations that provide general compensators based on belief in the supernatural, and Stark thinks that if we keep this simple truth in mind, there can be little doubt that religions will persist—under the conditions of modernity or otherwise. In the words of Stark and Bainbridge,

> So long as humans intensely seek certain rewards of great magnitude that remain unavailable through direct actions, they will be able to obtain credible compensators only from sources predicated on the supernatural. In this market, no purely naturalistic ideologies can compete. Systems of thought that reject the supernatural lack all means to promise credibly such rewards as eternal life in any fashion. Similarly naturalistic philosophies can argue that statements such as "What is the meaning of life?" or "What is the purpose of the universe?" are meaningless utterances. But they cannot provide answers to these questions in the terms in which they are asked. (1985: 7–8)

With this perspective in mind, Stark argues that the process of secularization should be conceived of as a recurring and cyclical phenomenon. Secularization is not a uniquely modern development that entails the eventual demise of religion. Rather, it should be understood in terms of the periodic collapse of support for certain dominant forms of religion as they become complacent and overly accommodated to non-religious features of the societies in which they developed. Secularization should not be confused with the loss of all need for supernatural compensators, but should be associated with the failure of established religions to provide sufficiently vivid and consistent supernatural compensators. As such, secularization is an intrinsic and limiting feature of all religious economies, guaranteeing the periodic renewal of religious institutions.

This renewal may come in the form of revival, which Stark associates with the formation of religious **sects**, or of innovation, which he associates with the

---

11.2

Sociology in Action
New Religious Life and the Internet

Religion is abundantly present on the Internet. Every major world religion is represented, major and minor Christian denominations, almost all new religious movements, thousands of specific churches. Countless Web pages are operated by individual believers, self-declared gurus, prophets, shamans, apostates, and other moral entrepreneurs. In addition, the Internet has spawned its own religious creations, from megasites of cyberspirituality to virtual "churches" and strictly online religions. To this mix, we can add numerous commercial sites wishing to turn a profit on our spiritual appetites, providing us with religious news, selling us religious paraphernalia, and acting as network nodes for links to hundreds of other sites. There are also sites launched to educate the public or to pursue a diverse array of religious causes (for example, sites based on university courses or anti-cult crusades).

On the Internet, people can read about religion, talk with others about religion, download religious texts and documents, buy religious books and artifacts, take virtual tours of galleries of religious art or the interiors of religious buildings, search scriptures using electronic indexes, locate churches and religious centres, vote on organizational propositions, see images of their religious leaders, watch video clips, and listen to religious music, sermons, prayers, testimonials, and discourses. They can also participate in rituals or meditation sessions, share intercessory prayers, or undertake virtual pilgrimages. Soon they may even be able to feel the texture of objects appearing on their screen or smell the aroma of the virtual incense burning on the computer-generated altar to their gods. The technology exists to simulate both.

The Pew Internet and American Life Project reports that approximately 3 million Americans turn to the Internet each day to meet their spiritual and religious need (Larsen, 2001), and 28 million Americans say they have used the Internet for religious purposes at some time.

continued

Every religion can benefit from being online, but the Internet has proved to be especially beneficial for the thousands of new religious movements operating around the world. In this and others ways, the Internet may be a new and significant force for religious change, magnifying the religious pluralism that is developing in our societies. Never has it been so easy for new religious ideas to gain a public voice. Anyone with a small investment in some computer hardware, software, and training can soon mount a Web page and operate it at little expense. With the right placement, the page may become rapidly available to a potential audience of millions.

The Internet is expanding at an astronomically rapid rate, and most users are drawn from the very segments of society that new religions wish to contact in their quest to mobilize resources (that is, to acquire members with money, skills, and influence). There is a pronounced overlap between those who have joined new religions in the last few decades—relatively well-educated, if somewhat disaffected, middle-class young adults—and the primary users of the Internet. Through the Internet, new religions can circumvent the political and commercial control of the conventional broadcast media by social elites intent on maintaining the status quo.

The Internet provides an unparalleled means for people to stay in touch with each other. New religious communities can be formed and operate over vast geographical distances, as 24-hour contact can be maintained in a relatively inexpensive manner. The monthly newsletter can be supplemented or even replaced by daily messages of inspiration and instruction, with the added possibility of immediate interaction between the leadership and distant followers, and between followers themselves. The Internet also opens up the possibility of much more direct and frequent contact between representatives of new religious organizations and other potentially helpful members of society, such as scholars of religion, advocates of civil rights, and journalists. This networking can greatly enhance the ability of such groups to rally allies in the face of legal challenges, negative media reports, government persecution, and the other crises that arise from time to time.

The relative anonymity of communicating online allows new religious movements to circumvent the social constraints and biases born of systems of social stratification and of ethnic and cultural differences. The anonymity can be used to great advantage by groups intent on fashioning a new global community of individuals united above all else by their shared beliefs and interests.

――――――

SOURCE: Adapted for this volume from Lorne L. Dawson, "Doing Religion in Cyberspace: The Promise and the Perils," *Council of Societies for the Study of Religion Bulletin*, 30, no. 1 (2001): 3–9, and Lorne L. Dawson, "Religion and the Internet: Presence, Problems, and Prospects," in Peter Antes, Armin Geertz, and Randi Warne, eds, *New Approaches to the Study of Religion* (Berlin: Verlag de Gruyter, 2003).

creation of **cults** or new religious movements. *Sects* are offshoots of mainstream religions that are seeking to recapture the purity of some tradition and to reform the world on this basis. *Cults* are groups that introduce more unconventional and often totally new religious ideas into a society, often with the intent of initiating an even more revolutionary change in the character of the society.

All of the great religious traditions of the contemporary world began as either sects or cults, and with time they will likely be replaced by others. In the course of a few centuries, for instance, the tiny minority of the followers of Jesus expanded to become the official religion of the Roman Empire, with hundreds of millions of devotees. Likewise, in the early nineteenth century, Methodists were a ridiculed sectarian minority in the United States, yet by the early twentieth century they were the dominant Protestant denomination. Today their numbers are in steady decline, and the more fundamentalist Southern Baptists have become the single largest Protestant denomination. Stark and his colleagues have attempted to painstakingly account for the diverse social factors and processes that precipitated these shifts in religious allegiance, both great and small (Finke and Stark, 1992; Stark, 1996).

In addition to postulating the importance of a relatively steady "demand" for religion at the individual level, undercutting the assumption that the decline of certain institutions is indicative of the complete secularization of society, Stark and his colleagues (Finke and Stark, 1992; Stark and Finke, 2002; Stark and Innacconne, 1994) have argued that many of the differences in rates of secularization detected between countries can be accounted for by examining how religion is "supplied." This so-called **supply-side theory** argues, contrary to Berger, that pluralism acts as a stimulus to religious growth by encouraging competition between religious groups, like companies struggling for a share of a market. Competition makes the leadership of the religions more responsive to the needs of the people, resulting in higher levels of religiosity overall. This is why the United States, one of the most modern nations in the world, is still a very religious society. The guarantee of religious freedom provided by the First Amendment of the US Constitution has fostered a diverse and competitive religious market.

In many European countries, however, various Christian denominations acquired a more or less full monopoly (for example, the Catholic Church in Italy, the Lutheran Church in Germany, the Anglican Church in England). These established churches became complacent because they were able to suppress any effective competition, often with the official help of the governments of these nations. They were stripped of any incentive to remain responsive to the changing needs of their constituencies, and in modern times these societies have become largely secular. The veracity of this supposition has been put to the test through various empirical studies, generating considerable controversy (for example, Finke, 1997; Finke, Guest, and Stark, 1996; Froese, 2001; Olsen, 1999). But while many sociologists are now persuaded of the value of Stark's arguments, the jury is still out and a final verdict has yet to be rendered.

Steve Bruce (2001), for example, is a vocal critic of both Berger and Stark and a staunch proponent of secularization theory. He thinks that Berger was too quick to recant his views and doubts that the data will support Stark's alternative theories. Briefly stated, he argues that the so-called revival of religion in the United States is likely to be a short-lived and shallow affair. Secularization, he stresses, is the by-product of certain larger social processes associated with modernization, such as **urbanization** and the advancement of knowledge (that is, a scientific world view). In both regards, the United States simply lags behind its European counterparts. The United States, for example, "did not reach until the 1920s the degree of urbanization of Britain in the 1850s" (Bruce, 2001: 89). As the social conditions in America come to parallel those of Europe, secularization will follow. "There is certainly considerable evidence," Bruce insists, "that church membership and attendance is now declining in the United States" (Hadaway, Marler, and Chaves, 1993, cited in Bruce, 2001). Moreover, as several other prominent scholars have argued before (for example, Luckmann, 1967; Wilson, 1966), the religion of Americans has been secularized from within. It is a diluted and comfortable religion of conformism that offers broad support to the most basic cultural values of the United States without really demanding much from its practitioners. In other words, it is a pale ghost of its former self, and even the recent turn to the religious right has rapidly dissipated as the new evangelicals become increasingly like everyone else in their behaviour, if not in their stated ideology.

Likewise, in the developing world, the resurgence of religion is tied to social conditions of either rebellion or repression. In the face of the political, economic, and cultural threats posed by **globalization**, religion has become once again a potent force for the protection of **ethnicity** and national sovereignty. Its use is facilitated, moreover, by the absence of any liberal democratic order in most of these societies. They need not support any significant religious pluralism—one of Berger's original forces of secularization—in the name of democracy. But historically, Bruce is confident, this is a transitory state of affairs that will change as these societies are compelled to find their place in a new global order marked at its heart by the attributes of the Western societies. At present, it is theoretically inappropriate to contrast the state of religion in the developed and developing worlds, since the social conditions of these nations differ so much. Secularization theory can only be said to be defeated when religion truly persists in nations where the elements of modernity have been comparably reproduced. In truly modern and secularized societies, such as Germany, Britain, the Netherlands, and Denmark, there are no signs of a return to religion, despite the formal creation of conditions of religious pluralism and the introduction of many new minority religions. The data are not congruent with Stark's expectations, but they continue to offer support for Berger's original theory of secularization.

In the end, scholars are awaiting the data that will demonstrate whether the continued religiousness of Americans is an exceptional state of affairs, defying the slow but steady secularization of the world, or whether the continued secularity of Western European nations is the exceptional case, defying a world that always has been and will continue to be religious.

But what about the Canadian situation? How does the evidence of our attitudes and behaviour factor into the equation? We share much of our cultural experience and religious history with the United States, and until recently our religious profiles were very similar. But since the 1960s, the religious habits of Canadians have come to resemble those of Western Europeans. We seem to fall betwixt and between the American and the European cases. Does our religiosity hold the key to determining whether it is the Americans or the Europeans that are exceptional?

The Religious Life of Contemporary Canadians

The prognosis for organized and conventional religion in Canada has been quite bleak for several decades. Beginning in the 1960s, all of the major indices of religious membership and activity began to decline steadily. Yet in his latest detailed analysis of religion in Canada, Reginald Bibby (2002) finds some evidence of rejuvenation. Moreover, as Berger stresses and as Bibby has consistently documented in

the Canadian context (1987, 1993), the religiosity of individuals has not significantly diminished with time. Most Canadians, like their British and European counterparts (Davie, 1994, 2002), still display an apparent interest in religious concerns even though they have stopped going to church.

Beginning in the 1960s, Canadian and American churches experienced what Wade Clark Roof and William McKinney (1987) aptly call "the collapse of the middle." In both nations, the large mainline and liberal Protestant denominations that had dominated religious life started to lose members and to experience declining attendance at services. These groups had held the middle ground on a religious spectrum for almost two centuries, with more radical and largely new or alternative religions on the left, and more conservative, even fundamentalist, religious orientations on the right. In the United States, the Congregational, Episcopalian, Presbyterian, and Methodist churches suffered the blow, along with the more doctrinally liberal segments of the Lutheran and Baptist churches. In Canada, the Anglican, Presbyterian, Lutheran, and United churches felt the losses. The collapse in support was more precipitous in Canada, however, and its consequences more severe since the vast majority of Canadians belonged to these few Protestant churches or to the Catholic Church, which has experienced serious declines as well (see Table 11.2).

In the United States, the decline of the mainline Protestant denominations was balanced by a remarkable and unexpected increase in religious activity on the right, and even some modest growth on the left (for example, the rise of such diverse new religious movements as neo-paganism/witchcraft and various imported Eastern religions). In Canada, however, no

Table 11.2 **Religious Identification of Canadians, 1871–2001 (Percentage of Total Population)**

	1871	1901	1931	1961	1991	2001
Protestant	56	56	54	49	36	29
Roman Catholic	42	42	41	47	46	43
Eastern Orthodox	<1	<1	1	1	1	2
Jewish	<1	<1	1	1	1	1
Other faiths	2	2	2	1	3	5
No religion	<1	<1	<1	<1	12	16

SOURCES: Reginald Bibby, *Restless Gods: The Renaissance of Religion in Canada* (Toronto: Stoddart, 2002), 85; Statistics Canada, 2001 census data.

such compensation occurred. Weekly churchgoing for the mainline Protestant denominations in Canada dropped from 35 per cent in the 1950s to 23 per cent in the 1970s, and to a mere 14 per cent in 1990s (Bibby, 2002: 20). Attendance at conservative services in Canada dipped slightly during this period as well, but by 1990 had returned to the levels of the 1950s (49 per cent). Unlike in the United States, there was no sweeping turn to the right in religious matters in the 1980s. There was, however, a modest yet significant increase in the actual percentage of Canadians involved in more conservative churches (for example, various Baptist and Pentecostal groups), which grew by about 8 per cent in the 1990s. But very few Canadians turned to any of the alternative religions identified with the left end of the religious spectrum (Bibby, 2002: 62–4).

Roman Catholic levels of attendance fell equally precipitously in Canada, from a high of 83 per cent in 1957 to 33 per cent in 1990 (see Table 11.1, p. 285). Measures of Catholicism in Canada, though, are complicated by the cultural differences between Quebec and the rest of the country. Figures that were once consistently higher inside Quebec than outside the province are now consistently the reverse, with non-Québécois Catholics displaying higher levels of religiosity.

Overall church attendance figures in Canada have dropped from a high of 53 per cent in 1957 to a low of 19 per cent in 2000 (Bibby, 2002: 75). This figure is still significantly higher than the single-digit figures common in most Western European nations and Britain (Davie, 2000), but it presents a startling contrast with the figure of approximately 40 per cent regular service attendance that Americans have maintained with some consistency for the last 50 years (Greeley, 1989).

Can we account for these differences using Stark's theories? Clearly, Canada is not simply a more modern nation than the United States. Could the answer lie then with Stark's supply-side notions and the variant degrees of religious pluralism historically fostered in each nation? Americans have long spread their religious allegiance over a much greater array of religious choices. Hundreds of denominations have flourished throughout their history, and they have given birth to several successful new religions (for example, the Mormons, the Seventh Day Adventists, the Jehovah's Witnesses, and Pentecostalism). The religious history of Canada, however, has been marked by what the British sociologist David Martin (2000) calls "shadow

A Jewish boy performing an essential rite of passage into manhood, his bar mitzvah ceremony. (Michael Rumack)

establishments." No single church has been formally established in Canada as the state religion since the mid-nineteenth century, but the extended colonial ties with Britain in English Canada did secure the pre-eminence of the Anglican and Presbyterian churches among the nation's economic, political, and social elites. These few churches, along with the United Church (which was formed out of elements of the Methodist, Presbyterian, and Congregational churches in 1923) have monopolized Protestant religious life in Canada. In Quebec, the Catholic Church exerted an overwhelming control over almost all aspects of life until quite recently. Catholicism was synonymous with the French Canadian identity, protecting the culture of the province from the incursion of the larger Anglo-American society of North America. Perhaps these historical differences contributed to the reduced religious vitality of contemporary Canadians?

Later developments lend some support to this supposition. In Quebec, for example, everything changed dramatically with the Quiet Revolution of the 1960s, when a secular form of Quebec nationalism began to systematically displace the church's control over education, health care, and other aspects of social welfare. Within 30 years, Quebec was transformed from one of the most religious societies in the world to one of the least religious. Today Quebec most resembles Europe in its secularity, a result in line with Stark's assumptions about the negative consequences of religious monopolies.

The same explanation may hold true for the increased secularization of English Canada relative to the United States. In this case, however, we are dealing with a lesser measure of religious monopoly, one offset by a degree of denominationalism. Seeing themselves as denominations, and not universal churches with a right to impose their beliefs on others, most religious groups in English Canada were content to recognize that they represented but one of many ways of embodying the truth of Christianity. This hybrid situation may account for the betwixt-and-between status of Canada in considering the arguments for either the European and the American exceptions to secularization. At this stage it is still too early to tell what will transpire in Canada, and there are many other complex factors to consider (see, for example, Beyer, 1997, 2000; Reimer, 1995). Clearly, though, as the Canadian sociologist Peter Beyer (1997, 2000) asserts, there is no single "master trend" for religion in modernity. Regionally specific and unique developmental patterns have to be taken into consideration.

At the institutional level, Canada appears to be secularized, though Bibby has raised some doubts in *Restless Gods* (2002). He notes, for example, that by 2000, church attendance figures in Canada had stopped declining, and in fact the liberal Protestant denominations had begun to post some modest increases in membership and attendance figures (see Table 11.1, p. 285). Moreover, Canadian churches in general were maintaining or even increasing the levels of participation of teens and other young people in their activities. But the single most significant factor currently giving sociologists pause is the persistent strength of measures of individual or private religiosity in Canada and the rest of the Western world. People may be "unchurched," but it is far from clear that they have become irreligious.

In his repeated surveys of the religious views of Canadians (begun in 1974), Bibby has documented certain constants other than the decline in church attendance. First, most Canadians continue to identify themselves with some specific religious group—usually that of their parents and grandparents—even if they no longer participate in most of its activities. They show little inclination, moreover, to switch from this traditional religious identity. Second, most Canadians state that they will continue to use the religion with which they identify to perform various important rites of passage in their lives, like baptisms, marriages, and funerals. Third, most Canadians say they believe in God (see Table 11.3) and that they think God cares about them.

Fourth, most Canadians continue to ask themselves such fundamentally religious questions as what happens after death, why is there suffering in the world, and what is the purpose of life. But what is more, almost half of all Canadians say they have actually experienced God's presence in their lives (see Table 11.4), and 74 per cent acknowledge that they pray privately, with 3 in 10 saying they do so daily. In light of these and other kinds of longitudinal results, Bibby concludes,

> The empirical data are decisive: God has not disappeared from the lives of the vast majority of Canadians. The average people we pass on sidewalks and roadways and see in supermarkets and malls may not often say it out loud, but most of them believe in God, converse with God, and in nearly one in two cases think they have experienced the presence of God. That's a lot of people. These are not anomalous beliefs, practices, and experiences. (2002: 164)

But what are we to make of these findings? Similar data have been produced for Britain and Europe (Davie 1994, 2002) and for the "unchurched" in the United States (Roof, 1999). Are these results definitive disproof of the secularization thesis? Or, as Bruce would argue, are they merely evidence of a process of cultural lag, of resistance to social change that will eventually succumb to a more secular world view? Only time, of course, will tell.

In this regard, however, Bibby's analysis of the Canadian context did uncover one disturbing trend: Canadians are just as likely to reflect on the ultimate questions of life today as 30 years ago; "however, in each case, the proportion who are 'often' thinking about these issues is down from the mid-70s, while the proportion who are 'no longer' reflecting on them is up" (2002: 133). The shift, moreover, is statistically significant.

The "no longer" response does not necessarily mean, though, that people have found answers to their questions (presumably secular answers). It may simply mean, Bibby suggests, that they lack the time and energy in our busy world to reflect on these

Table 11.3   **Belief in God in Canada, 1985–2000 (Percentage of Total Population)**

"Do you believe that God exists?"	1985	1990	1995	2000
Yes	84	82	80	81
Yes, I definitely do.	61	56	57	49
Yes, I think so.	23	26	23	32
No, I don't think so.	10	10	11	13
No, I definitely do not think so.	6	8	9	6

SOURCES: Reginald Bibby, *Restless Gods: The Renaissance of Religion in Canada* (Toronto: Stoddart, 2002), 140; Bibby, Project Canada Survey Series.

Table 11.4   **Claims of Experiencing God, 1975–2000 (Percentage of Total Population)**

"Do you believe that you have experienced God's presence?"	1975[a]	1980[a]	1985	1990	1995	2000
Yes	48	43	44	43	41	47
Yes, I definitely do.	22	21	25	20	20	20
Yes, I think so.	26	22	19	23	21	27
No	52	57	56	57	59	53
No, I don't think so.	–	–	32	31	33	31
No, I definitely do not.	–	–	24	26	26	22

[a] In 1975 and 1980, the question read, "Have you ever had a feeling that you somehow were in the presence of God?" with the response options, "Yes, I'm sure I have," "Yes, I think I have," and "No."
SOURCE: Reginald Bibby, *Restless Gods: The Renaissance of Religion in Canada* (Toronto: Stoddart, 2002), 147; Project Canada Survey Series.

ultimate concerns. Or they may have stopped asking the questions because they are unsatisfied with or even just unaware of any viable answers. The latter possibility would lend support to Stark's hypothesis, linking the signs of secularization to a failure in the system of religious supply, and not to a decline in the demand for religion. But this shift could be equally evidence of the creeping secularization of society, as Bruce would presume. After all, the percentage of Canadians claiming to have "no religion" has been steadily increasing, moving from 12 per cent in 1991 to 16 per cent in 2001 (Statistics Canada, 2001 census data). Even in the United States this figure has doubled in the last decade, reaching an all-time high of 14 per cent. For the first time in US history, the overall increase in religious affiliation did not keep pace with the rate of population growth (8.8 per cent, compared to 13.2 per cent; Smith, 2002).

But the increase in the "no religion" category, Bibby and others (for example, Hout and Fischer, 2002) argue, may be deceptive. The category is like a revolving door, with more members flowing constantly in and out than staying. Data suggest that the increasing numbers reflect an increase in the proportion of the population in a process of transition in their lives and in a temporary condition of religious disaffiliation more than they do a sheer increase in true religious dropouts. Those claiming no religious affiliation are more likely to be young and also, in many cases, in the process of switching religious affiliation rather than of leaving religion behind altogether. With age and the onset of family responsibilities, or the completion of other major disruptions such as geographic migrations, many of them will push their way through the revolving door again back to a religious affiliation.

Of course, all analyses of religion in the Western world must now also contend with a new reality of religious pluralism. While most Canadians, Europeans, and Americans remain overwhelmingly Christian—at least nominally—there are growing communities of Hindus, Buddhists, Muslims, and those of many other faiths. At this point it is unclear

Contrary to some popular misperceptions, the non-Christian component of Canada's population is still statistically low. However, the rise of largely Eastern religions in Canada is symbolically significant—it is part of a growing awareness of the influence of other global cultures on Canada's future. Here, a Muslim man shares a tender moment with his wife to view the crescent moon that will signal the beginning of Ramadan (Pat Shannahan/*The Arizona Republic*).

how their presence will alter the overall pattern of religious life in Western societies. New ways of being religious, born in part of the influence of these new religious communities, are emerging in Canada and elsewhere. Perhaps these recent additions to the competitive market of religious options will work to reduce or reverse the effects of secularization, as Stark's theory suggests. But with the passage of time, the followers of these imported traditions may, like most of their Christian counterparts, simply become less religious or even non-religious.

The Future of Religion

For thousands of years, humankind has been deeply religious and almost every aspect of social life has borne a religious significance. Little has fundamentally changed in the fate of individuals and nations. We still live with uncertainty, fear, disease, and death. We still yearn to be blessed and somehow spared from the harsh realities of human existence. We find it difficult to live with the knowledge of our demise and

seek some eternal happiness or peace. Religious beliefs still play a key role in assuring the civility of our societies. Religion has not disappeared from our world—not even from the most scientific and prosperous parts.

Viewing matters from one perspective, there is little reason to doubt that the inhabitants of the late twenty-first century will be as religious, in some sense. But from another perspective, we must pause to consider just how much things have changed in a historically short period of time. In just a few centuries, religion has fallen from its place of pre-eminence amongst social institutions to become only one of many segmented aspects of our lives. It persists in the hearts and minds of most people, but it no longer exerts much influence over our education, business choices, social activities, or commitments. We do not choose our political leaders because of their religious convictions, nor are the religious orientations of our neighbours of much concern to us. The face of religion has changed in the modern Western world, and probably for good (short of a complete socio-economic collapse). But it is far too early to tell what the real consequences will be of the changes religion is undergoing, even with regard to the very existence of religion. Care must be taken to realize that elsewhere the face of religion has changed little.

As cautioned in the introduction to this chapter, the view from Canada is far from universal. More traditional, conservative, supernatural, and collectively oriented religious movements are spreading rapidly and gaining strength throughout the world. Religion may have become a very individual and private affair in much of the Western world, but fundamentalist styles of Islam and evangelical and Pentecostal styles of Christianity are ascendant in many parts of Africa, Latin America, and Asia. Where the populations of the world are growing the fastest, so are the most traditional and fervent forms of religious life. Religion is bound to play an increasingly important role in the clash of interests and sensibilities between the developed and developing worlds over the course of the next century (see Jenkins, 2002).

11.3

Human Diversity
The New Religious Diversity

The religious landscape of North America is changing as Muslim mosques, Hindu and Buddhist temples, and Sikh gurdwaras begin to appear in Canadian and American cities. More people immigrated to the United States between the 1960s and the 1990s than during the so-called heyday of immigration at the height of the Industrial Revolution from 1890 to 1920. But now the immigrants are coming from India, Pakistan, China, Indonesia, Korea, and other countries throughout Asia and the Middle East, not from Europe. As these millions of people settle into their new lives in their adopted, yet still strange, homelands, they have brought their religious traditions with them.

As sociologists have long recognized, religious organizations commonly play a crucial role in helping immigrants to maintain their cultural traditions while providing the physical and social support required to make the transition. In fact, in the face of a foreign society in which immigrants' language is not spoken or their customs known and respected, religious beliefs and practices often surge to the fore as a bulwark of cultural identity. For a generation or two, the devotion of immigrants is likely to be greater than that of people in their native lands. But with time, assimilation frequently sets in and many members of later generations enter more completely into the dominant culture, often through marriage to people of other faiths and cultures.

For the Canadian communities into which these new immigrants have moved, though, things have changed forever. On any street in Montreal, Toronto, Winnipeg, Edmonton, or Vancouver, a Catholic church is as likely to have a Gujarati Hindu temple as its neighbour as it is a Lutheran church. This new visible presence of other traditions from around the world is inevitably changing the cultural and religious consciousness of Canadians. It is part of the process of globalization happening all around us. The national policies and rhetoric of multiculturalism are taking concrete form in unusual yet inspiring ways, in the elaborate facades of the Hindu temples and the large and shining domes of the Muslim mosques being built in our cities. Canadians are learning to accept and understand a much wider array of religious traditions, and some are even choosing to practise them. As the Christian legacy of Canada fades in the face of secularization, our strong and persistent curiosity about religious and spiritual issues is finding new avenues of expression. There is no going back to the narrow Judeo-Christian heritage that shaped the first centuries of our nation. As Canadian life is increasingly infused with the practices of cultures from around the world, and as people are exposed on a daily basis to distant lands through mass communications, air travel, and business contacts, a new and unparalleled religious diversity is slated for our future.

The consequences of this diversity are as yet unknown. But in recent years, scholars have begun

continued

to turn their attention to the study of these groups (for example, the Pluralism Project led by Diana Eck at Harvard University; see <www.pluralism.org>). Many important studies have been completed, though much more research is required (see, for example, Ebaugh and Chafetz, 2000; McLellan, 1999; Warner and Wittner, 1998).

All the same, we must be careful not to exaggerate the changes underway. In 2001, only about 5 per cent of the Canadian population were Hindus, Buddhists, Muslims, Sikhs, or members of other non-Christian religions. The Canadian census reveals that this was true of 2 per cent of Canadians in 1871 (Bibby, 2002: 85). The rate of growth is steadily increasing, but the real numbers are still quite small. The recent growth of these groups in the United States has been more rapid, but they still constitute only a small fraction of Americans. They constituted 0.8 per cent of the population in the late 1970s and about 2.6 per cent of the population in 2000 (see Smith, 2002: 578). To gain some perspective, it might be noted that the membership of the 12th largest Christian denomination in the United States, the United Church of Christ, is about the same as the entire American Muslim population (1.7 million and 1.5–1.9 million people, respectively). With 62 million Catholics alone, for example, it will be some time before these new religions have a statistically significant impact on the United States (Glenmary Research Center, 2002).

Nevertheless, the change that is underway is already forcing our dominant institutions to adapt (for example, legal, medical, and educational institutions), especially in cities like Toronto, where, for example, over 254,000 Muslims now live. These institutions are being drawn increasingly into the dialogue of religious differences and similarities as they attempt to serve the needs of a new range of Canadians.

☐ Questions for Critical Thought

1. How would you define *religion*?
2. Are there aspects of religion that just cannot be measured or analyzed by the social sciences?
3. Can you describe a recent situation in which religion acted primarily as an agent of social control?
4. Have you ever experienced the social effervescence that Durkheim says is crucial to religion? Under what circumstances, and what was it like?
5. If you attend religious services with some regularity, why? If you do not, why not?
6. Do you think Stark's supply-side theory of secularization explains why church attendance has dropped off so sharply in Canada?
7. Bibby reports that half of all Canadians claim to have experienced God's presence in their lives. How would we go about investigating what this really means?
8. Judging by events happening in the world today, do you think that religion is going to play a significant role in social developments in the twenty-first century?

☐ Recommended Readings

Peter L. Berger, *The Sacred Canopy: Elements of a Sociological Theory* (New York: Doubleday, 1967).

This modern classic has exerted a tremendous influence on the study of religion. Berger delineates one of the most fundamental theories of the basic nature and social function of religion and provides a classic statement of the theory of secularization, developing the ironic Weberian theme that Christianity sowed the seeds of its own destruction.

Reginald W. Bibby, *Restless Gods: The Renaissance of Religion in Canada* (Toronto: Stoddart, 2002).

This is one of a series of books written by this Canadian sociologist providing a detailed overview of the religious beliefs and practices of contemporary Canadians based on comprehensive and longitudinal survey data. Bibby provides an effective summary of his earlier findings. The latest data indicates that the declining fortunes of mainstream religions in Canada may be reversing itself.

Lorne L. Dawson, *Comprehending Cults: The Sociology of New Religious Movements* (Toronto: Oxford University Press, 1998).

This book provides a concise overview of the results and insights of the social-scientific study of new religious movements since the onset of the contemporary controversy over cults in the 1960s, including questions of brainwashing, violence, and cultural significance.

Russell T. McCutcheon, ed., *The Insider/Outsider Problem in the Study of Religion: A Reader* (New York: Cassell, 1999).

This comprehensive collection of classic and contemporary essays provides a stimulating overview of the serious methodological challenges faced by social scientists seeking to assess and explain so subjective a phenomenon as religion.

H. Richard Niebuhr, *Christ and Culture* (New York: Harper, 1951).

This seminal book by one of America's earliest and most gifted sociologists of religion, who was also a theologian, neatly captures the paradoxical and perplexing nature of the relationship between religions and their surrounding cultures. Niebuhr describes five different scenarios, relating them to elements of Christian scripture and doctrine, different historical traditions, and prominent spokespeople: Christ against culture, the Christ of culture, Christ above culture, Christ and culture in paradox, and Christ the transformer of culture.

Wade Clark Roof, *Spiritual Marketplace: Baby Boomers and the Remaking of American Religion* (Princeton, NJ: Princeton University Press, 1999).

This book provides one of the best overviews of religious life in the contemporary United States, using extensive survey research data and detailed interviews. Roof argues that the religious culture of America has fragmented into five distinct subcultures: dogmatists, born-again Christians, mainstream believers, metaphysical believers and seekers, and secularists.

Rodney Stark and Roger Finke, *Acts of Faith: Explaining the Human Side of Religion* (Berkeley: University of California Press, 2000).

This book provides an excellent and very readable overview of the "religious economies" approach to the study of the most basic elements of religious life and the heated debate over secularization. Religious preferences and behaviour are framed in terms of our understanding of broader human decision-making processes.

Max Weber, *The Protestant Ethic and the Spirit of Capitalism*, translated by Talcott Parsons. (New York: Scribner, [1904–5] 1958).

Weber argues that the Protestant Reformation had a profound and unanticipated impact on the modern world. The Protestant quest for personal salvation set in place a world view that stimulated the development of the economic ethos undergirding the rise of the capitalist system that dominates all aspects of life throughout the contemporary world.

☐ Recommended Web Sites

Academic Info

www.academicinfo.net

This non-profit academic reference service provides access to many pages listing Web sites that deal with most religious groups present in North America and a wide variety of related religious topics (under the headings Humanities and Social Science).

Beliefnet

www.beliefnet.com

This is the largest and best-known commercial 'zine site dedicated exclusively to religion, with many features designed to educate and entertain the public and to sell religious goods of all kinds. This sophisticated site has regular columnists and special essays by experts; covers religion in the news; profiles groups, festivals, and places; reviews books; discusses TV shows, movies, and other Web sites; and has numerous chat lines dedicated to different religious foci.

The Cauldron

www.ecauldron.com

This large and sophisticated US-based neo-pagan Web site is meant to meet every possible need of the committed and the curious, with feature articles and forums on every aspects of belief and practice and on the integration of paganism into American religious and popular culture. Internet Relay Chat (IRC) rooms and links to hundreds of other similar pages are available.

The First Church of Cyberspace

www.godweb.org

This is one of the first and most successful efforts to create a virtual Christian community, or at least a church presence that is exclusively online. It offers visitors a wide array of traditional church services, sermons, prayer groups, Biblical studies, Biblical texts and indices, movie reviews, book reviews, chat rooms, and information on Christian developments from around the world.

Ontario Consultants on Religious Tolerance

www.religioustolerance.org

This private effort has received international acclaim for its efforts to promote religious understanding by providing profiles of many different religious groups, including new religious movements, and careful information and discussion of many controversial religious topics (for example, assisted suicide, evolution, and creation science).

Religion in the News

www.trincoll.edu/depts/csrpl/RIN.htm

The Web site for Religion in the News, a serial academic publication of the Leonard E. Greenberg Center for the Study of Religion in Public Life at Trinity College, Hartford, Connecticut, provides links to numerous articles and books published on a very wide array of religious topics by academics and journalists.

The Religious Movements Homepage

http://religiousmovements.lib.virginia.edu

The Religious Movements Homepage at the University of Virginia is an excellent source of information on a wide array of new religious movements (NRMs) and for essays on aspects of the study of such controversial groups. The page was created by a prominent sociologist of religion, the late Jeffrey Hadden, and contains many contributions from his students.

Wiccan Church of Canada

www.wcc.on.ca

The Wiccan Church of Canada is one of thousands of neo-pagan groups operating in North America. The Web site is designed to provide basic information on this group and to provide links to the wider neo-pagan community.

12

Peter R. Sinclair

> > >

Politics and Political Movements

© Dick Hemingway

☐ Learning Objectives

In this chapter, you will:

- be introduced to concepts that help illuminate political life

- become aware of different forms of the contemporary state

- come to appreciate the value of comparing different societies

- review and evaluate competing perspectives on democratic societies

- consider the global dimensions and implications of many political issues

- grasp why women, the poor, and minority ethnic groups have been poorly represented in political life

- appreciate the forces that generate internal and international terrorism

- understand why many problems require answers at a regional or even global level and why solutions are difficult to put into practice

Introduction

11 September 2001. On this day, international terrorism shocked North America with new ferocity and massive loss of life. Four planes were hijacked after taking off from US airports. Their pilots were replaced at the controls by men bent on a suicide mission to destroy core symbols of American power and to kill as many civilians as possible. Two hijacked jets ripped into first the north and then the south towers of New York City's World Trade Center. About one hour after the first strike, a third plane smashed into the Pentagon, the Washington, DC, home base of the US military, with the subsequent loss of almost 200 lives, including those on the plane. Meanwhile, raging fires weakened key parts of the superstructures of the twin towers, which collapsed in clouds of debris within half an hour of each other. Although many by this time had escaped to the streets, nearly 2,800 employees, passengers, and rescue workers perished in this devastating spectacle. Minutes after the collapse of the south tower, the fourth plane crashed into a Pennsylvania field, probably after a struggle on board, as hijackers tried to fly it to Washington.

As the events unfolded, it became evident that Islamic extremists conducted the attacks to strike back at the United States and international capitalism for supporting regimes they perceived as corrupt and immoral. When the United States became convinced that Osama bin Laden's al-Qaeda network had orchestrated the assaults from its sanctuary in Afghanistan, American and allied forces first bombed that country and then joined Afghans on the ground to attack both the Taliban (the fundamentalist Islamic rulers of Afghanistan) and al-Qaeda. President George W. Bush demanded that all countries support his "War on Terror," and received backing from most Islamic states, including Pakistan. By early December, the Taliban regime had collapsed and al-Qaeda forces had dispersed into the mountains, possibly to Pakistan and other countries where they might find refuge.

After the United States sustained such a violent and successful attack on its own territory, there could be little doubt that the scale of response would be enormous and that the inevitable anti-terrorist measures would disrupt movements of people and products, especially across borders. Long delays occurred on the busy crossing points between the United States and Canada. Stock markets plunged. Many people cancelled all but essential travel. Airlines, the travel industry, and all those linked to it suffered from declining business. In these ways, the terrorists were successful, but US policy and the views of the general population probably hardened after the attacks. There was no immediate sign of rethinking the directions of international capitalism or US foreign policy in ways more sympathetic to poor countries and particularly to Palestinians, as al-Qaeda supporters desired.

September 11 and its aftermath were dramatic and extraordinary political events, but politics enters into everyone's life every day in much more routine ways because there is almost nothing we do that the state does not in some way limit or regulate. Through its laws, regulations, and system of enforcement, the state influences people's lives from the cradle to the grave. At the same time, the state's power is under threat from **globalization** trends, terrorist opposition, popular disenchantment, and environmental disasters, to name only some of the most pressing problems. Despite the obvious importance of politics, people are unequally involved and their interests unevenly satisfied. This chapter provides sociological concepts and perspectives that should help explain politics and the state in Canada and elsewhere.

US foreign policy has come under attack in recent years. In the aftermath of 11 September 2001, the United States hunted down potential terrorists in Afghanistan, forced a regime change in that country, and revisited Iraq. Many peace movements around the world protested the war with Iraq. In this photograph, a man protests by diving onto riot police at the entrance to the Al-Azhar mosque in Cairo. The demonstration came after a leading cleric in the Muslim world expressed sympathy for the Iraqi people. (Marwan Naamani/Agence France-Presse/GettyImages)

Core Concepts

Politics and Power

Politics is the process by which individuals and groups act to promote their interests, often in conflict with others. It is intimately connected to **power**. In all spheres of action, power reflects the extent to which available resources both constrain and enable people's actions (Giddens, 1979). Resources provide the means for action, but they also provide a limit on what action is possible. Following Max Weber ([1908] 1978), one of sociology's outstanding social theorists of the early twentieth century, *power* is often defined as the ability of a person or group to achieve their objectives, even when opposed. Power typically becomes concentrated in society because some people consistently have greater discretion in controlling what others do (Barnes, 1988). However, in some situations power is more or less equal, as in most friendships.

Thus power is about capacity to act in a desired way, and politics is the process of mobilizing these capacities. Politics is most visible when it involves struggle between opposing forces, but it is also evident in what people do to avoid conflict and maintain their domination. Examples include controlling agendas and the timing of decisions, even how other people define their interests (Lukes, 1974). John Gaventa (1980) demonstrated the way power was maintained for generations in his investigation of why Appalachian miners remained politically inactive,

---

12.1

Sociology in Action
The Impact of Research on Political Practice: The Aalborg Project

Social research can have an effect on what is studied by helping to change the way people conduct their affairs. Bent Flyvbjerg's investigation of Aalborg's transportation system (1998) uncovered how effectively the local business elite was able to bypass formal democratic processes and achieve its objectives over a period of 15 years. However, Flyvbjerg (2001) was also committed to research that would be critical and reflexive. This required placing the results of his research back into the political arena in the hope that improvements might take place—here, in the functioning of democracy. Flyvbjerg therefore presented his results in the mass media and in public meetings. For example, he demonstrated that, contrary to expectations, traffic accidents in the centre of Aalborg increased over the life of the plan without officials apparently noticing, and that "the increase in accidents was caused by city officials allowing the rationality of the Chamber of Industry and Commerce to slowly, surely, and one-sidedly, influence and undermine the rationality of the Aalborg project" (Flyvbjerg, 2001: 157).

Initially, those whose positions were threatened by his evidence challenged Flyvbjerg by claiming his information was inaccurate, but a determined defence of that evidence was eventually accepted by the alderman responsible for city planning. After that, dialogue developed. *Dialogue* is understood as a respectful exchange of ideas, a requirement of the democratic process, in contrast with mere rhetoric and polemic, which impede informed judgment.

As the public debate proceeded, the alderman and his officials realized that reports about the research were influencing the public and that the Aalborg plan had to change. They could no longer defend what was demonstrably not working, especially as the project was by this time receiving much international attention. A new plan emerged based on an open democratic process. The city government invited a variety of interest groups to join the planning and implementation processes. The European Union, inspired by Flyvbjerg's research and determination that it should be noticed outside the academy, recognized this new practice by commending Aalborg for its innovative, democratic planning process.

IN THE FIRST PERSON

I went to the University of Aberdeen in 1964 thinking I wanted to study how people behaved. A year later I discovered the new subject of sociology, which captured me immediately with its focus on social relationships and issues of social justice. More important, I was forced to challenge many beliefs I assumed to be true, to recognize that other ways of behaving were plausible and sometimes preferable. Since then, over many years, I have been rewarded by countless opportunities to research and teach about things that excite me—such as how people can act collectively to challenge what disturbs them in society; how inequality affects the way people conduct their lives; why people have destroyed so many of the natural resources on which they depend. One of the many rewarding aspects of doing sociology is the opportunity to help young people achieve their potential and challenge what is taken for granted. –PETER R. SINCLAIR

despite much poverty, from the late nineteenth century until 1975. Apart from brief periods when recessions weakened the position of landowners and mine operators, this local elite wielded effective power. In particular, the poor miners and their families accepted existing conditions because their opponents controlled not only vital resources—jobs, houses, land, stores, access to medical facilities, even the local electoral process—but also the opinion-forming institutions of the area: schools, churches, and the media.

An excellent example of the difficulty of challenging power holders is Bent Flyvbjerg's study (1998) of the politics of urban planning in Aalborg, Denmark. Flyvbjerg provides careful documentation of the ill-fated attempt to reduce the use of private cars in the centre of Aalborg and to make conditions more favourable for other forms of transportation. This study investigates the process of winning and losing, how reason is argued and manipulated in the exercise of power. Local business people believed that restrictions on automobiles would reduce their sales. Through the Chamber of Industry, they prevented measures to control cars while supporting aids to buses, bicyclists, and pedestrians. Much of this activity was covert, unnoticed by the general public. In the end, the environment and virtually every citizen lost out when all forms of traffic increased. Yet this study paradoxically shows the practical value of sociology.

Power is often hidden in relationships. For power to be observed, those subject to it must actively resist. However, opposition will be rare if people believe they have no chance of successfully resisting the demands being placed on them; and it will not appear when power holders enjoy **authority**, which may be

defined as power considered legitimate by those subject to it.

Types of Authority

To hold authority over others is clearly a critical resource in the conduct of politics. Where authority is widely accepted, politics will likely follow peaceful, established patterns, but when it does not exist, intense conflicts are probable sooner or later. In order to understand how authority becomes established, the work of Max Weber, almost a century ago, remains important. Weber ([1908] 1978) identified three types of authority according to the grounds on which it was accepted by those subject to it. These types seldom appear in pure form because actual relationships usually involve combinations.

Traditional authority is evident when people obey because that is the way things have always been done. The power holder enjoys "the sanctity of immemorial traditions" (Weber, [1908] 1978, vol. 1: 215) and may expect obedience as long as these established rules are followed. Examples include chiefs and elders who ruled tribal societies by customary practice and acceptance of their rights. Authority of this type is more secure when it is grounded in the belief that it derives from a revered spiritual source. Thus, to oppose one's leader would also be to oppose one's god.

Charismatic authority rests on belief in the exceptional qualities of an individual person, someone of exemplary or heroic character who reveals how life will unfold, perhaps involving new social **values** and patterns of conduct. The person with charisma is thought to be able to resolve problems beyond the capacity of ordinary people and may build a devoted following, sometimes rooted in religious faith, as with the Christian prophets, or in secular **ideologies**, as with Mao Zedong and Adolf Hitler. Charismatic leaders are innovative, even revolutionary, but their authority is fragile, being dependent on their personal qualities and the appearance of results.

Rational-legal authority is based on formally established rules, procedures, and expertise in which an individual's acknowledged right to command is limited to his or her formal position. Personal characteristics of both the office holder and those subject to command are irrelevant to the conduct of business. It is expected that each person will be treated as any other, which gives rise to formal procedures both for appointment to positions and for the treatment of citizens. This form of authority is characteristic of bureaucratic structures, both public and private, where those in higher-ranked positions may command those in lower positions within the limits of their jurisdiction. Thus, the manager who attempts to obtain sexual services from a secretary engages in behaviour that is considered illegitimate in that context. Specialized knowledge or expertise is another modern basis of authority, as when a physician persuades a patient to endure unpleasant and undignified procedures that the patient does not fully understand.

Modern states develop bureaucratic structures based on claims to rational-legal authority, though backed by the capacity to draw on the means of force should there be opposition. Of course, bureaucratic officials, in practice, are at times corrupt (which means that some people are treated with special favour in return for unofficial personal payments) or obstructionist. These departures from the rules weaken the legitimacy of the **bureaucracy** and may increase the likelihood of radical opposition to the regime in control of the state.

Although power and politics are dimensions of all **social relationships**, "politics" in common use refers, in the first instance, to processes of government and regulation within and between modern states. It is this more specific understanding of politics that will be developed in this chapter.

Political institutions are established rules and procedures for the conduct of political affairs, including the government of society. They constitute a network of power relationships. Specialized political institutions were evident in some form in most earli-er societies but became more complex in the industrial countries of the modern world, on which we focus here. There is no uniform course of development, but several important trends can be identified: increasing scale of government, growing political intervention in social affairs, the rise of the nation-state, and various forms of bureaucratic administration (Bottomore, 1979). These political institutions constitute networks of power that we can analyze in light of their internal structures and their links to the rest of society. Special interest groups, **social movements**, and political parties connect various segments of the public to the state, which is the core political frame of contemporary complex societies.

In modern societies, state institutions are both objectives of political struggle and resources in these struggles. In Weber's famous definition, **the state** is "a human community that (successfully) claims the monopoly of the legitimate use of physical force within a given territory" ([1922] 1946: 78). Residents consider the use of force to be acceptable only when state leaders call upon it, and probably only when it is applied according to widely held rules. However, it is common for physical coercion to be deployed within a particular territory without that force being viewed as legitimate by most residents. Tyrants, dictators, and zealots can rule effectively for long periods. Unless we insist that states exist only when rule is legitimate, another definition is called for. Thus *the state* may be considered to be that set of procedures and organizations concerned with creating, administering, and enforcing rules or decisions for conduct within a given territory. Here, legitimacy is not assumed.

Pre-industrial states were usually rudimentary in form, for example, extensions of the household of a ruler. They were also small, as reflected in the Greek city-states. **Monarchy** is rule by a single individual who claims legitimacy based on royal lineage. Today's monarchs, as in Canada, Britain, and the Netherlands, have survived the transition to democratic constitutions, but their powers are only formal, their practice essentially ceremonial.

Modern nation-states certainly vary in scale, but they are typically much more complex, with their legislatures, governments, public bureaucracies, police, judiciary, and military components. Remembering the complexity and scale of these states, it is misleading to assume that "the state" is coherently unified; in practice, the parts are loosely integrated and often work at cross-purposes. Canada's federal Department

12.2

Human Diversity
State Fragmentation: Fisheries Policy and Competing Political Interests

The Canadian state is certainly not a homogeneous, unified structure, as is illustrated by the frequent disputes arising from the fishery. Who can catch fish, when, by what means, and how much is a federal responsibility in Canada, while the licensing of processing establishments is a provincial right. Ideally, processing capacity and available fish resources would be closely matched, but this is never easy, and is often impossible when the two levels of government have competing objectives.

Since the cod moratorium of the 1990s, the federal Department of Fisheries and Oceans has preferred a cautious approach to management of fish resources. The provincial government of Newfoundland and Labrador agrees with protecting the stocks, but at the same time responds to local pressures to maintain employment by licensing more plants for shrimp and crab than are required to harvest what is available. This creates pressure to expand production to a level dangerous for the species or to subsidize the fishery in some way, which goes against the fashionable position that government should be less involved in economic affairs.

It would be much easier to limit the fishery if the rural areas of the province depended less on it. This implies the need for a co-ordinated regional economic development strategy, with both levels of government and their various departments working

to a common plan. However, achieving this has always been a daunting task. For example, in the mid-1980s, the interests of Newfoundland and Labrador favoured tough action against France to protect fish stocks while trying to solve the international boundary dispute between the two countries. Both Canada and France claimed extended jurisdiction of the area around St Pierre and Miquelon, but the federal government moved cautiously to avoid open conflict with France that might also have alienated Quebec even more from the federal government.

Early in 1987, agreement was reached at a meeting from which Brian Mulroney, the Conservative prime minister, excluded Newfoundland's Conservative government, led by Brian Peckford. Scarce fish resources were allocated to France with no clear commitment from France to resolve the boundary dispute. Having been offered an apology for the way the process was handled and a promise that there would be no future exclusion of Newfoundland and Labrador, Premier Peckford responded in typical style: "To hell with the process. It doesn't make any difference if we're there while they sell the shop on us or whether we're home. They sold the shop. So don't give me this business of apologising to me for not inviting me" (*Evening Telegram*, 30 January 1987).

---

of Finance, for example, may wish to reduce taxes at the same time as the Department of Health and Welfare is pushing for a better-funded health care system. The federal structure also creates layers of government with overlapping jurisdictions and potential conflicts.

The Emergence of Modern States

It is challenging to explain why societies developed the different types of institutions that characterize

their political lives. Why, for instance, has liberal democracy remained so firmly entrenched in Sweden and the United States while it was so weak in Germany and Italy earlier in the twentieth century that it was overthrown by fascism? Why did China and Russia choose socialism while India opted for the capitalist, democratic route? Why have so many attempts at nation-building ended in military dictatorship and other forms of authoritarian government? Although no one has answered all these questions adequately, several impressive attempts have been made.

Moore's Alternate Paths

Among the seminal works of political sociology is Barrington Moore's investigation of the conditions that led to the major forms of the modern state: democracy, fascism, and communism. Moore's *Social Origins of Dictatorship and Democracy* (1969) is a comparative assessment of these alternate paths. The key examples of the capitalist path to democracy are Britain, France, the United States, and, more recently and less securely, India. The path to fascism is exemplified by Germany and Japan in the second quarter of the twentieth century. Moore takes the former Soviet Union and the People's Republic of China as the essential illustrations of the path to communist development. He explains the various paths in terms of the relationships among the agrarian classes. Particularly relevant to life in Canada is Moore's identification of the conditions for the emergence of democracy, which he saw as involving the elimination of arbitrary government and mass participation in the making of rules.

According to Moore, the first condition is that neither the monarchy nor the landed aristocracy should be able to dominate each other consistently. A central power must bring some semblance of order to the nobility, yet where the Crown holds absolute power for too long, democracy cannot flourish. Moore cited the histories of China, Russia, and Germany in support of this point.

Second, in the absence of urban dwellers to counteract the landed aristocracy when it challenges royal power, democratic impulses falter. In Moore's own words, "No bourgeois, no democracy" (1969: 418). In Germany, for example, the weakness of the towns led to a lack of pressure to expand the scope of aristocratic demands in a democratic direction. In Russia, the **bourgeoisie** was too weak to become the country's dominant political force; hence, Russia had little chance of developing **capitalism** in either a liberal democratic or a reactionary fascist framework.

Next, the development of commercial agriculture by the landed aristocracy is a key to democratic resistance to the monarchy. In England, the nobles became commercial farmers, displacing the peasantry. This social change provided the basis of common interests between the nobility and the urban bourgeoisie. Where landowners maintain an agrarian labour force in conditions resembling serfdom, as in Prussia, the result of their alliance with the bourgeoisie is more likely to be fascism. When this alliance cannot be formed because the bourgeoisie is too weak, peasant-based communist revolution is possible, as in China. The experiences of France and the United States provide further evidence that different forms of commercial agriculture are associated with different paths to democracy.

The fourth condition is that there should be no massive reservoir of peasants that might be mobilized as capitalism develops, either to fascist ends or in a communist movement. The United States never had a "peasant problem," while in England the peasantry was drastically reduced in numbers. The considerable size of the peasantry was an important reason for the instability of democracy in France during the nineteenth and twentieth centuries.

The final condition is that a revolutionary break with the past should occur. In this context, Moore points to the English Civil War, the French Revolution, and the American Civil War as vital components of democratic development. Without such a break, democratic tendencies will not become strongly entrenched. Only when such radical changes are combined with the conditions previously discussed will democracy result. Under other conditions, such as those in Russia and China, communist systems may triumph.

Moore was reluctant to generalize from these conditions to evaluate the fate of contemporary societies because he was sensitive to the fact that the early development of some societies necessarily changes the circumstances encountered by others. Nevertheless, his analysis remains a significant achievement.

Skocpol's Theory of Social Revolutions

Theda Skocpol also stresses the importance of **social revolutions**, which she defines as "rapid, basic transformations of a society's state and class structures" (1979: 4). Her theory is based on an examination of the French, Russian, and Chinese revolutions, with additional reference to Germany, Japan, and England. Skocpol treats states as key parts of the **social structure** that contribute to bringing about social change. She also stresses a society's international environment far more than Moore, arguing that modern social revolutions occur only in countries situated in disadvantaged positions in the international arena. This international context is increasingly important.

Like Moore, Skocpol places great weight on the actions of the peasantry. She demonstrates that France,

Russia, and China were each characterized by conditions favourable to both political crisis and peasant revolt. For instance, Russia before 1917 was a bureaucratic, absolutist state dominated by the czar, who claimed to rule by divine right. Its nobility was politically weak, its agriculture backward. Conflicts with other societies placed Russia under pressure by showing up its military and economic weakness. Despite the land reforms of the nineteenth and twentieth centuries that eliminated feudalism, rents and redemption payments continued to impoverish the peasants. However, through their close-knit village communities, they could be mobilized against the existing order. Peasant revolts against private landed property contributed to the defeat of the state in 1917 and helped bring the Bolsheviks to power. Internal pressure alone could not bring down the czarist state, which stumbled into its final crisis as a result of military defeats during World War I. Wisely, Skocpol does not conclude her analysis with the rise to power of a new regime but recognizes that the process of revolutionary state-building can last for decades. In her three cases, it was encouraged by popular mobilization against counter-revolutionaries and foreign powers. The outcome was states that were larger, more centralized, more bureaucratic, and more concerned to mobilize the masses than the ones they replaced.

Despite the majestic sweep of Skocpol's analysis and the range of evidence mustered in support, she leaves room for argument and extension. First, the differences in both the origin and the outcome of the three main cases are considerable. It is necessary to recognize, for example, that the success of the Chinese Communists depended on their mobilization of the peasantry, whereas the Bolsheviks had no significant rural organization. Indeed, Skocpol pays too little attention to the urban, industrial roots of the Russian Revolution. Furthermore, general theories of nation-building are difficult to square with the historically specific factors that condition each case. Finally, Skocpol almost wholly neglects the role of creative human action because of her emphasis on the general structural conditions of change.

Modern State Institutions

The structure of states varies in the degree to which power is centralized, civil rights are equally distributed, opposition is permitted, and military forces are subject to civilian control—key dimensions for the analysis of state political institutions. The forms of the state are usefully summarized as *authoritarian*, *totalitarian*, and *liberal-democratic*. Since the nineteenth century, the importance of the idea of nationhood to many cultures means that a society within the territorial boundaries of a state is often referred to as a *nation-state*, even though state and national boundaries rarely coincide perfectly. We shall see that attempts to establish truly national states have often generated severe conflict in the last 50 years.

Authoritarian States

In authoritarian states, public opposition is forbidden and the population as a whole is under great pressure to accept and comply with the expectations of political leaders. At a minimum, authoritarian leaders insist on compliance in all public life and depend on control of military force to maintain their positions if challenged.

Absolutist monarchies, which combine tradition and force to control the population, were common in pre-industrial societies in which the labour of ordinary people supported an elite. Although this type of state became rare in the late twentieth century, one example was the regime of the shah of Iran prior to that country's Islamic revolution of 1979. Some contemporary states, such as Saudi Arabia, come close to this model.

Military dictatorships have frequently taken power in Asian, African, and Latin American countries following their independence from colonial rule. Usually these seizures are claimed to be temporary measures until corruption or ethnic conflicts can be solved. Nigeria, Haiti, Myanmar, and Argentina are among many examples. Military regimes lack popular legitimacy and may be short lived. At times, experimental democratic regimes and military dictatorships replace each other in a cyclical pattern.

Totalitarian States

Totalitarianism is more extreme than authoritarianism because it involves intervening in and controlling all aspects of both public and private life. It demands cultural homogeneity in every important respect. Nazi Germany is considered an exemplar of totalitarianism in which the Nazi Party (the National Socialist German Workers' Party) mobilized cultural institutions (mass media, schools, religion) to promote its ideals and eliminated any opposition through imprisonment and genocide of the Jewish people and others. Such states usually function in alliance with established classes and corporations, although the rhetoric of their leaders may be populist; for example, they may appeal to the anger of ordinary people, who may be suffering economic pain or political humiliation, by selecting visible minorities as targets for extremist action. Hitler brought the Nazi Party to power by appealing to nationalists who felt humiliated by the country's defeat in World War I and to middle-class Germans who felt threatened by the economic problems that followed the war and culminated in the Depression of the 1930s. Nazis also appealed to workers, but with less success. Once in power, a compromise with big business was soon worked out and the assault on liberty accelerated.

Socialist states, of which the former Soviet Union is the prime example, are totalitarian but ideologically quite different from those already discussed in that they are committed to a revolutionary transformation of capitalism (hence the rationalization for controlling all political, cultural, and economic institutions without permitting open dissent) in order to break the old order and bring a new socialist society to life. In the Soviet Union, most productive property was collectively owned, but control was centralized in the bureaucracy of the Communist Party rather than dispersed among collectives or workers.

In practice, totalitarian homogeneity never existed in the Soviet Union. Although the Soviet state was highly centralized, it was not a monolithic entity that excluded all debate and dispute. Even in the years before Mikhail Gorbachev's leadership (1985–91), interest groups and factions struggled for control within the Communist Party. There was, for example, long-standing competition between advocates of a more decentralized economic system and those who believed that modern information-processing technologies could permit centralized planning to a high degree, even in a complex industrial economy. Until the 1980s, the latter position dominated, but the rise of Mikhail Gorbachev and his commitment to a more decentralized structure—to the reform of state socialism from within—changed the balance, with serious consequences for the whole system.

Liberal-Democratic States

Literally, *democracy* means rule by the people, but who is to count as the people and how ruling takes place can vary enormously. *Direct democracy*, in which all citizens discuss and vote on all issues of importance to them, can function effectively only in small settings such as utopian communities or the classical Greek city-states. That said, liberal-democratic states are characterized by institutions that allow representation of the views of ordinary citizens through political parties that compete for the power to govern. These states may be *constitutional monarchies*, like Norway and Canada, in which the head of state is a hereditary position, or *republics*, like France and the United States, in which the head of state is elected.

At the heart of democracies are their election practices. These electoral institutions are quite varied. Some create legislatures by electing members from small areas (*constituencies*) within the state. In a sense, such societies (such as the United Kingdom and Canada) conduct a set of mini-elections all at the same time. Other democracies count votes for the whole society and candidates are elected from a party list in proportion to the party's share of the total votes cast. These *proportional representation* systems are found in many countries, including Israel and Italy.

The rapid spread of democracy has been one of the world's great dramas over the last 50 years. As Table 12.1 indicates, democratization proceeded rapidly in the twentieth century. In 1900, no society qualified as fully democratic because the first democracies of Europe, North America, Australia, and New Zealand restricted voting rights to men. After 1945, many societies emerged from colonial rule, sometimes to continuous democratic politics (like India), sometimes to unstable democracies with periods of military rule (like Nigeria). In addition, many Latin American states formally established in the nineteenth century did not transform effectively to democratic institutions until the latter part of the twentieth century. Although China continues to try to maintain authoritarian central control in political life while opening the economy to market rules, it has proven exceptionally difficult to restrict individual freedom to the market place in socialist societies.

After 1989, the spread of democracy accelerated for several years with the dramatic appearance of fledgling democratic political institutions when the Soviet Union and its East European allies collapsed. Following 70 years of control, once popular sentiments, unconvinced by decades of persuasion, were unleashed, communist institutions were swept away. Although few commentators foresaw the end of the

Table 12.1 **Political Development, States and Colonies, 1900–2000**

	1900	1950	2000
Democracy[a]	120 (62.5%)	22 (14.3%)	0
Restricted democratic practice[a]	16 (8.3%)	21 (13.6%)	25 (19.2%)
Constitutional monarchy	0	9 (5.8%)	19 (14.6%)
Traditional monarchy	10 (5.2%)	4 (2.6%)	6 (4.6%)
Absolute monarchy	0	2 (1.3%)	5 (3.8%)
Authoritarian regime	39 (20.3%)	10 (6.5%)	0
Totalitarian regime	5 (2.6%)	12 (7.8%)	0
Colonial dependency	0	43 (27.9%)	55 (42.3%)
Protectorate	2 (1.0%)	31 (20.1%)	20 (15.4%)
Total	**192**	**154**	**130**

[a] Freedom House defines democracies as competitive party systems in which "opposition parties have a legitimate chance of attaining power or participating in power," whereas restricted democratic practices are systems that preclude "meaningful challenge" to ruling parties.

SOURCE: Freedom House, Democracy's Century report, 1999, <www.freedomhouse.org>, accessed 16 July 2003. Reprinted by permission of Freedom House.

USSR until it was practically upon us, with hindsight it is possible to suggest plausible factors leading to its collapse. Perhaps the most significant of these are the internal contradiction of state socialism and the lack of legitimacy. The contradiction lay between the need to raise productivity and living standards, which increasingly required more individual initiative and "company" autonomy in some kind of market system, and the need to maintain central control of the social structure (Sinclair, 1982). A system created on the basis of bureaucratic control and centralized planning could not easily be reconciled with the decentralization required by effective local initiatives. Openness and criticism could not be contained once genuinely released. The second factor, lack of legitimacy, had to do with popular frustration resulting from inadequate material living conditions in comparison with the advanced capitalist societies, resentment against authoritarian rule, and the suppression of ethnic and religious cultural identities. In the case of the nations of Eastern Europe, hostility toward the USSR as a colonizing power was an additional factor.

By 1989, it was clear that Gorbachev would not maintain Soviet influence in Eastern Europe by force, and populist democratic pressures in all the satellite nations swept the old Communist parties from power. In the Soviet Union itself, both reformers, who felt that change was too limited, and old socialists, who feared loss of power and, perhaps genuinely, the harshness of the free market system, challenged Gorbachev's power. In 1991, Boris Yeltsin spearheaded popular resistance to old-style socialists who had attempted to unseat Gorbachev, but these victorious radicals then deprived Gorbachev of effective power. The old USSR was dead. In its place are Russia, Ukraine, and other republics in which somewhat fragile democratic institutions have been established and a capitalist economic structure is emerging.

Perspectives on the Democratic State

Sociologists have attempted to explain the politics of the modern state by analyzing the connection between political institutions and the **social groups** of which society is composed. Sociological theories of the state revolve around the question of whose interests are represented in institutions and actual policies. (See Table 12.2 for summary statements.) Do all these approaches provide part of the answer, or does the evidence fit some better than others?

Old Foes

The Ruling Elite

Until the 1970s, the chief contending perspectives stressed either elite domination or pluralism. The

Table 12.2 **Key Features of Perspectives on Liberal-Democratic States**

	Social Bias of the State	Basis of Political Power	Possibility of Major Change
Power/Ruling elite	Captive of the elite: leading members of state, military, and especially economic elite	Common socialization process and control of key political resources	Highly unlikely because the mass public lacks effective organization
Pluralism/Elite competition	Neutral arena for debate: wide range of interest groups and public as a whole benefit	Success in persuading electorates in open competition plus interest group mobilization	Normal rotation of parties and effective interest groups; no structural change
Neo-Marxism	Serves the capitalist class and, to a lesser extent, the service class	Control of wealth and, indirectly, of the political elite	Unlikely but occasionally possible through revolutionary class action
Autonomous state	State elite and more powerful interest groups	Control of means of force, taxation, and votes	Possible if balance of resources shifts among key social groups
Feminism	Reflect male values and organizations; state helps maintain patriarchy	Male control of institutional patterns; limited participation by women	Unlikely without radical transformation of gender attitudes

"ruling elite" approach pointed to a small clique that effectively dominated political decisions on all matters that were central interests of its members. C. Wright Mills argued for the existence of a power elite at the national level in the United States— "those political, economic and military circles which as an intricate set of overlapping cliques share decisions having at least national consequences" (1956: 18). This power elite was not a fixed group whose members, in conspiratorial fashion, made all decisions; rather, it was composed of people who knew each other, shared an upper-class background, and consulted each other on issues of fundamental importance to society. Other researchers identified elites that effectively controlled decision making at the local level (Hunter, 1953). Thus, the vision of elite domination encompassed all levels of the state.

Mills believed that the corporate elite was the most powerful segment of the power elite. Closer to Marx's concept of the ruling class is William Domhoff (1990), who believes that the corporate wealthy (about 1 per cent of the US population) are able to limit government to actions that serve the interests of the capitalist class. Similarly, Wallace Clement (1975) describes at length a ruling class in Canada intimately interconnected at the highest levels of corporate

power and between private boardrooms and the national government.

The image of the state implicit in "ruling elite" theory is one that puts little emphasis on administration. Instead, it focuses on policy, which is linked to the interests of those who hold key institutional positions. In all cases, this theory agrees that the interests of ordinary people are ignored whenever they might clash with those of the elite. Without explicitly writing about the state, these theorists create a vision of the state as necessarily anti-democratic. The state becomes nothing more than a means of domination, even when policy is couched in formally democratic procedures.

Pluralism and Elite Competition

Mills and his followers wrote partly in criticism of pluralism, whose advocates presented a benign view of American democracy as a forum in which any person or group had a fair chance of being represented. In turn, they themselves were attacked by those identifying a pluralist structure in US politics. Robert Dahl (1961), for example, cautioned that Mills had merely pointed out a group with high potential for control but had failed to demonstrate that this group actually dominated decision making. Furthermore,

Dahl insisted that only issues on which a clear difference of position could be observed in public debate ought to be considered. He also adopted the restrictive view that power is not exercised in situations where people are persuaded by others to adopt their attitudes. Dahl's own research, particularly in the city of New Haven, Connecticut, led him to conclude that democracy was alive and well in the America of the 1950s.

The pluralist approach recognizes that modern states all have intermediate organizations between government and the people—namely, parties and interest or lobby groups, which represent those with particular issues to promote in the state. Interest groups attempt to influence parties but rarely offer their own candidates for election because their objectives are limited to particular issues. Pluralists claim that no one interest is able to dominate the state and that democracy is protected by the competition between interests. Political leaders will be swayed by mass opinions because of their desire to win elections.

Evaluation

If pluralism is correct, the more disadvantaged groups in society (workers, women, minorities, and the poor) will not consistently lose to other groups. The pluralist position is justified to the extent that these groups sometimes achieve their objectives. Rights to organize and strike, extension of the franchise to women, equal-pay legislation, medicare, language legislation, land claims agreements with Aboriginal peoples, unemployment insurance, and welfare state payments are among the most important state actions that point to an element of pluralism in the Canadian system. This system might be viewed as one of elite competition for popular support. However, these policies could also be interpreted as elite concessions, implemented because they were socially and politically expedient. Clearly, an extreme ruling elite perspective is unwarranted, but so is the uncritical image of a political system functioning without bias.

A fundamental problem for the pluralist perspective is that men and elites dominate political parties, the key groups in the political system. Of course, there is no assured link between social background and political views. As A. Paul Williams (1989) shows in his study of Canada's political elite, a person's social background is no guarantee that he or she will understand or support the interests typical of that group. Nevertheless, it is a disadvantage for any group to have to rely on the sympathetic perceptions of

others. In research in the 1980s, Neil Guppy, Sabrina Freeman, and Shari Buchan (1987) found that the New Democratic Party (NDP) elected more people from lower-status groups than the other parties but that the middle class still predominated.

As Figure 12.1 reveals, representation in Parliament shows a strong class bias that has persisted throughout Canada's history. White-collar workers in routine jobs (clerical and sales) and blue-collar workers, the majority of the population in the twentieth century, have always been severely underrepresented, whereas business and middle-class professionals have dominated all parliaments. The increasing proportion of people from business and administration reflects the growing significance of corporate managers. Recently, the number of lawyers in office has

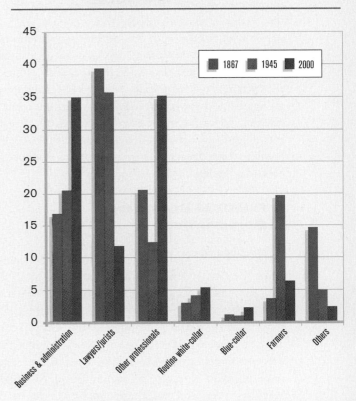

Figure 12.1 **Occupations of Members of Parliament, Canada, 1867, 1945, and 2000 (Percentage of Total Membership)**

SOURCE: Calculated from Senators and Members, Historical Information, Library of Parliament, Information and Documentation Branch; available at <www.parl.gc.ca/information/about/people/House/mpshist.asp?lang=E&param=nm&id=A>, accessed 16 July 2003.

declined sharply while that of other professional groups, mainly educators and social scientists, has increased.

The extent to which Canada's tiny capitalist class occupies the pinnacles of state power has also been the subject of considerable research by such sociologists as John Porter (1965), Clement (1975), Denis Olsen (1980), and John Fox and Michael Ornstein (1986), although much of this work is now dated. During the nineteenth century, the wealthy were often directly represented in the state apparatus; in the late twentieth century, this became less common, but connections were still close.

For 1946–77, Fox and Ornstein (1986) investigated the convergence between those in leading state positions and those sitting on the boards of Canada's largest corporations. At the federal level, they examined the Cabinet, deputy ministers, major Crown corporations, the Senate, senior courts, and the governor general; at the provincial level, cabinets, deputy ministers, major Crown corporations, and lieutenant governors. In addition, they looked at the 20 largest universities and the 15 largest hospitals. They found that, "overall, more than 3300 ties connect the 148 state organizations and 302 private organizations" (1986: 489–90). Manufacturing and finance firms were especially well connected to the federal cabinet, the Senate, and the state bureaucracy. Provincial governments were much less likely than the federal government to be linked to corporations. Moreover, the degree of convergence increased substantially over the three decades. The weight of this evidence is behind a "ruling elite" position.

Political Economy Perspectives

Neo-Marxism

Since the late 1960s, political economy perspectives have dominated discussions about the state, which is seen as the core of the political system. For the most part, modern thinkers abandoned the old Marxist view, associated with Vladimir Ilyich Lenin, that the state was merely the instrument of capital designed to solve periodic problems of accumulation. Although they have disputed the degree to which the state should be seen as the captive of capital, neo-Marxists usually consider the state to be structured or even programmed so that it acts in the long-term interests of capitalists as a class. Consequently, these authors de-emphasize the evidence that workers appear not to be against capitalism, and see reformist labour or social democratic parties as fulfilling a need for capitalism to make concessions in order to maintain legitimacy and continuity. Similar to ruling elite theory, the liberal-democratic processes are thought to function at a secondary level in the power structure.

Nicos Poulantzas (1978) developed the neo-Marxist perspective most fully, arguing that the state must be relatively autonomous from class conflict in the production process if it is to serve the needs of the dominant class. Here, *autonomy* does not mean independence from class control, but rather that the state is not directly representing dominant class interests. The key role of the state is to attain cohesion by "individualizing" the workers—that is, by contributing to their sense of **identity** as individuals and as part of a nation rather than as members of a class. Legal and ideological structures resting on claims of equality among citizens conceal from workers the fact that they are engaged in class relations. To achieve this outcome, the state may act to protect certain economic interests of the dominated classes, but it never challenges the political power of the dominant class. The state may have to resist certain short-term demands of capitalists (for example, reduced taxes and reduced public spending) to meet the long-term needs of capitalism as a whole (for example, maintaining an appropriately educated labour force). From this perspective, the expansion of public welfare against capitalist opposition is interpreted as a move to shore up the future of capitalism by smoothing over some of the discontent engendered by unemployment, poor health care, and unequal access to education.

The Partially Autonomous State

Skocpol (1979) and Fred Block (1980), among others, put forward another theory of the state. These theorists claim a genuinely independent source of power for state officials based on the resources of the state that these officials control. This position challenges Marxist theory by claiming, first, that the continuation of capitalism is not necessary; second, that other forms of state or institutional action might meet the "needs" of capitalism; and, third, that much state action is opposed by those for whom it is thought to be essential.

Block's answer to the key question of why state managers should act in the interests of capitalism is that they need capitalists to continue investing, or the state will lose income and political legitimacy.

Nevertheless, state intervention often takes a form opposed by capital, because the state is forced to respond to working-class political pressure and because state managers have an interest in expanding their sphere of influence. Depending on the relative flow of power among these groups, state policies can be expected to oscillate. In this model, the state becomes a third effective force, although it is tied to the perpetuation of capitalist interests.

In a more radical version of this thesis, Skocpol argues persuasively that the state should be recognized as a "structure with a logic and interests of its own not necessarily equivalent to, or fused with the interests of the dominant class in society or the full set of member groups in the polity" (1979: 27). Here we are directed to the interests of state actors themselves, as well as to the process of policy formation, to explain the policy that is actually produced. Skocpol does acknowledge that the state often protects dominant class interests, but not in all circumstances—in particular, not when such protection would threaten political stability. Hence, according to Skocpol, "the state's own fundamental interest in maintaining sheer physical order and political peace may lead it—especially in periods of crisis—to enforce concessions to subordinate class demands" (1979: 30). Skocpol charges neo-Marxists with a failure to accord sufficient independence to state and party and with an unjustified insistence that the state must work toward the reproduction of capitalism. Without accepting the idea that politics is a free-for-all competition among equals, this position goes some way toward the pluralist interpretation by recognizing that the capitalist class is not consistently dominant.

Evaluation

As indicated earlier, Canadian data show that the links between capital and the state are substantial—certainly substantial enough to permit direct input of capitalist interests into the state arena. Fox and Ornstein conclude, however, that "the data demonstrate nothing like a fusion of state and capital" (1986: 502). Thus, a simplistic view of the state as the instrument of capital will not hold true. Power can, of course, be exercised indirectly when interest groups lobby government and appeal to popular opinion. For example, David Langille (1987) claims that the most powerful corporate group, the Business Council on National Interests, was the effective architect of Canada's free trade policy, while Jack Richardson (1992) demonstrates how this policy fits squarely with the interests of finance capital.

What are the implications for state policy and practice? On the basis of their exhaustive study of Canadian industrial policy, Michael Atkinson and William Coleman (1989) claim that Canada, unlike societies such as France, has not developed a tradition of strong state intervention. They suggest that Canadian business and political elites share critical values on such matters as minimizing state intervention, that industrial policy is largely consistent with business interests, and that the organization of political representation tends to render agrarian and labour interests ineffective. This is not to deny considerable variation, particularly by industrial sector. Peter Sinclair's research on fisheries policy (1987) shows, for example, that the interests of small inshore fishermen in Atlantic Canada have been partly protected by a state that both limited the access of corporate fishing companies to critical stocks and provided subsidies or income support to small operators.

The state elite is not a mere tool of capital. One reason for the independence of the state elite is that capitalists seldom present a united front on specific policies; another is that the state controls such key resources for independent action as legal authority, lawful force, and information. The elite accommodates deprived groups to some degree in order to guarantee the legitimacy and stability of the political structure in which their own careers are located. That said, it is also true that the ideological compatibility between the state elite and Canadian capitalists, together with the complementarity of their interest in maintaining the social structure from which they benefit, works to inhibit radical institutional change. Thirty years ago, Robert Presthus argued that the unequal distribution of political resources permits those with a vested interest in the status quo to enjoy more meaningful and successful political participation. His crisp conclusion remains valid: "The perhaps inevitable inequalities of political resources among interest groups mean that government, to some extent, is pushed into the anomalous position of defending the strong against the weak" (1973: 349).

Feminist Perspectives

Most theories of the state focus on class issues to the exclusion of **gender** and **ethnicity**. By contrast, feminist theory makes gender a central component in the analysis of politics and the state, as it does for social life generally. Specifically, the **feminist perspective** has brought attention to the state as a contributor to the subordination of women and as an institution permeated by gender inequality. However, there is no single feminist position. Judith Allen (1990), for example, has even asserted that feminists have no need for a theory of the state because the concept of the state is too vague and unitary to be applicable to women's political strategies, which must focus on specific local conditions or "sites."

Nonetheless, other feminists have considered state theory important. In a critical influential paper, Mary McIntosh (1978) argues that the state supports a system in which men control women in the household, where they work without pay to maintain capitalism's labour force, and from which they can be drawn as needed to supply cheap labour. Referring mainly to the United Kingdom, McIntosh reviews the ways in which the state indirectly subordinates women by staying out of certain areas such as family life, which are left to the control of men, and through legislation, such as husbands' tax allowance, which privileges employed, married men. In a sense, McIntosh contends, women are hidden in the family or household to serve the needs of men and capitalism.

Jill Quadagno claims, with justification, that the explanation of the development of the welfare state has emphasized class analysis, while ignoring the welfare state's "organization around gender" (1990: 14). Feminist theorists often claim that welfare programs maintain male dominance insofar as their rules of eligibility favour male breadwinners. Women are more often subject to means tests for social assistance programs, whereas men are more likely to qualify for universal entitlement programs. However, Quadagno notes that some social programs could advance women's interests by reducing their dependence on men. But the development of "gender-equal policies" requires women to become mobilized as effective political actors. The latter point is effectively supported by Quadagno's analysis of the defeat of the US Family Assistance Plan in 1972. Had it been implemented, this program would have improved the economic position of both women and blacks in the southern states.

Quadagno's view is consistent with the work of Varda Burstyn (1983), a Canadian feminist, who also identifies the state as acting to maintain domination both by capitalism and by men. Burstyn explains the gender-biased actions of the state largely by the massive extent to which men occupy higher-level state positions. The most extreme bias in the state's structure is the inadequate representation of women.

Canadian women did not achieve federal voting rights until 1918—in Quebec, not until 1940. The 65 women elected between 1921 and 1984 amount to 0.8 per cent of all elected members of the House of Commons (Brodie, 1985: 2–4). Since then, the situation has improved, with women constituting 21.1 per cent of MPs in 2002 (Library of Parliament, 2002), the same as their share of Cabinet positions. Still, Sylvia Bashevkin's generalization that the more powerful the position, the fewer the women (1985) remains apt for both party and state. Only one woman has been prime minister—Kim Campbell, for several months in 1993 until her Conservative government was defeated.

Does representation matter? While there is no reason to expect women to hold different views than men on many issues, it is more likely that the interests of women would be effectively represented if they were present in decision-making positions. Manon Tremblay's analysis of women in Parliament in the mid-1990s (Tremblay, 1998) gives some support to this position. Although women's issues (women's rights and traditional areas of women's involvement, such as elder care) were marginal in House activities, when discussion did take place women were more involved than men. MPs who were women gave greater importance than did men to women's issues; they were more likely to report interest in these matters and to feel that they should be given priority. Yet differences were moderate. Regardless of whether or not women would be better protected by greater political participation, their absence from positions of power is unacceptable, since it seems to rest purely on the ascriptive criterion of gender.

The position of Canadian women in politics is intermediate when compared with other societies, as Table 12.3 demonstrates. In the Scandinavian countries and the Netherlands, women fare much better, holding over 35 per cent of electoral seats in 2003, while the United States, with 14 per cent, did not rank in the top 50. Women have also made substantial advances since the 1980s in holding executive positions. As of December 1990, women headed just 6 of the United Nation's 159 member states, while in 93 countries women held no ministerial positions (United Nations, 1990: 31). Since then, it has been much more common to find a woman holding the highest office. Thus, between 1990 and 2000, 36 women were elected as heads of state (Lewis, 2002). In European Union countries, women held an average of 24.6 per cent of Cabinet positions in 2001, with parity actually achieved in Sweden (FCZB, 2001).

Table 12.3 **Women as Percentage of Legislatures, Most Recent Election, Regions and Selected Countries, Ranked by Lower House Representation**

	Lower or Combined House	Upper House
Countries		
1 Sweden	45.3	–
2 Denmark	38.0	–
3 Finland	37.5	–
4 Netherlands	36.7	26.7
5 Norway	36.4	–
6 Cuba	36.0	–
7 Belgium	35.3	–
8 Costa Rica	35.1	–
9 Austria	33.9	21.0
10 Germany	32.2	33.3
36 Canada	20.6	32.4
59 United States	14.3	13.0
Regions		
1 Nordic countries	39.7	–
2 Americas	17.7	17.2
3 Europe: OSCE[a] members including Nordic countries	17.7	14.5
4 Europe: OSCE members excluding Nordic countries	15.6	14.5
5 Asia	15.4	13.8
6 Sub-Saharan Africa	14.1	15.6
7 Pacific	12.1	25.9
8 Arab states	5.9	3.6

[a] Organization for Security and Co-operation in Europe.
SOURCE: Inter-parliamentary Union, *Women in National Parliaments*; data available at <www.ipu.org/wmn.e/classif.htm>.

Women are dismantling the bastions of male political dominance, but the process is slow and depends on reorienting attitudes toward gender roles. The **socialization** process must change before this form of discrimination will disappear. Although some men are sensitive to women's issues, male-controlled legislatures in Canada and elsewhere have been slow to act on many matters of importance to women. Can it be purely coincidental that women are primarily responsible for child care prior to school but that the state provides inadequate assistance for mothers who wish to be employed? As of 2003, there was still no national daycare policy. Publicly funded daycare facilities do not meet the demand. Furthermore, child care workers are unable to earn the professional salaries that would justify the necessary training and commitment. In the labour market generally, part-time workers are disproportionately women and receive inferior job protection. Legislation that would end pay discrimination in the private sector based on

gender has been slow to arrive and is difficult to enforce. These are only a few examples of the gender-related problems that remain to be solved in Canada and most other societies.

Democracy and Politics in Canada

Party Politics

A **political party** is an organization dedicated to winning political power by controlling government. In liberal democracies, this means winning a general election. Canada is a federation with a complex structure in which the powers of legislation are divided between federal and provincial governments. The organization of parties mirrors this institutional arrangement, and securing as much electoral support as possible within this structure is the key to their success.

At the federal level, only the Liberal and Progressive Conservative parties have ever governed, and the Liberal Party has been dominant. This is evident in Figure 12.2, which shows party support since the 1949 election. Until the 1990s, these two parties competed with each other for control of the state by following a brokerage strategy in which the parties would attempt to appeal to diverse social groups in order to establish a winning combination. Usually, this meant avoiding controversial ideological issues and adopting broadly similar positions on major issues. An exception was the 1988 election campaign in which the Conservatives championed free trade and claimed victory after a bitter struggle.

The Co-operative Commonwealth Federation (CCF) and its successor, the NDP, have taken positions similar to European labour and social democratic parties but have never succeeded at the federal level in gaining Ontario-based support outside several industrial or peripheral areas. In Quebec, the CCF/NDP has completely failed to establish itself. With this weak performance in the most populated provinces, the CCF/NDP has been unable to exceed 20 per cent of the vote after more than 50 years of campaigning. Since 1988, the party has fallen in popularity to under 10 per cent as the rise of neo-conservatism pushed some NDP voters to prop up the Liberal centre. The NDP has consistently failed to translate its support in provincial elections into equivalent federal votes, with the exceptions of Saskatchewan, Manitoba, and BC. This may be due to a perception that the provincial NDP governments, especially in Ontario, could not enact sufficient legislation to favour the interests to which the party has appeared committed (workers, the poor, minorities, and women). Also, the party's more popular policies, such

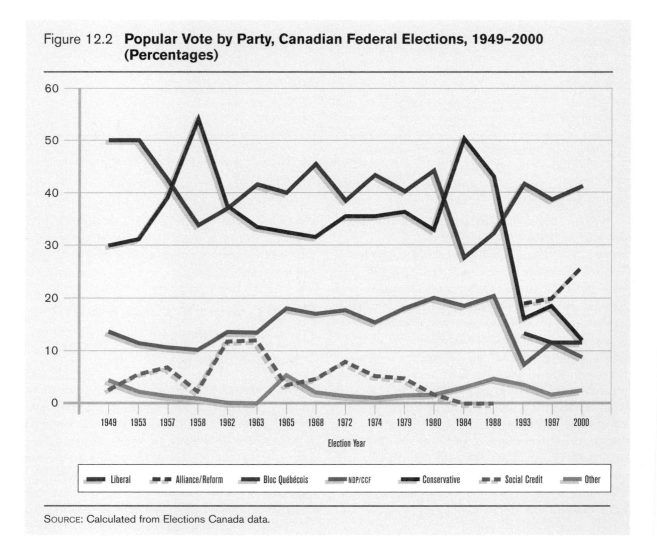

Figure 12.2 **Popular Vote by Party, Canadian Federal Elections, 1949–2000 (Percentages)**

SOURCE: Calculated from Elections Canada data.

as medicare and subsequent support for public health systems, were adopted by the mainstream parties when it was expedient to do so.

In the 1990s, several important new parties emerged in federal politics. The Bloc Québécois, paradoxically, has represented separatist voters in the national parliament since 1993, but this party, like the provincial Parti Québécois, is social democratic as well as nationalist. That makes it quite different from the other newcomer to federal politics, the Canadian Alliance, which began its existence as the Reform Party. The Alliance is a socially conservative, populist party that emerged from Alberta and spread eastward with decreasing success after Manitoba except for pockets of support in Ontario and the Maritimes. It has fared well in British Columbia. The populist dimension is reflected in the party's formal commitment to direct democracy and members' control of the organization, although this has seldom been evident in practice, despite sharp attacks on the elitist practices of established parties. The Alliance found core support among Canadians who want lower taxes, reduced public spending, a smaller state presence in their lives, a more punitive approach to crime control, curtailment of abortion rights, and more restrictive immigration policies. This Canadian version of the New Right agenda climbed to 25 per cent of popular support in the election of 2000, but the party lost favour as a result of a bitter internal struggle, ultimately successful in 2002, to remove Stockwell Day from the leadership. The chief casualty of the emergence of the Alliance has been the Progressive Conservative Party, whose support plummeted after 1988 to a level not much greater than that of the NDP. Its only hope of revival would be as the vehicle to unite the right, which seems plausible given the disarray of the more radical alternative.

The Electoral System

Canada's electoral system has several advantages. Citizens may be able to approach their local area's member of parliament (MP), although it would be impossible for everyone actually to do so. More important, this system usually produces a majority, and thus a stable government. But it clearly makes some people's votes more influential than others, depending on where they live, and often produces a parliament that does not reflect the wishes of the population as a whole.

Most people vote for the party rather than for the individual candidate. The electoral system, however, provides no assurance that the party receiving the most votes over the whole country will win the election. If two parties have roughly equal total support but one party has voters equally distributed and the other much more concentrated, the party with equal distribution will certainly win. In fact, it can win even if its total votes are fewer, as has happened several times in Canadian history. Thus, the majority does not necessarily elect the governing party. Indeed, in only 4 of the 17 elections between 1949 and 2000 did the governing party receive more than 50 per cent of all votes. Moreover, since it is rare for more than 75 per cent of those eligible to vote actually to cast a ballot, there has never been a Canadian government voted to office by a majority of citizens.

None of this makes Canada unusual. Rule by minorities occurs because more than two parties contest the elections, and the system of competition in constituencies spread across the country means that popular vote does not translate directly into representation in Parliament. In three elections (1957, 1962, and 1979), the Progressive Conservatives formed the government after having received fewer votes than the Liberals.

Figure 12.3 shows that in the election of 2000, the Liberal Party translated 40.8 per cent of the votes cast into 57.1 per cent of the seats. Getting more than 40 per cent is usually enough to assure success. Except for the Bloc Québécois, all the smaller parties received a higher percentage of the vote than seats. The Bloc's vote was highly concentrated in a few ridings, many of which it won. The other parties, especially the Progressive Conservatives, had moderate support widely scattered across constituencies with the consequence that they could win few seats. The Conservatives had greater popular support in Canada than the Bloc Québécois but won only 12 seats compared with the Bloc's 38. The constituency system often leaves supporters of minority parties with little or no representation. It is especially difficult for new parties to be successful in this system because they have difficulty translating their support into seats and political visibility. Thus, a party that obtains 10 per cent of the votes may not win a single seat unless those votes are concentrated in a few ridings. This discourages participation and makes it difficult for new parties to become established and considered as viable options by the electorate as a whole.

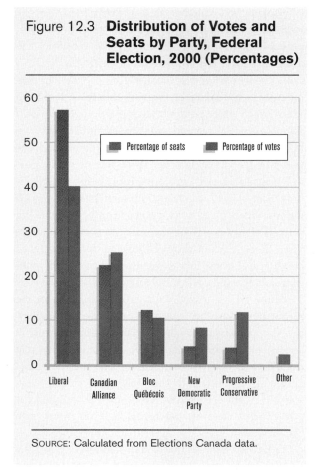

Figure 12.3   **Distribution of Votes and Seats by Party, Federal Election, 2000 (Percentages)**

SOURCE: Calculated from Elections Canada data.

Proportional representation is designed to avoid these problems. Had such a system functioned in Canada with the same voting distributions, the country would have had a minority or coalition government in 2000 and in 12 other elections from 1949 until then. Political compromises would have been necessary, but many societies achieve stable governments with election by proportional representation. Usually, a party must obtain a minimum of 5 per cent of electoral support in order to obtain any seats; this prevents excessive fragmentation of the legislature. Because the party that governs and benefits from the present system would have to support a change, it is extremely unlikely that Canadians will adopt a more representative system in the foreseeable future.

Political Participation

Participation in the political process varies from informal discussion, listening to media reports, and voting to more demanding activities such as attend-ing meetings, assisting with campaigns, contacting politicians in order to influence them, even running for office. For most Canadians, political participation is limited to discussion and voting for candidates to the various levels of government. However, it appears that the public is becoming increasingly cynical about politicians; turnout at elections is falling, with federal elections now attracting about 70 per cent of eligible voters.

Sociologists are interested in the social characteristics that may influence participation. However, a great deal of research has demonstrated that there is no necessary link between a person's social background and the party he or she supports. Harold Clarke's team (1991) examined the variables of class, gender, ethnicity, religion, region, community size, and age, and found that they all have some effect on Canadians' voting preferences, but much less than political variables such as prior voting record, concern about immediate issues, and the image of the party leader. Nonetheless, in 2000 the Liberal Party could not have won without the strong support outside Quebec of Catholics (54 per cent) and Canadians of non-European ethnicity (70 per cent; Gidengil et al., 2001: 28). Region was more critical than it had been in earlier elections, with the Alliance powerful west of Ontario (where Liberals were much weaker) but unable to break through in eastern Canada, where Conservatives and especially Liberals were stronger. Women supported the NDP much more than did men, whereas men were more drawn to the Alliance. Age and language were critical to voting in Quebec, where those under 55 and francophones were more likely to support the Bloc Québécois.

Class is not a defining force in contemporary Canadian politics, but economic issues and beliefs do influence the choices of many voters. Thus, outside Quebec, those who believed in giving increased priority to market forces were more attracted to the Alliance and Conservative parties in 2000, while those with the opposite view favoured Liberals and the NDP; social conservatives preferred the Alliance to the Conservative Party (Gidengil et al., 2001).

A crude theory in which voting behaviour inevitably follows from social experience is obviously untenable. A more useful sociological account, influenced by **symbolic interactionist** theory, starts from the assumption that voting is an interpretive action to which people carry assumptions from their prior experience, filtered through their social positions and possibly their previous commitments to a party. Usually they have incomplete information and incomplete understanding of how the political system operates. Typically, the strongest parties play down social issues and try to emphasize the quality of their leaders (or record in office) to cope with whatever problems exist. To achieve overall victory, care will be taken not to appear too closely linked to the interests of any particular group. In the end, voters make choices that respond only partially to social and cultural factors. Of course, for decades in Quebec, the priority of cultural concerns and the issue of independence has made political life more ideological and socially influenced. Nonetheless, voting does not really determine state policy—it provides legitimization for those who control it.

Neo-conservatism and Privatization

After decades of expansion of the welfare state and standards of living, many countries faced problems of inflation, lower economic growth, and budget deficits in the 1970s and 1980s. Continued demands for better public education and health care were incompatible with pressure to reduce taxes. Many states seemed to be suffering from or on the brink of what some called a "crisis of legitimation" (Habermas, 1975; Offe, 1984). With welfare state policies under severe stress, political space opened up for more conservative policies. These policies stressed eliminating public deficits by reducing expenditure, stimulating the economy by cutting taxes, and withdrawing the state

---

 12.3

Open for Discussion
Controversy over Health Care Reform

According to various polls, Canadians consider protection of the health care system to be a priority for public action. Nevertheless, a national poll in 2001 reported that 56.6 per cent were generally satisfied with the existing system and 81.7 per cent were content with services they had received in the previous five years. The main problems that respondents perceived were poor management, inadequate financing, and staff shortages. A majority believed the Canadian system to be superior to that of the United States and were against privatization of hospitals (Leger Marketing, 2001: 2–6).

Although problems are often recognized, many Canadians resist major changes that might affect universal access, especially a reduction in the services that are currently paid from state treasuries. Canadian health care is not, for the most part, socialized because most health care professionals work in private practice or for independent hospital boards. About 30 per cent of services are not covered by public medicare. Access to health services could be privatized by eliminating state payments so that patients would have to rely on their own resources or a private insurance plan.

The key issue here is whether or not social inequality would affect availability of health care if public services were reduced and access determined by capacity to pay the market rate for the service. Opponents clearly believe this to be the case and prefer other solutions to existing problems. In 2002, the Romanow Commission investigated alternatives prior to the federal government's announcing its plan of action. Preliminary evidence of public opinion on these options indicates that most prefer system reform with a focus on preventative medicine, but nearly half would be willing to accept more private-sector participation (Decima Research, 2002). By 2002, the most radical plan to date to alter the existing system was put forward by Ralph Klein's government in Alberta, which planned to contract out certain services from public hospitals to private clinics. By 1994–5, Alberta had already moved to allow physicians to bill the state for certain core services and to privately sell additional services to their patients. These plans have been bitterly attacked by those concerned about inequities in the emerging health care system.

from the economy by privatizing existing public enterprises and contracting to the private sector for services previously provided by public employees. Sometimes **privatization** sales have been legitimized as contributions to debt reduction. The promotion of "free" market forces and a smaller state is at the core of this new conservatism, which has found favour with many voters, especially those who would benefit from tax reductions and who have the capacity to purchase services for themselves.

In Canada, this trend has been evident not only in the rise of the Canadian Alliance, but also in practices of various provincial governments, especially Conservatives in Ontario (under Mike Harris) and Alberta (Ralph Klein) and Liberals in British Campbell (Gordon Campbell). However, all levels of government have participated to some degree. For example, the federal government sold Air Canada to the private sector, and most of PetroCanada, the highly successful national oil company, can now be purchased on the stock market. Airport security was subcontracted prior to the terrorist attacks of 11 September 2001. The privatization of basic public goods, such as power and water supply, is proving to be controversial: many people are concerned that prices will fall in the long term once supply is in corporate hands. Thus, the decision to sell Ontario Hydro in a mammoth public share offering proved difficult to implement in 2002 as citizen groups mobilized in opposition.

Certainly among the most critical issues is the reform and increased privatization of health care, which was on the political agenda for some years and subject of several investigations, most recently the Romanow Commission on the Future of Health Care in Canada, which reported in 2002. As of 2003, the federal government insisted that it would use its power to maintain standards across Canada, including universal access. Nevertheless, there have been signs of creeping privatization, especially in Alberta, and considerable dispute between the federal government and the more conservative provincial administrations. Canadians worry about what is happening to their health care system when they see so many publicized delays in accessing specialist services and when hospital emergency rooms are frequently overflowing. The 2003 SARS outbreak in Toronto again brought such concerns to the forefront as the hospital system appeared close to collapse. Several hospitals had to be diverted from their normal activities, and medical staff were required to function under dangerous and stressful conditions. Some are convinced that privatization or a two-tier system is necessary, while others prefer a reform of the existing system and the injection of the necessary funds to make it work properly.

Challenging Issues and Political Movements

Political movements are social movements that challenge established state policies and practices in order to bring about social and political changes. Their objectives can vary from moderate reform to radical overhaul of **social institutions**. Similarly, the means vary widely from conventional interest group or party activities to protests outside the existing political norms, including campaigns of violence. **Terrorism** occurs when physical violence is directed against civilians, without regard for who will suffer, in order to promote political objectives. This section reviews a critically important political movement in Canada: Quebec separatism, which has a complex history that includes both peaceful opposition and terrorism.

The Quebec Question: Maîtres chez nous?

It is difficult to create a cohesive nation-state in which a large minority speaks a different language and remains committed to continuing its different culture. To some extent, Canada's federal structure allows for these differences, but the movement for an independent Quebec has threatened to split Canada apart for 40 years.

In the 1950s, a new Quebec started to emerge from a society that had been church-dominated, elitist, and uncomfortable with urban industrial development. Quebec's Quiet Revolution accelerated in the 1960s as the francophone majority became better educated and determined to push ahead with a modern society that would be French-speaking (McRoberts, 1988). Hence the famous provincial Liberal campaign slogan of 1962: "*maîtres chez nous*"—"masters in our own house." Quebec became much more secular and urbanized, but many Québécois felt that more radical changes were necessary to ensure their survival as a distinct, francophone society surrounded by anglophones.

The moderate, federalist segment was led by Liberals, and it brought Pierre Trudeau into the political limelight in 1968 as the champion of an officially bilingual Canada, shortly after the government released the report of the Royal Commission on Bilingualism and Biculturalism (Canada, 1967). The key legislation was the Official Languages Act (1969), which was designed to ensure that public services would be available all over Canada in both languages. One by-product was that bilingualism became critical for higher-level positions in the civil service, which made it easier for Québécois to rise in the bureaucracy.

Although opposed by many anglophones, this accommodation to Quebec's cultural interests did not satisfy a growing force of nationalists who believed that the only solution was for Quebec to become sovereign, that is, to be politically independent and thus in charge of all its own institutions. The most extreme position was taken by a small group known as the FLQ (Front de Libération du Québec), which adopted terrorist means from 1963 to 1970 with a campaign of bombings culminating in the kidnapping of British diplomat James Cross and the murder of Pierre Laporte, Quebec's minister of labour.

Although the FLQ was crushed when Trudeau implemented the War Measures Act in 1970, the idea that Quebec required greater independence than was possible within Canada gained ground. Thus the Parti Québécois (PQ), dedicated to separatism and generally sympathetic to aspirations of the newly politicized working class, swelled from a minor movement in the late 1960s until it achieved power in 1976 under its charismatic leader, René Lévesque. The PQ moved quickly to introduce legislation that made French the only official language in Quebec and required the children of immigrants and of Canadians moving from other provinces to be educated in French. Anglophones and English business flowed out of the province, but 60 per cent of voters rejected sovereignty association in the divisive referendum of 1980.

Once more in office, Trudeau's response was to repatriate the Constitution complete with a new Charter of Rights and Freedoms that failed to win support in Quebec. Later, having promised to introduce changes satisfactory to Quebec, the new Conservative government promoted an agreement that increased Quebec's powers (including the right to opt out of federal legislation) and recognized that it was a distinct society. This agreement, the Meech Lake Accord (1987), was almost ratified by the legislatures of the country but collapsed in Manitoba when Elijah Harper's decisive vote went against it in frustration over the failure of Aboriginal peoples to achieve their similar objectives.

Jean Chrétien celebrates the twentieth anniversary of the Canadian Charter of Rights and Freedoms. (CP/Jonathan Hayward)

Clearly, further action was required, and the process of constitutional reform continued, with many public meetings culminating in the Charlottetown Accord, which included greater rights for both Quebec and Aboriginal peoples. However, a disenchanted public defeated the subsequent referendum in 1992. The rejection of the Charlottetown Accord prompted a strong showing by the separatist movement in the 1993 federal election.

The PQ returned to office in Quebec, and in 1995 held a second referendum in which its proposal for negotiated independence was defeated by the narrowest of margins—50.58 per cent to 49.42 per cent. At this time, some form of separation appeared almost inevitable, but subsequent years were bedevilled with economic and social problems for the government. Both the PQ and separatism in general lost their attraction as opponents made ground with claims that Quebec would suffer excessive economic damage as a separate state. Premier Jacques Parizeau also blamed the "ethnic" vote for the referendum defeat and quickly resigned amid tremendous furor. Lucien Bouchard, the popular leader of the federal Bloc Québécois, became the new PQ leader but resisted any attempt to call another referendum until winning conditions were present—not when the government was engaged in struggles with labour to reduce public spending and services. Discouraged by internal party conflict and especially signs of anti-Semitic views within the party, Bouchard resigned from the premiership. His more radical successor, Bernard Landry, failed to hold the movement's support. In 2002, its future looked shaky as previously invincible seats were lost in by-elections and polls showed little support for independence. Indeed, in 2003, the Liberals, under the leadership of Jean Charest, won a clear majority of seats based on 44.9 per cent of the popular vote. However, the underlying problems have not been resolved and a revival of separatism is certainly possible unless Canadians can find a way to accommodate the interests of Quebec inside Canada.

Loss of Legitimacy and Terrorist Opposition

When people believe that their opinions are unwanted and that they can never achieve their objectives by working through the political institutions of their society, established political life has no legitimacy for them. If their commitment is high, they may feel that they have no option but to try any means possible and that the means are justified by the failure of existing authorities. Indiscriminate violence directed against civilians is intended to pressure power holders to meet the objectives of terrorists and so avoid chaos for and harm to citizens. Perhaps most common are movements to promote independence of ethnic or nationalist groups. Well-known examples are the Irish Republican Army, Basque nationalists operating in Spain, Kashmiri independence groups, and the Tamils of Sri Lanka. Many parts of the world are unsafe, and many thousands die each year in violent conflicts, usually but not exclusively in less developed countries (see Figure 12.4). Canada has not been free of this problem, as we have seen in the previous section.

Colombia provides an example of this national or internal terrorism, which has changed its focus and lost popular support there after four decades of conflict and over 100,000 deaths. Perhaps because these deaths have occurred over a long time in small numbers per incident, Colombian violence has attracted less attention than its importance warrants, given the threat it poses to South America's oldest democracy.

The roots of crisis include a political system that had to cope with long-standing regional political struggles, from which emerged an elite compromise between liberals and conservatives that effectively eliminated the masses from political life. In a country that was difficult to unite physically and where local power holders could raise private armies, violence became a normal way of settling disputes. Leftist radicals, both socialist and populist, felt that there was no option in the 1960s but to start a guerrilla campaign against the state. However, in later years, some were reabsorbed into institutional politics, while others turned to the drug trade to finance ongoing struggle against paramilitary forces as well as the army. These paramilitaries sometimes allied with the state against the left, sometimes with drug barons against the state. By the 1990s, the former populist guerrillas had become indistinguishable in practice from drug criminals, and their political objectives seemed simply to achieve a resolution that would solidify their power and acquisition of wealth. Kidnappings, murders, bombings, and brutal attacks on state personnel continued even as peace negotiations were taking place spasmodically from 1999 to 2002. The guerrillas lost almost all their public sympathy, and President Andrés Pastrana was compelled to end negotiations in February 2002.

International terrorism differs only in its focus and visibility through the mass media. In the early twenty-first century, the most evident examples are Palestinian attempts to counter the superior military power of Israel and the radical Islamic militants who were behind the events of 11 September 2001. Suicide bombings and hijacking of airliners are difficult to understand for most people and extremely hard to prevent. Real danger exists that the level of control and surveillance of the affairs and movements of ordinary people in response to the desire to avoid terrorist attacks will endanger personal freedoms and change the nature of the society for the worse.

Figure 12.4 **Armed Conflicts in 2002**

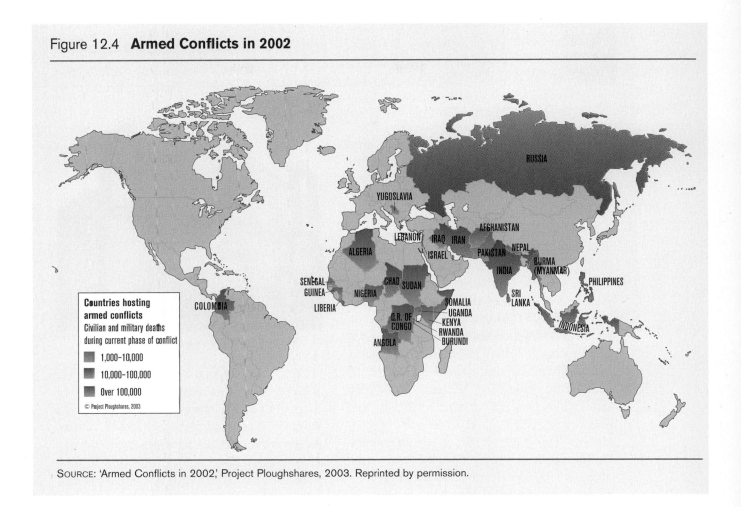

SOURCE: 'Armed Conflicts in 2002,' Project Ploughshares, 2003. Reprinted by permission.

Environmental Degradation: Coping with Climate Change

Since the 1960s, alarm bells have been ringing about the way economic activity has changed and degraded the environment. Non-renewable resources, such as fossil fuels and minerals, have been extracted at an increasing rate to power industrial economies. The pursuit of raw materials and the sprawl of asphalt have destroyed natural habitats. Renewable resources have been taken without, in many cases, the necessary management action to replenish them. Industrial production and consumption pollute the air, soil, and water. Among the most serious problems that have come to the forefront is a gradual warming of the earth's atmosphere, which most knowledgeable scientists trace to the greenhouse gas effect—carbon dioxide, methane, and nitrous oxide produced by industrialization. Conversely, forests, which absorb carbon dioxide from the atmosphere, have been seriously depleted.

The solution to the greenhouse gas problem requires international co-ordination to reduce emissions. Everyone will benefit, but costs will vary. This is a major problem that illustrates the continued power of the nation-state: compliance with any international agreement must be voluntary in the absence of any means of enforcement. By 1992, scientific concern about climate change had become so widespread that a Framework Convention on Climate Change was established in which the key strategy was to stabilize greenhouse gases at 1990 levels by the year 2000. Although 166 states, including Canada, had signed the agreement by February 2003, and another 22 had indicated their acceptance, most failed to come close to its objectives. The 1997 Kyoto Protocol provides more advanced objectives—specifically, that the developed societies would reduce their emissions to 5.2 per cent less than those prevailing in 1990. Canada was slated for a 6 per cent reduction (Bernstein and Gore, 2001).

12.4

Global Issues

Colombia: "Everybody Is Full of Terror"

Choco is Colombia's poorest province and a battleground for terrorist actions. In May 2002, 119 civilians, including many children, were killed in the little jungle town of Bellavista when a crude mortar exploded in the church where they were hiding to avoid conflict between paramilitary forces and the guerrilla group FARC (the Revolutionary Armed Forces of Colombia). FARC claimed that the civilian deaths were accidental, but this attack appears to have shaken any external political support that FARC had managed to retain up to that time. A few days later, President Pastrana and top officials visited the remote scene, which government troops failed to reach in time to intervene: "Awed by the evidence of the savage attack—empty storefronts, abandoned homes, war-battered buildings—nobody said a word as they walked down the rubble-filled streets in gloomy silence. 'Everybody is full of terror,' Emiliano Perera, mayor of nearby Vigía del Fuerte, said afterward" (*Miami Herald*, 19 May 2002).

Two main guerrilla groups, FARC and ELN (the National Liberation Army), as well as paramilitary forces that have operated in Colombia for decades, use terror and intimidation in order to establish their economic and political power. By 2002, their combined forces were estimated at 32,000, up from about 12,000 in 1990. Civil war has been no stranger in the history of this geographically splintered country, but the failure to peacefully resolve political disputes gradually turned into a struggle for power in which ideals of social justice played no role. The conflict claimed an estimated 3,500 lives in 2001 and at least 200,000 over its full history.

(© Frances Robles/The Miami Herald)

More than 30 years ago, groups of left-wing activists became so frustrated with what they considered as elite domination of politics to the exclusion, in practice, of the interests of ordinary people that they began guerrilla actions to bring about change. The inability of the army to suppress them led to the formation of equally violent private armies or paramilitaries, later joined into the United Self-Defence Force. By the 1980s, the main guerrilla groups had become involved in the drug trade in order to finance their activities in what had become a political stalemate with no negotiated end in sight. Colombia's other internal war was being waged against the drug cartels, whose leaders also used terrorism to try to influence state action. Whatever idealistic values promoted initial guerrilla tactics and brought some measure of support inside and outside Colombia evaporated as the revolutionary forces turned into opportunistic seekers of power and wealth (Wagner, 2002).

Citing his refusal to endanger the profits of US corporations, President George W. Bush stated, prior to the Bonn meeting on climate change in 2001, that the United States would not ratify the Kyoto Protocol: "The Kyoto treaty would severely damage the United States' economy, and I don't accept that. I accept the alternative we put out, that we can grow our economy and, at the same time, through technologies, improve our environment" (United States, White House, 2002). The president's statement was a reaction to a report prepared by the Environmental Protection Agency (EPA), which acknowledged that human action was responsible for global warming. A year later, the US government was still apparently resisting the scientific evidence by pressuring the EPA to change statements on climate change in its most recent report.

In December 2002, Canada finally agreed to support the Kyoto agreement despite the resistance of several provinces, spearheaded by Alberta, which feared the effect on oil and gas revenues and, more generally, that Canadian companies will be at a disadvantage until and unless the United States ratifies the treaty—all for a control program that will have little impact. Thus, "Alberta has warned that Canadian ratification of the Kyoto Accord could cost the economy up to $40 billion, drastically higher than estimates by the federal government" (CBC News, 2002). Since fossil fuels burned in the **developed countries** account for most greenhouse gases, it is no surprise that resistance should come from those who might experience economic contraction if severe measures are taken.

Despite the opposition of some governments and of industry, the environmental movement has been growing in Canada; citizens are concerned about global warming and doing their part to protect the atmosphere. Thus, by 2000, 72 per cent of Canadians were willing to assume a worst-case scenario and take action without waiting for further evidence. This was an increase from 61 per cent in 1997. Residents of Quebec were the most supportive (81 per cent) while residents of Alberta and Saskatchewan, Canada's main oil provinces, were least supportive (57 and 59 per cent, respectively; Environics International, 2000).

Who will pay the costs of coping with climate change is a tricky political issue. In this regard, Kyoto places a greater burden on the developed countries, which were most responsible for creating the problem. Ultimately, new energy sources that do not depend on fossil fuels will need to be introduced on a massive scale. Voluntary measures have little chance of working, and the task is becoming ever greater: Canada's actual emissions are expected, on the present course, to exceed its Kyoto commitment by 27 per cent in 2010 (Bernstein and Gore, 2001: 30).

Conclusion: Future Developments

Politics in Canada and around the globe are changing quickly as the people of various societies grapple with major technological, environmental, and social forces that are impinging on their lives. Consider, for example, the capacity to manipulate, even to create, living forms that is based on scientists' discovery of DNA structures and how they may be changed. Already various genetically engineered food products have entered the marketplace, although public resistance has been mobilized, especially in Europe. Proponents point to security of food supply and improved product characteristics. Insofar as they are successful, ownership of this knowledge will generate more centralized control. The landscape and wildlife are also likely to change; the possibility of manufacturing a forest without natural reproduction and without natural undergrowth may have profound effects on the environment as well as on people (Bailey, Sinclair, and Dubois, forthcoming). The same cloning technologies make it possible to create animal life and raise the possibility of radical intervention in human reproduction and health care. While long-term effects are debated, the critical political questions are who is in control and what will be permitted.

In the early twenty-first century, there are forces that imply decentralization and fragmentation as cultural groups struggle for political autonomy (like Quebec) and as others advocate a smaller role for the state in many ways, from privatization to more partnerships with non-state actors. Probably these forces are weaker than the integrating, regionalizing, and even globalizing tendencies associated with high-speed communication, cultural diffusion of tastes and values, an international division of labour, corporate concentration, world-level environmental problems, North–South inequality, and new or more powerful transnational organizations.

Does this globalization mean the eclipse of the state (Strange, 1996)? Most likely not within the next 20 years. So far, despite the tendencies mentioned, there is little sign that any global decisions, whether taken in political centres such as the United Nations or by other assemblies such as inclusive meetings on AIDS or climate change, can be effective if the most powerful states are unwilling to support them. International organizations such as the World Bank have been able to exert tremendous pressure on debtor countries to mould their domestic policies in return for continued support. The World Trade Organization (WTO) is a key centre of international policy formation; it is binding on its members and its free market orientation is consistent with the policy of the United States. In contrast, the Kyoto Protocol is drastically weakened without US participation.

Regional concentration appears a more powerful force than globalization as such. Regional economic integration through organizations such as the European Union and agreements such as the North American Free Trade Agreement (NAFTA) is certainly a challenge to the capacity of smaller states to influence investment decisions and the functioning of their more local labour markets. The largest transnational corporations operate in any part of the globe where profit is likely and they can put great pressure on smaller states to provide conditions attractive to their business. But there is nothing fundamentally new in this. Moreover, as Grace Skogstad (2000) points out, the changing context need not leave states, even smaller ones, helpless; rather, they may expand policy development into new areas such as information technology.

We live in difficult and dangerous times in which no country is truly isolated from external economic, cultural, and political forces. To that extent, life is internationalized, if not fully globalized. Violent conflicts spill over national borders. Even the powerhouse of world affairs, the United States, is not immune to the most determined assaults of radicals willing to resort to any means. This has placed great pressure on states to control cross-border movement and harmonize policy, including between the United States and Canada (Cilluffo, 2001). In such a situation, Canada, as the weaker state, is put under great pressure to compromise and adjust to the wishes of the United States. Maintaining the civil rights of all people is one of the greatest political challenges that societies face in the early twentieth century.

☐ Questions for Critical Thought

1. Discuss the ways in which authority can be exercised, providing examples. What sources of bias, if any, can be observed in the organization of the Canadian state?
2. Electoral institutions ensure that political leaders are responsive to the interests of the population as a whole. Do you agree or disagree with this statement?
3. What changes have occurred since 1980 in women's participation in the legislatures and cabinets of liberal democracies? Discuss some of the differences you observe. How would you explain these findings?
4. Assume that a new royal commission into the current status of women has been established (a Royal Commission on the Status of Women did report in 1970). Write a brief in which you argue for or against changes in the political process with regard to promoting women's involvement in politics. Compare the current circumstances with what the previous study indicated.
5. Select an issue that has been important during the last year in the province or municipality where you live. Using media sources try to determine who was able to exercise power. What theory of the state best explains what you observed?
6. Collect information on the size of public-sector employment relative to private-sector employment in Canada's provinces. Try to explain any variations among the provinces.
7. Select any five Western democracies. Find out the percentage of electors who voted in at least three general elections since 1970. Try to account for any differences you observe.

☐ Recommended Readings

Michael M. Atkinson and William D. Coleman, *The State, Business, and Industrial Change in Canada* (Toronto: University of Toronto Press, 1989).
Atkinson and Coleman present an excellent case study of Canadian policy and interest groups.
Bent Flyvbjerg, *Rationality and Power: Democracy in Practice*, translated by Steven Sampson (Chicago: University of Chicago Press, 1998).
This is an outstanding case study of power in action as a Danish city attempted to grapple with competing demands of business, citizen mobility, and protection of the environment.
Murray Knuttila and Wendee Kubik, *State Theories: Classical, Global and Feminist Perspectives*, 3rd edn (Halifax, NS: Fernwood, 2000).
State Theories is a thorough review of recent theorizing about the state.

Jacques Lévesque, *The Enigma of 1989: the ussr and the Liberation of Eastern Europe*, translated by Keith Martin (Berkeley: University of California Press, 1997).

> Lévesque provides a valuable account of the collapse of state socialism in the Soviet Union and Soviet-influenced areas.

Kenneth McRoberts, *Quebec: Social Change and Political Crisis*, 3rd edn (Toronto: McClelland & Stewart, 1988).

> Grounded in the history of Quebec, this is a sympathetic and insightful account of Quebec politics.

Theda Skocpol, *States and Social Revolutions: A Comparative Analysis of France, Russia, and China* (Cambridge: Cambridge University Press, 1979).

> Skocpol's is an outstanding theoretical and empirical contribution to theories of the state and revolution.

Grace Skogstad, "Globalization and Public Policy," *Canadian Journal of Political Science*, 33 (2000): 805–28.

> This article provides insightful commentary on the complex issues around globalization and its implications for state policy, with special attention to Canada.

Manon Tremblay and Caroline Andrew, eds, *Women and Political Representation in Canada* (Ottawa: University of Ottawa Press, 1998).

> This collection is a useful overview of issues that are particularly significant for women.

☐ Recommended Web Sites

Canada's Parliament
www.parl.gc.ca

> This government Web site provides information on the conduct of parliamentary life and on members of the two houses of Parliament.

Canadian Election Study (ces)
www.fas.umontreal.ca/pol/ces-eec/ces.html

> The results of investigations into the 1997 and 2000 federal elections may be obtained at this site, from which various academic presentations may be downloaded.

Comparative Study of Electoral Systems
www.umich.edu/~cses/

> This University of Michigan site maintains an extensive data base of US and international election studies.

Electionworld.org
www.electionworld.org

> Here you can find results of national elections around the world and links to the Web sites of political parties, including all parties represented in Canada's House of Commons. The site is updated monthly.

Google News Canada
http://news.google.ca

> This Web site allows access to a vast database of newspaper articles and news agency reports on any subject.

Peace Pledge Union
www.ppu.org.uk/war/

> Here you can click sections of a world map and receive summary information on wars and violent conflict since 1945.

United Nations
www.un.org

> The United Nations provides a vast range of information about its activities, as well as databases and bibliographies.

Women in National Parliaments
www.ipu.org/wmn-e/world.htm

> The Inter-parliamentary Union's Web site contains extensive, regularly updated information on women's political participation.

13

John Veugelers
and Randle Hart

\> \> \>

Social Movements

© Dick Hemingway

☐ Learning Objectives

In this chapter, you will:

- see how social movements are studied sociologically

- review the theoretical approaches to the study of social movements

- read about key debates within the study of social movements

- see how empirical research is used to test and criticize social movement theories

- learn how social movements are embedded in national and international (global) politics

- understand why social movements have historical importance in the process of social change

Introduction

Writing in the nineteenth century about political associations, Alexis de Tocqueville noted that "citizens who are individually powerless do not very clearly anticipate the strength that they may acquire by uniting together" ([1835] 1945: vol. 2, 124). De Tocqueville had identified a curious feature of society: when powerless people lend time, energy, and material resources to an ideological cause, their combined efforts create a new reality with a life and force of its own. This reality becomes a **social movement**. Examples of present-day social movements include women's, peace, gay and lesbian, anti-nuclear, labour, environmental, ethnic, and regionalist movements.

A social movement is a group. Thus, it is more than the sum of the individuals forming it. As a consequence, social movements may take a direction contrary to their members' wishes. Surprisingly, some social movements even betray their supporters by adapting to a social system once seen as corrupt or unresponsive. Others disappear as a result of internal bickering or government repression even though their members' grievances persist.

Since social movements are groups, what they say and do may not reflect their members' attitudes. Furthermore, a psychological analysis of a social movement's members will reveal little about the movement's origins and development, its effect on the social order, or the causes of its successes and failures. A social movement is a distinctive social reality for which sociology offers appropriate tools of analysis.

This chapter opens by looking at the characteristics of social movements. It next considers theoretical approaches to social movements, then examines four social movements of the nineteenth and twentieth centuries. The chapter ends with a discussion about social movements in today's global context.

What Is a Social Movement?

Ideal-typically, a social movement depends on the actions of non-elite members of society, those people who have relatively little or no control over major economic, symbolic, political, or military resources—in short, over anything scarce that, if controlled, gives one power over others.

People form a social movement when they voluntarily work together to influence the distribution of social goods. A *social good* is anything that a particular

society values. Familiar examples include money, honour, peace, security, citizenship, leisure time, political power, and divine grace. There are probably no universal social goods, because no two societies have exactly the same set of values. Furthermore, social goods vary historically. They emerge and disappear as values change or traditions lose relevance (Walzer, 1983).

Social goods are scarce—in part, that is why they are valuable—and some individuals or groups get more of them than others do. How people make sense of such inequalities depends on **ideologies**, sets of ideas that justify how social goods are distributed. *Dominant ideologies* defend existing inequalities by making them seem right. *Counter-ideologies* challenge

Demonstrations belong to a repertoire of contention that also includes strikes, violent action, and civil disobedience. These may have influence on public opinion, government policies, or business practices. In this photograph, citizens are protesting in front of the Ontario legislature against cuts to the public education system. (© Dick Hemingway)

the justice of the existing social system, promote alternative values and goals, and present a plan for change. Promoting counter-ideologies is a goal of social movements.

Social movements try to achieve change through the voluntary co-operation of the relatively powerless. These people may contribute financial or other material resources, recruit new members, or spread a counter-ideology. They may also participate in strikes, sit-ins, boycotts, demonstrations, protest marches, violent action, or civil disobedience. The efforts of social movements can be focused on changing attitudes, everyday practices, public opinion, or the policies and procedures of business and government.

Environmental movements, for example, have the basic impacts set forth in Figure 13.1. Social change through collective action involves dynamic and complex processes: social movements affect individuals and political policies, but they are also influenced by them. As Figure 13.1 shows, environmental problems are usually identified by natural scientists. Once a problem of this kind is identified, the environmental movement may choose to address the issue. It may lobby the government or appeal to individuals' sense of moral indignation. In some instances, an environmental organization may choose to run in democratic elections, thus forming a political party with ecological issues as its main concern.

Social movements are easier to understand when compared and contrasted with other phenomena studied by sociologists (Diani, 1992). A *social trend*, for example, is simply a changing pattern of social behaviour, whereas a social movement is a co-operative effort to achieve social change from below. The rising labour market participation of women is a social trend; a group of volunteers who fight for gender equality is a social movement. Certainly, social movements influence some social trends. For instance, feminist movements may encourage the trend for women to enter the paid workforce. However, many social trends—such as changing fashions or unemployment patterns—may be scarcely affected by social movements.

A *pressure group* is an organization that aims to influence large institutions, particularly **the state**. A social movement is one kind of pressure group. However, other pressure groups—known as *interest groups*—represent the specific concerns of farmers, employers, medical doctors, ethnic groups, and so on. Interest groups restrict their membership and rely heavily on a professional staff rather than volunteers. Moreover, recognition by the government often gives them semi-official or even official status. Like social movements, interest groups use public opinion to put pressure on political or economic elites. But membership in social movements is more open, and their ideologies typically appeal to people from different walks of life.

Since social movements depend on voluntary participation, they are *voluntary associations*. However, not all voluntary associations seek deeper changes in the distribution of social goods. Some provide social or health services; others organize leisure activities or unite the followers of a spiritual doctrine. Voluntary associations that only help people to accept or enjoy the existing social system are not social movements.

While social movements try to change the distribution of social goods, **political parties** try to win and keep political power. In principle, a social movement becomes a political party when it fields candidates in elections. The Green parties in Germany, France, and Italy, for example, have grown out of environmental movements in these countries. In practice, the difference between social movements and political parties is sometimes hazy. Parties that have grown out of social movements often retain features from their past. They may be more sectarian or rely heavily on grassroots supporters. These features foster a strong party identity, but they may also discourage outsiders from joining.

Figure 13.1 **The Impact of Environmental Movements**

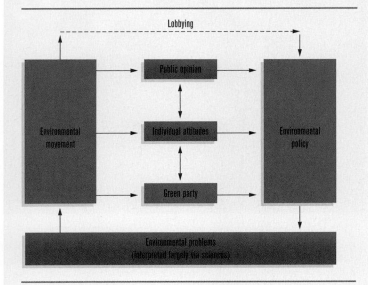

SOURCE: Dieter Rucht, "The Impact of Environmental Movements in Western Societies," in *How Social Movements Matter*, Marco Giugni, et al. eds (Minneapolis: University of Minnesota Press, 1999), 214.

Finally, not all groups with non-elite, voluntary members who aim to reallocate social goods are necessarily social movements. A *counter-movement* may have all of the characteristics of a social movement, but with one important difference: a counter-movement arises *in response to* a social movement. Three conditions must be met for counter-movements to appear:

13.1

Sociology in Action
Reality Check

A year ago today, he was on the front lines of demonstrations at the Summit of the Americas in Quebec City, wearing a gas mask and hurling live tear-gas canisters back at Sûreté du Québec riot police. Now, he's a cook in Old Montreal, flipping crêpes for US tourists, his plans for the next step in the struggle against global capitalism put on the back burner for a summer job. Welcome to the reality check of Octavio Elias Munguia, 23. "You can't always be radical in life," said the soft-spoken university graduate, an immigrant from El Salvador who grew up francophone in Montreal. "At the end of the day, you have to pay the rent." Like the tens of thousands of other young people who took to the streets of the capital last April 20 to 23 to protest against negotiations for the Free Trade Area of the Americas, Munguia came away with some hard lessons:

1. Rubber bullets hurt (he got two in the back and one in the leg).
2. Protest doesn't work miracles overnight.
3. The hardest part of the struggle is getting people's attention.

"Quebec City changed my life," Munguia said this week between shifts at the restaurant. "Even if it didn't change anything in reality—because, you know, poverty still exists—at least it told me I wasn't alone in wanting a better world."

Last year's summit drew together the heads of state of all 34 countries of North, Central and South America (except Cuba) for three days of talk and declarations on the subject of extending free trade across the hemisphere. At the time, the 500-page draft text of the agreement they were negotiating had still not been made public, and so the event was a lightning rod for protesters upset by the official secrecy of the process. For three days they rallied behind the formidable barricade erected to keep them at bay—a 3.8-kilometre-long steel fence that only reinforced the perception the FTAA was an elitist exercise under siege.

"The protests didn't put a stop to anything," said Professor Dorval Brunelle, who teaches sociology at the Université du Québec à Montréal and has followed the FTAA process closely. "The FTAA negotiations are like any other—a permanent state of affairs."

Since Quebec City, "the debate has come out of the closed circle in which it was confined, and now the FTAA is no longer like a state secret," added Pierre Beaudet, director of the Montreal-based group Alternatives. "And another positive impact is that governments really got the message that they have to be more responsive and be concerned about democracy." Take, for example, the Inter-American Democracy Charter that the summit leaders pledged themselves to in their closing statement. Finally signed formally on Sept. 11 in Lima (and obscured by that bad historical timing), the agreement enshrines the rule of law, separation of powers and free and fair elections throughout Latin America. Would it have been drafted and adopted if it hadn't been for the protests in Quebec City? Probably not, the activists believe.

———

SOURCE: Jeff Heinrich, "Reality Check: A year ago, tear gas was billowing at the Summit of the Americas in Quebec City. Today, we look at how its plans have developed . . . or not developed," *The Gazette*, 20 Apr. 2002. Reprinted with permission of The Gazette.

IN THE FIRST PERSON

I was first introduced to the study of social movements by William K. Carroll, a sociology professor at the University of Victoria, and I was lucky enough to be admitted into his senior-level sociology seminar, though I had been studying Canadian literature and had very little experience in sociology. With work, I became acclimatized to the sociological imagination and learned how to analyze the social world with a critical eye. I was hooked: I practically ran to the Registrar's office to declare a major in sociology. I remained at the University of Victoria to study for my master's degree in sociology and participated in an interdisciplinary program in cultural, social, and political thought. I continue to be inspired by the possibilities of the sociological study of social movements at the University of Toronto. –RANDLE HART

1. A social movement must be seen as successful (or as gaining success).
2. A social movement's goals must be seen as a threat to another group.
3. Allies must be available to support mobilization of the counter-movement.

While some counter-movements (such as the National Rifle Association) wish to defend the status quo against a perceived threat by social movements, others (such as the anti-abortion movement) emerge when a state or government agency has ambiguous policies or is internally divided on a particular social issue (Meyer and Staggenborg, 1996).

To sum up: A social movement is an organization that co-ordinates the voluntary actions of non-elite members of society and that offers a program for changing the way society distributes social goods. Though social movements are pressure groups, they differ from interest groups because they have open recruitment, rely on volunteers, and are based outside of elite circles. Social movements are also voluntary associations, but their commitment to social change sets them apart from groups whose main goal is to organize and provide charity, leisure activities, spiritual guidance, and so forth. Unlike political parties, moreover, social movements do not strive for political office. Social movements direct their grievances against the existing distribution of social goods. Counter-movements, by contrast, direct their grievances against the potential success of social movements. Finally, social movements are groups. Hence, knowing the beliefs and behaviours of individual members gives only partial insight into the nature of a social movement.

Theoretical Approaches

Different beliefs about society separate the four main approaches to social movements. The **breakdown approach** assumes that stability is the basis of social order and that **culture** is the major determinant of action. The **resource mobilization approach** assumes that social order is based on competition and conflict and that interests are the fundamental cause of action. The **identity-based approach** and the **political process approach** draw selectively from the other two. Both assume that social order rests on an unsteady resolution of conflict and that culture is the major determinant of action. Table 13.1 summarizes the assumptions that underlie these four perspectives.

The Breakdown Approach

The breakdown approach builds on a view of society developed by the French sociologist Émile Durkheim (1858–1917) and later by the American founder of **structural functionalism**, Talcott Parsons (1902–79). Both thought that shared **norms** and **values** hold society together. The breakdown approach holds that rapid, thorough, or uneven change in society weakens the social bonds that promote social order. Social disintegration, in turn, encourages the formation of groups advocating radical change.

Relative Deprivation Theory

The assumptions of the breakdown approach underlie **relative deprivation theory**, which claims that radical social movements result from feelings of fear and frustration. According to James C. Davies (1962),

Table 13.1 **Approaches to the Study of Social Movements**

		Primary Cause of Social Action	
		Culture	Interests
Underlying Societal Dynamic	Consensus	• breakdown approach	• *undeveloped approach*
	Conflict	• identity-based approach • political process approach	• resource mobilization approach

revolutions and rebellions are preceded by two phases. The first phase is characterized by economic and social progress. More and more social goods become available—food becomes more plentiful, for example, or the rights of citizens expand—and expectations rise. But if a sharp reversal follows—if food suddenly becomes scarce and costly, or if authorities ban opposition parties and the free press after a period of liberalization—rising expectations are no longer met. In the second phase, the gap between what people expect and what they actually get grows ever wider. Rebellion results when anxiety and frustration become widespread and intense.

Critics of relative deprivation theory point out that the most frustrated members of society are not the only people who fight for radical change. Revolutions, especially successful ones, are often led and supported by people from the middle and upper classes. Moreover, relative deprivation theory does not provide a convincing link between people's feelings and revolution. Surely the people of Haiti, for instance, have endured many decades of anxiety and frustration under brutal dictatorships. Yet their dissatisfaction has not led to revolution. A great deal must happen before individual grievances will translate into major changes such as the toppling of a political regime.

Systemic Theory

Like relative deprivation theory, Neil Smelser's **systemic theory** highlights the role of social breakdown in the growth of social movements. But instead of focusing on individuals, as relative deprivation theory does, Smelser looks at society as a whole. He sees society as a set of linked elements that work to maintain stability. Social movements reflect the breakdown of stability, but they do not form unless six conditions are met (Smelser, 1963):

1. *Structural conduciveness*. Social conditions must give people a chance to unite for change. If people remain isolated, they cannot pool their efforts.

2. *Structural strain*. The dominant ideology must be viewed with dissatisfaction or uncertainty.

3. *Growth and spread of a generalized belief*. Potential participants in social movements must share a counter-ideology that binds them together.

4. *A precipitating factor*. This is the straw that breaks the camel's back—some event so serious that people finally decide to fight for change.

5. *Mobilization*. People's readiness for action must have an outlet; they must be able to join a social movement.

6. *The response of authorities*. Because the state is so powerful, its response affects a social movement's chances of survival and success.

Smelser's systemic theory improves on relative deprivation theory. It corrects the overemphasis on individuals by specifying group and societal factors involved in the rise of social movements. Moreover, systemic theory recognizes that shared grievances alone will not bind protesters together. For a movement to last, protesters must share a counter-ideology, a set of ideas that gives them guidelines to work together for change. Finally, the theory brings mobilization into the picture. Personal dissatisfaction alone will not form a social movement, no matter how widespread the grievance.

Unfortunately, Smelser's theory rests partly on circular reasoning. An example of circular reasoning would be as follows: Suppose you ask someone to explain what caused hail, and the person replies, "It's frozen rain." Because hail and frozen rain are the same thing, your respondent's reply is not an explanation, but merely a restatement using different words. Hence, your question has been left unanswered.

Smelser does something similar, though less glaringly. On the one hand, he defines social mobilization for action as a response to strain on generalized belief (1963). But he also lists mobilization for action, strain, and generalized belief among the six factors that explain social movements. In this respect, his theory is a restatement of what needs to be explained, not an explanation (Aya, 1990).

Criticisms of the Breakdown Approach

The breakdown approach has also been criticized for forgetting that value consensus and social stability result partly from relations of domination. As Barrington Moore, Jr, observes, "To maintain and transmit a value system, human beings are punched, bullied, sent to jail, thrown into concentration camps, cajoled, bribed, made into heroes, encouraged to read newspapers, stood up against the wall and shot, and sometimes even taught sociology" (1966: 486). Contrary to the assumptions of the breakdown approach, social conflict may be a normal feature of social life. If this is so, then the breakdown of value consensus and stability may not explain the formation of social movements.

Breakdown theory has also been accused of treating social movements as ailments. This charge arose during the 1960s, a time when social movements supported by mainstream members of society were flourishing in Western democracies. Many sociologists welcomed the new movements against war, racism, sexism, pollution, bureaucracy, and the educational system as positive signs of healthy protest against injustice and alienation.

Finally, critics have argued it is misleading to treat social movements as outbursts of uncontainable emotion. Experience suggests that participation in social movements may involve the same kind of calm and rational decision making found in other areas of life. This interpretation underlies the resource mobilization approach.

The Resource Mobilization Approach

The resource mobilization approach challenges the image of social movements as unusual, impermanent, or disorderly. Instead, it assumes that social movements are quite similar to other organizations. They are managed by leaders whose decisions are no less calculating than anyone else's. Some sociologists go so far as to treat social movement organizers as entrepreneurs who have a "product" to sell.

Unlike business entrepreneurs, however, social movement entrepreneurs must deal with *free-riding*—non-cooperation in the attainment of a good that will be available to all members of the community. For movement leaders, the solution is to make their "product" appealing in the competitive market for potential members' time, energy, and resources. From this perspective, social movement propaganda is a form of marketing that advertises the benefits of joining (Jenkins, 1983).

Proponents of the resource mobilization approach argue that the breakdown approach is wrong in assuming that satisfaction with the social order is the normal state of affairs. Instead, dissatisfaction is built into society. There will always be people with grievances because social goods are unequally distributed. But grievances alone do not make a social movement. What social movements do is lift grievances out of the shadows, giving them ideological form and propelling them into public life.

The resource mobilization approach puts power at the centre of analysis. **Power** is not something one has: one can only be in a position that confers power, for power means having the ability to carry out one's wishes. As the German sociologist Max Weber (1864–1920) put it, power refers to a person's or group's chance of fulfilling their goals even when others would have it otherwise ([1908] 1978: 926).

The source of power is control over resources. Control creates *leverage*, the ability to get others to do what one wants. What represents a resource in any given situation varies, but three kinds of power stand out. One is *economic power*, which is based on control over the means of material production: land, energy, capital, technology, labour, factories, raw materials, and so forth. Another is *political power*, based on control over the legitimate means of violence: the police and the armed forces. A third is *ideological power*, which is based on control over the means of producing and disseminating **symbols**: schools, churches, newspapers, publishing houses, television and radio, film and advertising companies, and the like. The resource base for each of the three kinds of power differs. Nonetheless, control over any resource allows elites to shape the lives of the powerless.

Social movements must compete against other **social institutions** for the scarce resources necessary to start and operate an organization. The resource mobilization approach therefore searches for the social conditions that affect social movements' control over resources, and focuses on the strategies that translate power into success.

There are two perspectives on resource mobilization: the utilitarian and political conflict perspectives (Ramirez, 1981). While both assume that actors (whether individuals or groups) are rational and seek

Open for Discussion
The Free-Rider Problem

The Fresh Air Coalition is fighting for a reduction in the toxic emissions of Steel City. If the group meets its goal, all of Steel City's citizens will breathe cleaner air: it would be impossible to give the cleaner air only to people who had joined the Fresh Air Coalition, while everyone else—the people who didn't attend the protest rallies, write letters to newspapers and politicians, or contribute to the Fresh Air Coalition's fundraising plant sale—got the same dirty air as before.

Assuming the citizens of Steel City are self-interested, it doesn't make sense for them to join the Fresh Air Coalition. They are free riders: they will benefit even if they don't help, because collective goods such as clean air cannot be divided.

What can the Fresh Air Coalition do? According to free-rider theory, groups can foster co-operation through selective incentives. The Fresh Air Coalition can make co-operation worthwhile by providing rewards. So, in addition to fighting for clean air, the leaders of the Fresh Air Coalition will be sure to organize social events—picnics, parties, camping weekends—that attract and keep members by satisfying their immediate self-interest.

---

to maximize self-interest, each addresses somewhat different problems.

The Utilitarian Perspective

The **utilitarian perspective** focuses on how individuals promote their own interests. The free-rider problem is a central concern, with this perspective asking how and why selective incentives attract volunteers and cut down on free-riding. It also studies the relationships between social movements and how rewards motivate social movement entrepreneurs.

Critics of the utilitarian perspective have stressed the limited applicability of the free-rider problem. The assumption that social movements attract support only by providing selective incentives may misconstrue people's reasons for joining. Instead, people may join a movement simply because it seems headed for success. Or they may join because they identify with other members of the social movement and believe the group will benefit if its members work together (Barry, [1970] 1978). Finally, norms of fairness may override concerns about efficiency. Pressures to conform may lead people to join social movements, irrespective of selective incentives (Elster, 1989). Such considerations are ruled out by an exclusive focus on the free-rider problem. The utilitarian perspective forgets that people are ruled by more than self-interest. Further, it forgets that social movements are groups, so they cannot be explained by individualistic decisions alone.

The Political Conflict Perspective

The **political conflict perspective** focuses on how parts of society (typically **classes**) promote collective interests. Although not a Marxist approach, it tends to stress issues central to the Marxist tradition: working-class mobilization, class conflict, and revolution. Hence, analysis from this perspective usually tries to explain the origins of class **solidarity**. Studies in the political conflict tradition also search for factors that determine the success and failure of class-based movements, including class alliances, pre-existing social ties that foster communication and group action, and ties with other groups and political authorities.

In recent decades, sociologists who work from the political conflict perspective have reduced an earlier emphasis on class strength and class alliances. Simultaneously, they have lent more attention to the state. Because it is so powerful, the state can tip the balance in favour of one class over another. Thus, domestic and international events that affect the state may decide the fate of a revolution.

By *the state*, sociologists mean what we commonly call "the government"—the set of institutions responsible for defending the polity, making and carrying out its laws and public programs, and promoting its interests in foreign affairs. The sociological relevance of the state stems from its domination and influence over social relations. This power is rooted in the state's monopoly over the legitimate use of violence and is expressed in the ability to extract taxes, print money, make and enforce laws, conduct foreign policy, and distribute political office and public funds. Such a high degree of power crucially shapes the milieu in which social movements emerge, mature, and meet with success or failure.

To be sure, the state's power over society differs greatly according to the type of regime, whether monarchy, dictatorship, or democracy. Its power also varies between regimes of the same type. The welfare state is stronger in Sweden than in the United States, for instance, even though both are democracies. History matters as well. Between the 1940s and the 1970s, democratic states increasingly intervened in the economy and provided an ever greater range of welfare services. Finally, the strength of the state varies across different areas of society. For example, the state may control the educational system but leave religious institutions alone.

What do these observations imply? A thorough analysis of social movements will pay attention to the state's power, and a subtle analysis of social movements will respect the complexity of state–society relations.

Criticisms of the Resource Mobilization Approach

The resource mobilization approach represents a clear advance over the breakdown approach. It underscores the normality of social movements by drawing attention to their similarities with other organizations. Nevertheless, this approach has some shortcomings too.

First, it runs the danger of missing some important differences between social movements and other organizations. Few sociologists still believe that social movements are irrational, exotic, or unusual. However, many are beginning to realize that social movements differ from other types of organizations. They have different resources, career cycles, and relationships with government authorities as well as with other social movements. They also exhibit distinctive modes of acting, organizing, and communicating (Tarrow, 1988).

The image of human action conveyed by the resource mobilization approach has also been criticized as too voluntaristic. It exaggerates the extent to which social movements reflect careful planning and successful strategy. People often behave with vague or conflicting goals in mind. Like any other **social group**, a successful social movement probably does

things the participants never intended in the first place. Further, the goals of social movements often emerge and change as situations evolve.

The voluntarism of the resource mobilization approach contains another drawback: this approach neglects political and international contexts. These matter, for they shape a social movement's chances for success. Devoting greater attention to warfare and the role of the state is one remedy for this oversight (Skocpol, 1979). Critics also point to a more fundamental weakness of the resource mobilization approach: it neglects the manner in which culture shapes—and is shaped by—participation in social movements.

The Identity-Based Approach

The identity-based approach squarely confronts the resource mobilization approach's neglect of culture. Major intellectual influences on this approach include neo-Marxists who have treated ideas and consciousness as stakes in class and political struggle, such as the Italian Antonio Gramsci (1891–1937) and theorists associated with Germany's Frankfurt School (Held, 1980). According to the identity-based approach, dominant interpretations of reality uphold class, gender, racial, and other inequalities. Progressive social movements must therefore challenge the dominant culture.

The identity-based approach criticizes the resource mobilization approach for forgetting that neither the goals of social movements nor the way they calculate the best means of achieving them is self-evident. Norms and values are created in and by social movements. Hence, the formation of social movements' goals needs to be explained (Nedelmann, 1991). Moreover, the resource mobilization approach takes for granted the sense of community that creates **identity** and a willingness to work together. How people define themselves depends very much on whom they identify with—on what community, with its unique norms and values, they feel they belong to. Effective social movements redefine identities by changing or reinforcing people's sense of community.

The New Social Movements

The *new social movement (NSM)* perspective focuses largely upon identity. It proposes that social movements can be laboratories for more progressive forms of **social interaction** (Melucci, 1989). The breakdown and resource mobilization approaches define the success of social movements in terms of change in economic or political institutions. The NSM approach defines success differently. To be sure, it does not deny the desirability of change in dominant institutions. However, the more important struggle takes place in civil society, those areas of social interaction that stand largely outside of the state and the market. In fact, theorists claim that new social movements have come about since the 1960s because state and economic practices have increasingly encroached on people's everyday lives. Slogans such as "the personal is political" are meant to express how everyday life is pervaded by government and corporate activities, as well as by dominant cultural ideas that create inequality.

According to this approach, civil society offers greater chances for freedom, equality, and *participatory democracy*, a system of decision making in which all members of a group exercise control over group decisions. Indeed, new social movements are, in part, characterized by institutional arrangements wherein their members try to organize according to the ideals of equal participation. This is what social movements are good at, and striving for other kinds of success risks perverting these ideals (Cohen, 1985).

Generally, new social movements are said to be distinctive from previous forms of collective action. The appearance of these new social movements may be explained by a value shift (Inglehart, 1990b). With relative economic and political stability in Western societies, the cultural value of social goods has changed. In the past, social movements were concerned primarily with the redistribution of social goods that provided sustenance and security, such as money, job security, and welfare rights. The new social movements, in contrast, are said to be concerned primarily with cultural recognition. In other words, these movements attempt to have their subcultural practices understood and in some cases legitimated by the dominant culture.

The work of French sociologist Alain Touraine (1981) exemplifies the identity-based approach. Touraine originally studied the French workers' movement, but during the 1960s, he became interested in the feminist, student, peace, and ecological movements. Unlike movements promoting the interests of a specific group, these new social movements had goals based on more universal values. They also displayed an innovative interest in participatory democracy. Touraine has urged sociologists analyzing social movements to follow an *intervention approach*—that is, to abandon professional detachment and contribute to social change by actively sharing insights and ideas with the people they are studying.

Criticisms of the Identity-Based Approach

Like resource mobilization approaches, the identity-based approach tends to be voluntaristic in its emphasis on people's potential for actively challenging and changing society. It focuses on altering the shared understandings that maintain patterns of domination. Consequently, it too often ignores the structures of economic and political opportunity that shape the destinies of social movements.

Also, while identity-based theories lean toward abstraction in their language and scope, identity-based studies tend to be descriptive and narrowly focused. These characteristics point to a gap between theory and research. Ideally, good sociological theory guides research by providing useful questions, hypotheses, and models, and good research seeks to test, correct, or refine theory. The identity-based approach suffers because theory and empirical study sometime stand so far apart.

The Political Process Approach

While the breakdown, resource mobilization, and identity-based approaches have been very useful for understanding social movements, in recent years scholars have attempted to create a synthesis. The political process approach is generally attributed to Peter Eisinger's study of movements during the 1960s (1973). Eisinger argued that collective action depends on the structure of local political opportunities at the institutional and governmental levels. Charles Tilly (1978), an early proponent of the political process approach, built on this idea by showing how nation-states can manipulate the political terrain to stymie the activities of social movements. Tilly argues that the rise of nation-states gave rise to the national social movements of the early modern era in Europe. New political ideas that helped to create nation-states also generated grievances that led people to act collectively. These national social movements had characteristics that set them apart from previous forms of collective action (see also Tarrow, 1998).

The political process approach assumes that the *polity* (the political field) can be characterized by its opportunities and constraints. *Opportunities* involve almost anything that provides reasons and resources for people to mobilize—so long as the political climate is not so oppressive that people cannot mobilize without fear or great difficulty. Political opportunities may include economic crises, laws ensuring the right to assemble, a history of previous collective action, even accidents that show the need for social change. *Constraints* include anything within the polity that may act as a barrier to the mobilization and survival of a social movement. Political constraints include a repressive police state, inexperience with collective action, even a lack of communication among social movement participants. Opportunities and constraints go hand in hand: no polity is completely open or completely closed.

The breakdown approach assumes that some form of social or political crisis is needed for people to act collectively. By contrast, the political process approach assumes that collective action is an ongoing social phenomenon. In other words, the breakdown approach assumes that social movements arise from *outside* the polity but enter the political terrain when there are reasons to do so. Conversely, the political process approach assumes that social movements have a historical position *within* the polity and that the frequency of social movement activity changes according to opportunities and constraints (Tarrow, 1998).

Fluctuations in the opportunities and constraints that influence the incidence of collective action creates a *cycle of contention* (Tarrow, 1998). A rise in the cycle means that social movements have created or met new opportunities and have made room for the rise of other movements. Figure 13.2 shows the rise and decline of collective action by Canadian Aboriginal bands from 1981 to 2000 (Wilkes, 2001). Protest events among Native groups in Canada rose dramatically between 1989 and 1991, peaking in 1990. This increase can be attributed to 1990's 78-day Kanienkah armed uprising in Oka, Quebec, over municipal plans to convert a Mohawk burial ground into a golf course. In support of the Kahnawake, Akwesasne, and Kanesatake, bands across Canada increased their protest activities.

Like the resource mobilization approach, the political process model focuses on institutions. Specifically, this approach looks at *mobilizing structures*, which include levels of informal and formal organization (McCarthy, 1996). An example of **informal organization** is a friendship network. When the cycle of contention is at its lowest point—when there are relatively few (or no) active social movement organizations—the network of friendships among demobi-

Slogans such as "the personal is political" are meant to draw attention to the ways in which everyday life is pervaded by dominant values that promote inequality. Environmental, feminist, gay and lesbian, peace, and anti-poverty organizations in British Columbia and other provinces have formed coalitions based on shared understandings of social injustice. (© Dick Hemingway)

lized movement participants keeps the spirit of collective action alive. These latent, or buried, networks explain why social movements arise when political opportunities appear and when constraints are eased (Melucci, 1989). Although informal communication alone cannot give rise to a social movement, it can become an important resource for mobilization.

The analysis of **formal organization** looks at the inner dynamics of social movements. These generally include leadership structures, flows of communication, the entry and exit of members, and the means of identifying, obtaining, and utilizing resources. By studying mobilizing structures, sociologists can understand the institutional processes whereby movements rise, persist, and decline.

The study of social movement organizations also includes inter-organization dynamics, such as *movement coalitions*. A coalition results when two or more social movement organizations share resources, such as information, in the course of pursuing a common good. Coalitions can be temporary or enduring, and they can bridge different types of movements. Environmental, feminist, gay and lesbian, labour, peace, and anti-poverty organizations in British Columbia, for example, have formed coalitions based on shared understandings of social injustice (Carroll and Ratner, 1996).

According to the identity-based approach, social movements develop subcultural understandings of the world. These understandings form the basis for identifying and acting on social grievances. These also provide movement participants with the resources needed to create activist identities.

The political process approach uses frame analysis to analyze the ways in which movements create novel understandings of the world. Drawing on Irving Goffman's concept of framing processes (see Goffman, 1986), *collective action frames* are "action-oriented sets of beliefs and meanings that inspire and legitimate the activities and campaigns of a social movement organization" (Benford and Snow, 2000: 614). Collective action frames are the communal understandings of a social movement, and these understandings are used to identify and promote grievances. The process whereby individuals come to adopt the ideology and methods of a particular movement organization is called *frame alignment* (Snow et al., 1986).

Collective action frames are also used to identify appropriate forms of protest. Table 13.2 shows the frequency of types of protest among Native bands in Canada between 1981 and 2000. Clearly, road blockades were the most common protest strategy during this period. In part, this may be due to framing processes: the popularity of roadblocks as a tactic may arise from the cultural significance of this form of protest. As more Native groups block roadways to express their grievances, this form of protest becomes more strongly associated with their social movement. Other Native bands then become more likely to adopt the same tactic.

Finally, social movements may use collective action frames as strategic resources. To mobilize general support for their cause, movements promote their own ideologies in the wider culture. If a social movement's framing of injustice and its solution are accepted in society, then it has created its own political

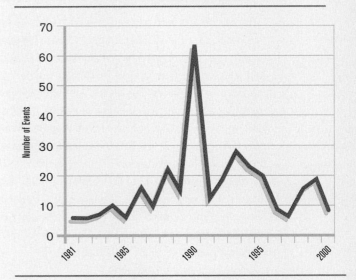

Figure 13.2 **Number of First Nations Protest Collective Events by Year, 1981–2000, Canada**

SOURCE: Rima Wilkes, *Competition or Colonialism? An Analysis of Two Theories of Ethnic Collective Action,* PhD dissertation, University of Toronto, 2001.

opportunities. If a movement is unsuccessful, however, it risks adding to its own difficulties.

Criticism of the Political Process Approach

One strength of the political process approach is its simultaneous focus on structural, institutional, and cultural conditions. Ideally, such a perspective should provide a robust account of social movement processes. As William Gamson and David Meyer observe, however, the political process model has been "used to explain so much, it may ultimately explain nothing at all" (1996: 275). While somewhat overstating their case, these critics are concerned that if variable after variable is included in the model, the explanation is no longer parsimonious. The model loses simplicity and thus its explanatory appeal.

Doug McAdam (1996) provides two solutions to this problem. First, he suggests restricting this concept to include only four variables:

• the openness of the state
• the stability of alliances among elite members of society
• support within the elite for a particular movement
• the level of state repression

13.3

Human Diversity
Activism After 11 September

This story starts with planes flying into buildings on the other coast, in another country. It was just over a year ago, and in the heady months that followed, our elected representatives in Ottawa rushed to approve anti-terrorism legislation intended to protect Canada's national security. In recent months, two Vancouver Island activists found themselves on the wrong side of the Royal Canadian Mounted Police unit created to enforce that legislation.

Early in the morning on September 21, the RCMP's anti-terrorism force, the Integrated National Security Enforcement Team (INSET), followed an anonymous tip and raided John Rampanen's family's empty home in a Port Alberni suburb. They were looking for unauthorized guns.

The INSET team didn't discover anything at the home, says Rampanen, but later, when they found him and his family at his parents' house, they made "veiled threats towards the safety of our children." He plans to lodge a formal complaint about the threats. While Rampanen sees the need for the police to investigate such serious allegations as possession of illegal weapons, he says, "It baffles me that they would be so aggressive in their approach."

As a member of the West Coast Warriors, an Aboriginal activist group, Rampanen has figured prominently in high-profile confrontations at Cheam on the Fraser River and at Burnt Church in New Brunswick. He also delivers drug and alcohol education programs to First Nations communities. The warriors don't shy from confrontation, he says, but they aren't terrorists and it doesn't make sense for them to be under the scrutiny of INSET. "It's been over three weeks now, and I still don't understand."

David Barbarash, former spokesperson for the Animal Liberation Front [ALF], had two computers, computer disks, videos, photos, files, papers, and other documents seized from his home and office in Courtenay on July 30, by INSET officers. He says he understands only too well why INSET might take an interest in activists. "It used to be people could take these kinds of actions and they'd be labeled protesters," he says. "At some point in time there was a move to criminalize dissent. What's happening now, post-September 11, is it's shifted again. Now we're not even criminals, we're terrorists."

The July raid on Barbarash's property stemmed from an ALF action in Maine three years earlier. A group there broke into hunting clubs, spray-painted messages on walls, broke windows and stole stuffed animal heads which they later "returned to their natural environment to rest in peace." Damage was estimated at $8,700.

Barbarash acknowledges that the ALF actions were criminal, but stresses the group doesn't physically harm anyone and that what he calls "economic sabotage" has a long, dignified history that can be traced back to the Boston Tea Party and further.

As with other animal rights actions, Barbarash received information from sources he says he does not know, and has no way to contact, and communicated their message to the media. "I'm not committing any crimes, I'm simply voicing my support for these kinds of activities," he says. "I don't see why our resources should be spent in this way, as if this is some kind of terrorist activity. I think it's outrageous."

"Lets face it," says Barbarash. "This is Canada. There isn't a lot of terrorism." So instead of infiltrating al-Qaeda sleeper cells, he says, INSET officers are being used to investigate more mundane criminal matters.

"When they're going after people like me who just speak to the media, it's pretty pathetic," he says. "They've got to justify their expense account somehow."

SOURCE: Abridged from Andrew MacLeod, "Anti-terrorism Police Harass Island Activists," *Monday Magazine* 28, 43: 24–30 Oct. 2002.

Table 13.2 **Frequency of Types of Protest Among Native Bands in Canada, 1981–2000**

	Number	Percentage
Road blockade	114	36.08
March/demonstration	86	27.22
Train and boat blockade	19	6.01
Boycott	18	5.70
Occupation of land	17	5.38
Illegal fishing/logging	17	5.38
Occupation of building	11	3.45
Hunger strike	5	1.58
Toll booth	5	1.58
(Non-strategic) Violence	4	1.26
Withdrawal from school	3	0.95
English signs changed	2	0.63
Illegal gambling	2	0.63
Invitation of foreign ambassadors	2	0.63
Eviction of police and non-natives	2	0.63
Dam diversion	2	0.63
Destruction of property	2	0.63
Other	5	1.58
Total	**316**	**100.00**

SOURCE: Rima Wilkes, *Competition or Colonialism? An Analysis of Two Theories of Ethnic Collective Action*, unpublished PhD dissertation (University of Toronto, 2001), 72.

Second, McAdam argues that opportunities and constraints are different for each type of social movement. For example, the elements of the political structure that give rise to revolutionary movements will likely be different from those that give rise to identity-based movements. Revolutionary movements are likely to identify most of their political opportunities within the state system, whereas identity-based movements are likely to find most of their opportunities within the cultural practices of civil society (McAdam, 1996).

The Analysis of Social Movements

At one time, sociologists argued that successful movements promote their supporters' interests. Nowadays such explanations are rejected, for they fail to recognize that interests are themselves cultural constructs. Moreover, a movement's supporters often have only a schematic or confused understanding of its ideology. But the compelling question remains: Why do some movements succeed, while others fail? To help find an answer to this question, we will examine four social movements: the Canadian women's movement, agrar-

ian social movements in Canada, Nazism in Germany, and socialism in Western Europe.

Unity and Diversity in the Canadian Women's Movement

Social movements need both diversity and unity. In the history of the Canadian women's movement, diversity of membership and experience has helped the movement adapt to a range of situations. Diversity has also encouraged recognition of the many faces of gender inequality. By maintaining a stock of alternative views and ideas, ideological diversity readies the movement for social change. Unity, in turn, gives the movement strength. A one-woman strike, boycott, or sit-in scarcely represents a threat to dominant institutions. But women who are individually powerless gain leverage by acting together. Unified, they can disrupt patriarchal institutions and pressure authorities into finding new solutions.

Though diversity and unity are both beneficial, they pull social movements in opposite directions. Diversity tends to impede unity and may lead to factionalism. Unity tends to suppress diversity and may stifle flexibility and innovation. As in any complex social arrangement, there can be no either/or choice for social movements: survival and efficacy dictate a balance between diversity and unity. The story of the first and second waves of the Canadian women's movement illustrates this dilemma.

The first wave of **feminism** in Canada began in the late nineteenth century and ended in 1918. During this period, women formed organizations for the protection and education of young single women, such as the Anglican Girls Friendly Society and the Young Women's Christian Association (YMCA). Women's groups also protested against child labour and poor working conditions and pressed for health and welfare reforms.

Feminists of the first wave differed in their religious, class, and ethnic backgrounds. While many were Protestant, others were not. Anglo-Saxon women from the middle and upper classes predominated, especially among the leadership, and language divided anglophone and francophone feminists. Moreover, women's organizations had diverse goals.

But the battle for women's voting rights unified the movement. One of the earliest women's groups in Canada, the Toronto Women's Literary Club (soon renamed the Women's Suffrage Association), was founded in 1876. By 1916, women had won the right to vote in provincial elections in Alberta, Saskatchewan, and Manitoba. Other provinces soon followed, and Canadian women finally received the federal franchise in 1918.

As with many other social movements, success led to decline. The fight for voting rights had given the women's movement a common goal. When this goal was attained, the movement lost unity and momentum. Certainly, women did not stop pushing for change after winning the right to vote. Some worked within the labour movement; others continued to fight for social reform or female political representation. Yet after 1918, the Canadian women's movement became fragmented, and four decades would pass before it regained strength (Wilson, 1991).

The second wave of the movement rose out of the peace, student, and civil rights movements of the 1960s. In some cases, organizations advanced the women's cause by branching out. For example, a Toronto organization called the Voice of Women (VOW) was founded in 1960 as a peace group. But the VOW gradually adopted other women's issues, and by 1964 it was promoting the legalization of birth control.

The social movements of the 1960s also spurred women in other ways. Women in the student move-ment came to realize that many male activists were sexist. This drove home the extent of gender inequality and the need to organize apart from men. Through the New Left movement, women discovered that socialism helped make sense of gender inequality. More generally, the cultural upheaval of the 1960s encouraged women to question their position in private and public life.

As a distinct women's movement emerged in the late 1960s and early 1970s, so did internal diversity. Some members were revolutionary Marxists, while others were socialists, liberals, or radical feminists. At times, those who favoured grassroots activism criticized those who worked through high-profile official committees such as the Canadian Advisory Council on the Status of Women. The specific concerns of lesbian, non-white, immigrant, or Native women were often ignored or marginalized by mainstream women's groups. Finally, issues of language and separatism split women's organizations in Quebec from those in the rest of Canada.

Still, the movement found bases for unity. In 1970, a cross-Canada caravan for the repeal of the abortion law attracted much publicity. The caravan collected thousands of petition signatures, showing women what could be achieved through collective action. Since then, other coalitions have formed around the issues of daycare, violence against women, labour, and poverty. Women's groups have also worked together on International Women's Day celebrations.

During both its first and second waves, then, the Canadian women's movement has organized around many issues. The diversity of its concerns and perspectives not only reflects the many faces of gender inequality, but also promotes a diffusion of the movement's ideas and its survival in the face of changing social conditions. However, serious internal arguments may exhaust activists. Although factions permit the coexistence of different constituencies, they draw attention and energy away from common interests that can unite diverse organizations. When the time for action comes, a movement may lose effectiveness if its factions do not set aside their differences. At the same time, the success of the women's movement, like that of all social movements, also depends on balancing the trade-offs between diversity and unity (Briskin, 1992).

Today, the women's movement in Canada remains very active. Many feminists organizations now practise "equality in difference," a philosophy that recognizes that social diversity itself can be used to build solidarity and maintain unity. In other words, the very fact that all women experience unique and particular forms of economic, ethnic, racial, or sexual oppression becomes a unifying issue. For example, the National Action Committee on the Status of Women recognizes that no single gender issue simultaneously affects all women in all places. This organization recognizes a plethora of issues and uses them to create coalitions with other women's groups, both in Canada and around the world. Creating unity and solidarity through diversity entails non-hierarchical thinking: no single gender issue is thought to be more important than another.

The Roots of Agrarian Protest in Canada

A study by Canadian sociologist Robert J. Brym (1980) shows why regional differences between farming economies have affected agrarian social movements in Canada. The ideology and popularity of these movements and their links with other social groups all depend on the type of farming found in each region. Brym's study examines regional differences in agrarian protest by comparing farming economies in Alberta, Saskatchewan, and New Brunswick during the Depression years.

During the 1930s, agrarian protest grew rapidly in the Prairie provinces, but not in New Brunswick. Much of this difference can be explained by the degree to which farmers' livelihoods were affected by the market. In the west, farmers concentrated on producing beef or wheat, both for the rest of Canada and for export. Hence, western ranchers and wheat farmers faced similar economic pressures. Eastern Canada set the tariffs on manufactured goods, the rates for railroad freight and bank credit, even the prices of beef and wheat. United by common economic interests, western farmers responded by creating marketing, consumer, and other voluntary associations that stressed co-operation.

In New Brunswick, by contrast, farmers practised mixed agriculture. Their primary productive goal was meeting their economic needs without selling what they produced or buying what they needed—strictly speaking, they were peasants rather than farmers. Since changes in market prices hardly affected them, they had little reason to defend themselves by forming co-operatives. Historical and geographical factors also mattered. While the dominance of shipping and timber interests had hampered the commercialization of agriculture in New Brunswick, the province's poor soil and rugged terrain confined farming to river valleys and the coastline. Finally, New Brunswick farmers were not only more isolated than those in the west, they also had much smaller debts. Farmers in New Brunswick were therefore much less likely to form associations. In 1939, for instance, membership in farmers' co-operatives per 1,000 rural residents over 14 years of age was 32 in New Brunswick, compared with 326 in Alberta and 789 in Saskatchewan (Brym, 1980: 346).

Thus, the greater radicalism of western farmers stemmed from high solidarity and a loss of control over their **means of production**. But the two western provinces diverged in their approach to agrarian protest. Alberta's Social Credit Party was right-wing, while Saskatchewan's CCF (Co-operative Commonwealth Federation, the predecessor of today's New Democratic Party) was left-wing. What accounts for this divergence?

In Alberta, a leftist agrarian party known as the United Farmers of Alberta excluded small-town merchants and others seen as exploiters of farmers. During the difficult Depression years of the 1930s, however, co-operation between farmers and merchants increased when they saw that their economic fortunes were connected—if farmers did badly, so would local businesses, and vice versa. With the support of right-wing merchants, teachers, professionals, and preachers, the new Social Credit Party spread from Calgary to the small towns of southwestern Alberta. Eventually, Social Credit reached farmers and won their support too, but the party never lost the right-wing ideology of its urban roots.

In Saskatchewan, on the other hand, the CCF maintained strong ties between farmers and the left-wing urban working class. Of the CCF leadership, 53 per cent were farmers and 17 per cent workers, while of the Social Credit Party 24 per cent were farmers and none were workers (Brym 1980: 350). Thus, the differing class backgrounds of the farmers' allies helps to explain differences in the ideologies of agrarian movements in Saskatchewan and Alberta.

Brym's study suggests that economic factors affect the formation of social movements, as well as affecting which ideological direction they take. Agricultural producers such as prairie farmers are more likely to protest if there is a downturn in the capitalist economy because their livelihood, unlike that of producers in New Brunswick, depends on the market. Furthermore, the organization of a protest movement is hampered when potential supporters lack pre-existing social ties or work in isolation from other potential supporters. Finally, the alliances of a social movement affect both its ideology and its chances of success.

The history of agrarian protest in Alberta is linked to a more recent development in Canadian politics, the rise of the Canadian Alliance. This party began as the Reform Party in 1987, and won a staggering 52 seats in the 1993 national election. In many ways, the Reform Party was a protest party. It provided critical opposition to the Progressive Conservatives while appealing to western Canadians' sense of regional pride. Although there are many variables that determined the rise and success of the Canadian Alliance, the early organizers of the Reform Party were able to draw upon a right-wing, populist ideology that had already been created and maintained by Alberta's Social Credit Party. In other words, the ideological conditions that made it possible for the rise of a new national conservative party were set many years earlier. Indeed, the Reform Party and the Social Credit Party shared similar bases of support: just prior to the 1993 election, surveys indicated that Alberta's farmers were much more likely than any other group in that province to vote for the Reform Party (Harrison and Krahn, 1995).

The Spread of Nazism

How did so many ordinary Germans come to support the Nazis in the early 1930s? A once-popular explanation, known as **mass-society theory**, holds that the strong social bonds inherent in rural family and village life create psychological security. Modern cities, by contrast, are said to contain masses of individuals uprooted from community and tradition. Feeling lonely and desperate, these isolated individuals readily succumb to extremist movements. Nazism relieved the psychological anxieties of such people with its easy solutions, utopian promises, scapegoating of Jews, and emotion-charged mass gatherings. Mass-society theory also emphasizes the strong manipulative potential of the modern **mass media** and claims that intolerant ideologies such as Nazism attract marginalized members of the working class (Kornhauser, 1959).

Mass-society theory exhibits the chief deficiency of the breakdown approach: a failure to show a plausible connection between subjective feelings and the spread of a **political movement**. Surely the Nazis' rise to power required more than supporters who felt isolated and disoriented. Moreover, if mass-society theory is true, why did Nazi-style movements not emerge in other modern societies experiencing social strains similar to Germany's?

These issues have been addressed by a number of studies that conclude that Nazism could not have developed among a mass of isolated individuals (Birnbaum, 1988; Hamilton, 1982; Koshar, 1986). Indeed, these studies show that mass-society theory is wrong in assuming that the solidarity of rural communities raised a barrier to Nazism. In the important German election of July 31, 1932, the proportion of voters supporting the Nazis (the National Socialist Party) was lowest in cities and highest in small communities. In fact, in some villages, all the votes went to the Nazi party. Further, there is no evidence that marginalized working-class people were especially likely to support the Nazis, as mass-society theory claims. To be sure, this question remains unresolved, for the class background of individuals who voted for the Nazis is poorly understood. Nevertheless, electoral support for the Nazis was lower in predominantly working-class districts. This does not prove conclusively that working-class people were less likely to support the Nazis—people from more than one social class may inhabit a district. However, the class pattern of regional voting certainly casts doubt on the mass-society thesis. One other finding has also contributed to the search for an alternative explanation: the fact that the Nazis received far fewer votes in Catholic areas but far more where Protestants predominated.

The spread of Nazism is better explained by first looking at economic conditions in the early 1930s. Like many other countries, Germany was experiencing an economic depression so severe that citizens were eager for new options. In the United States, Depression-era voters turned to the Democratic Party. In the Scandinavian countries, support for socialist parties rose sharply, while in Canada and Britain, voters elected the Conservative parties. Since people exposed to the difficult conditions of the Great Depression wanted substantial change, anti-democratic ideologies also gained strength, especially where liberalism was weak. However, the direction of change was not predetermined. Some countries turned sharply to the left, and even in Germany the left (the Communists and the Social Democrats) presented a radical alternative that attracted many.

But Germany finally turned to the far right, above all because of the effectiveness of Nazi activists. Many were veterans of World War I who had retained military values of comradeship, discipline, obedience, and honour. Rapidly demobilized by the thousands after the Versailles Treaty, they were never reintegrated into German society. These men harboured a wide-ranging resentment against Jews, materialism, democracy, communism, and capitalism. Through persuasion, intimidation, and thuggery, and by adjusting their propaganda to different audiences, they worked to win support for the Nazis. Elements of the German press also helped by presenting the Nazi cause in a favourable light.

Contrary to the claims of mass-society theory, social ties actually helped the Nazis. It was through their social ties that activists spread the Nazi message and recruited supporters. Nazi activists targeted local leaders and organizations such as clubs, associations, and farmers' and religious groups. These targets were of pivotal importance because of their ties with potential Nazi supporters. If Nazi activists could convert an influential local dignitary or organization leader, then ordinary citizens or organization members were likely to follow. The preponderance of the Protestant vote for the Nazis, especially in the countryside, therefore reflects the activists' success in winning over Protestant religious organizations.

Interestingly, the strength of social ties also explains some of the Nazis' difficulties during the early 1930s. The Catholic Church and strong working-class organizations in the cities resisted Nazi activism. They limited the spread of Nazi support, and even organized anti-Nazi resistance. The Nazis were aware of this, and after taking power in 1933 they replaced independent organizations such as unions and youth groups with ones they controlled. The Nazis recognized that the control of social ties amounted to the domination of German society.

Selection for Socialism

The preceding explanations have focused on the roles played by activists, social ties, class alliances, and economic interests. As a comparative study of socialism by Robert Wuthnow (1989) demonstrates, political alliances and the nature of the regime also influence the nature and fortune of ideological movements.

The hope that **capitalism** will one day give way to collective ownership of the means of economic production lies at the heart of socialist doctrines. To this, **Marxism** added two further tenets: first, the belief that class conflict drives history and, second, faith in the industrial working class—the **proletariat**—as the agent of historical progress. While the names of Karl Marx and Friedrich Engels are closely associated with socialism, *socialism* and *Marxism* are not synonymous. Various currents of socialist thought had already appeared in Europe by the 1830s and 1840s, and many variants continued to flourish outside of Marxism. Moreover, the ideas of Marx and Engels themselves continued to develop long after they wrote the *Communist Manifesto* in 1848.

European intellectuals were not the only advocates of socialist ideas. Indeed, in some ways they were less influential than the many newspapers and associations affiliated with the movement. Eventually, political parties became the principal promoters of socialism in nineteenth-century Europe. The puzzling question is why some socialist parties in Western Europe were much more successful than others.

Consider the vote for socialist parties prior to World War I. Western European countries fell into three categories on the basis of the level of electoral support for the socialists: *low*, where the socialists got under 15 per cent of the popular vote; *medium*, where they got 15 to 25 per cent; and *high*, where they got over 25 per cent (see Table 13.3). The socialists' electoral performance was a good indicator of their

Table 13.3 **Support for Socialist Parties in Western Europe Prior to 1914**

Low Support	Medium Support	High Support
Great Britain	France	Germany
Italy	The Netherlands	Sweden
Spain	Norway	Belgium
		Denmark

SOURCE: Based on Robert Wuthnow, *Communities of Discourse: Ideology and Social Structure in the Reformation, the Enlightenment, and European Socialism* (Cambridge, MA: Harvard University Press, 1989).

strength in other key areas as well, including party membership, newspaper and book publishing, and the sponsorship of clubs, educational programs, and benevolent societies.

If economic conditions alone affected the success of socialist movements, pre-1914 voting for socialist parties ought to have been stronger in industrialized countries with large working classes. However, voting for the socialists was very low in Great Britain and moderate in France, even though both societies were highly industrialized relative to the rest of Europe. Clearly, industrialization and the presence of a large working class do not adequately explain variations in socialist success.

Wuthnow argues for "the importance of state structures in addition to economic conditions in accounting for the success of the socialist movement" (1989: 446). The main factors he cites are the nature of the regime and the balance of political forces. In a conservative aristocratic regime such as Germany's, the mainly middle-class liberal political parties were weak, unable to forge strong alliances with the industrial working class. Socialist organizers in Germany thus faced less competition in recruiting and organizing the working class. The situation in Belgium paralleled that in Germany. Rule was in the hands of an alliance between industrialists and a monarchic oligarchy. Belgian socialists were also helped by anti-union laws that stifled other working-class organizations. In France, Great Britain, and the Netherlands, by contrast, liberal institutions and forces were well established by the late nineteenth century. Liberalism and healthy trade unions undercut the socialists' attempt to capture the working-class vote in these nations.

In the Scandinavian countries, the conservative aristocracy was relatively weak by the end of the nineteenth century, but it retained some influence in the towns and cities. In the countryside, the farmers supported liberal parties, especially in Denmark and Norway. Because the conservatives were on the wane and the liberal parties were young and more strongly rooted in the countryside, socialists in Scandinavia had a good chance of organizing the new urban working class.

Economic factors carried more weight in Italy and Spain, where late industrialization delayed the formation of a working class. To be sure, Italy's socialists made rapid gains after 1898, especially in the industrialized northern regions. Still, they faced strong competition from the church, the liberal parties, and the unions. In Spain, the liberal parties were disorganized, but the socialists had to compete against the anarcho-syndicalists. They also faced a movement for regional autonomy in Catalonia, one of Spain's chief industrial areas. The Catalan movement blocked the socialists by uniting workers with other classes in the region.

European socialism was thus stronger where liberals were weak and industrialists and conservatives were united (Germany and Belgium) or where conservatives and liberals kept each other in check (Scandinavia). Socialism was weaker where conservatives were weak and liberal forces won significant working-class support (France and Britain). In Italy and Spain, socialism remained weak because of late industrialization. More generally, Wuthnow's study (1989) shows that the nature of the regime and the type of alliances struck by different political forces crucially affected the socialist movement's chances for success before World War I.

Is the Future of Social Movements Global?

The world is going through an accelerated bout of **globalization**. While this is hardly new, some sociologists claim the level of global interdependence and the scale of global interaction are becoming more complex too. Capital and commodities, information and ideas, people and their cultures are criss-crossing the globe, and these interactions are changing the world's societies.

Many social movements recognize that globalization is changing the political terrain. New opportunities and constraints are appearing that force social movements to adapt their strategies, resources, and ideologies. Recall Charles Tilly's research (1978) on the development of the nation-state in Europe: the rise of new forms of social protest was a product of the rise of nations. Will globalization also give rise to new, global forms of protest?

Some environmental organizations, such as Greenpeace International, Amnesty International, and the Sea Shepherd Society, as well as a variety of anti-globalization movements, claim to operate in a global polity. These organizations take the globe as their site of struggle while simultaneously operating in specific locations. In other words, organizations such as these claim to "think globally but act locally." Their strategy is clear: concerted efforts in locations throughout the world will alter the negative social and environmental effects of globalization.

The link between globalization and social movements has not gone unnoticed by sociologists. German sociologist Ulrich Beck (1996) claims that globalization creates opportunities for new forms of collective action that operate outside the politics of the nation-state, in the politics of what Beck calls a "world risk society." Beck suggests that ordinary people in all societies have been socialized to understand that the modern world is full of human-created hazards. Widely publicized dangers, such as the radioactive cloud that drifted from a nuclear reactor in Chernobyl (in Ukraine, at that time part of the Soviet Union) to the rest of Europe in 1986, have forced people to acknowledge that many political issues transcend borders. For Beck, the emerging recognition of global risks marks a new reality for social movements.

Greenpeace International is a good example of a global, or *transnational*, social movement that appears to have adapted to this world risk society. Greenpeace originated in the late 1960s, and its earliest members were environmental activists from Canada and the United States. From the start, this environmental movement was concerned with global issues and it organized protests throughout the world.

Greenpeace has developed its own political opportunities by creating unique forms of global diplomacy (Beck, 1996). It often operates outside the boundaries of the nation-state, such as on the high seas, where individual nations have no legal jurisdiction (Magnusson, 1990). Conscious of the influence of the international media, Greenpeace rallies support by organizing global boycotts that challenge governments and corporations to change their environmental policies and practices. Through these media events, Greenpeace attempts to stir up moral indignation while recognizing that different cultures have various understandings and experiences of global environmental dangers (Eyerman and Jamison, 1989).

Not all sociologists agree that globalization has created a fundamentally new political reality. Leslie Sklair (1994) argues that global politics are very much like national politics, simply on a larger scale. For Sklair, organizations such as Greenpeace International mirror the organizational structures of transnational corporations. He suggests that the global environmental movement consists of transnational environmental organizations whose professional members make up a global environmental elite. This elite plays an ideological game with the transna-

February 2003 saw worldwide peace rallies in opposition to the war expected to be waged by the United States against Iraq. In a global outpouring of anti-war sentiment, millions of protestors gathered in all of the capitals of America's traditional allies: London, Rome, Paris, and Ottawa. In this photograph, anti-war activists brave −30 degree Celsius temperatures to protest against any Canadian involvement in a possible war with Iraq. (Jonathan Hayward/CP)

tional corporate and governmental elite: each side attempts to have its version of the environmental reality accepted as the truth. For Sklair, this is politics as usual.

Sociologists also question whether the rise of supranational organizations, such as the European

13.4

Global Issues
The Clayoquot Standoff

The tourist board markets British Columbia as "Super, Natural," a Pacific Eden full of lush rainforests and forgotten inlets harbouring killer whales and inexhaustible salmon runs. That wild, virginal image began fading in Clayoquot Sound, on the west coast of Vancouver Island, as loggers and environmentalists battled over the giant cedars and Sitka spruce that have stood on the West Coast since before the time of Columbus.

In the summer of 1993, more than 800 protesters were charged by police after trying to block loggers' attempts to start felling the old-growth stands of Clayoquot Sound. The loggers had the legal right to do so, since the provincial government has decided that 62 per cent of the 270,000 hectare area should be opened up for a timber harvest by forestry giant MacMillan Bloedel Ltd. The rest was to be preserved. The protesters, ranging from teenagers with nose-rings to pensioners in cable-knit sweaters, were carted off in one of the biggest mass arrests in Canadian history. In the courts, some received unexpectedly harsh sentences: up to 60 days in jail and fines as high as $3,000.

But the battle was far from over. Though the environmentalists found themselves on the wrong side of the law, they testified in court that they had the moral high ground. Some used a character in one of Dr Seuss's children's books to illustrate what they viewed as a spiritual quest to save the forests from greedy timber conglomerates: "I am the Lorax, I speak for the trees." They settled in outside the Vancouver headquarters of MacMillan Bloedel, where they were to be found most lunch hours, toting billboards in a legal picket. One group planned to take a stump from Clayoquot Sound on a European protest tour in the spring of 1994.

The message of the environmental groups was simple: Forestry companies have been criminally negligent in their stewardship of British Columbia's forestry resource, turning the province into the "Brazil of the North." As a result, they do not deserve to be trusted with the logging of Clayoquot Sound, the largest coastal temperate lowland rainforest left in the world. Those in Ireland and Scotland were cut down long ago.

MacMillan Bloedel's response was that the environmentalists simply want to stop logging. Period. Dennis Fitzgerald, a company spokesman, commented, "I've yet to see them approve of a logging plan anywhere." To fight back, the forestry industry began doing its own politicking and myth-building. To prove that MacMillan Bloedel is sensitive to the environment, Fitzgerald pointed out that clearcuts no longer stretch over 80 to 100 hectares of forest land, creating eyesores that leave tourists gasping. In the previous five years, the forestry industry reduced clearcuts to between 30 and 40 hectares. MacMillan Bloedel has also stated that it can log in Clayoquot Sound forever, since it will cut at a rate that will give seedlings 80 to 100 years to grow before the chainsaws return.

Ironically, both sides said they want the same thing: sustainable development, the buzzword of the decade. That is easy to overlook, however, given the din of loggers' chainsaws and the TV-savvy theatrics of the environmentalists blocking logging roads.

SOURCE: Adapted from Miro Cernetig, "The Clayoquot Standoff," *Report on Business* (Jan. 1994), 31–2. Reprinted with permission from The Globe and Mail.

Union (EU), will bring about new forms of collective action that link activists across national boundaries. Although the EU does constitute a new political terrain, Doug Imig and Sidney Tarrow (2001) have found that collective action in Europe remains strongly rooted within the nation-state. While Europeans have many grievances against the EU, most protest against it is domestic rather than transnational. This may simply indicate that activists have yet to develop new transnational strategies and linkages. Nevertheless, domestic politics remain a viable political arena for voicing concerns about the EU (Imig and Tarrow, 2001).

Today the world is more intricately connected than in the past. A variety of new social issues have arisen as a result, and there are now social movements that attack globalization. Each has to identify guilty institutions and actors, however, and states and corporations remain the best choice because they are largely responsible for the policies and practices that promote globalization.

Generally, two characteristics are needed for a social movement to be truly global. First, a social movement must frame its grievances as global grievances. Many environmental organizations do this. By framing environmental risks as global risks, the environmental movement hopes to demonstrate that environmental degradation affects everyone. Second, to be global a social movement needs to have a worldwide membership and organizational structure. On a global scale, membership and frame alignment are probably supported by communication technologies such as e-mail and the Internet. Alternatively, a global movement can arise through a long-term coalition or network of movement organizations. For example, indigenous peoples across North and South America, Australia, and New Zealand have united against the ongoing effects of colonialism and to ensure that the rights of indigenous populations are recognized.

Conclusion

Sociologists seek to explain how and why social movements form, continue, and dissolve. Comparative studies of movements can help to determine whether or not any common features point to a general explanation or whether existing explanations hold for different situations. And historical studies reveal how social movements change over time.

Figure 13.3 depicts the changes in protest repertoires in Western Europe and North America. Early forms of collective action were poorly organized and relatively sporadic. Often their grievances were tied to local affairs, and thus their targets were usually local elites. With the rise of nation-states, however, new kinds of social movements appeared. These movements were highly organized and often identified social issues that stemmed from structural conditions such as economic inequality and narrow political representation. They also routinized protest activities: different social movements learned to apply similar methods of protest, such as the mass demonstration. The rise of NSMs in the second half of the twentieth century marks another change. These movements are more concerned with gaining cultural recognition than with the redistribution of social goods. So even though NSMs tend to use traditional forms of protest, they are more concerned with the politics of everyday life than with the traditional politics of governance.

While issues and methods of protest have changed over time, the success of collective action is always linked to the social and political climate. In other words, social and political changes can create opportunities for social movements, or they can create con-

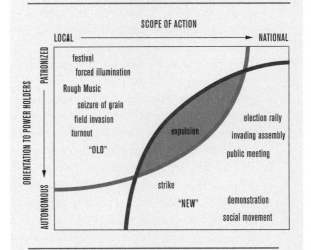

Figure 13.3 "Old" and "New" Repertoires in Western Europe and North America

SOURCE: Charles Tilly, "Speaking Your Mind Without Elections, Surveys, or Social Movements," *Public Opinion Quarterly*, 47(4): 461–78, 1983. Reprinted by permission of the University of Chicago Press.

straints. According to a theory developed by Herbert Kitschelt (1993), present conditions in Canada have created opportunities that may lead to an increase in social movement activity. To understand why, short- and long-term social movement dynamics must be distinguished. Support for social movements usually rises when political parties and interest groups fail to channel citizens' demands. Social movements can then mobilize support, attract resources, and forge alliances among protest groups. However, according to Kitschelt, this surge in social movement activity peaks as resources dwindle, as political parties begin to take up citizens' concerns, and as people's interest in collective mobilization wanes. Social movement activity then falls, only to rise again the next time organizers capitalize on frustration with parties and interest groups. In other words, the short-term pattern of movement activity is cyclical.

The long-term trend, by contrast, is toward an increase in the number of social movements. In the wealthy capitalist democracies, social movement activity has grown steadily since the 1960s. Established parties and politicians have proven increasingly incapable of providing satisfactory solu-

tions to such issues as nuclear power, toxic waste disposal, resource management, abortion rights, pornography, and equal rights. Today, many Canadians share a distrust of established politicians, political parties, and interest groups. The heavy "No" vote in the constitutional referendum of 1992, the Conservative Party's brutal fall from power in 1993, and the rise of protest parties in Quebec (the Bloc Québécois) and western Canada (the Reform Party and its successor, the Canadian Alliance) all signal citizens' disenchantment with the political establishment. The extent of citizen discontent should not be exaggerated, however. Recent federal elections have shown that an established party like the Liberals can still attract much support. Nevertheless, many burning public questions—citizen participation, gender, and environmental, ethnic, and Native rights issues—often elude both parties and interest groups. The current climate in Canada therefore favours an expansion of social movement activity. Of course, whether organizers will actually exploit this situation remains to be seen. The outcome will depend on social movement leaders and on the political establishment's ability to co-opt them.

☐ Questions for Critical Thought

1. Does economic prosperity encourage or hinder the formation of protest movements? Consider the experience of Canada in the 1930s and the 1960s, or compare capitalist countries in Latin America today.

2. Many people today believe that social movements offer better prospects for democratic participation than political parties or interest groups. However, Roberto Michels's "iron law of oligarchy" says that organization discourages democratic participation because resources, expertise, and status tend to flow to leaders. Have new social movements (NSMs) successfully broken the iron law of oligarchy? If you were organizing a social movement, what kind of safeguards would you put in place to prevent an oligarchy from forming?

3. Find an ideological statement from a social movement, such as a flyer or leaflet, a brochure or members' newsletter, a Web site, or an interview with a movement representative. What are the movement's ideals, goals, and plan of action? What social goods does the statement value, disparage, or neglect? How does the statement use emotional appeals to make its message more persuasive? Is the movement offering selective incentives to attract new members? What kinds of people are most and least likely to be persuaded by this statement?

4. Select a chapter of *Political Man* (1981) by Seymour Martin Lipset and write a critique of it based on your sociological understanding of social movements.

5. The political process approach attempts to determine how political opportunities and constraints influence social movement activities. Do you think that McAdam's proposal to restrict the definition of these concepts is useful, or is it too narrow? As an aid, look over the case studies in this chapter and try to identify the most important political opportunities and constraints.

6. All sociological theories make **ontological** assumptions. In other words, theorizing about the social world requires particular assumptions about how it operates (for example, social conflict versus social consensus). How can empirical research on social movements be used to refute or confirm the ontological assumptions of social movement theories?

7. A counter-movement is generally understood to be a response to a social movement. Find an example of a counter-movement and compare it with its associated social movement. What do you think are the main differences? Are there similarities that you think are of sociological importance? What social movement theory do you think is the most appropriate for understanding the relationship between these two forms of collective action?

8. Social movements disseminate ideas and hope to influence the general public. What is the role of the media in this process? How might new media technologies change social movement strategies, processes, and internal organization?

☐ Recommended Readings

Brian Barry, *Sociologists, Economists and Democracy* (Chicago: University of Chicago Press, [1970] 1978).
This lucid review and critique of "rational choice" and cultural approaches remains pertinent to theoretical debates on social movements raging among sociologists and a good source for readers interested in exploring structural functionalism, the role of values, and the free-rider problem.

William K. Carroll, ed., *Organizing Dissent: Contemporary Social Movements in Theory and Practice*, 2nd edn (Toronto: Garamond, 1997).
The ideological stance, choice of subject matter, analytical styles, and emphasis on identity-based approaches found in this edited volume exemplify the dominant trends in studies of Canadian social movements.

Mario Diani and Jon Eyerman, eds, *Studying Collective Action* (London: Sage, 1992).
This collection of articles by prominent social movement researchers provides detailed discussion of methodological problems in the study of social movements.

Todd Gitlin, *The Whole World Is Watching: Mass Media in the Making and Unmaking of the New Left* (Berkeley: University of California Press, 1980).
Gitlin's vivid account shows why the modern mass media are a mixed blessing for social movements.

Barrington Moore, Jr, *Social Origins of Dictatorship and Democracy: Lord and Peasant in the Making of the Modern World* (Boston: Beacon, 1966).
A classic of historical-comparative sociology, this ambitious, closely argued work connects class alliances and regime outcomes in England, France, the United States, China, Japan, and India.

Theda Skocpol, *States and Social Revolutions: A Comparative Analysis of France, Russia, and China* (Cambridge: Cambridge University Press, 1979).
Skocpol's influential study, which was written partly in rebuttal to Barrington Moore's *Social Origins of Dictatorship and Democracy*, helped to renew interest in the sociological role of the state and the ideas of Max Weber.

Sidney Tarrow, *Power in Movements: Social Movements and Contentious Politics*, 2nd edn (New York: Cambridge University Press, 1998).
An up-to-date survey of social movement studies, written by a scholar versed in theory and empirical work on both sides of the Atlantic.

Eric R. Wolf, *Peasant Wars of the Twentieth Century* (New York: Harper & Row, 1969).
Peasant rebellion and revolt in Mexico, Russia, China, Vietnam, Algeria, and Cuba are explained in terms of the penetration of capitalism.

□ Recommended Web Sites

American Sociological Association, Section on Collective Behavior and Social Movements
www.asanet.org/sectioncbsm

This a good starting place for more information on the sociological study of social movements. Read *Critical Mass*, the section's newsletter, to be informed of new publications, conferences, and the latest research.

Assembly of First Nations
www.afn.ca

This very comprehensive site contains detailed information about social issues pertaining to Canada's First Nations.

Canadian Lesbian & Gay Archives (CLGA)
www.clga.ca/archives/

This site provides information that relates to lesbian, gay, bisexual, and transgender movements. Its focus is mostly Canadian, but the archive also provides plenty of information from around the world.

Canadian Race Relations Foundation
www.crr.ca

The Canadian Race Relations Foundation's primary goal is to end race- and ethnic-based discrimination in Canada. This Web site provides information about current issues and research.

Centre for Social Justice
www.socialjustice.org

This organization was established in 1997 and is based in Toronto. Its goals are to foster national and international social change through research and advocacy.

Global Solidarity Dialogue
www.antenna.nl/~waterman/dialogue.html

This is a good starting place for information on global social movements. The site provides research, news, and discussion on social movements throughout the world, as well as information on globalization.

Greenpeace Canada
www.greenpeace.ca

This site provides information about Greenpeace's past and current campaigns. Peruse the site and try to establish how this organization frames environmental issues.

National Action Committee on the Status of Women
www.nac-cca.ca

NAC is the largest women's movement organization in Canada. This site provides the history of the organization, and it presents current issues and discussion about equity issues in Canada.

part **four**

> > >

Social Inequality

This part is about social inequalities associated with social class, gender, and ethnicity and race. These inequalities are central to the way Canadian society and most other societies are structured. No one can hope to fully understand the way a society works without understanding how its main social inequalities operate, because they affect so many aspects of social life.

14

Julie Ann McMullin

> > >

Class and Status Inequality

© Bill Whittman

□ Learning Objectives

In this chapter, you will:

- seek to understand Marxist conceptualizations of social class
- examine Weberian conceptualizations of social class
- differentiate between Marxist and Weberian conceptualizations of social class
- learn about the feminist critique of social class
- explore the relationship between social class and inequality in paid work, education, and health
- come to understand why "class matters"

Introduction

Kimberly Rogers was born into a working-class family in Sudbury, Ontario, on 20 July 1961. She was raised by her mother and her stepfather, third in a line of four sisters. At the age of 18, Kimberly left Sudbury for Toronto, where she worked as a waitress, as a bartender, and as a receptionist. While working in Toronto, she also went to school and completed her high school diploma.

In 1996, she left Toronto and an abusive relationship, and returned to Sudbury. Upon returning to Sudbury, Kimberly could not find work and applied for social assistance. In the fall of 1996, Kimberly registered in the correctional services workers program at Cambrian College. She later changed programs and continued her studies in the social services program, from which she graduated near the top of her class, in the spring of 2000. By all accounts, she was a model student. As one of her teachers remarked, "She was such an ambitious student . . . very thorough in her work and very supportive of others, which made her extremely popular with her classmates" (MacKinnon and Lacey, 2001: F1).

In order to pay for her education, Kimberly received student loans while receiving benefits under the general welfare program. This violated Ontario provincial law because the general welfare program does not permit recipients to receive student loans, nor does the Ontario Student Assistance Program (OSAP) permit its recipients to receive welfare.

In November 1999, OSAP uncovered the fact that Kimberly had been receiving both OSAP loans and general welfare, and suspended her loan for the remainder of the academic year. Kimberly had to rely on two small grants obtained through the college to pay her tuition and books, and on charity for food. Because of her actions, Kimberly was also unable to benefit from the OSAP loan-forgiveness program, and would have to repay the loan in its entirety (approximately $30,000) upon graduation. Ontario Works also began an investigation into Kimberly's actions and, in September 2000, she was charged with welfare fraud.

In April 2001, Kimberly pled guilty to the fraud charge. The judge sentenced her to six months' house arrest and required her to pay restitution to welfare for the amount of benefits she received while she was in college, approximately $13,000. Because of her conviction for welfare fraud, Kimberly Rogers was automatically suspended from receiving social assistance for a period of three months. A new regulation, which came into force on 1 April 2000, required that persons convicted of welfare fraud committed prior to 1 April 2000 be suspended for a three- or six-month period, and that persons convicted of welfare fraud committed after 1 April 2000 be subject to a lifetime ban.

As a result of her conviction, Kimberly Rogers was required to stay in her apartment at all times, except for attending medical and religious appointments and for a three-hour period on Wednesday mornings, during which time she could run errands and buy groceries. But Kimberly Rogers had no money to buy the necessities of life. Even after her lawyers succeeded in having the court lift the ban on her benefits, her monthly benefits were reduced to collect a portion of the amount owing under the restitution order. After rent was taken into account, Kimberly Rogers was left with about $18 per month to buy food.

On 9 August 2001, while under house arrest, Kimberly Rogers died. She was eight months pregnant. Sudbury was suffering through a second week of temperatures over 30 degrees Celsius and Kimberly's unairconditioned apartment was on the top floor of an old house. Responding to her death, Kimberly's lawyer stated that "she would have been better off if she had committed a violent crime and been sent to prison. . . . If sentenced to jail, she would have had the necessities of life, she would have had access to medications. If something had happened to her, it wouldn't have been two days before her body was found" (MacKinnon and Lacey, 2001: F1).

On 20 December 2002, after a three-month coroner's inquest into her death, a coroner's jury determined that Kimberly Rogers had committed suicide. The jury heard testimony from an expert witness in suicidology, who explained that the suspension from benefits, the house arrest, the effects of a criminal conviction—which would effectively act as a bar from employment in the social work field—had acted as a crushing weight on Kimberly Rogers's spirit and played a decisive role in the decision to take her own life. At the conclusion of the inquest, the jury issued 14 recommendations, which they felt would prevent future deaths in similar circumstances. The recommendations included that the government remove the three-month, six-month, and lifetime bans for conviction of welfare fraud from the legislation and that it increase welfare rates to reflect the actual costs of shelter and basic needs. The government's response was a flat refusal (Income Security Advocacy Centre).

IN THE FIRST PERSON

I went to university wanting to become a social worker and save the world. In my first year of undergraduate studies at the University of Western Ontario, I took both introductory social work and sociology. My social work class put me to sleep, but my sociology class was exciting, thanks largely to the excellent teaching skills of Professor Lesley Harman. The lectures in this class set off bells in my mind as I learned that inequality had more to do with the structure of opportunities than with intelligence or ambition. A lot of things happened after Sociology 020 that influenced my decision to become a sociologist. But the thing that inspired me most was my strong belief that, compared to other disciplines, graduate training in sociology would give me a superior set of skills with which to understand social worlds. –JULIE MCMULLIN

Activist groups use Kimberly's death as political leverage in their fight against poverty and inequality. These groups blame the policies of an ultraconservative Ontario government for Kimberly's death. Indeed, the election of Mike Harris and his neoconservative government in 1995 led to a 21.6 per cent cut to welfare benefits, a radical dismantling of welfare services, the institution of the Ontario Works Act and the workfare program, massive cuts to social spending, and the deregulation of labour and other markets (Walkom, 1997). These social policy changes triggered massive protest movements. For instance, the Ontario Federation of Labour (OFL) sponsored Days of Action in most of Ontario's major cities, with participants from women's groups, unions, anti-poverty groups, and others (Munro, 1997). These were political strikes in which workers stayed "away from their jobs not to make a point during negotiations in their own work-places or for their own contracts, but for the express purpose of making a point with an elected government" (Munro, 1997: 129). Clearly, this was not a government for the working-class people or those who were otherwise disadvantaged. As Kimberly Rogers's experiences demonstrate, this was a government whose policies helped the rich get richer and the poor get poorer.

Social class, a structural pillar of inequality in Canadian society, influenced Kimberly Rogers's opportunities and experiences from the moment of her birth. It is not unusual, for instance, for people from working-class backgrounds to finish their education at the end of high school and to work at jobs such as bartending; their opportunities for anything else are often severely restricted. That Kimberly needed to rely on social assistance in the first place is also linked to her social class background.

This chapter considers the relationship between social class and inequality. From its inception, social class has been an important concept in sociology. Much has been written on the relationship between social class and politics and **social movements** (Curtis, Grabb, and Chui, 1999), voting behaviour (Andersen and Heath, 2002), educational attainment (Ali and Grabb, 1998), family (Bradbury, 1990; Fox, 2001b; Luxton, 1980), the nature of paid work (Rinehart, 1996), the process of professionalization (Adams, 2000), health (Davies and McAlpine, 1998; Turner and Avison, forthcoming), income (Allahar and Côté, 1998), **race** (Allahar, 1995), **gender** (Adams, 1998), and retirement (Myles, 1989; Street and Connidis, 2001). Yet, within this body of work, there is considerable debate about what **class** is and how best to conceptualize it. Hence, the first part of this chapter deals with various conceptualizations of social class. The second part of this chapter then considers the ways in which social class has been measured in the sociological literature and puts forth a working definition of *social class*.

I will next examine the relationship between social class and social inequality. Although many of the topics just listed touch on issues of inequality, it is well beyond the scope of this chapter to discuss all of them. Instead, the focus will be on paid work, education, and health. Finally, I will conclude this chapter by briefly considering an ongoing debate in sociology: Does class matter?

Open for Discussion
The Lessons of Kimberly Rogers's Death

It was sweltering hot this time last year when Kimberly Rogers, 40 years old and eight months pregnant, died in her Sudbury apartment. She was serving a six-month sentence of house arrest after pleading guilty to defrauding the Ontario Works program (she'd collected welfare while receiving student loans to cover her studies in the social services program at Cambrian College). . . .

What has society learned?

Ontario's welfare rates remain as low as they have been since they were cut by 21.6 per cent in 1995 (there hasn't even been a cost of living adjustment). A single person still receives a maximum of $520 per month.

Just months before Kimberly's death, Ontario introduced further amendments to its social assistance laws. Now, for anyone convicted of welfare fraud committed after April, 2000, there is a lifetime ban. Those convicted can never receive welfare again. Ever. Not even if they need it to survive. The fiscal savings that result from clamping down on welfare remain a greater political priority to government than the lives of citizens who are left without shelter and food.

And the Ontario government is still crowing about the success of "workfare" in helping welfare recipients return to work. But the reality is different: Instead of integrating people into the new, knowledge-based economy, workfare is geared toward pushing people into low-paying, insecure jobs.

Still, some things have changed.

Opposition to the province's treatment of welfare recipients is growing. To date, 10 Ontario municipalities have passed resolutions to oppose the lifetime ban. Recently, the Court of Appeal determined that the province can't discriminate against welfare recipients simply because they are welfare recipients and dependent on government programs for support—in other words, a government does not have carte blanche to impose stricter conditions on welfare recipients than any other citizen. And later this year the Ontario Superior Court will consider the cases of three people who are appealing their lifetime welfare-benefit bans.

What the government did to Kimberly Rogers, it did in the name of Ontario's citizens. So her case forces all citizens to think about what kind of society we want. One that truly gives us all opportunities to participate in all aspects of society? Or one that condemns the most vulnerable to die alone? We cannot ignore these questions even if we wish to: An inquest into Kimberly Rogers's death is set to begin Oct. 7.

SOURCE: Exerted from JoAnne Frenschkowski, "We've Learned Little from Kimberly Rogers's Death," *The Globe and Mail* (9 Aug. 2002). Reprinted by permission of JoAnne Frenschkowski, staff lawyer, Income Advocacy Centre.

What Is Social Class?

First-year sociology students are often perplexed when they discover that they are not members of the middle class, as they had been led to believe, even though their family income was sufficient to afford them with the necessities of life and a university education. Unlike lay conceptions of social class that focus on income, sociologists define *social class* in relation to the paid work that people do. The general idea that people can be members of the working class without being aware that they are is a situation some-

times referred to as **false consciousness**. Members of the working class who are living in a state of false consciousness have not developed a revolutionary, collective sense of their plight in a capitalist world (Hunter, 1981:47–8).

As students try to make sense of their "new" social class, a second thing they learn about is **social structure**. In learning about social structures, students begin to understand that individuals are poor not because they are lazy or stupid but because they are not afforded the same opportunities as others. Social life does not provide a level playing field for its players. Tommy Douglas (then premier of Saskatchewan) nicely made this point at the beginning of one of his political speeches when he said, "'Everyone for himself,' yelled the elephant, as he danced among the chickens" (cited in Hunter, 1981: 211). Kimberly Rogers was a chicken. She was a straight-A student who was an ambitious and hard worker. She died, in part, because she was poor.

Sociologists talk a lot about *social structures* in their work, but there is no single definition of them. Some argue that **social institutions**, such as the family and the educational system, are social structures. Others use the term *social structure* to refer to relatively long-lasting patterns that emerge among elements of society that may or may not be directly observable (Abercrombie, Hill, and Turner, 2000). It is in the latter sense that the term **structure** is used in this chapter. Hence, *social structure* refers to how society is organized according to patterns of deeply held **beliefs**, of various **roles** and responsibilities of its members, and of sets of social behaviours. Social class may then be considered a social structure because our positioning within the social class system organizes and influences everything that we do. This idea will be developed throughout this chapter, but for now it is important to understand that the terms *social class* and *social structure* are highly interrelated.

Debates about how best to conceptualize social class stem from the sociological traditions of Karl Marx and Max Weber, both of whom might arguably be considered **conflict theorists**. The next sections consider these debates and outline the key themes that emerge from conflict and feminist accounts of social class.

Themes from Conflict Approaches to Social Class

Many of the debates about how to conceptualize social class stem from the work of Karl Marx and the subsequent critiques and elaborations of his views. Interestingly, although Marx discussed social class at length in his work, nowhere in his writings did he provide us with a succinct definition of what he meant by *social class*. Instead, scholars have had to piece together what they think he meant by the term from the various contexts in which Marx uses the concept. A now-famous quotation from the *Communist Manifesto* is often used in such assessments. Marx and Friedrich Engels wrote,

The history of all hitherto existing society is the history of class struggles. Freeman and slave, patrician and plebeian, lord and serf, guildmaster and journeyman, in a word, oppressor and oppressed. . . . Our epoch, the epoch of the bourgeoisie, possesses, however, this distinctive feature: It has simplified class antagonisms. Society as a whole is more and more splitting up into two great hostile camps, into two great classes directly facing each other—bourgeoisie and proletariat. ([1848] 1983: 203–4)

In these few lines, Marx emphasizes two issues that are central to his work on social class: first, he argues that society is characterized more by conflict than by harmony; second, he suggests that a distinctive feature of **capitalism** is the segregation of society into two central classes.

Few conflict theorists would disagree with Marx's view that society is characterized more by conflict than by harmony. Since the onset of industrial capitalism, workers and owners have fought over working conditions, pay, benefits, required hours of work, and so on (MacDowell, Sefton, and Radforth, 1992; Morton, 1998). Today, struggles continue over job security within the context of globalized economies and the rights of workers in **developing countries**.

The point on which scholars disagree is whether Marx's dichotomous conception of class is—or ever was—accurate. Some argue that these two basic class divisions still exist (Braverman, 1974), while others suggest that Marx's two-class conceptualization needs elaboration (Wright, 1997). Still others argue that Marx's two-category system was simply a theoretical abstraction and that he was well aware of the presence of middling classes and of the historical complexities of class formation (Giddens, 1971). Although such debates are interesting, they are complex and, as yet, unresolved. Hence, rather than delving into debates about how many classes there currently are in Canada, it is more fruitful to discuss the themes that are central to Marxist conceptualizations of social class.

First, Marx and Marxists argue that class is a social relation. Marx believed that society is divided into social classes that are defined by their relationship to the principal **means of production** in society (Giddens, 1971; Zeitlin, 1990). *Relations of production* refers to the idea that individuals who engage in production processes have various rights and powers over the resources that are used in production processes (see Wright, 1999). Under capitalism, those who own the means of the production (the **bour-**

Much inequality theory, from Marx to Weber, discusses the proletariat, or working class, but few people realize the devastating and long-lasting effects of such labour ghettoization. This working-class residence, close to Nova Scotia's defunct Sydney Steel Mill, captures the devastation. (CP/Andrew Vaughan)

geoisie) exploit labourers (the **proletariat**), who have little choice but to sell their **labour power** to the bourgeoisie in order to survive. For Marx, class is not an economic relation but a social one. Hence, unequal access to the rights and powers associated with productive resources are class relations (Wright, 1999).

A second feature of Marxist accounts of class relations concerns who controls production processes (Poulantzas, 1975; Wright, 1997). *Control* refers to a specific form of authority. **Authority**, in turn, is connected to issues of **power**. More will be said on power as we move into a discussion of Weberian accounts of social class. For now, it is important to note that class relations reflect the amount of control that people have, over themselves and others, in doing the work that they do to achieve their means of subsistence. In other words, class relations reflect the rel-

ative amount of control that a person has over production processes.

Third, Marxists generally agree that **exploitation** is a central component of social class relations. According to Eric Olin Wright, class-based exploitation occurs if the following criteria are met:

1. *The inverse interdependence principle.* The material welfare of one group of people causally depends upon the material deprivations of another.
2. *The exclusion principle.* The inverse interdependence in (1) depends upon the exclusion of the exploited from access to certain productive resources, usually backed by property rights.
3. *The appropriation principle.* Exclusion generates material advantage to exploiters because it enables them to appropriate the labor effort of the exploited. (Wright, 1997: 10)

If the first of these two conditions are met, "non-exploitative economic oppression" (Wright, 1999: 11) occurs, but it is not technically a situation of class exploitation as such. Exploitation exists only when all three principles are operating simultaneously.

Note the relational component in each of these exploitation principles. Explicit in these statements is the idea that class exploitation involves **social interaction**. This interaction is structured by sets of productive social relations that serve to bind exploiters to the exploited (Wright, 1997). Class exploitation also highlights the presence of inherent conflict in class relations. Put simply, in a profit-driven capitalist system, owners want their workers to work longer and harder than the workers would freely choose to do. Hence, class conflict results, not simply over wage levels, but also over how much "work effort" is expected (Wright, 1997: 18).

In summary, Marxist accounts of social class focus on the relationships between those who appropriate the labour of others to make a profit and those who need to sell their labour power. Furthermore, class relations may be assessed through the concepts of exploitation and control. As we have noted, control is related to power. Hence, one similarity between Marxist and Weberian scholarship, as we shall see, is that both schools agree that power is a central dimension of class relations. Weberians, however, have a somewhat different understanding of power than do Marxists, and Weberians focus more on distribution than on exploitation in their assessment of social class.

For Weber, classes are groups of people who share a common class situation. In *Economy and Society*, Weber defines *class situation* as the

> typical chances of material provision, external position, and personal destiny in life which depend on the degree and nature of the power, or lack of power, to dispose of goods or qualifications for employment and the ways in which, within a given economic order, such goods or qualifications for employment can be utilised as a source of income or revenue. ([1908] 1978: 57)

For Weber, class situations are market situations, and "a class is simply an aggregate of people sharing common 'situations' in the market" (Grabb, 2002: 51–2).

Weber further argues that there are three types of classes: property classes, income classes, and social classes. A *property class* is one in which differences in property ownership determine class situations. An *income class* is one in which "the chances of utilising goods or services on the market determines the class situation" (Weber, [1908] 1978: 57). A *social class* is a combination of the class situations created by property and income, whereby mobility between the social classes is a typical occurrence within either an individual lifetime or over successive generations.

Weber identified four main social classes: (1) the working class as a whole; (2) the petite bourgeoisie; (3) propertyless intellectuals, technicians, commercial workers, and officials who may be socially different from one another depending on the cost of their training; and (4) classes privileged because of property or education. Although these social class distinctions are similar to those put forth by Marx (except with regard to the emphasis on education and the cost of training), Weber employs a different method in assigning groups of individuals to each class. For Weber, the emphasis is on the distribution of resources, whereas Marx is mainly concerned with the social relations of production.

Parties and status groups are other pillars of social power according to Weber. By **parties**, Weber means voluntary associations that organize for the collective pursuit of interests, such as political parties or lobbying groups. **Status** reflects an individual's position in society according to the relative prestige, esteem, or honour they are afforded (Clark, 1995; Turner, 1988). Samuel Clark (1995) argues that status varies along four dimensions: differentiation, criteria, ascription, and institutionalization. The meanings of these variables are summarized in Table 14.1.

Notably, Clark argues that status is a form of power—the "power to elicit respect" (Clark, 1995: 15). A **status group** comprises a number of individuals who share a common status situation. Status groups "are organized to maintain or expand their social privileges by a mechanism of social closure to protect existing monopolies of the privilege against outsiders, and by usurpation to expand the benefits by reference to proximate or superior status groups" (Turner, 1988: 8). Thus, although members of a particular class may not be aware of their common situation, members of a status group usually are (Giddens, 1971; Grabb, 2002). And although classes, status groups, and parties sometimes overlap, this is not always the case. In Weberian scholarship, each is analytically distinct and central to class analysis (Weber, [1908] 1978; see also Giddens, 1971; Grabb, 2002).

Weber's assessment of status groups and parties and the analytical importance that he attaches to these

Table 14.1 **Samuel Clark's Status Variables**

Differentiation	The extent to which status is differentiated from other kinds of power, especially economic, cultural, political, and military power.
Criteria	What characteristics or possessions are accorded status (for example, wealth, erudition, military valour, athletic ability).
Ascription	Whether status is ascribed hereditarily.
Institutionalization	The extent to which stable norms and values regulate the distribution of status and the rights and duties associated with it.

SOURCE: Samuel Clark, *State and Status: The Rise of the State and Aristocratic Power in Western Europe* (Montreal and Kingston: McGill-Queen's University Press, 1995), 17. Reprinted by permission.

multiple bases of power point to the fundamental difference between his analysis of class and that of Marx. According to Weber, although status groups and parties are analytically distinct from classes, they are central to class analysis (Giddens, 1971; Grabb, 2002). For Weber ([1908] 1978), *status situations* are distinct but related to class situations; this term refers to the social status, prestige, and esteem that are associated with a social position. Unlike Marx, who believed that power is held by those who own the means of production, Weber felt that certain people in high-status groups derive power by virtue of their social position rather than through economic control.

The analytical importance that Weber attaches to the concept of power is evident in the preceding discussion. Unlike Marx, who believed that power relations are structural and cannot be separated from class relations, Weber defines **power** as "every possibility within a social relationship of imposing one's own will, even against opposition, without regard to the basis of this possibility" ([1908] 1978: 38).

He goes on to clarify this broad definition of *power* by introducing the concept of *domination*. Domination exists in social relationships in which one actor (or group of actors) comes to expect that his or her orders will be followed by others or a group of others (Weber, [1908] 1978). *Domination* is a specific power relation in which "regular patterns of inequality are established whereby the subordinate group (or individual) accepts that position in a sustained arrangement, obeying the commands of the dominant group (or individual)" (Grabb, 2002: 60). Weber states that although relations of domination are usually at work within associations or in cases in which an individual has an executive staff, other non-economic situations are also characteristic of relations of domination. One

of the examples Weber mentions in this regard is that the head of the household exercises domination over the members of the household "even though he does not have an executive staff" ([1908] 1978: 39).

Three themes emerge from Weber's conceptualization of class that separate his work from that of Marx. The first is Weber's insistence that classes, class situations, parties, and status groups must all be considered if we are to understand the class structures of societies. The second is Weber's emphasis on and view of power. Marx felt that power was derived from an economic base and was largely structural. Weber, on the other hand, saw power as a multi-faceted concept that could be derived from many sources and has both structural and individual dimensions. Finally, unlike the social-relational approach to class in Marxist sociology, Weber focuses far more on distributional issues. For Weber, the ability of people to gain access to scarce resources such as income and education is central to class analysis.

Drawing on Weberian scholarship, Canadian sociologist Edward Grabb's work on social inequality and social class is worth considering. According to Grabb, power is the "differential capacity to command resources, which gives rise to structured asymmetric relations of domination and subordination among social actors" (2002: 224–5). In an elaborate scheme of power, domination, and social inequality, Grabb (2002) suggests that there are three means of power—control of material resources, control of people, and control of ideas—which correspond primarily with economic structures, political structures, and ideological structures respectively (see Figure 14.1). These structures of power are crossed by class and non-class bases of inequality that represent the "human content" of power relations.

Figure 14.1 **Edward Grabb's Theoretical Framework on Social Inequality**

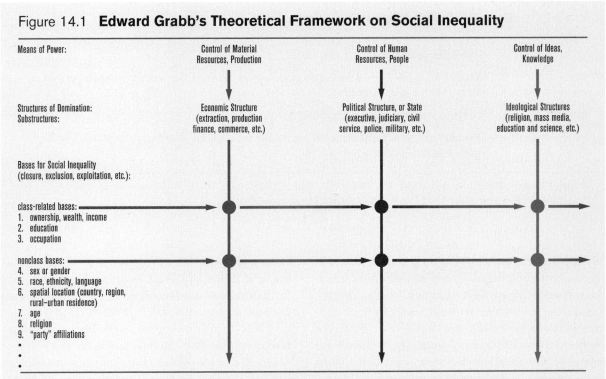

SOURCE: 'The Major Means of Power, Structures of Domination, and Bases for Social Inequality' from *Theories of Social Inequality*, Fourth Edition, by Edward Grabb. © 2002. Reprinted with permission of Nelson, a division of Thomson Learning: www.thomsonrights.com. Fax 800-730-2215.

Grabb defines *class* on the basis of ownership, education, and occupation. For Grabb, these factors represent a synthesis of the key concepts in class analysis. *Ownership* includes ownership of property but also material possessions and income. *Education* comprises credentials and knowledge. *Occupation* includes distinctions such as manual versus non-manual labour, but also includes issues of skill. Grabb further suggests that, although classes should not be considered in static terms because they vary over time and space (that is, historically and in different regions and countries), there tend to be three main class categories in modern capitalist systems: an upper class, a heterogeneous central category, and a working class. Grabb defines the *working class* as those who do not own capital, who have no special skills or credentials, and who sell their labour to make a living. The *upper class* is made up mostly of capital owners, although individuals with significant political or ideological power fall into this category as well. The *middle class* is a diverse group that may or may not have limited ownership but that is mostly distinguishable from the working class on the basis of credentials.

According to Grabb (2002), the means of power (economic, political, and ideological) are differentially distributed along class lines. Of course, people in the upper classes control the means of material production or the economic structure by virtue of their ownership of the means of production. Middle classes may have some economic power depending on whether their incomes are sufficient to purchase desirable consumer goods and to the extent that their occupation confers upon them a certain amount of authority or autonomy. And working classes tend not to have economic power at all. In Grabb's scheme, class also crosses political and ideological structures of power. Hence, those in the upper class, by virtue of their capital, high levels of education, and good occupations, tend to control political and ideological institutions such as the judiciary and educational systems. Those in the working class tend not to have ideological or political power, and those in the middle vary in the extent to which they hold such power, again on the basis of class-related factors.

Grabb's work holds a great deal of appeal to those who assume that Marxist conceptions of social class do not go far enough in explaining social inequality and that social inequality is, instead, a multi-faceted phenomenon. Why? Because the central focus in his framework is on power, not class. The inherent problem with theories of inequality that begin with issues of class is that other bases of inequality, such as gender, race, ethnicity, and age, carry less theoretical significance. Indeed, **feminist** scholarship has been critical of the literature on social class for this reason.

Feminist Approaches to Social Class

Many theorists have worked to perfect the concept of social class. Researchers strive for a specific delineation of social class that corrects what they see as limitations in the classical work. But except among feminist sociologists and a few others (for example, Carroll, 1987; Cuneo, 1985), the exclusion of women and gender from class analysis has not traditionally been considered a theoretical limitation. Rather, if the social class of women is mentioned at all, it has been assessed using categories of analysis that were established to study men (Fox, 1989). Unwaged wives are assumed to take on their husband's social class, whereas women involved in the paid labour force are classed like men in what is assumed to be a gender-neutral class system (Acker, 1980, 1988, 1990; Fox, 1989).

Indeed, gender relations are intertwined with class relations in modern industrial capitalism. Particularly telling are the following research findings: (1) Housework and child care, which women are primarily responsible for, are productive activities that are important for capitalist production (Fox, ed., 1980). Hence, "ignoring gender relations in general, and household labour in particular, produces distorted analyses of 'the economy'" (Fox, 1989: 123). (2) Women are segregated into low-paying jobs both across and within broad occupational classifications (Bielby and Baron, 1984; Fox and Fox, 1986, 1987). (3) This segregation cannot be explained by status-attainment variables (England, 1982; England et al., 1988). (4) The relations between men and women at work are often antagonistic (Cockburn, 1983; Milkman, 1987). And (5) the responsibilities that women have to their families are inextricably bound to their work lives: wives are more likely than husbands to work at home or to take time off of work to care for a sick child (Hochschild and Machung, 1989; Michelson, 1983), and their wages are influenced by the amount of time they spend engaged in household labour (Coverman, 1983; Shelton and Firestone, 1989).

Although this research demonstrates the prevalence of gender inequality within capitalism, feminists disagree over how these findings should be interpreted. Specifically, there is a theoretical debate among feminists over whether **patriarchy** (male dominance) and capitalism are two systems of oppression that serve to subordinate women (this is called *dual-systems theory*) or whether women's oppression can be best understood by theorizing about a single system of inequality that simultaneously considers gender and social class relations. Patriarchy, an essential concept in dual-systems theories (see Hartmann, 1981), is at the heart of the feminist debates over the appropriateness of single- and dual-systems approaches.

Patriarchy refers to "the system of practices, arrangements and social relations that ensure biological reproduction, child rearing, and the reproduction of gendered subjectivity" (Fox, 1988: 175). The term *patriarchy* has served a useful purpose in feminist theory because it gave women (although arguably only white, middle-class women) a political voice and also because it corrected some of the flaws of omission that were prevalent in social theory before the 1970s (that is, women were generally invisible; Acker, 1989). However, the concept of patriarchy is limiting in several respects.

Radical feminists conceptualize patriarchy as a "universal, trans-historical and trans-cultural phenomenon; women were everywhere oppressed by men in more or less the same ways" (Acker, 1989: 235). The tendency in this view is to reduce male oppression of women to biological essentialism, and it is limiting because it does not consider historical or contemporary variations in women's situations (Acker, 1989). In light of these problems, dual-systems theorists attempted to conceptualize a system of patriarchy that was linked to household production. The tendency in this approach was to view patriarchy as a system of domination that operates alongside and interacts with the political-economic system. The roots of patriarchy are thought to be located within the reproductive sphere of the family, whereas the roots of the political-economic system are located in the **mode of production** (Acker, 1989; Fox, 1989). Thus, although surprising given its Marxist roots, this perspective considers gender in a more Weberian manner, as one of several sources of inequality.

Recognizing these problems, some feminists have argued against using the concept of patriarchy (Acker, 1989; Fox, 1988). These researchers argue for a single-system approach whereby the oppression of women cannot be separated from issues of social class. This requires a reconceptualization of social class that adequately considers gendered processes as they structure the class system (Acker, 1988, 1990; Fox, 1989).

Taking issue with dual-systems theory, Joan Acker (1988), for instance, sets out to develop a single-system theory of social relations that places equal emphasis on gender and social class. According to Acker, this requires a reformulation of Marx's conception of class that is best done by taking the social relations of distribution as well as the social relations of production into account. Relations of distribution "are sequences of linked actions through which people share the necessities of survival" (Acker, 1988: 478). According to Acker, the fact that there has always been a sexual division of labour suggests that in all known societies, the relations of distribution are influenced by gender and take on a gendered meaning. Gendered relations of distribution in capitalist society are historically rooted and they are transformed (like the relations of production) as the means of production change.

Acker suggests that the wage, which is rooted in the relations of production, is the essential component of distribution in capitalist society. The wage has developed historically as a gendered phenomenon because women have always been paid less than men and because gendered job segregation is typical. Thus, "the wage and the work contexts within which it is earned are gendered in ways that re-create women's relative disadvantage" (Acker, 1988: 483).

Personal relations, marital relations, and state relations are the gendered processes through which distribution occurs. According to Acker, *personal relations of distribution* are held together by emotional bonds, usually between blood relatives, and are dependent upon the wage. As a result of both the gender-based division of labour and the **ideology** of the family wage, gender serves to organize the personal relations of distribution. In its simplest form, this system requires that at least part of the male wage is distributed to women, who then redistribute it to the dependents in their families. The personal relations of distribution also often extend beyond the household. In instances where economic hardships are typical, women often maintain extensive kinship networks by means of which survival is ensured through the allocation of resources across households. Among the economically advantaged, gender-based personal relations of distribution also occur, helping to ensure the stability and reproduction of class (Acker, 1988).

Marital relations are the central component of distribution for married women who do not work for pay and are thus dependent upon their husbands for their wage. According to Acker, unwaged housewives are connected to the production process through their husbands' wages. Although they share common standards of living with their husbands, they do not assume the same class because their situations, experiences, and activities are different. Unwaged wives have little control over their economic situation, although Acker (1988) suggests that this control likely varies by the men's and women's class.

State relations of distribution are the final type of distribution arrangement that Acker (1988) considers. The state relations of distribution are based in laws and governmental policies that have historically been developed in gendered ways. Policies and laws, established to alleviate the financial burden of the working class when the market fails, are based on gendered ideologies supporting the "male breadwinner/ dependent housewife" ideal. This renders some groups of women—those who remain unmarried, single mothers, poor working women—particularly disadvantaged. Women are further disadvantaged by the gendered nature of entitlement regulations because many social security programs are based on the labour-force experiences of men.

For Acker (1988), the culmination of these gendered relations structures social class. Conceptualizing class in this way allows unwaged persons to be included in the class structure. According to Acker, the aim of class analysis should not be to classify people into different categories; rather, class should be considered as "processes that produce contradiction, conflict, and different life experiences" (Acker, 1988: 496). Thus, in order to fully understand the "links between gender and class, divisions must be changed. One way to do this is to see class as rooted in relations of distribution (as well as in relations of production) that necessarily embed gender, both as ideology and material inequality" (Acker, 1988: 496).

Acker (2000) expands her analysis to include race and ethnic relations. Acker argues that to fully understand how class is gendered and racialized, a rethinking of class is necessary. This rethinking, according to Acker, should be informed first by a concept of class "anchored within a larger notion of the economic than is now used" (2000: 54). This idea corresponds with Acker's promotion of a conceptualization of class whereby class relations encompass relations of distribution and production. Second, class, gender, race, and ethnicity must be understood from the standpoints of many different people within these categories (see Smith, 1987). In other words, the experiences of men and women of different classes and of different racial and ethnic groups need to inform class analysis. Third, class is not simply an abstraction into which people can be placed. Rather, it is an "active accomplishment" (Acker, 2000: 53). Everything that people do and say is influenced by their class relations. Class is accomplished by people in interaction with one another. And fourth, class, race and ethnicity, and gender mutually constitute one another. That is, through structural processes and through processes of cultural representation and social interaction, race and ethnicity, class, and gender shape one another; they cannot be considered separately. **Identity** and meaning are not shaped simply by whether one is a man or black or middle class, but by the interacting influence of all three of these things (see also Glenn, 2000).

To summarize, a central problem in much of the traditional class analysis and the key point of the feminist critique of social class is that the study of class has focused far too much on the relations of production (Acker, 1988, 2000). Feminist scholars argue that class relations are social relations that extend beyond the arena of production and that Marxist approaches that conceptualize social class simply as a relation of production are too restrictive. This is true, in part, because traditional class analysis excludes far too many people who are not directly linked to production processes, such as homemakers and retired individuals. Notably, scholars have tried to reconcile this problem by attributing the social class of husbands to homemakers and by assigning a class to retired persons based on their pre-retirement status. However, these approaches are unsatisfactory because they do not capture important distributive and status differences between a housewife and her husband or between a retired autoworker and her employed counterpart (see Acker, 1988; Estes, 1999).

With these caveats in mind, the remainder of this chapter will nonetheless focus on social class as it has been traditionally defined and conceptualized. The difficulties associated with rethinking social class in light of gender, race, ethnic, and age relations are far too complex for an introductory chapter on social class and inequality. Readers should refer to the chapters on gender, ethnicity, and race for more detail about how these factors structure social inequality.

Defining and Measuring Social Class

Researchers study social class using both quantitative and qualitative methods. Qualitative approaches to social class often draw on the insights of **symbolic interactionism** and place emphasis on issues of meaning, experience, and identity. Such assessments do not attempt to succinctly categorize people into various classes but are instead concerned with the meaning, identity, and experiences of one class in relation to another. Qualitative historical work, for instance, has examined processes of class formation (Comninel, 1987) and how class relations structure professionalization projects (Adams, 1998, 2000). Using observation or in-depth interviewing techniques, other studies have explored the meaning and experiences of class relations in workplaces (Gannagé, 1986; Reiter, 1996; Rinehart, Huxley, and Robertson, 1994) and in schools (Willis, 1977).

Quantitative work on social class tends to focus either on how class affects various outcomes of social inequality or on how the class structure has changed over time. Social class is defined differently depending on which of these particular focuses is at the heart of the research. In work on social inequality, for instance, proxies of social class (that is, such factors as income, education, and occupation that indirectly measure social class), derived from **structural functionalist** approaches to stratification, tend to be used.

Social stratification approaches to social class have been very influential, particularly in American sociology. Stratification approaches conceptualize inequality as a hierarchal order (Davis and Moore, 1945) in which individuals are grouped into strata on the basis of their socio-economic status (SES) as measured through indicators such as income, education, or occupation. As a result, inequality tends to be conceptualized at the level of individual difference rather than in relational terms or on the basis of class structures (Grabb, 2002; Tilly, 1998).

Traditionally, stratification approaches have assumed that the rank ordering of people into socially defined strata is a universal and functionally necessary dimension of society (Davis and Moore, 1945). In other words, an ordering of people according to their worth, variously defined, is required for the smooth functioning of society. Certain positions in society are more valued than others because of the high level of skill that is attached to them. Only a few people can attain the skills required to fulfill these positions, and such attainment requires significant time commitment for the appropriate training. People who choose to invest the time in such training deserve higher-status positions in society and the resultant rewards attached to these positions. Furthermore, there is general agreement or consensus among the members of society that such stratification systems are acceptable (Davis and Moore, 1945).

There are two underlying assumptions in stratification research that set it apart from the Marxist and Weberian approaches to inequality. First is the tendency in stratification research to overemphasize the extent to which society operates on the basis of consensus rather than conflict. Second, and related to the first, is the underemphasis in stratification research on issues of power and exploitation (see Grabb, 2002, for an extensive discussion of these issues).

The identification of problematic assumptions in stratification research has not, however, led to its demise. Instead, it remains influential in studies of inequality and informs much empirical research on the subject. Michael Grimes (1991) argues that many researchers apply stratification measures to the study of class inequality either because they remain committed to certain aspects of functionalist thought or because stratification measures are often used in large surveys. It is important to clarify that stratification researchers do not suggest that they are studying class; class researchers, although they sometimes do stratification research, make the distinction between the two (Grabb, 2002). The point that Grimes makes is nonetheless an important one and stems, perhaps, from a more general observation that researchers whose primary interest lies outside of class and stratification analysis tend to convolute the two approaches. This propensity is most likely a result of the significant overlap between the various social factors that are examined in these approaches. For instance, occupation, defined in various ways, tends to be at the core of research on social class regardless of theoretical perspective. Further, there is a general concern in all conceptual frameworks about the distribution of scarce resources such as income, education, and skill. Hence, the tendency to use stratification measures as indicators of social class likely stems from the continued use of traditional measurements in survey research and also from the fact that the indicators of social class are quite similar, regardless of theoretical perspective.

There is little doubt that stratification measures tell us something about class-based inequality. However, these indicators cannot fully capture the extent to which social class matters in contemporary Canadian society. Instead, a relational understanding of social class is necessary. Such an understanding of social class follows a long tradition in Marxist sociology that suggests that class is not merely an economic relation. Rather, social class manifests itself as people from various classes interact with one another in productive relations. Researchers who are concerned with the macro implications of the organization of the social relations of production **operationalize** social class using concepts such as power, exploitation, oppression, property ownership, and so on, that are central in Marxist and Weberian scholarship.

Wright's work is an example of how social class can be assessed quantitatively in this way. For the past 20 years, Wright and his colleagues have been developing a typology of social class that relies on measures of occupation, authority, skill, and the number of employees who work at a particular locale (see Figure 14.2). This latter classification category reflects the number of people who are under the authority of each particular class location. For example, managers tend to have many employees over whom they have authority and dominance, while non-managers have authority over no one. Owners are separated from employees in this scheme and are differentiated from one another only on the basis of how many employees they have. Hence, owners who have only a few employees are thought to be different from those who have many and from those who have none. Employees, on the other hand, are differentiated on the basis of number of other employees, skills, and authority. Expert managers have high levels of authority and of skill and tend to supervise many employees. They stand in most stark contrast to non-skilled workers, who have no authority or skill and who supervise no employees.

In this typology, the cells do not represent classes as such, but rather refer to class locations within the capitalist class structure. The distinction here is a subtle but important one that allows Wright to cover all of his bases. Unlike an earlier version of this framework, in which he refers to the various groupings in this model as classes (Wright, 1985), in his more recent work Wright makes it clear that these cells represent class locations within an overriding framework of class relations. By doing this, Wright can stay true to a Marxist version of class relations in which exploitation is at the core while at the same time identifying contradictory places within class relations that individuals occupy.

Figure 14.2   **Eric Olin Wright's Class Divisions**

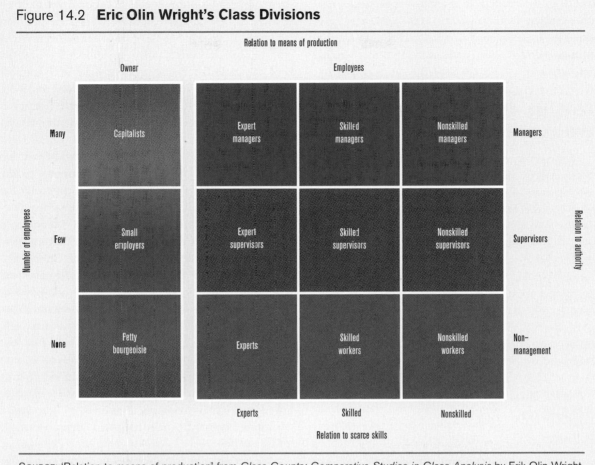

SOURCE: 'Relation to means of production' from *Class Counts: Comparative Studies in Class Analysis* by Erik Olin Wright (Cambridge: Cambridge University Press, 1997). Reprinted by permission of Cambridge University Press.

Class has thus been used in many ways in sociological thought. For the purpose of this chapter, stratification measures will be used to assess the relationship between social class and each of income, education, and health. To assess class structure, a modified, more parsimonious version of Wright's conceptualization, as it is put forth by Wallace Clement and John Myles (1994), will be used. Clement and Myles developed a four-class model in which the *capitalist-executive class* controls both the labour power of others and the means of production (see Table 14.2). The *old middle class*—the "petite bourgeoisie" in Marxist terminology—commands the means of production but not the labour power of others. The *new middle class* controls the labour power of others but not the means of production. And, finally, the *working class* commands neither the labour power of others nor the means of production. The advantage of this approach to social

Table 14.2   **Clement and Myles's Conceptualization of Social Class**

	Command Labour Power of Others	
Command Means of Production	**Yes**	**No**
Yes	Capitalist-executive	Old middle class
No	New middle class	Working class

SOURCE: Wallace Clement and John Myles, *Relations of Ruling: Class and Gender in Postindustrial Societies* (Montreal: McGill-Queen's University Press, 1994), 16.

class lies in its simplicity; it accurately reflects the "relations of ruling" in Canada while at the same time eliminating the unnecessary and often tedious class location distinctions that are contained within Wright's approach.

Social Class and Inequality

Social inequality reflects relatively long-lasting differences between individuals or groups of people that have substantial implications for individual lives, especially "for the rights or opportunities they exercise and the rewards or privileges they enjoy" (Grabb, 2002: 1–2; see also Pampel, 1998). So, for example, people who are a part of the working class earn less money, have less fulfilling jobs, do not have the same educational opportunities available to them, and have worse health than do people from the middle and upper classes. The next sections consider the relationship between social class and each of paid work, education, and health.

Paid Work, Income, and Poverty

Marx argued that as capitalism evolved, there would be an increasing polarization of workers into two central classes, the proletariat and the bourgeoisie. This polarization would involve at least three things: (1) a reduction in the proportion of small business owners and hence a shrinking of the old middle class; (2) increasing proportions of income going to the owners of large businesses and a reduction in the earnings of middle-class workers; and (3) continued deskilling of work and corresponding increases in the **alienation** of workers (Conley, 1999). We will consider each of these issues.

Class Structure in Canada

According to Clement and Myles's definition of social class, a slight majority of employed Canadians in the early 1980s formed the working class (57.6 per cent), almost 25 per cent formed the new middle class, 11.3 per cent the old middle class, and 6.2 per cent the capitalist-executive class (1994: 19).

Since the early twentieth century, the proportion of Canada's class structure comprising small business owners has declined considerably (Clement and Myles, 1994). Between the 1930s and the early 1970s, for instance, the proportion of the workforce com-

prising small business owners declined from approximately 25 per cent to between 10 and 12 per cent (Conley, 1999: 24). Much of this decline occurred in the agricultural sector, where advances in farm technology made the business of small farming unprofitable (Clement and Myles, 1994; Conley, 1999). Nonetheless, for much of the twentieth century it appeared as if Marx's prediction regarding the shrinking middle class was right.

Since the mid-1970s, however, this trend has reversed. Indeed, the most significant change in the class structure over the past 20 years in particular has been the increase in the proportion of the class structure that is held by the old middle class. Clement and Myles report that the level of non-agricultural self-employment increased from 5.8 per cent in 1975 to 7.4 per cent in 1990 (1994: 42). When self-employed owners of incorporated businesses are included in this measure, the old middle class made up about 14 per cent of the total labour force in the early 1980s (Lin et al., 1999: 15). By 1997, 17.8 per cent of the total labour force were self-employed in both incorporated and unincorporated businesses (Lin et al., 1999: 15). The majority of those who are self-employed either work on their own or hire fewer than three employees (Clement and Myles, 1994: 49; Hughes, 1999).

Reactions to recent increases in the proportion of employed Canadians who primarily constitute the old middle class have been mixed. On the one hand, some hail these changes as positive. According to this school of thought, small business owners are free of the control of large capitalist enterprises and as a result have more autonomy in their work. Their conditions of work are less alienating, and this is a positive development of post-industrial capitalism. Others have argued that, far from being a positive occurrence, the rise of small business owners is the result of workplace restructuring whereby workers lose their jobs and are forced to earn a living without some of the rewards (such as pensions and benefits) that are associated with employment in large companies (see Clement and Myles, 1994, for an overview of these opinions). This suggests that the conditions under which one becomes a small business owner are important considerations when discussing the social implications associated with higher proportions of workers in the "old" middle class.

Notably, the old middle class still includes a relatively small proportion of employed workers. Workers in the new middle class and the working class encompass the overwhelming majority in the Canadian class structure—82.5 per cent, according to Clement and Myles (1994: 19). The next two sections consider the income, skill, and alienation that are associated with these classes.

Income and Poverty

There is a strong correlation between social class and income. Working-class jobs pay less than middle-class jobs, and owners of capital tend to have higher incomes than others (Krahn and Lowe, 1998). For instance, in 1995, average annual earnings in Canada for managers ($41,352), teachers ($35,330), and medical and health professionals ($34,410) were much higher than were the average annual earnings for clerical and service workers ($21,825 and $17,160, respectively; Krahn and Low, 1998: 96–7). These earnings stand in stark contrast to the incomes of the chief executive officers (CEOs) of large companies. In 1996, the CEOs of Canada's 100 largest corporations all earned over $700,000 (Krahn and Lowe, 1998). Notably, a strong correlation between social class and income does not mean that it is a perfect correlation. There are certain jobs that, based on the definitions of social class found above, would be considered working-class jobs even though they command a relatively high wage. For example, assembly-line workers in any of the "big three" auto manufacturing plants are part of the working class, but because they are members of a relatively strong union they are paid a good wage and have good benefits.

Owners and executives of capital clearly have much higher incomes than do workers. The question that remains unanswered is whether there has been an increasing polarization of income over time. One way to address this issue is to divide Canadians into equal groups (typically either deciles or quintiles) on the basis of their income, calculate the proportion of the total income in Canada that each group accounts for, and then examine whether that proportion changed over time. In 1996, 44.5 per cent of all before-tax income was concentrated in the top quintile of the Canadian population, 24.7 per cent in the fourth quintile, 16.3 per cent in the third (middle) quintile, 10 per cent in the second quintile, and only 4.6 per cent in the lowest quintile. Between 1951 and 1996, there was a 2.9 per cent shift from the second and third quintiles to the two highest quintiles, while the proportion of income concentrated in the lowest quintile remained relatively stable. Moreover, between 1981 and 1996, the second, third, and fourth quintiles lost 2.8 per cent

of their before-tax income, a total of $14 billion, to the upper quintile (Urmetzer and Guppy, 1999: 59). These figures support the idea that there is increasing polarization of income in Canada.

The proportion of total before-tax income that is concentrated in the lowest quintile has remained relatively stable since 1951. What these figures do not tell us is that this stability has been maintained largely through government transfers such as tax credits, social assistance, and unemployment insurance. Indeed, for low-income families, the proportion of their total income from labour market earnings has declined since the 1970s (Picot and Myles, 1995). Hence, income polarization is not as serious as it could be because government policies are in place to ensure more equitable income distributions in Canada (Ross, Shillington, and Lochhead, 1994). But how equitable is a system in which the lowest quintile receives only 4.6 per cent of all before-tax income? And how equitable is a system in which the $14-billion gain made in the upper quintile during the 1980s and 1990s is equivalent to the amount of money it would take to eliminate poverty in Canada (Osberg, 1992)?

Poverty is a serious social problem in Canada. The National Council of Welfare reports that although poverty rates declined between 1998 and 1999, there were still more people living in poverty in 1999 than there were in 1989. Approximately 16 per cent of Canadians lived in poverty in 1999; poverty rates for families are about 12 per cent, and for unattached individuals they are around 39 per cent (National Council of Welfare, 2002: 4).

Poverty rates vary on the basis of gender, family status, age, immigrant and minority status, education, and labour-force attachment. For instance, in 1999, the poverty rate for single-parent mothers was 51.8 per cent—more than four times the poverty rate for all families (National Council of Welfare, 2002: 15). Unattached women under the age of 65 are more likely to live in poverty than are their male counterparts (42.3 per cent versus 33.2 per cent), as are unattached women who are aged 65 and over (48.5 per cent versus 31.9 per cent) (National Council of Welfare, 2002: 18–19). Children (18.7 per cent) and the elderly (17.7 per cent) are somewhat more likely to be poor than are all Canadians (16 per cent) (National Council of Welfare, 2002: 10–12).

Gainful employment significantly reduces poverty rates among both unattached individuals and families. Yet more than 40 per cent of families who were living

14.2

Human Diversity
Images of Child Poverty in Canada

Dirty, bare feet dangle over a licence plate in Prince Albert, Sask. A child plays with a lone tricycle on a cracked driveway in Winnipeg.

Those are images of some of the 1.3 million children in Canada who live in poverty, whose existence a group called PhotoSensitive is documenting in a cross-Canada exhibit.

The show was launched yesterday, in conjunction with a report on child poverty, released by Campaign 2000, that says nearly one in five children [was] living in poverty in 1999, compared with one in seven in 1989.

Campaign 2000 is a coalition of organizations formed to ensure that a 1989 House of Commons resolution to end child poverty by 2000 was implemented, a result still far from being realized, co-ordinator Laurel Rothman said.

"We are no closer [to ending child poverty]," she said. "In 1989, we were at one in seven children living in poverty. Now we're at almost one in five."

Ms Rothman said what is disturbing is that child poverty was prevalent even during the economic prosperity of the late 1990s.

"Governments have the option in the boom years of investing in children. Instead they took the strategy of cutting taxes, and in many cases, social services."

The report says that despite a strong economy between 1998 and 1999, the child-poverty rate dropped only slightly to 18.5 per cent from 19 per cent. And with the latest economic downturn, "those numbers are going to rocket up again," Ms Rothman said.

One positive number in the bulletin is the decrease in the depth of poverty, said Andrew Jackson, research director for the Canadian Council on Social Development, which compiled the data from several Statistics Canada studies.

In 1999, poor families saw an improvement of more than $500 in their depth of poverty over the previous year (to $9,073 below the poverty line in 1999 from $9,597 in 1998), but the gap between the rich and the poor in Canada is still far too wide, Ms Rothman said.

The report makes several recommendations to government, including the development of a national housing strategy.

And the photographs by the 24 members of PhotoSensitive remind people of the "faces behind the numbers," Andrew Stawicki, photographer and founder of PhotoSensitive, said.

Samantha naps in the attic apartment she shares with her mother and three brothers in Edmonton. They will be moving soon. (Chris Schwarz)

SOURCE: Allison Dunfield, "In 1989 We Were at One in Seven Children Living in Poverty. Now We're at Almost One in Five," *Globe and Mail* (27 Nov. 2001), A11.

in poverty in 1999 were headed by people who were employed. Compared to the total Canadian population (29.5 per cent), higher proportions of immigrant visible minorities (42.5 per cent) and Aboriginal people living off-reserve (49.4 per cent) lived in poverty for at least one year between 1993 and 1998. Finally, the poverty rate for single-parent mothers who worked full-time for the full year was still 19.7 per cent (National Council of Welfare, 2002: 6–7).

Poverty rates also vary from province to province. Newfoundland and Labrador has the highest poverty rate (20.7 per cent), followed closely by Quebec (19.5 per cent) and Manitoba (18.5 per cent). Ontario has the lowest poverty rate (13.5 per cent), followed by Prince Edward Island (14.7 per cent), New Brunswick (15.1 percent) and Alberta (15.2 per cent) (National Council of Welfare, 2002: 42). Provincial variations in poverty rates are a result of regional differences in economic structures, provincial inconsistencies in gov-ernment policies regarding social welfare transfers, and access to other social and economic resources (National Council of Welfare, 2002).

Good Jobs/Bad Jobs

You will recall that Marx's third prediction with respect to the polarization of classes was that as capitalism developed, jobs would become increasingly deskilled and alienated. Indeed, skill and alienation are two characteristics of paid work that vary depending on social class. Generally, working-class jobs are characterized by low levels of skill required to do the job and by often corresponding high levels of alienation, whereas jobs held by those in the "new middle class" and the "old middle class" tend to require more skill and to be more intrinsically rewarding. That said, for Marx's prediction to be supported, we must see evidence that middle-class jobs have become increasingly deskilled.

In 1974, Harry Braverman published his classic book *Labor and Monopoly Capitalism*. Taking issue with those who argued that rising white-collar employment was a positive effect of post-industrialism that resulted in an increasingly large middle class, Braverman convincingly argued that most white-collar jobs (such as clerical and retail jobs) should be considered working-class, not middle-class. White-collar jobs, Braverman argued, were increasingly being deskilled and organized according to **scientific management** techniques, thereby eliminating most of the control and autonomy that workers may have had over their work. Advances in new technolo-

gies contributed to this process by giving managers sophisticated tools through which they can monitor their employees' work. For example, before the advent of computerized cash registers, cashiers needed to know how to make change. Now cash registers inform cashiers how much change they need to give a customer. Further, cash registers can now monitor the speed of keystrokes and the number of customers that a cashier serves per hour. Managers, in turn, use this information in employee job performance evaluations. Hence, new technology has been used both to deskill the work process and to monitor and control it.

One year before Braverman published his book, Daniel Bell published what was to become an influential text on post-industrial society. Unlike Braverman, who argued that occupations were becoming increasingly deskilled, Bell (1973) looked to the future and argued that knowledge, and hence skill, would become a highly valued commodity in post-industrial society. According to Bell, knowledge would be a basis of power much as the ownership of property had traditionally been, and knowledge workers would form a significant class (both in number and in power) in their own right. Bell argued that as the proportion of knowledge workers grew, the historical trend toward the polarization of society into two central classes, the bourgeoisie and the proletariat, would lose speed.

In the 30 years since Bell and Braverman published their books, debates have ensued over which thesis better explains the relationship between skill and class structure in post-industrial society. Although such debates are far from resolved, Clement and Myles are worth quoting at length on the issue. They note that the debate has unfolded as follows:

> We face either a postindustrial Nirvana of knowledge where everyone will be a brain surgeon, artist, or philosopher (Bell) or, alternatively, a post-industrial Hades where we shall be doomed to labour mindlessly in the service of capital (Braverman). When drawn in these terms, the historical debate is now no debate at all. Bell is the clear winner. Although much less than a knowledge revolution, the net result of the shift to services has been to increase the requirements for people to think on the job. (1994: 72)

In Canada, 42 per cent of jobs in the post-industrial service sector are skilled compared to only 26 per cent of those in the goods and distribution sector. And 55 per cent of "new middle class" jobs are skilled, compared to only 23 per cent of working-class jobs (Clement and Myles, 1994: 76). Clement and Myles point out that the growth in the service sector has brought both skilled and unskilled jobs, but they underscore the fact that in Canada and the United States, unskilled service jobs are often entry jobs for new workers rather than serving as a basis for working-class formation. This—combined with the fact that these service jobs are now often exit jobs for older workers who have been displaced, discouraged, restructured, or retired early—suggests that age may play a more significant role in labour market inequality in the years to come. Nonetheless, the point is that although the conditions of work in contemporary Canadian capitalism are far from ideal, the proletarianization of the labour force as predicted by Braverman has not occurred even though skilled jobs are concentrated in the new middle and executive classes (Clement and Myles, 1994).

In summary, considering debates about the deskilling of work in post-industrial capitalism, about whether the middle class is shrinking, and about the distribution of income and poverty, there is no consensus among sociologists about whether the class structure of Canadian society has become increasingly polarized. On the one hand, overall increases in the skill levels associated with many jobs and recent increases in the number of self-employed small business owners suggests that the polarization thesis is incorrect. On the other hand, huge inequities in the distribution of income in Canada cannot be ignored. Furthermore, regardless of where one comes down on the debate about overall class polarization, the fact is that compared to "middle-class" jobs, working-class jobs are characterized by low levels of income and other benefits, low levels of autonomy and control in the work process, poor working conditions, low levels of skill, and high levels of alienation. The combination of these things creates social disadvantage for members of the working class relative to members of the middle classes, which carries over to other social domains. Education and health are two areas of sociological study that stand out as sites of class-based inequality.

Education

Many Canadians believe that education is a vehicle through which occupational and income advantages may be attained (Wotherspoon, 1998). Over the last 30 years, more education has come to be required to perform jobs that were done well without as much education in years past (for example, needing a high school degree to work at an auto manufacturing plant). But regardless of this "credential inflation" (Baer, 1999), there remain strong correlations between education, occupation, and income in Canada (Hunter and Leiper, 1993).

Typically, highly educated people are employed in well-paid jobs (Little, 1995) that have relatively high degrees of autonomy and authority associated with them (Butlin and Oderkirk, 1996). Of course, we have all either heard about or met a taxi driver who holds a PhD or a high school dropout who is the well-paid owner of a successful business. These examples illustrate that, just as with grammar, there are exceptions to the rules. Often there are other extraneous factors that account for these exceptions. For instance, in the case of the well-educated taxi driver, recent immigration status may affect his or her job prospects because of discriminatory hiring criteria (for example, a hiring requirement of Canadian education or work experience).

In light of the relationship between educational attainment and economic advantage, sociologists have long been concerned with the social determinants of educational attainment. Social class background, usually measured using SES indicators, is one such determinant. Two key measures of educational attainment are often considered in this regard: (1) whether young people complete high school and (2) whether they continue with postsecondary education.

On average, Canadians are among the most educated people in the world (Looker and Lowe, 2001). High school completion rates continued to increase throughout the 1990s such that only 12 per cent of 20-year-olds did not complete high school in 1999, as compared to 18 per cent in 1991 (Bowlby and McMullen, 2002). The more educated parents are, the more likely their children are to complete high school (Bowlby and McMullen, 2002). Figure 14.3 shows data for 18- to 20-year-olds from the Canadian 2000 Youth in Transition Survey. Here we see that the highest proportion of both high school graduates (34.7 per cent) and high school dropouts (45.2 per cent) have at least one parent who graduated from high school. However, among those who have at least one parent who has completed either a college or university program, the proportion of graduates is twice the proportion of dropouts (56.6 per cent versus 27.9 per cent). Among youth whose parents had not graduated from high school, the proportion of dropouts is three times the proportion of graduates (26.9 per cent versus 8.7 per cent). Furthermore, approximately 7 out of every 10 dropouts, compared to 4 out of 10 graduates, had parents who did not complete high school (Bowlby and McMullen, 2002: 31).

Similarly, mothers' and fathers' occupations are correlated with whether youth graduate from or drop out of high school. Mothers of high school dropouts were more likely to be working in sales and service jobs or in primary, processing, manufacturing, and utilities jobs. Mothers of graduates were more likely to be working in social science, government, art, culture, health, and applied science jobs. Fathers of dropouts were more likely to be working in trades, transport, and equipment-operating jobs, whereas fathers of graduates were more likely to be working in management jobs (Bowlby and McMullen, 2002).

Approximately 65 per cent of high school graduates enter postsecondary educational institutions in Canada (Looker and Lowe, 2001: 4). Among youth, the higher parents' measures of SES, the higher their children's expectations regarding postsecondary educational attainment (Looker and Lowe, 2001). Plans to attend college or university are correlated with whether youth actually attend such institutions. Hence, educational attainment, including participation in college and university programs after high school completion, is also influenced by class background, regardless of how it is measured (Ali and Grabb, 1998; Wotherspoon, 1998). Several studies have shown that financial situation is listed by youth as a key barrier to pursuing postsecondary studies (Bowlby and McMullen, 2002; see Looker and Lowe, 2001, for an overview). Furthermore, youth who are from families in the highest SES quartile are much more likely to attend university than are those in the lowest SES quartile (Chippendale, 2002; Statistics Canada and CMEC, 2000).

The preceding findings demonstrate that there is clear a relationship between parents' SES and children's educational attainment. A combination of economic, social, and cultural factors help to explain the relationship between SES and educational attainment (Davies, 1999). In the first place, if parents are poorly educated and have low-paying jobs, families may not be able to afford to keep children in school. Poor families may need their children to drop out of high school and work to help with the family economy. In

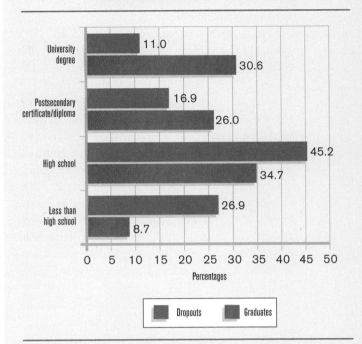

Figure 14.3   **Highest Education Attainment of Parents or Guardians of Dropouts and Graduates**

SOURCE: Adapted from Jeffrey Bowlby and Kathryn McMullen, *At a Crossroads: First Results for the 18–20-Year-Old Cohort of the Youth in Transition Survey 2002* (Ottawa: Statistics Canada, 2002), Catalogue 81-591, January 2002, 31.

other situations, parents may not be able to help with the costs of postsecondary education, and the thought of excessive debt upon school completion may dissuade youth from continuing their studies. Notably, neither of these situations is likely to improve in the short term as rates of child poverty and the costs of postsecondary education continue to rise.

Besides economic factors, other social factors intersect with SES and social class to play a role in educational attainment. To the extent that children and youth of similar SES and social class backgrounds are segregated into schools based on community residence, they will develop social ties with other children and youth of similar backgrounds. Lack of exposure to middle- and upper-class children and their parents limits access to **social capital**, the resources that are available through our connections to others. In other words, working-class children and youth may not have access to the information gained through social capital that is required for them to succeed in their educational careers. For instance, whereas middle-class children can turn to their parents and friends to learn about the intricacies of the educational system, working-class children do not have those social resources available to them and may not know how to find answers to questions that would help them succeed within school environments.

Finally, **cultural capital** also plays a role in educational attainment. Cultural capital is derived mostly from education and reflects middle- and upper-class values, attitudes, and beliefs regarding various aspects of social life. If education and related activities such as reading, discussing politics, and learning about the world and music are valued within a family and by the individuals within it, high levels of educational attainment are more likely. Working-class families tend not to expose their children to these activities to the extent that middle- and upper-class families do. Hence, the value of education is often not as strongly held in working-class families as it is in middle-class families, and working-class children may not be as inclined to continue with their education as a result.

Health

According to the World Health Organization, *health* is broadly defined as "a state of complete physical, mental, and social well-being and not merely the absence of disease or infirmity" (2003), which suggests that multiple measures of health need to be examined in order to fully understand health and inequality. Income, status, and class advantages lead to better health outcomes within and across countries. Recent media and policy attention regarding the HIV/AIDS epidemics in developing countries suggests that **developed countries** need to pay more attention to the "have-nots" who live beyond our national borders. Indeed, mortality and **morbidity rates** tend to be higher in developing than in developed countries, and biotechnology researchers are in search of methods to reduce the health gap between rich and poor countries.

Among the many indicators of health, mortality is one of the most studied. There is a well-known and consistent relationship between SES and mortality. Individuals who have lower incomes and less education tend to have lower life expectancies than do individuals who have higher incomes and who are better educated (Mustard et al., 1997; Williams and Collins, 1995). Recent evidence suggests that the

mortality gap between the rich and the poor is widening; this has been attributed to the more rapid gains for those with high SES relative to those with lower SES (Williams and Collins, 1995).

Recently, researchers have argued that beyond the simple relationship between SES and mortality, a socio-economic "gradient" also influences mortality. This *gradient effect* reflects the research finding that regions characterized by high levels of income inequality have higher death rates than do regions in which the income distribution is more equal. This suggests that the experience of disadvantage relative to others in a particular locale has an effect on mortality rates that cannot be explained by SES alone (Kawachi et al., 1999).

Morbidity generally refers to the presence of illness or disease, chronic symptoms, and general malaise. Regardless of how it is measured, there is also a strong and consistent relationship between SES and morbidity such that those who are more disadvantaged experience higher levels of morbidity (Cairney, 1999; Humphries and van Doorslaer, 2000; Jette, Crawford, and Tennstedt, 1996; MacMillan et al., 1996; Mao, Ugnat, and White, 2000; Williams and Collins, 1995). Regional disparities regarding income and poverty have also been found to influence the experience of morbidity (Guernsey et al., 2000). Besides these differences in mortality and morbidity, individuals in lower-SES groups suffer poorer mental health (measured either as the presence of mental illness or as more generalized distress) than do those in higher-SES groups (Turner and Avison, forthcoming). Although there are debates about whether low SES causes poor mental health or whether poor mental health causes low SES, the correlation is strong.

What explains the strong and consistent relationship between SES and these various measures of health? People with lower levels of income and education and those employed in working-class occupations are more likely to experience malnutrition, disproportionately lack knowledge of health care practices, and are more often exposed to dangerous working and living environments. All of these things negatively affect health status. As well, research has shown that SES is associated with access to health care services even in countries such as Canada that have "universal" health care systems (Newbold, 1998).

Conclusion: Does Class Matter?

For decades, sociologists have quibbled over the relevance of social class as a marker of inequality (Clark and Lipset, 1991; Nisbet, 1959; Pakulski and Waters, 1996). Some argue that because false consciousness is so widespread within contemporary capitalism, political distinctions between the middle class and the working class have become negligible. Others suggest that because some working-class jobs are well paid, distributive distinctions between the classes are becoming less significant. Still others purport that because most people report that they are members of the middle class not the working class, and because working conditions are better now than they were a century ago, class is losing its significance as a basis of inequality in Canada and other Western industrialized nations (Pakulski and Waters, 1996). Indeed, Jan Pakulski and Malcolm Waters (1996) have gone as far as to proclaim the "death" of class.

The claims in support of the "death of class" are true to a certain extent. Indeed, the fact that many students first discover their working-class backgrounds in their first year of university may add some support to the argument that class does not matter. As well, the conditions of, and rewards for, work have mostly improved over the last century. Social security systems are better now than they were during the rise of industrial capitalism in Canada, which has reduced the risk associated with working-class membership.

That said, it is also true that after students are given social class as an explanatory tool, they understand better the circumstances of their lives. Furthermore, if given a choice, most employees would choose to work in non-working-class occupations that are better paid, more autonomous, and less alienating; working-class parents are not able to provide their children with the same educational opportunities that are afforded to middle-class children; and there are unique health risks associated with being a member of the working class. The culmination of this information suggests that although the nature of class-based inequality has changed over time, class remains alive and well.

☐ Questions for Critical Thought

1. Some may argue that no one but Kimberly Rogers was to blame for her death. Others would argue that structural circumstances and social policy at least contributed to it. Compare and contrast these views. Which better explains Rogers's death?
2. Based on what you have learned in this and the preceding chapters, how many social classes are there in contemporary Canadian society? Which makes more sense today, a Weberian or a Marxist view of social class?
3. Discuss the feminist critique of social class. How can social class be reconceptualized so that the experiences of women are fully integrated into a theoretical framework of social class?
4. Why are sociologists concerned about the polarization of social classes? In other words, what are the social implications of a shrinking middle class and a swelling working class?
5. Under the conditions of contemporary capitalism, does small business ownership hold the same appeal as it did for Marx? In other words, assuming that alienation is reduced substantially or even eliminated for small business owners, are there other things that may matter more to one's overall well-being in contemporary capitalism? If so, why do so many Canadians dream of being self-employed?
6. Are there policies that could be put in place that could eliminate poverty? What might some of these policies be? Is the elimination of poverty a desirable social outcome?
7. Are there policies that could be put in place that could eliminate the relationship between social class and education? What might some of these policies be? Is educational equality a desirable social outcome?
8. Are there policies that could be put in place that could eliminate the relationship between social class and health? What might some of these policies be? Is health equality a desirable social outcome?

☐ Recommended Readings

Joan Acker, "Class, Gender, and the Relations of Distribution," *Signs*, 13 (1988): 473–97.

This seminal article tackles the complexities of integrating gender, class, patriarchy, and capitalism into a single system of inequality.

Wallace Clement and John Myles, *Relations of Ruling: Class and Gender in Postindustrial Societies* (Montreal: McGill-Queen's University Press, 1994).

This book applies Wright's conceptualization of social class in an analysis of class and gender inequality. Although it focuses primarily on Canada, there are also cross-national comparisons with the United States, Norway, Sweden, and Finland.

James E. Curtis, Edward G. Grabb, and Neil L. Guppy, eds, *Social Inequality in Canada: Patterns, Problems, and Policies* (Scarborough, ON: Prentice-Hall Allyn and Bacon, 1999).

This is an excellent source of information on various aspects of social inequality in Canada.

Bonnie Fox, "The Feminist Challenge: A Reconsideration of Social Inequality and Economic Development," in Robert J. Brym with Bonnie Fox, *From Culture to Power: The Sociology of English Canada* (Toronto: Oxford University Press, 1989), 120–67.

This chapter provides an excellent overview and analysis of how feminist scholarship provides a more complete understanding of social inequality and development than do "male-stream" approaches.

Edward G. Grabb, *Theories of Social Inequality*, 4th edn (Toronto: Harcourt, 2002).

Grabb provides an excellent overview and analysis of classical and contemporary theories of social inequality.

Heidi Hartmann, "The Unhappy Marriage of Marxism and Feminism: Towards a More Progressive Union," in *The Unhappy Marriage of Marxism and Feminism: A Debate on Class and Patriarchy*, edited by Lydia Sargent (London: Pluto, 1981), 2–41.

This classic socialist-feminist article brings together, in a dual-systems theory, issues of patriarchy and capitalism.

Desmond Morton, *Working People: An Illustrated History of the Canadian Labour Movement*, 4th edn (Montreal: McGill-Queen's University Press, 1998).

This is a great resource book that explores the evolution of the labour movement in Canada from the late nineteenth century until the 1990s.

Erik Olin Wright, *Class Counts: Comparative Studies in Class Analysis* (Cambridge: Cambridge University Press, 1997).

This comprehensive book outlines Wright's ideas on social class.

☐ Recommended Web Sites

Canadian Labour Congress (CLC)

www.clc-ctc.ca

Labour-related publications, media releases, and the history of the CLC are among the many resources available on this site.

Canadian Policy Research Networks

www.cprn.ca

This is a excellent source of information regarding the relationship between social policy and social inequality.

Eric Olin Wright

www.ssc.wisc.edu/~wright/

Wright's home page includes an up-to-date listing of his publications, many of which can be downloaded from this site.

Income Security Advocacy Centre

www.incomesecurity.org/index_html

This is an excellent source for more information on the Kimberly Rogers case.

Human Resources and Development Canada, Children and Youth

www.hrdc-drhc.gc.ca/menu/youth_child.shtml

Explore this site to learn about child poverty and the social welfare transfers that are in place to benefit poor children.

Human Resources and Development Canada, National Homelessness Initiative

www21.hrdc-drhc.gc.ca/home/index_e.asp

Information is available on this site on the problem of homelessness among Canadians.

National Council on Welfare

www.ncwcnbes.net

This site includes facts and reports on poverty in Canada and information about poverty myths.

Statistics Canada

www.statcan.ca

A wealth of statistical information about income and employment status in Canada is available here.

World Health Organization (WHO)

www.who.int

The WHO Web site provides definitions of health and world reports about various health topics.

15

Pat Armstrong

> > >

Gender Relations

© Digital Vision

☐ Learning Objectives

In this chapter, you will:

- learn that biology alone does not account for differences between males and females

- see how ideologies, child-rearing practices, the division of labour by sex, the education system, and the media all influence the physiology, behaviour, and perceptions of both sexes

- examine the segregation of the labour force, the political arena, and medical services by sex

- consider why the life experiences of women are different from and more limited than those of men

- study the issues of housework and caregiving

- consider the changing personal relationships between men and women

- take into account the effect of changing gender relations on men

Introduction

"Is it a boy or a girl?" This is the first question asked of new parents. The answer is critical because it has profound implications for an individual's choices and possibilities throughout life.

All known cultures have distinguished between male and female. Furthermore, in all cultures the distinctions have provided the basis for divisions of not only labour, but also most other activities. The distinctions made between **genders** and the divisions of labour have varied enormously through time and across cultures, however, because such distinctions exist within a **social environment**. They result more from social relations and social structures than from biologically determined differences.

This chapter examines gender distinctions and the relations between males and females in Canadian society. We open with a discussion of what is known about biological differences and their implications for behaviour and relationships. Next we turn to the evidence on sex-specific patterns in behaviour, education, and occupations, evaluating alternative explanations for the established patterns. Finally, we outline some strategies for altering these patterns and reshaping the relations between the sexes in Canada.

Theories of the Sexes

From one perspective, clear biological distinctions exist between the sexes—men bring home the bacon, while women produce babies, feed and nurture them—and it is these that determine what people can be when they grow up. Many sociologists, however, see clear lines to be drawn between distinctions that are biologically determined and those that are socially learned—in short, between nature and nurture. Twenty years ago, Marlene Mackie explained that "sex is the biological dichotomy between females and males. It is determined at conception and is, for the most part, unalterable. Gender, on the other hand, is what is socially recognized as femininity and masculinity" (1983: 1). By differentiating between **sex** and **gender**, sociologists sought to stress the **social construction** of distinctions between the sexes. But these terms raised their own problems. First, they implied that biological factors can be separated from social factors and that biological differences are firmly established. Second, they also implied that biology is unchanging, outside history and influence. Third, the distinction suggested that biology is irrelevant to

an understanding of social distinctions between males and females.

In an effort to overcome these problems, *gender* has, in the intervening years, increasingly became the only term used. However, the growing popularity of the new genetics and biotechnology has once again encouraged an emphasis on biological differences between the sexes (Grant, 1998). The rest of this section will examine each of the problems in determining biological differences, explaining why it is not always easy to differentiate between sex and gender, biology and learning.

Separating the Boys from the Girls

People throughout the ages have debated the biological differences between the sexes, and they continue to do so today despite extensive research. A 1993 CBC series based on the book *Brain Sex* (Moir and Jessel, 1989) stressed the **biological determinist** side. A more recent article in *Maclean's* magazine begins, "If there is a gene for murder, it is a safe bet it will be found first in someone who carries XY chromosomes. That is, a man. There may be no such gene. Many experts insist violence is learned, not inherited" (Wood and Kar, 2000: 5). Clearly the issue is far from settled (Blustain, 2000).

Most people would agree that hair length and high heels are socially created distinctions. Fewer would reach a consensus about which aspects of motherhood have biological links. Moreover, some would argue that women are "naturally" homemakers, men "naturally" breadwinners. Finally, while most would agree that women and men have different genitals, this difference alone cannot be used to divide all people into two categories. Indeed, the Olympic Committee considers visible genitals so unreliable in establishing sex that they reject the distinction as a basis for determining who may compete in the women's games.

Science provides few definitive answers to many points in the debate over biological differences. There is little consensus in the vast research and literature on the topic. The lack of agreement reflects both the problems encountered in conducting the research and the more fundamental problem inherent in the assumption that nature and nurture can be isolated from one another.

Research into human biological differences linked to behaviour is difficult for several reasons. First, children begin learning at birth, if not before, so we cannot be entirely certain that the behaviour even of newborns is innate. Second, while infants have a very limited repertoire for study, as they expand their activities they also increase their opportunities to learn. Moreover, the older the subjects, the more likely they are to respond in terms of their own **values** and expectations. In any event, there are severe restrictions on the kind and amount of experimentation permitted on humans, whatever their age. Third, even when genes or hormones or other biological factors are determined to be different in males and females, there is little basis for assuming that these differences translate into particular behaviours. Perhaps most important, researchers themselves cannot escape their own learning, which helps structure how they do research and interpret results as well as what they accept as evidence (Fausto-Sterling, 2000; Messing, 1998).

Research on other species encounters similar problems, even though there are fewer restrictions placed on it. Other animals, such as rodents and birds, learn just as humans do, and there is enormous variety in their behaviour. Males are not universal breadwinners or heroes, and in some species, mothers eat their young. Moreover, researchers' values come into play here, too, often guiding them to select the evidence that best supports their own **hypotheses** (Blustain, 2000). While there are many things to be learned from studying other animals, we cannot be confident that anything we might argue as being innate in another species will be so in humans, for the simple reason that humans are qualitatively different from other species.

Such difficulties have led many observers to contend that an answer to "Nature or nurture?" can never be found, because the wrong question is being asked. Anne Fausto-Sterling has argued that it is impossible to determine which aspects of our behaviour are biologically determined, because "an individual's capacities emerge from a web of interactions between the biological being and the social environment. . . . Biology may in some manner condition behavior, but behavior in turn can alter one's physiology. Furthermore, any particular behaviour may have many different causes" (1985: 8). This is why, as she has said more recently (Fausto-Sterling, 2000), even with the latest techniques, scientists still disagree about differences and their impact. These debates are not surprising because people do not exist outside their social environment, and what are often called

"biological processes" are influenced by that environment. Jogging or stress may delay a menstrual cycle; tight jeans or a radio carried too often below the waist may reduce sperm counts. The more often women run in marathons, the closer they come to matching the men; the more often men spend their days sitting in office chairs, the less muscle-bound they become.

To argue that nature cannot easily be separated from nurture is not to argue that there are no biological components to people's behaviour or that there are no gender differences that can be related to biological factors. Rather, it is to assert that biological components have no predetermined meaning or value and that they are not unalterable.

The Sexes: What's the Difference?

Researchers do agree on some sex differences. While both sexes have 23 pairs of chromosomes, in most females one pair is made up of two X chromosomes; in most males one pair consists of an X and a Y chromosome. The Y chromosome must be present for the embryonic sex glands to develop in a male direction. Furthermore, hormones must be present in both sexes for either males or females to reach sexual maturity. Although estrogens are often called "female" hormones and androgens "male" hormones, both sexes secrete both types of hormones—"what differs is the ratio of estrogen to androgen in the two sexes" (Rose, Kamin, and Lewontin, 1984: 151). Between them, the XX and XY chromosomes and the hormones are responsible for the different reproductive capacities of women (menstruation, gestation, and lactation) and men (semen production and impregnation).

It is at this point that agreement ends. Debates rage over the implications of the differences in chromosomes, hormonal ratios, and reproductive capacities for male and female behaviour and possibilities (see, for example, Bancroft, 2002).

The Genetic Perspective

Sociobiologists and others who are convinced that biology determines a wide range of behaviour attribute a powerful effect to the lone Y chromosome. Different researchers working from this perspective have argued that the genetic makeup of men makes them more intelligent than women, superior in visual-spatial abilities and mathematical skills, or more aggressive and dominant. It has also been suggested that women's double X chromosome creates a maternal instinct and makes females more intuitive, tricky, nurturant, and moral than men. For supporters of the genetic perspective, then, the hierarchical structure of society and the sexual division of labour are the natural and inevitable result of biological differences (Geary, 1998; Geary and Flinn, 2000).

So is what is often called the **double standard** in sexual practices. That is, men have a natural sexuality that results, in the words of David Barash, from the "biologically based need to inject their sperm into as many women as possible" (cited in Messing, 1987: 112). Some have concluded, on the basis of this viewpoint, that rape and violence against women have biological roots: the men cannot help themselves any more than women can stop being nurturant and deceitful. In the eyes of these theorists, women are destined to be mommies and men bosses. Moreover, women should expect to be dominated and sexually harassed.

Study after study has challenged these notions (Fausto-Sterling, 2000; Rose, Kamin, and Lewontin, 1984). Research in countries other than Canada, for example, reveals an astonishing variety in gender rela-

tions that seems to deny biological determinism. Margaret Lock (1998) found that the physical manifestations of menopause vary across cultures, R.A. Anderson and colleagues (1999) that testosterone replacement had a different impact on male sexuality in Hong Kong than it did in North America.

Within Canadian society, too, considerable differences are evident in gender behaviour over the course of history. Elizabeth Mitchell, for instance, examined Prairie households at the turn of the century and concluded that "there is no question at all of inequality; the partners have several departments, equally important, and the husband is the first to admit how much he owes his wife, and to own that the burden falls on her heaviest" ([1915] 1981: 48). Mitchell also maintains that city life served to create inequalities and make women subordinate in ways we see today. In addition, **First Nations** families have a long tradition of female independence and of community participation in child rearing (Cassidy, Lord, and Mandell, 2001).

To sum up, research has not revealed any simple dichotomy between the sexes or any direct link between genetics or hormones and the behaviour patterns attributed to each sex. Sociobiology has not

---

 15.1

Global Issues
Changing Views of Men

While most of the research and writing on changing relations between the sexes has focused on women, in the last two decades there has been a flurry of publications that look at emerging patterns for men. Analysis of advertising offers just one example of this trend.

In her examination of the representation of males in advertising, Judith Posner (1987) found that the new male is smaller, has a less pronounced jaw, and is more likely to smile. He is also more likely to be found undressing or partially dressed, and he appears more vulnerable. Yet Posner concludes that this does not reflect a move toward equality, but rather demonstrates "the increasing commercialization of sexuality" for both men and women (1987: 188).

In another analysis of advertising, Andrew Wernick argues that as women have moved into the labour force, men have become more involved in private consumption; this change has been reflected in "a steady drive to incorporate male clothing into fashion, and mounting efforts to sell men all manner of personal-care products, from toothpaste and bath oil to hair dye and make-up" (1987: 279). Wernick suggests that men are being subjected to the same kind of "intense consumerization as women and are no longer defined as breadwinners" (279). More recently, however, Varda Burstyn (1999) has argued that both advertising in sports and the practice of sport promotes what she calls "hypermasculinity."

succeeded in demonstrating "that a genetically based human nature or genetically based sex differences exist" (Lowe, 1983: 13). The variability across cultures, the minor differences between the sexes in any particular culture, and the variations in patterns within the sexes all challenge notions of simple genetic determinism.

The Hormonal Perspective

Instead of attributing predetermined sex differences to genes, others have looked to hormones as causal agents (Moir and Jessel, 1992). Supporters of this perspective argue that different levels of hormones affect the brain, resulting for males in higher intelligence, more ambition and drive, and more aggressive behaviour. The effect on women is seen as far more negative, inasmuch as menstruation and menopause are viewed as incapacitating them, making them unsuitable for many kinds of work.

Again, research has provided very limited support for this viewpoint. Although the injection of hormones might influence a rodent brain in ways that encourage mating behaviour, in non-human primates it does not create the same results (Lowe, 1983). In the words of Fausto-Sterling, "the evidence that male hormones control aggression in humans and other primates ranges from weak to non-existent" (1985: 45). A survey of research has concluded that "there is no known causal relationship between sex hormone levels and other traits, such as intelligence, intuition, and creativity" (Richardson, 1988: 149). Indeed, Lynda Birke (1999) cites evidence that hormone production itself is influenced by the social environment.

Reproductive Capacity

Some feminist theorists have looked to reproductive capacities, rather than to genes or hormones, to explain differences between the sexes. Mary O'Brien, for example, has argued that the very different parts women and men play in reproduction lead to different forms of consciousness and to men's efforts to control women: "Women's reproductive consciousness is a consciousness that the child is hers, but also a consciousness that she herself was born of a woman's labour, that labour confirms genetic coherence and species continuity. Male reproductive consciousness is splintered and discontinuous, and cannot be mediated within reproductive process" (1981: 59). In O'Brien's view, men experience reproduction mainly as alienation of their male seed, which in turn motivates them to seek control over both mother and child.

This kind of theoretical argument is much more difficult to examine through scientific research than those that attribute sex differences to genes or hormones. What is clear is that the effects of reproductive capacities, like those of genes or hormones, cannot be understood outside the context of time and place. How women experience childbirth, for instance, is related to the available technology and medical care, nutrition, and social support. These factors can transform not only how women feel about giving birth, but also the very biology of the birth process. Women's reproductive capacity makes the consequences of sexual intercourse different for women and men, especially in the absence of safe, effective birth control (Armstrong and Armstrong, 1983a; Hamilton, 1978) and different for women from different racial and cultural groups (Cassidy, Lord, and Mandell, 2001). Moreover, the consequences are different today than in our grandmothers' time, not only because contemporary women have a better chance of avoiding childbirth, but also because they have a better chance of surviving it. The development of relatively effective birth control has made the implications of sexual intercourse more similar for both sexes and has thereby contributed to changes in sexual practices and in the double standard. In turn, these social changes have affected the workings of our bodies and the meaning of what are often called "biological processes."

The recent spread of HIV/AIDS provides another example of the complex relationship between biology and social environment. In making men more vulnerable to the long-term consequences of their sexual activities, HIV/AIDS has altered the sexual practices of at least some men. Furthermore, at least today, AIDS can be controlled primarily by changes in **social relationships** and social practices, not through biological means.

In the end, we are left to conclude that biology cannot be separated from the social environment that influences both its meaning and its structure. Biology is not an independent variable. Moreover, "female" and "male" do not constitute opposite sexes. Women and men share both genes and hormones. They differ mainly in reproductive capacities, and the significance of these differences is primarily socially, rather than biologically, structured. Furthermore, "human biology and behavior are anything but immutable. Stimulate the brain, and neurons branch out to form new connections. Arouse the senses, and hormonal levels change. Exercise the muscles, and the body becomes stronger and sleeker" (Hales, 2000: 9). As Judith Lorber and Susan Farrell point out, "it makes more sense to talk of genders, not simply gender, because being a woman and being a man change from one generation to the next and are different for different racial, ethnic, and religious groups, as well as for the members of different social classes" (1991: 1). This does not mean that biology is irrelevant. What it does mean is that sex differences cannot be attributed to biology alone.

Growing Up Feminine or Masculine

When parents answer the question about the sex of their new child, they trigger a range of social responses that have very little to do with genes, hormones, or reproductive capacities. Sex distinctions are a central part of the content and structure of child-rearing practices in the home, and they are just as integral to the content and structure of **social institutions**, such as the formal education system and the **mass media**. The distinctions are reinforced by the dominant **ideology** manifested in all these social contexts. This is not to suggest that children and adults are mere passive recipients or transmitters of ideas and practices. Through interaction with their social and physical worlds, people alter them as well as their ideas about them. Nevertheless, child-rearing practices, educational systems, and dominant ideologies have a powerful influence on the pace and nature of social change, as well as on the distinctions made between males and females.

The Influence of the Home

Once we know the sex identification of a child, we know what toys to bring, what clothes to buy, what colour to paint the baby's room, what stories to read, what games to play, how rough we can be, how much we should talk to the newborn, and what kind of name the child will have, although what is considered appropriate varies with culture (Mackie, 1993). In recent years, unisex clothes, toys, and hairstyles have become popular, and many parents are attempting to raise their children in what is termed a "non-sexist" manner. Despite some important changes, however, many differences based on sex still persist.

Parents tend to spend more time interacting with little girls, while they not only tend to leave boys alone more often, but also punish them more often.

Boys are more likely to have computers and to be shown how to operate them so they can play their adventure games. Girls tend to be more closely supervised, especially when they reach adolescence. Boys are seldom allowed to wear dresses and are taught rough, physical games such as football. Girls are seldom given footballs or guns to play with, but are taught how to play house and dress Barbie in ball gowns. Toughness, aggression, and emotional control are rewarded in boys and sanctioned in girls (Kilmarten, 1994). When tasks are assigned in the house, boys are told to take out the garbage and shovel the walk, girls to clean the toilet and wash the floor—though more boys are helping with the dishes and operating the microwave. As Jane Gaskell's research on Canadian adolescents shows, the division of household labour contributes to the shared view among young men and women that "young women will add work outside the home to their domestic work" (2001: 229).

These child-rearing practices help shape the physiology, behaviour, and perceptions of both sexes. Girls and boys learn different skills and develop in different ways. Playing with computers and construction equipment encourages males to develop visual-spatial and mathematical skills. Playing hockey encourages them to be aggressive and dominant. Shovelling snow and lugging garbage develop strength and foster muscle growth. At the same time, playing with dolls encourages girls to develop verbal and relational skills. The wearing of stacked heels discourages a range of physical activities, while cleaning toilets contributes little to muscle growth. Close supervision limits adventurousness and encourages passivity or trickery.

These differences in experience also lead females and males to view themselves and the other sex in particular ways. Research undertaken for the Royal Commission on the Status of Women found that children "were more certain about the meaning of masculinity and femininity when they thought in terms of potential jobs or relations than when they thought in terms of personality dispositions" (Lambert, 1971: 69). What they experience in the area of jobs is a division by sex in which the tasks assigned to females have less value, are less interesting, and have less potential than those done by men. What they experience in the area of relations is greater freedom, more choices, and more **power** for males than for females.

It is in the context of child care that such division along gender lines is most evident. Even though a

Inside and outside of the home, mothers are still considered the primary caregivers. (www.harrycutting.com)

ture classes in ways that encourage girls to focus on courses leading to clerical jobs or other similar work associated with women (Gaskell, 1992; Gaskell and Willinsky, 1995). At the same time, they frequently structure sports in ways that help boys move in other directions and encourage them to be dominant. As former Olympic runner Bruce Kidd makes clear,

> by giving males exciting opportunities, preaching that the qualities they learn from them are "masculine," and preventing girls and women from learning in the same situations, sports confirm the prejudice that males are a breed apart. By encouraging us to spend our most creative and engrossing moments as children and our favorite forms of recreation as adults in the company of other males, they condition us to trust each other more than women. (1987: 255)

The very place of women in the educational system is also instructive for the young. Most principals are men. While most elementary school teachers are women, the higher the level, the greater the number of male teachers. Although university programs have long abandoned a quota on the number of women admitted, many less visible barriers remain in place. Women in postsecondary education are still concentrated in health, education, and the social sciences, while the number of women in science and technology remains low relative to their enrolment in other fields (Statistics Canada, 2000).

Various women's groups—some of them made up of teachers—have exposed and successfully attacked such practices. More women are now principals and greater numbers of men teach in elementary schools, though the latter trend may well be more a reflection of higher wages and scarce employment than of feminist action. When quotas on female enrolments were removed, women rushed to take places in faculties of law, medicine, and dentistry. Indeed, in some institutions women now constitute the majority of those enrolled in such traditionally male-dominated programs. Career counsellors discuss non-traditional job possibilities with students, and new courses introduce counsellors to more alternatives for women.

Research revealing the way girls were encouraged to see paid work as secondary to the "real" work as mothers has been used to bring about some changes within the classroom. Indeed, there are now concerns being raised that girls are doing much better in traditional male subjects, leaving the boys behind.

majority of women now work in the labour force and men help more than they used to with the children, women still bear the primary responsibility for child care (Frederick, 1995; Ghalam, 2000; Sinclair and Felt, 1992). Some theorists (Chodorow, 1978; Pollack, 1998) have argued that this aspect of the division of labour has profound implications for the psyches of females and males. Given that women are child-rearers, females can continue to identify with their mothers and can feel comfortable with intimate or nurturant relations. Men, on the other hand, can find **identity** only by separating themselves from the caregiver. This painful separation helps create the urge to dominate women and to repress intimate or nurturant behaviour.

Although this explanation simplifies the complex and often contradictory process of gender development (Connell, 1995), it nevertheless draws our attention to the importance of the division of labour in forming gender distinctions in children. It also suggests the implications of these differences for the perceptions of males and females throughout life.

The Influence of the Educational System

Even if parents try to raise their children in a social environment patterned on equal relations between the sexes, once children enter the educational system they are exposed to sex distinctions and relations in which women are subordinate. Schools often struc-

However, there is evidence that there is still a **hidden curriculum** that silently encourages girls and boys in different directions (Bourne, McCoy, and Novogrodsky, 1997).

The Influence of the Media

Gender divisions are reflected in and reinforced by the majority of books, magazines, videos games, music, television programs—in short, all the media. Research a decade ago showed that in television and film there were only half as many parts for women as there were for men (Armstrong, 1991). Women were much less likely than men to be portrayed as the initiators of adventures or as the rescuers in the action. They were more often evaluated primarily in terms of their youth, beauty, and ability to attract a man, while men were more often evaluated in terms of their skills, courage, and ability to capture women (Robinson and Salamon, 1987). The major preoccupation of women of any age in many programs and much music remains being attractive to a man.

The content of some textbooks and some television programs and films has changed. Women are now far more likely to be portrayed as employed outside the home in such fields as medicine or law and as taking the initiative in sexual relationships (changes that reflect a new reality). Nevertheless, in books, as in other media, men are still more powerful and more plentiful, and they are in the society as well. Pictures of gatherings of world leaders make this very clear.

The Influence of Ideologies

The practices in the home, the educational system, and the media cannot be separated from the dominant ideologies in a society. Indeed, in many ways they constitute those ideologies. But ideologies are not static—they are constantly being transformed as experiences and interests change. Ideas that do not coincide with people's life experiences or that make little sense of people's lives are difficult to maintain.

Feminist sociologist Dorothy Smith makes it clear that women "have historically and in the present been excluded from the production of forms of thought, images, and symbols in which their experience and social relations are expressed and ordered" (1975: 353). She goes on to argue that women "have never controlled the material or social means to the making of a tradition among themselves or to acting as equals in the ongoing discourse of intellectuals" (353).

While many would argue that women have developed some specifically female ideologies, few would challenge the notion that men have been in a far better position than women to have their views of the world and its workings prevail. This has been the case even in the home, traditionally the woman's sphere, because it is men who have most often provided the primary monetary support. Moreover, the male view of the place of both men and women is likely to reaffirm the dominance of men, given their continuing superior place in the home, the educational system, and the media.

Although women do not control what Smith calls "the means of mental production" (1975: 355), they have nonetheless developed their own perspectives from their own life experiences. For instance, the traditional notion of women focusing exclusively on the home no longer makes sense in light of women's actual experiences. As women gain power in every social institution, their views are likely to become more visible and shared by men. Nevertheless, while, in 1995, 41 per cent of women disagreed with the notion that what most women want is home and family, this was the case for only 34 per cent of men (Ghalam, 2000: 72).

Ideologies, child-rearing practices, the division of labour by sex, the education system, and the media all work together to shape infants into feminine and masculine adults. At the same time, children and adults of both sexes are shaping the practices and ideas of society in response to changes in their daily experiences and the structure of their lives.

The Division of Labour by Sex

Gender divisions are still most obvious in the context of work. Men and women tend to do different work, in different places, for different wages. These differences in work not only create both limits and possibilities, but also help shape the ideas of members of each sex about themselves. In turn, work itself is shaped by the ideas people bring with them to the job, by employers' demands, and by people's responsibilities outside their paid labour.

Paid Work

Like clothing and hairstyles, women and men's paid work has become increasingly similar in recent years. Women have been moving into the labour force in greater numbers, so the gap between male and female participation rates has been narrowing. In 1976, 42 per cent of women and 73 per cent of men were counted as employed; women constituted just over one-third of the labour market. By 1999, the official employment rates were 55 per cent for women and 67 per cent for men, with women forming 46 per cent of the labour market (Statistics Canada, 2000: 116). These figures actually underestimate the number of women employed at some point during the year and hide significant variations by marital status, citizenship status, race, and culture (Statistics Canada, 2000).

Most of the increase in female labour-force participation is accounted for by the movement of married women into the labour market, largely in response to family economic need. Even married women with young children are keeping their paid jobs. In 1999, two-thirds of women with preschool-aged children were in the labour force. Edward Pryor points out that between 1971 and 1981 the income of wives "was the significant factor in preventing family income from declining in real dollars," although "by 1979–81, increases in wives' income were no longer able to offset the decline in husbands' average income" (1984: 102). By the end of the 1990s, wives' income accounted for nearly one-third of household income in dual-earner families (Statistics Canada, 2000: 140). Without wives' income, the number of families living in poverty would increase by three-quarters of a million and many more would suffer significant setbacks in lifestyle (Statistics Canada, 2000: 146).

Furthermore, a growing number of women have taken jobs traditionally done by men. According to Katherine Marshall, "during the 1971–1981 period, the proportional representation of women increased in all but 1 of the 34 professions identified as male-dominated" (1987: 8). The largest percentage increases were in management, law, veterinary work, and engineering, while the largest numerical increases were in management, pharmacy, law, postsecondary teaching, and medicine (Marshall, 1987). This invasion into male-dominated domains was not limited to the professions, but extended to construction, agriculture, mining, and forestry. A few women even acquired licences to operate their own fishing boats. The pace of the movement of women into these occupations has slowed since then, but women do still move into male-dominated fields.

As more women have entered the labour force and followed patterns similar to men's, more of them have joined unions. Indeed, women's unionization rate grew throughout the 1970s and 1980s, while that of men declined. However, the number of employees grew in the 1990s faster than the rate of unionization. By 2001, only 30 per cent of men and women belonged to unions (Statistics Canada, 2002d: 1).

Despite these widely publicized gains, most women have remained doing women's work at women's wages; few have had a choice about taking on paid employment. And many face additional barriers linked to their race, age, or geographical location (Das Gupta, 1996; Statistics Canada, 2000). In 1999, one-quarter of all employed women still did clerical work, and women accounted for 80 per cent of all clerical workers. Another one in three women did sales or service work (Statistics Canada, 2000: 128). Table 15.1 shows that 30 per cent of women have work in business, finance, and administrative occupations, but only 6 per cent of women have managerial jobs. While women account for nearly 80 per cent of those in health occupations, they constitute less than 20 per cent of those in natural and applied sciences. In other words, over half of employed women are segregated into traditionally female clerical, sales, and service employment, as opposed to 26 per cent of men.

Thus, although some women moved into traditional male areas, the labour force still remained highly segregated. According to the 1996 census, nearly two-thirds of employed women worked in the 40 jobs in which women accounted for 70 per cent or more of the workers. Men were significantly more dispersed and dominated more job categories—67 of them (Armstrong, 2000: 41, 43).

Not only do women and men do different jobs, they often do them in different places. Three-quarters of those employed in the goods-producing industries were male, while more than half of those working in community, business, and personal services were female (see Table 15.2). Women are also more likely than men to do paid work in their homes. If men do work out of their homes, they are far more likely than women to be their own bosses.

Women also have a greater tendency to work part-time or part of the year. As Table 15.3 indicates, women account for nearly 70 per cent of those employed part-time, a pattern that has changed little over the years. Although the proportion of women employed full-time in the labour force has increased over recent years, it is still the case that over one-quarter have only part-time paid work.

Shorter work weeks and fewer years of paid employment help account for women's lower wages.

Table 15.1 Female Labour Force by Occupation, 1996 Census

	Number	% Female	% of All Female
Management occupations	408,885	31.7	6.2
Business, finance, and administrative occupations	1,951,680	71.8	29.8
Natural and applied sciences and related occupations	127,080	17.8	1.9
Health occupations	566,625	78.8	8.7
Occupations in social science, education, government service, and religion	581,670	59.6	8.9
Occupations in art, culture, recreation, and sport	206,390	53.4	3.2
Sales and service occupations	2,114,920	56.8	32.3
Trades, transport, and equipment operators and related occupations	122,100	6.0	1.9
Occupations unique to primary industry	146,670	21.5	2.2
Occupations unique to processing, manufacturing, and utilities	323,030	29.6	4.9

SOURCE: Statistics Canada, "Experienced Labour Force 15 Years and over by Occupation and Sex, 1996 Census, Census Metropolitan Areas" adapted from Statistics Canada web site <http://www.statcan.ca/english/Pgdb/labor45a.htm>, accessed 8 August 2003.

Table 15.2 Female Labour Force by Industry, 1996 Census

	Numbers[a] (000s)	% Female	% of All Female[a]
Goods-producing sector	907.6	23.5	13.2
Agriculture	112.8	30.3	1.6
Forestry, fishing, mining, oil, and gas	44.5	15.7	0.6
Utilities	26.1	22.4	0.4
Construction	88.4	10.9	1.3
Manufacturing	635.7	27.9	9.3
Services-producing sector	5,952.8	53.9	86.8
Trade	1,120.2	48.3	16.3
Transportation and warehousing	177.8	22.8	2.6
Finance, insurance, real estate, and leasing	512.2	59.1	7.5
Professional, scientific, and technical services	408.3	43.2	6.0
Management of companies and administrative and other support services	254.0	46.5	3.7
Educational services	631.6	64.8	9.2
Health care and social assistance	1,237.7	81.1	18.0
Information, culture, and recreation	317.6	47.7	4.6
Accommodation and food services	570.1	59.3	8.3
Other services	366.7	52.7	5.3
Public administration	356.5	46.8	5.2

[a] Columns may not add up to totals or to 100 because of rounding.
SOURCE: Adapted from Statistics Canada web site <http://www.statcan.ca/english/Pgdb/labor10b.htm>, accessed 5 August 2003.

But this is only part of the story. In 1999, women's average wages were 64.1 per cent of men's—not much improvement over the decade (see Table 15.4). Even full-time wages for women averaged only 72 per cent of full-time wages for men (Akyeampong, 2001: 53).

Census data for 1996 indicate that 80 per cent of those in the 10 highest-paying occupations are male, while nearly three-quarters of those in the 10 lowest-paying occupations are female (Statistics Canada, 1993: 10–11). Table 15.5 offers a graphic illustration

Table 15.3 **Full-Time and Part-Time Employment in Canada, 1997–2001**

	1997		2001	
	% Female	**% of All Females**	**% Female**	**% of All Females**
Full-time	39.7	70.6	41.1	72.9
15–24 years	40.3	7.1	42.8	7.9
25–44 years	40.9	42.1	41.9	40.5
45 years and over	37.4	21.4	39.5	24.5
Part-time	69.9	29.4	69.1	27.1
15–24 years	56.7	8.5	56.6	8.2
25–44 years	80.4	13.0	79.7	10.9
45 years and over	72.5	7.9	72.5	8.0

SOURCE: Adapted from Statistics Canada web site <http://www.statcan.ca/english/Pgdb/labor12.htm>, accessed 5 August 2003.

Table 15.4 **Average Earnings by Sex and Work Pattern, 1999 (Constant 1999 Dollars)**

	Women	**Men**	**Earnings Ratio (%)**
1990	20,318	33,997	59.8
1991	20,320	33,054	61.5
1992	21,016	32,930	63.8
1993	20,770	32,316	64.3
1994	20,984	33,748	62.2
1995	21,449	32,988	65.0
1996	21,244	32,901	64.6
1997	21,380	33,700	63.4
1998	22,384	34,769	64.4
1999	22,535	35,169	64.1

SOURCE: Adapted from Statistics Canada web site <http://www.statcan.ca/english/Pgdb/labor01a.htm>, accessed 5 August 2003.

of the wage gap in these top jobs. Although large numbers of women have moved into what is classified as managerial and professional work, they earn significantly less than the men in the same occupational categories. The largest wage gaps are in the male-dominated groups. Although unions have helped close the wage gap in some occupational groups, this is not the case for the primarily non-unionized occupations listed in Table 15.5.

One result of women's lower wages is less power, both within and outside the household. Another is their far greater economic dependence on marriage, to the extent that many women are only a man away from poverty: "In 1997, 2.8 million women, 19 per cent of the total female population, were living in low-income situations, compared with 16 per cent of the male population" (Statistics Canada, 2000: 137). The difference is accounted for by senior women and lone-parent moth-

ers. On the other hand, there are now more women who can leave an unhappy marriage because they have a job that pays them enough to survive on their own.

The fact that men and women do different jobs for different wages means that they often have different life experiences and possibilities. Women are more likely than men to work in jobs that are dull, repetitious, and boring, with little opportunity for training or advancement (Armstrong and Armstrong, 1983b, 1993). As Figure 15.1 shows, women are more likely to be in employment that includes part-time work (less than 30 hours per week), second jobs, and self-employment. It is interesting to note that across the different age groups, close to 50 per cent of wives have such employment. This reflects an ongoing need for wives to supplement family income and, at the same time, fulfill all their family and household responsibilities.

Table 15.5 **10 Highest-Paid Occupations, 1995**

	Both Sexes	% Women	Average Earnings ($) Both Sexes	Men	Women
Total–10 highest-paying occupations	197,735	20	92,735	99,605	64,719
Judges	1,765	23	126,246	128,791	117,707
Specialist physicians	12,560	26	123,976	137,019	86,086
General practitioners and family physicians	21,670	26	107,620	116,750	81,512
Dentists	8,530	18	102,433	109,187	71,587
Senior managers–goods production, utilities, transportation, and construction	35,510	8	99,360	102,971	58,463
Senior managers–financial, communications carriers, and other business services	23,055	17	99,117	104,715	71,270
Lawyers and Quebec notaries	44,385	29	81,617	89,353	60,930
Senior managers–trade, broadcasting, and other services n.e.c.	28,665	14	79,200	84,237	48,651
Primary production managers (except agriculture)	7,075	6	76,701	78,421	48,479
Securities agents, investment dealers, and traders	14,520	34	75,911	90,391	47,323

SOURCE: Adapted from Statistics Canada, "Number of Earners Who Worked Full Year, Full Time in 1995 in the 25 Highest Paying and 25 Lowest Paying Occupations and Their Average Earnings by Sex, for Canada, 1995 (20% Sample Data)"; available at <http://www.statcan.ca/english/census96/may12/t2.htm>, accessed 8 August 2003.

Men and women also tend to face different health hazards in their paid work. Men are more likely to suffer visible physical injury, women to be exposed to cumulative, invisible hazards that are difficult to trace directly to employment. These tend to create effects such as nervousness, headache, and irritability that are often blamed on female physiology rather than on working conditions (Messing, 1998). Another hazard of the workplace that women are far more likely than men to face is **sexual harassment** (Duffy and Cohen, 2001). To quote Marlene Kadar, "sexual harassment is almost expected in job ghetto areas where women represent the service and clerical occupations. Here women are most vulnerable to a supervisor's or a co-worker's explicit or implicit demands" (1988: 337). In one important aspect, however, women's and men's jobs are very similar. While both girls and boys are likely to have female care-givers, both men and women are likely to have male bosses.

Research in both the United States (Hochschild, 1989) and Canada has shown that the structure of men's jobs can have a significant effect on family life and gender relations. For example, Meg Luxton's interviews in Flin Flon, Manitoba (1983), show how shift work disrupts social life, making it very difficult for couples to participate together in regularly organized community activities. The frustrations the men interviewed felt over their mining jobs were often brought home and "taken out" on their wives; they were also reflected in disrupted sleep patterns. Luxton's more recent study of families in Hamilton, Ontario, shows such patterns continue (Luxton and Corman, 2001).

The structure of women's paid work likewise affects gender relations in the home. A study con-

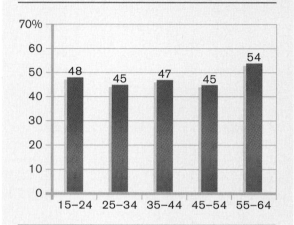

Figure 15.1   **Age of Wives with Children, 2000, Percentage of Each Age Group with Non-traditional Employment**

SOURCE: Roger Sauve, "Tracking the Links Between Jobs and Family Job, family and Stress Among Husbands, Wives and Lone Parents 15–64 from 1990–2000," *Connections* (2002).

Women entering the workforce have to face not only often unchallenging jobs and lower wages, but also the possibility of sexual harassment, whether explicit or implicit. (www.harrycutting.com)

ducted in Toronto suggests that the entry of women into full-time work has profound consequences for relationships—one woman explained, "My husband works evenings, from 5 p.m. until 1:30 or 2 a.m. My work hours are from 7 a.m. until 4 p.m. We avoid child care expenses and it gives the kids enough time to spend with both parents" (Johnson, 1986: 18). Such arrangements may allow children to spend more time with their parents, but they don't leave the parents much time to spend with each other. In their study of Toronto women, Ann Duffy, Nancy Mandell, and Norene Pupo found that many women who had paid work "describe such burn-out symptoms as chronic fatigue, depression, apathy, irritability and anxiety" (1989: 37). These symptoms are bound to affect the relationships of couples. A decade later, Bonnie Fox still found that "parenthood has meant increased differences between the lives of women and men with respect to responsibility, work and time," regardless of whether both had paid employment (2001c: 296).

On the positive side, as employment patterns grow more similar for both sexes, women and men can share their work experiences, which may serve to bring a couple closer together. Parenthood is also more shared. More research is necessary before we have a clear idea about how the conditions of women's and men's work are reflected in their relationships. More research is also necessary on how the work of women and men in different classes, racial and cultural groups, age groups, and locations affects gender relations.

Unpaid Work

Unpaid work, like paid work, is segregated. Women not only do different work than men, they also do more work. As Figure 15.2 shows, regardless of the employment arrangement between the spouses, women do more housework than their husbands.

Study after study has shown that women and men do different kinds and amounts of labour in the home. Research conducted in the 1970s in Vancouver concluded that "most married women do the regular, necessary and time-consuming tasks in the household every day" (Meissner et al., 1975: 431) and that "when men's workload and regular housework are plotted against their own job hours . . . and compared with

15.2

Sociology in Action
More Work for Mother

More and more women are taking on paid work in addition to their domestic work. The most recent data indicate that the overwhelming majority of married women had paid work at some time during the year. This second job has important consequences for women and for their relations with men. Research conducted by Graham Lowe for the Canadian Advisory Council on the Status of Women (1989) concluded that 80 percent of women's illness can be attributed to the stress caused by their double day of paid and unpaid work. This stress may have an impact on relationships with men. When asked if her husband helped at home, one secretary replied:

Are you kidding? That's why I had a big fight with my husband last week because I was fed up. He was complaining about this and that and I turned around and gave it to him. I said, "I work seven hours a day. I come home, I make supper, I clean up." I said, "I do work before I leave in the morning. All weekend I'm working like crazy to get the house clean." I said, "You've got the nerve to tell me not to use the bathroom because you want to use it in the morning."

SOURCE: Pat Armstrong and Hugh Armstrong, *The Double Ghetto: Canadian Women and their Segregated Work* (Toronto: Oxford University Press, 2001), 207.

the data for women, men always work less than women" (429). On the basis of their Newfoundland research, Peter Sinclair and Lawrence Felt report that women's "routine housework declines somewhat as hours of employment increase. . . . It is hardly possible for men to reduce their participation" because they are already doing so little (1992: 67).

Luxton's research in Flin Flon, Manitoba (1983), indicates that when husbands do take over work in the home, they tend to do tasks with clearly defined boundaries or those that are the least boring or monotonous. On the basis of a study in Halifax, Nova Scotia, Susan Shaw (1988) suggests that this is why men tend to define cooking and home chores as leisure. Moreover, men's contribution does not seem to significantly reduce women's domestic workload. For example, men are helping more with the children, but the father frequently "plays with them and tells them stories and other nice things" while the mother performs most of the personal services and other tasks associated with child rearing (Luxton, 1983: 37).

Even when women have paid jobs outside the home, they still do most of the domestic work. In his Toronto study, William Michelson found that wives do three times as much household work as their husbands: "In families where the wife has a part-time job, this ratio is approximately 5 to 1, and it increases to

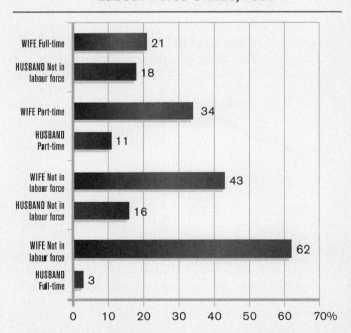

Figure 15.2 **Percentage of Spouse 15+ with Children Who Do 30 or More Hours of Unpaid Housework per Week by Labour-Force Status, 1996**

Labour-Force Status	Percentage
WIFE Full-time	21
HUSBAND Not in labour force	18
WIFE Part-time	34
HUSBAND Part-time	11
WIFE Not in labour force	43
HUSBAND Not in labour force	16
WIFE Not in labour force	62
HUSBAND Full-time	3

SOURCE: Roger Sauve, "Tracking the Links Between Jobs and Family Job, family and Stress Among Husbands, Wives and Lone Parents 15–64 from 1990–2000," *Connections* (2002).

6.7 to 1 when the wife is employed" (1985: 65). In other words, when wives take on paid work, they take on an additional job and get very little help from their husbands. Susan Clark and Andrew Harvey's Halifax research indicates that "at the present time it appears that the wife does most of the adapting; she reduces her household work and leisure hours quite significantly and is more likely than her husband to hold a part-time job" (1976: 64). Studies among unemployed men in Northern Ontario (Wilkinson, 1992) and among immigrant men in Toronto (Haddad and Lam, 1988) do indicate that some men increase their workload when they are unemployed or when their spouses take on paid work, but a clear division of both amounts and types of labour remains. There is little indication that things have changed significantly since this research was done. In 1996, two-thirds of those doing less than 5 hours a week of unpaid housework were men while over 80 per cent of those doing 60 or more hours were women (Statistics Canada, 2003b). And "women's share of unpaid work hours has remained quite stable since the early 1960s," in spite of their growing labour-force participation (Statistics Canada, 2000: 97).

Although women with relatively high-paying careers can afford to hire other women to do much of the domestic work, any remaining tasks are still divided by sex and done disproportionately by women. In her study of career women, Isabella Bassett reports that "close to half the career women polled say cleaning the house, grocery shopping, and doing the laundry are their responsibility, and over half say the same about cooking. This traditional division of labour applies also to the so-called 'male' jobs: two-thirds of career women say household repairs and maintenance are their husband's duties in their households" (1985: 144).

Women take primary responsibility for the sick, disabled, and elderly as well. As daughters, mothers, partners, friends, or volunteers, women are the overwhelming majority of unpaid primary caregivers and spend more time than men providing care. As Figure 15.3 shows, women are expected to take time off from work to take care of sick children or other child-related problems. This in turn greatly hinders the women's ability to advance or be promoted in the workplace.

Women are also much more likely than men to do personal tasks such as bathing and toileting, while men are more likely to do household maintenance tasks (Frederick and Fast, 1999; Morris et al., 1999). Moreover, women's caregiving workloads are increasing as governments across Canada reduce hospital and other institutional care (Armstrong et al., 2001). In situations in which women and men provide support to people outside the home, the former tend to do the regular and time-consuming chores such as housework and babysitting, while the latter help with yardwork and transportation. Similar divisions appear in volunteer work. Women work longer hours than men at volunteer jobs, and they are more likely than men to provide personal care. Men who do volunteer work are most likely to coach male teams or to raise and handle funds.

Like paid work, women's and men's unpaid work is often done in different places and under different conditions, resulting in different experiences. Again, women's domestic work tends to be boring and repetitious, as well as fraught with hidden health hazards and the real possibility of sexual harassment. Thus, "while differences in degree exist among social classes and ethnic groups, women and men in heterosexual partnerships continue to encounter essentially unequal experiences of married life" (Mandell, 2001: 204). We know less about equality in other kinds of partnerships, however.

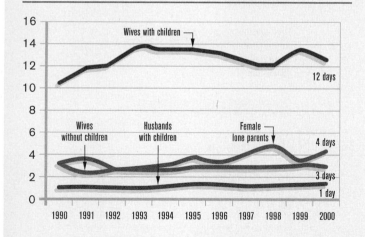

Figure 15.3 Days Lost for Personal and Family Reasons Excluding Maternity

SOURCE: Roger Sauve, "Tracking the Links Between Jobs and Family Job, family and Stress Among Husbands, Wives and Lone Parents 15–64 from 1990–2000," *Connections* (2002).

Community and Social Life

Relationships between men and women can be said to be characterized by both change and the persistence of traditional patterns of behaviour—in brief, by ambiguity. The "dating game," politics, and medical services all provide examples of both emerging and lingering patterns in relations between the sexes.

Dating and Sexual Relations

Women are now more likely to pay their own way and open their own doors, and they are even more likely to take the initiative in sexual activity (Wilson, 2001). Women are also, as far as we can tell from the research, more likely today to engage in premarital or extramarital sex than they were in the past. However, young women are still more likely to justify having sexual relationships on the basis of love, while young men are far more likely to refer to physical grounds for sex.

The old double standard for female and male sexual behaviour has weakened significantly but not disappeared entirely with the advent of better contraceptives and new ideas about women's place. According to a 1992 Gallup Poll, while 74 per cent of men did not think premarital sex was wrong, this was the case for only 65 per cent of the women. The persistence of the double standard may be related to the failure to develop completely effective and safe birth control techniques and to educate young people about their proper use. The spread of HIV/AIDS may serve to destroy the double standard, however. Both men and women are being educated about and encouraged to use condoms. Moreover, as pointed out earlier, AIDS has given men in particular cause for concern about the consequences of casual sex and may therefore make their sexual practices more similar to those of women, who have had to worry throughout history about the results of sexual contact. AIDS has also contributed to more public discussion of homosexual relationships.

Both the availability of contraception and women's participation in the labour force have given women greater choice about whether, when, and whom to marry. They also have more choice to enter lesbian relationships, although severe pressure against such relationships remains. Men now have greater choice as well because they do not have to assume the main financial burden of maintaining a household when they marry

or have children. These changes may help to explain why more and more couples are living in conjugal relationships outside of marriage. Couples may live together without marriage because they want to see whether they are compatible, because they cannot marry for a variety of reasons, to save money, or because they reject the notion of marriage. Living together does not necessarily mean a rejection of marriage, however—many of these couples do marry eventually.

Politics

Women have gained many legal and political rights since the turn of the century, including the right to vote and to be elected or appointed to political office. These rights have, in turn, helped to change laws related to equal opportunity for paid employment, to equal pay, and to property rights, to name but a few (Boyd, 1997; Brodie, 1996).

Women not only vote, they also run for office. The number of women who hold political office has grown enormously in recent decades. Canada's first female prime minister, Kim Campbell, was elected in 1993, and as of 2003, one woman had served as provincial premier. The active participation of women in politics has significantly altered relations within legislatures, regulatory bodies, and the courts, as well as altering legislation itself. Women's concerns and perspectives are more often taken into account.

But in the political arena, too, the sexes frequently remain segregated. Although women have participated at all levels of government, the largest proportion of women is found in municipal politics, the lowest level of decision making. Her study of municipal politics led Kathryn Kopinak to conclude that "women candidates and elected officials occupy positions of greater strength than men on several political dimensions," but also to suggest that this may be related to their smaller numbers at the higher levels (1988: 385). Little has changed in the intervening years. Furthermore, within municipal politics, women are segregated into traditional areas such as school boards, where they can oversee what is happening to the children. The balance of power is shifting, but the seats at the top are still reserved mainly for the men.

Medical Services

Relations between the sexes in the area of medical services are also changing, albeit very slowly. There are still significant differences in the treatment of women and men, reflecting old ideas about the relations between the sexes and about women's proper place. Most research is still done on male subjects and then generalized to women, and even less research is done on differences among women (Manzer, 2001). Men are less likely than women to use health care services (Health Reports, 2001); when they do, they are more likely to be treated as if they have a "real," biologically based medical problem. Ruth Cooperstock and Henry Lennard found that "women consistently receive twice the proportion of prescriptions for tranquilizers as do men" (1987: 314). Such prescriptions have been justified as a way of supporting social relationships, especially those based on sex. The prescription of tranquilizers to women is also "consistent with the culturally accepted view that it is the role of the wife to control the tensions created by a difficult marriage": Valium is used "as an aid in the maintenance of the nurturing, caring role" (Cooperstock and Lennard, 1987: 318).

Women's greater use of health services, which is related largely to their reproductive capacity, serves to reinforce the notion of dependency and the need for medical management. But as women move into the labour force and attain higher levels of education, traditional medical approaches are coming under attack—from men as well as women. Men now tend to be present not only at the births of their children, but also at prenatal classes. Such developments also influence relations between the sexes, often serving to bring women and men closer together as they share aspects of childbearing and other life experiences.

Explanations for Inequality: Making Connections

There is at least one woman and one man in every occupational category. Some women are bosses; others are sexual harassers. Some men stay at home and take responsibility for household chores and child care, while most never harass women or batter their wives. These facts reinforce the view that biology is not a major factor determining the division of labour by sex.

Nonetheless, biology is far from irrelevant. The fact that women, not men, have babies does make a difference in society. Childbirth and child rearing are separate from paid work. Because women bear children and because people have created a distinction

between different kinds of work, women are to some extent limited from participating in the labour force in the same way as men.

The differences are exaggerated by women's low wages and by the scarcity and high cost of child care. In addition, "licensed or regulated family daycare is still a rarity in Canada" (Baker, 2001b: 110). Good child care is not only difficult to find, it is also expensive. Daycare fees average almost half the average female wage. Consequently, the families most likely to enjoy access to such care still have "either an income high enough to pay for the service or an income low enough to qualify for subsidy" (Status of Women Canada, 1986: 72). For the many families who cannot afford or find daycare, it often makes economic sense for the woman to stay at home because she earns the lower wages. The young working-class Vancouver women interviewed by Gaskell (1992: 80) often said they would prefer working for pay to staying home with the children but saw little hope of having their male partners stay at home instead, given women's wages. Fewer women are dropping out of the labour force when they have children and more men provide care, but if anyone leaves the workforce to provide child care, it is almost always the female partner. As pointed out earlier, the same is true when elderly parents and disabled adult children require care. This type of work interruption can serve to boost men's earning potential and to reduce that of women—or at least be used as an excuse to do so.

Women's reproductive capacity and the social arrangements that turn this resource into a liability are not the only factors in the continuing division of labour by sex. The dominant ideology also plays a role. And this ideology is changing, especially for the younger generations. By 1995, the vast majority of women and men under the age of 24 thought paid work was important to personal happiness; however, over half of the men and women surveyed also thought growing children would suffer if both parents were employed (Ghalam, 2000: 70–1). Furthermore, many employers remain convinced that women are physically and mentally suited to some jobs and not others. Career women surveyed by Bassett (1985) cited sex **discrimination** as the most important factor contributing to their failure to win top jobs. Similarly, a Calgary study found that women in male-dominated professions had to work harder to establish authority, and it was assumed they had "greater split loyalties between work and home than their male

15.3 Open for Discussion
The High Cost of an Interrupted Career

Statistics Canada data reveal that women who interrupt their careers in order to fulfill family responsibilities suffer in terms of pay and promotion. Meanwhile, being married can raise a man's income by 30 per cent. In 1997, married women earned only 68 per cent of married men's wages (Statistics Canada, 2000: 157). When this research was made public, it was suggested that it should be used to convince judges to award higher settlements to women when marriages end in divorce.

Yet career interruptions explain only part of the gap in pay and promotion. A Statistics Canada study concludes,

> Despite the addition of a rich variety of workplace variables, a substantial portion

of the gender wage gap remains baffling. After accounting for differences in worker characteristics, women's hourly wage rate is 83.9 per cent of the men's average. . . . Once differences in the characteristics of the workplace to which men and women belong are controlled for, women's average hourly wage rate is 86.9 per cent of men's average. . . . The inclusion of industry and occupation yield considerably larger adjusted gender pay differentials: women earn roughly 91.6 per cent of comparable men. (Drolet, 2001: 42)

In other words, various forms of discrimination combine to create these inequalities.

---

peers" (Falkenberg, 1988: 77). A recent *Psychology Today* article reports that "women in male-dominated fields are so intimidated by their work environment that they tend to play down certain typically female traits" (2000: 18). For their part, many women have learned by example and experience that men and women do different work, and this notion has become part of their world view (Gaskell, 1992).

But economic need and the need of employers for employees can overturn ideology. Many married women move into the labour market because their families need the money, but during most of this century, single women have relied on paid work for personal economic survival. Women who are single parents depend either on wages or on welfare, given that the majority of women do not get support payments after separation but they do get the children (Galarneau and Sturrock, 1997). In addition, employers' need for people with the skills women have traditionally learned, as well as for cheap, often part-time, labour, has increased (see Table 15.3, p. 394). Women have thus provided what Patricia Connelly (1978) described as a "reserve army"—a large number of workers who are available and who compete with others in their group for the jobs they can get.

Women's subordinate position in the labour market has reinforced their responsibility for domestic work. At the same time, women's domestic responsibilities

have reinforced their subordinate position in the market. As women have gained both experience and income—at the same time suffering from the competing demands of paid and unpaid work—their ideas have changed. The resulting protests against male-dominated society and its ideology have changed both society and some of its dominant ideas.

Although large divergences remain, male and female life experiences have become more similar in recent years. Shared experiences open up new possibilities for more egalitarian relationships—though they may also create new areas of tension.

Strategies for Change

Many women (and some men) have developed a variety of strategies for change. Individual women have pushed men to do more domestic labour. They have entered the labour market, striven for interesting and well-paid jobs, and fought to end discrimination in the workplace. They have had the courage to publicize such previously hidden crimes as sexual harassment, wife abuse, and sexual assault, and to charge men—even their own husbands—with them.

Collectively, many women have worked—sometimes together with men—to create the conditions in which such individual efforts are possible and effective and to alter the structures that keep women subordinate. Women have succeeded in pressuring governments to pass laws recognizing women's equal contribution to marriage, mandating equal pay for work of equal value, providing maternity leave for employed women, and making job discrimination, sexual harassment, and the sexual assault of wives by their own husbands offences. Women have often succeeded in encouraging schools to develop new materials for classroom use that represent women doing more than domestic and secretarial work. Largely as a result of women's efforts, many of the practices (such as quotas) that prevented many women from entering such programs as law, medicine, and engineering have been ended. Women have also developed education programs to expand female skills and to provide information on birth control and self-protection. They have opened homes for battered women, rape crisis centres, and daycare centres. They have fought for affirmative action programs and for women's right to be heard in union affairs . . . and much more.

At the same time, men have started men's support groups and developed organizations intended to reduce violence against women. Increasing numbers of men are also seeking custody of their children and advocating equal rights for same-sex couples. They have actively worked to include the issues raised by the women's movement in classroom discussions and media presentations. More men are taking courses that teach them domestic skills, though few have enrolled in traditionally female university programs such as nursing and domestic science. Some men have taken on their share of domestic work or opted to stay at home to care for the children.

Certain of these strategies have been successful in altering patterns and relations; many have not. Both men and women have resisted changes in gender relations (Cockburn, 1991; Faludi, 1991, 1999). Men in general and employers in particular have too much at stake to willingly alter the status quo. It cannot be denied, however, that relations between women and men have been fundamentally altered over the past few decades. Some men have learned the joys of child care, the skills involved in domestic work, the strengths of female managers, the value of egalitarian relationships, the relief of not being the sole breadwinner, the negative consequences of sexual harassment and unprotected sex. It can no longer be assumed that a girl will be a mother and homemaker, or a boy a breadwinner and hero. Nor can it be assumed that all families will consist of partners of different sexes living with their own biological children.

Looking Ahead

Canadian society has been undergoing a fundamental economic restructuring that is bound to have a profound effect on gender relations. Jobs in resource-based industries, manufacturing, construction, and wholesale trade have disappeared, or at least become much less secure, in the face of free trade, new technologies, and new managerial strategies. Most of these jobs were held by men, and many were highly paid, unionized, full-time, and relatively permanent. Moreover, their existence was critical in making possible what is often called the "traditional" family, with mother at home and father in the workforce.

While jobs have become more precarious in the male-dominated areas, job growth has been in the service sector, where women dominate and where much of the work is part-time or short-term, insecure, and without union protection. Many service-sector jobs were created by **the state**, especially in health, social services, and education, where women dominate. But governments are now cutting back, and many of these jobs have disappeared or become precarious.

These developments have important consequences for both sexes. First of all, women and men are increasingly finding themselves in direct competition for work in all fields. Second, men's employment patterns are becoming more like women's as more men take part-time and short-term jobs in the sectors in which women have traditionally worked and in which more women have full-time employment. A third result is that, with men less able to be breadwinners, there is even greater pressure on women to take paid work.

These changes in the labour market could lead to greater equality. Men's taking on of women's traditional paid work may develop more of the skills and personality traits relevant to family care; part-time workers may have more time to spend at home. As a result, domestic labour may become more equally shared as many women and men have more time to devote to household work. At the same time, women who become the family breadwinner may better understand the pressures men face; they may also acquire more power and more of the characteristics men develop as a consequence of their paid work.

On the other hand, the same changes could aggravate tensions between the sexes. Competition for scarce wage labour could lead to bitter confrontations

The daily struggles of mothers to balance work and child care are further exacerbated by recent governmental reductions in hospital and institutional care. (GettyImages/Photodisc)

between men and women. Indeed, there has already been some backlash against employment and pay equity programs, as well as against public-sector jobs. Women's lower wages mean that families dependent on a female breadwinner sink into poverty. Women are taking on more child care, elder care, and domestic work as a result of cutbacks in government services. Government restructuring of social programs is creating an equality deficit in many areas because many more women than men were dependent on such programs (Day and Brodsky, 1998). The decision of most provinces to close some institutions for those with disabilities means that more women provide home care for those previously institutionalized. At the same time, men who can no longer make a significant contribution to family economic support may leave because they are unable to face what many regard as their failure to act like men. Both tendencies—greater equality and greater tension—are evident today. Which one will prevail depends largely on the responses of men and women themselves.

Conclusion

Relations between women and men have been characterized by both change and lack of change in recent years. Although women have gained certain important rights, greater access to traditionally male-dominated institutions and jobs, and some protection from abuse, they still bear the primary load in domestic work, have lower wages than men, and face a double standard in many relationships. Put another way, although more men are helping with the housework and child care, learning to express their emotions, and treating women as equals, men still dominate the most prestigious jobs in the labour force and seldom take on an equal share of caring work.

Biologically predetermined characteristics provide little explanation for these patterns, both because there are few clearly established biological distinctions between the sexes and because biological factors are influenced by the social and physical environments. Social structures and work relations provide much more useful explanations for both change and lack of change in gender relations. These institutions and interactions are now undergoing significant changes themselves, changes that will have profound consequences for how men and women view one another. But these consequences are not predetermined. They will depend greatly on decisions and actions taken by women and men, individually and collectively, to shape their own lives.

☐ Questions for Critical Thought

1. Why is it disturbing when we cannot readily determine a person's sex? Do you feel this should be disturbing?
2. Do you think it is possible to separate nature from nurture, biology from culture? Explain your reasoning.
3. Do clothes and hairstyles for males and females mean similar behaviour?
4. Do we expect the same behaviour from a black man and a white man, a rich woman and a poor woman? Why or why not?
5. Discuss the effect of HIV/AIDS on the double standard in sexual behaviour.
6. How can women's continuing responsibility for domestic work when they take on full-time employment be explained?
7. Select an article from a magazine directed at a female audience, and one from a magazine intended for a male audience. Compare the magazines with respect to the portrayal of women and men themselves and the portrayal of the relations between the sexes.

☐ Recommended Readings

Pat Armstrong and Hugh Armstrong, *The Double Ghetto: Canadian Women and Their Segregated Work* (Toronto: McClelland & Stewart, 1994).
Linking women's paid and unpaid work, this book examines different explanations for patterns in women's jobs.

Martha Bailey, ed., "Domestic Partnerships," *Canadian Journal of Family Law*, 17, no. 1 (2000).
This special issue explores various aspects of same-sex partnerships.

Tania Das Gupta, *Racism and Paid Work* (Toronto: Garamond, 1996).
This book sets out a theoretical framework for understanding class, racism, and gender at work. It uses nursing and the garment industry to illustrate this framework.

Meg Luxton and June Corman, *Getting By in Hard Times: Gendered Labour at Home and on the Job* (Toronto: University of Toronto Press, 2001).
Based on interviews with household members in Hamilton, Ontario, this book connects class and gender relations, family forms, labour markets, and the process of capital accumulation.

Karen Messing, *One-Eyed Science: Occupational Health and Women Workers* (Philadelphia: Temple University Press, 1998).
This book reveals how different work leads to different health hazards and how these differences are perceived and treated.

Statistics Canada, *Women in Canada 2000: A Gender-Based Statistical Report* (Ottawa: Statistics Canada, 2000).
This compilation of data on the status, health, education, income, and family status of women is accompanied by useful, descriptive text. There are also important chapters on Aboriginal and immigrant women, visible minority women, and senior women.

Stephen M. Whitehead and Frank J. Barrett, eds, *The Masculinities Reader* (Oxford: Blackwell, 2000).
The articles brought together in this text provide an overview of issues linked to being male in North American society.

☐ Recommended Web Sites

Canadian Centre for Policy Research

http://policyalternatives.ca

> The Canadian Centre for Policy Research published policy papers and research on Canadian issues. Much of the material on this Web site takes gender into account.

Canadian Policy Research Networks

www.cprn.ca

> The Canadian Policy Research Networks regularly produce research reports on families, on health, and on work. Their research includes a gender-based analysis of the data.

Canadian Social Research Links

www.canadiansocialresearch.net

> This accessible and current Web site provides information on social programs in Canada, usually offering links to other sites and sources that provide details. Many of these links are to gender-specific programs.

Centres of Excellence for Women's Health

www.cewh-cesf.ca

> This Web site offers access to a wide range of materials on women's health issues. Women's health is broadly defined to include factors that influence health as well as male/female differences in health.

Statistics Canada

www.statcan.ca

> Statistics Canada provides reliable data on the Canadian population. Almost all of its data is reported by sex, and a variety of research studies on gender are available.

Status of Women Canada (swc)

www.swc-cfc.gc.ca

> SWC is the federal government department that promotes gender equality and the full participation of women in the economic, social, cultural, and political life of the country. SWC focuses its work in three areas: improving women's economic autonomy and well-being, eliminating systemic violence against women and children, and advancing women's human rights.

Women Watch

www.un.org/womenwatch/

> The United Nations Convention on the Elimination of Discrimination Against Women can be found on this site, along with routes to a variety of documents the United Nations produces on the current situation of women in the world.

World Health Organization (WHO)

www.who.int

> The World Health Organization monitors patterns in population and health around the world. Much of its material reports on issues by gender, and some of its research is gender-specific.

16

Michael Rosenberg

> > >

Ethnic and Race Relations

© Bill Whittman

☐ Learning Objectives

In this chapter, you will:

- become familiar with the sociological concepts of ethnicity and race and with some of the theories sociologists have developed to explain these phenomena

- come to understand the role of ethnic and racial groups in the evolution of Canadian society

- identify some of the major issues and concerns regarding immigration and the retention of ethnic identities in Canadian society

- examine the ways in which ethnicity and race can intersect with other social factors, such as gender and politics

- identify some fundamental patterns of relations among Canadians (bilingualism and multiculturalism) that are based on ethnic identity and diversity

- consider the difference between prejudice, discrimination, and racism, and the impact of each on Canadian society

Introduction

In Canada, ethnic and racial diversity is a fact of life. Canada accepts more immigrants on a proportional basis than any other industrialized country, and the people who come to Canada are members of all of the major ethnic and racial groups to be found in the world. In the 2001 census, Canadians indicated more than 200 distinct ethnic origins, including such new groups (for Canada) as Kosovars, Azerbaijani, Nepali, Kashmiri, Yoruba, Ashanti, and Maya and Carib Indians (Statistics Canada, 2003a). Canadians, it would seem, value diversity and enjoy the blend of cultures, languages, and practices it promotes, especially in the large urban areas where most of the recent immigrants are to be found.

Canada has always been a culturally plural society. Founded as a political union of two **ethnic groups**, the British and the French, contemporary Canada owes its constitutional and political structure (as well as some of its problems) largely to the union of these two distinct groups. As a result, **ethnicity** and ethnic group relations hold a special place in Canadian society. Of course, pluralism does not necessarily mean that all groups are treated equally, nor that all have the opportunity to participate fully in the society, as the history of Canada's Native peoples makes clear. Still, Canadians have dealt with most of their group conflicts without violence, and those individuals who oppose ethnic or cultural diversity seem to be a minority among Canadians.

This acceptance of diversity does not seem to be true in many other parts of the world. Ethnic and racial differences, along with differences of religion, language, and national identity, are the bases for animosity, **discrimination**, and violence in many nations. Violence or institutionalized discrimination persists in the relations between Protestants and Catholics in Northern Ireland, between Hindus and Muslims in India, between indigenous peoples and the government in Mexico, between Romanians and Gypsies in Romania. Almost every day, we can read in

Pluralism does not necessarily mean that all groups are treated equally or that all have the opportunity to fully participate in society. The history of Canada's Aboriginal peoples illustrates this fact. This photograph, taken from a *Globe and Mail* special series called "Canada's Apartheid," illustrates an Inuit couple frustrated by their experiences of racism. (Fred Lum/*The Globe and Mail*)

newspapers of conflict somewhere in the world between tribal, cultural, or racial groups.

All of this global upsurge of ethnic identification and conflict has been somewhat surprising to most sociologists because for a long time social scientists had assumed that ethnicity would be of declining significance in any modern, industrial society. Industrialization itself, it was thought, would lead to the breakdown of racial and ethnic distinctions as new sources of solidarity—and of conflict—arose. Many Marxists, for example, argued that **class** differences supersede ethnic divisions and that in time all workers, regardless of race or ethnicity, would come to realize that they share the same interests in opposition to the interests of capitalists. Industrial theorists, too, had argued that ethnic differences would diminish with the spread of modernization. In this case, occupational, professional, or educational **statuses** were expected to replace ethnic identity in relations among individuals.

Neither of these seem to have happened. Indeed, some of the most violent and bitter ethnic conflicts are found in former communist countries, such as Russia, Yugoslavia, and Romania, where the previous Marxist governments worked hard for many years to eradicate ethnic differences. In addition, such highly industrialized nations as Britain, Germany, and France have been the scene for the rise of new racist movements, such as the National Front in France, the British National Party in Britain, and the Republican Party in Germany. Even in the United States, the most industrialized of all nations, race persists as the most fundamental dividing line in the society (Smelser, Wilson, and Mitchell, 2001).

Given the rapid social, economic, cultural, and technological transformations found around the world, such as **globalization** and transnationalism, Canada's ethnic and racial diversity may serve as a model of what the whole world will be like in the near future. This makes it all the more urgent that we understand the nature of that diversity and the impact it has on all Canadians. How are our economy, our political system, and our lifestyles changed by immigration? How are the relations among citizens affected? Are all groups able to participate equally in the fundamental institutions of the country, or are some treated as second-class citizens? Do most Canadians wish to perpetuate diversity, or would they prefer the development of a new consensus among Canadians with respect to language, culture, values, and civic rights? Answering these questions has become a priority for many Canadian social scientists.

But before we can discuss these issues in detail, we must first define our terms and explain what is meant by *ethnicity*, *ethnic groups*, and *ethnic group relations*.

Defining *Ethnicity* and *Race*

It would be convenient to be able to give a clear and unambiguous definition of *ethnicity*. Unfortunately, it is not possible. Like many other sociological concepts, ethnicity is the subject of much disagreement. This is not surprising because ethnicity is a relational phenomenon emerging from the patterns of **social relationships** among and interactions between people and groups. It can take many forms and display many characteristics, nor does it play the same role in Indonesia, in Switzerland, and in Canada.

Nevertheless, ethnicity does possess some key features. In its broadest sense, *ethnicity* refers to sets of social relationships—particularly class, status, or power relationships—defined as being based on inherited biological differences. The noted German sociologist Max Weber ([1908] 1978) therefore defined *ethnicity* as the sets of social distinctions by which groups differentiate themselves from one another on the basis of presumed biological ties. Members of such groups have a sense of themselves as a common "people" separate and distinct from others.

This biologically legitimated claim to form a "people" is crucial. While sociologists and anthropologists often consider cultural distinctions to be just as intimately tied into ethnicity as is biology, cultural distinctiveness is not sufficient to characterize an ethnic group. If it were, then "intellectuals," for example, would constitute an ethnic group in many societies. This is not to say that intellectuals have never come to form an ethnic group, but they have done so only after redefining common biological origin as the basis of their solidarity. This last point illustrates another crucial sociological feature of ethnicity: common biological origin need not be real—as long as it is believed to be real (Smith, 1988).

While most claims to ethnic distinctiveness may be biological, the **symbolic markers** used to differentiate groups are rarely biological, with the extremely important exception of racial distinctions. Instead, the indicators of ethnicity used as symbolic markers are usually cultural (De Vos and Romannuci-Ross, 1982; Geertz, 1973). In Canada, for instance, language is a particularly important symbolic marker for both francophones and anglophones. The preservation of the French language has been a source of pride for francophones, while the use of English was for a long time regarded as a sign of higher status by anglophones. Many other groups in Canada, too, consider language an important component of **identity**. Greek, Hungarian, Italians, Polish, and Ukrainian Canadians, for example, consider speaking their ethnic language, if only at home, extremely important for retaining their ethnic identity. Jeffrey Reitz (1980) has found evidence suggesting that they are right. Other symbolic markers are religion, attachment to a homeland, a sense of common history, festivals and ceremonies, traditions, even ethnic food or dress.

As noted above, while most symbolic markers are cultural, racial distinctions make use of supposed biological markers. In this case, sociologists use the term *race* rather than *ethnicity* when referring to a group. A *race* is a group that is defined on the basis of perceived physical differences such as skin colour.

Clearly, race and ethnicity are related concepts, and not too long ago it was common to treat ethnic groups as racially distinct. That is why, for instance, the British and French used to be referred to as the two "founding races" of Canada. The contemporary use of the term *race* differs from *ethnicity* in that racial groups are considered to be those whose perceived physical difference play a greater role than cultural differences as a symbolic marker in setting group boundaries. Blacks in Canada, for example, come from many cultural backgrounds. Some were born and raised in Canada, others in the United States; some come from Haiti, others from Jamaica, still others from Africa. To the degree that we treat them all as a single group on the basis of skin colour alone, however, they constitute a racial group.

It is essential to keep in mind that the existence of distinct and definite biological races is largely a myth. Sociologists are interested in the social, not the physical, significance of race. To sociologists, race is a symbolic marker by which individuals categorize themselves and others into different groups. Indeed, it is questionable whether the term *race* is still a useful one because its use may imply that it refers to real, rather than symbolic, distinctions (Mason, 1999). In Canada, the term *visible minority* has come to replace *race* in designating groups having a perceived physical difference from the white Europeans who make up the majority of Canada's population. Use of the newer term has the advantage of allowing us to avoid the negative emotional significance often attached to the term *race* and to

regard groups that seem physically distinct primarily as ethnic groups.

People differ in the degree to which their ethnicity plays an important role in their lives or in their identity. Ethnic groups defined largely by religion, such as Hutterites or Doukhabours, and groups whose physical or cultural traits make them conspicuous tend to see ethnicity as highly relevant. Such groups often come to form an *ethnic community*; that is, they develop a set of ethnic institutions based on common interests and identities. An ethnic community may try to close itself off as much as possible from the broader society. This is the case with the Hutterites, who form relatively isolated agricultural communities. Usually, however, an ethnic community is a *partial community*, organized around key institutions, such as an ethnic church, a school, or a political lobby group. Even the family can serve as a key institution in an ethnic community. A partial community is embedded in the broader society; most of its members work and live among people who do not belong to their ethnic group. Ethnic interests and identities, then, must compete with other interests and identities, such as those based on occupation, religion, gender, or status.

For some individuals, ethnicity has diminished to the point where it is a minor component of their identity, important only at ethnic festivals or family celebrations, when they cheer their homeland's sports victories or fear for it in time of war. Such people may not form an ethnic community in any meaningful sense, but we can still speak of them as an *ethnic group* to the degree that they are potentially capable of organizing and acting upon their ethnic interests or identity. An ethnic group, like an ethnic community, may have some central institutions, but these are unlikely to have been established by the group itself as specifically ethnic institutions. "National" churches, for example, may serve as a focus for group activity, as may ethnic stores, restaurants, or even travel agencies.

Finally, there are people for whom ethnicity is completely irrelevant. Such individuals may well be counted as part of an ethnic category, however. An *ethnic category* is a strictly objective measure of how many people have some particular ethnic origin, regardless of whether they identify with their ethnicity. An individual whose ancestors came from Ireland in the 1840s may consider himself or herself Canadian, or even Québécois(e), but may well be counted among those of "Irish" ethnicity in census statistics.

Theories of Ethnicity

While there are many theories of ethnicity, most tend to fall into two broad categories: pluralistic and remedial. We will now look at each of these in turn.

Pluralistic Theories

Pluralistic theories see ethnic and racial differences among people as natural or inevitable. Their adherents maintain that there have always been and will always be ethnic distinctions between groups.

Many types of pluralistic theories exist. *Sociobiologists* such as Pierre Van den Berghe (1987), for example, see ethnic groups as based on genetically determined processes of kin selection and reproductive success. *Primordialists*, including John Stack, Jr (1986), view ethnic differences as based on emotional ties to others with whom an individual identifies and shares a sense of kinship. American sociologists often link ethnicity to politics, and some argue that ethnic distinctions will exist as long as people form groups to compete for control over public institutions and political entitlements (Bell, 1975; Glazer and Moynihan, 1975).

Perhaps the most influential pluralistic theory is that of Fredrik Barth (1969), whose argument is that ethnic differences are a consequence of the patterns of **social interaction** that generate boundaries among people. By an *ethnic group boundary*, Barth means a "structuring of interaction" that divides people into groups (1969: 16). Ethnic boundaries make use of markers to indicate who is or is not a member of the ethnic group. Patterns of interaction will differ when an individual deals with fellow group members rather than non-members, says Barth, because membership "implies a sharing of criteria for evaluation and judgment . . . [and] the assumption that the two are fundamentally 'playing the same game'" (1969: 15). By contrast, identifying others as non-members "implies a recognition of limitations on shared understandings, differences in criteria for judgment of value and performance, and a restriction of interaction to sectors of assumed common understanding and mutual interest" (15).

Barth's approach has changed the way most sociologists—whether they are pluralists or not—think about ethnicity. Barth showed that an ethnic group cannot be examined in isolation because ethnic groups are always organized around patterns of interaction. As Barth himself put it, "to the extent that actors use ethnic identities to categorize themselves and others for purposes of interaction, they form ethnic groups in [an] organizational sense" (1969: 13–14). Ethnic groups are then seen as forms of social organization, and the issue of how and why ethnic groups are formed becomes an issue of how and why group boundaries are created and maintained.

This perspective is particularly useful because Barth does not assume that any particular set of ethnic group distinctions or ethnic institutions is natural. Instead, ethnicity can be understood only in a specific context, because it reflects the patterns of social relationships among the particular sets of people found in that context. Barth's approach is similar to what is known as the *emergent identity approach*, because it examines how and why the symbolic markers of ethnic identity evolve over time (Yancey, Ericksen, and Juliani, 1976).

Remedial Theories

Remedial theories tend to treat ethnicity as a characteristic of a class or industrial society. While they largely discount the importance of ethnicity in modern societies, remedial theorists nevertheless try to explain how or why ethnicity may be of (temporary) relevance under certain conditions. They argue that ethnic differences are not inevitable but arise from class differences or cultural factors that inhibit economic rationality.

Remedial theories, like pluralistic theories, come in many varieties. *Class theories* tend to link ethnic or racial differences to differences centred on labour. According to the *split labour market theory* described by Edna Bonacich (1972), for example, employers take advantage of ethnic distinctions by paying some workers (who belong to a particular ethnic group) more and others (who belong to another group) less. The inequity is used to explain ethnic antagonisms, since higher-paid workers will attempt to exclude the lower paid. Conflict over access to and control over jobs therefore leads to racial or ethnic conflict.

The theory of *internal colonialism* is another explanation of the relevance of ethnicity in a modern economy. As Susan Olzack explains this approach, "an internal colony exists to the extent that a richer and culturally dominant core dominates an ethnically identified periphery" (1983: 359). In this way, the core region is able to take advantage of the economic and political weakness of the peripheral region. The resources and raw materials of the peripheral region may be obtained at reduced cost, while workers in the peripheral area can be used as cheap labour. The result is resentment among the exploited "ethnics," which can lead to nationalist or separatist movements. This approach is little used by Canadian sociologists, since Canada as a whole can be viewed as peripheral to the United States. It has, however, been used by James Frideres (1988) to account for the disadvantaged position of Native groups in Canada.

One remedial approach that is particularly popular in Canada looks at the role of **the state** in defining and promoting ethnic distinctions. Leo Panitch (1977) has suggested that the Canadian state played a particularly central role in the country's economic and social development. State policies such as official bilingualism and official **multiculturalism** have not only promoted ethnic distinctions, they have actually defined them. The federal government's policy has been to treat ethnic groups as primarily cultural groups, rather than as religious, national, political, or economic groups. Daiva Stasiulis (1980) has argued that this policy has caused many groups to redefine themselves and has also allowed the state to control ethnic group activities and to determine ethnic group leaders by how and to whom it disburses grants. Peter Li suggests that the policy allows for "managing race and ethnic relations within a state apparatus . . . through fiscal control of ethnic associations whereby the nature, duration, and amount of grants that ethnic associations receive fall in line with the officially defined priorities of multicultural programs" (1988: 132). Versions of this approach have been used by Terry Wotherspoon and Vic Satzewich (1993) to understand the relations between Native groups and the state, by Michael Rosenberg and Jack Jedwab (1992) to identify organizational differences between major ethnic groups in Montreal, and by Raymond Breton (1984, 1989) to examine the impact of state policy on ethnic identity and concerted group action.

A popular remedial approach in the United States is the theory of *symbolic ethnicity*—ethnicity that has becomes purely a matter of personal identification and that has little or no impact upon how people live their lives or relate to each other. Herbert Gans (1979) introduced the concept to resolve a seeming paradox in American social life: the resurgence of ethnicity in a society where people's lives have come increasingly to be alike. Third-, fourth-, or fifth-generation Italian, Polish, or Greek Americans have little that distinguishes them from one another, yet a so-called ethnic revival began in the United States in the late 1960s. In a sense, the phenomenon should not pose a paradox—as the real distinctions among people diminish, it is not surprising that those few distinctions that remain become more important, more central to group or personal identity. This can be seen in Quebec in the contemporary emphasis on the French language as the mark of a distinctive Québécois identity while the other characteristics that once served as distinguishing marks of Quebec society, such as a rural lifestyle and a commitment to Catholic institutions, have all but disappeared.

The assumption underlying the concept of symbolic ethnicity as used by Gans seems to be that if ethnicity is merely symbolic, then it loses both its impact upon everyday life and its ability to divide American society. In effect, ethnicity becomes purely a matter of personal sentiments. This theory is much less popular among Canadian sociologists because it does not reflect the corporate character of many ethnic groups in Canadian society or the links between ethnicity and inequality. Furthermore, as the example of the role played by the French language in Quebec demonstrates, ethnic differences that are "only" symbolic can be as important as any others.

Ethnicity in the Canadian Context

The resurgence of ethnicity has been something of a surprise to most sociologists. It may be, however, that Canadian sociologists are less surprised than others. Sociologists in this country have long acknowledged the significance of ethnicity in Canadian society and have been at the forefront of theory and research on ethnic phenomena.

Ethnic and racial groups are more likely to take an institutional form in Canada than in the United States, Britain, or Germany. The reason lies in two factors: the special role played by ethnicity in Canadian society, and the official policies of bilingualism and multiculturalism, initiated and promoted by the federal and various provincial governments. These two factors have caused Canadian sociologists to direct much of their attention to two issues: the connection between ethnicity and inequality in Canadian society, and the integration—or lack of integration—of ethnic groups and communities into Canadian society.

John Porter's description of Canadian society as a **vertical mosaic** (1965) stimulated research into the link between ethnicity and inequality. Porter asserts that an individual's ethnicity defined his or her "place" within Canada's stratification system. Immigrants and their children had little social mobility. Most people in Canada tended to retain their ethnic *entrance status*, that is, their occupational, educational, or social status upon first arrival. Porter's data showed that the groups of British and French origin dominated Canadian society with respect to economics, politics, and status. Other groups fell into place in what was effectively an ethnically divided stratification system—the vertical mosaic—that promoted ethnic community organization. As a result, the various minority ethnic groups imitated the earlier example of the French and the British by treating ethnicity less as a matter of individual sentiment than as a form of collective organization designed to meet collective interests.

Hubert Guindon (1967) argues that the cleavage between British and French had a structural impact on the development, nature, and context of ethnic inter-group relations. Following the British Conquest, a pattern of ethnic and religious institutional self-segregation developed between the British and French communities, resulting in two parallel societies. While they did interact somewhat in the areas of politics and work, the two groups maintained a rigorous separation in terms of language, education, religion, residence, and marriage. Although the popular description of Canada's British and French communities as "two solitudes" ignores the important realities of class, status, and political divisions within each of what are often called the **charter groups**, there is nevertheless a sense in which each has lived in a world of its own.

It may equally be said that the other minority ethnic groups have formed solitudes of their own. This is certainly true for the Native peoples, whose isolation on reserves kept them outside the economic and political mainstream of Canadian society. Each of the other major ethnic groups imitated—to a greater or lesser degree—the pattern of institutional self-segregation they found in Canada. Throughout much of Canada's history, the cultural and physical separation of British and French created a climate for newly arriving immigrant groups, a separation that fostered and preserved the differences between them and thereby promoted institutional development within them.

Breton (1964) suggests that the high level of institutional development within ethnic communities explains the lack of integration among ethnic groups in Canada. The idea of institutional development inspired Breton's article on **institutional completeness** (1964), a measure of the degree to which a community offers a range of services to its members. According to Breton, full institutional completeness implies that "members would never have to make use of native institutions for the satisfaction of any of their needs" (1964: 194). By focusing on the level and type of social organization found among ethnic groups, Breton initiated an examination of ethnic groups in Canada as organized communities (Breton, 1978, 1983, 1984; Breton et al., 1977, 1990).

Does Porter's thesis of the vertical mosaic still reflect the reality of inequality in Canada? This is a hotly debated question—one to which we will return later in this chapter. What is beyond debate is that, as Porter demonstrated, ethnic communities are always elements in some system of stratification. John Rex (1987) notes that they are embedded in a social context in which significant social forces, such as class relations or political interests, cut across the commonalities. Breton (1978) suggests that, in a society such as Canada, an ethnic community is usually a partial community, one whose members have diverse interests, who participate in other, often competing institutions, and who take on multiple and distinct identities. Most people's participation in their ethnic community is a sometime thing, as the salience of their ethnic identity ebbs and flows with the circumstances in which they find themselves. These circumstances are often situations of group conflict, because ethnic communities are among the more important means by which group conflict is expressed. They provide the resources used to compete for political, economic, and cultural advantages.

Ethnicity and Politics

As mentioned previously, the state in Canada has tended to define ethnic groups as primarily cultural, through such policies as official bilingualism and multiculturalism. But the political character of ethnic group organization cannot be overlooked. Indeed, federal government policy has unintentionally promoted the political character of ethnic group organizations through its funding strategies. Funds tend to be disbursed to umbrella organizations, whose membership is composed of other organizations, rather than to individuals or specialized institutions. Examples of umbrella organizations are the Canadian Jewish Congress, the National Association of

Canadians of Origin in India, and the National Congress of Italian Canadians.

Because of the relationship that umbrella organizations evolve with government agencies, they come to serve as points of contact between the ethnic community and the state. The receipt of funds legitimates them as the representative of their ethnic community in the eyes of both the community and the government. Prominent members of umbrella organizations will be invited to join consultative committees or commissions, to participate in workshops, and to help to legitimate government policy. These individuals may also come to lobby on behalf of their group's interests, and, to the degree that they are seen as "official" representatives of their communities, their views may influence government policy.

There has been, then, a slow but steady reshaping of some ethnic institutions, from cultural institutions to representatives of political interest groups. Moreover, different groups sharing common political goals may unite. In Quebec, for example, the key umbrella organizations of the Greek, Italian, and Jewish Canadian communities have worked together in recent years on political issues. They have prepared joint submissions and briefs, formed joint committees, and organized common community political events. Unified action has given these groups far more influence with the government than they could have achieved alone, even if they had separately supported the same policies. Unity provides greater strength—and it clearly identifies the joint structures as political. Politicians have come to recognize the political strength of ethnic organizations and try to curry favour with them in the hope that it will be translated into votes at election time.

Not all groups share equal access to such resources as political advantage, of course. Important differences between groups result from their time of arrival in Canada and the type of reception they experienced.

Ethnicity and Gender

Gender plays a multi-faceted role in society, and the intersection of gender and ethnicity raises numerous questions that address a wide variety of issues (see, for example, Stasiulis, 1999). Many of these issues, however, are only just beginning to be acknowledged by social scientists. Until quite recently, gender issues were ignored by researchers studying ethnicity, just as gender was ignored in much of sociology. Indeed, minority women researchers suggest that the con-

cerns of immigrant and minority women have been largely overlooked by what they call "mainstream"— that is, white, middle-class—feminists (Petrovic, 2000). There is now growing recognition of the interconnections of gender, ethnicity, and Canadian society in the areas of immigration policy, the workplace, and the home (Stasiulis, 1999). In looking at the connection between gender and ethnicity, then, it is important to acknowledge the diversity of women and to realize that the problems women face and the solutions they require are not the same for all (Ralston, 2000).

Stasiulis asserts that Canadian immigration policy has tended to make women "dependent on husbands, fathers, and other male relatives, and . . . restricted [in] opportunities to learn the official languages" (1990: 291). Living in a new and unfamiliar country, often unable to speak the local language, with few friends to provide assistance or offer practical advice, and with little knowledge of the social services available, the lives of immigrant and refugee women are often highly centred on their families and husbands. Immigration policies can leave women trapped in abusive situations from which they do not know how to escape.

Married women often have to work long hours at low pay to supplement the family's income. Nevertheless, many find that their husbands also expect them to take on all the traditional household tasks, which are perceived to be "women's work"— cooking, cleaning, and child care, and other roles, such as serving as "domestic brokers," "organizing and pooling resources . . . to maintain themselves and their families" (Henry, 1994: 60). In addition, there are often domestic tensions caused by the frustrations felt by both men and women as a result of having to work at jobs that are much lower in pay and status than their skills or education would lead them to expect. Frustration can lead to conflict, sometimes even domestic violence. Immigrant women are more vulnerable in such a situation because, as we have seen, they are more dependent on their husbands and more centred on the family.

Like many other Canadians, immigrants participate in a gendered division of labour in the workplace. Historically, immigrant women have tended to work in low-paying, low-status jobs in manufacturing or domestic service. These are precisely the kinds of jobs in which they are most likely to be exploited. Domestics, for example, are usually paid the minimum wage, and many are expected to work extra hours for little or no pay (Bakan and Stasiulis, 1997). In manufacturing, many immigrant women work in factories, some of them illegally, many of them not unionized. These women have no job security, may be paid below minimum wage, and are expected to work over 40 hours a week. Such **exploitation** is possible because immigrant women are unfamiliar with Canadian law and unaware of the existence of agencies designed to protect their rights. Those who are aware of these agencies may still avoid them because they are unable to speak one of the official languages, or simply because they are distrustful of or intimidated by people they see as "officials." Given these circumstances, it is not surprising that many fear unemployment more than exploitation.

Native women have distinctive concerns of their own, some of which came to the fore during the constitutional debate of the early 1990s. While the male Native leadership advocated the precedence of Aboriginal rights over the Canadian Charter of Rights and Freedoms, the Native Women's Association of Canada argued that Aboriginal rights must not supersede federally guaranteed equal rights for Native women (Krosenbrink-Gelissen, 1993).

Prior to 1985, for instance, as a result of gender discrimination in the Indian Act, Indian women who married non-Indian men lost their Indian status and their right to own property and reside on a reserve. The same was not true for Indian men who married non-Native women. When Indian women took legal action to end this discrimination, they found that the official Native organizations—all dominated by men— opposed their position. Thus, many Native women feel they have not received fair and equitable treatment from Native organizations and have not had their concerns taken seriously. They even fear that Native self-government might cause them to lose their rights under Canada's constitution without granting them equal rights within the Native community. Lilianne Krosenbrink-Gelissen notes that, for this reason, many Native women "oppose the position that [self-government] must be entrenched unconditionally, without a guarantee of gender equality rights" (1993: 361).

For immigrant women, too, community support is often lacking. Research by Amanda McIntyre and Michael Rosenberg (2000) on a number of ethnic women's organizations in Montreal found that these groups were often refused money or support by their local ethnic community umbrella organizations. Frequently people in the community—both men and women—viewed women's organizations as having

only one goal, that of "breaking up families." They ignored or disregarded the many programs and services these organizations tried to initiate. Ironically, women active in these organizations sometimes reported that they also received little support from mainstream feminists. Feminist groups defined the organizations as "ethnic" rather than "women's" organizations (McIntyre and Rosenberg, 2000).

The links between gender and ethnicity require a new way of thinking about many of the issues related to ethnicity. Indeed, as Stasiulis (1990) suggests, it forces feminists as well to question their ethnocentric views of women and the positions that women should be taking on a wide variety of issues.

Patterns of Immigration to Canada

In December 2002, *Maclean's* magazine had a cover story on immigration asking the question, how many is too many (Janigan, 2002)? This is not a new question. Indeed, it is the question that has set the context for Canadian immigration policy since Confederation (Palmer, 1991). Although immigration has been a major force in shaping Canadian society, Canada, unlike the United States, is not now and never has been a "nation of immigrants." Immigration has not only played a different and far lesser role in building Canadian society, it has also had a different meaning in the Canadian context.

In the United States, immigrants played a crucial role in the industrialization and modernization of American society, especially in the period between 1880 and 1925. Arriving in huge numbers to fill the enormous demand for labour created by American industry, they were expected not only to merge into American society, but also to contribute to the creation of a new, dynamic society. The United States was a nation of immigrants not only in a numerical sense, but in the central, symbolic, and creative role assigned to immigration. The so-called American dream was a dream of both achieving personal success and finding a place in American society, being accepted as a full-fledged US citizen. This dream reflected the **melting-pot** ideology that assumed that immigrants would discard all the traditions and distinctions they brought with them, including their ethnic language and national identity, and become nothing other than Americans.

To some extent, the dream and the melting pot were no more than myths. Many immigrants found life in the United States to be one of unending poverty, toil, and exploitation. Some groups, such as blacks and Asians, were entirely excluded from the melting pot. Yet some immigrants found real opportunities, and even those who never "made it" in their own lifetimes could still look forward to having their children take advantage of the opportunities they themselves were denied.

Why did immigration never have the same central role in Canadian society? The answer, as so often happens, lies in the attitudes and preferences of the two charter groups, both of which dominated Canada and neither of which sought either to incorporate the other or to absorb new immigrants. The British and the French are known as *charter groups* because they have a special status in Canada, one entrenched in the Canadian constitution, and have effectively determined the dominant cultural characteristics of Canada. Each group has special rights and privileges, especially with regard to the language used in the legislatures, courts, and schools.

At Confederation, almost all Canadians were of either French or British origin. The two groups saw Canada as a political union between them. The goal of immigration was not to alter this political equation, but to provide the human "raw materials" needed to run the factories or farm the land. Immigrants were viewed as fulfilling primarily an economic function; they were acceptable to the majority groups only so long as they were considered neither a cultural nor an economic threat. Simply put, an Italian coming to the United States became an American, but an Italian coming to Canada became an Italian Canadian.

Traditional Immigration

At every stage of Canada's evolution, national immigration policy has preferred certain groups over others. Initially, migrants from Britain or Northern Europe were favoured. This was still reflected in the ethnic composition of Canada's population as late as 1991, as shown in Figure 16.1. Canadians believed that the British and Northern Europeans would best fit into Canadian society with respect to culture, race, economics—even adaptation to the Canadian winter. Immigration of non-whites was discouraged, and immigration policy before the late 1960s was racist and exclusionary. The history of migration to Canada for the first century after Confederation was a history of European migration.

Even so, not all Europeans were viewed as equal; nor were they equally welcomed. Early policy discouraged immigrants from Eastern and Southern Europe. It was only the failure to attract sufficient immigrants from Britain and Northern Europe that forced the government to recruit from elsewhere. Beginning in about 1880, Eastern Europeans were

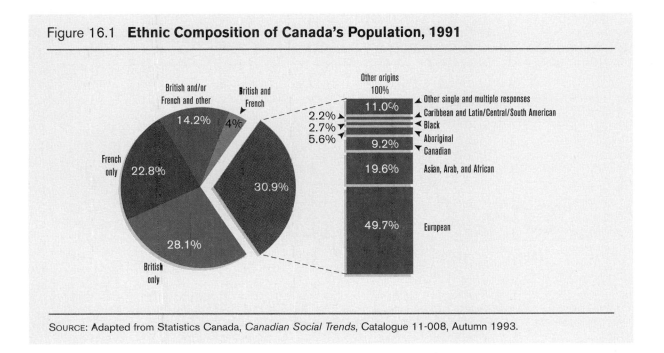

Figure 16.1 **Ethnic Composition of Canada's Population, 1991**

SOURCE: Adapted from Statistics Canada, *Canadian Social Trends*, Catalogue 11-008, Autumn 1993.

encouraged to come to Canada to farm the West. Ukrainians, Russians, and Poles came in large numbers because of the terrible economic conditions in their homelands at that time. By the turn of the century, Southern Europeans, notably Italians, began arriving to work as manual labourers in the rapidly expanding and industrializing cities of central Canada.

Even between 1900 and 1930, when immigration rates were high, as shown in Figure 16.2, Canada's population did not increase dramatically as a result. One reason is that many of the new immigrants simply left Canada; some 50 per cent either moved on to the United States or returned to their homelands. Another factor was the high death rate among immigrants at the turn of the century. Montreal, where many of the early immigrants settled, was an unhealthy city with poor medical facilities. Paul-André Linteau, René Durocher, and Jean-Claude Robert (1983) have pointed out that malnutrition and disease killed large numbers of immigrants who were impoverished and had no family or friends to help them through hard times.

The most significant factor was the first—the departure of so many of the new immigrants. Why did they leave? Why would people coming from what were often extremely harsh economic or political circumstances not find Canada an attractive place to live? Part of the answer has to do with the enormous pull of the United States, the attraction of the American dream of equality and opportunity for all. Immigrants to Canada not only found themselves overworked and underpaid, but also realized that the charter groups dominated society and that not all groups were politically or economically equal here.

Another reason for this pattern of emigration was the indifference, or sometimes outright hostility, of Canadians toward the new arrivals. The isolation of Catholic Quebec promoted a distancing from (if not animosity toward) immigrants, who were seen as weakening the French Catholic character of the province. The British, for their part, were unwilling to absorb immigrants from Eastern and Southern Europe. Their desire was to "keep Canada British," not to have Canada imitate the cultural hodgepodge of the United States.

Attitudes toward immigration became more positive after World War II, a time of economic prosperity when there was a significant demand for the labour that immigrants could provide. By the 1950s, most Canadians no longer looked upon European immigrants as racially different or inferior, but rather as generally desirable. However, immigration from Europe failed to keep up with Canada's demand for labour by the mid-1960s because the economies of Western European countries, initially devastated by the war, had improved dramatically. At the same time, Eastern European countries, now under the control of communist governments, blocked emigration.

Figure 16.2 **Immigration Numbers in Historical Perspective, 1860–2001**

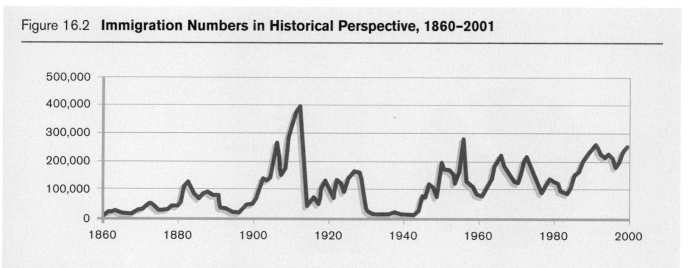

SOURCE: From Citizenship and Immigration Canada's *Immigration Overview, Facts and Figures 2001*, <http://www.cic.gc.ca>. Adapted with the permission of the Minister of Public Works and Government Services Canada, 2003.

The New Immigration

Immigration patterns have changed substantially since the late 1960s. Immigrants, once almost exclusively European in origin, are coming in increasing numbers from areas outside of Europe, particularly Asia. In 2001, China, India, Pakistan, the Philippines, and Korea were the top five source countries for immigrants to Canada. Indeed, 16 per cent of all immigrants that year came from China, 11 per cent from India, and 6 per cent from Pakistan; altogether over 42 per cent of that year's immigrants came from the top five countries. The top European source country in 2001 was Romania, from which about 5,600 immigrants arrived, making up only a little more than 2 per cent of all immigrants. Table 16.1 compares the top source countries for Canadian immigrants in the 1990s with those for immigrants who arrived before 1961.

One result is that more immigrants than ever before are members of visible minorities—almost 4 million in 2001, nearly 13.5 per cent of Canada's population. Such people face different problems from those being encountered by European immigrants, problems compounded by several other trends. Almost all immigrants end up in cities; indeed, almost 77 per cent of those who came to Canada in 2001 went to live in Toronto, Vancouver, or Montreal. Toronto by itself received 125,061 immigrants in 2001, almost 50 per cent of the total. This concentra-

tion means that visible minorities are, so to speak, more visible than ever in some parts of Canada; at the same time, they remain largely invisible, and therefore unknown, elsewhere.

Moreover, immigration is on the rise after a decline in the mid-1980s—from just over 84,000 in 1985 to over 250,000 in 2001, as Table 16.2 indicates. This increase, combined with the high level of concentration, means that many urban residents are immigrants—44 per cent of the population in Metropolitan Toronto, over 2 million people, almost 800,000 of those having arrived since 1990.

It makes little sense, then, to refer to immigration to "Canada," since most of Canada does not participate in this immigration. Table 16.3 indicates that few immigrants in 2001 chose to live elsewhere in Canada. Only 404 immigrants came to live in all of Newfoundland, only 1,709 in Saskatchewan, and only about 5,000 in Quebec outside of Montreal—about the same number as selected Manitoba. In contrast, more than 445,000 immigrants arrived in the Toronto area between 1996 and 2001. This rate of immigration puts enormous strains on the infrastructure of the Toronto region, as well as raising issues of settlement and the adequate provision of services for the new arrivals. Language training alone is a major undertaking, with 45 per cent of the new arrivals in 2001 speaking neither English nor French. If immigrants are to get decent jobs, interact with others, and

Table 16.1 Top 10 Countries of Birth, Canada, 2001[a]

	Immigrated Before 1961			Immigrated 1991–2001[b]	
	Number	%		Number	%
Total immigrants	894,466	100.0	Total immigrants	1,830,680	100.0
United Kingdom	217,175	24.3	China, People's Republic of	197,360	10.8
Italy	147,320	16.5	India	156,120	8.5
Germany	96,770	10.8	Philippines	122,010	6.7
Netherlands	79,170	8.9	Hong Kong, Special Administrative Region	118,385	6.5
Poland	44,340	5.0	Sri Lanka	62,590	3.4
United States	34,810	3.9	Pakistan	52,990	3.2
Hungary	27,425	3.1	Taiwan	53,755	2.9
Ukraine	21,240	2.4	United States	52,440	2.8
Greece	20,755	2.3	Iran	47,080	2.6
China, People's Republic of	15,850	1.8	Poland	43,370	2.4

[a] Population counts are rounded to the nearest 5.
[b] Includes data up to 15 May 2001.
SOURCE: Adapted from Statistics Canada, *Canada's Ethnocultural Portrait: The Changing Mosaic*, 2001 Census (Analysis series), Catalogue 96F0030, <http://www.statcan.ca/english/IPS/Data/96F0030XIE2001008.htm>.

Since the 1960s, immigrants have been coming to Canada from non-European countries. In 2001, 16 per cent of immigrants came from China, 11 per cent from India, and 6 per cent from Pakistan. These photos depict two thriving communities in Toronto: Chinatown and Little India, the Southeast Asian community in Toronto's east end. (© Megan Mueller)

Table 16.2 **Total Immigration to Canada, 1980–2001**

	Number of Immigrants
1980	143,135
1981	128,639
1982	121,176
1983	89,188
1984	88,271
1985	84,334
1986	99,325
1987	151,999
1988	161,494
1989	191,493
1990	216,396
1991	232,744
1992	254,817
1993	256,741
1994	224,364
1995	212,859
1996	226,039
1997	216,014
1998	174,159
1999	189,922
2000	227,313
2001	250,346

SOURCE: Communication Branch, Citizenship and Immigration Canada, *Facts and Figures 2001* (Ottawa: Citizenship and Immigration Canada, 2002).

fully understand their rights, they must be able to speak one of the official languages. Moreover, if immigrants are allowed into Canada in order to benefit the country economically, demographically, and culturally, then most parts of the country do not get to share in that benefit.

Both the numbers and the concentration of immigrants in urban areas tend to perpetuate various problems of integration. One such problem is that, by remaining in the cities, immigrants are contributing to the regionalization of Canada, whose large cities are coming to have very different characteristics from other areas. For example, 88 per cent of Quebec's immigrants live in Montreal, making up 18.4 per cent of the city's population. By contrast, immigrants make up just 2.9 per cent of Quebec City's population, and 1.5 per cent of a city like Trois-Rivières. Since Montreal is also the only major centre in Quebec with a high concentration of anglophones, it may be said that in Quebec, ethnic and linguistic diversity is a characteristic only of Montreal. Indeed, many Montrealers feel that their city is quite different from the rest of Quebec, while many Québécois who do not live in Montreal fear that the city is losing its "French face" (Statistics Canada, 2003a: 58).

Table 16.3 **Distribution of 1990s Immigrants Compared with Distribution of Total Population, 2001[a]**

	1990s Immigrants (%)	Total Population in Canada (%)	Ratio of 1990s Immigrants to Total Population[b]
Canada	100.0	100.0	–
Newfoundland and Labrador	0.1	1.7	0.1
Prince Edward Island	0.0	0.5	0.1
Nova Scotia	0.6	3.0	0.2
New Brunswick	0.2	2.4	0.1
Quebec	13.4	24.0	0.6
Ontario	55.8	38.1	1.5
Manitoba	1.8	3.7	0.5
Saskatchewan	0.5	3.2	0.2
Alberta	7.1	9.9	0.7
British Columbia	20.2	13.1	1.5
Yukon Territory	0.0	0.1	0.4
Northwest Territories	0.0	0.1	0.3
Nunavut	0.0	0.1	0.1

[a] Columns may not add up to totals because of rounding; 0's also represent rounded figures.

[b] This ratio shows whether the proportion of 1990s immigrants living in a given province or territory is higher than the proportion of the total population living in that province or territory. For example, if 5 per cent of 1990s immigrants live in a given province and the same proportion (5 per cent) of the total population lives there, then the ratio will be 1.0.

SOURCE: Adapted from Statistics Canada, *Canada's Ethnocultural Portrait: The Changing Mosaic*, 2001 Census (Analysis series), Catalogue 96F0030, <http://www.statcan.ca/english/IPS/Data/96F0030XIE2001008.htm>.

16.1

Global Issues

Migration in International Context

Migration, whether of immigrants, refugees, or "guest workers," has become a major international phenomenon in the contemporary world. Recently, the United Nations Population Division estimated that there were 175 million people who could be classified as migrants, double the number in 1975. (*Migrants* are defined by the United Nations as persons who have been residing outside of their country of birth for at least 12 months.) Most of these migrants, 56 million, are in Europe, another 50 million in Asia, and 41 million in North America, including 35 million in the United States and almost 6 million in Canada (United Nations Population Division, 2002: 2).

Because Canada has a high rate of immigration, most Canadians do not realize that immigration is severely restricted by many other nations. Those that do allow immigration usually allow only a limited number of people to arrive in any given year. Germany, for example, enacted a law in 2003 that allows in 50,000 people a year, in contrast to the Canadian immigration target for 2003 of 220,000 to 245,000. Like Germany, many European countries have passed legislation further restricting immigration and the possibility of naturalization (that is, becoming citizens). They have a long history of allowing "foreigners" to enter their countries as labourers, but not of granting them the right to settle permanently or to become citizens. Many countries outside of Europe, too, have large numbers of migrants who neither expect to, nor will be allowed to, become citizens.

continued

In Canada, we do expect immigrants to become full-fledged members of the society. We expect them to work at the same jobs as other Canadians, to have most of the same rights and entitlements as Canadian citizens, and to become citizens themselves (Bloemraad, 2002). Indeed, Canada allows immigrants to become citizens after only three years of residence. In contrast, Germany requires "foreigners" to have resided in Germany for 15 years in order to apply for naturalization (Martin, 2002). Even then, they must meet more stringent criteria than those applied in Canada for new citizens. In the Netherlands, immigrants must take 1,000 hours of courses in Dutch language and citizenship within their first year of residence and pay a fee equivalent to about $9,000, half of which is refunded upon completing the course. The leader of one major political party in the Netherlands has argued that foreigners who refuse to integrate should be deported (*Migration News*, January 2003). In Britain, immigrants must take a course on "Britishness" that includes "instruction in modern family life and the need for tolerance of different ethnic groups" (*Migration News*, December 2002). Clearly, such countries do not value "multiculturalism."

Citizenship makes a significant difference in many countries around the world. In most countries, migrants do not have the same rights as citizens, nor are they entitled to the same services or protection of the law. In France, for example, non–European Union citizens are restricted from working in certain sectors, including government-owned industries; they also may not work as pharmacists, as architects, or in 50 other professions. Given these kinds of restrictions, it is not surprising that unemployment rates for non-citizens in the European Union are twice as high as for citizens. Non-citizens are also subject to the arbitrary whim of legislative and regulative agencies. Recently, the government of Saudi Arabia decided that "foreigners" would no longer be allowed to drive taxis, putting 50,000 people out of work.

Generally speaking, migrants in many nations are often economically exploited and subjected to discrimination; they may even be physically abused. Human Rights Watch (<www.hrw.org>), for example, has documented cases of beatings and other forms of "cruel, inhuman, or degrading treatment" directed at suspected illegal North African migrants (including children) by Spanish authorities (see Bustamente, 2002, for a general discussion of human rights issues with respect to migrants). In dramatic contrast to Canadian procedures, many countries routinely detain illegal immigrants or refugee claimants. Riots in French and Australian detention centres have received widespread media attention, but migrants are treated even worse in many countries around the world. Even legal migrants may have to pay bribes to government officials to be allowed to remain in their place of work.

While many Canadians are somewhat concerned about the current high levels of immigration, they do not have the strong negative attitudes toward migrants typically found elsewhere. A poll conducted in November 2002 by the Institute of Conflict Research at Bielefeld University indicated that "52 per cent of men and 58 per cent of women agreed that Germany has too many foreigners, and 24 per cent of men and 31 per cent of women believed foreigners should leave Germany in times of high unemployment" (*Migration News*, January 2003). Anti-immigrant sentiment is also strong in Italy. The mayor of Treviso, an industrial town near Venice, "removed park benches to discourage 'non-European hang-abouts,' and had the shanty homes of legal immigrant workers razed" (*Migration News*, October 2002). Similar attitudes can be found elsewhere in Europe.

Under the circumstances, we can see why Canada and the United States are so desirable as destinations for migrants. Despite the problems immigrants and refugees may face in these countries, they know that their reception elsewhere can be much worse.

This concentration in cities also causes problems for the immigrants themselves, who would be in a better position to compete for jobs if their distribution were more even. Li (2000) found that immigrants made up over 32 per cent of the labour market in metropolitan areas that had over 1 million people. Furthermore, housing costs and the cost of living in general are higher in the cities; at the time of writing, this is particularly true of Vancouver and Toronto. Finally, concentration may promote **racism** or **prejudice**. Because relatively few Canadians come to know new immigrants, perceptions of them outside of urban centres may be based on stereotypes that are rarely challenged by reality.

Another trend in immigration is that recent immigrants tend to have more education than previous generations of immigrants. In fact, Arnold deSilva (1992) has found that they are better educated than the general population in Canada. This development is a result of immigration policy, which favours those with a high level of education or with job skills that are needed in the labour force. That outcome will also be affected by the existing demand for specific skills, the level of unemployment, and other job-related factors, as well as by the degree to which discrimination is present in the society.

Patterns of Inter-group Relations in Canada

How are the new immigration trends affecting Canadian society? Not all of the effects are visible yet, but the new immigration is certainly affecting the patterns of relationships among Canada's ethnic groups. In recent years, these patterns have largely been directed by the state, particularly through its promotion of official bilingualism and multiculturalism. Both policies may, however, need to be redefined to reflect the changing ethnic, cultural, and linguistic reality of Canadian society.

Bilingualism

Sociologists often speak of the unintended consequences of social actions and policies. The issues surrounding ethnic group relations in Canada serve as examples of such unintended consequences.

In theory, official bilingualism—the government policy of providing services everywhere in Canada in both official languages—seems like a good idea. All Canadians, whether English- or French-speaking, should feel at home anywhere in Canada. They should feel secure in the knowledge that their government institutions will be able to serve them in their own language, that these institutions are theirs. The net result of bilingualism should be to promote Canadians' sense of identification with the country as a whole, and thereby to promote national unity.

Yet it has been argued by Guindon (1983) and others that official bilingualism has divided rather than united Canadians. Like any policy designed to please everyone, it seems to have ended up pleasing almost no one. It certainly fails to meet the aspirations of most francophone Québécois, while simultaneously creating tensions and animosities among anglophones, especially those Westerners who are members of non-British minority groups.

Canada's bilingualism policy emerged out of an attempt to deal with the "problem of Quebec." By 1960, the start of the Quiet Revolution, many Québécois felt dissatisfied with the constitutional, political, and fiscal arrangements in Canada, which they perceived as having negative effects on Quebec society and on the status of its francophone citizens. The response of the federal government was to establish the Royal Commission on Bilingualism and Biculturalism in 1963. The commission's task was to "recommend what steps should be taken to develop the Canadian Confederation on the basis of an equal partnership between two founding races, taking into account the contribution made by other ethnic groups to the cultural enrichment of Canada and the measures that should be taken to safeguard that contribution" (Royal Commission on Bilingualism and Biculturalism, 1970: 3).

Canada's constitutional and linguistic problems have not ended; the commission may be said to have failed in its task. Perhaps it did so largely because it defined the key problem in the relationship between the English and French as one of language and thereby failed to address the many other concerns of Quebec—constitutional, political, and economic. This failure made the commission and its proposals largely irrelevant to most Québécois. Even worse, the solution offered—the federal policy of official bilingualism—served to aggravate rather than solve the real problems, including the linguistic ones. The idea behind bilingualism was that it would allow Québécois to feel at home anywhere in Canada because French services would be available everywhere. A francophone resident of Quebec passing through Moose Jaw, Saskatchewan, for example, would be able to use French in a post office. But Québécois were not complaining about the status of French outside of Quebec—they were complaining about their own status within Quebec.

Bilingualism is not popular in Quebec. Some Québécois assert that, in practice, what bilingualism really means is that francophones are encouraged to learn English. Census data for 2001, almost 40 years after the creation of the royal commission, tend to support such a view. The data show that slightly over 17 per cent of Canadians are bilingual, including about 43 per cent of francophones but only 9 per cent of anglophones. Moreover, given that over 65 per cent of the Québécois are unilingual francophones, many francophones feel that a policy that promotes

16.2

Sociology in Action
Québécois Nationalism

When we look at ethnic distinctions between Canadians, we must inevitably deal with the issue of Quebec and its relation to the rest of Canada. Quebec is not only a province of Canada; in a very real sense, it is also a distinct society within Canada (Fournier, Rosenberg, and White, 1997). It is one, moreover, which may well choose, at some future date, to separate entirely from Canada.

Québécois nationalism is a volatile phenomenon. There are times when it seems quiescent, other times when it flares up and presents a real threat to Canadian unity. Recent surveys suggest that support for sovereignty is on the decline in Quebec (Centre for Research and Information on Canada, 2001; Ekos Research, 1999). Yet in two federal by-elections held in Quebec in December 2002, the Bloc Québécois, a party committed to Quebec sovereignty, was victorious. Although the Parti Québécois lost power in the 2003 provincial election, many Québécois, even those supporting federalism, seem to see sovereignty as an option that must, at the very least, be kept in reserve.

The issue of Quebec separation is not a new one. It has been a part of Canada's political history, and has helped shape Canada's political structure, from the time of Confederation on.

Québécois nationalism took its modern form between 1960 and 1966, the years of the Quiet Revolution, which were characterized by a profound reorientation of Quebec state action and policy. The provincial government initiated a broad series of reforms in a wide range of areas. The reforms were of two types, structural and ideological. Structural changes included the establishment of a Ministry of Education and the implementation of the Quebec Pension Plan. Ideological reforms expressed a new conception of the state as the leading actor in the process of transforming Quebec into a modern, self-assured, and democratic society capable of controlling its own destiny.

The society that emerged from the Quiet Revolution was substantially different from that which preceded it. Quebec's key institutions—in particular the state—had been radically transformed. The state expanded its influence into almost every sector of Quebec society. During this period, much of Quebec's francophone population had came to equate the promotion of their collective identity with the empowerment of the state (Guindon, 1968). The Québécois, as they began to call themselves, felt that in the state and its agencies they finally had the collective tools with which to build their future society. But what type of society would it be? How would it fit into Canada's political and economic structure? Was a fully developed Quebec society even possible within the confines of the Canadian federation? These questions raised new debates and generated new disagreements within the Québécois community, giving urgent priority to issues of nationalism and language (Monière, 1981).

Language played a significant role in the debates for a number of reasons. First of all, French had always been a key part of the francophone community's collective sense of self, the symbolic marker that identifies them as a coherent collectivity distinct from most other Canadians. The preservation of the French language despite 200 years of British domination has been a major accomplishment of the francophone Québécois, a shared source of pride in the past and a collective point of concern for the future. One point on which almost all francophone Québécois agreed, then, was that the new Quebec society being built should be a French society.

Language is also a contentious issue in Quebec because of demographic changes affecting the francophone population. The high birth rates that had characterized the francophone community for 200 years went into a steep decline. The declining birth rate caused widespread concern because it seemed to pose a threat to the continued survival of Quebec as a French society. The influx of non-francophone immigrants reinforced the proportionate decline of the francophone Québécois population since most of these new immigrants chose English as their language of work and the language of education for their children. Many immigrants believed that job opportunities and higher status were more accessible to anglophones than to francophones. Nationalists concluded that if it was to survive as a French society, Quebec would have to expand the use of French by immigrants.

In 1976, the election of the Parti Québécois put into power a party committed to building Quebec as a French society. A year later, Bill 101 was passed by the National Assembly (the provincial legislative body). The new law presented a vision of Quebec as a francophone society in which government took a central role in promoting the language. The French language, Bill 101 asserts, is "the distinctive language of a people that is in the majority French-speaking [and] is the instrument by which that people has articulated its identity." The issues of nationalism and language had become intertwined.

bilingualism disadvantages them by effectively locking them out of jobs or obstructing promotion to senior positions. Even many francophones who do speak English also feel disadvantaged; they find it insulting to be required to know English in order to get a job within their own overwhelmingly francophone community. As Quebec's Bill 101 expresses it, the consensus among most Québécois is that French—and only French—is to be the "normal and everyday language of work, instruction, commerce and business" in Quebec.

Francophones outside of Quebec, however, do benefit from official bilingualism. Since they are a minority in all provinces but Quebec, official bilingualism serves to protect their linguistic rights and provides them with services and job opportunities. Anglophones within Quebec, 66 per cent of whom are bilingual, also benefit from the federal policy.

Outside of Quebec, many anglophones dislike bilingualism, complaining that they are having French forced upon them on signs and packaging or in government services. In fact, they are not having French forced upon them at all; bilingual signs and services do not replace English, but merely add French. Why is there such resentment about the presence of French?

Breton suggests that the federal government has been engaged in attempting the "reconstruction of the symbolic system and . . . the redistribution of social status among linguistic and ethnocultural groups in Canadian society" (1984: 134). The effect of the policy of bilingualism has been to raise the status of francophones outside of Quebec by giving their language a special status. This, in turn, has had the unintended effect of lowering the relative status of other groups. In western Canada, where groups such as Ukrainians outnumber the French, these groups see official bilingualism as implying that the government considers the French more important than they are. The result is resentment—what Breton (1984) calls "status anxieties" and "cultural tensions."

Bilingualism, then, has solved few existing problems but has instead created problems of its own. Indeed, Breton (1984) argues that it was the resentment aroused by the bilingualism policy that forced the government to initiate yet another policy: official multiculturalism.

Multiculturalism

Like bilingualism, official multiculturalism—the government policy of promoting tolerance among cultural groups and helping them preserve the values and traditions important to them—seems a good thing in principle. Who could be opposed to the aims it espouses? Yet, once again, many people question whether an official policy of multiculturalism is truly beneficial or whether it instead engenders strains in Canadian society and divisions between Canadians.

Multiculturalism became an official government policy in 1971, under Prime Minister Pierre Trudeau, who pointed out in a House of Commons debate that "although there are two official languages, there is no official culture." The federal government then proposed a series of initiatives to promote cultural diversity and tolerance.

How real is cultural tolerance in practice, and how real should it be? Jean Leonard Elliot and Augie Fleras (1992) cite the example of a bullfight organized by a Portuguese group in Ontario. Many Canadians would consider a bullfight to be the cruel mistreatment of an animal; it is, in fact, illegal under Canada's laws. Should it nevertheless be tolerated as part of the Portuguese culture? According to Elliott and Fleras, "We need to ask about the limits of multicultural tolerance. Which cultural differences can be absorbed within a multicultural society without undermining incontestable values and beliefs? The dilemma is self-evident: too many differences can create anarchic conditions which inhibit the effective functioning of a social system. Too many restrictions makes a mockery of multicultural principles" (1992: 293).

Multiculturalism is an inherently limited policy because the focus is on ethnic groups as cultural groups and because the activities it promotes are cultural activities. As noted earlier, the policy has given the federal government what some regard to be unwarranted control over which sorts of activities are legitimate for a given group and over who is recognized as an appropriate representative of the group. The result is yet another unintended effect: the politicization of ethnic groups and the corresponding alteration of the equation between government and ethnic communities.

Despite the restrictions in the government's policies on multiculturalism, Canadians tend to be ambivalent about the whole idea. Canadians pride themselves on being a tolerant people who respect others' cultures and traditions and are willing to accept cultural pluralism. Nevertheless, many would like to see a more unified country whose people are committed to being "Canadians" rather than retaining their ethnic languages or loyalties (Kalin and Berry, 1994). Ambivalence about ethnicity shows up in the data gathered by Breton, who found that among members of ethnic groups in Toronto, "a majority of most groups feel that the loss of traditions, customs, or language is a problem . . . [yet] a majority also feel that members of their group should blend and not form communities" (1990: 213).

This ambivalence has its sources in various sociological factors. First, as we have seen, the ambiguous government definitions and policies related to ethnicity seem to have aggravated the ethnic tensions they were designed to ease. Related to this is a shift in the meanings assigned to ethnic groups, from primarily cultural groups to political interest groups. The most dramatic example is offered by the Native peoples, who have organized to become a highly visible political force in Canada. Another factor is the new immigration, along with the degree to which Canadians are willing to accept visible minorities as full-fledged members of their society.

Significantly, multiculturalism may no longer reflect the reality of a society in which more and more people see themselves as "Canadian" rather than as members of minority cultural groups. In the 2001 census, almost 40 per cent of the population—well over 11 million people—indicated their ethnic origin to be "Canadian." This is in contrast to 1991, when only about 4 per cent of the people reported their ethnic identity to be Canadian on the census forms, and 1996, when that figure rose to 19 per cent. This change may reflect many factors, but it does indicate that many people in Canada are coming to identify themselves in a new way, one in which their ethnic origin is less significant than their attachment to Canada.

Also, there has been an increase in intermarriages, which has an impact upon the notion of ethnic culture implicit in multicultural policy. The assumption is that every Canadian is tied into a specific and distinct heritage culture. Intermarriage not only ties each person, at least to some extent, into the ethnic culture of their spouse, it means that children have multiple ethnic backgrounds. In 2001, about 11 million people reported having multiple ethnic backgrounds. For such people, policies designed to enhance or maintain ethnic identification may have little significance. Still, groups are not equally likely to intermarry: most intermarriages occur among people of European ancestry.

Prejudice and Discrimination

The distinction between *prejudice* and *discrimination* is a distinction between attitude and action. Racism is a form of discrimination.

Prejudice

Prejudice refers to the prejudgment of an individual on the basis of stereotyped characteristics assumed to be common to all members of that individual's group. A prejudice describes someone's attitudes toward a group; it will not necessarily determine how he or she behaves toward that group. To believe that all Native people are alcoholics, that all Newfoundlanders are stupid, or that all Americans are arrogant is prejudice based on acceptance of stereotypes and myths. The term *prejudice* denotes that such stereotypes and myths cause people to decide in advance what a certain person will be like based on knowing no more than that individual's ethnic group or appearance.

Are Canadians free of ethnic or racial prejudices? The evidence is that we are not. If anything, says Peter Pineo (1977), Canada seems to be a society with strong, distinctive attitudes toward different ethnic and racial groups. John Berry, Rudolf Kalin, and Donald Taylor (1977) found that most Canadians, whatever their ethnic group, tend to have a positive perception of and positive attitudes toward the two charter groups. This finding comes as no surprise considering the dominant political, economic, and symbolic role played by the British and French in Canadian society. These groups have served as role models for most other Canadians, providing an image of what it means to be a Canadian. To sum up, Canadians have a positive prejudice in favour of the charter groups.

What about other groups? Here again, we can identify a positive prejudice, at least in how each group views itself. Groups sees themselves to be very much like the charter groups, characterizing them- selves as "decent," "friendly," "trustworthy," and "clean" (Berry, Kalin, and Taylor, 1977). But more negative attitudes can also be found. Canadians gen-

erally see the visible minorities in the least positive light, with Native people, blacks, and East Indians (South Asians) at the very bottom. Berry, Kalin, and Taylor (1977) found that East Indians, for example, received low scores for being "hardworking," "Canadian," or "clean," the implication being that they are viewed as "lazy," "foreign," and "dirty."

Research done in 1991 showed that most Canadians report themselves to be "comfortable" when in the presence of British-origin Canadians but that the level of comfort decreased significantly for many when in the presence of Muslims, Indo-Pakistanis, or Sikhs (Driedger and Reid, 2000). This type of prejudice is not necessarily a problem in soci- ety as long as it is not transformed into the differen- tial treatment of individuals and groups. There is always the danger, though, that prejudice will result in discrimination.

Discrimination

Discrimination refers to the action of treating an indi- vidual differently—usually unfairly—because of his or her membership in a particular group or category. Discrimination is based on prejudice, not on the

Are Canadians free of ethnic and racial prejudices? The evidence is that we are not. This photograph documents the case in which parents were split over whether to allow 12-year-old Sikh pupil Gurbaj Singh to wear his kirpan, a ceremonial dagger, to a Montreal school. (CP/Ryan Remiorz)

objective features of the individual or groups being discriminated against. Consider an example. As noted earlier, recent immigrants to Canada tend to be well educated and relatively highly skilled. Yet they frequently fail to find work in the occupations for which they have been trained, being forced instead to accept menial, low-status jobs. Patricia Tomic and Ricardo Trumper (1992) give the example of two Chilean economists who, on coming to Canada, found themselves offered jobs as shipping clerks.

Discrimination comes in many forms, some more insidious than others. Blatant discrimination was seen in 1982 in Montreal when a taxi company fired more than 20 Haitian cab drivers. The company announced that the drivers were not being fired because they did not do their job properly, but because the public refused to take cabs driven by Haitians. It claimed to have received many complaints from the public that the Haitians did not know their way around the city and frequently got lost, that their cabs were "dirty" and "smelled," that they were rude, and that they spoke in an "incomprehensible" French. Although the drivers were rehired after extensive media coverage and a public outcry, the incident made evident the degree of prejudice and discrimination in Montreal. Such cases are relatively easy to deal with precisely because they are so obvious. Should public opinion fail to end the discrimination, then human rights legislation and government agencies will do so. Blatant discrimination may pose problems for particular individuals, but as long as instances remain few in number, it does not constitute a problem for society.

Perhaps the most insidious of all forms of discrimination is **institutional** or **structural discrimination**, discrimination that is actually built into the structure of an institution or its method of operation. For example, in a time of economic recession, workers in a company are likely to be laid off on the basis of seniority. Since new immigrants are likely to be at the bottom of the seniority list, they are most vulnerable to losing their jobs. Indeed, the more recently an immigrant arrived, the more likely he or she is to be unemployed (Citizenship and Immigration Canada, 1998). However, immigrants generally have lower **unemployment rates** than do the Canadian-born—in 1986, the figures were 8.2 per cent for immigrants and 10.8 per cent for the native-born Canadians (de Silva, 1992: 11). Unemployment rates among immigrants in the same year were 11.5 per cent for those who arrived between 1978 and 1982

and 16 per cent for those who arrived between 1983 and 1986. It is sometimes claimed that high levels of immigration lead to high levels of unemployment, but the figures do not bear this out. What is clear is that it is the most recent immigrants who are likeliest to be unemployed.

Another example of **institutional discrimination** is the failure to recognize the credentials of an immigrant professional. The discrimination may not be intentional but may simply reflect the local professional association's difficulty in evaluating whether the foreign credentials are equivalent to Canadian standards. Intentional or not, the effect is to discriminate against immigrants. Yet another example is the common requirement of having a college diploma for a relatively unskilled job, a requirement that penalizes members of poorer minority groups, who are less likely to have completed college. Because these forms of discrimination are hidden or can be justified on the basis of "good reasons," they are often very hard to eliminate.

Most Canadians recognize that there is some degree of prejudice in society, but they think of Canada as a land that is largely free of discrimination. Unfortunately, many researchers, such as Subhas Ramcharan (1982), show that this is simply not so. Given the above-mentioned pattern of institutional self-segregation of ethnic groups, which characterizes most ethnic group relations, institutional discrimination is not only common, but acceptable to most Canadians. Indeed, institutional self-segregation can be characterized as **systemic discrimination** because it is built into the very fabric of Canadian life. Most Canadians prefer to live their lives in communities where they encounter people like themselves. They prefer to deal with doctors, lawyers, bank managers, politicians, and police officers from their own or what they consider to be a similar ethnic group. Systemic discrimination may not be intended; it may simply be the consequence of the preference of ethnic group members to do business with their "own kind." Still, the result is that immigrants, especially members of visible minorities, do not have the same opportunity to obtain jobs or gain the trust of the established group.

This type of systemic discrimination promotes the establishment of an *ethnic sub-economy*, which Morton Weinfeld describes as "a network of economic relationships which may link employees, employers, consumers, buyers and sellers, of a specific ethnic group" (1983: 8). The sub-economy provides jobs and opportunities for members of an ethnic community. However, Norbert Wiley (1967) has pointed out that it can also serve as a mobility trap when ethnic group members find themselves locked into it and out of the larger economy.

Racism

Racism can be defined as a belief that one racial group is superior to others. Racists believe that differences in physical appearance serve as an index to a wide variety of other differences—for instance, in personality characteristics, intelligence, honesty, reliability, law-abidingness, and so on. Racism in this sense has probably always existed; it is likely that there have always been people or groups that regarded themselves as superior to everyone else. Racism in the modern sense is different, however; it categorizes groups strictly on the basis of physical appearance and offers a "scientific" basis for claims to superiority.

Scientific racism is the attempt to categorize human groups into distinct biological classes forming an evolutionary, intellectual, and moral continuum. The theory of scientific racism emerged in the nineteenth century. It helped justify European colonialism and imperialism by seeming to promise a scientific basis for racism that was absolute and impervious to moral, ethical, or religious debate. In its essentials, as developed in Western Europe and the United States, the theory holds that the different races resulted from a differential rate of evolution among the peoples of the world. Thus, while some races have evolved to a higher level of "humanness," others remain in a lower evolutionary state. Scientific racists argue that it was evolution, not the actions of human beings, that condemned the "inferior" races to low status and to the supervision of the superior.

In Canada, scientific racism was combined with a number of other **ideologies** that served to reinforce one another. British imperialism, for example, to which many Canadians subscribed, viewed the British as culturally and institutionally superior and therefore best qualified to shoulder the "white man's burden" of civilizing, and of course ruling, "inferior"

16.3

Human Diversity
Racism and Institutional Discrimination in Canada: The Case of the Chinese

The treatment of Canada's Chinese immigrants has always served as an index of the country's racial and ethnic "climate." Prior to 1948, Canada's treatment of the Chinese was unquestionably racist and the Chinese experienced more systematic, institutional discrimination than did any other immigrant group in Canada. Since then, they have experienced a dramatic level of upward social mobility and become one of Canada's most "successful" ethnic groups. Yet racism and misunderstandings persist and Chinese immigrants continue to face a wide variety of problems in trying to integrate into Canadian society.

It is not difficult to document the extraordinary level of racism and discrimination directed at the Chinese before 1948, particularly in British Columbia. For example, it was only in 1948 that Chinese Canadians in British Columbia finally received the right to vote in both provincial and fed-

eral elections. Indeed, beginning about 1875, legislation in British Columbia had excluded the Chinese from buying Crown land or working as miners, loggers, fishermen, civil servants, pharmacists, or lawyers. The Chinese were not allowed to serve on a jury, to be admitted to provincial homes for the aged, or to obtain a liquor licence. Similar legislation was enacted by a number of other provincial governments. (Li, 1988, and Wickberg, 1982, provide a good summary of the discriminatory and racist legislation directed at the Chinese.)

The federal government, too, sought to discourage Chinese immigration to Canada, imposing a head tax of $50 on Chinese immigrants in 1885, a tax increased to a forbidding $500 by 1903. An even more explicitly restrictive law, the Chinese Immigration Act, was passed in 1923. Until 1947, this act excluded almost all new Chinese immigrants.

continued

This catalogue of anti-Chinese legislation is a mix of economic restrictions, such as prohibiting the Chinese from working as fishermen, and "symbolic" restrictions that identified the Chinese as second-class citizens, such as prohibiting them from jury duty. This mix reflects the combination of economic and racist fears that fuelled the animosity against the Chinese.

The economic animosity against the Chinese is easy to document. That the Chinese were a cheap and reliable labour force is shown by the preference given them as workers in building the Canadian Pacific railway. This, however, led to fears that cheap Chinese labour would take away jobs from British Columbia workers and undermine "the position of skilled labour" (Comack, 1985: 75), especially after the completion of the railway. As industrial unions began to form in the 1890s, opposition to cheap Chinese labour became organized and politically popular.

Additionally, racist sentiment viewed the Chinese as morally and mentally inferior to whites and as unfit to participate in Canadian society. This racism was tinged with fear of the "yellow peril," the belief that the Chinese were bent on world conquest. Racists such as Edmonton judge Emily Murphy, for example, claimed that opium and other narcotics were being used in an international conspiracy by "foreigners" to bring "about the downfall of the white race" (quoted in Green, 1986: 32). William Lyon Mackenzie King, sent to Vancouver in 1907 to investigate an anti-Oriental riot, urged the federal government to prohibit the recreational use of narcotics in Canada. "To be indifferent to the growth of such an evil in Canada," King said, "would be inconsistent with those principles of morality which ought to govern the conduct of a Christian nation" (quoted in Green, 1986: 27).

Today, these attitudes and fears seem remarkably dated to most Canadians. Positive attitudes toward the Chinese as "allies" developed during World War II, and racist and discriminatory legislation was largely scrapped by the late 1940s. Since then, Chinese Canadians have become a success story in socio-economic terms. They are better educated than the average Canadian, have a higher income, are more likely to own their own homes, and are more likely to work as professionals. Asians, including Chinese, are coming to Canada in record numbers and are bringing much-needed skills—and money—with them.

Yet racism is far from gone. Headlines in newspapers and magazines, for example, proclaim the danger posed to Canadians by the "new" Asian gangs. Asian immigrants are accused of taking away jobs from "Canadians" and of raising the housing costs in Vancouver. Foreign Chinese students are portrayed as taking away places in universities from Canadians. Some Quebec nationalists accuse the Chinese of being cliquish and of refusing to integrate into Quebec's French culture. Surveys show that many Canadians believe that immigrants, especially visible minorities, are entering Canada too fast and in too high numbers (Ekos Research Associates, 2002).

Nevertheless, most Canadians do recognize that immigrants are making valuable contributions to Canada. These contributions cannot be measured in strictly quantitative terms or only in the short run. Canada needs not only workers and investors, it also needs the vitality, skills, motivation, and creativity that immigrants bring. As long as immigrants such as the Chinese continue to come to Canada, all of us can be sure that the climate of relations among all Canadians will continue to be a good one.

There is little question that immigrants such as the Chinese are making important contributions to Canadian society and that they have much to offer to Canada. Yet if people do not feel welcome and if they are not given a chance to participate fully in our society, they will cease to come and those already here will leave. This might please racists, but it would impoverish the rest of us. If immigrants cannot find a home here, we must wonder if the divisions dividing the country can ever be resolved.

Racism has always been a part of Canadian society. In this historical photograph, dated 1942, Vancouver police harass a Japanese man and confiscate his vehicle. After Pearl Harbor, Canada expelled or interned 22,000 Japanese immigrants and Japanese Canadians. (Vancouver Public Library, Special Collection, VPL 1362)

races. Canadians combined this viewpoint with a sense of moral superiority to the United States, which was seen as a land of unrestrained greed, crime, and vice, characteristics linked to its open immigration policy.

Canadian racists also evolved an ideology of their own that equated life in the north with racial superiority. Because of the harsh Canadian winters, they argued, only the northern "races," such as the Anglo-Saxons, Scandinavians, and Germans, could survive in Canada. They went so far as to claim that it was Canada's climate that made its people hard-working, self-reliant, and honest. Again, this perspective was contrasted with a negative image of the United States, whose population was seen as lazy, impulsive, and disorderly, partly as a result of the influence of the warmer American climate (Berger, 1966).

Racism is a form of discrimination. How, then, is it to be differentiated from other forms of discrimination? There is, of course, overt racism, such as that promoted by white supremacist groups. Few Canadians belong to or support such clearly racist groups, however, so racism in Canadian society tends to be less overt. Instead, racism often takes the form of institutional or systemic discrimination. These, as we noted, work in ways which are not intentionally discriminatory, although people with racist views can take advantage of institutional practices and policies to cover up racial discrimination.

Today, Canada is at the forefront of attempts to prevent racial or other forms of discrimination, whether intentional or not. Employment equity programs and other forms of affirmative action are designed to produce what is termed "equality of result." The federal government and the provincial governments have encouraged the civil service and Crown corporations to hire women, French Canadians, Native people, visible minorities, and the disabled in numbers reflecting their percentage of the population (Abella, 1984; Weinfeld, 1981). In Quebec, for example, an Act Respecting Equal Access to Employment in Public Bodies came into effect in 2001, requiring measures to increase the representation in public bodies of "target groups" such as visible minorities.

Discrimination in Canadian Society

Have the programs for combating discrimination worked? Or is Canada still characterized by the vertical mosaic? To what extent are new immigrants or visible minorities discriminated against in contemporary Canada? As noted before, these remain matters of contention among social scientists.

Immigrants almost always enter a new country at a disadvantage. They may not know the language of the new country or be familiar with the customs and routine expectations of the host society. They are likely to be unaware of their legal rights, as well as of the agencies to which they can turn for assistance. They may have difficulty getting their credentials or qualifications recognized. They will lack a network of friends and contacts for support, work, or assistance. They will often have to start at the bottom, whatever their qualifications, in order to prove themselves. Low in seniority or in a subordinate position, they may feel vulnerable at work and may accept lower wages, longer hours, or worse conditions than they are entitled to. None of these obstacles necessarily implies discrimination. Rather, they are all a consequence of the structural disadvantages facing new immigrants. Discrimination is a valid explanation only if these disadvantages are unevenly distributed among new immigrants or if they persist for some groups and not for others.

In this regard, the evidence concerning the prevalence of discrimination is inconsistent. Clearly, however, differences do exist. The questions are what they really mean and whether they will persist. DeSilva's examination of 1986 census data (1992) led him to conclude that there is no significant discrimination against visible minorities in Canada and that, over time, most immigrants achieve income equality with Canadian-born workers. DeSilva does admit, however, that immigrants from East Asia and the Caribbean do not seem to achieve income equality and that the education and work experience obtained by immigrants before coming to Canada seem to count less then education and work experience within Canada.

However, DeSilva's data assume that members of visible minorities are invariably foreign-born, effectively ignoring the existence of Canadian-born members of visible minority groups. Li (2000) examined the data from the 1996 census, comparing immigrants with native-born Canadians of the same gender, racial origin, and urban location. He found that immigrant men and women "earned either the same or more than their native-born counterparts of the same racial background" (Li, 2000: 304). Li, however, then took into account such factors as experience and language ability and found that the earnings "advantage" of immigrants disappeared. In fact, he found that immigrant women, whether or not members of visible minorities, had a significant earnings disadvantage, as did immigrant visible-minority men, whereas non-visible-minority immigrant men had a much smaller income disadvantage. (See Table 16.4.)

Li's data indicate a more significant earnings disadvantage than that found by earlier researchers, such as Monica Boyd (1992), who examined 1986 data. Li's analysis made use of different assumptions, but it may also reflect the increasing earnings disadvantage of more recent immigrants. A recent report on the economic performance of immigrants (CIC, IMDB Profile Series, May 1999) indicates that whereas immigrants with a university degree had employment earnings 20 per cent above the Canadian average in 1981 after only one year in Canada, such immigrants had a 30 per cent earnings disadvantage by 1992. The relative earnings of recent refugees has also deteriorated compared to average Canadians, with refugees in 1992 earning 35 per cent less relative to the Canadian average than in the 1980s (CIC, 1998).

These figures are all the more discouraging when we recognize that current policy promotes the immigration of skilled workers and professionals. The proportion of immigrants arriving prior to 1986 without a level of education or credentials equivalent to native-born Canadians was much greater than today. Yet while recent immigrants have a higher level of education and better credentials than those in the past, they are making less money. Credentials are of no benefit if they are not recognized, and *Maclean's* (Janigan, 2002) reports that there are over 344,000 people in Canada whose foreign credentials are not recognized.

It is obvious that being an immigrant, and especially a member of a visible minority, makes a difference. Put together, these data suggest that the lower income of visible minorities results mainly from structural disadvantages and from their relatively recent time of arrival rather than from overt discrimination. Support for this can be found in the fact that the longer immigrants have resided in Canada, the more likely they are to have an income equal to or greater than the Canadian average (see Figure 16.3).

Table 16.4 Earnings of Immigrants and Native-Born Canadians as Percentage of Earnings of Native-Born Non-visible-minority for Men, for Four CMA Levels, 1996

	Gross Earnings		Net Earnings After Adjusting for Individual Characteristics[a]		Net Earnings After for Adjusting Individual and Market Characteristics[b]	
	Native-Born Canadian	Immigrant	Native-Born Canadian	Immigrant	Native-Born Canadian	Immigrant
Not CMA						
Non-visible minority						
Male	$28,122	122%	$29,590	86%	$31,657	88%
Female	61%	70%	73%	52%	75%	56%
Visible minority						
Male	77%	106%	98%	87%	99%	89%
Female	62%	61%	83%	62%	85%	66%
Small CMA (<500,000)						
Non-visible minority						
Male	$32,821	120%	$31,936	90%	$32,565	89%
Female	62%	66%	71%	53%	71%	52%
Visible minority						
Male	71%	86%	96%	76%	96%	75%
Female	51%	52%	77%	57%	77%	56%
Medium CMA (500,000–999,999)						
Non-visible minority						
Male	$33,182	114%	$31,679	89%	$31,657	88%
Female	62%	63%	72%	52%	72%	50%
Visible minority						
Male	56%	73%	85%	65%	84%	64%
Female	46%	51%	80%	54%	79%	53%
Large CMA (1,000,000+)						
Non-visible minority						
Male	$36,082	106%	$33,954	85%	$31,913	82%
Female	68%	68%	74%	56%	72%	51%
Visible minority						
Male	60%	75%	88%	67%	85%	62%
Female	45%	56%	79%	56%	75%	51%

[a] Net earnings are adjusted earnings after differences in individual characteristics and differences in market characteristics have been taken into account. Individual characteristics include industry of work, occupation, full-time or part-time work, years of schooling, years of work experience, experience squared, number of weeks worked, official languages ability, and number of years since immigrated to Canada for immigrants (native-born = 0).

[b] Market characteristics include the level of unemployment in the person's region of residence and the size of immigrants' population as a percentage of the region's total population.

SOURCE: Peter Li, "Earnings Disparities Between Immigrants and Native-Born Canadians," *Canadian Review of Sociology and Anthropology*, 37 (2000): 303.

Figure 16.3 does not differentiate visible-minority immigrants from others. Research by Francis Henry and Effie Ginzberg (1990) attempted to uncover discrimination against visible minorities in a more direct way. These researchers arranged for equally qualified blacks and whites apply for jobs in Toronto in 1984. They found that whites were favoured 3:1, with 27 job offers made to whites and only 9 to blacks. This is clear evidence of discrimination. On the other hand, a replication of the study in 1989 had different results, with blacks slightly favoured in job offers: 20 compared with 18 offers to whites (Economic Council of Canada, 1991: 30).

Like more recent immigrants, many European immigrants arriving in the 1950s and 1960s found themselves near the bottom of the occupational and income hierarchy. Yet the evidence suggests that they have in large measure been able to move beyond their entrance status. A study by Wsevolod Isajiw, Aysan Sev'er, and Leo Driedger (1993) compared German, Italian, Jewish, and Ukrainian Canadians in Toronto and found that, in all four cases, there had been significant occupational and educational mobility between the first-, second-, and third-generation group members. Hugh Lautard

and Neil Guppy approached the issue from another angle, looking at the index of occupational dissimilarity among ethnic groups. In their words, the index of occupational dissimilarity is the "percentage of the ethnic group which would have to have a different occupation in order for there to be no difference between the occupational distribution of the group and the rest of the labour force" (1990: 200). Their figures show that the index of occupational dissimilarity declined for most major ethnic groups between 1961 (when Porter gathered much of his data) and 1986. For Italian Canadians, for example, declined from 40 to 24, for Jewish Canadians from 59 to 49.

Despite these findings, it would be unrealistic to paint a rosy picture of eventual equality for all. Occupational dissimilarity may have diminished, but it still exists. Remember, too, that not all discrimination is intentional. Institutional and systemic discrimination remain problems in Canada inasmuch as they are built into the very fabric of our society. In difficult economic times, for example, employers might prefer hiring members of visible minorities on the assumption that they could pay them less or provide them with fewer benefits.

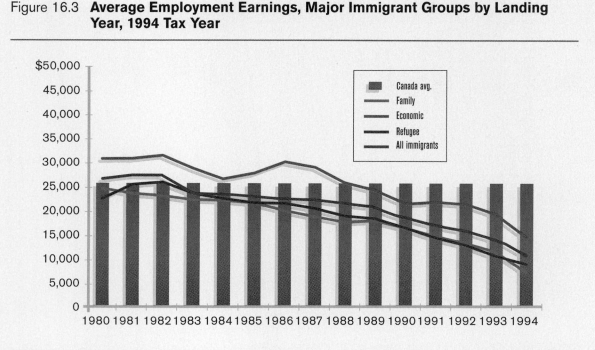

Figure 16.3 **Average Employment Earnings, Major Immigrant Groups by Landing Year, 1994 Tax Year**

SOURCE: Citizenship and Immigration Canada, web site, <http://www.cic.gc.ca/english/srr/pdf/res4bi.pdf>. Adapted with the permission of the Minister of Public Works and Government Services Canada, 2003.

Canada as a whole is characterized by income inequality. The "average" income simply masks the distinctions of poverty and wealth found in our society. An ethnic group's success in achieving an "equal" income simply reflects that this group is just as unequal as Canadians are as a whole.

Ethnicity and the Future of Canada

Can Canadians overcome their regional, ethnic, and linguistic differences in order to keep the country together? Or will the differences that have for so long shaped Canadian society eventually tear it apart? There are no easy answers to these questions. Past policies intended to ease the differences do not seem to have been effective. And while few Canadians expect the resulting problems to be resolved by violence, recent history might give us pause. The 1990 confrontation between Natives and police at Oka, Quebec, near the Kanesatake reserve, escalated very quickly. A police officer was killed, troops were brought in, and a series of ugly incidents erupted outside the area, including the blocking of a bridge by Mohawks near Montreal and the stoning of Mohawks' vehicles by whites. Given the intensity of these reactions, what if Quebec were to choose to separate from the rest of Canada? Most Canadians assume the separation would be peaceful. However, there would inevitably there would be disputes over jurisdictions, money, perhaps even borders. How would these disagreements be resolved in an emotionally charged atmosphere?

Discrimination is another problem related to ethnicity. While Canada remains one of the most tolerant and pluralistic societies in the world, there are disturbing signs that racism, if not more prevalent, is now more acceptable. Canadian society seems to be coping well with institutional and systemic discrimination and racism. However, what is to be done about avowedly racist groups? Should their members be censored or charged with promoting hatred? In answering these questions, we inevitable run into questions of rights. It is hard to make sure that in trying to protect the rights of some, we do not endanger the rights of others. Serving to complicate the situation is the fact that court action against racists serves to give them free publicity and thereby helps them disseminate their ideas.

It is clear that the Canadian dilemma of trying to keep together a nation composed of people divided by ethnicity, language, and even region will not soon be resolved. Yet Canadians have so far shown a remarkable ability to handle these divisions with very little recourse to violence, oppressive legislation, or the suspension of rights. Perhaps the best solution is to try to understand the different kinds of people who make up this country and make them all feel that they are equally at home in Canada.

Conclusion

Because of Canada's origin as a political union of two distinct groups—the British and the French—ethnicity and ethnic differences have always played a special role in Canadian society. Contention between the two charter groups has been a part of Canada's history since their first arrival. More recently, the Native peoples have been engaged in political action, with a view to achieving self-government. Understanding such issues requires an awareness of ethnicity and its role in Canadian society.

Ethnicity refers to the social distinctions whereby groups differentiate themselves from one another on the basis of presumed biological ties. Distinctions are justified on the basis of symbolic markers such as appearance, language, or religion. When the symbolic markers are biological, sociologists use the term *race* to refer to a group.

An *ethnic group* exists to the extent that people are capable of organizing and acting upon their ethnic interests or identity. An *ethnic community* is a group that has evolved an overlapping set of common interests, institutions, and identities. Even people for whom ethnicity is irrelevant may be counted as part of an *ethnic category*, a strictly objective measure of how many people are of a given ethnic origin.

Most theories of ethnicity are either pluralistic theories or remedial. Pluralistic theories see ethnic or racial differences among people as natural or inevitable. Remedial theories tend to treat ethnicity as a characteristic of a class or an industrial society. While they largely discount the role of ethnicity in modern societies, they still try to explain how or why ethnicity may be relevant under certain conditions. The most influential pluralistic theory is that of Barth, who argued that ethnic differences are a consequence of the patterns of social interaction among people that generate boundaries among them. The most popular remedial approach in Canada is to look at the role of the state in defining and promoting ethnic distinctions.

Two issues have dominated Canadian sociologists' research on ethnicity: the connection between ethnicity and inequality in Canada, and the integration of ethnic groups and communities into Canadian society. Porter's description of Canadian society as a vertical mosaic initiated research interest in the link between ethnicity and inequality. Porter's work showed that ethnic groups in Canada have been encouraged to retain their distinctive identity and culture and have thereby been locked into accepting limited economic opportunities and retaining their entrance status. Breton's work on institutional completeness gave sociologists an essential tool for measuring an ethnic community's integration into Canadian society and initiated an examination of ethnic groups in Canada as organized communities.

While Canadians pride themselves on being tolerant, prejudice, discrimination, and racism may all be found to some degree in Canadian society. Institutional discrimination, which is built into the very structure and operation of society's institutions, is particularly difficult to eradicate.

Canadian immigration policy has always favoured certain groups over others, initially, migrants from Britain or Northern Europe. Immigration policy before the late 1960s was racist and exclusionary. Since then, immigration patterns have changed substantially, with more immigrants coming to Canada from non-European, especially Asian, countries. As a result, more immigrants than ever are members of visible minorities, who face different problems from those faced by earlier European immigrants.

Inter-group relations in Canada have evolved in a context of bilingualism and multiculturalism. While these official policies were intended to ease tensions between ethnic groups, both have met with only limited success. Currently, transnationalism and the increase in the number of Canadians having multiple ethnic origins are changing the pattern of relations among Canadians. These new patterns are evolving in ways which may soon make both bilingualism and multiculturalism outdated as policies.

The most recent research concludes that ethnicity still makes a difference in such factors as income; however, gender often makes more of a difference. The data suggest that the lower income of visible minorities is mainly the result of structural disadvantages and their relatively recent time of arrival, rather than of discrimination.

☐ Questions for Critical Thought

1. Suppose you could decide who should or should not be admitted to Canada as an immigrant. On what factors would you base your decisions for admitting immigrants? What factors would you use to keep people out?

2. Would you prefer to be identified as a Canadian or as a member of an ethnic or racial group? Is your own ethnic or racial identity relevant to your everyday life? Are there particular circumstances in which it becomes more relevant?

3. Do you agree that Native peoples should have some form of self-government? Should Aboriginal rights be given precedence over Canada's constitution and laws? Is Native self-government compatible with women's entrenched equal rights?

4. Are most Canadians racially or ethnically prejudiced? Is it necessary that people be prejudiced for minority groups to suffer discrimination? Can you think of examples of discrimination that may be unintentional but that have negative consequences anyway?

5. Why do ethnic differences appear to be increasing in significance worldwide? Is the world changing in ways that make ethnic identity more relevant to people?

6. Religious and national differences seem to be a source of much conflict in the world today. Do you think ethnic or racial attachments differ in kind from religious or nationalist differences, or are they all part of some broader category of social differentiation? How can we go about overcoming such differences?

7. The extraordinary movement of peoples we see today can be expected to continue and even expand in the future. What kinds of changes might this make necessary in how we relate to one another locally, nationally, and globally?

8. Immigrants to Canada are far more likely to obtain Canadian citizenship within the minimum prescribed time than are immigrants to the United States. Why do you think that is? Do immigrants feel a greater need for political and constitutional protections in Canada than in the United States?

□ Recommended Readings

Vered Amit-Talai and Caroline Knowles, *Re-situating Identities: The Politics of Race, Ethnicity and Culture* **(Peterborough, ON: Broadview, 1996).**

This reader is one of many new books and collections that are attempting to re-examine and rethink the phenomenon of ethnicity in light of the fundamental social changes that are transforming relations among individuals and groups. This particular collection focuses on transformations of identity both in Canada and elsewhere in the world.

Raymond Breton, *The Governance of Ethnic Communities: Political Structures and Processes in Canada* **(New York: Greenwood, 1991).**

This important book by one of the most influential and respected researchers on ethnicity in Canada examines the way in which the nation's ethnic communities are organized and govern themselves.

Alan C. Cairns, *Citizens Plus: Aboriginal Peoples and the Canadian State* **(Vancouver: University of British Columbia Press, 2000).**

One of Canada's most thoughtful and elegant writers on politics and the state examines the issue of Aboriginal relations with the rest of Canada. In this book, Cairns is less concerned with providing data than with putting forth an argument that all Canadians, including Aboriginal peoples, need to develop a sense of common identity and institutions that can foster common citizenship.

Richard Jenkins, *Rethinking Ethnicity: Arguments and Explorations* **(London: Sage, 1997).**

A systematic, in-depth discussion of the pluralist/social constructionist view of ethnicity, enriched by fascinating discussions of Northern Ireland and of the connections between culture and power.

Madeline Kalbach and Warren E. Kalbach, *Perspectives on Ethnicity in Canada* **(Toronto: Harcourt, 2000).**

A first-class collection of readings on Canadian ethnicity covering a wide spectrum of topics.

Peter S. Li, *The Chinese in Canada,* **2nd edn (Toronto: Oxford University Press, 1998).**

This book remains an essential examination of one of Canada's most significant ethnic groups. This is one of the few books to examine an ethnic group in the context of its interactions with others, especially the impact of racism on the development of the Chinese Canadian community.

Aihwa Ong, *Flexible Citizenship: The Cultural Logics of Transnationality* **(Durham, NC: Duke University Press, 1999).**

In this remarkable book, Ong examines various facets of Chinese migration, linking this movement to cultural, economic, political, and other forms of social change.

John Porter, *The Vertical Mosaic: An Analysis of Social Class and Power in Canada* **(Toronto: University of Toronto Press, 1965).**

The classic statement on the relationship between ethnicity and inequality in Canadian society. While much of the data are now dated, the discussion has remained relevant to much contemporary research.

☐ Recommended Web Sites

Citizenship and Immigration Canada

www.cic.gc.ca

This is the official source of government data on immigration and citizenship issues, and the only site where you can get information on immigration that is more up to date than the census. It is also a source of practical information for people seeking to immigrate to Canada and of government policies and plans.

Ethnic Community Organization Project

http://lrpro.hypermart.net/index2.htm

This site outlines one particular investigation into the sociology of ethnicity. It is a useful site to see how the theory of sociology is investigated in practice.

International Organization for Migration

www.iom.int

This site collects a wide variety of information and material from around the world. More than a newsletter, it is a gateway to many other sites and sources of information.

Metropolis Canada

http://canada.metropolis.net/

This is another example of the extraordinary wealth of material available on the Internet, as well as of how Canadian sites set an example for the rest of the world. The Metropolis project is an international interdisciplinary program of research on migration, integration, and cultural diversity.

Migration News

migration.ucdavis.edu/mn/

This monthly online newsletter is an excellent source of concise, up-to-date information on migration and immigration issues and events.

Statistics Canada

www.statcan.ca

Canadians are extraordinarily lucky to have this source of high-quality data available. There is a wealth of information available at this user-friendly Web site on a broad a set of topics, including all of the census information. This is also a good source of learning resources and information about statistics.

Transnational Communities Programme

www.transcomm.ox.ac.uk

Located at Oxford University, the Transcomm Programme has generated a wealth of material written by major scholars and available on the Web site. The material on this site is written at an advanced level.

United Nations Refugee Agency

www.unhcr.ch

The United Nations has a number of useful Web sites devoted to various aspects of migration and ethnicity. This one is focused on refugees and provides excellent, up-to-date information in a pleasing format. The issue of refugees is an urgent one in the world today—everyone ought to familiarize themselves with this site.

part five

Canadian Society and the Global Context

This part is about Canada's place in a global context and the implications of this for Canadians. Today, we humans are trying to find ways of achieving peace in a world pulled apart by ideologies, racial and cultural conflicts, and competition for scarce natural resources. We are all connected in global networks of organizations, institutions, markets, and alliances. The fate of humanity depends on how willingly and well we can co-operate despite a poor history of past peaceful co-operation. Sociology may have a role to play in showing how groups and nations can work together, in search of Durkheim's organic solidarity.

17

Michael R. Smith

> > >

Global Society

© Bill Whittman

□ Learning Objectives

In this chapter, you will:

- identify the major international organizations that are the focus for much of the debate on globalization

- learn the four main forms of globalization: international political agreements, trade and capital flows, the mobility of populations, and cultural diffusion

- distinguish between globalization effects in rich and poor countries

- see how constraint on policy choice is present whether countries enter into treaties or not

- see that overall, there is little evidence of net and aggregate harmful effects of globalization, and there is some evidence of positive effects

- examine how "global cities" play a critical role in the globalization process

- explore the two main forms of the cultural diffusion argument

- set current concerns with globalization within a broader historical context

Introduction

On 12 August 1999, a group of about 200 people vandalized a McDonald's restaurant that was under construction in Millau, southern France. They were led by José Bové, a sheep farmer from the region. Bové is a different sort of farmer. He spent most of his childhood in Berkeley, California, while his French parents were teaching at the University of California, before returning to France at the age of 15. Prior to the McDonald's incident, he had led several agriculture-related protests—to recover agricultural land used by the French military, to ban the feeding of growth hormones to calves, to destroy a stock of transgenic (genetically modified) corn. He was in Seattle in 1999 to protest at a World Trade Organization (WTO) meeting, and returned to North America to protest at another one in Quebec City in 2001. In 2002, while awaiting the outcome of his appeal against a prison sentence for the McDonald's incident, he led a group in Brazil that, among other things, pulled up crops of genetically modified corn and soybeans. Bové has become a symbol of anti-globalization protest. His targets reflect a number of the areas of concern about the process.

There is the WTO itself. Created through negotiations between governments, it enforces international trade rules on member countries. Anti-globalization protesters criticize the lack of citizen involvement in such negotiations, claiming that corporations have privileged access to governments so that treaties reflect corporate interests rather than the interests of the broader population.

Countries use tariffs (taxes on imported goods), quotas (restrictions on the quality of incoming goods), and subsidies (cash transfers or tax relief) to protect domestic producers. The WTO's assumption is that international trade is a good thing, that tariffs, quotas, and subsidies obstruct international trade. The WTO is a forum for negotiating their reduction or elimination.

The WTO also has a quasi-judicial responsibility. Governments that think that other countries protect their industries in ways that are incompatible with treaty obligations can appeal to the WTO, which then rules on the matter and prescribes sanctions to impose on the offending country, usually including the right to impose retaliatory tariffs. For example, when in response to steel industry lobbying the United States government imposed a 30 per cent tariff on steel imports, the European Union responded by appealing to the WTO. All this limits national policy autonomy. Thus, a country like France that uses subsidies to maintain a strong national movie industry is likely to run afoul of the WTO. Bové and others regard this as an inappropriate limit on national policy autonomy.

Then there is the issue of health and safety. In the 1990s, some people in Britain developed a human variant of bovine spongiform encephalitis (BSE, or "mad cow disease"), apparently from the consumption of meat from British cattle. Other countries responded by closing their markets to British beef imports on health grounds. WTO regulations permitted this. Other health or safety issues are less clear. In North America, for example, hormones are often added to livestock feed to accelerate growth. This is less common in Europe. Several European governments claim that hormone-fed beef is a health hazard to those who consume it. North American producers contest that claim, arguing that European cattle producers are asserting this health effect as a pretext, that the real European objective is to protect domestic producers against more efficient North American competition. Bové and others contest the right of the WTO to adjudicate this sort of issue.

Finally, there is a broader resistance to the diffusion of a foreign **culture**, particularly US culture. Bové can wax lyrical on the virtues of small-scale local production and high-quality food. On his own farm, he produces one particular culinary gem: Roquefort cheese. The contrast with the industrial agriculture and standardized distribution that underpins the success of McDonald's Corporation is obvious. Bové and his supporters vandalized a McDonald's because they regarded it as a symbol of the intrusion of American culture.

Clearly, Bové is not enthused by globalization, at least in its current form. The same animus with respect to globalization that has expressed itself in his political career stimulates much of the academic, and quasi-academic, debate on the subject. It is an area of diatribes. On one side of the debate, globalization (in its current form) is iniquity incarnate (see, for example, Klein, 1999). On the other side, critics of globalization are treated as fools or knaves, or both (for example, Burtless, 1998). Let us try to bring some detachment to the issue.

17.1

Open for Discussion
The International Monetary Fund (IMF)

Before World War II, there had been a period of competitive currency devaluations that reduced international trade. The Bretton Woods negotiators established the IMF to address this problem.

Countries can maintain or create jobs by exporting goods to other countries. How much they export will depend, in part, on the prices of the goods they produce. There are two ways of cutting the prices of export goods. First, producers can reduce the costs of production in the country's own currency. Thus, Canadian manufacturers might use energy or labour more efficiently. Alternatively, the country's currency can be devalued. The Canadian dollar depreciated by about 35 per cent between 1974 and 2002. This led American consumers to buy more Canadian goods than they would otherwise have done. The devaluation has reduced the price of Canadian products in US dollars. Think about this in terms of the current relative cost of snowboarding to an American paying in US dollars for a visit to a Canadian ski mountain as opposed to a Canadian paying for a visit to a US ski mountain.

During the Great Depression of the 1930s, many people lost their jobs in Europe and North America. Several countries tried to create employment by devaluing their currencies. But any advantage gained if one country devalues its currency is lost if its commercial rivals devalue their currencies. Something like this happened during the 1930s—there was a wave of competitive devaluations (Kindleberger, 1986). The Bretton Woods negotiators concluded that export industries had been damaged and jobs destroyed by competitive devaluations. The reason for this is that exporting and importing are much riskier where prices are subject to substantial change through relative currency price changes.

The IMF was set up to deal with this problem. Suppose, for example, that an early frost damages the coffee crop of a Third World country that is substantially dependent on coffee exports. This is likely to cause a temporary fall in government revenues since there will be less income to tax. This fall in revenue would be likely to lead to a government deficit. And government deficits tend to put pressure on currency values. (Part of the decline of the Canadian dollar from the 1970s to now is probably explained by the large deficits of Canadian governments from the mid-1970s until the early 1990s.) So where there is temporary pressure on a country's currency, the IMF may make a loan to that country—at less than commercial interest rates—to allow its government to cover the temporary revenue shortfall.

This is fairly non-controversial. The problem occurs where the government of a country like, say, Argentina, accumulates a large debt over a substantial period of time. The IMF may still make a loan to help the Argentinian government deal with its problems, but in such cases the IMF is mandated to encourage governments to adopt "sound economic policies." This usually means reductions in government expenditures, balancing budgets, and privatization. The rationale for privatization is that loss-making government-run enterprises contribute to government debt. The IMF also assumes that private ownership implies improved efficiency. It makes these sorts of policies conditions for the receipt of a loan.

But cutting government expenditures usually means reducing education and welfare spending, and privatization sometimes leads to layoffs. There are sometimes real costs for significant parts of the populations of countries receiving IMF loans. It is these that generate the hostility of anti-globalization protesters toward the IMF.

What Is Globalization?

There is much debate on what **globalization** means (see Guillén, 2001), but the underlying idea is fairly clear: international processes intrude on the preferences and behaviour of national and local populations. The word *intrusion* is chosen deliberately: it has a pejorative connotation. In much of the relevant writing, so does *globalization*. That writing often associates globalization with the loss of things that ought to be valued. Beyond this, things get more complicated, as globalization takes many forms. We will consider globalization as political arrangement, as economic process, as mobility and transnational **social networks**, and as cultural diffusion.

Globalization as Political Arrangement

After World War II, the United States and Britain—and, to a lesser extent, other countries—negotiated the framework for subsequent international economic arrangements. They produced the Bretton Woods agreement, named after the resort in New Hampshire where the main negotiations took place. Bretton Woods created the International Monetary Fund and the World Bank. Each has become a *bête noire* to anti-globalization protesters.

The IMF and the World Bank encourage "**sound economic policies**" in the **Third World**, usually including cuts to government expenditures and the reinforcement of the private sector. The WTO (successor to the General Agreement on Tariffs and Trade, GATT) acts to limit the discretion of governments with respect to tariffs, quotas, and subsidies. Critics oppose these organizations because of their definition of "sound economic policies" and also because of the role of rich, powerful countries in their design. The Bretton Woods agreement was only one of several proposed arrangements for managing post-war international trade, but the relative economic power of the United States after World War II meant that its preferences largely prevailed (Skidelsky, 2000). The IMF, World Bank, and WTO commitments to market solutions reflect the policy preferences of a set of Western nations—in particular, the United States.

Moreover, beyond international organizations, outcomes are also shaped by naked **power**. Take the softwood lumber dispute between Canada and the United States. For a number of reasons, but particularly because of the depreciation of the Canadian dollar, the US lumber industry has lost market share to Canadian producers. In response, it has pressured US politicians to look hard at Canadian practices, claiming that, in violation of trade rules, Canadian governments have found ways to subsidize the industry. Using threats, the US government has forced Canada to adopt policies that raise the price of lumber exports into the United States, including, at various times, both export taxes and quotas (Grafton, Lynch, and Nelson, 1998).

International agreements limit the policy choices of the countries that sign them. Some of the passions that this arouses are clearly expressed in these photographs. A protestor shouts at the police; Quebec City, Summit of the Americas protests, April 2001. The police response follows. (Dru Oja Jay/Dominionpaper.ca)

IN THE FIRST PERSON

I was drawn into sociology because it engaged the sorts of larger issues of inequality, efficiency, and fairness that interested me when I was a student. I've remained a sociologist because the discipline provides a broad enough tent to accommodate the various interests that I've since developed and followed. My approach to sociology has been substantially shaped by my colleagues at McGill, and by others whose work I know and admire. The lesson that I've drawn from those colleagues is that facts matter. It's easy to construct large, general theories of the social and economic world. People do so all the time. Good tests of theories, however, require lots of hard work. So they're less abundant. We need more of them. Using one research method or another, that's what I work on. –MICHAEL SMITH

 17.2

Global Issues
The World Bank

After World War II, the large European countries were in appalling financial shape. But global growth depended on their return to financial health. Countries such as the United States and Canada were in better economic shape but needed European countries rich enough to absorb their exports. The International Bank for Reconstruction and Development (IBRD) was the policy response to this problem. It was created to provide loans to governments to fund investments in devastated European countries—say, the reconstruction of a rail network.

The World Bank evolved out of the IBRD, which is now one part of the World Bank Group. But its mission has changed. By the mid-1950s, European countries had substantially recovered, so the IBRD shifted to providing loans to "credit-worthy poor countries." It was reoriented to the Third World.

Other elements of the World Bank Group, with the dates of their establishment, are the International Financial Corporation (1956), which helps to finance the private sector in the Third World; the International Development Association (1960), which funds programs to alleviate long-term poverty (in recent years, it has, for example, funded female education and anti-AIDS programs); the International Centre for Settlement of Investment Disputes (1966), which mediates disputes between private investors and countries (for example, a dispute involving the claim by a private company that the government of Albania expropriated its property); and the Multilateral Investment Guarantee Agency (1988), which encourages private-sector investments in Third World countries by providing insurance against political risk (such as civil war).

Like those of the IMF, these purposes seem entirely worthy. But the IBRD directs its loans to "credit-worthy countries." This puts pressure on borrowers to balance their budgets. At the same time, the International Finance Corporation, the Multilateral Investment Guarantee Agency, and the International Centre for Settlement of Investment Disputes are all designed to reinforce the private sector. Those who would prefer a larger role for the public sector in development might object to this.

Globalization as Economic Process

Consider, first, rich countries. Trade exposes owners and employees to competition. Third World competitors mostly pay markedly lower wages. They may either drive rich-country producers out of business or force them to cut the wages of their employees in order to compete (Wood, 1994).

Then there are **multinational corporations**. Nortel, Bombardier, and Inco are Canadian examples. Other things being equal, managers of these companies are likely to locate factories and offices where costs are lower and the political environment more congenial. Low taxes, less restrictive labour laws, and government reticence to intervene in the economy are likely to attract them. So, in competition for investment, countries may cut taxes, reduce services, weaken labour laws (health and safety regulations, statutory protections against dismissal, trade-union protections), and refrain from other policies offensive to foreign investors.

There are also enormous flows of **finance capital** between countries. So-called **hot money** usually accumulates in countries where interest rates are higher and the local currency more stable (Sassen, 2002). This also limits policy options. Government policies designed to stimulate the economy normally involve lower interest rates, but lower interest rates may lead to a flight of "hot money" out of the country as investors seek the highest rate (for a given level of political and economic stability).

A government confronting a high **unemployment rate** may wish to reduce interest rates, hoping that doing so will create jobs. Lower interest rates imply lower mortgage payments, which stimulate the housing market. Lower rates also reduce entrepreneurs' cost of borrowing, which encourages job-creating investment. But interest-rate reductions may precipitate a decline in the value of a country's currency. For various reasons, a government may be reluctant to see the value of its currency fall. Insofar as this is the case, it may avoid policies that lead to a reduction in interest rates (Andrews, 1994). Thus, the unemployment rate in Canada in the early 1990s was well over 10 per cent, but the government of the time did not substantially stimulate the economy. It chose instead policies that had the effect of supporting the value of the Canadian dollar, and the unemployment rate rose fairly dramatically (see Fortin, 1996). The anti-globalization interpretation of this is that Canadian government policy was limited by the development of an international market for capital, with ever-larger flows of "hot money" between countries.

Parallel damage may be inflicted on the Third World. Despite lower labour costs, Third World producers are sometimes undercut by exports from rich countries. Here is a particularly pathetic example: rich-country charities receive donations of second-hand clothes, but "with more donations than they can use, the charities unload their surplus on wholesalers who buy it in the West for a few pennies a pound, then ship it [to Zambia] and sell bales of it to . . . street retailers at a markup of 300 to 400 per cent" (Jeter, 2002:A1). The local population buys the goods for reasons of both price and taste. Items with sports logos are particularly popular in some African markets. There used to be relatively lively textile and apparel industries in Zambia. These have now been seriously damaged by competition from second-hand European and North American goods.

Most damage to domestic industries in Third World countries, however, comes from **capital-intensive** industries. Capital-intensive production in rich countries—particularly agriculture—can often lead to lower sale prices, despite the relatively high cost of labour in the rich countries. The effects are compounded where agriculture is heavily subsidized, as is the case for many US and European agricultural products. Some development analysts believe that it is only possible for Third World countries to develop their own industries if those industries are protected or encouraged—with tariffs, quotas, or subsidies. But doing so would go against the policy preferences of the WTO, the World Bank, and the IMF, all of which press for liberalized trade and have sanctions available if a country chooses protectionism.

This brings us to the Third World and capital markets. Lenders often regard Third World countries as too risky for investment, so those countries are compelled to turn to international organizations—the World Bank or, during financial crises, the IMF—as sources of loans or as guarantors of private-sector loans. But these loans come with strings attached, of the sort discussed earlier—requirements that markets be opened and that the country adopt a "sound economic policy."

Globalization as Mobility and Transnational Social Networks

Products imported from the Third World might force down rich-country wages, but migration from the Third World to rich countries may have the same effect. In either case, wages of unskilled (usually meaning poorly educated) employees in rich countries are most likely to be affected. There has been a large unskilled migration into the United States, both legal and illegal. One result of this is competition between poorly educated Latin American migrants and, disproportionately, poorly educated African Americans. Some think that this competition has forced down wages of unskilled workers in the United States—of African Americans in particular (Stevans, 1998).

The Canadian situation is a little different. A points system determines eligibility for some immigrant classes. Would-be migrants are given points for education and in-demand skills (as well as other things). Those with enough points are admitted. This system for selecting immigrants is thought to have reduced the magnitude of unskilled immigration to Canada (but see Reitz, 1998). Europe has also experienced post-war migrations. The fundamental point, though, is that international migration—mainly from poor to rich countries—is a common experience across rich countries.

These migrations create transnational social networks. Most migrants settle in cities. The main destinations of migrants to Canada are Toronto, Montreal, and Vancouver, where they create their own communities, sometimes retaining close ties with other members of their family or ethnic group in other cities in the world. The same thing happens on a larger scale in New York, Los Angeles, and London. This creates what Alejandro Portes (1997) calls *transnational communities*, with identities and economic interests shaped by their inter-city relations.

At the other end of the social scale, claims Saskia Sassen (2002), international cities develop a distinctive elite. This elite manages international commercial flows—the movements of goods, services, and capital that have become these cities' main economic vocation—and, to some degree, becomes detached from national loyalties. Bankers in London engaged in the financing of international trade, for example, become less concerned with British domestic policy issues. Rather, their transnational economic and social ties become increasingly important (Sassen, 2002; see also Arthurs, 1999, on Canada).

Globalization as Cultural Diffusion

Hollywood is the most conspicuous worldwide projector of a particular culture, through the process called **cultural diffusion**. The US movie and television industry has aggressively marketed itself throughout the Americas and Europe (Segrave, 1998). It probably shapes the world views of receiving populations. What Hollywood projects is heterogeneous (it is a long way from Woody Allen to Clint Eastwood to Arnold Schwarzenegger), but it is unlikely to reflect the range of preferences and opinions in the rest of the world. It must substantially embody cultural judgments, knowledge, or ignorance of those producing movies and television. Hollywood's ignorance extends even to its most immediate northern neighbour; Pierre Berton (1975) describes one film that took place during a blizzard in Saskatchewan—in July!

American cultural influence is not confined to Hollywood. US universities train graduate students from the rest of the world and produce a disproportionate share of the world's academic output. US multinational companies transmit employment practices to other countries (Merten, 1997). That is to say, American multinational corporations have similar ways of hiring (recruitment and evaluation methods), of promoting, and of dealing with grievances (among other things). When they set up branches in Belgium, or Brazil, or Barbados, they bring those practices with them. They change the culture of employment in those countries. To varying degrees, so do multinationals based in other countries.

The Effect of Globalizing Mechanisms

Two linked themes run through this discussion so far. One is that globalization is a homogenizing process. Political, economic, and cultural pressures create societies that look increasingly similar. Such homogenization may be regarded as undesirable in general—a process through which the diversity and richness of cultures is replaced with the grey monotone of a standard international practice. A displacement of consumption from, say, Roquefort cheese or similarly distinctive products to McDonald's might be a symbol of this process. The other theme specifies what seem to be identifiably bad outcomes of the

American cultural influence extends across the globe. This striking photograph was taken in an open-air market in Kabul, Afghanistan. Even in countries where America is not favoured, an impressive array of US-made running shoes are ready for sale. (Steve McCurry/Magnum Photos)

globalization process. The destruction of Zambia's indigenous clothing industry might be an example of this. The limits placed on government choices of economic and social policy by international organizations and by international trade and capital flows are often also regarded in this way.

Consider the four broad globalizing mechanisms identified above in light of these concerns.

Treaties and International Organizations

Constraint in Principle

International organizations and common markets are created through treaties. Treaties are international contracts, so, like the contracts associated with a mortgage, a marriage, or a mutual fund purchase, they impose constraints on signatories. Further, sovereign nations can sign or not sign such agreements. Several European countries, for example, chose not to become members of the European Economic Community (now the European Union, EU) when it was first created. Some (in 2003, Norway, Switzerland, and Iceland) still remain outside it. Had the 1987 federal election in Canada gone differently—and it could easily have done so—the Canada–US free trade agreement (FTA) would not have been signed. The initiative to create the North American Free Trade Agreement (NAFTA) came from the United States and Mexico. The Canadian government inserted itself into the process when it seemed it would be left out (Robert, 2000)—it was concerned that a NAFTA without Canada might mean that Mexico would replace Canada as the principal trading partner of the United States.

Of course, a picture of sovereign governments free to choose between courses of action would be a gross misrepresentation. Self-defence motivated the Canadian government to negotiate the FTA. Rising protectionist sentiment in the United States in the 1980s led to threats of unilateral imposition of tariffs and quotas. The FTA was conceived to shelter Canadian exporters from this protectionist wave. The threat of protectionism, then, constrained the Canadian government to pursue a trade agreement.

Similarly, Third World countries that borrow from the World Bank, or rich or poor countries that borrow from the IMF, do so because other options seem less appealing. There is no such thing as unconstrained choice. Still, there is some choice. The core of the debate on globalization is about whether or not the amount of constraint has increased.

Constraint in Practice

Do the sorts of treaties associated with globalization imply increased levels of constraint? To answer this question we need first to determine as compared to *when* constraint might have increased.

Consider these two examples. From 1876 to 1884, King Leopold of Belgium created his own personal second kingdom, in what became the Congo, ushering in a period of spectacular brutality (Anstey, 1966; Hochschild, 1998). Indigenous males were conscripted into the production of rubber, or their lives were disrupted as they fled the Belgian troops sent to conscript them. Among other atrocious acts, mutilation was used as a form of labour discipline. In areas of British conquest in southern Africa, European farmers displaced the indigenous population. That population was then subjected to taxes. The idea was that the need to pay taxes in cash would force the native population to seek employment on settler farms (Crush, 1987). Coercive activities of various sorts were common across the various European empires in Africa and elsewhere. *This* was constraint.

Treaties and international organizations, moreover, are often methods for escaping or limiting other sorts of constraint. Take, for example, the case of the Bretton Woods agreement of 1944. Part of it committed signatories to maintain approximately fixed rates of exchange between their currencies. This ruled out (or made more difficult) one particular policy choice: competitive devaluation. Bretton Woods was a means for escaping the macroeconomic policy constraints imposed by competitive devaluations, with which governments had to deal during the inter-war period.

Treaties, then, embody chosen constraints. How binding are those constraints? Post-war trade agreements were supposed to create a level playing field across countries, so that only the most efficient producers would thrive, irrespective of country of location.

But consider the following case. In 1999, a Taiwanese computer chip company proposed siting a plant in a suburb of Montreal. As encouragement, the

Quebec government agreed to invest \$400,000 in it, offered a tax holiday worth about a billion dollars and training grants of several million dollars. The municipality targeted offered half the cost of necessary infrastructure investments, with water supplied at a discount. Further subsidies were sought from the federal government, but that support, in the amounts sought, was not forthcoming and the project was dropped. All these promises—and this is the important point—were made despite the fact that they were probably inconsistent with international trade agreements to which Canada is a signatory. This example is not unique (Smith, 2001b).

Canada is not alone in evading trade treaty obligations. It may offend less than other rich countries. The United States aggressively subsidizes its agriculture and in March 2002 imposed a 30 per cent tariff on steel imports that was ruled illegal by the WTO, a year later. The European Union is no better. Treaties do constrain signatories, but it is important to understand that the degree of compliance is highly variable. Further evidence of this is the substantial body of legal writings dealing precisely with the problem of increasing the likelihood of treaty compliance. We live in a world where treaty violation is frequent (Chayes and Chayes, 1995).

Governments regularly confront choices. On the one hand, there is the possibility of inconsistent mutual regulation through a treaty. On the other hand, there is the possibility of inconsistent mutual regulation in the absence of a treaty. The latter, no-treaty, situation will often involve a tit-for-tat approach to disputes—one country limits trade to protect its vulnerable industries, another country punishes the first country by closing off its domestic market to the first country's major export industries, and so on. Or countries might consecutively devalue their currencies, as during the inter-war period. Or they might do both.

Constraint is present in both situations. What matters is the relative benefits of different kinds of constraint. Since treaties spell out rules for international relations, they will usually be preferable. Rules mean that treaty implications for signatories are relatively predictable, except where treaty enforcement is very inconsistent indeed. Critics of the IMF, the World Bank, and the WTO say interesting things about harmful consequences of their actions. However, in the final analysis, our judgment of them and other international organizations requires the specification of feasible alternative arrangements, and their consequences.

17.3

Open for Discussion
Protectionism vs Free Trade

Tariffs, quotas, and subsidies are all forms of protectionism. *Tariffs* are taxes imposed on goods when they enter a country. They raise prices to importers and therefore to consumers. *Quotas* limit the quantity supplied of the goods to which they are applied. A reduced supply usually also implies a higher price. Why would anyone favour policies that increase the prices of goods? *Government subsidies* involve the transfer of income from those who pay taxes to the private owners of the firms receiving the subsidies. Why might taxpayers wish to enrich other private owners—often foreign—most of whom are very rich? Here are some arguments for one or another of these protectionist measures:

1. The removal of tariffs or quotas exposes a previously protected industry to low-cost foreign competition. Many consumers will benefit from lower prices, but the benefit per consumer is likely to be small. In contrast, industry employees will likely suffer large costs. Either their pay will be cut to match the competition, or they will lose their jobs. This implies a transfer of income from producers to consumers.

2. Protectionist measures might be adopted to punish another country that already has quotas, high tariffs, or industrial subsidies. This can encourage another country to change its policies. Recent increases in subsidies to agricultural producers in the United States might be seen as retaliation against even higher subsidies in the European Union.

3. Already-established firms have an advantage: they have invested in plant and equipment over a long period of time, developed local expertise in production processes, and created networks of suppliers and customers. For a new entrant to an industry to match all this would be very costly indeed. Consequently, a country might protect domestic producers for the first decades of their operation so that they can build up to a competitive scale of operation. This is called the *infant industry argument*. It suggests that transitional protection is appropriate.

4. It is in the interests of countries to have high-technology industries because profits and wages in them are higher than in other industries. This is because of monopoly power. Scale economies in the aircraft industry, for example, are so large that, worldwide, only a small number of producers is feasible. Patents legalize pharmaceutical monopolies for specified numbers of years. Even without patent rights, the knowledge frontier of high-technology industries is continually being pushed outward so that technology and products are progressively improved. This makes it hard to enter an industry or, if a new firm does so, to catch up. Most countries recognize this. Japan protected its computer industry for many years. European governments have subsidized Airbus Industries. In such an environment, protectionism may be necessary to assure a high-technology industry presence (see Johnson, Tyson, and Zysman, 1990).

There are, of course, pro–free trade responses to each of these arguments:

1. It is better to liberalize trade and provide temporary help (unemployment insurance, retraining) to those who lose their jobs through foreign competition.

2. Retaliation against the protectionism of others leads to a mutually harmful tit-for-tat spiral.

3. In practice, protected "infant industries" rarely "grow up."

4. High-technology industries are not as distinctive as the protagonists of protectionism claim.

Trade and Investment: Rich Countries

Critics of globalization tend to focus on two negative consequences for rich countries of increased trade and more mobile investment. One suggests that increased trade—particularly with the Third World—worsens the pay and employment situation of the less skilled and of workers in general. Another argues that, to create an investment-friendly environment and attract increasingly footloose capital, rich countries adopt less generous social policies. This is the "**race to the bottom**" argument.

Employment and Wages

Most trade is between rich countries. Roughly speaking, the world's rich countries are members of the Organisation for Economic Co-operation and Development (OECD). Figure 17.1 shows that from 1970 to 1998, over two-thirds of imports into OECD countries originated in other OECD countries. There was no downward trend in the share of OECD-originating imports. Finally, imports from members of the Organization of the Petroleum Exporting Countries (OPEC) account for a significant share of total non-OECD imports. But the bulk of imports from these countries is petroleum. Few OECD countries compete in the oil market.

But perhaps the variation in pay levels between rich countries is sufficient to undermine Canadian

and US wages. For example, the gap between wages in Canada and the United States, on the one hand, and Greece and Portugal, on the other, is fairly wide. In fact, however, the evidence seems to suggest that trade is not forcing down wages in richer countries.

It is price competition that is supposed to put pressure on the wages of richer countries. Low-wage countries should be able to sell into high-wage countries at a lower price. But were this process underway, one might expect those industries in rich countries exposed to more trade to be less able to raise their prices than industries exposed to less trade or altogether sheltered from trade. They might even be forced to lower them. Research on both the United States and Europe, however, suggests that there is no link between the amount of trade in the goods of a particular industry and price trends in that industry (Slaughter and Swagel, 1997). In fact, rich-country prices have proven to be robust in the face of international competition. This suggests that trade exerts little pressure on rich-country wages.

Then there is the effect of trade on unemployment. For Canada, a good test of this is provided by events following the FTA and NAFTA (Smith, 2001b), which came into force on 1 January 1988 and 1 January 1994, respectively. Each reduced barriers to competition with the United States. The second also reduced barriers with Mexico, a low-income country. Unemployment in Canada did rise after the FTA, but the FTA's implementation coincided with a recession—unemployment rose elsewhere at the same time. NAFTA, in contrast, was implemented in the early part of an upswing in the economy. Unemployment was falling before it was signed and continued to fall after it was signed. There is evidence, however, that the largest post-FTA declines in employment were concentrated in industries that had been subject to the largest tariff cuts. All this suggests that some workers lost their jobs because of the trade agreements but that the agreements' aggregate net effect on unemployment was negligible.

But if particular workers were damaged by these agreements, perhaps this is evidence of trade's generally harmful effect on unskilled employees in particular? Rising earnings inequality is usually cited in support of this interpretation (e.g., Bernard and Jensen, 2000). It is sometimes thought to reflect the downward pressure on the earnings of the unskilled (the uneducated) exerted by Third World competition. But only a small number of countries—in particular the United States and the United Kingdom—

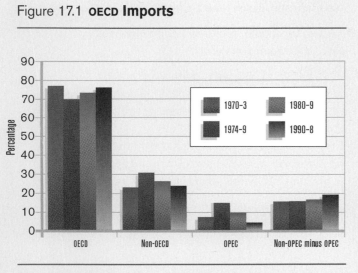

Figure 17.1 OECD Imports

SOURCE: Based on Organisation for Economic Co-operation and Development (OECD), *OECD Historical Statistics, 1970–1999* (Paris: OECD, 2001), 118.

have experienced large and sustained increases in earnings inequality (Atkinson, 2000; Card and DiNardo, 2002; Wolfson and Murphy, 1998). Earnings inequality rose in Canada from about 1975 to about 1985 and has been stable or falling since (Card and DiNardo, 2002; Wolfson and Murphy, 1998). In still other countries—Italy and Germany—there was no increase at all (Atkinson, 2000). Yet all of these countries have been exposed to globalization. Further, earnings inequality stopped rising in the United States in about 1993 while world trade continued to increase.

The Race to the Bottom

Social programs rest on tax collections. But corporations are lured by cuts in corporate taxes and in the income taxes to which high-earning managers are liable. So, it is argued, competitive tax cuts cause cuts to social programs.

This argument is plausible. But the available evidence tends not to support it. Nancy Olewiler (1999) has found that there were large differences between OECD countries in the tax rates imposed on corporations and individuals, that there were large differences between tax rates in Canada and the United States, that there was no evidence of a convergence in tax rates over time across OECD countries, and that taxes had tended to rise rather than fall in the periods studied.

Consistent with this, huge social policy divergences persist. The income protection provided to those who lose their jobs, get sick, or incur hard-to-manage family obligations (for example, those of single mothers), remain much more generous in Sweden and Germany, say, than in the United States. There is a substantial literature that documents the persistence of social policy variation despite globalization (see, for example, Kitschelt, 1999). Figure 17.2 shows just how wide the variation in social spending remains, with social spending as a percent of GDP (gross domestic product) in Sweden about twice that of Japan. Note, furthermore, the variation in methods of social spending: all Norway's involves direct spending by the government, whereas about one-quarter of spending in the United States involves private social benefits, either legally stipulated (such as occupational health and safety premiums) or voluntarily provided (such as employer-funded pensions).

What Prevents Convergence?

Given the criticisms of globalization, one might wonder why international trade and investment with the

Crowded bridges crossing the Canada–US border reflect the enormous volume of trade between the two countries, a volume that increased after the FTA and NAFTA. But Canada depends more heavily on its trade with the United States than the United States depends on Canada. This is an important source of policy constraint. (KRYK ARTS)

Third World does not lead to rising unemployment and falling wages among unskilled workers in rich countries.

One reason is that the magnitudes of the economic changes associated with globalization are often exaggerated. Paul Hirst and Grahame Thompson (1996) have observed that only at the beginning of the 1990s did trade as a percentage of GDP equal and begin to exceed the figure for 1913. And William Watson (1999) notes that in some countries, including Canada, investment as a percentage of GDP was much larger in the late nineteenth and early twentieth centuries than it is currently. Some caution, then, is warranted with respect to the novelty of the globalization process.

Another reason is that in capitalist economies many jobs are both destroyed and created (Davis, Haltiwanger, and Schuh, 1996). Changing technology and tastes, as well as globalization, lead to declines in employment in some firms and industries. These

Figure 17.2 **Net Public and Private Social Expenditures as a Percentage of GDP**

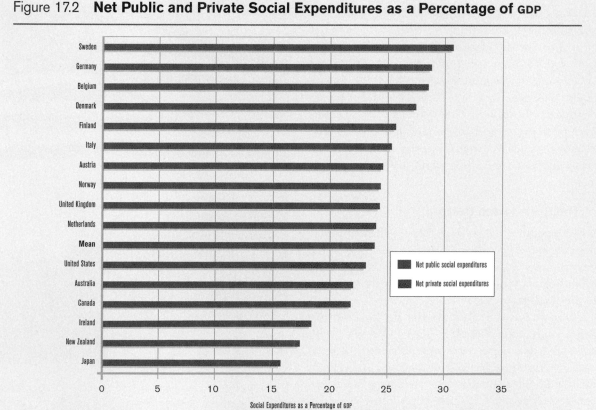

ᵃ Social benefits include old-age cash benefits, disability cash benefits, occupational injury and disease benefits, sickness benefits, services for the elderly and the disabled, survivors' benefits, family cash benefits, family services, active labour market policies, unemployment compensation, housing benefits, public health expenditures, and other contingencies, such as cash benefits to those on low incomes.
SOURCE: Willem Adema, *Net Public Social Expenditures* (Paris: OECD, 2001), 27–8.

declines in employment sometimes involve layoffs, but they are also often managed through attrition. The same changes in technology, taste, and opportunities on the international market, however, lead to expansions in employment in other sectors. As a result, while particular groups of employees may be harmed by globalization (as was the case for the FTA in Canada), the aggregate effect may be modest.

Still another reason is that many governments of countries with greater exposure to the international market have chosen to invest more heavily in social programs than have those with less exposure. Other things being equal, trade as a percentage of GDP is higher in small countries such as the Netherlands, Belgium, Sweden, and Canada than it is in large countries such as Germany, the United Kingdom, or, in particular, the United States (perhaps because of economies of scale). At the same time, social programs are, on average, more generous in the first set

of countries than in the second (though Germany diverges from the second group pattern).

What explains this association? Dani Rodrik (1997) notes that countries with a large share of their economy engaged in trade are likely to be particularly hard hit during downturns in the economic activity of their principal trading partners. To compensate for this vulnerability, governments of small countries like the Netherlands have developed generous welfare states. In their case, globalization has led to more generous social policy rather than to a race to the bottom.

A final problem with the "race to the bottom" argument is that the "bottom" may not be the outcome preferred by managers of multinational corporations. Suppose that you are a manager of a multinational company. What factors might affect your decision with respect to where to locate your head office? You would certainly prefer a reasonably safe city—it is harder to recruit and keep high-quality employees who confront a significant likelihood of being mugged, assaulted, or burgled. So investments in a police force are required, as well, probably, as investments in social programs that provide a living standard adequate to reduce the likelihood that the poor will feel inclined to mug, assault, or burgle. Since few people enjoy being solicited by beggars or passing people sleeping in doorways, you may want to see some programs established to help the homeless.

In addition, you almost certainly do not want to be exposed to infectious diseases. Investments in public health reduce the likelihood of contracting, say, tuberculosis. You would want traffic jams kept under control. In a large **metropolitan area**, that would require (very costly) investments in mass transit. You might also like to see a rich cultural life in your city. Universities tend to elevate the cultural lives of their host cities. Even in the United States, universities are substantially funded through taxes. If you want an opera, ballet, symphony orchestra, a set of museums, and a theatre district, you would also have to expect to be taxed to make possible subsidies to these cultural institutions. Along these lines, there are more high-paid head office jobs in New York City than in, say, Birmingham, Alabama. Taxes are markedly lower in Birmingham than in New York, but so are public services. Many would think that the quality of life is also inferior in Birmingham. The preservation of better jobs certainly requires some public spending, possibly a lot of it.

Trade and Investment: Poor Countries

What about the Third World? Is the case of the Zambian apparel industry exemplary? The answer to this question is yes—and no.

The Indian textile industry in the early nineteenth century provides a classic example of destructive trade. It was destroyed by competition from Britain, causing considerable suffering among local weavers (Rothermund, 1993). Contemporary writers within the "fair trade" tradition are convinced that there are many more such examples (for example, Suranovic, 1997). It is clear that the export from the United States and Europe of (often subsidized) agricultural products makes more difficult the development of a viable commercial agriculture in several Third World countries. That is the "yes" part of the answer.

But the issue is complicated. In an exhaustive review of evidence, Peter Lindert and Jeffrey Williamson (2001) show that, over two centuries, between-country inequality has risen. By the mid-1990s, the gap between rich and poor countries was greater than it had been at the beginning of the nineteenth century. Clearly, this rise coincides with a huge increase in economic integration at the international level. Is this evidence of the harmful effects on poor countries of globalization?

Not really. The long-term rise in inequality between countries originates in the improvement in average incomes in those countries that integrated into the world economy. Inequality rose as the European countries that created the modern world economy became rich after 1600. It increased further as countries like Japan, Taiwan, Singapore, Korea, Mexico, and Brazil opened up to the world economy and competed successfully. Japan's success in the 1980s in the export of automobiles and consumer electronics would be a good example of this. Japan, Taiwan, and countries like them became richer than did the Third World countries that failed to integrate themselves into the global economy. At the same time, other poor-country economies remained closed. Where that was the case, their populations failed to get any richer. This pattern is reflected in Figure 17.3.

Trends in inequality within Third World countries that have opened themselves to the international market provide further evidence consistent with this interpretation. Inequality has risen within the so-called East Asian tigers as well as in China, Mexico, and Brazil. This is, in part, because regions that are more integrated into the world economy have become richer while the regions that have not been integrated remain as poor as they ever were. For example, it is in the southern coastal part of China, where export industries are located, that incomes are rising. In the interior and the north, which remain largely unintegrated into the world economy, incomes have failed to rise. The Chiapas region in Mexico provides another interesting case. There is significant political unrest there—and it is also a region where persistent poverty coincides with relative exclusion from the international economy, as compared to other parts of the country (Lynn, 2002).

For both the Third World and for rich countries, then, the character of the economic effects of globalization seems broadly similar. Some workers (and their families) have been harmed by processes associated with globalization—for example, weavers in the nineteenth-century Indian textile industry, agricultural producers in Third World countries excluded from commercial markets by cheap food imports from rich countries, and many employees in the apparel industries of rich countries since World War II.

But it is difficult to discern harmful net and aggregate economic effects of globalization. On the contrary, international trade has been the main route to the relative prosperity of the currently richer countries in the world economy. Nor does the evidence yet suggest that trade and investment flows lead to a race to the bottom in social policy, in part because relatively generous social programs and other forms of government spending may often be a requisite for trade and investment, at least where higher-paid jobs are involved.

Social Networks and the Movement of Populations

"Global Cities" and Global Networks

Globalization disperses economic activity across countries. This creates a problem of co-ordination (Sassen, 1991, 1998, 2002). The international flow of goods and contracts and the financing of that flow require "a system for the provision of such inputs as planning, top-level management, and specialized business services" (Sassen, 1991: 29). These inputs are most efficiently co-ordinated within a small number of very large cities. New York, London, and Tokyo are at the top of the global hierarchy of cities providing this co-ordination. Toronto falls in the upper part of the hierarchy, with Montreal some way behind.

The development of **global cities** has created two sorts of network, each globally oriented. One is made up of the economic decision makers in global cities—bankers, specialists in commercial insurance, international lawyers, brokers of various kinds, and so on. Because in their day-to-day work they deal with issues that are international, and because that implies that they are part of international social networks, their political orientations also tend to be international. Their loyalties shift toward their international network and away from the nation-state in which they are located.

The second network is quite different. It is made up of those at the bottom of the hierarchy within global cities. In these cities, immigrants from Third World countries create an ethnic underclass at the bottom of the social hierarchy. Several mechanisms are involved in this. Traditional ways of life have been disrupted by the spread to the Third World of commercial agriculture and resource extraction (mining and logging) to supply rich countries with coffee, sugar, lumber, bauxite, and so on. Direct foreign investment has created manufacturing jobs in Third World cities, further disrupting traditional ways of life. Manufacturing plants often disproportionately

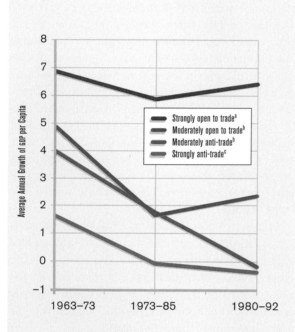

Figure 17.3 **Trade Policy and the Third World**

Average Annual Growth of GDP per Capita

Legend:
- Strongly open to trade[a]
- Moderately open to trade[b]
- Moderately anti-trade[b]
- Strongly anti-trade[c]

Periods: 1963–73, 1973–85, 1980–92

[a] [Strongly open] Hong Kong, South Korea, and Singapore.
[b] [Strongly anti-trade] 1963–73: Argentina, Bangladesh, Burundi, Chile, Dominican Republic, Ethiopia, Ghana, India, Pakistan, Peru, Sri Lanka, Sudan, Tanzania, Turkey, Uruguay, and Zambia. In the two later periods, Chile, Pakistan, Sri Lanka, and Turkey became more open, while Bolivia, Madagascar, and Nigeria joined the strongly anti-trade group.
[c] The composition of the intermediate groups can be found in the original World Bank source used by Lindert and Williamson.
SOURCE: Peter H. Lindert and Jeffrey G. Williamson, *Does Globalization Make the World More Unequal?* (Cambridge, MA: National Bureau of Economic Research, 2001).

recruit young women. The geographic mobility entailed loosens the traditional ties of those women, making more likely further, overseas, migration. Direct foreign investment in the Third World, then, creates a population pool detached from the social roots that would be likely to keep them in their countries of origin. These are the potential migrants.

Then there is the character of the demand for labour in the global city. Those who co-ordinate global economic flows have high incomes. They consume lots of personal services; "the increase in the numbers of expensive restaurants, luxury housing, luxury hotels, gourmet shops, boutiques, French hand laundries, and special cleaners that ornament the urban landscape illustrates this trend" (Sassen, 1991: 9). Many of these activities are both labour intensive and poorly paid. They provide jobs that immigrants are willing, and that native labour is unwilling, to fill.

The immigrants filling these low-paid service-sector jobs are usually distinguished by skin colour, language, or both. They tend to be the objects of **discrimination**. Imperfectly integrated into the host society because of discrimination, immigrants retain their loyalties to family and former neighbours in their countries of origin. They, too, are part of larger transnational networks. Once immigrant communities get established in a global city, they facilitate the migration of others by providing information, cash, sponsorship (for example, through the family reunification component of Canadian immigration policy), contacts, or employment. The result of all this is immigrant communities that are substantially estranged from their host society but that remain part of, and contribute to, the nurturing of a dense pattern of social relations with their countries of origin.

In Sassen's account, these ties with the country of origin often provide economic opportunity to migrants. They can use the ties to develop more or less lucrative business relationships. They can involve themselves in the import and export of goods from their home countries. Relatives brought in to work in family businesses provide both cheap and reliable labour. Like the elites, the immigrants in global cities develop an extra-national orientation, but, obviously, for different reasons.

Global Cities and Global Networks: Hypotheses and Evidence

According to Sassen, then, globalization challenges the nation-state. It does so by creating core groups at both the top and the bottom of the hierarchy, groups whose political orientation is shaped by international networks rather than country of residence.

There is a further effect that connects with the discussion earlier. In rich countries, the development of an elite that prospers through the co-ordination of global interchanges and of an underclass largely made up of immigrants increases inequality. The gap between the business elite and the ethnic underclass means that global cities are highly unequal. Since the global business elite earn very high salaries and the ethnic underclass very low ones, it also tends to increase inequality in the broader society.

The evidence shows that the volume of international financial flows and direct investment has increased over several decades. Someone must be managing them. A significant share of a variety of specialized business services *is* concentrated in the cities that Sassen identifies as being "global"—though an increase in the concentration of those services in global cities over recent decades is less clear.

But, as we have seen, the evidence on trends in earnings inequality is much more mixed (M. Smith, 1999). There have been increases in some societies, but not in all of them. The clearest increase took place in the United States, but even there the level of inequality stopped increasing after 1993 (Card and DiNardo, 2002).

Jeffrey Reitz (1998) has compared the effects of immigration on inequality within cities in three countries—the United States, Canada, and Australia. He shows that outcomes depend heavily on the particular institutional environment within which immigration takes place. Immigrants, in fact, do relatively (but not absolutely) worse in the United States. That is, their income difference with the native population is larger in the United States than it is in Canada and Australia. This is because stronger unions and higher minimum wages prop up immigrant earnings in these latter two countries. Sassen may have overgeneralized the particular case of the United States.

Where the possible effects of immigration on the employment and earnings of the domestic working class are concerned, on balance, the evidence tends to suggest that there may be a negative effect on the least skilled, but that it is very small indeed (e.g., Borjas, Freeman, and Katz, 1997).

This raises a further interesting question: How is it that such a large flow of mainly unskilled immigrants can have such a small effect on the wages and employment probabilities of native unskilled workers? Gregory DeFreitas (1998) proposes the following explanations. The arrival of immigrants increases not only the supply of labour, but also the demand for all sorts of goods being produced by non-immigrants. The proportion of the self-employed among immigrants is also high. Many create their own jobs. In addition, and related to the sort of argument made by Sassen, immigrants often occupy jobs that native labour avoids. Many of these jobs would remain unfilled for longer, or not be created at all, were immigrants unavailable to occupy them. Overall, the evidence tends to suggest smaller employment and wage effects of immigration than some of the writing inspired by Sassen would suggest.

Note also that, as compared to earlier periods of history in immigrant-receiving countries like Canada and the United States, immigrants are a fairly small percentage of the total population. In Canada in the decade before World War I, for example, immigrants made up almost 30 per cent of the population; the equivalent current figure is about 17 per cent (Badets and Chui, 1994: 9; Marr, 1992: 19). Canada experienced a larger immigrant "shock" at the beginning of the twentieth century than at the end of it.

As for the question of the location of loyalty within global cities, the political orientations of powerful city elites may shift from the national to the global. They may, for example, become preoccupied with the elimination of obstacles to international trade and investment flows. The sequence of liberalizing policies associated with the GATT and its successor, the WTO, as well as the creation of regional trade associations and agreements such as the EU and NAFTA, would be broadly consistent with this. But protectionist forces remain strong in all countries, including the United States. Because the small size of their domestic markets requires that they engage heavily in trade, much of the pressure to restrict discretionary protectionism originates in countries such as Canada and Australia, where the leading global cities are *not* located.

With respect to the political orientation of immigrants at the lower end of the income distribution, Portes (Portes, 1999; Portes, Guarnizo, and Landolt, 1999) has made the following observations. First, immigrant groups vary in the extent to which their members remain oriented to their country of origin. Second, they are more likely to do so where the group was formed by a political convulsion, leading to the simultaneous migration of large numbers of people (for example, Cubans in the United States); where the group arrives with a culture that provides it with the skills and motivations to develop businesses with contacts to the homeland; where the group confronts fairly clear discrimination in the destination country; and where the government of the country of origin expends funds and effort to develop and maintain ties with expatriate communities.

Third, concerns with the "cultural integrity and solidarity of the receiving society" are probably exaggerated (Portes, 1999: 469). Foreign-born people make up only 17 per cent of the population in Canada, and under 10 per cent in the United States. Even if their relationship to the host society is problematic, as an aggregate, immigrants are fragmented into their different ethnicities so that it is hard for them to avoid converging with the majority (host) culture to some degree. Finally, where the cultivation of transnational commercial activities enriches members of a particular immigrant group, it decreases the likelihood of the development of a hostile, adversarial culture within subsequent generations.

Cultural Homogenization

Causes of Cultural Convergence

While some writers have worried about the fragmentation of cultures within countries as a result of immigration, others have worried that a process of standardization has been underway *across* countries. Two different mechanisms might produce this outcome. There are general processes to which many societies are exposed that might lead to the development of shared **beliefs** and behaviours. Or the United States may be a particular, overwhelming source of standardizing cultural practices. What processes might be producing standardization across countries?

First, **capitalism** itself has standardizing effects. It implies common economic and social structures—property ownership, a labour force with varying skills, banks and stockbrokers that mobilize and transfer capital, and so on (Holton, 1998; see also Bromley, 1999).

Second, countries have used force to impose cultural practices on other countries. When they decolonized, France and Britain bequeathed boundaries, education systems, civil services, and government institutions to a range of countries in Africa and the Middle East. Modern Japanese institutions bear the heavy stamp of practices imposed by the United States after World War II.

Third, increasing living standards—wherever they occur—shift popular preoccupations. Most of the population in Western countries has a sufficiently high income that it does not have to worry about the prospects of malnutrition, starvation, or homelessness. The quality of life therefore becomes more salient.

People worry about personal development, cultural enrichment, and consumption more generally. Moreover, the development and spread of **education** and **mass media** increases average political skills within the population. A better-informed populace is better able to hold political leaders accountable. Consequently, these shifts in preoccupations get translated into policies consistent with the changed

---

17.4

Global Issues
Edward Said and "Orientalism"

When forced to encounter them, people have to make sense of each other's cultures. Across regions and countries, those cultures often seem strikingly different. Making sense of culture will always require simplification. Whatever English Canadian culture might be, it is almost certainly somewhat different in Newfoundland and in Alberta. Within Newfoundland, custom and practice are likely to vary from an upper-middle-class district of St John's to, say, Corner Brook, or Fogo. Each level of aggregation requires a greater degree of simplification.

Simplification is always likely to create misleading impressions. These misleading impressions may or may not be pernicious. But they are particularly likely to be pernicious where there is a large power asymmetry between two cultures. This is the starting point for Edward Said's much-celebrated *Orientalism* (1978). There is a long history of European attempts to apprehend the Middle East—the "Orient" upon which Said focuses. That attempt has involved a combination of academic enquiry into, and casual observation of, the languages, customs, and politics of the region. The interpretations generated in this way, in turn, have shaped Western government policies.

Nineteenth-century philological researchers concluded that European languages originated in Semitic languages of the Middle East. But whereas European languages had continued to evolve, the Semitic languages remained in a state of "arrested development" (Said, 1978:

145). Said's point is that this presumption of European superiority pervades subsequent Orientalist writing. For example, he makes much of distinctly crass and vulgar comments on Arab women by the otherwise distinguished French novelist Gustave Flaubert, which rested on casual observations made during his travels in the Orient.

Said's general thrust, it should be clear, is to demonstrate that the Orientalist intellectual tradition established for Western statesmen the inferiority of the Arab world relative to the West. It provided a legitimation for forceful interventions by European powers in the Middle East. Thus, there was a "theme of Europe teaching the Orient the meaning of liberty" (Said, 1978: 172). Interventions in the Middle East using force could be justified as part and parcel of the "White man's burden," to use Rudyard Kipling's nineteenth-century expression.

While the bulk of Said's book deals with the construction of the idea of the Orient in France and Britain, in the last part of it he argues that the same condescending tradition informs post–World War II US policy in the region. The general point here is that the attempt to diffuse cultures has sometimes involved brute force—armies dispatched, monarchies toppled, and systems of education and government inspired by Western European or American ideas imposed on local populations, whether they wanted them or not.

preferences. This has happened (with lags) across rich industrial countries (Inglehart, 1977, 1990a).

Fourth, there is a large volume of more specialized communication between nations—publications, conferences, diplomatic transactions—that are concerned with a range of broader political issues. Since there is no single power centre, no world government, controlling those communications, multiple models get introduced into political debate. For John Meyer (for example, Meyer, 2000), this has allowed many non-governmental organizations (NGOs) to insert themselves into political debate and develop alternative policy models that sometimes change government policy. Examples of this are the emergence to policy salience at the international level of both the issue of human rights and environmental concerns, producing more or less binding international agreements (the Kyoto Accord), coercive political measures (NATO's bombing of the former Yugoslavia), and shared policy priorities (a commitment to create the education system required by a "knowledge society"). These are a source of social, economic, and political convergence.

Fifth, the policies of many governments in the 1980s shifted to the right, Patricia Marchak (1991) argues, in response to the concerted urging of a set of think-tanks located in several countries, but with links among them. The Cato Institute in the United States, the Kiel Institute in West Germany, the Mont Pélerin Society in Geneva, the Institute for Economic Affairs in Britain, and the Fraser Institute in Canada celebrated and advocated free market solutions to problems, or what they saw as problems. They continue to do so. This common, well-financed network, Marchak claims, generated policy convergence across countries. There was **privatization** (in Canada, for example, the CN railroad network was privatized). There was deregulation, in particular of financial markets. And by the 1990s, many countries had scaled down the magnitude of government expenditures, or were trying to.

Alternatively, increasing similarities across countries may reflect US hegemony. There is a rising volume of communication between countries using the Internet (Holton, 1998). A disproportionate share of it is in English. This increases the value of the language and the exposure to ideas and preferences originating in English-language media. But while the English language is the primary medium of communication in several societies (including Canada), the sheer volume of communication originating in the United States arguably swamps all other sources.

Table 17.1, which summarizes shares of cultural imports into Canada by country or region of origin, documents the relative dominance of the United States.

Businesses and consecutive US administrations have deliberately attempted to break down regulatory obstacles to US cultural products. Jack Valenti, for one, president of the Motion Picture Association, a US lobby group, is an indefatigable crusader for the removal of barriers to the entry of US-produced films (McCarthy, 2002). From Henry Ford to McDonald's, the success of the mass marketing of US companies has transformed the tastes and behaviour of consumers and the menu of business models from which investors can draw (Fantasia, 1995; Ritzer, 2000). Some part of whatever cultural convergence may be taking place is likely to reflect the sheer pervasiveness of the United States and its institutions.

Still, there is no consensus that cultural convergence is taking place, let alone on the origins of that convergence, whether in processes common across countries or in US cultural hegemony.

Trying to Make a Judgment

The following things can reasonably be said. Ronald Inglehart (1990a) has assembled a significant body of longitudinal attitudinal data from surveys conducted in rich countries. These data do tend to suggest some shift to a wider preoccupation with quality-of-life issues, evidence of cultural convergence in rich countries. However, there has been a growth in nationalist sentiments in a number of countries and regions—in Quebec, in the Basque region in Spain, in Scotland within the United Kingdom, and, tragically, in a virulent form in the Balkans. Nationalism can be viewed as a forcible assertion of distinctness (Anderson, 1983). It suggests exactly the opposite of cultural convergence. So, for that matter, does the flow of migrants into global cities, where those migrants retain strong connections not only within their migrant communities but also with their countries of origin. Moreover, since many of those migrants are flowing into the United States and shaping US culture, it seems implausible to argue that cultural diffusion is a one-way street.

The case for cultural convergence or for US cultural hegemony is not overwhelming. However, in a thoughtful article on this, Christoph Brumann says that it strikes him "how much the general debate relies on ad hoc impressions instead of more systematic empirical observation" (1998: 498), but that

Table 17.1 **Shares of Cultural Imports[a] into Canada, 1996–2000**

	Share (%)[b]					% Change 1996 to 2000
	1996	1997	1998	1999	2000	
North America						
United States	85.5	85.5	84.2	83.4	82.2	−3.9
Other	0.2	0.3	0.4	0.4	0.6	200.0
Total North America	85.7	85.8	84.6	83.8	82.8	−3.4
Western Europe						
United Kingdom	3.0	3.3	3.5	3.3	3.6	20.0
France	3.3	3.3	3.6	3.6	3.6	9.1
Germany	0.8	0.6	0.8	0.8	0.8	0.0
Other	2.5	1.9	2.0	2.2	1.9	−24.0
Total Western Europe	9.6	9.1	9.9	9.9	9.9	3.0
Asia	4.1	4.5	4.8	5.5	6.4	56.1
Other Regions[c]	0.6	0.7	0.7	0.8	0.9	50.0
Total	**100.0**	**100.0**	**100.0**	**100.0**	**100.0**	

[a] "Cultural industries" are defined as books and printing services, newspapers and periodicals, other written materials, music and other recordings, printed music, visual arts, architectural plans, other pictorial material, advertising material, and exposed film.

[b] Columns may not add up to 100 because of rounding.

[c] "Other regions" include European countries not listed above, Middle East, Africa, Central and South America, and the Antilles.

Source: Cindy Carter and Michel Durand, "Market Opportunities: International Trade of Culture Goods and Services," *Forum on Culture,* 12 (2000): 7.

"pending further empirical support, I still think that a slow *decrease* in the total number of distinct cultural elements or traits . . . paralleling a rampant *increase* of the possible as well as the actual *combinations* of these elements is the best working hypothesis about current world cultural developments" (499).

What Brumann means by this is that modern communications diffuse cultural traits (a process called **cultural diffusion**) between countries (hence the "*combinations*") but that the number of traits tends to decline as the diffused traits replace or modify others in the recipient countries. Popular music in many countries, for example, absorbs musical characteristics from other countries, creating new combinations that appear across those countries. But some of the original national musical forms disappear as these combinations replace them. This is well illustrated by the conservation work of several late-nineteenth- and early-twentieth-century European composers. Leoš Janáček and Zoltán Kodály in Czechoslovakia, Béla Bartók in Hungary, and Gustav Holst and Ralph Vaughan Williams in England all travelled to the countryside of their respective countries to discover and record examples of folk musical forms. They feared the loss of their national musical traditions because of the cultural dominance of Germany, Italy, and France (Schonberg, 1997). Even in France, which has resisted US cultural influences with some vigour, American cinema, cuisine, language, and management practices now exist alongside what might be regarded as "authentic" French forms (Gordon and Meunier, 2001). It is likely that, in some cases, the US forms replace, as well as exist alongside, French forms. Or it is possible that existing forms are displaced by new, Franco-American ones.

This conclusion about cultural diffusion seems plausible. But the evidence will not support a claim that goes beyond plausibility.

Conclusion

Different groups of humans have been bumping into each other throughout human history. Thirty thousand years ago, Neanderthals were driven to extinction through contact and competition with the earliest form of modern humans, the Cro-Magnons (Balter, 2001). Two thousand years ago, the Roman Empire was influencing lives from Western Europe to the Middle East (Gibbon, [1776–88] 1994). Five hundred years ago, a set of European explorers (Magellan, Columbus, Champlain, and others) pushed farther the limits of Western influence (Fernández Armesto, 1995). One hundred years ago, the European empires were attempting to regulate—and were certainly disrupting—lives in areas of conquest spanning the globe (Samson, 2001). The time in-between those events was filled with contact and disruption, often involving amounts of taken-for-granted brutality that challenge modern sensibilities. All this is to say that the facts of contact, constraint, and disruption do not in themselves make distinct what we call contemporary globalization.

What is clearly distinctive about modern relations between individuals and organizations in different countries is the speed and capacity of communication. "Hot money" flows are usually seen as the clearest expression of this (but see Smith, 2001a). More important, though, is the fact that modern communications have enhanced the degree to which control can be effectively exercised over large distances and have made it possible to run a multinational corporation, in which a single organization can co-ordinate production and marketing in different countries. This seems not to imply homogeneity of social and economic policies across countries, but there are strong reasons to believe that the multinational corporation *is* an effective vehicle for diffusing both business practices and tastes. One need not endorse Bové's actions to recognize that the McDonald's Corporation has changed consumer preferences in a wide range of countries and that in doing so it is forcing indigenous competitors in those countries to change their way of doing business.

Still, it remains clear that the idea of a global society is a chimera, an illusion. It certainly does not yet exist, and there is no prospect of it in the medium term. The range of social and economic forms remains huge, the WTO and the IMF notwithstanding. What we do confront, as in the past, is a set of international influences and options that constitute both constraints and possibilities. An intelligent reaction to the processes associated with globalization involves discussion of which responses to those constraints are most sensible and which options should be embraced.

☐ Questions for Critical Thought

1. Four components of globalization have been identified: political arrangements, economic processes, the mobility of populations, and cultural diffusion. Do they all have to move in the same directions? For example, is it possible to have common practices created by treaties and liberalized trade while populations are prevented from moving and cultures are protected against processes of diffusion from elsewhere?

2. Would Third World countries be better off without the IMF and the World Bank?

3. Is it sensible to expect investors to always prefer lower taxes? If not, for what purposes are they likely to favour taxes, and for what purposes are they likely to oppose them?

4. Sassen argues that the development of global cities changes the political context in the countries in which the cities are located. Suppose her analysis is correct. Do you judge the implications of her analysis to be good, bad, or neutral? For whom?

5. Over the post-war period, treaties and the international organizations those treaties have created (such as the WTO) have been designed to limit the capacity of governments to use law (through tariffs and quotas) and taxpayers' money (through subsidies) to protect their domestic industries from international competition. Suppose those treaties and international organizations did not exist. Who would gain and who would lose?

6. The Third World is filled with desperately poor people who work at very low wages. In a context of free trade, how is it possible for rich-country employees to keep their jobs?

7. How do the processes associated with globalization affect labour markets and social policy in rich countries?

8. Does Hollywood matter? If so, how?

☐ Recommended Readings

Gary Burtless, *Globophobia: Confronting Fears About Open Trade* (Washington, DC: Brookings Institution, 1998).

> Most economists hold favourable views of globalization. This book is one example, providing a generally non-technical and empirical examination of the subject.

Thomas J. Courchene, ed., *Room to Manoeuvre? Globalization and Policy Convergence* (Montreal: McGill-Queen's University Press, 1999).

> This is an excellent collection of essays dealing with the implications for Canada of trade agreements and technology, including suggestions by William Watson that the claims about globalization are overstated.

Mauro Guillén, "Is Globalization Civilizing, Destructive or Feeble? A Critique of Five Key Debates in the Social Science Literature," *Annual Review of Sociology*, 27 (2001): 235–60.

> This is a quite even-handed treatment of the issue by a sociologist who allows that the process may be thought of as going back "to the dawn of history."

Robert J. Holton, *Globalization and the Nation-State* (New York: St Martin's, 1998).

> This excellent, balanced treatment of globalization contains a very useful analysis of the process of cultural diffusion.

Naomi Klein, *No Logo: Taking Aim at the Brand Bullies* (New York: Picador, 1999).

> This book made Naomi Klein famous. It opposes a number of features of "corporate rule," including the effects of marketing by multinationals of culture, of globalization on the characteristics of jobs, and of commerce on cities.

John W. Meyer, John Boli, George M. Thomas, and Francisco Ramirez, "World Society and the Nation-State," *American Journal of Sociology*, 103 (1997): 144–81.

> Many sociologists are convinced that there is a world culture developing that includes a concern with human rights, democratic forms, and various sorts of entitlements. This article provides a reasonably clear exposition of this position.

Saskia Sassen, *The Global City* (Princeton, NJ: Princeton University Press, 1991).

> Sassen is the main source on the social and political consequences of international migration. She attributes large political and economic effects to it.

Adrian Wood, *North–South Trade, Employment and Inequality* (Oxford, UK: Clarendon, 1994).

> This is the classic statement on the effects of trade liberalization and competition from the Third World on unskilled wages in rich countries.

☐ Recommended Web Sites

Canadian Heritage
www.pch.gc.ca

> The mandate of the government department Canadian Heritage is to promote Canadian culture, which in practice often means finding ways of resisting US culture. For example, the site lists ways that the department subsidizes the Canadian film, magazine, and book publishing industries.

Council of Canadians
www.canadians.org

> This nationalist organization has been uniformly hostile to the two North American trade agreements. Its Web site provides a good guide to the range of preoccupations of skeptics of the benefits of a more integrated world economy. See, in particular, the discussion of water as a tradable commodity.

Culture et Communications Québec

www.mcc.gouv.qc.ca

This is the Web site of the Ministry of Culture of the Government of Quebec. While the federal government is promoting Canadian culture in general, the Quebec government is, for the most part, promoting French-language culture in particular.

Fair Trade Watch

www.fairtradewatch.org

This Web site maintained by the United Steel Workers of America provides useful, though unsympathetic, information on the WTO and other international organizations and agreements. It can also be used as a glossary for trade jargon.

International Monetary Fund (IMF)

www.imf.org

This site provides a summary description of the organization, as well as reports on its recent loans to countries and on the conditions imposed on the countries in exchange for the loans.

Motion Picture Association of America (MPAA)

www.mpaa.org

The Motion Picture Association of America is a tireless advocate of the removal of obstacles to the diffusion of that quintessential vehicle for the diffusion of American culture, the cinema. It is also concerned with the protection of copyright.

World Bank

www.worldbank.org

The World Bank is as unpopular with anti-globalization protesters as the IMF, and its Web site provides some evidence of its concern with its image.

World Trade Organization (WTO)

www.wto.org

The WTO provides both a forum for the negotiation of liberalized trade and investment and a quasi-judicial apparatus issuing judgments on complaints about infractions of trade laws. This Web site is an extremely useful source on what the WTO actually does.

18

Frank Trovato

> > >

Population and Society

© Bill Whittman

☐ Learning Objectives

In this chapter, you will:

- learn the definition of *demography* and the balancing equation for population change

- explore various demographic phenomena, the aggregate expressions of individual behaviour, conditioned by culture and social structure

- see how the "population explosion" is a relatively recent phenomenon

- study the demographic transition theory, which summarizes the long-term historical trends in birth and death rates and population growth in three stages

- compare the demographic transition histories of industrialized and developing countries

- explore the implications of Malthusian theory of population growth and available resources

- consider the Marxist perspective on overpopulation

- examine the growth of Canada's population and changing life expectancies over the last century and into the future

Introduction

At just over 6 billion, the population of the world in 2003 is growing at a rate of 1.3 per cent per annum. At this rate of growth, the population increases by about 82 million persons annually. Some scholars view figures such as these with alarm because of the potentially devastating impact continued growth might have on the long-term sustainability of the planet's environment and resources. More optimistic pronouncements in the literature suggest that population growth may actually serve as a stimulus to economic growth and, indirectly, to human well-being. As we shall see, a number of competing perspectives exist on the question of population and its relationship to resources and human welfare.

To demographers—scientists who study the **census** and vital statistics of societies—the term *population* encompasses a number of interrelated dimensions. Samuel Preston, Patrick Heuveline, and Michel Guillot (2001) define *population* as a collection of persons, alive at a specified point in time, that meets certain criteria, of which national and geographic boundaries are two of the most obvious. As a collectivity, a population persists through time even though its members are continuously changing as a result of *attrition* (losses through out-migration and death) and *accession* (gains through births and immigration). A population also entails the aggregate of persons who have ever been alive in a designated national or geographic area, and possibly those yet to be born there. Populations can be projected into the future by using mathematical procedures guided by sound assumptions concerning anticipated changes in fertility, mortality, and migration.

Demographers study the growth, distribution, and development of populations with respect to their geographic concentration and compositional characteristics, of which age, sex, and marital status are especially relevant (though other characteristics such as language, religion, and ethnicity are also important). The natural processes of fertility and mortality, plus *net migration* (the net exchange between numbers of incoming and outgoing migrants) determine change in population size for a specified area or territory over some defined time interval. This is illustrated with the **demographic components equation**:

$$P_{t2} - P_{t1} = (B_{t1,t2} - D_{t1,t2}) + (IN_{t1,t2} - OUT_{t1,t2})$$

Letting P_{t1} and P_{t2} represent the population at the beginning and the end of some specified time interval, the change over this period $(P_{t2} - P_{t1})$ is a function of the difference between births and deaths $(B_{t1,t2} - D_{t1,t2})$ plus the net exchange between the numbers of immigrants $(IN_{t1,t2})$ and emigrants $(OUT_{t1,t2})$ during the interval. The component $(B_{t1,t2} - D_{t1,t2})$ represents natural increase because it measures the difference between the two natural processes of births and deaths; net migration is measured by the term $(IN_{t1,t2} - OUT_{t1,t2})$.

Populations also change as a result of the reclassification of people across distinct **statuses**. Examples of reclassification include a change in marital status from single to married or from married to divorced. The distribution of the population in accordance with characteristics such as age and sex is also subject to change as a function of changes in fertility, mortality, and migration.

Demographic Change and Social Change

Aggregate demographic phenomena are the collective expression of individual behaviour conditioned by cultural **norms** and **social structure** (Davis and van den Oever, 1982). Often, novel behaviours develop into widespread demographic phenomena. One such behaviour concerns the growing preference among recent generations of youth to form cohabiting unions rather than marriages. In Canada during the early part of the 1970s, only about 17 per cent of couples entering their first union were common-law relationships. By the early 1980s, the corresponding figure had risen to 40.5 per cent. During the later part of the 1980s, over half of all first-union couples were common-law (Wu, 2000: 51). Coinciding with the generalized acceptance of cohabitation, there has been a precipitous decline in the total marriage rate of single persons, and the median age at marriage has been going up.

Other examples may be used to illustrate the interconnectedness of demographic factors with societal change. One could, for instance, discuss the evolution of Canadian society into a multicultural and multiracial nation as a function of shifts in the regional origins of immigrants, from the once dominant European sending areas to the current predominance of Asia, Africa, and South America as sending regions.

We could also examine how the majority of today's population is alive because of the mortality improvements that took place at the turn of the twentieth century in the industrialized world. As a result of

IN THE FIRST PERSON

When I first entered university, my intention was to eventually study architecture. However, during my first year, I became interested in population studies, a subfield of sociology. I went on to do graduate work in this field and obtained the PhD in 1983. This area of sociology has held my interest for two important reasons: first, it is highly applied and therefore of practical use in a vast array of areas, from urban planning to forecasting future markets, public policy analysis, and health care planning for governments. Second, demography is immensely interesting because of its interdisciplinary nature and the intellectual challenges it offers.

–FRANK TROVATO

many developments in public health, medicine, and standards of living in the early twentieth century, newborns at that time enjoyed unprecedented gains in survival probabilities over earlier generations in history. Under preceding historical conditions, large proportions of infants and children succumbed to the ravages of infectious and parasitic diseases. Improved socio-economic conditions and public health programs helped babies and young children overcome the dangerous stages of infancy and early childhood. More infants and children would live to adulthood to eventually have their own children, who would later bear progeny of their own under even more favourable health conditions. Kevin White and Samuel Preston (1996) show that approximately half of the population alive today in the United States owe their existence to twentieth-century mortality improvements. In other words, half of the current population would never have been born had it not been for the significant progress in health and disease prevention that took place around the turn of the twentieth century.

David Herlihy (1997) gives another interesting account of how demography and social structural change are related. He describes how mortality conditions in European history helped provoke lasting social-structural and cultural transformations in Western society. Among other things, he attributes to the black death (the bubonic plague) that struck Europe in 1348 and several times into the fifteenth century, indirect responsibility for the development of the national university system in Europe and for the rise of nationalism. The population of Europe may have been reduced by two-thirds between 1320 and 1420 as a result of this highly infectious disease.

Under the spectre of early death, many wealthy people bequeathed their fortunes to institutions such as the church and the educational system. This helped the creation of new national universities throughout Europe. As many of the teachers in the newly created universities were at first unfamiliar with Latin (the language of higher learning at that time), they used the local languages in their teaching. This, according to Herlihy, stimulated the development of strong nationalistic sentiments in the population and the eventual rise of nationalism in Europe.

World Population

The current population of the world and its projected future must be understood in the broader context of human history. Ansley Coale (1974) divides population history into two broad segments of time: the first, from the beginning of humanity to around 1750 CE, was a very long era of slow population growth; the second, relatively brief in broad historical terms, is one of explosive gains in human numbers. According to Coale (1974: 17), the estimated average annual growth rate between 8000 BCE and 1 CE was only 0.036 per year. Between 1 CE and 1750, the average rate of growth rose to 0.056 per cent, and from 1750 to 1800 it went up to 0.44 per cent. In modern times, the trajectory of population growth has followed an exponential pattern (1, 2, 4, 8, 16, . . .): since the early nineteenth century, each successive billion of world population has arrived in considerably less time than the previous one. It took humanity until about 1750 CE to reach a population size of approximately 800 million. The first billion of population occurred in

1804, the second 123 years later in 1927. Thirty-four years beyond that point, the world witnessed its third billion. The 4 billion mark was reached in 1974, only 14 years later, and 13 years passed before the earth welcomed its 5-billionth person in 1987 (Birg, 1995: 85; United Nations Population Division, 1999: 8). In 1999, the globe's population turned 6 billion. In 2003, the population of the world was 6.3 billion (Population Reference Bureau, 2003). (See also Figure 18.1.)

Figure 18.1 **The World Population Explosion**

Most of the world's population increase has taken place in the past two centuries. It took hundreds of thousands of years for the human race to reach its 1960 total of about 3 billion people. But in the 40 years that followed, it grew by another 3 billion people, to its present total of over 6 billion.

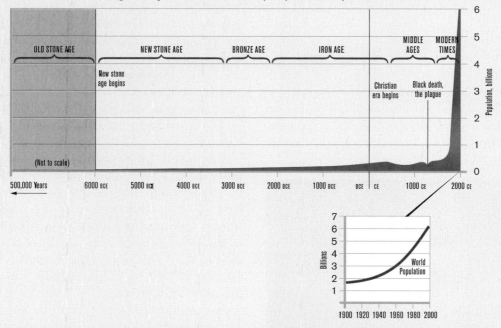

SOURCE: Adapted from Glenn Trewartha, *A Geography of Population: World Patterns* (New York: Wiley, 1969), 29.

World Population Growth Through Broad Historical Periods and Projections

Historical Period/Interval	Estimated population at the end of period	Estimated average annual growth rate (%) at the end of each period, or between periods	Years to add 1 billion
1 million BC–8000 BC	8 million	0.010[a]	
8000 BC–AD 1	300 million	0.036[a]	
AD1–AD 1750	800 million	0.056[a]	
1804	1 billion	0.400[a]	all of humanity to 1804
1927	2 billion	0.540[a]	123
1950	2.5 billion	0.800[a]	–
1960	3 billion	1.7–2.0[b]	33
1974	4 billion	2.0–1.8[b]	14
1987	5 billion	1.8–1.6[b]	13
1999	6 billion	1.6–1.4[b]	12
2013 (projected)	7 billion	1.100[c]	14
2022 (projected)	8 billion	0.900[c]	15
2042 (projected)	9 billion	0.500[c]	26

[a]Estimated average population or average rate of growth at the end of the period.
[b]Range of growth rates between specified periods.
[c]Estimated.
Note: for the years 2013, 2028, and 2054, the projected populations are based on the UN 2000 medium variant revision of world population prospects (United Nations, 2001).
SOURCES: Adapted from Coale (1974); Trewartha (1969); Bongaarts and Bulatao (2000); Population Reference Bureau (World Population Data Sheets, various years).

World population growth rates peaked at just over 2.0 per cent during the 1960s and early 1970s. In recent decades the growth rate has been declining to its present level of 1.3 per cent (Population Reference Bureau, 2003). This trend is expected to proceed into the foreseeable future, such that by the year 2050, the growth rate of the world might be as low as 0.5 per cent per year—a rate of growth not seen since the 1920s (Bongaarts and Bulatao, 2000: 20; Eberstad, 1997; Lutz, 1994). This remarkable reduction will come about as a result of anticipated declines in fertility and mortality over the next half century. The latest medium variant projection of the United Nations (a projection that assumes change in fertility and mortality thought to be most likely) assumes that the total fertility rate at the world level will decline from 2.83 children per woman in 1995–2000 to about 2.02 children per woman in 2045–50. The change in **life expectancy at birth** during this same period is expected to be from 65 years in 1995–2000 to 74 years in 2045–50 (United Nations, 2003: 1). This "central" scenario projection suggests a population in 2050 of just under 9 billion (see Table 18.1).

During this century, population growth will occur unevenly across the major regions of the world. Most of the projected growth will take place in the **developing countries**, especially in the poorest nations, where rates of natural increase are currently in the range of between 1.6 and 2.5 per cent annually. Though fertility has been declining in many developing countries, natural increase remains high because of the faster pace of the mortality declines. Africa's share of the world's population will increase rapidly, regardless of its devastating experience with the HIV/AIDS epidemic (Eberstadt, 1997). The growth rate for the **developed countries** is only 0.1 per cent per year; in nations such as Germany, Italy, and Japan, annual rates of natural increase have been close to zero or even slightly negative (Population Reference Bureau, 2002).

Some of the anticipated population growth for the world over the next 50 years is unavoidable. Even if current fertility rates worldwide were to decline suddenly to the replacement level of 2.1 children per woman, substantial population growth would occur, at least until about the third decade of this century (Eberstadt, 1997). This unavoidable growth is due to the powerful effects of **population momentum** (Bongaarts and Bulatao, 2000; Lutz, 1994). That is, because of past high fertility and mortality declines, the proportion of the world's population in the reproductive ages (roughly ages 15–49) has been growing and is expected to continue to grow over the next several decades. Even with their much reduced fertility rates, today's large parental cohorts will be bringing more babies into the world than ever before. Indeed, even the "low variant" projection by the United Nations (2003), which assumes large declines in fertility, shows a population of about 7.4 billion in 2050 (see Table 18.1). But under this low variant, the population of the world would peak in around 2030, then start a course of indefinite decline. That is, the 7.409 billion number in 2050 under the "low variant" scenario would be part of a downward trend in world population (Eberstadt, 1977). Of course, we must recognize that predicting population growth is an inexact science; the projections depend largely on changes in fertility, which can be a rather unpredictable **variable**. Even small changes in fertility can have dramatic effects on the results.

Most industrialized nations have been experiencing a baby dearth in recent years. In Italy, the pope has urged the population to have more children in order to solve the "birth rate problem." In Spain, women are being asked to reproduce for the sake of the nation. (Vince Streano/CORBIS/Magmaphoto.com)

Table 18.1 **Estimated and Projected Population (Millions) of the World, Major Development Groups and Major Areas, 1950, 2000, and 2050, According to Fertility Variants[a]**

	Estimated population		Population in 2050			
	1950	2000	Low fertility	Medium fertility	High fertility	Constant fertility
World[b]	**2,519**	**6,071**	**7,409**	**8,919**	**10,633**	**12,754**
More developed regions	813 (32.3%)	1,194 (19.7%)	1,084 (14.6%)	1,220 (13.7%)	1370 (12.9%)	1,185 (9.3%)
Less developed regions	1,706 (67.7%)	4,877 (80.3%)	6,325 (85.4%)	7,699 (86.3%)	9,263 (87.1%)	11,568 (90.7%)
Least developed countries	200	668	1,417	1,675	1,960	3,019
Other less developed countries	1,505	4,209	4,908	6,025	7,303	8,549
Africa	221 (8.8%)	796 (13.1%)	1,516 (20.5%)	1,803 (20.3%)	2,122 (20.0%)	3,279 (25.7%)
Asia	1,398 (55.5%)	3,680 (60.6%)	4,274 (57.7%)	5,222 (58.5%)	6,318 (59.4%)	7,333 (57.5%)
Europe	547 (21.7%)	728 (12.0%)	565 (7.6%)	632 (7.1%)	705 (6.6%)	597 (4.7%)
Latin America/Caribbean	167 (6.6%)	520 (8.6%)	623 (8.4%)	768 (8.6%)	924 (8.7%)	1,032 (8.1%)
North America	172 (6.8%)	316 (5.2%)	391 (5.3%)	448 (5.0%)	512 (4.8%)	453 (3.6%)
Oceania	13 (0.5%)	31 (0.5%)	40 (0.5%)	46 (0.5%)	52 (0.5%)	58 (0.5%)

[a] The United Nations has incorporated varying fertility and mortality assumptions for the world, its major regions, and development groups. Given the varying demographic conditions prevailing across the regions, assumptions regarding expected changes in fertility and mortality over the projection period would differ accordingly. Totals may appear inaccurate because of rounding.

[b] The sum of least developed and other less developed countries adds up to the total population for the less developed countries. The sum of the six regions adds up to the overall world total population.

SOURCE: United Nations, *World Population Prospects: The 2002 Revision* (New York: UN Department of Economic and Social Affairs Population Division, 2003), 18–21.

Over the course of this century, all populations in the world will become older, the result of decades of fertility declines worldwide. Countries with more rapid and sustained fertility reductions will experience greater degrees of demographic aging. For example, Italy, with one of the lowest fertility rates in the world, will see its potential support ratio—the number of persons of working age (15–64) per older person—drop by the year 2050 to less than 2, from its current ratio of about 4. For the Republic of Korea—a society that has also been experiencing rapid fertility declines—the fall in the magnitude of its potential support ratio will be even more dramatic. The United Nations has estimated that this country's potential support ratio of 12.62 in 1995 will likely reduce to between 2 and 3 by 2050 (United Nations, 2000: 7).

In 2050, it is anticipated that the world will see 16 per cent of its population being over the age of 65. (In 2000, the percentage was close to 7.) Seniors will account for almost 26 per cent of the population in the industrial countries, while in the developing regions as a whole, this proportion will rise to 15 per cent (Bongaarts and Bulatao, 2000: 23; United Nations, 2002: 48).

Age Compositions of Developed and Developing Countries

The different demographic experiences of the developed and developing countries are reflected in their

Owing to decades of very low fertility, the industrialized countries are experiencing significant growth in their senior citizen populations. This trend is expected to intensify during this century. (© David Turnley/CORBIS/Magmaphoto.com)

respective **age compositions**. Fertility plays a greater role than mortality in determining the age composition of a population (Coale, 1964; Coale and Hoover, 1958; Frejka, 1973; Keyfitz, 1968). The higher a population's fertility, the larger the percentage of the population in the younger ages. The developing countries have relatively young populations. Low-fertility societies, on the other hand, will have proportionately fewer people in the younger ages and relatively more in the older ages (see Figure 18.2).

The age distribution of the developed countries manifests a slow-growing population, with relatively few people below age 15. Sustained low fertility rates in these countries are responsible for this. On the other hand, the age distribution of the developing countries characterizes a rapidly growing population, approximating the shape of a pyramid: a wide base and a narrow top. In comparison to the developed countries, a large proportion of their population is under the age of 15, and their distribution narrows considerably with increasing age.

Owing to decades of high fertility and rapid population growth, these societies will soon witness huge waves of young people seeking productive work

Figure 18.2 **Comparison of Age Structures: Population by Age, Sex, and Development**

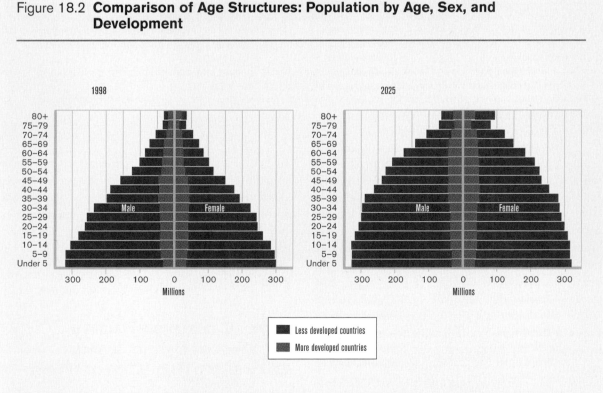

SOURCE: US Bureau of the census, International Data Base.

18.1

Open for Discussion
Sex Ratio Imbalances and the Marriage Market

A population's age distribution mirrors its experience with respect to fertility, mortality, and migration. The **sex ratio** measures the balance of males and females in a population (males/females = 100). A sex ratio of 100 indicates an equal number of males and females, whereas a ratio below 100 denotes that the number of women exceeds the number of men. Values in excess of 100 mean there are more men than there are women.

In most populations, the overall sex ratio is usually just below 100. This is due to the interplay of three demographic factors: (1) the sex ratio at birth favors males, as for every 100 baby girls, there are usually 105 baby boys; (2) in most populations, the death rates for males are greater than the death rates for females; (3) in some populations, males have greater rates of emigration than do females. Distortions in the overall sex ratio can occur from any or all of these conditions. Severe distortions in these factors can cause the sex ratio to be substantially above or below 100. For instance, in a balanced population, a sudden influx of male workers might raise the sex ratio. On the other hand, a large-scale emigration of males could have the opposite effect.

Sex ratio imbalances can also occur in specific age categories. In some situations, the marriage market (that is, the balance of eligible young men to eligible young women) is affected as a result of either a shortage or a surplus of males or females in the prime marriageable ages. This type of phenomenon is not uncommon. For example, it has been reported recently that in China there is a serious deficit of young women for the number of eligible young men to marry—the number of young men is much greater than that of potential brides (Tuljapurkar, Li, and Feldman, 1995).

According to demographers, this problem stems from the Chinese government's implementation of the one-child policy, initiated in the late 1970s. The Chinese have a traditional preference for sons. Given the government's one-child directive, over the past several decades many couples, it is suspected, have been resorting to sex-selective abortion to ensure having a sole male child (Tuljapurkar, Li, and Feldman, 1995). As explained in the following article, over the course of two or more decades, this situation has helped produce in China a highly distorted marriage market: too few young women for marriage to eligible young men.

With Women So Scarce, What Can Men Do?
Years of female infanticide help shatter the taboo on incestuous marriages

Liu Dehai and Hai Hongmei's matrimonial bed is laid with a thick quilt embroidered with the characters for "double happiness," words meant to augur good fortune for just-married Chinese couples. This should be a room of joy and hope, but Liu's mother doesn't want anyone investigating too closely. "Please," she says, "do not speak of this room." The marriage of Liu and Hai is a subject of shame, for they are not just husband and wife; they are also first cousins.

Their marriage, and others of cousins and even siblings, is the latest consequence of China's profound shortage of females. For two decades, the government has tried to control population by limiting most rural families to one child, two if the first is a girl. Because boys are prized in rural areas—they can work the land and give more support to their families—this has led many couples to abort female fetuses, kill newborn daughters or neglect them to death. The result: China, according to the World Health Organization, is short 50 million females. The first wave of children born under the policy is reaching marriageable age, and there are far too few brides to go around. The most desperate bachelors have taken to marrying relatives. In a few places, the practice has become so common, the communities are referred to as "incest villages."

continued

Liu Dehai never imagined he would marry his shy first cousin Hai. Though intramarriage was common in imperial days, it is taboo in modern China. But at age 20, with his friends already paired off, Liu found himself the odd man out. His parents, farmers in the village of Nanliang in Shaanxi province, could not raise the $2,000 required to attract a woman to Nanliang to marry their son. With so many men to choose from, women are loath to settle in hardscrabble villages like Nanliang. Desperate, Liu's mother contacted her sister and requested a favor: Could she ask Hai to be Liu's bride? Young women like Hai are not apt to defy their parents. And so Liu and Hai were wed.

While a recent U.S. study concluded that the odds of first cousins producing children with birth defects may have been overstated, the risk is still almost double that for unrelated couples. Denizens of the incest villages see ample evidence of this. Near the city of Yan'an, a brother and sister squat in the mud-brick slums, signing a secret language to each other: both Cao Shuai and Cao Jing were born deaf, to parents who are first cousins. Early this year in Yan'an county, a severely retarded newborn girl was found abandoned beside a road. Her parents, it turned out, were brother and sister.

The female shortage in China is only worsening. In 2000, 900,000 fewer female births were recorded than should have been, based on male births. In 1990 the shortfall was 500,000. Some of that owes to parents giving up daughters for adoption without registering their birth. But population experts at the Chinese Academy of Social Sciences in Beijing estimate that up to one-third of the girls are missing because of gender-based abortions. Rural Chinese women also tend to breast-feed girls for shorter periods, providing less hope for survival. Chinese demographers estimate that in some rural areas, 80 per cent of children ages 5 to 10 are boys.

In Shaanxi's Qiaogou village, children play under a dusty apple tree. The noise is the raucous glee of boys being boys. There is only one girl among them. Asked what he thinks his future will hold, Xiaochun, 7, replies, "I'll get married and be a good farmer, of course." Where will he get a wife? "I think in other villages far away, there are many more girls," Xiaochun says. "I will get my wife from there." Across China, millions of boys are hoping the same thing, but only a few will ever meet the woman of their dreams.

———

SOURCE: Hannah Beech/Nanliang, "With Women So Scarce, What Can Men Do?" *Time*, 1 July 2002, 8. ©TIME Inc. Reprinted by permission.

(Cleland, 1996). This demographic condition may present itself as a once-in-a-lifetime opportunity for the developing countries. Assuming that sufficient work is made available, a youthful labour force would help boost productivity, economic growth, and prosperity. Failure to seize this opportunity may provoke extreme social unrest and political instability in these countries. Widening regional inequalities in wealth and resources would help promote illegal and clandestine migrations, possibly exacerbating existing political tensions between nations (Clarke, 1996; Cleland, 1996; Homer-Dixon, Boutwell, and Rathjens, 1993; McCarthy, 2001; Meadows, Meadows, and Randers, 1992; Peterson, 1999; Pimentel and Pimentel, 1999).

Theories of Population Change

Two influential themes can be identified in the literature regarding the interrelationship of population and resources. The first proposes that curbing population growth is essential for maintaining a healthy balance between human numbers, resources, and the sustainability of the environment; the second characterizes population as a minor or inconsequential factor in such matters. Thomas Malthus and Karl Marx (with Friedrich Engels) are the principal thinkers representing these opposing views. Before examining their ideas, let us review another influential theory of population dynamics: the demographic transition theory.

18.2

Global Issues
Youth in the International Labour Market

As the world's population surges past the six-billion mark . . . 700 million young people will enter the labour force in developing countries—more than the entire work force of the developed world in 1990—the United Nations says.

And as the largest-ever group of young people enters its child-bearing and working years, the number of people over the age of 65 continues to swell as health and longevity improve, according to the UN's annual State of the World Population report. . . .

If jobs can be found or created for the global bulge of one billion people between the ages of 15 and 24—the result of past high fertility—there is a chance to increase human capital so that the dependent young and elderly age groups can be better cared for, the report said.

But without investment in jobs for the young, better education for children, especially girls, and better health care for both young and old, social unrest and instability are inevitable.

"The rapid growth of young and old 'new generations' is challenging societies' ability to provide education and health care for the young, and social, medical and financial support for the elderly," the report says. . . .

Some developing nations, particularly in Southern Asia and Northern Africa, could reap an economic windfall in the next couple of decades as the bulge in 15- to 24-year-olds swells the work force in comparison to dependent age groups, the report says.

To avoid squandering this one-time "demographic bonus," these countries will have to ensure their young people can find jobs and don't start families too soon.

Stan Bernstein, chief author of the UN report and a research adviser at the UN Population Fund, said developing countries need both private and public, domestic and international investment in their basic social services to ensure they don't miss this "window of opportunity."

It is in the interest of wealthier nations and private companies to make this investment, Mr

Global Population Growth by Age Group

Although fertility rates have declined, better medical care means infant mortality has fallen and people are living longer. The result—the population continues to grow.

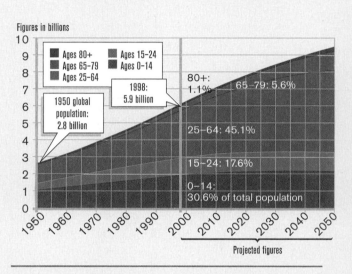

SOURCE: : United Nations, *State of the World Population Report*.

Bernstein said in a phone interview from New York yesterday.

"These countries, if given the opportunity to accelerate their development now, are going to be significant economic, trade and social partners in the future. It's a win-win situation."

However, with most developed nations steadily reducing the amount of foreign aid they provide, and cutting their own social-service budgets, other sources of investment are needed. . . .

At the other end of the age spectrum, a rapidly growing population over the age of 60—578 million this year—is seeing more years of healthy life, is able to work longer and is moving toward greater independence from grown children. . . .

SOURCE: From Jane Gadd, "Record Numbers of Youth Will Seek Work: UN," *The Globe and Mail*, 2 Sept. 1998. Peprinted with permission from the Globe and Mail.

Demographic Transition Theory

The **demographic transition** theory was first developed on the basis of the experience of Western European countries with respect to their historical pattern of change in birth and death rates in the context of socio-economic modernization. In general terms, the theory can also describe the situation of the developing countries, though the structural conditions underlying changes in vital rates are recognized as being substantially different from the European case (Kirk, 1996; Teitelbaum, 1975). The demographic transition of Western societies entailed three successive stages: (1) a pre-transitional period of high birth and death rates with very low population growth; (2) a transitional phase of high fertility, declining death rates, and explosive growth; (3) a final stage of low mortality and fertility and low natural increase. (The second stage may be divided into early and late Stage 2.) By the early 1940s, most European societies had completed their demographic transitions. (See Figure 18.3.)

Crude birth and death rates in the ancient world probably fluctuated between 35 and 45 per 1,000 population (Coale, 1974: 18). With gradual improvements in agriculture and better standards of living, the death rate declined, though fertility remained high. During the second stage, the excess of births over deaths was responsible for the modern rise of population—the so-called population explosion (McKeown, 1976). With gradual modernization and socio-economic development, during the middle and later parts of the nineteenth century, birth rates in Europe began to fall, first in France and then in other countries. In the early 1930s, Western nations had attained their lowest birth rates up to that point in their histories; the death rate was also quite low by historical standards, and a new demographic equilibrium had been reached. In pre-transition times, the low growth rates were the result of humans' lack of control over nature and acceptance of fate; the end of the demographic transition came from incremental successes over nature—agricultural development, industrialization, **urbanization**, economic growth, and modern science and medicine.

Figure 18.3 The Classical Demographic Transition Model and Corresponding Conceptual Types of Society

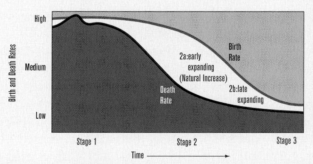

Stage	Fertility	Mortality	Population Growth	Economy
1. Pre-industrial	High, fluctuating	High, fluctuating (low life expectancy)	Static to very low	Primitive or agrarian
2. Early industrial	High	Falling	High, explosive	Mixed
3. Modern urban industrial	Controlled: low to moderate to sub-replacement levels	Low (high life expectancy)	Low to moderate to negative	Urban industrial to post-industrial

SOURCE: Adapted from Glenn Trewartha, *A Geography of Population: World Patterns* (New York: Wiley, 1969), 45, 47.

Modifications to Demographic Transition Theory

Coale (1969, 1973) undertook an extensive investigation to re-examine the causes of the European fertility transition. Theorists had proposed that in pre-transitional societies, conscious use of family limitation was absent, that economic development and urbanization preceded the onset of fertility declines, and that a drop in mortality always occurred prior to any long-term drop in the birth rate (Davis, 1945; Notestein, 1945; Thompson, 1929, 1944). But some of the empirical evidence uncovered by Coale failed to support some of these propositions. For instance, one important discovery was that economic development is not always a precondition for a society to experience the onset of sustained declines in fertility (though economic development would help speed up the transition). Coale concluded that sustained fertility declines in a society would take place when three preconditions were met: (1) fertility decisions by couples must be within the calculus of conscious choice; that is, cultural and religious norms do not forbid couples to practise family planning, nor do they promote large families; (2) reduced fertility must be viewed by couples as economically advantageous; and (3) effective methods of fertility control must be known and available to couples (Coale, 1969, 1973; Coale and Watkins, 1986).

Having long completed their mortality and fertility transitions, the industrialized countries have gained widespread economic success; their populations enjoy a great deal of social and economic security and well-being. Couples in these societies see little need to have large families. In many developing countries, however, entrenched cultural norms and traditions favour high fertility; parents tend to view children as a source of security in an insecure environment (Cain, 1983; Caldwell, 1976). Nevertheless, over recent decades much progress has been made in raising the prevalence levels of contraceptive practices. Organized family planning programs have played a major role in this trend (Caldwell, Phillips, and Barkat-e-Khuda, 2002). New evidence suggests a growing number of developing nations are now approaching the end of their demographic transitions, and others in the poorer regions of the world (for example, sub-Saharan Africa) have recently begun their fertility transitions (Bulatao, 1998; Bulatao and Casterline, 2001).

Demographic Transitions of Industrialized and Developing Countries

Figure 18.4 displays in schematic form the demographic transitions of the West and of the contemporary developing countries, the latter subdivided into "transitional" and "delayed transition" societies.

Figure 18.4 Schematic Representation of Demographic Transition: Western, Delayed, and Transitional Models

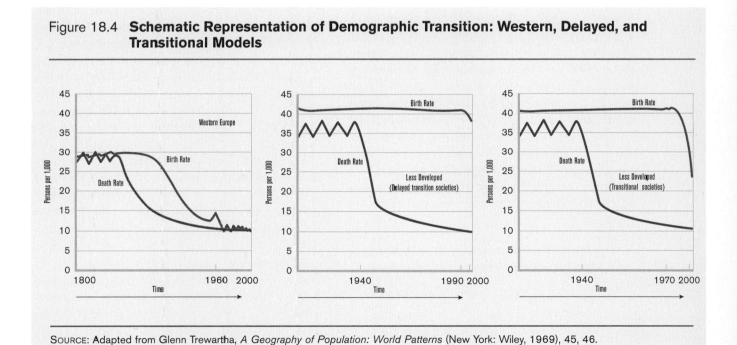

SOURCE: Adapted from Glenn Trewartha, *A Geography of Population: World Patterns* (New York: Wiley, 1969), 45, 46.

Examples of transitional populations are India, Turkey, China, Indonesia, Taiwan, Thailand, Mexico, and countries in Latin America and the Caribbean. Delayed transition societies are found in sub-Saharan Africa, southern Africa, and southwest Asia (for example, Afghanistan, Pakistan, and Bangladesh). In both these cases, mortality reductions have been fairly rapid. In the European historical context, health improvements occurred more gradually in response to incremental socio-economic advancements and economic modernization. In the developing countries, declining death rates have been achieved through family planning, public health programs, and other medical interventions offered by the industrialized countries (Preston, 1986b).

Malthusian Theory

Thomas Malthus (1766–1883) was an ordained Anglican minister and professor of political economy in England. His most famous work, *An Essay on the Principle of Population*, was published in 1798. This important treatise has had a lasting influence on subsequent theorizing about population matters. At the time that Malthus wrote his *Essay*, a number of scholars had already contributed serious thoughts on the question of population and resources. For instance, the Enlightenment theorists Jean-Jacques Rousseau, Marie-Jean-Antoine-Nicolas de Caritat marquis de Condorcet, and William Godwin viewed population growth as a positive development (Overbeek, 1974). A growing population would help stimulate economic growth, and with further advances in civilization, there would be a natural tendency for subsistence to increase faster than population. Malthus reacted strongly to such optimistic views; he was less optimistic about mankind's capacity to maintain a sustainable balance between available resources and population growth. He set out to warn humanity about the dangers of unchecked population growth.

Citing directly from the work of Malthus, Alan Macfarlane identifies three fundamental themes in the *Essay*:

The first is that human beings are very strongly motivated by a desire for sexual intercourse:

"The passion between the sexes has appeared in every age to be so nearly the same, that it may always be considered, in algebraic language, as a given quantity.

"All else being equal, men and women will mate as soon as possible after puberty. If such mating is only permitted within marriage,

"Such is the disposition to marry, particularly in very young people, that, if the difficulties of providing for a family were entirely removed, very few would remain single at twenty-two . . . . "

The second fact is the high fertility of humans. If this high fertility is combined with a reasonable rate of mortality, such early and frequent mating will lead to rapid population growth. . . . The third fact is that economic resources, and in particular food production, cannot keep pace with this population growth within a basically agrarian economy largely dependent on human labour. This is due to the law of diminishing marginal returns. While there may be periods when rates of growth in agriculture rise to three or four per cent *per annum*, which is equivalent to a doubling of food in a generation, such periods cannot be sustained for more than a few decades. (Macfarlane, 1997: 12–13)

Malthus assumed that there is an inherent tendency in humans to increase in numbers beyond the means of subsistence available to them. Mankind, he argued, lives at the brink of subsistence. Population, left unchecked, tends to double once every generation; it thus follows a geometric, or exponential, progression (1, 2, 4, 8, 16, 32, . . .). The food supply, on the other hand, tends to grow arithmetically (1, 2, 4, 6, 8, 10, . . .). Under this scenario, in the long term, population would eventually outstrip food and other essential resources.

As a solution to this problem, Malthus proposed that population could be kept in equilibrium through the activation of two different mechanisms. The first is what he called *positive checks* (also referred to as *vice and misery*). These are conditions that raise the death rate and thus serve to reduce population—famine, pestilence, war, and disease. The second, and more desirable alternative, would be widespread exercise of *preventive checks* (also referred to as *moral restraint*) to curb population growth—the imposition of the human will to deliberately curtail reproduction through celibacy, postponed marriage, and sexual abstinence. By postponing marriage until people were in an adequate position to maintain a family, individuals and society would both gain economically:

by working longer before marriage, people would save more of their incomes, thus helping to reduce poverty and raise the overall level of well-being. Malthus considered abortion and contraception to be immoral.

Criticism of Malthusian Theory

Malthusian theory has provoked strong reactions. One criticism is that Malthus failed to fully appreciate the resilience of humanity when faced with difficult problems. Throughout history, humanity has shown a remarkable ability to solve many of its predicaments. Writers point out that progress in science, technology, and socio-economic well-being has evolved in tandem with explosive population growth and that the agricultural and industrial revolutions arose in response to problems and demands arising from a rapidly growing population (Boserup, 1965, 1981; Fogel and Costa, 1997; Simon, 1995, 1996).

Malthus suggested that population and food supply must be in balance. But exactly what constitutes an "optimum" population size is difficult, if not impossible to specify. Perceptions of the "optimal," in this sense, are highly dependent on available resources to a society, as well as on consumption patterns and the degree of economic activity and production. Consumption and production are closely tied to a society's cultural standards for material comfort and demand for consumer products. As described by Paul Ehrlich and J.P. Holdren (1971), the potential impact of population on the environment is multiplicative. That is, the effect of the population depends partly on its size and growth, but also on a society's level of affluence and technological complexity. In a slow-growing population with strong material expectations, the potential for environmental and resource depletion may be greater than in a fast-growing population with lower levels of material aspirations and technological sophistication. The more developed the society, the higher the expected standard for "basic" necessities. As material aspirations rise, so do levels of consumption and expenditures by the public. Increased consumer demand for material goods spurs economic activity; greater levels of economic activity heighten the risk of environmental damage because of increased pollution and resource depletion (Ehrlich and Ehrlich, 1970, 1990).

It has been proposed that industrial societies may be facing an inversion of the Malthusian scenario (Woolmington, 1985). In these societies, overpopulation is no longer the threat Malthus advocated.

Rather, the seeds of systemic instability in these societies may lie more in their reliance on endless economic growth and consumption. Rather than population pressing on resources, as was proposed by Malthus, the economy now presses the population to consume—economic growth and stability depend on this. However, in the long term, the spiral of consumption and production may not be sustainable in slow-growing or declining populations (Woolmington, 1985).

Finally, Malthus's insistence on the unacceptability of birth control is inconsistent with his advocacy of curbing rapid population growth. The reality is that people throughout the centuries have always resorted to some means of birth control at one time or another. As stated by Eric Ross,

> Malthus recognized that a desire for children could be moderated by human reason and ingenuity, but failed to advocate any particular method, including non-coital sex, *coitus interruptus*, abortion and contraception, and actually branded them as "vice" or "improper acts." Nevertheless, one of these so-called vices—*coitus interruptus*, or "withdrawal" . . . continued to be one of the most popular and effective forms of contraception well into the second half of the twentieth century . . . largely because it was safe, free and remarkably effective. (1998: 3)

The Marxist Perspective on Population

Marxist scholars have refuted the Malthusian principles. They contend that population is a secondary issue to the pernicious problems of widespread economic inequality and poverty. Large families arise from poverty. With Friedrich Engels, Marx advocated the elimination of hunger, poverty, and human suffering through the radical restructuring of society to ensure the equitable distribution of wealth and resources (Marx and Engels, [1845–6] 1970). As for poor developing nations, their population predicament can be traced to their relative economic deprivation. In response to Malthus's principle that population grows geometrically, it also the case that scientific and technological solutions tend to progress geometrically. Scientific and technological progress could be used to relieve human suffering.

The Marxist perspective is grounded in the idea that socio-economic inequality is a root cause of human problems and suffering. However, in matters

Is the poverty shown in this photograph a result of overpopulation or of unequal access to resources and opportunities? This is a shantytown just outside of the commercial district in Buenos Aires, Argentina. (Mariana Bazo/Reuters)

of population control, Marxist skepticism toward the role of population in human problems is now largely ignored (Petersen, 1989). China—a communist state—has outwardly rejected the Marxist doctrine of population. Chinese officials have recognized that slowing population growth through concerted family planning policies is, in the long term, essential to societal well-being (Bulatao, 1998; Caldwell, Phillips, and Barkat-e-Khuda, 2002; Haberland and Measham, 2002). With few exceptions, developing countries now embrace population policies that are consistent with neo-Malthusian principles. Family planning and reproductive health programs are recognized by governments as critical means in their quest to curb population growth.

Contemporary Perspectives on Population

Neo-Malthusian scholars—the contemporary followers of Malthus—believe that the world's population has been growing too fast and that the planet is already close to reaching critical ecological limits. Unlike Malthus, however, neo-Malthusians view contraception and family planning as a key element in population control (Ehrlich and Ehrlich, 1990). The neo-Malthusian perspective inherently implies that the world would be a better and safer place if it contained fewer people. An expanding population in conjunction with excessive consumerism and economic production will, in the long term, lead to the depletion of essential resources and to ecological breakdown.

Neo-Marxist scholars place less emphasis on the centrality of population as a source of human predicaments. Focusing on population as the root cause of human suffering obscures the reality that the world is divided into wealthy and relatively poor regions and that this divide is widening rather than narrowing. Neo-Marxists alert us to the extreme consumerism of wealthy regions and their overwhelming economic and political influence over less advantaged nations. It is also argued that the **globalization** of capital—seen by many other observers as the key to emulating the "success story" of the West—often exacerbates, rather than diminishes, socio-economic disparities within and across societies. Investigations by neo-Marxist scholars tend to focus their analyses on regional inequalities in resources and wealth and on the political and economic dependence of developing countries on the developed nations. Some nations enjoy inordinate power and influence over others (Gregory and Piché, 1983; Wimberley, 1990). In this connection, Andre Gunder Frank (1991) has coined the phrase "the underdevelopment of development" to refer to the overwhelming influence and control the world's major economic powers hold over the developing countries. Development, it is argued, serves mostly the interests of the most powerful nations. Aid received by the poor nations comes at the cost of being in a persistent state of dependence on the providers.

Other writers concerned with the complex interactions of population, environment, and resources take a revisionist stance on such questions. Revisionists are neither neo-Marxists nor neo-Malthusians (Ahlburg, 1998; Cincotta and Engelman, 1997; Clarke, 1996; Evans, 1998; Furedi, 1997; National Research Council, 1986). Julian Simon (1995, 1996), for instance, has written that population growth historically has been, on balance, beneficial to humankind—people are the "ultimate resource," Simon contends.

The US National Research Council's report on population, environment, and resources (1986) exemplifies a revisionist perspective. This committee has proclaimed that, in some cases, population may have no discernable relationship to some of the problems that are often attributed to it. The report also concludes that population's relationship to depletion of exhaustible resources is statistically weak and often exaggerated. Indeed, income growth and excessive consumption are more important factors in this sense: a world with rapid population growth but slow increases in income might experience slower resource depletion than one with a stationary population but rapid increase in income. It was also found that reduced rates of population growth would increase the rate of return to labour and help bring down income inequality in a country.

The National Research Council committee also suggests that while rapid population growth is directly related to the growth of large cities in the **Third World**, its role in urban problems is most likely secondary. Ineffective or misguided government policies may play a more important role in the development of urban problems. Moreover, the committee has noted that although it is often assumed in the literature that reducing population growth leads to a reduction in poverty and income inequality, in fact this relationship holds to a certain point only. For instance, if the population of Bangladesh were halved, its status as a poor nation would not change appreciably; it would move from being the second poorest nation in the world to thirteenth poorest (National Research Council, 1986). Many factors beyond rapid population growth are responsible for poverty (Keyfitz, 1993).

Canada's Population: An Overview

Components of Growth

Canada is the second largest territory in the world (only Russia is larger). It is a sparsely populated country. Its population density in 2001 was 3.3 inhabitants per square kilometre, one of the lowest in the world. According to the 2001 census, Canada's population was just over 30 million (Statistics Canada, 2003d). At the time of its first national census, in 1851, the country had only 2.4 million residents. In the 1931 census, Canada recorded its first 10 million inhabitants. By 1967, the population had grown to over 20 million (Statistics Canada, 2003d).

What is the role of the demographic components of fertility, mortality, and migration in this development? Table 18.2 looks at the components of population growth from 1851–61 to 1991–6, as well as the population count from the 2001 census. Historically, natural increase has been the principal driving force behind population growth (Beaujot and McQuillan, 1982). However, since the middle of the 1980s, the contribution of net migration has been rising in prominence to explain intercensal population growth. Declining birth rates coupled with rising levels of international migration account for this fact. Between 1986 and 2001, natural increase and net migration have practically converged, each accounting for half of the intercensal population growth. This situation highlights the rising importance of immigration for the long-term maintenance of Canada's population in a context of subreplacement fertility.

Table 18.2 **Canada's Population and Demographic Growth Components (Thousands)**

	Census Population at the End of Period[a]	Total Population Growth[b]	Births	Deaths	Immigration	Emigration
1851–61	3,230	793	1,281	670	352	170
1861–71	3,689	459	1,370	760	260	410
1871–81	4,325	636	1,480	790	350	404
1881–91	4,833	508	1,524	870	680	826
1891–1901	5,371	538	1,548	880	250	380
1901–11	7,207	1,836	1,925	900	1,550	740
1911–21	8,788	1,581	2,340	1,070	1,400	1,089
1921–31	10,377	1,589	2,415	1,055	1,200	970
1931–41	11,507	1,130	2,294	1,072	149	241
1941–51[c]	13,648	2,141	3,186	1,214	548	379
1951–6	16,081	2,433	2,106	633	783	185
1956–61	18,238	2,157	2,362	687	760	278
1961–6	20,015	1,777	2,249	731	539	280
1966–71[d]	21,568	1,553	1,856	766	890	427
1971–6	23,450	1,882	1,755	824	1,053	358
1976–81	24,820	1,371	1,820	843	771	278
1981–6	26,101	1,280	1,872	885	677	278
1986–91	28,031	1,930	1,933	946	1,199	213
1991–6	29,672	1,641	1,936	1,024	1,137	229
1996–2001	31,111	1,439	1,704	1,095	1,051	270

[a] Population estimates are based on census counts.

[b] *Total population growth* is the difference in census population counts at the end and beginning of each period.

[c] Beginning in 1951, Newfoundland is included.

[d] Beginning in 1971: The population estimates are based on census counts adjusted for net undercount and the reference date is July 1 instead of Census day (the 1 July 1971 population adjusted for net census undercount is 21,962,100). Immigration figures include landed immigrants, returning Canadians, and the net change in the number of non-permanent residents. Population growth calculated using the components will produce a different figure than is reported in table. Beginning in 1971, the emigration figures are "residual" estimates and include the errors in the other three growth components–births, deaths, and emigration–as well as errors in the census counts.

SOURCE: Adapted from Statistics Canada, Demography Division, <www.statcan.ca/english/Pgdb/defodemo.htm>.

Mortality

Changes in human mortality can be monitored by examining measures such as the crude death rate, life expectancy, and infant mortality. The *crude death rate* is the number of deaths in a given year divided by the mid-year population, usually expressed per 1,000 population. Canada's crude death rate in 2001 was 7 per 1,000 population. Since the early 1920s, Canada has witnessed a steady decline in its crude death rate, from 11.6 per 1,000 population in 1921 to 10.1 in 1941 and 7.7 in 1961, the latter being very close to the 2002 rate.

Unfortunately, the crude death rate is not the best indicator of mortality conditions in a society as it fails to take into account the confounding effects of age composition. In some cases, reliance on this measure can seriously distort comparative analyses of mortality. Measures such as life expectancy at birth and the infant mortality rate provide more accurate accounts of mortality conditions as they mirror a society's overall level of socio-economic development and standard of living. *Life expectancy at birth* represents the average number of years of life remaining for a newborn baby under prevailing mortality conditions in society. *Infant mortality* is defined as the number of deaths of infants in a given year divided by the number of live births in that year. These two measures are inversely related: when infant mortality is high, life expectancy at age zero will be relatively low, and vice versa. In 2002, Canadians (men and women combined) enjoyed a life expectancy at birth of 79 years. By comparison, the corresponding life expectancy for Mexicans was 75 years. Closely tied to this survival gap is the wide discrepancy in the infant mortality rates of these two societies—5.3 infant deaths per 1,000 live births in Canada versus 25.0 in Mexico (Population Reference Bureau, 2002).

In general, women live longer than men (El-Badry, 1969; Vallin, 1983). The literature emphasizes the interaction of biology and environment as the underlying basis of this differential (Gove, 1973; Nathanson, 1984; Perls and Frets, 1998). The Population Reference Bureau (2002) reports that life expectancies for men and women in the more developed regions of the world are 72 and 79, respectively. For the less developed countries (excluding China), the corresponding expectancies at birth are much lower—61 and 64 years, respectively. During the

1990s there were some setbacks in life expectancy gains in sub-Saharan Africa (comprising eastern, central, western, and southern Africa but not North Africa) because of the HIV/AIDS epidemic, periodic famines, and social unrest (Lamptey et al., 2002).

Epidemiological Transition

In Canada and in other advanced societies, the vast majority of deaths on an annual basis are accounted by a few leading "killers"—cardiovascular disease, cancer, accidents, and violence. Infectious and parasitic diseases such as typhus, cholera, smallpox, and tuberculosis are rare causes of premature mortality. In the past, these ailments predominated as leading killers, over the chronic, degenerative, and "man-made" causes of death (Omran, 1971). In 1921, out of 67,722 deaths in Canada, malignant neoplasms and diseases of the circulatory system accounted for 20.9 per cent of all deaths. Of the 210,733 deaths recorded in 1991, these same diseases represented

18.3

Global Issues
HIV/AIDS in the African Context

In many parts of Africa, the combination of demographic and social-structural problems serve to maintain high birth rates and thus rapid population growth. There is political instability, poor living standards, and frequent food crises. Recurrent epidemics of influenza, tuberculosis, whooping cough, measles, chicken pox, typhoid fever, intestinal diseases, cholera, malaria, yellow fever, sexually transmitted diseases, and malnutrition are common. And though not nearly as prevalent as in the industrialized countries, cancer and heart disease are on the rise (Kibirige, 1997; Olshansky et al., 1997). Adding to this heavy health burden is the grave problem of the HIV/AIDS epidemic.

Unlike the situation in the West, where most HIV cases arise as a result of homosexual contact and through blood contamination by means of blood transfusions and shared intravenous needles, the main mechanism for the African epidemic is heterosexual transmission (Caldwell and Caldwell, 1996; Lamptey et al., 2002).

According to the Population Reference Bureau (2001: 2), an astounding 36 per cent of Botswana's 15- to 49-year-olds live with the disease. In Lesotho, Swaziland, and Zimbabwe, approximately 25 per cent of adults in these prime ages have HIV. Namibia, South Africa, and Zambia each have prevalence rates of 20 per cent among adults ages 15 to 49. In another nine sub-Saharan African countries, over 10 per cent of adults aged 15 to 49 are infected. South Africa has the highest number of adults living with the virus, at about 4.1 million. Nearly 3 million Ethiopian adults live with HIV. Outside of sub-Saharan Africa, the largest numbers of people infected with HIV or living with AIDS are in India, at 3.5 million.

The United Nations (2001: 12–13) has estimated that in the 35 most affected countries in Africa, life expectancy at birth was 48.3 years in 1995–2000–6.5 years less than it would have been in the absence of AIDS. The population of these countries if projected to 2015 will be 84 million (10 per cent) less than it would have been (United Nations, 2001: 12–13).

continued

World AIDS Snapshot

Most of the globe's 40 million people infected with HIV live in sub-Saharan Africa and South and Southeast Asia, as reflected in the ranking below, which is based on 2001 data from the Joint United Nations Program on HIV/AIDS. There are five major strains of HIV, which are also called *clades*. Although more than one clade can usually be found in any given area, the map highlights the predominant clade affecting each region. The boundaries between prevailing clades are not exact; they change frequently.

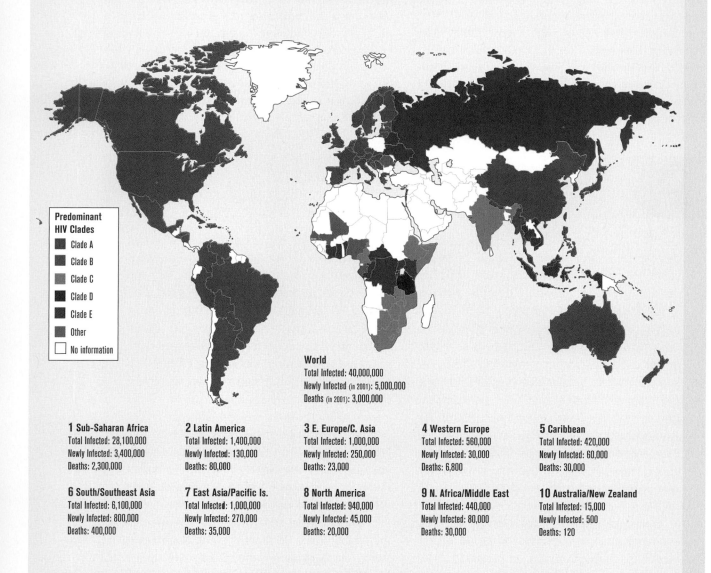

Predominant HIV Clades
- Clade A
- Clade B
- Clade C
- Clade D
- Clade E
- Other
- No information

World
Total Infected: 40,000,000
Newly Infected (in 2001): 5,000,000
Deaths (in 2001): 3,000,000

1 Sub-Saharan Africa
Total Infected: 28,100,000
Newly Infected: 3,400,000
Deaths: 2,300,000

2 Latin America
Total Infected: 1,400,000
Newly Infected: 130,000
Deaths: 80,000

3 E. Europe/C. Asia
Total Infected: 1,000,000
Newly Infected: 250,000
Deaths: 23,000

4 Western Europe
Total Infected: 560,000
Newly Infected: 30,000
Deaths: 6,800

5 Caribbean
Total Infected: 420,000
Newly Infected: 60,000
Deaths: 30,000

6 South/Southeast Asia
Total Infected: 6,100,000
Newly Infected: 800,000
Deaths: 400,000

7 East Asia/Pacific Is.
Total Infected: 1,000,000
Newly Infected: 270,000
Deaths: 35,000

8 North America
Total Infected: 940,000
Newly Infected: 45,000
Deaths: 20,000

9 N. Africa/Middle East
Total Infected: 440,000
Newly Infected: 80,000
Deaths: 30,000

10 Australia/New Zealand
Total Infected: 15,000
Newly Infected: 500
Deaths: 120

SOURCE: Laurie Grace, *Scientific American* (June 2002), 41. Reprinted by permission of Laurie Grace.

66.5 per cent of this total (McVey and Kalbach, 1995: 206).

The historical shift in Canada's cause-of-death distribution is part of a general phenomenon that all societies typically undergo in the context of their demographic and socio-economic transformations. Abdal Omran's *epidemiological transition theory* (1971) states that industrialized societies have gone through three epidemiological stages: (1) During stage one, in prehistoric times, life was ruled by Malthusian positive checks—famine, misery, pestilence. Life was brutish and short; infectious and parasitic diseases were the leading killers, along with violence and accidents. (2) With the advent of the modern era, the development of agriculture, better systems of food production, and general improvements in the standard of living, humanity developed the ability to resist many infectious diseases, and people lived on average longer than in the preceding stage. This period of epidemiological history in the Western world, "the stage of receding pandemics," began around 1750 CE and ended around the turn of the twentieth century. (3) The third stage, that of "man-made and degenerative diseases," began in the 1930s; its main feature was a rising dominance of the chronic and degenerative ailments, such as cancer and heart disease, as the leading killers. Infectious and parasitic diseases receded in relative importance in claiming lives on an annual basis. During this stage, accidents, violence, and suicide also took a prominent position as causes of premature mortality, though overall life expectancy reached unprecedented levels, in the vicinity of 70 years.

At present, the industrialized societies of Western Europe, North America, Japan, Australia, and New Zealand are situated in the fourth stage of epidemiological transition (Olshansky and Ault, 1986). Essential features of this stage include (1) life expectancy at birth in excess of 70 years, (2) continuation of cancer and heart disease as the leading causes of death, (3) increased survival by people with these conditions as a result of effective medical therapies and interventions, (4) unprecedented survival improvements among the old, and (5) the compression (postponement) of the majority of deaths on an annual basis to the advanced ages, as relatively few deaths take place in infancy, early childhood, and young adulthood; over two-thirds of all deaths occur at the ages beyond 65 (Kannisto et al., 1994). Some analysts believe that these societies are now close to attaining the maximum attainable average lifespan for humans (Fries, 1980; Olshansky, Carnes, and Cassel, 1990).

Fertility

The most basic measure of fertility is the *crude birth rate* (CBR), the number of births in a given year divided by the mid-year population times 1,000. Currently, the Canadian crude birth rate is 11 per 1,000 population—the lowest in the history of the country (Bélanger, 2002: 20). Between the early part of the 1920s and the present, some of the highest crude birth rates were recorded during the peak years of the **baby boom**, the period between the end of World War II and 1966. Between 1947 and 1966, a total of 8,571,376 babies were born, constituting the largest generation in the history of this country (Foot and Stoffman, 1998: 24–5; Romaniuc, 1984: 121–2). From 1966 onward, Canada experienced a **baby bust** followed by a more recent period of sub-replacement fertility levels (Bélanger, 2002; Grindstaff, 1975, 1994; Romaniuc, 1984, 1994).

There have been other low-fertility periods in Canadian history. In 1933, births in Canada had fallen to a low point, with only 229,791 registered that year. One year after the cessation of the war (that is, in 1947), the number of newborns rose to 372,589, a 62 per cent jump from 1933. A steady increase in births occurred during the 1950s, peaking at 479,275 in 1959, at the height of the baby boom. As the 1960s unfolded, Canadians embarked on a long-term trend toward having smaller families. By 1966, the eve of Canada's centennial, the decline was underway; 387,710 babies were born that year, a 19 per cent decline from 1959. The annual numbers of births kept dropping until 1990, when for the first time since 1966, more than 400,000 babies were born. But this was a temporary surge; 1993 saw a return to fewer babies being born (388,394), and the number dropped even further in 2000, to 327,882, the lowest since 1946 (Statistics Canada, 2002b: 2).

The *total fertility rate* (TFR) measures the number of children a woman would bear throughout her reproductive lifetime if she experienced the prevailing age-specific birth rates in a given period. In 1959, at the peak of the baby boom period, the TFR had climbed to 3.94. But by 1966, it had reduced to 2.81 children per woman. The year 1972 marks an important turning point in Canadian fertility: the TFR fell for the first time to below 2.1, the number of children needed to ensure long-term replacement of the generations. Canada's total fertility rate in 2000 was 1.49, the lowest in the country's history (Statistics Canada, 2002b: 2). If this trend persists, the future of the

Canadian population is a precarious one. Other industrialized nations share this prospect as a result of their common pattern of subreplacement fertility (United Nations, 2000a).

Explanations of Fertility Change

The baby boom and baby bust phenomena were precipitated by changes in the *intermediate variables*—a set of variables through which social, cultural, and biological factors operate to determine a society's overall fertility rate (Davis and Blake, 1956). John Bongaarts (1978) has shown that four of these intermediate variables (also known as *proximate determinants*) account for most of the fertility variation across societies: the extent of non-marriage (the higher the number of people who remain unmarried, the lower the overall fertility), the level of contraceptive use (the greater the use of contraception, the lower the fertility), the degree to which abortion is practised (high rates of abortion translate into reduced overall fertility), and the level of postpartum amenorrhea (the longer women breastfeed their babies, the later the return of ovulation, and hence the lower the societal fertility rate). Changes in the extent of marriage and contraceptive use have played leading roles in the historical rise and fall of the Canadian birth rate (Grindstaff, 1975, 1994, 1995; Romaniuc, 1984). Sociological, cultural, and economic factors have also played an important role in the observed changes in Canadian fertility, though indirectly, through the proximate determinants.

The Baby Boom

Following the marriage downturn of the early 1930s associated with the economic depression, the number of Canadians marrying rose substantially during the 1940s. Although the Canadian marriage rate has followed an uneven historical trend, between 1940 and the late 1950s it was well above the rates recorded for the 1920s and the early 1930s.

According to Richard Easterlin (1969, 1980), the economic recovery and prosperity of the post-war period was a major factor explaining the rise of marriage and early procreation among young couples during the baby-boom period. Young men could find abundant work, and their prospects in the labour market looked exceptionally promising. As well, the major institutions—the church, the economy, and **the state**—provided the individual with a strong sense of security and stability, as governments were in the midst of creating safety-net systems to enhance

the welfare of their populations (universal health care, education, employment insurance, and so on). As well, the church exerted a strong moral influence on the people, reinforcing pro-natalist values. These conditions promoted early marriage and childbearing (Ariès, 1980; Lesthaeghe and Surkyn, 1988; Simon, 1980). As described by Easterlin (1969, 1980), demographic conditions in the post-war period were also favourable. The relatively small cohorts of young male workers, born during the low-fertility period of the 1930s, would enter the labour market in the late 1940s and 1950s, a period of increased demand for workers in a rapidly expanding economy.

Changes in **gender roles** also contributed to the baby-boom phenomenon. In her study of the "feminine mystique," Betty Friedan (1963) outlined the tendency of women in the 1950s to be preoccupied with marriage to a successful husband, motherhood, and a new home in the suburbs. Their self-concept was tied to this "mystique," presented and reinforced by the society. Early marriage and early parenthood were therefore common. The male role was predominantly that of the breadwinner. This traditional system of gender roles began to collapse in the 1960s and was eventually supplanted by a more egalitarian system.

At the outset of the 1960s, women began their "flight" from domesticity, seeking to redefine themselves as full participants in the economic and educational spheres of society. In 1951, only slightly more than 20 per cent of Canadian women of working age held paid jobs. By 1960, the proportion of women in the paid labour force rose to almost 29 per cent, and it increased over 38 per cent in the following decade. With the advent of the 1980s and the 1990s, the proportion of women working was fast approaching 60 per cent (Mills and Trovato, 2001: 108; Romaniuc, 1994: 221). The rise of female employment has been most pronounced among those in the prime childbearing ages of 20–34 (Beaujot et al., 1995). Improvements in birth-control methods helped women gain greater control of their reproductive and productive lives (Davis, 1984; Davis and van den Oever, 1982; Murphy, 1993).

Women have been pursuing higher levels of education, careers, and jobs. In the new sex-role system, men are no longer the sole economic providers. In a growing number of Canadian families, the earnings of wives now equal or exceed those of their husbands. During the early 1970s, wives' earnings exceeding or equalling those of their husbands characterized only about 6 per cent of working couples in Canada. By

1997, this proportion had changed to 25 per cent (Grindstaff and Trovato, 1990: 236; Little, 2000: A2).

The Baby Bust

Economists have enunciated theories to help explain the current low-fertility environment of post-industrial societies. A central postulate of economic theories of the family concerns the rising material and non-material costs of parenting (Becker, 1960; Willis, 1987). Easterlin's cyclical theory (1969, 1980) also suggests that there is an interaction of economic factors with demographic and sociological variables in the explanation of family change. As described by Easterlin, the baby boom and the baby bust represent a natural sequence in a self-regulatory process, whereby periods of low fertility give rise to periods of high fertility, and vice versa. The driving forces for this cyclical pattern include economic and sociological forces—how well the economy performs in meeting the material aspirations of young adults, the size of one's birth cohort, and the strength of material preferences among young people of parental age.

The baby bust resulted from the growing gap between high material aspirations among the baby-boom cohorts and declining socio-economic opportunities for these cohorts as compared to their parental generation. As well, the large size of the baby-boom cohorts would represent a further source of insecurity among this generation. In an uncertain economic environment, large cohorts do not fare as well as small cohorts in finding permanent work and in gaining job promotions. The labour pool is large, as is the number of persons seeking advancement in the workplace. These conditions have instilled in young people a reluctance to enter matrimony, and among the married a tendency to postpone having children. One common strategy adopted by couples is to delay childbearing and to have a completed family size of one or two children on the average. This allows couples to maximize their socio-economic opportunities while fulfilling their parental obligations (Ram and Rahim, 1993).

Following theoretical premises developed by Gary Becker (1960), William Butz and Michael Ward (1979) have suggested that low fertility rates in advanced societies in recent decades are linked to the rising value of time for women. Unlike in the past, most women are now gainfully employed in the labour market. This means that the economic value of their time is now greater. Having children therefore means having to forgo not only potential income, but also career opportunities. Looking at the United States as a case study, Butz and Ward determined that a rise in the average incomes of males induces couples to have more children, presumably because of greater affordability. The same trend for women was found to be inversely associated with fertility, overriding the positive income effect of men. This finding is explained in terms of women's rising opportunity costs, such as lost career opportunities, associated with having children. Besides material considerations, there are also psychic costs—the perceived complications and stresses associated with having to care for children while often maintaining a job or career, and the restricted freedom that goes along with being a parent.

Sociologically based explanations of fertility decline are grounded on the assumption that social change is largely a function of *diffusion processes*, whereby new ideas and values gradually spread throughout the society and supplant old ones. Such theories recognize the important interactions of structural and economic forces with ideational factors. The traditional sources of authority in matters of family and procreation—religion, community, **extended family**—have weakened considerably in recent decades. Individualism is now the dominant ethos guiding personal actions (Ariès, 1980; Keyfitz, 1986; Lesthaeghe and Surkyn, 1988; Preston, 1986a; Simon, 1980; Trovato, 1988b; Van de Kaa, 1987). Contemporary values, attitudes, and lifestyles seem incompatible with early marriage and raising large families, as the pro-natalist forces of the past have given way to the small family ideal of the present. According to Ron Lesthaeghe and Johan Surkyn (1988), during the baby-boom period, people generally felt optimistic about their economic future. However, there now exists among the young a generalized skepticism of **social institutions**, including traditional marriage. Cohabitation, for instance, is seen by the young of today as a less restrictive form of sexual union than traditional marriage. In the postmodern society, diverse family forms are increasingly tolerated and accepted. It is no longer unusual for young couples to consciously avoid having children or for individuals to forgo matrimony altogether.

To summarize, social forces of germane importance in explaining the persisting pattern of sub-replacement fertility in industrialized societies are (1) the rise of individualism as a dominant aspect of our **culture**, which emphasizes detachment of the individual from traditional sources of regulation such as religion; (2) the rise of a consumerist **ideology** emphasizing strong material preferences and aspirations over early marriage and family building; (3) increasing levels of divorce and the growing preference of the young to enter alternative living arrangements rather than legal marriage; and (4) the sex-role revolution and the increasing levels of emancipation of women and men from traditional roles, allowing people a wide range of alternatives to traditional roles as sources of self-fulfillment.

Demographic and Societal Implications of Subreplacement Fertility

For a society, one of the most profound long-term outcomes of continued low fertility is demographic aging. The 2001 Canadian census confirms that the median age of the population—the point where exactly one-half of the population is older and the other half is younger—is 37.6. The 1996 census showed a median age of 25.4. In 1901 it was only 22.7 years (National Post, 2002: A9). The Canadian situation is not unique; other industrialized nations are experiencing the same trend, as denoted by the following population median ages in 2001: United States, 35.5; Germany, 40.1; France, 37.6; Italy, 40.2; Japan, 41.2. For the world, the median age in 2001 was 26.5 (National Post, 2002: A9).

Figure 18.5 shows a typology of age pyramids, juxtaposed with Canada's actual and projected population age structure to 2036. This typology outlines in schematic form the long-term progression of expected change in the age pyramids of societies as they pass through their demographic transitions. The *true pyramid* has a wide base and a narrow top, typical of rapidly growing populations with characteristically high reproductive rates and a high percentage of the population below age 15. Some developing nations exemplify this structure, particularly those in sub-Saharan Africa and parts of Asia (for example, Kenya and Afghanistan). The *constrictive pyramid* is indicative of populations experiencing continued declines in fertility. A number of developing nations have recently begun sustained fertility declines; for this reason, their population pyramids will eventually take on the look of something intermediate to the true and constrictive types. With continued fertility declines, the transitional societies will in time enter a stage at which the shape of their population structures will approximate those of the industrialized nations, whose age pyramids are gradually approaching the *stationary* form. The Canadian population has gone through this evolution and is projected to attain the stationary form in 2036.

On a practical level, a youthful population means that government have to plan and devote considerable resources to the needs of children and youth. In an aging society, the dependency burden shifts gradually from the youth to the elderly. Central in such a context are issues related to retirement planning, pension security and management, and adequate provision of geriatric health care and services. The greying of the population is bound to play a critical role in shaping the long-term collective futures of Canada and other demographically mature societies. An article in one of Canada's major newspapers on the recently released 2001 census figure begins by saying that as a consequence of the aging trend, "Canadians could face delayed retirement, even higher health-care costs, more school closings and a shortage of skilled workers" (Lewington, 2002). According to Peter Peterson (1999), in some societies, demographic aging will induce growing pressures on the old age retirement benefit system as the costs of maintaining it will escalate to unprecedented levels. Widening public pension deficits could consume the economic savings of the developed world. As well, reforms of health care systems will be needed to take into account the growing health needs of an aging population. The growth of the "old-old" component (the population 85 and older) will be much faster than that of the "young old" (65–84). In the long term, these societies will be facing an unprecedented economic burden on their working-age populations as the proportion in the working ages shrinks while that of old age dependents keeps growing. Demographically mature societies will require large numbers of immigrants to supplement their diminishing labour-force populations (Kennedy, 1993; United Nations, 2000b; United Nations Economic Commission for Europe, 1992).

Migration

Canada is a country made up almost exclusively of immigrants and their descendants. The history of the nation is closely tied to immigration (C. Brown, 2002). Currently, about 18 per cent of our population is first-generation immigrants.

Immigration to Canada has fluctuated significantly over the years. In 1852, this country welcomed 29,307 people; in 1913, there were 400,000 newcomers—an annual figure not yet surpassed. Since

Figure 18.5 Typological Age-Sex Pyramids and Actual and Projected Age-Sex Pyramids of Canada, 1881, 1921, 1951, 1991, 2011, and 2036

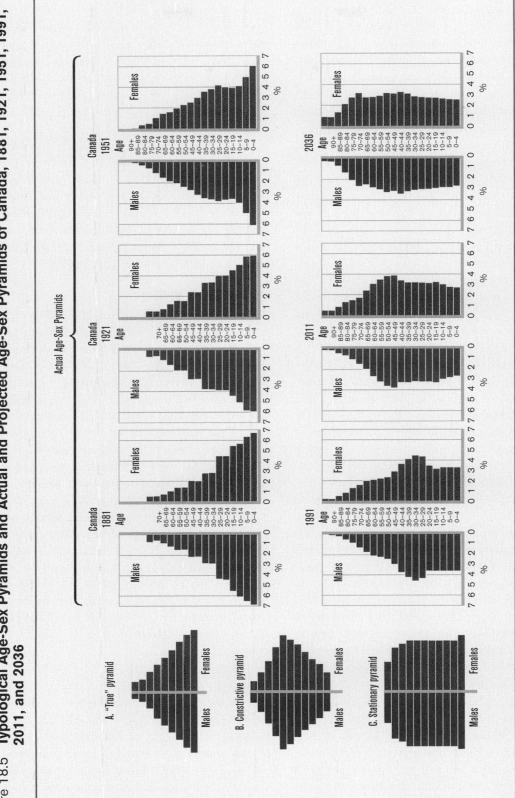

Source: Adapted from Bertrand Desjardins, *Population Aging and the Elderly: Demographic Analysis* (Ottawa: Statistics Canada, 1993), 18; C.W. Kammayer and Helen L. Ginn, *An Introduction to Population*, 2nd edn (Chicago: Dorsey, 1986), 89.

the early 1970s, immigration levels have been in the range of 80,000 to 250,000 per year. Fluctuations in the annual immigration levels are set by government, usually in response to economic conditions and other policy considerations. From the time of Confederation to 1967, more than 8 million people were admitted to Canada (McVey and Kalbach, 1995: 83). Until recently, most immigrants were from Britain, other northwestern European areas, and the United States. After World War II, immigration started to diversify, with large waves of Italians, Germans, Hungarians, Dutch, and Portuguese. Since the early part of the 1970s, the major source areas have been Asia, South America, the Caribbean, Central America, and Eastern Europe (McVey and Kalbach, 1995; Samuel, 1990).

Immigration has been a significant factor in the growth of Canadian cities (Stone, 1967). The majority of immigrants settle in the largest metropolitan areas of Ontario (about 50 per cent), British Columbia (15 per cent), and Quebec (15 per cent). This rank order of preference has remained fairly stable over time (Bélanger, 2002; Dumas, 1990); it reflects variations in economic and social pulls across Canada's regions. The more economically advantaged locations receive the majority of immigrants. According to Statistics Canada (2003c), one-third of the Canadian population in 2001 was concentrated in the **census metropolitan areas** (CMAs) of Toronto (4.7 million), Montreal (3.4 million), and Vancouver (2 million). Thus, over 60 per cent of new Canadians make their homes in these three areas of the country.

Studies on immigrants' internal migration patterns indicate little movement out of the large urban areas of the country (Trovato, 1988a). The general reluctance of immigrants to relocate to smaller centres in Canada is largely due to the combined effects of economic and social advantages large cities afford and to the strong attraction represented by immigrant ethnic communities in large urban locations. The presence of like ethnic members provides material and psychological comfort and support to immigrants (Breton, 1964; McDonald and McDonald, 1964; Trovato, 1988a).

Between 1951 and 2000, almost 15 million people in Canada moved interprovincially (Bélanger, 2002; Dumas, 1990). Internal migration is predominantly from the economically disadvantaged to the economically prosperous regions. The literature describes this as a *core/periphery* phenomenon: under-

developed regions (the periphery) export people, and economically developed areas (the core) import labour (Massey et al., 1993). Core/periphery migratory systems arise from unequal regional development. In the Canadian case, the Atlantic region has been a net loser in terms of migration; Ontario, British Columbia, and Alberta have been net gainers (see Table 18.3). However, economic conditions across these regions fluctuate periodically. Boom periods translate into large net migration gains, while declining economic conditions usually provoke high rates of out-migration. During the mid- to late 1990s, Ontario underwent a downturn in its economy, while Alberta enjoyed a period of booming conditions. Not surprisingly, Alberta gained people through net migration. Ontario's recent economic recovery means that this province is now attracting many internal migrants (Bélanger, 2002).

Factors of Migration

People are more prone to changing residence during certain stages of the life cycle. The intensity of life-cycle events is greatest in the young adult years, particularly between the ages of 20 and 34. Indeed, besides sex and marital status, one of the most predictive variables for migration is age—a variable that is strongly correlated with life-cycle stage (Lee, 1966; Rogers and Willekens, 1981).

During childhood, the predominant basis of relocation is tied to family migration decisions. In the late teens up to the early thirties, this stage of the life cycle involves a number of important life events for most people, such as graduating from high school, attending university or college, postsecondary graduation, entering the labour force, and marriage. These types of events often dictate having to relocate (for example, for a job in another city). The likelihood of migration diminishes considerably after the late thirties and early forties as during this part of life, persons are established with work and family.

Conclusion

Population is the foundational base of society and its subsystems. The social world cannot be understood in isolation of demography, nor can demography be properly understood devoid of a proper understanding of society. Given the centrality of population to the study of society, sociologists pay particular attention to the dynamics of population change. Fertility, mortality, and migration are the basic demographic

Table 18.3 **Interprovincial Migratory Balance in Canada over Five Decades, 1950 to 2000**

	1951–60	1961–70	1971–80	1981–90	1991–5	1996–2000	1991–2000
Newfoundland	−9,816	−34,557	−20,840	−30,626	−19,814	−32,590	−52,404
Prince Edward Island	−7,938	−5,732	2,927	378	1,414	194	1,608
Nova Scotia	−28,851	−43,521	4,165	3,331	−4,415	−4,412	−8,827
New Brunswick	−25,360	−45,277	6,441	−5,915	−3,094	−7,269	−10,363
Quebec	−72,877	−142,594	−234,163	−122,143	−50,758	−71,509	−122,267
Ontario	148,036	236,081	−96,391	184,649	−42,570	57,698	15,128
Manitoba	−40,587	−64,161	−68,977	−37,968	−26,558	−19,563	−46,121
Saskatchewan	−87,938	−123,492	−50,603	−67,475	−28,917	−22,631	−51,548
Alberta	32,858	30,022	244,991	−61,203	5,753	134,470	140,223
British Columbia	93,075	192,713	216,486	144,345	169,608	−27,452	142,156
Yukon and Northwest Territories[a]	−600	519	−4,036	−7,373	−649	−6,936	−7,585
Total movements	**2,962,004**	**3,660,061**	**3,849,741**	**3,168,426**	**1,482,443**	**1,471,878**	**2,954,321**

[a] Includes data for Nunavut beginning in 1992.

SOURCE: Alain Bélanger, *Report on the Demographic Situation in Canada 2001: Current Demographic Analysis* (Ottawa: Statistics Canada 2002), 58; Jean Dumas, *Report on the Demographic Situation in Canada 1990* (Ottawa: Statistics Canada, Demography Division, 1990), 106.

variables. In combination, they determine whether a population experiences growth, stability, or decline. Aggregate change in fertility, mortality, and migration results from change in individual behaviour in accordance with conditions in the social structure.

The history of the human population can be subdivided into two broad stages: a very long period of very slow growth, from the beginning of humankind to about 1750 CE, followed by a relatively recent phase of explosive growth. As a legacy of the population explosion that took place in the modern era and currently ongoing in many developing countries, the world faces challenges heretofore unforeseen in the history of humanity. The earth's population (just over 6 billion in 2003) is expected to reach 9 billion by the year 2050. Most of the projected growth will be in the developing countries, particularly in Africa and also in Asia and Latin America. Some of the developing countries are close to completing their demographic transitions; others are just beginning to experience sustained fertility declines after decades of mortality reductions.

Three demographic trends seem inevitable over the course of this new century: the population of the world will become older; the developing countries will grow much more than the developed countries; and there will be intense pressure on highly industrialized countries to accommodate an even larger share of immigrants from developing countries than they do currently. The implications of this eventuality will be far-reaching: with increased immigration, the highly industrialized receiving nations will become even more racially and ethnically heterogeneous. Given its relatively long history of immigration and its multicultural orientation, Canada seems well positioned to deal with this reality. For the countries that are relatively new immigrant-receiving societies in Western Europe (many of which until recently were sending nations), the adjustment process to this emerging reality poses difficult challenges. Their conceptions of nationhood may need to be modified in view of the changing racial and ethnic composition of their societies.

☐ Questions for Critical Thought

1. Describe how populations change. What are the demographic components of change?
2. What is atypical about the current stage of the demographic history of the world? Describe the relationship of demographic transition to the history and projected future of the human population. Are there any certainties about the future population of the world?
3. Assess the theories of Malthus and Marx on the matter of population and its relationship to contemporary issues concerning resources and the environment. Discuss how contemporary perspectives on population matters relate to the Malthusian and Marxist theories of population.
4. What are some of some sociological determinants of fertility change over the last half century in Canada?
5. What is the relative importance of fertility and mortality in determining the age distribution of a population?
6. Explain how the epidemiological profile of Canadian society differs today from that of the early part of the century.
7. Why do immigrants to Canada prefer to settle in the largest metropolitan areas of the country?
8. Regional inequalities in socio-economic development explain differential migratory flows within Canada. Explain.
9. What are some of the social and economic implications of increased immigration for the future of Canadian society and other receiving countries in the Western world?

☐ Recommended Readings

Roderic Beaujot and Kevin McQuillan, *Growth and Dualism: The Demographic Development of Canadian Society* (Toronto: Gage, 1982).
This book is an important introduction to Canada's population. The authors' historical overview of the development of Canada's population is particularly insightful.

John I. Clarke, *The Future of Population* (London: Phoenix, 1997).
This is an excellent introduction to some of the most critical issues concerning the population of the world.

David K. Foot with Daniel Stoffman, *Boom, Bust and Echo 2000: Profiting from the Demographic Shift in the New Millennium* (Toronto: Macfarlane Walter & Ross, 1998).
The revised edition of this best-selling book examines many potential practical applications of demography to business. It gives a wide range of insights on how demographic shifts affect key sectors of the economy, from the state of the housing market to consumer demand for sports, travel, leisure, and financial investing.

Wayne McVey, Jr, and Warren E. Kalbach, *Canadian Population* (Toronto: Nelson, 1995).
This is an updated version of a classic text first published in the early 1970s. It gives technical and substantive explanation of demographic concepts, with specific reference to Canada.

Anatole Romaniuc, *Fertility in Canada: From Baby-Boom to Baby-Bust* (Ottawa: Statistics Canada, 1984).
Although this study's primary focus is on Canadian fertility, the theories and explanations reviewed by the author have broader application to the other industrialized countries.

W.W. Rostow, *The Great Population Spike and After: Reflections on the 21st Century* (New York: Oxford University Press, 1998).
The author takes a careful look at the populations of the industrial and developing countries, how they have been changing, and how they will change over the course of the new millennium. Rostow examines key challenges the industrialized societies are likely to face in the near future as the populations of emerging economies will assert a greater influence on the global economy while the industrial societies face the prospect of depopulation.

Frank Trovato, ed., *Population and Society: Selected Readings* (Toronto: Oxford University Press, 2002).
Twenty-five readings are presented, covering a broad range of topics central to the field of population studies. These selected works emphasize the interrelation between population, culture, and social structure.

David Yaukey, *Demography: The Study of Human Population* (New York: St Martin's, 1985).
This is a lucid and authoritative introductory exposition on the discipline of demography.

☐ Recommended Web Sites

Health Canada: Population Health

www.hc-sc.gc.ca/hppb/phdd/docs/social/
Mortality and other population health information on Canadians can be found at the Health Canada Web site.

POPLINE Digital Services

www.jhuccp.org/popline
POPLINE is an important online bibliographic database on population research and related topics, based at Johns Hopkins University.

Population Index

http://popindex.princeton.edu
This very useful and comprehensive bibliographic source for population research and related disciplines is no longer published in print form.

Population Reference Bureau

www.prb.org
The Population Reference Bureau issues a series of excellent publications on a regular basis, including *Population Bulletin* and the annual *World Population Data Sheet*.

Statistics Canada

www.statcan.ca
Statistics Canada is the authoritative source for Canadian census and other population data.

United Nations Population Division

www.unpopulation.org
The *United Nations Demographic Yearbook* contains a wealth of demographic information by country; it comes out on a yearly basis. Another key product from the United Nations is the *Human Development Report*.

The United States Bureau of the Census

www.census.gov
This is one of the best sources of demographic information for the United States and other countries. Check out their population clock, which gives continuous updates on the population of the world.

World Health Organization

www.who.int/en/index.html
Another important source of mortality data is the *World Health Organization Statistics Annual*. This publication contains deaths by cause, age, and sex for a large number of countries. The WHO publishes these tables on a yearly basis.

19

William Michelson

> > >

Cities and Urbanization

© Bill Whitman

☐ Learning Objectives

In this chapter, you will:

- see how the existence and prevalence of cities reflects societal and world conditions
- examine the extent to which and ways that cities affect people's characteristic behaviours
- begin to understand how built environments facilitate and constrain everyday life
- examine characteristic parts of cities and their potential patterns
- learn what cities are intended to do as social organizations
- study the basis for conflict and change within cities
- consider the known implications of different forms of municipal structure and of their restructuring
- gain an appreciation of Canadian cities in historical and comparative perspective

Introduction

> Remember: for every urban problem, there is a solution that is clear, simple, and wrong.
> —Terry Nichols Clark

The three-quarters of Canadians living in urban areas are bombarded with glib remedies for the difficulties cities and city-dwellers regularly undergo. Everyone has an opinion. Some of these opinions are informed. Sociologists have assembled considerable knowledge gained from their long-standing application of sociological perspectives and research tools to cities. Moreover, sociological insights on cities are highly diverse and complementary.

Sociologists' fields of interest in cities run the gamut from the place of cities in society to the interiors of dwelling units. The effects of industrialization and de-industrialization, why women feel safe in some places and unsafe in others, the allure of shopping centres for youth, the rationales for regional government—all are valid matters for study within urban sociology. But an understanding of one phenomenon does not automatically explain others. No single theory is sufficient to describe, explain, or solve all problems. A mixture of sociological perspectives is needed to help us understand and deal with the many unique, challenging situations in urban life.

Cities and urbanization will therefore be viewed in this chapter according to four perspectives. The first of these is **urbanization**: the nature, extent, and distribution of cities in the larger society or nation. The second perspective is **urbanism**: behaviour patterns associated with cities. The third is **ecology**: the internal makeup and patterning of cities. Our final perspective is **structural analysis**, which focuses on the functions cities perform, as well as on who has what effect on the decisions and outcomes involving cities.

Individually and together, these perspectives help us to understand cities and to deal more adequately with their woes. Canadians may also understand their urban conditions in the context of historical and international perspectives.

Urbanization

We are all familiar with cities from current observations and personal experiences. The concept of urbanization, however, focuses our attention on the place of cities in the greater society, from nation to nation, and over time.

The First Cities

The emergence of cities in about 3500 BCE truly represented something new under the sun. Perhaps the most elementary conception of a city is that it must contain at least some non-agricultural workers. The effect of cities on the rest of the society was therefore immediate and direct: the rural sector had to grow a surplus of food to feed the urbanites. Creating stable and predictable agricultural surpluses required simultaneous developments throughout the whole society in technology and **social structure** in geographic areas, such as Mesopotamia and the Indus Valley, that could support intensive agriculture (Adams, 1966).

Technological innovations of importance for urbanization included irrigation; bronze metallurgy for ploughing and cutting instruments; animal husbandry for use in agriculture; stone mortars; the selective cultivation of rich, non-perishable foods such as grains and dates; wheeled carts and sailing vessels for transport; and building bricks for permanent settlements.

Like technology, social organization evolved, and the division of labour beyond age and sex became a legacy to later cities and societies. One aspect of the enhanced division of labour was *vertical stratification—* differentiation in the degrees of responsibility and power. For instance, it became the responsibility of some individuals to see to it, by providing technological support and controlling delivery, that the farmers produced surpluses for the non-agricultural workers. Another aspect of the division of labour was *horizontal stratification*—different job specializations even at the same level of power and prestige. Full-time soldiers, artists, and producers of consumer goods appeared in the urban settlements, while farmers could become ever more specialized. From the beginning, then, cities had heterogeneous populations with complex, usually coercive relationships with the rest of society. Although the farmers did obtain products and the often-dubious benefits of laws and protection, they relinquished some of their food under terms beyond their control.

This relationship between urban and rural people may appear current. However, there have been enormous changes over time in the balance between the two groups, reflecting developments in the central elements of technology and social organization. For example, technology was at first barely adequate for producing the necessary food surplus; 50 to 90 farmers were needed to produce enough surplus food

IN THE FIRST PERSON

As an undergraduate, I sampled a number of different subjects before concluding that sociology addressed more comprehensive and thoroughgoing questions about the real world, while the attempt to answer them also brought in aspects of the scientific method. During an academic year spent in Denmark, I became more sensitive to how social structure could vary from what I had previously experienced. I was particularly intrigued by the rationales for city planning and housing and the forms they took in the Copenhagen area. But subsequent university courses in urban sociology, while interesting, failed to deal with either the creation or the human implications of such built environments. Filling this vacuum became my goal for a continuing program of conceptual thought and research.

–WILLIAM MICHELSON

for 1 urbanite. Today, a single farmer in a technologically developed country produces food for about 9 urbanites.

In the first few thousand years after the appearance of cities, even the largest urban settlements were very small. Archeological evidence suggests the largest had populations of between 5,000 and 30,000. Their size was limited by the distance over which labour-intensive transportation technology could bring food from outlying areas, by how far coercion could be extended, and by the state of sanitation and public health. With refinements in technology and social structure, some ancient cities grew much larger. Athens had about 150,000 residents in 500 BCE. At its height, Rome grew to between 250,000 and 1 million inhabitants. But despite the existence of such city-states, which often dominated vast tributary areas, the kind of urbanization we know today did not develop until many centuries later—after the Middle Ages.

Paths to Urban Development

The development of industry based on non-living energy sources such as coal and steam is commonly given credit for a substantial shift in the population balance from rural to urban. Powered industry reflected societal developments in technology and accentuated the division of labour. The same advances in science and engineering that made possible large-scale factories with machinery also led to innovations in agricultural technology that enabled fewer farm workers to grow food more intensively and on larger holdings.

In technologically advanced societies, a surplus of agricultural labour therefore became available for newly emerging, specialized city jobs. These workers were pushed from the countryside and pulled to cities. They became specialists in housing, food, transportation, financial services, warehousing distribution, and much more; several specialists were needed to provide the services and supplies for every factory worker. This led to a growth in urban population by what is called the *multiplier effect*—population growth several times the number accounted for by factory workers alone.

Technically, observers think of urbanization as the proportion of a nation's population living in settlements of a certain minimum size, usually defined as 5,000 and over. Just two centuries ago, only about 3 per cent of the world's population lived in settlements of 500 or more inhabitants. A city about the size of the current Vancouver metropolitan area would have been the largest in the world. Today's technologically advanced nations have urbanization levels exceeding 75 per cent.

If you look at the development of urbanization in historical perspective, as in the timeline represented by Figure 19.1, you see that it took many thousands of years of human life for the prerequisites for cities to occur and then to lead to the establishment of urban settlements in various parts of the world. The ingredients of modern cities have only become known in the last few minutes in the day of mankind. Indeed, the predominantly urban society is largely a phenomenon only of the past 60 years of the 50,000 or so of known human history. During this recent time, however, the tempo of technological innovation

Figure 19.1   **Timeline of Significant Events in the Development of Urbanization**[a]

50,000+ BCE	Human life
3,500– 1000 BCE	First cities. 3500 BCE, in the Fertile Crescent of Persia; 3000 BCE, Thebes and Memphis, Egypt; 2500 BCE, Indus River settlements, India; 2500 BCE. Yellow River settlements, China; 1000 BCE, Meso-America (Peru)
500 BCE– 500 CE	City-states of Carthage, Athens, Sparta, and Rome
750– 1400 CE	Dark Ages, feudalism (decline of most European cities)
1400– 1700 CE	Renaissance, nation–states, capitalism, guilds, revival of trade
1700– 1900 CE	Industrialization in parts of the world
1900+ CE	Electricity, metropolitan cities, megalopolises, automobiles, air travel, electronic data processing, mega–cities, global cities ...

[a]Not to scale.

to 39.9 for less developed regions. Canada is just about on this level, with 77.1 per cent urbanization, as is the United States, with 77.2 per cent (see Table 19.1). Although this represents a relatively steady level of urbanization for the more developed nations in the past 20 years, it is an increase of about one-third in the urbanization levels of less developed nation during this recent time (Gold, 2002: 3).

Table 19.1 shows that the highly industrialized continents of the Americas, Europe, and Oceania all have mean urbanization levels of over 70 per cent, compared to much lower levels for Africa and Asia. The former levels, however, have been relatively steady for two decades, while the latter levels have increased by about one-third during this time, suggesting the possibility of future international convergence in the spread of urbanization.

Nonetheless, a concentration on such large land masses obscures differences in levels of industrialization within them. Hence, a focus on national urbanization levels shows that Western Europe has some of the highest levels in the world (for example, Belgium at 97.3 per cent, the United Kingdom at 89.5 per cent), while some nations in Eastern Europe have less urbanization (for example, Romania at 56.2 per cent, Croatia at 57.7 per cent). Australia and New Zealand are at the 85 per cent level, while the smaller islands in Oceania bring down the regional mean level. Japan has a markedly higher urbanization rate than many other Asian nations that have not as yet achieved the same level of industrialization (United Nations Centre for Human Settlements, 2001).

Nations with low urbanization rates may nonetheless have very large cities. Indeed, as Table 19.2 indicates, many of the largest cities in the world

and societal adaptation has grown phenomenally. Considering that powered industry only came about in the eighteenth century, electricity in the nineteenth, and the automobile, telephone, radio, television, airplane, computer, nuclear power, and much more even later, it is increasingly difficult to predict or imagine what cities and society will be like even in the next decade.

Canada and the United States belong to a club of industrial nations with reasonably similar, high rates of urbanization. According to the United Nations Centre for Human Settlements (2001), the more developed nations of the world had a mean urbanization level of 76.0 per cent in the year 2000, compared

Table 19.1   **Levels of Urbanization by Continent, 2000**

	Level of Urbanization in 2000 (%)
North America	77.2%
Latin America	75.3%
Europe	74.8%
Oceania	70.2%
Africa	39.9%
Asia	36.7%

SOURCE: Derived from United Nations Centre for Human Settlements (HABITAT), *Cities in a Globalizing World: Global Report on Human Settlements 2001* (London: Earthscan, 2001), Table A2.

are found in less developed nations. The economic and technological contexts in which cities become established are important to understanding their size and distribution within their nations.

The urban population in Western industrial societies is distributed quite evenly across a number of reasonably sized settlements, as capital and technology are diffused. In less developed nations, it is concentrated in the single very large metropolis in the country or in a region. Most of the extremely large cities in the **Third World**, such as Bombay, Calcutta, and Shanghai, were centres from which foreign imperial powers exported the nation's or region's raw materials for industrial production in the home countries. This was called *imperialism*. Mattei Dogon and John Kasarda (1988) suggest that these urban settlements grew to such size as obvious destinations for the rural poor, despite the virtual absence of an industrial economic base in both the cities and the countries at large. Urban populations in such situations are typically underemployed, poor, and predominantly male.

When more people reside in a city than would be expected from its economic base, *overurbanization* is said to occur. Then, when the technology and infrastructure catch up to overurbanized cities that are already large, they become huge. Cities of 10 million or more persons are called **mega-cities**, and the majority of them are in less developed nations. Often their expansion is accompanied by environmental degradations of many kinds: air, water, hazardous wastes, road accidents, and noise (Hardoy, Mitlin, and Satterthwaite, 2001).

Globalization and Global Cities

Although industrialization is held largely responsible for high rates of urbanization, it is argued that the recent trend of **globalization**, in which corporations have expanded their focus to production and sales in many nations of the world, exporting investment capital to take advantage of lower-paid employees in other nations and non-traditional markets for the resulting products, has led to added growth and wealth in a few cities with extensive development of corporate organization, finance, telecommunications, and air transportation. These favoured cities, known as **global cities**, manifest high levels of technology. As David Thorns puts it, "Global cities are now the key sites for the control, coordination, processing and distribution of knowledge that makes them the engines of growth within the present stage of capitalist development" (2002: 54). They are vital centres for the flow of information, direction, and money, and they do not have to be on the doorstep of the heavy industries they indirectly control and co-ordinate. Global cities reflect the presence of interacting financial enterprises through highly concentrated and prominent office buildings (Castells, 1989; Sassen, 1991).

Saskia Sassen (1991) argues that such cities as New York, London, and Tokyo have achieved more prominence than their manufacturing base might suggest, while large cities based more fully on manufacturing (such as Detroit in the United States and Manchester in England) do not gain global status because they do not need the same degree of white-collar employment right at hand. Toronto is considered a minor global city, and Vancouver is active in this respect on the Pacific Rim. One might well consider whether globalization can be viewed as a modern form of imperialism, in which profits and consumer products flow from around the world to the home country rather than raw materials for home-country industries and their wage workers.

Table 19.2 **The 20 Largest Cities in the World in 2000**	
	Population (in millions)
1. Tokyo	26.4
2. Mexico City	18.1
3. Bombay	18.1
4. São Paulo	17.8
5. New York City	16.6
6. Lagos	13.4
7. Los Angeles	13.1
8. Calcutta	12.9
9. Shanghai	12.9
10. Buenos Aires	12.6
11. Dhaka	12.3
12. Karachi	11.8
13. Delhi	11.2
14. Jakarta	11.0
15. Osaka	11.0
16. Metro Manila	10.9
17. Beijing	10.8
18. Rio de Janeiro	10.6
19. Cairo	10.6
20. Seoul	9.9
44. Toronto	4.7
68. Montreal	3.4

SOURCE: Adapted from David C. Thorns, *The Transformation of Cities: Urban Theory and Urban Life* (New York: Palgrave Macmillan, 2002), 54.

Sociology in Action
The Gap Between the Real World and Formal Measures

Documenting various aspects of urbanization demonstrates many of the measurement challenges facing sociologists more generally. For example, the basic measure of urbanization—the percentage of persons in a nation living in urban areas—depends on a standard definition of what constitutes an *urban area*. In some nations, it means a municipality of 5,000 persons. In others, the threshold is only 1,000 persons, while in yet others, it is as high as 10,000 persons. Beijing, for example, is known to have at least 3 million undocumented residents on top of the nearly 11 million officially reported as legal residents.

The degree to which census organizations are able to accurately count urban and rural populations is variable. The size of large cities also reflects how wide an area of settlement is considered to be part of a given city. Urban regions—larger than a named municipality—are often considered a logical unit on which to present city size figures. But how such regions are defined and then measured varies greatly from place to place and from time to time. Mexico City, for example, might be considered the world's largest city were different approaches to measurement taken. Therefore, descriptive and analytic numbers should be understood in terms of the best efforts of researchers and knowledge of the criteria they employ, rather than as absolutely objective and fully comparable facts.

In Canada, as in the United States, economic factors pull people to cities rather than push them away from rural areas, and women typically outnumber men in the urban context. Figure 19.2 shows that, as of 2001, the majority of people in every Canadian province and territory except Prince Edward Island and Nunavut were city-dwellers. Thus, high levels of urbanization are not confined to Ontario and Quebec, with their predominant cities. The overall urbanization rate documented by the 2001 census in Canada is 79.7 per cent. The relatively large recent growth of Toronto and Vancouver is related to major global functions, while cities such as Winnipeg, Montreal, and Hamilton, though still major centres within the Canadian context, lack the same level of international roles with which to boost their employment and population.

Urbanism

One of the reasons sociologists are interested in cities is the popular belief that life in cities differs from life in other forms of settlements. Research findings over many years have shown that the issue is subtler than simple urban–rural differences. The path to understanding urbanism is a good example of the conver-

gence of different theories and the research done to document them.

Classical Approaches

Early approaches to urbanism seemed to make the assumption that urban contexts cause certain forms of behaviour in a very direct way. This viewpoint is known as *determinism*, since it presupposes that a given set of conditions determines behavioural outcomes.

Does life in an urban context differ systematically from that in a rural context? Many classical analysts have thought so. Gideon Sjoberg (1960), for example, found that job specialization and the complexity of production and marketing that accompanied industrialization required standardization in weights, measures, currencies, pricing, and financial interaction. For the system to work, rational, exact actions became necessary. Other theorists, such as Max Weber, Sir Henry Maine, Ferdinand Tönnies, and Émile Durkheim, used different words but made similar observations that urban life is more likely to involve rational, universalistic, impersonal, and logistically oriented behaviours than had been the case in earlier rural settings. Noting that German urbanites had to pay constant attention to contextual signals—lights,

Figure 19.2 **Urbanization of Canada, by Province and Territory, 2001**

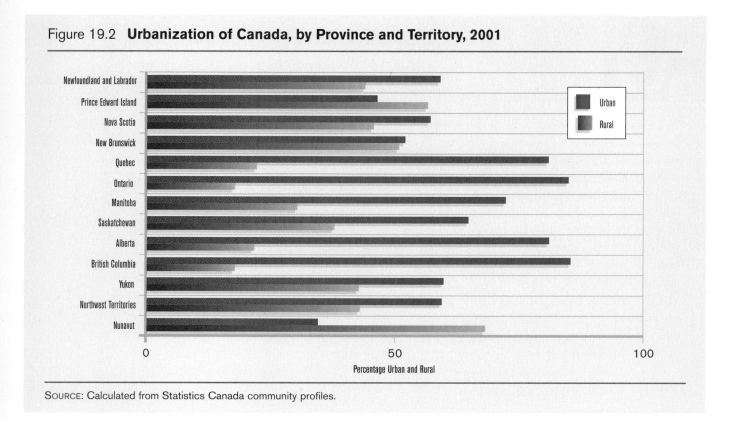

SOURCE: Calculated from Statistics Canada community profiles.

signs, footsteps, whistles, and the like—Georg Simmel (1950a) summarized these observations by saying that the head, rather than the heart, dictates most urban behaviours.

The best-known ideas on urbanism may be attributed to Louis Wirth's 1938 article "Urbanism as a Way of Life." Wirth believed that cities have three defining characteristics—large numbers of inhabitants, high densities, and heterogeneous populations—each accounting for important aspects of an urban way of life. Large numbers lead to the impossibility of knowing all persons, and hence to the relative absence of intimacy in most interpersonal relationships. Human relations become segmented into many largely anonymous, superficial, transitory contacts. At the same time, high density fosters human diversification and specialization. Social distance is established to maintain personal space in response to the inescapable presence of close physical contact with diverse persons. Nonetheless, accentuated friction inevitably arises, and formal means of **social control**—notably, uniformed police—assume prominence in cities. Despite, or perhaps because of, such close proximity, complex patterns of segregation take shape. Finally, heterogeneity makes it difficult for individuals to be constricted by rigid social struc-

tures, as in rural areas. Urban individuals more often find themselves in varied social settings and groups. Both upward and downward mobility, with the resultant greater feelings of instability and insecurity, are more likely in cities.

Although classical approaches to urbanism never achieved total consensus, their legacy was sobering. Any societal gains derived from greater division of labour, rationality, and personal freedom seemed to be counterbalanced by unending suspicion, distrust, and isolation.

Modern Social-Psychological Approaches

Modern social psychologists have been particularly taken with the earlier theoretical themes dealing with urban life as situated in the impersonal presence of great numbers of strangers, some of whom represent annoyance at the least, and, more seriously, risk. Lyn Lofland wrote a valuable analysis of how people relate to each other in cities, with the germane title, *A World of Strangers* (1973). In it, she stresses that people minimize interpersonal interaction as a way to maximize public order (that is, safety). In recent work (Lofland, 1998), she delves into how urbanites have a love-hate relationship with public spaces. She suggests that even though people potentially access unparalleled experiences in the congregating spaces of large cities, the public realm has been largely neglected, given the ambivalence urbanites have about contact with strangers.

Stanley Milgram made a noteworthy development of Simmel's notion of impersonal signals bombarding urbanites. Using modern systems analysis, Milgram characterizes urban life as sensory overload: "City life, as we experience it, constitutes a continuous set of encounters with overload, and of resultant adaptations" (1970: 1462). He goes on to describe a variety of ways in which urbanites cope with overload. All of them are literally textbook examples of the *Gesellschaft* side of Tönnies's classical theoretical dichotomy between *Gemeinschaft* and *Gesellschaft*—figuratively, "heart" versus "head"—as describing **social interaction** in societies.

One common strategy for coping with overload is to tune out what is found to be overburdening: anything from drunks through poverty to negative consequences of public- or private-sector policies or practices that benefit only some. Increasing numbers of people live literally on the streets of Canada. Many citizens have taken active ameliorative roles in food drives, food banks, and night patrols for the homeless, but the context of everyday life for many involves passively working around difficult situations.

In another coping strategy, urbanites are said to avoid aiding strangers who need help, in order to avoid trouble themselves. Much research followed the public shock that resulted when, in 1964, Kitty Genovese was murdered after appealing for help outside the windows of at least 38 onlooking neighbours in a New York City apartment house. The research suggested that the more people are there, the less likely any individual is to intervene. People are more likely to intervene if they feel that they are needed in the absence of others.

Urbanites also minimize involvement by taking action to remove themselves from easy contact with strangers. They buy telephone answering devices or subscribe to voice mail services, institute scripted menus to provide information, fail to list their telephone numbers (this is certainly the case for ubiquitous cell phones), filter visitors through secretaries and assistants, travel by private automobile, and live in segregated (and, increasingly, guarded) buildings and **neighbourhoods**. Ironically, at the same time, the same people are in greater contact than ever with those they know, through the medium of electronic mail.

People use a range of coping procedures in public places. They pretend not to see each other (for example, on beaches) and tolerate other lifestyles except where these represent clear and present dangers. They follow unspoken but definite rules about how much distance to keep from others for particular purposes,

Urban life in a world of strangers: a subway station. (William Michelson)

where they sit (for example, on buses or in libraries), and the way they walk (Hall, 1966; Sommer, 1969).

Urbanites, however, are not totally isolated beings. There are public settings where people come to expect to interact with other persons in ways that they don't during most public encounters. Churches, bars, and sporting events, for example, all provide the opportunity for positive interactions among persons with similar interests and objectives.

People wanting to communicate to others their personal **identity**, once relied on clothing in general, and uniforms in particular, to provide a basis for secure interaction without previous personal acquaintance. In smaller settings, the family name was noteworthy, and it still is in some circles. However, in urban circles in which consumer goods like clothing are rampant and family connections may be obscure, personal credentials (transcripts, credit cards, and so on) and home addresses help complete the introduction, for good and for ill. According to Janet Abu-Lughod, "the larger neighborhood or even the city can take on an important symbolic and social meaning, serving as a source of identity ('I come from Grosse Pointe')" (1991: 338).

The Subcultural Theory of Urban Life

Is it really some aspect of the city that calls for coping behaviours such as those described by Milgram? Albert Reiss, Jr (1959), found that the anonymous, segmented, and impersonal relations noted by Wirth reflected occupation more than residence. For instance, men living in rural areas with non-farm jobs had daily contact patterns resembling those of their urban counterparts.

In contrast to the deterministic approach of the classical thinkers, other sociologists adopt a *compositional* perspective, according to which behaviour reflects the composition of the population. Herbert Gans (1967), for example, explains suburban behaviour not in terms of the physical nature of the area, but in terms of the social class background and life-cycle characteristics of the population in the suburb he studied. The nature and extent of their contact with neighbours, their participation in organizations, and their interest in schools all reflected middle-class backgrounds and the presence of families with young children. In short, exponents of the compositional approach believe that urban life reflects the most salient features (for example, class, ethnic background

or race, religion, age, and sex) of the particular population groups living in particular cities or their constituent parts.

In *The Urban Experience* (1976), Claude Fischer attempts to reconcile deterministic and compositional theories and to go beyond them. Fischer argues that Wirth was right in stressing the significance of large numbers of persons in cities. But Fischer does not see the numbers as providing various direct effects; rather, he considers their primary importance as providing the nucleus for various specialized **subcultures** within cities. It is the particular compositions of the various subcultures that influence so-called urban lifestyles.

Fischer calls his approach the *subcultural theory* of urban life. Which subcultures become significant in a given city depends upon many macroscopic characteristics of cities: their economic base, sources of migration, climate, and more. Within highly urbanized societies, cities of different sizes and in different locations may be functionally specialized. This does not mean that they are monolithic in terms of their activities or resident populations, but there are distinct tendencies regarding who chooses to live and work there and, hence, which subcultures take root. It is unusual for even a city specializing in industry to have more than 25 per cent of its jobs in manufacturing because of the need for complementary and supportive activities, yet the difference between 25 per cent and 10 per cent spells a big difference in the critical mass of a blue-collar subculture. Hamilton, Ontario, with its huge steel mills, differs substantially in its ways of life from nearby London, an insurance and financial centre—not to mention from Victoria, British Columbia, with its combination of government jobs, retirees, mild weather, and afternoon tea. However, the largest national cities tend to be diverse economically, with their population size supporting varied subcultures and lifestyles. It takes a Toronto, not a Truro, to supply the critical masses for creating the world's most ethnically diverse city, where the varied ethnic communities enjoy rich cultural lives and where these cultural groups exist side by side with youth, yuppie, gay, sports, criminal, and endless other subcultures.

Does Fischer's subcultural theory invalidate the generalizations made by urban social psychologists about such problems as overload, anonymity, and coping adaptations? In subsequent work, Fischer (1982) shows that the personal contact patterns of urbanites are more firmly concentrated in specialized

19.2

Human Diversity
Gender and the Everyday Use of Urban Contexts

Regularities in the way people manage their interactions with others in public areas become most evident in times of social change. It is then that unstated assumptions are challenged and that the implications of emerging behaviours are felt most strongly. It is perhaps noteworthy in this connection that some of the most dramatic episodes in the long-term trend toward greater racial integration have focused on the shared use of public facilities: buses, beaches, and bathrooms. While such facilities are a tangential part of everyday life, they strongly symbolize differential assumptions about who mingles with whom, where, and for what purpose.

One of the major social changes of the past 20 years is the increase in the proportion of women with young children who undertake paid employment. Their numbers have risen from a minority (clearly thought of as an exception to the norm of women staying home to care for children) to a majority approaching 70 per cent, even among mothers of preschool children. Among the many explanations for the change are greater support for gender equality, higher education among women, increases in the cost of living (particularly of housing), a rising divorce rate, and a growing incidence of childbirth among single women. Much attention is given to how women balance traditional household responsibilities and the demands of the paid employment sector, as well as to the availability of child care and other relevant support facilities.

A relatively neglected aspect of the growing employment of mothers is the revolution in women's use of non-traditional urban spaces and their interaction with other people there. When women were more likely to "stay home," far more emphasis was placed on the nature of their neighbourhoods. The local area was a cocoon, containing (to the extent that could be arranged) the "right" kind of neighbours and stores in a setting con-

ducive to safety. Errands away from home occurred during the day, unless a woman's husband accompanied her. When not with their husbands, therefore, women spent much time alone, with their children, or with immediate neighbours. For employed women, the pattern of daily life is very different. Relatively little time is spent with neighbours (less than was previously spent with relatives), but much more is spent with other types of people on the job. Most women now spend a significant part of the day in non-domestic settings, usually outside their own neighbourhoods, and they travel at non-traditional times on non-traditional routes, usually without spousal accompaniment.

Past understandings about whom people meet, how they differentiate themselves, and who might be found in what location (and for what purpose) are in a state of flux. The results are ambiguity, concern, and, unfortunately, danger. Adaptation to social change lags behind the overt change itself. How long will it take for women to be able to travel safely home from work, through areas where women aren't expected to be out after dark?

A major national study in 1993 by Statistics Canada found that over 80 per cent of women feared entering parking garages, 76 per cent worried about using public transportation after dark, and 60 per cent were afraid to walk in their neighbourhoods after dark. In her report on the Statistics Canada data, Rosemary Speirs notes, "42 per cent said they have no choice in walking alone on dark streets at least weekly. Young women living in large cities are most fearful of situations in which they are alone after dark" (1993: A29).

Perhaps it is not surprising that both sociologists and geographers have recently discovered this neglected aspect of the interaction between social change and urban space (Hanson, 1992; Michelson, 1994, 1997a).

19.3

Open for Discussion
Diversity, Stereotyping, and Hiring

Both selective interaction and avoidance behaviours accompany urbanism. Identification with those like oneself and distrust of those very different can lead to stereotyping and social problems. The situation is particularly problematical when those with power and authority are not sufficiently sensitive to the nuances of subcultures that are different from their own. The widespread issue as to whether police officers profile members of minority groups would not be as keen if subcultures were not perceived as significantly separate. Recognition of these problems underlies current attempts to incorporate minorities more fully into police and fire departments and into the teaching profession, as well as to expand human rights programs.

groupings (which in cities means subcultures) than those of people living in smaller communities and rural areas. Similarly, big-city dwellers are likely to trust their closest neighbours but not urbanites in general.

Ecology

You have already seen much evidence that urban behaviour patterns reflect subcultural cleavages. You might therefore expect that the physical structure of cities will reflect and reinforce these patterns. Examining the city in ecological terms strongly supports such an expectation. We know that most cities are made up of distinct parts. The ecological perspective addresses the nature of these parts and what kinds of patterns they form.

Cities, Suburbs, and Metropolitan Areas

While urbanization levels in Canada show that Canadians live predominantly in cities, they do not reveal in what types of settlements or where within them we live. Do most Canadians live in large or small cities, in central cities or suburbs?

A common pattern in technologically advanced societies has been the buildup of population beyond the borders of older cities and into newer municipalities immediately adjacent. These are commonly called *suburbs*, although the word is often applied to areas that simply look newer and less crowded than the centres of the traditional cities. Montreal and Vancouver, for example, have many suburbs, while much of Calgary and Edmonton appears suburban.

Large cities and their suburbs may represent different municipalities, but in terms of everyday behaviour and economic activity, they form an entity known as a **metropolitan area**. Many people live in one part of a metropolitan area and work in another; there is, for instance, an active interchange between Vancouver and New Westminster.

Statistics Canada defines a **census metropolitan area (CMA)** as an area comprising one or more large cities (totalling at least 100,000 inhabitants at the previous census) in the centre (the urban core) together with surrounding areas that are economically and socially integrated on a day-to-day basis with the urban core (1992: 29). On the basis of these criteria, some CMAs include a central city and many municipalities extending a considerable distance from the urban core, while others consist of a single municipality. The makeup of a CMA reflects the size of the urban area, its history, and the amount of land suitable for expansion under the control of the central city. Toronto extends as a functional entity almost as far as Hamilton (that is, through Oakville), while Saskatoon not only includes nearly all the residents in its vicinity but also controls undeveloped land for future development. There are 27 CMAs in Canada. Although these metropolitan areas take up only a tiny fraction of the land in Canada, they were home to more than 19 million of Canada's 2001 population of 30 million—just short of two-thirds of the national population (Statistics Canada, 2001 census data). Canada's urban population is not dispersed into many small cities and towns across the landscape—it is highly concentrated in metropolitan areas.

Many people have an image of the city as an older municipality with a high density and buildings

that are large and striking or old and grey. The suburbs are, somehow, something else. This view, however, needs revision. Most residents of Canadian and
American metropolitan areas are suburbanites, even
if we discount the great numbers of people in the
newer cities—largely in the western regions of both
countries—who live in typically suburban conditions. Table 19.3 presents Canadian CMAs with about
300,000 residents or more in order of size, indicating
the breakdown of the population by residence in
either the central city or suburban municipalities.
The final column shows that the suburban segments
of all CMAs but Kitchener, Ontario, have grown
between 1991 and 2001, continuing previous trends
in the distribution of population within metropolitan areas. This distribution is essential to an understanding of the pattern of local areas and lifestyles in
metropolitan areas. Whereas people previously
focused on the central city and spoke in stereotyped
terms about the suburbs and suburbanites, now it is
essential to recognize that a major and still-growing
share of the urban population lives outside of traditional central cities.

Metropolitan Population and Land-Use Patterns

How are people and their subcultures patterned
within metropolitan areas? Several theories have been
proposed to answer this question.

From studies of Chicago, Ernest Burgess (1925)
identified the *concentric ring* land-use and stratification
pattern of cities. At the heart of this pattern is the
central business district (CBD), consisting of the principal private- and public-sector offices, department
stores, and hotels. The CBD is serviced by public transit to make it the most accessible place in the city.
Burgess assumed that the CBD would be the only
major centre in the city and that it would continue
to grow indefinitely. Because of this growth, the land
around the CBD would be held speculatively for
future profit. Before upgrading, the *zones in transition*
would be used, without maintenance or improvement, for rooming houses, transient hotels, and
other impermanent uses. They would contain the
poorest, newest migrants, the criminal element, and
prostitutes—all subcultures requiring short-term

Table 19.3   Distribution of Population in Canada's Largest Census Metropolitan Areas in Central City (Cities) and Suburban Portions, 2001

	Total Population in 2001	Population in Central City or Cities (%)	Population in Suburbs (%)	Change in Suburban Percentage (1991–2001)
1. Toronto	4,682,897	14[a]	83	+2
2. Montreal	3,426,350	30	70	+3
3. Vancouver	1,986,965	27	73	+2
4. Ottawa-Hull	1,063,664	38[b]	62	+3
5. Calgary	951,395	92	8	+2
6. Edmonton	937,845	71	29	+2
7. Winnipeg	672,274	92	8	+2
8. Quebec City	682,757	25	75	+1
9. Hamilton	662,401	50	50	+3
10. London	432,451	77	23	+2
11. Kitchener	414,284	67	33	–
12. St Catharines–Niagara	377,009	55[c]	45	+8
13. Halifax	359,183	33[d]	67	+2
14. Victoria	311,902	24	76	+1
15. Windsor	307,877	68	32	+5
16. Oshawa	296,208	47	53	+7

[a] Central city is the original City of Toronto before amalgamation in 1998.
[b] Central city is the original City of Ottawa before amalgamation, plus Hull.
[c] Central city is St Catharines plus Niagara Falls.
[d] Central city is taken as Halifax and does not include Dartmouth.
Source: Calculated from Statistics Canada community profiles.

affordable housing and, in many cases, anonymity. The more regularized sectors of the population would be distributed in rings around both the CBD and the zones in transition, in proportion to their ability to pay for greater amounts of land increasingly far from these two areas, as well as for the cost and time involved in longer commutes. Thus, working-class communities would be surrounded by the middle class, which in turn would be surrounded by the upper class. In short, according to Burgess, major land uses would claim the city centre through market-mechanism competition, while residential areas would be distributed at varying distances from the CBD according to income.

Another member of the Chicago School of urban sociology, Robert E. Park (1925), labelled as "**community**" the forms of behaviour thought to arise because "birds of a feather flock together." Within a given ring, local communities that were homogeneous by ethnic or religious background would form within boundaries formed by major streets, railways, parks, and the like. Park called these communities *natural areas* because no one rationally planned their location—they were simply a function of land value (thought to lie beyond the control of individuals) and incidental boundaries. According to this view, it was the physical proximity of people to one another in the natural area by which the critical mass of people in subcultures could exercise a strong influence on individual behaviour.

Unfortunately, the concentric ring pattern is far from universal; it has been demonstrated to exist in few places outside Chicago. Indeed, in many settings outside the United States, the rich occupy the city centres while the poor are left outside of the benefits of urban infrastructure.

Ironically, it was right in Chicago that another researcher, Homer Hoyt (1939), discovered a rather different pattern. Hoyt's *sectors* resemble pieces of a pie, extending from the centre outward without interruption. Hoyt noted that certain amenities, such as waterfront parks, and eyesores, such as freight railways, extended outward. People of means would try to live within view of the amenities; those of few means would follow the tracks; still others would locate themselves in-between. One side of town would become better than another, if only because it was upwind from centrally located industries.

A third approach is Chauncy Harris and Edward Ullman's *multiple nuclei theory* (1945), which states that each land use or subculture is located according to unique criteria having to do with the proximity of other land uses. Heavy industry, for example, wants to be near railroads and highways but doesn't need to be as accessible to consumers as do retailing land uses. Head offices draw fine restaurants, banks, and law offices to their vicinity, while universities attract fast-food chains and bookstores. The result is a city with many diverse centres whose locations are not in a fixed geometric pattern.

Toronto's central business district, with a zone in transition clearly visible at its edges. (William Michelson)

Central London, England. There's no law that CBDS must emphasize skyscrapers. The London Eye ferris wheel towers over the CBD. (William Michelson)

A statistical process called *factorial ecology* lets sociologists analyze census statistics for local areas of a given city in order to determine the patterns shown by such dimensions. Robert Murdie (1969) drew a number of conclusions in his pioneering analysis of Metro Toronto: that family size increased with distance from the centre, that social class segregation was in sectors from the centre outward, and that **ethnic groups** lived in unique clusters of multiple nuclei. He demonstrated that a single city could show several different patterns, depending on the criterion. No one pattern of land use characterizes all cities.

Neighbourhood and Community

The various approaches discussed so far might lead you to conclude that every city-dweller lives in a tightly knit neighbourhood made up of people similar in social class, family size, and ethnicity. While this is not the case, it is true that the concepts of neighbourhood and community help to clarify urban settlement patterns. A *neighbourhood* is a specific physical area within a city that may or may not have formal boundaries, though people may have an image of it even without any consensus on its exact territory. *Community* refers to tangible interpersonal contact patterns; the term has primarily social connotations.

Traditionally, neighbourhood and community were synonymous. In the old days, or in small communities, people centred their interpersonal relationships within the physical areas where they lived. According to the deterministic view of urbanism, this kind of community was lost in the city. However, later researchers, such as Gans (1962), found extremely strong ethnic subcultures in cities, subcultures that appeared to re-establish the identity between community and neighbourhood. Barry Wellman and Barry Leighton (1979) declared community regained. More penetrating analyses of interpersonal networks went on to show that many people in cities have specific types of contact patterns that often reflect subcultures but that have no reference to the boundaries of neighbourhoods (Wellman, 1979; Wellman, Carrington, and Hall, 1988). Close associates may be all over the map but may easily be reached by telephone or computer, or met at work, bars, parties, or conventions. Melvin Webber (1963) called this phenomenon *community without propinquity*; Wellman and Leighton (1979) termed it *community liberated* or *unbound*.

Urban neighbourhoods take various forms, starting with the *ideal type*, where everybody interacts with everyone else (Hallman, 1984; Wireman, 1984). A *conscious neighbourhood* is something that developers and designers work to achieve in newly built areas by trying to construct unifying **symbols**, so that residents will treat the area well and interact with each other. Clarence Perry (1966) created the *neighbourhood unit plan* in 1927. It was an area of about 400 homes surrounded by traffic arteries but with only local roads inside, focusing on an elementary school and communal facilities. Although Perry's plan has been shown to be ineffective in its most grandiose social-engineering objectives (because people often have greater interpersonal loyalties elsewhere), it has been highly influential in suburban development. The most common urban neighbourhoods represent what Morris Janowitz (1952) called the *community of limited liability*. People recognize that they live in a specific area that has identifiable institutions, yet it is the limit to neither their contact patterns nor their everyday activities.

A Closer Look at Selected Urban Neighbourhoods

Within the inner cities, planners have noted the crucial differences between slums and low-income ethnic subcultural neighbourhoods. The former, typified by the *skid row* (or *skid road*), is what Burgess meant by his "zones in transition." People go to such areas to avoid contact, usually for short periods. Intense personal networks are uncommon, and there is little or no proprietary interest in buildings or neighbourhood areas apart from their pragmatic short-term function. Skid rows contrast greatly in their interpersonal communities with other areas that may also have older buildings, poor maintenance, and poor people but where well-established kinship and neighbourhood relationships exist. Gans (1962) and William Whyte (1943) have written extremely detailed accounts of the high degree of organization in two Italian American communities in central Boston. Gans called such neighbourhoods *urban villages*, a term fitting many neighbourhoods with ethnic communities in Canadian cities, including Italian (Sidlofsky, 1969), Jewish (Shaffir, 1974), and Portuguese communities (Anderson, 1974).

A phenomenon studied by David Ley (1991), which is now more than a decade old, is *gentrification*. To take Donald Rosenthal's description (1980), upper-middle-class professionals move into and transform formerly working-class areas of the central city. Gentrification is well developed in Canada, the United States, Britain, and other nations. The trend shows certain characteristics: it occurs less frequently in new cities, its extent is highly variable, and it normally occurs in cities with centralized white-collar and professional jobs, where the suburbs are extending farther and farther, and where the housing stock in one or more relatively central areas is fundamentally sound and has aesthetic potential and historical interest.

The gentrification process begins when relatively wealthy individuals purchase, restore, and modernize the older buildings in a given neighbourhood for personal use or for sale at enormous markups. As more members of the upper middle class move in, the neighbourhood changes. Local businesses shift toward the tastes of well-heeled adults; trendy restaurants, health food stores, art galleries, computer boutiques, and similar concerns appear. In Toronto, a formerly rundown area known for decades as Cabbagetown has, with gentrification, assumed the more upscale name of Don Vale.

While some Canadian cities have witnessed the slow but mellow transformation of existing neighbourhoods through gentrification, the subsequent condominium boom is more obvious. This currently ongoing boom in the larger cities involves a radical intensification of building, both in the central cities and in suburbs, whereby land that is underutilized is covered by (usually) high-rise buildings, in which apartments are created for purchase. In some instances, ground-level space is rented to commercial enterprises such as grocers, coffee shops, and home furnishing stores. Many people purchase condo units for speculative purposes, with the result that these units become an informal part of the rental market—but expanding only the more expensive part of the market, not adding generally affordable rental housing to scarce supply. Although the condo boom is upgrading the urban streetscape and expanding the tax base for cities, neither this nor gentrification offers any hope to the less affluent segment of the population. Vacated housing does not work its way down to use by the destitute in Canadian cities that are expanding.

The suburbs also provide a diversity of urban neighbourhoods. The old suburban stereotypes came from studies of middle- and upper-middle-class areas. But other segments of the population seek suburban residence as well; many blue-collar families have sought affordable housing away from what some regard as disreputable elements in the central city. S.D. Clark (1966) has pointed out that suburban lifestyles end up reflecting diversity in the composition of their residential populations. The urban development legislation accompanying the early years of the experiment in metropolitan government (about 1953–80) led to the accommodation of great numbers of immigrants in high-rise apartments throughout what were then the suburban reaches of Toronto, even while more traditional suburban neighbourhoods with single family homes were also being built.

Two new trends have appeared in the past decade. One is the *edge city*. This is the creation of highly concentrated business, commercial, and high-technology centres on lower-cost land on the fringes of urban areas, which suburbanites find easier to access than the traditional central business district. The edge city becomes a competitor to the original central city, with comparative economic advantages and an absence of central-city costs and difficulties. Joel Garreau (1992) describes edge cities in such different places as Boston, the state of New Jersey, Washington, DC, and Atlanta. Edge cities are surely evident north and west of Toronto and south of Vancouver.

Another trend emerging in the United States is in the development of occasional planned towns under the guiding theories of the *new urbanism* (Duany, Plater-Zyberk, and Speck, 2000). These are towns or settlements on the outer fringes or away entirely from existing cities, built with a unifying design reflecting a period of historical gentility and emphasizing public spaces to be shared by wealthy owners of the private homes built according to the plan. They have become refuges for affluent people seeking alternatives to contemporary cities. The solution found here to urban problems is to ignore them in congenial company elsewhere. In the southern United States, Georgian architecture is popular. The city of Seaside, Florida, is an early icon of the new urbanism. The Disney Corporation has created a rendition of this kind of development in a new town they call Celebration, which has been criticized for over-regimentation and control by the developer and a lack of diversity resulting from the deliberate unavailability of affordable housing (Gold, 2002). A subdivision called Cornell built according to new urbanist principles has been built in the suburban belt north of Toronto; after much discussion, Victorian architecture was chosen, as found historically in Cabbagetown/Don Vale.

Computer technology and advances in market analysis have led to the study of the social and residential characteristics of Americans living within areas defined by zip code. As documented by Abu-Lughod (1991), the researchers ended up with 40 types of residential clusters throughout American urban areas, ranging in nomenclature from Blue-Blood Estates through Emergent Minorities to Hard Scrabble. Both urban Americans and Canadians are surrounded by great variations in residential neighbourhoods.

Third World nations, whose large cities typically receive immigrants fleeing rural poverty, add another suburban variation, the *shantytown* (also known as the *favela* or *bidonville*). A shantytown is built in extremely short order with a miscellany of salvaged materials on found land in poorly accessible areas outside of the city proper. It has little or no infrastructure and is an illegal first foothold giving residents some access to the city without the requirements of money, jobs, or legitimacy. Planners and other observers despair of these communities, but development agencies have learned that the most responsible reaction is to try to help the residents by installing such basic aspects of infrastructure as sewage, water, and electricity. As the economic situation of the shantytown dwellers starts to improve, so does their quality of life, and mobility to the city becomes a possibility (Van Vliet, Huttman, and Fava, 1985).

These glimpses of selected urban neighbourhoods have been extremely brief. Still, they serve to prove that a huge variety of factors—far more than just the growth of the central business district—accounts for differentiation among metropolitan areas. Many kinds of rational human intervention establish and change local areas, beyond the invisible reach of land economics. Developers cultivate new neighbourhood images; real estate agents help reinforce or change the composition of older ones. Banks and insurance companies can influence who enters, leaves, and stays in neighbourhoods through their lending and insuring policies. Planning and zoning activities affect stability and change, while ratepayers' associations, tenant groups, and trade organizations influence planning and zoning bodies.

The variation in neighbourhood mix is accentuated by a non-random distribution of population in residential space. Affordability is linked to socioeconomic status. Different types of housing and location come with different **household** structures; families with children often have different criteria for choosing housing than do elderly persons and couples. People with the same backgrounds are more likely to live together than not, and this is clearly exemplified in ethnicity, whether by choice or by compulsion.

Paul Jargowsky's work in the United States (1996) suggests the presence of economic and racial segregation working together. Many areas in American central cities and inner suburbs are designated as high-poverty areas (where 40 per cent or more of residents are in poverty) but distinguished as being black ghettos, Hispanic barrios, or white slums—different names according to the nature of the occupants.

Ethnic segregation in Canadian cities is omnipresent but not as constant in its characteristics and locations as that in US cities. There is a tradition in Halifax of black versus white residential clustering. Montreal is residentially divided between French, English, and allophone. Toronto finds distinct but certainly not total ethnic clustering of Portuguese, Jews, Italians, Chinese, East Indians, Maltese, Ukrainians, Greeks, Russians, and many other groups. In Vancouver, the Chinese ethnic population has traditionally been residentially segregated, though now it is assuming a significant proportion of the population. One group, Native Canadians, is significantly segregated in many cities.

Although there is much clustering in Canadian cities by ethnicity, this does not mean that a great proportion of single groups are necessarily in a single place or in the central city. Different ages and economic levels of groups such as Chinese, Jews, and Italians may be found in different types of housing, locations, and levels of prosperity throughout the Toronto area, for example.

Some groupings comes about as an expression of education and lifestyle. Jon Caulfield (1994), for example, shows how clustering in Canada can occur as a result of willed human action, or human agency, over time by like-minded people, rather than as a function of determination by either economics or external parties.

Built Environments, Health, and Behaviour

The components of the urban pattern are many and complex, as are the forces influencing them. Nevertheless, the social composition of sub-areas of cities is not the only influence on human behaviour within urban settlements. The built environment and the organization of its infrastructure also have important effects. In many instances, both the design and the planning of buildings, neighbourhoods, and cities can facilitate or constrain behaviours.

The Design of Housing and Other Institutions

Families differing in age, composition, size, and ethnic background choose or are forced to live in homes that vary by size, density, layout, and amenities. Apart from **status** and identity connotations, does it matter who lives where?

Numerous studies have confirmed that housing design does have an effect on people's lives (Arias, 1993; Marcus and Sarkissian, 1986). Research on married couples living in high-rise apartments and single family homes in both downtown and suburban areas of Metro Toronto (Michelson, 1977a) concludes that behaviours differed because of the respective opportunities in housing.

Research by C. Ray Jeffery (1971) and Oscar Newman (1972) has also suggested that enlightened designs for residential buildings and grounds can help prevent such crimes as vandalism and muggings, which occur where perpetrators believe they can get away with them. For example, apartment houses with stairways out of the public view provide opportunities for muggings; glass-walled stairways, in contrast, take away an intruder's protection. Long, anonymous hallways make it possible for strangers to lurk unchallenged, unlike small apartment groupings, where residents are more likely to know each other and their respective guests. Well-lit, open lobbies situated within view of many apartments are less of a target than those that are out of sight. By extension, Robert Gifford (1987) has commented that it takes no stretch of the imagination to consider what difference the amount and design of space in schools, hospitals, offices, and factories can make to the people there.

It is becoming more common to conduct a safety audit in and around multiple-family dwelling areas, office buildings, universities, and transit systems. The intention is to learn from those who use these facilities the circumstances in which they feel afraid of being victimized, so that appropriate environmental changes might be made. Women's safety has become a particular concern. Toronto's subway system, for example, has responded by creating designated waiting areas on the platforms. These are monitored by television cameras and are positioned to be adjacent to the cars in oncoming trains in which the conductors are stationed.

Neighbourhood Design

Neighbourhoods have been shown to be of considerable salience to housewives, children, and others whose daily routines or resources restrict them to the areas where they live. Consider children. The scope of their world starts with a crib or room and expands slowly; only with their teenage years does it typically expand beyond their neighbourhoods for independent activities, and even then only by the grace of adults in the absence of good public transportation (Michelson and Roberts, 1979).

From the time they can walk until they are considered capable of negotiating the greater urban context, children are expected to conduct the sum of their daily non-school or non-daycare play and social interaction within their own neighbourhoods. How safe are these areas—from adults and from other children, from automobiles, from pollutants? What is there for the children to do? If play areas are provided, under what weather conditions can they be used? Are the play areas physically safe, interesting, available to all relevant age groups? To what extent can parents observe and control their child's situation from their dwelling unit? Is the child's play restricted by parental availability for supervision? Numerous guidelines have been set out suggesting how local neighbourhood designs can fruitfully accommodate the needs of families with children (Marcus and Sarkissian, 1986).

Comparative international research has confirmed the importance of local area characteristics in the daily lives of children, even as the particular characteristics of such neighbourhoods vary greatly from country to country, as do the **cultures** in which the children grow up (Chawla, 2002).

There has been a resurgence of research attention in recent years to the characteristics of local areas within cities. Some of this has been with respect to the risks encountered by relatively fragile sectors of the population such as children and the elderly from environmental perils. Air pollution, heavy traffic, vermin, and hazardous waste are distributed no more randomly than are the population groups most exposed to them. As a result, disease and accidents affect more greatly the sectors of the population with fewer economic means to have choices in where to live (Fitzgerald and LaGory, 2000).

Furthermore, research has shown that some decision makers in both the private and the public sector consciously decide to locate noxious land uses (euphemistically known as "locally unwanted land uses," or LULUs) proximate to those population groups least able to defend themselves politically against them (Bryant and Mohai, 1992). In the United States, such **discrimination** has been largely directed against African Americans. In Canada, the spotlight on powerless groups has been less specifically focused (but see Michelson, 1997a). Native Canadians have observed more than their share of this decision making. Attention to such practices goes under the academic heading of environmental justice.

Considerable attention is also being given to the aggregate social characteristics of local areas within cities, just as was the case 80 years ago in Chicago with the work of Robert Park and his colleagues at the University of Chicago. The concentration of people, problems, and varying availability and quality of support facilities is being explored in books with titles like *Place Matters*. Peter Dreier, John Mollenkopf, and Todd Swanstrom, for example, start a book with that title as follows:

> Where we live makes a big difference in the quality of our lives, and how the places in which we live function has a big impact on the quality of our society. The evidence shows that places are becoming more unequal. Economic classes are becoming more spatially separate from each other, with the rich increasingly living with other rich people and the poor with other poor. The latter are concentrated in central cities and distressed inner suburbs, and the former are in exclusive central-city neighborhoods and more distant suburbs. (2001: 1)

Contemporary researchers at the University of Chicago have developed modern methods to assess the aggregate social characteristics of local areas (Raudenbush and Sampson, 1999; Sampson and Raudenbush, 1999).

Macro Urban Design and Organization

It is somewhat difficult to grasp how urban design on a scale greater than the neighbourhood affects individual behaviour. The Swedish geographer Torsten Hägerstrand (1970) has fortunately provided some insight into this matter, as has Tommy Carlstein (1978). The spatial dimensions of the greater urban area—that is, the degree of mixture or separation of

its land uses, its densities, and the layout and operation of private and public transportation—are *capability constraints* that serve to make combining different daily activities such as work, shopping, and entertainment either easier or harder to manage. The time dimensions of community—working hours, school and daycare hours, medical and bank hours, delivery hours, the opening and closing times of stores, services, and bureaucracies, and so forth—are *authority constraints* that likewise impinge on what people can do on a given day. These two types of constraints combine with others to limit daily activity and to serve as the basis for habit formation (Cullen, 1978; Van Paasen, 1981).

Much literature has been devoted to the relative disconnect between the changing lives of women and the spatial and temporal dimensions of cities at the macro level (for example, Altman and Churchman, 1994; Hayden, 1984; Kleniewski, 2002). Although women are given credit for long-term devotion to ameliorating the conditions of others in cities (Spain, 2001), their own gradual change of roles from the home to jobs and careers runs in the face of long suburban distances and land-use segregation and transportation deficits, made more daunting by relatively unchanged responsibilities for child care and domestic work (Palm and Pred, 1974; Wekerle, 1984; Wekerle and Rutherford, 1987). More women are now working at home in response (as men are doing, too), but women continue to encounter greater daily stress resulting from the continued need to reconcile occupational and domestic responsibilities, even at home (Michelson, 1998).

Structural Analysis

Cities do not consist "merely" of people and their behaviours occurring in and between land uses. The land uses have to be made, transportation and infrastructure have to be built, and decisions have to be made and funds made available so that the whole complex can be provided and maintained. For this reason, a *socio-spatial* approach to cities has been advocated in recent years (Gottdiener and Hutchison, 2000). Cities do not appear and run without social organization and process.

Cities must take collective action with respect to both social and physical policies. They must make decisions about which political jurisdictions are relevant, which actions to take, whose interests are to be served, and who will take initiatives. Cities are formed and are granted their powers and responsibilities according to the laws and decisions of the provincial and federal governments in Canada and of the state and federal governments in the United States. In short, what cities do and how they do it are functions of the attitudes and actions of higher levels of government.

Schools have traditionally been organized at the municipal level and have always accounted for the greatest portion of municipal spending. Among other long-standing municipal responsibilities are police and fire protection; public works such as roads, parks, water, and sewage; and public health, including the prevention of epidemics, the maintenance of sanitary standards, and, more recently, pollution control. Planning, transportation, recreation, child care, and welfare have become increasingly important municipal responsibilities. Performing these varied functions are government bureaucracies that oversee the writing, processing, and maintenance of by-laws, records,

permits, licences, and so on, as well as the collection of taxes and the payment of bills.

Figure 19.3 shows the allocation of the average Toronto residential property-tax payment for various long-standing and recent types of municipal responsibilities. There are many, diverse categories of function. Even though education financing has been assumed by the provincial government in Ontario in exchange for a downloading of other functions to the municipality, the half of the provincial education budget still collected as part of municipal property taxes is about three times the amount of the second largest expenditure, that for police services, and many more times the amount of all the lesser municipal budget items. The innovation accompanying the transfer of the education component of the property tax to provincial auspices is that the funds collected in Toronto need not be—and are not—targeted for the direct benefit of Toronto's children.

Figure 19.3 **Payment by Average Residential Property Owner in Toronto (2002) for Types of Municipal Expenditures**

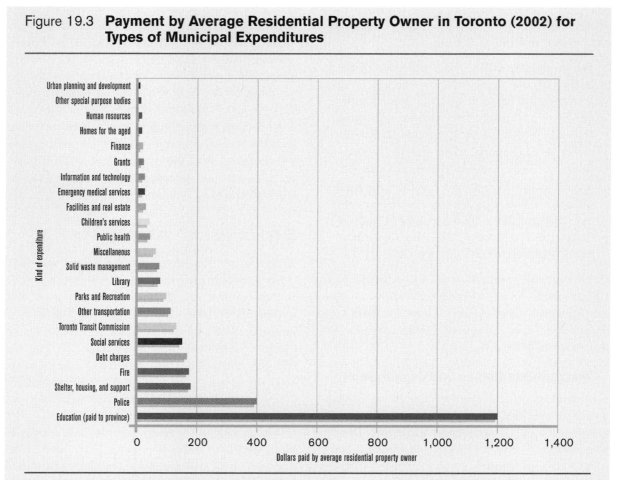

SOURCE: Derived from City of Toronto, *City Budget 2002*, available at <www.city.toronto.on.ca/budget2002>, accessed 24 June 2003; City of Toronto, *City Budget 2003*, available at <www.toronto.ca/budget2003>, accessed 24 June 2003.

Conflicts Within the System

It is possible to view the functioning of municipal government as a harmonious application of rational laws—but only by doing no more than reading descriptions of how the system is formally structured and by never attending a meeting of city council. There are several reasons why urban structure should be viewed through a conflict perspective, in which disagreements emerge naturally within the system.

The primary source of conflict is that the money required for what cities do is always limited, so different functions have to compete for funds. For instance, in a given year, a new daycare centre may have to compete with a new stadium, or with the basic maintenance of existing facilities and services. Or, perhaps, none of these can be done if a higher level of government changes the rules of the game.

Second, municipalities have a mandate to preserve and enhance health, welfare, and safety, providing the greatest good for the greatest number. However, specific issues typically carry costs and benefits that affect different sectors of the population differentially. Employed mothers (not to speak of their children and spouses) are most affected by decisions related to child care, while the construction of stadiums affects the development and hospitality industries more directly. When any decision is made, one part of town may receive the benefits and another the costs. For example, building a superhighway from a suburb to the city centre provides greater access for suburbanites but gives the highway itself and more cars and pollution to the central area.

Our final point brings us back to the matter of funds, specifically, to their transfer. In response to difficulties and inequities in financing many municipal programs, governmental structures in Canada and the United States have adapted to raising money at higher, more broadly based levels, transferring it downward to guarantee that essential programs are provided regardless of varying local resources. But when **ideologies** and budgets are less generous, transfers decline or disappear altogether. Declining transfers leave lower levels of government with decisions as to how to manage responsibilities on which people have come to depend, without the financial support that stimulated their creation and growth. The level and perhaps the very continuation of local services are at stake. In such a situation, conflict arises between levels of government and between program sectors.

This conflict is exacerbated even more when the higher level of government constrains its grants as a result of lowering income taxes. In this situation, relatively affluent people gain economically while those most dependent on municipal programs have no way to replace those programs.

Such a situation is more than theoretical within Canada: over the past decade, federal grants to provinces have declined at the same time that some provinces restructured their support to municipalities because of ideological priorities.

Power

Into this diversity of interests enters the exercise of **power**—the ability of individuals or groups to get others to do what they want them to do. The formal structure of government grants power to elected representatives and to those who implement policies and laws. However, sociological studies by Willis Hawley and Frederick Wirt (1968) and by William G. Domhoff (1980), among others, have documented a host of ways in which this formal system is swayed by informal power structures. Power has been found to be centralized in the hands of a few in some cities and dispersed among different interest groups in others. Obviously, no two cities are the same in this regard, given the range of conditions in each. Norton Long (1958) has argued persuasively that the city is an "ecology of games," meaning that the outcome of any policy issue is never totally predictable. Each issue will draw a unique combination of protagonists whose influence and power are cast in different combinations upon the formal decision makers. According to this view, urban politics is kaleidoscopic, forming a different pattern with various combinations of elements each time.

Roger Friedland and Donald Palmer (1984) and William Tabb and Larry Sawers (1984) have suggested that, in this context, one should focus primarily on major actors in the economic system and on associated motives for profit and control. A convincing case has been made that there is a coalition of persons believing in and usually benefiting personally from continuous urban growth, which they unflaggingly foster. John Logan and Harvey Molotch (1987) have called this neo-Marxist view the *urban growth machine*. Analyses of Toronto by James Lorimer (1978) and many others have placed the interests of large property owners at the centre. Recent transaction patterns in Vancouver indicate that the urban growth machine there is increasingly fuelled from outside of Canada.

It is ironic that the production of numerous costly new buildings by the urban growth machine, creating upward pricing pressures throughout the urban real estate market, has been accompanied by an unprecedented increase in the number of homeless people. Homelessness is all the more serious because most people in North America have assumed that it can't happen here (Bingham, Green, and White, 1987). David Hulchanski (1991) reminds us of the important point that what's good for the functioning of the economic market is not necessarily positive for the objectives of social welfare in cities. Homelessness has spread from older men to women, children, and whole families, in part related to policies in both the private and public sectors that undermine job security and rates of pay.

There is no questioning the presence and impact of economic forces and factors. Nonetheless, economics do not always win. Many decisions made in recent decades in Montreal, Vancouver, Toronto, and other cities have gone in the opposite direction from what an ideologically pure economic determinist perspective would have predicted.

The Scope of Urban Functions and Organization

In metropolitan areas, many municipalities exist side by side. Should decisions and operations be kept close to home in each municipality, where the local population can exercise the greatest degree of control for its particular interests? Or should they be the responsibility of the higher level of the metropolitan area?

Many functions and responsibilities of municipal government transcend boundaries. Polluted water or toxic emissions in one municipality have tangible effects in other jurisdictions; pollution is seldom a local concern. Roads, policing, and licensing would be chaotic without clear organization and co-ordination at higher levels.

While the different parts of a metropolitan area may share responsibility for many activities, their historical boundaries can divide efforts to solve problems facing the area as a whole. For instance, the tax money that can be gathered by an individual municipality has traditionally reflected its wealth and the intensity of activity within its borders. Research has shown that many people differentiate clearly between adjacent municipalities (Michelson, 1997b) and that they

choose where to live in view of the long-standing images of different municipalities (Weiher, 1991). But the needs of a given municipality for funds for such operations as education, welfare, and police and fire protection are not always in line with its tax base. Indeed, the relationship is often inverse: municipalities with poor and aging populations may need greater levels of service yet have less of a basis for raising money.

The purely fiscal solution to the inequitable availability of funds is to let higher levels of government (federal or provincial) collect taxes and provide grants to municipalities with special needs. But even when the funding tap is flowing, objectives can be distorted in actual operation. School financing, for example, relies more and more on provincial grants in response to local inequities. However, the strings attached often bind the recipients more than they might wish—perhaps by requirements for larger student–teacher ratios or for curriculum reforms to reflect the ideology of the provincial government of the day. Even when grants have few strings, benefits do not always go where intended. Federal transfers for higher education can end up in more mundane coffers, for instance.

Metropolitan Government

One structural response to municipal conflicts and inequities is the creation of metropolitan government. A higher level of government is superimposed on existing municipalities, which can remain as they were or be reconfigured. The metropolitan level carries out the functions for which higher-level co-ordination and financing are needed. The functions chosen vary with both place and time.

Examples of metropolitan government abound in Canada. Metropolitan Toronto was formed in 1953 to care for water, sewage, arteries, parks, school financing, welfare, co-ordinated planning, policing, business licensing, and air-pollution control. The metropolitan government was run—until it was abolished by the provincial government in 1998—by a council elected from wards in the various municipalities and a chairperson elected by council members. Metro collected tax money from its constituent cities and boroughs and distributed it where needed. Periodic reviews increased the powers of the metropolitan government and decreased those of the lower-level municipalities. The metropolitan government of Winnipeg was given even more responsibility, while that of Montreal had less. The power of the Greater Vancouver Regional District has waxed and waned over the decades.

The turn of the century has seen considerable restructuring of municipal government in Ontario and Quebec. In Toronto, the recommendations of a royal commission to abolish the boundaries of the Metro government and to extend the functions of a metropolitan government to the larger area now constituting the de facto Toronto area, while maintaining the lower-level municipalities as a form of direct democracy, were countermanded by the government of Ontario, which instead abolished the local municipalities and created, in 1998, a unified City of Toronto with the existing Metro boundaries, in the process all but ignoring the presence of a larger population outside those boundaries than inside. Although many of the functions of the new, larger City of Toronto were already being carried out at the Metro level, the job of governing was made more difficult by the downloading of increasingly costly services from the provincial level in return only for the province's assuming the untraditional role of paying (what turned out to be only half) the costs of schools while controlling school budgets entirely. Ottawa and Hamilton were also compelled to implement a consolidation of existing municipalities into a single, larger one. The looser federation of the City of Montreal and its surrounding suburbs was consolidated on 1 January 2002 into a single City of Montreal.

The sociological lessons of informal systems should not be forgotten when formal solutions are evaluated—even such a highly rational structure as metropolitan government is affected by human interests and influences.

Other Structural Solutions

In situations in which people fear alterations in municipal jurisdictions but urgently require area-wide services, special authorities, commissions, or districts are commonly set up. These entities are charged with specific responsibilities. Depending on their location and function, they might have taxation rights or public subsidies, as well as the right to charge the public for services. Such bodies are usually shielded from the direct control or scrutiny of city officials. They generally function more efficiently than local municipal services but are often more remote from constituency demands as well.

Nonetheless, even when a good match is made between types of needs and governmental level and structures, governments may not be adequately responsive, if only because of a lack of appropriate information and communication. Eric Klinenberg

(2002), for example, documents the disconnect between disadvantaged residents of Chicago and the government when a long, severe heat wave hit the city. The government had difficulty recognizing how poor, old, minority-group residents of the city were hindered in taking adaptive survival steps to protect themselves against the searing heat. As a result, many people died in the absence of a prompt public response to the heat wave.

Evidently, there is no perfect form of government, though some are surely better suited to achieve certain needs than others. Sociological examination of municipal experiences with different structures is a resource that all too often goes untapped by decision makers with their own agendas. In deciding what is most appropriate, certain factors must always be taken into consideration: what needs to be done, what type of structure is appropriate for achieving each objective, and what interests are mobilized in the de facto operation.

Urban Planning in Structural Perspective

Planning is a profession practised by members of municipal staffs or by private consultants hired to contribute services and reports; planners are not elected officials. In most municipalities, planning is found within a number of city structures. It may be done in a separate city department, parallel to public works or licensing; it may be advisory to the mayor; or it may take place under the supervision of an elected or selected commission that reports to city council. Planning activities usually also take place within other organizations, including transit agencies, school boards, and public housing agencies.

Planners help to create long-range, comprehensive plans that, if adopted by city governments, should facilitate the orderly growth of cities. They also help in designing transportation networks. In addition, they are highly visible in planning interventions within existing city areas.

Urban renewal occurs when the nature or use of an area changes and improvements are made to buildings and/or land use. City officials disapprove of areas whose property values and, hence, tax-base potential are low. When existing buildings or activities are considered outdated or no longer viable and are unlikely to be changed by means of private-sector initiatives, cities often intervene. One form of urban renewal is *redevelopment*. A block or larger area is levelled, and a new land use is arranged in co-operation with public- or private-sector organizations. Another is *rehabilitation*, in which existing buildings are modernized and either resold or rented at higher levels.

American cities have seen much publicly planned and implemented renewal of residential and commercial areas. By contrast, major Canadian projects have tended toward the reuse of former industrial sites and railroad yards. The False Creek area of Vancouver, for example, was built on redeveloped railway lands adjacent to the downtown core. It provides housing with considerable amenities for families varying in income and structure. The St Lawrence housing development in downtown Toronto was built on disused industrial land.

Public initiative in urban renewal depends greatly on the health of the economy. For example, an area adjacent to the St Lawrence housing development was rejected for a similar use. The reasons offered were the much greater potential costs for decontamination than originally estimated and the site's loca-

tion on a 150-year flood plain (that is, the area is considered subject to flooding once every 150 years). Yet private redevelopment in the same site was permitted to proceed. Toronto locations whose site characteristics are very similar but that promise commercial-level returns, positive effects on the value of surrounding land, or international prestige are being enthusiastically supported for redevelopment. The situation is much the same in Vancouver: prospective redevelopment has been transferred from the public sector to private capital, drawing on investment funds flowing from Hong Kong.

To sum up, when money is short, support for sports and entertainment arenas, convention centres, or hotels is much greater than support for housing. The urban growth machine is common in cities throughout North America. This approach to planning has been referred to as the creation of a "Fantasy City" (Hannigan, 1998)

Not all planning activities involve such radical intervention as redevelopment or even rehabilita-

The Yaletown Urban Renewal Project on the north shore of False Creek, Vancouver. (© Steve Allen/ BrandX/MAGMA)

tion—preventive medicine is preferable to surgery. Much planning activity is devoted to liaisons with specific neighbourhoods in hopes that minor site-by-site improvements, such as off-street parking, can maintain or upgrade existing areas.

Yet, whatever they do, planners are caught in a strange structural position. Their recommendations always involve economic benefits to some parties and losses to others. Moreover, they have no political decision-making power. R.E. Pahl (1970) points out that influences on the essentially redistributive processes with which planners deal can enter the decision-making process above their heads and from outside the formal decision-making structure. Furthermore, while planners may honestly support the point of view of neighbourhood residents and groups, deviation from their employers' positions may be at the risk of their own jobs.

Ambiguity about the role of planners and their conflicts with other interest groups concerned with urban developmental decisions during times of municipal austerity have led to threats to cut out planning functions entirely, as was debated in Cincinnati, Ohio, at the end of 2002.

Citizen Participation

It is commonly felt that citizens need to express their interests to those in power in an organized and active way, just as large corporate groups do. The best-known approach to citizen participation is that of the late Saul Alinsky and his many North American followers, documented by Donald Reitzes and Dietrich Reitzes (1987). Their *conflict approach* recognizes the difficulty of inducing largely apolitical people to unite in a public stand on technical matters. The answer, according to Alinsky, lies in the uniting effect of conflict. People will join together during a crisis. Trained conflict agents are brought in to discover (or invent) problems besetting the local community that could bring them into conflict with others (often the city government). Through such conflict, latent power can be mobilized to pursue planning interests. The problem in this approach lies in the difficulty of keeping organizational momentum after the main conflict is resolved.

An alternative to the conflict approach is the *coalition approach*, in which an effort is made to create a local citizens' group, perhaps a ratepayers' association or tenants' union. Rather than acting independently, such groups join with other interests and organiza-

tions for mutual support. It is true that they gain a broader base of support and can wield considerable influence. But it is unclear how broad a coalition can be if interests within it eventually clash over issues.

There are many other techniques developed for citizen participation. Some using videotaped opinions were developed in Canada. Given that planners have technical expertise and that elected city officials represent the people, it may seem surprising that so many efforts appear necessary to represent the ordinary Canadian's interests in planning issues. Once again, however, we must keep in mind the diversity of persons and interests in urban areas, and recall that informal processes occur within formal institutional structures. Organizational innovation and animation are often essential if the legitimate needs and wants of citizens are to be promoted to the same extent as those of strong economic interests.

Nonetheless, recent research on environmental justice shows that even successful citizen participation in conflictual planning situations may consume huge amounts of time and emotional cost—something that ordinary people are less equipped to endure than are large corporations with professional support (Roberts and Toffolon-Weiss, 2001). It is a measure of the decision-making apparatus as to what it demands of citizens to make their voices and interests heard.

Conclusion

The diversity in nature and scale of urban considerations and problems taxes the scope of the **sociological imagination**. This chapter itself is very much a summary. No single sociological theory or perspective addresses all urban problems or phenomena. No two matters are likely to draw on the same combination of factors for their solution or understanding. Yet it is useful to start thinking through questions about cities and urban living in light of the logic of four perspectives: urbanization, urbanism, ecology, and structural analysis.

No matter which of these perspectives is taken, cities are not immutable structures with predictably deterministic effects on human beings. They are a part of societies and of social changes, reflecting the conscious actions of people like you and me. Cities may be large and complex, but—for good or for ill—they are subject to human agency and organization. In many respects, cities mirror on an impressive scale the interacting agendas of individuals, groups, cultures, and nations. As in other areas of sociological inquiry, analysis and research help clarify what goes on around us and provide a basis for shaping contexts and structures in useful ways. It remains for everyone to benefit from such knowledge by taking conscious steps for the common good.

There is now so much known about cities and how they function that it is unconscionable for informed citizens to allow charismatic advocates to provide solutions that are clear, simple, and wrong.

☐ Questions for Critical Thought

1. Has the coercive relationship of city-dwellers to those living in their hinterlands changed materially over the span of history? If so, in what ways? Why?
2. What role does technology plan in contemporary urbanization and in the growth or decline of specific Canadian cities?
3. Do you think that everyday interpersonal behaviour varies more in an urban–rural comparison or between critical masses of subcultures within cities?
4. What are the largest subcultures in your area? Do they have different ways of life that make an impact on the city?
5. How would you describe the macro-spatial pattern or infrastructure of the city you know best? What differences in everyday life are possible outcomes of the opportunities and constraints presented by this pattern or infrastructure?
6. If you were an architect, to what extent would your residential designs vary according to specific characteristics of the people expected to live there? What differences in characteristics are significant in this regard? How would your designs vary accordingly?
7. If you were a city planner, to what extent would you take gender differences into account in your plans for the city? What aspects of the city do you think are pertinent in this regard?
8. Evaluate the governmental structures (and restructuring) of cities you know in terms of how effectively they can carry out what cities are expected to do.

☐ Recommended Readings

Leo Driedger, *The Urban Factor: Sociology of Canadian Cities* (Toronto: Oxford University Press, 1991).
Although somewhat dated, this text provides excellent perspectives and data on urban Canada. These data are particularly strong concerning the ecological shapes of Canadian cities and distributions of population within them.

**Kevin Fitzgerald and Mark LaGory, *Unhealthy Places: The Ecology of Risk in the Urban Landscape* (New York: Routledge, 2000*).*
This is an unusual and pioneering examination of some sources of physical and social risk in cities. It shows how exposure to risks is greater among otherwise disadvantaged segments of urban populations.

John Hannigan, *Fantasy City: Pleasure and Profit in the Postmodern Metropolis* (New York: Routledge, 1998).
John Hannigan gives many examples of how cities are persuaded to solve their fiscal and land-use problems by giving priority to the creation of entertainment districts catering to tourists.

Nancy Kleniewski, *Cities, Change, and Conflict: A Political Economy of Urban Life* (Belmont, CA: Wadsworth, 2002).
This is a textbook on urban sociology that heavily emphasizes the structural aspects of the field. It details many of the ways in which decisions are made that impact the nature of urban development.

Lyn H. Lofland, *The Public Realm: Exploring the City's Quintessential Social Territory* (New York: Aldine de Gruyter, 1998).

> Lyn Lofland is one of the leading students of urbanism. In this recent book, she examines in a thorough and engaging way how people adapt to urban spaces.

Kevin Lynch, ed. *Growing Up in Cities* (Cambridge, MA: MIT Press, 1977).

> Written by an acknowledged great among city planning researchers, this book examines with great sensitivity how children use cities and urban spaces. It is based on interviews with and observations of children in contrasting areas of the world.

David C. Thorns, *The Transformation of Cities: Urban Theory and Urban Life* (New York: Palgrave Macmillan, 2002).

> This is a sophisticated, well-written book on how cities have changed as result of recent global trends. It is particularly strong in its international content, perspectives, and documentation.

United Nations Centre for Human Settlements (HABITAT), *Cities in a Globalizing World* (London: Earthscan, 2001).

> The United Nations has made available a treasure chest of information on cities throughout the world. It provides detailed documentation for any number of specific interests and inquiries concerning urbanization.

☐ Recommended Web Sites

American Planning Association
www.planning.org

> This organization makes available the latest thinking on urban planning and issues on its site.

Canadian Institute of Planners
www.cip-icu.ca

> The Canadian Institute of Planners provides practical, up-to-date information on urban issues.

The Community Web
www.commurb.org

> The Web site of the American Sociological Association's Section on Community and Urban Sociology has a section of featured writings and photographs about contemporary topics and issues.

Earth from Space
http://earth.jsc.nasa.gov/sseop/efs/city.htm

> This site contains stunning birds-eye views of a number of North American and international cities. Montreal and Vancouver are included.

Metropolis
www.metropolis.org

> The World Association of the Major Metropolises provides interesting information about metropolises and their problems and prospects.

Statistics Canada
www.statcan.ca

> Increasing amounts of information and data about Canadian communities, cities, and urbanization are available from Statistics Canada.

United Nations Centre for Human Settlements
www.unchs.org

> The United Nations Centre for Human Settlements (HABITAT) provides information about housing and infrastructural considerations.

20

Rowland Lorimer and
Richard Smith

> > >

Mass Media and Technology

© PhotoDisc, Inc.

☐ Learning Objectives

In this chapter, you will:

- gain an overall understanding of how technology shapes the mass media and how the mass media influence society

- learn how communication is a social process

- redefine the mass media to take into account both established media and the Internet

- study Marshall McLuhan's and Harold Innis's theories of how communication and its associated technology influence society

- read a historical account of the development of radio, its technology, and some major elements of its influence on Canadian society

- consider the operation of television and the major ways in which it affects society

- learn significant features of newly developing technology and how they are revolutionizing the music industry

- read about the development of the Internet and learn how it is affecting social activity

Introduction

Back in ancient history, when once you left your home no one could reach you by phone. The only source of **information** was printed texts in libraries. Movies were shown only in movie theatres, and the only way of getting a document to Australia was by post. In the past 20 years, all that has changed. And the changes have affected society fundamentally. The purpose of this chapter is to explore the extent and dynamics of technological change that affects **communication** in society and, as a result, changes the **mass media**, which, in turn, change society.

We might begin with a brief example of the extent to which technological change and media form are interwoven in our society. As this chapter will review in depth media forms such as radio, television, and the Internet, we will draw our example here from an important but often unremarked form of mass media—the telephone.

The telephone, when it first emerged, was not what we know today. In fact, it was very much a solution looking for a problem, and many commentators thought that it had no future at all. The giant telegraph company Western Union famously turned down a proposal to buy the Bell telephone patents, ostensibly because the new invention would never amount to anything.

Given this lack of interest at first, various entrepreneurs experimented with the **technology** in a variety of ways, some of which had nothing to do with calling someone on a telephone. Telephone technology was used to distribute music programs and to provide news services on a subscription basis; it was even sold as a long-distance intercom. The various subscription news and entertainment programs were never that successful, as they were soon supplanted by the just-emerging radio technology. And the point-to-point uses of telephones, which had also been a target market for radio pioneers, were soon much more viable, as the airwaves became saturated with radio stations.

More important, people became used to the concept of picking up a telephone and talking to someone who wasn't in the room. They found it very useful. Although initially targeted at the businessperson, telephones soon made their way into the house, and their popularity soared. A telephone is now considered an essential part of the North American household, and most of us would never consider living without one (although increasingly this phone is a mobile one). Along the way, the telephone has gone

Today's multimedia cell phone. When the idea was first hatched, many thought it had no future at all. (Courtesy: Nokia)

from being a medium with no determined type of use, to a mass medium used for news and entertainment, to a personal medium. With the advent of digital high-bandwidth multimedia wireless telephones, the telephone is being transformed again, returning to the fold of mass media technologies.

These changes in the use of the telephone are examples of the way in which technology and mass communication co-evolve. That is, changes in one enable or require changes in the other, and vice versa. In the telephone world, for example, the development of the mechanical telephone switch became absolutely necessary as predictions of telephone growth began to outpace the population—it was estimated at one point that in order to switch all those calls, every young woman in North America (women did most of this work) would have to be a telephone operator. As you continue through this chapter, you will see several other examples of technical, economic, and political forces that combine and interact to shape the forms of media and the society that they reflect.

The previous chapter examined urbanization and the urban nature of Canadian society. Much about that urban environment is possible only because of technology—how many people could live in Toronto without the subway, for example? Or electricity? Our mass media are similarly dependent upon and affected by technology and technological change.

This chapter will begin by putting some definitions in place and then look at the past (the history of radio technology and its influence on society), the present (the impact of television technology in its current and evolving operations, and their influence on society), the changing present (in the music industry), and the future (the effects of Internet technology as it evolves, and its likely direction of evolution). In a concluding section, we will make brief mention of media form theory and analysis as first put forward by Harold Innis and Marshall McLuhan.

Defining the Media

The *mass media* are technologically based communication institutions. To understand the influence of technology, we need to define both *communication* and *technology*.

Defining Communication

It would be possible to communicate messages without technology. Human beings have built-in encoding capabilities (voice) and decoding capabilities (ears). But these have relatively short range and are relatively impermanent, storytelling aside. In order to communicate in ways that reach farther in time and space, we employ technology. These technologies have evolved over time to let us reach farther and faster than ever before.

The technologies of the pre-electric and electronic eras included printing and such things as the semaphore telegraph (Rowland, 1999). The technologies of the nineteenth century, in the form of steam-powered printing presses and newspapers delivered by train, had a dramatic effect on communication processes, and brought in what has been known as *mass media*. The world of electric communication (for example, by radio or telegraph) and electronic communication (for example, by computer) has both extended the reach and enhanced the quality of the mass media.

Scholars who study this process range from those who are concerned with the way in which the technology works (engineers, typically) to those who look at the impact on society (communication scholars and sociologists of the media). For both of these groups, a simple formula developed in the 1940s has come to serve as a framework for study. It looks something like Figure 20.1.

Out of this formula comes the following definition: *Communication* is the process by which a message, including the content or meaning, is encoded, transmitted, and decoded and how that message, including the content and meaning, is transformed by that three-part process.

Defining Technology

If communication is a three-part process, what is *technology*? Langdon Winner (1977), reflecting general thinking in this area, proposes that technology is composed of three elements:

1. pieces of apparatus,
2. techniques of operation to make the apparatus work (we might say "professional practice"), and
3. **social institutions** within which technical activities take place (we might say "receptive social institutions open to using machines").

So conceived, a printing press in the hands of a group that cannot operate it, or locked up and made inaccessible by a ruler or a government, is but a piece of iron.

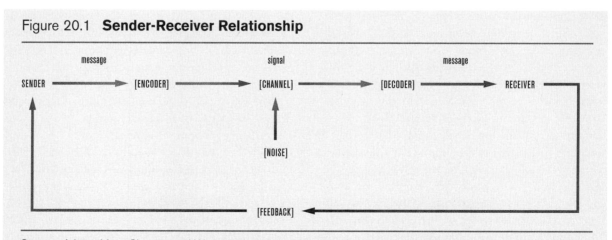

Figure 20.1 **Sender-Receiver Relationship**

SOURCE: Adapted from Shannon and Weaver's theory of communication model, available at <http://www.gslis.utexas.edu/~lis382pd/sp203/Shannon.pdf>, accessed 23 July 2003.

IN THE FIRST PERSON

My interest in the social implications of communication media and technology dates from my university days and a paper I wrote as an undergraduate on a new technology called "teletext." This technology, called Telidon in Canada, has long since been displaced by the Internet and it's easy to see why. In my study of the technology, I noticed that it was very unequal with regard to the creators and the consumers of information on the system. The creators used special terminals that cost an enormous amount of money, whereas the consumers used less expensive terminals, connected to their TV sets, to select from a list of available items. Recognizing a structural imbalance in the way the technology was configured sparked an interest in studying new media that has lasted to this day.
—RICHARD SMITH

In a way, technology is an artifact of instrumental thought. Technology starts with an idea and manifests that idea in a device to achieve a transformation. An idea develops from a world view, for instance, that instrumental action by human beings to transform the world in a certain way and within a certain realm is both possible and legitimate. Technology is developed and applied when people accept that such human intervention is possible, legitimate, and advantageous and when they understand both the principles and the specifics of the operation of the machine (otherwise, they can do nothing when it breaks down). Technology is used by society when social institutions are active in adopting, if not developing, machines to facilitate instrumental action.

In sum, *technology* is the combined elements of apparatus, techniques of operation, and receptive social institutions that allows its users (usually human beings) to transform the environment.

With these two definitions—*communication* and *technology*—in hand, we are now ready to examine mass communication and the mass media, which are, effectively, the combination of communication and technology in order to reach large groups of people very quickly.

Mass Communication/The Mass Media

The integration of technology with communication across society as a whole creates both the process of mass communication and the institutions that allow for mass communication, the mass media.

Step back two paces. If we were to carry forward the social definition of *communication* from the previous section, we would conceive of *mass communication* as communication on a mass (or societal) scale, in other words, as a lot of messages being encoded, sent, and decoded. Some of mass communication is exactly that—a lot of people talking on the telephone, sending and receiving e-mail, and writing and receiving letters, along with some of the mass media phone companies, Internet service providers (ISPs), and the post office.

Interestingly, however, until very recently the accepted meaning of *mass communication* did not describe that process at all. Nor were phone companies and post offices seen to be the dominant mass media. What was, and still is, more often termed *mass communication* is the communication that happens by means of mass media institutions that produce and distribute movies, large daily newspapers, and TV and radio programs. Tim O'Sullivan and colleagues, writing in 1983 in *Key Concepts in Communication* prior to the development of the Internet and CD-ROM games, capture that type of mass communication quite well: "Mass communication is the practice and product of providing leisure entertainment and information to an unknown audience by means of corporately financed, industrially produced, state-regulated, high technology, privately consumed commodities in the modern print, screen, audio and broadcast media" (131). The *mass media*, they say, is "usually understood as newspapers, magazines, cinema, television, radio and advertising; sometimes including book publishing (especially popular fiction) and music (the pop industry)" (O'Sullivan et al., 1983: 130).

At the time of providing that definition, O'Sullivan and colleagues pointed out that this usage of the term *mass communication* had the potential to

IN THE FIRST PERSON

I never really expected to end up doing research and writing about communication. But with a PhD in cognitive/educational psychology at the tender age of 24, I still had some maturing to do. I began to realize that psychology was a behavioural rather than a social science. Spurred on by a year at Oxford, reading and listening to social anthropologists, I shifted my attention away from the dynamics of thinking and toward the media that carry ideas to members of society. Once oriented toward the media, I focused initially on ownership and policy, but before too long found myself examining technology. Today I am ever more involved in technological innovation aimed at making technology work for society rather than just pursuers of profit. –ROWLAND LORIMER

mislead. They advised that the word *mass* encouraged many to think of the audience as a vast, undifferentiated agglomeration of unthinking individuals, likely to behave in a non-rational—if not irrational—manner. This conception of the audience is misleading. In reality, those who watch television or read newspapers or go to movies are a heterogeneous group who bring many different contexts ("encoding envelopes") to any message. Moreover, O'Sullivan and colleagues added, the word *communication* tends to mask the social and industrial nature of the media and promotes a tendency to think of them as analogous to interpersonal communication, that is, communication on a mass scale. Back in 1983, with these caveats in place, their definition (and others essentially the same) was generally accepted and was widely used.

Times—and technology—have changed. Beginning in about 1990, when Internet use began to migrate from science communication to the wider world, the possibilities for person-to-person communication on a mass scale expanded dramatically. Suddenly it became possible to post an e-mail message to an address anywhere in the world that had an e-mail system, where the message would await access by the user. In quick succession, a number of platform-independent technologies replaced basic text-exchange protocols (notably Mosaic and the World Wide Web) so that by 2000, digital files of any type—text, sound, image—could be exchanged between any computer user and any other computer user for an insignificant (for most in the Western world) cost. Moreover, with the deployment of World Wide Web technology, the foundations of centralized mass com-

munication (that is, corporate-financed, industrially produced, state-regulated, high-technology institutions) as the only form of mass communication began to unravel.

By 2000, it had also become possible for any person with a bit of effort and little more expense than a computer, some software, and Internet access to create a Web site that was accessible around the world. In other words, while the Internet started off as a means for person-to-person communication (on a mass scale), as the business community embraced the Internet for commercial purposes, and with the success of Web technology, the Internet became both a mass person-to-person communication system and a mass (decentralized) broadcast system. That is to say, it allowed anyone who wished to to create content for next to nothing and to make that content available (broadcast it) to the world. Given that millions were anxious to do just that (and for other reasons as well), search engines were developed to facilitate finding information, thereby adding substantially to the effectiveness of the technology as a means of mass communication.

These changes are far more significant than people, including members of the media and media theorists, generally recognize. In a sense, these changes expose O'Sullivan and colleagues' caveats to be an awareness of an inadequacy of the mass communication system at a particular stage in its evolution. In a way, they anticipated the future, but they could not imagine technology developing that would allow interpersonal communication on a mass scale. No one did, except Marshall McLuhan (who will be discussed later in this chapter), and few fully understood or believed what McLuhan actually claimed. So, reflective of their time (and then-current usage of the term), they defined *mass communication* not as mass communication at all, but rather as the mass distribution of centrally produced information and entertainment products.

The last 10 years of technological change have set in place communication on a mass scale. As a consequence, mass communication and hence the mass media have been transformed so fundamentally that both must be redefined.

Mass Communication (Re)Defined

Mass communication is

1. the production and distribution of centrally produced information or entertainment products by means of modern technology,
2. the decentralized production of and provision of access to information or entertainment on the Internet (think Web sites), and
3. decentralized media-based point-to-point interaction on a mass scale through, for example, telephone, the mail, e-mail, pagers, two-way radio, and fax.

Mass Media (Re)Defined

The *mass media* are institutions and their associated technology and practices that allow for

1. the centralized production and distribution of information and entertainment (for example, newspapers, magazines, film, movie theatres, television, radio, advertising, and games; sometimes including book publishing, especially popular fiction, and music, especially the pop industry);
2. provision of wide access to information and entertainment created by individuals and institutions; and
3. provision of communication services to individuals and institutions.

The new definitions of *mass communication* and *mass media* are very significant insofar as they reorient mass communication and the mass media. That reorientation takes the previously dominant instance of centralized production and dissemination of information and entertainment products and diminishes it to one element of a three-element system. Moreover, it elevates person-to-person communication and wide access to many different informational and entertaining creations. In so doing, it makes Internet activities, Web sites, cell-phone telephony, e-mailing, and a host

of other activities prime objects of study within communications and sociology.

One caveat: as James Curran (1982) points out, the mass media are really a subset of centralized mass communication—such a list does not include all instances of centralized mass communication. Buildings, pictures, statues, coins, banners, stained glass, songs, medallions, and rituals of all kinds are mass media in that they involve institutions communicating with members of society. Today they remain media of centralized mass communication, but we do not often talk about them as "mass media" institutions.

Canada and Mass Communication

Canadians are great believers in the value of mass communications technology. Both federal and provincial governments have funded the development of a sophisticated technological infrastructure that has often surpassed that of the United States. For example, Canada was the first nation in the world to launch a non-military communications satellite. Also, as of 2003, our high-speed Internet backbone was 60 times faster than that of the United States. This strong belief in communications technology inspired Duncan McKie—not an unbiased observer in that he was the co-author of *Canada's Information Highway* (McKie and Angus, 1994)—to comment, "Just as our lumber, minerals and fisheries were accessed through the public infrastructure of canals, rail and highways, the new infrastructure must be extended to a resource as precious to Canada's growth. Those Canadians who live outside the reach of the high-speed Internet have a wealth of talent and imagination to offer other Canadians and the world" (2001: A21).

McKie's statements echo throughout Canadian history, beginning with John A. Macdonald's building of a national telegraph system and railway and extending through the creation of a national radio system, national television, and national data communications and Internet infrastructure. Indeed, the continuous struggle to establish a truly national newspaper and a national newspaper chain can also been seen as a belief in the value of communications to nationhood.

Radio Broadcasting Yesterday

Unlike printing and its institutions, which began with the invention of moveable type by Johannes Gutenberg in about 1450, **broadcasting** did not evolve slowly over several hundred years. Rather, as a result of the activities of various inventors—particularly Guglielmo Marconi (who made his first transatlantic transmission on 12 December 1901 from the United Kingdom to Signal Hill in St John's, Newfoundland) and a Canadian, Reginald Fessenden—broadcasting burst suddenly upon the scene. Fessenden was the first to broadcast a sound (his violin-playing to sailors at sea) by superimposing it on radio wave. This was at a time when Marconi was content with using the radio to send the dots and dashes of the telegraph. (For students interested in further reading on the history of broadcasting technology, especially in the context of later technological developments such as the Internet, Wade Rowland's *Spirit of the Web* [1999] is an excellent source of information.)

But the invention of broadcasting is not wholly described by making reference to the concoction of devices developed by inventors. Broadcasting is a social practice that makes use of particular technology. In a closed society, Marconi could easily have been suppressed, jailed, or murdered by the state. The same could apply to Fessenden and others who followed. In the context of an open and dynamic—indeed, technology-entranced—society, broadcasting was able to establish itself quickly. In fact, Marconi, an Italian, sought out a receptive country, Great Britain, with its vast navy, to invest in the development of radio technology that could provide real-time communication with people at a distance.

Marconi saw his apparatus as a point-to-point (that is, land-to-ship) communication device. Indeed, he went to some length in an attempt to compensate for the fact that the medium itself was a broadcast to anyone with reception equipment. He took out restrictive patents on the sending and receiving equipment he invented. He leased rather than sold his equipment. He trained and licensed all operators, and he required that radio operators be employed by him rather than by the organization for which they provided communications services. In contrast to Marconi's activities and point of view, Fessenden's violin-playing to ships at sea embraced radio's broadcast potential. The extension of the model of the telegraph to wireless communication froze elementary radio-signal generation and transmission techniques to maintain radio as a point-to-point device. Even the use of Morse code can be seen as a means for restricting the use of radio communications and working against its broadcast characteristics.

Had radio been restricted to a point-to-point medium, the world would have been filled with multitudes of radio transmitters and receivers (called *transceivers*). Indeed, such transceivers exist, in the form of two-way radios or walkie-talkies. You see people using them at large ski resorts, contacting their friends and arranging to meet at a certain place at a certain time. But the potential for broadcast seemed irrepressible. Even those who were interested primarily in radio's point-to-point capacity toyed with broadcast. The Canadian National Railway was an early broadcaster.

In addition to its capacity for broadcast and the lack of deterioration of the signal no matter how many people listened, another factor played a role in encouraging radio's development as a broadcast technology—the cost of the technology for production and dissemination of content. Within a few years of its development, so cheap was the technology to broadcast and receive radio signals that almost any community of more than 500 could afford to have its own station if it really wanted. Alternatively, powerful transmitters could be built to cover vast areas, as the CBC did with its transmitter in the small town of Watrous, Saskatchewan. The conductivity of the alkali soil of the region turned out to be perfect for radio, and Watrous became the key CBC transmission station for the farming communities of the prairies.

By the 1920s, radio stations had come into existence in North America. Each station sent out a signal in all directions from a tall antenna on a frequency of its choosing. Suddenly, the isolation of remote farms, especially in winter, was lifted. But just as it was lifted, the space left was filled with a near-cacophony of voices. Canadian listeners had two difficulties in the early years: the first was receiving one clear signal without the interference of another signal from another station; the second was finding a Canadian signal that was not overpowered by a usually more powerful US signal, especially at night when signals bounce off the ionosphere and travel much farther. For these reasons and, in prior years, because Marconi had managed to create an effective monopoly on radio transmission, national governments first decided to become involved and then later strengthened their involvement as regulators of radio; they did so by declaring the airwaves (the electromagnetic spectrum used by radio) to be a public resource.

The first to commercialize radio were the hardware manufacturers. Their specific problem was to persuade people to listen to the radio and, secondly, to find a way to pay for the cost of creating broadcasts. Their initial strategy was to create the programs themselves to encourage people to purchase radios and to demonstrate the viability of the technology as a popular medium to potential investors and advertisers. Over the course of a decade or so, aided by the ability of radio stations to broadcast events live from afar, listenership increased.

As the number of listeners increased, program producers were able to interest manufacturers—especially soap manufacturers anxious to promote their products to large audiences—to underwrite the costs of creating programs. Government-employed engineers found ways to decrease interference by allocating signals at certain frequencies. And governments or their agencies (in Canada, the Canadian Radio-television and Telecommunications Commission, or **CRTC**) played a critical role by dividing up the radio spectrum so that the ability of one national or local community to have a radio station was not precluded by the existence of another, larger nearby national or local community. Today, with the virtual ubiquity of cable and satellite and with **digitization**, signal interference is increasingly less of an issue.

In response to this technology, to its cost, to its capacity, and to its regulatory environment, a wide range of entrepreneurs set up radio stations in various communities. The political economy of radio broadcasting was such that, over the years as program formulas became more established, the more ambitious of the radio entrepreneurs were able to identify economies of scale (for example, national news programming serving all stations within the owned group, or programming formulas that would work within any large metropolis). Once they realized that these economies of scale could be achieved, they were able to acquire chains of radio stations and pay owners of single stations more than they could ever expect to earn on their own. In Canada, those who were successful on a relatively small scale, such as the Moffat family of Winnipeg, were able to accumulate nearly $1 billion in the space of a lifetime. The most successful, the Thomson family, was able to catapult itself into a hereditary peership and membership among the 10 most wealthy people in the world.

This historical glimpse at radio illustrates how technology is not mere apparatus but social practice. That is, while Marconi seemed to want a point-to-point technology, others, and seemingly society in general, wanted broadcast. Once Fessenden had demonstrated that radio waves could carry sound, and others later found ways that received signals could have their fidelity preserved and signal amplified, and still others (governments and advertisers) were brought in to underwrite the costs of programming, broadcasting was underway. Cost entered the equation, as did infrastructure, in the form of such basics as electricity. Radio could have never become a popular medium of communication if radio sets had been prohibitively expensive. Likewise, without readily available electricity, the uptake of radio would have been far slower.

Radio practice integrated itself with existing social practices and institutions. Programs began as talking newspapers and extensions of vaudeville. Had governments not seen the advantage of being able to speak to the nation, and had advertising not reached a point where manufacturers could conceive of courting national audiences by sponsoring programs, radios would have been prohibitively expensive. A comparison with the state-controlled development of radio in Britain, with its annual licence fees for owners of receivers, demonstrates how one socio-technical form leads not only to a different technology management structure, but also to different content. For example, the development of rock 'n' roll and the derivative popular culture embraced by young audiences was slowed significantly by state control of radio in Britain and, at the same time, hastened by pirate radio transmitters on ships anchored in international waters.

The greater enthusiasm of the United States for technology seems to have given it significant advantage not just in the development of hardware, but also in the development of derivative industries such as popular music. Herbert Schiller (1984) has argued that this embrace of technology by the United States is part of its overall imperialist strategy. Less condemnatorily, one might certainly attribute the ubiquity of US popular culture around the world to the American embrace of communications technology of all kinds and the opportunities thereby created for derivative leisure product manufacture and distribution. It is also possible to view US communications and information policy, stressing the free flow of information—that is, the right of individuals anywhere to have access to US broadcasting—as a natural extension of the interests of the entertainment industries that have been built around the almost total and enthusiastic embrace of communications and, indeed, all technology by the United States. Certainly, in the early years, initial policy was formed on the basis of the potential (broadcasting) and the limitations (signal interference) of the machinery.

Of particular interest in Canada was the struggle over the ownership of broadcasting stations. The slogan developed by Graham Spry and Alan Plaunt of the Canadian Radio League was "the state or the United States." Much has been written about the beginnings of radio in Canada (Nash, 1994; Peers, 1969; Weir, 1965). In a nutshell, US interests in collaboration with Canadian radio-station owners argued for private ownership. Others, spearheaded by the Radio League, argued for the British model of state ownership. A royal commission was set up, chaired by Sir John Aird, a former head of the Canadian Imperial Bank of Commerce. Aird heard the concerns of those who appeared before the commission and, in his 1929 report, interpreted their statements in favour of Canadian participation and content as a desire for public ownership, that is, ownership by an arm's-length government agency with funding coming from taxpayers through the government. When Conservative prime minister R.B. Bennett introduced the first broadcasting act of 1932, he stated,

> First of all, this country must be assured of complete Canadian control of broadcasting from Canadian sources, free from interference or influence. Without such control radio broadcasting can never become a great agency for the communication of matters of national concern and for the diffusion of national thought and ideals, and without such control it can never be the agency by which national consciousness may be fostered and sustained and national unity still further strengthened. . . .
>
> Secondly, no other scheme than that of public ownership can ensure to the people of this country, without regard to class or place, equal enjoyment of the benefits and pleasures of radio broadcasting. Private broadcasting must necessarily discriminate between densely and sparsely populated areas. This is not a correctable fault in private ownership; it is an inescapable and inherent demerit of that system of radio broadcasting. (quoted in Bird, 1988: 112)

What Canada got was a mixed system of public and private ownership that, in the past two decades, has tilted toward greater private ownership and hence commercialization, especially in television.

Overall, as a media form, radio brought to Canada a variety of social forces. It brought a social integration by means of a capacity for delivering both information and entertainment to urban communities, small towns, and rural residences. It built on the railroad to bind the nation together with ideas and images, personalities and national events. Once spectrum management created room for Canadian signals, and once the Canadian government opted for mixed public and private ownership, Canada began to be shaped by its own messages and by a concern with integrating all Canadians of various cultures, regions, ages, and tastes into a common social space. Radio was a respite from isolation in rural areas and provided a social fabric as represented in the concerns and creativity of radio producers. Radio also laid the foundations for television.

Television Today

Television, of course, is the world's other major broadcast mass medium. With a historical analysis of radio in place, and with the understanding that, historically, many of the same technological and policy issues affected television as much as they did radio, we will turn to the modern day and discuss how television technology is affecting the operation of television. (See also Canada, House of Commons, Standing Committee on Heritage, 2003.)

Canada threw in its lot with the United States in the early years of television by adopting the same picture standard, rejecting the slightly superior standard of Britain and most of Europe. The North American standard was NTSC (National Television Standards Committee). The European standard was PAL (phase alternating line), except for France, which adopted SECAM-L (*sequential couleur avec mémoire*) as its standard. This means that Canadian television sets were capable of receiving US signals. And while Dallas Smythe (1981) has argued that Canada could have maintained its cultural sovereignty more successfully by creating an incompatible standard for television in North America, popular resentment of such a decision by many Canadians would have defeated any government. Moreover, Canadians would just have acquired two television sets—one to receive Canadian signals and one to receive US signals.

The pace of development of television was quick enough for its time in history, but when looked at in the context of the pace of today's developments in communications, it seems positively plodding. The federal government funded the development of a national television network, CBC Television, in the 1950s, on the foundation created for radio. The government, through the CRTC (then known as the Canadian Radio Television Commission), also allowed private television to develop in local markets and allowed a national private-sector network, CTV, to evolve. However, it restricted ownership in individual stations to Canadians (at a level of 80 per cent) and the level of ownership any one group could have in CTV.

The CRTC declined for several years to decide whether cable television would be allowed. But eventually it allowed individual entrepreneurs in many different communities to found local cable companies, which they used to import and distribute US programming, sometimes the same material that the CBC or CTV had purchased for distribution in Canada. This necessitated a policy pirouette called **simultaneous program substitution**, in which the Canadian signal with its ads was substituted for the US signal so that the Canadian broadcasters could claim the whole audience and thus attract higher revenues from advertisers. This is why Canadians rarely get to see the ads that make their first—sometimes their only—public appearance on the day of the Superbowl.

Over the years, because technology allowed for economies of scale, industry pressure persuaded the CRTC to allow increased concentration of ownership. Following the pattern set with radio, the more aggressive of the cable entrepreneurs, especially Ted Rogers and J.R. Shaw, bought out the smaller operators and formed themselves into multimedia conglomerates (see Figure 20.2).

Eventually, the CRTC allowed other local television stations to be brought together under one owner, Izzy Asper. Asper found ways of forming a major television empire based on multiple ownership of stations. His company, CanWest Global, now owns not only television stations but also a good number of Canada's major English-language daily newspapers and some French-language ones as well—the *Toronto Star* and the *Globe and Mail* are notable exceptions (see Lorimer and Gasher, 2003).

CTV is now controlled by one group, Corus (see Figure 20.3). CanWest Global is a second national network. Rogers and Shaw dominate the cable industry in English Canada, in contrast to the hundreds of small operators that began cable services in their communities.

In an era of **globalization**, concentration of ownership is hardly news. Yet in television—as in all communications industries—concentration of ownership has grown more rapidly than in many other industries. One reason is technology. In most industries, after development and plant setup costs, there are continuing manufacturing costs for each item produced—say, each pair of shoes—and the product is literally consumed (and thereby destroyed over time) by the initial purchaser. Even "pre-owned" luxury cars have been partially consumed by their first owners. The transmission technology of communications, combined with the properties of the very products themselves, results in very limited manufacturing costs for each new copy produced or broadcast made. In broadcasting, there are no copies that are consumed. The program is produced and a signal sent out for any qualified viewer to receive.

In broadcasting, a program is not consumed in the fire of any single person's imagination but rather lives for another day to be shown to another with no deterioration. Whether the audience is 1,000 or 1,000,000, the cost of the broadcast is the same, except if the audience lives in a widely dispersed area and the signal must be relayed or the signal strength increased. In the worst case—which is still far more advantageous to producers than the best case in many other industries—each copy costs a small amount to deliver the content to the consumer. CDs, for example, cost less than one dollar for the reproduction of each copy. The showing of a movie adds only a small amount of wear and tear to the copy. A radio station playing music, or a TV station running a movie, needs only two or three people to broadcast to as many as care to tune in. This means that the financial rewards of concentration of ownership are far higher, especially in the non-print communications industries, than they are in most other manufacturing.

In short, technology has been instrumental in encouraging concentration of ownership in the mass media. That same technology has encouraged—at least until the last decade, when the number of available channels began to expand—a narrow range of programs. How? By lavishing funds on production—obtaining imaginative, high-jolt-per-minute scripts, hiring good and beautiful actors, shooting in exotic locations. The US-dominated industry has weaned audiences on high production values, selling programs into new national markets for next to nothing, while local producers attempt to compete with programming that has production budgets less than 5 per cent

Figure 20.2 **Ownership Chart for Rogers**

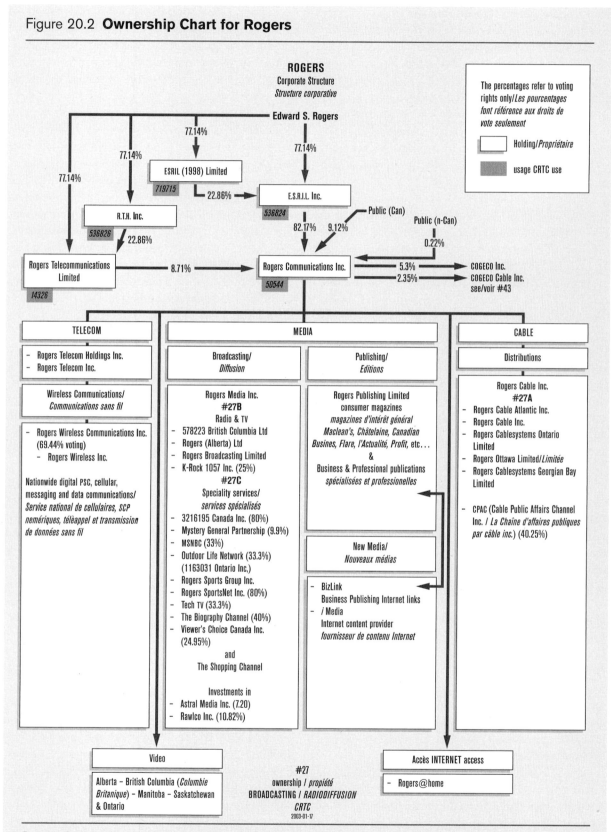

SOURCE: Canadian Radio-television and Telecommunications Commission, <http://www.crtc.gc.ca/ownership/cht27.pdf>, accessed 23 July 2003. Reproduced with the permission of the Minister of Public Works and Government Services Canada, 2003.

Figure 20.3 **Ownership Chart for Corus**

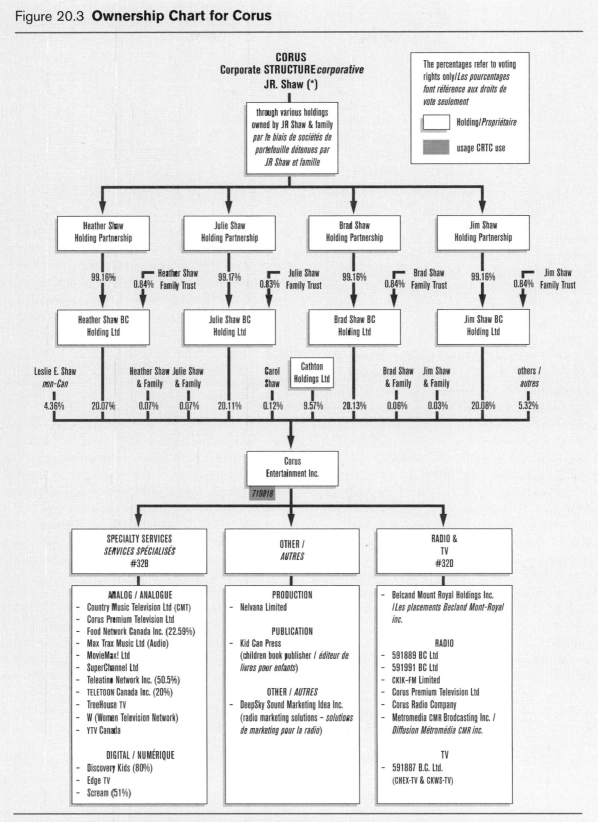

SOURCE: Canadian Radio-television and Telecommunications Commission, <http://www.crtc.gc.ca/ownership/cht32.pdf>, accessed 23 July 2003. Reproduced with the permission of the Minister of Public Works and Government Services Canada, 2003.

of those of the major producers. Such competition has been a major disincentive to the production of new programs over the purchase of existing ones.

In Canada, and in many other countries, this has led to limited domestic content and, in Canada specifically, to a major effort by the CRTC to force Canadian producers to create Canadian programs. In response, the industry has put further pressure on the CRTC to allow concentration of ownership so that the costs of production can be earned back by means of full access to all Canadians. Communications technology has also encouraged a growing preoccupation with movie and sports celebrities whose vast salaries are purely a function of the low cost of worldwide broadcasting. The visuality of television and movies has fostered the development of cosmetic surgery, the most vivid examples being Cher, Michael Jackson, and Pamela Anderson. It has also led to the evolution of idealized body types and the spread of health disorders such as anorexia based on what is photogenic.

Television technology has favoured the development of endorsed and designer products whose market success depends on the endorsement of celebrities over the quality of the product. The advertising industry cajoles and threatens us into participating in endorsed products by injecting those products into desirable lifestyle ads. In an illustration of celebrity endorsement, in her debut into men's hockey (in Finland), Canadian female hockey player Hayley Wickenheiser's clothes were paid for by Adidas, her car provided by Volkswagen (on which was a department store ad—they probably helped out, too), and her hotel accommodations provided by Radisson.

Communications technology, led by television, has favoured the election of telegenic presidents and prime ministers. It has focused the attention of the citizenry on devils, fools, and saints—personalities from Osama bin Laden through Stockwell Day to Mother Teresa and Bono. Indeed, television technology has raised the stakes of conflict. Greenpeace taught the world how a small group, in concert with the media, can disrupt the concentrated power of large corporations and governments by portraying that power as bullying by a Goliath. The media-captured crashing of two large fuel-filled planes into the symbols of worldwide capitalism represented in the twin towers of the World Trade Center taught us about the tentacles of Western **values**—in part through the media—of the resentment of those values by some, and of the ability of a few to affect the entire world by using the media to expose the vulnerability of the citadels of power. Nothing since the sinking of the *Titanic* at the beginning of the era of radio has so shocked the industrialized world.

This, then, describes the current technological communications order within which we are living, where television plays a predominant role. However, the leading edge in television technology and the reformation of the mass media is elsewhere.

The digitization of electronic communication and the shift of transmission from electrons to light within optical fibres have changed the mass media fundamentally. *The Economist* captures the latter quite strikingly:

> Some scientists are dissatisfied with electrons. This seems ungrateful. Electrons have served mankind well as carriers of energy; they have become adept as shufflers of information. Some of their attributes, however, offend purists. They have mass, which makes them a bit sluggish. They have electric charges, which means they interfere with one another. Fortunately, there is something better around, something with no mass, no charge, and no rival when it comes to speed: light. (1991: 87)

Once communications engineers began working with light, the possibilities seemed endless. Light pulses could be sent at 300,000 kilometres per second, switched to go one way then the other, in nanoseconds. Multiple signals could be sent down the same fibre by a variety of means, the latest being by changing colour, that is, *wavelength*. By coating the insides of the glass fibre with rare earths, the engineers were able to build in chemical amplifiers for the signal. The whole thing was and is quite fantastic.

Digitization is no less fantastic than nanotechnology. Fidelity is preserved by digitization in both sound and picture. The arrival of digital signals has hugely diminished the amount of "noise" that people have to tune out. A computer is exceedingly good at telling a 1 from a 0 and can even be fed information about the signal to provide further hints (checksums and error correction). Digital signals are also much easier to compress, hence the 500-channel universe and MP3s. Interference has moved from being a problem between different users of the same section of the radio spectrum to being a problem between sectors of society who wish to make use of the airwaves. Spectrum allocation requires a careful balancing of needs, taking into account the military, commercial, and hobbyist interests.

The point is not to understand the dynamics of the technology itself but to understand the reverberations of the 500-channel universe in society. Like passing phrases such as the "information highway," the "500-channel universe" is a sound bite that means that communications technology has reached the stage where the possibilities for broadcast and reception of signals is essentially limitless. Combined with communication satellites, there is no technological reason why you could not receive in your home any signal from any broadcaster. The cost of rerunning a channel in Canada that broadcasts at a previous time in China, India, Australia, or Russia is relatively trivial. Similarly, the CRTC can no longer cite a lack of broadcast spectrum space for a new signal and therefore favour what it sees to be the most socially beneficial proposal for a new channel.

In short, technology has cleared the way for any number of channels, and the CRTC has felt it appropriate to grant many licences to operate. So expanded has the universe of available channels become that at the beginning of 2001, a survey conducted on a group of new specialty channels showed that many were registering fewer than 10,000 viewers on an average evening. Many Web sites are doing far better than that. A bottom-line figure for any viable programming is about 50,000. The less-than-10,000 figure indicates a tremendous audience fragmentation. It is also a sign that the system may have reached the limit in terms of viable program supply.

There is another level to the social meaning of the 500-channel universe. It is that the mass media are moving away from a restricted club of producers, all with substantial revenues, to an open market in which almost anyone will be able to participate as a supplier of programming. Indeed, with the miniaturization and decrease in cost of recording technology (a broadcast-quality TV camera can now, in 2003, be bought for less than $5,000) and the development of audio- and video-streaming technology (technology to be discussed in the next section), we are effectively there now. The question is, what impact does this technological breakthrough have on content, audiences, policy, and nations, particularly Canada?

The answer is that restricted choice (as a result of limiting technology) effectively led to a centralized point-to-many-points broadcasting system and to a definition of mass communication in terms that reflected the technology of the day. Such a system was accepted (and probably encouraged) by the thinking within the industrialized nations of the world because it extended the past. Prior to electronic communication, the mass media were restricted by location (for example, churches) and physical distribution (newspapers). News from far-off places was exotic and was the province of specialty services—in the twentieth century, of international news agencies such as Reuters. The centralized mass media reflected and preserved the hierarchical organization of the most democratic of societies. It allowed for and increased the plurality of the elites—politicians, business leaders, intellectuals, the church and other social service organizations, the health, legal, and engineering professions, and media celebrities—but it maintained, or at least it did not threaten, those elites or the integrity of existing communities and their physical, and hence cultural, spatially organized geography.

Opening the market to all players, as communications technology is doing, has created opportunity on the production side. An increased number of channels has opened up the market to a greater number of producers, and Canada's television production industry has benefited. Television needs product. Canadian producers have product and are finding markets for it. Any programming that has some dramatic tension in it is likely to find buyers in a whole host of countries that do not have the wealth to found a television production industry. Canadian programming also benefits in certain countries from not being American.

Opening the market to all players can, however, also be seen as the weakening of nations and communities as we know them. And nationalists in Canada are likely to see the weakening of regulation and the strengthening of market forces as the arbiter of mass media content as threatening to Canadian **culture** and perhaps to Canadian nationhood. Indeed, governments around the world are now developing a concern for social cohesion in part in reaction to weakening centralized mass communications systems that bring citizens of a nation together. (Other major factors such as globalization and new mixes of ethnicities within nations are also major contributors to a need to consider how social cohesion can be maintained.)

The impact of communications technology on Canadian culture is difficult to foretell. What is certain is that the fragmentation of the audience caused by increased channel choice is a distinct reality, and the Knitting Channel—the joke of the 500-channel universe—is a distinct possibility.

What is equally certain is that such fragmentation will not privilege national or geographical organization of communities—the Canadian Knitting Channel is not a distinct possibility. In short, the division of channels into focused content—individual sports, women's health, physics education, and so on—will favour the formation and strengthening of communities of interest and will weaken geographically based communities if such communities are based on geography alone. Yet if such communities are founded on deeper values, such as concern with the creation of a healthy social environment for the raising of children, then a restructured, more diverse mass media will be as kind to those values to as any others.

As the previous sentence indicates, there are many other social forces outside those of the mass media that are continually at play in weaving the fabric of society. Within communications, technology is only one influencing factor. The never-ending search for profit by the private sector and the somewhat more fitful attention of politicians to culture and the national interest are also key factors in determining the role of the mass media and how they contribute to culture. Were technology and economics the only critical factors in the newspaper industry, there would be no national newspaper chain, only a single national paper telecommunicated to printing plants across the nation and, perhaps, single-community papers. Indeed, were there no restrictions on newspaper ownership, technology would favour distillation down to only a few North American newspapers. In other words, technology in itself is an inadequate and insufficient dictator of the social form of the mass media and their content. Even the technology of the Internet, which favours wide participation, may be nullified or ruled out by other factors—financial interest, policy, and audience choice.

As a technological form, television introduced the world of the eye, a world dominated by visuality, to Canada and the world. Telegenic politicians, entertainers, and even news readers came to dominate, as did larger and larger owners. Economies of scale, together with high production costs, encouraged centralization through concentration of ownership as well as the importation of US programs rather than the production of domestic programs. In combination with visuality, television encouraged the development and worship of celebrity and further concentrations of wealth and power. More recently, with technological change in and reduced costs of signal delivery and program production, television markets have been opening to wider participation by ordinary citizens. While these developments favour citizen participation, they also tend to favour a diminution of the national presence.

The Changing Music Industry of Today

Before turning to the Internet, we should really take a look at sound recording—the music industry—partly because it is being so greatly affected by technological change. (For those interested in understanding the ins and outs of the music business, in the US at least, a good reference is Sidney Shemel and William Krasilovsky's *This Business of Music*, 2003).

Each of the cultural industries is undergoing some change as a result of digital technology. Film is beginning to be delivered through digital signals to computers for in-home viewing. In 2000 and 2001, it appeared as if electronic books ("e-books") were going to revolutionize the book publishing industry in the same way that online magazines such as Salon.com were going to replace print magazines.

The recording industry is dominated by five large companies: Vivendi Universal, Sony, Bertelsmann's BMG Music Group, AOL Time Warner's Warner Music Group, and EMI Group PLC. These companies have developed an industry that signs up a considerable array of talent and, while giving them a break into potential stardom, manages to get most bands to sign contracts that effectively make them indentured labourers. That is to say, if they do gain some fame, vast amounts of money go to the record company and small amounts go to the band. So unfair is the system that aging stars such as Sir Elton John periodically resolve not to record ever again. On the other hand, Michael Jackson is now in control of some early Beatles songs. Others, such as Bruce Springsteen, Prince, and George Michael, go for several years without recording because they get wound up in legal disputes that prevent them from issuing any new material.

On the consumer side, the record companies are equally unfair players. For example, in 2002, the five majors were hit with a lawsuit in the United States that focused on price-fixing (Globe and Mail, 2002). They (and their co-defendant retailers, Tower Records, Musicland, and Trans World Entertainment) agreed to an out-of-court settlement of $108 million (US) in fines plus the distribution of CDs worth $121 million to public entities and non-profit organizations. Nor does the matter end there. In recent years, agents of recording companies have been visiting community centres where dances are held

20.1

Open for Discussion
"Cultural Industries"

In Canada, the term *cultural industries* is used to accurately describe the relationship between a culture and those businesses that produce such products as music, books, magazines, movies and television programs. It draws attention to the fact that these products derive from and reflect the culture within which they are created. In the United States, the term *cultural industries* is not used, essentially because the large film studios, music recording companies, and publishers have a vested interested in denying that they have anything to do with culture. By calling themselves "entertainment companies," they wish to downplay the roots that books, magazines, music and movies have in the producing culture and hence to trivialize the impact of their cultural values on other societies. The "entertainment" industries (and, through lobbying, also the US government) then extend this naming and stance to claim the right, on the basis of free trade agreements, to sell their products into any country where individuals might wish to buy them.

This stance, which underlies the high levels of US movies, books, magazines, videos, and music in Canada, accounts for much of Canadian government support for cultural industries and broadcasting. Thus, for example, radio stations are required to play a certain minimum level of Canadian content. Their performance with regard to Canadian content can be found in *Our Cultural Sovereignty* (Canada, House of Commons, Standing Committee on Heritage, 2003). In the book industry, no foreign company is allowed to set up a book business in Canada without being able to demonstrate net benefits to Canadians. In magazines, foreign publications can sell only 18 per cent of their advertising space to firms that wish to reach Canadian audiences. If they wish to sell more, they must set up a Canadian business. In movies, companies that do not have distribution arms must distribute their films using the services of a Canadian-owned distributor. In broadcasting, foreign ownership is restricted to less than half of a broadcasting company through combined direct and indirect ownership.

demanding that these centres pay royalties for the songs that they play. The result: the community centres have taken to playing the radio in order to avoid royalty payments.

On the side of technology is the famous fight between the record companies and Napster, an online service that allowed individuals to download music files and thereby obtain free copies of songs. The court-mandated closure of Napster only seems to have scattered the Recording Industry Association of America's targets and resulted in ever-increasing levels of downloading of music files. In mid-2003, the Recording Industry Association of America decided to go beyond its pursuit of companies that facilitate the sharing of music files and began proceedings against some individuals who shared significant numbers of files, with the implication that it would eventually get around to everyone. How realistic this is, with over 60 million users of file-sharing software, remains to be seen. It may have the opposite effect,

driving the activity further underground. On the other hand, initiatives such as the iTunes Music Store, launched by Apple, suggest that there is demand for reasonably priced music for downloading, as users downloaded and paid for millions of songs in the weeks following the launch.

The issue with the downloading of songs is not complex. It is clear that technology is now in place to allow the online purchase of songs. However, the record labels are profoundly disinclined to deliver music in that manner, essentially because they fear that one person will order a song and pay for it and then copy it to 100 of his or her closest friends (and complete strangers, for that matter). While there is little doubt that some level of leakage would occur, what the record labels are struggling to do is embrace the new technology and create a product that is packaged and priced in such a way that people would prefer to buy it rather than acquire it at second or third hand. After all, if marketers can persuade people to purchase water in plastic bottles, and if other companies can persuade members of the public to pay 5 to 10 times more for a pair of jeans that differs from its cheaper cousins only in the tag that is attached, then it would be surprising indeed if recording companies could not find a way to do business on the Internet. Note that this is a very fast-evolving situation. Between the time this chapter was drafted and the book was published, Apple had put in place a system for the purchase of songs from major labels. Also, increasingly, the major labels are being challenged by independent record companies.

As a social phenomenon, the tension that exists between normal social behaviour—sharing a song with a friend or making a copy to play to a class—and the desire of copyright holders to exploit what they see as their intellectual property is interesting indeed. That tension is being played out everywhere in society. It is found in the music business and other cultural industries; in food production, where patented life forms are owned by companies such as Monsanto; in the drug industries, where public health systems face ever-increasing costs; in clothing manufacture, where fabrics are patented.

Intellectual property law is the foundation of the information and communications economy. If creators are not recompensed for intellectual work, then innovation will cease and the information economy will grind to a halt. However, and equally, if intellectual property owners push too hard, then the information economy will grind to a halt. Just imagine if the music companies demanded to be allowed to monitor a person's brain to determine what songs were going around in his or her head and then demanded a royalty that was automatically deducted from the person's bank account. Perhaps the only way to fight back would be by means of a class action suit classifying the songs as deliberate viruses designed to lodge themselves in our brains. Absurd? Not as much as you might think.

As a cultural industry that is being greatly transformed by technological developments in its media form, it is easy to see at this early stage how concentration of ownership in music is threatened. Radio in Canada is also profoundly affected by policy, specifically what is generally known as the "30 per cent Canadian-content policy," even though the requirements the CRTC puts on radio stations varies and for popular music is generally 35 per cent. The obvious efficiencies of online distribution of content may give sufficient advantage to individual artists and new

recording companies that in 10 years the big five will be a spent force. On the other hand, they may scramble, adapt, and survive. In terms of content, the media form that is music should lead to greater diversity in music and performers, yet the continuing influence of visuality (through movies and television) will counter that diversity. With respect to Canadian society, we should expect to see a continued strengthening of Canadian artists and, maybe, of Canadian record companies.

The Internet

Canadians have actively participated from the earliest days in the Internet; some key elements of Internet technology were pioneered or fostered here. Several widely available Internet timelines and histories of the technology chronicle significant Canadian contributions (see Zakon, 2003).

Against a background of enthusiasm for communications technology, the Canadian government very early on saw potential for Internet technology; it has pushed a strong policy agenda that has emphasized the extension of connectivity to remote and rural communities and the building of high-speed backbone links across the country. Canadian universities, entrepreneurs, and the general public have all contributed to the creation of an Internet "communication ecology" that is supportive of and includes many media elements (see Carroll and Broadhead, 1994). Internet technologies, like any other technology, shape the format of communication media, content, the audience, and policy.

The Technology of the Possible

At its heart, the Internet is a way for computers and other devices to interconnect with one another. Until the advent of the Internet, connecting computers from different manufacturers was difficult if not impossible. They were, therefore, used mainly as stand-alone devices and not for communication.

The original motivation for connecting computers was practical: to share scarce computational resources. Although it seems incredible now, there was a time when there weren't enough computers to go around, and people had to share them. This aspect was almost immediately eclipsed by the ability to share thoughts and ideas through e-mail, in chat rooms, through Web pages, and by downloading music, programs, and more (see Zakon, 2003).

The Internet is a collection of co-operating technologies that are largely based on what are known as **open standards**. These technologies allow connectivity, and they include everything from the wires and fibres, to the electrical and optical signals on those connections, to the applications that we use every day, such as Web browsers, instant-messaging clients, and e-mail programs.

Open standards means that software developers around the world are given the information they need to create software and hardware that will be interoperable with the existing parts of the network. This open system, with programmers building on the work of others, has made for rapid development and a hectic pace of change as new technologies are made available and the basic features of the Internet are enhanced. The result is that the Internet becomes ever more powerful and ever more valuable to users and to society.

As a result of open systems technology, the evolutionary path of Internet technologies has been visible to all who care to look. Most apparent has been the influence of those who first adopt and use the new technology. It is they who have most dramatically shaped its growth and development. Such **early adopters** were able to do this in large part because of decisions made early in the history of the Internet (Rogers, 1995). The pioneers of the technology established patterns and foundations for subsequent developments.

The history of the World Wide Web is illustrative of that process. As the World Wide Web evolved from a simple tool used within one organization to a global industry with literally billions of pages in existence, user involvement in shaping and directing change has been key to its evolving form. While many industries conduct market research on the desires and habits of their users (the colours and features found in cars, for example, represent the outcome of considerable research), the role of the users has been more active in the evolution of the Internet. That role has been and remains more like a collective production of many thousands of user/developers, from professionals to beginners. For example, some of the largest and most well known Internet technologies today—Google, Yahoo, and ICQ, to name just a few—had their origins as student projects.

The result is that the best interests of the political or economic elite in society are not at the forefront of Internet development. Music-sharing technologies like Napster and Gnutella have challenged the interests of the music and other industries and, in the case of Napster, have been shut down because they have been judged to infringe other people's rights or privileges. The development and widespread use of those technologies can be traced in large part to the open standards and hence non-industrial interests they reflect.

The Internet and Mass Communication

At its inception, the Internet allowed people to connect to computers to perform calculations. The linking of computers quickly evolved into a means of sharing ideas. The sharing of ideas took off in a way that sharing calculating power never did: according to Todd Campbell, "by 1976 e-mail had become the raison d'être of the new network" (Campbell, 1998).

The mass distribution of single messages arrived on the Internet very early as well, although it was not initially recognized as such by major media outlets. The "bulletin board" or "netnews" format, still active today, was, in some ways, a precursor to the active news sites maintained by major media outlets today. Like many early Internet technologies, however, it was most useful to an expert and had limited appeal to a newcomer. The interface was text only, and much of the functionality assumed prior knowledge of the technology. In other words, if you hadn't used it before, or you weren't the kind of person willing to dig into the manuals or read the source code to figure things out, you wouldn't be able to use these tools without training.

Nevertheless, these early forms of news shaped today's practices for interacting with the news online. For example, the principle of allowing a reply to a news posting emerged early on. The assumption made by the small cadres of expert users designing the system was that the reader would have something interesting to say in response to a posting. Most postings, of course, were of a technical nature, and fellow techies could be expected to have opinions and views on everything that happened.

In fact, those opinions and views sometimes escalated into heated debates, called "flame wars" (named after a comic-book character who would turn into a pillar of flame after saying "Flame on"). This pattern of extreme response, whether in e-mail or netnews, is also part of the Internet heritage.

From the beginning, and as a result of its openness, Internet technology has been shaped to be interactive—immediate replies are the norm even on flashier Web-based news sites—and users have come to expect that kind of interactivity through regular use and history.

Internet users don't adhere to a schedule like television or radio viewers, so the media forms have evolved into short items, text-heavy news stories that can be popped up from a Web page, or streaming audio-video pages when the visitor arrives rather than run continuously waiting for users to arrive. New technologies, such as the Ananova computer-generated newsreader, have also been developed to address these challenges. Ananova reads the news for you, in a computer-generated voice and with a computer-generated face, whenever you click on "her" site.

In short, the biases of the Internet pioneers, the organization of their work—in a public forum with a public tool—and the built-in characteristics of the technology shaped the design and roll-out of the technology, which in turn shaped the nature of the interactional patterns of subsequent users.

The Internet can be distinguished from the traditional media in another, significant way. The Internet, together with computers, has made it possible to put all media in digital form and to make the resulting digital files available through a high-speed network. The ability to digitize everything and thus for all media to be integrated one with another and communicated using the same system is called *convergence*.

Early attempts at taking advantage of digitization were not entirely successful. Newspapers were among the first to take advantage of the new media technology. Reporters were required to create digital files that could be imported into a page layout format so newspaper owners could take advantage of the productivity enhancements that digital news creation and printing offered. By creating digital files, newspapers were well positioned to beam their papers into local printing plants and also to deliver their content on the Internet. Not very many of them took advantage of the latter until the arrival of the World Wide Web, but once friendly browsers appeared, newspaper Web sites began to spring up all over. This marked an early instance of repurposing content for a different mode of delivery, here by the Internet rather than by the early morning newspaper carrier. Television and radio stations were not as well positioned for such a transformation, and their necessarily higher bandwidth requirements—sending audio or video through the Net typically requires customers to have a high-speed connection—restricted their ability to repurpose their content.

The past few years, however, have seen remarkable transformations in the computerization and digitization of the radio and television newsrooms. This digitization, coupled with a ever-growing population of subscribers to so-called broadband Internet services, such as through cable modems and digital subscriber lines (DSL), has made the online radio or television station not only possible but (potentially) profitable. As a result, impressive offerings from CNN, the BBC, and our own CBC are now available online, complete with streaming live audio and video feeds. The audio is still tinged with the artifacts of a compressed signal, and the video windows are usually grainy and small, but they are available and are proving the viability of the medium.

These initial forays into online delivery have also enabled broadcasters to experiment with hybrid formats—not just delivering existing content over a new "pipe," but taking advantage of the hypertextual interface to connect background information, follow-ups to ongoing stories, and permanent links to important archival information. It has also allowed the CBC, for example, to accept audio and video files for broadcast that are sent in by listeners (see <http://120seconds.com> and <http://NewMusicCanada.com>).

For the most part, the grandiose visions for a converged media future have not (yet) come to pass. The signature event of this era, the purchase of Time Warner by the Internet company America Online (AOL), has not resulted in the so-called synergistic benefits to the consumer or to the bottom line of the merged entity. In fact, the merged company is less stable than Time Warner ever was. Nevertheless, the potential impact of an endlessly changeable information transmission form does continue to attract both new entrants with dreams of the future and existing media companies looking for new markets.

In the case of convergence, a social observer might note how technological possibility encouraged a mindset that drove the evolution of business forms, both large and small, that were vulnerable to collapse when overstated projections of growth and markets failed to materialize. An interesting point, however, is that while many companies have collapsed and many investors lost money on the stock market, the transition to a digital information system and the evolution of the Internet continues.

The Audience and the Internet

Technological form and social practice are in a constant see-saw of change. The Internet is no exception. The history of broadcast television has been characterized by a series of technological changes—colour television, cable TV, the remote control, the VCR, satellite television, and, most recently, large-screen televisions, DVD players, digital satellites, digital cable, HDTV, and Internet television. At the same time, the appetite of the audience has been changing. TV viewers appear to want more and more diverse programming; they tolerated and then developed a need for fast-action editing and "jump cuts"; they began to use the VCR to time-shift their viewing because of busy schedules; they developed a curiosity for news and programs from afar, and a willingness to pay for premium content that is differentiated from the regular broadcast fare.

In the context of television, one might ask, which way did the influence flow? Did the profusion of channels make the remote control an option people would pay for? Or was people's resistance to getting up to change the channel the motivation to develop and market a remote control for televisions? Did the remote control device "create" the practice of channel-flipping and a nation of couch potatoes?

It would be simplistic to say that any of the technological changes caused one or more social changes, just as it is almost impossible—without careful and thoughtful case studies—to trace with certainty the process by which a technological innovation is pursued and brought to market because of perceived or potential market need. The literature on the social construction of technology has done some of these studies, most famously with the bicycle, and has produced numerous examples of the complex and iterative set of social and technical negotiations that take place along the way to a new technological form or social practice making use of that technology (MacKenzie and Wajcman, 1999).

Some Internet examples of this complex and iterative social and technical negotiations include the extent to which Internet users, long accustomed to interactive modes of communication such as e-mail and bulletin boards, are adopting and popularizing media outlets that provide a place for feedback and commentary. The Slashdot phenomenon, in which a community of technologically adept—and apparently highly opinionated—self-described "nerds" engage in vociferous and lively online debate on almost every new item related to technology, is a perfect example of this, as is the current craze for web log (or "blog") sites (see <www.slashdot.com> and <www.blogger-.com>). Careful observation of audience/participant behaviour led some young entrepreneurs to build on the popularity of Internet relay chat (IRC) and create a simpler and centralized service called ICQ (named in the style of the medium, in which shorthand and nicknames are based on sometimes cryptic abbreviations—in this case "I seek you"). It is enormously popular and has helped define a whole genre of Internet use called *instant messaging*.

The audience and the technology for Internet media continue to evolve. As more people subscribe to broadband, the potential for listening to Internet content becomes more viable, and inevitably the medium will allow us to watch television-like material on our computer—that is, if people have an appetite for it. The online pornography industry, based on an obvious demand, pioneered many aspects of the Internet as we know it today, including secure credit card transactions, compressed streaming video, and elaborate pop-up windows. Future Internet evolution will also follow the money and the desire.

Technology and Policy

When a new technology enables new social action, policy decisions can't be far behind, either to foster or to inhibit that behaviour. The Internet was widely seen as a tool that could bring greater educational and economic opportunities to remote areas, and has thus been targeted for expansion and promotion by the federal and many provincial governments since the early 1990s. Programs include federal programs such as Connecting Communities (subsidies for community networks), SchoolNet (a program to bring computers and networks into schools), and CANARIE's CA*net (an infrastructure program to enhance the technical underpinnings of Internet service). Provincial programs have also been created to build infrastructure, encourage computer and network use in schools, and put government online.

At the same time, Internet technologies have made possible numerous antisocial activities, ranging from pornography and hate mail to sharing recipes for bomb-making. These, too, have been the targets of a variety of policy initiatives or revisions to existing laws to ensure that these laws are applicable to new situations. Sometimes the policies are purely economic, as in copyright provisions that cover digital works or the acceptability of digital signatures.

As a communications technology, the Internet has a special place in a democratic society. The free exchange of ideas and information is considered a cornerstone of democratic politics, and various initiatives have been launched with the explicit goal of taking advantage of this power. These range from major government information-distribution Web sites to experiments with online voting.

Internet technologies even have a growing role in the formation of policy, with electronic communication with constituents and policy experts emerging as an important source of input and a forum for debate. Certain groups with a policy-making agenda, such as the Electronic Frontier Foundation of Canada (<www.efc.ca>), have made key issues relating to information technology the cornerstones of their lobbying and information activities—freedom of speech, security of online data, rights to own and operate **cryptographic** software. Cryptographic software enables computer users to create secure, password-protected copies of documents. The power of modern computers and the dissemination of the enabling software in the form of free—albeit somewhat technically challenging to use—software, means that secrecy, something formerly only within reach of the wealthy or powerful, is now in reach of the computer-using person. The Internet allows those documents to be circulated, creating a form of secret communication that is, for all intents and purposes, uncrackable. In the fall of 2002, Canadian women and women's equality-seeking organizations were invited to use the Internet to share their opinions, experience, and knowledge of the Internet. This consultation had four topics: participation, impact, empowerment, and strategies. (See <http://consult.womenspace.ca/> for another example of the use of online technologies, in this case the Web and Web-based discussion boards, to gather, focus, and deliver political messages.)

A Likely Internet Future and the Influence of the Internet on Canadian Society

Dozens of corporate executives and government policy makers would love to know where the Internet is headed. At one time in the late 1990s, the answer seemed clear: Internet technology would spread to every home and business in the land, it would be capable of carrying and therefore displacing all existing forms of media, and it would be the platform for remarkable social and economic transformation. The dot-com meltdown, coupled with a general cooling to overblown predictions of social transformation, has displaced that vision with a general uncertainty.

In the summer of 2002, it was revealed that a growing number of people were dropping their Internet connections, slowing the rate of growth in connected households (Kapica, 2002). The torrent of unsolicited commercial e-mail (UCE, or spam) that flooded mailboxes in 2002 has also begun to cause more and more people to question the value of this supposed salvation technology. It certainly is clear that Internet business, or e-commerce, is not the panacea to commercial enterprises and that normal business practices still matter.

As usual, neither the utopian nor the dystopian vision represents a likely future. It was inevitable—given the overblown claims—that the Internet wouldn't live up to expectations. Nevertheless, it is an important communication technology and it is here to stay.

Although the potential has yet to be fully realized, two key features of Internet technology seem poised to contribute something unique to our ability to understand mass media. The first feature of the Internet that could reshape media as we know them is the *addressability* of the medium—the possibility of sending a message to a particular person through the Internet. Previous broadcast media, such as radio, television, and newspaper and journal publishing, lacked this ability to personalize the message. The telephone can provide personal connections, but scaling personal connections up to levels where one message is sent to thousands is an enormous undertaking, as anyone who has participated in a political campaign or even tried to reschedule a soccer game knows full well.

The Internet reduces the cost and effort of sending a personal message to hundredths of a cent, well below even the most efficient mass mailing. At present these features are being exploited mainly by spammers, but their use as forms of media goes well before unsolicited commercial e-mail. The antecedent technology can be found in newsletters and mailing lists, which formed one of the first social uses (after e-mail) of Internet technologies. These mass-but-not-mass messages are now finely honed with technologies that allow you to see who has received your message, whether recipients click on any of the embedded links, and even whether they forward it to someone else. A company from Vancouver, innovative info, specializes in this field and sees in it great potential for connecting people, ideas, and issues—not just selling stuff.

In fact, it is this companion ability—the ability to instantly reply to Internet messages—that most distinguishes the Internet from prior forms of media. When people receive Internet messages, they not only have the ability to reply, they *expect* to have that ability. With this sort of technology and this sort of social understanding, it is possible to design an action campaign that will be enormously effective, rapid to deploy, and extremely efficient. As such it may finally pierce the barrier put up by the (mostly reasonable) critics who claim direct democracy is unwieldy and inefficient. Even if we don't see that sort of use for the technology in the near term, we could very well see a redefinition—both technically and socially—of what we all understand as media. The audience of the future will not be content to lie back and be washed over by messages meant for the average person, but instead will be receiving messages targeted to them with the expectation that they can engage in a conversation for fun, for extracting further information, or for taking action. Who knows? We may just take the media as something for participation and not just for persuasion and distraction.

Conclusion: Theory of Technology

This chapter does not put theory up front and then discuss phenomena within the context of that theory. This is partly because we—the authors of this chapter—are not sociologists. Partly it is because we believe that it is more important to explore phenomena in and of themselves and to follow that exploration with a briefer exploration of what theory can offer to extend our understanding. At the same time, and somewhat in contradiction to this stance, we realize that any exploration of any topic begins with a set of assumptions and hence with a theory.

The theory that extends our understanding of technology and the mass media goes under at least two names. It is known as the *Toronto School* and also as *media form theory*. Its best-known proponents are two Canadians, Harold Innis and Marshall McLuhan.

Innis came first, with three books that developed out of his study of the influence of resource extraction on the development of Canadian society (the fur trade, the fishery, and the timber trade). In his later years, he expanded his thought to communication in three books, *Empire and Communication* (1950), *The Bias of Communication* (1951), and *Changing Concepts of Time* (1952). In those books, Innis put forward the notion that the dominant mode of communication in societies is a formative influence on the nature of those societies.

Innis was particularly enamoured with oral societies such as classical Greece and with how literacy fundamentally transformed the Roman Empire. Marshall McLuhan latched on to Innis's ideas and wrote with amazing prescience about the development of electronic society. In two books, *The Gutenberg Galaxy* (1962) and *Understanding Media* (1964), he noted how the linearity, logicality, and conceptuality of print culture was being replaced with the image, an all-at-oneness, and a globalized familiarity.

Like it or not, McLuhan claimed, with all its advantages and disadvantages, we are living in a single world, a global village, or, as the space travellers have it, a blue sphere hurtling through the heavens. The 11 September 2001 attack on the Pentagon in Washington, DC, and on the twin towers of the World Trade Center in New York brought home to the world, and especially to US citizens, the reality of the global village and of the resentment felt by some of the power of others, especially that of the United States.

McLuhan's famous saying "the medium is the message" (1964) captures his perspective well. It means that if you want to understand the impact of a particular means of communication on society, look at the dynamics of the medium itself, not the content of the message it carries. Print, McLuhan (1964) argued, makes us think and reason. Radio tunes us in to the voice and a projected persona of the person at the other end of the microphone. It also allows us to carry on a variety of activities. TV turns us into couch potatoes, demanding our eyes and ears (but often not much of our brains). In leading with the image, it creates a world of beautiful people.

In this essay, we have favoured a media form perspective, although from time to time we have stepped away from that perspective. Overall, we have examined the social form of technology created as a result of the interaction of social institutions and technology to produce a certain social result. We have explored how four media forms—radio, television, sound recording, and the Internet—have favoured certain preoccupations, how they have encouraged certain types of content, certain forms of ownership, and certain kinds of social processes that encourage certain other social developments, including ones designed to work against the expansion of the interests of currently dominant producers.

In the next chapter, on environment and the social world, you will encounter numerous examples of both the natural and the built (human-created) environment and how we have affected and are being affected by that environment. In many ways the media is an environment for the social aspects of human beings, and it must be constructed, respected, and maintained, with the same care.

Media and the influences that derive from their forms do not act alone, but rather evolve out of an overall social process that favours their very existence as well as complements their inherent biases. The mass media amplify—they reflect and help reinforce the social formations that are part of society. They also bring messages that we need to know, and they convey information that we often do not want to hear, whether they be the complaints of those who see themselves as dispossessed or, as in the case of the pornographers, the exploitation of human desires. Their technologies derive from human inventiveness within a rewarding social context and the applications of those technologies both reinforce the status quo and challenge it.

☐ Questions for Critical Thought

1. Think of a number of quite different people, for example, a child, a parent, a brother or sister, a very dear grandmother, an intimate friend, a person in authority whom you do not know, a person who does not speak your language, a person you intensely dislike, an arrogant person, a shy person. Write down beside each how you would tell them something personal and likely to be embarrassing to them, such as that they have horrible-smelling breath or a tear in an awkward place in their clothes. Try, then, to describe the dynamics of formulating the same message to these different people and why you chose to do what you thought you would do.

2. Traditionally, with the centralized mass media, the state has played a regulatory role by requiring, for example, that each broadcasting outlet come forward with a "promise of performance" in which the broadcaster outlines the nature of the social contribution that it is prepared to make to the community. As Web sites proliferate, should the government extend its regulation to require Web broadcasters to make a social contribution?

3. Construct an inventory of the ways in which electronic communication affects your life.

4. What other theoretical points of view can you find in other chapters of this text that relevant to the study of the media, to understanding the social influence of technology and the mass media?

5. What do you think would happen to these regulations if foreign owners were allowed to own and control Canadian radio stations?

6. Canadian radio and television, in combination with movies, magazines, books, and other media, have consistently inundated Canada with American content. What do you see to be the future for Canadian programming?

7. Do you believe that television will continue to be dominated by beautiful celebrities and commercial interests? How might things change? Is webcasting an important factor?

8. Describe your patterns of consumption of recorded music. How have they changed as a result of the Internet? How much illegal copying have you done in the past year? If you were advising the music industry, how would you suggest that it take advantage of the Internet?

9. How could you make better use of the Internet for your academic work, to pursue your interests? How do you see the Internet evolving?

□ Recommended Readings

Manuel Castells, *The Internet Galaxy: Reflections on the Internet, Business, and Society* (New York: Oxford University Press, 2001).

> Manuel Castells is better known for his enormous tome *The Rise of the Network Society*, but this slim volume neatly captures many of those earlier themes and brings his earlier writing into a form more suited to a pragmatic audience. Castells covers topics from the culture of the Internet to the digital divide and politics on the Net.

Sherry Devereux Ferguson and Leslie Regan Shade, eds, *Civic Discourse and Cultural Politics in Canada: A Cacophony of Voices* (Westport, CT: Ablex, 2002).

> This book is a good illustration of the third part of the mass media, communication on a large scale. The essays encompass discourses on the constitution, cultural sovereignty, feminism, globalization, the Internet, marginal communities, nationalism, and Native people.

Harold Innis, *The Bias of Communication*, with an introduction by Marshall McLuhan (Toronto: University of Toronto Press, [1951] 1964).

> Innis's lasting legacy is the focus Canadian scholars put on three questions: How do specific communications technologies operate? What assumptions do they take from and contribute to society? What forms of power do they encourage?

Rowland Lorimer and Mike Gasher, *Mass Communication in Canada*, 5th edn (Toronto: Oxford University Press, 2003).

> This is the foundation text to many introductory courses on mass communication in Canada. In this edition, the authors provide an overview of the communications industry as well as key elements of the policy process that governs it.

Marshall McLuhan, *Understanding Media: The Extensions of Man* (New York: McGraw-Hill, 1964).

> McLuhan's enigmatic writing style notwithstanding, this book remains one of the cornerstone documents for an understanding of Canadian perspectives on media and technology.

Paul Mayer, ed., *Computer Media and Communication: A Reader* (Oxford: Oxford University Press, 1999).

> Mayer's reader covers the essentials of computers as media, with a section on history that sets the stage and then a set of "systematic studies" that provide insights into current and emerging issues for those who use computers as a form of media.

Wade Rowland, *Spirit of the Web: The Age of Information from Telegraph to Internet* (Toronto: Key Porter, 1999).

> Rowland's breezy style and plethora of historical anecdotes makes this history of the Age of Information seem to race by. The premise, that there is much we can learn about the present age by looking at the past, is a sound one.

Bodhan Szuchewycz and Jeannette Sloniowski, eds, *Canadian Communications: Issues in Contemporary Media and Culture*, 2nd edn (Toronto: Prentice Hall, 2002).

> This is a diverse set of sources, newspapers, policy documents, speeches, and so on, with an annotation for each entry. The general topics covered are language, cultural forms, the news, representations, policy and regulation, and advertising.

□ Recommended Web Sites

Canadian Heritage
www.canadianheritage.gc.ca

> This government department site provides information on government programs for books, magazines, sound recording, and film. It also provides links to studies of the industry. From their front page: "Canadian Heritage is responsible for national policies and programs that promote Canadian content, foster cultural participation, active citizenship and participation in Canada's civic life, and strengthen connections among Canadians."

The Canadian Radio-television and Telecommunications Commission (CRTC)

www.crtc.gc.ca

> The CRTC's Web site is an essential stopping place for those concerned with broadcast media and telecommunications issues in Canada. The site contains links to documents that spell out the current law governing radio, television, cable television, and data communication (including Internet) companies. As well, reports and calls for comments on current issues are listed on the site.

CIOS McLuhan Website

www.cios.org/encyclopedia/mcluhan/m/m.html

> Together with Harold Innis, Marshall McLuhan raised the profile of a uniquely Canadian approach to the study of media and technology. This site provides an engaging and wide-ranging set of "probes" (a word McLuhan would have approved of) on the work of McLuhan as well as more recent developments in the world of media and society.

Electronic Frontier Canada

www.efc.ca

> The Canadian division of the Electronic Frontier Foundation (EFF) was set up, in their words, to "ensure that the principles embodied in the Canadian Charter of Rights and Freedoms remain protected as new computing, communications, and information technologies are introduced into Canadian society."

Information Highway Advisory Council

http://e-com.ic.gc.ca/english/strat/doc/september1995.pdf

> Although somewhat dated in the fast-moving and turbulent world of the Internet, this report and the research documents that supported it provide a window into government thinking about the Internet and the background to much that has happened since. It is hosted on Industry Canada's Web site, Strategis <www.strategic.gc.ca>, another important starting point for the study of media technologies in Canada.

Media Awareness Network

www.media-awareness.ca

> This site provides readers with introductory material as well as numerous links to organizations and supporting documents for issues related to the media in Canada. Its primary audience is the younger reader, but many of the links and supporting documents are suited to any reader.

Netfuture: Technology and Human Responsibility

www.netfuture.org

> Steven Talbott's Netfuture is a welcome antidote to our often uncritical and endlessly sympathetic press coverage of technology and society. Thoughtful, provocative, and wonderfully down-to-earth, Netfuture brings Talbott together some of the best of our current world's commentators, including Langdon Winner, for a debate that will leave you wondering for a long time.

Vancouver Independent Media Centre

http://vancouver.indymedia.org/

> This site represents an excellent example of the use of new technologies in the construction of new forms of mass media. The indymedia Web sites (there are dozens of them) are supported through a collective effort both on the technical side—developing software to enable the sites— and on the content site—independent commentators contribute stories, and there is considerable commentary and debate on every page.

21

G. Keith Warriner

> > >

The Environment

© PhotoDisc, Inc.

☐ Learning Objectives

In this chapter, you will:

- examine global population growth and its relationship to poverty and development
- differentiate theories of environmental sociology and their basic assumptions
- critically assess terms such as *sustainable development*, *scarcity*, and *carrying capacity*
- be introduced to the theory of risk society
- come to understand the social constructionist perspective as it is applied in environmental sociology
- study the distribution of environmental benefits and impacts
- differentiate the various sides of the environmental movement

Introduction

Saving the environment is often in the forefront of public concern, but few people associate sociology with the study of environmental problems. Typically, we assume that overcoming these problems requires an understanding of the natural world and knowledge of biology, chemistry, physics, bioengineering, and geography, areas in which sociologists tend to have little expertise. In fact, students are often surprised to learn that a field of sociology associated with the study of environmental issues even exists.

No one denies that science and technology play vital roles in the fight to protect the environment. However, it takes only a little thought to appreciate the very significant connection between social conditions and environmental quality. Take the recent debate over the Kyoto Protocol. This international agreement was negotiated between more than 160 countries in 1997, establishing targets for the reduction of gases believed to be contributing to global climate change. Global warming may have very significant social implications for the future, eradicating some low-lying Pacific island nations, altering agriculture and food consumption patterns in the world, and triggering catastrophic regional weather disturbances with resulting economic disaster and human destruction. The natural sciences of physics, chemistry, biology, and geography are all closely associated with attempts to understand global warming, but almost all agree that human society is among the root causes of global climate change, as well as being very significantly affected by it. Industrialization, population growth, and even the eating habits of much of the world all are to a degree responsible for the production of greenhouse gases that lead to global warming. Greenhouse gases, therefore, exist as one of the largely human-induced environmental problems that threaten the **carrying capacity** of Earth, its ability to provide the resources to sustain all of humankind.

That human beings contribute to environmental problems through our social systems comes as no surprise. But the issue of global warming is sociologically far more profound than simply that humans contribute to it. A contentious debate over whether global warming even exists has scientists, business leaders, policy makers, and environmentalists all vying for the media's and the public's acceptance of their side's version of the extent and nature of the climate change problem, an example of how even so-called objectively determined environmental problems are **social constructions**.

In addition, how societies define global warming affects responses. In Canada, some groups argue that achieving Kyoto's emissions-reduction targets will be prohibitively expensive and harmful to Canadian economic competitiveness. Finally, the Kyoto Protocol is responsible, to a degree, for rekindling long-standing regional tensions in Canada, reflected largely by Alberta's strong opposition to the federal government's ratification of the convention. Hence, there are sociological implications surrounding every point in the global climate change question, from debates over whether global warming even exists to who is responsible, what can be done, and how the costs of solutions will be shared. The sociological complexity of the climate change issue means that science and technology alone are not likely to solve the environmental problem of global warming.

The example of climate change is typical of the societal debate around most environmental problems, and over the last several decades the field of environmental science has become interdisciplinary, spanning the natural and social sciences. Researchers, policy makers, and environmentalists have all come to accept that the complexity of the environment defies the ability of any single field of science to solve environmental problems. Environmental sociology makes its contribution by seeking to understand those aspects of societies, organizations, and people that contribute to environmental degradation, as well as by assessing the prospects for social change necessary for improving environmental quality.

Environmental sociologists have tended to draw upon the traditional theories and approaches of sociology and at the same time to challenge and suggest alternatives to certain of sociology's basic assumptions. Thus, not only the subject matter of environmental sociology but also its approaches are somewhat unorthodox within the broader field of sociology.

This chapter opens with a look at the basic assumptions of environmental sociology and at its origins, then examines the theory and practice of environmental sociology. Various topics of current relevance to research in the discipline are described in the following section, with an emphasis on sustainable development. Next, we look at the environmental movement, its history and contemporary forms. The chapter closes with a discussion of the future of the environment and the global changes affecting it.

The Basics of Environmental Sociology

Environmental sociology as a distinctive subfield of the larger discipline is generally acknowledged as having originated in the mid-1960s in connection with the rise of the environmental movement. Sociologists of the day were nothing short of fascinated by this rich, new **social movement** that emerged in the United States during the late 1960s and rapidly spread worldwide.

Environmentalism among US college students of the 1960s was as much a result of the social climate of American society as of any startling understanding of or revelation about environmental concerns (Hays, 1987). The long wave of economic prosperity following World War II helped to deflect the attention of youth from material concerns to social conditions, particularly the uneven distribution of political and economic power. This new awareness, together with obvious environmental problems such as smog and the influence of Rachel Carson's *Silent Spring* (1962), which detailed the effects of pesticides on the environment and human health, made environmental protection a cause. Two earlier causes, the civil rights and anti-war movements, provided the backdrop, helping the environmental movement's leadership to gain experience in activism and providing the organizational framework needed to launch a successful new movement. According to Craig Humphrey and Frederick Buttel,

> Students who participated in [these] causes registered limited successes, but they were reaching political impasses with respect to ending racism and the Vietnam War. As successes became more elusive, the movements became more radical in their ideologies and tactics. Universities were polarized. Pivotal events such as the Santa Barbara oil spill then directed the anticorporate predilections of the civil rights and antiwar activists to another area of importance for human survival, the problems of pollution, resource depletion and eventually energy. (1982: 7–8)

As the environmental movement escalated, leading to such events as the first Earth Day in 1970, many sociologists became interested in studying it. The field of social movements has long been important in sociology, and the environmental movement allowed sociologists to bring established theories and approaches to an exciting new social phenomenon. Some researchers investigated the composition of the movement and the **ideologies** and tactics of its participants (Dunlap and Gale, 1972). Others questioned how the environmental movement had so successfully supplanted the civil rights and anti-war movements (Gale, 1972; Morrison, Hornback, and Warner, 1972). Still others applied theories of social problems to environmental concerns (Albrecht and Mauss, 1975).

Along with the environmental movement, the development of environmental sociology was aided by the theoretical tradition of **human ecology**. Developed by Robert Park and Ernest Burgess of the Chicago School of sociology of the 1920s and 1930s, human ecology was the prevailing sociological tradition prior to being supplanted by the **structural functionalism** of Talcott Parsons and Robert Merton in the 1940s (Michelson, 1976). For environmental sociology, the legacy of human ecology provided a theoretical perspective capable of being reactivated at the moment when the environmental movement crystallized a broadly based sociological interest in the environment. The approach allowed an optimistic vision of applied problem solving based on functional adaptation to dominate the field of environmental sociology at its inception.

A third and final formative influence for environmental sociology was rural sociology (Humphrey and Buttel, 1982). Rural sociologists tend to be involved with applied, quantitative research aimed at problem solving in rural settings; they frequently work with interdisciplinary teams of planners, geographers, economists, wildlife managers, and agronomists. Their interest in such matters as rural communities, agriculture, urban–rural migration, and underdevelopment in the **Third World** creates inevitable contact with resource development and its consequences, including the pollution caused by new human settlement, modern agricultural practices, and economic growth. The result was that when the environment came to the forefront of public concern in the mid-1970s, there already existed an experienced body of professional researchers in rural sociology who were in a position to deal with environmental problems.

As is usually the case for sociologists in other subfields of the discipline, environmental sociologists tend to be diverse with respect to their research interests, theoretical approaches, and methodological practices. Nevertheless, there are a number of shared assumptions. Environmental sociology studies the interrelationships between society and the environment. The focus is on the relationship between human social organization and the physical environment. This focus effectively amounts to an important distinction between environmental sociology and other sociological fields to do with the definition of *environment*. Within sociology, the term *environment* generally refers to a socio-cultural or symbolic system—a particular social context, its organizational framework, and the relationships among and meanings shared by the individuals involved. Sociologists have been reluctant to extend the term to include the physical environment, preferring to leave this usage to natural scientists. Environmental sociology, however, seeks to consider *environment* as both a physical entity and a socio-cultural (symbolic) phenomenon. This does not mean that environmental sociologists are scientific experts; indeed, their work has sometimes been challenged on the grounds of their naïveté in the natural sciences. What it does mean is that environmental sociology typically acknowledges physical environmental factors along with socio-cultural factors as vital for understanding the (physical) environmental consequences of social organization, as well as for predicting such organization. This position is not without controversy, resulting in sociology's "essential dualism," according to Alan Irwin (2001: 3), meaning that environmental sociologists are critical of their colleagues from other sociological fields for treating the physical environment as little more than backdrop to social activity or a context in which it occurs, while in turn they are themselves criticized for advocating a scientific approach that seems impossible because it is too encompassing.

Environmental sociologists agree that environmental issues are by and large social problems, even though these problems often affect the biophysical world of animals, plants, landforms, and water, while other social problems affect humans almost exclusively. This may seem obvious, but it requires further consideration. Environmental problems, like other social problems such as war, crime, and inequality, exist and persist largely because of the way societies and the global social order are organized. Consider, for instance, the fact that modern industrial and post-industrial societies contain within their central logic the enhancement of such **values** as individualism, universalism, and achievement. These values are part of the **socialization** of citizens, and they result in both social differentiation and material abundance. At the same time, the positive values attached to eco-nomic growth and structural differentiation fuel an expansionist society. The expansionist tendency, in turn, causes myriad environmental problems. This does not have to be so—the environmental problems associated with the "treadmill of production," as it has been labelled by sociologist Allan Schnaiberg (1980: 227), could be avoided, but to do so would involve a fundamental change in ideology.

Too often there has been a tendency to see environmental problems as inevitable consequences of the process of modernization. People have a tendency to consider social processes and structures as being beyond their ability to change. From this perspective, many are satisfied with a rearguard action to keep environmental problems in check, without believing that they can be eliminated altogether. Moreover, societies tend to adapt to scarcities imposed by environmental destruction rather than seek fundamental social change. Environmental sociologists want to challenge these attitudes. They argue that the environment has fallen victim to a process of collective social definition that accepts the inevitability of environmental damage and that simultaneously fails to question the social system that allows it—a system that in itself is neither right, best, nor inevitable. Society can choose to deal with environmental problems, as with other social problems, through deliberate social change. Achieving environmental integrity may mean sacrifices, but it is a choice people can make.

A complication arises in that environmental issues are likely to be the focus of conflict between competing **social groups**. Resources such as air and water tend to be considered common property, freely available to everyone and having economic, recreational, and aesthetic uses. But competition for such resources often arises. The net result is to make solutions to environmental problems all the more difficult, since the usual response of the authorities has been to compromise environmental integrity in order to satisfy competing social demands.

Chief among the social processes and structures questioned by environmental sociology are the benefits of economic growth. In the past, sociologists, together with other scientists, tended to be enamoured of social progress, which was regarded as the means for achieving uniform prosperity and thereby eliminating **class** differences. Today's environmental sociologists are of two minds. On the one hand, economic expansion has adverse consequences for the environment: pollution, waste, and the destruction of non-renewable resources. On the other hand, the expansion of economic markets, besides helping to provide economic and social well-being, also provides the prosperity societies need in order to deal with environmental problems. The conundrum of economic growth versus environmental protection has been recognized by Schnaiberg (1975) as the "socio-environmental dialectic." Schnaiberg points out that economic policies that are "regressive" in their effects—that is, that lead to reductions in economic benefits because of stagnant or negative growth—are more likely to result in environmental policies that are less sensitive to the environment. When times are hard, politicians, encouraged by corporations, see stimulating the economy as the first priority, with environmental protection being put on hold. Hence, there are grounds for believing that a healthy, growing economy is needed for environmental preservation.

Support for this viewpoint was offered by the report of the 1987 World Commission on the Environment and Development, *Our Common Future*, which strongly supported the principle of **sustainable development**. According to this principle, it is only through significant improvements in the economic conditions of developing nations that global ecological disaster can be averted. Sustainable development approaches have emerged to become indispensable to economic planning at many levels, but at a cost of falling well short of providing a set of agreed-to "best practices," operating principles, and goals. Professing support for the environment while doing little about it is one way many projects gain political and public approval. On these grounds, while still acknowledging the importance of a healthy economy for environmental matters, most environmental sociologists remain skeptical about the wisdom of constant economic expansion, especially in the guise of sustainable development, and advocate both redirection and some curtailment in growth.

The Environment and Ecological Scarcity

Issues of ecological scarcity have long been of considerable interest to environmental sociologists. *Scarcity* has to do with problems associated with the overuse of natural resources, leading to their exhaustion, or with their waste or destruction by contamination or misuse. The immense reliance of societies on natural resources and the extent to which this

reliance influences social arrangements as well as prospects for social change often go unrecognized. Sociological interest in resource scarcity therefore addresses questions of world population growth, global carrying capacity limits, and the relationship between development and scarcity.

Population Growth

There are presently more people living on Earth than throughout all of human history. It took over 1 million years for the population to reach 1 billion, around the mid-nineteenth century. In the century and a half since then, the figure has grown to approximately 6.2 billion (in 2002). Some 75 million people are added each year, at a rate of over 2 people per second. Although the rate of world population increase is slowing, the absolute amount of growth continues to be substantial. By 2050, the world's population will increase by more than half again its size today, to 9.3 billion people (US Bureau of the Census, 1999: 9).

These startling statistics explain why Earth's population has been likened to a time bomb threatening to destroy the planet. Population pressure is regarded as one of the most serious environmental threats, contributing to resource exhaustion, destroying species and habitat, causing pollution, and taxing the capacity of agricultural systems. It is a major factor in such diverse ecological disasters as famines in Africa, global warming, acid rain, the garbage crisis, and the spread of disease. While we have not yet arrived at the theoretical limits for food production on the planet, they will be reached by the year 2100, with a projected population of 11.2 billion (World Commission on Environment and Development, 1987: 98–9).

The most serious environmental problems affect mainly the more than 5 billion people in the developing countries of Latin America, Africa, and Asia— 80 per cent of the global population (see Figure 21.1). It is here, among the 172 nations classified by the United Nations as "less developed countries" (LDCs), that 99 per cent of global population natural increase—the difference between numbers of births and numbers of deaths—occurs. By the end of the first quarter of the twenty-second century, the world's more developed countries (MDCs) will begin experiencing negative natural increase, and all of the global population increase will come from the less developed world (US Bureau of the Census, 1999: 10). It is not surprising, then, that environmental scientists and population experts generally agree that the way

Figure 21.1   **Potential Exposure to Health Risks from Environmental Threats: Developing Countries**

This map portrays the geographic distribution of various environmental threats to health. It conveys the extent of environmental threats to health in developing countries, which stem from both biological risks associated with poverty and chemical risks associated with industrialization.

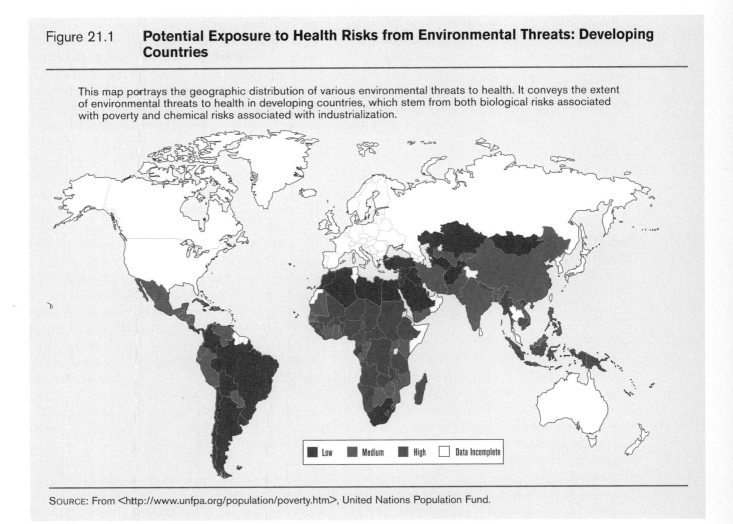

Low   Medium   High   Data Incomplete

SOURCE: From <http://www.unfpa.org/population/poverty.htm>, United Nations Population Fund.

to avoid reaching the limits of the global carrying capacity is to reduce the birth rates of developing nations.

How can the differences in birth rates between developed and developing nations be accounted for? The **demographic transition** theory is widely used to explain the dynamic relationship between fertility and mortality, which is based on economic and social progress in societies (Notestein, 1967). During the first stage, *pre-transition*, a society experiences high rates of both fertility and mortality. Medicine, science, and agriculture are not sufficiently developed to keep deaths from disease, injury, starvation, or childbirth in check, while lack of contraception means fertility remains high. Births are offset by deaths, so natural increase is slow and the population remains stable or grows slowly. At the second stage, *transition*, mortality rates decline due to scientific and technological advances, while fertility rates remain high. Births outstrip deaths, so the population grows rapidly. In the final stage of the demographic transition, *post-transition*, the death rate remains low, but the birth rate also decreases because of contraception and societal changes. Births are again offset by deaths, so natural increase is low, and the population remains stable or grows slowly.

After the post–World War II **baby boom** (1947 to 1966), industrialized nations moved rapidly into the third stage of the demographic transition and remain there today. The social bases for this transition are quite clear. The modernization process in these countries was accompanied by improvements in sanitation, nutrition, water, medicine, housing, and social programs, all of which help to increase **life expectancy** substantially. The reasons for the corresponding decline in fertility are more difficult to pin down. They probably centre on changes in institutional structures and cultural and personal values. Examples of the former are the entry of women into the workforce, which tends to be associated with later marriage and childbearing, and the rise of the nuclear family, which made the services of extended-family members for child care less available. Examples of changes in values include the preference of many couples for emphasizing the quality of their children's upbringing instead of having large families and the tendency for children to remain dependent on their parents into early adulthood.

Developing countries have also benefited to some extent from the same technological and social improvements. However, mortality rates remain high in comparison with the developed world. Moreover, these societies are still largely agrarian and based on the extended family. Large numbers of children are needed to guarantee the economic survival of the family by working and performing household tasks, as well as to support the parents in old age. In some cases, an entire family may be carried by an exceptional child, who is given access to higher education and a secure, well-paying job. Although birth control is widely available and, in many cases, strongly encouraged by **the state**, a variety of compelling cultural, religious, and lifestyle reasons militate against contraception. As a result of all these factors, fertility levels have remained relatively high, and most developing nations remain at the second stage of the demographic transition, with fertility outpacing mortality.

At present, only some 20 to 30 per cent of the world population has attained the stable third stage. A significant question for social scientists concerns the prospects for the remainder of the world reaching post-transition. It is generally felt that for this change to occur, the requisite social and cultural conditions of industrialization must first appear, including a complex division of labour, more labour specialization and increased employment opportunity, and a more efficient system of agricultural production capable of freeing families from the necessity of providing just their own basic needs. But long-standing relations of inequality between developed and developing countries, stemming from colonialism and from both political and economic imperialism, have distorted and weakened the ability of poorer nations to move toward full-fledged industrialization. Without the accompanying fundamental improvements, the chance of reducing birth rates is small.

Some gains have been made through programs of public education about birth control, the dispensing of free contraceptives, and coercion by the state through laws enforcing birth-control policies, most notably in China. However, as noted, contraception

has had limited success. Sociologists such as Karen Michaelson (1981) have suggested that the main reason these countries remain in the transitional stage is poverty. Bearing many children to support the family is seen as the only option for escape. Thus, the most direct means of solving the world population problem is to eradicate poverty, as difficult as this may be. Environmental planners have increasingly come to accept this argument. Both the 1987 report of the World Commission on Environment and Development, chaired by Norwegian prime minister Gro Harlem Brundtland, and the 1992 and 2002 United Nations conferences on environment and development (the "Earth Summits") have based their recommendations on the same proposition.

Only improvements to the economies of developing nations that help them move to the final stage of the demographic transition will end the poverty underlying high birth rates. It is clear that programs for economic improvement will require co-operation between developed and developing nations. But many factors stand in the way. Industrialized nations have traditionally benefited from access to cheap resources and labour in Third World countries, and so have contributed greatly to their economic problems. Furthermore, wealthier nations laud their overseas investments in developing countries as helpful, but studies show that there is no guarantee that the benefits will be shared equally in the face of historically rigid class divisions and traditional concentrations of wealth among a tiny elite. Industrialized nations may also view economic improvements in less developed countries as a potential threat. For all these reasons, the task of altering socio-economic arrangements in these countries—giving families a greater measure of financial security and more control over their lives—is daunting. But without a more equitable distribution of economic, social, and technological benefits, people in developing nations will have little incentive for having fewer children, and the world will have little hope of achieving environmental integrity by defusing the population bomb.

The Limits to Growth

The concept of limits to growth—the extent of the planet's ability to sustain its population—is an important basis for much environmentalism and for the scientific arguments underlying conservationism. The metaphor of "Spaceship Earth" readily evokes the image of a shimmering orb floating in the vast void of space, reminding us of both the fragility of the planet and our dependence upon it.

That Earth's natural resources are finite is accepted by almost everyone. Nonetheless, debate has raged for decades about how to ascertain the ecological limits of the planet and pinpoint their implications for economic growth. The controversy is highly significant, since it influences much of present-day resource use and planning, including population planning. Some observers, including ecologist Paul Ehrlich (1981) and sociologist William Catton (1980), believe that Earth's capacity to sustain itself in the face of population expansion and resource exploitation is rapidly nearing the limit and that ecological collapse is a possibility unless growth is curbed very soon. Others, such as economist Julian Simon (1981), regard this perspective as needlessly alarmist, arguing against any immediate, or even long-term, crisis and claiming that resources are abundant and people have the inventiveness to adapt to shortages. The continuum of environmental concern defined by these two poles is the basis of calls for either continued economic expansion or economic restriction.

The controversy over the issue of limits to growth was initiated by the publication in 1972 of a study entitled *The Limits to Growth* (Meadows et al., 1972). The research team attempted to model the interplay among five factors affected by economic growth on the planet: population, agricultural production, natural resources, industrial production, and pollution. One assumption of the model was that the components of the system grow exponentially (2, 4, 8, 16, 32, . . .). Another was that the five variables affect one another reciprocally though feedback loops of cause and effect. As you can see in Figure 21.2, the model is highly complex.

The model was used to generate the baseline projection of outcomes on the five variables until the year 2100, given the assumption that no significant changes in human values or in global population and economic functioning would occur over the next 50 years. The results were startling. According to the model, sometime before 2100, "overshoot"—the team's term for ecological disaster—was imminent. By the middle of the twenty-first century, the world's population would overtake food production and resources. The resultant predicted collapse of the industrial system would, in all likelihood, be followed by famine, poverty, war, and significant population loss.

When assumptions about values, population, and the economy were changed, more optimistic models resulted. Still, even when the team assumed inexhaustible natural resources, a 75 per cent reduction in pollution, perfect birth control, and more output from food production, global ecological collapse was still predicted, although it would be delayed until after the twenty-second century. The most optimistic (and preferred) model was premised on significant changes in population and industrial growth occurring before the end of the twentieth century. In this model, equilibrium or sustainability was achieved and ecological disaster was avoided.

The release of the study unleashed intense debate between its supporters and critics. The latter pointed to the naïveté of certain of the model's assumptions and the inadequacies of many of its measures. Nevertheless, *The Limits to Growth* generated an international furor over environmental issues. In so doing, it had a notable impact as a warning against unchecked growth and was responsible for creating much of today's widespread opposition to economic expansion.

The growth versus no growth debate remains central to discussion on the environment. But the debate has become anything but clear cut. Some scientists who favour continued expansion have close ties to the environmental movement. Their argument is that growth is essential for ameliorating the conditions of the poor in the Third World, that it will lead to reduced population growth and ultimately to the preservation of soil, water, and other resources. An extension of this argument is that, even in industrialized nations, limits on growth will have the most adverse effects on the working class and the poor. Yet another view is that economic growth is necessary to provide the profits to invest in technologies for reducing waste and controlling pollution. Thus, where economic growth and environmental quality were once considered irreconcilable, this is no longer the case. Nor can the proponents of growth or no growth be easily located along the continuum of environmental concern.

Sustainable Development

The concept of sustainable development grew out of the perspective that economic development and environmental conservation are compatible goals. First appearing during the 1972 United Nations Conference on the Human Environment in Stockholm, the principle gained widespread support over the three decades that followed while being the

Figure 21.2 The World Model from *The Limits to Growth*

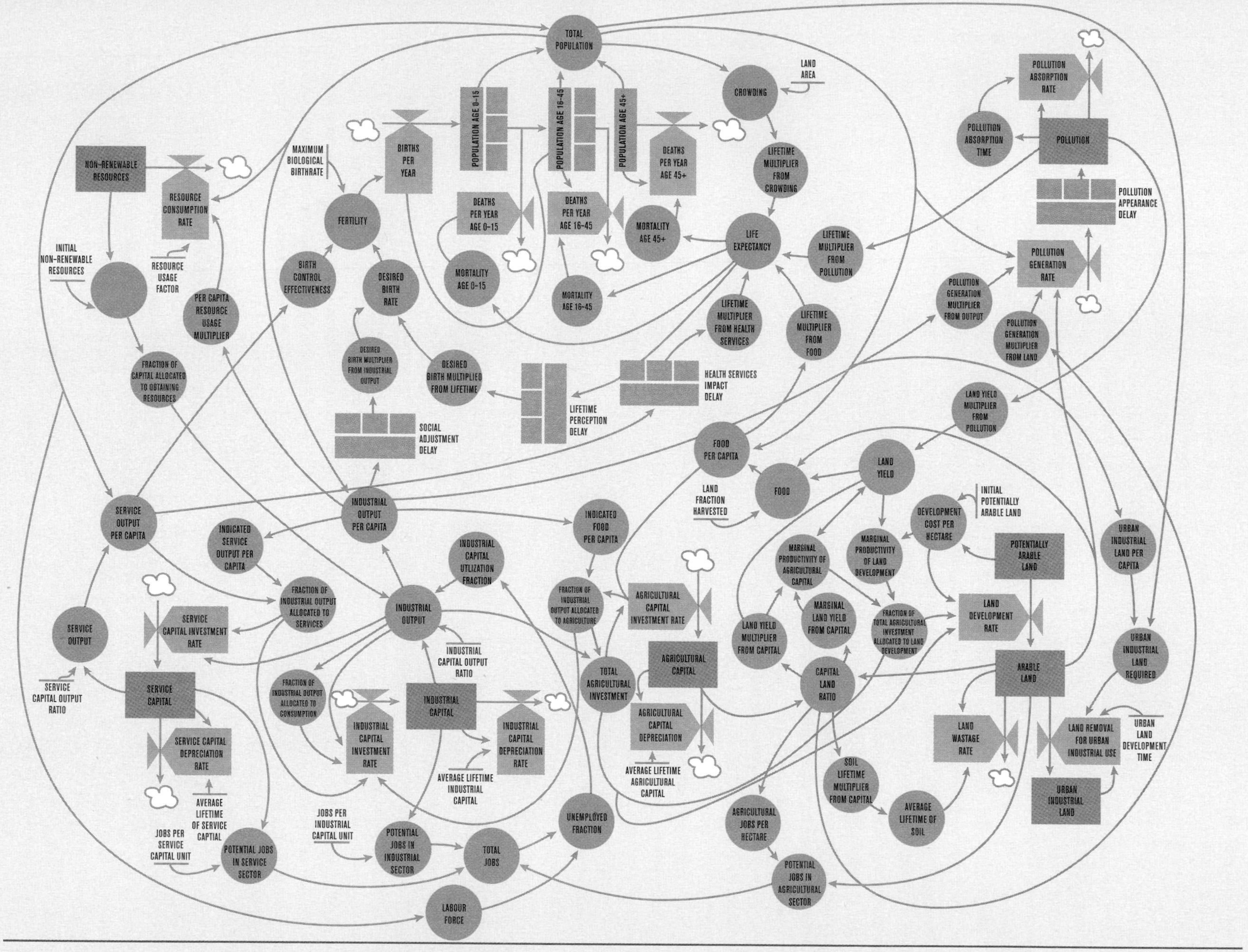

SOURCE: Donella Meadows, Dennis L. Meadows, Jorgen Randers, and William Behrens III, *The Limits to Growth* (New York: Universe, 1972), 101–3. By permission of Donella Meadows.

focus of various international conferences and reviews, including the 1987 Brundtland Commission and the 1992 and 2002 Earth Summits. *Sustainable development* calls for the conciliation of several apparently competing ends: environmental integrity; the protection of ecosystems and biodiversity, and the meeting of human needs; and positive economic growth and equitable distribution of the benefits of the environment and resources among social classes and across nations. While the idea of the existence of ecological limits is clearly ingrained in sustainable development, and while there is an insistence on strict resource husbandry, the principle is unabashedly pro-development. In the words of the 1987 World Commission on Environment and Development,

> Growth has not set limits in terms of population or resource use beyond which lies ecological disaster. Different limits hold for the use of energy, materials, water and land. Many of these will manifest themselves in the form of rising costs and diminishing returns, rather than in the form of any sudden loss of a resource base. The accumulation of knowledge and development of technology can enhance the carrying capacity of the resource base. But ultimate limits there are, and sustainability must ensure equitable access to the constrained resource and reorient technological efforts to relieve pressure. (45)

After initial enthusiasm, certain environmentalists have come to regard sustainable development with skepticism. Some see it as no more than a legitimization of development under the guise of assisting the poor. An extension of this view is that sustainable development is an excuse for further incursions by Western nations into the Third World for the sole purpose of profit. In the words of Wolfgang Sachs, "Capital, bureaucracy and science . . . the venerable trinity of Western Modernization declare themselves indispensable to the new crisis and promise to prevent the worst through better engineering, integrated planning and sophisticated models" (1991: 257). Finally, there are those who claim that the principles of ecology, together with the scientific community, are being co-opted to support the further destruction of nature on the grounds of scientific rationality.

The Environment and Social Theory

Environmental sociology has its theoretical bases in several sociological traditions. Among these is the field of *human ecology*, a sociological perspective with important ties to the work of Émile Durkheim. More recently, human ecology has been revised for the insights it provides for environmental sociology. Another theoretical topic debated by environmental sociologists concerns whether their field should be seen as constituting a paradigm shift for sociology in general. The division between the order and conflict schools so prevalent elsewhere in sociology is also a characteristic feature of environmental sociology. More generally, there has been broad debate over the relevance of sociology's classical theoretical traditions to the study of environmental issues. Contemporary theoretical approaches include the concept of the **risk society**, developed by Ulrich Beck. Finally, **social constructionism**, a perspective found elsewhere in sociology, has developed to become a prominent approach within environmental sociology. In this section, we review these theoretical positions.

Human Ecology

The science of ecology is central to the study of environmental issues; *human ecology* is the application of the same approach to sociological analyses. Human ecology emerged under the direction of Robert Park and Ernest Burgess at the University of Chicago during the 1920s (Park and Burgess, 1921; Park and McKenzie, 1925; Theodorson, 1961, 1982). Much as the science of ecology studies plant and animal communities, human ecology sought to explain human spatial and temporal organization by concentrating on the dynamic processes of competition and succession that influence human social organization. Park and Burgess and their students concentrated on studying how Chicago's rapidly changing society physically accommodated increases in population and changes in the industrial and cultural organization of the city. Their approach, and that of their successors, was to focus on symbiosis, the dynamic interdependencies that bind people together in communities and lead to particular living arrangements.

In developing the concept of human ecology, Park was greatly influenced by Durkheim's *The Division of Labor in Society* ([1893] 1964). Durkheim addressed

21.1

Global Issues
Energetics

Energetics is the study of the flow of solar energy through the biosphere, and especially of the various processes by which it is transformed into other forms of energy capable of performing work for humans. As early as 1955, sociologist Fred Cottrell noted that modern societies have developed without a full appreciation of their dependence on the energy resources of the physical environment. Cottrell recognized that the forms of energy used by a given society influence its organization and ideological characteristics. Each transformation from lower to higher energy forms throughout history (for example, wood to coal to hydro-electricity) has been accompanied by fundamental changes in the social, economic, political, and psychological makeup of the society.

In short, most people fail to realize that the survival of any society depends on its characteristic energy flows. Disruptions in these flows foreshadow social dislocation and change. "Energy crises" are no new phenomenon. In the eighteenth century, for instance, the depletion of wood in England provided the stimulus for the development of coal and steam as energy resources, which in turn led to the Industrial Revolution with its massive social disruptions.

The 1973 oil embargo of the Organization of the Petroleum Exporting Countries (OPEC) was responsible for rekindling sociological interest in energetics. The resulting body of microsociological research focused on energy consumption and programs as sociologists responded to the energy crisis by attempting to demonstrate the relevance of their work in solving or helping to avoid future energy shortages. Other studies examined such matters as the beliefs and attitudes of energy consumers about conservation and pricing programs, the effectiveness of information campaigns on changing attitudes, the social-demographic correlates of reduced energy use, and the relationship between attitudes and conservation behaviours. Still other researchers focused on

general issues of energy policy for society, particularly on alternative forms of energy.

In this connection, a distinction is often made between "hard" and "soft" energy paths. *Hard energy paths* involve the generation and distribution of energy through large-scale, centralized production systems relying mainly on non-renewable energy forms such as oil, gas, coal, and nuclear energy. Such systems prevail in the industrialized world today. *Soft energy paths* comprise systems relying mainly on renewable energy sources: solar power, wind, tidal power, hydro-electricity, and energy from biomass; these systems also involve conservation and recycling. Because of the nature of these fuels, these systems are more likely to be small and decentralized; examples include solar panels on a building, a community hydro-electric dam, and windmills. The essence of a soft energy path is to use the resources available locally to produce energy to be consumed locally.

the development of social complexity from human population growth and density. As populations grow, the threat to available resources is crucial from a sociological viewpoint because it leads to competition and conflict. Problems of resource scarcity can therefore affect societal organization.

Durkheim's work was appealing to early human ecologists because of their interest in *sustenance activities*—the routine functions necessary to ensure the survival of a population from generation to generation (Hawley, 1950). Humans have a greater capacity for adapting to resource scarcity than any other organism, an ability labelled *competitive co-operation*. Adaptive responses include reductions in per capita consumption, increases in production through technology or more intensive resource exploitation, changes to distribution networks, and decreases in competition because of emigration from the community or an increased division of labour (Micklin, 1973; Schnore, 1958). Through such adaptive mechanisms, involving reciprocal cause-and-effect processes between the population and its vital resources, a state of equilibrium is reached. Park and Burgess (1921) postulated that competition and co-operation are the key forms of human exchange by which organized populations seek to maintain equilibrium within a dynamic environment.

Park and Burgess's theory underwent significant revision beginning in the mid-1950s to correct what are commonly regarded as major shortcomings: an overemphasis on the spatial arrangements of populations at the expense of understanding societal–environmental relations, and the neglect of **culture** and values (Dunlap and Catton, 1979a, 1979b; Hawley, 1981). Moreover, while highly influenced by the conceptual approaches and terminology of ecology, early human ecologists concentrated on human social organization and patterns and did not include other species or aspects of the natural world in their analyses. They therefore veered away from a concern about environmental issues. During the 1950s, the *ecological complex* (Duncan and Schnore, 1959; Hawley, 1950), which viewed societies as being constituted of four interrelated dimensions—population, organization, environment, and technology (POET)—substantially revised the conceptual basis of human ecology. But even after this reformulation, human ecologists continued to use the concept of environment in socio-cultural, symbolic terms (Dunlap and Catton, 1983; Michelson, 1976).

Human Exemptionalism and the New Environmental Paradigm

Paradigms are organizing metatheoretical (that is, broad and comprehensive) frameworks of understanding based on a set of shared assumptions by practitioners in a given field. Because paradigmatic assumptions are widely shared, they tend not to be questioned. At the same time, they influence the direction and scope of the field by defining the nature of both the questions asked and those that are resisted (Kuhn, 1970).

Sociology has long been characterized by paradigmatic divisions that have led to hot debates. Environmental sociology was at the centre of one such paradigmatic clash in the early 1980s, one that has never been fully resolved. In several influential articles, William Catton and Riley Dunlap (Catton and Dunlap, 1978, 1980; Dunlap and Catton, 1979a, 1983) forcefully advanced the thesis that "the numerous competing theoretical perspectives in contemporary sociology—e.g., functionalism, symbolic interactionism, ethnomethodology, conflict theory, Marxism, and so forth—are prone to exaggerate their differences from each other" (1978: 42). That is, Catton and Dunlap argued that, while purporting to be paradigms in their own right, all these approaches were really variants of a larger paradigm. The basis of their similarity was their "shared anthropocentrism." The authors argued that this assumption—that humans are separate from and superior to other things in nature—is the product of 500 years of Western culture in which societies have behaved as though nature existed primarily for human use (Dunlap and Catton, 1983; White, 1967). Catton and Dunlap referred to this world view as the **human exemptionalism paradigm (HEP)**, arguing that it comprises several assumptions that sociologists, regardless of their orientation, implicitly accept (see Table 21.1). This failure, even in the face of the contradictions suggested by contemporary environmental events, suggested that sociologists were unequipped to deal meaningfully with ecological problems.

For Catton and Dunlap, the assumptions and approaches of the newly emerging environmental sociology constituted a paradigm shift, or a challenge to orthodox sociology. A paradigm shift occurs in science when a previously unrecognized framework of understanding replaces the dominant world view and

Table 21.1   **A Comparison of the Human Exemptionalism Paradigm and the New Ecological Paradigm**

Assumptions	Human Exemptionalism Paradigm (HEP)		New Ecological Paradigm (NEP)	
About the nature of human beings	HEP$_1$	Humans have cultural heritage in addition to (and distinct from) their generic inheritance, and so are quite unlike all other animal species.	NEP$_1$	While humans have exceptional characteristics (culture, technology, etc.), they remain one among many species that are interdependently involved in the global ecosystem.
About social causation	HEP$_2$	Social and cultural factors (including technology) are the major determinants of human affairs.	NEP$_2$	Human affairs are influenced not by social and cultural factors, but also by intricate linkages of cause, effect, and feedback in the web of nature; purposive human actions therefore have many unintended consequences.
About the context of human society	HEP$_3$	Social and cultural environments are the crucial context for human affairs, and the biophysical environment is largely irrelevant.	NEP$_3$	Humans live in and are dependent upon a finite biophysical environment which imposes potent physical and biological restraints on human affairs.
About constraints on human society	HEP$_4$	Culture is cumulative; therefore, technological and social progress can continue indefinitely, making all social problems ultimately solvable.	NEP$_4$	Although human inventiveness and the powers derived from it may seem for a while to extend carrying capacity limits, ecological laws cannot be repealed.

Source: William Catton, Jr, and Riley Dunlap, "A New Ecological Paradigm for Post-exuberant Society," *American Behavioral Scientist*, 24 (1980), 34.

redirects the given field on a qualitatively new course involving different research propositions and methods. Catton and Dunlap referred to the new approach as the **new environmental paradigm (NEP)**. Its assumptions are compared to those of the human exemptionalism paradigm in Table 21.1. The essential difference between them can be summed up as anthropocentrism (HEP) versus ecocentrism (NEP).

According to the NEP's supporters, sociologists and others who adopt the NEP world view must limit their faith in the ability of social progress and culture to overcome contemporary social problems, including environmental problems, while striving to appreciate the realities of humans within nature. Moreover, environmental problems cannot just be expected to go away; rather, societies must learn to minimize the environmental harm they inflict and be willing to rely less on nature to increase material comforts and prosperity. Since human society and nature can never really be separated, the implication for sociology in general is that the NEP should be accepted as the only framework within which sociologists can understand the laws that shape the development of modern soci-

eties. Therefore, according to Catton and Dunlap, the HEP/NEP distinction should be recognized as the principal paradigmatic cleavage in sociology; moreover, the HEP should be considered obsolete.

NEP vs Classical Sociological Theory

The debate over HEP and NEP and whether environmental sociology constitutes a paradigm shift for sociology as a whole has raised further questions over the relevance of classical sociological theory for understanding environmental problems. One concern is whether the HEP/NEP distinction should be regarded as anything but a further manifestation of the long-running theoretical debate in sociology over order versus conflict. Many environmental sociologists, including Frederick Buttel (1976) and Craig Humphrey (Humphrey and Buttel, 1982), disagreed with Catton and Dunlap's belief that environmental sociology represented a paradigm shift. Instead, they argued that environmental sociology is still characterized by paradigmatic cleavages, primarily between structural functionalism (order) and **Marxism** and neo-Marxism (conflict). The two approaches offer competing views on both the social origins of environmental problems and their solutions.

The structural functionalist school of sociology, stressing the rational functioning of society, has been summarized by Buttel (1976). The image of society is that of a social system with needs. Individual actors and institutions within the system have competing needs, and the state acts as an impartial arbitrator to smooth out differences and relieve stress and misalignment. From this perspective, environmental problems are associated with the process of modernization or progress. The positive functions associated with the needs of economic growth, abundance, and social stratification sometimes get out of hand, leading to environmental harm. Social reform or adjustment is then called for. The public's values must be modified, usually through public education, so that society may remain within its survival base and adapt to environmental exigencies. Protective environmental legislation is also enacted. The goal is to create an environmental ethos based on rights and the rational use of resources. Appropriate environmental use is maintained through state laws, social **norms**, and collective action. Possible adverse distributional effects on certain social groups as a result of environmental laws are regarded as the unfortunate, but necessary, trade-off for protection of the resource base, and they are not seriously questioned.

By contrast, the conflict approach takes the view that environmental problems are irrationalities within the capitalist system leading to societal contradictions (Schnaiberg, 1980). The key proposition here is that economic growth under **capitalism** has been a historical necessity in order to allow the corporate class to maintain its dominant position and its control of private property. Class struggle is the permanent condition of society, with the state favouring and promoting the interests of the upper classes. Everyone must work so that capitalists may receive profits. Growth is mandatory, and the environment is the victim. Arrangements for maintaining growth and profits—including planned obsolescence, disposable products, private transportation, and the military—promote waste and excessive resource exploitation and lead to environmental destruction. In short, Marxists and neo-Marxists see environmental destruction as inherent in capitalism. The working class cannot help because of its powerlessness, the control of the state, and the co-optation of workers

through high wages earned at the expense of the environment. Orthodox approaches to solving environmental problems do not help since the necessary social reorganization will be resisted. **Conflict theorists** tend to be hostile to reform solutions, arguing that they do not treat the root causes of environmental destruction and mislead the public into believing something is being done. Environmental laws and regulations passed by elites call for only "reasonable" conservation, whose conditions are most easily met by large corporations, so that wealth and power are further concentrated. Finally, the costs of such reforms are carried mainly by the poor and the working class through losses of resource jobs and through higher prices and taxes for environmental protection.

After reading these summaries of the order and conflict approaches, you may agree with Buttel and Humphrey that the HEP and the NEP are nothing other than a new expression of these classical approaches. Such a conclusion would refute Catton and Dunlap's view that environmental sociology represents a paradigm shift in sociology. Moreover, the order/conflict controversy raises questions about the evidence for environmental damage by various political-economic systems. Following the collapse of the Soviet bloc in 1989, it became abundantly clear, if it was not already known, that neither communist (conflict perspective) nor capitalist (order perspective) societies are manifestly different in regards to environmental sensitivity—all industrialized nations share the environmental problems associated with industrial technologies.

Finally, the debate over HEP/NEP versus order/conflict provokes further questions concerning the benefits of classical theoretical approaches in sociology for understanding and addressing environmental problems. It has already been noted that the Durkheimian tradition was important to the formulation of early human ecology, which helped to guide the new field of environmental sociology at its beginnings. But human ecology is not without its critics, and today, despite recent reformulation, it is largely seen as relevant only in certain areas of study of the built (that is, urban) environment. By and large, the classical theorists, Marx, Weber, and Durkheim—so important for their contributions to the conceptual foundations of much of sociology—do not appear nearly so relevant to the field of environmental sociology (Goldblatt, 1996; Redclift and Benton, 1994).

Weber, for example, is known to have vigorously opposed the inclusion of "naturalistic or biologistic concepts" within the conceptual framework of sociology, partly in order to enhance the status of sociology as a new and separate discipline, as well as to avoid any decent into **biological determinism** (Stehr and Grundmann, 1996). Durkheim's dictum that all human circumstances could be eventually explained through knowledge of "social facts" is further evidence of the tendency for the classical theorists to see a clear separation between the social and the natural worlds (Redclift and Woodgate, 1994).

The Marxist approach of dialectical materialism, which includes among its arguments the logic that new ideas can only be achieved through knowledge of the real, or material, world, has been quite relevant to the developments of a critical new branch of environmental philosophy known as "green" political thought (for example, Dickens, 1992, 1996; Eckersley, 1992), which is of interest to many environmental sociologists. As well, Marx did argue that natural conditions, such as climate and region, contribute to the division of labour, while both he and Friedrich Engels were forceful in their condemnation of capitalism for its appalling effects on the health and living conditions of workers ([1867] 1967) .

Nevertheless, the tendencies of the founders of sociology were, for the most part, to focus on distinguishing between social and natural conditions while emphasizing the social and ignoring the dynamic interplay between the two. For this reason, environmental sociology has not benefited from the classical writings to the degree found elsewhere in sociology, and there is ongoing and pressing need for new theories for understanding this relationship. The risk society as outlined by Ulrich Beck and social constructionist applications for the analysis of environmental problems are two areas of significant new theoretical development within environmental sociology.

The Risk Society

Ulrich Beck's conception of the risk society was initially outlined in *Risk Society: Towards a New Modernity* (1992). Originally published in German in 1986, this text has had considerable impact in sociology as well as in the social sciences and philosophy in general, while also drawing wide public debate and media attention.

The central thesis of the risk society concerns the evolution toward a new modernity, referred to by Beck as "late modernity" (1992: 10), reflecting social change on a global scale. The impetus for this transformation is risk, hence the term *risk society*. According to this theory, the world has evolved beyond the industrial state, with its successor, later modernity or postmodernity, being essentially the outcome of the success of the period preceding it. For affluent Western societies, the success of industrialization has meant, in practical terms, the end of scarcity. Wealth, science, and technology combine to provide for the needs of those in prosperous countries. At the same time, however, there is a multitude of problems, or *risks*, that individuals must face on a daily basis, which can be traced directly to industrialization. These involve all sorts of uncertainties—to do with changing workplace and gender roles, the nature of the family, social class relations, crime, environmental dangers, and more—all confronting the individual and for which there are no obvious solutions. This creates uncertainty, doubt, and confusion.

How should people respond? In industrial society, the primary concern involved the distribution of "goods," with class action as the resulting collective response to inequities. Within late modernity, however, the concern is with the distribution of the "bads"—the risks and dangers confronting individuals, which are the by-products of the success of industrialization. Social class and class relations are no longer relevant to the extent they once were. Rather, the defining perception is with respect to one's risk position. In a class-based society, one's material position determines consciousness, making one aware of one's access, along with that of others, to scarce resources and being prepared to act collectively to secure a greater share. In a risk-based society, consciousness around issues of risk defines individual well-being and the struggle to exist. With this comes a decline in importance of structures like social class that previously served to support a direction to be taken on the person's behalf, while at the same time there is increased emphasis on the individualization of the actor, who now is forced to choose from a range of ambiguous options.

Reflexive modernity is the term used to describe the response to this new reality. Problems faced by individuals are no longer clearly externally imposed (for example, resource scarcities), nor are solutions founded on some kind of "natural" order (for example, gender roles). Instead, we must reflect on our options, while struggling to make the best choice. Uncertainty, **alienation**, and loneliness may result. Where alliances exist, they are less likely to be defined on socio-economic grounds, and they are more likely to be ideologically determined and "strategic," as in the example of the European Green party, in which the anti-establishment forces of the environmental, feminist, and anti-nuclear movements combine to form a pragmatic alliance in opposition to the traditional parties. Thus, while modernity has freed Western society from material want, we are confronted with new challenges and fewer guideposts to understanding.

Reflexive modernity must also be considered in light of the new and ambiguous role of science. Science and technology are irrevocably tied to the success of industrialization. Hence, science is in part responsible for the growth of hazards and risks, while at the same time it is the body called on to provide knowledge claims needed to overcome or avoid risk (Dietz, Frey, and Rosa, 2002). However, in the period of late modernity, the notion of the existence of simple truth and certainty seems naïve. One only has to reflect briefly on the scientific debates and controversies that have raged over such issues as global warming, genetically modified foods, ozone depletion, hazardous waste, acid rain, and the risks of nuclear energy to realize that there is no single scientific position on these issues, or even an agreed-to set of facts. Rather, scientific knowledge is often revealed to be a body of contested claims, with the supremacy of any position largely linked to the skills of its advocates and their resources for advancing it, more so than to evidence of any overt truth. This absence of a clear and unequivocal knowledge system means that science, rather than solving the problems of the risk society, only adds to them by increasing uncertainty.

The premise of the risk society advanced by Beck has very important implications with respect to the study of environmental problems by environmental sociologists. On the one hand, the theory represents a serious challenge to what has emerged as the most widely supported position on how to deal with the environmental crisis, that of sustainable development. The logic of sustainable development sees the need for fine-tuning of the existing system. Industrialization and development are not in themselves considered inimical to environmental preservation. Indeed, the position typically is that economic development needs to be expanded, especially in the case of the Third World, while still adhering to sustainability principles. Notwithstanding the lack of any widely agreed-to model of sustainability, even 25 years after the publication of *Our Common Future* (World Commission on Environment and Development,

1987), the sustainable development thesis is in stark contradiction to the risk society. The underlying assumption on which sustainable development is based is that the existing system can cope. The risk society represents an entirely different perspective, that of a society imbued with uncertainty and self-doubt. On what grounds, Beck asks, is society likely to right itself and overcome environmental risks? The continued expansion of industry and development in the name of prosperity only increases environmental risk rather than solving it, and science, the henchman of this advancement, increases the odds of risk further while proving incapable of providing solutions or reducing uncertainty.

The risk society thesis has numerous other implications for society and the environment. It strongly emphasizes the interconnections between society and nature, rejecting any anthropocentric tendency to see humans as distinct from and superior to nature while requiring us to question conventional assumptions about both society and nature. The theory is one of epochal-level change, and preparation for this new age requires challenging social traditions and taken-for-granted conventional ways of life. This invites uncertainty, but living with risk and ambiguity is something that each one of us must learn to accept (Beck, 1992).

In addition, there are profound implications for existing **social institutions** and social actions in connection with the risk society. Beck is generally hostile to any notion of existing institutions—government, corporations—responding effectively to the environmental crisis. Rooted to an earlier age, they are insensitive and ill suited for dealing with contemporary problems of such complexity. Generally, political systems create more problems than they solve. Where progress has occurred, it has been in the guise of environmental movements, coalitions, and local networks. This therefore calls for new forms of political action that rely on grassroots protest and for strategic alliances demanding more openness and access to the decision-making process while at the same time bypassing existing political systems, parties, and the civil service.

Social Constructionism and Environmental Sociology

Social constructionism is a perspective often applied in other areas of sociology, one that has recently become established within environmental sociology as well.

This establishment has stirred new debates. Social constructionism argues that social reality is more a matter of perception than of objective determination (Best, 1989, 1993; Blumer, 1971; Spector and Kituse, 1977). In other words, reality is what we think it is rather than what it is. While most people assume social problems are recognized and dealt with because their existence is obvious, social constructionists argue that such recognition only occurs following a process of negotiation by which the "reality" of the problem becomes recognized. What is real is contested among parties with competing claims struggling to frame their version of the situation in order that the broader public will come to accept it. In these negotiations, the media play an important role, allowing the means for claims to be reported and providing important interpretation and emphasis, which may assist one or another of the competing parties to be successful in defining the problem and the approaches for dealing with it.

Social constructionism has been widely applied in sociology in areas such crime and deviance, homelessness, gender inequality, sexual orientation, illness and health care, and race and ethnicity. The perspective is appealing to some environmental sociologists, as well. John Hannigan's 1995 book on the topic, for example, argues that the "successful construction" of environmental problems requires that six conditions be met:

1. scientific "authority for and validation of claim" by parties
2. the existence of "popularisers" who can bridge environmentalism and science
3. media attention in which the problem is framed as novel and important
4. the dramatization of the problem "in symbolic and visual terms"
5. economic "incentives for taking positive action"
6. the emergence of an "institutional sponsor who can ensure both legitimacy and continuity" (55)

In other words, an environmental problem is only the result of the success of the claims-making of those who advocate its existence. The implication here concerns the sociological process that underlies the "discovery" of the environmental problem. Social dynamics replace objective existence of scientific risk as the object of scholarly interest since the social process is the basis for what we believe the problem to be.

Does this make sense when environmental problems are associated with such catastrophic threats that the very life of the planet is considered at risk? The social constructionist approach has provided abundant insight with respect to a variety of environmental debates, including global warming, acid rain, ozone depletion, environmental racism, **globalization** in general, and a host of local and regional industrial contamination and development debates. Examine any recent environmental controversy in your community and you will likely be able to apply a social constructionist perspective. Issues such as new industrial development, chemical contamination, or the siting of a landfill invariably pit residents, politicians, factory managers, government officials, and scientific experts against one another in a struggle to get their version of "the truth" accepted. The media provide the means for broadcasting the competing views, while also arbitrating what will be presented. Science has an authoritative voice in these debates, but all sides struggle to mount compelling scientific and/or moral/emotional arguments, and it is unlikely that science alone will determine the outcome. The result may be perceived by many as objective truth, but it is clear that such so-called reality is largely a social product.

Concerns over social constructionist analyses as applied to environmental problems have been expressed by a number of environmental sociologists, including Ted Benton (1994), Dunlap and W. Richard Catton (1994), Raymond Murphy (1994), and Peter Dickens (1996). These authors argue that there are objective, independent, and physical qualities to environmental problems that cannot be accounted for simply on the grounds of being "social constructions." For example, chemical contamination of groundwater from industry and radiation from nuclear energy each constitute an absolute and deadly threat to individuals and should not be treated simply as perceived concerns. Murphy accuses social constructionists within environmental sociology of having lost touch with nature and "gone overboard" (1994: 970), and Benton laments the "over-socialized" view of environmental risks by social constructionists (1994: 44). Further, these "realist" critics consider environmental sociology to be positioned to assist in overcoming environmental problems, and express alarm over whether the constructionist perspective is deflecting scholarly interest away from such work by focusing only on the moral and political issues surrounding the way a problem becomes defined.

Environmental social constructionists respond by noting that their position is not strict constructionism, as sometimes found in other areas of sociology

(Burningham and Cooper, 1999). Such extreme **relativism** sees all reality in terms of linguistic and social constructs and is of interest mainly to such areas of theoretical reasoning as postmodernism, areas that have little following within environmental sociology. Rather, for environmental sociology, the constructionist approach has been a more mild relativism, or *contextual constructionism*, which attempts to draw attention to the social processes involved in the development of societal recognition and response to environmental problems but does not claim that environmental problems do not objectively exist. For example, numerous sociological studies have reviewed the political discourse around the acid rain debate, along with the process by which scientists came to accept its existence and impacts (Zehr, 1994), and while there was strong interest in studying how the denials around acid rain were overcome, there was always recognition of the existence of dying lakes and forests and a desire to help end this.

The Environment and Social Movements

Fascinated by the environmental movement from its inception, environmental sociologists continue to be deeply interested in it. It has proven to be among the most successful and enduring social movements of all time. Few other recent movements can match it in terms of sustained activity, size of following, and ability to affect the lives of so many people. It has even changed our language, with such terms as *NIMBY* ("not in my back yard") and *environmentally friendly product* entering the vernacular. The first Earth Day, staged 22 April 1970, was impressive, drawing some 20 million people (Dunlap and Gale, 1972), and Earth Day has since grown to become an international annual event—Earth Week, celebrated in 180 countries. Today few people admit to not supporting environmentalism; in fact, most people claim to be environmentalists (Dunlap, 1992). The environmental lobby, institutionalized as a significant player in government decision making, is further evidence of the movement's impressive success.

The environmental movement has changed significantly over the years, often appearing to share little with its student-activist beginnings. The movement seems less angry today, but at the same time far more meticulous and deliberate in its approaches, often more at home in the corridors of power than on the protest line. The discussion that follows offers a look at the several strands of the contemporary environmental movement.

Progressive Conservation

Contemporary environmentalism traces its roots to the **progressive conservation** movement of the late-nineteenth-century United States (Fox, 1985; O'Riordan, 1971). Led by such reformers as Gifford Pinchot and John Muir, the founder of the Sierra Club, progressive conservation was a reaction against the unchecked destruction of nature during this period of freewheeling capitalism. The wanton environmental damage caused by private ownership of resources led to widespread public support for placing limits on the private use of land. Progressive conservation was instrumental in the creation of the national parks system in the United States, the increase of government control over public lands, and the founding of such conservation groups as the Sierra Club and the Audubon Society.

Reflecting a period in which science and technology were revered, progressive conservation sought to formulate and implement "scientific management" of the environment. Two alternative science-based approaches to environmental management emerged. The preservationists, led by John Muir, advocated setting aside and protecting wilderness so that its natural, aesthetic, recreational, and scientific values could remain undisturbed for the benefit of future generations. Consumptive wildlife users, on the other hand, promoted conservation for utilitarian ends. Led by Pinchot and supported by President Theodore Roosevelt, this group wanted lands to be set aside mainly for recreational needs, but also for logging, mining, and grazing. American conservation policies in the early twentieth century tried to accommodate both sides of the debate through the creation of a liberal policy of greater government control over both private enterprise and public lands.

Mainstream Environmentalism

One legacy of the progressive conservation movement was the legitimization of government involvement in the economy and the environment. The responsibility for maintaining some balance between environmental preservation and economic growth is mainly the province of government planners and politicians. Hence, progressive conservation set the scene for the current relationship between business and government. The main beneficiaries of this policy are the large corporations, which, while gaining controlled access to resources, have paid little in resource rents. Some observers regard the sustainable development movement as a new expression of the principle of consumptive wildlife use. Meanwhile, the voices of the early preservationists, calling for environmental protection on moral, scientific, and aesthetic grounds, have largely gone unheard.

According to Robert Cameron Mitchell, Angela Mertig, and Dunlap (1992), the other legacy of progressive conservation can be seen in the relationship between contemporary mainstream environmentalists and the government. Early preservationists quickly learned that they had to co-operate with the consumptive wildlife users and the Roosevelt administration or they would have little hope of making progress toward environmental protection. By now, environmentalists have become highly skilled at working as partners with government and developers in reaching compromise on environmental decisions. The inevitable result is trade-offs on preferred environmental solutions. Rik Scarce (1990: 15) reports that most environmental organizations admit to having no specific approach or plan for the environment other than saving what they can. Such muddling through has resulted in some checks on development, but also in serious environmental losses. Rarely have the mainstream environmental groups been in a position to claim complete victory in their efforts to stop a development or save an ecosystem.

Contemporary mainstream environmentalism is increasingly in the form of inside lobbying, politicking, and consultation, and relies mainly on its well-organized bureaucracies for success (Mertig, Dunlap, and Morrison, 2002). The leaders tend to be highly educated environmental professionals, often having backgrounds in public administration or environmental law and holding permanent, salaried positions. Fundraising and research are essential to successful competition with large corporations over the fate of resources. The individual member is far more likely to write a cheque or the occasional letter to an elected representative than to take part in a sit-in or blockade.

Many mainstream environmentalists argue that it has only been through these increasingly well-organized, well-funded, professional organizations that environmental review and assessment have become a permanent part of economic planning. Critics such as William Devall (1992) have suggested, however, that these same organizations are too accommodating to development interests, their leaders too close to their opposite numbers in business and government and too secure in their professional status. Still others are critical of mainstream environmentalism in general, arguing that it has long suffered from elitism. Various writers have pointed out the middle- or upper-class origins and high educational levels of environmental leaders and members of mainstream environmental organizations (Humphrey and Buttel, 1982; Morrison and Dunlap, 1986). However, it is also important to note that supporters of the environmental movement—if not those actually involved in it—tend to be drawn widely from across the social class spectrum (Mertig and Dunlap, 2001). A related criticism levelled at mainstream environmentalism is that the programs or policies advocated may lead to reductions in resource-based jobs or even in wholesale plant closures because of the high costs of environmental regulation or the protection of a given wilderness area (Schnaiberg, 1975). Such economic events are likely to have the most adverse effects on the working class and the poor.

The New Ecologies

Mainstream environmentalism is one wing of the larger environmental movement, which includes various alternatives. The *new ecologies* are a range of approaches within environmentalism with a number of features. First, they are all critical of mainstream environmentalism for its failure to address ecological problems by taking into account the systems of dominance in social relations that help to create those problems. Inequality among nations and regions serves to enhance competition for scarce resources and thereby increases environmental harm. The new ecologies argue that the key to solving environmental problems is the promotion of social equity and self-determination, which will allow peoples and nations to meet their human needs while maintaining ecological integrity (Gardner and Roseland, 1989).

Another distinguishing feature of the new ecologies, according to Nicholas Freudenberg and Carol Steinsapir (1992), is their devolved character. Hierarchical relations of authority between the membership and leaders or between the branches of each organization are rejected as being inconsistent with the prevailing thesis of human equality with nature rather than domination over it. This essentially eco-centric (and preservationist) stance is yet another characteristic of these groups, which tend to be sharply critical of any anthropocentric tendency to "manage" the environment—an approach mainstream environmentalists seem all too willing to accept.

Finally, the new ecologies tend to outline specific principles for environmental reform consistent with their broad vision of the human–nature relationship, rather than simply muddling through. They are also far less willing than the mainstream to accommodate solutions in the interest of political and economic expediencies. Indeed, some radical arms of the new ecologies movement advocate the use of illegal, even violent, actions in order to win environmental disputes. While these radicals are in the minority, mainstream environmentalists admit to having been helped by them in reaching compromises more favourable to the environment—they appear reasonable in comparison to the unbending demands and extremism of the radicals (Scarce, 1990).

Thus far, we have enumerated the similarities among the new ecologies. Now we look at three of these movements in order to highlight their differences.

Eco-feminism

Eco-feminism represents the partnership of ecology and feminism. It is founded mainly upon shared opposition to hierarchy and domination. Feminists argue that the subordination of women by men has been achieved through the ability of men to employ conceptual frameworks that place women at a disadvantage. According to Val Plumwood (1992), these include hierarchical frameworks that justify inequality; dualism, which justifies exclusion and separation; and rationality, which justifies logic and control. By advancing these three conceptual preferences, men have succeeded in legitimizing their domination over both women and nature.

The logic of domination holds that by virtue of the distinctiveness of men from nature and of men from women, together with the greater rationality of men, the domination of men over both women and nature is reasonable. In other words, eco-feminists argue that exactly the same male-controlled value system is used to justify both patriarchal human relations and the exploitation of nature.

Feminism and environmentalism connect, then, at the point of recognizing the similarities in the ways men treat women and nature. If one form of domination—of men over women—is wrong, then all forms of domination are wrong, including that of humans over nature. To be a feminist therefore compels one to be an environmentalist. Moreover, eco-feminists argue, inasmuch as environmentalists recognize and reject the domination of men over nature, they must also reject the domination of men over women. Therefore, all environmentalists must be feminists (Warren, 1990).

Social Ecology

Social ecology has become a major pillar of philosophical thought in contemporary environmentalism. Founder Murray Bookchin (1989) has articulated this philosophy over two decades. *Social ecology* advances a holistic world view of the human–nature partnership, one based on community. Bookchin identifies the dualism and domination informing current human–nature relations as products of human ideology and culture through which society has come to be defined as distinct from and superior to nature. While he acknowledges that culture and technology do distinguish society from nature, Bookchin rejects the idea that they are separate. Rather, society springs from nature, reworking it into the human experience. Society always has a naturalistic dimension, and social ecology is largely involved with attempting to describe how both the connectedness and the divergences between society and nature occur. Appropriate technology, reconstruction of damaged ecosystems, and human creativity will combine with equity and social justice to produce an ecological society in which human culture and nature are mutually supportive and evolve together. Social ecology envisions a society in harmony with nature, combining human-scale sustainable settlement, ecological balance, community self-reliance, and participatory democracy.

Deep Ecology

Deep ecology is among the most intriguing of the new ecologies, as well as the most controversial. The name was coined in 1973 by Norwegian philosopher Arne Naess. Defining contemporary environmentalism as "shallow" ecology, Naess (1973) argued that its advocacy of social reforms to curb problems of pollution and resource depletion identifies it as concerned mainly with protecting the health and affluence of the developed countries. By contrast, *deep ecology* is concerned with the root causes of environmental crisis and inspired by the understanding derived through personal experiences as humans in nature. The most distinctive aspect of deep ecology is its biocentric emphasis. Deep ecologists hold all forms of life dear, raising non-human life forms beyond the human. Therefore, while deep ecology shares with the other new ecologies the rejection of anthropocentrism, it goes beyond the humanistic, ecocentric ecology of human–nature coexistence. Deep ecologists desire humans to have the least possible effect on the planet and respect ecological integrity above all else (Tokar, 1988).

Deep ecology also places heavy emphasis on self-realization, the extension of the environmentally conscious individual's self beyond his or her personal needs to include the environment as a whole. The idea that human insight and experience are enhanced by contact with nature follows logically from biocentrism.

Deep ecologists believe that an important practical consequence of self-realization is the obligation to strive actively to prevent environmental destruction. The emphasis on direct action has particularly inspired the best-known of the deep ecology groups, Earth First!, which advocates the use of whatever means are necessary to save wilderness areas. Earth First! has garnered much attention—and criticism—for the use of ecological sabotage ("ecotage"), illegal force intended to block actions perceived as harming the environment (Taylor, 1991). "Monkey wrenching"—disruption by such covert and unlawful means as removing survey stakes, destroying machinery, or spiking trees—is controversial even within Earth First! These tactics stand in sharp contrast with the more widely accepted civil disobedience strategies of other radical environmentalists. *Civil disobedience* involves public protest for a cause, and while the marches or blockades may result in the protesters' being charged with civil crimes, there is a strong commitment to non-violence.

Grassroots Environmentalism

While the roots of environmentalism date back to the preservationist movement of the nineteenth century, it was the publication of Rachel Carson's *Silent Spring* in 1962 that led to human health risks' assuming significance along with conservation and preservation as environmental goals. The current era of environmentalism has increasingly focused on the dangers associated with industrial pollution and placement of pollution sources in residential communities. Recent years have seen the emergence of new grassroots forms of environmentalism with this as the mandate.

The Toxic Waste Movement

The toxic waste movement is a branch of environmentalism unlike either the mainstream environmental movement or the new ecologies. On the one hand, the well-funded and organized mainstream environmental organizations, such as the Sierra Club, rely on professional leadership and a skilled staff, along with well-placed connections within the power structure, savvy insight into the political process, and a large public base of followers willing to provide financial support or to lend their voices to back a cause. On the other hand, the new ecologies are far less resourced but are inspired and maintained by the ideology and shared values of the members.

The toxic waste movement reflects few of the tendencies of either of these more general arms of the environmental movement. The movement is, in a sense, all the disputes and protests by myriad groups opposed to perceived environmental threats present in their own communities and neighbourhoods. Diffuse in its focus, the toxic waste movement is associated with all manner of protest against everything from proposed developments, such as a new landfill, factory, or highway, to those connected with pollution caused by an existing industry. What unites the toxic waste movement is a common focus on perceived health threats to the community. The movement is intrinsically grassroots in its composition and approach, constituted typically of groups of formerly uninvolved citizens now struggling in their cause to stop a development or clean up pollution while facing the efficient and well-funded opposition of industry and/or government.

The toxic waste movement may be the fastest growing branch of environmentalism (Szasz, 1994). It is also in many ways far less distinguishable than the other types of environmentalism. For one thing, there is little in the way of national organizing bodies, or even communication among the various local groups. This extreme decentralization means that local protesters have very few resources, outside of their own means, on which to draw in developing their plans of opposition. Mainstream environmental organizations typically employ professional social movement organizers in order to guide their agendas, but local toxic waste protesters rarely have the backgrounds or resources required to mount a well-managed and effective campaign. Valuable skills may be learned

21.2

Sociology in Action
Cancer City

The only thing missing from disaster is the bodies on the streets of Whitney Pier.

On a drive through the neighborhood, the quiet homes reveal no clues about the hundreds who have died prematurely over the years.

But those who live here can tell you how cancer and heart disease have stalked this area for decades.

"Heart attack and cancer in these houses here," says Eric Brophy, 65, pointing to a group of homes along Lingan Road.

"My wife, who died 2-1/2 years ago, this was her grandfather's home. Her aunt who lived in this house died of cancer. Her dad died of a heart attack. He was 58."

Pointing a stubby finger down the road, Mr Brophy indicates yet another home.

"The Hotter girl that I mentioned, she lived in this house. That was cancer."

He continues to drive, hooded eyes focused on memories.

"Cancer through there. I know there was cancer here, I don't know the years. This is where my wife grew up. My wife was 56 when she died. She died of cancer."

House after house. Street after street. Block after block.

Why?

Finding the answer is what drives the health studies working group of the Joint Action Group, a community-driven effort to clean up the largest toxic waste site in North America.

For almost 90 years, smoke stacks at Sydney Steel belched carcinogens daily over Sydney, blanketing Whitney Pier and adjoining neighborhoods.

The mill's coke ovens were torn down a decade ago, but the pollution stayed.

Leachate from a hilltop municipal dump still flows into the 50-hectare coke ovens site, mixing with the heavily contaminated soil and bedrock.

The resulting chemical cocktail—a witch's brew of heavy metals, poisonous hydrocarbons and other toxins—creeps steadily downhill, finally draining into the infamous tar ponds, two pools holding 700,000 tonnes of hazardous goo, including 50,000 tonnes of PCBs.

Since the tar ponds are actually a tidal estuary, every day the ocean flushes more contaminants out to sea.

"Last week I buried a second family member in a year from cancer," says Michelle Gardiner, a young, expectant mother and interim chair of the health studies group. "I live with the same things that people in this community do, but I want the truth."

Ms Gardiner, who lives in Ashby, bordering Whitney Pier, leans forward, her voice weary yet earnest.

"What a legacy to pass on to this baby I'm carrying right now. 'You were born in the cancer capital.' I'm sorry, there's so much else at risk here. There's a future."

Despite dozens of studies done through the years, scientists and JAG officials agree there's not enough evidence to conclusively identify what's causing the health problems.

Only one report has ever been published in the scientific literature, a 1985 study by Health Canada scientist Yang Mao on mortality in Cape Breton County.

Using death certificate data from 1971 to 1983, Mr Mao's team found rates of cancer and circulatory disease higher than the provincial average among both men and women, particularly in Sydney.

While the link between environmental factors and health remains largely unstudied, a 1987 provincial study of lifestyle factors associated with cancer and heart disease found many Cape Breton County residents smoked too much, had poor diets, were overweight and did not exercise enough.

That report is derisively known in Sydney as the Broccoli Study because of a perception the

continued

study concluded local residents needed to eat more broccoli.

Meanwhile, studies in other parts of the world—Pennsylvania, the United Kingdom and Ontario—have established a link between coke oven emissions and cancer, especially of the lungs.

But, explains Don Ferguson, Health Canada's director general for the Atlantic region, more studies are needed to determine the precise role that pollution played in the Sydney area.

"Exposed to what? Through what conditions? For what period of time?" Mr Ferguson said. "In order to get to 'what happened', you need to know these three things."

Even when all the studies are complete, he said, the best you'll be able to say is that there's a high probability that exposure to hazardous waste contributed to the high rates of cancer and other diseases.

"The reality is you will probably never find the smoking gun because health is impacted by genetics, it's impacted by lifestyle and, clearly, environmental and occupational exposures."

JAG members acknowledge that scientifically proving a connection between pollution and disease might be extremely difficult.

Still, they're determined to try.

At JAG's request, two Health Canada scientists launched a multiyear study in May, reviewing cancer mortality and incidence rates over a 30-year period, as well as reproductive health outcomes, including birth defects.

The first results, to be released in late September, will show some diseases are definitely more common in Sydney than the rest of the province, says team co-leader Pierre Band.

Other disease rates are higher in Cape Breton County than Nova Scotia, and higher still in Sydney, he said.

"At the end, we'll have a reasonably complete picture of what stands out," Mr Band said. "And based on that, one would then need to develop other studies to try and answer why."

Finding answers will likely take three to five years, he said.

"I have no problem with three to five years, if it's done right," Ms Gardiner said. "We deserve to know what the hell is going on."

The coke ovens site, bordering Whitney Pier, is largely barren today.

Two towering smokestacks still rise from the ground like bleached ribs. A rusting warehouse stands in the distance.

On the northwest corner of the site, a large steel tank similar to those used at refineries sits beside a gravel ramp once used by dump trucks.

Inside are some 4,000 tonnes of toxic liquid and sludge, including lead, mercury, various hydrocarbons and PCBs.

When the coke ovens were demolished in 1988, 16 other tanks belonging to the coal tar company Domtar were torn down and their contents transferred to the largest remaining tank.

"It's full, right to the top," said Mike Britten, JAG's overall program coordinator. "Every time it rains and the wind blows, the material blows over the side.

continued

"You can see the black staining down along the side of the tank from the hydrocarbons."

The tank's structural integrity is unknown, he said. Removing the tank's top in 1988 to simplify dumping weakened the structure. And the tank was not designed for its current contents.

Discussions on removing the tank and its contents are under way, he said. "I'd say this fall that tank would be gone."

But what if the tank ruptured?

There would be a public outcry and an emergency cleanup, say both Mr Britten and Germaine LeMoine, public information officer for JAG.

But it's Mr Britten's frank assessment of the relative impact of the contamination that speaks volumes about the size of the overall problem.

You'd be adding 4,000 tonnes to literally millions of tonnes of contamination already in the ground, he said.

"In the big picture, given a couple of days, you probably wouldn't even see it."

Conveying the immensity of the problem to the public is a challenge, say JAG members.

"The tar ponds are barely one-fifteenth of the problem," said Francois Sirois, a member of JAG's environmental data gathering and remedial options working group.

Including the heavily contaminated soil at the coke ovens site and surrounding areas, "you're looking at up to 10 million tonnes of potentially contaminated sediment."

The tar ponds have been extensively tested, but officials say they know little about the rest of the site.

That problem is compounded by the roughly 13 kilometers of steel pipe, used to carry byproducts like benzene, still buried underground.

"If you were operating a high hoe [used for excavating], would you want to start digging in the coke ovens [site] not knowing what's down there?" asks John Steele, a member of JAG's environmental group.

"And [if] you run into a benzene line or possibly a pocket of coke ovens gas that might be in there—Boom!"

JAG must also evaluate various methods for cleaning up the mess, Mr Sirois said.

People are already sending in ideas for disposal, including firing the mess into space aboard a rocket, Ms LeMoine said. "For every idea, there are 10 behind it."

The cleanup will take decades, Mr Sirois said, and afterwards the area will only be suitable for industrial use, not housing.

"You can't, with the fact the bedrock is contaminated.

"You can't dig into that bedrock forever. It would be prohibitive. You'd have to be blasting in the middle of Sydney to break up the rock.

"Not possible."

Source: Paul Schneidereit, *Halifax Herald* (26 July 1998).

---

as the protest develops, but as these campaigns are often also short lived, such knowledge may not be passed on.

What is characteristic of the toxic waste movement is the high proportion of its members who are women and homemakers, minorities, and those from lower socio-economic backgrounds (Brown and Masterson-Allen, 1994). Toxic waste activists also tend to be older, politically conservative, and trusting of existing institutions, laws, and regulations. The movement's high composition of women and homemakers is in keeping with its principal focus on preserving human health, especially that of children, in the face of an immediate threat from a nearby development or pollution source. These groups' membership is on average less educated than that found within mainstream environmentalism and the new ecologies, and their protests are more emotional than those of these other groups, which prefer to emphasize rational opposition based on scientific and legal evidence.

Unlike the new ecologies, ideology is not a prominent factor relating to either the formation or the reasoning of toxic waste groups. Toxic waste activists are motivated by the presence of a nearby environmental threat and are conditioned by their experiences in responding to it. Initially apolitical and naïve in the art of protest, the lessons learned at the hands of the authorities and corporations may compel a loss of innocence leading to personal transformations (Aronson, 1993). Along with bringing lifestyle and value changes, such personal reconsideration may also prompt new skepticism about the political process, along with mistrust of the authorities, business, and scientific experts.

Grassroots toxic waste protest is often dismissed as NIMBYism by those who disagree with its ends, and it is true that it often does appear that self-interest is an underlying motivation on which such protests are based. Nevertheless, if the threat is real, why should self-interest depreciate the legitimacy of the group's goal? It is also the case that a general increase within society in concerns over health risk from pollution and development is helping to move the toxic waste movement toward a more formally defined foundation of support and new allegiances. This is seen, for example, in connection with the general movement to supplant NIMBY with NIABY—"not in anyone's back yard"—indicative of the reduced emphasis on self-interest, as well as with LULU ("locally unwanted land uses"), reflective of the greater sensitivity to the broader public interest currently sought in the development of many municipal land use plans (Freudenburg and Pastor, 1992).

Environmental Justice

Recently, another new grassroots movement, known as the **environmental justice** (EJ) movement, has emerged, with an agenda going beyond the traditional concerns of conservation and preservation common to most environmentalism. The EJ movement has ties to the toxic waste movement, but is also altering the focus of environmentalism generally to include broader concerns with regard to the societal inequities that result from industrial facility siting and industrial development. Lois Gibbs, a leader in the fight over the chemical contamination of the Love Canal neighbourhood in Niagara Falls, New York, and founder of the Citizens' Clearing House for Hazardous Waste, has written,

This movement, in hundreds of local and regional organizations, is typically led by women, working-class people, and people of color. Many, particularly the women, have never been involved in any political issue before and have been galvanized primarily by their concern for their children's safety. . . . Although these leaders became involved because of a single issue or problem, they quickly recognized the interconnections with other injustices they face daily. They realise that the root of their problem is the lack of organized political power, deteriorating neighborhood conditions, poverty and race. . . . As a result, these leaders now build bridges with civil-rights and labor organizations, housing groups, and those fighting for adequate health care for all. . . . As they battle with various bureaucracies to resolve the crisis that brought them together, they begin to identify links among issues and build an even broader coalition for change. . . . These new alliances and cooperative work can achieve real democracy. (1993: ix–x)

While the environmental movement has long been concerned with the risks to human health from industrial pollution, it is only recently that awareness has developed over the distributional risks associate with these effects. Various US studies have documented the inequitable distribution of environmental hazard (Bryant and Mohai, 1992; Bullard, 1990; Hofrichter, 1993), showing, for the most part, that low-income and racial-minority populations are disproportionately being affected by poor environmental quality resulting from exposure to industrial pollution, workplace pollution, and contaminated water and lands. A similar finding for low income and the likelihood of exposure to contamination risk was found in a comparison of pollution sites across Toronto, Hamilton, and Niagara Falls, Ontario (Nabalamba, 2001), and lower socio-economic status has often been found to be a prevalent condition within Canada's worst-polluted neighbourhoods.

Various explanations revolve around the processes that result in the inequitable distribution of environmental burdens. One position reflects economic or market dynamics, suggesting that "sound" business decisions and the need to reduce costs may be grounds for locating potentially polluting industrial facilities (Kriesel, Centner, and Keeler, 1996; Oakes, 1996). It points to economic efficiency within the marketplace as the central criterion that guides what

21.3

Human Diversity
Environmental Justice

Much of the environmental justice literature is based on US findings. In a Canadian study, Alice Nabalamba (2001) focuses on Southern Ontario, in particular, Toronto, Hamilton, and the Niagara region. Using 1996 data from the Canadian census and municipal records, Nabalamba investigates the link between visible-minority status, socio-economic status, and the location of pollution sources. Five types of polluted sites were included: contaminated sites, industrial discharges, hazardous waste treatment and storage facilities, polychlorinated biphenyl (PCB) storage and treatment facilities, and other waste treatment, disposal, and storage facilities.

Nabalamba found that "people of lower socio-economic means were more likely than the general population to live near a pollution source and industrial land use" (2001: 141). Visible-minority status was also related to increased exposure to certain types of pollution sources, but the relationship is clouded by the lower socio-economic status of many visible minority groups. The location of pollution sources was related to decreased real estate values, decreased home ownership (versus renting), and the age of housing. The relationship between pollution siting and older, poorer neigh-bourhoods reflects a lack of political and organizational clout to defend against these types of uses. Therefore, Nabalamba predicts, future siting of these kinds of facilities will continue to effect these types of neighbourhoods more so than wealthier, newer, and "whiter" areas.

(Waite Air Photos Inc.)

results as the unfair distribution of environmental risks to the poor. Industry's desire to minimize costs specifically associated with land or property values is seen as a major contributing factor to the disproportionate exposure to environmental pollutants. The suggestion is that this unequal risk occurs because cost-efficient industrial areas with low property values are also likely to be near areas with low residential property values or affordable housing and therefore a concentration of low-income populations.

Another rationale given for why the poor face greater pollution risk is the "path of least resistance" argument (Higgins, 1994; Hofrichter, 1993). This suggests that low-income and minority communities end up with a disproportionate share of disposal and polluting industrial facilities and poor environmental quality in general because they have less political clout than the more affluent communities.

Finally, a more contentious explanation cites "environmental racism" among private-industry and government decision makers as being behind the disparities found in the uneven distribution of polluting industrial facilities (Bryant and Mohai, 1992; Bullard, 1994). This position draws largely on interpretations of evidence from the United States that show race to be a major factor in who is likely to be exposed to pollution risk. Hence, it is concluded that when race stands out as being significantly associated with the location of new disposal and polluting industrial facilities, it is racism that is influencing the decision-making process.

Conclusion

It is evident that the environment and social change are profoundly intertwined. The relationship cuts both ways: either societies will change to achieve environmental integrity, or they will be changed by environmental contamination and resource depletion. Social change on behalf of the environment is therefore one of the most pressing global issues.

If sociology can be said to make one substantial contribution to the understanding of ecological crisis, it is the recognition that environmental problems are social products. This understanding goes beyond descriptions of how individuals or firms contribute to environmental degradation, and the solutions suggested involve more than promoting more environmentally responsible behaviours or technologies. While such approaches may help deal with an immediate situation, they ultimately do more harm than good by deflecting attention from the real roots of environmental problems and the discovery of long-term solutions.

In short, social systems must change in order that global disaster may be averted. Buttel and Peter Taylor (1992) have pointed out that one promising development in this direction has been the globalization of environmental discourse. The 1972 UN conference on the environment held in Stockholm initiated the process, helping to shift the attention of governments to the global nature of environmental problems, boosting public concern for the environment, and spawning a number of treaties and other institutional innovations to reduce marine pollution, control acid rain, protect the atmosphere, and preserve wetlands.

Almost as important as the actual steps taken to check environmental damage has been the extension of such talks to include global social relations and their connection to environmental threats. The 1972 conference dealt mainly with industrial pollution in the developed world, but at the Earth Summits held two and three decades later, Third World development, sovereignty, foreign aid, poverty, debt, and social justice were central to the negotiations. Indeed, these issues had become so dominant by the time of the 2002 Earth Summit, held in South Africa, that the United States refused even to attend, arguing that the process had been "hijacked" by anti-globalization interests.

It is now widely accepted that the eradication of Third World poverty is among the keys to solving environmental problems. Yet this realization has served to kindle both old and new tensions between industrialized and developing nations. The former continue to promote such traditional mechanisms for economic improvement as foreign investment, new trading relations, and foreign aid. In some cases, it has been suggested that foreign assistance be tied to population control or environmental improvements. Third World countries tend to be deeply suspicious of such tactics, referring to them as environmental colonialism and arguing they are little more than a new version of the historical patterns of domination that have been responsible for most underdevelopment. The refusal also by the United States to sign the biodiversity convention at the 1992 Earth Summit in Rio de Janeiro, on the grounds that it could restrict US international commercial interests, was widely interpreted as demonstrating a willingness to abandon the environment if its protection involved any threat to the existing global distribution of power.

Developing countries are also sensitive to any threats to their sovereignty perceived to result from intrusive foreign aid or investment, and are distrustful of the World Bank, the International Monetary Fund, the Food and Agriculture Organization, and other global bodies traditionally involved with Third World programs. Finally, many developing countries have crushing foreign debts and are compelled to earn hard currency through the export of raw resources or agricultural products in demand in industrialized nations. The harvesting of the resources and the farming practices used to grow the crops often cause considerable environmental damage while doing little to improve the long-term economic prospects of poorer countries.

Another source of tension is the fact that the industrialized nations have failed to demonstrate sufficient financial commitment to solving global environmental problems. It has been estimated that a total of $600 billion (US) annually would be needed in order to make progress toward the environmental improvements outlined in the work plan, Agenda 21, agreed to by the 150 nations attending the 1992 Earth Summit. Of this total, $125 billion was expected to come through development assistance or loan relief from the industrialized world. These amounts have never been pledged, and foreign aid still remains a controversial, and largely low-priority, item for countries such as Canada and the United States.

On a smaller scale, the principle of sustainable development is becoming ingrained in the policy and planning frameworks of both developed and less developed countries. Many herald this tendency as a breakthrough in attitudes toward the environment. Others are more skeptical, suggesting that the concept of sustainable development may be hijacked by development interests and used to legitimize unnecessary economic expansion. These critics cite the Business Council for Sustainable Development, created at the 1992 Rio summit and comprising 48 CEOs from the world's corporations. The council was intended to represent business interests in global sustainable development negotiations and to sensitize world business leaders to issues of development and the environment. However, its many detractors regard the council as demonstrating all too clearly the real interests the sustainable development movement will serve.

The potential for deflecting such a hijacking, if one is planned, could rest with the success of the new ecologies and grassroots environmentalism. The intensely participatory focus of these organizations, together with their high levels of commitment to local control of ecosystems, could go far toward curtailing economically driven environmental exploitation. As noted earlier, the influence of such movements in environmental planning is increasing, and if Ulrich Beck's risk society thesis is correct, then such involvement is destined to grow. The new ecologies' less conventional approaches to environmental planning are also considered to represent the new forms of thinking necessary for achieving true sustainable development (Gardner and Roseland, 1989). By reflecting alternatives to current forms of social organization and changing environmental values and aspirations, contemporary environmentalism may be in the vanguard of social change on behalf of both the environment and social improvement generally.

☐ Questions for Critical Thought

1. Despite the recognition that significant environmental problems persist, there still exists a spirit of optimism in many quarters, a feeling that humankind is making progress toward environmental quality. Should we be optimistic or pessimistic about the view that societies are succeeding in overcoming environmental problems?

2. Environmental sociologists argue that ecological problems are social problems; that is, they exist because of the nature of social arrangements and social organization. Discuss this idea by selecting one or more environmental problems and suggesting how they might have been avoided or reduced if alternative social arrangements had existed.

3. The concept of sustainable development is key to much economic planning, but its critics often argue that it is being used mainly as a rationale for allowing more economic growth at the expense of the environment. Can economic growth and environmental quality coexist, in your opinion? Is sustainable development the answer for saving the planet?

4. When, if ever, is illegal protest, such as the ecotage practised by Earth First!, justifiable for protecting the environment?

5. Eco-feminists see similarities between environmentalists' fight to preserve the environment and women's struggle to achieve equality. Do you agree that there is a connection between these two social movements? Should all feminists be environmentalists, and vice versa?

6. Population growth is frequently likened to an ecological time bomb and one of the most virulent threats to the future of the planet. Are such claims valid? What are the various side to this controversy? Discuss ways in which the global population problem could be solved.

7. Social constructionists see environmental problems as relying on the extent to which these are recognized and validated by the greater society in terms of the form of response provided. How helpful is this in alleviating environmental problems? Consider environmental controversies at both the local and international levels. How does the constructionist viewpoint contribute to their understanding?

8. How valid is the claim that being poor or a member of an ethnic minority increases environmental threat in Canada? Is inequitable distribution of environmental hazard inevitable? Discuss, drawing on examples from your community.

9. Ulrich Beck's theory of the risk society is a challenge to conventional thinking with regard both to the organization of society in the twenty-first century and to how environmental problems are viewed. How could Beck's theory alter the course of environmentalism and the manner by which environmental problems are addressed?

☐ Recommended Readings

Ronald Bailey, *Eco-scam: The False Prophets of Ecological Apocalypse* (New York: St Martin's, 1993).
Not everyone agrees with environmentalism, and some are adamant in being strongly critical of its claims, particularly with respect to carrying capacity, or Earth's ability to sustain its resource base. This book is a response to environmentalism's assumptions, claiming that environmentalist alarmism and extremism are actually serving to undermine the future of the planet.

Phil Brown and Edwin J. Mikkelsen, *No Safe Place: Toxic Waste, Leukemia and Community Action* (Berkeley, CA: University of California Press, 1990).
This book analyzes the civil protest that occurred in connection to the childhood leukemia cluster discovered in Woburn, Massachusetts, which was linked to industrial waste carcinogens that leaked into the community's water supply. The resulting protest and legal case was one of the most comprehensive community actions ever taken in connection with a toxic waste problem. The story was later the subject of the 1998 movie *A Civil Action,* starring John Travolta.

Robert D. Bullard, *Dumping in Dixie: Race, Class and Environmental Quality* (Boulder, CO: Westview, 1990).
This series of case studies on five Southern black communities chronicles the increased environmental risks associated with being poor, black, and female in the United States, and is one of the principal works leading to the development of the field of environmental social justice.

Rachel Carson, *Silent Spring* (Boston: Houghton Mifflin, 1962).
Carson's book, the first widely read analysis of the environmental and health risks associated with modern agricultural herbicides and pesticides, created a wave of public concern when first published and helped launch the modern environmental movement.

Paul R. Ehrlich, *The Population Bomb* (New York: Ballantine, 1968).
Ehrlich's book was among the first analyses of the global ecological consequences of overpopulation. It received widespread attention for its prediction of imminent ecological collapse, leading to the founding of the zero population growth (ZPG) movement.

Lois Gibbs, *Love Canal: My Story* (Albany: State University of New York Press, 1982).
Love Canal is the most famous incidence of chemical hazardous waste contamination in the United States and of the struggle of neighbourhood residents to have it recognized. This book is the autobiography of local housewife Lois Gibbs, who emerged as the leader of the struggle to have the contamination recognized and compensation provided to its victims.

Robert Hunter, *Warriors of the Rainbow: A Chronicle of the Greenpeace Movement* (New York: Holt, Rinehart and Winston, 1979).
This is an account by one of its founders of the early days of the Greenpeace Society, launched in 1969 in Vancouver, British Columbia.

Rik Scarce, *Eco-Warriors: Understanding the Radical Environmental Movement* (Chicago: Noble, 1990).
Scarce reviews the histories, actions, and philosophies of the various groups constituting the radical arm of contemporary environmentalism, including Greenpeace, Earth First!, the Sea Shepherds, and Animal Liberation.

Allan Schnaiberg and Kenneth Alan Gould, *Environment and Society: The Enduring Conflict* (New York: St Martin's, 1994).
Schnaiberg is the foremost conflict-oriented environmental sociologist, whose earlier book, *The Environment: From Surplus to Scarcity* (1980), largely defined the critical approach in environmental sociology. This more recent book updates those ideas in the context of sustainable development.

Mathis Wackernagel and William Rees, *Our Ecological Footprint: Reducing Human Impact on the Earth* (Gabriola Island, BC: New Catalyst, 1996).

This book introduces the metaphor of the *ecological footprint*, a term used to refer to the productive land needed in order to sustain different lifestyles. If everyone in the world lived like the average Canadian in terms of their consumption patterns, housing, and transportation, we would need two additional planets to provide for all our needs. This books provides an accounting measure by which each individual can measure his or her own ecological footprint.

☐ Recommended Web Sites

Center for Health, Environment and Justice

www.chej.org

This Web site is an online extension of the public campaign to promote environmental justice through community action and public awareness of toxins. The site provides information and practical advice on community mobilization against toxic products, processes, and wastes.

David Suzuki Foundation

www.davidsuzuki.org

Canada's most famous environmentalist, David Suzuki, began a foundation in 1990 that focuses on climate change, biodiversity, and forest and fishery issues. The Web site offers information on public action and advocacy, a regular column by Dr Suzuki, and media releases and community events information.

Earth Day Network Ecological Footprint Quiz

www.earthday.net/footprint/index.asp

A number of Web sites allow online calculation of your ecological footprint, the amount of productive land needed to sustain an individual's lifestyle. This one from the Earth Day organization calculates your ecological footprint based on information you provide on your consumption, housing, and travel patterns.

Environmental Defence Canada

www.edcanada.org

This charitable organization, with broad-based membership and university, private, and corporate sponsorship, advocates community and individual actions on environmental problems. Its Web site contains links to its newsletter, action alerts, and media releases.

Greenpeace

www.greenpeace.ca

Greenpeace's Web site provides information on its various campaigns as well as public information guides and press releases on environmental problems.

Institute for Deep Ecology

www.deep-ecology.org

Deep-ecology.org offers readings and discussion about the philosophy of deep ecology, as well as current press releases on environmental issues with an international focus.

The Pembina Institute

www.pembina.org

This Canadian-based organization states on its Web site, "the Institute's major policy research and education programs are in the areas of sustainable energy, climate change, environmental governance, ecological fiscal reform, sustainability indicators, and the environmental impacts of the energy industry."

United Nations Environmental Programme

www.unep.org

The UNEP Web site offers access to maps, UN publications, and many databases from various sources, including the World Bank, UNICEF, UNESCO, and UNPOP. Databases can be downloaded in many different formats.

part **Six**

> > >

Sociological Theory and Methods

Several types of theories and research procedures have been discussed throughout the chapters of this book. The purpose of the two chapters in part VI is to bring these different approaches together, to carefully compare and contrast them, first for sociological theory, then for research methods.

22

Joseph M. Bryant

> > >

Sociological Theory

© PhotoDisc, Inc.

☐ Learning Objectives

In this chapter, you will:

- learn how and why the social sciences differ from the natural sciences

- see how sociological theories can be comprehended in terms of their basic assumptions about the nature of social reality, as expressed in the two main traditions: the structure and the agency perspectives

- explore key concepts and contributions of the structuralist tradition—in Marx's historical materialism, Weber's sociology of world history, and Durkheim's functionalism

- survey key concepts and contributions of the agency tradition—Mead's symbolic interactionism, Goffman's dramaturgy, Schütz's phenomenology, Garfinkel's ethnomethodology, and the exchange and rational choice perspectives

- consider how feminism has challenged the biases of "male-stream" social science

- study how the current challenge is to integrate the structure and agency perspectives

Introduction

If you were asked to provide an example of a scientific **theory**, which one would you choose? The leading candidates would undoubtedly be drawn from the natural sciences: Charles Darwin's theory of evolution, the laws of thermodynamics, Albert Einstein's theory of relativity. But what if you were required to furnish an example from the social sciences? Some of you would refer to the ideas of Sigmund Freud, whose views on sexuality and personality formation have entered widely into popular culture. Others might mention an axiom drawn from economics, as issues of unemployment and inflation are routinely discussed in the media. Some might cite Karl Marx, whose theories of social change and class conflict inspired a series of revolutions—in Russia and China, most notably—that transformed world history. It is unlikely, however, that many of you would agree that these examples are as "scientific" as those found in the natural sciences. After all, is it not the case that many psychologists now reject the theories of Freud, that economists are in perpetual squabble, and that Marx's prophecies of the demise of capitalism have not been fulfilled?

Getting One's Bearings: On Science and Theory, Natural and Social

In comparison to the natural sciences, the social sciences do exhibit more persistent discord and controversy. But why so? Answers range from dismissals that the social sciences are not "true" sciences at all to countering claims that they will become so over time, as they develop in imitation of the older natural sciences. Ironically, both these views share an assumption that science is a uniform way of knowing and that the procedures found in physics and chemistry set the standards to follow. Most scientists today would not accept such a view, for the differences between the various sciences are no less important than the formal similarities they share.

Science is a social practice that uses systematic methods of investigation—observation, measurement, and analysis—in order to develop verifiable knowledge. But knowledge about what? It is here that diversity takes over, for each of the sciences specializes in exploring quite distinct subject matters: physical, chemical, biological, psychological, and soci-ological. Because the natural and social worlds are complex and diverse, many different sciences are required, and each will adopt modes of analysis and explanation that correspond to the particular realities being investigated.

All scientific work is ultimately guided by *first principles*. These are the assumptions scientists make about two basic concerns: (1) the specific "what" that is being studied (this is called **ontology**) and (2) the particular "how" of acquiring knowledge about it (known as **epistemology**). *Ontology* is concerned with identifying the kinds of things that exist, and with specifying their basic constitution and causal powers. *Epistemology* is concerned with how knowledge of those things is to be obtained. Ontology specifies how the parts, processes, and relations of things make them what they are. Epistemology specifies the relations between the perceiving subject (the knower) and the perceived object (the known).

Consider a brief illustration. What is the ontology—the "what"—of this book? On first appearances, it is a solid compound of paper, ink, and glue. No physicist would settle for that characterization, however, for the book is ultimately composed of a whirling mass of particles. We know of the phenomenal properties of things—how they "appear," as large or small, solid or liquid, rough or smooth—through our senses, primarily by seeing and touching. Science, however, is about penetrating beyond the appearances of things to their essences, to the underlying mechanisms and forces that cause things to happen and that give a patterned order to realities, both natural and social. By the use of various instruments and methods, the sciences "look deeper," so to speak, and so we come to know things at a theoretical level that is non-apparent at the level of common sense or ordinary perception (see Figure 22.1).

The division of the sciences into two subsets—the natural-physical and the social-cultural—reflects the fact that they investigate different ontological realities (different objects and processes), and so confront distinct epistemological challenges in *how* they establish their claims to knowledge (see Table 22.1).

Natural phenomena—physical, chemical, biological—are said to be **objective**, in that their properties and relations occur by necessity or circumstance, given their constitution and combinations. Earthquakes, thunderstorms, an eclipse of the sun or moon, a gene-tic mutation, the spread of a virus, the growth and decay of living organisms, the movement of the oceanic currents—all such processes occur

IN THE FIRST PERSON

As a kid, I was always fascinated by history and the diversity of human existence displayed in books, films, documentaries—even comics and toy soldiers! My family moved around quite a bit, so I realized early on that different places brought one into contact with different peoples and cultures. How could all this diversity be explained? By sociology, of course! As an undergraduate, I took two courses that really opened my eyes. One was on the history of sociological theory, which introduced me to the ideas of Marx and Weber, Veblen, Mead, Mannheim, Goffman, and others, and enabled me to begin seeing how human beings are "made" by the social worlds they themselves are busy creating. The second course, on social movements, suggested that we are not prisoners of the pasts we inherit, but have some capacity to reform or even revolutionize the institutions and customs that thwart our aspirations for justice, freedom, and decency. Using sociology to make sense of history, and using history to deepen and enrich our sociological imagination—that's a fascination that continues.

—JOSEPH M. BRYANT

objectively as a result of the properties and causal relations of the things involved. In explaining how and why planets orbit, cells divide, species evolve, or atoms combine, no *subjective* or personal desire, belief, or motive ever needs to be considered. And because natural phenomena are ontologically objective, it is often possible in the natural sciences to provide explanations of *universal deductive scope* (in the logical form, for every *x*, if *y*, then *p*).

Social phenomena, in contrast, are both objective and subjective, in that human beings are not only created by the cultural worlds they inhabit, they also create those worlds through their interactions. We are socialized in conformity with existing traditions, but we also have a capacity to reflect, to innovate, and so

to change our social arrangements. In everyday life, each of us functions within an already established world of institutions, technologies, and customs, but we do so with thoughts and attitudes in mind. Social realities, in other words, exist not just *materially*, as objects and arrangements of various sorts, but also *mentally*, in the meanings and values that human beings assign to those objects.

Subjective states of consciousness—desire, belief, motive—will thus be at the core of any understanding of the human social condition, for our actions take the form of meaningful reactions to culturally defined and interpreted situations. A revolution, for example, will not occur automatically whenever a fixed percentage of the population falls below the

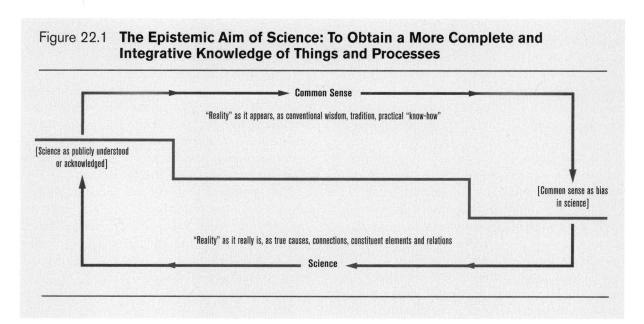

Figure 22.1 **The Epistemic Aim of Science: To Obtain a More Complete and Integrative Knowledge of Things and Processes**

Common Sense

"Reality" as it appears, as conventional wisdom, tradition, practical "know-how"

[Science as publicly understood or acknowledged]

[Common sense as bias in science]

"Reality" as it really is, as true causes, connections, constituent elements and relations

Science

Table 22.1	**Ontological and Epistemological Foundations of the Sciences**	
	Natural Sciences	**Social Sciences**
Ontology (theory of the nature of the different kinds of being)	• Natural phenomena are objective (matter and energy) • Things happen according to causal necessity, force of circumstance, the "laws of nature"	• Social phenomena are objective and subjective (material and mental) • Things happen according to the meaningful and interpretive responses of human beings to the social situations they encounter and create
Epistemology (theory of the nature of knowledge)	• Natural phenomena are known from the "outside," through observable measurement • The perceiving subject and the perceived object are non-identical	• Social phenomena are known on the basis of both "external" observable measurement and "internal" intersubjective understanding • With human beings studying human beings, there is a subject–object identity

poverty line, or whenever elite corruption crosses a certain threshold. It will happen only when groups of people feel unjustly exploited or oppressed and are able to organize to challenge the established system. An inner-city teenager, failing in school and facing bleak employment prospects, may experience peer pressure to join a criminal gang, but that choice is not determined for him. It can be countered by other considerations, such as strong family ties or religious commitment. Because social phenomena combine the material and the mental, and because they arise out of the meaningful responses of reflective (thinking) human agents to existing circumstances, theoretical explanations in the social sciences tend to be of *context-dependent and probabilistic scope* (for most *x*'s in situation *y*, there is a tendency for *p*).

Consider an example that involves both a natural and a social dimension. Because of advances in biology and medicine, we now know that illness and disease are caused mainly by natural occurrences, such as bacterial infections, the ingestion of cancer-causing substances, and so on. In the pre-modern age, however, people did not possess that knowledge, nor did they view their existence in scientific terms. They interpreted ailments quite differently, as signs of divine punishment or demonic possession, or as harmful curses invoked by personal enemies. Most of us today adhere to a scientific-medical definition of illness, and so we follow a *logic of action* (a "way" of doing things) that differs significantly from the healing efforts of those who do not share that perspective. If you were to experience severe chest pains right now, you probably wouldn't think that a visit to a religious shrine or a witch-doctor is in order, or that the discomfort is a divine warning against any further

study of sociology. As this comparison of differing world views on illness indicates, it is the *social definition of reality*—the world we collectively imagine or "construct" through meaningful, conscious activity—that informs and directs human action.

What, then, of the epistemological differences between the natural and social sciences? Most fundamentally, a situation in which human beings study the social life of other human beings constitutes a knowledge relationship very different from situations in which human beings study plants or particles. In this regard, the social sciences operate under a hazard and a privilege.

Our hazard? In investigating the human social condition, it is quite difficult to preserve our objectivity or value neutrality, even in our role as investigators, for we too are inescapably a part of that reality. Being human—all too human—we are prone to carrying into our research the preconceptions and prejudices we have acquired as socialized members of our societies. To set aside our gender identities, our class interests, or our political orientations is no easy matter, even after professional training has alerted us to these tendencies in ourselves. Herein lies *the problem of subjectivity*—of socially produced bias possibly influencing and distorting what we see and how we interpret it.

As human beings, however, we do possess some "insider" familiarity with the social realities we are investigating. Jealousy, fear, ambition, love, hatred—these are widely shared experiences, in family life, in the domains of work, war, and politics, in religious practices, and so on. A social scientist—who likewise lives within a socially established world of institutions and customs—thus has a capacity to identify with and to grasp the emotional and cognitive states that orient the actions of other human beings. This is our epistemic advantage: the possibility of *intersubjectivity*, of relating to and comprehending the meaningful actions of others by situating or placing their conduct within the complex of beliefs, values, and institutions that constitute their social realities. Through intersubjective understanding, one can appreciate, for example, why it would "make sense" for someone who contracts an illness in a pre-modern society to make offerings to the spirits, just as it is reasonable for us, given our own perspective, to allow white-coated strangers to slice us open or inject needles into our bodies.

The epistemological procedure of the natural sciences is to discover the workings of nature by breaking it apart—through the dissection of plants and animals, chemical processing, smashing atoms, and so on. The social sciences, in contrast, take what people say and do, and try to determine the meanings and purposes that render those actions understandable or sensible, given the social situations in which the actors are operating.

We can now account for the higher disputation levels in the social sciences. Our problem, simply stated, is that we social scientists have not yet reached a consensus on our *first principles*—our ontological and epistemological assumptions. The plurality of theoretical perspectives you will encounter in this chapter reflects the fact that the various schools and traditions not only think of social reality in different terms, they also disagree over how knowledge of the social world can be reliably obtained.

Perhaps the most difficult question that can be asked in sociology is also the most basic: What is **society**? We use the term in everyday speech, but what is its actual ontological status? Is society the sum or aggregate of the individuals that make it up? Or is it something over and above this, a structural reality with distinct causal powers—that is, a kind of actor itself? Is it just a convenient label, or an active force or entity? Similarly, when we speak of "the economy" or "racist culture" or "religious fundamentalism," what exactly are we referring to? Is it scientifically legitimate to endow collective concepts with a capacity for action—to make them, rather than individual humans, responsible for action—as when we assert that "capitalism is destroying the environment," "nationalist ideologies are fomenting ethnic civil wars," or "the patriarchal family promotes gender inequalities detrimental to women"?

The social sciences remain divided on these questions, which have been the focus of debate for centuries. Over that time, two polar or opposing ontological perspectives have become established. One, called **nominalism**, holds that only flesh-and-blood individuals are real and have the capacity to act. Collective concepts such as "the mafia" or "the media" are, for nominalists, mere figures of speech, and consist only of the joined or combined actions of individuals. The other ontological position, **social realism**, maintains that collective concepts refer to independent, emergent realities, which, in social life, take the form of relational structures that exert causal influence on individual lives.

Nominalism, as a scientific strategy, inclines toward **reductionism**: wholes or totalities are explained by "reducing" them to the properties of their constituent parts. For example, a bureaucracy is the sum of the individual personnel who staff and run it. Nominalists generally insist that **macro** phenomena—institutions like the state or economy, and large-scale collective processes like revolutions or religious movements—are to be explained in **micro** terms, as the associated, co-ordinated actions of individuals. Expressed in logic, a reductionist explanation takes the form, $T = P1 + P2 + P3 \ldots$, where a totality T is the aggregation of its parts P.

Social realism, in contrast, proceeds from the **doctrine of emergence**: when individual elements combine and associate, new realities are created by those interactions. For example, a bureaucracy is more than its personnel—it is a relational reality, or structure, that shapes the thoughts and actions of the individuals operating within it. For social realists, macro phenomena are not only active forces in their own right, they also largely determine what occurs at the micro level. In logic, this principle is expressed in the form, $T > P1 + P2 + P3 \ldots + (P1 \times P2 \times P3 \ldots)$, signifying that a totality is more than the sum and interaction of its parts and that it has macro-systemic properties that condition the micro elements.

As ideas about the nature of social reality, nominalism and social realism represent opposing tendencies along a scale or continuum and serve to provide orienting assumptions for social scientific research (see Table 22.2). Indeed, on the basis of these polar ontological positions, the history of sociology can be written as a history of two sociologies: a nominalist, or micro, tradition advancing theories of agency, and a realist, or macro, tradition advocating theories of structure.

22.1 Sociology in Action
Georg Simmel's Dyads and Triads

One of the classic illustrations of the doctrine of emergence—the idea that when individual elements combine and associate, new realities are created by those interactions—was offered by the German sociologist Georg Simmel (1858–1918).

In a famous discussion in 1908, Simmel (1950b) showed that an association or relationship between two units, a *dyad*, is qualitatively transformed whenever a third unit is added, forming a *triad*. Entirely new possibilities for action now become possible, such as mediation, whereby one unit acts impartially to resolve conflicts between the other two; *tertius gaudens*, or "the third who enjoys," whereby

one unit benefits from the jealous attention and competitive favours of the other two; and *divide et impera*, "divide and rule," whereby one unit actively promotes rivalry and distrust between the other two so as to gain a dominating, controlling position.

Triads are thus structurally different from dyads, and it is the relational configuration of three units (how they relate to each other)—not their simple addition—that is sociologically decisive. Simmel's insights apply equally to intimate interpersonal relations (such as between friends, lovers, and spouses) and to arrangements between and within larger associations, such as nation-states and bureaucracies.

Table 22.2   Orienting Ontologies of the Rival Traditions in Sociology

◄——— **Ontological Continuum** ———►

Nominalism ◄————————————————► Social Realism	
• Emphasizes individual action, human agency	• Emphasizes structures, social systems
• Sees reality as an ongoing construction, a negotiated flow or process between interacting individuals	• Sees reality as a totality, objectified in institutions and culture
• Proceeds from the micro level of face-to-face interaction	• Proceeds from the macro level, focusing on the impact of social structures on individual actors
• *Reductionism*: Macro structures are the temporary joint-actions of individuals	• *Doctrine of emergence*: Social structures are the enduring by-products of past interactions by individual agents, and the preconditions for present and future social actions

---

Each of these orientations captures something important about social life, for do we not exist both as active subjects and as conditioned objects? Every **social structure**, after all, is a product of past and present human agency, and every human agent has been socialized by established institutions and cultural conventions. Human beings are thus caught up in a social-historical loop, an ongoing process in which we reproduce the social structures that have conditioned the kinds of people that we are and that we become, but also a process in which we change those arrangements over time, through our interactions and our conscious creativity. Nominalists are thus correct

to insist that only individuals can truly "act," and that "structures are what people do." Social realists, however, are no less correct when they note that the "individual" is a misleading abstraction, inasmuch as all the terms that apply to acting individuals are already social, already structured. Thus, "parent" implies a kinship institution, "priest" entails a religious order, "corporate executive" presupposes an economic system, "queen" a political structure, "student" an educational system, and so on, for every identifying **status**. Individuals simply do not exist independently of the social relations in which they develop and operate.

Ultimately at issue in the structure-versus-agency controversy is the question of human freedom. Are we the authors of our individual and collective destinies, or are our choices already limited by the social identities we have inherited? Are the historical forces and social conditions that shape our worlds largely beyond, or within, our rational control?

These questions permit no fixed or simple answers. Some moments of history are more open to change than others, some societies and institutions are more dynamic and flexible, and some individuals and groups hold positions and resources that afford them a greater autonomy, a greater personal control. In an important sense, sociology is an investigation into the diverse and changing limits of and possibilities for human freedom. Where theories of agency tend to accentuate creative initiatives and the fluid nature of interaction, theories of structure tend to accentuate conditioned responses and the formation of socialized role players who conform within established systems. This tension between fulfilling social requirements and evading or protesting against them is part of the common human experience, as reflection on the stories of our own lives should confirm. Identifying and explaining the many surface and hidden plot lines of all the many life stories, characterizing the major and marginal players and the various social scenes and stages on which they enact their roles—that is sociology's unending assignment.

One more introductory remark: a *scientific theory* is an integrated set of concepts and statements that specify relations of ordered dependence and causal connection between phenomena. The word *theory* comes from *theória*, an ancient Greek word meaning "to see or observe." Theories in the most basic sense are thus "ways of seeing," which is to say that theoretical perspectives highlight certain connections and patterns among the realities investigated. That means, of course, that "ways of seeing" are also "ways of *not* seeing." As a proverb has it, to gaze at particular trees is to miss the forest—concentrate on the forest, and you neglect the trees. Most social science controversies arise out of this, for our theories tend to be selective and partial, even when they aspire to be comprehensive.

This section can thus be closed on an encouraging note. The rival theoretical traditions you will encounter should not be evaluated in terms of their absolute truth or falseness. The real issue is their range or scope of validity, that is, how one-sided or balanced they are and how well they apply across different times and places.

Theoretical Perspectives in Sociology

Though there have been many different schools of thought in the long history of reflection on the human condition, most of the major modern contributions can be located within the "two sociologies" framework we will review here. That is, theories either tend to emphasize the structural properties of social life or they concentrate on the dynamics of interaction and agency. For theories of structure, the key questions centre on how societies and institutions are constituted and change, and how they organize and condition the groups and individuals within them. For theories of agency, the key questions centre on how individual "selves" are formed and how social relationships are constructed and transformed by their meaningful interactions.

Figure 22.2 presents an ontological mapping of the major theories of the structure and agency perspectives, disclosing their locations on the nominalism–social realism continuum that we reviewed in Table 22.2.

Theories of Structure

In this section, we will examine some of the major contributions to our understanding of macro social phenomena, such as the organization of societies, the links between institutions and cultural traditions, and the dynamics of social-historical change.

Marxism

Karl Marx is widely known as the intellectual founder of modern communism, a philosopher whose ideas inspired political movements, revolutions, and social reforms that did much to shape the world we live in today. Besides being a revolutionary, Marx was a thinker of profound originality, whose contributions to the study of history and the workings of the capitalist system are still important.

Marx's sociology is founded upon what is called a *materialist* conception of history. Human affairs, he insisted, are not driven principally by political values or religious beliefs (as had been maintained in various *idealist* philosophies), but by material factors, above all by an ongoing need to produce the necessities of life: food, shelter, clothing. Human existence is possible only through collective labour, and the survival of any group or community is dependent on this

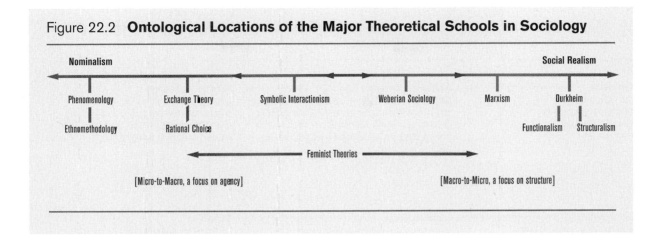

Figure 22.2 **Ontological Locations of the Major Theoretical Schools in Sociology**

Nominalism ← → Social Realism

Phenomenology   Exchange Theory   Symbolic Interactionism   Weberian Sociology   Marxism   Durkheim

Ethnomethodology   Rational Choice   Functionalism   Structuralism

← Feminist Theories →

[Micro-to-Macro, a focus on agency]   [Macro-to-Micro, a focus on structure]

Karl Marx (1818–83), German-born social theorist and political activist. (Marx/Engels Image Library)

co-ordinated practical activity. How communities produce will thus determine how their societies are organized, what kinds of human beings they become, and how they express and define themselves culturally. Marx's materialism does not discount the importance of ideas and values (what he called *social consciousness*); it is simply that those ideal factors are to be explained in connection with their origins and functions in productive practices.

Marx's core concept is the **mode of production**, which refers to the arrangements humans establish in the collective task of extracting from nature the essentials of life. Each mode of production in history is organized by the specific forces or means used and by the legal-political relations directing their use.

The *productive forces* consist chiefly of three components: the tools and instruments used in the work process (that is, all invented technologies, from the stone axe to the microchip); the patterns of social labour (from handicraft to assembly-line processes); and the available natural resources. The *relations of production* are essentially proprietary; they specify the rights of ownership and control of the productive forces. Differences in who possesses what result in a division of *classes*, usually featuring a dominant or ruling class that owns the land, the animals, the factories, the machines, and so on, and various dispossessed classes that are compelled to labour and produce for the benefit of their oppressors.

According to Marx, the mode of production forms the organizing foundation, or *base*, of any particular society, the other institutions of which—government, law, religion, art—make up its *superstructure*. "The mode of production of material life," Marx insisted in 1859, "determines the general character of the social, political, and intellectual processes of life" (1956: 51). How communities are governed, how family life is ordered, what kinds of values and ideas people hold—all such superstructural phenomena are conditioned by the economic structure of the society in question.

Marx identified several modes of production in world history, each characterized by a particular level of development in productive forces and by corresponding legal-political relations (see Figure 22.3).

Once communities pass beyond the egalitarian primitive-communal phase, conditions of hereditary

Figure 22.3   Major Modes of Production in Historical Sequence, Identifying Social Organization, Economic System, and Class Structure[a]

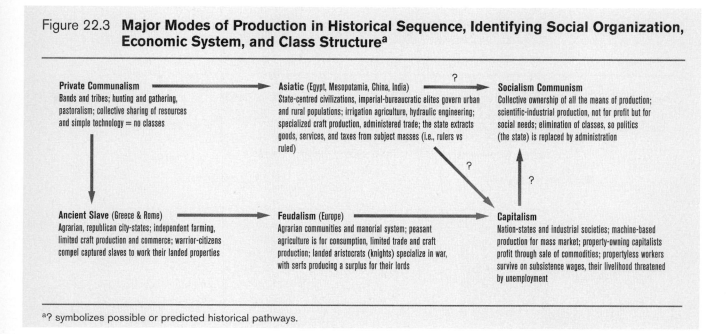

[a]? symbolizes possible or predicted historical pathways.

inequality enter into their arrangements. Property rights, social privileges, and coercive powers are claimed and exercised by certain groups at the expense of others. Marx and his colleague, Friedrich Engels, announced this thesis on the famous opening page of *The Communist Manifesto*, published in 1848:

> The history of all hitherto existing society is the history of class struggles. Freeman and slave, patrician and plebeian, lord and serf, guild-master and journeyman, in a word, oppressor and oppres-sed, stood in constant opposition to one another, carried on an uninterrupted, now hidden, now open fight, a fight that each time ended either in a revolutionary reconstitution of society at large, or in the common ruin of the contending classes. ([1848] 1948: 1)

Exploitation is thus the defining relationship between classes. The owners of property extract from the primary producers a *surplus*—a disproportionate share of the material wealth that frees the dominant classes from the burden of producing for themselves. This appropriation enables them to exercise leadership and control in war, politics, art, and religion. Just how the exploiting classes extract that surplus varies with the mode of production. In the agriculturally based Asiatic, ancient, and feudal modes, the subject masses, slaves, and serfs were compelled to toil for their masters by threat of force, and they delivered specified quantities of produce and labour services.

But under **capitalism**, Marx notes, the exploitation is less direct and is partially concealed by the complex intricacies of industrial production: here the workers create *surplus value* (rather than merely a *surplus*), by receiving less in the form of wages than the exchange value of the commodities they produce—a monetary differential that enables capitalists to garner profits through sales in the market.

The dominance of the ruling classes is based on their ownership of the means of material production, but this also enables them to control the means of "mental production." As Marx noted in 1845, "the ideas of the ruling class are, in every age, the ruling ideas: i.e., the class that is the dominant *material* force in society is at the same time its dominant *intellectual* force" (1956: 78).

What are these ruling ideas? They are **ideologies**—systems of norms, values, and beliefs that legitimize or justify the supremacy of the ruling classes and that rationalize the subordination of the labouring classes. Such ideologies typically sanctify the established social order by invoking nature, divine approval, or the alleged superior merits of the privileged. By controlling the media of cultural expression, the dominant classes are able to represent reality in terms beneficial to themselves and thus to impress subordinates with displays of achievement in the arts and in fields of higher learning. As a result, oppressed classes tend to partially internalize and defer to the ruling ideologies of their oppressors, a situation Marx termed **false consciousness**. Political resistance is possible only when subordinate classes reject those ideologies and forge instead *class consciousness*, an awareness of their exploited status and of their common interests in overthrowing an unjust system.

Revolutionary political developments occur in conjunction with changes in the productive base, as new technologies and working arrangements begin to destabilize the established hierarchies. Marx believed that just such a situation was arising within capitalism. The tremendous productive capacities of modern science and industry are able to solve the historic problem of scarcity—of universally satisfying basic human material needs. But so long as the private property system maintains vast disparities in the distribution of wealth and resources, there will be luxury for the few and continued misery for the many.

Marx, principally in his three volumes of *Capital* (*Das Kapital*, [1867] 1967), traced the boom–recession cycle of capitalist economies to this structural inequality: millions are hungry and homeless around the globe not because the means to feed and house them are lacking, but because they cannot be fed and housed within the limits set by the private profit motive—hence the paradox of massive layoffs and unemployment despite the public need for expanded production. Marx argued that this "contradiction" would intensify over time, and that the working class would organize politically and overthrow the capitalist system, whether by armed revolution or through the ballot box. Private ownership of the **means of production** would be abolished and production redirected to serve "the social needs of all" rather than "the private interests of the few." Under socialism/communism, classes would disappear, the state would "wither away" (in Marx's famous phrase of 1875), and human beings would at last be free to develop their full humanity and creative potential.

Marx's sociology provides a powerful light on the complex dynamics of world history, but his vision of a future society free from want and oppression now seems hopelessly utopian. Yet even if it is, he nonetheless bestowed upon social science a necessary critical edge. As he himself memorably commented in 1845, "philosophers have only interpreted the world in various ways; what matters is to change it" (1956: 69).

Max Weber's Historical Sociology

For sheer breadth and depth of learning, the German sociologist Max Weber has few peers. His writings—though left incomplete at the time of his death in 1920—contain nothing less than a sociology of world history. At the core of Weber's research lay one overriding question: how and why did capitalism originate in Western Europe in the sixteenth and seventeenth centuries, rather than in the advanced civilizations of China, India, or the Muslim world? Weber was following in Marx's tracks, respectful of his predecessor's insights but convinced that additional perspectives were required for explaining developments and histories so complex, so consequential.

The best introduction to Weber's project is his early and most famous work, *The Protestant Ethic and the Spirit of Capitalism*, published in 1904. As the title indicates, Weber was investigating a connection between two cultural developments: a new religious ethos and changing economic values. The rise of capitalism, Weber argues, could not be explained solely in terms of technological advances and class conflict. Social life must always be viewed in terms of multiple determinations—economic, political, military, religious, and so on—which change in their influence over time and place. He acknowledged that the origins of modern capitalism lay primarily in certain economic innovations: the introduction of machines, the harnessing of new sources of energy, the technological displacement of peasants from the land, rationalized accounting,

Max Weber (1864–1920), celebrated German scholar and one of the founders of modern sociology. (The Granger Collection, New York)

and the factory system. He rightfully held, however, that a comprehensive explanation must also incorporate non-economic factors.

Weber ([1904] 1958) argued that the Protestant Reformation, by introducing religious values that affirmed worldly activity, contributed significantly to the consolidation of the new economic order. This was not, he stressed, the intention of the leading reformers, Martin Luther (1483–1546) and John Calvin (1509–64). These "protestors" were spiritual men, distressed by what they saw as the corruption of Christianity by the church's seemingly limitless appetite for wealth and power. In breaking with Roman Catholic tradition, however, the reformers were forced to create new standards of religiosity.

Central to the Protestant view was the idea that individuals must reach God directly, through their own personal faith and holiness—and not through the sacraments administered by the church. No bishop or priest could control the means of salvation by assigning penances and selling indulgences to free people from their sins. God's revealed word must therefore be made available to all, and so the Latin Bible was translated into English, French, German, and other vernacular (everyday) languages, thereby breaking the church's monopoly over scripture.

With personal faith now holding the key to salvation, the early Lutherans, Calvinists, and Puritans came to view disciplined work as a "calling," a form of religious devotion to God. Diligent and dutiful in the labours God had assigned, these Protestants did not believe in building ornate churches filled with gold and fine art, in adorning themselves in luxurious clothing, or in dining on rich foods in houses of splendour. Against these worldly vanities, they practised *asceticism*, a frugal lifestyle of sober, methodical piety.

As Weber ([1904] 1958) observed, this new "**Protestant ethic**," while religious in inspiration, provided a powerful stimulus for and legitimation of economic pursuits. Not only was work redefined as a spiritual vocation, but savings and investment were encouraged, as the faithful shunned all conspicuous consumption. Success in business came to be seen as a *sign of election*—an indication that one was predestined for heaven. What greater support could an emerging economic system obtain, Weber asked, than religious sanctification? The relationship between Protestantism and capitalism was not one of simple cause and effect, but one of *elective affinity*, a situation in which originally distinct but compatible lines of development intersect to produce an intensified synthesis or fusing.

Broadening the scope of his analysis, Weber turned to the major spiritual traditions of the East. He examined Confucianism and Taoism in *The Religion of China* ([1916] 1951), Hinduism and Buddhism in *The Religion of India* ([1916–17] 1958). Here again, Weber was interested in charting the multiple linkages between religious, political, and economic institutions. Since China and India had each developed an advanced civilization, with large urban populations, craft specialization, far-flung trading networks, and numerous scientific-technological advances, the question of why these conditions did not lead to a capitalist "breakthrough" was puzzling.

Weber, following Marx, recognizes that the Asian tradition of powerful, centralized states—which had arisen in connection with the management of complex irrigation agriculture, located in the major river valleys—meant that economic life in the East operated under the political control of imperial bureaucrats. Another "brake," however, was provided by the Asian religions, which did not assign high spiritual value to worldly affairs. Eastern religiosity tends to emphasize meditation, the attainment of inner bliss and purity, or transcendent union with the divine—an orientation Weber terms *other-worldly mysticism*. In the eyes of a Mandarin, a Brahmin, or a mystic, to devote oneself to economic affairs is unspiritual, even polluting.

Protestant ministers, in contrast, would openly encourage Christians "to gain and save all that they can," and to "labour to be rich for God." Beginning with the monotheistic teachings of the Hebrews, examined by Weber in *Ancient Judaism* ([1917–19] 1952), the Western religious tradition did not promote a spiritual devaluation of the world, for the world had been created by an all-powerful personal deity. The cause of misfortune and suffering is human sin, and so the prime religious task is not to transcend or escape a flawed or meaningless world through mystical meditation, but to transform sinful hearts through holy actions within God's providential creation. For Weber, it is this *inner-worldly asceticism* that accounts for the active "restless rationalism" so characteristic of Western culture, its unrestrained drive for progress and world mastery.

Recognizing that religious definitions of the world powerfully influence the organization of social life, Weber, in his collected studies in *The Sociology of Religion* ([1920–1] 1963), develops a theoretical model to explain how such traditions arise. All religious movements pass through two formative stages: genesis and diffusion. The creation of new religious world views is the inspired work of charismatics or virtuosi—extraordinary figures such as Moses and the Hebrew prophets, the Buddha, Lao-Tzu, Jesus, and Muhammad. As they announce new visions of the divine and new ways of salvation, disciples are drawn to these charismatics.

Next comes the phase of preaching and converting others to the fledgling faith or practice; this requires that the message be adjusted to the needs of potential followers. Weber believed that religions could secure mass followings only if the original teachings were modified to permit easy compliance, since most people are not capable of the intense religiosity characteristic of the highly committed. The social success of a new religion thus brings on a compromise or moderation of spiritual requirements—a circumstance that alienates the purists or rigorists, who in turn start a new round of religious change by calling for a higher spirituality. For Weber, religious history is largely cyclical: religious movements typically begin as sects of enthusiastic devotees, and then—if they are socially successful—develop into churches that address the more limited needs and capabilities of the masses, thereby setting the stage for a new round of sectarian reforms.

Like Marx, Weber believed that societies are organized in terms of **power**—what he called *relations of domination* ([1908] 1978). Unlike Marx, he did not believe that economic inequalities were always and everywhere of primary influence. Weber insisted that power is derived from multiple sources, material as well as ideological. Through the control of diverse social and natural resources, some groups and strata are able to establish positions of authority and privilege.

Weber held that class, status, and party were the principal channels along which power flows. *Class inequalities* derive from the differential ownership of property, and also from the market opportunities that follow from differences in labour-skill levels. *Status inequalities* derive from styles of life, most strongly in association with ethnic, racial, or religious identities. As for *party*, this refers to the formation of organizations that recruit individuals in order to gain political power, whether through armed violence or electoral victories. Control over economic, cultural, military, and political resources thus leads to different forms of domination. Living in a military dictatorship or in a religious one is quite different from living in a socie-ty dominated by class inequalities or one organized on a discriminatory ethnic basis.

Weber's concern with political forms of domination is illustrated most clearly in his analysis of bureaucracy. A **bureaucracy** is an organization featuring a hierarchical, pyramidal chain of authority, with specialized offices of jurisdiction. Duties are based on written regulations and filed information (reports, data). The bureaucrat is a functionary: he or she operates by implementing the rules and by processing individuals and cases as "types" and "categories." Depersonalization is thus the very hallmark of bureaucratic procedure. In terms of administrative efficiency, however, and as an instrument of control, bureaucracy is unrivalled, and so it spreads wherever social life grows in scale and complexity—in economics, politics, warfare, education, religion, science, medicine.

The fate of the modern world, Weber feared, was one of increasing bureaucratization, a trend he saw relentlessly erecting "a prison-house of future bondage," an "iron cage" that would reduce the human experience to forced regimentation. Marx's humanistic expectations for socialism were utopian, Weber argued, for socializing the means of production would lead to a totalitarian state, a situation in which the "administrators" would reign unchecked by any competing powers. As the Nazi and communist dictatorships of the twentieth century tragically confirm, Weber's fears were well founded. The fact that we now share our lives with that most efficient of processing and monitoring machines—the computer—only confirms the continuing relevance of Weber's concerns about the prospects for freedom in a bureaucratized world.

Durkheim and the Functionalist Tradition

No figure in the history of sociology contributed more to its professional development than Émile Durkheim. He was among the first to offer university courses in sociology, and in 1898 he founded one of its most influential journals, *L'Année sociologique*. It was this French scholar's self-appointed mission to legitimize the science of sociology at a time when it was barely acknowledged in academic circles.

Durkheim insisted that social reality is a reality *sui generis* ("of its own kind"), ontologically distinct from the facts studied by biology and psychology. In *The Rules of Sociological Method*, published in 1895, Durkheim attempts to define the scope of sociology and to provide a manual for proper scientific procedure. Rejecting all reductionist/nominalist approaches, Durkheim stresses that social reality is an emergent, objective order that transcends the level of acting individuals. Each of us enters into, and thereafter confronts, a ready-made world of institutions, customs, moral traditions—a society within which we are socialized and constituted as social beings. Social facts are thus to be studied as things, as collective arrangements and ideas that are external to and coercive of the individuals functioning within a community. For Durkheim, the ontological primacy of society is central: it surpasses each individual in time and space, and imposes on each person "ways of acting and thinking which it has consecrated with its prestige" ([1895] 1964: 102).

What each individual thinks and values is informed by the **collective consciousness**, a system of shared symbols, beliefs, and sentiments. The binding force and complexity of this *conscience collective* will vary with the organization of the society in question. In simple societies, with only a rudimentary division of labour, the collective consciousness will be powerful and uniform; in complex societies, it will be more diffuse and internally diverse.

How a community reacts to crime and deviance, Durkheim ([1893] 1964) observes, reveals what kind of collective consciousness is at work. In undifferen-

Émile Durkheim (1858–1916), French academic and influential pioneer in sociological theory and method. (Bettmann/CORBIS/Magmaphoto.com)

tiated societies, there is *repressive law*, which imposes harsh and violent punishments upon even minor infractions, because deviance of any sort scandalizes the homogeneous community and offends against the rigid moral order that preserves it. In complex societies, in contrast, there is *restitutive law*, a system of fines and sanctions that seeks to restore order whenever it breaks down and that tolerates a wider divergence of personal opinion and conduct, in recognition of the greater diversity within the society.

Durkheim's famous study *Suicide*, published in 1897, best exemplifies his theoretical perspective. The topic would appear to pose a major challenge for sociological analysis, for is not self-murder a private act, with the individual as both willing victim and perpetrator? Through a careful scrutiny of suicide statistics, however, Durkheim proves that social factors operate even here, at the very moment when an individual is contemplating the voluntary termination of his or her existence.

Contrary to the claims of various biological and psychological theories, Durkheim ([1897] 1951) found that suicide rates do not vary directly with racial and ethnic factors, or with insanity and alcoholism; nor is contagion, or "copy-cat" practices, much in evidence. What the statistics do reveal is that suicidal tendencies are strongly influenced by social relationships—specifically, by the degree of *solidarity* and *normative integration* that can be found in an individual's life situation. That is, individuals are prone to suicidal acts in inverse proportion to the strength of their social ties (to kin, friends, community) and to their adherence to the collective consciousness.

In modern societies, individuals tend to be more autonomous and independent, left on their own to succeed or fail, while also being less committed and less bound to traditional norms and values. This situation, Durkheim argues, is conducive to two characteristic modern forms of self-murder: *egoistic suicide*, which arises from the stresses of excessive individualism, a loss of group cohesion and solidarity, and *anomic suicide*, which arises from moral confusion or anarchy, an absence of binding norms and values. More rarely, where social bonds are exceedingly strong, instances of *altruistic suicide* occur (as in the sacrificial efforts by parents to save their children, or by soldiers to save their comrades and country). And where the cultural norms are too binding and restrictive, instances of *fatalistic suicide* are found (as among slaves, or prisoners condemned to long terms of incarceration). As Durkheim's classification tellingly reveals, suicide is a highly personal act, but it occurs as a result of social forces, which variously shield or support us in our in times of difficulty or leave us exposed to the ravages of loneliness, uncertainty, and despair.

Durkheim's last major work, *The Elementary Forms of Religious Life*, published in 1912, provides a brilliant synthesis of his sociological vision. In this influential study, Durkheim seeks to explain the social origins and functions of religious belief—one of the main components of the collective consciousness. He begins by defining *religion* as "a unified system of beliefs and practices regarding things that are sacred" ([1912] 1995: 44). The *sacred*, in this definition, involves symbols, images, objects, and rites that invoke feelings of reverence and awe; it forms a special realm set apart from the profane world of everyday objects and affairs. All religions, Durkheim argues, are ultimately founded upon this distinction between the sacred and the profane, and so the sociological task is to explain how and why a sense of the sacred arises.

Examining the ethnographic records about the earliest forms of human society—the aboriginal clans and tribes of Australia and North America—Durkheim notes that each clan or tribe offers veneration to a totemic object that also symbolized the community itself. In the totem's spirit, the worshippers acknowledge the existence of a superior, superhuman force. This feeling of dependence and attachment is real, Durkheim insists, not imaginary. Religious devotees are mistaken only in the true identity of the "sacred being" they worship: it is not a god or spirit, but the collective powers of the society in which they live and upon which they depend. Society is that greater force that transcends each individual, for as it compels obedience to its rules, it provides identity and security and so gives meaning and purpose to our lives.

Durkheim insists that religions are socially produced and communicated, and that people experience the sacred most dramatically during social gatherings, such as festivals and ceremonials. With celebrative dance and chanting, individuals are carried away in a group-induced ecstasy, a **collective effervescence** that is expressive of their membership in a power greater than themselves. Society, then, is the true "god"—the basis for our existence and the moral force that imparts to us our values and ideals.

As societies change, Durkheim reasons, so will human representations of the divine, for each deity is really only a symbolic totem of how the group conceives of itself. Religions thus provide an essential sta-

bilizing force in social life, for while "their apparent function is to strengthen the bonds attaching the believer to his god, they at the same time really strengthen the bonds attaching the individual to the society of which he is a member, since the god is only a figurative expression of the society" ([1912] 1995: 226).

Durkheim's intellectual legacy remains highly influential. In France, his ideas provided the basis for the theoretical perspective known as *structuralism*. Though many-sided and supported by diverse thinkers, such as the anthropologist Claude Lévi-Strauss and the philosopher Michel Foucault, this perspective follows Durkheim in giving priority to the social arrangements that shape and constrain action and that confine human thought and imagination to what is "thinkable" within structurally determined *mentalités sociales*.

Durkheim's ideas were no less central in the development of the English and American tradition known as *functionalism*, which flourished in the social sciences from the 1920s through the 1960s. The initial elaboration of functionalist analysis came with early anthropological field research, as contact with other cultures soon yielded a major discovery. However "strange" local customs might appear to European eyes, closer examination typically revealed what is called their *adaptive utility*.

Bronislaw Malinowski's famous studies of the Trobrianders (1922), for example, showed that these island people resorted to magical rituals in preparation for deep-sea fishing but not for lagoon fishing. Why the difference? Because it is a highly dangerous venture to sail in open waters, whereas inshore operations are low-risk and easily managed. The Trobrianders employ magic strategically as a way of allaying fears and anxieties in domains beyond their control, thereby enabling them to carry out certain essential tasks.

Why do the Hopi periodically engage in the rain dance when it appears inconsistent in yielding the desired meteorological effects? Because the true function of this ceremonial is to provide a means for reinforcing group identity and solidarity. Why do Hindus regard their cattle as sacred and proscribe the eating of beef as taboo? Not for the professed spiritual reasons, according to functionalist thought, but because a living cow is far more useful as a source of milk and traction power than as meat, while its dung provides valuable fertilizer and fuel—hence the urgent social need to shield this animal religiously from the ravenous appetite of the human carnivore.

Countless other anthropological studies suggest much the same pattern: of the customs and institutions that exist in social life, most appear to contribute to *system maintenance*.

In sociology, the functionalist line was championed by the American scholars Talcott Parsons (1902–79) and Robert Merton (1910–2003) and their legion of Harvard-trained students. According to Parsons (1951), social life must be understood in terms of its systemic properties. Society itself forms a *social system*, comprising various differentiated and interdependent subsystems (economic, political, educational, religious, and so on). Each institutional subsystem likewise features specialized parts and functions. The family, for example, consists of various structured units, or **roles** (parents, children, relatives), whose specialized responsibilities are assigned to fulfill system needs, such as sexual and emotional bonding and socialization of the young. Order or integration within the complex set of institutions that constitute a society is provided by a common **value** system—cultural norms and beliefs that develop in harmony with the needs of the social structure.

Perhaps the most revealing application of this kind of analysis is the functional theory of stratification, put forward in 1945 by Kingsley Davis and Wilbert Moore. On appearances, it is difficult to see how inequalities in wealth and power could contribute to the adaptability of a society, given that disparities between "haves" and "have-nots" are commonly at the root of major social problems and revolutionary conflicts. For Davis and Moore, however, the persistence and apparent universality of inequality implies that inequality must serve a system-enhancing function. The unequal distribution of resources, they reason, operates as a necessary motivational mechanism. By assigning greater rewards to the most vital and demanding positions—in government, the economy, health care, and so on—competition and effort are stimulated. "Social inequality," they conclude, "is thus an unconsciously evolved device by which societies insure that the most important positions are conscientiously filled by the most qualified persons" (Davis and Moore, 1945: 243). Those at the top thus deserve to be there, and inequalities keep the whole system running optimally.

The conservative bias in this perspective is easily identified. The basic assumption—that whatever exists is functionally adaptive—neglects entirely all questions of power and exploitation within a social system. It was to purge functionalism of such excesses that Robert Merton (1967) offered significant revisions to the theory. Merton recognized that customs and practices could also become dysfunctional, leading to social disorder and chaos. Strong religious commitment, for example, might prove adaptive in certain respects, but it could also trigger violent conflict in societies with competing faiths. Moreover, talk about "system needs" presents an overly unified and homogenized picture of social reality—but, in reality, what might prove beneficial for some groups could be detrimental to others. Nor should sociologists assume that the mere existence of a practice or custom attests to its indispensability, for functional alternatives are always possible. Contemporary functionalist analysis has thus become far more open to the conflictual and competitive side of social life than the original "consensus and harmony" version.

Theories of Agency

In this section we will highlight some of the major contributions to our understanding of micro social phenomena, such as the nature and development of "minds" and "selves," the dynamics of face-to-face interaction, and the construction of "multiple realities" through symbolic communication.

Symbolic Interactionism

Human beings are self-aware agents who create their lives—their societies—through ongoing processes of interaction with other selves. That statement conveys the basic ontological premise of **symbolic interactionism**. For sociologists working in this tradition, *Homo sapiens* is a species whose existence is constructed through communicative interaction, based on the creation and use of **symbols**—objects or acts that represent and convey meanings, such as a uniform, a clenched fist, a spoken or written word.

It was the American philosopher George Herbert Mead (1863–1931) who formulated the core principles of this perspective. In *Mind, Self, and Society*, published posthumously in 1934, Mead shows that the individual is a social construct and that society is, in turn, the creation of socialized, interacting individuals. Mead's starting point is a rejection of *behaviourism*, a reductionist psychology that viewed human beings as mere products of their environment, organically conditioned to react in fixed ways to positive and negative stimuli. Mead argues that a stimulus–response model misses the true nature of the social act, for humans do not respond directly to external stimuli (like the dogs, rats, and pigeons studied in behaviourist research); rather, they assign meanings to and interpret those stimuli.

Consider the role of fashion in conveying sexual messages. When viewed today, the clothing and hairstyles of the 1960s and 1970s are often seen as odd or comical; in their own time, however, they were judged attractive, even sexy. What counts as a stimulus, then, is largely determined by the cultural meanings that are assigned to the symbols we reflect upon. Human beings do not so much "behave" in conditioned ways as "act" purposefully, pursuing goals by making sense of their situations in light of the ideas they deliberate over in their minds.

How do we become self-aware agents? Each of us enters life, Mead (1934) notes, as a bio-psychic organism—a bundle of nerves, sensations, and unfocused impulses. Through cultural learning (**socialization**), those organic properties are gradually disciplined and transformed into emotions, perceptions, ambitions, and principles. That process cannot be understood, Mead insists, unless we recognize that "mind" and "self"—the two essential attributes of any cultured personality—are not biological endowments, but social emergents, developmental by-products or creations of interaction. The body is not a self, nor is the brain a mind. Individuals can become "minded selves" only in a social context, through symbolic interaction with others.

So what is **mind**, and what goes on in there? As an activity or process, *mind* is simply conscious thought. But how is thought possible? If you reflect on your own thinking right now, you will realize that thought occurs by means of "self-talk," or inner conversation. And what is conversation? It is a form of symbolic communication employing *language*, a socially created system of vocal and written designations or "gestures" called *words*, which are used to symbolize and make possible shared experiences. And how is language acquired? It is imparted through socialization, as parents, siblings, teachers, and others offer instruction in the use of their particular linguistic system. Mead's key discovery is that our minds come from the outside, from society, for we develop a capacity for thought only to the extent that we internalize the social product that is language, our principal means of accessing and communicating about the worlds we live in.

As our brains (the "hardware") acquire the linguistic codes (the "software") that make minds ("computation") possible, another important development is underway: the emergence of a **self**. For Mead, the defining property of a self is its capacity to reflect on its own actions or status, to take on the perspective of both subject and object. This reflective capacity is not innate or instinctive—we are not born with it—but arises only through an extended process of interactive learning. Mead (1934) identifies three critical stages in the social genesis of the self: (1) the *preparatory* stage, in which small children begin to imitate or mimic the actions of significant others; (2) the *play* stage, in which children "take the role of the other," as in hide-and-seek; and (3) the *game* stage, in which children learn to place themselves in multiple roles, co-ordinating their actions with others on a team, as in hockey or baseball. At each successive stage, a child is developing an expanded capacity to step outside of pure subjectivity, pure ego, and reflect on actions in the light of how others might judge them. Mead's colleague, Charles Horton Cooley (1864–1929) coined the term **looking-glass self** to capture this notion—that we form our self-concept largely through the "mirrored reflections" of ourselves that we see in the reactions of others (1902).

For Mead, the self is fully attained when one can take on the collective attitudes of one's community or society, what he calls the **generalized other**. As we mature as social beings, our minds come to encompass an ever-widening "internalized audience" or reference group, with which we carry on "inner dialogue" in the process of planning the actions that express our sense of self, as our identities are constructed through **social interaction**.

In the symbolic interactionist perspective, mind, self, and society constitute three ongoing, interrelated processes. No sociologist has contributed more to the elaboration of this framework than the Canadian-born Erving Goffman (1922–82). Beginning with *The Presentation of Self in Everyday Life*, published in 1959, Goffman attempted to situate the "minded self" in various interaction settings, documenting the habits, cons, and stratagems people use in "presenting themselves" in the hectic course of daily living. Adapting Shakespeare's famous metaphor "all the world's a stage, and all the men and women merely players," Goffman styled his sociology the *dramaturgical* perspective. In this view, social life is a ritualized drama, and we are all struggling actors, artfully staging performances before the varied audiences that make up the theatres of our existence.

According to Goffman (1959), interaction is driven by **impression management**, the efforts of participants to advance "definitions of the situation" favourable to their interests and self-image. This imperative applies to panhandling beggars no less than to corporate executives. Delivering a successful performance is partly a matter of effective staging, through the use of props and timing. More important, an actor must control the flow of information, not only the "expressions given" (the verbal declarations made), but also—and this requires much greater acting skill—the "expressions given off," as conveyed by the individual's body language and manner of delivery.

In a romantic encounter, for example, a suitor selects an appropriate time and setting (candlelight dinner, soft music), and attempts to persuade the other person that he or she is both sincerely interested and personally worthy. If the expressions given off do not match those deliberately given, the performance can go awry. Excessive perspiration, a nervous speech pattern, blushing, the averting of eye contact—there are many such signs and cues that audiences look for in assessing performances. But even when insincerity or delivery flaws are detected, norms of tact usually preserve a "veneer of consensus," as actors and audience alike have an interest in avoiding the mutual embarrassments caused by making a scene. That is why, when the smiling waiter asks, "How was your dinner?" most of us reply, "Fine," even if we've just eaten a lousy meal, and with cutlery less sparkling than we would have liked.

One of Goffman's major achievements was to show how micro interaction rituals are highly structured or patterned. Performances, he notes (1959), are typically regionalized in terms of *backstage* and *frontstage* settings. Closed to audiences, the back stage is where we do the preparatory work, donning costume and makeup, rehearsing the act prior to its delivery frontstage. In many cases, one is part of a *performance team*, joined to others with whom one collaborates in staging a performance (for example, a married couple entertaining dinner guests, or a work crew during a visit by management). Members of teams learn to maintain staging secrets and to bolster solidarity by making jokes about their audiences. Preserving team loyalty and co-ordination is of great importance in *social establishments*, places where people gather regularly to deliver and receive services, such as restaurants, hospitals, schools, or the workplace.

More restrictive is life inside *total institutions*, places where selected individuals are cut off from the wider society and subjected to administered control, as in prisons or the military. In *Asylums*, published in 1961, Goffman investigates the incarcerated world of mental patients and exposes the dehumanizing practices routinely employed by staff against inmates. The professionals maintain a public "front" stressing humane care for their patients, but behind the walls, inmates are subjected to beatings, deprivations, and humiliations—what Goffman calls "degradations of self"—

22.2

Human Diversity
Stigma

One of Erving Goffman's most important and poignant works is *Stigma: Notes on the Management of Spoiled Identity*, published in 1963. Here Goffman explores the interaction strategies and rituals that are adopted by the "stigmatized," those persons who are "disqualified from full social acceptance" (1963: v) owing to their possession of a discrediting social attribute, such as a physical abnormality or disability, a character flaw, or their membership in a disprivileged group (as with persecuted racial, ethnic, and religious minorities). Goffman shows how social acts of classification— carried out by "the normals" who hold the power to impose their standards and prejudices—significantly limits and burdens the life chances of those who are seen to be different or deviant. For an analysis of what it feels like to be an ex-con, a prostitute, an addict, blind or deaf, a stutterer, a despised ethnic, or an amputee, living in a world where one must conceal shameful secrets, live reclusively, or simply grin and bear the stares and verbal abuse, Goffman's dramaturgical insights yield a profound understanding.

which are carried out in the interests of bureaucratic order and efficiency. This disjunction between therapy and control gives rise to the creation by those who are oppressed of an alternative system, an "underlife" with rules of their own making that allow for a measure of autonomy and dignity, as well as defiance against the staff.

At the other end of the spectrum from total institutions are fleeting *encounters*. Yet here too order prevails. In *Behavior in Public Places*, published in 1963, Goffman examines such phenomena as waiting in line, riding mass transit, walking on crowded streets, and using public washroom facilities. In all such cases, people employ routines to minimize interpersonal contact with the strangers in their midst. We try to space our bodies properly, look away, or pretend not to hear adjacent conversations—and if contact is inadvertently made, we quickly seek to mend the breach with standardized apologies or excuses.

Ultimately, Goffman's work presents a disturbing image of social life—a world where the arts of impression management take precedence over honest communication, where contrived appearances prove more rewarding than poorly dramatized substance. We appear to be trapped in an unending con game, where the self is little more than "a product of the scene that comes off," a continuously changing "dramatic effect" that varies according to setting and performance. Is it merely chance, Goffman (1959) asks, that the word *person* derives from *persona*, the Latin word for "mask"?

Phenomenology and Ethnomethodology

Human agency is meaningful and rule-governed, but how is it that meanings and rules come to be established? According to proponents of phenomenology and ethnomethodology, mainstream sociology has largely ignored the everyday processes by which social practices are constructed and achieved by the participants themselves. With all our abstract scientific talk about social structures, institutions, roles, and cultural systems, we have failed to attend to how real people actually experience the worlds they inhabit.

For followers of *phenomenology*, the analysis of human consciousness is a primary task, for social reality is a *phenomenal* reality—that is, it *is* only what it *appears* to be to the minds of those experiencing it. As reality is interpreted and defined, so it is experienced. Consider astrology. People who are convinced that the stars govern individual destinies allow their belief to have that practical effect; they order their affairs in line with horoscope tables. Practices follow

from beliefs, thereby reaffirming those beliefs through compliance with them.

Phenomenologists refer to this experiential reality as the **lifeworld**—the shared or intersubjective world of common-sense perceptions and pragmatic actions. As the German philosopher Edmund Husserl (1859–1938) observed, what characterizes a lifeworld for its participants is its seeming "naturalness" or obvious facticity; it is taken for granted on the basis of **common-sense knowledge** shared by the members. For scientists to understand these phenomenal lifeworlds, they must suspend, or "bracket," their own conceptions and treat what they observe as strange or alien. Only by removing our preconceptions can we see how all the many diverse lifeworlds are collaboratively made to seem natural rather than created.

The sociologist Alfred Schütz (1899–1959) provides a framework for understanding the construction of lifeworlds in *The Phenomenology of the Social World*, first published in 1932. Schütz notes that all interpretations of reality are based on the "stocks of knowledge" we inherit from predecessors, which we extend through our own experiences of living in worlds that are already defined for us. Because our actions are ordered in reference to these common-sense knowledge frames, it follows that social life will feature *multiple realities*, or distinct domains of experience, such as the world of work, the domestic scene, play, religious life, and so on.

Some lifeworlds are framed by a key status or identity—mystic, criminal, addict, child, rich, poor, soldier, scientist, artist. Each status or identity operates according to distinctive sensibilities and assumptions. What serves to hold a lifeworld together for its members is a consensus of understanding, based on the intersubjective character of routine, everyday consciousness. That is, people sharing a lifeworld function on the basis of suspending doubt that it could be other than what their stock of knowledge specifies. This is termed by Schütz the **naturalistic attitude**, and it is grounded in several tendencies:

- *A reciprocity of perspectives.* We assume that those we interact with in our lifeworlds share our view of reality. Strangers, in contrast, seem "strange" to us precisely because we do not presume that they share our basic assumptions.
- *The objectivity of appearances.* What appears is real, not a figment of the imagination.
- *Typifications.* We navigate through life by relating present situations to what we have typically experienced before.

- *Glossing.* Our lifeworld experiences come to us in partial fragments or signals, which we interpret as indicators of some unseen complex or totality. For instance, a patient sees diplomas in a doctor's office, the shelves of medical books, and presumes or fills in that these signs indicate a proper professional training.

How individual actors actually make use of their "common stocks of knowledge" is the chief research focus of *ethnomethodology*. This perspective—a study of the practical methods used by ordinary "folk" (*ethnos* in Greek) in constructing their lifeworlds—was founded by Harold Garfinkel (b. 1917). In his *Studies in Ethnomethodology*, published in 1967, Garfinkel attempts to identify the underlying, tacit rules that make orderly interaction possible. To that end, he introduces an experimental method called *breaching*, which involves "making trouble" by disregarding or violating the common-sense understandings that govern routine interactions.

Garfinkel's research assistants were instructed to go out and "act strangely": they would bargain for items in department stores; they would act like lodgers when living with their own families; in conversations, they would request full explanations for statements of obvious meaning. The result? At first, people would attempt to rationalize the odd behaviour—the action was a joke, a misunderstanding, or perhaps the person was under psychological strain. But as violations of the taken-for-granted normality continued, people reacted with anger, even stress. For Garfinkel and his followers, breaching thus discloses the "fragility of reality"—a consensus that is upheld more by default than by the conscious value commitments celebrated in functionalist theory.

What ethnomethodological studies also reveal is that order, or "sense," is collaboratively made on a local, ongoing basis. Participants relate to each other in a sort of shorthand, by offering cues that are *indexical* in expression, that are meaningful only in lived context. An insightful illustration of this is provided in Joan Emerson's study of gynecological exams (1970). Gynecology is a domain in which medical and sexual meanings are in tension, particularly whenever the physician is male. Emerson notes that this tension is diffused or minimized by the examination setting, the medical equipment, the presence of a nurse, and the use of scientific terms for the genital region. On occasion, however, patients do express considerable embarrassment or overt sexual arousal. This requires "neutralization techniques," such as humour or re-definitions in terms of pain, anxiety, or ticklishness. Overall, Emerson shows how the participants "negotiate the process" by offering indexical expressions that endorse the medical meaning of their shared situation while suppressing the possible sexual dimension. But as recent media reports and lawsuits regarding predatory and harassing behaviour by some physicians confirm, crossing the professional line stands as a ready temptation in these situations, where even the choice of a word can redefine the realities that are experienced.

Ethnomethodologists today have largely abandoned the breaching experiment as ethically questionable; they now concentrate on providing detailed descriptions of various micro interaction settings. How do newspaper stories get composed? How do scientists make discoveries in the lab? How does one learn to play jazz music? How do people make talk in everyday conversation? A recurrent finding in all this research is that human beings do not mechanically implement rules or rigidly adhere to norms. We routinely make sense as we go, using our inherited stocks of knowledge as orientation or reference. In the ethnomethodological perspective, the actor is no puppet or "cultural dope," but a skilled constructor of reality.

Exchange Theory and Rational Choice

Are there universal causes of human action? Do unvarying laws govern our social relations? Most social scientists remain skeptical of such notions, recognizing the remarkable historical and cultural diversity that has been displayed by our inventive, imaginative species. But some schools of thought—those taking the natural sciences as their model—presume otherwise, insisting instead that the variability is merely apparent or inconsequential: human action, like all things in the natural world, is caused by certain universal tendencies.

One such perspective is *exchange theory*, first put forward by the American sociologist George Homans (1910–89). Reviving the behaviourist doctrine of conditioning through positive and negative reinforcers, Homans proceeded to fuse the stimulus–response model with the supply–demand principles of classical economics. In *Social Behavior: Its Elementary Forms* (1961), Homans openly advocates a reductionist approach, insisting that social phenomena can be explained by psychological laws.

According to Homans, human beings are egoistic creatures, propelled to action by self-interest. The social relations they establish are thus designed to facilitate the exchange of valued goods and services. In these transactions, individuals seek to maximize rewards and minimize costs, thereby securing "profit." This calculating quest for gain is allegedly ever-present, whether in the workplace, in leisure activities, in love affairs, in religion, in scientific pursuits, or in family life. The function or cause of any activity, Homans insists, is its expected "payoff."

In recent years, the exchange viewpoint has resurfaced in more elaborate guise as *rational choice theory*. This, too, is a reductionist sociology, which insists that cultures and social structures are the by-products of the combined or aggregated actions of individuals seeking to maximize rewards. *Rationality* is here defined as the pursuit of self-interest, which is determined by cost-benefit calculations.

In order to explain human actions, four key factors must be identified and measured. First, an actor's *hierarchy of preferences* needs to be established. That is, what are the particular *utilities*, or rewards, valued—money, esteem, eternal salvation, power, leisure, sexual gratification—and how are they ranked? Second, *opportunity costs* need to be considered. These are what an actor risks or sacrifices in the quest for any particular utility. For instance, career advancement might entail neglecting one's family life; cheating to pass an exam might result in expulsion. Third, there are various *institutional constraints* on action. For example, in a society that features ethnic or gender discrimination, individuals will be subject to various advantages and disadvantages largely on the basis of their group identity. The fourth key determinant is information. In order to chart a rational course of action, an individual requires extensive knowledge about the market situation he or she faces, the capabilities of competitors, and the like. Because the available information varies in quality and reliability, there will always be some margin for erroneous calculation. Rational choice theorists accordingly attribute instances of non-optimizing behaviour to faulty or incomplete information, not to an actor's inclination to subordinate self-interest to traditional norms and collective goals.

Let us consider a few examples of rational choice interpretation (see Friedman and Hechter, 1988). Why are the elderly overrepresented in attendance at religious services? Because salvation ranks as a strong preference for those who are closer to death. In addition, elderly people have fewer things to do in life, so the cost of making time for a sermon or two is not very significant. Why is corruption among police officers and prison guards so rampant? Because deal-making with criminals brings extra rewards in the form of bribes and kickbacks, while also facilitating control. Moreover, there is limited opportunity for supervisors to monitor actions on the beat or in the pen, and so detection is not a high opportunity cost. Why is there racial discrimination in the economy? Racism on the part of employers is unlikely, according to rational choice theory, since racist hiring practices are economically irrational, entailing both higher wage costs and a restriction of the talent pool. The discrimination must therefore derive from other workers, who rationally seek to preserve advantages for their own group. Why do young people commit more crimes proportionally than older age groups? Because they have less to lose if apprehended, whereas adults typically risk careers, family, years of life (of which fewer remain), and so on. Why have industrial workers so far failed to stage a revolution against capitalism? Because each worker realizes that risks are entailed by personal involvement, and so contributes only minimally in time and effort, hoping to benefit as free-riders from a revolution that others will sacrifice for.

If you had trouble with some of the assertions and reasoning offered in the preceding examples, don't feel alarmed. There are a great many critics of the "sociology-as-economics-as-psychology" school who find that its claims are questionable or partial at best. Most fundamentally, by starting with the individual actor, rational choice theory provides no way of explaining why social value preferences exhibit such tremendous diversity and change—why materialistic interests prevail here and now, while spiritual interests prevail there and then; why a sexual revolution takes place in one society, while religious fundamentalism gains ground elsewhere. Human beings are, to be sure, attentive to self-interest, and they are often strategic in their pursuit of goals. However, as we have learned from the symbolic interactionist perspective, minds and selves are not natural givens but social emergents. What counts for rationality, and what passes as a preferential utility, is likewise socially constructed.

The Feminist Critique and Corrective

Did it escape your notice that the theories we have discussed were all formulated by men? If you are a female, probably not; if a male, it probably did. That differential reaction discloses an important sociological fact: perception is selective, and it is highly dependent upon one's socialization and location in existing hierarchies of power and privilege. The social worlds of males and females are shared and overlap, but they are not identical or equal. Until quite recently, women were largely excluded from the domains of knowledge production, just as they have been denied equal opportunities in other public arenas. In understanding the social practice called *science*, that historic inequity is very relevant.

As the struggle for women's liberation gained momentum over the course of the twentieth century, female intellectuals began offering incisive criticisms of male-oriented, or *androcentric*, claims to knowledge and truth. Groundbreaking works such as Simone de Beauvoir's *The Second Sex* ([1949] 1957), Betty Friedan's *The Feminine Mystique* (1963), and Kate Millett's *Sexual Politics* (1970) exposed various biases in male definitions and appraisals of reality. Eventually these critical efforts came together in a general political and intellectual framework known as **feminism**.

As feminist political action made progress in opening up career paths and educational opportunities for women, feminism as an intellectual force began to challenge male monopolies in the fields of science. Feminist scholarly journals were founded, university curricula and textbooks were reworked to incorporate women's issues, and increasing numbers of female academics carried out research that illumined hitherto-neglected dimensions of gender-structured realities. This many-sided development constituted nothing less than a revolution in scientific practice and consciousness.

The feminist critique of "male-stream" social science proceeds on interrelated epistemological and ontological fronts, challenging both what is studied and how it is studied. With regard to establishing "objective" accounts of social life, feminist scholars have shown that, historically, male researchers and theorists tended to see the world from a male, not a neutral or a balanced, perspective. In sociological studies of the family, for example, it was thought to be both natural and functional for the man to reign as a "breadwinning authority figure" while the woman contributed as a "nurturing homemaker." Sigmund Freud's psychoanalytic theories of personality formation are all grounded in an assumption that females are essentially castrated males, suffering from "penis envy." Economists offered elaborate models regarding

production and exchange, yet failed to appreciate that unpaid domestic labour by women sustains all economic systems. In studies of politics, religion, and other institutions, much the same bias can be detected: practices and norms that had been socially constructed—and largely expressive of male interests and power—were viewed as "natural" or "functional." And that, of course, is one of the prime functions of ideology: to justify or conceal the inequities and injustices of established arrangements by making what is historically and socially constructed appear universal or necessary, "in the nature of things." Even in the linguistic packaging of scientific knowledge, the tendency to employ strictly masculine terms of reference—*man* instead of *humanity*, masculine pronouns (*he* and *his*) rather than feminine ones (*she* and *her*)—contributed to misrepresentation.

These epistemological problems were compounded by an equally serious ontological shortcoming. Our understanding of social reality has been partial and skewed, for female experiences have been either invisible or marginal in most social-scientific research. Can any sociology of religion be valid or comprehensive if it does not take into account that the major world faiths were all created and defined by males, who have continued to monopolize spiritual authority? Can any sociology of war be realistic if rape and female enslavement are given only passing mention? Can political sociology properly analyze relations of domination and control without attending to the long-standing exclusion of women from the forums of public power? Can the sociology of science accurately grasp the dynamics of knowledge creation without taking into account that the laboratory has been largely an all-male preserve? Can studies of the mass media properly assess and explicate the nature of our pervasive consumer culture if it goes unrecognized that media moguls, executives, and "ad-men" are, for the most part, just that—men? In short, the historic inattention to the experiences and forced social exclusions of the female half of our species has resulted in significant gaps and distortions in our knowledge of most social institutions and practices.

For feminists, these deficiencies in scholarship are related to a more basic social condition: the widespread and enduring reality of **patriarchy**, an institutional and cultural system of male domination that has empowered men to control and limit female possibilities, restricting both their minds and their bodies. The historical origins of patriarchal domination date back thousands of years, to the creation of the

22.3

Open for Discussion
The Woman's Bible

One of the most influential and important contributions to the rise of feminist thought is Elizabeth Cady Stanton's *The Woman's Bible*, published in 1895. Regarding traditional religions as a principal bulwark for male domination, Stanton offers a critical commentary on select passages from the Jewish Old Testament and the Christian New Testament, to illustrate how these texts promote and enshrine patriarchal values and prejudices.

Scandalizing her contemporaries, Stanton did not shirk from asking the most direct questions of the sacred scriptures, including this one: "If a Heavenly Father was necessary, why not a Heavenly Mother?" For Stanton, religions were largely created by and for men, and if women were ever to secure equality and justice, they must first free themselves from the negative images and stereotypes that originated millennia ago, with the ideological myth of the temptress Eve and the gullible Adam, and a paradise that was lost owing to a woman's sinful duplicity.

---

first complex civilizations. With the rise of the state, private property, urbanization, writing, professional militarism, and a growing division of labour, human communities began to develop ever-widening internal disparities in wealth, power, and privilege. Accompanying that mounting inequality and stratification was a general deterioration in the social position of women—a fall from the general egalitarianism and co-operative parity they tended (and continue) to enjoy in band and tribal arrangements and in many horticultural-pastoral societies.

As a consequence of centuries-old traditions of patriarchal domination, the social worlds we presently inhabit are organized in terms of *gender inequalities*, cultural specifications—largely created by men—of what biological sex differences supposedly require. There are established male and female "psychologies," patterns of play and patterns of work, role expectations, moral ("double") standards, occupational opportunities, and so on. From our personal self-images on up to the most powerful institutional structures that will determine the ecological fate of our planet, gender is a fundamental sociological factor. Explicating and exposing the **social construction** of patriarchal-gendered realities is thus a basic concern of feminist theory and research.

Unlike the various sociological schools and traditions we have examined, feminist scholarship does not fit into any specific ontological or epistemological box. Feminists typically draw upon select theoretical frameworks—most commonly, Marxism, symbolic interactionism, phenomenology, and ethnomethodology—which they modify and expand to incorporate their concerns with gender-based realities. As a consequence of this analytical diversity, feminism is no monolith, and there is considerable debate about the directions to follow for the future.

Fundamentally at issue is the question of whether feminism represents an "alternative way of knowing" or a scientific corrective. Those arguing for a distinctive "feminist truth" insist that science—with its detachment and categorical logic—is inherently masculine and therefore incapable of dealing with female experiences and interests. Most, however, disagree with this rejectionist position, and argue that the norms of science—the principles of objectivity, factual proof, and theoretical consistency—actually encourage the correction of flawed scientific practices. After all, is it not the case that feminism has emerged historically from *within* the tradition of science and critical rationalism, and does it not base many of its corrective claims on the charge that androcentric science is "bad" science? In that regard, the progressive incorporation of feminist insights and concerns should result in a more balanced, comprehensive, more truly scientific sociology.

Future Prospects and Ongoing Challenges

Sociological theory must continue to shed light on how personal destinies are connected with the institutional and cultural structures of social life and on how these relations intersect with historical and global processes of change. Ongoing theoretical work in sociology is therefore principally concerned with integrating the "two sociologies"—the structure and agency perspectives. By combining the insights of structuralist approaches with those contained in the various agency perspectives, we attain a deeper understanding of how selves and societies are mutually created, constituted, and transformed over time.

One highly promising effort at synthesis in this regard is *historical sociology*, which proceeds on a recognition that social action is always structurally situated and that cultures, institutions, and social roles are temporal (or, time-relative) phenomena that change dynamically as a consequence of ongoing human interaction. As we learn more fully about how the past reaches into the present and about how the social penetrates into the psychological, we gain a greater sense of both where we're coming from and where we're at, thereby enhancing our awareness of the possibilities for progressive changes ahead—"where we're heading." For sociology to make continued progress in that emancipatory direction, however, two temptations must be resisted.

The first of these is the allure of *reductionism*—the tendency to seek simplified answers for the complexities of social life. Here the main challenge is posed by *sociobiology*, which holds that genes rather than cultures are in control of human destinies. Against this, one needs to raise a fundamental logical objection: change and diversity cannot be explained by invoking relative constants, things that change very little at all. Empires, for example, don't fall because the biological makeup of the ruling classes suddenly deteriorates, and genes don't abruptly mutate favourably when immigrants leave behind oppressive or impoverished conditions to find success and prosperity elsewhere. Indeed, for the past 40,000 years or so, the biology of *Homo sapiens* has not undergone any significant alteration, and yet over that time we have created vastly different social worlds, remarkably variable forms of personhood. Humanity's biological and sociocultural clocks simply do not keep time in tandem.

The other temptation is to respond to the seeming babble of competing voices by denying the very possibility of science. Such is the thrust of *postmodernism*, a radical subjectivist stance that holds that all knowledge is fabricated and all truths are local. Here, too, the reply can be brief. Though the methods of science are not flawless in practice, the principles of critical rationalism—subjecting arguments to empirical tests, demanding logical consistency, remaining open to new perspectives—provide rules of procedure that remain our best bet in the ongoing quest for objective knowledge. Science is not inherently partisan or ideological, nor is it identical with poetry, rhetoric, religion, or politics—though these aspects can be present in actual scientific work. The challenge is to remain vigilant against such tendencies, and indeed, a new speciality—the sociological study of scientific practice—arose precisely out of that concern. Science, more than any other form of knowledge, is an enterprise with a remarkable capacity for self-correction.

Conclusion

Scientific theories seek to specify key relations of dependence and order among phenomena. By identifying causal connections, theories enable us to see and understand how processes unfold in patterned ways. In sociology—the most comprehensive of the social sciences—we investigate many diverse phenomena, from the micro situations of interacting "minded selves" to the macro transformations of institutions and entire societies. Theoretical pluralism is a logical consequence of this diversity of research interests.

There have been two pervasive theoretical approaches in sociology. One tradition features theories of social structure, which focus primarily on systems and institutions and on how these govern the thoughts and practices of the actors living within them. The other tradition features theories of social action or agency, which focus primarily on the social construction of situational realities through the interactions of minded selves. Structure–agency, micro–macro, nominalism–social realism: these are the basic polarities in sociological theory, the major points of contention in ongoing debate. As we have observed, however, our theoretical approaches tend to be more complementary than contradictory, for social reality is inherently dualistic or dialectical: human beings are the "creators" of their social worlds, and also the "products" of those worlds. The different theoretical perspectives offered in sociology enable us to better understand how selves and societies are mutually implicated, dynamically changing constructions.

☐ Questions for Critical Thought

1. The debate over whether the social sciences should or can be modelled after the natural sciences is of long duration. What reasons can you think of—pro as well as con—in addressing that issue? Organize your points in reference to both ontology (the object of study) and epistemology (the nature of knowledge).
2. Marxists emphasize class inequalities and conflict in their sociology, while functionalists emphasize order and consensus based on shared value systems. Which perspective offers a more realistic picture of Canadian society? State your reasons.
3. Max Weber feared the suppression of personal freedoms by the relentless march of bureaucratization. How is your life constrained or limited by bureaucratic controls and regulations? What social forces or groups control the bureaucracies?
4. The famous wit and writer Oscar Wilde once said, "Most people *are* other people; their thoughts are someone else's opinions." Try rephrasing that statement in the sociological languages of Marxism, symbolic interactionism, and phenomenology.
5. How were you "socially constructed"? Perform a kind of sociological archeology on your personal identity, uncovering the accumulated layers of your "mind" and "self." Specify the sources from which your thoughts, values, and self-image derive.
6. Using Goffman's dramaturgical perspective as a guide, write up a report on a single day in your life, identifying all backstage and frontstage settings, all efforts at impression management, the various "masks" you tried on, and so on. How much was "con," and how much was sincere and genuine? Is that distinction meaningful?
7. The exchange/rational choice model of egoistic, calculating individualists has been criticized for offering a narrow characterization of human beings. Does that charge appear valid or invalid? Do you believe there is such a thing as "human nature," or do different societies create significantly different kinds or types of human beings?
8. Feminists maintain that our social worlds are fundamentally structured in terms of gender inequalities. Identify three key institutions that are based upon such differentiation. Identify three patriarchal features in our culture.

☐ Recommended Readings

Lewis Coser, *Masters of Sociological Thought: Ideas in Social and Historical Context*, 2nd edn (New York: Harcourt, 1977).

This is a reader-friendly text that provides lucid summaries of the key contributions of the major theorists. Informative biographical vignettes are offered, and ideas are clarified by relating them to the contexts in which they emerged.

Anthony Giddens, *Central Problems in Social Theory: Action, Structure, and Contradiction in Social Analysis* (Berkeley: University of California Press, 1979).

Giddens's book is perhaps the best place to start for getting a handle on contemporary debates, with much attention given to the necessity of integrating the agency and structure perspectives.

Gerda Lerner, *The Creation of Patriarchy* (New York: Oxford University Press, 1986).

Lerner provides a fascinating historical sociology of the key processes in the rise and consolidation of patriarchal forms of domination in Western civilization.

Peter Manicas, *A History and Philosophy of the Social Sciences* (New York: Basil Blackwell, 1987).

This is a highly informative treatment of the key ontological and epistemological problems in social science.

Theda Skocpol, ed., *Vision and Method in Historical Sociology* (Cambridge: Cambridge University Press, 1984).

Skocpol's is a most useful introduction to and analysis of the renewal of historical sociology. The book explores the works of nine prominent scholars who draw upon and extend the Marx–Weber legacy of grounding theory in history and of explicating history in sociological terms.

Bryan S. Turner, ed., *The Blackwell Companion to Social Theory* (Oxford: Blackwell, 2000).

This collection of informative essays covers classical legacies and contemporary themes.

Malcolm Waters, *Modern Sociological Theory* (London: Sage, 1994).

This innovative text is organized around themes and debates rather than thinkers and schools. Theories of agency, structure, rationality, culture, power, gender, and inequality are explored.

Irving Zeitlin, *Ideology and the Development of Sociological Theory*, 7th edn (Englewood Cliffs, NJ: Prentice-Hall, 2001).

This influential study charts the development of modern theory in connection with two decisive debates: the romantic-conservative reaction to the reformist principles of the Enlightenment, and the sociological response to Marx's historical materialism and politics of revolutionary emancipation.

☐ Recommended Web Sites

A Celebration of Women Writers
http://digital.library.upenn.edu/women

A Celebration of Women Writers provides biographies and selected writings from women authors of all genres—from poetry to philosophy—dating from antiquity to the present, and global in scope.

Cybertheory: Sociological Theory on the Internet
www.cla.sc.edu/socy/faculty/deflem/Cybertheory.htm

This is an excellent guide to theory sources and sites on the Internet, with a wonderful array of links.

The Émile Durkheim Archive
http://durkheim.itgo.com

The Durkheim Archive, for undergraduates, offers key passages from his major studies on religion, crime, suicide, and so on.

Marxists.org Internet Archive
www.marxists.org

This comprehensive site features the complete works of Marx and Engels, the writings of some 60 other major and minor Marxist authors, a history of Marxism, an encyclopedia, a subject archive, and a study guide.

The Mead Project
http://spartan.ac.brocku.ca/%7Elward/

This extremely valuable site featuring virtually all of Mead's writings, along with many texts from other major contributors to social psychology, such as John Dewey, William James, Charles Horton Cooley, and William Isaac Thomas. Commentaries, references, and links are supplied.

Sociosite: Sociological Theories and Perspectives
www2.fmg.uva.nl/sociosite/topics/theory.html

This general theory site covers the major perspectives and also has a linked alphabetical listing of famous sociologists.

Verstehen: Max Weber's HomePage
www.faculty.rsu.edu/~felwell/Theorists/Weber/Whome.htm

Here you will find clear summaries of Weber's major studies, along with accompanying quoted passages.

www Virtual Library: Sociology: Sociological Theory and Theorists
www.mcmaster.ca/socscidocs/w3virtsoclib/theories.htm

This site includes selected texts of major theorists.

23

Bruce Arai

> > >

Research Methods

© PhotoDisc, Inc.

☐ Learning Objectives

In this chapter, you will:

- become familiar with the traditional model of science and with the more sophisticated model that has superseded it

- differentiate between quantitative and qualitative approaches to sociology

- differentiate between validity and reliability

- appreciate the importance of ethics in sociological research

- learn the different approaches to validity in qualitative and quantitative methods

- explore the influence of feminist theory on sociological methods

- gain a better grasp of social survey design

- learn about field research, interviewing, and ethnographic research

- study the different types of existing data and how they are analyzed

Introduction

In the previous chapter, you read about the major theories that sociologists use to understand social life. In this chapter, we focus on the methods that sociologists use to collect the data that have informed these theories and produced the many findings you have read about throughout this text. Among other things, you will learn about the debate over the scientific status of the discipline of sociology, the major techniques of data collection, and the influence of research ethics and the rise of feminism on sociological research methods.

Sociology departments in Canada belong to many different faculties. At your university or college, is the sociology department located in the faculty of arts, the faculty of social sciences, or somewhere else? This may seem like an unimportant issue, but it gives you some indication of the different ways in which sociology is perceived. Many sociologists think of sociology as a science or a social science, others view it as an arts or humanities discipline, and still others choose not to categorize it at all.

How we view sociology is important for this chapter because the methods that we use to produce sociological knowledge are intimately related to whether it is seen as a science, an art, or something else. Viewed as a science, sociological research is often designed to measure and quantify social life; this is called *quantitative sociology*. Viewed as an art or humanity, sociological research is often designed to get at the rich meanings that people attribute to their lives; this is called *qualitative sociology*. This distinction between quantitative and qualitative sociology is not absolute, and many sociologists prefer not to use it. It is used occasionally in this chapter to organize the discussion, and also to show how the distinction itself has become irrelevant to some scholars. The chapter begins by exploring a scientific view of sociology, because the founders of the discipline certainly thought of it this way and because it is still one of the most dominant views of the discipline today. The scientific view of sociology is also used as a backdrop for understanding other perspectives on the discipline.

Sociology as a Science

We often imagine that a science has several distinguishing characteristics (see Figure 23.1), including these:

How we view sociology is important because the methods that we use to produce sociological knowledge are related to whether we see sociology as a science or an art. (© Dick Hemingway)

- Knowledge is based only on facts.
- Facts are part of the real world and can be observed.
- When making scientific observations, we do not let our personal emotions or biases interfere with our observations; this is called *objectivity*.
- We usually use the scientific method, including experiments, to collect and analyze data and to draw conclusions.
- Science gives us the best understanding of the way the world works. In other words, if we follow the proper procedures of science, we will discover the truth about the world, and this truth will be better than other truths.

We usually base these ideas on what we think of as "real science"—something like physics, astronomy, chemistry, or perhaps biology. Compared to these fields of study, sociology seems to be a lesser science, perhaps not even a science at all. It is debatable whether any social science can ever live up to the rigorous standards of scientific inquiry set by these other disciplines. So it is not just sociology that fails

Figure 23.1 **The Traditional View of Sociology as a Science**

"NOW *THAT'S* THE SIGN OF A VERY ADVANCED CULTURE!"

to meet the standards; so do the other social sciences, including psychology, economics, and political science.

However, the perception that the social sciences are lesser sciences than their more hard-nosed cousins is based largely on an outdated, unrealistic understanding of what actually happens in disciplines like physics, astronomy, chemistry, and biology. As Sandra Harding (1986) has argued, what physicists actually do when they do physics is only one very particular way of doing science, and it is not clear that most sciences follow this model. Instead, there are a great many ways of doing science, and what physicists do is only one of them. Stanley Lieberson (Lieberson and Lynn, 2002), a past president of the American Sociological Association, has recently argued that sociologists should not model themselves on what happens in physics because the subject matters are too different. What we should be doing is paying more attention to what biologists are doing and using biology as a more appropriate model of how we might do sociology scientifically.

If we look at what scientists actually do and the methods they use to produce their scientific claims, whether it is in chemistry, biology, sociology, or economics, we see that there are many different ways of doing science. Not all of them involve experiments, or even the collection of data. Some science can be done with only a paper and pencil. Sociologists, anthropologists, and others who have studied the

actual behaviour of scientists have shown convincingly that the production of scientific knowledge depends heavily on things like informal negotiations between scientists, drama, and rituals (Latour and Woolgar, 1987; Lynch, 1985). In other words, it is not just the scientific method and **objective** observations that lead to scientific conclusions.

Additionally, completely objective observations of the world are impossible. Nobody can separate himself or herself completely from his or her prior knowledge of the world when making observations. Indeed, it is impossible to even make observations of the world, much less record them and communicate them to others, without knowing a language. And since languages are not unbiased, accurate reflections of the world, the fact that we have to make and express our observations of the world through language makes total objectivity impossible (see Chalmers, 1999).

This would seem to be a serious threat to the possibility of science in general. Scientific findings should not be influenced by the emotions, thoughts, prejudices, or language of any individual scientist. Instead, they are supposed to be true, accurate recordings of the real world. So does this make science impossible?

One answer is "yes," and some people argue that if objectivity is impossible, then science is impossible. The reason for this opinion is that without the claim to objective knowledge, science ceases to be a distinctive form of inquiry. We should abandon science, or at least alter it radically. This point of view is often associated with **relativism**—the belief that there is no ultimate truth.

But another answer is "no," that it is possible for sociology and other forms of inquiry to be scientific. The reason for this opinion is that the criticisms of objectivity, convincing as they are, do not undermine science because objectivity is not a necessary condition for something to be called "scientific." All that we require is that science be defined as "guidelines or rules of thumb or conventions that produce claims that are defensible when called upon, though not perfect" (Goldenberg, 1992: 19). The "eight items or less" rule in grocery stores, seen in Figure 23.2, is simply a rule we use to make our lives easier. The rules we use in science are more important than eight items or less, but they are not ultimate commandments.

What this means in practical terms is that sociologists can and do develop rules for what constitutes "good sociology" and for how it can be differentiated from "bad sociology." Physicists, chemists, and

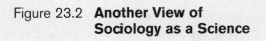

Figure 23.2 **Another View of Sociology as a Science**

"9.....10.....11......12......"

psychologists do the same thing, developing rules for "good" and "bad" physics, chemistry, and psychology. Many of these rules concern the proper methods used to collect, record, and analyze data. We will cover some of these basic rules or conventions in the next two sections of this chapter, on the connections between theory and research and on the major techniques of sociological research.

Theory and Research

For most sociologists, it is important that their research be closely connected with a **theory** or set of theories. Briefly, *theories* are abstract ideas about the world. Most sociological research is designed to evaluate a theory, either by testing it or by exploring the applicability of a theory to different situations. As can be seen throughout the many chapters in this text, sociologists investigate substantive problems and try to use their theories to help them understand these problems better. For instance, sociologists may be interested in understanding crime, the family, the environment, or education, and they will almost always use their theories to provide a deeper appreciation of these issues.

Sociologists use theories as models or conceptual maps of how the world works, and they use research methods to gather data that are relevant to these theories. So theories and methods are always intertwined in the research process. There are hundreds of different theories in sociology, but most of them can be grouped into the four main theoretical perspectives that can be found throughout this text: structural functionalism, conflict theory, symbolic interactionism, and feminism. But theories cannot be tested directly, because they are only abstract ideas. Theories must be translated into observable ideas before they can be tested. This process of translation is called **operationalization**.

Operationalization

Operationalization is the process of translating theories and concepts into hypotheses and variables. *Theories* are abstract ideas, composed of concepts. **Concepts** are single ideas. Usually, theories explain how two or more concepts are related to each other. For instance, as discussed in chapter 14 on class and status inequality, Karl Marx used concepts such as "alienation," "exploitation," and "class" to construct an abstract explanation (theory) of capitalism.

Once we have a theory, we need some way to test it. The problem is, we are not able to test theories directly. We need an observable equivalent of a theory, or at least a set of observable statements that are consistent with our theory. These are called **hypotheses**. In the same way that theories express relationships between concepts, hypotheses express relationships between variables. Unlike the typical definition of a hypothesis as simply an "educated guess," it is important to point out that hypotheses must be observable or testable. This means they must be composed of or express relationships between variables.

Variables are the empirical or observable equivalent of concepts. The two key points about a variable are that it must be observable and that it must have a range of different values it can take on. For instance, ethnicity, age, years of schooling, and annual income are variables. We can collect information on all of these items (that is, they are observable), and people can have different ages, ethnicities, and so on. "French," "45 years old," "12 years of schooling," and "$50,000 per year" are not variables because although these are observable, they do not vary. They are *values* of variables, not variables in themselves, and it is important not to confuse the two.

In most cases, our hypotheses contain a minimum of two types of variables: independent variables and dependent variables. *Independent variables* are roughly equivalent to causes, and *dependent variables* are roughly equivalent to effects. Another way to keep these straight is to remember that the value of a dependent variable *depends upon* the value of an independent variable. For instance, if you wanted to investigate differences between the average earnings of men and women, then sex or gender would be the independent variable and earnings would be the dependent variable. This is because peoples' earnings may *depend upon* their gender. Indeed, it is easy to keep the independent and dependent variables straight in this example because it makes no sense to say that a person's gender can depend upon their earnings.

Validity and Reliability

In the process of operationalizing our theories and concepts into variables and hypotheses, it is important that this process of translation be as clean as possible. That is, we want to ensure that our variables and hypotheses accurately reflect our theories and concepts. In particular, we want to ensure that when we go out and collect our data, we are using measures that are both valid and reliable. The most important step in this process is the construction of *operational definitions* of our concepts. These are definitions that specify what we are going to observe, how we are going to make our observations, and how we are going to differentiate observations from non-observations (or how we will know which possible elements to exclude from our study).

Validity

The **validity** of an empirical indicator refers to the degree to which it represents the concept with which it is associated. A valid measure is one that adequately represents the concept, and an invalid measure is one that does not. However, there is no firm line between valid and invalid indicators. Instead, the validity of an indicator is always a matter of degree. Some measures are more valid indicators of one concept than are others.

The validity of a measure is also always related to the concept it is supposed to capture. That is, there are no valid or invalid measures as such. Rather, a measure can be perfectly valid in relation to one concept but invalid for another. For instance, sociologists often

use a person's years of schooling as an indicator of their educational attainment, and most sociologists consider it a valid (if imperfect) indicator of this concept. However, a person's years of schooling is not a valid indicator of their ethnic origin.

It is probably fairly obvious to you that a person's years of schooling is a better indicator of their educational attainment than of their ethnicity. But this is really only one of several validity criteria, one called *face validity*. An indicator has high face validity when it seems to fit nicely with our mental image of the concept it is supposed to measure. There are several other types of validity that are often used in social sciences research, but we will only cover two more of them here.

Construct validity assesses how well an indicator of one concept performs against indicators that measure other, related concepts. A measure with high construct validity will behave as expected in relation to indicators of these other concepts. For example, you may be interested in the concept of political involvement, and you may choose to use the number of political rallies or events that a person attended in the past year as a measure of this involvement. You might also think that a person's political involvement should be positively related to his or her level of political awareness, and you could develop an awareness score for your respondents based on their answers to a series of questions about politics and current events. If you find that people's scores on your political awareness measure correlate well with the number of rallies and events they have attended, then your measure of political involvement probably has good construct validity.

The *content validity* of a measure refers to the degree to which that measure captures the various meanings of a concept. A measure with high content validity will cover all or most of the meanings of a concept without overlapping onto other concepts. For example, one commonly used measure of educational attainment in high school is a student's score in math, or sometimes the difference between a student's math scores in Grade 10 and in Grade 12 (Morgan and Sorensen, 1999). These variables have reasonably high content validity for the concept of math ability but fairly low content validity for concepts like intelligence and school success. School success is often measured by a student's overall average, and IQ is sometimes used to measure intelligence.

In addition to discussing the content and construct validity of specific measures or variables, sociologists also talk about two types of overall validity of a piece of research: the external and internal validity of a study also need to be established.

The *external validity* of a piece of research refers to the extent to which the results from that research can be generalized to a larger population (that is, the generalizability of the findings beyond, or external to, the specific **sample** used in the study). The two main areas of concern in establishing external validity are the proper selection of the sample of people or elements to be studied and the specific techniques used in the research. Ensuring that a sample is chosen using a properly random procedure usually satisfies concerns about sample selection. The threat from the procedures themselves is most commonly that there may be a reason to suspect that the results are a product of something in the study itself and not completely reflective of real-life situations. In other words, if there is a reason to think that people acted or answered differently during the research than they would in real life, then there is a threat to the external validity of the study. For instance, people may answer questions differently if they know they are being tape-recorded, and people may act differently simply because a researcher is present.

The *internal validity* of a study concerns the degree to which the conclusions from the study are actually supported by the data and methods that were used. Internal validity is threatened when the effects that are attributed to specific variables or processes in the study (for example, the effect of more education on the amount of money a person earns in his or her first job) are actually produced by other factors. For instance, if people perform better on a math test after taking a math class than they did on a test before taking the class, it might be tempting to conclude that the class was a good one because peoples' grades went up. However, there are many other reasons why math grades might have gone up, including the fact that the students will have a better idea of the types of questions that will be asked on the second test than they did on the first one. If these and other factors are not accounted for in the research, then the internal validity of the study is lower than it could be (Campbell and Stanley, 1970).

Reliability

The **reliability** of a measurement process refers to its level of consistency. A reliable measurement process is one that produces the same measurements of the same phenomenon again and again. For instance, you can get a sense of the reliability of a supermarket scale by weighing an apple on it several times in succession. If you get very similar weights each time, the scale is reliable. However, if you get very different weights each time, it is not. In sociology, assessing the reliability of our measurement processes is rarely this straightforward. The details of these assessment procedures are beyond the scope of this chapter, but you can learn more about them in sociology research methods courses.

 23.1

Open for Discussion
Validity and Reliability in Sociological Research

Sociologists do research to find out about the social world they live in. Sometimes they are interested in finding out more about a specific group, such as the members of a particular church or protest group, and sometimes they want to know more about the population of an entire nation. Some topics, like how a particular protest group started, are best studied using qualitative methods, such as interviews or participant observation. Other topics, like the effects of ethnicity on educational attainment, are best studied using quantitative methods, such as national surveys and statistical analysis.

Regardless of the topic or method, sociologists always want to ensure that their findings are both valid and reliable. However, they may establish these properties in very different ways. Quantitative sociologists tend to emphasize logic and statistical tests to establish validity and reliability, while qualitative sociologists tend to emphasize the depth of understanding they are able to achieve. Notice that despite these differences, the goal of accurate and trustworthy results (or valid and reliable results) is the same.

Another Approach to Validity and Reliability

There is also another way of assessing the validity and reliability of our measurement processes. This approach is most often associated with qualitative research, and it is based on the depth of understanding that a researcher has of her or his topic. In this approach, researchers usually refer to the validity and reliability of their findings rather than to their measurement processes, in part because many qualitative researchers do not see themselves as "measuring" social phenomena so much as they see themselves as "recording" or "understanding" them. Indeed, there is often a hesitancy to use the terms *validity* and *reliability* because they are closely associated with the idea of precise, often quantitative, measurement.

One of the main goals of a great deal of qualitative research is to gain a better understanding of the topic or group being studied. But in order to acquire this better understanding, it is important that the results of the research be both valid and reliable. The reason is simply that we cannot have a better understanding of the topic if our results are unreliable and invalid. Wendy Griswold (1987), for instance, has developed a sophisticated model for assessing the validity of qualitative cultural data.

To achieve a level of validity and reliability in qualitative research, we do not usually engage in an extensive process of testing the different dimensions of validity and reliability like we do in quantitative research. Instead, we establish it by making a convincing argument that we have properly understood our topic or group. In other words, we demonstrate to our readers that we have gained enough understanding of our topic to ensure that our results are valid. We do this in several ways, including spending enough time with the people we are studying to fully understand their point of view, interviewing group members until we begin to see the same ideas come up again and again, or conducting extensive analyses of written records and documents on our topic of interest. (For a readable and irreverent discussion of these issues in qualitative research, see Stoddart, 1986.)

Bias and Error

Even with solid conceptualization and operationalization, a study can be threatened by the existence of both biases and errors. Although these words, *biases* and *errors*, are often used interchangeably in everyday conversations, they have two distinctly different meanings in social science research.

Error refers to the unintentional, accidental mistakes that inevitably creep into a piece of research. These errors are often referred to as "random errors," reflecting the understanding that these mistakes are unintentional and unpredictable. Random errors have many sources, including having the wrong people participate in research, respondents making mistakes when they fill out a survey or answer questions, errors in coding (the process of preparing data for analysis), and errors in analysis. There are ways of checking for some types of random errors, but there are no foolproof checks that will catch all of them. Obviously, our goal is to minimize the number of random errors in our research.

Bias is different from *error*—it refers to systematic inaccuracies in our data or analysis. Biases are usually unintentional, but they can be more serious than errors because they distort our findings in systematic ways. They also have multiple sources, but most researchers are concerned primarily about *respondent biases*. Two of the most common forms of respondent bias are *acquiescence bias*, where respondents simply check off answers to questions without thinking about them, and *social desirability bias*, where they try to answer questions the way they think the researcher wants them to instead of answering the way they want to themselves.

Even though *bias* and *error* mean two different things in social science research, something that starts out as a random error can turn into a systematic bias. For instance, when entering data from a survey into a computer, numbers are usually used to refer to different possible answers to each question. So instead of entering "French" or "Korean" for a person's ethnic background, a researcher will arbitrarily assign numbers to these categories (1 for French and 2 for Korean, for instance) and then enter the numbers into the computer. If during the course of entering the data a researcher mistakenly starts to enter the number 2 for people who are French, the data will be systematically biased.

Research Techniques

Having covered many of the more general issues in social scientific research, we now turn our attention to some of the specific techniques that sociologists and other social scientists use to conduct research. Again, this chapter will not cover these in great detail but rather try to give you a sense of what these techniques are, and when and how they are used. Before doing so, let us return for a moment to the traditional vision of what methods a scientist might use.

A popular image is that the primary method scientists use to conduct research is the experiment. However, even in the natural sciences, experiments are often the exception rather than the rule. A great deal of biology, astronomy, and other sciences is not done—and, in many cases, cannot be done—experimentally. Nevertheless, the image persists, and has traditionally been the standard against which science of all types, natural or social, has been measured.

The main advantage of experiments is that (1) they provide a controlled environment in which it is possible to (2) manipulate specific factors in an attempt to determine their effect on an outcome. Experiments can show the effects of one variable on another variable quite convincingly because of these two features.

However, sociologists do not use experiments very often for two reasons. First, we cannot manipulate many of the variables we are interested in, for either practical or ethical reasons. Sociologists are often interested in the effects of variables like gender, ethnicity, and social class on other variables like educational outcomes, earnings, or health status. But it is neither ethical nor practical to alter peoples' ethnicity or gender just so we can observe what happens to their educational outcomes. Nor can we simply move a person from an upper-class home into a lower-class home (or vice versa) just so we can find out what effect this might have on his or her eventual choice of career.

Second, one of the enduring criticisms of experiments is that it is not always clear that what happens under the controlled conditions of an experiment will also happen when we try to apply our findings to the "real world" (that is, external validity). For instance, many of the experiments in medical research are done first on rats and other animals, and it is always a question whether or not what happens to rats will also happen to humans. Similarly, in social-scientific research, it is never clear that what we observe in a controlled social experiment will also happen to people in their daily lives. Yet it is what happens in the real world that is often of most interest to sociologists. So the findings from a social experiment are often not interesting for us until it can be shown that the results are relevant in the real world as well.

Despite the fact that sociologists do not use experiments very often, the logic of the experiment still dominates at least one of the major techniques of sociological research. Surveys almost always collect a great deal of extra information from respondents in an attempt to recreate the controlled environment of the experiment after the fact. Surveys are often referred to as *quasi-experimental* designs because they are only able to construct a controlled environment after the data have been collected. In other words, in true experiments the controlled conditions are set in place and then the experiment is allowed to run, while in quasi-experiments observations of "naturally occurring" phenomena are made and an attempt is made to remove the effects of confounding variables during the analysis stage.

Surveys

Surveys are the most widely used technique in social-scientific research. Sociologists, economists, political scientists, psychologists, and others use them regularly (Gray and Guppy, 2003). They are an excellent way to gather data on large populations that cannot be studied effectively in a face-to-face manner. The goals of almost all social-scientific surveys are to produce detailed data that will allow researchers to describe the characteristics of the group under study, to test theories about that group, and to generalize results beyond just those people who responded to the survey.

You have probably participated in a survey or opinion poll before, although perhaps not in one used for social-scientific research. Many polls done by political parties or polling organizations to find out about the political preferences of the electorate are very well done. The need to be able to generalize results from a sample of people up to the preferences of voters is extremely important, and consequently most of these organizations put a great deal of effort into constructing and administering their polls properly. The one disadvantage of many of these polls is that they are often very focused on time-sensitive issues or candidates, so they are only useful for a limited range of social-scientific research topics. However, studies of voting behaviour and other political processes have profited immensely from public opinion polls.

But many "surveys" are done for purposes other than social-scientific research, and most of these will not produce data that are amenable to social science research. Designing and administering a good survey is much more difficult than it seems, but respondents rarely see all of the work that goes into producing a good survey. This may partly explain why surveys seem easy to create, and it may also contribute to the proliferation of pseudo-surveys in many different forms.

Pseudo-surveys

A great deal of marketing and customer satisfaction research does not meet the standards of a social-scientific survey, despite the fact that generalizable results remain an important goal. That is, companies do this research only in order to find out what their customers and potential customers want and do not want to see in their products and services. But if their results apply only to the specific people who answered the survey and not to their customers and potential customers more generally, then they have very limited value. The usual problem in these surveys is that not enough attention is paid to the selection of the people to whom the survey will be sent or administered or to ensuring that enough of the surveys are actually returned. Both of these factors jeopardize the generalizability of the results.

Typically, a customer satisfaction survey will be sent to a selection of customers, perhaps all customers during the past year, in the hope that some of these customers will send it back. But the keys to being able to generalize the results of a survey are that the sample be chosen using a randomized selection procedure and that enough people return the completed survey to ensure that there are no important differences between people who did and did not return it. Unless the company chooses its sample randomly, the results will apply only to those who actually answered the survey.

Moreover, it is not unusual for a company to send a survey to all of its customers and to get only 20 per cent of them back. Why did so many people not return it, and are these people different from those who did return it? Some people probably moved and did not get it, but others probably did not return it because they were unhappy with the service or product they received. To improve a product or service, you need this "negative" information as much as or more than the positive information from the people who did respond.

You have probably also seen TV shows that ask you to register your opinion about something covered in the show by phone or Web site. You may have also seen people in shopping malls asking passersby for

their opinions, or come across a survey on an Internet site, or read a mail-in questionnaire in a magazine. Sometimes the results of these questionnaires are released with outrageous claims, like "46 per cent of Canadians think X." The problem with many of these questionnaires is that respondents are chosen based on convenience and luck rather than at random. After all, the respondents to these questionnaires have to watch the TV show, read the magazine, or be in the mall in order to find out about the survey in the first place, and these groups of people are not necessarily representative of the larger population. Indeed, one of the main purposes of TV and radio shows, magazines and newspapers, and shopping malls is to appeal to specific, and often unique, parts of the population. So clearly the results of any of these polls are not generalizable to larger populations.

A relatively new class of pseudo-surveys comprises push polls, sales pitches disguised as surveys, questionnaires designed to create mailing lists, and other gimmicks. *Push polls* are often phone interviews that are designed to influence rather than record public opinion by "pushing" people into believing certain things. Political parties (or lobby groups) often run them to spread damaging facts or rumours about opposing candidates. The hope is that the bad publicity will push people into supporting their favoured candidates.

Some companies also use surveys as a cover for their sales pitches. These take many forms, but often people are called and asked to participate in a survey about their buying habits, or perhaps about their concerns about their health or the environment. Then, a week or two later, they get calls from companies selling products that fit their buying habits.

To alleviate some of the confusion around surveys and pseudo-surveys, and also to remove the derogatory connotation of the latter category, it is useful to distinguish between surveys and questionnaires. The pseudo-surveys mentioned above can be classified as questionnaires, but not as surveys. A *questionnaire* is any set of questions that is administered to a group of people. A *survey*, on the other hand, is a properly designed set of questions that is systematically administered to a randomly chosen sample from a population. In other words, all surveys are questionnaires, but not all questionnaires meet the standards of being a survey. What sets a survey apart are the design of the questions, the goal of collecting data rather than manipulating people, the method of administration, and how the sample is chosen.

Constructing Survey Questions

Having summarized what social scientific surveys are not, it is also important to describe some of the key characteristics of a good survey. Surveys consist mainly of questions, and there are many issues to consider in designing good survey questions (see Table 23.1 for a summary of key points to consider when constructing survey questions).

At first glance, it might seem that designing good questions for a survey would be easy. The reality is that it is quite difficult—sociologists can spend months just trying to figure out what questions they will ask, how they will word them, and the order in which they will ask them. One of the reasons that it is so difficult is because each question must be unambiguous for both the respondent and the researcher. A question with several different interpretations is not useful because respondents may answer it in a different way than is intended by the researcher. Similarly, questions that are too complicated for respondents to answer, or that presume a level of knowledge that respondents do not have, will not produce useful data. There are many, many issues to consider in designing good questions and the order they appear on the questionnaire, but we will only talk about four of them in this chapter.

First, sociologists must avoid the use of double-barrelled questions in surveys. *Double-barrelled questions* are those that have two or more referents or subjects, and that can therefore be answered in different ways. For instance, "Do you think that the government should increase taxes so that it can spend more on environmental protection?" is a double-barrelled question, and not one that should be used on a survey. The problem is that a yes or no answer to this question is not easy to interpret. A "yes" may mean that a person agrees with the whole statement, or it may mean that he or she agrees only with the environmental protection component or only with the increasing taxes component. A "no" may mean that the person disagrees with increased taxes but may nonetheless want more environmental protection, or it may mean that he or she disagrees with the entire statement. The trouble is, a researcher will not know which of these interpretations is correct for any individual respondent. The way to avoid this confusion is to use two separate questions, one for tax increases and one for environmental spending.

A second problem occurs when researchers do not pay sufficient attention to respondents' abilities to answer questions accurately. It may seem straightforward to ask a person how much he or she earned last

---

Table 23.1 Guidelines for Designing Good Survey Questions

Focus	Each question should have one specific topic. Questions with more than one topic are difficult to answer, and the answers are often ambiguous.
Brevity	Generally, shorter questions are preferable to longer questions. They are easier to understand for respondents. An important exception to this guideline is when asking about threatening topics, where longer questions are often preferable.
Clarity	Use clear, understandable words and avoid jargon. This is especially important for general audiences, but if you are surveying a distinctive group or population (such as lawyers), then specialized language is often preferable.
Bias	Avoid biased words, phrases, statements, and questions. If one answer to a question is more likely or is more socially acceptable than others, then the question is probably biased and should be reworded. For instance, if you are asking people about their religious preferences, do not use words like "ungodly," "heathen," or "fanatic" in your questions, or else you will bias your answers.
Relevance	Ensure that the questions you ask of your respondents are relevant to them and to your research. Also, in most surveys, some questions will not be relevant to all respondents; filter questions allow people to skip questions that are not pertinent to them. For instance, if you want to know why some people did not complete high school, you should first filter out high school graduates and ask them not to answer the questions about not completing high school.

SOURCE: Adapted from George Gray and Neil Guppy, *Successful Surveys: Research Methods and Practice*, 3rd edn (Toronto: Nelson Thomson, 2003).

year, but very few people know to the actual dollar how much they earned over the last 12 months. And even fewer people will be willing to look it up on their latest tax return. So while you can ask people for their specific annual income, most of the answers you get will be wrong. Some people round off their income to the nearest $1,000, others round it off to the nearest $5,000, and others simply guess at the actual dollar amount. You then have no way of correcting for these different reporting procedures. The solution is to offer people categories, because people often know to the nearest $5,000 or $10,000 how much they earn in a year.

Third, in some surveys, it is necessary to ask people about uncomfortable topics, topics that they may perceive as threatening. Surveys of criminal activity, sexual practices, and criminal victimization often require researchers to ask threatening questions. However, it is impossible to predict how individuals will react to any question, and even the most innocuous question may be perceived as threatening. Generally speaking, asking people about their incomes is perceived as somewhat threatening, and care must be exercised in how you ask about this.

There are a number of strategies for reducing the threat of questions, including making the behaviour or attitude you are asking about appear "normal" by asking about it in hypothetical terms, or asking about it as one of a series of questions. For instance, instead of asking people directly if they have been victims of crime, you could ask people about how they feel about their own safety, how much media coverage of criminal activity they receive, and then whether or not they have been victimized. No single strategy will work for every question, topic, or sample.

Finally, the order in which you ask questions can have a significant effect on respondents' answers, and even on whether or not they will complete the survey. As a general rule, it is better to ask threatening questions near the end rather than at the beginning of a survey. There are two reasons for this. First, by asking easier questions up front, researchers have an opportunity to establish a rapport with the respondent, in phone and interview surveys through conversation, and in paper surveys through identifying with the topics and issues on the survey. Second, if threatening questions turn off respondents so much that they refuse to participate further in the research, then at least they have completed part of the survey already. If this happens at the beginning of the survey, no usable data are collected at all.

Random Sampling, Sample Size, and Response Rates

The idea of choosing samples using a random procedure was emphasized in the discussion of pseudo-surveys. The reason that random sampling is so important is that it is the only way that we can be confident that our sample is representative of (that is, that it looks like) the population we are interested in. If our sample is representative, then we can be fairly confident that the patterns we find among our sample will also be present in the larger population. If it is not representative, then we have no idea if what we found in our sample is also present in our population. Using a proper randomization procedure ensures that we do not deliberately bias our sample and guards against any unintentional biases that may creep into our selection process. And although randomization does not guarantee that our sample will be representative, by minimizing both intentional and unintentional biases we maximize our chances that the sample will be representative. Additionally, randomization does not solve all problems in sociological research, and is not even always appropriate or necessary in field research.

There are many procedures for choosing a truly random sample, but they are all based on the principle that each person (or element) in a population has an equal (and non-zero) chance of being selected into the sample. The simplest random-sampling procedure is known as *simple random sampling*: each person in a population is put in a list and then a proportion of them are chosen from this list completely at random. The usual way of ensuring that people are chosen at random is to use a table of random numbers either to select all of the people or to select the starting point in the list from which the sample will be chosen.

Actually, the adjective "simple" in "simple random sampling" does not refer to the degree of difficulty—simple random samples are quite difficult to construct. Generating truly random samples is not as easy as is suggested in Figure 23.3. The problem lies not in choosing the actual people or elements but in constructing a complete list of every person or element in the population. For this reason, other sampling techniques such as stratified sampling and cluster sampling are often used to choose samples, even by large government agencies like Statistics Canada.

It is also important to consider the issue of sample size in designing a proper survey. How big a sample do you need in order to be able to generalize your

Figure 23.3 **Randomization**

"FILE THESE IN RANDOM ORDER LIKE YOU USUALLY DO."

results? Actually, this is the wrong question to ask—it is not the size of the sample but rather how it is chosen that determines how confident you can be that your results are applicable to the population. That is, even a very large sample, if it is not chosen randomly, offers no guarantee about the generalizability of the results. On the other hand, a small sample, properly chosen, can produce very good results. So never assume that because a sample is large it must be representative. Always make sure you find out about how the sample was chosen before making any judgments about its generalizability.

Another crucial factor in determining the generalizability of survey results is how many people from the original sample actually complete the survey. This percentage is called the *response rate*, and is an important, although not the only, issue to consider in determining the generalizability of the results of a survey. The reason it is important is that unless a large proportion of the people in the original sample actually complete the survey, it is quite possible that the people who do not respond to it are different from those who do respond.

Field Research

In surveys, the primary aim is to collect quantitative or numerical data that can be generalized to a larger population. In contrast, field researchers are concerned about collecting qualitative or non-numerical

data that may or may not be generalized to a larger population. In field research, the aim is to collect rich, nuanced data by going into the "field" to observe and talk to people directly. Researchers will often spend time getting to know their subjects, in order to be able to capture their world view. Some of the classic sociological field studies, such as William Whyte's *Street Corner Society* (1943) and Elliot Liebow's *Tell Them Who I Am* (1993), are vivid portrayals of what life is like for certain groups of people—in the former case, the members of a lower-class urban community, and in the latter case, of homeless women.

There are actually several separate techniques that fall under the rubric of field research. These include participant observation or ethnography, in-depth interviewing, and documentary analysis. In many studies, more than one of these techniques is used.

Ethnographic or Participant Observation Research

In *ethnographic* or *participant observation research*, the researcher participates in the daily activities of his or her research subjects, usually for an extended period of time. This may include accompanying them on their daily activities (such as following police officers on patrol), interviews and discussions about their lives, and occasionally even living with them. During these activities, researchers take field notes (or recordings) either during or after an episode in the field.

A good example of participant observation research is Rebecca Tardy's study (2000) of how mothers interact with each other in a "moms and tots" playgroup to construct ideas about what a good mother is, and of how closely they match that ideal. Tardy participated in a playgroup of mothers and toddlers in a small community in the southern United States over a 14-week period. As is typical of participant observation research, Tardy did not have a rigid research design that she followed strictly over the time she was in the field. Rather, her main interest was in the women's conversations about health care and how they used these conversations to define, alter, and reconstruct ideas about "good mothers." She did not direct the women's conversations or ask them to focus their talk on particular issues. Instead, she simply participated in the playgroup and allowed the conversations to occur naturally. She found that women's understandings of good mothers centred on a few very particular health issues and on a heightened concern for their babies.

Tardy's research is interesting for several reasons, but two are particularly relevant to her use of participant observation. First, her use of Erving Goffman's dramaturgical theoretical approach (in which the metaphors of the theatre are used to understand social life) made participant observation a particularly appropriate method (Goffman, 1959). It allowed her to observe interactions as they occurred and to relate these data directly to some of Goffman's points about how people present themselves differently when they are in more public interactions (frontstage) than when they are in more private interactions (backstage).

Second, by focusing on naturally occurring conversations, Tardy was able to show how cultural ideals about things like motherhood and good mothers are embedded in and recreated by seemingly mundane discussions among mothers. In other words, ideals about good mothers do not just appear out of nowhere and exert pressure on people through "norms" or "society." Instead, ideals about good mothers get defined, interpreted, and reconstructed by actual people in actual interactions.

In-depth Interviews

In-depth interviews are another popular field research technique and are often used in conjunction with participant observation. *In-depth interviews* are extensive interviews that are often tape-recorded and later transcribed into text. In some cases, these interviews are highly structured and neither the researchers nor the respondents are permitted to deviate from a specific set of questions. At the other extreme, unstructured interviews may seem like ordinary conversations in which researchers and respondents simply explore topics as they arise. In many cases, researchers use semi-structured in-depth interviews that ask all respondents a basic set of questions but that also allow participants to explore other topics and issues. Striking the right balance between structured and unstructured questions can pose problems for sociologists, as can asking the right questions.

Like Tardy, Elizabeth Murphy (2000) investigated the connections between health care conversations and ideals about good mothers. Obviously, field research techniques can be used to investigate many more issues than motherhood, but Murphy's and Tardy's research provide a nice illustration of how different field methods can be used to study the same topic. Murphy used theories about how people understand and respond to risks as the basis of her research on breastfeeding and motherhood. She

interviewed 36 British mothers six times each, from one month before the birth of their babies to two years after birth. Each interview was semi-structured. In Murphy's sample, 31 women breastfed their babies initially, but only 6 were still breastfeeding four months after birth. This is interesting in light of current medical advice about the importance of exclusively breastfeeding infants for at least four months. Did the women in this study who stopped breastfeeding before four months think of themselves as bad mothers? Or were they able to set aside this medical advice and still think of themselves as good mothers? Murphy found that almost all of the women who had stopped breastfeeding recognized formula feeding as inferior but that none of them perceived this as a threat to their status as good mothers. Rather, they were able to justify their decisions because other people were at least partly—and, in many cases, primarily—responsible for the switch to formula feeding. The interviews revealed that some women encountered health care workers who were unsupportive of breastfeeding or who did not diagnose medical or mechanical problems that prevented breastfeeding. Other women had babies who were either uncooperative or could not do it because of "incompetence" (Murphy, 2000: 317).

One of the strengths of Murphy's research is the flexibility of her semi-structured interview technique. By directing the women to discuss their breastfeeding decisions and then following their leads, Murphy was able to gain a much deeper understanding of these choices. Had she not imposed some structure on the interviews, it is possible that the women might not have talked about their breastfeeding choices at all. Instead, her research presents us with a better understanding of how women can reconcile individual decisions to stop breastfeeding with seemingly contradictory ideals about "good motherhood."

Documentation

In some field studies, researchers will have access not only to people, but also to documents. This is more common when studying formal organizations like police forces or law firms, but can also be true when studying churches, political groups, and even families. These documents (case records, files, posters, diaries, even photos) can be analyzed to provide a more complete picture of the group under study.

The elaborate procedures needed to choose a sample for a survey are not necessary for selecting the research site and the sample in field research. Strictly following a randomization protocol is only necessary if statistical analysis and generalization are the goal of the research. Field research is done to gain greater understanding through the collection of detailed data, not through generalization. Nevertheless, it is important to choose both the research site and the subjects or informants carefully.

Conducting Field Research

The first criterion in choosing a site for field research is obviously the topic of study. A field study of lawyers or police officers will likely take place at the offices and squad rooms of the respective groups. Choosing which offices and squad rooms to study depends on many factors, including which ones will be the most useful for the purposes of the research. But there is also a practical element in much field research. That is, the actual choice of research site can come down to which law offices or squad rooms will grant access. This is not a criticism of field research but a recognition of the realities facing scholars doing this kind of research.

Once the site has been chosen, the issues of whom to talk to, what types of data to record, and how long to stay in the field become important. Some things can be planned in advance, but many things are often decided during the course of the field research. The selection of key informants—those people who will be most valuable in the course of the study—cannot always be made beforehand. Similarly, figuring out what to write down in field notes, whom to quote, and which observations to record cannot always be determined until after the research has begun.

Deciding when to leave the field is almost always determined during the course of the research. Most researchers stay in the field until they get a sense that they are not gaining much new information. In many cases, researchers decide to leave the field when they find that the data they are getting from new informants merely repeats what they have learned from previous informants. This is often taken as a sign that the researcher has reached a deep enough level of understanding to be confident that he or she will not learn much from further time in the field.

This flexibility during the course of the study is one of the great advantages of field research over survey research. Mistakes in research design and the pursuit of new and unexpected opportunities are possible in field research but are not usually possible in quantitative survey research. Once a survey has been designed, pre-tested, and administered to a sample, it is impractical to recall the survey to make changes. This is one of the reasons why pre-testing is so important in surveys.

Existing Data

In both surveys and field research, sociologists are involved in collecting new, original data. However, a great deal of sociological research is also done with data that already exist. There are several different types of existing data, and they are amenable to different modes of analysis. Some of the major types of existing data are official statistics and surveys done by other researchers; books, magazines, newspapers, and other media; case files and records; and historical documents.

Secondary Data Analysis

The analysis of official statistics and existing surveys (also known as *secondary data analysis*) has grown immensely with the development of computers and statistical software packages. It is now one of the most common forms of research reported in the major sociological journals, such as the *American Journal of Sociology* and the *American Sociological Review*. Statistical analyses of existing surveys can also be found in almost every issue of the *Canadian Journal of Sociology* and the *Canadian Review of Sociology and Anthropology* for at least the past 10 years.

Quantitative data are often presented in tables like Table 23.2. Tables can be designed in many different ways, and the type of information that is presented in a table will determine the types of comparisons that can be made. In Table 23.2, on marital status in Canada, comparisons can be made within or across the values of marital status (for example, how many people are married versus single), by sex, and across five different years.

As an example, we can see that the number of divorced males has increased by over 93,000 between 1997 and 2001 ($641,734 - 547,914 = 93,820$) and the number of divorced females has risen by over 125,000 ($868,037 - 742,671 = 125,366$), while the numbers of married men and women have increased by 87,500 and 106,136 respectively. However, the table does not tell us anything about why these numbers may have changed, nor can we make any comparisons with the number of married and divorced people in other countries.

In Table 23.3, though, comparisons between countries are possible. Some of these results may seem surprising, depending on your impressions of high

Table 23.2 **Population by Marital Status and Sex, Canada, 1998–2002**

	1998	1999	2000	2001	2002
Total					
Both sexes	30,248,412	30,499,323	30,770,834	31,110,565	31,413,990
Male	14,978,787	15,107,404	15,236,964	15,405,773	15,552,644
Female	15,269,625	15,401,919	15,543,870	15,704,792	15,861,346
Single					
Both sexes	12,797,263	12,911,946	13,031,272	13,175,106	13,304,129
Male	6,849,478	6,912,620	6,979,618	7,059,481	7,131,973
Female	5,947,785	5,999,326	6,051,654	6,115,625	6,172,156
Married[a]					
Both sexes	12,979,263	12,911,946	13,031,272	13,175,106	13,304,129
Male	7,299,132	7,337,226	7,381,266	7,431,522	7,476,537
Female	7,331,041	7,374,567	7,425,428	7,482,244	7,541,593
Widowed					
Both sexes	1,489,388	1,503,843	1,518,633	1,534,232	1,550,367
Male	263,490	269,220	274,910	280,748	286,940
Female	1,225,898	1,234,623	1,243,723	1,253,484	1,263,427
Divorced					
Both sexes	1,331,588	1,381,741	1,434,235	1,487,461	1,541,364
Male	566,687	588,338	611,170	634,022	657,194
Female	764,901	793,403	823,065	853,439	884,170

[a] Includes persons legally married, legally married and separated, and living in common-law unions.
SOURCE: Statistics Canada, CANSIM database <http://cansim2.statcan.ca>, Table 051–0010.

school graduation rates here in Canada versus other countries. Many media portrayals of the US school system would suggest that it is inferior to the Canadian system, yet the United States has a higher graduation rate than Canada.

However, this table also reveals some of the problems that may be present in tables, especially those presenting data from different countries. First, the school systems vary widely between countries, and despite careful efforts by the Organisation for Economic Co-operation and Development (OECD) to standardize the data, all of these numbers should be treated with caution. That is, many of these numbers could change significantly depending on the way in which graduates are counted, and especially on how each country reports its data to the OECD. Second, data may simply not be available, as in the case of Slovakia in Table 23.3.

Personal computers, statistical software packages, and the ready availability of many national and international data sets have made secondary data analysis possible for almost every social scientist. The advantages of secondary analyses are that the coverage of the data is broad and that the hard work involved in constructing and administering a survey has already been done, usually by an agency with far more expertise and resources than most individual researchers. The disadvantages are that the data collected are often not precise enough to test the specific ideas that researchers are interested in and that the learning curve associated with mastering the techniques to analyze the data properly is potentially steep.

Historical Research and Content Analysis

The analysis of historical documents, print and other media, and records and case materials can be done by several methods. The two most common forms of analysis are probably historical research and content analysis. Historical sociology relies on *historical research* into all kinds of historical documents, from organizational records, old newspapers, and magazines to speeches and sermons, letters and diaries, and even interviews with people who participated in the

Table 23.3	Percentage of 25- to 64-Year-Olds Graduating from Upper Secondary (High School) Programs, by Country, 1998
	Percentage Graduating from Upper Secondary
Canada	79.7
Mexico	21.2
United States	86.5
Japan	79.9
Korea	65.4
Australia	56.0
New Zealand	72.7
Belgium	56.7
Czech Republic	85.3
Denmark	78.4
Finland	68.3
France	60.7
Germany	83.8
Hungary	63.3
Italy	41.0
The Netherlands	64.3
Norway	83.0
Poland	54.3
Portugal	20.1
Spain	32.9
Slovakia	–
Sweden	76.1
Turkey	17.7
United Kingdom	60.2
OECD Mean	61.2

SOURCE: Organisation for Economic Co-operation and Development (OECD), <http://www.oecd.org/pdf/M00019000/M00019568.pdf>, accessed 30 June 2003. Reprinted by permission.

All sociologists engaged in research will use libraries extensively to find out information about their topic. But for historical sociologists, libraries often also contain the data they are interested in, such as letters, diaries, newspapers, magazines, and records of speeches. (© Dick Hemingway)

events of interest. In *content analysis*, documents such as newspapers, magazines, TV shows, and case records are subjected to careful sampling and analysis procedures to reveal patterns.

One of the major issues facing historical sociologists is that someone or some organization has created the records used in their analyses, but the potential biases and reasons for recording the information in the documents are not always clear. Further, over time some documents get lost or destroyed, so the historical sociologist must be aware that the existing documents may not give a complete picture of the events or time period under study. Why have certain documents survived while others have not? Also, is there any significance to the ordering or cataloguing of the

documents? These and other issues must be dealt with continually in historical research.

Content analysis can be done in a number of ways, but it usually involves taking a sample of relevant documents and then subjecting these documents to a rigorous procedure of identifying and classifying particular features, words, or images in these documents. For instance, in studying political posters, content analysis could be used to determine whether the posters from particular parties put more emphasis on the positive aspects of their own party or the negative aspects of other parties. These results could then be used to better understand styles of political campaigning in a particular country or time period. In *manifest content analysis*, words, phrases, or images are counted to provide a sense of the importance of different ideas in the documents. In *latent content analysis*, researchers focus less on specific word or phrase counts and more on the themes that are implicit in the documents.

Selecting a Research Method

To summarize, all of the methods described here are used by sociologists to collect data on particular research problems, and they use theories to help them understand or solve these problems. Any of these methods can be used to investigate problems from any of the theoretical perspectives encountered in this text, although some methods are almost never used in some perspectives. For instance, symbolic interactionists rarely if ever use quantitative surveys, while most conflict theorists prefer surveys to participant observation.

So how do you know which method to use with which theory or theoretical perspective? A complete answer to this question is beyond the scope of this chapter, but the general rule of thumb in sociology has been that you let the problem determine the method. For example, if you want to find out something about the national divorce rate and how divorced people differ from those who remain married, then you need a method, like a survey, that will give you data from people all over the country. But if you want to find out how nurses manage the many pressures of their jobs, then participant observation is an appropriate method.

As with any rule of thumb, though, there are exceptions. And as Sheldon Goldenberg (1992) and others have argued, letting the problem determine the method is not as straightforward as it seems. The main reason for this is that sociologists often become much more comfortable using one technique or another. They may then frame their research questions in ways that allow them to use those familiar techniques. In other words, many researchers "load the dice," and the methods that they are comfortable with tend to determine the questions they investigate.

The Context of Sociological Research

So far in this chapter, we have discussed the scientific status of sociology, the connection between theory and research, and some of the major research techniques used by sociologists, but we have said little about the context in which this research takes place. In this final section, we will consider three of the many possible issues that affect the way in which sociologists do their research: the different purposes of sociological research, the rise of feminism and feminist methods, and research ethics.

Purposes of Research

Sociological research can be done for several different purposes. Some research is *exploratory* or descriptive, where the goal is to find out more about a particular group or topic. For instance, research on homeschoolers (people who educate their children at home) is often exploratory because not much is

known yet about this particular group (Arai, 2000). Other studies are designed to be *explanatory*. Usually, these studies test different theories about some phenomenon against each other to determine which theory provides the best explanation. Explanatory studies may also test whether a theory developed from one group or time period applies to another group or time period. A good example of an explanatory study is Stephen Morgan and Aage Sorensen's test of James Coleman's "social capital" theory applied to why students in Catholic high schools tend to outperform students from public high schools (1999).

Other research aims to be able to predict future patterns of behaviour. Many early studies of criminal recidivism (convicted criminals' committing of further offences after being released from prison) were designed to enable people to make better predictions about which criminals would be more likely to re-offend once they were released from jail. Note that although they are often related, prediction and explanation are not the same thing. It is fairly easy to predict that night will follow day, but this does not mean that night causes or explains day.

Still other research aims to empower the group being studied. In the past, anthropologists would often become very involved with the concerns of the people they studied and would become advocates for that group. This was generally frowned upon, and anthropologists were accused of "going native"—becoming one of the people they were studying—instead of actually studying them. But nowadays, many researchers specifically want to empower the people they study. For instance, *participatory action research*, in which researchers are guided at least as much by the goals and wishes of their respondents as they are by their own theoretical concerns, has become more popular in sociology and other disciplines, such as psychology and social work. In Canada, there are even government grants available specifically for social-scientific research that is guided primarily by the needs and concerns of community groups rather than by the academic concerns of the researchers.

Feminism and Research Methods

The goal of empowering the people being studied is also an important component in feminist research. **Feminism** has had an enormous impact on many disciplines, including sociology. This influence has affected the topics that sociologists study, the perspectives they use to study them, and even the methods they use. The topics and perspectives influenced by feminism are covered in other chapters in this book, but it is important here to mention the influence of feminism on research methods in sociology.

Over the last 30 or so years, feminists have increasingly criticized the visions of science that inform the methods used by social scientists to study the world (Harding, 1986). In particular, the values of objectivity and detachment from the subjects that underlie a scientific view of the world have been heavily criticized on two grounds. First, these values are often associated with men, while attributes like emotionality and intuition that are supposedly non-scientific are often associated with women. The implication is that a scientific view of the world, based as it is on the "male" characteristics of reason and objectivity, is a better way to understand the world than a typically female view, which is coloured by emotion and irrationality. The result of this has been a systematic exclusion of women from science and the subordination of women's perspectives on the world to those of men.

Second, feminists and others have shown convincingly that a detached, unbiased science of society is not possible. Much of this demonstration is based on some of the criticisms of objectivity outlined in the first section of this chapter. Social scientists all have biases, and to claim a position of objectivity is simply to hide one's biases. It is far more preferable, for feminists and for others, to acknowledge biases up front than to hide them behind a curtain of supposed objectivity (Loughlin, 1993).

One of the hallmarks of feminism is the recognition and even the celebration of diversity. Feminists have responded to the challenge of science in several different ways. Some feminists have deliberately abandoned science of any sort, preferring the contradictions of relativism to the straitjacket of science. Others have done the opposite, trying to apply the rules of science as precisely as possible to show that science can be a useful tool in eradicating the suppression of women.

Still others have worked to articulate a feminist "standpoint" theory that takes the lived experiences of women as the critical starting point for a less distorted understanding of the world than that produced through science (Smith, 1990). Briefly, the standpoint of women is crucial for better understanding because of the unique positions of women as research subjects and of women as scientists. Women as subjects, largely excluded from mainstream society, can provide a less tainted view of the world because they are on the outside looking in. Women as researchers also have a privileged standpoint because they can both understand the experience of exclusion and work with the women they study to empower them to make positive changes in their lives.

This diversity means that there is no single method that can be properly called a "feminist

23.2

Human Diversity
Feminist Research Methods in Sociology

Theories and research methods are intimately connected in all sociological research. This connection has led to speculation about the existence of a distinct feminist method, given the importance of feminist theory in sociology. Looking at the literature, it is clear that feminists have used all of the major research techniques in sociology. In other words, feminists have used a diversity of methods in their research, and there is no single method that can only be used with feminist theory. For instance, Rebecca Tardy (2000) and Elizabeth Murphy (2000) both examined the subject of motherhood, but each used a different method.

"LET ME PUT IT THIS WAY, HAZEL. I'M NO LONGER GENDER-SPECIFIC."

method." Indeed, most feminists would reject any attempt to create a singular feminist method as an example of more male-centred, or *androcentric*, thinking. Feminists use a variety of methods. But what often sets their research apart from that of other researchers are a commitment to the empowerment of their research participants, and the modification or rejection of social-scientific methods to meaningfully incorporate women into the philosophy and practice of social science research.

Research Ethics

The final topic to be covered in this chapter is the ethics of social research. This topic, like many of the previous ones, is too broad and complicated to cover in any detail in a chapter like this, but it is possible to provide a summary of some of the main issues confronting researchers. It is a topic with increasing relevance in the social sciences, but also one with a long history.

A crucial point in the history of research ethics in the social and natural sciences was the Nuremberg trials of Nazi doctors and concentration camp officials after World War II. One of the problems was that research performed on prisoners in these camps had produced valuable insights into human physiology, but only as a result of the prisoners' having been subjected to some truly horrible experiments (Guillebaud, 2002). The stark contrast between the acquisition of knowledge and the protection of research subjects has guided the development of ethical principles for social and natural scientific research ever since.

In North America, one of the most important principles of research ethics to arise from these trials is the principle of *voluntary participation*. This means that people can be asked to participate in any piece of research, regardless of its potential damage, as long as they voluntarily agree to be a part of that research. People must not be coerced or tricked into participating, and they must be able to withdraw from the study at any time, without penalty.

The principle of voluntary participation cannot be fully realized unless its complementary principle of *informed consent* is also present. Potential participants must give their consent to participate in the research with a full knowledge of the potential costs and benefits to themselves and to the researchers. Indeed, participation cannot be voluntary unless a person is fully informed about the research before giving his or her consent.

One of the implications of informed consent is that research should be designed without deceiving the subjects unnecessarily. If deception is used, it must be absolutely necessary to the project and the benefits of the research must outweigh the harms associated with the deception. In most cases in sociology, this is not a problem, but there are topics that require the use of deception. For instance, studying people's discriminatory attitudes is often not possible without deception. One way of doing this that has been particularly successful is to have people evaluate fictitious résumés of job applicants on which all of the details of the résumé are the same except for the gender of the applicant. The idea is to determine whether or not people evaluate the abilities of men and women differently based not on their reported abilities but simply on their gender. Telling people that the gender of the applicants will be switched around beforehand would defeat the purpose of the study (Foschi, Lai, and Sigerson, 1994).

The identity of research participants must also be protected in North America, either through an assurance of *confidentiality* or through *anonymity*. Sometimes these terms are used interchangeably, but they are actually quite different. To assure participants of anonymity, a researcher must not even collect identifying information about his or her respondents. This is really only possible in mail-in surveys. In most interviews, field research, and telephone surveys, researchers have either met their participants or possess identifying information about them.

It is more common to assure respondents of confidentiality, whereby identifying information is collected but deliberately withheld in the publication of any results. This is possible in all types of research, but note that the protection of a subject's identity is weaker with confidentiality than it is with anonymity. For instance, researchers asked by a court to reveal the identities of their subjects may have to decide between breaking a promise to their subjects or disobeying a court order. But if they have not collected identifying information about participants, they will have nothing to reveal.

Many researchers are now getting around the potential conflict of confidential information by promising to keep subjects' identities secret unless they are ordered to reveal them by court order. This has certainly weakened the confidentiality protections in many studies, but it arguably allows potential subjects to make a more informed decision about participating in the research in the first place.

A final principle that is often attributed to the Nuremberg trials is that research should not involve any unnecessary harm to the participants. The Nazi doctors were completely unconcerned about the well-being of their subjects and did not take any precautions to protect them from harm. Most researchers find this abhorrent and do not inflict any more harm on their subjects than is absolutely necessary. In most sociological research, the greatest harm to participants is the time they have to spend talking to researchers, filling out surveys or diaries, or allowing them into their lives. However, there are instances in which real psychological damage can occur, and researchers have an obligation to be aware of this and guard against it.

Conclusion

The purpose of this chapter has been to introduce to you some of the major methods that sociologists use in their research and to some of the issues they face when conducting that research. A simplistic understanding of science is not helpful, for sociology or any other science. But a more sophisticated view of science does underpin how many sociologists view their discipline, although some sociologists reject the idea that sociology is a science at all. Nevertheless, establishing the validity and reliability of our results remains important to almost all sociologists.

The three main techniques—surveys, field research, and the analysis of existing data—were then reviewed, and the chapter ended with a discussion of research ethics and the influence of feminism on sociological methods. And while it has not been possible to cover all topics in detail in this chapter, you should have a better appreciation for both the difficulties and the joys of finding out about the world sociologically.

☐ Questions for Critical Thought

1. What was your understanding of science before reading this chapter? How has it changed?
2. When you read about a social-scientific finding in the newspaper, what kinds of evidence convince you of the veracity of those findings? In other words, do you need quantitative, statistical results, are you convinced by detailed accounts of individuals, or are both equally convincing?
3. If you were going to investigate the effects of a person's ethnicity on his or her educational attainment across Canada, what method would be most appropriate? Why?
4. If you wanted to find out more about the motivations of parents who send their children to a particular private religious school, what methods would be most appropriate? Justify your answer.
5. Outline the two different approaches to establishing validity.
6. Summarize the criticisms of science outlined in this chapter. Which one is most convincing, and why?
7. It was argued in this chapter that there is no single feminist method. Do you agree with this? Why or why not?
8. It is often difficult to distinguish between a survey and a pseudo-survey, especially if you are a respondent rather than a researcher. Summarize the key points necessary for a proper social-scientific survey and how these are violated in each of the types of pseudo-surveys discussed in this chapter.

☐ Recommended Readings

Earl Babbie, *The Basics of Social Research*, 2nd edn (Toronto: Wadsworth Thomson Learning, 2002).

Babbie's books are used in more research methods courses across North America than those of any other author. This one is a comprehensive treatment of research methods.

Bruce Berg, *Qualitative Research Methods for the Social Sciences*, 4th edn (Boston: Allyn and Bacon, 2001).

Berg's book is the current standard for qualitative research methods courses.

Sheldon Goldenberg, *Thinking Methodologically* (New York: HarperCollins, 1992).

This sophisticated research methods text is more difficult to read than the other texts listed here, but is well worth the effort.

George Gray and Neil Guppy, *Successful Surveys: Research Methods in Practice*, 3rd edn (Toronto: Nelson, 2003).

Gray and Guppy have written an accessible and comprehensive introduction to survey research methods. The book can be used as a step-by-step guide for conducting a basic survey.

Sandra Harding, *The Science Question in Feminism* (Ithaca, NY: Cornell University Press, 1986).

This is arguably Harding's most influential book, although most of her writings have had a significant impact. It begins with the issue of the underrepresentation of women in science and moves to the issue of the sexist nature of science more generally.

Don G. McTavish and Herman Loether, *Social Research: An Evolving Process*, 2nd edn (Boston: Allyn and Bacon, 2002).

Another popular methods book, this one is more focused on quantitative methods than qualitative methods. Loether and McTavish have also written statistics texts that have been used in many social statistics courses across North America.

Charles Ragin, *Constructing Social Research: The Unity and Diversity of Method* (Thousand Oaks, CA: Sage, 1994).

Ragin's book covers the main topics of social research but it is shorter and less comprehensive than Babbie, Goldenberg, or McTavish and Loether. Nevertheless, it is an excellent introduction to social research methods.

Shulamit Reinharz with Lynn Davidman, *Feminist Methods in Social Research* (New York: Oxford University Press, 1992).

Reinharz's book is the starting point for informed discussions of feminist methods. By reading this book first, you'll have a better appreciation of the more recent writings on feminist methods, many of which cite this book as a key source.

☐ Recommended Web Sites

Inter-university Consortium for Political and Social Research
www.icpsr.umich.edu

This is one of the first—and one of the best—social science data archives in the world. As a college or university student, you can use many of the datasets from the ICPSR for class and research purposes, at no charge.

Organisation for Economic Co-operation and Development (OECD)
www.oecd.org

The OECD collects data on economic, political, social, environmental, and industrial conditions in member countries (including Canada) and non-member countries (particularly developing countries). Data, publications (online and paper), and special reports are all available at this site.

PAR-L: A Canadian Electronic Feminist Network
www.unb.ca/PAR-L/

PAR-L (Policy, Action, Research List) is a network of feminist groups and individuals engaged in research and policy discussions on women. This site is a great collection of links to feminist and advocacy organizations, as well as to publications and resources on feminist issues in Canada.

Qualpage
www.qualitativeresearch.uga.edu/QualPage/

This site is dedicated to qualitative methods. It lists new books, conferences, and many other resources for people interested in qualitative research.

Research Methods Resources on the www
www.slais.ubc.ca/resources/research_methods/content.htm

This useful site lists both qualitative and quantitative methods resources, originally developed at the University of British Columbia library. Resources include online books, data, journals, and more.

Society for the Study of Symbolic Interaction (SSSI)
http://sun.soci.niu.edu/~sssi/

This society is open to anyone interested in qualitative social science research and, in particular, symbolic interactionist research. The society publishes a journal and holds annual meetings at which members and others present their work. The journal *Symbolic Interaction* publishes high-quality qualitative research.

Statistics Canada
www.statcan.ca

This is one of the most useful sites on the Internet for Canadian sociologists. Many of the surveys listed at this site can be used for class projects and research papers through your university or college, at no charge to you. Ask at your computing centre or library for details on the Data Liberation Initiative. If you only go to one of the sites listed here, make it this one.

US Census Bureau
www.census.gov

Like Statistics Canada, the US Census Bureau provides a wealth of resources and data, some of it free to use. You can also order publications, view them online, and download some US data from this site.

References

Abella, Rosalie. 1984. *Equality in Employment: A Royal Commission Report*. Ottawa: Commission on Equality in Employment.

Abercrombie, Nicholas, Stephen Hill, and Bryan S. Turner. 2000. *The Penguin Dictionary of Sociology*, 4th edn. London: Penguin.

Abu-Lughod, Janet L. 1991. *Changing Cities: Urban Sociology*. New York: HarperCollins.

Acker, Joan. 1980. "Women and Stratification: A Review of Recent Literature." *Contemporary Sociology*, 9: 25–34.

———. 1988. "Class, Gender, and the Relations of Distribution." *Signs*, 13: 473–97.

———. 1989. "The Problem with Patriarchy." *Sociology*, 23: 235–40.

———. 1990. "Hierarchies, Jobs, and Bodies: A Theory of Gendered Organizations." *Gender and Society*, 4: 139–58.

———. 1991. "Hierarchy, Jobs, Bodies: A Theory of Gendered Organizations." In *The Social Construction of Gender*, edited by Judith Lorber and Susan Farrell, 162–79. Newbury Park, CA: Sage, 1991.

———. 2000. "Rewriting Class, Race, and Gender: Problems in Feminist Rethinking." In *Revisioning Gender*, edited by Myra Marx Ferree, Judith Lorber, and Beth Hess, 44–69. New York: AltaMira.

Acker, Sandra. 1999. *The Realities of Teachers' Work: Never a Dull Moment*. London: Cassell.

Adams, Tracey L. 1998. "Combining Gender, Class, and Race: Structuring Relations in the Ontario Dental Profession." *Gender and Society*, 12: 578–97.

———. 2000. *A Dentist and a Gentleman: Gender and the Rise of Dentistry in Ontario*. Toronto: University of Toronto Press.

Adams, Robert M. 1966. *The Evolution of Urban Society*. Chicago: Aldine.

Adler, Patricia A., and Peter Adler. 1995. "Dynamics of Inclusion and Exclusion in Preadolescent Cliques." *Social Psychology Quarterly*, 58, no. 3: 145–62.

Agnew, Robert. 1985. "A Revised Strain Theory of Delinquency." *Social Forces*, 64, no. 1: 151–67.

Agnew, Robert, and Lisa Broidy. 1997. "Gender and Crime: A General Strain Theory Perspective." *Journal of Research in Crime and Delinquency*, 34: 275–306.

Ahlburg, Dennis A. 1998. "Julian Simon and the Population Growth Debate." *Population and Development Review*, 24: 317–27.

Akyeampong, Ernest B. 2001. "Fact Sheet on Unionization." *Perspectives on Labour and Income*, 13, no. 3: 46–54.

Albas, Dan, and Cheryl Albas. 1993. "Disclaimer Mannerisms of Students: How to Avoid Being Labelled as Cheaters." *Canadian Review of Sociology and Anthropology*, 30: 451–67.

———. 1995. "Avoiding the Label of Cheater During Exams." In *Sociology Everyday Life: A Reader*, 2nd edn, edited by Lorne Tepperman and James Curtis, 217–23. Toronto: McGraw-Hill.

———. 2003. "Aces and Bombers: The Post-exam Impression Management Strategies of Students." In *A Social World: Classic and Contemporary Sociological Readings*, 3rd edn, edited by Ramón S. Guerra and Robert Lee Maril, 27–36. Boston: Pearson Custom Publishing.

Albrecht, Stan L., and Armand L. Mauss. 1975. "The Environment as a Social Problem." In *Social Problems as Social Movements*, edited by Armand L. Mauss, 556–605. Philadelphia: Lippincott.

Albury, Rebecca M. 1999. *The Politics of Reproduction*. Sydney, Australia: Allen and Unwin.

Ali, Jennifer, and Edward Grabb. 1998. "Ethnic Origin, Class Origin and Educational Attainment in Canada: Further Evidence on the Mosaic Thesis." *Journal of Canadian Studies*, 33: 3–21.

Allahar, Anton L. 1995. *Sociology and the Periphery: Theories and Issues*, 2nd edn. Toronto: Garamond.

Allahar, Anton L., and James E. Côté. 1998. *Richer and Poorer: The Structure of Inequality in Canada*. Toronto: Lorimer.

Allcorn, Seth. 1997. "Parallel Virtual Organizations: Managing and Working in the Virtual Workplace." *Administration and Society*, 29: 412–39.

Allen, Judith. 1990. "Do We Need a Theory of the State?" In *Playing the State: Australian Feminist Interventions*, edited by Sophie Watson, 21–37. London: Verso.

Altheide, David. 1997. "The New Media, the Problem Frame and the Production of Fear." *Sociological Quarterly*, 38: 645–66.

Altman, Dennis. 1986. *AIDS in the Mind of America*. New York: Doubleday–Anchor.

Altman, Irwin, and Arza Churchman, eds. 1994. *Women and the Environment*. New York: Plenum.

Alvarez, Rodolfo. 2001. "The Social Problem as an Enterprise: Values as a Defining Factor." *Social Problems*, 48: 3–10.

Alwin, Duane F. 1984. "Trends in Parental Socialization, Detroit, 1958–1983." *American Journal of Sociology*, 90: 359–82.

———. 1990. "Historical Changes in Parental Orientations to Children." In *Sociological Studies of Child Development*, vol. 3, edited by Patricia Adler and Peter Adler, 65–86. Greenwich, CT: JAI Press.

Amato, P.R., and S.J. Rezac. 1994. "Contact with Non-resident Parents, Interparental Conflict, and Children's Behavior." *Journal of Family Issues*, 15: 191–207.

Andersen, Robert, and Anthony Heath. 2002. "Class Matters: The Persisting Effects of Contextual Social Class on Individual Voting in Britain, 1964–97." *European Sociological Review*, 18: 125–38.

Anderson, Benedict. 1983. *Imagined Communities: Reflections on the Origin and Spread of Nationalism*. London: Verso.

Anderson, Grace. 1974. *Networks of Contact: The Portuguese and Toronto*. Waterloo, ON: Wilfrid Laurier University Press.

Anderson, R.A., et al. 1999. "7a-Merhyl-19-Notestosterone (MENT) Maintains Sexual Behavior and More in Hypogonad Men." *Journal of Clinical Endocrinology and Metabolism*, 78: 711–16.

Andres Bellamy, Lesley. 1993. "Life Trajectories, Action, and Negotiating the Transition from High School." In *Transitions: Schooling and Employment in Canada*, edited by Paul Anisef and Paul Axelrod, 136–57. Toronto: Thompson Educational.

Andrews, David M. 1994. "Capital Mobility and State Autonomy: Toward a Structural Theory of International Monetary Relations." *International Studies Quarterly*, 38: 193–218.

Anisef, Paul, Paul Axelrod, Etta Baichman-Anisef, Carl James, and Anton Turritin. 2000. *Opportunity and Uncertainty: Life Course Experiences of the Class of '73*. Toronto: University of Toronto Press.

Anstey, Roger. 1966. *King Leopold's Legacy: The Congo Under Belgian Rule, 1908–1960*. London: Oxford University Press.

Antonovsky, Aaron. 1979. *Health, Stress and Coping*. San Francisco: Jossey-Bass.

Apple, Michael W. 1997. "What Postmodernists Forget: Cultural Capital and Official Knowledge." In *Education: Culture, Economy, and Society*, edited by A.H. Halsey, Hugh Lauder, Phillip Brown, and Amy Stuart Wells, 595–604. New York: Oxford University Press.

Appleton, Lynn M. 1995. "Rethinking Medicalization: Alcoholism and Anomalies." In *Images of Issues: Typifying Contemporary Social Problems*, 2nd edn, edited by Joel Best, 59–80. New York: Aldine de Gruyter.

Arai, A. Bruce. 2000. "Changing Motivations for Homeschooling in Canada." *Canadian Journal of Education*, 25, no. 3: 204–17.

Arat-Koc, Sedef. 1990. "Importing Housewives: Non-citizen Domestic Workers and the Crisis of the Domestic Sphere in Canada." In *Through the Kitchen Window: The Politics of Home and Family*, 2nd edn, edited by Meg Luxton, Harriet Rosenberg, and Sedef Arat-Koc, 81–103. Toronto: Garamond.

Archibald, W. Peter. 1976. "Face-to-Face: The Alienating Effects of Class, Status and Power Divisions." *American Sociological Review*, 41: 819–37.

———. 1978. *Social Psychology as Political Economy*. Toronto: McGraw-Hill Ryerson.

Arias, Ernesto, ed. 1993. *The Meaning and Use of Housing*. Aldershot, UK: Avebury.

Ariès, Philippe. 1980. "Two Successive Motivations for Declining Birth Rates in the West." *Population and Development Review*, 6: 645–50.

Armstrong, Pat. 1991. "Understanding the Numbers: Women in the Film and Television Industry." In *Toronto Women in Film and Television, Changing Focus: The Future for Women in the Canadian Film and Television Industry*, 3–38. Toronto: Toronto Women in Film and Television.

Armstrong, Pat, Carol Amaratunga, Jocelyne Bernier, Karen Grant, Ann Pederson, and Kay Willson, eds. 2001. *Exposing Privatization: Women and Health Reform in Canada*. Aurora, ON: Garamond.

Armstrong, Pat, and Hugh Armstrong. 1983a. "Beyond Sexless Class and Classless Sex." *Studies in Political Economy*, 10, Winter: 7–43.

———. 1983b. *A Working Majority: What Women Must Do for Pay*. Ottawa: Canadian Advisory Council on the Status of Women.

———. 1993. *The Double Ghetto: Canadian Women and Their Segregated Work*. Toronto: McClelland & Stewart.

Aronson, Hal. 1993. "Becoming an Environmental Activist: The Process of Transformation from Everyday Life into Making History in the Hazardous Waste Movement." *Journal of Political and Military Sociology*, 1: 63–80.

Arthurs, Harry. 1999. "Constitutionalizing Neo-conservatism and Regional Economic Integration." In *Room to Manoeuvre? Globalization and Policy Convergence*, edited by Thomas J. Courchene, 17–74. Montreal: McGill-Queen's University Press.

Atkinson, Anthony B. 2000. *Increased Income Inequality in OECD Countries and the Redistributive Impact of the Government Budget*. Helsinki: World Institute for Development Economics Research, United Nations University.

Atkinson, Michael M., and William D. Coleman. 1989. *The State, Business, and Industrial Change in Canada*. Toronto: University of Toronto Press.

Atwood, Margaret. [1968] 1994. *The Edible Woman*. Toronto: McClelland & Stewart.

Axelrod, Paul. 1997. *The Promise of Schooling: Education in Canada, 1800–1914*. Toronto: University of Toronto Press.

Aya, Rod. 1990. *Rethinking Revolutions and Collective Violence: Studies on Concept, Theory, and Method*. Amsterdam: Het Spinhuis.

Babbie, Earl R. 1988. *The Sociological Spirit: Critical Essays in a Critical Science*. Belmont, CA: Wadsworth.

Badets, Jane, and Tina W.L. Chui. 1994. *Canada's Changing Immigrant Population*. Ottawa: Statistics Canada.

Baer, Doug. 1999. "Educational Credentials and the Changing Occupational Structure." In *Social Inequality in Canada: Patterns, Problems, and Policies*, edited by James E. Curtis, Edward G. Grabb, and Neil L. Guppy, 92–106. Scarborough, ON: Prentice-Hall Allyn and Bacon.

Bafoil, François. 1998. "Weber critique de Marx: Elements d'une interpretation de la crise des systèmes bureaucratiques communistes." *L'Année sociologique*, 48: 385–415.

Bailey, Conner, Peter R. Sinclair, and Mark Dubois. Forthcoming. "Genetic Engineering of Trees: Forecasting Social Consequences." *Society and Natural Resources*.

Baines, Carol T., Patricia M. Evans, and Sheila Neysmith, eds. 1998. *Women's Caring: Feminist Perspectives on Social Welfare*, 2nd edn. Toronto: Oxford University Press.

Baird, P. 1997. "Individual Interests, Societal Interests, and Reproductive Technologies." *Perspectives in Biology and Medicine*, 40: 440–52.

Bakan, Abigail, and Daiva K. Stasiulis. 1994. "Foreign Domestic Worker Policy in Canada and the Social

Boundaries of Modern Citizenship." *Science and Society*, 58, no. 1: 7–33.

———. 1997. *Not One of the Family: Foreign Domestic Workers in Canada*. Toronto: University of Toronto Press.

Baker, Maureen. 1995. *Canadian Family Policies: Cross-national Comparisons*. Toronto: University of Toronto Press.

———. 2001a. *Families, Labour and Love: Family Diversity in a Changing World*. Vancouver: University of British Columbia Press.

———. 2001b. "Paid and Unpaid Work: How Do Families Divide Their Labour?" In *Families: Changing Trends in Canada*, 4th edn, edited by Maureen Baker, 96–115. Toronto: McGraw-Hill Ryerson.

Baker, Maureen, and David Tippin. 1999. *Poverty, Social Assistance and the Employability of Mothers: Restructuring Welfare States*. Toronto: University of Toronto Press.

Bales, Robert F. 1950. *Interaction Process Analysis: A Method for the Study of Small Groups*. Chicago: University of Chicago Press.

Balter, Michael. 2001. "What—or Who—Did in the Neanderthals?" *Science*, 293: 1980–1.

Bancroft, John. 2002. "Biological Factors in Human Sexuality." *Journal of Sex Research*, 39: 15–21.

Bandura, Albert. 1973. *Aggression: A Social Learning Analysis*. Englewood Cliffs, NJ: Prentice-Hall.

Barnes, Barry. 1988. *The Nature of Power*. Cambridge, UK: Polity.

Barry, Brian. [1970] 1978. *Sociologists, Economists and Democracy*. Chicago: University of Chicago Press.

Barth, Fredrik, ed. 1969. *Ethnic Groups and Boundaries: The Social Organization of Culture Difference*. Boston: Little, Brown.

Bartsch, Robert, Theresa Burnett, Tommye Diller, and Elizabeth Rankin-Williams. 2000. "Gender Representation in Television Commercials: Updating an Update." *Sex Roles*, 43: 735–43.

Bashevkin, Sylvia. 1985. *Toeing the Lines: Women and Party Politics in English Canada*. Toronto: University of Toronto Press.

Bassett, Isabella. 1985. *The Bassett Report*. Toronto: Collins.

Baumrind, Diana. 1971. "Current Patterns of Parental Authority." *Developmental Psychology Monographs*, 4: 1–107.

Baxter, Janine. 2000. "The Joys and Justice of Housework." *Sociology*, 34: 609–31.

Beaujot, Roderic. 2000. *Earning and Caring in Canadian Families*. Peterborough, ON: Broadview.

Beaujot, Roderic, Ellen M. Gee, R. Fernando, and Z.R. Ravanera. 1995. *Family over the Life Course: Current Demographic Analysis*. Ottawa: Statistics Canada, Demography Division.

Beaujot, Roderic, and Kevin McQuillan. 1982. *Growth and Dualism: The Demographic Development of Canadian Society*. Toronto: Gage.

Beauvoir, Simone de. [1949] 1957. *The Second Sex*. Translated by H.M. Parshley. New York: Vintage.

Beck, Ulrich. 1992. *Risk Society: Towards a New Modernity*. Translated by Mark Ritter. London: Sage.

———. 1996. "World Risk Society as Cosmopolitan Society? Ecological Questions in a Framework of Manufactured Uncertainties." *Theory, Culture, and Society*, 13, no. 4: 1–32.

Becker, Gary. 1960. "An Economic Analysis of Fertility." In *Demographic and Economic Change in Developed Countries: A Conference of the Universities–National Bureau Committee for Economic Research*, 209–40. Princeton, NJ: Princeton University Press.

Becker, Howard. 1952. "Social Class Variations in the Teacher–Student Relationship." *Journal of Educational Sociology*, 25: 451–65.

———. 1963. *Outsiders: Studies in the Sociology of Deviance*. New York: Free Press.

———. 1982. *Art Worlds*. Berkeley: University of California Press.

Beck-Gernsheim, Elisabeth. 2002. *Reinventing the Family: In Search of New Lifestyles*. Cambridge, MA: Polity.

Beiser, Morton, Feng Hou, Ilian Hyman, and Michel Tousignant. 1999. "Immigrant Mental Health." Human Resources Development Canada, *Applied Research Bulletin*, Fall: 20–2.

Bélanger, Alain. 2002. *Report on the Demographic Situation in Canada 2001: Current Demographic Analysis*. Ottawa: Statistics Canada.

Belknap, Joanne. 1996. *The Invisible Woman: Gender, Crime and Justice*. Belmont, CA: Wadsworth.

Bell, Daniel. 1973. *The Coming of Post-industrial Society*. New York: Basic Books.

———. 1975. "Ethnicity and Social Change." In *Ethnicity: Theory and Experience*, edited by Nathan Glazer and Daniel P. Moynihan with Corinne Saposs Schelling, 141–74. Cambridge, MA: Harvard University Press.

———. 1979. *The Cultural Contradictions of Capitalism*. 2nd edn. London: Heinemann.

Bellah, Robert. 1996. *Habits of the Heart: Individualism and Commitment in American Life*. Berkeley: University of California Press.

Belsky, Jay. 1985. "Exploring Individual Differences in Marital Change Across the Transition to Parenthood: The Role of Violated Expectations." *Journal of Marriage and the Family*, 47: 1037–44.

Bendix, Reinhard. 1956. *Work and Authority in Industry*. New York: Harper and Row.

Benford, Robert D., and David A. Snow. 2000. "Framing Processes and Social Movements: An Overview and Assessment." *Annual Review of Sociology*, 26: 611–39.

Bensman, Joseph. 1987. "Mediterranean and Total Bureau–cracies: Some Additions to the Weberian Theory of Bureaucracy." *International Journal of Politics, Culture and Society*, 1, no. 1: 62–78.

Benton, Ted. 1994. "Biology and Social Theory in the Environmental Debate." In *Social Theory and the Global Environment*, edited by Michael Redclift and Ted Benton, 28–50. London: Routledge.

Berger, Carl. 1966. "The True North Strong and Free." In *Nationalism in Canada*, edited by Peter Russell, 3–26. Toronto: McGraw-Hill Ryerson.

Berger, Peter L. 1967. *The Sacred Canopy: Elements of a Sociological Theory of Religion.* Garden City, NY: Doubleday.

———, ed. 1999. *The Desecularization of the World: Resurgent Religion and World Politics.* Grand Rapids, MI: Eerdmans.

Berger, Peter, and Brigitte Berger. 1975. *Sociology: A Biographical Approach.* 2nd edn. New York: Basic Books.

Berger, Peter, and Thomas Luckmann. 1966. *The Social Construction of Reality: Treatise in the Sociology of Knowledge.* Garden City, NY: Anchor.

Bernard, Andrew B., and J. Bradford Jensen. 2000. "Understanding Increasing *and* Decreasing Wage Inequality." In *The Impact of International Trade on Wages,* edited by Robert C. Feenstra, 227–61. Chicago: University of Chicago Press.

Bernstein, Basil. 1977. "Class and Pedagogies: Visible and Invisible." In *Power and Ideology in Education,* edited by Jerome Karabel and A.H. Halsey, 511–34. New York: Oxford University Press.

Bernstein, Steven, and Christopher Gore. 2001. "Policy Implications of the Kyoto Protocol for Canada." *ISUMA Canadian Journal of Policy Research,* 2, no. 4: 26–36.

Berry, John W., Rudolf Kalin, and Donald M. Taylor. 1977. *Multiculturalism and Ethnic Attitudes in Canada.* Ottawa: Minister of Supply and Services.

Berton, Pierre. 1975. *Hollywood's Canada: The Americanization of Our National Image.* Toronto: McClelland & Stewart.

Berwick, Donald. 2002. "We All Have AIDS: Case for Reducing the Cost of HIV Drugs to Zero." *British Medical Journal,* 324: 214–8.

Best, Joel. 1989. "Extending the Constructionist Perspective: A Conclusion—and an Introduction." In *Images of Issues: Typifying Contemporary Social Problems,* edited by Joel Best, 243–53. New York: Aldine de Gruyter.

———. 1993. "But Seriously Folks: The Limitations of the Strict Constructionist Interpretation of Social Problems." In *Reconsidering Social Constructionism: Debates in Social Problems Theory,* edited by James A. Holstein and Gale Miller, 129–47. New York: Aldine de Gruyter.

———. 1999. *Random Violence: How We Talk About New Crime and New Victims.* Berkeley: University of California Press.

———. 2001. *Damned Lies and Statistics: Untangling Numbers from Media, Politicians and Activists.* Berkeley: University of California Press.

Beyer, Peter. 1997. "Religious Vitality in Canada: The Complementarity of Religious Market and Secularization Perspectives." *Journal for the Scientific Study of Religion,* 36: 272–88.

———. 2000. "Modern Forms of the Religious Life: Denomination, Church and Invisible Religion in Canada, the United States, and Europe." In *Rethinking Church, State, and Modernity: Canada Between Europe and America,* edited by David Lyon and Marguerite Van Die, 189–210. Toronto: University of Toronto Press.

Bibby, Reginald. 1987. *Fragmented Gods: The Poverty and Potential of Religion in Canada.* Toronto: Irwin.

———. 1993. *Unknown Gods: The Ongoing Story of Religion in Canada.* Toronto: Stoddart.

———. 2001. *Canada's Teens: Today, Yesterday and Tomorrow.* Toronto: Stoddart.

———. 2002. *Restless Gods: The Renaissance of Religion in Canada.* Toronto: Stoddart.

Bielby, William, and James Baron. 1984. "Men and Women at Work: Sex Segregation and Statistical Discrimination." *American Journal of Sociology,* 91: 759–99.

Bies, Robert J., and Thomas M. Tripp. 1996. "Beyond Distrust: 'Getting Even' and the Need for Revenge." In *Trust in Organizations: Frontiers of Theory and Research,* edited by Roderick M. Kramer and Tom R. Tyler, 246–60. Thousand Oaks, CA: Sage.

Bingham, Richard D., Roy E. Green, and Sammis B. White, eds. 1987. *The Homeless in Contemporary Society.* Beverly Hills, CA: Sage.

Bird, Roger, ed. 1988. *Documents of Canadian Broadcasting.* Ottawa: Carleton University Press.

Birg, Herwig. 1995. *World Population Projections for the 21st Century: Theoretical Interpretations and Quantitative Simulations.* Frankfurt: Campus Verlag; New York: St Martin's.

Birke, Lynda. 1999. *Biology, Bodies and Feminism.* Edinburgh: Edinburgh University Press.

Birnbaum, Pierre. 1988. *States and Collective Action: The European Experience.* Cambridge: Cambridge University Press.

Bittman, Michael, and Jocelyn Pixley. 1997. *The Double Life of the Family: Myth, Hope and Experience.* Sydney, Australia: Allen & Unwin.

Blackledge, David, and Barry Hunt. 1985. *Sociological Interpretations of Education.* London: Routledge.

Blackwell, Judith C. 1992. "Mental Illness." In *Deviance: Conformity and Control in Canadian Society,* edited by Vincent F. Sacco, 172–202. Scarborough, ON: Prentice-Hall.

Blau, Peter M. 1963. *The Dynamics of Bureaucracy.* Chicago: University of Chicago Press.

Bliss, Michael. 1991. *Plague: A Story of Smallpox in Montreal.* Toronto: HarperCollins.

———. 1992. *Banting: A Biography.* 2nd edn. Toronto: University of Toronto Press.

Block, Fred. 1980. "Beyond Relative Autonomy: State Managers as Historical Subjects." In *The Socialist Register, 1980,* edited by Ralph Miliband and John Saville, 227–40. London: Merlin.

Bloemraad, Irene. 2002. "The North American Naturalization Gap: An Institutional Approach to Citizenship Acquisition in the United States and Canada." *International Migration Review,* 36: 193–228.

Blumer, Herbert. 1937. "Social Psychology." In *Man and Society: A Substantive Introduction to the Social Sciences,* edited by E.P. Schmidt, 148–98. New York: Prentice-Hall.

———. 1969. *Symbolic Interactionism: Perspective and Method.* Englewood Cliffs, NJ: Prentice-Hall.

———. 1971. "Social Problems as Collective Behavior." *Social Problems,* 8: 298–396.

Blustain, Sarah. 2000. "The New Gender Wars." *Psychology Today*, Nov./Dec.: 43–8.

Bohm, Robert M. 1997. *A Primer on Crime and Delinquency*. Belmont, CA: Wadsworth.

Bonacich, Edna. 1972. "A Theory of Ethnic Antagonism: The Split Labor Market." *American Sociological Review*, 37: 547–59.

Bongaarts, John. 1978. "A Framework for Analyzing the Proximate Determinants of Fertility." *Population and Development Review*, 4, no. 1: 105–32.

Bongaarts, John, and Rodolfo Bulatao, eds. 2000. *Beyond Six Billion: Forecasting the World's Population*. Washington, DC: National Academy Press.

Bookchin, Murray. 1989. *Remaking Society*. Montreal: Black Rose.

Booth, Alan, and John N. Edwards. 1990. "Transmission of Marital and Family Quality over the Generations: The Effect of Parental Divorce and Unhappiness." *Journal of Divorce*, 13: 41–58.

Boritch, Helen. 1997. *Fallen Women: Women, Crime and Criminal Justice in Canada*. Toronto: Nelson.

Borjas, George J., Richard B. Freeman, and Lawrence F. Katz. 1997. "How Much Do Immigration and Trade Affect Labor Market Outcomes?" *Brookings Papers on Economic Activity*, 1: 1–67.

Boserup, Ester. 1965. *The Conditions of Agricultural Growth: The Economics of Agrarian Change Under Population Pressure*. Chicago: Aldine.

———. 1981. *Population and Technological Change: A Study of Long-Term Trends*. Chicago: University of Chicago Press.

Boston Women's Health Collective. 1971. *Our Bodies, Our Selves*. Toronto: New Hogtown Press.

Bottomore, Tom. 1979. *Political Sociology*. London: Hutchinson University Press.

Bouchard, Brigitte, and John Zhao. 2000. "University Education: Recent Trends in Participation, Accessibility and Returns." *Education Quarterly Review*, 6, no. 4: 24–32.

Bourdieu, Pierre. [1979] 1984. *Distinction: A Social Critique of the Judgement of Taste*. Translated by Richard Nice. London: Routledge.

———. 1997a. "The Forms of Capital." Translated by Richard Nice. In *Education: Culture, Economy, and Society*, edited by A.H. Halsey, Hugh Lauder, Phillip Brown, and Amy Stuart Wells, 46–58. Oxford: Oxford University Press.

———. 1997b. "From the Royal House to the State's Logic: A Model of the Genesis of the Bureaucratic Field / De la maison du roi a la raison d'état: un modèle de la genese du champ bureaucratique." *Actes de la recherché en sciences sociales*, 118, June: 55–68.

Bourdieu, Pierre, and Jean-Claude Passeron. 1979. *The Inheritors: French Students and Their Relations to Culture*. Translated by Richard Nice. Chicago: University of Chicago Press.

Bourne, Paul, Liza McCoy, and Myra Novogrodsky, eds. 1997. "Gender and Schooling." *Orbit*, 28, no. 1: special issue.

Bowlby, Jeffrey, and Kathryn McMullen. 2002. *At a Cross-roads: First Results for the 18- to 20-Year-Old Cohort of the Youth in Transition Survey*. Ottawa: Human Resources Development Canada.

Bowles, Samuel, and Herbert Gintis. 1976. *Schooling in Capitalist America: Education Reform and the Contradictions of Economic Life*. New York: Basic Books.

Boyd, Monica. 1992. "Gender, Visible Minority, and Immigrant Earnings Inequality: Reassessing an Employment Equity Premise." In *Deconstructing a Nation: Immigration, Multiculturalism, and Racism in '90s Canada*, edited by Vic Satzewich, 279–321. Halifax, NS: Fernwood.

———. 1999. "Integrating Gender, Language and Visible Minority Groups." In *Immigrant Canada: Demographic, Economic and Social Challenges*, edited by Shiva S. Halli and Leo Driedger, 282–306. Toronto: University of Toronto Press.

Boyd, Susan B., ed. 1997. *Challenging the Public/Private Divide: Feminism, Law and Public Policy*. Toronto: University of Toronto Press.

Bozeman, Barry, and Hal G. Rainey. 1998. "Organizational Rules and the 'Bureaucratic Personality'." *American Journal of Political Science*, 42: 163–89.

Bradbury, Bettina. 1990. "The Fragmented Family: Family Strategies in the Face of Death, Illness, and Poverty, Montreal, 1860–1885." In *Childhood and Family in Canadian History*, edited by Joy Parr, 109–28. Toronto: McClelland & Stewart.

———. 1993. *Working Families: Age, Gender, and Daily Survival in Industrializing Montreal*. Toronto: McClelland & Stewart.

———. 2001. "Social, Economic, and Cultural Origins of Contemporary Families." In *Families: Changing Trends in Canada*, 4th edn, edited by Maureen Baker, 69–95. Toronto: McGraw-Hill Ryerson.

Braithewaite, John. 1979. *Inequality, Crime and Public Policy*. London: Routledge and Kegan Paul.

Braverman, Harry. 1974. *Labor and Monopoly Capital: The Degradation of Work in the Twentieth Century*. New York: Monthly Review Press.

Breton, Raymond. 1964. "Institutional Completeness of Ethnic Communities and the Personal Relations of Immigrants." *American Journal of Sociology*, 70: 193–205.

———. 1978. "Stratification and Conflict Between Ethnolinguistic Communities with Different Social Structures." *Canadian Review of Sociology and Anthropology*, 15: 148–57.

———. 1983. "West Indian, Chinese and European Ethnic Groups in Toronto: Perceptions of Problems and Resources." In *Two Nations, Many Cultures: Ethnic Groups in Canada*, edited by Jean Leonard Elliott, 425–43. Scarborough, ON: Prentice-Hall.

———. 1984. "The Production and Allocation of Symbolic Resources: An Analysis of the Linguistic and Ethnocultural Fields in Canada." *Canadian Review of Sociology and Anthropology*, 21: 123–44.

———. 1989. "The Vesting of Ethnic Interests in State Institutions." In *Multiculturalism and Intergroup Relations*, edited by James S. Frideres, 35–55. New York: Greenwood.

———. 1990. "The Ethnic Group as a Political Resource in Relation to Problems of Incorporation: Perceptions and Attitudes." In Raymond Breton, Wsevolod W. Isajiw, Warren E. Kalbach, and Jeffrey G. Reitz, *Ethnic Identity and Equality: Varieties of Experience in a Canadian City*, 196–255. Toronto: University of Toronto Press.

Breton, Raymond, Jean Burnet, Norbert Hartmann, Wsevolod Isajiw, and Jos Lennards. 1977. "The Impact of Ethnic Groups on Canadian Society: Research Issues." In *Identities: The Impact of Ethnicity on Canadian Society*, edited by Wsevolod Isajiw, 191–213. Toronto: Peter Martin.

Breton, Raymond, Wsevolod Isajiw, Warren Kalbach, and Jeffrey G. Reitz. 1990. *Ethnic Identity and Equality: Varieties of Experience in a Canadian City*. Toronto: University of Toronto Press.

Briskin, Linda. 1992. "Socialist Feminism: From the Standpoint of Practice." In *Feminism in Action: Studies in Political Economy*, edited by M. Patricia Connelly and Pat Armstrong, 267–93. Toronto: Canadian Scholars' Press.

Brock, Deborah R. 1998. *Making Work, Making Trouble: Prostitution as a Social Problem*. Toronto: University of Toronto Press.

Brodie, Janine. 1985. *Women and Politics in Canada*. Toronto: McGraw-Hill Ryerson.

———, ed. 1996. *Women and Canadian Public Policy*. Toronto: Harcourt Brace.

Bromley, David G., and Anson D. Shupe, Jr. 1981. *Strange Gods: The Great American Cult Scare*. Boston: Beacon.

Bromley, Simon. 1999. "Marxism and Globalization." In *Marxism and Social Science*, edited by Andrew Gamble, David Marsh, and Tony Tant, 280–301. Urbana: University of Illinois Press.

Brook, Barbara. 1999. *Feminist Perspectives on the Body*. London: Longman.

Brower, Ralph S., and Mitchel Y. Abolafia. 1997. "Bureaucratic Politics: The View from Below." *Journal of Public Administration Research and Theory*, 7: 305–31.

Brown, Craig, ed. 2002. *The Illustrated History of Canada*. Toronto: Key Porter.

Brown, Louise. 2002. "Two-Tier Grade Schooling Feared." *Toronto Star*, 31 May, A1, A26.

Brown, Phil, and Susan Masterson-Allen. 1994. "The Toxic Waste Movement: A New Type of Activism." *Society and Natural Resources*, 7: 269–87.

Bruce, Steve. 1996. *Religion in the Modern World*. Oxford: Oxford University Press.

———. 2001. "The Curious Case of the Unnecessary Recantation: Berger and Secularization." In *Peter Berger and the Study of Religion*, edited by Linda Woodhead, 87–100. London: Routledge.

Brumann, Christoph. 1998. "The Anthropological Study of Globalization: Towards an Agenda for the Second Phase." *Anthropos*, 93: 495–506.

Bryant, Bunyon, and Paul Mohai, eds. 1992. *Race and the Incidence of Environmental Hazard: A Time for Discourse*. Boulder, CO: Westview.

Bryant, Heather. 1990. *The Infertility Dilemma: Reproductive Technologies and Prevention*. Ottawa: Canadian Advisory Council on the Status of Women.

Brym, Robert J. 1980. "Regional Social Structure and Agrarian Radicalism in Canada: Alberta, Saskatchewan and New Brunswick." In *People, Power and Process: A Reader*, edited by Alexander Himelfarb and C. James Richardson, 344–53. Toronto: McGraw-Hill Ryerson.

Bulatao, Rodolfo. 1998. *The Value of Family Planning Programs in Developing Countries*. Santa Monica, CA: Rand.

Bulatao, Rodolfo, and John Casterline, eds. 2001. "Global Fertility Transition." *Population and Development Review*, 27 (suppl.).

Bullard, Robert. 1990. *Dumping in Dixie: Race, Class and Environmental Quality*. Boulder, CO: Westview.

Bullock, Cathy Ferrand, and Jason Culbert. 2002. "Coverage of Domestic Violence Fatalities by Newspapers in Washington State." *Journal of Interpersonal Violence*, 17: 475–99.

Burgess, Ernest. 1925. "The Growth of the City: An Introduction to a Research Project." In *The City*, edited by Robert E. Park, Ernest Burgess, and R. McKenzie, 47–62. Chicago: University of Chicago Press.

Burningham, Kate, and Geoff Cooper. 1999. "Being Constructive: Social Constructionism and the Environment." *Sociology*, 33: 297–316.

Burstyn, Varda. 1983. "Masculine Domination and the State." In *The Socialist Register, 1983*, edited by Ralph Miliband and John Saville, 45–89. London: Merlin.

———. 1999. *The Rites of Men: Manhood, Politics and the Culture of Sport*. Toronto: University of Toronto Press.

Burt, Ronald S., and Marc Knez. 1996. "Trust and Third-Party Gossip." In *Trust in Organizations: Frontiers of Theory and Research*, edited by Roderick M. Kramer and Tom R. Tyler, 68–89. Thousand Oaks, CA: Sage.

Burtless, Gary. 1998. *Globaphobia: Confronting Fears About Open Trade*. Washington, DC: Brookings Institution.

Bush, Diane Mitsch, and Roberta G. Simmons. 1981. "Socialization Processes over the Life Course." In *Social Psychology: Sociological Perspectives*, edited by Morris Rosenberg and Ralph Turner, 133–64. New York: Basic Books.

Bussière, Patrick, Fernando Cartwright, Robert Crocker, Xin Ma, Jillian Oderkirk, and Yanhong Zhang. 2001. *Measuring Up: The Performance of Canada's Youth in Reading, Mathematics and Science*. Ottawa: Statistics Canada.

Bustamente, Jorge A. 2002. "Immigrants' Vulnerability as Subjects of Human Rights." *International Migration Review*, 36: 333–54.

Butler, Judith. 1992. "Contingent Foundations: Feminism and the Question of 'Postmodernism'." In *Feminists Theorize the Political*, edited by Judith Butler and Joan W. Scott, 3–21. New York: Routledge.

Butlin, George, and Jillian Oderkirk. 1996. *Educational Attainment: A Key to Autonomy and Authority in the Workplace*. Ottawa: Statistics Canada.

Buttel, Frederick. 1976. "Social Science and the Environment: Competing Theories." *Social Science Quarterly*, 57: 307–23.

Buttel, Frederick, and Peter J. Taylor. 1992. "Environmental Sociology and Global Environmental Change: A Critical Assessment." *Society and Natural Resources*, 5: 211–30.

Butters, Jennifer, and Patricia Erickson. 2002. "Addictions as Deviant Behaviour: Normalizing the Pleasures of Intoxication." In *New Perspectives on Deviance: The Construction of Deviance in Everyday Life*, edited by Lori G. Beaman, 67–84. Toronto: Prentice-Hall Allyn and Bacon.

Butz, William P., and Michael P. Ward. 1979. "The Emergence of Countercyclical US Fertility." *American Economic Review*, 69: 318–28.

Cain, Mead. 1983. "Fertility as an Adjustment to Risk." *Population and Development Review*, 9: 688–702.

Cairney, John. 1999. "Socio-economic Status and Self-Rated Health Among Older Canadians." *Canadian Journal on Aging*, 19: 456–77.

Caldwell, John C. 1976. "Toward a Restatement of Demographic Transition Theory." *Population and Development Review*, 2: 321–66.

Caldwell, John C., and Pat Caldwell. 1996. "The African AIDS Epidemic." *Scientific American*, March: 62–8.

Caldwell, John, James F. Phillips, and Barkat-e-Khuda, eds. 2002. "Family Planning Programs in the Twenty-First Century." *Studies in Family Planning*, 33, no. 1: special issue.

Calliste, Agnes. 1993. "Sleeping Car Porters in Canada: An Ethnically Submerged Split Labour Market." In *Work in Canada: Readings in the Sociology of Work and Industry*, edited by Graham S. Lowe and Harvey Krahn, 139–53. Scarborough, ON: Nelson.

Calvert, Barbara, and Warren R. Stanton. 1992. "Perceptions of Parenthood: Similarities and Differences Between 15-Year-Old Girls and Boys." *Adolescence*, 27: 315–28.

Campbell, Donald T., and Julian C. Stanley. 1970. *Experimental and Quasi-experimental designs for Research.* Chicago: Rand McNally.

Campbell, Todd. 1998. "The First E-mail Message: Who Sent It and What It Said." *PreText*, March. Available at <www.pretext.com/mar98/features/story2.htm>, accessed 25 June 2003.

Campey, John. 2002. "Immigrant Children in Our Classrooms: Beyond ESL." *Education Canada*, 42, no. 3 (Summer): 44–7.

Canada. House of Commons. Standing Committee on Heritage. 2003. *Our Cultural Sovereignty: The Second Century of Canadian Broadcasting.* Ottawa: Speaker of the House of Commons.

Canada. Royal Commission on Bilingualism and Biculturalism. 1967. *Report of the Royal Commission on Bilingualism and Biculturalism.* Ottawa: Queen's Printer.

Canadian Health Services Research Foundation. 2001. "Myth: The Aging Population Will Overwhelm the Healthcare System." Ottawa: Canadian Health Services Research Foundation.

———. 2002. "Myth: For-Profit Ownership of Facilities Would Lead to Better Health Care." Ottawa: Canadian Health Services Research Foundation.

Canadian Institute of Child Health. 1994. *The Health of Canada's Children: A CICH Profile.* Ottawa: Canadian Institute on Child Health.

Card, David E., and John DiNardo. 2002. *Skill Biased Technological Change and Rising Wage Inequality: Some Problems and Puzzles.* Cambridge, MA: National Bureau of Economic Research.

Carley, Kathleen. 1989. "The Value of Cognitive Foundations for Dynamic Social Theory." *Journal of Mathematical Sociology*, 14, nos 2–3: 171–208.

———. 1991. "A Theory of Group Stability." *American Sociological Review*, 56: 331–54.

Carlstein, Tommy. 1978. "A Time-Geographic Approach to Time Allocation and Socio-ecological Systems." In *Public Policy in Temporal Perspective*, edited by William Michelson, 69–82. The Hague: Mouton.

Carre, Dominique, and Sylvie Craipeau. 1996. "Entre delocalisation et mobilité: analyse des strategies entrepreneuriales de teletravail." *Technologies de l'information et société*, 8: 333–54.

Carroll, Jim, and Rick Broadhead. 1994. *The Canadian Internet Handbook.* Scarborough, ON: Prentice Hall.

Carroll, William K. 1987. "Which Women Are More Proletarianized Than Men?" *Canadian Review of Sociology and Anthropology*, 24: 465–95.

Carroll, William K., and Robert S. Ratner. 1996. "Master Framing and Cross-movement Networking in Contemporary Social Movements." *Sociological Quarterly*, 37: 601–25.

Carson, Rachel. 1962. *Silent Spring.* Boston: Houghton Mifflin.

Cassidy, Barbara, Robina Lord, and Nancy Mandell. 2001. "Silenced and Forgotten Women: Race, Poverty and Disability." In *Feminist Issues: Race, Class and Sexuality*, 3rd edn, edited by Nancy Mandell, 75–107. Toronto: Prentice-Hall.

Castellano, Marlene Brant, Lynne Davis, and Louise Lahache. 2000. "Conclusion: Fulfilling the Promise." In *Aboriginal Education: Fulfilling the Promise*, edited by Marlene Brant Castellano, Lynne Davis, and Louise Lahache, 251–5. Vancouver: University of British Columbia Press.

Castells, Manuel. 1989. *The Informational City: Information Technology, Economic Restructuring, and the Urban-Regional Process.* Cambridge, MA: MIT Press.

Catton, William, Jr. 1980. *Overshoot: The Ecological Basis of Revolutionary Change.* Urbana: University of Illinois Press.

Catton, William, Jr, and Riley Dunlap. 1978. "Environmental Sociology: A New Paradigm." *American Sociologist*, 13: 41–9.

———. 1980. "A New Ecological Paradigm for Post-exuberant Sociology." *American Behavioral Scientist*, 24: 15–47.

Caulfield, Jon. 1994. *City Form and Everyday Life: Toronto's Gentrification and Critical Social Practice.* Toronto: University of Toronto Press.

CBC News. 2002. "Alberta Oil Industry Predicts Losses After Kyoto." 22 February. Available at <http://cbc.ca/stories/2002/02/22/kyoto_alberta020222>, accessed 11 June 2003.

Centre for Research and Information on Canada. 2001. "Quebec Sovereignty: An Outdated Idea." [Press release]. Ottawa: Centre for Research and Information on Canada.

Chalmers, A.F. 1999. *What Is This Thing Called Science? An Assessment of the Nature and Status of Science and Its Methods.* 3rd edn. Indianapolis, IN: Hackett.

Chappell, Neena L., and Nina L. Colwill. 1981. "Medical Schools as Agents of Professional Socialization." *Canadian Review of Sociology and Anthropology*, 18, no. 1: 67–79.

Chasteen, Amy L. 2001. "Constructing Rape: Feminism, Change, and Women's Everyday Understandings of Sexual Assault." *Sociological Spectrum*, 21: 101–39.

Chawla, Louise. 2002. *Growing Up in an Urbanising World.* London: Earthscan.

Chayes, Abram, and Antonia Chayes. 1995. *The New Sovereignty: Compliance with International Regulatory Agreements.* Cambridge, MA: Harvard University Press.

Chesney-Lind, Medea. 1997. *The Female Offender: Girls, Women and Crime.* Thousand Oaks, CA: Sage.

Chippendale, Nigel. 2002. *Access to Post-secondary Education in Canada: Facts and Gaps: Conference Report.* Ottawa: Canadian Policy Research Networks for the Canadian Millennium Scholarship Foundation. Available at <www.cprn.ca/en/doc.cfm?doc=59>, accessed 19 June 2003.

Chodorow, Nancy. 1978. *The Reproduction of Mothering.* Berkeley: University of California Press.

———. 1989. *Feminism and Psychoanalytic Theory.* New Haven: Yale University Press.

Christiano, Kevin J., William H. Swatos, Jr, and Peter Kivisto. 2002. *Sociology of Religion: Contemporary Developments.* Walnut Creek, CA: AltaMira.

Chubb, John E., and Terry M. Moe. 1990. *Politics, Markets, and America's Schools.* Washington, DC: Brookings Institution.

Cilluffo, Frank J. 2001. "Terrorism and the Canada–US Border." *ISUMA Canadian Journal of Policy Research*, 2, no. 4: 104–10.

Cincotta, Richard P., and Roberta Engelman. 1997. *Economics and Rapid Change: The Influence of Population Growth.* Washington: Population Action International.

Citizenship and Immigration Canada. 1998. *The Economic Performance of Immigrants: Immigration Category Perspective.* Available at <www.cic.gc.ca/english/srr/research/res3aiii.html>, accessed 26 July 2003.

———. 1999. *The Economic Performance of Immigrants: Education Perspective.* Available at <www.cic.gc.ca/english/srr/research/res3aii.html>, accessed 26 July 2003.

———. 2001. *Canada's Recent Immigrants: A Comparative Portrait Based on the 1996 Census.* Available at <www.cic.gc.ca/english/srr/research/res3ci.html>, accessed 26 July 2003.

Clark, S.D. 1966. *The Suburban Society.* Toronto: University of Toronto Press.

———. 1995. *State and Status: The Rise of the State and Aristocratic Power in Western Europe.* Montreal: McGill-Queen's University Press.

Clark, Susan, and Andrew S. Harvey. 1976. "The Sexual Division of Labour: The Use of Time." *Atlantis*, 2, no. 1: 46–65.

Clark, Terry, and Seymour Martin Lipset. 1991. "Are Social Classes Dying?" *International Sociology*, 6: 397–410.

Clark, Warren. 2000. "Education." *Canadian Social Trends*, Winter: 3–7.

Clarke, Harold D., Jane Jensen, Lawrence Leduc, and Jon H. Pammett. 1991. *Absent Mandate: The Politics of Discontent in Canada.* 2nd edn. Toronto: Gage.

Clarke, John I. 1996. "The Impact of Population Change on Environment: An Overview." In *Resources and Population: Natural, Institutional, and Demographic Dimensions of Development*, edited by Bernardo Colombo, Paul Demeny, and Max F. Perutz, 244–68. Oxford, UK: Clarendon.

Clarke, Juanne N. 2000. *Health, Illness, and Medicine in Canada.* Toronto: Oxford University Press.

Cleland, John. 1996. "Population Growth in the 21st Century: Cause for Crisis or Celebration?" *Tropical Medicine and International Health*, 1, no. 1: 15–26.

Clement, Wallace. 1975. *The Canadian Corporate Elite.* Toronto: McClelland and Stewart.

———. 1988. "The Labour Process." In *Understanding Canadian Society*, edited by James Curtis and Lorne Tepperman, 161–84. Toronto: McGraw-Hill Ryerson.

Clement, Wallace, and John Myles. 1994. *Relations of Ruling: Class and Gender in Postindustrial Societies.* Montreal: McGill-Queen's University Press.

Clevedon, Gordon, and Michael Krashinsky. 2001. *Our Children's Future: Child Care Policy in Canada.* Toronto: University of Toronto Press.

Cloward, Richard A., and Lloyd E. Ohlin. 1960. *Delinquency and Opportunity: A Theory of Delinquent Gangs.* New York: Free Press.

Coale, Ansley J. 1964. "How a Population Ages or Grows Younger." In *Population: The Vital Revolution*, edited by Ronald Freedman, 47–58. Chicago: Aldine.

———. 1969. "The Decline of Fertility in Europe from the French Revolution to World War II." In *Fertility and Family Planning: A World View*, edited by S.J. Berhman, Leslie Corsa, and Ronald Freedman, 3–24. Ann Arbor: University of Michigan Press.

———. 1973. "The Demographic Transition Reconsidered." In International Union for the Study of Population, *Proceedings of the International Population Conference*, vol. 1, 53–72. Liège, Belgium.

———. 1974. "The History of the Human Population." *Scientific American*, special issue: 15–25.

Coale, Ansley J., and Edgar M. Hoover. 1958. *Population Growth and Economic Development in Low-Income Countries.* Princeton, NJ: Princeton University Press.

Coale, Ansley J., and Susan Cotts Watkins, eds. 1986. *The*

Decline of Fertility in Europe: The Revised Proceedings of a Conference on the Princeton European Fertility Project. Princeton, NJ: Princeton University Press.

Coats, Patricia B., and Steven Overman. 1992. "Childhood Play Experiences of Women in Traditional and Nontraditional Professions." *Sex Roles*, 26, nos 7/8: 261–71.

Cockburn, Cynthia. 1983. *Brothers: Male Dominance and Technological Change.* London: Pluto.

———. 1990. "Men's Power in Organizations." In *Men, Masculinity and Social Theory*, edited by Jeff Hearn and David Morgan, 72–89. London: Unwin Hyman.

———. 1991. *In the Way of Women: Men's Resistances to Sex Equality in Organization.* Ithaca, NY: ILR Press.

Cockett, Monica, and John Tripp. 1994. *The Exeter Family Study: Family Breakdown and Its Impact on Children.* Exeter, UK: University of Exeter Press.

Cohen, Albert K. 1966. *Deviance and Control.* Englewood Cliffs, NJ: Prentice-Hall.

Cohen, J.L., and J.H. Davis. 1973. "Effects of Audience Status, Evaluation, and Time of Action on Performance with Hidden-Word Problems." *Journal of Personality and Social Psychology*, 27: 74–85.

Cohen, Jean L. 1985. "Strategy or Identity: New Theoretical Paradigms and Contemporary Social Movements." *Social Research*, 53: 663–716.

Coker, Naaz. 2001. *Racism in Medicine.* London: King's Fund.

Coleman, James W. 1987. "Toward an Integrated Theory of White Collar Crime." *American Journal of Sociology*, 93: 406–39.

Collier, Gary, Henry L. Minton, and Graham Reynolds. 1991. *Currents of Thought in American Social Psychology.* New York: Oxford University Press.

Collins, Randall. 1979. *The Credential Society: An Historical Sociology of Education and Stratification.* New York: Academic Press.

Comack, A. Elizabeth. 1985. "The Origins of Canadian Drug Legislation: Labelling Versus Class Analysis." In *The New Criminologies in Canada: State, Crime, and Control*, edited by Tom Fleming, 65–86. Toronto: Oxford University Press.

Comninel, George C. 1987. *Rethinking the French Revolution: Marxism and the Revisionist Challenge.* New York: Verso.

Conley, James. 1999. "Working-Class Formation in Twentieth-Century Canada." In *Social Inequality in Canada: Patterns, Problems, and Policies*, edited by James E. Curtis, Edward G. Grabb, and Neil L. Guppy, 20–34. Scarborough, ON: Prentice-Hall Allyn and Bacon.

Connell, R.W. 1995. *Masculinities.* Berkeley: University of California Press.

Connelly, Patricia M. 1978. *Last Hired, First Fired.* Toronto: Women's Press.

Conrad, Peter, and Joseph Schneider. 1980. *Deviance and Medicalization: From Badness to Sickness.* St Louis, MO: Mosby.

Constant, David, Lee Sproull, and Sara Kiesler. 1996. "The Kindness of Strangers: The Usefulness of Electronic Weak Ties for Technical Advice." *Organization Science*, 7, no. 2: 119–35.

Cook, J. 2001. "Practical Guide to Medical Education." *Pharmaceutical Marketing*, 6: 14–22.

Cooley, Charles Horton. 1902. *Human Nature and Social Order.* New York: Scribner.

———. [1909] 1962. *Social Organization: A Study of the Larger Mind.* Glencoe, IL: Free Press.

Cooperstock, Ruth, and Henry Lennard. 1987. "Role Strain and Tranquilizer Use." In *Health and Canadian Society: Sociological Perspectives*, 2nd edn, edited by David Coburn, Carl D'Arcy, George M. Torrance, and Peter New, 314–32. Markham, ON: Fitzhenry & Whiteside.

Cottrell, Fred. 1955. *Energy and Society.* New York: McGraw-Hill.

Council of Ministers of Education, Canada. 1996. *Enhancing the Role of Teachers in a Changing World.* Report in response to the International Survey in Preparation for the Forty-Fifth Session of the International Conference on Education. Toronto: Council of Ministers of Education, Canada.

———. 2001. *The Development of Education in Canada: Report of Canada.* Toronto: Council of Ministers of Education, Canada.

Coverman, Shelly. 1983. "Gender, Domestic Labour Time and Wage Inequality." *American Sociological Review*, 48: 623–37.

Crockett, Lisa, Mike Losoff, and Anne C. Petersen. 1984. "Perceptions of the Peer Group and Friendship in Early Adolescence." *Journal of Early Adolescence*, 4, no. 2: 155–81.

Crompton, Susan. 2000. "Health." *Canadian Social Trends*, 59: 12–17.

Crossley, Michelle L. 2002. "The Perils of Health Promotion and the 'Barebacking' Backlash." *Health*, 6, no. 1: 47–68.

Crozier, Michel. 1964. *The Bureaucratic Phenomenon.* Chicago: University of Chicago Press.

Crush, Jonathan. 1987. *The Struggle for Swazi Labour, 1890–1920.* Kingston, ON: McGill-Queen's University Press.

Cullen, Ian. 1978. "The Treatment of Time in the Explanation of Spatial Behavior." In *Human Activity and Time Geography*, edited by Tommy Carlstein, Don Parkes, and Nigel Thrift, 27–38. New York: Halstead.

Cuneo, Carl. 1985. "Have Women Become More Proletarianized Than Men?" *Canadian Review of Sociology and Anthropology*, 22: 465–95.

———. 1990. *Pay Equity: The Labour-Feminist Challenge.* Toronto: Oxford University Press.

Cunningham, Mick. 2001. "The Influence of Parental Attitudes and Behaviors on Children's Attitudes Toward Gender and Household Labor in Early Adulthood." *Journal of Marriage and the Family*, 63, no. 1: 111–23.

Curra, John. 2000. *The Relativity of Deviance.* Thousand Oaks, CA: Sage.

Curran, James. 1982. "Communications, Power, and Social Order." In *Culture, Society, and the Media*, edited by Michael Gurevitch, et al. London: Edwin Arnold.

Currie, Dawn. 1988. "Starvation Amidst Abundance: Female Adolescents and Anorexia." In *Sociology of Health Care in Canada*, edited by B. Singh Bolaria and Harley D. Dickinson, 198–215. Toronto: Harcourt, Brace, Jovanovich.

Curtis, James, Edward Grabb, and Tina Chui. 1999. "Public Participation, Protest, and Social Inequality." In *Social Inequality in Canada: Patterns, Problems, and Policies*, edited by James E. Curtis, Edward G. Grabb, and Neil L. Guppy, 371–86. Scarborough, ON: Prentice-Hall Allyn and Bacon.

Dahl, Robert. 1961. *Who Governs? Democracy and Power in an American City*. New Haven, CT: Yale University Press.

Das, Mallika. 2000. "Men and Women in Indian Magazine Advertisements: A Preliminary Report." *Sex Roles*, 43: 699–717.

Das Gupta, Tania. 1996. *Racism and Paid Work*. Toronto: Garamond.

Davey, Ian E. 1978. "The Rhythm of Work and the Rhythm of School." In *Egerton Ryerson and His Times*, edited by Neil McDonald and Alf Chaiton, 221–53. Toronto: Macmillan.

Davidson, James, and Dean Knudsen. 1977. "A New Approach to Religious Commitment." *Sociological Focus*, 10, no. 2: 151–73.

Davie, Grace. 1994. *Religion in Britain Since 1945: Believing Without Belonging*. Oxford: Blackwell.

———. 2000. *Religion in Modern Europe: A Memory Mutates*. Oxford: Oxford University Press.

Davies, James C. 1962. "Toward a Theory of Revolution." *American Sociological Review*, 27: 5–19.

Davies, Lorraine, and Patricia Jane Carrier. 1999. "The Importance of Power Relations for the Division of Household Labour." *Canadian Journal of Sociology*, 24: 35–51.

Davies, Lorraine, and Donna McAlpine. 1998. "The Significance of Family, Work, and Power Relations for Mothers' Mental Health." *Canadian Journal of Sociology*, 23: 368–88.

Davies, Scott. 1999. "Stubborn Disparities: Explaining Class Inequalities in Schooling." In *Social Inequality in Canada: Patterns, Problems, and Policies*, edited by James E. Curtis, Edward G. Grabb, and Neil L. Guppy, 138–50. Scarborough, ON: Prentice-Hall Allyn and Bacon.

Davies, Scott, Janice Aurini, and Linda Quirke. 2002. "New Markets for Private Education in Canada." *Education Canada*, 42, no. 3 (Fall): 36–8.

Davis, Charles R. 1996. "The Administrative Rational Model and Public Organization Theory." *Administration and Society*, 28: 39–60.

Davis, Kingsley. 1945. "The World Demographic Transition." *Annals of American Academy of Political and Social Sciences*, 237: 1–11.

———. 1984. "Wives and Work: The Sex Role Revolution and Its Consequences." *Population and Development Review*, 8: 495–511.

Davis, Kingsley, and Judith Blake. 1956. "Social Structure and Fertility: An Analytic Framework." *Economic Development and Cultural Change*, 4, no. 4: 211–35.

Davis, Kingsley, and Wilbert E. Moore. 1945. "Some Principles of Stratification." *American Sociological Review*, 10: 242–9.

Davis, Kingsley, and Pietronella van den Oever. 1982. "Demographic Foundations of New Sex Roles." *Population and Development Review*, 8: 495–512.

Davis, Steven J., John C. Haltiwanger, and Scott Schuh. 1996. *Job Creation and Destruction*. Cambridge, MA: MIT Press.

Dawe, Alan. 1970. "Two Sociologies." *British Journal of Sociology*, 21: 207–18.

Day, Shelagh, and Gwen Brodsky. 1998. *Women and the Equality Deficit: The Impact of Restructuring Canada's Social Programs*. Ottawa: Status of Women Canada.

de la Torre, Isabel. 1997. "La formacion y las organizaciones. Los acuerdos nacionales de formacion continua." *Revista Espanola de Investigaciones Sociologicas*, 77–8, Jan.–June: 15–33.

de Tocqueville, Alexis. [1835] 1945. *Democracy in America*. New York: Vintage.

De Vos, George, and Lola Romanucci-Ross. 1982. *Ethnic Identity: Cultural Continuities and Change*. Chicago: University of Chicago Press.

Decima Research. 2002. "Canadians Favour Fundamental Changes to Health Care System over Other Romanow Commission Options." Press release, 7 March (Ottawa).

DeFreitas, Gregory. 1998. "Immigration, Inequality, and Policy Alternatives." In *Globalization and Progressive Economic Policy*, edited by Dean Baker, Gerald Epstein, and Robert Pollin, 337–56. Cambridge: Cambridge University Press.

Dei, George J. Sefa. 1996. *Anti-racism Education: Theory and Practice*. Halifax, NS: Fernwood.

Dei, George J. Sefa, Irma Marcia James, Leeno Luke Karumanchery, Sonia James-Wilson, and Jasmin Zine. 2000. *Removing the Margins: The Challenges and Possibilities of Inclusive Schooling*. Toronto: Canadian Scholars' Press.

DeKeseredy, Walter. 2001. "Patterns of Family Violence." In *Families: Changing Trends in Canada*, 4th edn, edited by Maureen Baker. Toronto: McGraw-Hill Ryerson.

Dempsey, Ken. 1999. "Resistance and Change: Trying to Get Husbands to Do More Housework." Paper presented at the Australian Sociologists Association Annual Meetings, Monash University.

———. 2002. "Who Gets the Best Deal from Marriage: Men or Women?" *Journal of Sociology*, 38, no. 2: 91–110.

DeNora, Tia. 1991. "Musical Patronage and Social Change in Beethoven's Vienna." *American Journal of Sociology*, 97: 310–46.

Dery, David. 1998. "'Papereality' and Learning in Bureaucratic Organizations." *Administration and Society*, 29: 677–89.

DeSilva, Arnold. 1992. *Earnings of Immigrants: A Comparative Analysis*. Ottawa: Economic Council of Canada.

Deutschmann, Linda. 1998. *Deviance and Social Control*. Toronto: Nelson.

Devall, William B. 1992. "Deep Ecology and Radical Environmentalism." In *American Environmentalism*, edited by Riley Dunlap and Angela G. Mertig, 51–62. Philadelphia: Taylor and Francis.

Devereaux, P.J., Peter T.L. Choi, Christina Lacchetti, Bruce Weaver, Holger J. Schünemann, Ted Haines, John N. Lavis, Brydon J.B. Grant, David R.S. Haslam, Mohit Bhandari, Terrence Sullivan, Deborah J. Cook, Stephen D. Walter, Maureen Meade, Humaira Khan, Neera Bhatnagar, and Gordon H. Guyatt. 2002. "A Systematic Review and Meta-analysis of Studies Comparing Mortality Rates of Private For-Profit and Private Not-for-Profit Hospitals." *Canadian Medical Association Journal*, 166: 1399–1406.

Dhalla, Irfan A., Jeff C. Kwong, David L. Streiner, Ralph E. Baddour, Andrea Waddell, and Ian Johnson. 2002. "Characteristics of First-Year Students in Canadian Medical Schools." *Canadian Medical Association Journal*, 166: 1029–35.

Di Martino, Vittorio. 1996. "Télétravail: à la recherche des règles d'or." *Technologies de l'information et société*, 8: 355–71.

Diani, Mario. 1992. "The Concept of Social Movement." *Sociological Review*, 40: 1–25.

Dickens, Peter. 1992. *Society and Nature: Towards a Green Social Theory*. Hemel Hempstead, UK: Harvester Wheatsheaf.

———. 1996. *Reconstructing Nature: Alienation, Emancipation and the Division of Labour*. London: Routledge.

Diekman, Andreas, Monika Jungbauer-Gans, Heinz Krassnig, and Sigrid Lorenz. 1996. "Social Status and Aggression: A Field Study Analyzed by Survival Analysis." *Journal of Social Psychology*, 136: 761–8.

Dietz, Thomas, R. Scott Frey, and Eugene A. Rosa. 2002. "Risk, Technology and Society." In *Handbook of Environmental Sociology*, edited by Riley Dunlap and William Michelson, 329–69. Westport, CT: Greenwood.

Dobash, R. Emerson, Russell P. Dobash, Margo Wilson, and Martin Daly. 1992. "The Myth of Sexual Symmetry in Marital Violence." *Social Problems*, 39: 71–91.

Dogon, Mattei, and John Kasarda, eds. 1988. *The Metropolis Era*. Beverly Hills, CA: Sage.

Doherty, Gillian, Martha Friendly, and Mab Oloman. 1998. *Women's Support, Women's Work: Child Care in an Era of Deficit Reduction, Devolution, Downsizing and Deregulation*. Ottawa: Status of Women Canada.

Domhoff, G. William, ed. 1980. *Power Structure Research*. Beverly Hills, CA: Sage.

———. 1990. *The Power Elite and the State: How Policy Is Made in America*. Hawthorne, NY: Aldine de Gruyter.

Doob, Anthony N., and Alan E. Gross. 1968. "Status of Frustrator as an Inhibitor of Horn-Honking Responses." *Journal of Social Psychology*, 76: 213–18.

Dooley, Martin. 1995. "Lone-Mother Families and Social Assistance Policy in Canada." In *Family Matters: New Policies for Divorce, Lone Mothers, and Child Poverty*, edited by Martin Dooley, Ross Finnie, Shelley A. Phipps, and Nancy Naylor, 35–104. Toronto: C.D. Howe Institute.

Doyal, Lesley. 1995. *What Makes Women Sick: Gender and the Political Economy of Health*. New Brunswick, NJ: Rutgers University Press.

Dreeben, Robert. 1968. *On What Is Learned in School*. Reading, MA: Addison-Wesley.

Dreier, Peter, John Mollenkopf, and Todd Swanstrom. 2001. *Place Matters: Metropolitics for the Twenty-First Century*. Lawrence: University Press of Kansas.

Driedger, Leo, and Angus Reid. 2000. "Public Opinion on Visible Minorities." In *Race and Racism: Canada's Challenge*, edited by Leo Driedger and Shiva S. Halli, 152–71. Ottawa: Carleton University Press.

Drolet, Marie. 2001. *The Persistent Gap: New Evidence on the Canadian Gender Wage Gap*. Ottawa: Statistics Canada.

Duany, Andres, Elizabeth Plater-Zyberk, and Jeff Speck. 2000. *Suburban Nation: The Rise of Sprawl and the Decline of the American Dream*. Boston: North Point.

Duffy, Ann, and Rina Cohen. 2001. "Violence Against Women: The Struggle Persists." In *Feminist Issues: Race, Class and Sexuality*, edited by Nancy Mandell, 134–65. Toronto: Prentice-Hall.

Duffy, Ann, Dan Glenday, and Norene Pupo. 1997. *Good Jobs, Bad Jobs, No Jobs: The Transformation of Work in the 21st Century*. Toronto: Harcourt Brace.

Duffy, Ann, Nancy Mandell, and Norene Pupo. 1989. *Few Choices: Women, Work and Family*. Toronto: Garamond.

Duffy, Ann, and Norene Pupo. 1992. *Part-Time Paradox: Connecting Gender, Work and Family*. Toronto: McClelland & Stewart.

Dumas, Jean. 1990. *Report on the Demographic Situation in Canada 1990*. Ottawa: Statistics Canada, Demography Division.

Duncan, Otis Dudley. 1985. *Notes on Social Measurement: Historical and Critical*. New York: Russell Sage Foundation.

Duncan, Otis Dudley, and Leo F. Schnore. 1959. "Cultural, Behavioral and Ecological Perspectives in the Study of Social Organization." *American Journal of Sociology*, 65: 132–45.

Dunlap, Riley. 1992. "Trends in Public Opinion Toward Environmental Issues: 1965–1990." In *American Environmentalism*, edited by Riley Dunlap and Angela G. Mertig, 89–116. Philadelphia: Taylor and Francis.

Dunlap, Riley, and W. Richard Catton. 1994. "Struggling with Human Exemptionalism: The Rise, Decline and Revitalization of Environmental Sociology." *American Sociologist*, 25 (Spring): 5–30.

Dunlap, Riley, and William Catton, Jr. 1979a. "Environmental Sociology." *Annual Review of Sociology*, 5: 243–73.

———. 1979b. "Environmental Sociology: A Framework

for Analysis." In *Progress in Resource Management and Environmental Planning*, edited by Timothy O'Riordan and R.C. d'Arge, 1: 57–85. Chichester, UK: Wiley.

———. 1983. "What Environmental Sociologists Have in Common (Whether Concerned with 'Built' or 'Natural' Environments)." *Sociological Inquiry*, 53, nos 2/3: 113–15.

Dunlap, Riley, and Richard P. Gale. 1972. "Politics and Ecology: A Political Profile of Student Eco-activists." *Youth and Society*, 3: 379–97.

Dunn, Judy. 1986. "Growing Up in a Family World: Issues in the Study of Social Development in Young Children." In *Children of Social Worlds: Development in a Social Context*, edited by Martin Richards and Paul Light, 98–115. Cambridge, UK: Polity Press.

Durkheim, Émile. [1893] 1964. *The Division of Labor in Society*. Translated by George Simpson. New York: Free Press.

———. [1895] 1964. *The Rules of Sociological Method*. Translated by S. Solovay and John Mueller. New York: Free Press.

———. [1897] 1951. *Suicide: A Study in Sociology*. Translated by John A. Spaulding and George Simpson. New York: Free Press.

———. [1912] 1965. *The Elementary Forms of Religious Life*. Translated by Joseph Ward Swain. New York: Free Press.

———. [1912] 1995. *The Elementary Forms of Religious Life*. Translated by Karen E. Fields. New York: Free Press.

———. [1922] 1956. *Education and Society*. Translated by Sherwood W. Fox. Glencoe, IL: Free Press.

Dworkin, Ronald W. 2001. "The Medicalization of Unhappiness." *The Public Interest*, Summer: 85–99.

Easterlin, Richard A. 1969. "Towards a Socio-economic Theory of Fertility: A Survey of Recent Research on Economic Factors in American Fertility." In *Fertility and Family Planning: A World View*, edited by S.J. Berhman, Leslie Corsa, and Ronald Freedman, 127–56. Ann Arbor: University of Michigan Press.

———. 1980. *Birth and Fortune: The Impact of Numbers on Personal Welfare*. New York: Basic Books.

Ebaugh, Helen. 1988. *Becoming an Ex: The Process of Role Exit*. Chicago: University of Chicago Press.

Ebaugh, Helen Rose, and Janet Saltzman Chafetz, eds. 2000. *Religion and the New Immigrants*. Walnut Creek, CA: AltaMira.

Eberstadt, Nicholas. 1997. "World Population Implosion?" *The Public Interest*, 129: 3–20.

Eckersley, Robyn. 1992. *Environmentalism and Political Theory: Toward an Ecocentric Approach*. Albany: State University of New York Press.

Economic Council of Canada. 1991. *New Faces in the Crowd: Economic and Social Impact of Immigration*. Ottawa: Economic Council of Canada.

Economist. 1991. *The Economist*, 6 July, 87.

Edwards, Nigel, Mary Jane Kornacki, and Jack Silversin. 2002. "Unhappy Doctors: What Are the Causes and What Can Be Done?" *British Medical Journal*, 324: 835–8.

Edwards, Richard. 1979. *Contested Terrain: The Transformation of the Workplace in the Twentieth Century*. New York: Basic Books.

Ehrenreich, Barbara. 2001. *Nickel and Dimed: On (Not) Getting By in America*. New York: Henry Holt.

Ehrlich, Paul R. 1981. "Environmental Disruption: Implications for the Social Sciences." *Social Science Quarterly*, 62, no. 1: 7–22.

Ehrlich, Paul R., and Anne H. Ehrlich. 1970. *Population, Resources, Environment: Issues in Human Ecology*. San Francisco: Freeman.

———. 1990. *The Population Explosion*. London: Hutchinson.

Ehrlich, Paul R., and J.P. Holdren. 1971. "The Impact of Population Growth." *Science*, 171: 1212–7.

Eichler, Margit. 1996. "The Impact of New Reproductive and Genetic Technologies on Families." In *Families: Changing Trends in Canada*, 3rd edn, edited by Maureen Baker, 104–18. Toronto: McGraw-Hill Ryerson.

———. 1997. *Family Shifts: Families, Policies, and Gender Equality*. Toronto: Oxford University Press, 1997.

Eisenberg, David M., Roger B. Davis, Susan L. Ettner, Scott Appel, Sonja Wilkey, Maria Van Rompay, and Ronald C. Kessler. 1998. "Trends in Alternative Medicine Use in the United States, 1990–1997: Results of a Follow-up National Survey." *Journal of the American Medical Association*, 280: 1569–75.

Eisinger, Peter K. 1973. "The Conditions of Protest Behaviour in American Cities." *American Political Science Review*, 67: 11–28.

Ekos Research Associates. 1999. "Federal Liberals Riding High, Sovereignty Movement Dormant." [Press Release]. Ottawa: Ekos Research Associates.

———. 2002. *CBC/Ekos Poll: Public Attitudes Towards Immigration*. Ottawa: Ekos Research Associates.

El-Badry, M.A. 1969. "Higher Female Than Male Mortality in Some Countries of South Asia: A Digest." *Journal of the American Statistical Association*, 64: 1234–44.

Eliade, Mircea. 1969. *The Quest: History and Meaning in Religion*. Chicago: University of Chicago Press.

Elias, Norbert. 1994. *The Civilizing Process*. Translated by Edmund Jephcott. Oxford: Blackwell.

Elizabeth, Vivienne. 2000. "Cohabitation, Marriage, and the Unruly Consequences of 'Difference'." *Gender and Society*, 14, no. 1: 87–100.

Elliot, Faith Robertson. 1996. *Gender, Family, and Society*. London: Macmillan.

Elliott, Jean Leonard, and Augie Fleras. 1992. *Unequal Relations: An Introduction to Race and Ethnic Dynamics in Canada*. Scarborough, ON: Prentice-Hall.

Elliott, J., and M. Richards. 1991. "Parental Divorce and the Life Chances of Children." *Family Law*, 481–4.

Elster, Jon. 1989. *The Cement of Society: A Study of Social Order*. Cambridge: Cambridge University Press.

Emerson, Joan. 1970. "Behavior in Private Places: Sustaining Definitions of Reality in Gynecological

Examinations." In *Recent Sociology 2*, edited by Hans P. Dreitzel, 73–97. London: Macmillan.

Emery, Robert. 1994. "Psychological Research on Children, Parents, and Divorce." In *Renegotiating Family Relationships: Divorce, Child Custody, and Mediation*, edited by Robert Emery, 194–217. New York: Guildford.

Engels, Friedrich. [1845] 1994. *The Condition of the Working Class in England*. Translated by W.O. Henderson and W.H. Chaloner. Stanford, CA: Stanford University Press.

———. [1882] 1942. *The Origin of the Family, Private Property and the State*. New York: International Publishers.

England, Paula. 1982. "The Failure of Human Capital Theory to Explain Occupational Sex Segregation." *Journal of Human Resources*, 17: 358–70.

England, Paula, George Farkas, Barbara Kilbourne, and Thomas Dou. 1988. "Explaining Occupational Sex Segregation and Wages: Findings from a Model with Fixed Effects." *American Sociological Review*, 53: 544–58.

Ennett, Susan T., and Karl E. Bauman. 1996. "Adolescent Social Networks: School, Demographic, and Longitudinal Considerations." *Journal of Adolescent Research*, 11: 194–215.

Entwistle, N.J., and D. Entwistle. 1970. "The Relationship Between Personality, Study Methods, and Academic Performance', *British Journal of Educational Psychology*, 40: 131–40.

Entwisle, Doris, and Leslie Hayduk. 1988. "Lasting Effects of Elementary School." *Sociology of Education*, 61: 147–59.

Environics International. 2000. "Canadian Opinion on Climate Change Action in Advance of COP-6." Available at <www.rockies.ca/election/Environics_Climate_eFlash.pdf>, accessed 16 July 2003.

Epstein, Debbie, Jannette Elwood, Valerie Hey, and Janet Maw. 1997. *Failing Boys? Issues in Gender and Achievement*. Buckingham, UK: Open University Press.

Erasmus, Georges. 2002. "Why Can't We Talk." Excerpted from the 2002 Lafontaine-Baldwin Lecture. *Globe and Mail*, 9 March, F6–7.

Erikson, Erik. 1982. *The Life Cycle Completed: A Review*. New York: Norton.

Erikson, Kai T. 1966. *Wayward Puritans: A Study in the Sociology of Deviance*. New York: Wiley.

Ermann, M. David, and Richard J. Lundman. 1996. "Corporate and Governmental Deviance: Origins, Patterns, and Reactions." In *Corporate and Governmental Deviance: Problems of Organizational Behavior in Contemporary Society*, edited by M. David Ermann and Richard J. Lundman, 3–44. New York: Oxford University Press.

Estes, Carroll L. 1999. "The New Political Economy of Aging: Introduction and Critique." In *Critical Gerontology: Perspectives from Political and Moral Economy*, edited by Meredith Minkler and Carroll L. Estes, 17–35. Amityville, NY: Baywood.

Evans, L.T. 1998. *Feeding the Ten Billion: Plants and Population Growth*. Cambridge: Cambridge University Press.

Eyerman, Ron, and Andrew Jamison. 1989. "Environmental Knowledge as an Organizational Weapon: The Case of Greenpeace." *Social Science Information*, 28, no. 1: 99–119.

Ezzell, Carol. 2002. "Hope in a Vial: Will There Be an AIDS Vaccine Anytime Soon?" *Scientific American*, June: 38–45.

Falkenberg, Loren. 1988. "The Perceptions of Women Working in Male-Dominated Professions." *Canadian Journal of Atlantic Studies*, June: 77–83.

Faludi, Susan. 1991. *Backlash: The Undeclared War Against American Women*. New York: Doubleday–Anchor.

———. 1999. *Stiffed: The Betrayal of the American Man*. New York: HarperCollins.

Fantasia, Rick. 1995. "Fast Food in France." *Theory and Society*, 24: 201–33.

Fausto-Sterling, Anne. 1985. *Myths of Gender*. New York: Basic Books.

———. 2000. *Sexing the Body: Gender Politics and the Construction of Sexuality*. New York: Basic Books.

Feld, Scott L. 1982. "Social Structural Determinants of Similarity Among Associates." *American Sociological Review*, 47: 797–801.

Ferguson, Kathy E. 1984. *The Feminist Case Against Bureaucracy*. Philadelphia: Temple University Press.

Fernández Armesto, Felipe, ed. 1995. *The European Opportunity*. Aldershot, UK: Variorum.

Filion, Normand. 1998. "The Management of Self-Discipline: Social Norms and Cultural Surveillance." Paper presented at the annual meeting of the International Sociological Association.

Fineman, Martha A. 1995. *The Neutered Mother, the Sexual Family, and Other Twentieth Century Tragedies*. New York: Routledge.

Finke, Roger. 1997. "The Consequences of Religious Competition: Supply-Side Explanations for Religious Change." In *Rational Choice Theory and Religion: Summary and Assessment*, edited by Lawrence A. Young, 45–64. New York: Routledge.

Finke, Roger, A. Guest, and Rodney Stark. 1996. "Mobilizing Local Religious Markets: Religious Pluralism in the Empire State, 1855 to 1865." *American Sociological Review*, 61: 203–18.

Finke, Roger, and Rodney Stark. 1992. *The Churching of America, 1776–1990*. New Brunswick, NJ: Rutgers University Press.

Fischer, Claude S. 1976. *The Urban Experience*. New York: Harcourt Brace Jovanovich.

———. 1982. *To Dwell Among Friends: Personal Networks in Town and City*. Chicago: University of Chicago Press.

Fitzgerald, Kevin, and Mark LaGory. 2000. *Unhealthy Places: The Ecology of Risk in the Urban Landscape*. New York: Routledge.

Flood, Gavin. 1999. *Beyond Phenomenology: Rethinking the Study of Religion*. London: Cassell.

Flyvbjerg, Bent. 1998. *Rationality and Power: Democracy in Practice*. Chicago: University of Chicago Press.

———. 2001. *Making Social Science Matter*. Cambridge:

Cambridge University Press.

Fogel, Robert W., and Dora L. Costa. 1997. "A Theory of Technophysio Evolution, with Some Implications for Forecasting Population, Health Care Costs, and Pension Costs." *Demography*, 34: 49–66.

Foot, David, with Daniel Stoffman. 1998. *Boom, Bust and Echo 2000: Profiting from the Demographic Shift in the New Millennium*. Toronto: Macfarlane Walter & Ross.

Fortin, Pierre. 1996. "The Great Canadian Slump." *Canadian Journal of Economics*, 29: 761–87.

Foschi, Martha, Larissa Lai, and Kirsten Sigerson. 1994. "Gender and Double Standards in the Assessment of Job Applicants." *Social Psychology Quarterly*, 57: 326–39.

Fournier, Marcel, Michael Rosenberg, and Deena White, eds. 1997. *Quebec Society: Critical Issues*. Scarborough, ON: Prentice-Hall Canada.

Fox, Bonnie, ed. 1980. *Hidden in the Household: Women's Domestic Labour Under Capitalism*. Toronto: Women's Press.

———. 1988. "Conceptualizing 'Patriarchy'." *Canadian Review of Sociology and Anthropology*, 25: 163–83.

———. 1989. "The Feminist Challenge: A Reconsideration of Social Inequality and Economic Development." In Robert J. Brym with Bonnie J. Fox, *From Culture to Power: The Sociology of English Canada*, 120–67. Toronto: Oxford University Press.

———, ed. 2001a. *Family Patterns, Gender Relations*. 2nd edn. Toronto: Oxford University Press.

———. 2001b. "The Formative Years: How Parenthood Creates Gender." *Canadian Review of Sociology and Anthropology*, 38: 373–90.

———. 2001c. "Reproducing Difference: Changes in the Lives of Partners Becoming Parents." In *Family Patterns, Gender Relations*, 2nd edn, edited by Bonnie Fox, 217–302. Toronto: Oxford University Press.

Fox, Bonnie, and John Fox. 1986. "Women in the Labour Market, 1931–1981: Exclusion and Competition." *Canadian Review of Sociology and Anthropology*, 23: 1–21.

———. 1987. "Occupational Gender Segregation of the Canadian Labour Force, 1931–1981." *Canadian Review of Sociology and Anthropology*, 24: 374–97.

Fox, Bonnie, and Pamela Sugiman. 1999. "Flexible Work, Flexible Workers: The Restructuring of Clerical Work in a Large Telecommunications Company." *Studies in Political Economy*, 60: 59–84.

Fox, James Alan, and Jack Levin. 2001. *The Will to Kill: Making Sense of Senseless Murder*. Boston: Allyn and Bacon.

Fox, John, and Michael Ornstein. 1986. "The Canadian State and Corporate Elites in the Post-war Period." *Canadian Review of Sociology and Anthropology*, 23: 481–506.

Fox, Stephen. 1985. *The American Conservation Movement: John Muir and His Legacy*. Madison: University of Wisconsin Press.

Frank, Andre Gunder. 1991. "The Underdevelopment of Development." *Scandinavian Journal of Development Alternatives*, 10, no. 3: 5–72.

Fraser, Nancy. 1997. "After the Family Wage: A Postindustrial Thought Experiment." In Nancy Fraser, *Justice Interruptus: Critical Reflections on the 'Postsocialist' Condition*, 41–66. New York: Routledge.

Fraser, Nancy, and Linda Nicholson. 1990. "Social Criticism Without Philosophy: An Encounter Between Feminism and Postmodernism." In *Feminism/Postmodernism*, edited by Linda Nicholson, 19–38. London: Routledge.

Frauen Computer Zentrum Berlin (FCZB). 2001. "European Database: Women in Decision-Making. Fact Sheet: Women in the National Governments of the EU-Member States—2001." Available at <www.db-decision.de/FactSheets/FactSheets_E.htm>, accessed 11 June 2003.

Frederick, Judith. 1995. *As Time Goes By . . . : Time Use of Canadians*. Ottawa: Statistics Canada.

Frederick, Judith, and Janet E. Fast. 1999. "Eldercare in Canada: Who Does How Much?" *Canadian Social Trends*, Autumn: 27–30.

Frederick, Judith, and Jason Hamel. 1998. "Canadian Attitudes to Divorce." *Canadian Social Trends*, no. 48: 6–11.

Freidson, Eliot. 1970. *The Profession of Medicine: A Study in the Sociology of Applied Knowledge*. New York: Harper and Row.

Freire, Paulo. 1970. *Pedagogy of the Oppressed*. Translated by Myra Bergman Ramos. New York: Herder and Herder.

Frejka, Tomas. 1973. *The Future of Population Growth: Alternative Paths to Equilibrium*. New York: Wiley.

Freud, Sigmund. [1923] 1974. *The Ego and the Id*. Translated by James Strachey. London: Hogarth.

———. [1927] 1961. *The Future of an Illusion*. Translated by James Strachey. New York: Norton.

———. [1938] 1973. *An Outline of Psychoanalysis*. Translated by James Strachey. London: Hogarth.

Freudenberg, Nicholas, and Carol Steinsapir. 1992. "Not in Our Backyards: The Grassroots Environmental Movement." In *American Environmentalism*, edited by Riley Dunlap and Angela G. Mertig, 27–38. Philadelphia: Taylor and Francis.

Freudenburg, William, and Susan Pastor. 1992. "NIMBYs and LULUs: Stalking the Syndromes." *Journal of Social Issues*, 48, no. 4: 39–61.

Frideres, James S. 1988. *Native Peoples in Canada: Contemporary Conflicts*. Scarborough, ON: Prentice-Hall.

Friedan, Betty. 1963. *The Feminine Mystique*. New York: Norton.

Friedland, Roger, and Donald Palmer. 1984. "Park Place and Main Street: Business and the Urban Power Structure." *Annual Review of Sociology*, 10: 394–416.

Friedman, Debra, and Michael Hechter. 1988. "The Contribution of Rational Choice Theory to Macrosociological Research." *Sociological Theory*, 6: 201–18.

Fries, James F. 1980. "Aging, Natural Death, and the Compression of Morbidity." *New England Journal of Medicine*, 303: 130–5.

Friesen, John W., and Virginia Lyons Friesen. 2001. *In Defense of Public Schools in North America*. Calgary, AB: Detselig.

Froese, Paul. 2001. "Hungary for Religion: A Supply-Side Interpretation of the Hungarian Religious Revival." *Journal for the Scientific Study of Religion*, 40: 251–68.

Fuller, Colleen. 1998. *Caring for Profit: How Corporations Are Taking Over Canada's Health Care System*. Vancouver: New Star.

Funder, Kathleen. 1996. *Remaking Families: Adaptation of Parents and Children to Divorce*. Melbourne, Australia: Australian Institute of Family Studies.

Furedi, Frank. 1997. *Population and Development: A Critical Introduction*. New York: St Martin's.

Furstenberg, Frank F., S. Philip Morgan, and Paul D. Allison. 1987. "Paternal Participation and Children's Well-Being After Marital Dissolution." *American Sociological Review*, 52: 695–701.

Galarneau, Diane, and Jim Sturrock. 1997. "Family Income After Separation." *Perspectives on Labour and Income*, 9, no. 2: 19–28.

Gale, Richard P. 1972. "From Sit-ins to Hike-ins: A Comparison of the Civil Rights and Environmental Movements." In *Social Behavior, Natural Resources and the Environment*, edited by William R. Burch, Jr, Neil H. Cheek, Jr, and Lee Taylor, 280–305. New York: Harper.

Gallup Organization. 1992. "70% Believe Premarital Sex Not Wrong." *Gallup Report*. 27 August.

Gamson, William A., and David S. Meyer. 1996. "Framing Political Opportunity." In *Comparative Perspectives on Social Movements: Political Opportunities, Mobilizing Structures, and Cultural Framing*, edited by Doug McAdam, John McCarthy, and Mayer Zald, 275–90. New York: Cambridge University Press.

Gannagé, Charlene. 1986. *Double Day, Double Bind: Women Garment Workers*. Toronto: Women's Press.

Gans, Herbert J. 1962. *The Urban Villagers: Group and Class in the Life of Italian-Americans*. New York: Free Press.

———. 1967. *The Levittowners: Ways of Life and Politics in a New Suburban Community*. New York: Pantheon.

———. 1979. "Symbolic Ethnicity: The Future of Ethnic Groups and Culture in America." *Ethnic and Racial Studies*, 2: 1–20.

Gardner, Julia, and Mark Roseland. 1989. "Thinking Globally: The Role of Social Equity in Sustainable Development." *Alternatives*, 16, no. 3: 26–35.

Garfinkel, Harold. 1956. "Conditions of Successful Status Degradation Ceremonies." *American Journal of Sociology*, 61: 420–4.

———. 1967. *Studies in Ethnomethodology*. Englewood Cliffs, NJ: Prentice-Hall.

———. 1997. "A Conception of and Experiments with 'Trust' as a Condition of Concerted Stable Actions." In *The Production of Social Reality: Essays and Readings in Social Interaction*, edited by J. O'Brien and P. Kollock, 396–407. Thousand Oaks, CA: Pine Forge Press.

Garreau, Joel. 1992. *Edge City: Life on the New Frontier*. New York: Anchor.

Garson, Barbara. 1972. *All the Livelong Day: The Meaning and Demeaning of Routine Work*. New York: Doubleday.

Gaskell, Jane. 1992. *Gender Matters from School to Work*. Milton Keynes, UK: Open University Press.

———. 1993. "Feminism and Its Impact on Educational Scholarship in Canada." In *Contemporary Educational Issues: The Canadian Mosaic*, 2nd edn, edited by Leonard L. Stewin and Stewart J.H. McCann, 145–60. Toronto: Copp Clark Pitman.

———. 2001. "The Reproduction of Family Life: Perspectives of Male and Female Adolescents." In *Family Patterns, Gender Relations*, 2nd edn, edited by Bonnie Fox, 217–32. Toronto: Oxford University Press.

Gaskell, Jane, and John Willinsky, eds. 1995. *Gender In/forms Curriculum: From Enrichment to Transformation*. Toronto: OISE Press.

Gaventa, John. 1980. *Power and Powerlessness: Quiescence and Rebellion in an Appalachian Valley*. Urbana: University of Illinois Press.

Geary, David. 1998. *Male, Female: The Evolution of Human Sexual Differences*. Washington, DC: American Psychological Association.

Geary, David C., and Mark V. Flinn. 2001. "Evolution of Human Parental Behavior and the Human Family." *Parenting, Science and Practice*, 1: 5–61.

Geertz, Clifford. 1957. "Ritual and Social Change: A Javanese Example." *American Anthropologist*, 59, no. 1: 32–54.

———. 1973. *The Interpretation of Cultures: Selected Essays*. New York: Basic Books.

Gergen, Kenneth. 2001. "From Mind to Relationship: The Emerging Challenge." *Education Canada*, 41, no. 1: 8–11.

Ghalam, Nancy. 2000. "Attitudes Toward Women, Work and Family." *Canadian Social Trends*, 3.

Ghosh, Sabriti. 2002. "AIDS in Canada." *Voices*, 9, no. 10: 1–3.

Gibbon, Edward. [1776–88] 1994. *The History of the Decline and Fall of the Roman Empire*. London: Allen Lane.

Gibbs, Lois. 1993. Foreword to *Toxic Struggles: The Theory and Practice of Environmental Justice*, edited by Richard Hofrichter, ix–xi. Philadelphia: New Society.

Giddens, Anthony. 1971. *Capitalism and Modern Social Theory: An Analysis of the Writings of Marx, Durkheim, and Max Weber*. Cambridge: Cambridge University Press.

———. 1979. *Selected Problems of Social Theory*. London: Macmillan.

———. 2000. *Introduction to Sociology*. 3rd edn. New York: Norton.

Gidengil, Elizabeth, André Blais, Richard Nadeau, and Neil Nevitte. 2001. "Making Sense of the Vote: The 2000 Canadian Election." Paper presented at the annual meeting of the Association for Canadian Studies in the United States.

Gidney, R.D. 1999. *From Hope to Harris: The Reshaping of Ontario's Schools*. Toronto: University of Toronto Press.

Gifford, Robert. 1987. *Environmental Psychology: Principles and Practice*. Toronto: Allyn & Bacon.

Gilbert, Neil. 1997. "Advocacy Research and Social Policy." *Crime and Justice*, 22: 101–48.

Gilligan, Carol. 1982. *In a Different Voice: Psychoanalytic Theory and Women's Development*. Cambridge, MA: Harvard University Press.

Giroux, Henri. 1997. *Pedagogy and the Politics of Hope: Theory, Culture, and Schooling: A Critical Reader*. Boulder, CO: Westview.

Glassner, Barry. 1999. *The Culture of Fear: Why Americans Are Afraid of the Wrong Things*. New York: Basic Books.

Glazer, Nathan, and Daniel P. Moynihan, eds. 1975. *Ethnicity: Theory and Experience*. Cambridge, MA: Harvard University Press.

Glenmary Research Center. 2002. "Religious Congregations and Membership: 2000." Available at <www.glenmary.org/grc/RCMS_2000/release.htm>, accessed 8 June 2003.

Glenn, Evelyn Nakano. 2000. "The Social Construction and Institutionalization of Gender and Race: An Integrative Framework." In *Revisioning Gender*, edited by Myra Marx Feree, Judith Lorber, and Beth B. Hess, 3–43. New York: AltaMira.

Globe and Mail. 2002. *Globe and Mail*, 1 Oct., B12.

Glock, Charles, and Rodney Stark. 1965. *Religion and Society in Tension*. Chicago: Rand McNally.

Goffman, Erving. 1959. *The Presentation of Self in Everyday Life*. Garden City, NY: Doubleday–Anchor.

———. 1961a. *Asylums: Essays on the Social Situation of Mental Patients and Other Inmates*. New York: Doubleday.

———. 1961b. *Encounters: Two Studies in the Sociology of Interaction*. Indianapolis, IN: Bobbs Merrill.

———. 1963a. *Behavior in Public Places: Notes on the Social Organization of Gatherings*. Glencoe, IL: Free Press.

———. 1963b. *Stigma: Notes on the Management of Spoiled Identity*. Englewood Cliffs, NJ: Prentice Hall.

———. 1967. *Interaction Ritual: Essays on Face to Face Behavior*. Garden City, NY: Anchor.

———. 1971. *Relations in Public: Microstudies of the Public Order*. New York: Basic Books.

———. 1986. *Frame Analysis: An Essay on the Organization of Experience*. Boston: Northeastern University Press.

Gold, Harry. 2002. *Urban Life and Society*. Upper Saddle River, NJ: Prentice Hall.

Goldblatt, David. 1996. *Social Theory and the Environment*. Cambridge, UK: Polity.

Goldenberg, Sheldon. 1992. *Thinking Methodologically*. New York: HarperCollins.

Goldthorpe, J.E. 1987. *Family Life in Western Societies: A Historical Sociology of Family Relationships in Britain and North America*. Cambridge: Cambridge University Press.

Goldthorpe, J.H., David Lockwood, Frank Bechhofer, and Jennifer Platt. 1969. *The Affluent Worker in the Class Structure*. Cambridge: Cambridge University Press.

Gomme, Ian McDermid. 2002. *The Shadow Line: Deviance and Crime in Canada*. Toronto: Nelson.

Goode, William J. 1960. "A Theory of Role Strain." *American Sociological Review*, 25: 483–96.

Gordon, Philip H., and Sophie Meunier. 2001. "Globalization and French Cultural Identity." *French Politics, Culture and Society*, 19: 22–41.

Gordon, Robert M., and Jacquelyn Nelson. 2000. "Crime, Ethnicity, and Immigration." In *Crime in Canadian Society*, 6th edn, edited by Robert A. Silverman, James J. Teevan, and Vincent F. Sacco. Toronto: Harcourt Brace.

Gorski, Philip S. 1995. "The Protestant Ethic and the Spirit of Bureaucracy." *American Sociological Review*, 60: 783–6.

Gorz, Andre. 1999. *Reclaiming Work: Beyond the Wage-Based Society*. Translated by Chris Turner. Cambridge: Polity.

Gottdiener, Mark, and Ray Hutchison. 2000. *The New Urban Sociology*. 2nd edn. Toronto: McGraw-Hill.

Gottfedson Michael, and Travis Hirschi. 1990. *A General Theory of Crime*. Palo Alto, CA: Stanford University Press.

Gove, Walter. 1973. "Sex, Marital Status and Mortality." *American Journal of Sociology*, 79: 45–67.

GPI Atlantic. n.d. "The Economic Value of Housework and Child Care." Available at <www.gpiatlantic.org/ab_housework.shtml>, accessed 27 May 2003.

Grabb, Edward G. 2002. *Theories of Social Inequality*. 4th edn. Toronto: Harcourt.

Grafton, R. Quentin, Robert W. Lynch, and Harry W. Nelson. 1998. "British Columbia's Stumpage System: Economic and Trade Policy Implications." *Canadian Public Policy*, 24 (suppl.): S41–50.

Graham, Hilary. 1984. *Women, Health and the Family*. Brighton, UK: Wheatsheaf.

Gramsci, Antonio. 1992. *Prison Notebooks*. Vol. 1. Translated by Joseph A. Buttigieg and Antonio Callari. New York: Columbia University Press.

Granovetter, Mark S. 1974. *Getting a Job: A Study of Contacts and Careers*. Cambridge, MA: Harvard University Press.

———. 1982. "Alienation Reconsidered: The Strength of Weak Ties." *Connections*, 5, no. 2: 4–16.

Grant, Karen. 1998. "It's All in Your Genes." In *Critical Thinking About Canadian Social Issues*, edited by Wayne Antony and Les Samuelson, 200–17. Halifax: Fernwood.

Gray, Gary, and Neil Guppy. 2003. *Successful Surveys: Research Methods and Practice*. 3rd edn. Toronto: Nelson Thomson.

Gray, Herman. 1989. "Popular Music as a Social Problem: A Social History of Claims Against Popular Music." In *Images of Issues: Typifying Contemporary Social Problems*, edited by Joel Best, 143–58. New York: Aldine de Gruyter.

Grbich, Carolyn. 1992. "Societal Response to Familial Role Change in Australia: Marginalisation or Social Change." *Journal of Comparative Family Studies*, 23, no. 1: 79–94.

Greeley, Andrew. 1989. *Religious Change in America*. Cambridge, MA: Harvard University Press.

Green, Leonard. 2000. "Attention-Deficit/Hyperactivity

Disorder: Constructing Deviance, Constructing Order." In *New Perspectives on Deviance: The Construction of Deviance in Everyday Life*, edited by Lori G. Beaman, 263–82. Toronto: Prentice-Hall Allyn and Bacon.

Green, Melvyn. 1986. "A History of Canadian Narcotics Control: The Formative Years." In *The Social Dimensions of Law*, edited by Neil Boyd, 24–40. Scarborough, ON: Prentice-Hall.

Gregory, J.W., and V. Piché. 1983. "Inequality and Mortality: Demographic Hypotheses Regarding Advanced and Peripheral Capitalism." *International Journal of Health Services*, 13: 89–106.

Grimes, Michael D. 1991. *Class in Twentieth-Century American Sociology: An Analysis of Theories and Measurement Strategies*. New York: Praeger.

Grindstaff, Carl F. 1975. "The Baby Bust: Changes in Fertility Patterns in Canada." *Canadian Studies in Population*, 2: 15–22.

———. 1994. "The Baby Bust Revisited: Canada's Continuing Pattern of Low Fertility." In *Perspectives on Canada's Population: An Introduction to Concepts and Issues*, edited by Frank Trovato and Carl F. Grindstaff, 168–72. Toronto: Oxford University Press.

———. 1995. "Canada's Continued Trend of Low Fertility." *Canadian Social Trends*, Winter: 12–16.

Grindstaff, Carl F., and Frank Trovato. 1990. "Junior Partners: Women's Contribution to Family Income in Canada." *Social Indicators Research*, 22: 229–53.

Griswold, Wendy. 1987. "A Methodological Framework for the Sociology of Culture." *Sociological Methodology*, 17: 1–35.

Grosjean, Michele, and Michele Lacoste. 1998. "L'oral et l'écrit dans les communications de travail ou les illusions du 'tout ecrit'." *Sociologie du travail*, 40: 439–61.

Gross, Edward, and Gregory P. Stone. 1981. "Embarrassment and the Analysis of Role Requirements." *American Journal of Sociology*, 70: 1–15.

Guernsey, Judith Read, Ron Dewar, Swarna Weerasinghe, Susan Kirkland, and Paul J. Veugelers. 2000. "Incidence of Cancer in Sydney and Cape Breton County, Nova Scotia 1979–1997." *Canadian Journal of Public Health*, 91: 285–92.

Guillebaud, Jean-Claude. 2002. "Definition of Man: What Is Left of the Nuremburg Code?" *Diogenes*, 195: 7–12.

Guillén, Mauro F. 2001. "Is Globalization Civilizing, Destructive or Feeble? A Critique of Five Key Debates in the Social Science Literature." *Annual Review of Sociology*, 27: 235–60.

Guindon, Hubert. 1967. "Two Cultures: An Essay on Nationalism, Class, and Ethnic Tension." In *Contemporary Canada*, edited by Richard Leach, 33–59. Durham, NC: Duke University Press.

———. 1968. "Social Unrest, Social Class and Quebec's Bureaucratic Revolution." In *Canadian Society: Sociological Perspectives*, edited by Bernard R. Blishen, Frank E. Jones, Kaspar D. Naegele, and John Porter, 702–10. Toronto: Macmillan.

———. 1983. "Quebec and the Canadian Question." In *An*

Introduction to Sociology, edited by M. Michael Rosenberg, William B. Shaffir, Allan Turowetz, and Morton Weinfeld, 619–42. Toronto: Methuen.

Guppy, Neil, and Scott Davies. 1998. *Education in Canada: Recent Trends and Future Challenges*. Ottawa: Statistics Canada.

Guppy, Neil, Sabrina Freeman, and Shari Buchan. 1987. "Representing Canadians: Changes in the Economic Backgrounds of Federal Politicians." *Canadian Review of Sociology and Anthropology*, 24: 417–30.

Gusfield, Joseph R. 1963. *Symbolic Crusade: Status Politics and the American Temperance Movement*. Urbana: University of Illinois Press.

———. 1981. *The Culture of Public Problems: Drinking-Driving and the Symbolic Order*. Chicago: University of Chicago Press.

———. 1989. "Constructing the Ownership of Social Problems: Fun and Profit in the Welfare State." *Social Problems*, 36: 431–41.

Haas, Jack, and William Shaffir. 1978. "The Professionalization of Medical Students: Developing Competence and a Cloak of Competence." In *Shaping Identity in Canadian Society*, edited by Jack Haas and William Shaffir. Englewood Cliffs, NJ: Prentice-Hall.

Haberland, Nicole, and Diana Measham, eds. 2002. *Responding to Cairo: Case Studies of Changing Practice in Reproductive Health and Family Planning*. New York: Population Council.

Habermas, Jürgen. 1975. *Legitimation Crisis*. Translated by Thomas McCarthy. Boston: Beacon.

———. 1984. *The Theory of Communicative Action*. 2 vols. Translated by Thomas McCarthy. Cambridge: Polity.

Hadaway, C. Kirk, Penny Long Marler, and Mark Chaves. 1993. "What the Polls Don't Tell Us: A Closer Look at United States Church Attendance." *American Sociological Review*, 58: 741–52.

———. 1998. "Overreporting Church Attendance in America: Evidence That Demands the Same Verdict." *American Sociological Review*, 63: 122–30.

Haddad, Tony, and Lawrence Lam. 1988. "Canadian Families—Men's Involvement in Family Work: A Case Study of Immigrant Men in Toronto." *International Journal of Comparative Sociology*, 29: 269–79.

Hagan, John, and Ruth D. Peterson, eds. 1995. *Crime and Inequality*. Stanford, CA: Stanford University Press.

Hägerstrand, Torsten. 1970. "What About People in Regional Science?" *Papers of the Regional Science Association*, 24: 7–21.

Hales, Dianne. 2000. *Just Like a Woman: How Gender Science Is Redefining What Makes Us Female*. New York: Bantam.

Hall, Edward T. 1966. *The Hidden Dimension*. Garden City, NY: Doubleday.

Hall, Emmett. 1964–5. *Report of the Royal Commission on Health Services*. Ottawa: Queen's Printer.

Hall, Stuart. 1980. "Encoding/Decoding." In *Culture, Media, Language*, edited by Stuart Hall, Dorothy Hobson, Andrew Lowe, and Paul Willis, 128–38. London:

Unwin Hyman.

———. 2000. "Conclusion: The Multi-cultural Questions." In *Un/settled Multiculturalism: Diasporas, Entanglements, "Transruptions,"* edited by Barnor Hesse. London: Zed Books.

Hallman, Howard W. 1984. *Neighborhoods: Their Place in Urban Life.* Beverly Hills, CA: Sage.

Hamilton, Richard F. 1982. *Who Voted for Hitler?* Princeton, NJ: Princeton University Press.

Hamilton, Roberta. 1978. *The Liberation of Women.* London: Allen and Unwin.

Handel, Gerald, ed. 1988. *Childhood Socialization.* New York: Aldine de Gruyter.

Haney, Banks, and Zimbardo. 1973.

Hannigan, John. 1995. *Environmental Sociology: A Social Constructionist Perspective.* London: Routledge.

———. 1998. *Fantasy City: Pleasure and Profit in the Postmodern Metropolis.* New York: Routledge.

Hanson, Susan. 1992. "Geography and Feminism: Worlds in Collision?" *Annals of the Association of American Geographers,* 82: 569–86.

Hardey, Michael. 2002. "The Story of My Illness: Personal Accounts of Illness on the Internet." *Health,* 6, no. 1: 31–46.

Harding, Sandra. 1986. *The Science Question in Feminism.* Ithaca, NY: Cornell University Press.

Hardoy, Jorge E., Diana Mitlin, and David Satterthwaite. 2001. *Environmental Problems in an Urbanizing World.* London: Earthscan.

Harris, Chauncy, and Edward L. Ullman. 1945. "The Nature of Cities." *Annals of the American Academy of Political and Social Science,* no. 242: 7–17.

Harrison, Trevor, and Harvey Krahn. 1995. "Populism and the Rise of the Reform Party in Alberta." *Canadian Review of Sociology and Anthropology,* 32: 127–50.

Hartmann, Heidi. 1981. "The Unhappy Marriage of Marxism and Feminism: Towards a More Progressive Union." In *The Unhappy Marriage of Marxism and Feminism: A Debate on Class and Patriarchy,* edited by Lydia Sargent, 2–41. London: Pluto.

Hartnagel, Timothy F. 2000. "Correlates of Criminal Behaviour." In *Criminology: A Canadian Perspective,* edited by Rick Linden, 94–136. Toronto: Harcourt.

Harvey, David. 1989. *The Condition of Postmodernity: An Enquiry into the Origins of Cultural Change.* New York: Routledge.

Hawley, Amos A. 1950. *Human Ecology: A Theory of Community Structure.* New York: Ronald Press.

———. 1981. *Urban Society.* 2nd edn. New York: Wiley.

Hawley, Willis, and Frederick M. Wirt. 1968. *The Search for Community Power.* Scarborough, ON: Prentice-Hall.

Hayden, Dolores. 1984. *Redesigning the American Dream.* New York: Norton.

Hays, Samuel. 1987. *Beauty, Health and Permanence: Environmental Politics in the United States, 1955–1985.* New York: Cambridge University Press.

Health Canada. 2003. *HIV/AIDS Epidemiology Update: HIV and AIDS Among Women in Canada.* Ottawa: Health Canada.

Health Reports. 2001. "Women's Health Needs." *Health Reports,* 12, no. 3: 34.

Heimer, Robert. 2002. *Social Problems: An Introduction to Critical Constructionism.* New York: Oxford University Press.

Held, David. 1980. *Introduction to Critical Theory: Horkheimer to Adorno.* Berkeley: University of California Press.

Helwig, David. 2000. "NWT Residents Are Accident Prone, Live Shorter Lives." *Canadian Medical Association Journal,* 162: 681–2.

Henry, Frances. 1994. *The Caribbean Diaspora in Toronto: Learning to Live with Racism.* Toronto: University of Toronto Press.

Henry, Frances, and Effie Ginzberg. 1985. *Who Gets the Work: A Test of Racial Discrimination in Employment.* Toronto: Urban Alliance on Race Relations and Social Planning Directorate.

———. 1990. "Racial Discrimination in Employment." In *Images of Canada: The Sociological Tradition,* edited by James Curtis and Lorne Tepperman, 302–9. Toronto: Prentice-Hall.

Herek, Gregory M. 2002. "Gender Gaps in Public Opinion About Lesbians and Gay Men." *Public Opinion Quarterly,* 66: 40–66.

Herlihy, David. 1997. *The Black Death and the Transformation of the West.* Cambridge, MA: Harvard University Press.

Hewitt, John P. 2000. *Self and Society: A Symbolic Interactionist Social Psychology.* 8th edn. Boston: Allyn and Bacon.

Hickman, B. 1988. "Men Wise Up to Bald Truth." *Australian,* 21 May: 4.

Hier, Sean P. 2002. "Raves, Risks and the Ecstasy Panic: A Case Study in the Subversive Nature of Moral Regulation." *Canadian Journal of Sociology,* 27: 33–52.

Higgins, Robert R. 1994. "Race, Pollution and the Mastery of Nature." *Environmental Ethics,* 16: 251–64.

Hilberg, Raul. 1996. "The Nazi Holocaust: Using Bureaucracies, Overcoming Psychological Barriers to Genocide." In *Corporate and Governmental Deviance: Problems of Organizational Behavior in Contemporary Society,* edited by M. David Ermann and Richard J. Lundman, 158–79. New York: Oxford University Press.

Hilgartner, Stephen, and Charles Bosk. 1988. "The Rise and Fall of Social Problems: A Public Arenas Model." *American Journal of Sociology,* 94: 53–78.

Hirschi, Travis. 1969. *Causes of Delinquency.* Berkeley: University of California Press.

Hirschi, Travis, and Michael Gottfredson. 1985. "Age and Crime, Logic and Scholarship: Comment on Greenberg." *American Journal of Sociology,* 91: 22–7.

Hirst, Paul, and Grahame Thompson. 1996. *Globalization in Question: The International Economy and the Possibilities of Governance.* Cambridge, UK: Polity.

Hobbes, Thomas. [1651] 1968. *Leviathan.* Baltimore, MD: Penguin.

Hochschild, Adam. 1998. *King Leopold's Ghost: A Story of Greed, Terror, and Heroism in Colonial Africa.* Boston: Houghton Mifflin.

Hochschild, Arlie. 1983. *The Managed Heart: Commercializa-*

tion of Human Feeling. Berkeley: University of California Press.

———. 1997. *The Time Bind: When Work Becomes Home and Home Becomes Work*. New York: Metropolitan Books.

———. 2001. "The Third Shift." In *Family Patterns, Gender Relations*, 2nd edn, edited by Bonnie J. Fox, 338–51. Toronto: Oxford University Press.

Hochschild, Arlie, with Anne Machung. 1989. *The Second Shift: Working Parents and the Revolution at Home*. New York: Viking.

Hodson, Randy. 2001. *Dignity at Work*. Cambridge: Cambridge University Press, 2001.

Hofrichter, Richard, ed. 1993. *Toxic Struggles: The Theory and Practice of Environmental Justice*. Philadelphia: New Society.

Holmes, Malcolm D., and Judith A. Antell. 2001. "The Social Construction of American Indian Drinking: Perceptions of American Indian and White Officials." *Sociological Quarterly*, 42: 151–73.

Holmes, Mark. 1998. *The Reformation of Canada's Schools: Breaking the Barriers to Parental Choice*. Montreal: McGill-Queen's University Press.

Holton, Robert J. 1998. *Globalization and the Nation-State*. New York: St Martin's.

Homans, George. 1951. "The Western Electric Researchers." In *Human Factors in Management*, edited by Schyler Dean Hoslett, 210–41. New York: Harper.

———. 1961. *Social Behavior: Its Elementary Forms*. New York: Harcourt, Brace, and World.

Homer-Dixon, Thomas F., Jeffrey H. Boutwell, and George W. Rathjens. 1993. "Environmental Change and Violent Conflict." *Scientific American*, February: 38–45.

Hope, Steven, Chris Power, and Bryan Rodgers. 1998. "The Relationship Between Parental Separation in Childhood and Problem Drinking in Adulthood." *Addiction*, 93: 505–14.

Hout, Michael, and Claude S. Fischer. 2002. "Why More Americans Have No Religious Preference: Politics and Generations." *American Sociological Review*, 67: 165–90.

Hoyt, Homer. 1939. *The Structure and Growth of Residential Neighborhoods in American Cities*. Washington, DC: Federal Housing Administration.

Hughes, Diane, and Deborah Johnson. 2001. "Correlates in Children's Experiences of Parents' Racial Socialization Behaviors." *Journal of Marriage and Family*, 63: 981–96.

Hughes, Everett C. 1945. "Dilemmas and Contradictions of Status." *American Journal of Sociology*, 50: 353–9.

Hughes, Karen. 1999. *Gender and Self-Employment in Canada: Assessing Trends and Policy Implications*. Ottawa: Canadian Policy Research Networks.

Hulchanski, David. 1991. "Social Welfare Versus Market Welfare." In *The Canadian City*, edited by Kent Gerecke, 207–16. Montreal: Black Rose.

Human Fertilisation and Embryology Authority (HFEA). 1997. *Sixth Annual Report*. United Kingdom: HFEA.

Human Resources Development Canada (HRDC). 2002. *Knowledge Matters: Skills and Learning for Canadians*. Hull, QC: Human Resources Development Canada.

Human Resources Development Canada (HRDC) and Statistics Canada. 1998. *High School May Not Be Enough: An Analysis of Results from the School Leavers Follow-up Survey 1995*. Ottawa: Minister of Public Works and Government Services Canada.

Humphrey, Craig R., and Frederick R. Buttel. 1982. *Environment, Energy and Society*. Belmont, CA: Wadsworth.

Humphreys, Laud. 1970. *Tearoom Trade: Impersonal Sex in Public Places*. Chicago: Aldine.

Humphries, Karin H., and Eddy van Doorslaer. 2000. "Income-Related Health Inequality in Canada." *Social Science and Medicine*, 50: 663–71.

Hunter, Alfred A. 1981. *Class Tells: On Social Inequality in Canada*. Toronto: Butterworths.

Hunter, Alfred A., and Jean McKenzie Leiper. 1993. "On Formal Education, Skills and Earnings: The Role of Educational Certificates in Earnings Determination." *Canadian Journal of Sociology*, 18: 21–42.

Hunter, Floyd. 1953. *Community Power Structure: A Study of Decision Makers*. Chapel Hill: University of North Carolina Press.

Hunter, James Davison. 1991. *Culture Wars: The Struggle to Define America*. New York: Basic Books.

Hurrelmann, Klaus, ed. 1989. *The Social World of Adolescents*. Berlin: Walter de Gruyter.

Idinopulos, Thomas A., and Edward A. Yonan, eds. 1994. *Religion and Reductionism*. Leiden, Netherlands: E.J. Brill.

Illich, Ivan. 1976. *Limits to Medicine: Medical Nemesis: The Expropriation of Health*. Toronto: McClelland & Stewart.

Imershein, Allen W., and Carroll L. Estes. 1996. "From Health Services to Medical Markets: The Commodity Transformation of Medical Production and the Non-profit Sector." *International Journal of Health Services*, 26: 221–38.

Imig, Doug, and Sidney Tarrow. 2001. "Mapping the Euro-peanization of Contention: Evidence from a Quantita-tive Data Analysis." In *Contentious Europeans: Protest and Politics in an Emerging Polity*, edited by Doug Imig and Sidney Tarrow, 27–49. New York: Rowman and Littlefield.

Income Security Advocacy Centre. 2002. "The Inquest into the Death of Kimberly Rogers." Available at <www.incomesecurity.org/index_html>.

Inglehart, Ronald. 1977. *The Silent Revolution: Changing Values and Political Styles Among Western Publics*. Princeton, NJ: Princeton University Press.

———. 1990a. *Culture Shift in Advanced Industrial Society*. Princeton, NJ: Princeton University Press.

———. 1990b. "Values, Ideology, and Cognitive Mobiliza-tion in New Social Movements." In *Challenging the Political Order*, edited by R.J. Dalton and M. Kuechler, 23–42. New York: Oxford University Press.

Innis, Harold A. 1950. *Empire and Communications*. Toronto: University of Toronto Press.

———. 1951. *The Bias of Communication*. Toronto: University of Toronto Press.

———. 1952. *Changing Concepts of Time.* Toronto: University of Toronto Press.

International Labour Organization. n.d. *Multinational Corporations.* Available at <www.itcilo.it/english/actrav/telearn/global/ilo/multinat/multinat.htm>, accessed 27 May 2003.

Irwin, Alan. 2001. *Sociology and the Environment.* Cambridge, UK: Polity.

Isajiw, Wsevolod W., Aysan Sev'er, and Leo Driedger. 1993. "Ethnic Identity and Social Mobility: A Test of the 'Drawback Model'." *Canadian Journal of Sociology*, 18: 177–96.

Jablin, Frederic M. 1984. "Assimilating New Members in Organizations." In *Communication Yearbook*, edited by R.N. Bostrom, 594–626. Newbury Park, CA: Sage.

Jackson, Andrew, and David Robinson. 2000. *Falling Behind: The State of Working Canada, 2000.* Ottawa: Canadian Centre for Policy Alternatives.

James, Daniel Lee, and Elizabeth A. Craft. 2002. "Protecting One's Self from a Stigmatized Disease . . . Once One Has It." *Deviant Behavior*, 23: 267–99.

Jamieson, Lynn. 1998. *Intimacy: Personal Relationships in Modern Societies.* Cambridge, MA: Polity.

Janigan, Mary. 2002. "Immigrants. How Many Is Too Many? Who Should Get In? Can We Tell Them Where to Live?" *Maclean's*, 16 December: 20–5.

Janis, Irving Lester. 1982. *Groupthink: Psychological Studies of Policy Decisions and Fiascoes.* 2nd edn. Boston: Houghton Mifflin.

Janowitz, Morris. 1952. *The Community Press in an Urban Setting.* Chicago: University of Chicago Press.

Jargowsky, Paul A. 1996. *Poverty and Place: Ghettos, Barrios, and the American City.* New York: Russell Sage Foundation.

Jeffery, C. Ray. 1971. *Crime Prevention Through Environmental Design.* Beverly Hills, CA: Sage.

Jenkins, J. Craig. 1983. "Resource Mobilization Theory and the Study of Social Movements." *Annual Review of Sociology*, 9: 527–53.

Jenkins, Philip. 1994. *Using Murder: The Social Construction of Serial Homicide.* New York: Aldine de Gruyter.

———. 2002. *The Next Christendom: The Coming of Global Christianity.* New York: Oxford University Press.

Jeter, Jon. 2002. "Zambia Reduced to a Flea-Market Economy: Cheap Foreign Imports Have Destroyed the Once Thriving Textile Industry." *Washington Post*, 22 April, A1.

Jette, Allan M., Sybil L. Crawford, and Sharon L. Tennstedt. 1996. "Toward Understanding Ethnic Differences in Late-Life Disability." *Research on Aging*, 18: 292–309.

Johnson, Chalmers, Laura D'Andrea Tyson, and John Zysman. 1990. *Politics and Productivity: How Japan's Development Strategy Works.* New York: Harper Business.

Johnson, Holly. 1990. "Wife Abuse." In *Canadian Social Trends*, edited by Craig McKie and Keith Thompson, 173–76. Toronto: Thompson Educational.

———. 1996. *Dangerous Domains: Violence Against Women in Canada.* Toronto: Nelson.

Johnson, Laura. 1986. *Working Families: Workplace Supports for Families.* Toronto: Working Families Project of the Social Planning Council of Metropolitan Toronto.

Johnson, Terence. 1972. *Professions and Power.* London: Macmillan, 1972.

Jones, Jennifer M., Susan Bennett, Marion P. Olmsted, Margaret L. Lawson, and Gary Rodin. 2001. "Disordered Eating Attitudes and Behaviours in Teenaged Girls: A School-Based Study." *Canadian Medical Association Journal*, 165: 547–52.

Junger, Marianne, Peter van der Heijden, and Carl Keane. 2001. "Interrelated Harms: Examining the Association Between Victimization, Accidents and Criminal Behaviour." *Injury Control and Safety Promotion*, 8, no. 1: 13–28.

Kachur, Jerrold L. 1999. "Quasi-Marketing Education: The Entrepreneurial State and Charter Schooling in Alberta." In *Citizens or Consumers? Social Policy in a Market Society*, edited by Dave Broad and Wayne Antony, 129–50. Halifax, NS: Fernwood.

Kachur, Jerrold L., and Trevor W. Harrison. 1999. "Introduction: Public Education, Globalization, and Democracy: Whither Alberta?" In *Contested Classrooms: Education, Globalization, and Democracy in Alberta*, edited by Trevor W. Harrison and Jerrold L. Kachur, xiii–xxxv. Edmonton: University of Alberta Press and Parkland Institute.

Kadar, Marlene. 1988. "Sexual Harassment as a Form of Social Control." In *Gender and Society*, edited by Arlene Tigar McLaren, 337–46. Toronto: Copp Clark Pitman.

Kalin, Rudolf, and John W. Berry. 1994. "Ethnic and Multicultural Attitudes." In *Ethnicity and Culture in Canada: The Research Landscape*, edited by J.W. Berry and J.A. Laponce, 293–321. Toronto: University of Toronto Press.

Kannisto, Vaino, Jens Lauritsen, A.R. Thatcher, and J.W. Vaupel. 1994. "Reflections in Mortality at Advanced Ages: Several Decades of Evidence from Advanced Countries." *Population and Development Review*, 20: 793–810.

Kanter, Rosabeth Moss. 1977. *Men and Women of the Corporation.* New York: Basic Books.

Kanungo, Shivraj. 1998. "An Empirical Study of Organizational Culture and Network-Based Computer Use." *Computers in Human Behavior*, 14, no. 1: 79–91.

Kapica, Jack. 2002. "Canadians Log In, Not Turned On, Drop Out." *Globe and Mail*, 8 Oct.

Kasper, Anne S., and Susan J. Ferguson, eds. 2000. *Breast Cancer: Society Shapes an Epidemic.* New York: St Martin's Press.

Kassebaum, Donald G., and Ellen R. Cutler. 1998. "On the Culture of Student Abuse in Medical School." *Academic Medicine*, 73: 1149–58.

Katzmarzyk, Peter T. 2002. "The Canadian Obesity Epidemic: 1995–1998." *Canadian Medical Association Journal*, 166: 1039–40.

Kawachi, Ichiro, Bruce P. Kennedy, Vanita Gupta, and Deborah Prothrow-Stith. 1999. "Women's Status and the Health of Women and Men: A View from the States." *Social Science and Medicine*, 48: 21–32.

Kelley, Maryellen R., and Susan Helper. 1997. "Inter-organizational Learning and the Environment: The Influences of Regional Agglomeration and Local Institutional Linkages on the Adoption of New Technologies." Paper presented at the annual meeting of the American Sociological Association.

Kennedy, Paul. 1993. *Preparing for the Twenty-First Century*. Toronto: HarperCollins.

Kenway, Jane, and Helen Modra. 1992. "Feminist Pedagogy and Emancipatory Possibilities." In *Feminisms and Critical Pedagogy*, edited by Carmen Luke and Jennifer Gore, 138–66. London: Routledge.

Kenway, Jane, Sue Willis, Jack Blackmore, and Leonnie Rennie. 1998. *Answering Back: Girls, Boys, and Feminism in Schools*. New York: Routledge.

Keyfitz, Nathan. 1968. *Introduction to the Mathematics of Population*. Reading, MA: Addison-Wesley.

———. 1986. "The Family That Does Not Reproduce Itself." *Population and Development Review*, 12 (suppl.): 139–54.

———. 1993. "Are There Ecological Limits to Population?" *Proceedings of the National Academy of Sciences USA*, 90: 6895–9.

Kibirige, Joachim S. 1997. "Population Growth, Poverty and Health." *Social Science and Medicine*, 45: 247–59.

Kidd, Bruce. 1987. "Sports and Masculinity." In *Beyond Patriarchy*, edited by Michael Kaufman, 250–65. Toronto: Oxford University Press.

Kiernan, Kathleen. 1997. *The Legacy of Parental Divorce: Social, Economic, and Demographic Experiences in Adulthood*. London: Centre for Analysis of Social Exclusion.

Kilgour, David. 1998. "From Informal Economy to Micro-enterprise: The Role of Microcredit." Address to Results/Résultats Canada convention, Ottawa, 24 October. Available at <www.david-kilgour.com/ssap/informal.htm>, accessed 4 July 2003.

Kilmarten, Christopher T. 1994. *The Masculine Self*. Toronto: Maxwell Macmillan.

Kindleberger, Charles P. 1986. *The World in Depression, 1929–1939*. Berkeley: University of California Press.

Kinney, David. 1993. "From Nerds to Normals: The Recovery of Identity Among Adolescents from Middle School to High School." *Sociology of Education*, 66: 21–40.

Kirk, Dudley. 1998. "Demographic Transition Theory." *Population Studies*, 50: 361–87.

Kiser, Edgar, and Joachim Schneider. 1995. "Rational Choice Versus Cultural Explanations of the Efficiency of the Prussian Tax System." *American Sociological Review*, 60: 787–91.

Kitschelt, Herbert. 1993. "Social Movements, Political Parties, and Democratic Theory." *Annals of the American Academy of Political and Social Science*, 528 (July): 13–29.

———, ed. 1999. *Continuity and Change in Contemporary Capitalism*. Cambridge: Cambridge University Press.

Klein, David M., and James M. White. 1996. *Family Theories: An Introduction*. Thousand Oaks, CA: Sage.

Klein, Naomi. 1999. *No Logo: Taking Aim at the Brand Bullies*. New York: Picador.

Kleniewski, Nancy. 2002. *Cities, Change, and Conflict: A Political Economy of Urban Life*. Belmont, CA: Wadsworth.

Klinenberg, Eric. 2002. *Heat Wave: A Social Autopsy of Disaster in Chicago*. Chicago: University of Chicago Press.

Knight, Rolf. 1996. *Indians at Work: An Informal History of Native Labour in British Columbia, 1858–1930*. Vancouver: New Star.

Knighton, Tamara, and Sheba Mirza. 2002. "Postsecondary Participation: The Effects of Parents' Education and Household Income." *Education Quarterly Review*, 8, no. 3: 25–31.

Kohn, Melvin L. 1977. *Class and Conformity: A Study of Values, with a Reassessment, 1977*. 2nd edn. Chicago: University of Chicago Press.

Kopinak, Kathryn. 1988. "Women in Canadian Municipal Politics: Two Steps Forward, One Step Back." In *Gender and Society*, edited by Arlene Tigar McLaren, 372–89. Toronto: Copp Clark Pitman.

Kornhauser, Ruth R. 1978. *Social Sources of Delinquency: An Appraisal of Analytic Models*. Chicago: University of Chicago Press.

Kornhauser, William. 1959. *The Politics of Mass Society*. Glencoe, IL: Free Press.

Kortenhaus, Carole, and Jack Demarest. 1993. "Gender Stereotyping in Children's Literature: An Update." *Sex Roles*, 28, nos 3/4: 219–33.

Koshar, Rudy. 1986. "Political Gangsters and Nazism: Some Comments on Richard Hamilton's Theory of Fascism." *Comparative Studies in Society and History*, 28: 785–93.

Krahn, Harvey J., and Graham S. Lowe. 1998. *Work, Industry, and Canadian Society*. 3rd edn. Toronto: Nelson.

Kriesel, Warren, Terrence J. Centner, and Andrew Keeler. 1996. "Neighborhood Exposure to Toxic Releases: Are There Racial Inequities?" *Growth and Change*, 27: 479–99.

Krosenbrink-Gelissen, Lilianne E. 1993. "The Canadian Constitution, the Charter, and Aboriginal Women's Rights: Conflicts and Dilemmas." *International Journal of Canadian Studies*, nos 7–8: 207–24.

Kuhn, Thomas S. 1970. *The Structure of Scientific Revolutions*. 2nd edn. Chicago: University of Chicago Press.

Kwong, Jeff C., Irfan A. Dhalla, David L. Streiner, Ralph E. Baddour, Andrea E. Waddell, and Ian L. Johnson. 2002. "Effects of Rising Tuition Fees on Medical School Class Composition and Financial Outlook." *Canadian Medical Association Journal*, 166: 1023–8.

Lambert, Ronald D. 1971. *Sex Role Imagery in Children*. Ottawa: Royal Commission on the Status of Women.

Lamont, Michele. 1992. *Money, Morals, and Manners: The Culture of the French and American Upper-Middle Class*. Chicago: University of Chicago Press.

Lamptey, Peter, Merywen Wigley, D. Carr, and Y. Collymore. 2002. "Facing the HIV/AIDS Epidemic." *Population Bulletin*, 57, no. 3.

Landy, Sarah, and Kwok Kwan Tam. 1996. "Yes, Parenting Does Make a Difference to the Development of Children in Canada." In Statistics Canada, *Growing Up in Canada*, 103–11. Ottawa: Human Resources Development Canada and Statistics Canada.

Langille, David. 1987. "The Business Council on National Issues and the Canadian State." *Studies in Political Economy*, 24: 41–85.

LaPrairie, Carol. 2002. "Aboriginal Over-representation in the Criminal Justice System: A Tale of Nine Cities." *Canadian Journal of Criminology*, 44: 181–208.

Larsen, Elena. 2001. *CyberFaith: How Americans Pursue Religion Online*. Washington, DC: Pew Internet & American Life Project. Available at <www.pewinternet.org/ reports/pdfs/PIP_CyberFaith_Report.pdf>, accessed 8 June 2003.

Larsen, Nick. 2000. "Prostitution: Deviant Activity or Legitimate Occupation." In *New Perspectives on Deviance: The Construction of Deviance in Everyday Life*, edited by Lori G. Beaman, 50–67. Toronto: Prentice-Hall Allyn and Bacon.

Latour, Bruno, and Steve Woolgar. 1987. *Laboratory Life: The Construction of Scientific Fact*. 2nd edn. Princeton, NJ: Princeton University Press.

Laufer, William S., and Freda Adler. 1994. *The Legacy of Anomie Theory: Advances in Criminological Theory*. New Brunswick, NJ: Transaction.

Lautard, Hugh, and Neil Guppy. 1990. "The Vertical Mosaic Revisited: Occupational Differentials Among Canadian Ethnic Groups." In *Race and Ethnic Relations in Canada*, edited by Peter S. Li, 189–208. Toronto: Oxford University Press.

Lawr, Douglas, and Robert Gidney, eds. 1973. *Educating Canadians: A Documentary History of Public Education*. Toronto: Van Nostrand Reinhold.

LeBlanc, J. Clarence. 1994. *Educating Canadians for the New Economy*. Working paper prepared for the Canadian Institute for Research on Regional Development. Moncton, NB: Canadian Institute for Research on Regional Development.

Lee, Everet. 1966. "A Theory of Migration." *Demography*, 3: 47–57.

Leger Marketing. 2001. "Canadian Perceptions of Their Health Care System." Canadian Press report, 22 June.

Lemert, Edwin. 1951. *Social Pathology: A Systematic Approach to the Theory of Sociopathic Behavior*. New York: McGraw-Hill.

Lenski, Gerhard E. 1966. *Power and Privilege: A Theory of Social Stratification*. New York: McGraw-Hill.

Lenski, Gerhard E., with Patrick Nolan and Jean Lenski. 1995. *Human Societies: An Introduction to Macrosociology*. 7th edn. New York: McGraw-Hill.

Leslie, Gerald, and Sheila K. Korman. 1989. *The Family in Social Context*. 7th edn. New York: Oxford University Press.

Lesthaeghe, Ron, and Johan Surkyn. 1988. "Cultural Dynamics and Economic Theories of Fertility Change." *Population and Development Review*, 14: 1–45.

Levin, Benjamin, and J. Anthony Riffel. 1997. *Schools and the Changing World: Struggling Toward the Future*. London: Falmer.

Lewicki, Roy J., and Barbara Benedict Bunker. 1996. "Developing and Maintaining Trust in Work Relationships." In *Trust in Organizations: Frontiers of Theory and Research*, edited by Roderick M. Kramer and Tom R. Tyler, 114–39. Thousand Oaks, CA: Sage.

Lewington, Jennifer. 2002. "Canada Facing Age Crunch." *Globe and Mail*, 17 July, A1, A8.

Lewis, David L. 1993. "Canada's Native Peoples and the Churches." In *The Sociology of Religion: A Canadian Focus*, edited by W.E. Hewitt, 235–51. Toronto: Butterworths.

Lewis, Jone Johnson. 2002. "Women Prime Ministers and Presidents: Twentieth Century." Women's History Guide. Available at <http://womenshistory.about.com/ library/weekly/aa010128a.htm>, accessed 11 June 2003.

Ley, David. 1991. "Gentrification: A Ten Year Overview." In *The Canadian City*, edited by Kent Gerecke, 181–96. Montreal: Black Rose.

Li, Peter S. 1988. *The Chinese in Canada*. Toronto: Oxford University Press.

———. 2000. "Earning Disparities Between Immigrants and Native-Born Canadians." *Canadian Review of Sociology and Anthropology*, 37: 289–311.

Library of Parliament. 2002. "Women—Party Standings in the House of Commons: Current List." Available at <www.parl.gc.ca/information/about/people/house/ StandingsHofCwm.asp>, accessed January 2003.

Lieberman, Seymour. 1956. "The Effects of Changes in Roles on the Attitudes of Role Occupants." *Human Relations*, 9: 385–402.

Lieberson, Stanley. 2000. *A Matter of Taste: How Names, Fashions, and Culture Change*. New Haven, CT: Yale University Press.

Lieberson, Stanley, and Freda B. Lynn. 2002. "Barking up the Wrong Branch: Scientific Alternatives to the Current Model of Sociological Science." *Annual Review of Sociology*, 28: 1–19.

Liebow, Elliot. 1993. *Tell Them Who I Am: The Lives of Homeless Women*. New York: Free Press.

Lin, Zhengxi, Janice Yates, and Garnett Picot. 1999. *Rising Self-employment in the Midst of High Unemployment: An Empirical Analysis of Recent Developments in Canada*. Ottawa: Statistics Canada.

Lindert, Peter H., and Jeffrey G. Williamson. 2001. *Does Globalization Make the World More Unequal?* Cambridge, MA: National Bureau of Economic Research.

Linteau, Paul-André, René Durocher, and Jean-Claude Robert. 1983. *Quebec: A History 1867–1929*. Toronto: Lorimer.

Linton, Ralph. 1936. *The Study of Man: An Introduction*. New York: Appleton-Century-Crofts.

Lipman, Ellen L., David R. Offord, and Martin D. Dooley. 1996. "What Do We Know About Children from

Single-Parent Families? Questions and Answers from the National Longitudinal Survey on Children." In *Growing Up in Canada*, 83–91. Ottawa: Human Resources Development Canada.

Lipset, Seymour Martin. 1981. *Political Man: The Social Bases of Politics*. 2nd edn. Baltimore: Johns Hopkins University Press.

———. 1990. *Continental Divide: The Values and Institutions of the United States and Canada*. New York: Routledge.

Little, Bruce. 2000. "Female Boomers Led March into the Paid Work Force." *Globe and Mail*, 14 February, A2.

Little, Don. 1995. "Earnings and Labour Force Status of 1990 Graduates." *Education Quarterly Review*, 2, no. 3: 10–20.

Livingstone, D.W. 1999. *The Education–Jobs Gap: Underemployment or Economic Democracy*. Toronto: Garamond.

Lock, Margaret. 1998. "Menopause: Lessons from Anthropology." *Psychosomatic Medicine*, 60: 410–19.

Lofland, Lyn H. 1973. *A World of Strangers: Order and Action in Urban Public Space*. New York: Basic Books.

———. 1998. *The Public Realm: Exploring the City's Quintessential Social Territory*. New York: Aldine de Gruyter.

Logan, John, and Harvey Molotch. 1987. *Urban Fortunes: The Political Economy of Place*. Berkeley: University of California Press.

Long, Norton. 1958. "The Local Community as an Ecology of Games." *American Journal of Sociology*, 64: 251–61.

Looker, E. Dianne, and Graham S. Lowe. 2001. *Post-secondary Access and Student Financial Aid in Canada: Current Knowledge and Research Gaps*. Ottawa: Canadian Policy Research Networks. Available at <www.cprn.ca/en/doc.cfm?doc=192>, accessed 19 June 2003.

Looker, E. Dianne, and Victor Thiessen. 1999. "Images of Work: Women's Work, Men's Work, Housework." *Canadian Journal of Sociology*, 24: 225–54.

Lorber, Judith, and Susan Farrell. 1991. *The Social Construction of Gender*. London: Sage.

Lorimer, James. 1978. *The Developers*. Toronto: Lorimer.

Lorimer, Rowland, and Mike Gasher. 2003. *Mass Communication in Canada*. 5th edn. Toronto: Oxford University Press.

Loseke, Donileen R. 1992. *The Battered Woman and Shelters: The Social Construction of Wife Abuse*. Albany: State University of New York Press.

———. 1999. *Thinking About Social Problems: An Introduction to Constructionist Perspectives*. New York: Aldine de Gruyter.

Losh-Hesselbart, Susan. 1987. "Development of Gender Roles." In *Handbook of Marriage and the Family*, edited by Marvin B. Sussman and Suzanne K. Steinmetz, 535–63. New York: Plenum.

Loughlin, Julia. 1993. "The Feminist Challenge to Social Studies of Science." In *Controversial Science: From Content to Contention*, edited by Thomas Brante, Steve Fuller, and William Lynch, 3–20. Albany: State University of New York Press.

Lowe, Graham S. 1987. *Women in the Administrative Revolution: The Feminization of Clerical Work*. Toronto: University of Toronto Press.

———. 1989. *Paid/Unpaid Work and Stress: New Directions in Research*. Ottawa: Canadian Advisory Council on the Status of Women.

———. 2000. *The Quality of Work: A People-Centred Agenda*. Toronto: Oxford University Press.

Lowe, Marion. 1983. "Sex Differences, Science and Society." In *The Technological Woman*, edited by Jan Zimmerman, 7–17. New York: Praeger.

Luckenbill, David F. 1977. "Criminal Homicide as a Situational Transaction." *Social Problems*, 25: 176–86.

Luckmann, Thomas. 1967. *Invisible Religion: The Problem of Religion in Modern Society*. New York: Macmillan.

Lukes, Steven. 1974. *Power: A Radical View*. London: Macmillan.

Lutz, Wolfgang, ed. 1994. *The Future Population of the World: What Can We Assume Today?* London: Earthscan.

Luxton, Meg. 1980. *More Than a Labour of Love*. Toronto: Women's Press.

———. 1983. "Two Hands for the Clock: Changing Patterns in the Gendered Division of Labour in the Home." *Studies in Political Economy*, 12: 27–44.

———. 2001. "Family Coping Strategies: Balancing Paid Employment and Domestic Labour." In *Family Patterns, Gender Relations*, 2nd edn, edited by Bonnie Fox, 318–37. Toronto: Oxford University Press.

Luxton, Meg, and June Corman. 2001. *Getting By in Hard Times: Gendered Labour at Home and on the Job*. Toronto: University of Toronto Press.

Lynch, Kathleen. 1989. *The Hidden Curriculum: Reproduction in Education, A Reappraisal*. London: Falmer.

Lynch, Michael. 1985. "Discipline and the Material Form of Images: An Analysis of Scientific Visibility." *Social Studies of Science*, 15, no. 1: 37–66.

Lynn, Stephen. 2002. *Zapata Lives! Histories and Cultural Politics in Southern Mexico*. Berkeley: University of California Press.

McAdam, Doug. 1996. "Conceptual Origins, Current Problems, Future Directions." In *Comparative Perspectives on Social Movements*, edited by Doug McAdam, John McCarthy, and Mayer Zald, 23–40. New York: Cambridge University Press.

McCarthy, John D. 1996. "Constraints and Opportunities in Adopting, Adapting, and Inventing." In *Comparative Perspectives on Social Movements*, edited by Doug McAdam, John McCarthy, and Mayer Zald, 141–51. New York: Cambridge University Press.

McCarthy, Kevin R. 2001. *World Population Shifts: Boom or Doom?* Santa Monica, CA: Rand.

McCarthy, Shawn. 2002. "Valenti Pitches to Film Makers." *Globe and Mail*, 8 February, A1.

Maccoby, Eleanor. 1992. "Trends in the Study of Socialization: Is There a Lewinian Heritage?" *Journal of Social Issues*, 48, no. 2: 171–86.

Maccoby, Eleanor, and Carole Jacklin. 1974. *The Psychology of Sex Differences*. Stanford, CA: Stanford University Press.

McCutcheon, Russell T., ed. 1999. *The Insider/Outsider Problem in the Study of Religion: A Reader.* New York: Cassell.

McDaniel, Susan. 1988. "Women's Roles, Reproduction and the New Reproductive Technologies: A New Stork Rising." In *Reconstructing the Canadian Family,* edited by Nancy Mandell and Ann Duffy, 175–206. Toronto: Butterworths.

McDaniel, Susan A., and Lorne Tepperman. 2000. *Close Relations: An Introduction to the Sociology of Families.* Toronto: Prentice-Hall Allyn and Bacon.

McDonald, John, and L.D. McDonald. 1964. "Chain Migration, Ethnic Neighborhood Formation and Social Relationships." *Milbank Memorial Fund Quarterly,* 42: 82–7.

MacDowell, Laurel Sefton, and Ian Radforth, eds. 1992. *Canadian Working Class History: Selected Readings.* Toronto: Canadian Scholars' Press.

Macfarlane, Alan. 1997. *The Savage Wars of Peace: England, Japan and the Malthusian Trap.* Oxford, UK: Blackwell.

McGregor, Douglas. 1960. *The Human Side of Enterprise.* New York: McGraw-Hill.

McIntosh, Mary. 1978. "The State and the Oppression of Women." In *Feminism and Materialism,* edited by Annette Kuhn and Ann Marie Wolpe, 254–89. London: Routledge and Kegan Paul.

McIntyre, Amanda, and Michael Rosenberg. 2000. *Ethnic Women's Organizations in Montreal.* Unpublished paper, Concordia University, Montreal.

MacKenzie, Donald, and Judy Wajcman, eds. 1999. *The Social Shaping of Technology: How the Refrigerator Got Its Hum.* Milton Keynes, UK: Open University Press.

McKeown, Thomas. 1976. *The Modern Rise of Population.* London: Edward Arnold.

McKie, Duncan. 2001. *Globe and Mail,* 13 Dec., A21.

McKie, Duncan, and Lis Angus. 2001. *Canada's Information Highway.* Ottawa: Industry Canada.

Mackie, Marlene. 1983. *Exploring Gender Relations.* Toronto: Butterworths.

———. 1987. *Constructing Women and Men: Gender Socialization.* Toronto: Holt Rinehart and Winston.

———. 1993. "Primary Socialization in Socio-cultural Context." In *Marriage and the Family in Canada Today,* 2nd edn, edited by G.N. Ramu, 96–112. Scarborough, ON: Prentice-Hall.

MacKinnon, Mark, and Keith Lacey. 2001. "Bleak House." *Globe and Mail,* 18 August, F1.

McLaren, Peter. 1998. *Life in Schools: An Introduction to Critical Pedagogy in the Foundations of Education,* 3rd edn. New York: Longman.

McLellan, Janet. 1999. *Many Petals of the Lotus: Five Asian Buddhist Communities in Toronto.* Toronto: University of Toronto Press.

McLorg, Penelope A., and Diane E. Taub. 1987. "Anorexia Nervosa and Bulimia: The Development of Deviant Identities." *Deviant Behavior,* 8: 177–89.

McLuhan, Marshall. 1962. *The Gutenberg Galaxy: The Making of Typographic Man.* Toronto: University of Toronto Press.

———. 1964. *Understanding Media: The Extensions of Man.* New York: McGraw-Hill.

McMahon, Anthony. 1999. *Taking Care of Men: Sexual Politics in the Public Mind.* Cambridge: Cambridge University Press.

MacMillan, Harriet L., Angus B. MacMillan, David R. Offord, and Jennifer L. Dingle. 1996. "Aboriginal Health." *Canadian Medical Association Journal,* 155: 1569–78.

McRoberts, Kenneth. 1988. *Quebec: Social Change and Political Crisis.* 3rd edn. Toronto: McClelland & Stewart.

McVey, Wayne, Jr, and Warren E. Kalbach. 1995. *Canadian Population.* Toronto: Nelson.

Magnusson, Warren. 1990. "Critical Social Movements: De-centring the State." In *Canadian Politics: An Introduction to the Discipline,* edited by Alain G. Gagnon and James P. Bickerton, 525–41. Peterborough, ON: Broadview.

Malinowski, Bronislaw. 1922. *Argonauts of the Western Pacific.* New York: Dutton.

Malthus, Thomas R. [1798] 1970. *An Essay on the Principle of Population.* Harmondsworth, UK: Penguin.

Mandell, Nancy. 2001. "Women, Families and Intimate Relations." In *Feminist Issues: Race, Class and Sexuality,* 3rd edn, edited by Nancy Mandell, 193–218. Toronto: Prentice-Hall.

Mankoff, Milton. 1971. "Societal Reaction and Career Deviance: A Critical Analysis." *Sociological Quarterly,* 12: 204–18.

Manzer, Jenny. 2001. "Clinical Guidelines Ignore Gender Differences." *Medical Post,* 37, no. 13: 2, 65.

Manzer, Ronald. 1994. *Public Schools and Political Ideas: Canadian Educational Policy in Historical Perspective.* Toronto: University of Toronto Press.

Mao, Y., J. Hu, A.M. Ugnat, and K. White. 2000. "Non-Hodgkin's Lymphoma and Occupational Exposure to Chemicals in Canada." *Annals of Oncology,* 11, suppl. 1: 69–73.

Maquiladora Solidarity Network. 2000. "Child Labour and the Rights of Youth." Available at <www.maquilasolidarity.org/resources/child/issuesheet.htm>, accessed 28 May 2003.

March, Karen. 2003. "Who Do I Look Like? Gaining a Sense of Self-Authenticity Through the Physical Reflections of Others." In *Inner Lives and Social Worlds: Readings in Social Psychology,* edited by J. Holstein and J. Gubriam, 317–23. New York: Oxford University Press.

Marchak, Patricia. 1991. *The Integrated Circus: The New Right and the Restructuring of Global Markets.* Montreal: McGill-Queen's University Press.

Marcil-Gratton, Nicole. 1998. *Growing Up with Mom and Dad? The Intricate Family Life Courses of Canadian Children.* Ottawa: Statistics Canada.

Marcus, Clare Cooper, and Wendy Sarkissian. 1986. *Housing as If People Mattered: Site Design Guidelines for Medium-Density Family Housing.* Berkeley: University of California Press.

Marmot, Michael G., Geffrey Rose, Martin Shipley, and P.J. Hamilton. 1978. "Employment Grade and Coronary Heart Disease in British Civil Servants." *Journal of Epidemiological Community Health*, 32: 244–9.

Marmot, Michael G., George Davey Smith, Stephen Stansfeld, Chandra Patel, Fiona North, Jenny Head, Ian White, Eric Brunner, and Amanda Feeney. 1991. "Health Inequalities Among British Civil Servants: The Whitehall II Study." *The Lancet*, 337: 1387–93.

Marr, William L. 1992. "Post-war Canadian Immigration Patterns." In *The Immigration Dilemma*, edited by Steven Globerman, 17–42. Vancouver: Fraser Institute.

Marsden, Peter V., Cynthia R. Cook, and Arne L. Kalleberg. 1996. "Bureaucratic Structures for Coordination and Control." In *Organizations in America: Analyzing Their Structures and Human Resource Practices*, edited by Arne L. Kalleberg, David Knoke, Peter V. Marsden, and Joe L. Spaeth, 69–86. Thousand Oaks, CA: Sage.

Marshall, Katherine. 1987. "Women in Male Dominated Professions." *Social Trends*, Winter: 7–11.

———. 1993. "Employed Parents and the Division of Labour." *Perspectives on Labour and Income*, 5, no. 3: 23–30.

———. 1994. "Balancing Work and Family Responsibilities." *Perspectives on Labour and Income*, 6, no. 1: 26–30.

———. 1998. "Stay-at-Home Dads." *Perspectives on Labour and Income*, 10, no. 1: 9–15.

Marshall, Sheree. 1995. "Ethnic Socialization of African American Children: Implications for Parenting, Identity Development, and Achievement." *Journal of Youth and Adolescence*, 24: 377–96.

Martin, David. 2000. "Canada in Comparative Perspective." In *Rethinking Church, State, and Modernity: Canada Between Europe and America*, edited by David Lyon and Marguerite Van Die, 23–33. Toronto: University of Toronto Press.

Martin, Linda, and Kerry Segrave. 1993. *Anti-Rock: The Opposition to Rock 'n' Roll*. New York: Da Capo Press.

Martin, Philip L. 2001. *Germany: Managing Migration in the 21st Century*. Unpublished paper, University of California–Davis, Comparative Immigration and Integration Program.

Marx, Karl. [1844] 1957. "Contribution to the Critique of Hegel's Philosophy of Right—Introduction." In *On Religion: Karl Marx and Friedrich Engels*. Moscow: Progress.

———. [1867] 1967. *Capital: A Critique of Political Economy*. New York: International Publishers.

———. 1956. *Selected Writings in Sociology and Social Philosophy*. Edited by T.B. Bottomore and Maximilien Rubel. Translated by T.B. Bottomore. New York: McGraw-Hill.

———. 1964. *The Economic and Philosophical Manuscripts of 1844*. Edited by Dirk J. Struik. Translated by Martin Milligan. New York: International Publishers.

Marx, Karl, and Friedrich Engels. [1845–6] 1970. *The German Ideology. Part I, with Selections from Parts 2 and 3*. Translated by C.J. Arthur. New York: International

Publishers.

———. [1848] 1948. *Manifesto of the Communist Party*. New York: International Publishers.

———. [1848] 1983. "Manifesto of the Communist Party." In *The Portable Karl Marx*, edited by Eugene Kamenka, 197–324. New York: Penguin.

Maslovski, Mikhail. 1996. "Max Weber's Concept of Patrimonialism and the Soviet System." *Sociological Review*, 44: 294–308.

Maslow, Abraham. 1954. *Motivation and Personality*. New York: Harper & Row.

Mason, David. 1999. "The Continuing Significance of Race? Teaching Ethnic and Racial Studies in Sociology." In *Ethnic and Racial Studies Today*, edited by Martin Bulmer and John Solomos, 13–28. London: Routledge.

Massey, Douglas S., Joaquin Arango, Graeme Hugo, Ali Kouauci, Adela Pellegrino, and J. Edward Taylor. 1993. "Theories of International Migration: A Review and Appraisal." *Population and Development Review*, 19: 431–65.

Matza, D., and Gresham Sykes. 1957. "Techniques of Neutralization: A Theory of Delinquency." *American Sociological Review*, 5: 1–12.

Maxim, Paul S., and Paul C. Whitehead. 1998. *Explaining Crime*, 4th edn. Newton, MA: Butterworth–Heinemann.

Mead, George Herbert. 1934. *Mind, Self, and Society from the Standpoint of a Social Behaviorist*. Chicago: University of Chicago Press.

Mead, Margaret. 1935. *Sex and Temperament in Three Primitive Societies*. New York: Dell.

Meadows, Donella H., Dennis L. Meadows, and Jorgen Randers. 1992. *Beyond the Limits: Confronting Global Collapse, Envisioning a Sustainable Future*. Post Mills, VT: Chelsea Green.

Meadows, Donella, Dennis L. Meadows, Jorgen Randers, and William H. Behrens III. 1972. *The Limits to Growth*. New York: Universe.

Meissner, Martin, Elizabeth Humphries, Scott Meis, and William Schell. 1975. "No Exit for Wives: Sexual Division of Labour and the Culmination of Household Demands." *Canadian Review of Sociology and Anthropology*, 12: 424–39.

Melucci, Alerbero. 1989. *Nomads of the Present: Social Movements and Individual Needs in Contemporary Society*. Philadelphia: Temple University Press.

Merry, Sally Engle. 1981. *Urban Danger: Life in a Neighborhood of Strangers*. Philadelphia: Temple University Press.

Merten, Hans-Joachim. 1997. '*Lex mercatoria*: A Self-Applying System Beyond National Law?" In *Global Law Without a State*, edited by Gunther Teubner, 31–43. Aldershot, UK: Dartmouth.

Mertig, Angela, and Riley Dunlap. 2001. "Environmentalism, New Social Movement and the New Class: A Cross-national Investigation." *Rural Sociology*, 66, no. 1: 113–36.

Mertig, Angela, Riley Dunlap, and Denton Morrison. 2002. "The Environmental Movement in the United States."

In *Handbook of Environmental Sociology*, edited by Riley Dunlap and William Michelson, 448–81. Westport, CT: Greenwood.

Merton, Robert K. 1938. "Social Structure and Anomie." *American Sociological Review*, 3: 672–82.

———. 1957. *Social Theory and Social Structure*. New York: Free Press.

Messing, Karen. 1987. "The Scientific Mystique: Can a White Lab Coat Guarantee Purity in the Search for Knowledge About the Nature of Women?" In *Women and Men: Interdisciplinary Readings on Gender*, edited by Greta Hofmann Nemiroff, 103–16. Toronto: Fitzhenry and Whiteside.

———. 1998. *One-Eyed Science: Occupational Health and Women Workers*. Philadelphia: Temple University Press.

Messner, Steven, and Richard Rosenfeld. 1997. *Crime and the American Dream*, 2nd edn. Belmont, CA: Wadsworth.

Meyer, David, and Suzanne Staggenborg. 1996. "Movements, Countermovements and the Structure of Political Opportunity." *American Journal of Sociology*, 101: 1628–60.

Meyer, John W. 2000. "Globalization: Sources and Effects on National States and Societies." *International Sociology*, 15: 233–48.

Meyerson, Debra, Karl E. Weick, and Roderick M. Kramer. 1996. "Swift Trust and Temporary Groups." In *Trust in Organizations: Frontiers of Theory and Research*, edited by Roderick M. Kramer and Tom R. Tyler, 166–95. Thousand Oaks, CA: Sage.

Michaelson, Karen L., ed. 1981. *And the Poor Get Children: Radical Perspectives on Population Dynamics*. New York: Monthly Review Press.

Michels, Robert. 1962. *Political Parties*. New York: Free Press.

Michelson, William. 1976. *Man and His Urban Environment: A Sociological Approach*. Reading, MA: Addison-Wesley.

———. 1983. *From Sun to Sun: Daily Obligations and Community Structure in the Lives of Employed Women and Their Families*. Totowa, NJ: Rowman and Allanheld.

———. 1985. *From Sun to Sun: Daily Obligations and Community Structure*. Toronto: Rowman and Allanhead.

———. 1994. "Everyday Life in Contextual Perspective." In *Women and the Environment*, edited by Irwin Altman and Arza Churchman, 17–42. New York: Plenum.

———. 1997a. "Integrating Environmental Factors into Multidimensional Analysis." In Seymour Wapner, Jack Demick, Takiji Yamamoto, and Takashi Takahashi, *Handbook of Japan–United States Environment-Behavior Research: Toward a Transactional Approach*, 149–59. New York: Plenum.

———. 1997b. "Municipal Boundaries and Prospective LULU Impacts." In *Research in Community Sociology*, edited by Dan A. Chekki, 7: 117–40. Greenwich, CT: JAI Press.

———. 1998. "Time Pressure and Human Agency in Home-Based Employment." *Society and Leisure*, 21: 455–72.

Michelson, William, and Ellis Roberts. 1979. "Children and the Urban Physical Environment." In *The Child in the City: Changes and Challenges*, edited by William Michelson, Saul Levine, and Anna-Rose Spina, 410–77. Toronto: University of Toronto Press.

Micklin, Michael, ed. 1973. *Population, Environment and Social Organization: Current Issues in Human Ecology*. Hinsdale, IL: Dryden.

Miethe, Terance D., and Richard C. McCorkle. 1998. *Crime Profiles: The Anatomy of Dangerous Persons, Places, and Situations*. Los Angeles: Roxbury.

Milgram, Stanley. 1970. "The Experience of Living in Cities." *Science*, 167: 1461–8.

Milkman, Ruth. 1987. *Gender at Work: The Dynamics of Job Segregation by Sex During World War II*. Chicago: University of Illinois Press.

Miller, Carol T., and Cheryl R. Kaiser. 2001. "A Theoretical Perspective on Coping with Stigma." *Journal of Social Issues*, 57, no. 1: 73–92.

Miller, Gale, and James A. Holstein. 1993. *Constructionist Controversies: Issues in Social Problems Theory*. New York: Aldine de Gruyter.

Miller, John R. 1996. *Singwaulk's Vision: A History of Native Residential Schools in Canada*. Toronto: University of Toronto Press.

Millett, Kate. 1970. *Sexual Politics*. New York: Avon.

Mills, C. Wright. 1956. *The Power Elite*. New York: Oxford University Press.

———. 1959. *The Sociological Imagination*. New York: Oxford University Press.

Mills, Melinda, and Frank Trovato. 2001. "The Effect of Pregnancy in Cohabiting Unions on Marriage in Canada, the Netherlands, and Latvia." *Statistical Journal of the United Nations Economic Commission for Europe*, 18: 103–18.

Mitchell, Ann. 1985. *Children in the Middle: Living Through Divorce*. London: Tavistock.

Mitchell, Elizabeth. [1915] 1981. *In Western Canada Before the War*. Saskatoon, SK: Western Producer Prairie Books.

Mitchell, Robert Cameron, Angela G. Mertig, and Riley E. Dunlap. 1992. "Twenty Years of Environmental Mobilization: Trends Among National Environmental Organizations." In *American Environmentalism*, edited by Riley Dunlap and Angela G. Mertig, 11–26. Philadelphia: Taylor and Francis.

Moir, Anne, and David Jessel. 1992. *Brain Sex: The Real Difference Between Men and Women*. London: Michael Joseph.

Mondschein, E.R., K.E. Adolph, and C.S. Tamis-LeMonda. 2000. "Gender Bias in Mothers' Expectations About Infant Crawling." *Journal of Experimental Child Psychology*: 77: 304–16.

Monière, Denis. 1981. *Ideologies in Quebec: The Historical Development*. Translated by Richard Howard. Toronto: University of Toronto Press.

Moodie, Susannah. [1852] 1995. *Roughing It in the Bush*. Toronto: McClelland & Stewart.

Moore, Barrington, Jr. 1966. *Social Origins of Dictatorship and Democracy: Lord and Peasant in the Making of the Modern World*. Boston: Beacon.

———. 1969. *Social Origins of Dictatorship and Democracy*. London: Peregrine.

Morell, Carolyn M. 1994. *Unwomanly Conduct: The Challenges of Intentional Childlessness*. New York: Routledge.

Morgan, Stephen, and Aage B. Sorensen. 1999. "Parental Networks, Social Closure and Mathematics Learning: A Test of Coleman's Social Capital Explanation of School Effects." *American Sociological Review*, 64: 661–81.

Morris, Marika, Jane Robinson, and Janet Simpson with Sherry Galey. 1999. *The Changing Nature of Home Care and Its Impact on Women's Vulnerability to Poverty*. Ottawa: Status of Women Canada.

Morrison, Denton, and Riley E. Dunlap. 1986. "Environmentalism and Elitism: A Conceptual and Empirical Analysis." *Environmental Management*, 10: 581–9.

Morrison, Denton, Kenneth E. Hornback, and W. Keith Warner. 1972. "The Environmental Movement: Some Preliminary Observations and Predictions." In *Social Behavior, Natural Resources and the Environment*, edited by William R. Burch, Jr, Neil H. Cheek, Jr, and Lee Taylor, 259–79. New York: Harper.

Morton, Desmond. 1998. *Working People: An Illustrated History of the Canadian Labour Movement*. 4th edn. Montreal: McGill-Queen's University Press.

Moynihan, Ray, Iona Heath, and David Henry. 2002. "Selling Sickness: The Pharmaceutical Industry and Disease Mongering." *British Medical Journal*, 324: 886–91.

Muncie, John, and Margaret Weatherell. 1995. "Family Policy and Political Discourse." In *Understanding the Family*, edited by John Muncie, Margaret Weatherell, Rudi Dallos, and Allan Cochrane, 39–80. London: Sage.

Munro, Marcella. 1997. "Ontario's 'Days of Action' and Strategic Choices for the Left in Canada." *Studies in Political Economy*, 53: 125–40.

Murdie, Robert. 1969. *Factorial Ecology of Metropolitan Toronto*. Department of Geography Research Paper 116. Chicago: University of Chicago.

Murdock, George. 1949. *Social Structure*. New York: Macmillan.

Murphy, Elizabeth. 2000. "Risk, Responsibility and Rhetoric in Infant Feeding." *Journal of Contemporary Ethnography*, 29: 291–325.

Murphy, Michael. 1993. "The Contraceptive Pill and Women's Employment as Factors in Fertility Change in Britain 1963–1980: A Challenge to the Conventional View." *Population Studies*, 7: 221–44.

Murphy, Raymond. 1994. "The Sociological Construction of Science Without Nature." *Sociology*, 28: 957–74.

Mustard, Cameron A., Shelley Derkson, Jean-Marie Berthelot, Michael Wolfson, and Leslie L. Roos. 1997. "Age-Specific Education and Income Gradients in Morbidity and Mortality in a Canadian Province." *Social Science and Medicine*, 45: 383–97.

Mustard, Fraser. 1999. "Health Care and Social Cohesion." In *Market Limits in Health Reform: Public Success, Private Failure*, edited by Daniel Drache and Terry Sullivan, 329–50. London: Routledge.

Myles, John. 1989. *Old Age in the Welfare State: The Political Economy of Public Pensions*. Rev. edn. Lawrence: University Press of Kansas.

Nabalamba, Alice. 2001. *Locating Risk: A Multivariate Analysis of the Spatial and Socio-demographic Characteristics of Pollution*. Unpublished PhD dissertation, University of Waterloo, Waterloo, ON.

Naess, Arne. 1973. "The Shallow and the Deep, Long Range Ecology Movement." *Inquiry*, 16: 95–100.

Nagel, Thomas. 1986. *The View from Nowhere*. New York: Oxford University Press.

Nakhaie, M. Reza, Robert A. Silverman, and Teresa C. LaGrange. 2000. "An Examination of Gender, Ethnicity, Class and Delinquency." *Canadian Journal of Sociology*, 25: 35–59.

Nanda, Serena. 1991. *Cultural Anthropology*. Belmont, CA: Wadsworth.

Nash, Knowlton. 1994. *The Microphone Wars: A History of Triumph and Betrayal at the CBC*. Toronto: McClelland & Stewart.

Nathanson, C.A. 1984. "Sex Differences in Mortality." *Annual Review of Sociology*, 10: 191–213.

Nathe, Patricia. 1978. "The Flux, Flow, and Effluvia of Bohemia." *Urban Life*, 6: 387–416.

National Council of Welfare. 2001–2. *The Cost of Poverty*. Ottawa: National Council of Welfare.

———. 2002. *Poverty Profile 1999*. Ottawa: Minister of Public Works and Government Services.

National Longitudinal Survey of Children and Youth (NLSCY). 1996. *Growing Up in Canada*. Ottawa: Human Resources Development Canada and Statistics Canada.

National Post. 2002. "Census: How You Fit into the National Picture." *National Post*, 17 July, A9.

National Research Council. Committee on Population and Working Group on Population Growth and Economic Development. 1986. *Population Growth and Economic Development: Policy Questions*. Washington, DC: National Academy Press.

Navarro, Véase Vicente. 1975. "The Industrialization of Fetishism or the Fetishism of Industrialization: A Critique of Ivan Illich." *Social Science and Medicine*, 9: 351–63.

———. 1999. *NWT Health Status Report*. Ottawa: Department of Health and Social Services, Statistics Canada.

Nedelmann, Birgitta. 1991. Review of *Ideology and the New Social Movements*, by Alan Scott. *Contemporary Sociology*, 20: 374–5.

Nelson, Adie, and Barrie W. Robinson. 2002. *Gender in Canada*. 2nd edn. Toronto: Pearson Educational.

Nelson, Fiona. 1999. "Maternal Identities, Maternal Practices and the Culture(s) of Motherhood." Paper presented at the annual meeting of the Canadian

Sociology and Anthropology Association.

Nett, Emily. 1981. "Canadian Families in Social-Historical Perspective." *Canadian Journal of Sociology*, 6: 239–60.

Newbold, K. Bruce. 1998. "Problems in Search of Solutions: Health and Canadian Aboriginals." *Journal of Community Health*, 23, no. 1: 59–73.

Newman, Oscar. 1972. *Defensible Space: Crime Prevention Through Urban Design*. New York: Macmillan.

Nicholson, Linda, and Steven Seidman. 1995. Introduction to *Social Postmodernism: Beyond Identity Politics*, edited by Linda Nicholson and Steven Seidman. Cambridge: Cambridge University Press.

Nielsen, Tracy. 2002. *Streets, Strangers and Solidarity: A Study of Lesbian Interaction in the Public Realm*. PhD dissertation, University of Manitoba, Winnipeg, MB.

Nisbet, Robert A. 1959. "The Decline and Fall of Social Class." *Pacific Sociological Review*, 2: 11–17.

Notestein, Frank. 1945. "Population: The Long View." In *Food for the World*, edited by Theodore W. Schultz, 36–57. Chicago: University of Chicago Press.

———. 1967. "The Population Crisis: Reasons for Hope." *Foreign Affairs*, 46, no. 1: 156–80.

Oakes, J.M. 1996. "A Longitudinal Analysis of Environmental Equity in Communities with Hazardous Waste Facilities." *Social Science Research*, 25: 125–48.

Obesity Canada. 2001. "What Is Obesity?" Available at <www.obesitycanada.com>, accessed 11 July 2003.

O'Brien, Mary. 1981. *The Politics of Reproduction*. London: Routledge & Kegan Paul.

Occhionero, Marisa Ferrari. 1996. "Rethinking Public Space and Power." *Revue internationale de sociologie / International Review of Sociology*, 6 (n.s.): 453–64.

O'Connor, Dennis R. 2002. *Report of the Walkerton Inquiry: The Events of May 2000 and Related Issues: Part One: A Summary*. Toronto: Ontario, Ministry of the Attorney General.

O'Connor, Julia S., Ann Shola Orloff, and Sheila Shaver. 1999. *States, Markets, Families: Gender Liberalism and Social Policy in Australia, Canada, Great Britain and the United States*. Cambridge: Cambridge University Press.

Offe, Claus. 1984. *Contradictions of the Welfare State*. Cambridge, MA: MIT Press.

Offer, Daniel, Eric Ostrov, Kenneth Howard, and Robert Atkinson. 1988. *The Teenage World: Adolescents' Self-Image in Ten Countries*. New York: Plenum.

O'Leary, K. Daniel, J. Barling, Ilena Arias, Alan Rosenbaum, J. Malone, and A. Tyree. 1989. "Prevalence and Stability of Physical Aggression Between Spouses: A Longitudinal Analysis." *Journal of Consulting and Clinical Psychology*, 57: 263–8.

Olewiler, Nancy. 1999. "National Tax Policy for an International Economy: Divergence in a Converging World?" In *Room to Manoeuvre? Globalization and Policy Convergence*, edited by Thomas J. Courchene, 345–72. Montreal: McGill-Queen's University Press.

Olsen, Daniel V.A. 1999. "Religious Pluralism and US Church Membership: A Reassessment." *Sociology of Religion*, 60: 149–73.

Olsen, Denis. 1980. *The State Elite*. Toronto: McClelland and Stewart.

Olshansky, S. Jay, and Brian A. Ault. 1986. "The Fourth Stage of the Epidemiological Transition: The Age of Delayed Degenerative Diseases." *Milbank Quarterly*, 46: 355–91.

Olshansky, S. Jay, Bruce A. Carnes, and Christine Cassel. 1990. "In Search of Methuselah: Estimating the Upper Limits to Human Longevity." *Science*, 250: 634–40.

Olshansky, S. Jay, Bruce Carnes, Richard G. Rogers, and Len Smith. 1997. "Infectious Diseases: New and Ancient Threats to World Health." *Population Bulletin*, 52, no. 2.

Olson, Mancur. 1965. *The Logic of Collective Action: Public Goods and the Theory of Groups*. Cambridge, MA: Harvard University Press.

Olzak, Susan. 1983. "Contemporary Ethnic Mobilization." *Annual Review of Sociology*, 9: 355–74.

Omran, Abdal R. 1971. "The Epidemiologic Transition." *Milbank Memorial Quarterly*, 49: 509–38.

Organisation for Economic Co-operation and Development (OECD). 2001. *OECD Economic Outlook 70 (December, 2001)*. Paris: OECD.

O'Riordan, T. 1971. "The Third American Environmental Conservation Movement: New Implications for Public Policy." *Journal of American Studies*, 5: 155–71.

Osberg, Lars. 1992. "Canada's Economic Performance: Inequality, Poverty, and Growth." In *False Promises: The Failure of Conservative Economics*, edited by Robert C. Allen and Gideon Rosenbluth, 39–52. Vancouver: New Star.

Osborne, Ken. 1999. *Education: A Guide to the Canadian School Debate: Or, Who Wants What and Why?* Toronto: Penguin.

O'Sullivan, Tim, John Hartley, Danny Saunders, and John Fiske. 1983. *Key Concepts in Communication*. London: Methuen.

Ottawa Citizen. 2002. "Aboriginals More Likely to Get AIDS, Study Shows." *Ottawa Citizen*, 8 June: A7.

Otto, Rudolph. 1923. *The Idea of the Holy*. Oxford: Oxford University Press.

Overbeek, Johannes. 1974. *History of Population Theories*. Rotterdam, The Netherlands: Rotterdam University Press.

Pahl, R.E. 1970. *Whose City? And Other Essays on Sociology and Planning*. New York: Longman.

Pais, José Machado. 2000. "Transitions and Youth Cultures: Forms and Performances." *International Social Science Journal*, 52: 219–33.

Pakulski, Jan, and Malcolm Walters. 1996. *The Death of Class*. London: Sage.

Paletta, Anna. 1992. "Today's Extended Families." *Canadian Social Trends*, Winter: 26–8.

Palm, Risa, and Alan Pred. 1974. *A Time-Geographic Perspective on Problems of Inequality for Women*. Institute of Urban and Regional Development Working Paper 236. Berkeley: University of California.

Palmer, Howard H. 1991. *Ethnicity and Politics in Canada*

Since Confederation. Ottawa: Canadian Historical Society.

Palys, Ted. n.d. "Russel Ogden v. SFU." Available at <http://www.sfu.ca/~palys/OgdenPge.htm>, accessed 15 July 2003.

Pampel, Fred C. 1998. *Aging, Social Inequality, and Public Policy.* Thousand Oaks, CA: Pine Forge.

Pandey, Sanjay K., and Stuart I. Bretschneider. 1997. "The Impact of Red Tape's Administrative Delay on Public Organizations' Interest in New Information Technologies." *Journal of Public Administration Research and Theory,* 7: 113–30.

Panitch, Leo, ed. 1977. *The Canadian State: Political Economy and Political Power.* Toronto: University of Toronto Press.

Park, Kristin. 2002. "Stigma Management Among the Voluntarily Childless." *Sociological Perspectives,* 45, no. 1: 21–45.

Park, Robert E. 1925. "The City: Suggestions for the Investigation of Human Behavior in the Urban Environment." In *The City,* edited by Robert E. Park, Ernest Burgess, and Roderick McKenzie, 1–46. Chicago: University of Chicago Press.

Park, Robert, and Ernest Burgess. 1921. *Introduction to the Science of Sociology.* Chicago: University of Chicago Press.

Park, Robert, and Roderick D. McKenzie, eds. 1925. *The City.* Chicago: University of Chicago Press.

Parsons, Talcott. 1949. *Essays in Sociological Theory.* New York: Free Press.

———. 1951. *The Social System.* Glencoe, IL: Free Press.

———. 1955. *Family, Socialization and Interaction Process.* New York: Free Press.

———. 1959. "The School Class as a Social System: Some of Its Functions in American Society." *Harvard Educational Review,* 29: 297–318.

Parsons, Talcott, and Robert F. Bales. 1955. *Family Socialization and Interaction Process.* New York: Free Press.

Pearce, Frank, and Laureen Snider, eds. 1995. *Corporate Crime: Contemporary Debates.* Toronto: University of Toronto Press.

Peers, Frank W. 1969. *The Politics of Canadian Broadcasting, 1920–1951.* Toronto: University of Toronto Press.

Perls, Thomas T., and Ruth C. Fretts. 1998. "Why Women Live Longer Than Men." *Scientific American Presents,* 9, no. 2: 100–3.

Perrow, Charles. 1972. *Complex Organizations: A Critical Essay.* Glenview, IL: Scott, Foresman.

Perry, Clarence. 1966. "The Neighborhood Unit Formula." In *Urban Housing,* edited by William Wheaton, 94–109. New York: Free Press.

Petersen, William. 1989. "Marxism and the Population Question: Theory and Practice." *Population and Development Review,* 14 (suppl.): 77–101.

Peterson, Peter G. 1999. "Grey Dawn: The Global Aging Crisis." *Foreign Affairs,* 78, no. 1: 42–55.

Peterson, Richard A. 1994. "Culture Studies Through the Production Perspective: Progress and Prospects." In

The Sociology of Culture: Emerging Theoretical Perspectives, edited by Diana Crane, 163–89. Oxford: Blackwell.

Petrovic, Edit. 2000. "Conceptualizing Gender, Race, and Ethnicity as a Field of Study." In *Perspectives on Ethnicity in Canada,* edited by Madeleine Kalbach and Warren Kalbach, 48–54. Toronto: Harcourt.

Pfohl, Stephen J. 1977. "The Discovery of Child Abuse." *Social Problems,* 24: 310–23.

Pfuhl, Erdwin H., and Stuart Henry. 1993. *The Deviance Process,* 3rd edn. New York: Aldine de Gruyter.

Picot, Garnett, and John Myles. 1995. *Social Transfers, Changing Family Structure, and Low Income Among Children.* Ottawa: Statistics Canada.

Piliavin, Erving, and S. Briar. 1964. "Police Encounters with Juveniles." *American Journal of Sociology,* 70: 206–14.

Pimentel, David, and Marcia Pimentel. 1999. "Population Growth, Environmental Resources and the Global Availability of Food." *Social Research,* 66: 417–28.

Pineo, Peter. 1977. "The Social Standing of Ethnic and Racial Groupings." *Canadian Review of Sociology and Anthropology,* 14: 147–57.

Plumwood, Val. 1992. "Feminism and Ecofeminism: Beyond the Dualistic Assumptions of Women, Men and Nature." *Ecologist,* 22, no. 1: 8–13.

Pollack, William. 1998. *Real Boys: Rescuing Our Sons from the Myths of Boyhood.* New York: Random House.

Pomerleau, Andrée, Daniel Bolduc, Gerard Malcuit, and Louise Cossess. 1990. "Pink or Blue: Environmental Gender Stereotypes in the First Two Years of Life." *Sex Roles,* 22: 359–67.

Population Reference Bureau. 1995. *World Population Data Sheet for 1995.* Washington, DC: Population Reference Bureau.

———. 2000. *World Population Data Sheet for 2000.* Washington, DC: Population Reference Bureau.

———. 2001. *World Population Data Sheet for 2001.* Washington, DC: Population Reference Bureau.

———. 2002. *World Population Data Sheet for 2002.* Washington, DC: Population Reference Bureau.

———. 2003. *World Population Data Sheet for 2003.* Washington, DC: Population Reference Bureau.

Porter, John. 1965. *The Vertical Mosaic: An Analysis of Social Class and Power in Canada.* Toronto: University of Toronto Press.

Portes, Alejandro. 1997. *Globalization from Below: The Rise of Transnational Communities.* Princeton, NJ: Centre for Migration and Development.

———. 1999. "Conclusion: Towards a New World: The Origins and Effects of Transnational Activities." *Ethnic and Racial Studies,* 22: 463–77.

Portes, Alejandro, Luis E. Guarnizo, and Patricia Landolt. 1999. "The Study of Transnationalism: Pitfalls and Promise of an Emergent Research Field." *Ethnic and Racial Studies,* 22: 217–37.

Posner, Judith. 1987. "The Objectified Male: The New Male Image in Advertising." In *Women and Men: Interdisciplinary Readings on Gender,* edited by Greta Hofmann Nemiroff, 180–8. Markham: Fitzhenry and Whiteside.

Potuchek, Jean L. 1997. *Who Supports the Family: Gender and Breadwinning in Dual-Earner Marriages.* Stanford, CA: Stanford University Press.

Poulantzas, Nicos. 1975. *Classes in Contemporary Capitalism.* Translated by David Fernbach. London: New Left Books.

———. 1978. *State, Power, Socialism.* Translated by Patrick Camiller. London: New Left Books.

Presthus, Robert V. 1973. *Elite Accommodation in Canadian Politics.* Toronto: Macmillan.

Preston, Samuel H. 1986a. "Changing Values and Falling Birth Rates." *Population and Development Review*, 12 (suppl.), 176–200.

———. 1986b. "Mortality and Development Revisited." *United Nations Population Bulletin*, 18: 34–40.

Preston, Samuel H., Patrick Heuveline, and Michel Guillot. 2001. *Demography.* Malden, MA: Blackwell.

Pringle, Rosemary. 1988. *Secretaries Talk: Sexuality, Power and Work.* London: Verso.

Prus, Robert. 1987. "Generic Social Processes: Maximizing Conceptual Development in Ethnographic Research." *Journal of Contemporary Ethnography*, 16: 250–93.

Pryor, Edward. 1984. "Canadian Husband–Wife Families: Labour Force Participation and Income Trends, 1971–1981." *Labour Force*, May: 93–109.

Pryor, Jan, and Bryan Rodgers. 2001. *Children in Changing Families: Life After Parental Separation.* Oxford: Blackwell.

Psychology Today. 2000. "Makeup vs. Math." *Psychology Today*, November/December: 18.

Quadagno, Jill. 1990. "Race, Class, and Gender in the US Welfare State." *American Sociological Review*, 55: 25–7.

Quine, Lyn. 1999. "Workplace Bullying in NHS Community Trust: Staff Questionnaire Survey." *British Medical Journal*, 318: 228–32.

———. 2002. "Workplace Bullying in Junior Doctors: Questionnaire Survey." *British Medical Journal*, 324: 878–9.

Raadschelders, Jos C.N. 1997. "Size and Organizational Differentiation in Historical Perspective." *Journal of Public Administration Research and Theory*, 7: 419–41.

Radway, Janice. 1984. *Reading the Romance: Women, Patriarchy and Popular Literature.* Chapel Hill: University of North Carolina Press.

Ralston, Helen. 2000. "Redefinition of South Asian Women." In *Race and Racism: Canada's Challenge*, edited by Leo Driedger and Shiva S. Halli, 204–34. Ottawa: Carleton University Press.

Ram, Bali. 1990. *New Trends in the Family: Demographic Facts and Figures.* Ottawa: Statistics Canada.

Ram, Bali, and Rahim. 1993. "Enduring Effects of Women's Early Employment Experiences on Child-Spacing: The Canadian Evidence." *Population Studies*, 47: 307–18.

Ramcharan, Subhas. 1982. *Racism: Nonwhites in Canada.* Toronto: Butterworths.

Ramirez, Francisco O. 1981. "Comparative Social Movements." *International Journal of Comparative Sociology*, 22: 3–21.

Ramsay, Patricia. 1999. *Making Friends in School: Promoting Peer Relationships in Early Childhood.* New York: Teachers College Press, Columbia University.

Raphael, Dennis. 2001. "From Increasing Poverty to Societal Disintegration: The Effects of Economic Inequality on the Health of Individuals and Communities." In *Unhealthy Times: The Political Economy of Health Care*, edited by Pat Armstrong, Hugh Armstrong, and David Coburn, 223–46. Toronto: Oxford University Press.

Raudenbush, Stephen, and Robert J. Sampson. 1999. "'Ecometrics': Toward a Science of Assessing Ecological Settings, with Application to the Systematic Social Observation of Neighborhoods." *Sociological Methodology*, 29: 1–41.

Redclift, Michael, and Ted Benton, eds. 1994. *Social Theory and the Global Environment.* London: Routledge.

Redclift, Michael, and Graham Woodgate. 1994. "Sociology and the Environment: Discordant Discourse?" In *Social Theory and the Global Environment*, edited by Michael Redclift and Ted Benton, 51–66. London: Routledge.

Reimer, Samuel H. 1995. "A Look at Cultural Effects on Religiosity: A Comparison Between Canada and the United States." *Journal for the Scientific Study of Religion*, 34: 445–57.

Reinarman, Craig. 1996. "The Social Construction of an Alcohol Problem." In *Constructing Crime: Perspectives on Making News and Social Problems*, edited by Gary W. Potter and Victor E. Kappeler, 193–220. Prospect Heights, IL: Waveland.

Reiss, Albert J., Jr. 1959. "Rural–Urban and Status Differences in Interpersonal Contacts." *American Journal of Sociology*, 65: 182–95.

Reiter, Ester. 1991. *Making Fast Food: From the Frying Pan into the Fire.* Montreal: McGill-Queen's University Press.

———. 1996. *Making Fast Food: From the Frying Pan into the Fryer.* 2nd edn. Montreal: McGill-Queen's University Press.

Reitz, Jeffrey G. 1980. *The Survival of Ethnic Groups.* Toronto: McGraw-Hill Ryerson.

———. 1998. *The Warmth of the Welcome: The Social Causes of Economic Success for Immigrants in Different Nations and Cities.* Boulder, CO: Westview.

Reitzes, Donald, and Dietrich Reitzes. 1987. *The Alinski Legacy: Alive and Kicking.* Greenwich, CT: JAI Press.

Rex, John. 1987. "The Role of Class Analysis in the Study of Race Relations: A Weberian Perspective." In *Theories of Race and Ethnic Relations*, edited by John Rex and David Mason, 64–83. Cambridge: Cambridge University Press.

Rice, Suzanne. 1996. "The Evolution of the Concept of Sexual Harassment." *Initiatives*, 57, no. 2: 1–14.

Richardson, Laurel. 1988. *The Dynamics of Sex and Gender.* New York: Harper and Row.

Richardson, R. Jack. 1992. "Free Trade: Why Did It Happen?" *Canadian Review of Sociology and Anthropology*, 29: 307–28.

Rifkin, Jeremy. 1995. *The End of Work: The Decline of the Global Labour Force and the Dawn of the Post-market Era.* New York: Putnam.

Rinehart, James. 2001. *The Tyranny of Work: Alienation and the Labour Process.* 4th edn. Toronto: Harcourt.

Rinehart, James, Christopher Huxley, and David Robertson. 1994. "Worker Commitment and Labour Management Relations Under Lean Production at CAMI." *Industrial Relations*, 49: 750–75.

Ritzer, George. 2000. *The McDonaldization of Society.* 3rd edn. Thousand Oaks, CA: Pine Forge.

Robert, Maryse. 2000. *Negotiating NAFTA: Explaining the Outcome in Culture, Textiles, Autos, and Pharmaceuticals.* Toronto: University of Toronto Press.

Roberts, J. Timmons, and Melissa M. Toffolon-Weiss. 2001. *Chronicles from the Environmental Justice Frontline.* Cambridge: Cambridge University Press.

Roberts, Keith. 1995. *Religion in Sociological Perspective.* 3rd edn. Belmont, CA: Wadsworth.

Robertson, Ann. 2001. "Biotechnology, Political Rationality and Discourses on Health Risk." *Health*, 5: 293–310.

Robertson, David, James Rinehart, Chris Huxley, Jeff Wareham, Herman Rosenfeld, A. McGough, and Steven Benedict. 1993. *The CAMI Report: Lean Production in a Unionized Auto Plant.* North York, ON: CAW Research, 1993.

Robertson, Heather-Jane. 1998. *No More Teachers, No More Books: The Commercialization of Canada's Schools.* Toronto: McClelland & Stewart.

Robinson, B.W., and E.D. Salamon. 1987. "Gender Role Socialization: A Review of the Literature." In *Gender Roles: Doing What Comes Naturally?* edited by E.D. Salamon and B.W. Robinson, 123–42. Toronto: Methuen.

Robinson, Tracy L. 2001. "White Mothers of Non-white Children." *Journal of Humanistic Counseling, Education and Development*, 40, no. 2: 171–85.

Rodgers, Bryan, and Jan Pryor. 1998. *Divorce and Separation: The Outcomes for Children.* York, UK: Joseph Rowntree Foundation.

Rodrik, Dani. 1997. *Has Globalization Gone Too Far?* Washington, DC: Institute for International Economics.

Rogan, Mary. 1999. "Acts of Faith." *Saturday Night*, 114, no. 5: 42–51.

Rogers, Andrei, and Frans J. Willekens, eds. 1981. *Migration and Settlement: A Multiregional Comparative Study.* Dordrecht, Germany: Reidel.

Rogers, Everett. 1995. *Diffusion of Innovations.* 4th edn. New York: Free Press.

Romaniuc, Anatole. 1984. *Current Demographic Analysis: Fertility in Canada: From Baby-Boom to Baby-Bust.* Ottawa: Statistics Canada.

———. 1994. "Fertility in Canada: Retrospective and Prospective." In *Perspectives on Canada's Population: An Introduction to Concepts and Issues*, edited by Frank Trovato and Carl F. Grindstaff, 213–30. Toronto: Oxford University Press.

Romanow, Roy J. 2002. *Building on Values: The Future of Health Care in Canada.* Final Report of the Royal Commission on the Future of Health Care in Canada. Ottawa: The Commission. Available at <http://www.hc-sc.gc.ca/english/care/romanow/hcc0086.html>, accessed 16 July 2003

Roof, Wade Clark. 1999. *Spiritual Marketplace: Baby Boomers and the Remaking of American Religion.* Princeton, NJ: Princeton University Press,.

Roof, Wade Clark, and William McKinney. 1987. *American Mainline Religion.* New Brunswick, NJ: Rutgers University Press.

Rose, Steven, Leon J. Kamin, and R.C. Lewontin. 1984. *Not in Our Genes: Biology, Ideology, and Human Nature.* New York: Penguin.

Rose, Vicki. 1974. "Rape as a Social Problem: A Byproduct of the Feminist Movement." *Social Problems*, 25: 75–89.

Rosenberg, M. Michael, and Jack Jedwab. 1992. "Institutional Completeness, Ethnic Organizational Style and the Role of the State: The Jewish, Italian and Greek Communities of Montreal." *Canadian Review of Sociology and Anthropology*, 29: 266–87.

Rosenthal, Carolyn J. 1985. "Kinkeeping in the Familial Division of Labour." *Journal of Marriage and the Family*, 47: 965–74.

Rosenthal, Donald B., ed. 1980. *Urban Revitalization.* Beverly Hills, CA: Sage.

Ross, David P., and Paul Roberts. 1999. *Income and Child Well-Being: A New Perspective on the Poverty Debate.* Ottawa: Canadian Council on Social Development.

Ross, David P., E. Richard Shillington, and Clarence Lochhead. 1994. *The Canadian Fact Book on Poverty 1994.* Ottawa: Canadian Council on Social Development.

Ross, Eric B. 1998. *The Malthus Factor: Poverty, Politics and Population in Capitalist Development.* London: Zed Books.

Rossi, Alice. 1984. "Gender and Parenthood." *American Sociological Review*, 49: 1–18.

Rotermann, Michelle. 2001. "Wired Young Canadians." *Canadian Social Trends*, Winter, 4–8.

Rothermund, Dietmar. 1993. *An Economic History of India: From Pre-colonial Times to 1991.* 2nd edn. London: Routledge.

Rowland, Wade. 1999. *Spirit of the Web: The Age of Information from Telegraph to Internet.* Toronto: Key Porter.

Royal Commission on Aboriginal Peoples. 1996. *Report of the Royal Commission on Aboriginal Peoples.* Vol. 3: *Gathering Strength.* Ottawa: The Commission.

Royal Commission on Bilingualism and Biculturalism. 1970. *Report of the Royal Commission on Bilingualism and Biculturalism.* Vol. 4. *The Cultural Contribution of the Other Ethnic Groups.* Ottawa: Queen's Printer.

Ruble, Diane N., and Carol Lynn Martin. 1998. "Gender Development." In *Handbook of Child Psychology*, 5th edn, edited by William Damon, 933–1016. New York: Wiley.

Sacco, Vincent F. 1992. "An Introduction to the Study of

Deviance and Control." In *Deviance: Conformity and Control in Canadian Society*, edited by Vincent F. Sacco, 1–48. Scarborough, ON: Prentice-Hall.

Sachs, Wolfgang. 1991. "Environment and Development: The Story of a Dangerous Liaison." *Ecologist*, 21: 252–7.

Sadovnick, Alan R., ed. 1995. *Knowledge and Pedagogy: The Sociology of Basil Bernstein*. Norwood, NJ: Ablex.

Said, Edward W. 1978. *Orientalism*. London: Routledge & Kegan Paul.

Salazar, Lilia P., Shirin M. Schuldermann, Eduard H. Schuldermann, and Cam-Loi Huynh. 2001. "Canadian Filipino Adolescents Report on Parental Socialization for School Involvement." *Canadian Ethnic Studies*, 33, no. 2: 52–76.

Sampson, Robert, and Steve Raudenbush. 1999. "Systematic Social Observation of Public Spaces: A New Look at Disorder in Urban Neighborhoods." *American Journal of Sociology*, 105: 603–51.

Samson, Jane, ed. 2001. *The British Empire*. New York: Oxford University Press.

Samuel, John T. 1990. "Third World Immigration and Multiculturalism." In *Ethnic Demography: Canadian Immigrant, Racial and Cultural Variations*, edited by Shiva S. Halli, Frank Trovato, and Leo Driedger, 383–414. Ottawa: Carleton University Press.

Sartorius, N. 2001. "The Economic and Social Burden of Depression." *Journal of Clinical Psychiatry*, 62 (suppl. 15): 8–11.

Sassen, Saskia. 1991. *The Global City: New York, London, Tokyo*. Princeton, NJ: Princeton University Press.

———. 1996. *Losing Control? Sovereignty in an Age of Globalization*. New York: Columbia University Press.

———. 2002. "Introduction: Locating Cities on Global Circuits." In *Global Networks: Linked Cities*, edited by Saskia Sassen, 1–36. New York: Routledge.

Sasson, Theodore. 1995. *Crime Talk: How Citizens Construct a Social Problem*. Hawthorne, NY: Aldine de Gruyter.

Scarce, Rik. 1990. *Eco-warriors: Understanding the Radical Environmental Movement*. Chicago: Noble.

Schecter, Tanya. 1998. *Race, Class, Women and the State: The Case of Domestic Labour*. Montreal: Black Rose.

Schiller, Herbert I. 1984. *Information and the Crisis Economy*. Norwood, NJ: Ablex.

Schissel, Bernard, and Terry Wotherspoon. 2003. *The Legacy of School for Aboriginal People: Education, Oppression, and Emancipation*. Toronto: Oxford University Press.

Schnaiberg, Allan. 1975. "Social Synthesis of the Societal–Environmental Dialectic: The Role of Distributional Impacts." *Social Science Quarterly*, 56: 5–20.

———. 1980. *The Environment: From Surplus to Scarcity*. New York: Oxford University Press.

Schnore, Leo F. 1958. "Social Morphology and Human Ecology." *American Journal of Sociology*, 63: 620–34.

Schonberg, Harold C. 1977. *The Lives of the Great Composers*. 3rd edn. New York: Norton.

Schur, Edwin. 1979. *Interpreting Deviance: A Sociological Introduction*. New York: Harper and Row.

Schütz, Alfred. [1932] 1967. *The Phenomenology of the Social World*. Translated by George Walsh and Frederick Lehnert. Evanston, IL: Northwestern University Press.

Scott, Marvin B., and Stanford M. Lyman. 1968. "Accounts." *American Sociological Review*, 33: 46–64.

Segrave, Kerry. 1998. *American Television Abroad: Hollywood's Attempt to Dominate World Television*. Jefferson, NC: McFarland.

Seiber, Timothy, and Andrew Gordon. 1981. *Children and Their Organizations*. Boston: G.K. Hall.

Seltzer, Judith, and Debra Kalmuss. 1988. "Socialization and Stress Explanations for Spouse Abuse." *Social Forces*, 67: 473–91.

Selznick, Philip. 1949. *TVA and the Grass Roots*. Berkeley: University of California Press.

Sennett, Richard. 1998. *The Corrosion of Character: The Personal Consequences of Work in the New Capitalism*. New York: Norton.

Shaffir, William. 1974. *Life in a Religious Community: The Lubavitcher Chassidim in Montreal*. Toronto: Holt, Rinehart and Winston.

Shaw, Susan. 1988. "Gender Difference in the Definition and Perception of Household Labour." *Family Relations*, 37: 333–7.

Shelton, Beth Anne, and Juanita Firestone. 1989. "Household Labor Time and the Gender Gap in Earnings." *Gender and Society*, 3, no. 1: 105–12.

Shelton, Beth Anne, and Daphne John. 1996. "The Division of Household Labor." *Annual Review of Sociology*, 22: 299–322.

Shemel, Sidney and William Krasilovsky. 2003. *This Business of Music: The Definitive Guide to the Music Industry for Publishers, Writers, Record Companies, Producers, Artists, Agents*. (8th edn.) New York: Billboard Publications.

Shively, JoEllen. 1992. "Cowboys and Indians: Perceptions of Western Films Among American Indians and Anglos." *American Sociological Review*, 57: 725–34.

Sidlofsky, Samuel. 1969. *Post-war Immigrants in the Changing Metropolis, with Special Reference to Toronto's Italian Population*. Unpublished PhD dissertation, University of Toronto.

Sieber, Sam. 1981. *Fatal Remedies: The Ironies of Social Intervention*. New York: Plenum.

Siegel, Lloyd, and Arthur Zitrin. 1978. "Transsexuals in the New York City Welfare Population: The Function of Illusion in Transsexuality." *Archives of Sexual Behavior*, 7: 285–90.

Silva, Elizabeth B., and Carol Smart, eds. 1999. *The New Family?* London: Sage.

Simmel, Georg. 1950a. "The Metropolis and Mental Life." In *The Sociology of Georg Simmel*, translated by Kurt Wolff, 400–27. New York: Free Press.

———. 1950b. *The Sociology of Georg Simmel*. Translated by Kurt Wolf. Glencoe, IL: Free Press.

———. 1957. "Fashion." *American Journal of Sociology*, 62: 541–58.

Simmons, J.L. 1969. *Deviants*. Berkeley, CA: Glendessary Press.

Simon, David R., and Frank E. Hagan. 1999. *White Collar Deviance*. Boston: Allyn and Bacon.

Simon, Herbert. 1986. *Decision Making and Problem Solving*. Washington, DC: National Academy Press.

———. 1997. *Administrative Behavior: A Study of Decision-Making Processes in Administrative Organizations*. 4th edn. New York: Free Press.

Simon, Julian. 1980. "Reproductive Behavior as Religious Practice." In *Determinants of Fertility Trends: Theories Re-examined*, edited by Charlotte Höhn and Rainer Mackensen, 133–45. Liège, Belgium: Ordina.

———. 1981. "Environnemental Disruption or Environnemental Improvement?" *Social Science Quarterly*, 62: 30–43.

———, ed. 1995. *The State of Humanity*. Cambridge, MA: Blackwell.

———. 1996. *The Ultimate Resource 2*. Princeton, NJ: Princeton University Press.

Sinclair, Peter R. 1982. "Towards a Class Analysis of Contemporary Socialist Agriculture." *Sociologia Ruralis*, 22: 122–39.

———. 1987. *State Intervention and the Newfoundland Fisheries*. Aldershot, UK: Avebury.

Sinclair, Peter, and Lawrence Felt. 1992. "Separate Worlds: Gender and Domestic Labour in an Isolated Fishing Region." *Canadian Review of Sociology and Anthropology*, 29: 55–71.

Singer, Dorothy, and Jerome Singer. 2001. *Handbook of Children and the Media*. Thousand Oaks, CA: Sage.

Sjoberg, Gideon. 1960. *The Preindustrial City: Past and Present*. New York: Free Press.

Skidelsky, Robert. 2000. *John Maynard Keynes: Fighting for Britain, 1937–1946*. London: Macmillan.

Skill Development Leave Task Force, 1983. *Learning a Living in Canada: Report to the Minister of Employment and Immigration Canada*. Ottawa: Employment and Immigration Canada.

Sklair, Leslie. 1994. "Global Sociology and Global Environmental Change." In *Social Theory and the Global Environment*, edited by Michael Redclift and Ted Benton, 205–27. New York: Routledge.

Skocpol, Theda. 1979. *States and Social Revolutions: A Comparative Analysis of France, Russia, and China*. Cambridge: Cambridge University Press.

Skogstad, Grace. 2000. "Globalization and Public Policy." *Canadian Journal of Political Science*, 33: 805–28.

Slaughter, Matthew J., and Phillip Swagel. 1997. *Does Globalization Lower Wages and Export Jobs?* International Monetary Fund Economic Issues 11. Washington, DC: International Monetary Fund.

Smelser, Neil J. 1963. *Theory of Collective Behavior*. New York: Free Press.

Smelser, Neil J., William Julius Wilson, and Faith Mitchell. 2001. *America Becoming: Racial Trends and Their Consequences*. Washington, DC: National Research Council Press.

Smith, Adam. [1776] 1976. *An Inquiry into the Nature and Causes of the Wealth of Nations*. Edited by W.B. Todd.

Oxford: Oxford University Press.

Smith, Anthony D. 1988. *The Ethnic Origin of Nations*. Oxford, UK: Basil Blackwell.

Smith, Dorothy. 1975. "Ideological Structures and How Women Are Excluded." *Canadian Review of Sociology and Anthropology*, 12: 353–69.

———. 1987. *The Everyday World as Problematic: A Feminist Sociology*. Boston: Northeastern University Press.

———. 1990. *The Conceptual Practices of Power: A Feminist Sociology of Knowledge*. Toronto: University of Toronto Press.

———. 1993. *Earnings of Men and Women*. Ottawa: Statistics Canada.

———. 1999. *Writing the Social: Critique, Theory, and Investigations*. Toronto: University of Toronto Press.

———. 2000. *Women in Canada 2000: A Gender-Based Statistical Report*. Ottawa: Statistics Canada.

Smith, Michael R. 1999. "What Is the Effect of Technological Change on Earnings Inequality?" *International Journal of Sociology and Social Policy*, 19: 24–59.

———. 2001a. "La mondialisation à-t-elle un effet important sur les marchés du travail des pays riches?" In *Une société monde? Les dynamiques de la mondialisation*, edited by Daniel Mercure, 201–14. Quebec City: Presses de l'Université Laval.

———. 2001b. "What Have the FTA and the NAFTA Done to the Canadian Labor Market?" *Forum for Social Economics*, 30: 25–50.

Smith, Philip. 2001. *Cultural Theory: An Introduction*. Oxford: Blackwell.

Smith, Raymond T. 1996. *The Matrifocal Family: Power, Pluralism and Politics*. New York: Routledge.

Smith, Tom W. 2002. "Religious Diversity in America: The Emergence of Muslims, Buddhists, Hindus, and Others." *Journal for the Scientific Study of Religion*, 41: 577–85.

Smith, Wilfred Cantwell. 1959. "Comparative Religion: Wither—and Why?" In *The History of Religions: Essays in Methodology*, edited by Mircea Eliade and Joseph M. Kitagawa, 31–58. Chicago: University of Chicago Press.

Smythe, Dallas. 1981. *Dependency Road: Communications, Capitalism, Consciousness and Canada*. Norwood, NJ: Ablex.

Snow, David A., and Leon Anderson. 1993. *Down on Their Luck: A Study of Homeless Street People*. Berkeley: University of California Press.

Snow, David A., E. Burke Rochford, Jr, Steven K. Worden, and Robert D. Benford. 1986. "Frame Alignment Processes, Mobilization, and Movement Participation." *American Sociological Review*, 51: 464–81.

Sommer, Robert. 1969. *Personal Space: The Behavioral Basis of Design*. Toronto: Prentice-Hall.

Sontag, Susan. 1978. *Illness as Metaphor*. New York: Farrar, Straus & Giroux.

Spain, Daphne. 2001. *How Women Saved the City*. Minneapolis: University of Minnesota Press.

Spector, Malcolm, and John I. Kitsuse. 1977. *Constructing

Social Problems. Menlo Park, CA: Cummings.

Speirs, Rosemary. 1993. "Violence Affects Half of Women, Study Says." *Toronto Star*, 19 November, A1, A29.

Spittler, Gerd. 1980. "Abstract Knowledge as a Basis of Power: The History of the Evolution of Bureaucratic Power in the Prussian Peasant State." *Kolner Zeitschrift fur Soziologie und Sozialpsychologie*, 32: 574–604.

Spitzer, Steven. 1975. "Toward a Marxian Theory of Deviance." *Social Problems*, 22: 638–51.

Stack, John F., Jr. 1986. "Ethnic Mobilization in World Politics: The Primordial Perspective." In *The Primordial Challenge: Ethnicity in the Contemporary World*, edited by John F. Stack, Jr, 1–11. New York: Greenwood.

Stanton, Elizabeth Cady. [1895] 1972. *The Woman's Bible.* New York: Arno.

Stark, Rodney. 1996. *The Rise of Christianity.* Princeton, NJ: Princeton University Press.

Stark, Rodney, and William Sims Bainbridge. 1985. *The Future of Religion.* Berkeley: University of California Press.

———. 1996. *A Theory of Religion.* New Brunswick, NJ: Rutgers University Press.

Stark, Rodney, and Roger Finke. 2000. *Acts of Faith: Explaining the Human Side of Religion.* Berkeley: University of California Press.

Stark, Rodney, and Laurence Innaccone. 1994. "A Supply-Side Reinterpretation of the 'Secularization' of Europe." *Journal for the Scientific Study of Religion*, 33: 230–52.

Stasiulis, Daiva. 1980. "The Political Structuring of Ethnic Community Action: A Reformulation." *Canadian Ethnic Studies*, 12: 19–44.

———. 1990. "Theorizing Connections: Gender, Race, Ethnicity, and Class." In *Race and Ethnic Relations in Canada*, edited by Peter S. Li, 269–305. Toronto: Oxford University Press.

———. 1999. "Feminist Intersectional Theorizing." In *Race and Ethnic Relations in Canada*, 2nd edn, edited by Peter S. Li, 347–97. Toronto: Oxford University Press.

Statistics Canada. 1973. *Education in Canada 1973.* Ottawa: Statistics Canada.

———. 1992. *Census Metropolitan Areas and Census Agglomerations: Population and Dwelling Counts.* Ottawa: Statistics Canada.

———. 1993. *Earnings of Men and Women.* Ottawa: Statistics Canada.

———. 1996a. *Canada Year Book 1997.* Ottawa: Statistics Canada.

———. 1996b. *Growing Up in Canada.* Ottawa: Human Resources Development Canada and Statistics Canada.

———. 1998a. *Characteristics of Dual-Earner Families 1996.* Ottawa: Statistics Canada.

———. 1998b. "1996 Census: Education, Mobility and Migration." *The Daily*, 14 April.

———. 1999a. *Annual Demographic Statistics.* Ottawa: Statistics Canada.

———. 1999b. *Canada Year Book 1999.* Ottawa: Statistics Canada.

———. 2001a. *Canada Year Book 2001.* Ottawa: Statistics Canada.

———. 2001b. *The Changing Profile of Canada's Labour Force.* Ottawa: Statistics Canada.

———. 2001c. "Internet Use on the Cusp of the 21st Century." *Canadian Social Trends*, Winter: 2–3.

———. 2001d. "Television Viewing." *The Daily*, 23 Oct.

———. 2002a. "Advance Statistics/Education at a Glance." *Education Quarterly Review*, 8, no. 3: 41–53.

———. 2002b. "Births: 2000." *The Daily*, 26 September.

———. 2002c. "Education at a Glance." *Education Quarterly Review*, 8, no. 4: 46–51.

———. 2002d. "Fact Sheet on Unionization." *Perspectives on Labour and Income*, 13, no. 3: 1–25.

———. 2002e. *Life Tables: Canada, Provinces and Territories 1995–1997.* Ottawa: Statistics Canada.

———. 2002f. "Perspectives on Labour and Income: Fact-Sheet on Unionization." Ottawa: Statistics Canada.

———. 2003a. *Canada's Ethnocultural Portrait: The Changing Mosaic.* Ottawa: Statistics Canada.

———. 2003b. "Population 15 Years and over by Hours Spent on Unpaid Housework, 1996 Census." Available at <http://www.statcan.ca.80/english/Pdgb/famil56_96a.htm>, accessed 5 August 2003.

———. 2003c. "Population of Census Metropolitan Areas." Available at <www.statcan.ca/english/Pgdb/demo05.htm>, accessed 17 July 2003.

———. 2003d. *A Profile of the Canadian Population: Where We Live.* Available at <http://geodepot.statcan.ca/Diss/Highlights/>, accessed 17 July 2003.

Statistics Canada and Council of Ministers of Education Canada (CMEC). 2000. *Education Indicators in Canada: Report of the Pan-Canadian Education Indicators Program 1999.* Available at <www.cmec.ca/stats/pceip/1999/Indicatorsite/index.html>, accessed 19 June 2003.

Statistics Canada and Human Resources Development Canada (HRDC). 2001. *A Report on Adult Education and Training in Canada: Learning a Living.* Ottawa: Statistics Canada and HRDC.

Status of Women Canada. 1986. *Report of the Task Force on Child Care.* Ottawa: Status of Women Canada.

Steffensmeier, Renee. 1982. "A Role Model of the Transition to Parenthood." *Journal of Marriage and the Family*, 44: 319–34.

Stehr, Nico, and R. Grundmann. 1996. *Classical Social Science Discourse and the Impact of Climate on Society.* Unpublished paper. Wall Institute for Advanced Studies, University of British Columbia, Vancouver, and Max-Planck-Institut für Gesellschaftsforchung, Köln.

Stern, Nicholas. 2002. "Keynote Address: A Strategy for Development." In *Annual World Bank Conference on Development Economics 2001/2002*, edited by Boris Pleskovic and Nicholas Stern, 11–35. Washington, DC: World Bank; New York: Oxford University Press.

Stevans, Lonnie K. 1998. "Assessing the Effect of the Occupational Crowding of Immigrants on the Real Wages of African American Workers." *Review of Black*

Political Economy, 26: 37–46.

Stevenson, Kathryn. 1999. "Family Characteristics of Problem Kids." *Canadian Social Trends*, 55, Winter: 2–6.

Stoddart, Kenneth. 1986. "The Presentation of Everyday Life: Some Textual Strategies for 'Adequate Ethnography'." *Urban Life*, 15, no. 1: 103–21.

Stokes, Randall, and John P. Hewitt. 1976. "Aligning Actions." *American Sociological Review*, 1: 838–49.

Stone, Gregory P. 1981. "Appearance and the Self: A Slightly Revised Version." In *Social Psychology Through Symbolic Interaction*, edited by Gregory P. Stone and Harvey A. Farberman, 187–202. New York: Wiley.

Stone, Leroy O. 1967. *Urban Development in Canada*. Ottawa: Dominion Bureau of Statistics.

Storey, Robert. 2002. *From Capitalism to Socialism*. Unpublished paper. McMaster University, Hamilton, ON.

Strange, Susan. 1996. *The Retreat of the State*. Cambridge: Cambridge University Press.

Strauss, Murray A., and Richard J. Gelles. 1990. *Physical Violence in American Families: Risk Factors and Adaptations to Violence in 8,145 Families*. New Brunswick, NJ: Transaction.

Street, Debra, and Ingrid Connidis. 2001. "Creeping Selectivity in Canadian Women's Pensions." In *Women, Work and Pensions: International Issues and Prospects*, edited by Jay Ginn, Debra Street, and Sara Arber, 158–78. Buckingham, UK: Open University Press.

Sugiman, Pamela. 1994. *Labour's Dilemma: The Gender Politics of Auto Workers in Canada, 1937–1979*. Toronto: University of Toronto Press.

———. 2001. "Privilege and Oppression: The Configuration of Race, Gender, and Class in Southern Ontario Auto Plants, 1939 to 1949." *Labour/Le Travail*, 47 (Spring): 83–113.

Suranovic, Steven M. 1997. "Why Economists Should Study Fairness." *Challenge*, 40: 109–24.

Sutherland, Edwin. 1947. *Principles of Criminology*. 4th edn. Chicago: Lippincott.

Sydie, Rosalind. 1987. "Sociology and Gender." In *An Introduction to Sociology*, edited by M. Michael Rosenberg, William B. Shaffir, Allan Turowetz, and Morton Weinfeld. Toronto: Methuen.

Szasz, Andrew. 1994. *Ecopopulism: Toxic Waste and the Movement for Environmental Justice*. Minneapolis, MI: University of Minneapolis Press.

Tabb, William K., and Larry Sawers. 1984. *Marxism and the Metropolis*. 2nd edn. New York: Oxford University Press.

Tannenbaum, Frank. 1938. *Crime and the Community*. Boston: Ginn and Company.

Tanner, Julian. 2001. *Teenage Troubles: Youth and Deviance in Canada*. 2nd edn. Toronto: Nelson.

Tannock, Stuart. 2001. *Youth at Work: The Unionized Fast-Food and Grocery Workplace*. Philadelphia: Temple University Press.

Tapscott, Don. 1998. *Growing Up Digital: The Rise of the Net Generation*. New York: McGraw-Hill.

Tardy, Rebecca. 2000. "But I Am a Good Mom: The Social Construction of Motherhood Through Health-Care Conversations." *Journal of Contemporary Ethnography*, 29: 433–73.

Tarrow, Sidney. 1988. "National Politics and Collective Action: Recent Theory and Research in Western Europe and the United States." *Annual Review of Sociology*, 14: 421–40.

———. 1998. *Power in Movements: Social Movements and Contentious Politics*. 2nd edn. New York: Cambridge University Press.

Taylor, Bron. 1991. "The Religion and Politics of Earth First!" *Ecologist*, 21: 258–66.

Taylor, Frederick W. 1911. *Principles of Scientific Management*. New York: Harper.

Teitelbaum, Michael S. 1975. "Relevance of Demographic Transition Theory for Developing Countries." *Science*, 2 May: 420–5.

Ten Bos, Réné. 1997. "Essai: Business Ethics and Bauman Ethics." *Organization Studies*, 18: 997–1014.

Theodorson, George A. 1961. *Studies in Human Ecology*. New York: Harper and Row.

———. 1982. *Urban Patterns: Studies in Human Ecology*. University Park: University of Pennsylvania Press.

Thio, Alex. 1998. *Deviant Behavior*. New York: Longman.

Thomas, Derrick. 2001. "Evolving Family Living Arrangements of Canada's Immigrants." *Canadian Social Trends*, Summer: 16–22.

Thomas, W.I., and D.S. Thomas. 1928. *The Child in America*. New York: Knopf.

Thompson, Kevin, and Leslie Heinberg. 1999. "The Media's Influence on Body Image Disturbance and Eating Disorders: We've Reviled Them, Now Can We Rehabilitate Them?" *Journal of Social Issues*, 55: 339–53.

Thompson, Warren S. 1929. "Population." *American Journal of Sociology*, 34: 959–75.

———. 1944. *Plenty of People*. Lancaster, PA: Jacques Cattel.

Thomson, Elizabeth, Sara McLanahan, and Roberta Curtin. 1992. "Family Structure, Gender and Parental Socialization." *Journal of Marriage and the Family*, 54: 368–78.

Thorne, Barry. 1982. "Feminist Rethinking of the Family: An Overview." In *Rethinking the Family: Some Feminist Questions*, edited by Barry Thorne with Marilyn Yalom, 1–24. New York: Longman.

Thorns, David C. 2002. *The Transformation of Cities: Urban Theory and Urban Life*. New York: Palgrave Macmillan.

Tilly, Charles. 1978. *From Mobilization to Revolution*. Reading, MA: Addison-Wesley.

———. 1998. *Durable Inequality*. Berkeley: University of California Press.

Titchkosky, Tanta. 2001. "Disability: A Rose by Any Other Name? 'People-First' Language in Canadian Society." *Canadian Review of Sociology and Anthropology*, 38, no. 2: 125–40.

Tokar, Brian. 1988. "Exploring the New Ecologies." *Alternatives*, 15, no. 4: 31–43.

Tomic, Patricia, and Ricardo Trumper. 1992. "Canada and the Streaming of Immigrants: A Personal Account of the Chilean Case." In *Deconstructing a Nation: Immigra-*

tion, Multiculturalism, and Racism in '90s Canada, edited by Vic Satzewich, 163–81. Halifax, NS: Fernwood.

Tönnies, Ferdinand. [1887] 1957. *Community and Society (Gemeinschaft und Gesellschaft)*. New York: Harper and Row.

Torres, Carlos Alberto. 1998. *Democracy, Education, and Multiculturalism: Dilemmas of Citizenship in a Global World*. Lanham, MD: Rowman and Littlefield.

Touraine, Alain. 1981. *The Voice and the Eye: An Analysis of Social Movements*. Cambridge: Cambridge University Press.

Traill, Catherine Parr. [1836] 1966. *The Backwoods of Canada*. Toronto: McClelland & Stewart.

Tremblay, Manon. 1998. "Do Female MPs Substantively Represent Women? A Study of Legislative Behaviour in Canada's 35th Parliament." *Canadian Journal of Political Science*, 31: 435–65.

Tremblay, Mark S., and J. Douglas Willms. 2000. "Secular Trends in the Body Mass Index of Canadian Children." *Canadian Medical Association Journal*, 163: 1429–33.

Tremblay, Richard E., Bernard Boulerice, Philip Harden, Pierre McDuff, Daniel Perusse, Robert Pihl, and Mark Zoccolillo. 1996. "Do Children in Canada Become More Aggressive as They Approach Adolescence?" In Statistics Canada, *Growing Up in Canada*, 127–38. Ottawa: HRDC and Statistics Canada.

Tremblay, Sylvain. 1999. "Illicit Drugs and Crime in Canada." In Canadian Centre for Justice Statistics, *The Juristat Reader: A Statistical Overview of the Canadian Justice System*, 253–65. Toronto: Thompson.

Trovato, Frank. 1988a. "The Interurban Mobility of the Foreign Born in Canada, 1976–81." *International Migration Review*, 22, no. 3: 59–86.

———. 1988b. "A Macrosociological Analysis of Change in the Marriage Rate: Canadian Women, 1921–25 to 1980–85." *Journal of Marriage and the Family*, 50: 507–21.

Troyer, Ronald, and Gerald Markle. 1983. *Cigarettes: The Battle over Smoking*. New Brunswick, NJ: Rutgers University Press.

Tuggle, Justin L., and Malcolm D. Holmes. 1997. "Blowing Smoke: Status Politics and the Shasta County Smoking Ban." *Deviant Behavior*, 18: 77–93.

Tuljapurkar, Shripad, Nan Li, and Marcus W. Feldman. 1995. "High Sex Ratios in China's Future." *Science*, 10 February: 874–6.

Turk, Austin T. 1976. "Law as a Weapon in Social Conflict." *Social Problems*, 23: 276–92.

Turner, Bryan S. 1988. *Status*. Minneapolis: University of Minnesota Press.

Turner, Jay R., and William R. Avison. Forthcoming. "Status Variations in Stress Exposure Among Young Adults: Implications for the Interpretation of Prior Research." *Journal of Health and Social Behaviour*.

Turner, Ralph. 1962. "Role-Taking: Process Versus Conformity." In *Human Behavior and Social Processes*, edited by Arnold Rose, 20–40. Boston: Houghton Mifflin.

Tylor, Edward. 1871. *Primitive Culture: Researches into the Development of Mythology, Philosophy, Religion, Language, Art and Custom*. London: John Murray.

———. 1903. *Primitive Culture: Researches into the Development of Mythology, Philosophy, Religion, Language, Art, and Custom*. Vol. 1. London: John Murphy.

Tyrell, Hartmann. 1981. "Is Weber's Type of Bureaucracy an Objective, True Type? Remarks on a Thesis by Renate Mayntz." *Zeitschrift fur Soziologie*.

UNAIDS. 2001a. *Children and Young People in a World of AIDS*. Geneva: Joint United Nations Programme on HIV/AIDS.

———. 2001b. "Gender and HIV Fact Sheet." Geneva: UNAIDS, Joint United Nations Programme on HIV/AIDS.

———. 2002. "Epidemiological Fact Sheets on HIV/AIDS and Sexually Transmitted Infections: Canada." Geneva: UNAIDS, Joint United Nations Programme on HIV/AIDS.

Ungar, S. [1986] 1992. "Self Mockery: An Alternative Format Self-Presentation." In *Sociological Slices: Introductory Readings from the Interactionist Perspective*, edited by Gary Alan Fine, John Johnson, and Harvey A. Farberman, 45–58. Greenwich, CT: JAI Press.

United Nations. 1990. *The World's Women: Trends and Statistics*. New York: United Nations.

———. 2000. *Replacement Migration*. New York: UN Population Division, Department of Economic and Social Affairs.

———. 2001. *World Population Prospects: The 2000 Revision*. 2 vols. New York: UN Department of Economic and Social Affairs Population Division.

———. 2002. *World Population Ageing: 1950–2050*. New York: UN Department of Economic and Social Affairs Population Division.

———. 2003. *World Population Prospects: The 2002 Revision*. Highlights. New York: UN Department of Economic and Social Affairs Population Division.

United Nations Centre for Human Settlements (HABITAT). 2001. *Cities in a Globalizing World*. London: Earthscan.

United Nations Economic Commission for Europe. 1992. *Demographic Causes and Economic Consequences of Population Aging*. Edited by George Stolnitz. New York: United Nations.

United Nations Population Division. 1999. *The World at Six Billion*. New York: United Nations.

———. 2002. *International Migration Report 2002*. New York: United Nations.

United States. Bureau of Census. 1999. *World Population Profile: 1998*. Report WP/98. Washington, DC: US Government Printing Office.

———. 2003. World POPClock Projection. Available at <www.census.gov/cgi-bin/ipc/popclockw>, accessed 9 July 2003.

United States. White House. 2002. "Remarks by the President to the Travel Pool." Available at <www.whitehouse.gov/news/releases/2002/06/20020604-16.html>, accessed 16 July 2003.

Urmetzer, Peter, and Neil Guppy. 1999. "Changing Income Inequality in Canada." In *Social Inequality in Canada: Patterns, Problems, and Policies*, edited by James E. Curtis, Edward G. Grabb, and Neil L. Guppy, 56–65. Scarborough, ON: Prentice-Hall Allyn and Bacon.

Ursel, Jane. 1992. *Private Lives, Public Policy: 100 Years of State Intervention in the Family*. Toronto: Women's Press.

Vallin, Jacques. 1983. "Sex Patterns of Mortality: A Comparative Study of Model Life Tables and Actual Situations with Special Reference to the Case of Algeria and France." In *Sex Differences in Mortality*, edited by Alan D. Lopez and Lado T. Ruzicka, 443–76. Canberra: Australian National University.

Van de Kaa, Dirk J. 1987. "Europe's Second Demographic Transition." *Population Bulletin*, 42, no. 1.

———. 1994. "The Second Demographic Transition Revisited: Theories and Expectations." In *Population and Family in the Low Countries 1993: Late Fertility and Other Current Issues*, edited by Gijs Beets, Hans van den Brekel, R. Cliquet, G. Dooghe, and J. de Jong Gierveld, 81–126. Lisse; Berwyn, PA: Swets & Zeitlinger.

Van den Berghe, Pierre L. 1987. *The Ethnic Phenomenon*. New York: Praeger.

Van Paasen, C. 1981. "The Philosophy of Geography: From Vidal to Hägerstrand." In *Space and Time Geography: Essays Dedicated to Torsten Hägerstrand*, edited by Alan Pred, 17–29. Lund, Sweden: Gleerup.

Van Vliet, Willem, Elizabeth Huttman, and Sylvia Fava, eds. 1985. *Housing Needs and Policy Approaches*. Durham, NC: Duke University Press.

van Wormer, Katherine Stuart, and Clemens Bartollas. 2000. *Women and the Criminal Justice System*. Boston: Allyn and Bacon.

Vanier Institute of the Family. 2000. *Profiling Canada's Families II*. Ottawa: Vanier Institute of the Family.

Veenstra, Gerry. 2001. "Social Capital and Health." *Canadian Journal of Policy Research*, 2: 1672–81.

Vold, George B. 1958. *Theoretical Criminology*. New York: Oxford University Press.

Vold, George B., Thomas J. Bernard, and Jeffrey B. Snipes. 2002. *Theoretical Criminology*. 5th edn. New York: Oxford University Press.

Vosko, Leah. 2000. *Temporary Work: The Gendered Rise of a Precarious Employment Relationship*. Toronto: University of Toronto Press.

Wagner, David. 1997. *The New Temperance: The American Obsession with Sin and Vice*. Boulder, CO: Westview.

Wagner, Nicoletta. 2002. "Wars Old and New in Colombia." NZZ online (Neue Zürcher Zeitung), 19 May. Available at <www.nzz.ch/english/editorials/2002/05/07_colombia.html>, accessed 16 July 2003.

Waksler, Frances. 1991. *Studying the Social Worlds of Children: Sociological Readings*. London: Falmer.

Walkom, Thomas. 1997. "The Harris Government: Restoration or Revolution?" In *The Government and Politics of Ontario*, 5th edn, edited by Graham White, 402–17. Toronto: University of Toronto Press.

Waller, Willard. [1932] 1965. *The Sociology of Teaching*. New York: Wiley.

Walzer, Michael. 1983. *Spheres of Justice: A Defense of Pluralism and Equality*. New York: Basic Books.

Waring, Marilyn. 1996. *Three Masquerades: Essays on Equality, Work and Human Rights*. Toronto: University of Toronto Press.

Warner, R. Stephen, and J.G. Wittner, eds. 1998. *Gatherings in Diaspora: Religious Communities and the New Immigration*. Philadelphia: Temple University Press.

Warren, Karen. 1990. "The Power and Promise of Ecological Feminism." *Environmental Ethics*, 12, no. 2: 125–46.

Watson, William. 1999. "Globalization and the Meaning of Canadian Life." In *Room to Manoeuvre? Globalization and Policy Convergence*, edited by Thomas J. Courchene, 259–70. Montreal: McGill-Queen's University Press.

Weatherall, Ann. 2002. *Gender, Language, and Discourse*. New York: Routledge.

Webber, Melvin M. 1963. "Order in Diversity: Community Without Propinquity." In *Cities and Space*, edited by Lowden Wingo, 23–54. Baltimore, MD: Johns Hopkins University Press.

Weber, Max. [1904] 1958. *The Protestant Ethic and The Spirit of Capitalism*. Translated by Talcott Parsons. New York: Scribner.

———. [1908] 1978. *Economy and Society*. Translated by Ephraim Fischoff. Berkeley: University of California Press.

———. [1916] 1951. *The Religion of China: Confucianism and Taoism*. Translated by H.H. Gerth. Glencoe, IL: Free Press.

———. [1916–17] 1958. *The Religion of India: The Sociology of Hinduism and Buddhism*. Translated by H.H. Gerth and Don Martindale. Glencoe: Free Press.

———. [1917–19] 1952. *Ancient Judaism*. Translated by H.H. Gerth and Don Martindale. Glencoe: Free Press.

———. [1920–1] 1963. *The Sociology of Religion*. Translated by E. Fischoff. Boston: Beacon Press.

———. [1922] 1946. *From Max Weber: Essays in Sociology*. Translated and edited by H.H. Gerth and C. Wright Mills. New York: Oxford University Press.

———. [1922] 1958. *Essays in Sociology*. Translated by H.H. Gerth and C. Wright Mills. New York: Oxford University Press.

———. [1922] 1963. *The Sociology of Religion*. Translated by Ephraim Fischoff. Boston: Beacon.

———. [1923] 1961. *General Economic History*. Translated by Frank H. Knight. New York: Collier.

Weeks, Jeffrey, Catherine Donovan, and Brian Heaphy. 1998. "Everyday Experiments: Narratives of Non-heterosexual Relationships." In *The New Family?* edited by Elizabeth B. Silva and Carol Smart, 83–99. London: Sage.

Weiher, Gregory R. 1991. *The Fractured Metropolis*. Albany: State University of New York Press.

Weinberg, E., and P. Deutschberger. 1963. "Some Dimensions of Altercasting." *Sociometry*, 26: 545–66.

Weinberg, Martin S. 1997. "The Nudist Management of

Respectability." In *The Production of Reality: Essays and Readings on Social Interaction*, 2nd edn, edited by Jodi O'Brien and Peter Kollock, 511–19. Thousand Oaks, CA: Pine Forge Press.

Weiner, Gaby. 1994. *Feminisms in Education: An Introduction.* Buckingham, UK: Open University Press.

Weinfeld, Morton. 1981. "The Development of Affirmative Action in Canada." *Canadian Ethnic Studies*, 13, no. 2: 23–39.

———. 1983. "The Ethnic Sub-economy: Explication and Analysis of a Case Study of the Jews of Montreal." *Contemporary Jewry*, 6: 6–25.

Weir, Ernest Austin. 1965. *The Struggle for National Broadcasting in Canada.* Toronto: McClelland & Stewart.

Wekerle, Gerda. 1984. "A Woman's Place Is in the City." *Antipode*, 16, no. 5: 11–19.

Wekerle, Gerda, and Brent Rutherford. 1987. "Employed Women in the Suburbs: Transportation Disadvantage in a Car-Centered Environment." *Alternatives*, 14: 49–54.

Wellman, Barry. 1979. "The Community Question: The Intimate Networks of East Yorkers." *American Journal of Sociology*, 84: 1201–31.

Wellman, Barry, Peter Carrington, and Alan Hall. 1988. "Networks and Personal Communities." In *Structural Sociology*, edited by S.D. Berkowitz and Barry Wellman. New York: Cambridge University Press.

Wellman, Barry, and Barry Leighton. 1979. "Networks, Neighborhoods, and Communities: Approaches to the Study of the Community Question." *Urban Affairs Quarterly*, 14: 363–90.

Werbner, Pnina, and Tariq Modood. 1997. *The Politics of Multiculturalism in the New Europe: Racism, Identity and Community.* London: Zed Books.

Wernick, Andrew. 1987. "From Voyeur to Narcissist: Imaging Men in Contemporary Advertising." In *Beyond Patriarchy*, edited by Michael Kaufman, 277–97. Toronto: Oxford University Press.

Wertham, Frederic. 1954. *Seduction of the Innocent.* New York: Rinehart.

West, G. Page, III, and G. Dale Meyer. 1997. "Communicated Knowledge as a Learning Foundation." *International Journal of Organizational Analysis*, 5: 25–58.

Westhues, Kenneth. 1982. *First Sociology.* New York: McGraw-Hill.

White, David Manning. 1950. "The 'Gatekeeper': A Case Study in the Selection of News." *Journalism Quarterly*, 27: 383–90.

White, Kevin M., and Samuel H. Preston. 1996. "How Many Americans Are Alive Because of Twentieth-Century Improvements in Mortality?" *Population and Development Review*, 22: 415–30.

White, Lynn, Jr. 1967. "The Historical Roots of Our Ecological Crisis." *Science*, 155: 1203–7.

Whyte, William Foote. 1943. *Street Corner Society: The Social Structure of an Italian Slum.* Chicago: University of Chicago Press.

———. 1949. "The Social Structure of the Restaurant."

American Journal of Sociology, 54: 302–8.

Wickberg, Edgar. 1982. *From China to Canada: A History of Chinese Communities in Canada.* Toronto: McClelland and Stewart.

Wiley, Norbert F. 1967. "The Ethnic Mobility Trap and Stratification Theory." *Social Problems*, 15: 147–59.

Wilkes, Rima. 2001. *Competition or Colonialism? An Analysis of Two Theories of Ethnic Collective Action.* Unpublished PhD dissertation, University of Toronto.

Wilkins, Russell, Owen Adams, and Anna Brancker. 1989. "Change in Mortality by Income in Urban Canada from 1971 to 1986." *Health Reports*, 1: 137–74.

Wilkinson, Derek. 1992. "Change in Household Division of Labour Following Unemployment in Elliot Lake." Paper presented to Learned Societies, Charlottetown, PEI.

Williams, A. Paul. 1989. "Social Origins and Elite Politics in Canada: The Impact of Background Differences on Attitudes Towards the Welfare State." *Canadian Journal of Sociology*, 14: 67–87.

Williams, David R., and Chiquita Collins. 1995. "U.S. Socioeconomic and Racial Differences in Health: Patterns and Explanations." *Annual Review of Sociology*, 21: 349–86.

Williams, Frank P., III, and Marilyn D. McShane, eds. 1994. *Criminological Theory.* 2nd edn. Englewood Cliffs, NJ: Prentice-Hall.

Willis, J.R. 1987. "What Have We Learned from the Economics of the Family?" *American Economic Review*, 77, no. 2: 68–81.

Willis, Paul. 1977. *Learning to Labour: How Working Class Kids Get Working Class Jobs.* Farnborough, UK: Saxon House.

Wilson, Bryan. 1966. *Religion in Secular Society.* London: Watts.

———. 1982. *Religion in Sociological Perspective.* Oxford: Oxford University Press.

Wilson, Susannah J. 1991. *Women, Families, and Work.* 3rd edn. Toronto: McGraw-Hill Ryerson.

———. 2001. "Intimacy and Commitment in Family Formation." In *Families: Changing Trends in Canada*, 4th edn, edited by Maureen Baker, 93–114. Toronto: McGraw-Hill Ryerson.

Wimberley, Dale W. 1990. "Investment Dependence and Alternative Explanations of Third World Mortality." *American Sociological Review*, 55: 75–91.

Winner, Langdon. 1977. *Autonomous Technology: Technics-out-of-Control as a Theme in Political Thought.* Cambridge, MA: MIT Press.

Wireman, Peggy. 1984. *Urban Neighborhoods, Networks, and Families.* Toronto: Lexington.

Wirth, Louis. 1938. "Urbanism as a Way of Life." *American Journal of Sociology*, 44: 1–24.

Witz, Anne. 1992. *Professions and Patriarchy.* London: Routledge.

Wolejszo, Stefan. 2002. *Gender Trouble and the Construction of Gender Identity on Internet Chat Sites.* MA thesis, University of Manitoba, Winnipeg, MB.

Wolfe, David A., and Meric S. Gertler. 2001. *The New Economy: An Overview*. Discussion paper produced for the Social Sciences and Humanities Research Council of Canada.

Wolfgang, Marvin, and Franco Ferracuti. 1967. *The Subculture of Violence: Towards an Integrated Theory in Criminology*. Beverly Hills, CA: Sage.

Wolfson, Michael C., and Brian B. Murphy. 1998. "New Views on Inequality and Trends in Canada and the United States." *Monthly Labor Review*, April: 3–23.

Wollstonecraft, Mary. [1792] 1986. *Vindication of the Rights of Women*. Middlesex, UK: Penguin.

Wood, Adrian. 1994. *North–South Trade, Employment and Inequality*. Oxford, UK: Clarendon.

Wood, Chris, with Rima Kar. 2000. "Why Do Men Do It?" *Maclean's*, 7 August: 5–7.

Woods, Peter. 1979. *The Divided School*. London: Routledge and Kegan Paul.

Woodward, Kath. 2003. *Understanding Identity*. London: Arnold.

Woolmington, Eric. 1985. "Small May Be Inevitable." *Australian Geographical Studies*, 23 (October): 195–207.

World Commission on Environment and Development. 1987. *Our Common Future*. New York: Oxford University Press.

World Health Organization (WHO). 1996. *Statistics Annual for 1995*. Geneva: WHO.

———. 2001. "Obesity Epidemic Puts Millions at Risk from Related Diseases." [Press release]. Geneva: World Health Organization.

———. 2003. "WHO Definition of Health." Available at <www.who.int/about/definition/en/>, accessed 19 June 2003.

Wortley, Scott. 1999. "A Northern Taboo: Research on Race, Crime and Criminal Justice in Canada." *Canadian Journal of Criminology*, 41: 261–74.

Wotherspoon, Terry. 1995. "The Incorporation of Public School Teachers into the Industrial Order: British Columbia in the First Half of the Twentieth Century." *Studies in Political Economy*, 46: 119–51.

———. 1998. *The Sociology of Education in Canada: Critical Perspectives*. Toronto: Oxford University Press.

———. 2000. "Transforming Canada's Education System: The Impact on Educational Inequalities, Opportunities, and Benefits." In *Social Issues and Contradictions in Canadian Society*, edited by B. Singh Bolaria, 250–72. Toronto: Harcourt Brace.

Wotherspoon, Terry, and Vic Satzewich. 1993. *First Nations: Race, Class and Gender Relations*. Toronto: Nelson.

Wright, Erik Olin. 1985. *Classes*. London: Verso.

———. 1997. *Class Counts: Comparative Studies in Class Analysis*. Cambridge: Cambridge University Press.

———. 1999. "Foundations of Class Analysis: A Marxist Perspective." Paper presented at the annual meeting of the American Sociological Association.

Wrong, Dennis. 1961. "The Oversocialized Concept of Man in Modern Sociology." *American Sociological Review*, 26: 183–93.

Wu, Zheng. 2000. *Cohabitation: A New Form of Family Living*. Toronto: Oxford University Press.

Wuthnow, Robert. 1989. *Communities of Discourse: Ideology and Social Structure in the Reformation, the Enlightenment, and European Socialism*. Cambridge, MA: Harvard University Press.

Yalnizyan, Armine. 1998. *The Growing Gap: A Report on the Growing Inequality Between Rich and Poor in Canada*. Toronto: Centre for Social Justice.

Yancey, William L., Eugene P. Ericksen, and Richard N. Juliani. 1976. "Emergent Ethnicity: A Review and Reformulation." *American Sociological Review*, 41: 391–403.

Yinger, Milton J. 1970. *The Scientific Study of Religion*. New York: Macmillan.

Zakon, Robert H. 2003. "Hobbes' Internet Timeline v6.0." Available at <www.zakon.org/robert/internet/timeline/>, accessed 25 June 2003.

Zang, Xiaowei. 1998. "Elite Transformation and Recruitment in Post-Mao China." *Journal of Political and Military Sociology*, 26, no. 1: 39–57.

Zehr, Stephen. 1994. "The Centrality of Scientists and the Transition of Interests in the U.S. Acid Rain Controversy." *Canadian Review of Sociology and Anthropology*, 31: 325–53.

Zeitlin, I.M. 1990. *Ideology and the Development of Sociological Theory*. 4th edn. Englewood Cliffs, NJ: Prentice-Hall.

Zimbardo, Philip G. 1972. "Pathology of Imprisonment." *Society*, 9: 4–8.

Zola, Irving Kenneth. 1972. "Medicine as an Institution of Social Control." *Sociological Review*, 20: 487–504.

Zucker, Lynne G., Michael R. Darby, Marilynn B. Brewer, and Yusheng Peng. 1996. "Collaboration Structure and Information Dilemmas in Biotechnology." In *Trust in Organizations: Frontiers of Theory and Research*, edited by Roderick M. Kramer and Tom R. Tyler, 90–113. Thousand Oaks, CA: Sage.

Glossary

Accountability   The expectation that public education, like other state-provided services, has clearly defined objectives that members of the public can identify and assess how well and how cost effectively they are being met.

Aesthetics   A system of rules for the appreciation of the beautiful.

Age composition   The distribution of the population with respect to age (and usually also sex); it is typically displayed graphically as a population pyramid.

Agents of socialization   Those groups in a child's environment that have the greatest effect on his or her socialization.

Alienation   A concept derived from Marx's analysis of the position of workers under capitalism, it refers to the separation of workers from the products of their labour, from the control of the work process, from owners, managers, and other workers, and even from themselves.

Allopathic medicine   Conventional medicine that treats by opposing, whether the germs, the bacteria, or other pathology.

Altercasting   The counterpart of impression management. In impression management actors self-cast, whereas in altercasting actors force on others identities that are in the altercaster's interests.

Anticipatory socialization   Explicit or implicit learning, in preparation for a future role; in Merton's definition, the acquisition of values and orientations found in statuses and groups in which one is not yet engaged but that one is likely to enter.

Authority   Power considered legitimate by those subject to it.

Baby boom, baby bust   The dramatic rise in the birth rate in Canada following World War II and lasting until well into the 1960s is called the *baby boom*. The continuing decline in fertility following the end of the baby boom in the industrialized world is called the *baby bust*.

Behavioural school   An approach within organizational theory that developed out of human relations theory and a psychological conception of human needs.

Beliefs   Any statement or part of a statement that describes an aspect of collective reality. Beliefs are ideas and explanations of what is commonly accepted as the truth. Beliefs may also be normative, saying what ought—or ought not—to be done.

Bilateral descent pattern   A system under which a newly married couple is considered part of both the bride's and the groom's kin groups.

Biological determinism   The view that nature dominates nurture.

Bourgeoisie   Owners of the means of production; the ruling class.

Breakdown approach   An approach to social movements that assumes that rapid, thorough, or uneven change in social institutions weakens social bonds and encourages the formation of groups advocating radical change.

Bride price   Money or property provided by a groom's parents to a bride's parents for permission for the groom to marry the bride.

Broadcasting   Sending a single signal to many people at once and on a schedule. A television station or radio station is in the business of broadcasting to a mass audience. In contrast, Web sites specialize in "narrowcasting" to small audiences.

Bureaucracy   A type of formal organization, found in government and private industry and in capitalist and socialist societies alike, that has the following six characteristics: a division of labour, a hierarchy of positions, a formal system of rules, a separation of the person from the office, hiring and promotion based on technical merit, and the protection of careers. Administrative efficiency is achieved by depersonalized treatment and mass processing of cases, as dictated by regulations and filed information.

Capital-intensive production   All production involves both labour and capital, but the proportions of the two used can vary considerably across different goods and services. In dollar terms, the inputs of capital into the production of aluminum are enormous (equipment, plant, electricity, bauxite) but the labour inputs are modest. This is a *capital-intensive* industry. In contrast, hairdressers use negligible amounts of capital equipment (a chair, scissors, a mirror). The bulk of the cost of that activity is labour. This is a *labour-intensive* industry.

Capitalism   An economic system characterized by a relationship of unequal economic exchange between capitalists (employers) and workers. Because they do not own the means of production, workers must sell their labour to employers in exchange for a wage or salary. Capitalism is a market-based system driven by the pursuit of profit for personal gain.

Carrying capacity   The ability of Earth to provide the resources to sustain all of humankind.

Census   A complete count of the population at one point in time, usually taken by a country every 5 or 10 years. The census is distinguished from the *vital statistics system*, a continuous registration system of births, deaths, marriages, and divorces.

Census family   Statistics Canada's definition of the family; includes married couples and cohabiting couples who have lived together for longer than one year, with or without never-married children, as well as single parents living with never-married children.

Census metropolitan areas (CMAs)   Large urban agglomerations, that is, a large number of urban centres geographically interconnected in relatively close proximity by systems of roadways.

Charismatic authority   Power considered legitimate because those subject to it believe in the exceptional qualities of an individual person, who appears exemplary or heroic and able to solve what others cannot.

Charter groups Canadians of British and French origin are known as *charter groups* because they have a special status entrenched in the Canadian constitution and have effectively determined the dominant cultural characteristics of Canada. Each of these groups has special rights and privileges, especially in terms of the language of the legislature, of the courts, and of education.

Claims-making The social constructionist process by which groups assert grievances about the troublesome character of people or their behaviour.

Class Inequality based on the distribution of material resources.

Coherence Interrelationships that link parts to make a whole.

Collective conscience, collective consciousness Durkheim's term for the collective intellectual property of a culture; something that we can all share in and contribute to but that no one person can know or possess. The cognitive-moral system of shared symbols, beliefs, and sentiments of a social group. Individuals think and feel what they learn and internalize as members of a collective. The content of the *conscience collective* is determined by the structural organization of the society in question.

Collective effervescence The experience of psychological excitement and empowerment that often happens to individuals caught up in large crowd activities such as political rallies, sporting events, or rock concerts.

Common-sense knowledge Facts of life accepted without being fully researched and understood.

Communication Purposeful exchange of information between two or more parties. A social view of communication inquires into the meanings and impacts of the content and form of communication, a technical view into the mechanisms and means of communicating.

Community Tangible interpersonal contact patterns.

Compensators Things that are provided in place of some real but unattainable goal or object, for example, the religious promise of life after death in lieu of actual immortality in one's present existence.

Concept An abstract idea that cannot be tested directly. Concepts can refer to anything, but in social research they usually refer to characteristics of individuals, groups, or artifacts, or to social processes. Some common sociological concepts include religiosity (strength of religious conviction), social class, and alienation.

Conflict theory A theoretical paradigm that emphasizes conflict and change as the regular and permanent features of society, because society is made up of various groups that wield varying amounts of power.

Control theory A category of explanation that maintains that people engage in deviant behaviour when the various controls that might be expected to prohibit them from doing so are weak or absent.

CRTC The Canadian Radio-television and Telecommunications Commission, which governs the broadcasting as well as the telecommunications business in Canada, setting the rules for operation based on principles of scarcity, public resource, and national importance.

Cryptography Techniques used to disguise messages and allow communication to occur in a secure, private way. Although encryption has a long history, the application of computers to this problem since World War II has meant an ever-escalating "arms race" between those who would try to hide things and those who would like to pry open those secret messages.

Cults Religious groups, usually very small, that have either been newly created or imported into a society from a quite different culture.

Cultural capital A term coined by Pierre Bourdieu for the cultural and linguistic competence, such as prestigious knowledge, tastes, preferences, and educational expertise and credentials, that individuals possess and that influences the likelihood of their educational and occupational success.

Cultural diffusion The process whereby the beliefs and customary behaviours of one society spread to, and are adopted within, another society.

Cultural support theory A category of explanation that argues that people become and remain deviant because the cultural environments in which they find themselves teach deviance and define such behaviour as appropriate.

Culture At its broadest, the sum total of the human-produced environment (the objects, artifacts, ideas, beliefs, and values that make up the symbolic and learned aspects of human society) as separate from the natural environment; more often refers to norms, values, beliefs, ideas, and meanings; an assumption that different societies are distinguished by their shared beliefs and customary behaviours; the products and services delivered by a number of industries—theatre, music, film, publishing, and so on.

Decoding See **Encoding and decoding**.

Demographic components equation A method of estimating population size by adding births, subtracting deaths, and adding net migration occurring in an interval of time, then adding the result to the population at the beginning of the interval; also knows as a *balancing equation*.

Demographic transition The process by which a country moves from high birth and death rates to low birth and death rates. The shift in fertility rates is often referred to as the *fertility transition*, while the complementary change in death rates is referred to as the *mortality transition*. The *epidemiological transition theory* is a complementary theory to demographic transition theory.

Developed countries The most industrialized countries of the world. According to the United Nations, these are the countries in Europe and in North America, as well as Australia, New Zealand, and Japan.

Developing countries All the countries not in the developed world. A subdivision of developing countries is the *least developed countries*, defined by the

United Nations as countries with annual incomes of less than $9,000 (US). See also **Third World**.

Deviance People, behaviours, and conditions that are subject to social control.

Digitization The process by which the (analog) world is described in computer-friendly terms of (digital) numbers, ones and zeros.

Discourse A way of talking about and conceptualizing an issue, presented through ideas, concepts, and vocabulary that recur in texts.

Discrimination An action whereby a person is treated differently, usually unfairly, because of his or her membership in a particular group or category.

Disease, illness, and sickness Distinguished from one another in the sociology of health, illness, and medicine. *Disease* is the disorder that is diagnosed by the physician. *Illness* is the personal experience of the person who acknowledges that he or she does not feel well. *Sickness* is the social action taken by a person as a result of illness or disease.

Doctrine of emergence A key ontological principle in the social realist perspective: new properties or realities are created by the combination of elements.

Double standard Expecting or requiring different behaviour from women and men, boys and girls.

Dowry Money or property provided by a bride's family upon her marriage to help obtain a suitable husband and to be used by her in case of divorce or widowhood.

Early adopter One of the social categories that describes how people participate in the diffusion of innovation.

Ecology In the context of urban studies, the internal makeup, patterning, and dynamics of cities. See also **human ecology**.

Education The process by which human beings learn and develop capacities through understanding of their social and natural environments, which takes place in both formal and informal settings.

Encoding and decoding The inclusion and subsequent interpretation of cues, meanings, and codes in cultural productions.

Environmental justice The branch of environmentalism that focuses on the inequitable distribution of environmental risks affecting the poor and racial minorities.

Epistemology Inquiry concerned with the nature of knowledge, how it is obtained, and the means for establishing its validity.

Ethnic group People sharing a common ethnic identity who are potentially capable of organizing and acting upon their ethnic interests.

Ethnicity Sets of social distinctions by which groups differentiate themselves from one another on the basis of presumed biological ties. Members of such groups have a sense of themselves as a common "people" separate and distinct from others.

Ethnocentric bias The tendency to think that the beliefs, values, and customs of one's own culture are universal (that is, that they can be applied to others).

Exploitation At the heart of Marxist sociology, the situation under capitalism in which the bourgeoisie takes advantage of the proletariat. Class-based exploitation occurs when the bourgeoisie appropriates the labour effort of the proletariat to create its own material advantage.

Extended family Several generations sharing a residence and co-operating economically.

Face The positive self-presentation projected by an individual.

False consciousness Condition in which the working class does not recognize its exploitation and oppression under capitalism.

Feminism A theoretical paradigm that focuses on causes and consequences of inequality between men and women, especially patriarchy and sexism.

Finance capital In contrast to *physical capital*, instruments that can be used to purchase physical capital—bank loans, equity (voting shares in a company), fixed interest bonds, and so on; the monetary expression of physical capital.

First Nations "Indians" in Canadian law; together with Métis and Inuit, they constitute Canada's Aboriginal peoples.

Flexible specialization Another component of the new flexible approach to management; involves multi-skilling, job rotation, the organization of workers into teams, and concentrated yet decentralized decision-making power within work organizations.

Formal organization A deliberately formed social group in which people, resources, and technologies are consciously co-ordinated through formalized roles, statuses, and relationships to achieve a division of labour intended to attain a specific set of objectives.

Gender Socially recognized distinctions of masculinity and femininity.

Gender stereotyping A belief about differences in the natural capabilities and attributes of women and men.

Generalized other In Mead's theory, the "internalized audience" with which we, as "minded selves," dialogue or converse during the reflective prelude to action. It represents the collective attitudes and sentiments of our society or group.

Global cities Cities favoured under globalization that are at high levels of technology, finance, and international transportation, serving as the focal points for multinational corporations but not for local manufacturing.

Globalization Worldwide control and co-ordination by large private-sector interests not constrained by local or national boundaries.

Globalization of work The relocation of production and consumption beyond national borders to various parts of the globe. It is done in the interest of increasing profits by decreasing labour costs and maximizing employer control of the larger work process.

Hawthorne effect The finding that when people know they are subjects of an important experiment and receive a large amount of special attention, they tend to behave the way they think the researchers expect them to.

Health   Defined by the World Health Organization (WHO) as a "state of complete physical, mental and social well-being" (2003).

Hidden curriculum   The understandings that students develop as a result of the institutional requirements and day-to-day realities they encounter in their schooling; typically refers to norms, such as competition, individualism, and obedience, as well as to a sense of one's place in school and social hierarchies.

Hot money   Liquid assets that can be turned into cash quickly and with negligible cost. They can, consequently, be moved between investment locations—including countries—rapidly and easily.

Household   Term used by Statistics Canada to refer to people sharing a dwelling, whether or not they are related by blood, adoption, or marriage.

Human capital   The notion that education, skills development, and other learning processes are investments that enhances our capacities. *Human capital theory* builds on this notion.

Human ecology   The science of ecology, as applied to sociological analyses. See also **ecology**.

Human exemptionalism paradigm (HEP)   The term used by Catton and Dunlap in arguing that the competing theoretical perspectives in sociology, including functionalism, conflict theory, and symbolic interactionism, all share a world view based on anthropocentrism.

Human relations school   An approach within organizational theory that focuses on relationships within informal groups and assumes that happy group relationships produce job satisfaction, which, in turn, produces high productivity.

Hypermasculinities   An excessive emphasis on practices associated with being male in any culture.

Hypotheses   Testable statements composed of at least two variables and how they are related.

Identity   The way in which we see ourselves and how others see us. How we view ourselves is a product of our history and of our interpretation of others' reactions to us. How others view us is termed *placement* and is other people's reactions to our projections of ourselves, which, in turn, is termed *announcement*.

Identity-based approach   An approach to social movements that assumes that dominant interpretations of reality preserve class, gender, racial, and other inequalities. The central task of social movements is to challenge and reformulate the dominant culture by reshaping identities.

Ideology   A system of beliefs, ideas, and norms, reflecting the interests and experiences of a group, class, or subculture, that legitimizes or justifies the existing unequal distribution of power and privilege; ways of seeing and of understanding the world and its actors. Ideologies function by making the social appear natural or functional rather than constructed for partisan interests and advantage.

Illness   See **Disease, illness, and sickness**.

Impression management   Goffman's term for the "dramatic moves" individuals make in trying to advance "definitions of the situation" favourable to their interests and self-image. It is achieved by carefully manipulating the elements of appearance, manner, and setting.

Informal economy   A wide range of legal and illegal economic activities that are not officially reported to the government.

Informal organization   Complex personal and informal networks that develop among people within a bureaucracy who interact on the job.

Information   According to Gregory Bateson, information is "the difference that makes a difference." In other words, it is a non-random signal that conveys intelligence or meaning.

Institutional completeness   A measure of the degree to which a community offers a range of services to its members.

Institutional discrimination   Discrimination that is built into how an institution is structured or how it operates.

Labour power   Marx argued that labour is work and labour power is the capacity to work. The only real power that the proletariat has under capitalism is the power to choose whether to work.

Labour process theory   A neo-Marxist approach to organizations and the conduct of work that focuses on the alienation of the worker and on power relationships between capitalists and workers.

Life expectancy at birth   The average number of years left to live for a newborn in a given period. Life expectancy is distinct from *life span*, which is the oldest age humans can attain.

Lifelong learning   The ongoing requirements for people to acquire new knowledge and capacities through learning that occurs in various levels and kinds of formal education as well as in other learning contexts; associated with increasing emphasis on the new economy and the continuing transitions that individuals undergo throughout their lives.

Lifeworld   A concept in phenomenology referring to the lived, intersubjective experiences of people sharing a way of life. It is characterized by taken-for-granted assumptions about their constructed social reality.

Looking-glass self   In Cooley's symbolic interactionist approach, the idea that self-concept is based on a person's perceptions of the opinions that others hold about him or her.

Macro   See Micro, macro.

Macrosociology   The study of social institutions and large social groups; the study of the processes that depict societies as a whole and of the social structural aspects of a given society.

Marxism   Based on the work of Karl Marx, the historical materialist school of thought that posits a structural explanation for historical change, namely, that the economic base of society determines change in all other realms.

Mass media Media that allow for communication on a large scale. In the past, these have been "one-way" communication messages, but the Internet is pioneering "two-way" mass media possibilities.

Mass-society theory An argument that holds that modern life creates isolated, disoriented individuals who are easily manipulated by the media and extremist politicians.

Master status A status characteristic that overrides other status characteristics. When a person is assigned a label of "deviant" (for example, "murderer," "drug addict," "cheater"), that label is usually read by others as signifying the most essential aspects of the individual's character.

Matrifocal A family system in which life is organized around the women, who earn most of the money and hold the family together (often in the absence of husbands/fathers).

Matrilineal descent The tracing of relationships and inheritance through the female line.

Means of production Wealth-generating property such as land, factories, and machinery.

Medicalization The tendency for more and more of life to be defined as relevant to medical diagnosis and treatment.

Mega-cities Cities of 10 million or more residents.

Melting pot An American ideology that assumes that immigrants should discard all of the traditions and distinctions they brought to the United States with them, such as their ethnic language or national identity, and become nothing but "Americans."

Metropolitan area With respect to everyday behaviour and economic activity, the unified entity formed on a de facto basis by a large city and its suburbs. See also **census metropolitan areas (CMAs)**.

Micro, macro Used analytically to distinguish small-scale, face-to-face interaction settings (*micro*) from institutional arrangements such as the economy or state and from large-scale collective processes like revolutions and religious movements (*macro*).

Microsociology The analysis of small groups and of the face-to-face interactions that occur within these groups in the everyday.

Mind In Mead's theory, a "social emergent" created through symbolic interaction, consisting of the ability to think, to carry on an internal conversation. Mind is made possible through the internalization of language.

Mode of production Marx's concept referring to the economic structure of society, consisting of the forces and relations of production. It is the "base" that conditions the "superstructure" of politics, law, religion, art, and so on.

Modified extended family Several generations not sharing a residence but living near each other and maintaining close social and economic contact.

Monarchy Rule by a single individual who claims legitimacy based on royal lineage.

Morbidity rate The sickness rate per a specified number of people over a specified period of time.

Mortality rate The death rate per a specified number of people over a specified period of time.

Multiculturalism *Official multiculturalism* is a government policy to promote tolerance among cultural groups and to assist ethnic groups in preserving the values and traditions that are important to them.

Multinational corporations Companies that have significant production facilities in more than one national jurisdiction. Those that become detached from any particular country, with loyalty to no country, are sometimes labelled *transnational corporations*.

Naturalistic attitude Schütz's term for the common-sense mindset of people inhabiting a lifeworld. It is grounded in an intersubjective agreement that their world is as it appears to the members of a group or community—that is, a collective suspension of doubt that permits a taken-for-granted practicality.

Negotiation A discussion intended to produce an agreement.

Neighbourhood A recognizable physical area within a city, with or without formal boundaries.

New economy A term used to highlight the shift in emphasis from industrial production within specific industries, firms, and nations to economic activities driven by information and high-level technologies, global competition, and international networks, and knowledge-based advancement.

New environmental paradigm (NEP) The term used by Catton and Dunlap in arguing that environmental sociology constitutes a paradigm shift within general sociology based on the understanding that human societies cannot be separate and distinct from nature.

Nominalism An ontological position that insists that only flesh-and-blood individuals are real and have the capacity to act; collective terms like "the state" or "economy" are mere verbal expressions and consist only of aggregated individual actions.

Non-standard work Jobs that are characterized by an increasingly tenuous or precarious relationship between employer and employee, including part-time employment, temporary employment, contract work, multiple job holding, and self-employment; also termed *contingent work* and *casual work*.

Norms The rules and expectations of appropriate behaviour under various social circumstances. Norms create social consequences that have the effect of regulating appearance and behaviour.

Nuclear family A husband, wife, and their children, sharing a common residence and co-operating economically.

Numerical flexibility Part of a new general managerial approach that rests on flexibility in employment; involves shrinking or eliminating the core workforce (in continuous, full-time positions) and replacing them with workers in non-standard employment.

Objective   Something is said to be *objective* if it is completely unaffected by the characteristics of the person or instrument that is observing it. "Objective" observations were used in the past to establish the truth of scientific theories until it became clear that completely objective observations are impossible.

Ontology   Inquiry that deals with the fundamental nature of things—of reality or existence—and that specifies the essential properties or characteristics of phenomena.

Open standards   These agreements on how (typically technical) things are to work and interoperate are published and circulated freely, and have proven to be important in ensuring widespread use and adoption of new technologies.

Operationalization   The translation of abstract theories and concepts into observable hypotheses and variables. Once our abstract ideas are operationalized, we can test them in a study.

Organization   A group of people participating in a division of labour that is co-ordinated by communication and leadership to achieve a common goal or goals; includes both *spontaneous* and *formal* organizations.

Paradigm   A set of assumptions used to view society and people's behaviour. A paradigm serves as a model for which questions sociologists should ask and how they should interpret the answers.

Parties   Voluntary associations that organize for the collective pursuit of interests such as political parties or lobbying groups; common in Weberian scholarship.

Patriarchy   A society or form of social organization oriented toward men and dominated by men, which has empowered men to control and limit female possibilities. For example, patriarchal families are families in which authority resides with males.

Patrilineal descent   The tracing of relationships and inheritance through the male line.

Pedagogy   Processes associated with the organization and practice of teaching; more generally, various kinds of interactions (and how these are understood and organized) in teaching/learning situations.

Political conflict perspective   A resource mobilization approach that focuses on how groups (typically classes) promote collective interests.

Political institutions   Established rules and procedures for the conduct of political affairs.

Political movements   Social movements that challenge established state policies and practices in order to bring about social and political changes.

Political party   An organization dedicated to winning political power by controlling government.

Political process approach   An approach that assumes that political constraints and opportunities influence the rise and fall of social movements, as well as their institutional organization.

Politics   The process in which individuals and groups act to promote their interests, often in conflict with others.

Polyandry   The practice of being legally married to more than one husband at a time.

Polygamy   The practice of being legally married to more than one spouse at a time.

Polygyny   The practice of being legally married to more than one wife at a time.

Population momentum   The tendency for population to keep growing even when the fertility rate drops to just the replacement level of 2.1 children per woman, as a consequence of a high proportion of persons in the childbearing ages.

Power   In Marxist sociology, a social relationship that has a material base. Those who own the means of production have the power to exploit workers through the appropriation of their labour efforts. In Weberian sociology, *power* is more broadly defined and can reflect an individual's or group's capacity to exert their will over others.

Prejudice   An attitude in which individuals are prejudged on the basis of stereotyped characteristics assumed to be common to all members of the individual's group.

Primary socialization   The most intense socialization, which occurs from birth to adolescence and which takes place in or is strongly influenced by the family.

Privatization   The movement away from a completely universally available and state-funded medical system to one that includes profit-making components.

Progressive conservation   The movement originating in the nineteenth century that sought to check environmental destruction caused by unbridled economic growth and that resulted in the founding of such modern environmental organizations as the Audubon Society and the Sierra Club.

Proletariat   People who sell their labour power to capitalists in return for a wage; the working class.

Protestant ethic thesis   Weber's argument that aspects of the Protestant religion originally imbued people with a sense of dedication to their work that helped lay the foundations for capitalism.

PYLL   "Potential years of life lost"; refers to premature mortality and taking into account the average age of death from a particular cause.

Race   A group that is defined on the basis of perceived physical differences, such as skin colour.

Race to the bottom   The outcome produced by competitive tax cutting motivated by the desire to attract (and keep) investors.

Racism   A belief that groups that differ in physical appearance also differ in personality characteristics, intelligence, honesty, reliability, law abidingness, and so on. *Racism* also implies a belief that these differences make one group superior to another.

Rationalization   In Weber's view, the movement away from mystical and religious interpretations of the world to the development of human thought and belief based on the systematic accumulation of evidence; associated with the emergence of impersonal authority.

Rational–legal authority   Power considered legitimate

because those subject to it believe commands are based on formally established rules, procedures, and certified expertise.

Reductionism An analytical strategy that explains wholes or totalities by reducing them to the aggregated properties of their constituent parts. Examples would be attempts to explain social facts in strict psychological terms (*behaviourism*) or as the consequence of underlying biological factors (*sociobiology*).

Relative deprivation theory A breakdown approach that claims that radical social movements result from people's subjective feelings of fear and frustration.

Relativism The idea that there is no single, unchangeable truth about anything. Instead, all things are either true or false only in relation to, or *relative* to, particular standards. Many sociologists who do not view sociology as a science do so partly because of the persuasiveness of relativism.

Reliability The consistency of a measure, indicator, or study. Note that *reliability* is different from *validity* and does not refer to the accuracy of a measure or study.

Resocialization The process of learning new roles in response to changes in life circumstances.

Resource mobilization approach An approach that assumes that social movements are quite similar to other organizations.

Risk society A theory of the new modernity that argues that perception of risk is modernity's defining feature, creating uncertainty and compelling individuals to seek new strategic allegiances.

Rites of passage Rituals performed by all cultures to mark major transitions in life; these rites usually display a three-part structure: a symbolically marked departure from an old identity or phase of life, a symbolically marked period of innocent non-involvement, and a symbolic incorporation into the rights and responsibilities of a new identity or phase of life.

Role expectations The expected characteristics and social behaviours of an individual in a particular position in society.

Role-making The continual improvising and revising of our actions as others' reactions to them change and are imputed.

Roles The specific duties and obligations expected of one who occupies a specific status.

Role-taking The construction in our mind of what others mean by their actions.

Sample The group of people or objects, drawn from the whole population, that will be studied. In quantitative research, a great deal of time and effort is devoted to the selection of truly random samples, while in qualitative research, samples are often selected based on the theoretical importance of the people or objects.

Schooling Processes that take place within formal educational institutions.

Scientific management A managerial method that rests on breaking up work processes into their smallest constituent parts in an effort to maximize efficiency in productivity, resulting in the separation of mental from manual labour and in the deskilling of workers; assumes that workers are motivated by economic rewards alone and that specialists know more than workers about how a task can most effectively be performed; also known as *Taylorism*.

Secondary socialization The ongoing lifelong process of socialization, based on the accumulated learning of childhood and adolescence.

Sects Religious groups, still usually relatively small, that comes into being as a result of a disagreement between the members of an established church.

Secularization The social process resulting in the declining presence and influence of religious beliefs, practices, symbols, and institutions.

Self In Mead's theory, an emergent entity with a capacity to be both a subject and an object, as reflected upon in one's own mind. In Goffman's dramaturgical theory, the self is more a shifting "dramatic effect," a staged product of the scenes one performs in.

Serial monogamy A pattern of marriage, divorce, and remarriage, resulting in having more than one spouse over a lifetime, but only one at a time.

Service economy The economic sector in which most Canadians are currently employed. In comparison to *primary industry* (which involves the extraction of natural resources) and *manufacturing* (which involves processing raw materials into usable goods and services), the service economy is based on the provision of services (as opposed to a tangible product) ranging widely from advertising and retailing to entertaining to generating and distributing information. Also called the *tertiary sector*.

Sex The biological differences between females and males, determined at conception.

Sex ratio The number of males in the relation to the number of females in a population. The *primary sex ratio* is the sex ratio at birth, which is typically in the range of about 105 baby boys per 100 baby girls. The *secondary sex ratio* is the sex ratio beyond infancy.

Sexual harassment Unwanted attention linked to the gender of the person receiving that attention.

Sickness See **Disease, illness, and sickness**.

Situated identity According to symbolic interactionist theory, social life is in a constant process of change, imposing, in turn, changes in, and new forms of, identity announcement and identity placement. A particular announcement–placement identity at any point in time is referred to as a *situated identity*.

Situated transaction A process of social interaction that lasts as long as the individuals find themselves in each other's company. As applied to the study of deviance, the concept of the situated transaction helps us to understand how deviant acts are social and not just individual products.

Social capital A concept widely thought to have been developed by American sociologist James Coleman in 1988, but discussed by Pierre Bourdieu in a similar way in the early 1980s; reflects the power that is derived from ties to social networks.

Social constructionism   The sociological theory that argues that social problems and issues are less objective conditions than they are collective social definitions based on how they are framed and interpreted.

Social control   The various and myriad ways in which members of social groups express their disapproval of people and behaviours. These include name-calling, ridicule, ostracism, incarceration, and even killing.

Social environment   The people and relationships that surround us.

Social group   A number of individuals, defined by formal or informal criteria of membership, who share a feeling of unity or are bound together in stable patterns of interaction; two or more individuals who have a specific common identity and who interact in a reciprocal social relationship.

Social institution   A stable, well-acknowledged pattern of social relationships that endures over time, including the family, the economy, education, politics, religion, the mass media, medicine, and science and technology. Social institutions are the result of an enduring set of ideas about how to accomplish various goals generally recognized as important in a society.

Social interaction   The process by which people act and react in relationships with others.

Social movement   The co-ordinated, voluntary action of non-elites (those people with no control over major resources) for the manifest purpose of changing the distribution of social goods.

Social networks   Based on kinship, friendship, or economic ties, these may include social transactions (shared recreation, communication, gift exchanges, mutual assistance) and shared tastes and values.

Social realism   The ontological position that collective terms—such as "patriarchy," the "economy," "the church"—correspond to real emergent entities, to structures that exert causal influence on individual lives.

Social relationships   Interactions of people in a society. Because people share culture and a sense of collective existence, these interactions will to some extent be recurrent and predictable.

Social reproduction   A range of unpaid activities that help to reproduce workforces daily and over generations; typically, though not exclusively, performed by women in the family household.

Social revolution   A rapid, fundamental transformation of a society's state and class structures, often accomplished through violent means.

Social structure   Patterns of behaviour or social relationships developed and accepted through time in a given group, organization, or society.

Social support   The various ways people support each other through interactions.

Socialization   The process by which people learn to become members of society. See also **primary social-** **ization; secondary socialization**.

Society   The largest collection of social relationships in which people live their lives. There are some very encompassing international relationships among nations too (such as the European Common Market or the North American Free Trade Agreement), but these cover only a narrow range of types of activities (for example, economic relationships) compared to societies.

Sociological imagination   The understanding of how personal experiences and troubles are interrelated with others' experiences and troubles as public or societal problems.

Sociology   The systematic study of social behaviours in human societies.

Socio-technical systems theory   An approach within organizational theory that holds that the social and technological aspects of an organization should be developed simultaneously. It also focuses on semi-autonomous work groups rather than on individual workers.

Solidarity   The quality of an integrated and well-functioning society that is brought into harmony through an adaptive cultural foundation.

"Sound economic policies"   As understood by a number of international economic organizations, these usually imply assurance that government budgets are not in deficit, a dominant role for the private sector in the provision of most goods and services, and policies of openness to trade.

Spontaneous organization   An organization that arises quickly to meet a single goal then disbands when that goal is achieved or perceived to be beyond reach, or when the organization becomes absorbed by a formal organization.

the State   Procedures and organizations concerned with creating, administering, and enforcing rules or decisions for conduct within a given territory.

Status   A socially defined position that a person holds in a given social group or organization, to which are attached certain rights, duties, and obligations. Note that *status* is a relational term, as each status exists only through its relation to one or more other statuses filled by other people.

Status degradation ceremony   The rituals by which the formal transition is made from non-deviant to deviant status. Examples include the criminal trial and the psychiatric hearing.

Status groups   Organized groups comprising people who have similar social status situations. These groups organize to maintain or expand their social privileges by excluding outsiders from their ranks and by trying to gain status recognition from other groups.

Strain theory   A category of explanation that seeks to understand how deviant behaviour results as people attempt to solve problems that the social structure presents to them.

Structural analysis or approach   An approach within

organizational theory in the Weberian tradition; focuses on the structural characteristics of organizations and their effect on the people within them; in the context of urban studies, the analysis of the functions cities perform, the size and shape of their governments, and who has what bearing on decisions and outcomes involving cities.

Structural discrimination See **institutional discrimination**.

Structural functionalism A theoretical paradigm that emphasizes the way each part of a society functions to fulfill the needs of society as a whole.

Structure The "concrete" elements of society that are embodied and enacted by things and people, in opposition to the cultural elements of society.

Subculture A subset of cultural traits of the larger society that also includes distinctive values, beliefs, norms, style of dress, and behaviour.

Supply-side theory The notion that the state of religion, like any other product available in a society, is determined as much by how it is being supplied as by the demand for the product.

Sustainable development The principle that economic growth and environmental conservation are compatible goals.

Symbolic ethnicity Ethnicity that has become purely a matter of personal identification and that has little or no impact upon how people live their lives or relate to one another.

Symbolic interactionism The study of the processes by which individuals interpret and respond to the actions of one another.

Symbolic markers Cultural manifestations of identity, such as language, nationality, or skin colour, that groups use either to generate a common identity or to differentiate themselves from others.

Symbols The heart of cultural systems, for with them we construct thought, ideas, and other ways of representing reality to others and to ourselves; gestures, artifacts, or language that represents something else.

Systemic discrimination Discrimination that is built into the very fabric of Canadian life, as in the case of institutional self-segregation.

Systemic theory A breakdown approach, advanced by Neil Smelser, that views society as a set of interrelated elements that work together to maintain stability.

Systems theory An approach within organizational theory that sees organizations as open systems and that views organizations and their goals as shaped by the interests of their participants and their environments.

Technology The practical things we as humans make and use, and the knowledge we require to build, maintain, and enhance them.

Terrorism Physical violence directed against civilians, without regard for who will suffer, in order to promote political objectives.

Theory An integrated set of concepts and statements that specify relations of ordered dependence and causal connection between phenomena. At the most general level, theories are perspectives, or ways of seeing, that conceptualize and highlight certain patterns and relations among complex realities. Theories are not tested directly. They may also be simple or complex: the more complex a theory, the more difficult it is to operationalize and test it.

Third World Poor countries. It is an element of a classification in which the First World was made up of Western Europe, North America, Australia, and New Zealand, the Second World of the various communist countries (the Soviet Union, the numerous Soviet satellites, and China), and the Third World of poorer countries in Asia, Africa, and Latin America. See also **developing countries**.

Totalitarianism Form of the state that involves intervening in and controlling all aspects of both public and private life.

Traditional authority Power considered legitimate because those subject to it believe that is the way things have always been done.

Transitions The pathways that people follow from family life, into and out of education, and into various jobs or other social situations throughout their life course.

Unemployment rate People are considered to be unemployed only if they do not have a job and are actively looking for a job. The unemployment rate is the number of people who meet those two conditions divided by the labour force (which includes both the employed and unemployed) expressed as a percentage. Those who do not have a job and are not looking for one are considered to be not in the labour force.

Urbanism Behaviour patterns associated with cities.

Urbanization The nature, extent, and distribution of cities in the larger society or nation.

Urban renewal A general term for improving buildings and land use; can include redevelopment, rehabilitation, or both.

Utilitarian perspective A resource mobilization approach that focuses on how individuals promote self-interest.

Validity The accuracy of a measure, indicator, or study. There are many different dimensions to validity. Validity can be established through formal tests, logic, or depth of understanding.

Values Shared ideas about how something is ranked in terms of its relative social desirability, worth, or goodness; what a group or society views as right and wrong, good and bad, desirable and undesirable.

Variable The operational or observable equivalent of concepts. Many concepts require more than one variable for proper operationalization. The key characteristic of variables is that there must be a range of different values that can be observed.

Vertical mosaic A view of Canadian society as constituting an ethnically divided stratification system, with the charter groups at the top, Native people at the bottom, and other ethnic immigrant groups fitting in depending upon their entrance status.

Contributors

Cheryl Albas is part-time associate professor at the University of Manitoba. She has an ongoing interest in higher education as it relates to university student life, where she is researching study types. Another area of interest is families and how the physical structure of households influences family interaction. In addition, she is involved in a long-term study of non-tenured faculty and the dynamics of knowledge production in university-based professional education. Her publications have appeared in *Handbook of Symbolic Interactionism* (2003) and the *Canadian Review of Sociology and Anthropology*.

Daniel Albas is professor of sociology at the University of Manitoba. His areas of interest include social psychology and non-verbal communication. He is currently studying university student study types and issues relative to academic integrity. His published works are included in a wide variety of national and international journals (including the *Journal of Cross-Cultural Psychology*, *Sociological Quarterly*, *Symbolic Interaction*, and the *Canadian Review of Sociology and Anthropology*) and in *Handbook of Symbolic Interactionism* (2003).

Bruce Arai is associate professor of sociology at Wilfrid Laurier University. His research interests are in the areas of economic sociology, environmental sociology, and the sociology of education. Recent publications have appeared in *Education Policy Analysis Archives*, the *Canadian Journal of Education*, the *Canadian Review of Sociology and Anthropology*, and *Organization and Environment*.

Pat Armstrong is co-author of such books on health care as *Vital Signs: Nursing in Transition* (1990), *Take Care: Warning Signals for Canada's Health System* (1994), *Wasting Away: The Undermining of Canadian Health Care* (1996), *Universal Health Care: What the United States Can Learn from Canada* (1998), and *Heal Thyself: Managing Health Care Reform* (2000). She has also published on a wide variety of issues related to women's work and to social policy. She currently holds a CHSRF/CIHR Chair in Health Services, is a partner in the National Network on Environments and Women's Health, and chairs a working group on health reform that crosses the Centres of Excellence for Women's Health. Her current research compares care management in Canada and the United States. She is involved as well with projects on nursing retention, on quality indicators, on gender-sensitive evidence, and on the health care labour force.

Maureen Baker is professor of sociology at the University of Auckland in New Zealand. She has previously taught in several Canadian universities, including the University of Toronto and McGill University, as well as in Australia. From 1984 to 1990, she worked as a senior researcher in Ottawa for the Canadian parliament, specializing in policy issues relating to families, women, and children. Professor Baker is the author

or editor of 13 books and over 60 articles on family trends, aging, adolescent women, cross-national family policies, women and work, and comparative restructuring. She has lived and worked in New Zealand since January 1998.

Shyon Baumann is assistant professor of sociology at the University of Toronto at Mississauga. He works in the areas of the sociology of art, culture, and the media. His current projects include an analysis of the intersection of racial and gender stereotypes in advertising. In addition, he has published articles on the history of the American film industry and tensions there between art and entertainment, and he is now working on a book on this topic.

Joseph M. Bryant teaches in the Department for the Study of Religion and in the Department of Sociology at the University of Toronto. His main areas of interest are historical sociology and the sociology of culture. He is the author of *Moral Codes and Social Structure in Ancient Greece* (1996), and his articles on sociological theory, ancient Greek social thought, and the rise of Christianity have appeared in a variety of journals, including the *Canadian Journal of Sociology*, the *British Journal of Sociology*, the *History of Political Thought*, and *Archives européennes de sociologie*. He is currently working on a book entitled *Principles of Historical Social Science: A Primer on Theory and Method*.

Juanne Nancarrow Clarke, a medical sociologist at Wilfrid Laurier University, is the author of *Health, Illness and Medicine in Canada* (3rd edn, 2000). One of her areas of research interest is the social construction of illness in the mass print media. Her current studies concern mass print media presentations of diseases such as cancer, heart disease, and AIDS and their portrayal in magazines and newspapers directed to audiences that differ in gender, social class, ethnicity, and age. Her daughter Lauren was diagnosed with leukemia in 1995, and subsequent to that Clarke has done research on parents whose children have cancer and has written a book, with her daughter, called *Finding Strength: A Mother and Daughter's Story of Childhood Cancer* (1999).

James Curtis is professor in the departments of Sociology and of Health Studies and Gerontology at the University of Waterloo, where he has taught introductory sociology for many years. Among other professional activities, he has served as editor of the *Canadian Review of Sociology and Anthropology* and is a member of Statistics Canada's Advisory Committee on Social Conditions. He received the Outstanding Contributions Award from the Canadian Sociology and Anthropology Association for his overall research contributions to sociology. His publications include collaborations on books for use by sociology students in the areas of introductory sociology, social problems, Canadian society, sociology of knowledge, social inequality, and physical activity and sport.

Lorne L. Dawson is associate professor of sociology and chair of the Department of Religious Studies at the University of Waterloo. He is the author and editor of several books, including *Comprehending Cults* (1998) and *Cults and New Religious Movements* (2003), and of many articles and book chapters on theoretical issues in the study of religion, the study of new religious movements, and religion and the Internet, with title such as "Modernism, Anti-Modernism, and Postmodernism: Struggling with the Cultural Significance of New Religious Movements" and "Researching Religion in Cyberspace: Issues and Strategies."

Randle Hart is a doctoral candidate in the Department of Sociology at the University of Toronto. His co-authored articles on aging, immigration, cohabitation and marriage, and health have appeared in the *Journal of Marriage and the Family*, the *Journal of Family Issues*, *Social Biology*, *Research on Aging*, and the *International Journal of Sociology*.

Rowland Lorimer is director of the Canadian Centre for Studies in Publishing and professor of communication at Simon Fraser University. He is current publisher and past editor of the *Canadian Journal of Communication*. He is author of several books, including *Mass Communication in Canada* (5th edn, 2003). He has served on the National Library Advisory Board and as president of the Association for Canadian Studies and the Canadian Association of Learned Journals. He is also author of numerous scholarly articles and several major reports on publishing for the Canadian government. For the past eight years, he has been working with Richard Smith on online book and scholarly journal publishing.

Julie McMullin is associate professor in the Department of Sociology at the University of Western Ontario. Her research explores how class, age, gender, ethnicity, and race structure inequality in paid work and families. She is also the author of *Understanding Inequality: Class, Age, Gender, Ethnicity, and Race in Canada* (2003).

William Michelson is S.D. Clark Professor of Sociology at University of Toronto. His long-standing research interests focus on how people's everyday contexts, such as housing and urban infrastructure, bear on their lives and life chances. His publications include *Man and his Urban Environment: A Sociological Approach* (2nd edn, 1976), *Environmental Choice, Human Behavior, and Residential Satisfaction* (1977), *From Sun to Sun: Daily Obligations and Community Structure in the Lives of Employed Women* (1985), and the *Handbook of Environmental Sociology* (2002, co-edited by Riley Dunlap). In 1994, he was elected to the Royal Society of Canada.

Richard John (Jack) Richardson, now deceased, made a tremendous contribution to Canadian sociology. He received his BA with high distinction (double gold medallist) from the University of Toronto in 1978, his MA in sociology the following year, and his PhD in sociology, also at the University of Toronto, in 1984. From 1985, Dr Richardson

was assistant professor at McMaster University in the Department of Sociology. Throughout his distinguished career, he won many awards; taught countless undergraduate classes in Canadian studies, organized behaviour, work and occupations, and research methods; and led many graduate-level courses in organizational sociology and comparative social systems. His main areas of interest were economic sociology, socio-economic change and development, social organization, formal organization, inter-corporate relations, and Canadian society. His publications include *The Social World* (1986), co-edited with Lorne Tepperman, and, the following year, *An Introduction to the Social World*, also co-edited with Lorne Tepperman. Dr Richardson also contributed to many books, including Robert Brym's *The Structure of the Canadian Capitalist Class* (1985), and to many esteemed journals, such as the *Canadian Journal of Sociology* and the *Canadian Review of Sociology and Anthropology*.

Michael Rosenberg has been a member of the Sociology Department at Dawson College from 1974 to 1997 and adjunct assistant professor at Concordia University since 1997. Dr Rosenberg has co-authored and edited several books, including *Social Deviance: An Integrated Approach* (1993) and *Quebec Society: Critical Issues* (1997). His previous research was on ethnicity and school system structure, and his current research is on the organizational capacity of ethnocultural minority groups in Montreal.

Vincent Sacco is professor in and former chair of the Department of Sociology, Queen's University. Prior to coming to Queen's, he was a member of the faculty of the School of Criminology at Simon Fraser University. His research interests relate to the causes of criminal victimization and media images of crime and deviance. His recent publications include co-authored books, such as *Crime Victims in Context* (1998) and *Advances in Criminological Theory* (2001), and articles in *International Journal of Law and Psychiatry* and *Criminologie*.

Peter R. Sinclair is University Research Professor at Memorial University of Newfoundland. His current research is in global commodity systems and local restructuring, information technology occupations, timber dependency in rural Alabama and western Newfoundland, and interdisciplinary ecosystems theory. He is author of *From Traps to Draggers: Domestic Commodity Production in Northwest Newfoundland, 1850–1982* (1985) and *State Intervention and the Newfoundland Fisheries* (1987), as well as co-author of many books, including *When the Fish Are Gone: Ecological Disaster and Fishers of Northwest Newfoundland* (1997). Over 100 of his refereed articles, book chapters, and book reviews have been published since 1970.

Michael Smith is professor of sociology at McGill University. He has published extensively on a range of issues that fall, broadly, under the heading of economic sociology. His recent publications dealing with issues of globalization include "La mondialisation: à-t-elle un effet important sur le marché du travail dans les pays riches?" in

Une société monde? Les dynamiques sociales de la mondialisation (2001) and "What Did the FTA and the NAFTA Do to the Canadian Labor Market?" in *Forum for Social Economics*.

Richard Smith is associate professor of communication at Simon Fraser University, director of the Centre for Policy Research on Science and Technology (CPROST) at SFU's Harbour Centre campus in downtown Vancouver, and a research scientist at the New Media Innovation Centre (NewMIC). He is a frequent commentator to the media on topics relating to information technology and society, in particular on issues relating to computers in education, new developments in wireless technology and mobility, and the Internet. He is also a founding member of the BC Advanced Systems Institute's business advisory board and sits on the advisory boards of several high-technology companies and non-profit societies.

Pamela Sugiman is associate professor in the Department of Sociology at McMaster University, where she teaches Introduction to Sociology and courses in gender relations. In the Arts and Science Programme at McMaster, she teaches in the are of diversity and multiculturalism. She is the author of *Labour's Dilemma: The Gender Politics of Auto Workers in Canada, 1937–1979* (1994) and of articles in several journals, including *Labour/Le Travail* and *Studies in Political Economy*. She is currently researching the internment experiences of Japanese Canadian Nisei women during World War II.

Lorne Tepperman, professor of sociology at the University of Toronto, has, for three decades, advised both public and private organizations in his role of applied sociologist. His co-authored and co-edited books on women's work and family lives—*Lives of Their Own: The Individualization of Adult Women's Lives* (1993), *Next of Kin: An International Reader on Changing Families* (1993), *The Futures of the Family* (1995), and *Close Relations: An Introduction to the Sociology of Families* (2000)—use Canadian and cross-national data to examine recent changes and project them into the future. His most recent work includes a co-authored book, *Social Problems: A Canadian Perspective* (2003), with James Curtis. He recently received the Outstanding Contributions Award from the Canadian Sociology and Anthropology Association for his overall research contributions to sociology.

Frank Trovato is professor of sociology at the University of Alberta, where he teaches introductory and advanced courses in demography and population studies. His publications include numerous articles in professional journals and three edited books. His research deals with topics spanning diverse aspects of demography and sociology: fertility, nuptiality, internal migration, immigrant health and mortality, sex and marital status differentials in mortality, and the social demography of racial, immigrant, and ethnic groups. Professor Trovato is president of the Canadian Population Society, the professional association of Canadian demographers outside of Quebec. He also reviews extensively for journals in the areas of population and general sociology, has served on the editorial boards of *Social Forces* and *Sociological Perspectives*, and is a former editor of *Canadian Studies in Population*.

John Veugelers is associate professor in the Department of Sociology at the University of Toronto. His previous research has focused on immigration politics and right-wing extremism in Canada and Europe, with recent articles appearing in *Current Sociology*, *Sociological Quarterly*, and the *Canadian Review of Sociology and Anthropology*. Under a project funded by the Social Sciences and Humanities Research Council of Canada, he is currently studying the politics of French repatriates from colonial North Africa. He was the recipient of an Outstanding Teaching Award from the University of Toronto in 2001.

G. Keith Warriner is associate professor and chair of the Department of Sociology, University of Waterloo. Dr Warriner's major research interests concern natural resources and environmental sociology, as well as research methods and statistics. His studies have examined energy conservation, the west coast commercial fishing industry, adaptation to change by Ontario tobacco farmers, public participation in environmental decision making, and grassroots environmental protest. His recent publications have investigated issues of environmental justice, urban dispersion and the housing preferences of city-dwellers, and bias contained in the measurement of socio-economic status by surveys.

Sue Wilson teaches in the School of Nutrition and is the associate dean of the Faculty of Community Services at Ryerson University. Her research interests include women's work, women's health, women at mid-life, students with dependent care responsibilities, the long-term effects of job loss, and breast cancer and spirituality. She has published a number of textbooks, including *Women, Work and Families* (4th edn, 1996), and several co-authored introductory and family sociology texts.

Terry Wotherspoon is professor of sociology and head of the Department of Sociology at the University of Saskatchewan, where he has worked since 1986. In addition to several years of teaching experience at elementary, secondary, and postsecondary levels, he has engaged in research and published widely on issues related to education, social policy, indigenous peoples, and social inequality in Canada. Among his many publications, he is co-author or co-editor of *First Nations: Race, Class and Gender Relations* (1993), *Multicultural Education in a Changing Global Economy: Canada and the Netherlands* (1995), and *The Legacy of School for Aboriginal People: Education, Oppression, and Emancipation* (2003). His book *The Sociology of Education in Canada: Critical Perspectives* (1998) received a book award from the Canadian Association for Foundations of Education. In 2002, his work was honoured by the Canadian Education Association with the presentation of a Whitworth Award for Educational Research.

List of Tables, Figures, and Boxes

Tables

Figures

Boxes

Author Index

Subject Index

Stop Press

> **Stop press** 1. Late news inserted in a newspaper after printing has begun. 2. A column in a newspaper reserved for this.
>
> — *The Oxford English Reference Dictionary*

Society never stops changing and neither does sociology, the academic discipline tasked with studying society. But there is a point when a textbook, by its very nature, *must* stop changing. That point comes when the proofs have been checked for one last time, all the illustrations and figures are in place, and the files have been sent to the printers in order that the physical book may be produced.

So it was with *Socology: A Canadian Perspective*. But the world rolls on, regardless of printers' and publishers' schedules, and there have been significant developments in many of the areas covered by the book since its first printing. In particular, a flood of information continues to be released by Statistics Canada, not only in the wake of the most recent census (results from which are already incorporated throughout the text) but also as part of its ongoing efforts to collect and disseminate important data about Canadian society. The question arose: How best to incorporate at least a sampling of this new information without having to wait the three or four years that usually pass before a new edition of a textbook is issued?

The answer came from the world of newspapers, where the "stop press"—a special insert comprising news that has broken since the rest of the newspaper was (to borrow another term from journalism) "put to bed"—boasts a long and honourable history. The eight pages that follow represent a "stop press" to *Sociology: A Canadian Perspective*, allowing the authors and publishers the opportunity to update important data and highlight what has changed since the book's first printing. By including the material here in the book itself, rather than on a separate Web page or in a booklet packaged with the text, we hope convenience to the reader is maximized and students and instructors alike will find it easy and enlightening to flip back and forth between the stop press and the original chapter in order to see how particular aspects of society have changed in even the relatively short period of time since the original version of the text was printed. As well, in some cases, readers are encouraged to exercise their "sociological imaginations" in pondering why particular changes have occurred.

CHAPTER 3   SOCIALIZATION

There has been considerable discussion in media circles in recent years that the rise of the Internet and of electronic gaming systems such as PlayStation has meant a reduction in the amount of television watched by children. Do you think a comparison of the 2002 Statistics Canada data with the previous year's data (p. 71) bears this thesis out?

Update to Figure 3.2	**Average Hours per Week of Television Viewing for Children and Teens in 2002, by Province** (p. 71)	
	Children 2 to 11 years	**Teens 12 to 17 years**
Canada	**14.6**	**13.7**
Newfoundland and Labrador	17.0	13.7
Prince Edward Island	15.7	15.7
Nova Scotia	16.1	15.9
New Brunswick	16.3	13.4
Quebec	14.7	14.4
Ontario	14.5	13.8
Manitoba	15.0	13.9
Saskatchewan	16.0	12.3
Alberta	14.2	12.4
British Columbia	13.1	12.5

SOURCE: Statistics Canada, "Average hours per week of television viewing, 2002" based on CANSIM data. Available at <http://www.statcan.ca/english/Pgdb/arts23.htm>, accessed 29 December 2004.

CHAPTER 4 ROLES AND IDENTITIES

On page 91, the text discusses *role competition*. The table below presents data that illustrates the text's observation that in Canadian society today, many workers, especially women, "are faced with choices between competing tasks and competing loyalties."

New Table **Percentage of "Double Shifters" Who Work a Full Year (49–52 weeks) and Also Do Unpaid Housework and/or Childcare and/or Senior Care Each Week, 1996 and 2001**

	1996	2001
Males doing 30+ hours per week of unpaid housework	6	6
Males providing 30+ hours per week of unpaid childcare	8	9
Males providing some senior care during week	15	16
Females doing 30+ hours per week of unpaid housework	18	16
Females providing 30+ hours per week of unpaid childcare	16	17
Females providing some senior care during week	20	22

Source: Vanier Institute of the Family, Profiling Canada's Families III (Ottawa: Vanier Institute of the Family, 2004), 124.

CHAPTER 6 DEVIANCE

Update to Figure 6.2 **Provincial Variations in Rates of Homicide (Number of Homicides per 100,000 Population), 2003**

NL	PE	NS	NB	QC	ON	MB	SK	AB	BC	YT	NT	NU
0.96	0.73	0.85	1.07	1.34	1.45	3.70	4.12	2.00	2.24	3.22	9.55	10.21

CHAPTER 7 FAMILIES

The updated table below expands on the information provided in Chapter 7 of the text, by providing a 20-year range of data that allows one to see changes in the types of families most common in society during the final two decades of the twentieth century.

Update to Table 7.1 **Types of Families in Canada, 1981, 1991, and 2001 (Percentages)** (p. 164)

Type of Family	1981	1991	2001
Legally married couples with children	55.0	48.2	41.4
Legally married couples without children	28.2	29.1	29.0
Lone-parent families	11.3	12.7	15.7
Common-law couples without children	3.7	5.8	7.5
Common-law couples with children	1.9	4.2	6.3
Same-sex couples as percentage of all couples	N/A[1]	N/A[1]	0.5

[1]Same-sex couples were counted for the first time in the 2001 census, and classified as common-law couples

Source: Vanier Institute of the Family, *Profiling Canada's Families III* (Ottawa: Vanier Institute of the Family, 2004), 40; Vanier Institute of the Family, *Profiling Canada's Families II* (Ottawa: Vanier Institute of the Family, 2000), 31; Statistics Canada, *Dwellings and Households: 1991 Census of Canada* (Cat. no. 93-311) (Ottawa: Statistics Canada, 1992), 130.

What, if anything, do you think are the causes and consequences of the differences in participation rates between the 1996 and 2001 data?

Update to Table 7.2 **Labour Force Participation Rates for Mothers and Fathers with Children Under 15 Years of Age, 2001 (Percentages)** (p. 171)

Family Type	Mother	Father
Single lone parent with youngest child under 6	60	76
Married parent with child under 6	71	83
Single lone parent with youngest child 6–14	76	94
Married parent with youngest child 6–14	81	94

Source: Vanier Institute of the Family, Profiling Canada's Families III (Ottawa: Vanier Institute of the Family, 2004), 74.

Note the changes in custody awards over this seven-year period.

Update to Figure 7.2 **Dependent Children by Party to Whom Custody Was Granted, 1995 and 2002** (p. 177)

	Party to whom court awarded custody of children (percentages)			
	Wife only	Joint custody – husband and wife	Husband only	Other
1995	67.6	21.4	10.9	0.2
2002	49.5	41.8	8.5	0.2

Source: Vanier Institute of the Family, Profiling Canada's Families III (Ottawa: Vanier Institute of the Family, 2004), 38.

The updated table below now provides comparative data about child poverty rates over a ten-year span.

Update to Table 7.3 **Child Poverty Rates[1] in Selected OECD Countries, Late-1980s to Early-2000s** (p. 178)

Country	Late-1980s to Early-1990s	Late-1990s to Early-2000s
Finland	2.3	2.8
Norway	5.2	3.4
Sweden	3.0	4.2
Belgium	3.8	7.7
Netherlands	8.1	9.8
Canada	15.3	14.9
United Kingdom	18.5	15.4
United States	24.3	21.9

[1]Child poverty rate is defined as the percentage of children living in families whose income is less than 50 percent of the median adjusted disposable income for all persons

Source: The United Nations Children's Fund (UNICEF), The State of the World's Children 2005 (New York: UNICEF, 2004), 28.

CHAPTER 8 EDUCATION

The updated figures below now provide data over a five-year period. While Internet access has increased enormously for all income levels, there remains a strong correlation between household income and Internet access levels.

Update to Figure 8.3 **Percentage of Canadian Households with Internet Access, 1999–2003, by Household Income** (p. 203)

	1999	2000	2001	2002	2003
All households	**28.7**	**40.1**	**48.7**	**51.4**	**54.5**
Lowest quartile ($23,000 or less)	10.9	16.5	22.6	25.1	26.7
Second quartile ($23,001 to $39,999)	18.0	31.2	40.0	39.9	44.6
Third quartile ($40,000 to $69,999)	32.4	47.4	56.4	62.3	64.7
Highest quartile ($70,000 and more)	53.5	65.4	75.8	78.4	81.9

Source: Statistics Canada, Internet Use in Canada (56F0003XIE) (Ottawa: Statistics Canada, 2004). Available at <http://www.statcan.ca/english/freepub/56F0003XIE/index.htm>, accessed 29 December 2004.

CHAPTER 9   WORK & INDUSTRY

The table in the text provides data for the period 1997-2002; the table below provides additional data for 2003-2004.

Update to Table 9.2   **Full- and Part-Time Employment by Gender and Age, 2003–2004 (Thousands)** (p. 231)

	2003	**2004**
Both sexes		
Total	15,746	16,021
15–24 years	2,407	2,422
25–44 years	7,673	7,694
45 years and over	5,666	5,908
Full-time	12,781	13,072
15–24 years	1,308	1,327
25–44 years	6,717	6,758
45 years and over	4,757	4,987
Part-time	2,965	2,949
15–24 years	1,099	1,094
25–44 years	956	937
45 years and over	909	918
Men		
Full-time	7,485	7,615
15–24 years	756	761
25–44 years	3,886	3,888
45 years and over	2,844	2,966
Part-time	922	916
15–24 years	465	465
25–44 years	200	191
45 years and over	258	260
Women		
Full-time	5,296	5,457
15–24 years	552	566
25–44 years	2,831	2,870
45 years and over	1,913	2,021
Part-time	2,043	2,033
15–24 years	635	629
25–44 years	757	745
45 years and over	652	658

Source: Statistics Canada, "Full-time and part-time employment by sex and age group (2003)," available at <http://www.statcan.ca/english/Pgdb/labor12.htm>, accessed 13 January 2005.

CHAPTER 10 – HEALTH ISSUES

The upward trend in life expectancy continued for both sexes in the final decade of the twentieth century, although the gap between female and male life expectancies, which had begun narrowing sometime after 1980, also continued to decrease. Females now have a life expectancy at birth of 5 years longer than males, down from a gap of 7 years in 1970-2. Updated data by province is also presented below.

Update to Table 10.2   **Life Expectancy at Birth (Years), over Time, by Province and by Gender** (p. 257)

	Both Sexes	**Males**	**Females**	**Difference**
2000–2	80	77	82	5
2000–2				
Newfoundland and Labrador	78	76	82	4
Prince Edward Island	79	76	81	5
Nova Scotia	79	76	82	6
New Brunswick	79	77	82	5
Quebec	79	77	82	5
Ontario	80	78	82	4
Manitoba	79	76	81	5

	Both Sexes	Males	Females	Difference
Saskatchewan	79	76	82	6
Alberta	80	77	82	5
British Columbia	81	78	83	5
Yukon[1]	77	74	80	6
Northwest Territories[1]	76	73	80	7
Nunavut[1]	69	67	70	3

[1]Data should be interpreted with caution due to small underlying counts of births and deaths.

Source: Adapted from Statistics Canada, "Life Expectancy at Birth," available online at <http://www.statcan.ca/english/Pgdb/health26.htm>, accessed 30 December 2004; Statistics Canada, *The Daily* (27 September 2004), available online at <http://www.statcan.ca/Daily/English/040927/d040927a.htm>, accessed 30 December 2004.

The updated table below not only provides 2004 data but looks further back into the past, providing data for 1975. One of the striking changes that has occurred over the last three decades is the near-doubling of drug expenditures as a percentage of total health spending.

Update to Table 10.3 **Total and Private Sector Canadian Health Expenditure by Use of Funds, 1975, 1990, and 2004** (p. 266)

	Total Health Expenditure			Private Sector Health Expenditure[1]		
	1975	1990	2004[2]	1975	1990	2004[2]
Hospitals	44.7	39.1	29.9	11.0	14.4	7.9
Other institutions	9.2	9.4	9.6	11.3	10.2	8.5
Physicians	15.1	15.2	12.9	0.9	0.6	0.7
Other professional	9.0	10.6	11.2	33.0	35.3	34.2
Drugs	8.8	11.4	16.7	31.7	29.9	33.8
Capital	4.4	3.5	4.5	5.5	2.5	3.5
Public health & administration	4.5	4.2	6.7	–	–	–
Other health spending	4.3	6.7	8.6	6.6	7.3	11.5
Total	100.0	100.0	100.0	23.8[3]	25.5[3]	30.1[3]

[1]Includes out-of-pocket expenditures made by individuals, claims paid by health insurance firms, private spending on health-related capital construction, and privately funded health research
[2]Forecast
[3]Represents percentage of total health expenditure

Source: Canadian Institute for Health Information, *National Health Expenditure Trends 1975–2004* (Ottawa: Canadian Institute for Health Information, 2004), 108–9, 114–15.

CHAPTER 12 POLITICS AND POLITICAL MOVEMENTS

The following table provides additional results from the June 2004 federal election, including results for the Green Party of Canada.

Update to Figure 12.2 **Popular Vote by Party, Canadian Federal Elections, 2004 (Percentages)** (p. 318)

Political Party	Percentage of Popular Vote in 2004
Liberal Party of Canada	36.7
Conservative Party of Canada	29.6
New Democratic Pary/CCF	15.7
Bloc Québécois	12.4
Green Party of Canada	4.3
Other	1.3

Source: Calculated from Elections Canada data (2004), available at <http://www.elections.ca>, accessed 16 January 2005.

CHAPTER 15 GENDER RELATIONS

The 2001 census data reveals the continuing evolution of the nature of female participation in the Canadian workforce. What do you think are the most significant changes since 1996?

Update to Table 15.1   Female Labour Force 15 Years and Over, by Occupation, 2001 (p. 389)

	Number of women	% female	% of total female labour force
Management occupations	574,380	35.4	7.9
Business, finance, and administrative occupations	2,016,255	72.8	27.8
Natural and applied sciences and related occupations	215,620	21.5	3.0
Health occupations	642,745	79.1	8.8
Occupations in social science, education, government service, and religion	667,340	62.4	9.2
Occupations in art, culture, recreation, and sport	235,560	54.1	3.2
Sales and service occupations	2,238,510	58.7	30.1
Trades, transport, and equipment operators and related occupations	157,845	7.2	2.2
Occupations unique to primary industry	153,460	23.0	2.1
Occupations unique to processing, manufacturing, and utilities	363,720	30.5	5.0

Source: Statistics Canada, "Experienced labour force 15 years and over by occupation and sex (2001 Census)," available at <http://www.statcan.ca/english/Pgdb/labor45a.htm>, accessed on 16 January 2005.

A similar evolution can be discerned when the data is examined as categorized by type of industry rather than by occupation.

Update to Table 15.2   Female Labour Force, by Industry, 2004 (p. 389)

	Number of women	% female	% of total female labour force
Goods-producing sector	**944.0**	**23.4**	**12.6**
Agriculture	99.2	29.7	1.3
Forestry, fishing, mining, oil, and gas	48.3	16.2	0.6
Utilities	34.7	26.4	0.5
Construction	114.9	11.7	1.5
Manufacturing	646.9	28.3	8.6
Services-producing sector	**6,545.5**	**54.6**	**87.4**
Trade	1,210.4	48.4	16.2
Transportation and warehousing	195.9	24.5	2.6
Finance, insurance, real estate, and leasing	574.7	58.4	7.7
Professional, scientific, and technical services	431.8	42.2	5.8
Business, building, and other support services	294.0	46.8	3.9
Educational services	695.0	65.9	9.3
Health care and social assistance	1,427.8	81.6	19.1
Information, culture, and recreation	351.8	48.8	4.7
Accommodation and food services	608.9	60.2	8.1
Other services	360.0	51.7	4.8
Public administration	395.4	48.2	5.3

Source: Statistics Canada, "Employment by industry and sex (2004)," available at <http://www.statcan.ca/english/Pgdb/labor10a.htm>, accessed 16 January 2005.

The table below updates Table 15.4 in the text to reflect data through 2002. Note that in the new table, all the figures have been restated in terms of constant 2002—not 1999—dollars.

Update to Table 15.4 Average Earnings by Sex, 1993–2002 (Constant 2002 Dollars) (p. 390)

	Women ($)	Men ($)	Earnings Ratio (%)
1993	22,300	34,700	64.1
1994	22,500	36,200	62.0
1995	23,000	35,400	64.8
1996	22,700	35,300	64.5
1997	22,900	36,200	63.3
1998	23,900	37,400	64.0
1999	24,200	37,800	64.0
2000	24,900	39,000	64.0
2001	25,100	39,100	64.1
2002	25,300	38,900	65.2

Source: Statistics Canada, "Average earnings by sex and work pattern," available at <http://www.statcan.ca/english/Pgdb/labor01a.htm>, accessed on 16 January 2005.

The table below updates the data in the text to the year 2000. Based on the data presented here, has the wage gap between the sexes in highly paid occupations narrowed or widened? What reasons might sociologists identify for such changes?

Update to Table 15.5 10 Highest-Paid Occupations, 2000 (p. 391)

	Number of workers	% Women	Average earnings ($) Both sexes	Women	Men	Earnings ratio (%)
Total – 10 highest-paying occupations	237,715	23.3				
Judges	1,825	24.4	142,518	131,663	146,008	90.2
Specialist physicians	12,480	30.8	141,597	98,383	160,833	61.2
Senior managers – financial, communications carriers, and other business services	40,919	21.5	130,802	90,622	141,829	63.9
General practitioners and family physicians	22,040	30.8	122,463	96,958	133,789	72.5
Dentists	8,710	22.9	118,350	82,254	129,104	63.7
Senior managers – goods production, utilities, transportation, and construction	44,630	11.6	115,623	75,267	120,914	62.2
Lawyers and Quebec notaries	47,290	31.0	103,287	77,451	114,894	67.4
Senior managers – trade, broadcasting, and other services, n.e.c.	37,690	17.8	101,176	67,161	108,527	61.8
Securities agents, investment dealers, and traders	17,765	36.8	98,919	55,299	124,290	44.5
Petroleum engineers	4,370	10.0	96,703	61,057	100,633	60.7

Source: Pay Equity Task Force, Pay Equity: A New Approach to a Fundamental Right (Ottawa: Department of Justice, 2004); available at <http://canada.justice.gc.ca/en/payeqsal/index.html>, accessed 16 January 2005.

CHAPTER 16 ETHNIC & RACE RELATIONS

Additional data for 2002 is provided below.

Update to Table 16.2 Total Immigration to Canada, 2002 (p. 414)

Year	Number of Immigrants
2002	229,091

Source: Policy, Planning and Research, Citizenship and Immigration Canada, Facts and Figures, Immigration Overview (Ottawa: Minister of Public Works and Government Services Canada, 2003), 3.

CHAPTER 19   CITIES & URBANIZATION

The expanded table below, which shows levels of urbanization from 1950 to 2003, with a further projection for the year 2030, illustrates the dramatic influx of people into the world's cities, especially in the developing world—a process that is expected to continue in the future. Note that the percentages given here for levels of urbanization in the year 2000 are slightly different from those in the original table in the text on page 489, because of ongoing adjustments in the sourcing and analysis of the data.

Update to Table 19.1   Levels of Urbanization by Continent (Percentages), 1950–2030 (Projected) (p. 489)

	1950	1975	2000	2003	2030
North America	63.9	73.8	79.1	80.2	86.9
Latin America & the Caribbean	41.9	61.2	75.5	76.8	84.6
Europe	51.2	66.0	72.7	73.0	79.6
Oceania	60.6	71.7	72.7	73.1	74.9
Asia	16.6	24.0	37.1	38.8	54.5
Africa	14.9	25.3	37.1	38.7	53.5

Source: United Nations Department of Economic and Social Affairs, Population Division, *World Urbanization Prospects: The 2003 Revision* (New York: United Nations, 2004), 7.

The increasing urbanization of the world alluded to above (and the changing nature of that urbanization) is shown in a different fashion below. In 1950, there was only one urban area in the world with a population exceeding 10 million—New York. In 2015, demographers project there will be 23 such "megacities," with New York only the 8th largest among them.

Update to Table 19.2   Cities with Populations of 10 million+, 1950, 1975, 2000, and 2015 (Projected) (Population in Millions) (p. 490)

1950		1975		2000		2015	
New York	12.3	Tokyo	19.8	Tokyo	26.4	Tokyo	26.4
		New York	15.9	Mexico City	18.1	Bombay	26.1
		Shanghai	11.4	Bombay	18.1	Lagos	23.2
		Mexico City	11.2	São Paulo	17.8	Dhaka	21.1
		São Paulo	10.0	New York	16.6	São Paulo	20.4
				Lagos	13.4	Karachi	19.2
				Los Angeles	13.1	Mexico City	19.2
				Calcutta	12.9	New York	17.4
				Shanghai	12.9	Jakarta	17.3
				Buenos Aires	12.6	Calcutta	17.3
				Dhaka	12.3	Delhi	16.8
				Karachi	11.8	Manila (Metro)	14.8
				Delhi	11.7	Shanghai	14.6
				Jakarta	11.0	Los Angeles	14.1
				Osaka	11.0	Buenos Aires	14.1
				Manila (Metro)	10.9	Cairo	13.8
				Beijing	10.8	Istanbul	12.5
				Rio de Janeiro	10.6	Beijing	12.3
				Cairo	10.6	Rio de Janeiro	11.9
						Osaka	11.0
						Tianjin	10.7
						Hyderabad	10.5
						Bangkok	10.1

Source: United Nations Human Settlements Program (UN-Habitat), *Urban Millennium: Special Session of the General Assembly for an Overall Review and Appraisal of the Implementation of the Habitat Agenda, 6-8 June 2001*; available at <http://www.unhabitat.org/istanbul+5/booklet4.pdf>, accessed 22 January 2005.

Canada, like the rest of the world, continues to grow more urbanized.

Update to Figure 19.2 Urbanization of Canada, by Province and Territory, 2003 (Percentages) (p. 492)

	CAN	NL	PE	NS	NB	QC	ON	MB	SK	AB	BC	YT	NY	NU
% of population living in an urban area	80	58	45	56	50	80	85	72	64	81	85	59	58	33
% of population living in a rural area	20	42	55	44	50	20	15	28	36	19	15	41	42	67

Source: Vanier Institute of the Family, *Profiling Canada's Families III* (Ottawa: Vanier Institute of the Family, 2004), 16.

CHAPTER 21 THE ENVIRONMENT

The following new table supplements and amplifies some of the discussion in Chapter 21.

New Table 21.1 Ecological Footprints[1] of Selected Countries, 2001

Region	Total Ecological Footprint (global ha/person)
Africa	**1.2**
Kenya	0.9
Nigeria	1.2
South Africa, Republic of	2.8
Asia-Pacific	**1.3**
Nepal	0.6
India	0.8
China	1.5
Japan	4.3
Australia	7.7
Middle East & Central Asia	**2.1**
Saudi Arabia	4.4
Israel	5.3
United Arab Emirates	9.9
Latin America & the Caribbean	**3.1**
Costa Rica	2.1
Brazil	2.2
Mexico	2.5
Central & Eastern Europe	**3.8**
Ukraine	3.3
Poland	3.6
Russian Federation	4.4
Czech Republic	5.0
Western Europe	**5.1**
Netherlands	4.7
Germany	4.8
United Kingdom	5.4
France	5.8
Sweden	7.0
North America	**9.2**
Canada	6.4
United States of America	9.5

[1]An ecological footprint is a measure, in units of global hectares, of how much biologically productive land and water area an individual, city, country, region, or humanity requires to produce the resources it consumes and to absorb the waste it generates.

Source: World Wildlife Fund for Nature (WWF), Living Planet Report 2004 (Gland, Switzerland: WWF-World Wildlife Fund for Nature, 2004), 24-30.